JOHN MAYNARD KEYNES

1883–1946

Economist, Philosopher, Statesman

ALSO BY ROBERT SKIDELSKY

Politicians and the Slump

English Progressive Schools

Oswald Mosley

John Maynard Keynes Vol. 1 – Hopes Betrayed

John Maynard Keynes Vol. 2 – The Economist as Saviour

John Maynard Keynes Vol. 3 – Fighting For Britain

Interests and Obsessions

The World After Communism

John Maynard Keynes and Lydia Keynes, portrait by William Roberts

Robert Skidelsky

John Maynard Keynes

1883–1946

Economist, Philosopher, Statesman

MACMILLAN

This compiled and abridged one-volume edition first published 2003 by Macmillan
an imprint of Pan Macmillan Ltd
Pan Macmillan, 20 New Wharf Road, London N1 9RR
Basingstoke and Oxford
Associated companies throughout the world
www.panmacmillan.com

ISBN 0 333 90312 9

A selection of material taken from
John Maynard Keynes Vol. 1 – Hopes Betrayed (1983)
John Maynard Keynes Vol. 2 – The Economist as Saviour (1992)
John Maynard Keynes Vol. 3 – Fighting For Britain (2000)

1 3 5 7 9 8 6 4 2

A CIP catalogue record for this book is available from
the British Library.

Typeset by SetSystems Ltd, Saffron Walden, Essex
Printed and bound in Great Britain by
Mackays of Chatham plc, Chatham, Kent

TO MY FAMILY

Contents

List of Illustrations

Frontispiece: John Maynard Keynes and Lydia Keynes, portrait by William Roberts. *(By courtesy of the National Portrait Gallery, London)*

Section Three

Acknowledgements

My most persistent debts have been to my family, to Warwick University, to my agent Michael Sissons, and to my publisher. Without their support and forbearance this biography would never have been written. I would also like to thank the following individuals who provided important help at different stages of the journey:

Robert Ackerman
Judith Allen
Christopher Allsop
Joseph Altham
Noel Annan
Dennis Arundell
Frederick Ashton
Peter Avery
Paul Bareau
Florence Bartoshevsky
Fred Bauman
James Beechey
Quentin Bell
B. S. Benedikz
Terence Benton
Edward Bernstein
Daniele Besomi
Mark Blaug
Charles Blitch
John Morton Blum
Mark Bonham Carter
James Boughton
Richard Brain
Richard Braithwaite
Neville Brown
Clark Brundin
Katherine Burk
Terence Burns
Rohan Butler
Jack Butterworth

David Calleo
Carmen Callil
Anna Carabelli
Damon Clark
Peter Clarke
H. S. Cobb
Ruth Cohen
Christopher Cook
Jacqueline Cox
Bruce Craig
Peter Croft
Paul Davidson
Phyllis Deane
Stanley Dennison
Meghnad Desai
Sue Donnelly
Margaret Drabble
Mrs M. P. G. Draper
H. J. Elcock
Jo Elwyn-Jones
H. J. Eysenck
Mrs Roland Falk
Iraci Fedelli
Andrew Filson
Penelope Fitzgerald
Jean Floud
Brian Follett
Lady Ford
James Fox
Milton Friedman

Nicholas Furbank
Mrs G. M. Furlong
Joy Gardner
Angelica Garnett
Henrietta Garnett
Richard Garnett
Peter Gautry
Donald Gillies
Francis Gladstone
Andrew Graham
Angus Graham
     Campbell
Duncan Grant
Joe Grice
Chris Guest
Frank Hahn
A. C. L. Hall
Michael Halls
Liam Halligan
Frances Anne Hardin
Mrs S. C. Harding
Daphne Harmer
Frederic Harmer
Geoffrey Harcourt
José Harris
Jennifer Hart
Mrs P. M. Hatfield
Dorothea Hauser
Clarissa Heald
Suzanne Helburn

Nico Henderson
Mavis Hicks
Polly Hill
Caroline Hobhouse
Niall Hobhouse
Martin Hollis
Michael Holroyd
John R. de S. Honey
Elisabeth Hope
Susan Hope-Jones
Bryan Hopkin
Alan Hopkins
James Horwitz
Michael Howard
David Hubback
Jeremy Hutchinson
Terence Hutchison
Michael Ignatieff
G. John Ikenberry
Elizabeth Inglis
Peter James
Charles Jones
Evan Jones
Peter Jones
Vijay Joshi
Richard Kahn
Nicky and Clarissa
    Kaldor
Trevor Kaye
Mrs Marion Kennball
    Cook
Lord Kennet
Anne Keynes
Geoffrey Keynes
Milo Keynes
Richard Keynes
Simon Keynes
Stephen Keynes
Alastair Kilmarnock
Harvey Klehr
Oliver Knox
Deepak Lal
Helen Langley
Hermione Lee

Robyn Lee
Clive Lennox
Paul Levy
Harry and Margaret
    Lintott
Ian and Dobs Little
Bruce Littleboy
Adrian Lyttleton
John Luce
R. A. Luce
Don McCarthy
Fiona MacCarthy
Donald MacDougall
Elizabeth McLeod
Harold Macmillan
Deirdre McMahon
R. D. McNaghten
R. E. Macpherson
Robin Mackworth-
    Young
James Marcouyeux
David Marquand
D. F. J. A. Mason
James Meade
Robin Medley
Alan Megill
Michael Meredith
Marcus Miller
Norman Miller
Rosalind Moad
Donald Moggridge
M. Moir
Gary Mongiovi
Georgina Morley
Basil Moore
David Morse
Nicholas and Verity
    Mosley
Nigel Nicolson
Kalin Nikolov
F. J. Norton
Roderick O'Donnell
Réné Olivieri
Peter Oppenheimer

F. T. Ostrander
Wayne Parsons
Donald Patinkin
George Peden
Mrs. I. Percival
Roland Philipps
Peter Plesch
D. S. Porter
Peter Proby
John Presley
David Rees
Susan Rendell
Timothy Renton
Tom Rivers
Priscilla Roberts
Austin Robinson
Joan Robinson
Paul Roche
Kenneth Rose
Richard Rose
S. P. Rosenbaum
Victor Rothschild
A. L. Rowse
Steven Runciman
Elizabeth Russell
George (Dadie)
    Rylands
Roger Sandilands
Arthur Schlesinger Jr.
Stephen Schuker
Raymond Seitz
George Shackle
Helena Shire
Richard Shone
Larry Siedentop
Hans Singer
Augusta Skidelsky
Boris Skidelsky
Edward Skidelsky
William Skidelsky
Quentin Skinner
Mark Skousen
Lola S. Sladits
Iain Smith

Frances Spalding
George and Zara Steiner
Marion Stewart
Geoffrey Stone
Patrick Strong
Charles Swithinbank
Gerard Tallock
Sam Tannenhaus
Ferdinando Targetti

Raymond Teichman
Tanya Thompson
Christopher and Baillie
   Tolkien
Lynn Turgeon
Federico Varese
Gillian Vincent
Julian Vinogradoff
Michael Vyvyan

Douglass Wass
Christopher Webb
Andrew Weller
Jean Whiter
David Wigdor
Bernard Williams
Phillip Williamson
Barbara Wootton
Richard Wright

I would also like to thank the following organisations and institutions for the help they have afforded me:

Arts Council of Great Britain
Australian National University
Bank of England
Birmingham University Library
The Bodleian Library, Oxford
   (Dept of Western Manuscripts)
British Library
   (Manuscript Section)
British Library of Political and
   Economic Science
Cambridge University Library
   (Dept of Manuscripts)
Cambridge University Registrary
Christchurch College, Oxford
Churchill College, Cambridge
Clifton College, Percival Library
Dulwich College,
   Wodehouse Library
Economic and Social Research
   Council
Eton College, College Library,
   College Debating Society
Franklin D. Roosevelt Library
Harvard University, Baker Library,
   University Library, Thomas
   Lamont Papers Trust
House of Lords, Library, Record
   Office
India Office Library

Johns Hopkins University, Bologna
   Center, School of Advanced
   International Studies
King's College, Cambridge
Lehrman Institute of New York
Library of Congress
   (Manuscript Division)
Marshall Library, Cambridge
Nuffield College, Oxford
Pembroke College, Cambridge
New York Public Library,
   Berg Collection
Phoenix Trust
Polytechnic of North London
Public Record Office, Kew
Royal Economic Society
Society of Authors
Strachey Trust
Sussex University Library
   (Manuscript Section)
Trinity College, Cambridge
Tuesday Club
University College Library, London
Warwick University
Yale University
York University, Borthwick Institute of
   Historical Research
Cambridge University Press Ltd
Jonathan Cape Ltd

Hamish Hamilton Ltd
William Heinemann Ltd
Hodder and Stoughton Ltd
Houghton Mifflin Co.
The Institute of Economic Affairs
The Macmillan Press Ltd

John Murray (Publishers) Ltd
Penguin Books
Virago Press Ltd

Thompson Henry Ltd

Introduction

This single-volume life of John Maynard Keynes has been delayed by the publication of my three-volume life. I put it that way because my original contract with Macmillan, dating from early 1970, was to write a single-volume, 150,000-word biography of Keynes, to be delivered 'not later than 31 December 1972'.

It seemed a good idea at the time. I thought of Keynes as the third volume of a different trilogy, which had started with my first book, *Politicians and the Slump*, published by Macmillan in 1967. This was an account of the response of Britain's Labour government of 1929–31 to the great depression – a shortened version of my D.Phil thesis, written at Oxford. The question it tried to answer was: why had a Labour government spurned the 'New Deal' to combat mass unemployment, suggested by one of its own ministers, Oswald Mosley, and one of its economic advisers, John Maynard Keynes? My 'trilogy', I thought, would be rapidly completed by single-volume lives of Mosley and Keynes, the two spurned economic radicals of the first book, one of whom went on to become a fascist, the other to revolutionise economic theory and policy. Mosley had never had anything decent written about him; Roy Harrod's official life of Keynes was twenty years old and showing its age. Mosley was soon finished and published. Keynes took thirty years to complete, ending up as three volumes.

What defence can I offer for such a prodigious achievement in tardiness? The first part of the defence is familiar to most biographers: problems of getting access to the papers. Although Sir Geoffrey Keynes, the deceased economist's brother, had given me permission to see Keynes's personal papers held at King's College, Cambridge, the economist Richard Kahn, who held copyright of Keynes's economic papers – then stored in the university's Marshall Library – refused me entry to his own treasure trove. The reason? A research student of his, Don Moggridge, was editing them for the Royal Economic Society's collected edition of the great man's writings – by coincidence being published by another branch of my own publisher, Macmillan – and nothing must be allowed to slow down this valuable project. No less a figure than Harold Macmillan, the ex-Prime Minister, interceded on my behalf, but to no avail. Lord Kahn's letter to Macmillan dated 9 February 1970 ends: 'The unfortunate fact is that just the wrong moment has been chosen for a new biography, in so far as it involves access to the economic papers.' Moggridge tried to cheer me up: he would not be long in finishing, and then I would be able to read the papers I wanted in the published *Collected Writings*. 'Rest assured', he wrote to me on 28 July 1970 'that it is not my life's work – not even half a decade's.' The volumes of the *Collected Writings* were still being churned out twelve years later, the last one of all in 1989. And Moggridge's own (single-volume) life of Keynes did not appear till 1992.

My contract with Macmillan stood, but the completion date was tacitly dropped. Since I was frustrated on the Keynes front, I took a university teaching job in the United States and finished my biography of Oswald Mosley.

At this point luck – or fate – took a hand. As a result of the controversy stirred up by my Mosley book (published by Macmillan in 1975), I narrowly failed to get tenure at the Johns Hopkins University's School of Advanced International Studies in Washington, DC. So my wife and I came back to England, after a delightful cut-off year in Bologna. Had I stayed in the United States, I am certain that I would never have written a full-length biography of Maynard Keynes. Back in England, I set about reviving the Keynes project. I would start work on the personal papers and the few already published volumes of the *Collected Writings* and hope that by the time I had finished writing about the early Keynes the papers of the later Keynes would be open to me. I was still thinking in terms of a single volume.

So in 1976 I started my serious research in Cambridge. I took notes in the King's College and university libraries (no photocopies were then allowed, pencils only) and got to know members of the Keynes family, friends of his like Dadie Rylands and Harry Lintott, and surviving colleagues like Joan and Austin Robinson, and Richard Kahn. In 1977 my wife and I and our two young children spent the first of many summers in the comfortable, rambling house of Nicky and Clarissa Kaldor at 2 Adams Road. Nicky, too, had worked with Keynes as a young man, and he loved discussing (or rather expounding) economics. He was then obsessed by the need to save the world from the evils of 'monetarism', and would develop this theme for many hours at a stretch. I would ask questions, which he probably attributed to ignorance or incompetence or both, but which gave him fresh opportunities to lambast Milton Friedman and other assorted 'neo-classical' economists and free-traders. Nicky suffered from narcolepsy, and would often fall asleep in full flow, only to resume ten or fifteen minutes later at exactly the point he had left off. He was a wonderful and generous teacher and friend, and I learnt a great deal from these tutorials, though I had a strong intuition that he was fighting a losing battle against the forces of darkness.

The biographer's most important relationship, apart from that with his subject, is with what Virginia Woolf called the 'widow' – the guardian of the

Great Man's memory. My two widows were Geoffrey Keynes and Richard Kahn. (Keynes's actual widow, the ballerina Lydia Lopokova, did not inherit any of the Keynes papers.) Sir Geoffrey had commissioned Roy Harrod to write his brother's 'official' biography in the late 1940s, and, despite having given me permission to see the personal papers at King's, saw no need for another 'life'. He was well into his eighties when I started my research, and there was no apparent abatement of his proverbial fierceness.

It took several years to gain Sir Geoffrey's confidence. There were two main problems to overcome. The first was that thinking about his brother re-opened too many family wounds. For all his great eminence as a surgeon and bibliophile, Geoffrey suffered from an incurable sense of inferiority in relation to Maynard. He also resented the fact that his parents had preferred Maynard to him. I used to send him articles about his brother I wrote in the early days of my research, and he once told me they caused him 'great pain' to read. I was not as tactful as I should have been. I regarded these ephemera as a way of trying out ideas. Geoffrey would treat them as final thoughts, and turn on me. He would withdraw permission for me to see the papers, and the whole relationship would have to be re-established.

The other problem was Maynard Keynes's homosexuality. What purpose did I have, Geoffrey once asked me, other than to tell the world his brother was a bugger? I replied that the world already knew this, since Michael Holroyd's biography of Lytton Strachey had been published in two volumes in 1967–8. My aim was to enfold Keynes's private life in his public achievement. Geoffrey was not convinced. The annoying thing was that whenever the press gave me a 'puff' it was this aspect that they found most titillating for their readers. Alan Watkins wrote a silly article in the *Observer* on 30 April 1978 saying I had been commissioned to write a life of Keynes 'between the sheets'. This confirmed Geoffrey's worst fears.

Gradually things improved, and by the time he died in 1982 we were on excellent terms. The way to Geoffrey's heart was through his library. He had one of the great private collections of antiquarian books, and when I visited him at Lammas House, near Cambridge, we would always spend some time looking over them. (One of his favourites was a first edition of Francis Bacon's *Essays* annotated by William Blake.) As he told me the history of each venerable volume, and how he had acquired it, the fierce old man would soften, and his face would light up in a charming smile. At such moments, one felt he was almost reconciled to the thought of painful revelations in store.

One summer evening he was driven over by his grandson Simon Keynes to have supper with us at Adams Road. I remember Geoffrey almost springing out of Simon's very low-slung MG sports car. He must have been ninety-three by then. His great age made him a figure of awe to our two boys. For some years afterwards, whenever we met anyone who looked old, the younger, William, would always ask: 'Is he as old as Sir Geoffrey Keynes?'

The keeper of the economic tablets was Richard Kahn, Keynes's 'favourite pupil', who had helped him with the *General Theory* and lived on at King's College, also very old, though not as old as Geoffrey, and, unlike Geoffrey, very deaf. His face was purple, and he had enormous whiskers growing out of his ears, but he had the sweetest of smiles. Now that I no longer badgered him about 'his' papers, he had become very friendly. The truth, which I did not know then, was that he had never liked Roy Harrod's biography of Keynes.

But he had his eccentricities. Whenever I appeared at King's College, he would greet me warmly in the Combination Room and ask me to come and see him 'for a long talk'. 'Only', he murmured, 'be sure to ring to make an appointment.'

One morning I rang him up. A voice at the other end said 'Richard Kahn'. I told him who I was. There were some piercing high-pitched whistling noises as his hearing aid was turned on, much audible shuffling of pages (as though of an engagement diary), and an appointment was arranged. It had seemed quite easy, and I told Nicky Kaldor that I would be seeing Kahn in two days' time. Nicky roared with laughter. 'Oh no, you won't. You wait and see.' Early on the morning of the appointed day, the telephone rang. 'This is Richard Kahn. I'm terribly sorry, but I find I have an engagement for this afternoon. Could you come at the same time next week?' This went on for most of one summer and I left Cambridge without our long talk.

When I returned for more research the following year, I ran into Richard by the library steps at King's. 'I think you have been avoiding me,' he said. I did eventually get my interview. It was a grey winter afternoon, and Richard gave me tea in his study above the King's College library. His desk was covered with enormous piles of yellowing paper which, I had no doubt, included several letters of mine. I was placed in a chair at some distance from him, which did not make conversation easy. As the afternoon wore on, the light faded, but Richard made no move towards the light switch. Eventually we sat facing each other in almost complete darkness. I would shout a question (several times) and finally a ghostly reply would waft towards me through the gloom.

By 1981 I was ready to start writing. Our family decamped to La Garde-Freinet in the south of France, where we had a house, followed by a van with a huge pile of books. I wrote my first two sentences on 1 September 1981. 'John Maynard Keynes was not just a man of establishments; but part of the elite of each establishment of which he was a member. There was scarcely a time in his life when he did not look down at the rest of England, and much of the world, from a great height.'

La Garde-Freinet, a wind-swept *village perché* in Provence, was by no means devoid of intellectual resources. Christopher Tolkien (son of J. R. R.) had escaped there with his wife Baillie from the Oxford world of Eng. Lit. The economist Ian Little and his wife Dobs, who was then fighting a brave, but losing, battle against cancer, had a house just outside the village. Nicky Kaldor had a holiday home. The two economists were far from seeing eye to eye, even on matters of theory. Indeed, it was from listening to them argue one lunch time at Lady Jane Heaton's that I got my insight that economics was a form of post-Christian theology, with economists as priests of warring sects. Lady Jane lived in some state in a converted chapel in the middle of the village. On either side of her at a long table in the crypt, Kaldor and Little played intellectual tennis of high quality. Nicky served and volleyed with great ferocity, but I noticed that Ian's passing shots were working well. The issue was: did Ricardo's theory of comparative advantage assume constant returns to scale? Yes, thundered Kaldor; no, parried Little. Lady Jane presided with a charming but glazed expression, helping them in turns to nourishing soup, which she ladled out from a large tureen.

Looking through my correspondence of this time, I am amazed that in April 1982 I still contemplated having a single-volume life ready for publication in 1983. It was not till 21 November 1982 that I broke the bad news to my agent, Michael Sissons: there could be a book in 1983, but it would only be the first volume of a two-volume set. The reason, I told him, was 'that there is still too much material constantly coming out, which requires mastering and in many cases rewriting of stuff already written'. Although my schedule had always been fanciful, this was true. It turned out that the 'economic papers', to which I finally gained access that autumn, contained masses of unpublished philosophical manuscripts, which were not being prepared for publication at all. It was a young Australian economist, Rod O'Donnell, who alerted me to their existence. Reading them for the first time not only caused me to rewrite (in a great hurry) a fundamental chapter in my first volume, but also sharpened my intuition that there were important connections to be made between Keynes's theories of ethics and probability and his economics. However, it was also true that the scale on which I was writing the life was totally inconsistent with a one-volume treatment.

The first volume was published in November 1983 to what are called 'glowing' reviews. What I felt I had succeeded in doing was rescuing the 'young' Keynes from the 'moist light' with which Harrod, according to Noel Annan – reviewing the Harrod book in the *Times Literary Supplement* of 23 February 1951 – had irradiated him. I was particularly pleased to get the following from Richard Kahn (1 June 1984): 'I found [your book] most impressive, interesting and beautifully written. You have taken enormous trouble, covering a much wider field than might have been expected.... I look forward to the further volumes.'

There was the rub. I had by this time decided that there must be three volumes, since I had only got Keynes up to 1919, or thirty-six, and barely started on his economics. But I still persisted in predicting that I would finish volume two by 1985. Barring the way stood the Keynesian Revolution, hardly an under-excavated topic. Thousands of articles and books had appeared analysing what Keynes had said, what he had meant to say, what he should have said, what others said he had said, etc. Where amidst all this exegesis did my comparative advantage lie? What value could I add?

II

Here begins the second round of my defence. As I got deeper into my work, I became obsessed with two questions: how does a historian write about an economist and what is the value of biography? Over the period I was writing about Keynes, many of the old conventions were breaking down. Historians' range was increasing as they were becoming better trained technically. Biographies were becoming franker, and biographers were becoming more self-conscious about their craft.

The answer to the first question was obvious: learn economics. I am amazed this had not occurred to me before I embarked on the project. I had picked up some economics while working on *Politicians and the Slump*. Marty Feldstein, who was at Nuffield College in the 1960s, had given me a textbook explanation of Keynesian theory, in diagrammatic form on a blackboard. But anything technical floored me, and the history of economic thought was a closed book. My real economic education started with 'tutorials' with Nicky Kaldor, conversations with Ian Little, reading standard textbooks, and attending economics classes in America. Reading Keynes himself was the greatest of all lessons in economics, especially for its revelation of how an economist's mind works. Three things drove me to cross the disciplinary divide: a conviction that I had to engage with Keynes's theories, a fear of making mistakes in discussing them, and a fascination with the way economists think. Reviewing *Politicians and the Slump*, Max Beloff had noticed 'a willingness unusual in historians to tackle the economic issues themselves' (*Daily Telegraph*, 30 November 1967). I could never take seriously the standard view that historians should take ideas as given, and confine themselves to their effects; or even worse, the Marxist-cum-Freudian view that ideas have no independent effects, but are themselves the effects of economic or psychological causes. If one accepts that ideas shape events, then a historian has to be able to describe the ideas or doctrines relevant to his topic as accurately as can a theologian, a philosopher, or an economist. If that requires a specialised training, so be it. Any account of Keynes's influence that failed to engage with his 'theology' would be seriously incomplete *as history*.

But in learning economics it was equally important not to lose one's historical bearings. It was important not to get bamboozled by economics, not to lose one's historian's sense that economic doctrines are heavily contextual, and that biography is above all about character and context not propositions. Even though there is a logical core to all economic thinking, a biographer of Keynes, nevertheless, always has to keep in his mind the question of why Keynes's doctrines succeeded in the world of action, while those of his opponents failed. This is a historical, not an economic, question. My own biographical enterprise spanned exactly the years when Keynesian economics was fading, and when it started to be possible for Keynes to be seen as a historical figure – as an exemplar and product of the virtues and defects of his age. Knowledge of economics is necessary to understand Keynes's 'theology' and that of the anti-Keynesians; a strong historical sense is necessary to maintain the requisite detachment from the theology. I am always pleased when a reviewer remarks that it is impossible to tell whether I am a Keynesian or non-Keynesian.

Learning enough economics to be able to give a good account of Keynes's theoretical journey and finding a way of writing about it that would not repel a non-specialist reader largely explain the nine-year delay between the appearance of the first and second volumes. Today, I would call myself an economically literate historian rather than an economist. In fact, I am schizophrenic in my attitude to the discipline. I am shocked by how little of economic argument most of my fellow historians understand; but equally shocked about how little feel for the springs of action and the life of societies most economists have. I now feel it to be a major fault of volume two of my Keynes trilogy that there was too much economics in it. I was too anxious to show the world that I could 'do' it.

Completion of the trilogy had to wait till the year 2000, eight years after the publication of volume two. I had got Keynes through his great book, *The General Theory of Employment, Interest and Money*; there were nine years only of his life to go, though these covered the years of his greatest public activity, during and immediately after the Second World War, and included his greatest practical achievement, the Bretton Woods Agreement of 1944. For this last gap between the volumes there is no defence, only explanation. Most of the 1990s was taken up with other activities. In 1991 I was made a life peer and became chairman of the Social Market Foundation. In 1994 I made my first trip to post-communist Russia and spent a year writing a short book, *The World After Communism* (published in the United States as *The Road from Serfdom*). From 1992 to 2001, I took the Conservative whip in the Lords. However, I played my political cards in such a cunning way that I was able to resign or get dismissed from all the political jobs to which I was appointed, which in due course precluded further offers. Thus the road to Keynes's death was kept open.

III

My explanations are not quite over, for I have not yet dealt with the problems peculiar to biography. The main issue is this: does a thinker's life have anything to do with his thought? And if so, what? In his obituary notice of Keynes, published in 1946, the Austrian economist Joseph Schumpeter had posed this question when he wrote: 'He was childless and his philosophy of life was essentially a short-run philosophy.' The discussion in my first volume of Keynes's homosexuality gave critics of Keynesian economics their chance. William (now Lord) Rees-Mogg argued in *The Times* of 10 November 1983 that Keynes's rejection of moral rules led him to reject the gold standard which provided an 'automatic control of monetary inflation'. Admirers of Keynesian economics moved, with a kind of reflex action, to insulate the 'thought' from the 'life'. Thus Maurice (now Lord) Peston wrote in the *New Statesman* of 9 December 1983 that 'it is obvious philosophical nonsense to suggest that there is a connection [between Keynes's sexuality and his economics]; the logical validity of a theory and its empirical relevance are independent of its progenitor. (What help is knowledge of the lives of Newton and Einstein in predicting the movements of the planets?)' Rees-Mogg and Peston, it seems to me, were guilty of opposite errors. The riposte to Rees-Mogg is that a correlation is not a cause, and to Peston that economics is not a science like physics.

The most powerful theory of the connection between life and work is Freud's, and Freud's theory of the mind has spawned masses of biographies of uneven quality. I have a temperamental antipathy to Freudian explanations of 'achievement'. It seems to me that they are incurably reductionist. They seem to give the biographer warrant not to take a person's ideas seriously or to discuss them in their own terms, but to see them as the expression of childhood trauma. In any event, I found the Freudian approach unhelpful in writing about Keynes. The specific psychological mechanism used by Freud to explain rebellion – the Oedipus complex – seemed to be irrelevant in Keynes's case, either as an explanation of Keynes's homosexuality or as an explanation of his revolutionary economics. He was a rebel against Victorian orthodoxies, but this was not a revolt against his father, or his family's values. Sociology offered a better clue. The idea of Keynes as an Edwardian who tried, by manipulating economic facts, to restore post-Victorian cheerfulness after the horrors of the First World War seemed to me, as it still does, a better biographical setting for Keynes's economics than any circumstances of his childhood.

I am more sympathetic to Freud's poetry than to his psychology. He had a tragic vision of life, and saw the suppression of the instinctual desires as the price of civilisation and progress. It is possible to write about Keynes in this way: duty triumphed over inclination; Bloomsbury was sacrificed to Whitehall. But even this is to get things off-beam. One has no sense of a tragic life, but of a supremely happy, successful and fulfilled one. Of Keynes one can say with great confidence that he succeeded in getting the best of all his possible worlds. It is significant that Freud, with his wealth of classical stereotypes, never writes about Odysseus, the classical hero, 'soft of speech, keen of wit, and prudent', whom Keynes most resembled.

I have some sympathy for the neo-Marxist view that Keynes was a product of his class and background and therefore tended to see the economic problem from a particular point of view – that of the 'educated bourgeoisie' located at the centre of a declining empire. One can add a great deal of sophistication to this kind of approach. But it does not absolve the biographer from taking Keynes's ideas seriously, and leaves out the value added by sheer genius, that residual of universal significance.

A work of genius is a complex object and there is light to be shed about what went into the making of it. Even in the case of scientific and mathematical achievement we can say a great deal about the existing state of knowledge, the problems it failed to address, why those problems were or had become interesting, the particular capacities which the solver brought to their solution. At the other extreme is a work of art which seems to have much more immediate roots in the personal life of the artist or writer. In between is the area in which Keynes worked, which was partly scientific, partly artistic. This gives a wide justification for a biographical approach. As I put it in the introduction to my first volume: 'If underlying Keynesian theory was Keynes's vision of his age, knowledge of his state of mind and the circumstances which formed it is essential, not only in order to understand how he came to see the world as he did, but also in order to pass judgement on the theory itself.'

That being said, I don't want to argue the case for biography on utilitarian grounds. People do, of course, read biography partly to understand what formed the character and work of an outstanding person. But they also read it because it is the oldest form of story-telling, which long antecedes fiction. We want to know, and seem always to have wanted to know, how famous people lived their lives and to hear the stories of their exploits and the great events in which they were involved. There is no diminution of this interest, which is why biography remains one of the most popular genres of reading today.

What, finally, is biography's relation to history? The famous lines from Ecclesiasticus that start 'Let us now praise famous men' were read at Keynes's memorial service in Westminster Abbey and it is in these terms that I have finally come to see him. This is a Great Person view of history. But this is my belief. Individuals do make a difference; Keynes made a difference. No doubt, all the separate influences are absorbed in the long course of history. But I doubt if any serious historian today would deny that great men are one of these 'separate influences'. This is the justification for writing about them.

IV

Born in 1883 and dying in 1946, the bulk of Keynes's professional life was framed by two world wars. At the beginning, he was an Edwardian optimist, convinced that automatic progress was steadily enlarging opportunities for more and more people to live the 'good life', as identified by his mentor, G. E. Moore, and his friends of the Bloomsbury Group. He ended his life bequeathing the world a theory, policies, and two international institutions (the International Monetary Fund and the International Bank for Reconstruction and Development) designed to strengthen the foundations of a free economy, so as to make it possible again for people to indulge the hopes with which he had grown up. In between, there was catastrophe and retrogression, starting in Europe and spreading to most of the rest of the world. Any just estimate of what he strove for and what he accomplished has to be placed in the context of this history.

Re-reading the three volumes of my original life in preparing this single-volume edition, I have become more aware than I was of how certain themes run insistently through Keynes's life, giving his thought an underlying unity, despite the many technical variations in its expression. In economics, his most persistent ideas concern the pervasiveness of uncertainty and the part it plays in preventing economies performing at anywhere near their potential, except at moments of 'excitement'; his conception of economies as 'sticky masses', rather than 'fluids', making their recovery from 'shocks' protracted, difficult, costly and incomplete; and his stress on the duty of governments to keep economic life up to the mark – at or near its best possibilities, when there is a reasonably full and efficient use of actual and potential resources.

It was the failure of what Keynes called the 'classical' theory to understand economic life in these terms – specifically, its ignoring of uncertainty, and its assumption that wages and prices were fluid – that led him to invent a new branch of economics, 'macroeconomics', a theory of output as a whole, which could exhibit any number of equilibria, or levels of activity. He claimed that classical theory was worked out on the assumption that there was no unemployment to explain; but this happy state happened not to be characteristic of 'the economic society in which we actually live'. If, however, the central controls which he proposed succeeded in maintaining full employment, then 'the classical theory comes into its own again from this point onwards'. That is, he had 'no objection' to the way the classical theory explained the allocation of *scarce* resources between different uses and factors, and, by extension, no objection to a competitive market system as the most powerful instrument for securing such efficient allocation (Keynes, *The General Theory of Employment, Interest and Money*, 1936, pp. 3, 378–80). Thus, even at his most radical, Keynes aimed at reconciliation between his new theory and the 'classical' theory, by assigning them to different *domains*: the first to explaining the level of output; the second to how it was divided up. By and large, these were the terms of the contract by which the Keynesian Revolution was combined with the inherited body of economics. The lack of theoretical 'fit' between the two domains, however – especially Keynes's failure to explain mass unemployment in terms of individual motives and actions, the units of 'classical' analysis – contributed to the unravelling of the Keynesian revolution in the 1970s and 1980s.

This is the aspect of Keynes's work which has received the most attention. It has made him one of the three or four greatest economists who have ever lived. But it does not exhaust his contribution to modern thought. He may also be interpreted as a philosopher of individualism on the defensive – in retreat from communism and fascism, as well as opposed to the rise of militant trade unionism and the growing concentration of indus-try. These were the concrete manifestations of that 'stickiness' of contempor-ary economies which made *laissez-faire* policies so dangerous for liberal statemanship. As Keynes put it in 1925: the economic system must not ask 'from the principle of diffusion more than it can perform'. In his undergrad-uate essay on Burke, Keynes criticised a political philosopher he otherwise admired for failing to distinguish between the 'central structure' of a free system which needed to be defended at all costs and the 'outworks' which could be surrendered. Keynes's philosophy of the 'Middle Way' (more aptly thought of as the intelligent way) deliberately aimed to surrender some of the 'outworks' of the individualist system to collectivism in order to protect its 'central structure'. How much of the 'outworks' needed to be surrendered to preserve a free society was the subject of a famous exchange between him and Hayek in 1944. Keynes's sense of urgency to lift the average standard of capitalist performance was fed by his sense of danger. As he also wrote in 1925, 'modern capitalism is absolutely irreligious, without internal union, without much public spirit, often, though not always, a mere conge-ries of possessors and pursuers. Such a system has to be immensely, not merely moderately, successful to survive.'

Keynes's determination to squeeze extra performance out of the capital-ist market system was also driven by the ethical strand in this thinking. The quicker the system could be got to deliver on its promise to produce wealth for all, the sooner would mankind be in a position to enjoy the 'good' life – to value the present over the future, ends over means, the good over the useful. Keynes's student allegiance to G. E. Moore's *ethical* standpoint was not a youthful aberration but a lifelong commitment. He returned to it most fully in his delightful essay 'Economic Possibilities for Our Grandchildren', first read to a group of Winchester schoolboys in 1928. Its message was that solving the 'economic problem' is a necessary, though not sufficient, condition of civilisation.

Keynes's economic philosophy is thus made up of three interdependent parts: his technical macroeconomics, his embattled political philosophy and his ultimate ethical purpose. With the ending of the main political threats to liberty, one may validly ask how much of his own 'central structure' is still needed. Today there is no rival to political liberalism in the developed world. So the political system can more easily bear the strains of economic volatility. However, volatility still brings substantial welfare losses. And each welfare loss curtails the possibility of the 'good life' now and postpones its enlargement to more people.

Of enduring value for technical economics is Keynes's attempt to explain in terms of economic theory how mass unemployment can arise and persist. It is the quest which keeps the Keynesian research programme alive in economics today, because there is still something to be explained. However, the quest in not pursued in quite the same way as it used to be, and 'classical' theory is not treated in the same way as Keynes treated it. It is now recognised that 'classical' theory failed to specify properly the institutional framework (including the monetary, banking, political and legal systems) in which its theory of the self-regulating economy was supposed to be true; in fact, that it lacked any theory of institutions at all. Keynes, too, took institutions as given, and sought to improve or stabilise expectations by means of counter-cyclical monetary and fiscal policy. Those who take uncertainty seriously now place more stress on building stabilising institutions than on trying to 'fine-tune' the business-cycle. Whether the mix of institutions, rules and policies required to steady the path of the market economy is regarded as simple, spare and easy to bring about or as very complex and difficult to set up is still a matter of debate. With the collapse of communism, the debate has acquired a global dimension. But the naivety of the classical theory has gone. Whatever economists think of Keynes, there are no pre-Keynesian economists left.

The BBC recently conducted a poll asking people to name the greatest Britons of all time. Winston Churchill came out first, with Princess Diana third. Keynes did not make it to the top hundred. Nor did any other economist, including Adam Smith. This is not surprising. The pantheon of great thinkers remains almost unknown to the general public. This class of historical actor does its work silently: they are the backroom boys of our civilisation. Their ideas permeate the atmosphere from which practical persons draw such intellectual nourishment as they do. But the source of this nourishment remains by and large obscure to them. Most people today believe that governments can and should prevent economic depressions, with their concomitant of mass unemployment. Not one in a thousand knows that this idea originated with Keynes; perhaps not one in a hundred thousand could give you a tolerably accurate idea of how Keynes thought governments should set about doing this. And I am thinking only of the English-speaking peoples. Of the great economists, Keynes came closest to being a 'celebrity' in his own lifetime. But even then his fame hardly extended beyond the circle of what he called 'the educated bourgeoisie' – which was, and remains, a tiny fraction of the population anywhere.

But, 'soon or late, it is ideas, not vested interests, which are dangerous for good or ill', Keynes wrote, in one of his most famous passages. I have often puzzled about the word 'dangerous'. Keynes was a most careful user of words. How can ideas be *dangerous* for good? A more obvious word would be 'powerful'; the thought behind it, that ideas have a stronger influence on events, for good or bad, than have interests. And this is how the passage is usually interpreted. But the word 'dangerous' adds a subtlety characteristic of Keynes: the thought that ignorance is dangerous, but that knowledge, too, is dangerous, because it tempts to *hubris* – the usurpation by men of divine powers – whose inevitable fruit is *nemesis*. That Keynes's great revolutionary manifesto *The General Theory of Employment, Interest and Money* should have ended on this oblique note of warning is striking testimony to a greatness that transcended economics. An intellect that could soar, seemingly without limit, accepted the discipline of earth-bound limits in the management of human affairs. This is the Keynes I love, and whose personality and achievements I have tried to convey.

V

This abridgement cuts about 40 per cent from the three-volume version. Cutting has been by eliminating and condensing material. Also there has been a fair amount of rewriting: resulting from second thoughts, correction of mistakes, welding together the joins between the volumes, and taking account of criticism and later research. So to some extent it is a new book, which stands on its own, and can be read for the first time as a unity. My hope is that it will attract new readers for whom three volumes on Keynes is simply too much.

ROBERT SKIDELSKY,
June 2003

PART ONE

DUTY AND GOODNESS

By far the most valuable things, which we know or can imagine, are certain states of consciousness, which may be roughly described as the pleasures of human intercourse and the enjoyment of beautiful objects ... That it is only for the sake of these things – in order that as much of them as possible may at some time exist – that anyone can be justified in performing any public or private duty; that they are the *raison d'etre* of virtue; that is they ... that form the rational ultimate end of human action and the sole criterion of social progress: these appear to be truths which have generally been overlooked.

G. E. Moore, Principia Ethica, pp. 188–9

1

Dynastic Origins

I. ANCESTORS

There was scarcely a time in his life when John Maynard Keynes did not look down at the rest of England, and much of the world, from a great height. He went to England's best school, Eton. He was an undergraduate and fellow of King's, one of Cambridge's top colleges. He served in the Treasury, the top home department of government. He was the intimate of one prime minister, and the counsellor of many. He was at the heart of England's economics establishment, and at the centre of its financial oligarchy. He was a member of the Bloomsbury Group, England's most potent cultural coterie. His communications with the educated public were always made from a position of unimpeachable authority. This position was largely achieved by the force of his dazzling intellect and by his practical genius. But he started life with considerable advantages which helped him slip easily into the parts for which his talents destined him. There was no nonsense about his being in the wrong place or having the wrong accent. Of his advantages the chief was being born at Cambridge, into a community of dons, the son of John Neville and Florence Ada Keynes.

When he was five his great-grandmother Jane Elizabeth Ford wrote to him, 'You will be expected to be very clever, having lived always in Cambridge.' The way the expectation was phrased is interesting. Today a Keynes would be expected to have brains because he was born a Keynes. But great-grandmother Ford wrote before the dynasty was established. Indeed all she would have known about the Keyneses was that they came from Wiltshire, that Maynard Keynes's grandfather had been a successful businessman, and that her grand-daughter Florence had married his son, a clever young Cambridge don called John Neville Keynes. Looking at the matter from the heights of provincial Nonconformity Jane Elizabeth Ford must have felt that there was something quite ordinary about the Keyneses.

Not till he was sixteen did her great-grandson have much cause to think otherwise. It was only at Eton that he discovered that the Keynes side of the family had some fairly impressive historical credentials. Working in the college library he constructed a family tree which started with the Keynes who came over with the Conqueror.

Something of the esoteric quality of Maynard Keynes's life is suggested by the name itself. When spelt right it is often mispronounced Keens; when pronounced right it is sometimes mis-spelt Canes. Such are the incidental penalties for having come from the otherwise desirable location of Cahagnes in the Calvados district of Normandy.[1] The name is probably derived from the late Latin word *casnus*, an oak, from which comes the modern French name *chêne*. William de Cahagnes was a vassal of Robert, Count (later Earl) of Mortain, half-brother to Duke William of Normandy. He fought at the battle of Hastings, and received from Earl Robert a number of estates totalling over 5000 acres. The main ones were at Dodford in Northampton-shire – mentioned as being in the possession of 'William de Cahagnes' in the Domesday Book – and at Horsted Keynes in Sussex. On William's death his estates went to his son and heir, Ralph; and on Ralph's death were divided between Ralph's three sons, Ralph, Hugh and William.[2]

The lines of the first two had died out by the fourteenth century. 'The Keyneses do not seem to have been a very warlike family,' wrote the schoolboy Maynard. Prudently 'they went into battle only when their absence was likely to bring about a monetary fine'. The exception was Ralph's third son, William, from whom Maynard Keynes claimed descent. He captured King Stephen at the battle of Lincoln in 1141. As a reward, he received the manor of Winkleigh (later Winkley Keynes) in Devon. About 1330, William's descendant John de Keynes married Isabella Wake, who brought a considerable estate in Somerset into the family. In the sixteenth and seventeenth centuries, the Keynes family, now based at Compton Pauncefoote in Somerset, remained Roman Catholics and loyal to the Stuarts – a double mistake which resulted in their losing all their property. Some of them became Jesuit priests. The most famous, John Keynes (1625–95), was Professor of Logic at the University of Liège. In 1683 he was appointed by the Pope to be Provincial of England and was one of Titus Oates's intended victims. According to Maynard Keynes 'it seems likely that he was partly responsible, by his bad advice, for the fall of James II'. He had an elder brother, Captain Alexander Keynes. 'He fought for Charles I in the civil war; and the last remnant of the family estates was lost by him in the Royalist cause. The family now sinks into obscurity, and the next two links cannot be fitted in with any certainty. Alexander had several sons, most of whom became Jesuits. But as far as I can make out his son Henry was the father of Richard Keynes, of Wareham.'[3]

The line to our subject runs without problem from this Richard Keynes who died in 1720. There are three more Richards, then a John Keynes, who was the father of another John Keynes, Maynard Keynes's grandfather. These descendants of Captain Alexander Keynes, if such they were, start off as Anglicans but soon become Baptists; they also turn up in Salisbury as ornamental plasterers and brushmakers. By this time, Maynard Keynes noted, 'the tradition of their more interesting past seems to have entirely died out'.[4]

Family trees are apt to be tedious except to members of the family and genealogists. Nor are they always illuminating from a biographical point of view, since the laws of heredity are so little understood. Who knows what Maynard Keynes actually 'inherited' from all these Keyneses? The justification for the above account is that the subject of this biography thought that he had a name to live up to.

If his father's family recalled to Maynard Keynes vanished squirearchal glories, his mother's summoned him to moral and intellectual effort. His maternal grandmother traced her descent back to a Sussex smuggler, Thomas Ford, killed by the King's men in 1768. But repentance was swift and permanent. The smuggler's son, David Everard Ford, became a Congregational minister, 'subject to fits of depression possibly caused by the religious problems arising out of his interest in the study of fossils'.[5] In 1834 his son, also David Everard (1797–1875), who became Congregational minister at Lymington, Hampshire, married Jane Elizabeth Down, 'a young woman of outstanding energy and ability' who was descended on her mother's side from two old west-country families, the Haydons and the Langdons. She bore him ten children; she also ran a girls' boarding school at Lymington. When David Ford moved to the Richmond Congregational church in Manchester in 1843, she restarted her boarding school with her second daughter, Ada Haydon Ford.

It was Ada Haydon Ford of the boarding school who married Maynard Keynes's maternal grandfather, John Brown. Born in 1830, the son of modest Lancashire business folk, Brown was apprenticed at fifteen to a printer. He decided to become a minister, apparently as a result of reading the religious tracts he set up in print. He took his London Matriculation, studied classics at Owen's College, Manchester, and got his London BA in 1851. In 1855 he became Congregational minister at Park Chapel, Cheetham Hill Road, Manchester, channelling his dramatic instincts into preaching. Running through Maynard's mother's family is a strain of didacticism and intellectual fancy lacking in the more recent Keyneses. The women especially had a strong capacity for moral indignation which Keynes may have inherited. But the ambience of the Brown and Keynes families alike was very much Chapel and Trade. They were middle class, even moneyed, but not yet gentlefolk as the Victorians understood the term.

II. JOHN NEVILLE KEYNES

It was Maynard Keynes's paternal grandfather, John Keynes of Salisbury, born in 1805, who restored the Keynes family fortune. Portraits of him as a youth and old man show a slight, spare figure, with shrewd eyes, an amused

mouth, and a general air of satisfaction. John Keynes's satisfaction was that
of the self-made man. Apprenticed in his father's brushmaking business at
eleven, he had built it up, by 1830, into a 'very lucrative manufactory'. But
'the soul of the flower', according to a gardening journal given to poetic
exuberance, 'lodged in his breast'. At seventeen he won his first prize – a
pair of sugar tongs – for his pinks. Determined to profit from his green
fingers he gave up bristles and turned to dahlias. His one-man dahlia
exhibition at Stonehenge in 1841 attracted thousands. This was the start of
his reputation, and the foundation of his fortune. Dahlias made him. Cleverly developing new strains, he helped promote the dahlia boom; when the
dahlia bubble burst, he switched with equal success to roses. As he prospered, John Keynes diversified into banking and other commercial activities.
Like most self-made Victorian businessmen he attributed his success in
life to hard work and religious principles. He said his life had been
happy because he had succeeded in all his enterprises, and sounded as if he
meant it.

John Keynes's success was remarkable enough, but it was to be eclipsed
by the performance of his son. He married twice. His first wife, Matilda
Blake, bore him a daughter, Fanny, who later married a successful grocer,
Edward Purchase. Matilda died of cholera and in 1851 John Keynes married
Anna Maynard Neville, who came from an Essex farming family. Their only
son, John Neville, Maynard's father, was born on 31 August 1852. If John
Keynes took the first steps towards the production of Maynard Keynes by
making money, John Neville took the decisive second step by getting himself
established at Cambridge. It is a painful story.

Neville, as he was always called, grew up in a comfortable house in
Castle Street, Salisbury, adjoining his father's nurseries. It seems to have
been an affectionate home. Neville's relationship with his father is now
difficult to reconstruct, though son always spoke of father with affection
and respect. John Keynes was a religious man, who believed in religion as a
moral discipline. His earliest surviving letter to his son dates from 21 January
1857: 'My dear little Neville is not going to be a naughty boy, the good Jesus
was never a naughty boy and you must try and be like him.' Religious
reinforcements were provided by John Keynes's mother who lived with
them till her death in 1869 at the age of ninety-four. In her deaf old age
she sat all day with a Bible on her knee, mouthing the words of the scriptures. There is no doubt that John Keynes put Neville under great pressure
to succeed academically, once he showed signs of being clever. Academic
success was the royal road out of trade; Neville, in any case, never shared
his father's horticultural interests. However, John Keynes was not all stern
Victorian paterfamilias. There was clearly a lighter, more companionable,
side to him. He was a man of hobbies: he had built his fortune on a hobby.
He and Neville played chess, Neville starting to beat him when he was
twelve. John Keynes would take his son up to London for the pantomime,

and later to plays and oratorios. From his father Neville thus got an ambiguous legacy. The pressure to succeed was there; but also the message that life was not wholly serious. Neville was to show the same divided character. He grew up with a pervasive anxiety, to which immersion in hobbies was his eventual answer.

Neville was very close to his mother. She died when he was well over fifty, and his grief was overwhelming. She was a warm, emotional, person, not stupid, but not intellectual and didactic as the women on Maynard's maternal side were apt to be. Nor had she any interest in social work. (She once tried to sell some Bibles, but never, we are told, repeated the experiment.) Also living at home was John Keynes's unmarried sister Aunt Mary, fussy, anxious and devoted to Neville. There was the usual complement of family friends, but the most important non-family influence on Neville was undoubtedly Henry Fawcett. Henry's father, William Fawcett, was an old Salisbury friend of John Keynes. In an appalling shooting accident he had blinded his twenty-five-year-old son, then a fellow of Trinity Hall, Cambridge. Undaunted, Henry Fawcett went on to become Professor of Political Economy at Cambridge in 1863, and Postmaster-General in Gladstone's government of 1880. It was an exemplary Victorian success story, in which individual courage and determination had triumphed over the most adverse circumstances. Fawcett's shining moral example was always before Neville as he struggled to fulfil his father's hopes in the face of much discouragement. Fawcett is also important in our story because it was he who set Neville's sights on Cambridge.

In 1864, when he was eleven, Neville started at Amersham Hall, a small, exclusive Dissenting academy of about a hundred boys at Caversham, near Reading, which under its headmaster Ebenezer West provided 'just the sort of education which was necessary to nullify the disabilities from which Nonconformity laboured in those days...'[6] There was no nonsense about games: John Keynes paid his £70 a year for examination results; though the boys were allowed to keep rabbits. Neville was prepared for the London University Matriculation, similar to modern GCSEs. Via this route Amersham Hall produced 'senior wranglers,* leading men in surgery, medicine, law, and literature'.[7]

How happy Neville was at Amersham Hall is difficult to say. When he went there he started the diary he was to keep till 1917, fifty-three years later. By fourteen he was top of his matriculation class in mathematics, and second in classics. From that point his scholastic career took off, though not without alarms. A school report of April 1869 thought that in the Matriculation there would be 'marks lost through nervousness'. And so it turned out. He passed the Matriculation examination that summer respectably,

* Those obtaining first-class honours in the mathematical tripos were known as wranglers. Tripos is the Cambridge term for the examination leading to an Honours degree.

but not brilliantly, being lucky to get a Gilchrist scholarship to University College London.

On 5 October 1869, soon after his seventeenth birthday, he took up residence at University Hall, Gordon Square, Bloomsbury, a hostel set up in 1849 for Nonconformist students. Amersham Hall provided much of its intake, and Neville came up with a group of Amersham Hall friends, including Henry Bond, Arthur Spokes and William Lord. Mostly the sons of self-made businessmen, his fellow students knew they were expected through education to break out of trade into more highly valued professional careers. University College catered for this goal. Its educational system was based on examinations of 'portentous length'.[8] And for Neville this was not the end. Fawcett 'advised me to go for two years to London, & then on to Cambridge'.[9] As an only son Neville carried the whole burden of his parents' hopes. He used to say later he had never worked so hard in his life as in his years at University College. The strain told on his health and his personality. He began to complain of headaches, toothaches and chest pains, so much so that his mother feared the worst. 'You are very precious to us you know my own dear boy', she wrote him, 'and if we were to lose you I should lose my all.'[10] Until seventeen he was 'quite a chatterbox'. After that he started to dry up. By the time he got to Cambridge he was complaining in true pedant's fashion of idle chatter.[11] Coincidentally, he stopped growing, remaining stuck at five foot four inches, short even by Victorian standards.

As soon as he came to London he started recording the number of hours he worked each day, adding them up to make a grand yearly total – a habit which persisted until he gave up his diary. At University College he managed a ten-hour day. Yet he still had time for his hobbies. He played tournament chess. He collected stamps. He took up fives. Each weekend he escaped into the fantasy world of the Victorian melodrama, comedy, pantomime, opera; sometimes with his father up in London on horticultural business. Female company was confined to the holidays: skating with Flossie Williams, croquet and whist with Minnie Todd. Abandoning himself to passion he kissed Minnie's hand, receiving a lock of hair in return. But soon he was 'enjoying' himself with Flossie 'as if there was no Minnie Todd in existence'.

In July 1870 Neville obtained a first-class in Part I of his BA. For Part II in October 1871 he took logic and moral philosophy honours, being placed first equal. The following summer he got into Pembroke College, Cambridge, winning the top mathematical scholarship worth £60. But the worst of his troubles was yet to come. The problem was he was in the wrong subject. He soon discovered that he hated mathematics. A better tripos for him would have been the moral sciences tripos, established in 1848, and recently made available as a first degree. However, not only were there hardly any scholarships in it (which is why Neville had entered Cambridge as a mathematics scholar), but he would have been very unlikely to get a fellowship by doing well in it, fellowships at the time being awarded almost exclusively for high places in the mathematical and classical triposes. The choice seemed to be between slaving away at mathematics which he disliked, or switching to moral sciences which held out no academic prospects. He could see only one escape: to leave Cambridge right away. He wrote two tormented letters to his parents on 19 and 20 October 1872. Would they take him away? They had 'perhaps naturally' overestimated his abilities. He was really fit only to be a solicitor, and had better start training for that straight away. 'I do not mind being laughed at & called a fool as I know I shall be. I think my best & bravest course will be to acknowledge an error which I now realise & manfully do that which I esteem most likely to turn out best for my future welfare'.[12] There was also the worry about being a financial burden to his father, already in his late sixties and in indifferent health.

His parents did not hesitate. On 22 October 1872 Neville noted laconically in his diary, 'They are very averse to my leaving Cambridge, so I have agreed to stay.' The plan was for him to persevere with mathematics till May 'and see how I liked it then'. But doing problems with Routh, Cambridge's renowned mathematical coach, filled him with despair. In the Christmas vacation he came to a decision. He wrote to his College tutor, C. E. Searle (later Master of Pembroke), that he meant to give up mathematics and read moral sciences instead. 'I did not ask for his advice, as I have quite made up my mind on the subject.' But the argument in Salisbury went on. Fawcett urged him to continue with mathematics. He returned to Cambridge on 21 January 1873 where a 'very bad attack of the blues commenced. I am seriously doubtful if I took the right step when I came to Cambridge. My faceache still continues.' The next day he saw Searle.

> He was very kind & by dint of saying he thought I shd get a fellowship, his advice, added to that of Mr. Fawcett & to what I know to be Father's wish, has at last prevailed upon me to continue reading Mathematics till May. I do not myself consider the step to be a wise one, & I cannot begin to work with any 'go', but at any rate I suppose I please others.

He struggled on with mathematics till the summer of 1873 and then, not liking it any better, was finally allowed to give it up. He did so in the belief that his fellowship chances were at an end.[13] That summer he started on his new intellectual regime. Up at college in the long vacation he annotated the first volume of Mill's *Principles of Political Economy* and 'enjoyed it immensely'.[14] On 31 August, his twenty-first birthday, he started shaving.

Neville started reading moral sciences at a very interesting moment in the history both of the degree and of the university. The ancient universities were in the course of being roused from their long slumber to a new sense of their responsibility to provide leadership in an age of industrialism, declining religious faith, rising democracy and intellectual ferment. Neville's

presence at Cambridge was itself a sign of their new hospitality to intellectual Nonconformity, previously excluded by Test Acts dating from the
seventeenth century. The moral sciences tripos at Cambridge was one of the
points of this awakening. It was attractive to scholars, because its component
studies – moral and political philosophy, logic, psychology and economics –
were all in a state of flux, offering opportunities for creative work. It was
attractive to students like Neville whose logical grasp exceeded their mathematical facility. And parts of the moral sciences – especially moral and
political philosophy and political economy – were coming to be seen as a
source of social wisdom, replacing some of the functions hitherto performed
by religion. Neville's switch to moral sciences determined the atmosphere in
which Maynard Keynes was to grow up. He was a product of the Cambridge
moral science tradition, in which Cambridge economics developed side by
side with Cambridge moral philosophy.

By the end of the 1860s, though still a small school, the moral sciences
were attracting able, dedicated young dons and a much better calibre of
student. Henry Sidgwick had moved over from classics; Alfred Marshall from
mathematics: both 'new dons' with a high sense of intellectual and pastoral
responsibility. William Cunningham, Herbert Foxwell, Frederic Maitland and
James Ward were distinguished graduates of the late 1860s and early 1870s;
Arthur Balfour, the future Conservative Prime Minister, took second-class
honours in the moral sciences in 1869.

Neville went to Henry Sidgwick for moral and political philosophy.
Sidgwick, who had resigned his fellowship at Trinity College in 1869 because
he could no longer subscribe to its 'dogmatic obligations', was a representative figure of the new age of intellectual doubt and high responsibility. He
tried to construct a coherent system of secular ethics to replace religion, but
his mind was far too critical for him to succeed. Neville, like almost everyone
else, was very much attracted by Sidgwick's appealing personality, perplexed
search for truth, and anxiety to do justice to every position; but, not himself
troubled by religious doubts, he was not drawn to Sidgwick's brand of
metaphysical speculation. Intellectually he was closer to Alfred Marshall,
fellow of St John's, who taught him economics. Marshall had moved from
mathematics to economics via ethics, which he abandoned as a waste of
time. He was soon, Neville reported, 'speaking very highly of some of the
papers I have done for him, even in lecture'.[15] Neville went to Foxwell,
another young fellow of St John's, for mental philosophy, and to John Venn,
fellow of Caius, for logic. He showed great ability in the latter, though he
thought some of Venn's lectures 'useless'.[16] At last in congenial intellectual
territory, his self-esteem recovered. 'Spokes [who had also come up to
Cambridge] informs me that he has heard my manner spoken of as very
conceited,' he confided to his diary.[17]

He continued to work at a furious pace in these years. He was never
again to show such mental energy. In addition to his Cambridge work, he

was also preparing for the London BSc, which he took in both parts, obtaining first-class honours in geology and chemistry in October 1874. C. E. Searle, his college tutor, advised him to try for the gold medal (awarded for top place) in the London MA examination in July 1875. He was only prevented from doing so by Fawcett, who advised him to postpone the attempt till after the tripos.[18] The object of all this extra-Cambridge work was to improve his fellowship chances. As if this were not enough, he was gripped by 'chess mania'. He played first board for the university chess team, and took part in tournaments blindfolded, even though this gave him headaches.[19]

The reward for six years of nerve-racking exertion came in December 1875. He was declared senior moralist – placed first in the first class of the moral science tripos.

The examiners agreed that he had 'a very clear mind', but lacked originality in philosophy. The fellowship was not yet in the bag. There was a vacancy at Pembroke, but there were sure to be other candidates. Neville took out extra insurance by sitting the London MA in June 1876, in political economy. Four days later he heard he could add the Gold Medal to the honorary fellowship which University College had already given him. Then on 10 August 1876 a 'Telegram came to say that I had been elected a Fellow of Pembroke ... unanimously & almost without discussion'.[20] It was a double family triumph, for two months later his father was installed as Mayor of Salisbury. Already in failing health, John Keynes had less than a year and a half to live.

Neville had achieved his ambition; but he must already have known that it was a precarious security, because the system of fellowship tenure was about to be reformed by government commissioners appointed in 1876. The chief reform, designed to eliminate the abuse whereby college fellows could draw life-time incomes without performing any duties, was to limit fellowships to six years.* In retrospect what is important about the period to 1882 is Neville's failure to build on his achievement as senior moralist. When the time came for him to quit Pembroke he had written nothing. As a result, his career choices were limited.

It is not easy to establish what went wrong. Although his highest marks were achieved in logic, he decided, under Marshall's influence, to specialise in economics. Twenty years later Marshall still regarded Neville as one of the two or three best students he had ever had. Marshall encouraged him to enter for the university's newly established Cobden Prize, even though the set topic, 'The Effects of Machinery on Wages' was uncongenial to him. The

---

* Existing fellows had a choice between continuing as fellows under the old statutes, provided they stayed unmarried, or putting themselves under the new ones. Certain college jobs, like that of treasurer, would also qualify for extended tenure. (See Phyllis Deane, *The Life and Times of J. Neville Keynes*, pp. 44–56.)

prize went to Joseph Shield Nicholson, who got a chair in Edinburgh on the strength of it. Failure to win the prize must have been a damaging blow to Neville's self-confidence.

Marshall's departure to the University College of Bristol in 1877 – he had had to resign his fellowship at St John's on his marriage to his student Mary Paley – took Neville away from economics, and he started lecturing on logic at a number of colleges, as well as the two new women's halls of residence, Girton and Newnham. This brought him into contact with the strange new species of women undergraduates just starting to establish itself at Cambridge. (Women were officially admitted to the tripos examinations in 1881, but not allowed to take their degrees till 1947.) One of the by-products of the higher education of women was the academic marriage. Marshall set the trend; and Neville followed in his footsteps. He was strongly attracted to women, and in particular to one of his students, the flirtatious Fanny Hoyle, who, however, proved too unstable to be a suitable marriage partner.

In October 1878, the seventeen-year-old Florence Ada Brown, eldest daughter of the Rev. John Brown, came to Newnham Hall. Seventy-three years later, on her ninetieth birthday, she recalled the experience in a BBC interview:

> Well, in those days Newnham was a Hall of Residence for only about thirty students. Our principal was Miss Clough – a great personality. She had been encouraged by Cambridge friends to become a pioneer of University education for women. And naturally she was most anxious that her flock should be well behaved.... For example, she wished us to be inconspicuous in our dress. But, unfortunately for poor dear Miss Clough, we were rather taken with the pre-Raphaelite style. And we liked to trail about in gowns of peacock blue and terracotta and orange.... Instead of being inconspicuous, we were observed of all observers![21]

Florence was the youngest of Miss Clough's charges: 'I came up feeling very shy and inexperienced.' But she did go out occasionally, under chaper-oned conditions, and one such occasion was a party at the hospitable house of the Bonds in Brookside. William Bond, a successful local grocer, knew John Brown, and was keeping a friendly eye on his daughter. His son, Henry Bond, had been through Amersham Hall and University College London with Neville, and was now, like him, a Cambridge graduate; his sister Annie had hopes of Neville. It was at Brookside that Neville and Florence met for the first time in December 1978. Emerging from the dream – which had turned into a nightmare – of his infatuation with Fanny Hoyle, Neville was open to a new attack of love. On 20 May 1880, he proposed to Florence, and she accepted.

III. FLORENCE ADA BROWN

The arrival of Florence at Newnham was a tribute to the power of Nonconformity to overcome the widespread Victorian prejudice against the education of women. Florence Ada, the eldest daughter of John Brown and Ada
Haydon Ford, was born in Manchester on 10 March 1861. Three years later
John Brown moved to Bedford with his wife and small daughter, to become
minister of Bunyan Meeting. Alice, Jessie, Walter, Harold and Kenneth were
added to the family later, Kenneth not until 1879.

At the Manse in Dame Alice Street, Bedford, a 'high standard of moral
and intellectual effort' was demanded of both sexes, such effort being helped
by the rigour of the environment. In her family memoir, Florence recalled a
big, draughty house, almost without heating, but filled with relics of John
Bunyan, one of the first ministers of the Bedford Meeting. In the winter the
River Ouse froze; so did the soap in the dish. The bedroom floors felt like
ice, and there were no eiderdowns or hot-water bottles.[22]

To make up for the lack of heating there were books and sermons.
Literary, political and theological interests flourished on both sides of the
family. Florence's father, John Brown, despite an increasingly patriarchal
appearance, was a companionable scholar, a man of reason, who quelled his
own religious doubts by extensive lecturing and research on the history and
doctrine of Nonconformity. His talks on Bunyan were expanded into a
popular biography, published in 1885. A fine preacher, he became the
Nonconformist 'bishop' of the area. Maynard Keynes's brother Geoffrey
remembered him 'in his pulpit high above the congregation, with his white
pointed beard, healthy pink face, and piercing blue eyes, preaching in his
silvery voice to a rapt audience below'.[23] A convinced and active Liberal in
politics, he would entertain his family with dramatic readings from Gladstone's speeches as Chancellor of the Exchequer.

Florence herself was a 'sadly delicate and nervous child' of whom
sympathetic friends would say 'her mother can never hope to rear her'.[24]
Her childhood was punctuated by intimations of mortality, as a succession
of aunts passed away, with much solemnity and prolonged mourning, to
higher things. There was a constant reminder, too, of duties to the poor in
the long row of almshouses which faced the Manse. Ada Haydon Brown was
busy in the London Missionary Society, the Charity Organisation Society
and Liberal politics. Like that of many late Victorians, Florence's sense of
social obligation would prove more durable than her religious faith.

It was above all her mother who placed Florence in a position to meet
the young don from Pembroke. A woman of 'active mind, unbounded energy

and a full share of her mother's passion for education',[25] Ada Brown set up a school in the Manse to give her daughters the education they could not otherwise have had.

With some outside help in languages and mathematics, Ada Brown was able to get her daughter through the Cambridge Local Examination well enough for her to gain a small exhibition at Newnham Hall to study for the Higher Local Examination – similar to modern A levels – to prepare her for teaching at her mother's school. By this time she in turn was helping her mother run Bunyan Meeting Sunday School. She may have come to Newnham shy and inexperienced, but as the eldest daughter of the Manse she had already tasted responsibility.

It is difficult to know Florence in the way one feels one can know Neville. Her long life stretches out before us as dry and factual as the two books she wrote in her old age on Cambridge and on the Brown–Keynes connection, the two circles in which she passed it. The facts and achievements are all there: but the personality behind them has been carefully hidden away. Obituaries of her are mainly catalogues of committees. Florence's energies and interests were too ample to be confined to the home. She came from a family devoted to improvement – their own and the world's. Her era, coinciding with the growth of public and voluntary philanthropy, gave her much more scope than her mother had had for participation in public affairs.

But this picture of the energetic public woman forever in pursuit of good causes does not give the right impression of her personality. She was clearly a woman who charmed and persuaded rather than bullied her colleagues. All her work, one local correspondent wrote on her death, 'was done with such graciousness and kindliness that everyone found it a pleasure to work with her'. To her children, noted *The Times'* obituarist, she was 'both a mother and a companion'. Florence was not the kind of mother whose love of humanity is so intense that she has no time for her family. She was not demonstrative in her affection, but left no doubt that her first loyalty was to her husband and her children.

There was something else which was to be very important in Maynard's relationship with her. Florence had been bred in a hard school. Like many English women of Nonconformist background, her sympathies and tastes were high-minded but narrow. Whole areas of aesthetic and emotional life were beyond her range. Yet she obstinately refused to become a period piece. She made her children's interests her own. More than Neville, whose flame flickered earlier than hers, she grew into the twentieth century with them. This enabled her to transcend her Victorianism – even to bridge, in an extraordinary way, the gulf between the Bedford Manse and Bloomsbury. It was because she could grow up with her children that they never outgrew home.

IV. A VICTORIAN ENGAGEMENT

About one-third of the pages of Neville's diary for 1881–2 have been torn out. The missing and mutilated record covers the period of Neville's transition from young bachelor don to prosperous paterfamilias, a veritable valley of despair, with Florence alone beckoning him on and up to safety.

Neville's father John Keynes died from stomach cancer in February 1878. He left assets worth over £40,000 – a substantial sum in those days. Of this, Neville's share came to £17,000, his sister Fanny's to £12,000. His widow, Anna, got £12,000 in a trust, plus the Salisbury house, the Keynes share in the Nurseries, and other businesses, which were sold off.[26] With an unearned income of about £800 a year, Neville was free to embark on marriage in substantial middle-class style – which meant a spacious home and an adequate supply of servants.

Soon after their engagement was announced, in May 1880, Florence passed her Higher Local Examination,* and went back to Bedford to help her mother run the School. There she continued to live until she married Neville two years later. He went to Bedford, less than an hour away by train, once every three weeks. She came to Cambridge occasionally to see him, staying at Brookside with the Bonds. They spent vacations together either at Bedford or at Salisbury.

For much of their courtship Neville was acutely depressed. Part of the cause was physical. On top of the toothaches which continued to plague him, he experienced headaches and colds which brought on attacks of acute hypochondria, against which he struggled in vain.[27] He was convinced that Florence was about to tie herself to an invalid whom she would have to nurse over an inevitably brief married life[28] – that is, if she herself survived. 'She is so often very poorly', his mother confided in him; 'she must be most delicate. I can't help sometimes feeling anxious about this – particularly as you are not strong. Still we must hope for the best.'[29] Anna Keynes and Neville were very close to each other. She wrote to him in 1882, 'You are *everything* to me. I thank God for such a son. You *do* make up in a great degree what I have lost in your beloved Father.'[30] To his disappointment at not being able to express his love for his mother adequately was now added the guilt of deserting her to get married. This was not helped by the fact that Anna Keynes found Florence unsympathetic. For her part Florence vetoed a proposal that his mother should come

* Florence did not take the tripos, even unofficially, as Mary Paley had done. She was not, therefore, a 'graduate' of Newnham.

to live with them after they got married.[31] As a properly educated girl Florence probably found Anna Keynes frivolous and more than a little uncultivated, being entirely devoid of the intellectual interests and social concerns which flourished on both sides of her own family. Not till the summer of 1881 were there signs that Anna Keynes was becoming reconciled to Neville's engagement, and to Florence herself.[32] In the winter of 1881–2 mother and son went on a farewell holiday together in France and Italy, Neville finding Monte Carlo 'the most delightful spot on the Riviera'.[33] The trip, he concluded on their return, 'had been a great satisfaction to me in so far as I have been with her, & have been able a little, I think, to manifest my love towards her'.[34]

Meetings with, and letters from, Florence, while often delightful, sometimes bred the suspicion that her love for him was not as passionate or constant as it should be. Such thoughts induced the despairing reflection that he was unworthy of her. At other times they made him angry and critical. She was unfeeling, fickle, ungrateful. On holiday in the summer of 1881 he treated her 'like a brute'.[35] Florence responded with spirit – 'Yes, you *are* a critical person. . . . I must make a study of your character in order to find out exactly what it is that makes continual criticism endurable'[36] – while doing her best to reassure him: 'You talk as if any discovery I might make of shortcomings might possibly alter my love for you. Why, it wd only give me an extra reason for hoping that you wd not be too hard on mine. I love you & always shall.'[37] Florence herself was torn by a conflict of loyalties between Neville whom she loved and her family and work in Bedford. But she was never in danger of drowning in his flood of despair. Inexperienced as she was, she sensed that she was the stronger, and that her task in marriage would be to nurse not his body but his confidence.

> I too do sometimes have misgivings, but I am not fond of gloomy thoughts – I have a way of putting them off for consideration at another opportunity and meanwhile they generally vanish. My misgivings always arise from a contemplation of myself and my powers. At times I have such a scorn for this self, that I think it only natural & fitting that you shd have the same feelings towards it – and that I don't like. These are the thoughts that I think better on the whole to put to one side, for I believe a morbid investigation into oneself hinders growth rather than helps it. . . .[38]

Although to the outside world Neville would appear as the competent man of business, it was Florence who would keep the partnership afloat.

Not only did Neville's relations with Florence keep him agitated, there was also the uncertainty surrounding his future career. It was during the engagement that Neville revealed to Florence what she came to regard as his main fault: lack of ambition. When they became engaged she had reason to believe that he was destined to climb to the top of the academic ladder. But it was not to be. Early in their engagement he took a career decision which was to prove decisive, though it need not have been. By the time they got engaged it had become clear that his fellowship would expire in 1882 under the new statutes – six years after his appointment. There were no academic jobs to be had immediately at Cambridge. But there was a job in university administration. In 1858 the University had set up a Local Examinations Syndicate or Committee to set and mark examination papers for grammar schoolboys. In 1873 another Syndicate had been set up to organise extramural lectures, as part of the University Extension Movement. The two syndicates had a single secretary, but each one had a separate assistant-secretary. At the beginning of 1881 the assistant-secretaryship of Examinations fell vacant. Most of his friends advised Keynes not to apply for it, but to concentrate on getting an academic job. A professorship in economics was going at University College London, following the death of W. S. Jevons. Marshall supplied him with a glowing reference, which even allowing for the exaggeration customary in such exercises shows the high hopes he had of him. When Neville was offered the administrative job, however, he decided to withdraw his application for the professorship, which went to Foxwell. His decision disappointed Florence.[39] The later successes of her children, especially Maynard, were to give her the pleasure which she never really got from Neville's career; while Neville, who had a superb, but unambitious, mind, was able to encourage his children without competing with them.

With a job in Cambridge came the need to find a Cambridge home. They decided to buy one about to be built in Harvey Road, as part of a new 'development' for married dons. Plans were approved in November 1881, and the house rose steadily through the winter and spring, signalling the start of a new life.

The marriage was set to coincide with the end of his Pembroke fellowship in 1882. Neville was becoming more pleased with the Browns. 'At last Jessie & I kiss each other as sisters & brother ought to do,' he noted in February 1882. He confessed he was growing very fond of Walter,[40] found the baby Kenneth 'engaging'[41] and was enjoying Mr Brown's preaching more and more. He found it restful.[42]

John Brown wrote to Florence that Neville was a 'dear good fellow' and that he was quite reconciled to her going. Florence had 'fits of hysterical crying',[43] and Ada Brown could not stop crying either.[44] There was much weeping in Salisbury too. On 17 July 1882 it was 'good-bye to Mother & Aunt Mary. I fear that to both it seems like the breaking up of the Salisbury home. But I trust that Mother at any rate will gain more than she loses by my marriage.' Anna Keynes's deepest feelings came out in a letter she wrote to Neville just after the wedding, in which she discussed coming to live in Cambridge:

Then again I shd get to know more of Florence. Like yourself she is very reticent, so that I cannot *quite* understand her. I am quite certain she does appreciate kindness – still one wd like a little more expression of it – and no doubt it will come in time. You know dear Neville what a loving and affectionate husband your dear Father was – all that love & affection I miss terribly – and the more so as time goes on – and this perhaps makes me more sensitive. Do you think that Florence wd be pleased for me to live in Cambridge? She has never *said* she shd like me to do so – neither has Mrs. Brown.... Now all this is between ourselves dearest Neville. It will all come right, I know, still.... I feel it a good opportunity just to say what I have all along felt. You know how much I rejoice in your happiness, and after all this is more to me than anything personal.[45]

As the wedding approached, Neville and Florence clung to each other for support. She affirmed her love in passionate prose;[46] he affirmed his in despondent verse.[47] She urged him not to harp on his unworthiness. He wrote, 'My darling one! But she does not know yet all she may have to suffer for my sake!'[48] On 12 August he ceased to be a fellow of Pembroke. But for 'misgivings, hard to vanquish or control' his happiness would have been complete. 'My dearest maiden will very soon be my darling wife. If only I can keep tolerably well....'[49]

Panic-stricken to the end, Neville led Florence to the altar on 15 August 1882. The ceremony in Bedford was very much a Brown occasion. The service, conducted by Florence's father, was 'deeply affecting by reason of its earnestness and simplicity'. (The bride, wearing a dress of ivory satin brocade, was an inch and a half taller than the bridegroom.) They then went to Switzerland for their honeymoon.

Their marriage lasted sixty-seven years, until Neville died in 1949 aged ninety-seven. To all appearances it was a perfect love-match. On the fourteenth anniversary of his wedding, Neville wrote in his diary: 'We are happier together.... than we have ever been before. But indeed all our married life has been a continuous period of happiness.' Three years later he wrote: 'Every year I congratulate myself more and more on the remarkable wisdom & foresight I shewed in the selection of my wife.' And indeed it is easy to believe that, without Florence's rocklike support and moral strength, the iron discipline which kept Neville at his work would have disintegrated long before it did. Whether Neville was an ideal husband for someone of Florence's temperament is less certain. As his life became gently becalmed, her ambitions inexorably transferred themselves from her husband to her sons.

Back in England from their honeymoon, they bought furnishings for their new home.[50] They slept their first night at 6 Harvey Road on 11 November 1882. By this time Florence, 'troubled with sickness more or less all day', had been told by her mother, 'what *was* the matter with her. We were both surprised.'[51] Now they were entranced by thoughts of parent-hood. On 18 February 1883: 'We are so happy. Are we *too* happy? Do we need the discipline of suffering? We think & talk a good deal about "the little mortal".'

On 5 June 1883, labour began at 3 a.m. Neville reported to his mother:

> At 9.30 I went & listened outside the door ... Florence was giving a slight groan every now & then (they say she was very brave) & at 9.45 I heard such a hullabaloo & Mrs. Brown just came to the door, & said that it was a boy. (This was rather a blow – I had wanted a girl – but I think *you* will be satisfied).... They say that the boy is the image of me. It's ugly enough.... Now what do you think of *John Maynard* for a name? That is what we propose....

John Brown wrote from Bedford, 'I like the name suggested – John Maynard Keynes sounds like the substantial name of the solid hero of a sensible novel.'[52]

2

Cambridge Civilisation: Sidgwick and Marshall

I. THE CRISIS IN AUTHORITY

Maynard Keynes was born into a certain civilisation at a particular moment of history, and was one of its foremost products. He inherited both its aspirations and its tensions. He grew up in the shadow of its great figures, notably Henry Sidgwick and Alfred Marshall, the teachers and colleagues of his father. His style of thought and way of life both bear Cambridge's unmistakable imprint. Roy Harrod, his first biographer, often talks about the 'presuppositions of No. 6 Harvey Road'. But the presuppositions of Cambridge civilisation are more fundamental. Much of Keynes's life will not make sense unless this inheritance is set out.

Intellectual life in Victorian Cambridge was shaped by the crisis and eventual decline of religious belief. The 1860s were the decade when Cambridge men lost their religious faith: Edward Carpenter, Leslie Stephen, Henry Sidgwick, Alfred Marshall, Arthur Balfour were all from the 'doubting class' of the 1860s. The decade opened with the consequences of Darwin's *Origin of Species*, published in 1859, and closed with the results of the Second Reform Act of 1867. Occurring more or less simultaneously, the death of God and the birth of mass democracy wonderfully concentrated men's minds on the problems of personal conduct and social order.

The Victorian order rested on Evangelical religion and social deference. On the rock of these 'givens', the English and Scottish thinkers of the Enlightenment had erected political, moral and economic philosophies based on the sovereignty of the individual, his interests and choices. They never imagined that these interests and choices would be worked out other than in the framework of Christendom, would be other than constrained and harmonised by the existing social structure. The threatened breakdown of this protective system left them with nothing but their individualism to fall back on; and they were immediately faced with an adding-up problem. What guarantee was there that the sum of individual choices would result in a desirable social outcome? What assurance was there – heavenly rewards having been eliminated – that individual happiness would coincide with social duty?

Of all the institutions, the ancient universities were the most directly affected by the crisis of Christian belief. Their intellectual activity had consisted largely of theological, or theologically based, speculation. They provided the Established Church with its clergymen. They were thus an integral support of the inherited social order. But how could they continue to perform their social function in a situation in which theology was losing its power to do moral and political work, and in which their graduates no longer sought careers in the Church – or at least in such profusion?

Such questions dominated the movement for university reform. One response was the opening of the universities to Dissenters, as a result of which Neville Keynes himself had got established at Cambridge. The fundamental motive for this was conservative – to prevent the emergence of a rival, or dissident, intellectual class. In this it was successful: with the exception of the small group of Fabians, no one who had not been to Oxford or Cambridge made much impact on English thought over the next sixty years; in great contrast to the previous sixty years, when most of the seminal intellectuals were outside the university world. Undoubtedly, the relatively inclusive character of the English notion of a gentleman helped this consolidation of intellectual property. No one would have called Neville Keynes anything but a gentleman, although his father had started work aged eleven as an apprentice brushmaker.

However, the unification of the intellectual class was only part of the answer to the decline of religion. What was required from it, or what many of its leading members set out to supply, was authoritative doctrine – authoritative in the sense of being able to command what Sidgwick called the 'unconstrained consent' of experts. Initially the task of producing such doctrine was left to philosophy, and particularly moral philosophy. It was moral philosophy which was expected to provide true beliefs for a secular age.

There were two main traditions in moral philosophy for the post-theological intellectuals to draw on: Intuitionism and Utilitarianism. Both had theological roots, but were capable of non-theological development, because both started with an appeal to human reason. The simplest way of distinguishing them is to say that Intuitionism claimed that certain ways of acting were right or wrong, whatever their results might be, whereas Utilitarianism said that conduct must be judged by results: good results being, in the Benthamite or hedonist version of Utilitarianism, results which increased human happiness. Two different aspects of human reason were thus being appealed to: in the first case, what might loosely be called conscience; in the second case, calculation. Both presupposed certain kinds of knowledge: Intuitionism, moral knowledge produced by a moral faculty; Utilitarianism, knowledge of consequences. A philosophy based on good motives confronted one which wanted good results.

This philosophic disagreement had considerable political implications.

Utilitarianism had a radical edge. Institutions or practices must be swept away or reformed if they failed to pass the test of utility. It was the natural creed of those outside the Establishment. By contrast, Intuitionism was Establishment doctrine. As William Paley, an early Utilitarian, saw it, any system of morality built on innate ideas 'will find out reasons and excuses for opinions and practices already established'. This was certainly John Stuart Mill's view, too. He called Intuitionism 'the great intellectual support of false doctrines and bad institutions'. By its aid, he wrote, 'every inveterate belief and every intense feeling, of which the origin is not remembered, is enabled to dispense with the obligation of justifying itself by reason'.[1] On their side leading Cambridge Intuitionists such as Adam Sedgwick and William Whewell, both of Trinity College, regarded the London-based Benthamites as dangerous subversives. To Sedgwick, Utilitarianism prepared men for 'violent and ill-timed inroads on the social system, and the perpetration of daring crimes'. To William Whewell, it destroyed the 'reverence which, handed down by the tradition of ... moral and religious teaching, had hitherto protected the accustomed forms of moral good'.[2] These polemics must not be taken too seriously: philosophical debate took place within the framework of a constitutional settlement which was generally acceptable, and within a theological tradition 'broad' (or exiguous) enough to satisfy most reasonable men. There was no real equivalent in nineteenth-century England to the Continental polarisation between reactionaries and liberals, clericals and anti-clericals. Intellectual energy which in much of the rest of Europe went into fighting for the forms of popular rule could in England be mobilised to limit its consequences.

In fact, the philosophical differences between the two schools could be resolved readily enough once their social perceptions had changed. After the middle of the nineteenth century intellectual Nonconformity, the main source of Utilitarian thinking, was being absorbed into the Establishment. Naturally the view from the inside was more attractive than the view from the outside. On the other hand, Intuitionists, seeing their theological supports crumbling, were more ready to accept the support of some overriding principle to which their Pandora's box of 'intuitions' could be related. Both sides were worried by the social question. In addition, historical, sociological and legal studies helped to bring the two views closer together, by emphasising the functional character of many institutions and customs which the earlier Enlightenment philosophers had been disposed to dismiss as mere superstitions. The result was the famous Victorian compromise, by which Intuitionists were persuaded to accept utility as the final test of doctrine and conduct; while Utilitarians agreed that existing social arrangements had some Utilitarian justification after all. By means of this philosophical merger the characteristic English tradition of improving conservatism received its adequate intellectual justification, and was able successfully to negotiate the industrial age. Even the working-class movement was compelled to pursue its political and industrial goals within a framework of ideas largely (though not exclusively) supplied by these intellectual representatives of property.

Yet the intellectual synthesis between the rival philosophical traditions was by no means perfect. Philosophic agreement was possible so long as the subject matter of discussion was society. The difficulty lay in the relationship between social and individual conduct. In the end it proved impossible to combine social and moral philosophy within a consistent non-theological framework of ideas. Social philosophy could not do without Utilitarianism; moral philosophy found it difficult to live with it.

To understand the way the difficulty presented itself one must recall certain features of the Victorian age. Put briefly, many aspects of Victorian life afforded the thinking person neither aesthetic satisfaction nor personal happiness. On the one hand, the division of labour between cultural and non-cultural activities had become much sharper. The old gentlemanly culture, which had included learning and the arts, now stood sharply opposed to the much expanded world of business, money-making, and politics. On the other hand, a generalised Puritan ethic had succeeded the morally more relaxed conditions of the eighteenth century; this made much greater moral demands on the individual in the name of social duty. On both counts Victorian civilisation paid a high price in cultural impoverishment and psychic strain for its material achievements and its social stability. Once theology ceased to provide for the thinking Victorian an axiomatic connection between morals and social requirements the tension between the ideals of civilised living and the 'needs' of society, between personal happiness and social obligation, came out into the open.

These tensions were at the heart of the university reform movement. The problem as it presented itself to the reformers was how to maintain cultural standards *and* serve the needs of a society organised round money-making. The solution adopted was to admit a more representative elite, but to educate it in the old gentlemanly culture.[3] Greek was kept as a compulsory entrance requirement; the curriculum, based on classics and (at Cambridge) mathematics, remained sternly non-vocational. By these means the universities ensured both that they would not be swamped by the sons of businessmen and (more importantly) that their graduates would not go into business life. Previously most of them had become clergymen. Now they went into education, public service and the learned professions. The upshot was to place at the head of British public life in the first half of the twentieth century men whose education had left them quite uncontaminated by knowledge of industrial society, and with an ingrained dislike of the profit motive. Whether this proved good or bad for Britain is still endlessly debated.[4] It had also, to a lesser extent, given Britain a ruling class which regarded public life as a diversion from more valuable private pursuits.

The growing feeling that private life should be distanced from public life, and was in some sense opposed to it, wrecked the philosophic attempt to reconcile the two. Specifically it destroyed John Stuart Mill's attempt to combine social and moral philosophy under the unifying principle of utility. In one sense, Mill was successful. Setting out to provide a 'unifying social doctrine' by incorporating the 'major positive views' of his Intuitionist critics,[5] he succeeded in giving Utilitarian justifications for many current social practices. Where Mill was much less successful was in linking his social doctrine with his morals.

Mill's *Autobiography* is a brilliant dissection of Victorianism's mid-life crisis. It raised two problems which are vital for understanding the Cambridge civilisation of Keynes's day. First, how is one to reconcile the claims of personal happiness and social duty when the two diverge? And is happiness or pleasure an adequate aim for human conduct? Are there not some things worth doing, some dispositions worth cultivating, which are valuable in themselves, irrespective of any Utilitarian justifications they might have? Is it not better to be Socrates dissatisfied than a fool satisfied?

What Mill succeeded in doing was to make Cambridge Benthamite in that aspect of its thought which related to social policy. Mill's Utilitarianism, Cambridge mathematics and Cambridge's Nonconformist conscience were the chief constituents in what became the Cambridge School of Economics, whose founder was Alfred Marshall. What Mill failed to do was to make Cambridge moral philosophy Benthamite. Henry Sidgwick, Marshall's great contemporary, tried but failed to repair Mill's breaches in the Benthamite fortress. His failure left the way open for G. E. Moore, drawing on certain other features of the Cambridge tradition, to construct a Cambridge School of Moral Philosophy which was anti-Benthamite. Social and moral philosophy as Cambridge conceived them had come apart and were never put back together again. Maynard Keynes spent his life zigzagging between the two.

II. THE CAMBRIDGE SETTING

In the context which interests us the two dominant figures in late Victorian Cambridge were Henry Sidgwick and Alfred Marshall. They were near contemporaries, Sidgwick being born in 1838, Marshall in 1842. They both taught for the moral sciences tripos. Sidgwick became Professor of Moral Philosophy in 1882. Marshall became Professor of Political Economy in 1885. Both inherited the problems of a collapsing theology and both engaged in essentially the same enterprise: the attempt to find authoritative theology-substitutes. Both realised that this attempt had to come to terms with the Victorian mood. Like Mill, they were both compromisers and synthesisers. But whereas Sidgwick's efforts were conceived in the sphere of ethics, Marshall concentrated his on a branch of applied ethics, which he took economics to be. This difference is accounted for by differences in intellectual equipment and temperament. Sidgwick was a classicist; Marshall was a mathematician. The loss of religious belief was also a much greater personal shock to Sidgwick than it was to Marshall. Sidgwick's ambition was thus the greater. It was nothing less than to attempt to substitute a secular philosophy for theology as the scientific foundation of all social and individual conduct. Marshall quickly realised that this attempt was doomed to failure. Economics, he saw, had a far greater potential for scientific development if it was detached from moral philosophy. In terms of the organisation of Cambridge studies this disagreement led to the long-drawn-out battle Marshall waged against Sidgwick to liberate economics from the moral sciences tripos, a battle which he won only after Sidgwick's death. Sidgwick lost the intellectual as well as the institutional battle. His *Methods of Ethics* (1874) was widely recognised, not least by himself, to have fallen short of the goals he had set, whereas Marshall's *Principles of Economics* (1890) was immediately accepted as authoritative. Yet Sidgwick's failure was by no means so complete as to deter others from attempting to place ethics on a scientific basis. For many intellectuals brought up on Christianity still felt the need for authoritative guidance on how to conduct their lives – which they did not get from economics.

Sidgwick was a man of considerable parts: the trouble was they did not fit. He spent his life trying to work out a philosophy which would make them do so; and failed. His contradictions could be reconciled only in eternity; and eternity was the one thing Sidgwick could not believe in. He was Carlyle's typical Victorian intellectual, 'devoid of faith, and terrified of scepticism'.

Born the son of an Anglican clergyman, Sidgwick took a double first in classics and mathematics at Cambridge in 1858. He became a fellow of Trinity College at a time when Mill's influence was at its height and when theology was in retreat. Not surprisingly he swallowed Mill's Utilitarianism and lost his faith, though not his need for it. Eventually he resigned his fellowship in 1869 after he found he could no longer subscribe to the Thirty-nine Articles of the Church of England. Sidgwick became one of the best-connected figures of his day, moving effortlessly – if not painlessly – between the several worlds of Victorian *Angst*. Through his sister's marriage to E. W. Benson, the future Archbishop of Canterbury, and his own to the sister of Arthur Balfour, the rising Conservative politician, he gained access to the worlds of high Anglicanism and high politics. But not even the Church and the Cecils in combination could tell him what he ought to do. The search for an answer to this question drove him into prodigies of inconclusive enquiry ranging from the Arabic language to investigation of psychic phenomena. In addition, he was deeply involved in the problems

of homosexual friends like John Addington Symonds, quoting poetry at
them and burning theirs. His mind is a window into the whole range of
Victorian infirmity.

This is certainly how he struck Maynard Keynes. In 1906 Keynes, who
had played golf occasionally with Sidgwick, wrote of him with wicked
accuracy: 'He never did anything but wonder whether Christianity was true
and prove that it wasn't and hope that it was.' To bring about a reconciliation
between private happiness and public duty Sidgwick felt he needed the
Christianity he could no longer believe in. When it came to the crunch he
would not sell his reason for a 'mess of mystical pottage'. But as a result
he remained, in his own words, a 'maimed intellect'.

Like Mill, Sidgwick thought that people ought to conduct their lives in
such a way as to promote the general happiness. But how could they be
justified in doing so at the expense of their own happiness? Then again
there were certain qualities, states of mind, ways of life he instinctively felt
were good or bad independently of whether they increased or diminished
his own, or the world's, happiness. These dilemmas are set forth formally,
but not satisfactorily resolved, in Sidgwick's *Methods of Ethics* published in
1874. The three 'methods' for reaching ethical judgements he calls Rational
Egoism, Intuitionism and Rational Benevolence.

Sidgwick called the relation between Rational Egoism (aiming at my own
happiness) and Rational Benevolence (aiming at the universal happiness) the
'profoundest problem of Ethics'. He thought that people ought to act in
accordance with the latter. But he could not persuade himself that it would
make them happy to do so. He wrote that 'the inseparable connection
between Utilitarian Duty and the greatest happiness of the individual who
conforms to it cannot satisfactorily be demonstrated on empirical grounds'.
The reason was that there was no 'empirical' evidence for the existence
of God. Divine sanctions 'would, of course, suffice to make it always in
everyone's interest to promote universal happiness to the best of his knowledge'.[6]

Sidgwick felt he had made more progress in resolving the second
dilemma, that between the claims of intuition and rational calculation.
Intuitionism, he said, was not opposed to Utilitarianism since the things we
think of as good also tend to make the world a happier place. Thus most of
our intuitive moral judgements and the moral rules deriving from them
could also be defended on utilitarian grounds.

Having established that immortality is a necessary condition of a coherent ethical system, Sidgwick spent much of the remainder of his life trying
to discover empirical evidence for its existence. He attempted to get in touch
with the dead, accepting the presidency of the Society for Psychical
Research. Unfortunately, the main result of these researches was 'a considerable enlargement of my conceptions of the possibilities of human credulity'.[7]
His election to the Knightbridge chair of moral philosophy at Cambridge in

1883 led to a mental crisis which is captured in the following excerpt from his journal:

> 28 January 1886:
> I have been facing the fact ... that we have not, and are never likely to have, empirical evidence of the existence of the individual after death. Soon, therefore, it will probably be my duty as a reasonable being – and especially as a professional philosopher – to consider on what basis the human individual ought to construct his life under these circumstances. Some fifteen years ago, when I was writing my book on Ethics, I was inclined to hold with Kant that we must *postulate* the continued existence of the soul, in order to effect that harmony of Duty with Happiness which seemed to me indispensable to rational moral life. At any rate I thought I might *provisionally* postulate it, while setting out in the serious search for empirical evidence. If I decide that this search is a failure, shall I finally and decisively make this postulate? Can I [do so] consistently with my whole view of truth and the method of its attainment? And if I answer 'no' to each of these questions, have I any ethical system at all? And if not, can I continue to be Professor ...?[8]

Sidgwick's failure to prove his 'postulate' of immortality came at a particularly worrying moment. The economic reversals of the 1880s caused the ominous word 'unemployment' to appear for the first time in *The Oxford English Dictionary* in 1888. The coincidence of economic troubles with the further extension of the franchise to the working-class in 1884–5, the terrorism and mass disaffection in Ireland, the revival of socialism, and the appearance of demagogues such as Parnell, Joseph Chamberlain and Lord Randolph Churchill, all pointed to a new and highly disturbing era in which ignorance and madness would take the place of reason in politics. The following quotation from Sidgwick's journal of 1885–6 needs to be set against Roy Harrod's picture of confidence in a 'strongly upward' trend in England's material development:[9]

> 26 January 1885:
> Reading the growth of England's commercial greatness rouses a mixture of curiosity and patriotic anxiety; it seems clear that we are past all culmination, relatively speaking, and it would be contrary to all historical precedents that we should not go down hill; but will it be by destructive, disastrous shocks, or gradual painless decline? That, I fear, is the only question of practical importance; but who can answer it?

Despite his inability to build a system, Sidgwick had made Cambridge Benthamite in its social reasoning. Perhaps this development was always inevitable in a university which had aimed to turn out mathematical rather than classical curates. But it had important consequences. Only a philosophy based on a hedonistic calculus could provide exact reasoning about social policy: Alfred Marshall was a product of Sidgwick's Cambridge. On the other hand, Sidgwick left moral philosophy in a mess. Intuitionist ideas revived, with an admixture of Hegelianism, in the more dynamic form of Idealism. But its headquarters were at Oxford rather than Cambridge; its high priests the Oxford philosophers Bradley and T. H. Green. Cambridge had become too critical, too empirical, to accept its ethics in metaphysical form. The way was open for G. E. Moore to construct a Cambridge system detached from both Benthamism and metaphysics. Moore was as much a product of Sidgwick's failure as was Marshall.

If Sidgwick transmitted nothing but doubts to his students, Alfred Marshall gave his students a sense of mission. Marshall was the founder of English academic economics, giving it a new scientific and moral authority which equipped it to take over at least part of the political work which theology had done, and which philosophy could not do.

Marshall was yet another product of the well-connected clerical families which colonised English intellectual life. At school he developed a flair for mathematics. This meant Cambridge, not Oxford, and in 1865 he graduated as second wrangler. The study of mathematics, however, had not yet interfered with his own or his family's plans for his ordination; and, as Maynard Keynes remarked in his beautifully written memorial of Marshall, 'the double character of scientist and preacher clung to him for the rest of his life'. Both played a part in moulding the Cambridge tradition of economics. The familiar crisis of religious doubt occurred only in the mid-1860s, and coincided with his first contacts with the Sidgwick circle, but 'after a quick struggle his religious beliefs dropped away and he became ... an agnostic'.[10] Marshall never felt he needed Christianity to support his ethics. He simply redirected his energies from the service of God to the service of economics. Walking through the slums and looking at the faces of the people, he convinced himself that morality is largely a function of economic circumstances, the betterment of which was, therefore, the most important condition for moral improvement.

In order to get economics into a position where it could serve as an engine of moral progress much reconstruction needed to be done. Marshall began his life's work as an economist at a time when the scientific foundations of the subject were being knocked away. The centrepiece of classical value theory, the theory that the price of a good depends on its cost of production, had been challenged by Jevons, and others, in the name of subjective utility. Much more threatening to economics than the confusion (or profusion) of theory was the crisis of method. The claim of economics to be a science with its own laws invariant through time and place was challenged on the one side by sociologists who claimed that it gave only a very partial account of human behaviour, and on the other hand by the German historical school which argued that each epoch was subject to its own laws of development which could be uncovered only by history. These issues were fought out in an environment in which it was not exactly clear who was or who was not an economist. By the early 1870s it appeared to Foxwell 'as if science had been replaced by war of opinion'.[11]

The moral authority of economics was also at a low ebb. The classical political economy founded by Adam Smith and his followers was out of tune with Victorian evangelicalism because it offered no scope for benevolent motives. Critics demanded the right to judge wealth-creating activities by ethical standards. Ethical concerns merged with political ones. The great Victorian moralists like Carlyle and Ruskin argued that social policy based on the teachings of classical economists would, by destroying existing social relations, produce anarchy and revolution. This touched a responsive Victorian chord.

Marshall was determined to restore order in the unruly universe of economics. In his inaugural lecture as professor of political economy at Cambridge, delivered in February 1885 and entitled 'The Present Condition of Economics', he set himself three tasks: to strengthen the scientific authority of economics; to align it with the Victorian moral and political mood; and to draw the best Cambridge men into the subject. For the twenty-three years of his occupancy of the Cambridge chair Marshall pursued them all as energetically as his hypochondria would allow.

Marshall was economics' greatest synthesiser. He reconciled the cost of production and subjective utility theories of value by his famous simile of the two blades of a pair of scissors, thus establishing continuity with the older doctrine whereas Jevons had sought revolution. He generalised the underlying proposition of value theory – that value is determined at the equilibrium point of demand and supply – to cover the theory of distribution and the theory of money, hitherto regarded as subject to separate laws. Marshall also played a key part in ending the methodological dispute. Economics was the science of 'measurable motives'. It claimed that there was an economic, or calculable, aspect to all activities, not that people's only aim was to increase their material wealth. He also nodded in the direction of the German historical school, though his own history was, according to J. S. Nicholson, 'vague, old-fashioned and excessively weak'.[12] Marshall's real originality lay in his treatment of time and partial equilibrium. This was to set Cambridge economics apart from all other schools. It allowed Maynard Keynes to conceive his 'general theory' forty years later. Finally, Marshall played a crucial role in making English economics a profession with a specialised training and agreed standards of performance. His main contribution to this end was to establish the Cambridge Economics Tripos in 1903.

Marshall achieved his second ambition – to align the reconstructed science with the ethical aspirations of the enlightened middle class – by inserting into his economics a theory of moral evolution. The agent of moral growth is no less than business life itself. Specifically, 'free industry and enterprise' are associated with the development of two sets of virtues:

energy, initiative, and enterprise; and rationality, frugality, industry, and honourable-dealing. Marshall also believed that improved material conditions automatically produced an improved – that is, more energetic and self-sacrificing – character-type, by having a direct effect on people's genes. The long-run effect of capitalism was to 'moralise' wants.

Marshall could not complain of being misunderstood. When his *Principles of Economics* appeared in 1890, its success, as Maynard Keynes wrote, was 'immediate and complete'.

Marshall's aim of attracting 'fresh strong beautiful youthful minds' to the study of economics was also eventually realised. By the 1920s over 200 Cambridge students were reading economics, by the 1980s there were 450.

Through Marshall's life and work the Victorian demand for authoritative social doctrine found one of its most important expressions in the Cambridge School of Economics. Maynard Keynes's relationship to that tradition is one of the central themes of this biography. That relationship was never unproblematic, because Marshall's achievement was incomplete. He had shown how the existing moral code could be made to serve society rather than God. But there was nothing in his work to show how it could be altered so as to make it possible for individuals to lead happier or more civilised lives. Marshall himself seems not to have felt any pressure to do so. But Sidgwick had; as had many other thinking Victorians. It was the reorganisation of personal life rather than the reorganisation of society which seemed the urgent problem for the next generation, especially once the social and economic clouds of the 1880s and 1890s had given way to the bright sunlight of the Edwardian age.

3

Growing up in Cambridge

I. 6 HARVEY ROAD

Born on 5 June 1883, Maynard Keynes was the first of three children: a sister, Margaret, was born on 4 February 1885, and a brother, Geoffrey, on 25 March 1887. He grew up at 6 Harvey Road, a house 'without charm or character'.[1] It was part of a new housing development for young married dons, on land owned by Caius College, then on the outskirts of the town. It was double-fronted, bay-windowed and depressing, of dark yellow brick – 'corpse bricks' as the children called them – and stood on four floors including the basement. The house was comfortable, but not excessively large, considering that with all the staff nine or ten people had to live in it.

The year Maynard was born, Neville bought the house next door, the idea being that his mother might come to live there. This plan did not materialise, Florence dreading the 'implicit criticisms on small matters which Mother does rather keep on about'.[2] Instead, Anna Keynes moved to Sidney Villa in nearby Bateman Street in 1885. Most Sundays Neville would take the children to have tea with her, falling happily asleep himself. Much later he colonised one room of the ground floor of 5 Harvey Road as his study, the rest of the house being let to academic families. His property acquisitions continued with the purchase of 55 Bateman Street, next door to his mother's, for £1070 in 1895.

There was nothing in the Keynes family home to stimulate the aesthetic sensibilities. Neville's father had bought pictures in Salisbury, but with the exception of a small George Morland they were unremarkable, even by Victorian standards. Florence and Neville rarely bought new ones, though in 1889 she hung an engraving by Fred Walker called *A Rainy Day* in the drawing room.[3] Nor was music then part of their lives, except for an occasional visit to a Gilbert and Sullivan, though Neville later collected records of operatic arias.

In place of Art there was Nature. Harvey Road itself adjoined open country. Florence later wrote, 'My children looked from their nursery window across "Bulman's field", where the drovers kept their cattle over the week-end, ready for the Monday market, and the lowing of cows was a familiar sound. With the exception of the houses in Station Road there was, indeed, little or nothing between us and the Gogs [Magog Hills].'[4] To get from Harvey Road to the town one walked, or took the horse-drawn tram or a hansom cab. Unlike grander Cambridge families, such as the Jebbs, the Keyneses did not have a carriage. Bicycles came in in the 1880s, but the Keyneses did not acquire any till 1895 when Maynard was given a free-wheel one for his twelfth birthday. He promptly collided with a hansom cab, damaging his little finger.[5] His parents' efforts to master cycling a year later were not successful either, Neville finding it almost impossible to get on and off, and Florence forgetting to put the brakes on. She fell off her bicycle so often that Neville tried to stop her using it.[6]

Neville and Florence liked to escape from the family in July for a fortnight in Scotland or Switzerland. Then for August and part of September the whole family would set off, children, servants, relations, to Norfolk, Devon, Yorkshire or Cornwall, renting a house for six weeks. Christmases would be spent at the Manse, Bedford, where there would be skating on the frozen Ouse and full observance of the Sabbath. Neville enjoyed these visits to his in-laws provided they kept off politics and religion.

Like most middle-class Victorians the Keyneses read a lot. Reading novels was the main family entertainment, much of it done aloud and for the whole family, especially on holidays. They read the Victorian classics, but also lighter writers like Anthony Hope and Rider Haggard. Both Neville and Florence found French literature unedifying, but they thought *Anna Karenina* 'a wonderful book'.[7] Neville was an enthusiastic playgoer in Cambridge and London. But his taste was conventional. Although he found Ibsen's plays 'very interesting', he couldn't be an Ibsenite, finding it imposs-ible to justify Nora's desertion of her husband and children in *A Doll's House*.[8] Life was enough of a vale of tears as it was, and one looked to Art for uplift or escape, not to add to one's depression.

Apart from the odd visit to the theatre or pantomime families had to entertain themselves. They were saved from boredom not only by reading but by a multitude of games and hobbies. With Neville hobbies amounted to an obsession. Not least of his virtues as a father was the ability to enter into his children's interests and make them his own, without taking them over. As a young, unmarried don he had played chess and tennis. These continued, though less intensely. He started Harvey Road Book and Whist Clubs.[9] At the age of three, Maynard was showing an interest in stamps, and on 20 March 1887 we find the significant entry in Neville's diary: 'In my old age [he was thirty-four] I have actually begun stamp collecting again.' By 1895, he had 8000 stamps, which Maynard valued for him at £2000.[10] In the evenings at Harvey Road he would arrange them lovingly while Florence read to him. Every Sunday morning he would lay a pile of his rejects on his study table, allowing the children to choose one in turn till the pile was exhausted. 'Armed with a catalogue they studied the values carefully and chose accordingly. In this way they learnt how to use a catalogue and acquired a considerable knowledge of other countries,' commented Florence didactically.[11] On 3 August 1895 there is the first reference to butterflying with Geoffrey and Margaret. Geoffrey was to add to this entomological enthusiasm a passion for collecting and classifying bones; his father helping him with the knowledge he had acquired in preparing for the London BSc. This collecting trait was later to be extended by both brothers, though not by the father, to books. Margaret was more interested in handicrafts, painting and gardening.

From 1892 dates the start of Neville's greatest passion of all, one which was to dominate his middle age. On 20 September his friend Henry Bond initiated him and Florence into the mysteries of golf, at Sheringham, Norfolk, in the pouring rain. Neville's diary entry, listing an 'uncommon lot of foozlers', was the first of dozens of such, often of enormous length, in which he struggled with the problem of his recalcitrant swing in much the same spirit as other Victorians wrestled with sin, and equally unavailingly. Neville managed to get Maynard keen on golf, an interest which proved more enduring than stamps, Maynard continuing to play golf with his father till the First World War. In the 1890s they often went out together to the links at Royston, a few miles from Cambridge; Maynard played a round there with Henry Sidgwick a few weeks before Sidgwick's death in 1900. In the 1900s Maynard would accompany his father on golfing holidays.

In the holidays the whole family would collaborate to produce a newspaper. A succession of these ran through the 1890s. Maynard and his father were both fascinated by word games, especially puns. They enjoyed exchanging Spoonerisms. Like many children who have little aptitude for games, Maynard was entranced by them in their statistical aspect. He compiled lists of batting and bowling averages. In 1896 he spent every spare summer afternoon at Fenner's Cricket Ground, which adjoined Harvey Road, watching the University play. He and his father relentlessly kept their golf scores. The measurable aspect of activities fascinated them both.

Servants were a permanent, indispensable part of the background of this world. For most of Maynard's childhood, the Keyneses had three: a cook, a parlour maid and a nursery maid. Temporary reinforcements would arrive during Florence's confinements and after delivery. In 1892, a governess, Miss Laxton, made her appearance. She stayed for two years, and was followed by two German successors. Mostly we know the servants only as names as they passed through Harvey Road on their way to unknown fates.

The German governesses, Fräulein Rotman and Fräulein Hubbe, gave Maynard a good grounding in German, which was to prove indispensable to him when he came to write his *Treatise on Probability*. Maynard grew up in a pro-German household. This was not unusual, particularly in educated circles. Germany was still the home of philosophy and science, not of the jackboot. Florence had spent several months with a pastor in Bonn, a friend of Dr Brown's, just before going up to Newnham. Margaret and Geoffrey would also spend a year in Germany in their late teens. The Keyneses were not unusual, either, in holding the French in fairly low esteem. Traces of this early conditioning come through in Maynard's adult opinions.

The Keynes life-style was sustained by an income which was never less than comfortable, and grew more so. Marshall thought that a family man 'whose brain has to undergo continuous great strain' needed £500 a year at least.[12] Neville and Florence started married life with £1000. Of this £600 was income from Neville's inherited capital (part of which now included the two houses at Harvey Road which had cost just over £2000); £400 came from his stipend as assistant secretary for examinations, and the fees he received for lecturing and examining. Tax was paid at the less than punitive rate of sixpence in the pound. There were no dependants to support, Anna Keynes being amply provided for with an income which came to £700 in 1891.[13] Neville usually managed to save £400 a year to add to capital. Out of the £600 they spent annually they could afford two substantial holidays. The expenses of these were not great. It cost about £5 a week to rent a big farmhouse in the summer. In 1889, Neville and Florence spent ten days in Belgium for £23 10s inclusive. A month in Switzerland in 1891 cost them £68.

As Maynard grew up his parents became steadily more affluent. Capital and earnings went up, while prices went down. By the late 1880s the Keyneses' annual income averaged £1400, and their expenditure £1000. In 1892, when Neville became secretary for local examinations, his salary went up to £500; in 1896, to £775. Neville was a nervous manager of his money. In the late 1870s, as a bachelor of independent means, he had invested part of it with Frank Tiffin, his boyhood friend from Salisbury, and an underwriter at Lloyd's. But Tiffin proved unreliable, and Neville, finding that the profits from underwriting failed to balance the 'worry and anxiety' of it, withdrew.[14] On 30 June 1888 he felt very worried by the fall in the price of tin, in which he had speculated to the tune of £600. By 1900 his capital had grown to over £24,000. With his mother's death in 1907, he inherited more money, and by 1908 he had £38,000. His temperament was such that with every downturn he saw ruin staring him in the face. But what strikes one today is how secure his position was. He just went on getting richer and richer without any great effort on his part.

Neville found his wealth all the more agreeable because his enjoyment of it was unclouded by any sense of guilt. With his Baptist background he started as a conventional Liberal in politics, though without any great passion for Reform. He had breakfasted with Gladstone in 1878 and knew his mother would be 'glad that such a good thing has fallen my way'. But he was too pessimistic and anxious by nature to make a convinced Liberal.[15] He thought Gladstone's first Home Rule Bill 'a thoroughly bad Bill' and Chamberlain and Hartington 'excellent' in their arguments against it.[16] On 8 June 1886 he noted in his diary, 'My faith in Gladstone is shattered; and I fear my faith in democracy, which was never very strong, will be shattered also.' Like many other Cambridge academic Liberals he voted Tory in 1886. In the 1890s he would have described himself as a Liberal Unionist; in the 1900s as a Liberal Imperialist. But for a long time his deepest instincts had been conservative. In 1898 as well as in 1900 he allowed his name to go forward on the Conservative as well as the Liberal ticket for elections to the University Council. His references to socialists, socialism and working men became increasingly unsympathetic, though never cholerically so.

One important root of his conservatism was his love of ceremonial. He was moved by the pageantry of politics, not by the issues. He was also something of a social snob. Encounters with, or even close proximity to, aristocrats produced a warm glow of satisfaction. He wrote to the eight-year-old Maynard: 'We have had the honour of travelling in the same train as the Archduchess Valerie, daughter of the Emperor of Austria.'[17] This is typical of the sentiment such figures evoked in him. It is in sharp contrast to Maynard's own generally irreverent and mocking attitude to figures in authority. But Maynard had something of the same overvaluation of out-ward forms, of inherited position. It was part of the psychological adaptation of the Nonconformist intelligentsia to life inside the Establishment.

Florence's Liberalism was of a more robust variety. Her instincts and family tradition alike moved her towards self-improvement and do-gooding. Once the joy of reading each other romantic poetry had worn off,[18] Florence took to night school, mothers' meetings and Marshall's lectures.[19] In the autumn of 1890 her own lectures on health to mothers drew far larger audiences than Neville's on logic to Girton girls. Florence was genuinely interested in medical matters. Her brother Walter and her sister Alice became doctors. She was deeply concerned about the health of her children, stuffing them with tonics and taking great precautions against draughts, possibly in reaction to the neglect of such things by her parents. In February 1895, her public life took a definite direction when she became Cambridge secretary of the Charity Organisation Society. From then onwards her social work expanded in true Brown fashion. 'What a devoted woman she is!' Neville wrote to Maynard at Eton five years later. 'If there is anything in heredity, her children certainly ought to have a sense of duty.'[20] But privately he chafed at Florence's sense of duty and was always trying to get her to do less public work. He hated it when she was not at home.[21] Neville was wholly a family man. Florence was a conscientious wife and mother, but she needed larger causes to engage her full sympathies. Here again, quite apart from what she herself accomplished, Maynard was able to give her the vicarious satisfaction she could not get from Neville. So from his family Maynard got a divided legacy, his father standing for the private pleasures, his mother for the public.

II. NEVILLE'S ANXIETY

By the time Maynard was ten, his father had become a full-time university administrator, and had switched his intellectual energies from his own academic work to worrying about his children's. Neville's failure to build on his achievement as senior moralist came as a great disappointment to his colleagues but was inherent in his temperament. Although his mind was judicial rather than creative (he would have been a fine judge or civil servant) the real barrier to a successful academic career was not lack of originality, but anxiety. Neville's life strategy was an attempt to reduce the pressure on himself. The tasks he set himself once he did not have to 'please others' were such as to minimise strain. Immersion in hobbies was one solution; immersion in work which was intellectually undemanding was another. Unlike Marshall, who early in life abandoned activities which 'led nowhere', Neville increasingly gave himself over to them. To put himself beyond the judgement of his intellectual peers, to be judged by less exacting standards, became his goal.

This was not achieved quickly. There were considerable expectations of vigorous intellectual performance, which Neville himself shared. With Maynard safely born, he started, on 5 July 1883, 'a small book of Problems and Exercises in Formal Logic' which had arisen out of his teaching. Writing with great speed, he had already completed sixty-two Problems by 14 July, poor Florence having to spend her holiday evenings doing them. By the 27th he was expanding the book to include Terms, Propositions and Syllogisms. In September it was almost finished. The experience had not been encouraging. He regretted his inability to do 'really sterling literary work'.[22] On 27 October he noted that James Ward had been 'rather crushing on the subject of my book. The best he wd say was that it was *accurate* – but that of course he would naturally anticipate from me.' *Studies and Exercises in Formal Logic* was published by Macmillan in February 1884 to a chorus of praise from his Cambridge friends. It had one novel feature: the attempt (in Part IV) to develop a kind of Boolean algebra within the framework of traditional logic, while avoiding the use of mathematical symbols. Neville believed that logical symbolism should stick as closely as possible to the language in which arguments are originally stated.[23] This was the hallmark of Cambridge's intellectual style; a style which Maynard Keynes inherited. Neville revised his book several times before the definitive edition of 1906. But he played no further part in the development of the subject. Within his range he had reached a dead-end.

What the book got him, as it was intended to do, was a university lectureship in moral sciences. His next book was also a by-product of a teaching commitment. In his diary of 16 February 1885 he wrote: 'I have decided to lecture at Oxford on the Methods of Political Economy; and I have an idea of writing a small book on the same subject. This wd be my work during the Long Vacation.' It was Marshall who had brought him back to economics. A letter from Oxford, where Marshall had gone after leaving Bristol, hinted at talents running to waste in the Examination Syndicate. In November 1884 Henry Fawcett died, and Marshall was elected to succeed him as Professor of Political Economy at Cambridge. This meant he had to leave Balliol College, Oxford, after a very successful four terms there. He summoned Keynes to succeed him, enlisting Florence's help, and inundated him with telegrams and letters. He was extremely anxious to establish an outpost of 'scientific' economics at Oxford, and considered that Neville, his best student, was the person to man it.

Marshall's energetic lobbying secured Neville the offer, from Balliol, of a temporary lectureship. Under this pressure Neville developed shooting pains in his chest, which made him wonder how much longer he had to live.[24] Finally he yielded to Marshall's urging sufficiently to agree to go to Oxford one day a week in the Hilary, or Summer, term of 1885. Oxford was definitely a finer town than Cambridge, Neville decided. His lecture audiences, composed largely of candidates for the Indian Civil Service Examination, were large and appreciative. But Neville never developed Marshall's zeal to fertilise Oxford's barren economic culture. Although Balliol under Jowett was, as Maynard Keynes later wrote, 'at its highest point of brilliance and fame', Neville never took to it. He disliked Oxford men; he felt that Balliol 'might have paid me rather more attention'.[25] The experiment was not repeated. After the Oxford visit Neville practically gave up teaching economics in Cambridge also, Marshall's return having reduced the demand for his services.

The book on which Neville embarked was essentially an exercise in the Marshallian art of harmonising the views of various schools in order to regain for economics what Foxwell called its 'rightful authority in legislation and affairs'. J. S. Nicholson complained in 1885 that what economics needed was not more discussions on method but 'useful applications of the right method'.[26] Keynes's reply was that until the methodological issue between the deductive, inductive and ethical schools had been resolved, economics could have no practical influence. The point had some validity in 1885. By 1891 when Neville's book appeared, the methodological issue was just a little *passé*. Neville's 350 pages were a definitive summing up of the terms of a contract or *modus vivendi* between the rival methodological persuasions which had already been established. His second book, no less than his first, 'killed' the subject – not least for him.

The book's long gestation – it took over five years – can be explained partly by the time taken up by Neville's other work, partly by the discouraging effect of criticisms. The Cambridge habit of circulating work in progress was designed for people with a more robust self-confidence than Neville had. By 1888 he had a first draft ready, which he showed to Marshall. Marshall dashed his hopes of early publication. He 'depressed me very much' Neville wrote in his diary on 21 April 1888. 'He practically wants me to give a year to studying the Germans and then to rewrite entirely.' The disaster was compounded by the fact that Neville did not read German. So Florence was set to work on the German economists. At the same time throughout 1888 and 1889 Marshall was sending Neville massive chunks of his own draft *Principles*. Keynes generously responded with long, conscientious comments, though in the opinion of one observer he was 'too diffident and self-deprecatory' to make a completely effective critic.[27] Partly as a result, Marshall's book surged on to publication in the summer of 1890, while Keynes's more slender effort lagged behind.

In January 1888 the Professor of Political Economy at Oxford, Bonamy Price, died. Marshall wrote quickly to Neville: 'I was very glad to hear you intend to be a candidate . . .' Neville commented: 'This is the first I had heard of it.' He reflected that 'it is rather unfortunate that my book is not yet published. On the other hand, I should feel leaving Cambridge & my work here horridly.'[28] Sidgwick, Ward and Marshall all advised him to stand. So did his father-in-law, Dr Brown, who felt 'that your present work in connection with the Local Exams is not commensurate with your intellectual power. . . .'[29] Foxwell urged him to stay put:

> Pray don't go. It is much better that a study should be concentrated in a particular place. There arise many of the same advantages as in the localisation of an industry. Your departure would leave a nasty ragged wound in our Moral Sciences organisation.

He continued in lighter vein:

> What is the use of being a settled family man if you are to drift from your moorings in this fashion! Think of the effect your move may have on your son. He may grow up flippantly epigrammatical, & end up becoming the proprietor of a Gutter Gazette, or the hero of a popular party, instead of emulating his father's noble example, becoming an accurate clear headed Cambridge man, spending a life in valuable & unpretentious service to his kind, dying beloved of his friends, venerated by the wise, & unknown to the masses as true merit & worth mostly are.[30]

Neville applied for the chair without hope, and seemed pleased enough when the economic historian Thorold Rogers got it.

But Marshall was not finished with his nagging. Plans were afoot to start an Economic Association (later the Royal Economic Society) with its professional journal (the first issue of the *Economic Journal* appeared in 1890).

Marshall wanted Keynes to edit it. Keynes declined. It would 'worry me beyond measure', he told Marshall.[31] Instead Edgeworth took it on. He was succeeded in 1911 by Maynard Keynes, who never shrank from such challenges. Edgeworth tried hard to get Neville to write, without success: 'Unfortunately I have not the pen of a ready writer, & I cannot do literary work of any kind quickly.'[32]

The Scope and Method of Political Economy was finally published by Macmillan in January 1891. Neville resolved the methodological dispute between the different schools into a matter of correct classification. He accepted the primacy of the deductive approach – 'the preliminary determination of the principal forces in operation and the deduction of their consequences'. But deductive conclusions needed to be tested and modified by history and statistics. The role of ethics was to provide standards for judging economic arrangements. The book was praised for being 'so widely read, so impartial, and exact'.[33] On the strength of it, Neville received a doctorate in science, four-year-old Geoffrey enquiring anxiously whether his father 'would still live with us when he was a doctor'.[34] Florence, who was largely responsible for the book's much noticed mastery of German sources, did not get an acknowledgement[35] – an omission her husband failed to repair in subsequent editions. Running through the encomiums was a sense of relief that the final word seemed to have been said. 'For we cannot conceal', wrote Edgeworth in the *Economic Journal*, 'a certain impatience at the continual reopening of a question on which authorities appear to be substantially ... agreed.'

In producing one book on pure logic and a second on applied, Neville had circumnavigated his intellectual interests. He was thirty-eight. He lived another sixty years. Apart from a few contributions to Inglis Palgrave's *Dictionary of Political Economy* and the odd essay, his pen was thenceforth confined to revising previous work, writing his diary and letters, and drafting minutes. Had he finished his second book earlier, and got a chair when he was still relatively open to the idea of moving, a sense of duty, if not intellectual energy, might have led him to write more books in his lucid, painstaking manner.

Perhaps he is to be admired, rather than pitied, for keeping silent when he had nothing to say. As it was, soon after the publication of *Scope and Method*, his chief at the Syndicate, G. F. Browne, was made a canon of St Paul's. In 1892, Neville succeeded him as Secretary for Local Examinations at a salary of £500 a year. Marshall finally acknowledged defeat. 'I never felt quite sure', he write to him, 'that the work was the right thing for you; but I was always sure that you were the right man for the work.'[36] Being master at Syndicate Building pleased Neville.[37] His administrative work now took up more and more of his time. Later that year he was elected to the Council of the University's Senate, on which Maynard later served. Six months later, he became its Honorary Secretary, and thereafter indispensable. Rejecting an offer of a professorship of political economy at the University of Chicago in 1894, Neville wrote back that he was 'far too firmly rooted at Cambridge to be able to think of moving'. He crossed out a final sentence, 'I feel I am settled here for life.'[38]

III. MAYNARD'S EARLY YEARS: 1883–1897

Both parents were besotted with baby Maynard: Neville felt he could watch him for hours on end, though typically worried that he might not grow up 'sturdy in mind and body'.[39] He was born tongue-tied.[40] A small operation enabled Florence to nurse him normally till he was weaned at nine months; but, whether or not as a result of this, he lisped slightly as an adult. On 24 March 1884 Neville wrote in his diary, 'Florence says she loves Baby so much that it is quite painful. For myself I can say that his smiles and his little arms put out to come to me constitute one of the greatest joys that I have ever had in my life.'

Doting on Maynard did not exclude chastising him for his misdemeanours. From Maynard's second to seventh year there are frequent slappings and even 'whippings'. Then they stop, presumably with the dawn of 'reason'. Maynard was whipped when 'he got a spirit of wickedness into him that would not let him be good'.[41] He and Geoffrey were both circumcised as young boys, apparently to stop them masturbating.[42] The date of these operations cannot be placed with certainty, but they were probably done in London in 1891 when Geoffrey was four and Maynard eight.[43]

Within the limits of the moralistic conventions of the day, Neville and Florence were loving and careful, even over-careful, parents. Neville's diary makes it clear that from the start he was fascinated by Maynard – more so than he was to be by his other two children. Florence, it seems, did not keep a diary, so it is difficult to discover her own feelings about her children, or what she was like as a mother: a deficiency not repaired by Geoffrey Keynes's memoirs in which Florence and Neville as parents get one unilluminating sentence.[44] It is by no means clear that Maynard was Florence's favourite. Interests and companionship bound her more closely to Margaret than to either of the boys. She was more shy than was Neville about showing her feelings. There was also this difference between father and mother: that as the children grew up his interests came to narrow increasingly on the family whereas hers broadened outwards to the community.

Maynard's feelings towards his mother naturally waxed and waned at different times. He felt particularly close to her between the ages of six and eight, tending at this time to distance himself from his father. It is in this period that he calls Florence his 'greatest friend in the world' and his 'city of refuge'; when looking at her alone makes him incredibly happy, when he wants to be exactly like her, never to leave her or, alternatively, wants Neville to choose a wife for him just like her. Appeals to his love for his mother can get him to be good when all others fail.[45] From 1891 Father starts to come much more into the picture. He and Maynard are drawn to each other by their love of stamps. From eight onwards, right through school, university and into adult life, Maynard's relationship with his father is the essential one. Later things changed again as his father withdrew into apathy. These are relationships which, most unusually, lasted for sixty-two years. There was plenty of time for each to adapt to the others' evolving personalities and interests.

As one might suppose, Maynard was closer to his sister Margaret than to his brother Geoffrey, a twenty-month gap being easier to bridge than a forty-five-month one. Margaret was the first outlet for his didactive urges. However, apart from the age difference, his mental development was much quicker than that of the other two, and this alone would have drawn him to older people. An early memory of Geoffrey's which obviously crystallised for him his childhood relationship with Maynard is of rushing up to embrace his brother when he got his Eton scholarship in 1897, only to be pushed impatiently aside.[46] Of relations near his own age Maynard was probably closest to 'Uncle' Kenneth, Florence's youngest brother, only four years his senior. Harvey Road was full of dons' children. But friends started to be important to Maynard only at Eton.

He was a thin, delicate, lanky child. Florence and Neville quickly concluded that he was not robust, an opinion shared by their family physician, Dr Wherry, 'a tall man with a melancholy face and manner'.[47] Suffering frequent sickness and diarrhoea in his first three years, and 'feverish attacks' from then onwards, Maynard grew up, his parents felt, with a mind too active for his enfeebled body. He was frequently taken away from school or let off school work. Part of the problem may have been caused by his uneven physical development. His childhood is punctuated by fierce spurts of growth which left him exhausted, and by the age of fourteen he was already taller than his father.

From the age of six Maynard was convinced that he was 'remarkably ugly. He thinks no one ever was quite so ugly.'[48] This was not just a childhood fancy, but as he told Lytton Strachey many years later was a 'fixed, constant, unalterable obsession' from which he had 'always' suffered. A photograph of Maynard taken with the other two children when he was twelve shows an appearance far removed from that physiognomy, described by George Eliot, 'in which it seems impossible to discern anything but the generic character of boyhood'; but it is far from unattractive. He had a most unusual face, intelligent, alert, full of personality, besides which his younger sister and brother seem merely pretty. The 'little shrimp' as his father called him, with the distinctive high cheekbones and the delicate hint of laughter in eyes and mouth, is already recognisably the father of the man.

Surrounded as he was by the conviction that he was bound to be clever, Maynard would have disappointed more people than great-grandmother Ford had he turned out not to be. There was no fear of that. Even before he was two, Florence worried about his 'working his brain too hard'.[49] Such was Maynard's reputation for precocity that years later his Cambridge colleague C. R. Fay wrote, 'I have heard that when a few months old he confuted his nurse who was urging him to drink a noxious medicine by a carefully reasoned argument which proved conclusively that the Elasticity of his Demand for the commodity in question was zero.' But most of the evidence of budding genius recorded by his father consists of no more than the bright remarks of a bright boy. There is certainly nothing approaching the John Stuart Mill standard of achievement. However, a connoisseur of precocity might savour the definition of interest given by the future economist at the age of four and a half: 'If I let you have a halfpenny & you kept it for a very long time you would have to give me back that halfpenny & another one too. That's interest.'[50] That his economic understanding was not complete is shown by his wonder that all the chairs (rather than shares) should come tumbling down after a warlike speech by Kaiser William II of Germany.[51] He developed the bright boy's habit of blurting out embarrassing things. As the family were leaving chapel one Sunday he said in a loud, clear voice, 'It's the prayers I dislike most.'[52] When one Easter at Kington Aunt Mary Keynes in a 'rare mistake for her' said ''*im* instead of *him*', Maynard at once remarked drily and seriously, 'I *think* "him" is spelt with an "h".' He was not quite six. Nor was he at all put out when his parents told him that it was wrong to hurt other people's feelings. 'Father & Mother often hurt *my* feelings,' he replied.[53] On his sixth birthday he reduced his sister Margaret to tears by proving to her that she was a *thing*. 'She wouldn't like to be nothing, and if she wasn't nothing she must be something, & if she was something she was a thing.' The logician W. E. Johnson, visiting the Keynes house, decided to pursue the conversation further. 'You call Margaret a thing,' he said, 'but can things talk? Is this table a thing?' 'Yes.' 'Well, it can't talk, and Margaret can talk.' Unabashed, Maynard replied, '*Some* things can't talk, but *some* things can.'

As an adult, Maynard looked back with affection on his father's circle:

In the first age of married society in Cambridge, when the narrow circle of the spouses-regnant of the Heads of Colleges and of a few wives of Professors was first extended, several of the most notable dons, particularly in the School of Moral Science, married students of Newnham. The double link between husbands and between wives bound together a small cultured society of great simplicity and distinction. This circle was at its full strength in my boyhood, and, when I was first old enough to be asked out to luncheon or dinner, it was to these houses that I went. I remember a homely, intellectual, atmosphere which it is harder to find in the swollen, heterogeneous Cambridge of to-day.[54]

Geoffrey adds that Maynard was 'ready from an early age to join in learned discussions'.[55] W. E. Johnson, who joined subtlety of mind to sweetness of disposition, was Neville's closest friend. His sister Hattie ran a Dame's school attended by Margaret and Geoffrey. Maynard remembers him and Neville discussing logical points over interminable lunches. The austere but charming Sidgwick with his white flowing beard was a golf as well as a dinner companion. Another friend was the philosopher and psychologist James Ward, 'a testy, irritable thing' as he called himself: the Keynes and Ward families would picnic together on the river in the summer. The bibliophile economist Herbert Foxwell, another friend, moved to Harvey Road on his marriage in 1898. The absurd but fascinating Alfred Marshall was a frequent visitor at 6 Harvey Road, not so much for dinner as for discussion. Neville's friends included economists from outside Cambridge too – James Bonar, Henry Wicksteed, Robert Giffen and Inglis Palgrave. It was no doubt the educational effects of such a society which great-grandmother Ford had in mind when she wrote to Maynard that 'You will be expected to be very clever, having lived always in Cambridge.'

When he was five and a half he started going to the kindergarten of the Perse School for Girls. By the end of 1889 he was showing 'talent' at arithmetic. But 'Maynard's nerves seem very much unstrung,' reported his worried father on 10 October 1889. 'He is constantly blinking his eyes & sometimes he turns them up in a dreadful way so that only the whites shew.' The twitchings had become so 'dreadful' by 30 October that he was briefly removed from school after Wherry had diagnosed Sydenham's chorea, or St Vitus's dance, probably an after-effect of the attack of rheumatic fever he had had in the summer. A year later, in December 1890, Maynard was showing 'power' at arithmetic; but then for some reason he was removed from the kindergarten for good and taught at home for a year.

In January 1892, he started as a day boy at St Faith's Preparatory School in the Trumpington Road. It was founded and run by Ralph Goodchild, a tough Victorian pedagogue who recognised 'scholarship material' when he saw it. Neville moved quickly and sensibly to stop Maynard being exploited:

It is clear [he wrote to Goodchild on 12 February 1892] that Maynard finds the afternoon work rather long. He sometimes comes home – as to-day – quite overdone. I shall be very much obliged if instead of being kept in to write out his mistakes he can come home directly school is over, & write out his mistakes in the evening. . . . He also complains of being knocked on the head with a ruler & having his wrists twisted by a boarder named Watson – two years older than himself – when they are left in the schoolroom together. The boy himself does not like the idea of my writing to you, & I shall therefore be glad if you will say nothing about it at present to Watson or the other boys. I will write to you further if I hear of anything of the kind happening again.

By March, his father noted that Maynard was 'very quick at Arithmetic and Algebra'. He concluded, though, that he was 'not likely to excel in sports any more than his Father did'.[56] The main problem was to resist Goodchild's efforts to hurry him along. Before he was ten, Maynard had finished Book I of Euclid, was doing quadratic equations in algebra and stocks in arithmetic, Ovid and continuous prose in Latin, and *Samson Agonistes* in English.[57]

Worried by the effects of all this on his health, his parents removed him to Bedford for the autumn of 1893, where his Brown grandmother reopened her schoolroom for his benefit. Mrs Brown was much struck by Maynard's 'general ability and the interest – quite beyond his years – wh. he shews in literature. She says he is very intense while at work, but finds steady application more difficult' – a standard comment about this time.[58] But Neville was not completely satisfied with the results of the Bedford experiment. 'Maynard has come back not quite up to the mark,' he noted on 2 January 1894. 'Perhaps Florence pays rather too much attention to his ailments, but at Bedford they go to the opposite extreme, paying no attention to his diet, & laughing at him when he professes himself not well.'

Nevertheless, it was after his return from Bedford that Maynard's scholastic work really took off. In July 1894 he came top for the first time in examination and classwork, after being coached by Neville in examination technique. His ascendancy, which was not shaken while he remained at St Faith's, was firmly based on mathematics, for which it was now accepted that he had a definite bent. From October 1894 he started two hours' extra coaching in it, four days a week. On 30 November his father noted that 'Maynard has himself discovered the method of squaring a number of two figures by applying the formula $(x + y)^2 = x^2 + 2xy + y^2$' – a first sign of the facility in algebra which would be his main strength as a mathematician. By December that year, his teacher Holt, himself a wrangler, reported that Maynard 'now and then does really brilliant work, but soon tires & has not the perseverance in the face of a difficulty'. The following July a relieved Neville noted that 'his work does not seem to be any great labour to him, & he seems much more robust than he used to be'. Extremely quick to grasp the point, Maynard was careless about details. Goodchild told Neville that 'work that may take two hours is finished in less than half the time given'. The annoying thing, Goodchild continued, was 'that he corrects his mistakes when I am looking them over before I have seen them myself'.[59] Maynard was so obsessed by his algebra at this time that in family prayers he found himself praying, 'Let Mother equal x and let Geoffrey equal y.'[60]

The days when he was bullied in the schoolroom had been left far behind. Already tall for his age, soon after his return from Bedford he started shooting up in height. When Goodchild wrote to Neville at the end of 1896 that Maynard stood 'head and shoulders above all the other boys in the school' he meant physically as well as mentally.

> There can be no doubt [his brother recalls] that ... he was regarded almost with awe by his schoolfellows. The stories of his slave, who walked behind him carrying his books in return for help and protection, and of the other boy with whom he had 'a commercial treaty', sealed with blood and enacting that he should not approach at any time nearer than fifteen yards, are not apocrypha. I can still name the second one.[61]

He established something of an ascendancy at Harvey Road, too. The whippings long forgotten, Maynard now stayed up late at night and disdained, in the holidays, to come down to breakfast before mid-morning. He worked with Neville in his study. When his parents went away on holiday, Maynard expertly sorted out their mail, Neville thanking 'My dear Private Secretary'. The basis of Maynard's domestic position was parental admiration which became more unstinted with each prize he notched up. 'I am already too proud of the dear boy,' Neville noted on 12 January 1897. 'My pride in him and my love for him feed each other.'

Despite worries about his increased stammering, his parents decided, at the end of 1896, to enter him for the Eton College Scholarship Examination in July the following year. Maynard would have gone to public school in any case – Goodchild advised Tonbridge – since his parents were no longer members of a Dissenting sect but part of the Establishment, and well pleased to be so. But it was Maynard's brains which opened up Eton for him, for his parents would never have dreamt of placing him among the aristocratic or wealthy Oppidans. Eton meant Eton College to which each year about fifteen boys were 'elected' on the results of a competitive examination. It was Maynard's first chance to measure himself against a cross-section of England's budding intellectual elite.

Neville, as can be imagined, was determined to leave nothing to chance. Special tutors were engaged. Father and son started getting up at seven every morning and working together before breakfast to accustom Maynard to the times of the scholarship papers. Not surprisingly Neville started to feel 'very tired'. To his depression whenever he dwelt on Maynard's prospects was added his 'grief to ... think that the dear boy will not in any case do his work very much longer with me in the study'.[62] By the time he, Florence and Maynard left for Eton on Monday 5 July, he was in a 'fearful state of worry'. To make matters worse their hotel in the High Street was 'frightfully noisy', so that he lay awake all night with his gloomy thoughts.

They all got up at 6.15 a.m. on Tuesday 6 July to send Maynard off to Upper School in good time for Latin Composition. Before Neville could start out to meet Maynard at the end of the paper, his son walked cheerfully into the hotel having finished it early. Latin Translation and Mathematics followed. Next morning, Maynard, dispatched to Greek Grammar fortified with Valentine's Beef Extract, was out early again. Harder Mathematics followed: he left the afternoon's Greek Translation early once more, complaining that 'the days seem dreadfully long'. His parents meanwhile had formed a most favourable impression of the manners of the Eton boys. On Thursday morning Maynard did Latin Verse, and the examination ended with the General Paper 'which didn't suit [him] very well'.[63]

Worrying about the examinations was followed by worrying about the results. Depressed by Goodchild's pessimistic appraisal of Maynard's examination notes, and alarmed by the lack of geniality of the Vice-Chancellor, one of the Eton examiners, Neville despaired. 'Well, the dear boy has I am sure done his best.' As no news came on Monday he and Florence gave up hope. It would have to be Tonbridge after all, or perhaps Rugby. And yet 'after visiting Eton we are the more keen about the school: & after all the expectations raised about the boy, we cannot think of his failing at his first public trial'. At last a telegram came at 5.30 p.m. 'Maynard 10th College Scholar'. His mathematics had pulled him through after all, and he was placed first equal in that subject. 'This was I think the most delightful telegram I ever received,' a thankful Neville wrote in his diary. 'My own successes never gave anything like the pleasure this has done.' It was to be the first of many such pleasures, for, however often his father revised his expectations upwards, Maynard was to be equal to them.

That summer, at Leigh Farm, Tintagel, Neville observed his five-foot-five-inch son with fond indulgence. 'Maynard', he wrote, 'is just now a curious combination – quite childish in some things, thoroughly entering into the simplest enjoyments such as Geoffrey or even younger children can share with him, while in other things he is thoroughly grown up, entering most sensibly and seriously into what are quite men's ideas.'[64] Goodchild wrote, 'He leaves me with a great reputation for every good quality.'

4

Eton

I. AN ETON EDUCATION

As Tenth King's Scholar Maynard was given a place in College for September 1897. As the time for him to go to Eton approached he became depressed and irritable. As if in protest he developed a heavy cold and so had to miss the start of his first half (at Eton a term was known as a 'half': three 'halves' made a whole). 'It is most unfortunate that the dear boy should not be able to put in an appearance at Eton on the proper day,' noted his father, worried equally about Maynard's health and the proprieties. Eventually Maynard was able to leave Cambridge with his mother on 26 September, four days late, still looking 'like an invalid'. The College matron, Miss Hackett, was not very welcoming. 'This is not a hospital,' she told Florence crossly. But one of the boys' maids, 'such a nice motherly woman', unpacked Maynard's clothes in his cubicle. Florence was relieved to find them all correct. On 4 October Maynard wrote to his brother:

> Dear Boff,
>   ... We feel [sic] baths with pipes which we call siphons. Any insubordination is punished by a whacking with one of these and it is called siphoning. I played to-day at the Wall Game for the first time. It is a most indescribable and extraordinary game and you dress in most indescribable and extraordinary costumes called Wallsacks.
>   Please tell mother that I received the box containing stockings and books to-day.
>   I remain
>   Your affectionate brother
>   JMK
> Hallelujah

One benefit of arriving late was that Maynard missed the new boys' traditional first encounter with the headmaster in Upper School. The Rev. Edmond Warre, immensely muscular and immensely Christian, always used the occasion to deliver a warning about the dangers of 'filth'; a warning made more impressive and mysterious by the fact that few other words in his discourse were audible.[1] Maynard's Brown grandmother moved quickly to fill the gap in his education. 'Never do or say anything you would feel ashamed of if your mother were by,' she wrote to him. With these traditional injunctions ringing in their ears, Maynard and the other boys of his 'election' submitted themselves to be reshaped into Etonians. He emerged five years later very recognisably the adult he was to be for the rest of his life. What sort of experience had it been?

He was outstandingly successful at Eton, and predominantly happy there. These facts help one understand the part he came to play in English life. Many gifted English middle-class boys have been made miserable by their parents or by their boarding-schools; some of them, as a result, become rebels. However true this may be of some middle-class experience it does not fit Keynes. He is an example of a 'first-rate intelligence' who never became an 'outlaw'.

One reason for this is clear. He never felt the need to rebel against his home. The values of his parents were scholarly and intellectual, not hearty; and he never repudiated this part of his legacy. But Eton, too, must take some of the credit. His experience there did not turn him into a rebel. Perhaps the most important reason was that all the seventy scholarship boys lived together in the same house – College – rather than being scattered round the school. In College his intelligence could grow in congenial company and an environment favourable to learning. And the existence of College itself helped leaven the rest of the school. Maynard never had to 'kick' against the rampant philistine and athletic values which reduce so many clever boys to a state of misery and boredom. At home, at Eton and later at King's College, Cambridge, the development of his mind was supported by the surrounding conditions, not twisted by them.

Eton never surrendered to the excesses of muscular Christianity. The school's very position, at the apex of the public-school world, permitted a more humane, less repressive, internal culture than was found elsewhere. Its parents took gentlemanly status more for granted, and exerted less pressure on the school to produce a standardised product. Enlightened schoolmasters like William Johnson and Oscar Browning, who believed in cultivating the mind and feelings rather than the body, could flourish, at least for a time, in remarkable independence of the headmaster, aided in this by another unique Eton institution, the tutorial system, whereby each pupil was assigned a tutor who oversaw his progress and provided general counselling. Above all, each boy (in College after his first year) had the wonderful boon of his own bedroom-study, which meant privacy. Right through the school there was less pressure to conform than in other public schools. Eton, as one old Etonian described it, was a place where 'you could think and love what you liked: only in external matters, in clothes, or in deportment, need you do as the others do'.[2]

There remained a considerable difference between College and Oppidan (fee-paying) Eton. College, in Bernard Crick's apt phrase, was 'an intellectual elite thrust into the heart of a social elite'.[3] One of the practical consequences of this was captured in a letter Maynard wrote home in his third year (28 January 1900):

> Goodhart [the Master in College] gave us a lecture after prayers yesterday on the growth of slackness and extravagance in imitation of the Oppidans in College.
>
> His points were quite sound: that Collegers would have to earn their own livings and therefore must work now; that those who can afford to be extravagant ought not to be in College, and that those who can't shouldn't.

The atmosphere of College was cerebral and unworldly. It tended to produce clergymen, scholars and schoolmasters; Oppidan Eton soldiers, statesmen, bankers. Tugs, as Collegers were known, were expected to work or 'sap' harder than Oppidans. They wore gowns for school, and surplices for chapel. They had their own sports ground, College Field, where they played an incomprehensible game, the Wall Game. They had their distinctive social organisation and vocabulary. Geographically College, in School Yard, was at the heart of the school, whereas the Oppidans had their houses in the town. Until his last couple of terms all Maynard's habitual interests, activities and friendships were College-centred. Even though he would do his schoolwork with Oppidans, he and the fellow Collegers of his election formed an intellectual minority at the top of each division, competing with each other for the prizes.

Two people above all shaped Maynard's life at Eton. The first was his tutor, Samuel Gurney Lubbock, newly returned to Eton himself as an assistant master, having taken a first in classics at King's College, Cambridge. Neville had selected him personally for the job, after making enquiries at King's. It was an excellent choice. Lubbock was a true gentleman scholar, with an ideal of all-round development. He immediately recognised in Maynard a boy with an exceptional range of ability and interests and encouraged him to spread himself. Maynard, who as we shall see was no instinctive admirer of authority, liked and respected his tutor. Lubbock's influence can be seen in Maynard's decision to try for King's College, Cambridge, and in his refusal to specialise in his strongest subject, mathematics. It was Lubbock, too, who planted his interest in medieval Latin poetry. The second shaper was Neville Keynes himself. 'Let us know each week how you are getting on with your work,' he wrote to Maynard soon after he arrived. Maynard obliged. In return he got back a stream of instruction on methods of study, examination technique, prose style and general conduct.

Neville soon got to know his son's academic, social and competitive situation in College almost as well as did Maynard himself. Maynard took Neville's academic advice, but he pursued his own intellectual interests independently. Above all, his rhythm of work was different. To Neville,

academic achievement was always associated with pain; to Maynard, it came
much more easily. As the prizes came flooding in Neville's tone gradually
changed from one of exhortation to one of awe: 'These things seem to come
to you whether you will or not,' he wrote on 4 February 1901.

II. THE SCHOOLBOY

There is much about Maynard's schooldays at Eton which is probably
beyond recall. We have a complete run of his school reports, of his letters
home. A number of his essays and notebooks survive. He kept a diary for
most of his last three years, much of it compiled later from his memory and
letters to his parents. From these we can get a fairly good idea of his mental
growth, his interests, his sporting activities, his opinions on a variety of
topics, his literary style and those aspects of his personality which he chose
to expose to his teachers and parents. On the other hand the quality of his
inner life, of his relations with his schoolfellows, has to be, at best, inferred
from very slender evidence. This was before Keynes and his friends
exchanged copious quantities of letters analysing their 'states of mind'. The
few letters which survive between Keynes and his schoolfriends are rather
impersonal. They give one the feeling that they could be read, if necessary,
by parents.

From his school reports Maynard emerges as a model pupil, with a
number of mental and personality traits repeatedly singled out for mention.
There was the speed at which he did his work, based on quickness in
grasping and retaining facts, and understanding essential points. His command of the English language is often noticed. Yet though his domination
of mathematics, based on exceptional facility in algebra, became so complete
that he had to be barred, in his third year, from the Problems Prize, no one
except Gilbert Harrison Hurst, his mathematics master, wanted him to
specialise in his strongest subject. Luxmoore, Eton's best-known classicist,
hoped that 'the more accurate sciences will not dry the readiness of his
sympathy and insight for more inspiring and human subjects. His little essay
on "Antigone" was not like the work of one made for mathematics' (April
1901).

Keynes was a prodigious prize-winner at Eton. He won ten in his first
year, eighteen in his second, eleven in his third: a total of sixty-three
volumes. He won all the school's main mathematical prizes, and even
managed to pick up a chemistry prize on the way. Yet what particularly
pleased Lubbock was the absence of any 'mercenary spirit' in Maynard's
work. He worked for the pleasure of the work not for the pleasure of

winning prizes. 'He is one of the very few who seems to appreciate the value and merits of the books he is working at' (December 1898). Here Geoffrey Keynes may give a somewhat one-sided view of his brother. Their father, he wrote, 'set great store by our marks and position in class, and this stimulated a sense of competition in Maynard, who enjoyed his own capacity of leaping ahead of other boys'.[4] The first part of this statement is undoubtedly true. Neville's letters to Maynard are full of remarks such as 'You didn't tell me how much you were behind Herringham and Bailey in the first fortnightly order in Classics' (28 February 1898); 'Ainger seems to be coming on well. You must not let him beat you in Trials' (12 May 1898). How far Maynard needed this competitive stimulus is open to question. The truth seems to be that Neville, influenced by his own experience, could never appreciate the intensity of the pleasure which Maynard got out of work for its own sake.

Two examples of this from his Eton time, which had nothing to do with prizes, are his researches into his family history, which occupied much of his fourth year, and his love of medieval poetry. Such diversions from the main line of his school work worried his father. All his life Maynard had this capacity for getting hooked on something which seemed a diversion from his main efforts, yet in the end enriched them. Extra-curricular interests give an added dimension to his economic writings.

Keynes's interests, in or out of class, were far from being confined to matters cerebral. At first Lubbock found his manner a trifle spinsterish, but by his second term was able to note, with relief, that he had 'become a little more boyish' (April 1898). Keynes, he wrote in August of that year, was 'thoroughly interested in Athletic and School matters'. His cricket performances were modest. 'My scores have been 5, 3, and 2,' he reported to Neville on 22 May 1898 with his usual precision. In his second summer he became a 'wet-bob', and enjoyed to the full the life on the river, languidly sculling up the Thames with his friends to favourite spots for a bathe and tea.

His ability to share the normal schoolboy enthusiasms made him less formidable, and thus less remote, to his schoolfellows. 'It says much for him', Lubbock wrote on 5 August 1899, 'that some very illiterate members of my pupil room, with whom he comes into contact, like and respect him a good deal.' Members of his election looked on him as a natural spokesman.[5] He was a little older than most of them, having come at fourteen, rather than thirteen. He was very tall which meant that he had to go straightaway into 'tails' – a black morning suit, black silk top hat, and white bow-tie. (Florence used to buy his ties by the gross, to wear once and throw away.) His voice had already broken: a Colleger remembers 'a rather tall, incredibly angular' boy singing 'Three Blue Bottles' at Chamber Singing 'with great gusto and entire indifference to tune'. At the end of his first half he was elected to Chamber Pop (College's junior debating society) and took an active part in its speechmaking, his father furnishing him with topics and technical advice. In his third half Maynard became Captain of Chamber, a

position which 'I don't at all dislike', he told Neville. There is no evidence of
teasing: Maynard's personality commanded respect from his peers.

He made an equally good impression on his teachers. His modesty of
disposition, his lack of priggishness, his thoroughness, his willingness to do
what was asked of him, were all noted and appreciated. He rarely got into
trouble with his boy seniors, managing to avoid being 'worked off' (caned)
till his fifth term, and then 'absolutely unjustly', he wrote in his diary on
3 July 1899. His one consistent failing in the eyes of the authorities was his
inability to get up in the mornings. This was his only sign of rebellion.

That Keynes was already less pleased with authority than authority was
with him comes out clearly in his letters home. They are full of sharp
comments directed at the stupidity or dullness of examiners, masters,
preachers, bursars, matrons, etc. Even at Eton he did not suffer fools gladly.
He always seems to have had a lower opinion of examiners than examiners
did of him. The one whose papers won him the Junior Mathematical Prize
in his first year should have been 'locked up as a dangerous lunatic', he
wrote home on 3 July 1898. This is already vintage Keynes. His constant
irritation with the College matron – 'the Hackett', as she was known –
earned him a rare parental reproof: 'You must not let her little foibles blind
you to her good points.' On 14 October 1900 he complained of the lack of
hot water: 'But what can you expect of a Bursar, who thinks such things
superfluous because he cannot remember any hot and cold water arrangements in the Ark, where he spent one of his summer holidays with his old
friend Noah?' The Bursar of King's was later to squirm beneath that withering scorn.

He liked masters who could instruct or amuse him, but hated being
bored. His *bête noire* on the teaching staff was 'Mike' Mitchell, a cricketing
fanatic, to whom he was 'up' in classics in his third summer. Maynard could
'hardly have imagined that a man could be so dull; anyhow I shall not suffer
from want of sleep this half' (6 May 1900). Two weeks later: 'we have not
yet succeeded in probing the depths of his ignorance. It must, I think, be
bottomless.' Mitchell's report struck the only sour note in the encomiums
showered on Maynard at school. 'Rather a provoking boy in School – reads
notes often when he ought to be attending to the lesson, apt to talk to his
neighbour unless severely repressed. He gives one the idea of regarding
himself as a privileged boy, with perhaps a little intellectual conceit.' This
strikes an authentic note: so many gifts and so much modesty as Lubbock
portrayed suggest an implausible perfection.

Preachers in chapel provoked in him most unchristian feelings. On
12 November 1899 he 'sat and squirmed for twenty-five minutes'. The
preacher 'was an archdeacon, but you must have guessed it. I think that he
can almost preach badly enough to become a bishop.' Four months later
(4 March 1900) he registered a 'revolting performance. They ought to make
him an archdeacon at once. He has got all the qualifications.' Preaching

offered unrivalled opportunities for sonorous nonsense. It combined the two things Maynard disliked most: imprecise thought and the waste of his time.

Keynes was already a precisian. He wanted exact meanings. 'What is the "imperishable plinth of things"?' he asked after reading one of Kipling's poems. He had a passion for exact information, particularly when expressed in numerical form. His letters are full of the lengths of poems, times of trains, people's heights and weights, his own temperatures, their rise and fall, his financial accounts and so on. In his diary he followed his father's habit of recording hours worked per day (mornings, afternoons and evenings), books read during the year, visits to theatres, annual accounts, even golf scores. He was constantly monitoring his own time, noting down how long it took him to do this or that. To Florence he wrote on 2 May 1902, 'This letter is a very creditable performance having not taken me more than 10 minutes by the clock.' At the end of 1901 he astonished his father with an article he had written for the *Eton Chronicle* at one minute's notice and which was in the printer's hands an hour later. 'The article,' commented Neville, 'is very ingenious; and the composition, considering the circumstances, is quite admirable in style and finish.' Maynard rushed through life with the clock ticking in his ear, yet rarely gave the impression of being hurried.

Many of his comments on life outside the school betray, as one would expect, a bias in favour of his own class, the 'educated bourgeoisie' as he later called it. His attitude to the royal persons who thronged Windsor was robustly irreverent. Neville's star-struck account of the visiting Swedish King at Cambridge – 'a magnificent-looking person – every inch a King' (15 May 1900) – contrasts with Maynard's much lighter descriptions of Kaiser Wilhelm II (26 November 1899): 'I was much impressed by his kingly bearing and his moustache was quite up to my expectations.' Neville was loyally anxious that Maynard should catch a glimpse of 'Her Majesty'. He finally saw the 'good lady' close up, but 'doubtless owing to the coldness of the day, her nose was unfortunately red' (20 May 1900). Not that he took greater pleasure in lower forms of life. 'Windsor has got an extraordinarily ruffianly population,' he wrote home on 26 November 1899. Visiting his sister Margaret at school in High Wycombe he deplored 'the entire absence of moderately wealthy middle class residences' in the town (2 November 1899). When the Australians managed to draw a Test match by scoring 89 in five and a half hours, Maynard commented: 'But what can you expect of a team of bricklayers and such like' (19 July 1899). The interesting thing about such attitudes is not that he held them at this time of his life but that they never changed much later. Aristocrats were absurd; the proletariat was always 'boorish'. The good things in life sprang from the middle class.

No economist has wielded the pen as well or to such effect as Maynard Keynes; and the distinctive Keynes touch is already beginning to show in his letters home, though not in his rather uninspired diary. His ability to go straight to the point was coupled with the realisation that the point was often absurd. He was already telling sly jokes, too. Anticipating the visit of the Kaiser in 1899 he wrote, 'Last time he was here he asked to see a boy swiped but the head excused himself on the ground that no one happened to be in need of punishment. William immediately offered to place a member of his suite at his service.' He delighted in verbal games, and bombarded his father with Spoonerisms: 'Mr Spooner seeing a gang of navvies at work remarked on "these sturdy tons of soil"' (1 October 1899).

Maynard's style was economical, direct, limpid. He wrote in short sentences and paragraphs, going from point to point. He almost never crossed out. He described events, but rarely people, and never states of mind. He found it much easier to record facts than to paint pictures, admitting, in another context, that 'I have no imagination' (17 February 1901). But he worried about what he called his 'telegraphic style'. On 20 November 1898 he wrote, 'I wish I could write a less disjointed letter.' Two days before his sixteenth birthday he wrote: 'I have just read my letter through and it is a beastly series of very short jerky sentences. How can I improve on it?' Neville replied (9 June 1899): 'I do not think that the composition of your letter was at all bad. There is indeed a distinctive merit in short sentences, if the transition from one to another is not too abrupt. That is a point you might attend to but I have no doubt that with practice you will attain to a good English style.' Fortunately, despite some tendency to high-table phrases – 'I have replied in the negative' – Maynard did not model his style on Neville's which, while lucid, is a good example of the academic pompous. He never did entirely master the problem of the transition from one argument, or level of argument, or one subject, to another. The reason is that his ideas and interests, like the different facets of his personality, tended to be kept in separate compartments. The virtue of the defect was his uncanny power of switching off one subject and turning to another with complete concentration. Without it, he would never have been able to do so many things, and so well. The penalty was a certain brittleness.

What the reports and letters home leave out is one side of his personality which was already very important and was to become centrally so: his need to give and receive affection. Maynard's first important friendships date from his time at Eton. In adolescence his feelings started to catch up with his intellect – not unusual in a clever boy. Some boys find their main emotional outlets in poetry or religion. Their feelings can be aroused by natural beauty or heroic exploits. Maynard was too rational and ironic to be much affected by such things. Poetry gave him genuine pleasure but it was as likely to produce statistical as spiritual ecstasies. Nor did chapel awaken religious feelings. True enough, he was moved by some of the hymns. He even seems to have been confirmed in his third year, at what he called an 'awful service' (31 March 1900). But he was never able to take religion seriously, regarding it as a strange aberration of the human mind. Even at school he delighted to

puncture his friends' religious beliefs by refuting arguments for the existence of God. With little capacity for poetic or aesthetic experience Maynard
came to concentrate his feelings on two points: his work and his friendships.
Both became highly charged for him. And there must have been pain as
well as happiness for him in them, especially in the latter. He was not a
pretty or handsome boy. Indeed, according to Geoffrey Winthrop Young,
who came to Eton as an assistant master in 1900, Maynard was 'distinctly
ugly at first sight, with lips projecting and seeming to push up the well-
formed nose and strong brows in slightly simian fashion'.[6] Probably as a
result of his appearance he was nicknamed 'Snout' by his friends. In fact this
impression of ugliness was soon dispelled. He had very expressive eyes, his
face, in animation, was attractive, and he had a sympathetic voice. Nevertheless, he was convinced of his own ugliness. Lack of physical confidence and
athletic prowess can be agony for a schoolboy, however clever; and this, too,
helped make those friendships which Maynard did form particularly important for him.

Naturally enough his early schoolfriends were boys from his own
election. Chief of these was Dillwyn Knox, with whom he 'messed' or took
his meals during several halves in his first four years.

'Dilly' was the second of four remarkable sons of a bishop. Although he
was two years younger than Maynard, he and Maynard were the cleverest
boys in their election. Dilly, who looked like a scarecrow, was Maynard's
main rival for Eton's mathematical honours; he was a brilliant, if narrow,
classical scholar. He was also much the most interesting of Maynard's
friends. The quality of their relationship is suggested by two letters Keynes
wrote a few years later. The first, dated Christmas Day 1905, was to Dilly
himself. He never sent it. It concluded, 'But ever since we first messed
together, even through the curious incidents which marked our last two
years at Eton, there has been a kind of affection between us. . . .'[7] The
incidents were almost certainly sexual. Some years later, Keynes told another
College friend, Swithinbank, about them. 'I've never seen any one so surprised and so jealous. Apparently, he longed to do likewise himself and had
never dared. . . .'[8]

III. THE BOER WAR

The responsibilities of empire were to dominate much of Maynard's third
year at Eton. 'I don't know what to think about the Transvaal business,' he
wrote to his father on 8 October 1899, 'but I think I am getting more and
more anti-war.' In his diary he wrote three days later: 'The Boer ultimatum

expired to-day at 3.10. Herringham who was up to Allcock took out his
watch at that hour and said "Please, sir, it's war". He got 200 lines and a
ticket.'

Keynes was at or near the centre of British government in two world
wars. Much of his life after 1914 was spent thinking about the national
interest and his own relation to it. In 1899 these kinds of questions forced
themselves on his mind for the first time. On the whole his schoolboy
attitudes foreshadow his later ones; they were, of course, largely the attitudes of his home.

His parents took a moderate position. 'Of course I want to win,' wrote
Florence on 20 October, 'but I confess I find it blood-curdling to read of
these white men killing each other – The Dervishes did not seem so bad – I
mean the slaughter of them.' Maynard wrote home on 22 October: 'I am no
more jingo than I was previously, but now that the war has begun, one must
perforce be reconciled to it.' His father agreed, and approved.

Soon the heavy losses the Boers inflicted on Buller swung the Keyneses
more firmly behind the war. 'Your mother & I dined on Monday evening
with the Marshalls,' Neville wrote to Maynard on 13 December. 'Prof.
Marshall is a pro-Boer & we find him very irritating.'

In the new half – and century – the war came directly into the lives of
Collegers. Herringham of Maynard's election left at sixteen to join the army.
On 29 January 1900 Maynard wrote 'After 12 the Head gave the upper part
of the school [a talk] on the subject of the Volunteers. He said that at a
national crisis like the present it is the duty of everyone to do what he can
to make himself efficient by joining the Volunteers.' He wrote to his parents:
'Am I to join? I am not keen & the drills will be a nuisance, but I am perfectly
willing to do so if I ought. It would be unpleasant to be the only non-
shooter.' His mother pondered the familiar dilemma between moral and
social duty, or how to reconcile the values of Bedford and Eton: 'As you
know,' she wrote on 4 February, 'we were never very anxious for you to join
the Volunteers, and we are no more anxious now – in fact, we prefer that
you should not. At the same time, if you feel that it would be the right thing
to do, and that you would be in an uncomfortable position if you did not
join, we shall raise no objection. . . .' Maynard took the robust line. 'I wavered
a little and hey presto! it was done – or rather it was not done. I think that
without your letter which amounted to a refusal I should have been
engulfed in this marvellous martial ardour that has seized the school. Some
say that patriotism requires one to join the useless Eton shooters, but it
seems to me the sort of patriotism that requires one to wave the Union Jack.'

The relief of Kimberley stirred Maynard's father to patriotic enthusiasm.
'There is one thing upon which the whole country is agreed,' he noted in
his diary of 18 March 1900, 'and that is admiration for Lord Roberts.' Under
the influence of this emotion he applied for £4000 of War Loan, though
securing only £500. Maynard took a more detached view: 'The Head is quite

dotty with war enthusiasm, and can't talk about anything else,' he wrote home on 18 February. 'He came in the other day to talk about grammar ... and told us that it was by persevering with such things that England's battles were won.' And to counterbalance his father's enthusiasm he wrote on 18 March, 'Roberts' triumphal procession through the Orange Free is grand, but I think that too much has been made of the joy with which the inhabitants of Bloemfontein received him; for, after all, the majority of those that are left are of British descent.'

On 19 May 1900 Maynard took part in the riotous celebrations over the relief of Mafeking, but kept his usual detached note in his letter home.

> The papers call it a 'fervent thanksgiving from the heart'. But I do not think we are such hypocrites here. Most of us know that Mafeking is a glorious pretext for a whole holiday and for throwing off all discipline. We do not break windows because we are mad with joy, but because we think that under the circumstances we can do so with impunity.

The celebrations of the Windsor 'mob' on the other hand struck a discordant note:

> The men were reeling drunk, and the women offensive & gross beyond words. It is a good thing it was Mafeking and not the Royal Borough of Windsor that was besieged.

He concluded, 'The town of Windsor is the fungus on the Royal oak.'[9]

In his essay, 'The English National Character', written in March 1901 against the background of the war, Maynard developed his conception of a proper patriotism. The typical Englishman, he said, was 'neither reactionary nor radical'. In this vein he endorses Kipling's view of the obtrusive patriot as a 'jelly bellied flag flapper', but 'no less to be abhorred', in his opinion, is the obtrustive 'patrophobist' who has, unfortunately, become a 'character-istic figure' of the time. 'It is in part a reaction against modern imperialism, in part the effect of an increased tolerance in thought and speech, but it is largely due to a certain love for the minority which seems to possess a certain class of Englishman'. Keynes was already the thinking patriot he was to remain. His imperial confidence survived the Boer War. He was too young to identify with the anti-imperialism of the older generation of anti-war Radicals like J. A. Hobson, especially as there was no pressure in that direction from home. Throughout his life he assumed the Empire as a fact of life and never showed the slightest interest in discarding it. At the same time he was too much of an economic liberal to develop any sympathy for the attempts of Joseph Chamberlain and others to weld it into an economic bloc. He never much deviated from the view that, all things being con-sidered, it was better to have Englishmen running the world than foreigners.

IV. GLITTERING PRIZES

By his fourth year, Maynard had reached the First Hundred, or what was, in effect, the Lower Sixth form. He was now free to specialise. Hurst, his mathematics master, wanted him to drop all his other subjects. This annoyed Maynard very much. His curiosity was expanding, not contracting. In classics he was up to Luxmoore, whose sarcastic manner he found wholly congenial, regretting only his tendency to set verses on such unpromising subjects as Nuts. He thoroughly enjoyed his History 'extras' with C. K. Marten on the Gunpowder Plot, wondering whether it was really a plot hatched by the authorities to discredit the Catholics. (He was full just then of his Jesuit ancestors whom he had discovered in the course of his researches into his family history, conducted on Sunday afternoons in the Fellows' Library.) In the summer half of 1901 Lubbock opened up yet another interest, when he and Maynard read together an 'extremely fine poem' by Bernard of Cluny, *De contemptu mundi*. 'Mediaeval Latin poetry is now one of his hobbies,' noted Neville in his diary of 22 June 1901. How could one think of giving all this up for mathematics? Hurst now had an additional argument. In June 1901, R. G. Hawtrey, ex-King's Scholar and future Treasury official, managed only 18th wrangler in the mathematics tripos. Hurst cited him as an awful warning of someone who had spread himself too thin. Maynard was unconvinced. Hawtrey, he wrote to Neville on 16 June 1901, was not a person of 'surpassing mathematical ability'; and anyhow it was ridiculous of Hurst to think that 'he has lost his soul in knowing something besides Mathematics'. Both observations offer a clue to Maynard's refusal to specialise; a refusal endorsed by his father who remembered, perhaps, his own sufferings as an undergraduate mathematician.

Maynard's interests extended to sport. He was not good at games, but neither was he a complete 'scug'. In the Michaelmas Half he played a primitive form of soccer known as Eton football. In the Second Half he would play an almost equally esoteric game called Eton Fives, originating centuries earlier from the pastime of banging a ball around in the spaces between the chapel wall and its buttresses. He took up racquets in 1900, finding it a 'very excellent game'. He also rowed, getting his College boating colours in February 1901. Competitive rowing in the icy wind and driving rain gave him little pleasure. He sensibly concluded that 'the labour and time involved in becoming a good oar is not commensurate with the advantage gained' and welcomed his 'promotion' to the *Monarch*, a boat for bad oars where one bought 'cultured ease by giving up ambition' (12 May 1901). Maynard loved going on the river with friends. In the summer he would also join other wet-bobs in a light-hearted game of cricket known as Aquatics, played in College Field.

But the sport which gave him the greatest thrill was the Wall Game. This was yet another of Eton's sports based on special geographical features, in this case the existence of a wall, a gate and a tree in a corner of College Field. From these landmarks generations of Collegers had fashioned a game of exquisite boredom for the spectator, but one which roused its participants to ecstasies of joy. Two sides formed a scrimmage against the wall, each one hoping to gain ground with the ball by pushing the other one back. Proceedings could be brought to a virtual halt by one player sitting on the ball for an inordinate length of time. Maynard thought it a 'glorious game'. Several afternoons a week he would return to his room, muddy, exhausted, exhilarated. Not even the 'awful' inability to breathe beneath a tangle of limbs and bodies dampened his enthusiasm for it; and he was wont to discuss with great seriousness, deploying finely balanced arguments, proposals for some minute change in the rules. Maynard was too light to make a really good 'wall', but his height and pluck made him a valuable player. Every 30 November, on St Andrew's Day, came the great annual game between College and Oppidan Eton, which resembled the battles on the Western Front in the First World War in the mighty exertions they inspired without visible gain of ground. Maynard was College's twelfth man in 1900. The following year he played regularly as College '2nd wall', once remaining on the ball for eight minutes in a prodigious display of valour against gigantic opponents. His parents came up to see him play on St Andrew's Day, 1901, without much pleasure: 'Maynard and the others looked frightfully exhausted,' Neville wrote in his diary. 'He said at one time he thought he was done, all the bully being on top of him and he could not either breathe or call out.' Lubbock was delighted that 'he was so keen about such things'.

Maynard was now a person of some consequence in College. In the Michaelmas Half of 1900 he 'messed' in great style with Hamilton, Dundas and Young in upper tea room, of which he was captain. 'Yesterday evening,' he wrote to Neville on 30 September, 'we ordered 3/- worth of cutlets for tea, then I had a sort of sausage roll business, concluding with some most superlative jam Young brought from home, and cake. This morning after porridge we had buttered eggs made from 15 eggs, then sardines and jam.' His mother worried about such indulgence. 'But, really, my dear son, you will be laying up a bilious attack in store for yourself if you go on like this.' The collapse a few weeks later took the form of boils on the knees, brought about by scratches which had become infected from the mud of the Wall Game. Maynard's blood, the doctor concluded, was not sound.[10] As throughout his life, Maynard's workload was kept going in face of uncertain health. He had measles in his second term, facial twitchings in his fourth. He was prone to mysterious fevers which he called his 'periodicals'. Florence and

Neville had no doubt that he was delicate. They urged him to wrap up against the cold, unwrap against the heat, avoid draughts. They bombarded him with tonics and dietary instructions. He must be sure to wear a large white cotton hat for rowing, Florence wrote on 25 July 1900, 'for I am sure it cannot be safe to have your head and neck exposed'. She signed herself 'your over-anxious mother'. Maynard never showed the slightest resentment at this nagging, which his good humour soon converted into a family joke.

In January 1901 his standing with his fellow Collegers was confirmed when he was elected to College Pop, or Debating Society, the third of his election to make it, behind Dundas and Hamilton. It met on Saturday evenings under its president in College Reading Room. As the name suggests, election was a mark of a boy's popularity with his seniors, since someone could be blackballed almost indefinitely. Maynard took an active part in its proceedings, making witty speeches on such subjects as 'This House would rather England be free than sober'. He also took a close interest in Private Business, at which members of College Pop decided on the regulations and policy of the Reading Room. The future economist appears in this comment on the practice of fining people for leaving their possessions in the room (3 March 1901): 'I do not think it is a good policy to make fines a source of revenue; it is an extremely vexatious form of indirect taxation and one which involves a considerable trouble in collection.... I should prefer a fixed subscription in lieu of fines.' By such a lofty appeal to general principle did Maynard hope to lessen his own contribution to the Reading Room's revenue, as a result of constantly leaving his fives gloves there. His administrative activities burgeoned in his last year. He found himself on the Library Committee, which expelled 112 books from the College Library; on the Committee of Management of the School Stores, in which capacity he spent hours carrying out an inventory of the school shop; and on the Committee of the Athletic Society. 'I am finding like you', he wrote to his father on 9 February 1902, 'that when I am appointed to a committee I am invariably made to do all the work.'

In these ways his Eton life remained full of interest and activity. There was no question of Maynard being bored at school, a common experience of many bright boys. He wished a day had thirty-six hours, a week fourteen days, he told his father, so that he could do justice to all his interests.[11] Apologising for the abrupt termination of one letter home he wrote, 'In a minute and a quarter my light has to be put out and I have many things do before then.' It was to be thus all his life.

Eton's two main school prizes were the Newcastle for classics and divinity, taken in March, and the Tomline for mathematics, taken in June. In his fourth year, Maynard decided to concentrate his efforts on the second. Neville took charge of the preparations with his usual thoroughness, recording in his diary (11 April 1901): 'Maynard is working steadily about 3 hours a day under my direction. I feel quite like a trainer, as if I were training him for a race or a prize fight.' The Tomline examination started on 5 June 1901, Maynard's eighteenth birthday. 'The Algebra and the Analytical Conics were ridiculously easy,' he told his father, 'but the Differential Calculus and Theory of Equations were I think distinctly harder than usual. . . . I went on the plan of looking up very little during the examination.' He and his father had decided that the contest lay between him and Dillwyn Knox; in fact, he won it quite comfortably, Knox only just managing the Select (those who gained a certain minimum number of marks). Knox, Maynard thought, had been undone by his mechanics and lack of lucidity. 'He has got one of the most confused brains I have ever come across,' he wrote to Neville on 15 June. 'Even in conversation he is wholly incapable of expressing the meaning he intends to convey; in addition to this he is quite abnormally untidy in his work & always forgets to write down the most necessary steps.'

When Geoffrey heard the news of Maynard's success he said, 'Poor fellow, he can't help it.' This was Maynard's biggest prize to date – £32 worth of books. He had already started buying books from David's second-hand bookstall in the Cambridge market, and was determined to take some of his prizes in non-regulation bindings (the rule was that they had to be bound in leather) in order to increase the quantity of his purchases. He finally got the headmaster to agree, and as a result was able to buy forty-five volumes. By the time he left Eton his book collection already numbered over 300, of which about half were school prizes. His leaving present to the College was a fine psalter owned by Nicholas Udall, an Eton headmaster of the 1530s.

The Tomline over, Maynard could relax for a few days with his friends on the river before the next bout of examinations. In the last week in July he 'perpetrated' thirty papers for the Cambridge Higher Certificate – the same examination Florence had taken at Newnham. The main bait was the Chamberlayne Prize, a £60 scholarship for four years, which Eton awarded to its candidate with the highest marks, and which would contribute to Maynard's university fees. Maynard had 'never worked so hard before', he told his father, adding characteristic details: 'Before last week I have never done more than 10 hours in a day or more than an average of 7½ for a week, but for the last week I had an average of 10½ hours a day and on Thursday I worked for 12½ hours.' He thought that the mathematics was much harder than in the Tomline. Nevertheless mathematics and history combined won him the overall first place, since he was way down in the classics. 'Even I', Lubbock wrote to Neville on 2 August 1901, 'was fairly dazzled by the actual result. It is an extraordinary performance. He certainly does command success to an amazing extent but then no one ever deserved it better. His way of accepting it is characteristic; just as quiet, frank, and modest as ever. . . . I hope he has not overdone himself.'

It was accepted that Maynard should try for a university scholarship in his last year. There was no problem about which university: 'I don't want to go to Oxford at any price' (24 November 1901). It had long been established that he should try for King's College, Cambridge, Eton's sister foundation. 'There is nowhere else worth going to at Cambridge,' Maynard finally decided.

The subject in which he should try for a scholarship was carefully discussed. Lubbock considered Maynard safe for a first-class honours in classics if he read it; Hurst thought he was certain to be in the first twelve wranglers in mathematics.[12] Mathematics, Maynard's stronger subject, was decided on; but even then there was a question whether he should take just the mathematics papers or offer some classics in addition, as he was allowed to do. Hurst wanted him to take the mathematics papers only. But Maynard had the truer instinct that he would appear more impressive if he offered a combination. In one sense, he was paying the price for his refusal to specialise. Yet that refusal was based on a shrewd suspicion that mathematics was not his life's vocation. What strikes one about these preparations is how little was left to chance. Maynard came up to take his scholarship in December like a perfectly trained racehorse, whose capacities, as those of his rivals, were exactly known, for a race whose every obstacle had been foreseen and prepared for. The result could be predicted within a small margin of error. All this was, of course, made possible by the closeness of the connection between a few schools and a few colleges.

Ninety-five candidates in classics and sixty in mathematics competed for ten open scholarships; of these four from each camp offered the other subject as well. In addition, there was a general essay question: Maynard wrote on 'Money'. Neville got into his usual flap. He thought Maynard had done badly in mechanics and differential calculus. He tried to pick up hints about his son's performance, and couldn't sleep at night. By 9 December he was out of his misery: Maynard would have won one of the closed scholarships in any case. The addition of his classics converted it into an open scholarship, worth £80. Of all the mathematicians, Neville was told, his essay was the only one worth reading. The Provost, Austen Leigh, wrote to Maynard: 'It is a special compliment, and you will get tuition free besides the £80, and also rooms rent free till your first degree.'[13] This was not the end of December's good news. 'You will scarcely believe me,' Maynard wrote to Neville on 15 December, 'I have been elected to Pop.' Pop, or the Eton Society to give it its proper name – not to be confused with College Pop – was Eton's most exclusive social club, of which Roy Harrod remarked, 'these young men govern the school for a time – as they expect.... or used to expect, to govern the country later.'[14] Maynard was an unusual choice since Pop was notoriously a society in which athletes dominated. Certainly, neither he nor Neville had expected the honour. With membership of this grand order went a whole set of sartorial and disciplinary privileges; but, though it widened somewhat Maynard's Etonian circle, his best friends remained Collegers.

Even now there was no thought of relaxation. Neville was already

planning the future. On 14 January 1902 he wrote in his diary: 'I have been
looking up the King's Statutes and find that Maynard will probably be
superannuated for a Fellowship after the Michaelmas T. 1908. I suppose he
will take his Tripos in 1905, and his C[ivil] S[ervice] Exam^n in 1906; so this
leaves a good margin for writing a Fellowship dissertation.' Thus the next
six years were mapped out. Meanwhile there was one prize at Eton which
Maynard had not yet won: the Newcastle, or divinity prize. 'You know
Theology is damned interesting', he told Dundas. He sat for it on 21 March
1902 without much hope, since there were better classical scholars than he
in for it. He did well enough to make the Select, in seventh place, his father
noting that this was the first time a Tomline Prizeman had done so since
1888. Neville worked out that Maynard had done best of his election at
Eton. Long ago, Neville recalled, Mrs Goodchild had said he 'was a genius',
with a particularly marked 'general ability', and these results proved it.[15]

In his last year at Eton Maynard emerged into the sunlit eminence
which English public schools briefly confer on their cleverest and most
popular boys, and compared to which the rest of life seems for many who
have attained it a long anti-climax. He was now one of the schoolboy rulers
of College, exercising, according to his father, 'a wholesome influence on
the Elections below his own'.[16] As a sixth former he was entrusted with
maintaining general school discipline. No doubt, too, he excited the usual
feelings of awe and envy from lesser mortals as he grandly sauntered round
the school grounds, white-waistcoated, and linked arm in arm with a fellow
member of Pop. He blossomed on Eton's public occasions with the sartorial
splendour they required – declaiming Burke's panegyric on Fox in February
Speeches in dress clothes, knee-breeches, and black silk stockings, appearing
on the Fourth of June in a 'perfect dove of a waistcoat – lavender with pale
pink spots'. His social success was, in a way, more remarkable than his
intellectual success, and as significant for the future. Maynard lacked the
famous Eton charm. But he already showed a remarkable ability to win
the respect and appreciation of the authorities and his schoolfellows. His
intelligence was neither narrow nor abrasive; it was at the disposal of the
community. And with it went a sympathetic, quietly authoritative manner,
which was very appealing. Later Maynard's arrogance grew more pronounced to those outside his circle. His values became more self-consciously
private. Yet the nature of his gifts continued to tether him to society. He
never lost the ability to get the best of both worlds – the respect of both his
intellectual and his social peers.

To this one should add the ability to retain the love of his friends.
Despite his public successes he remained at his best and happiest in small
groups. Two partly overlapping circles dominated his last two terms at
school. This first was made up of his College friends, notably Bernard
Swithinbank from his own election, Harold Butler from the election of 1896,
and Daniel Macmillan from the election of 1898. His second circle was the

Eton Literary Society which he and Harold Butler rescued from a moribund condition in February 1902, Maynard becoming its president. Other members included Charles Buxton and Humphrey Paul, both Oppidans, and Bernard Swithinbank from College. They met a couple of times a term to read each other papers on literary topics. His own contribution to the Society was a paper on Bernard of Cluny which he read on 3 May 1902. He had spent almost the whole of the Easter holiday researching and writing it, much to the consternation of Neville, who wanted him to restart his mathematics in preparation for Cambridge. The paper consists partly of literary and philological exegesis. But Maynard was as much attracted by the character as by the poetry of this Benedictine monk who forsook the world for the cloister, reading an expanded and revised version of the same paper a number of times later. His theme is the gentleman's choice: between the life of action and the life of contemplation; the vanity and corruption of this world and the 'calm and joy and light' of the celestial city. The style is excellent, if a little clipped, throughout. And one wonders whether it was a sense of self-recognition that prompted him to end his paper with the following lines from Bernard's *De contemptu mundi*:

> Not only those
> Who hold clear echoes of the voice divine
> Are honourable – they are blest, indeed,
> Whate'er the world has held – but those who hear
> Some fair faint echoes, though the crowd be deaf,
> And see the white gods' garments on the hills,
> Which the crowd sees not, though they may not find
> Fit music for their visions; they are blest,
> Not pitiable.

A day after he read this paper he wrote to his father: 'It has at any rate inspired Bernard the Luny [Bernard Swithinbank] with a desire to read the complete works of Bernard the Cluny.' A year younger than Maynard, though of the same election, Swithinbank, the son of an Anglican clergyman, had come to College two terms after him. As a result their paths had not crossed much academically or in College till Swithinbank was elected to College Pop in July 1901. After that their friendship grew quickly and in his last year Swithinbank was Maynard's best friend. In his speeches at College Pop Maynard half jokingly referred to the 'epigrammatic lips of Mr. Swithinbank' and praised him as 'that child of all that is best in the eighteenth century'.

Swithinbank, a fine classicist, was good-looking, vulnerable, unworldly: a combination which Maynard always found appealing. He regarded him as a delicate work of art, to be worshipped and protected against breakage. The same feelings inspired the two great later loves of his life – Duncan Grant and Lydia Lopokova. The chief 'object' of their joint attentions was Daniel

Macmillan, then sixteen, a clever, beautiful boy, who remained Maynard's lifelong friend and published all his books. Bernard Swithinbank later described the emotional atmosphere as he remembered it:

> In College emotion and desire were directed almost exclusively towards the male sex – I knew hardly anyone who ever thought of women. This does not mean that there was a great deal of 'vice'; indeed, it was looked on with disapproval, not untinged with envy, by the many who repressed their desires through shyness or virtue. M[aynard] shared the general feeling. I do not know that he was reputed to indulge in it. At Cambridge, he was deeply moved by Plato's pictures of passion spiritualized.[17]

Maynard's Eton life ended as strenuously as it had begun. He and other members of the Shakespeare Society performed part of *Much Ado about Nothing* for Fourth of June Speeches (Maynard acting Dogberry); Maynard also acted Acres opposite Harold Butler's Sir Lucius in an act of Sheridan's *The Rivals*. Early in July he was briefly ill with one of his 'irrational fevers', Swithinbank nursing him 'in a most devoted way'.[18] At the end of July 1902, much against his inclination but no doubt as an antidote to idleness, he retook the Cambridge Higher Certificate, once more coming out top, despite lack of preparation. He was now nineteen; Eton had no more to give him. On 30 July he wrote to Neville: 'I have just reached the very melancholy stage. Last night I received a vote of thanks in College Pop, a thing I desired perhaps more than anything else that remained to be got here – Eton has been much kinder to me than I have deserved.' Lubbock wrote:

> He leaves regretted by everyone who knows him. He has I think been lucky in his time here: the leading boys here during the last year or two seem to me to have been extremely nice: & well has he taken his part among them. He has no doubt a very fine mature mind, & he is not in the least overweighted by it as many boys of his age might be; I have rarely known any boy so clever, & yet so far removed from any trace of priggishness.... I fear it may be long before I have again a pupil who will combine ability & industry so well; of his character I will only say that I think he is a boy on whom one can depend entirely. With all his cleverness he accepts the duties put before him with the readiest obedience & without any questioning as to whether he himself after all does not know best.

5

The Cambridge Undergraduate

I. KING'S COLLEGE

At Cambridge Maynard experienced a philosophic and emotional awakening which shifted his values. He never lost his inherited sense of public duty but this was to be balanced by the claims of friendship and aesthetic experience. In this shift, King's College played an important part.

It had been founded by King Henry VI in 1441 as the sister foundation of Eton College. The king's intention was that 'our poor scholars of our Royal Foundation of St Mary's of Eton, after they had been sufficiently taught the first rudiments of grammar, shall be transferred thence to our aforesaid College of Cambridge .... there to be thoroughly instructed in the liberal arts ....' Four hundred years later this scheme was still in operation. King's College 'numbered seventy members, partly Fellows and partly scholars, varying inversely with each other.... An Eton Colleger went in due time to King's, if there was a vacancy for him, became a Fellow, took his degree without examination, and remained till the end of his days with increasing income and dignity unless he married or took a living.'[1] But what was potentially, at any rate, 'a magnificent system for the endowment of research' had by then become 'a sort of life-long rest-home' for those who had survived the horrors of Eton's Long Chamber.[2]

In the first half of the nineteenth century King's must have given the impression of a beautiful, but largely deserted, stately home. Two buildings of great splendour, the Chapel, completed in 1515, and the Fellows' (or Gibbs) Building dating from 1725, were set in beautiful parks and lawns. But there was no intellectual life, and few signs of physical life. Most of the fellows, having no teaching duties, were non-resident, though they continued to draw handsome dividends from the college's estates. The scholars never numbered more than a dozen or so.

Both Royal Foundations were wakened from their torpor by the magic wand of Victorian reform. The revival of King's dates from the 1850s, and was accomplished by a mixture of external pressure from Parliament, and the internal pressure of new arrivals from a reformed Eton. When Maynard arrived, King's was on the crest of a wave. 'The decade 1875–1884', he recalled much later, 'was a period of exceptional distinction, the full prestige of which the college was enjoying when I was young.'[3] By basing its intake on scholars, and by insisting that all its undergraduates took the tripos, King's deliberately set out to educate an academic elite. Of thirty-four undergraduates in residence in 1873, no fewer than nineteen obtained first-class honours. By the time Keynes came up King's had 30 fellows, 30 postgraduates and over 130 undergraduates (there were 3000 undergraduates altogether at Cambridge) and only Trinity and St John's, much larger colleges, rivalled it in academic and social prestige. But although there were the usual divisions into scholars and hearties, as well as Etonians (now reduced to 13 per cent) and the rest, he entered a society very similar to the one he had left – where intellectual values were prized and which had inherited from Eton a tradition of intimacy, and close contact between dons and students. King's fellows of the late nineteenth century were characteristically outstanding teachers rather than scholars.

The King's of Keynes's day was shaped above all by Oscar Browning. 'The O.B.' as he was known was Cambridge's most famous 'character'. 'A genius flawed by abysmal fatuity' is E. F. Benson's well-known, but inaccurate, pre-Freudian verdict. In fact O.B.'s genius – as an educator, for he had none as a scholar – was built on his 'flaw', the flaw being a love of boys. O.B. was one of the great Victorian survivors. His secret was his style. He was outrageous, bawdy, witty, catty, artless, snobbish, egotistical, affectionate, amorous, but not overtly lecherous. In that repressed era, when intimacy was sought but denied, O.B. broke down barriers: his absurdity made them seem absurd. His gift was to put all kinds of people at their ease. As a result he got and gave a good deal of affection without overstepping the limits of what was permissible, though his behaviour was certainly highly eccentric.

O.B.'s aim was to provide an education fit for statesmen. To this end he opposed the two main educational tendencies of his day – the worship of athletics and the trend to specialisation. Like his university colleague J. B. Seeley, Regius Professor of Modern History, he believed that the kind of education he had in mind could best be done through history and politics. Browning was appointed college tutor in history in 1880, and a university lecturer in 1883. In his day, King's became the college to go to for history, though O.B. was an indifferent tutor, sleeping soundly while his students read their essays. His didactic purpose depended not on exact scholarship or criticism but on a new relationship between dons and undergraduates. He founded his famous Political Society, instituted his Sunday evening 'At Homes', and associated himself with numerous undergraduate activities (as president of the University Bicycle Club he once crossed the Alps on a tricycle). As he had done while an assistant master at Eton, he took favoured pupils on the Continental grand tour to widen their cultural horizons. Nor was working-class education neglected. O.B. was founder and for eighteen years principal of the Cambridge Teachers Day Training College. He took an active interest in the Cambridge branch of the Navy League, his biographer H. E. Wortham recording that 'one of the many soft spots in his heart he kept for sailors'. He would take groups of them to see plays in London. He kept working-class youths as his servants. They slept in his room and scrubbed him in his bath; he taught them to play musical instruments. His importance in our story is not that he and Maynard were particularly close, but that the social atmosphere of King's in Maynard's time and for many years afterwards was largely O.B.'s doing.

In 1908, O.B., by then seventy-one, lost both his college post and his principalship of the Day Training College, on general grounds of age and specific grounds of non-performance of duties. He felt he had been badly treated, and though still a fellow of King's, decamped to Rome where he lived, 'a by no means extinct volcano',[4] till 1923. Maynard, by then also a fellow of King's, made it a point to keep up with him and help him with his tax problems. One of O.B.'s last letters to Maynard from Rome is dated 19 January 1918: 'I am engaged in the fascinating occupation of writing a History of the World – the only History worth writing,' O.B. wrote. He added, 'I like being 81.'

A less overpowering personality than O.B. was a bachelor history don called Goldsworthy Lowes Dickinson, a fellow since 1887. If O.B. represented, notionally at least, the outgoing spirit of the college – he stood unsuccessfully for Parliament three times – Goldie represented it in its aspect as shelter from the world. This was so by temperament, not conviction. He wanted to serve humanity; but he could never hit the right keys on his typewriter. So he retreated into King's, and erected, as he himself admitted, a philosophy on a defect. Needing to love, and be dominated by, heterosexual men, he depicted in his writing an ideal world united by the love of comrades. His most influential books were in the form of Socratic dialogues; he made his educational impact at King's not through formal instruction but through his Discussion Society modelled on a Platonic symposium. At meetings of this body, writes Esmé Wingfield-Stratford, a Kingsman of Keynes's time, 'a convention of cultivated irreverence' coexisted with 'an atmosphere of a certain Grecian suggestiveness'.

While setting a standard in cultivated discussion, Goldie lacked the power to move either to intellectual or to emotional passion. When in 1914 the great fire of war swept away his hopes for sweetness and light, he blamed himself 'since I could never so speak and act that men had to attend to me'. At King's, though, many did, like E. M. Forster, his friend and biographer, and his influence was overwhelmingly on the side of the private affections and allegiances. Like Sidgwick and Browning, Goldie was a characteristic late-Victorian intellectual in whom a vestigial sense of public duty was constantly at war with unfulfilled private passions; unable to separate them in his mind, he was unable also to bring them into harmony with each other.

There were many other dons who contributed their quota of distinction and eccentricity – Nathaniel Wedd, a classics tutor who affected red ties and blasphemy, J. E. Nixon, a famous hoarder of umbrellas, 'Monty' James, a bibliophile of immense erudition and pedantry, who entertained his favourite Etonians by reading them his own ghost stories. The main point is that King's, contrary to Browning's hopes, was never cut out to be a nursery for statesmen. It was 'a perfect forcing house of unique characters, varying between the extremes of greatness and absurdity'.[5] It could remain a perfect shelter for those too shy or eccentric to face the world: a society of clever, dotty inmates, provided with a continuing supply of charming and clever youths to stir atrophied emotions. Maynard Keynes, while appreciating to the full what King's had to offer, was built for a less cloistered existence. Nevertheless, King's became, with Eton, an object of his passionate loyalty, to be cherished and preserved by all the exertions of his practical intelligence.

II. THE FRESHMAN

In his first year he was lodged in a poky house in King's Lane.* A fellow freshman, Charles Rye Fay, later an economic historian, remembered a young man with 'a moustache and fancy waistcoat' inviting him to tea on his first day. 'My name's Keynes. What's yours?' A little later he told Fay: 'I've had a good look round the place and come to the conclusion that it's pretty inefficient'. Maynard's best friend at King's was another Lane freshman, Robin Furness, a clever, elegant, Rugbeian classical scholar, with an exceptional mastery of the obscene in the literature of all languages and ages. Another freshman inhabitant of the Lane was William Norton Page, a mathematical scholar, with whom Maynard went for coaching to Ernest Hobson, later Sadlerian Professor of Mathematics, and elder brother of J. A. Hobson, the unorthodox economist. For many years Maynard had a higher regard for the mathematician Hobson than for the economist Hobson.

No more than at Eton was Maynard prepared to be boxed into mathematics. He would not, he told his father, devote himself exclusively to it, even 'if he could thereby be Senior Wrangler'.[6] Soon after he arrived he went on a book-buying spree; he also took up rowing for the college. But above all he found himself in a society honeycombed with clubs and discussion groups, many of them based on King's and Trinity. Although some of them were at least up to the Etonian standard of exclusiveness, Maynard, who arrived with a big reputation in a small world, soon found himself besieged with invitations. There was Oscar Browning's Political Society and Dickinson's

* The Lane was demolished in 1967 to make way for the Keynes Building.

Discussion Society. There was the Trinity Essay Society at which, on 10 November 1902, he heard Lytton Strachey deliver what he called a 'most brilliant satire on Christianity' – probably his first sight of Strachey, then a third-year undergraduate. Soon Maynard was a member of four debating societies, one of them the Decemviri, made up of ten invited undergraduates from King's and Trinity.

Some mathematics was done in Maynard's first Christmas vacation; but this was coupled with a study of 'the works of Peter Abelard, my intention being, at present, to write a paper upon the aforesaid gent'.⁷ This essay, he told Swithinbank, still at Eton, was getting more and more unwieldy but 'never mind, I do it for my own amusement rather than for my hearers' and they may go to the devil'.⁸ The following term at a meeting of the King's Appenine Literary Society, Maynard read his paper on Abelard, the twelfth-century theologian, who had been the lover of Héloïse and was condemned for heresy at the instigation of Maynard's old hero Bernard of Cluny. What Maynard admired in Bernard were his ascetic ideals; what he praised in Peter Abelard was his belief in reason. He quoted his words: 'Not because God has taught it, is a thing to be believed. . . . but because it is proved to be so.' In his paper on Bernard Maynard had set up the conflict between monastic ideals and the life of action. In his paper on Peter Abelard he contrasted the claims of reason and love with those of faith and conventional morality. He was growing up into adulthood, and into the Edwardian age.

Maynard was as eager as ever to taste anything which seemed intellectually worthwhile. Thus in his second term he dragged Fay, reading history, to G. E. Moore's lectures on ethics and J. E. McTaggart's on metaphysics. McTaggart covered the metaphysical aspects of time, and soon Keynes was writing a paper on 'Time and Change' to be read to another King's society, the Parrhesiasts. He helped form a Baskerville Club with fellow book-collectors like Arthur Cole. He took up bridge with the old Etonian Stephen Gaselee. 'It is too much,' Neville noted disconsolately.

Neville himself opened up one avenue of escape from mathematics. He had made Maynard a life member of the Cambridge Union, or Debating Society, and on 4 November 1902 Maynard made his maiden speech – 'the bravest thing I ever did,' he told his father. *Granta*, the undergraduate newspaper, thought it excellent. So did the president of the Union, Edwin Montagu, who invited Maynard to deliver a speech 'from the paper' a fortnight later. Montagu, a rising Liberal politician, was Keynes's first and most important political patron. He was a hideously ugly man, whose ugliness, however, was redeemed by charm, a cynical intelligence and a passion for gossip. Maynard had much reason to be grateful to him in the early part of his career. At the Union, Montagu was more taken by Keynes's logic than by his delivery, which was not impressive. Keynes spoke regularly throughout his first year on the political subjects which were the staple of debates, and in June 1903 was elected to its Committee at his second attempt.

The lack of passion in Maynard's oratory reflected the lack of passion in his political beliefs. He joined the University Liberal Club, because the Liberals were the party of intelligence, not because he had any great enthusiasm for reform. Thus in May 1903 we find him at the Union opposing Home Rule for Ireland on practical grounds. He could speak much more eloquently when aroused, as he invariably was when the subject was Christianity and its iniquities. In his second term he and fellow Kingsman Jack Sheppard mobilised the forces of college anti-clericalism to stop the establishment of a High Church mission to the East End of London, one of the main outlets for the do-gooding impulses of the time. As he wrote to Swithinbank on 5 February 1903:

> Sheppard and I and several others helped to organise a regular opposition and we finally carried the College meeting by a majority of 75 to 25 that the scheme should be on a purely *secular* basis.... It was a tremendous triumph.... I had to make a speech before the Provost, almost the whole College, and a no. of dons....

Maynard's speech was remembered years later as a triumph of the forensic art.

His fellow anti-clerical John Tressider Sheppard, the son of a Baptist pastor in Balham and later Provost of King's, was one of the products of O.B.'s liberating touch. He became one of Cambridge's 'characters', declaiming and dancing his way though the Union, of which he became president. The Greek tragedies were his real love. His approach to them, as to life, was histrionic rather than scholarly; and he lectured on the pagan ethic with all the eloquence of the Baptist preacher. He was slight and cherubic when Maynard first knew him. Sheppard's first impression of Maynard was of 'sensitive, expressive hands and of the beauty of his eyes'. They soon became friends, and were to be lifelong colleagues.

Maynard's insatiable passion for everything except mathematics alarmed Neville. Hobson was adamant: Maynard must 'wear blinkers' if he was to do well in the tripos. 'Probably his heart is not in the subject,' wrote Neville in his diary, remembering his own disastrous first year. Although Maynard confessed to being 'sick of mathematics', telling his father that it was his 'worst subject',[9] it was Neville who suffered more than he did.

III. APOSTLES AND PHENOMENA

In the December of his first term Maynard received a visit from two tall young men, one thin and etiolated, with moustache and pince-nez, the other dark, with a long, mournful face. They introduced themselves as Mr Strachey and Mr Woolf. Sir Roy Harrod assures us that a lively conversation ensued. Maynard was supposed to have no inkling of their purpose, which was to consider his suitability for election to the University's most selective society, the Cambridge Conversazione Society, or Apostles. Its existence was meant to be secret, partly to avoid offence to friends of Apostles who were not themselves Apostolic, and partly as a means to privacy. But the secrecy was not total; more aspired than were chosen. Maynard would not have been hard to spot as an 'embryo' or likely recruit to a Society whose field of scrutiny was virtually confined to two colleges – Trinity and King's. Both abounded in Apostles, active and emeritus. Maynard would already have been known to most of them by his brilliant reputation at Eton, his exceptional scholarship performance, and as Neville's son. In his first term, Oscar Browning and Lowes Dickinson, both 'angels' or retired Apostles, had observed him approvingly. Sheppard, an undergraduate Apostle, had met him through the Cambridge Union. Following the visit by Strachey and Woolf he was subjected to a secret selection procedure organised by Strachey, who was secretary, consisting of breakfast and tea parties at which other Apostles would look him over. In these ways he was judged and found worthy. On Saturday 28 February 1903 he was initiated or 'born' into the Society with the usual paraphernalia of the secret curse and other time-hallowed rituals. Sheppard was his 'father' or sponsor. It was a rare honour for a freshman, but Maynard was a rare freshman.

Maynard was Apostle no. 243 in an unbroken sequence stretching back to George Tomlinson, the Society's founder, in 1820. The proceedings were very much what they had been in Sidgwick's day. Every Saturday evening in term time the active brethren would meet, behind locked doors, in the secretary's room. Angels would often join them, though not obliged to do so. A 'moderator' would read a paper on a topic previously agreed; it would be discussed by members, speaking from the 'hearthrug', in an order determined by lot, and a question arising from it put to the vote. These intellectual activities were accompanied by the consumption of anchovies on toast – known as 'whales' – and tea or coffee. The object and atmosphere of the meetings seem not to have varied much over time. They were summed up by Sidgwick as 'the pursuit of truth with absolute devotion and unreserve by a group of intimate friends'. The papers often had humorous titles, and serious themes were thought to be improved by witty and amusing treatment. Meeting every Saturday, and practically living in each other's rooms in the intervals, the Apostles were more like a family than a club. Their discussions were full of in-jokes, personal allusions, private meanings. Their talk was spiced with blasphemy and sexual innuendo, much as it had been at school.

Maynard's new companions were clever, philosophical, irreverent and unworldly. The active brethren at the time of his election consisted of three undergraduates from Trinity – Lytton Strachey, Saxon Sydney-Turner and Leonard Woolf – and two from King's – Jack Sheppard and Leonard Greenwood. Older Apostles like E. M. Forster, Ralph Hawtrey, A. R. Ainsworth and H. O. Meredith, all recent graduates of King's, often came up for meetings. Further back were the 'angels' of the 1890s, notably Charles Percy Sanger, Bertrand Russell, R. C. and G. M. Trevelyan, G. E. Moore, G. H. Hardy and Desmond MacCarthy, all from Trinity. Stretching further back were the Davies brothers (Theodore and Crompton), Roger Fry, J. Ellis McTaggart, Lowes Dickinson and A. N. Whitehead. The O.B. was the most ancient fount of Apostolic lore, and had donated a cedar trunk (known as the ark) in which the Society kept its records.

Membership of the Society affected Maynard's life in a profound way. Most obviously it gave him a new circle of friends; and one which was constantly replenished from the same source, as the Society gave 'birth' to new Apostles, to whose selection and cultivation Maynard gave considerable attention. Much of the rest of his life would be spent in the circle of Apostles, old and new, and their friends and relations. Two close Trinity friends of Lytton Strachey, though not themselves Apostles, must count as part of this circle – Thoby Stephen and Clive Bell. A little later they played a key part in creating that London extension of Apostolic Cambridge known as the Bloomsbury Group. Not that Maynard's old friends fell away immediately: Dilly Knox (who came to King's in 1904), Bernard Swithinbank and Daniel Macmillan (who both went to Balliol College, Oxford) remained his main links with his Eton past. He remained friendly with Furness and Fay, especially the former. But he had entered a new world, which became more vivid to him than his old one.

With a change in friends came a change in values. Part of it was no doubt due to growing self-awareness; but membership of the Society reinforced it. At Eton he had been a schoolboy with an exceptional range: a scientist with an 'artistic' side, an intellectual with a marked practical flair. After 1903 the partition of his life into a private and a public sphere becomes more obvious. On one side were ranged philosophy, aesthetics, friendship; on the other, political and practical affairs. It is also noticeable that from this time onwards he started to give much more priority to the first than to the second. This represented a choice of values. Maynard's genius shone through in whatever he did; but from 1903 onwards his passions were most deeply engaged by private aims, however 'pleasant', 'agreeable' or 'amusing' he found politics or administration. The priority he gave to the private sphere reflected a particular kind of conditioning which started with his membership of the Apostles. The Society gave him the opportunity, incentive and justification for becoming the kind of person he wanted to be.

The shift can be summed up in terms of the Society's own Kantian joke: it alone was 'real'; the rest of the world was 'phenomenal'. When McTaggart unexpectedly married late in life he assured the brethren that he was merely taking a 'phenomenal' wife: Maynard himself would refer to non-Apostles as 'phenomena'. What all this meant was that the world outside was regarded as less substantial, less worthy of attention than the Society's own collective life. It meant it was being judged by esoteric standards and found wanting. It was a joke with a serious twist.

Whence came the Society's potency, its ability to transform the lives of its members? How could a club which in many ways was 'a typical undergraduate debating society and typically silly'[10] have this effect? One should never underestimate the effect of secrecy. Much of what made the rest of the world seem alien sprang from this simple fact. Secrecy was a bond which greatly amplified the Society's life relative to its members' other interests. It is much easier, after all, to spend one's time with people from whom one does not have to keep large secrets; and spending much time with them reinforces whatever it was that first drew them together. Also important was the fact that membership was for life. Older Apostles did not simply disappear into their careers. They took wing – but often no further than to the nearest combination room whence they could maintain their involvement in the Society's affairs. From 1903 until 1908 or 1909, that is, from the age of twenty to twenty-five or twenty-six, most of Maynard's private life, talk and gossip had reference to the Society. Such a prolonged exposure to a small group of people of like mind can implant a lifelong stamp on one's values and attitudes.

Membership of the Society undoubtedly bred an attitude of superiority to the phenomenal world and its concerns. No member doubted that he was one of the pick of young Cambridge. 'It was owing to the existence of the Society that I soon got to know the people best worth knowing,' wrote Bertrand Russell.[11] Such self-perception was only partly accurate: as Stephen Toulmin has remarked, most of the great nineteenth-century Cambridge scientists – Darwin, Rayleigh, Jeans and Eddington – managed to slip through the net.[12] So did Galton and Karl Pearson, Alfred Marshall and Arthur Pigou. Nevertheless, it was all too easy to feel that one was living on a lofty, and lonely, eminence. 'Is it monomania – this colossal moral superiority that we feel?' wrote Maynard to Lytton Strachey a couple of years later. 'I get the feeling that most of the rest never see anything at all – too stupid or too wicked.'[13]

'The undergraduates who made it into the Cambridge Conversazione

Society', Toulmin writes, 'were (it seems) the ones who had a way with words. . . .' This is important. The Society's tradition was philosophical. From the days of Maurice and Sterling in the early nineteenth century through Henry Sidgwick to McTaggart and Moore, philosophy, especially moral philosophy, had been a leading preoccupation. The Society of Maynard's day contained Whitehead, McTaggart, Russell and Moore, all destined to be world-famous philosophers. It is hardly surprising that Maynard's first sustained intellectual interest should have been in philosophy rather than economics, though here we must add the influence of his own home and the endless discussions between his father and W. E. Johnston on logical problems. But the important point about this philosophic apprenticeship is that successive generations of Apostles, and Maynard's was no exception, emerged with tough-minded, and therefore robust, theories about how they should lead their own lives. Maynard's election to the Society was followed, six months later, by the publication of G. E. Moore's *Principia Ethica*, the most important book in his life. We will discuss the ethical beliefs he got from Moore in the next chapter. The point to note is that they were far from being the wishy-washy things which emerge from most student discussions over midnight coffee. They were capable of giving direction to lives. A second important interest of the Society in Maynard's time was aesthetic. Apostles like Desmond MacCarthy, H. O. Meredith, E. M. Forster, Saxon Sydney-Turner, Lytton Strachey and Sheppard, as well as Clive Bell and Thoby Stephen, were more interested in literature and painting than in philosophy as such. Nevertheless, their orientation to these things, the value they placed on them, the way in which they talked about them, was largely determined by philosophy and particularly by Moore's philosophy. Both streams, philosophic and aesthetic, flowed into the Society's 'search for truth' in Maynard's time, and his own papers to the Apostles can be broadly divided into these two groups. Economics was hardly represented at all. Nor was politics.

The focus of the Society's interests suggests another feature: its unworldliness. Most of the Apostles were dons: embryonic, actual or manqué. They were selected for membership precisely because they combined great cleverness with great unworldliness. The source of this unworldliness differed from case to case. G. E. Moore was a genuine saint, whose innocence was palpable. Lowes Dickinson was simply defeated by the world. Lytton Strachey, as his biographer Michael Holroyd remarked, was 'not unambitious only unconfident'. Another characteristic is more common. The Apostles of Maynard's day, with one or two exceptions, were distinctly deficient in charm and beauty, the qualities which tether people to society. Not only were they lacking, as Virginia Woolf later remarked, in 'physical splendour'; they had no small talk; they were arrogant, prickly, withdrawn. They compensated by the brilliance and fearlessness of their cerebration to each other, by the exaggerated unworldliness of their ideals, and by the inelastic standards by which they judged the human drama unfolding outside. They were men whose lives tended to be devoid of feminine company, except that of their female relations. This was a common Cambridge, even Victorian, pattern in young adulthood; but it was exaggerated by precisely those other features which cut off the Society from the world. In these ways the Society functioned as a 'protective coterie' for members who were too shy or awkward or clever to be fully comfortable in the world and who needed each other to sparkle or for social therapy. At the same time, one must not ignore the positive power of the unworldly ideal for clever young men bred both in the classics and gentlemanly ideals, to whom much of Victorian life seemed ugly and oppressive.

When two of the Cambridge Apostles of the 1930s, Guy Burgess and Anthony Blunt, were exposed as Soviet agents, there were strident editorials in the newspapers denouncing the consequences of people cutting themselves off from 'ordinary morality' to indulge their esoteric tastes. Yet the most striking thing about the Apostles is their quintessential *Englishness*. Their own exclusiveness was rooted in the larger exclusions of English life: exclusions which ensured their own membership was drawn from the small group which had survived an elaborate selection procedure which started with birth. Their own sense of special worthiness was echoed by every group in England which felt able to look down on some other group as deficient in the special virtue it felt itself to possess. They were a product of a very English reaction to industrial life, based on the cult of dead languages, chivalry, moral utopias and the rejection of commercial careers. They were a civilised response to the barbarities of English public-school education and the stifling moralism of English family life; and at the same time an expression of the peculiar English capacity for keeping its upper-class males in a state of petrified adolescence. Finally, they reflected one side of an ancient university civilisation – Cambridge's image of itself as a world of learning and beauty set in a land of barbarians and philistines. Theirs was the donnish ideal of Elysium on the Cam. Even so, from all that we have discovered so far, and from what we know of Maynard's career, it is clear that the Society appealed only to certain sides of his character. He could get enjoyment out of life in its more vigorous aspects.

With Maynard at Cambridge, his parents gave up the family's traditional August holiday: it was important that their elder son go on working at King's, which provided residential facilities for a six-week term in the long vacation. On 12 July 1903 he moved into his new rooms on Staircase A of Wilkins Building, facing the chapel. Neville and Florence bought him a new desk, no doubt to encourage mathematical endeavour. There were the usual interruptions. Eton friends came to stay; at the end of August he spent a week with Humphrey Paul in Sussex. He returned to Harvey Road where, he told Swithinbank, 'I am enjoying a useless existence in the study of electricity, dynamics, and golf.' He was also engaged on a compulsory essay on Dickens, which King's inflicted on its undergraduates. 'He is an author whom I am physically incapable of reading, so that I have to invent purely imaginary theories about him – and then find not unnaturally that I have no illustrations....' On 25 September he left with his father for a week of mathematics and double dummy bridge at Sheringham. Neville, who was having one of his attacks of 'golf pleurisy', noted that Maynard had quite 'recovered his driving power' by the end of the vacation.

He could have done with some of it at the Union where, on 24 November 1903, he defended free trade in a speech which, according to *Granta*, displayed 'such an utter lack of animation and rhetorical verve' that Neville contemplated lessons in voice production.[14] But Maynard had sufficiently increased the vigour of his delivery by the end of his second year to be elected secretary of the Union, thus ensuring his automatic ascent to the presidency. The free trade-protection controversy, which broke out in 1903 with Joseph Chamberlain's call for protection and imperial preference, stirred Maynard to economic as well as political activity: his father records him studying political economy in September 1903.[15] Like most Cambridge economists (Marshall headed a Free Trade Manifesto published in *The Times* on 15 August 1903 which confidently declared that no unemployment could result from an increase of imports) Maynard was a staunch free trader; in fact free trade was his only political cause before the First World War. 'Conservatism had died and been born again, a lower animal,' he told the Cambridge Union a little later.[16] To Swithinbank he wrote on 15 December: 'Sir, I hate all priests and protectionists.... Free Trade and free thought! Down with pontiffs and tariffs. Down with those who declare we are dumped and damned. Away with all schemes of redemption or retaliation.'

A further distraction that term had been Cambridge's triennial Greek play, in which Sheppard had clowned his way through the part of Peisthetaerus in Aristophanes' *Birds*. Hamilton, Swithinbank and Dundas came over from Oxford; Daniel Macmillan from Eton. 'The naughty boy had already been twice to the Greek play,' Neville noted on 27 November 1903. The next night he went again with Florence and the Eton party. 'Maynard cannot be doing much Mathematics,' his father observed on 2 December. 'For 14 consecutive days he has only one free evening.' But discipline was re-established in the holidays. To Swithinbank Maynard wrote on 22 December: 'All the term long I talk and behave and talk and am desperately normal. And in the vacation I sit and read and write and the most mad things come into my head and I pass through every variety of mood in a week.'

Family business of a more agreeable kind occupied Maynard in his next vacation. His sister Margaret, 'exceedingly pretty and winsome' in Neville's eyes, had been packed off to Germany in October 1903 after having failed her examinations at Wycombe Abbey. There she spent a miserable six months with an impoverished aristocrat, Baroness von Gissing. In mid-March 1904 Florence and Maynard set out to rescue her. It was his first trip to Germany and they did some sight-seeing, as well as visiting his old German governess, Fräulein Rotman, now married. From Dresden Maynard wrote to Swithinbank on 24 March:

> Every painter is here, but I find the Germans of the early sixteenth century most to my taste, – the Dürers, Holbeins, and Cranachs. I should like to analyse my reasons – if I have any. In Berlin we saw more pictures – especially one Holbein, and both here and there much statuary, Greek and Roman and later; at Berlin two most beautiful boys' busts of the Augustan period, and a most magnificent bust of Scipio Africanus – but the list is endless....

On his return Maynard read a paper on 'Beauty' to the Apostles (30 April 1904) in which he tried to show that it was better to love nature than pictures and statues, but statues were more beautiful, because more like nature, than pictures. A faithful enough account of middle-brow Victorian aesthetic theory, it does at least show that Maynard's interest in the visual arts antedated his connection with Bloomsbury.

On 5 June 1904 Maynard became twenty-one. He received a watch from Neville and Florence, and many other presents from members of the family. Although one part of his life had moved beyond the control, even knowledge, of his parents, their involvement in his future had not diminished. A report to Neville on Maynard's mathematics was moderately encouraging: 'He thinks the boy has not got stale ... as at one time he feared would be the case.' Far from reassured, Neville 'made some suggestions' for future work to Maynard's new coach, Leathem of St John's.[17] But the role of 6 Harvey Road was not confined to this. In term-time it was a second home. Each weekend Maynard would take his friends there for meals. What Neville and Florence made of the squeaky, disjointed Lytton and trembling Leonard Woolf is not recorded. But their hospitality was not of the prying sort. Manners held together the Victorian and Edwardian worlds even after their values had started to drift apart. No doubt Neville and Florence tried a little match-making. There were plenty of young women on Harvey Road occasions, daughters of Neville's colleagues, or students at Girton and Newnham, where he still lectured on logic. Neville, with his old-fashioned gallantry, was probably more interested in them than was Maynard. There were also the usual invitations to dances and balls, which Maynard either refused, or accepted with bad grace. He hated dancing. 'Thank heaven I have refused *all* parties this year,' he wrote to his sister Margaret on 23 December 1903; 'not a single dame has ensnared me....'

Maynard's Cambridge friends were now a mixture of Apostles and phenomena. In June 1904 he stayed with Fay in Liverpool, where Fay remembers his brilliant disproofs of Christianity and his execrable golf.[18] In the middle of July he spent what was meant to be a restful weekend with Bertrand Russell and his wife Alys in their cottage near Farnham. Twenty-six guests arrived unexpectedly.[19] Russell's *Principles of Mathematics* (1903) had just established him as one of the world's leading philosophers. To Lytton Strachey Keynes wrote, 'For hours on Saturday night Russell wiped the floor with a man called Leonard Hobhouse – a most superb display.'[20] Russell formed the highest opinion of Keynes's intellect. It was 'the sharpest and clearest that I have ever known. When I argued with him, I felt that I took my life in my hands, and I seldom emerged without feeling something of a fool.'[21] On 29 August 1904 Maynard set off for a week's walking tour in Wales, knapsack on back, with Leonard Woolf. They climbed Snowdon, staying on the way with Sanger and his wife Dora in Aberdaron. Maynard was never a great walker or climber. On this holiday, however, Leonard remembered him as an 'extraordinarily good companion' with whom he talked philosophy all day and played bezique in the evenings.[22] At Cambridge in the Michaelmas Term of 1904 Maynard took to walking on Sunday afternoons with the 'angel' George Trevelyan, also of Trinity, a historian and doughty walker of the old school. Maynard had just become both president of the Liberal Club and of the Cambridge Union, speaking in debates at both Oxford and Edinburgh. He also took a King's team to Eton to play College in the Wall Game. 'I do think Eton is the most astounding place in the world,' he wrote to Swithinbank on 5 November 1904, 'of all complex entities the most a priori improbable.' Trevelyan urged him to a political career. 'You are born to be a politician I should guess,' he told him – a judgement singularly lacking in perception.[23]

IV. STATES OF MIND

Maynard's best friend at Cambridge in his last undergraduate year was Giles Lytton Strachey. The future author of *Eminent Victorians* was then a postgraduate at Trinity, writing a dissertation on Warren Hastings. In one respect, Strachey was the most important friend Maynard ever had. He was the only one who ever exerted on him an appreciable moral authority. In the usual pattern of Maynard's close friendships, Maynard was the one who dominated. He was cleverer, more articulate, more worldly, more practical than his friends. As his achievements piled up, he came to be regarded (and to regard himself) as an arbiter on every subject. In his friendship with Strachey, the roles were reversed. Strachey was three years older than Keynes and a much more formed and definite character. He did not become a professional philosopher, but he had a sharp, analytical mind, even being able to hold his own with Russell. Strachey was a philosopher of the tastes and the emotions. Long after the intimate phase of their friendship ended in 1908, he retained his power to make Maynard feel morally uncomfortable.

Born into London's intellectual aristocracy, the eighth child of parents with strong connections with Indian administration, Strachey grew up into a 'very queer gentleman'. His appearance when Keynes first knew him was disconcerting, even to himself. He was long, thin, pale and disjointed, with spidery legs and arms; short-sighted, big-nosed, and with what his biographer calls 'calamitous equine teeth'. His voice never managed a decisive transition to a lower register, periods of deep masculine sound alternating with squeals in piping falsetto. His family home, 69 Lancaster Gate, Lytton himself described as 'a house afflicted with elephantiasis'. Here he grew up with six sisters, a brother, and numerous relations, all talking, usually simultaneously, with those piercing voices and exaggerated emphases which came to be recognised as Stracheyesque. His education had been alarmingly spasmodic, mainly due to the inattention of his mother, intervals of the bizarre alternating with long stretches of the substandard. The Trinity College porter was very suspicious when the spindly Lytton first presented himself at Cambridge in 1899. 'You'd never think he was the son of a general,' he remarked. Nor did most of his fellow undergraduates. Lytton Strachey soon retired with a few choice spirits into a network of tiny literary societies, from which he graduated, in 1902, into the Apostles.

Out of these unpromising ingredients, Strachey fashioned a personality of unusual authority, if limited appeal; he was able to impose himself on his intimates by the definiteness of his views and sheer weight of his mannerisms. The two were intimately connected: Strachey was one of those people able to put behind a particular outlook on life the whole weight of a 'character'. The key to his power was the style and tone of his utterance which, in its unusual stresses, its joky private vocabulary and its chilling silences, conveyed a world of approval and disapproval. Much later Keynes wrote that he 'used to hear the Stracheys talk about someone being "dim" forty years ago, and it was only after that that it came into general circulation. They also had another, more extreme expression for someone who was still worse than dim, who was so to speak perniciously dim. He would be known as a "death packet".' Strachey delighted to shock people out of Victorian taboos. Discussing sex differences with a dowager at a dinner party, he remarked, 'The whole matter turns, as in golf, on the question of holes and balls.' His subversive wit which was one of the joys of his conversation, his letters and later his biographies was similarly always in the service of his own set of values. These values were largely derived from G. E. Moore, but Strachey invested them with his own apparatus of certainty. People and activities were either inside or outside the pale. His descriptions of his friends and enemies were masterly; his dissection of their characters merciless. He loved clever people and that is one reason he loved Keynes. 'He analyses with amazing persistence and brilliance. I have never met so active a brain,' he told Leonard Woolf. 'His conversation is extraordinarily alert and very amusing. He's interested in people to a remarkable degree.'[24] On the other hand, he never entirely approved of Maynard. He did not think that, on the whole, he had a 'good character' – an assessment in which there was a good deal of jealousy, as we shall see. Maynard, though, worshipped Lytton, even if he must often have been made uncomfortable by him. He had reached the point in life where he was ready to be shocked out of the conventions of Harvey Road. He and Lytton could now indulge in a common taste for blasphemy and attractive young men.

Their friendship almost broke up soon after it had started, over competition for the affections of a young Trinity freshman called Arthur Lee Hobhouse. Hobhouse was a stunningly handsome product of Oppidan Eton. He was spotted by Strachey, who introduced him to Keynes as an 'embryo' or possible Apostle. To Woolf, now banished for seven years to an administrative post in Ceylon, Strachey enthused on 30 November 1904, 'Hobhouse is fair, with frizzy hair, a good complexion, an arched nose, and a very charming expression of countenance. His conversation is singularly coming on.... He's interested in metaphysics and people, he's not a Christian and he sees quite a lot of jokes. I'm rather in love with him, and Keynes who lunched with him today.... is convinced that he's all right.... he looks pink and delightful as embryos should.'[25] Largely as a result of Strachey's energetic canvassing, the agreement of the brethren (including the important assent of G. E. Moore) was secured for Hobhouse's election. However, Lytton soon discovered that Hobhouse was much fonder of Maynard than of him; and it was Maynard, in fact, who sponsored the new 'birth' on 18 February 1905. Hobhouse's defection (as Lytton saw it) was a damaging blow to his own feeble sexual confidence. He broke off relations with Maynard. 'He repels me so much', he wrote to Woolf in Ceylon, 'that I can hardly prevent myself ejaculating insults to his face.'

The election of Hobhouse to the Apostles has been interpreted as marking a new phase in the Society's history, one in which the criterion for election became good looks rather than mental or spiritual qualities. In his autobiography, Bertrand Russell wrote that following a 'long drawn out battle between George Trevelyan and Lytton Strachey.... homosexual relations among the members were for a time common, but in my day they were unknown'.[26] This is not only untrue in general, but is misleading insofar as it refers to the reasons for Hobhouse's election. Perhaps Strachey and Keynes were influenced mainly by his looks, but George Trevelyan favoured his election on different grounds. 'I am immensely glad about Hobhouse,' he wrote to Maynard in February 1905. 'I remember him very well and thought he had a *distinction* of mind which raised him above the other candidates.'[27]

Schoolboy experiments apart, Hobhouse was the first great love of Keynes's life. Over the next seventeen years he had several love affairs with men, one of them of central importance, as well as a certain amount of casual sex. There is no satisfactory explanation of homosexual tendencies. Both Maynard's brother and sister were bisexual. But what, if anything, there was in the family situation to produce homosexuality in all three is difficult to say. More suggestive is the fact that Maynard, and many young men similarly situated, passed their adolescence and much of their adult life in an environment which excluded women, apart from family, either as companions or as providers of conveniences and comforts. There was little need to break patterns of relationships established at home and at boarding school. Even so, the break would surely have been made had the urge to do so been strong enough.

Intellectual ex-public schoolboys sought through homosexuality contact with the normal and uncomplicated. Writing to Sheppard in 1903 about a young subaltern who had taken his fancy, Lytton Strachey observed: 'It is what all of Us – the terribly intelligent, the unhappy, the artistic, the divided, the overwhelmed – most intimately worship, and most passionately, most vainly, love.' It was easy to build on an inaptitude for ordinary human contact an ideology of a higher form of love. Keynes and Strachey had been brought up to believe that women were inferior – in mind and body. Love of young men was, they believed, ethically better than love of women. They built an ethical position – the 'Higher Sodomy' they called it – on a sexual preference. Keynes was fully alive to the dangers of his choice. Oscar Wilde's conviction and disgrace were recent memories. 'So long as no one has anything to do with the lower classes or people off the streets,' he wrote to Strachey on 20 June 1906, 'and there is some discretion in letters to neutrals, there's not a scrap of risk – or hardly a scrap.' In their letters to each other there was less need for discretion. Keynes and Strachey felt that later generations would regard them as pioneers, not criminals. They carefully preserved their correspondence and expected that one day its contents would become public knowledge.

In March 1905 Maynard, who was now coming up to his finals, completed his term as president of the Cambridge Union. His farewell speech attacking the Conservative government was, according to the *Cambridge Review*, 'in the retiring President's best style – cool, logical, yet full of regard primarily, and above all, for the highest and best moral principles of statesmanship.... We look forward to a great career for him in other circles.'[28] On 30 March he and Hobhouse left for a three-week 'working holiday' in Truro. In his letters home Maynard emphasised his preparations for the tripos. On 16 April he wrote: 'This is the most industrious week I have had this year. Astronomy finished, Solid Conics, Optics begun.... I am coming back next Thursday – in the meantime there is nothing to tell you – except that my morning hours would surprise you.' Maynard, a relieved Neville noted, 'seems to be having a quiet but pleasant time.'

Maynard revealed more of the true story of his three weeks at Truro in a letter written on 23 April from Harvey Road to Lytton Strachey, with whom wary relations had been restored:

> That episode is over; I wonder if you will ever know exactly what happened.... I swear I had no idea I was in for anything that would so utterly uproot me. It is absurd to suppose that you would believe the violence of the various feelings I have been through.
>
> However – perhaps you will gather a little when we meet. All I will say is that for the moment I am more madly in love with him than ever and that we have sailed into smooth waters – for how long I know not....
>
> He – without intermission – was ill in health and attempting to force himself to do more work than he was fit for.
>
> However, it was – *ethically* – the most valuable three weeks I have ever spent.

From the Royston Golf Club Maynard wrote to Hobhouse on 27 April:

> Despite your treasonable thoughts, I very much want to see you again. Yes, I have a clever head, a weak character, an affectionate disposition, and a repulsive appearance. My latest disease is novel reading; I have not had an attack for years, and now it has come to find me absolutely defenceless....
>
> Anyhow get well, keep honest, and – if possible – like me. If you never come to love, yet I shall have your sympathy – and that I want as much, at least, as the other.
>
> Your importunate, affectionate,
>
>   JMK

Hobhouse had not allowed any physical intimacies at Truro; as he later told Lytton Strachey's brother James, 'Whenever his [Keynes's] demonstrations of feeling became very intense I couldn't help suffering a revulsion in mine.' Maynard remembered that 'he [Hobhouse] used to lead me on with one hand, and then every three days tell me, for the sake of honesty and sincerity and to show he was apostolic, that he hated me'. On the anniversary of the Truro holiday, Keynes wrote Hobhouse a letter which he signed 'Your constant true love, JMK'. Memories of Truro still brought tears to his eyes; he doubted whether a second affair could ever have all the supremacies of a first. But gradually the intensity of his feeling faded in face of Hobhouse's limitations. 'He simply does not know what the thing means,' he told Lytton Strachey; he was 'devoid of passion'.

One of Maynard's most useful traits was his ability to switch off the last subject completely when his mind needed to be given to the next. With the approach of the tripos, Hobhouse was banished from his mind as the Harvey Road examination machinery went into action. His father resumed his familiar role. 'Maynard has planned out his work very methodically. There is a great amount of ground to be covered.' By 11 May Neville was starting to feel dispirited; on 15 May, the tripos started. 'I went round to Maynard's room early to make sure he was getting up.' At the end of the first week Neville was 'feeling very tired & depressed. . . . I think he is going to do badly, & I am oppressed by the idea that I ought not to have encouraged him to read mathematics at all. He has throughout found the subject irksome.'

At last it was all over. 'Maynard thinks he may be as high as twelfth wrangler; but I am afraid he is too sanguine.' Maynard had judged his final sprint to perfection. In his three years as an undergraduate he had done all he wanted, and still managed to come out twelfth wrangler. 'On the whole we are satisfied,' a relieved Neville wrote, 'though the boy might of course have done better had he devoted himself more exclusively to his mathematics. Most people congratulate me, a few condole (having expected him to get a Fellowship place). At King's they appear to be very well pleased. . . .' Neville could not quite reconcile himself to the result: 'I fancy Maynard was not very well or wisely taught for Tripos purposes. . . .'[29] In fact, Maynard had followed his father's programme almost to the letter. That he would not be a top wrangler had always been foreseen. Mathematics could finally be put aside for more interesting intellectual pursuits. On 28 June 1905 he started work on Marshall's *Principles of Economics*.

6

My Early Beliefs

I. G. E. MOORE AND *PRINCIPIA ETHICA*

On 9 September 1938 Maynard Keynes read a paper to Bloomsbury's Memoir Club called 'My Early Beliefs'. It was published posthumously by his friend David Garnett in 1949 and is also reproduced in volume X of his *Collected Writings*. It is a key document for understanding his life's work; and that for one main reason. He was close enough to the 'believing' generation to have a need for 'true beliefs'. This is perhaps the characteristic of his age which separates it most strikingly from our own. It is not so much that we have lost our beliefs as that we have lost the belief in the possibility of having true beliefs. And this must mean that our beliefs make less claim on us. The importance Keynes attached to the discovery of true beliefs, the amount of intellectual attention he devoted to the relation between belief and action, the constant need he felt for justifying his actions by reference to his beliefs, all presuppose a mental outlook which has virtually disappeared. It was an outlook which also enabled Keynes to exert moral authority. His calculations and actions were in the service of ends he believed to be true.

Philosophy provided the foundation of Keynes's life. It came before economics; and the philosophy of ends came before the philosophy of means. Keynes's philosophy was worked out between 1903 and 1906, in his last two years as an undergraduate, and in his postgraduate year. It was elaborated mainly in the circle of the Apostles, being conceived as a set of answers to the questions which chiefly interested them. Fortunately we do not have to rely entirely on his 1938 paper for an account of what that philosophy was. A number of essays and fragments have survived from these early years, in which we see him wrestling with the problems of value and conduct, his solutions to which are given retrospectively, not always accurately, and certainly not completely, in his Memoir Club paper.

The heart of this paper is an account of G. E. Moore's *Principia Ethica*, and the effect it had on him. His testimony on the latter point is unequivocal. 'Its effect on *us*,' Keynes said, 'and the talk which preceded and followed it, dominated, and perhaps still dominates, everything else.' He went on, 'It was exciting, exhilarating, the beginning of a new renaissance, the opening of a new heaven on earth.' These were not retrospective judgements. A few days after the publication of *Principia Ethica* he wrote to Swithinbank (7 October

1903): 'it is a stupendous and entrancing work, *the greatest* on the subject'. And on 21 February 1906 he wrote to Lytton Strachey: 'It is *impossible* to exaggerate the wonder and *originality* of Moore; people are beginning to talk as if he were only a kind of logic chopping eclectic. Oh why can't they see?'

Moore's *Principia Ethica* was a product of a time, place and personality. In philosophic terms, it can be seen as a continuation of the enterprise of moral philosophy from the point where Sidgwick had left it, which was in a mess. It inherited the problems which had given rise to Sidgwick's project, and tried, where Sidgwick felt he had failed, to overcome them – the threat that a Godless universe would usher in a 'cosmos of chaos', the inadequacy of hedonistic utilitarianism, the demand for a philosophy which would lighten the burden of conventional morality. Whether Moore made any real progress, or whether it was the case that 'what Sidgwick portrays as a failure Moore takes to be an enlightening and liberating discovery',[1] is still debated. For the moment, it is enough to note that Moore's disciples did feel that he had made progress, and in so doing had provided them with the 'rudiments of a true theory of ethic'.

The demand, which Moore's theory supplied, was for a rational justification of a rearrangement of values, such that duties could be attached to goods which the Apostles felt were valuable rather than to those which society felt were useful. A shift in outlook which had already occurred among the Cambridge Apostles was waiting to be legitimised. Moore's book was more a result of this shift than its cause, though he provided the rational weapons for its defence and reinforcement. The change in outlook had been described in a paper which Desmond MacCarthy read to the Society in December 1900. In it he contrasted his generation's attitude to life with that of its Apostolic predecessors. The key difference was that his generation took 'everything more *personally*' than they did. 'We see the relations of men to each other and to other aims on the whole less broadly.' The change was due, MacCarthy explained, to 'all institutions, the family, the state, laws of honour, etc., which have a claim on the individual . . . having failed to produce convincing proofs of their authority'. He went on:

> But there is another characteristic, which is the result of a shaken belief
> in rules of thumb and the usual aims in life, which also contributes
> directly to the greater interest taken in personal relations.
>   They [the previous generation] did *not* trust their immediate judg
> ments as completely as we do, which simplified for them the social as
> well as the other relations in life. They had more rules which they
> trusted to instead. . . .

MacCarthy is making the important point that the more one analyses, and the more one's analysis disintegrates the 'rules of thumb' and 'usual aims in life', the more one is forced to rely on 'immediate' judgements of

value. But such 'immediate' or what we would now call 'intuitive' judgements have precisely the effect of cutting one off from broad aims and
turning one towards a companionship with those who share one's own
particular intuitions. It was the increased importance of the 'state of personal
relations at any particular time' in relation to 'their other aims' that Mac-
Carthy found to be the distinguishing feature of the Apostolic brethren of
his day. 'The previous generation did not think less *of* their friends; but they
thought less *about* them, not less of friendship, but less of intimacy.'[2]
Moore's achievement was to provide a particular kind of language for
justifying this shift, for making people comfortable with it.

Moore's own personality played a vital part in this achievement. Leonard
Woolf called him a 'great man, the only great man I have ever met'.[3] He was
honoured not just for his qualities of mind, but for his charisma. Indeed, his
single-minded dedication to the pursuit of truth was part of that charisma.
Educated at Dulwich College in south London, he 'caught' religion so
intensely at the age of thirteen that for two years he would ask of all
doubtful cases, 'What would Jesus do?' The loss of his Christian faith was so
traumatic that he determined thereafter to question all propositions. In 1892
he came up to Trinity College, Cambridge, on a classics scholarship. After
two years he switched to the moral sciences, and in 1898 won a prize
fellowship at Trinity with a dissertation on Kant.

Moore was elected an Apostle in 1894. From the beginning his combination of looks, philosophising passion and obliviousness to ridicule had an
explosive effect on the Society. 'He was in those days beautiful and slim,'
writes Russell, 'with a look almost of inspiration, and with an intellect as
passionate as Spinoza's. He had a kind of almost exquisite purity.'[4] The
theme of Moore's opening remarks to the Apostles was that 'we should
spread scepticism until at last everybody knows that we can know absolutely
nothing'. At this point he was overcome with hysterical laughter. 'We all felt
electrified by him,' Russell continued to his fiancée Alys Pearsall Smith, 'as if
we had slumbered hitherto and never realised what fearless intellect pure
and unadulterated really means.' Three days later Russell wrote to Alys: 'I
find it impossible either to like or dislike him, because I have seen no trace
of humanity in him yet: but there is an odd exhilaration in talking to him:
his criticism is like the air of the High Alps.'[5]

Moore's scepticism was directed against both Idealism, represented in
the Society by McTaggart and Lowes Dickinson, and the utilitarian tradition
bequeathed by Sidgwick. In the McTaggart–Dickinson version of Idealism,
the Absolute was 'a state of communion of immortal souls in the perfect
love of friendship'.[6] Moore had no objection to this as an ideal – in fact his
own Heaven was very similar – but he could not accept a style of philosophising which attempted to deduce it from the existence of an unknowable
world: a theistic philosophy with God left out. Moore was equally disen-
chanted with the language and mood of utilitarianism. This comes out in a

comment on the Fabian Graham Wallas, whom he met in 1896: 'A beastly fool ... everything is to subserve his wretched utility – educating the masses! Educating them for what? He cannot tell you. He is the blind leader of the blind. ...'[7]

The secret of Moore's power as a philosopher was his literalness of mind. He took words seriously, especially the words used in everyday language. When people called something good or bad, beautiful or ugly, intelligent or stupid, he thought they meant just that, not something else; they were referring to *things* which were as real as any natural objects. Keynes wrote, 'Moore had a nightmare once in which he could not distinguish propositions from tables. But even when he was awake, he could not distinguish love and beauty and truth from the furniture. They took on the same definition of outline, the same stable, solid, objective qualities and commonsense reality.'[8] The motto of his *Principia Ethica* was taken from Bishop Butler: 'Everything is what it is, and not another thing.' The effect of Moore's methods of argument was devastating. 'What exactly do you mean?' was his favourite question; and if he got an unclear answer he would assume an air of amazement that anyone could be so idiotic. As Keynes remarked, he was adept in his use of the 'accents of infallibility'.[9] His stream of expostulations, his violent shaking of the head, his desperate attempts to light his pipe were all integral parts of his philosophical performance. With the aid of his pipes, his gestures, his tone and his arguments, Moore exorcised the spirit of Idealism from Cambridge. McTaggart was defeated, but unrepentant. He stuck to his Idealism for the comfort it gave him. All he would say was 'Well, anyway, I'm sure Moore is wrong.'[10] Lowes Dickinson gave up philosophy altogether. 'I'm fagged to death,' he wrote to R. C. Trevelyan in 1898, 'the result of a metaphysical talk with Moore. What a brain that fellow has! It desiccates mine! Dries up my lakes and seas. ... in arid tracts of sand.'[11]

Paul Levy is right to notice that much of Moore's authority derived from his character, which had in it something of the Divine Fool. He had no small talk: all statements were taken with immense seriousness. He had no sense of fancy: his mind, as Keynes put it, was unadorned. Equally impressive was the agony which his thought processes gave him, the anguish he suffered if he failed to communicate something which seemed to him supremely important. His philosophy, Keynes thought, was 'wrung out, squeezed with pain and contortion through a constipated rectum.' Levy has emphasised Moore's innocence. He confessed to the Society that when he came up to Cambridge he did not know that there would be a single man there who fornicated, or that sodomy was ever practised in modern times.[12] Knowledge that these things went on in Cambridge did not change his attitude to them. He remained a Puritan. Good states of mind always seemed to him to involve much pain. Such a man was easy to revere, difficult to feel cosy with. 'He is too remote for ease or intimacy,' Keynes wrote to Strachey on

20 December 1905, 'but one could hardly treat him as a stranger.' And a little later (25 January 1906), 'Moore has, for me, become too mythical for inclusion in the list [of lovable Apostles]. I seem to know him by description only, and he lives with Socrates, Shakespeare, and Tomlinson – the trinity of our holy faith.'

There were four main building blocks in Moore's ethical system. The first was the notion of the indefinability of good. Good is the name of a simple, non-natural property, analogous to 'yellow', which can be identified only by direct inspection or intuition. It is indefinable because, Moore argues in *Principia Ethica*, it can be shown that any attempt to define it – that is, to make it mean something else like 'pleasant' or 'beautiful' or 'more evolved' – breaks down. Of any state of affairs which is one of these things it can always still be asked whether it is good. Attempts to identify good with such other properties Moore called the 'naturalistic fallacy'. Much of the ground for these assertions had already been laid by Sidgwick. Common to both Sidgwick and Moore is the abandonment of the attempt to ground ethical philosophy in the facts of human nature – to infer what is desirable from what is desired. Moore just carries the process further by breaking the link Sidgwick had tried to keep between goodness and happiness.

Moore's second building block is the assertion, in his famous last chapter 'The Ideal', that the only things valuable in themselves are states of mind, of which the most valuable are 'the pleasures of human intercourse and the enjoyment of beautiful objects'.[13] Of the many implications of this view, one which may be immediately noticed is that mental states are given ethical priority over states of action.

The third element in Moore's system is the doctrine that right action is aimed at bringing about desirable states of affairs – at the limit those ultimately valuable states of consciousness. Moore wrote: 'It's only for the sake of those things – in order that as much of them as possible may at some time exist – that anyone can be justified in performing any public or private duty'.[14]

Finally, Moore's view that action should be aimed at bringing about desirable states of consciousness was qualified by the doctrine of organic unities, which stated that the best achievable states of affairs are bound to be 'complex wholes', the value of which do not add up to the sum of the value of their parts.[15] By this he meant that goods which on their own had a zero or even negative value might, in conjunction with intrinsically valuable goods (states of mind), form a whole of greater value than good states of mind on their own. The chief use of the principle of organic unities was to limit the power to sum goodness by adding up isolated states of consciousness. By including in the notion of good states of affairs attributes, including those of action, which were not themselves good, Moore left the door open for the 'usual aims' in life which MacCarthy had talked about.

As we have seen, the Apostles were looking for an ethic which could direct attention to ends other than the duties set before the Victorian gentleman. This Moore provided for them. He unshackled contemporary ethics from its connection with social utility and conventional morality by locating its ultimate ends in goods which stood apart from the Victorian scheme of life, and by making 'ought' correlative to these goods. By dropping hedonism and by proclaiming as intrinsically valuable dispositions and states of mind which Mill and Sidgwick had been forced to treat instrumentally he had evaded the problems which had wrecked their attempt at coherence. No one serious about achieving Moore's goods could take Victorian morality entirely seriously again. What Moore had not solved was the problem of how to relate his goods to the practical business of life, most of which had no connection with them. It turned out that Sidgwick's difficulty of effecting a harmony between the private and public sphere, between the good life and the useful life, had not been overcome by Moore: it had merely been restated in a new way.

II. KEYNES AND MOORE

In his 1938 Memoir Club paper Keynes said: 'Now what we got from Moore was by no means entirely what he offered us'. He and his friends 'accepted Moore's religion ... and discarded his morals'. By religion Keynes means 'one's attitude towards oneself and the ultimate', by morals 'one's attitude towards the outside world and the intermediate', a distinction which roughly corresponded to 'being good' and 'doing good'.[16]

Their religion was Moore's Ideal: 'Nothing mattered except states of mind ... chiefly our own. These states of mind were not associated with action or achievement or with consequences. They consisted in timeless, passionate states of contemplation and communion, largely unattached to 'before' and 'after'. The appropriate subjects of passionate contemplation and communion were a beloved person, the creation and enjoyment of aesthetic experience and the pursuit of knowledge. Of these love came a long way first. . . .' He and his friends were 'chiefly concerned with the salvation of our own souls. The divine resided within a closed circle'. The life of action was not part of the Ideal. With power, worldly success, ambition, with the 'economic motive and economic criterion', he and his circle were less concerned than was St Francis of Assisi 'who at least made a collection for the birds'.[17] Moore's religion was attractive to Keynes because he could see it as a latter-day version of the monastic ideal which had excited his admiration as a schoolboy. 'Thus we were brought up', Keynes concludes, 'with Plato's absorption in the good in itself, with a scholasticism which outdid St Thomas, in Calvinistic withdrawal from the pleasures and success of Vanity Fair, and oppressed with all the sorrows of Werther'.[18]

This was scarcely a grown-up religion. It is hard to see how it could have survived the process of growing up. Rather, what it did for its acolytes was to provide a standard of value against which to measure the usual aims of life. In this sense, it continued to be Keynes's Ideal. The older Keynes still accepted the 'fundamental intuitions' of *Principia Ethica*. 'We were amongst the first of our generation, perhaps alone amongst our generation to escape from the Benthamite tradition', with its 'over-valuation of the economic criterion'. This had protected 'the whole lot of us from the final *reductio ad absurdum* of Benthamism known as Marxism'.[19] But it was much too blinkered. It ignored 'certain powerful and valuable springs of feeling', both the blinder passions of the human heart and those to do with the 'order and pattern of life among communities'.[20]

This impinged on the question of morals. Moore's purpose, Keynes pointed out, had been to 'distinguish between goodness as an attribute of states of mind and rightness as an attribute of actions'. Moore's morals were based on the Victorian compromise between the 'Benthamite calculus' and 'the general rules of correct behaviour'. These morals, Keynes claimed, were rooted in a double error of reasoning. Moore's handling of the probabilistic calculus was 'riddled with fallacies'. and Moore's 'general rules' had little enough sanction except Christian 'hocus-pocus'. 'We entirely repudiated a personal liability on us to obey general rules. We claimed the right to judge every individual case on its merits, and the wisdom to do so successfully.... We repudiated entirely customary morals, conventions and traditional wisdom. We were, that is to say, in the strict sense of the term, immoralists'.[21]

The older Keynes thought this arrogance rested on a 'disastrously mistaken' view of human nature. He and his friends, repudiating original sin, had believed that human beings were sufficiently rational to be 'released from . . . inflexible rules of conduct, and left, from now onwards, to their own . . . reliable intuitions of the good'. This view ignored the fact that 'civilisation was a thin and precarious crust erected by the personality and will of the few, and only maintained by rules and conventions skilfully put across and guilefully preserved'.[22]

Keynes's 1938 story of his early beliefs did not find unanimous favour either with his own circle or with later writers when it was published posthumously in 1949. Some like Bertrand Russell and Leonard Woolf have been concerned to defend Moore from what they saw as Keynes's trivialization of his teaching: the doctrine of 'organic unities', they argued, led straight to the question of right conduct, and therefore concern with the affairs of the world.[23] Others, like Roy Harrod, R. B. Braithwaite, and Rod O'Donnell have been concerned to defend Keynes from his own account of how Moore's values affected him. It was not true of how he lived his life as a young man; it was even less true of his life as a whole. However, whereas

Harrod sees his life's work as proof that he escaped from Moore's 'cloistered and anaemic values',[24] Braithwaite and O'Donnell believe that Keynes was a faithful follower of Moore, but that Mooreism, whatever Keynes said, pointed Keynes towards a 'humane Utilitarianism'.[25] Others like the literary scholar F. R. Leavis claim that Keynes's memoir shows how trivial and immature Cambridge civilisation at the turn of the century had become.[26]

Most of these criticisms are too heavy-handed. Keynes's memoir was read to a special audience of friends, and certain liberties with strict truth for the sake of effect and amusement would have been natural. Also he was exaggerating the unwordliness of his generation in order to demonstrate to young hearers that there was more to life than Marx – while acknowledging the importance of their social concerns.

The real tests of the accuracy of Keynes's recollections are how he lived his life as a young man and how he and his friends interpreted Moore's philosophy at the time. To get a sense of the first, the reader is invited to read on. On the second, there is a great deal of evidence, mostly from his youthful notebooks and the unpublished papers he read to the Apostles. This shows that the young Keynes was indeed a passionate Mooreite. But it was a Mooreism adapted to the psychological needs of a group of privileged intellectuals imbued with the optimism of the new century, who did not expect the affairs of the world to make exorbitant demands on them and who expected their adult lives to be a continuation of student life.

III. KEYNES'S PHILOSOPHIC APPRENTICESHIP

The best introduction to Keynes's early writings is from some notes he made between July and September 1905, just after his tripos examination, which he called 'Miscellanea Ethica':

> My scheme of a complete ethical treatise would be somewhat thus: the first division would be twofold – into Speculative and Practical Ethics.
>
> Speculative Ethics would concern itself, in the first instance, with certain quasi-metaphysical or logical questions; it would establish the usage and significance of the more fundamental terms. Out of this would follow an analysis ... of the notion of 'good' in itself. It would, in fact, include (in Moore's words) 'Prolegomena to any future Ethics that can possibly pretend to be scientific'. Moore himself might be employed (at a small but sufficient salary) to write it under direction.
>
> Upon this basis could be raised a Catalogue Raisonné of fit objects and good feelings. Bad feelings would come in for their share of attention; and there would be very little in the field of experience or

of passion, which the writers could not introduce if they had the mind for it.

The nature of beauty and tragedy and love and attitude a man should have towards truth would prove of interest in the discussion, though the conclusions appear in the result no wiser than Aristotle's.

The second division – of Practical Ethics – would concern itself with conduct; it would investigate the difficult question of the probable grounds of action, and the curious connexion between 'probable' and 'ought'; and it would endeavour to formulate or rather to investigate existing general maxims, bearing in mind their strict relativity to particular circumstances. It would also concern itself with the means of producing (*a*) good feelings, (*b*) fit objects. Perhaps this division would be less interesting than that of Speculative Ethics, but it might attempt to answer such questions as the following: –

   (i) the nature and value of virtue
  (ii) the theory and methods of Education
 (iii) the theory and methods of Politics
 (iv) the practical expediency and proper limits of Egoism – i.e., the extent to which we ought to regard ourselves as ends and means respectively
  (v) the exceptions to the rule that truth stands first.

The whole would be printed in Baskerville type and published in 150 volumes.[27]

This passage sufficiently indicates that Keynes's interests were from the first concentrated on the connection between 'speculative' and 'practical' ethics and on the problems to which Moore's treatment of these connections gave rise.

His first target was Moore's doctrine of organic unities. Moore had said that good wholes consisted of good states of mind *plus* things which were not good in themselves. Thus the states of 'aesthetic enjoyment' and 'personal affection' were said to contain respectively material objects (things of beauty) and mental objects (qualities of intelligence) which it was good to contemplate. Keynes regarded these assertions as perverse: it might be desirable that such objects should exist, but they could not be part of ethical good, which consists solely of good states of mind. We have it on his testimony that 'one Saturday evening the principle of organic unity was abolished'.[28] When this momentous event took place is unknown, but it must have been before 1906. Keynes proposed a replacement, based on a distinction between goodness as an attribute of states of mind and 'fitness' as an attribute of objects. 'Mental states alone are good' [he wrote in 'A Theory of Beauty', 1905] 'those objects which inspire good feelings are fit.... Corresponding to every good feeling there is a fit object.... [A] fit object is one the contemplation of which *ought* to give rise to a state of mind which is good.'

Keynes was making a logical point: if feelings alone are good, objects cannot be good also. But his argument had a potential bearing on practical ethics: if good feelings required the presence of fit objects, then it was surely the task of practical ethics to create a universe of them. This consideration was reinforced by the importance which Keynes, following Moore, attached to *true* belief as an attribute of goodness: a universe of dunghills ought to inspire feelings of disgust or bad states of mind. Nevertheless, *at the time*, the 'abolition' of the doctrine of organic unities was surely intended to justify a concentration on the pursuit of good states of mind in isolation – exactly as Keynes had recalled in his Memoir.

This supposition is reinforced by Keynes's treatment of a related problem. Given that ethical good consists solely of states of mind, should our aim be to improve our own state of mind or the state of mind of the Universe? Moore had claimed that the latter was the only rational ethical aim. But this rejection, Keynes claimed, rested on assertion only. Against it were two powerful arguments. First, 'as we never have the opportunity of direct inspection [of other people's states of mind], it is impossible to tell what kinds of action increase the goodness of the Universe as a whole' (he declared in 'Miscellanea Ethica'). Secondly, Moore had failed to provide any rational grounds of obligation to pursue the universal good at the expense of one's own good. 'Are we not, each of us, an end to ourselves?' Keynes asked in a paper on 'Egoism' he read to the Apostles in 1906. Should a person make himself *bad* (that is, engage in politics) in order to improve others' states of mind? Keynes denied that Moore had improved on Sidgwick's treatment of the problem.

A third major difficulty in Moore's *Principia Ethica* lay in his confused theory of consequentialism – the doctrine that the rightness of an act is to be judged by its results, actual or expected. The question is: what kind of knowledge is necessary for a consequentialist system to be possible? The answer must be: knowledge of probabilities; hence the importance of Keynes's phrase in his introduction to 'Miscellanea Ethica', about the 'curious connexion between "probable" and "ought"'.

In the chapter of *Principia Ethica* entitled 'Ethics in Relation to Conduct', Moore followed Hume in basing all probabilistic knowledge on experience. It was then easy enough to show that experience was inadequate to generate knowledge of the probable effects of actions stretching into a remote future; and to conclude, with Hume, that, in the absence of such knowledge, custom or habit should be the 'great guide of human life'. This conservative conclusion stuck in the young Keynes's gullet. 'Before heaven', he recalled in 1938, 'we claimed to be our own judge in our own case'. Most of his leisure between 1906 and 1914 was spent in working out a theory of probability to justify this claim. His first discussion of the subject dates from 23 January 1904 when he read a paper to the Apostles called 'Ethics in Relation to Conduct'. This makes it clear that his interest rose directly out of the intellectual ferment caused by the appearance of *Principia Ethica*. This paper already contains the main idea of what was to become Keynes's *Treatise on Probability*, which was not published till 1921. It is, therefore, of key biographical importance.*

In his 1904 paper Keynes accused Moore of having the wrong theory of probability. His argument is as follows. If I say that 'A is more probable than B', I am not claiming that A will happen more often than B for certain, but that I have more evidence in favour of A than of B. If I know that A will produce more good than B in the immediate future, and have no more reason to suppose that it will produce bad effects than good effects in the longer future, then I have more evidence to support the view that A is the right thing to do than that B is. As Keynes put it: 'Ignorance can be no bar to the making of a statement with regard to probability'. Rather, it is a way of neutralising the unknown. By utilising the principle of indifference, or insufficient reason, Keynes was able to show that there were more probabilities than were dreamt of in Moore's philosophy.

The 1904 paper clearly points to Keynes's logical theory of probability in which probability is a property of propositions rather than events and is, like Moore's concept of 'good', intuitively known. Its intellectual provenance was Russell's view, in his *Principles of Mathematics* published in 1903, that logic was the foundation of philosophy, and that the foundational truths of ethics, mathematics and science were self-evident. In biographical terms, it can be seen as an attempt to justify individual decisions on personal morality within the general framework of consequentialism.

Thus far it cannot be said that Keynes has given a false account of his 'early beliefs' in his 1938 paper. His revisions to Mooreism aimed to enlarge the private relative to the public space. Those aspects of Moore's ethical system which tethered it to duty and the 'usual aims' of life were de-emphasised; those which encouraged concentration on the 'passionate mutual admirations of a clique of the elect', as Russell dismissively put it, were placed at the centre.

However, Keynes's 1905 plan for a 'complete ethical treatise' included a section on Practical Ethics, the domain of 'doing good' rather than 'being good'. His theory of probability could be applied to public action as well.

---

* Keynes's paper 'Ethics in Relation to Conduct' is filed under UA/19 in the Keynes Papers at King's College, Cambridge. It is undated. When the first volume of my biography of Keynes was published in 1983, I was under a promise not to reveal the source of my dating. This was supplied to me by Mr G. Lloyd, then Fellow and Tutor in classics at King's College, from the records of meetings of the Apostles, which were not open to researchers. This dating was subsequently challenged by D. E. Moggrige in his *Keynes: An Economist's Biography*, pp. 131–6, who suggests from internal evidence, that it was probably written in 1906. In his 1982 PhD dissertation *Keynes: Philosophy and Economics*, R. M. O'Donnell dated it 'around early 1904, probably before April' (p. 10); subsequently he adopted my dating.

Since Keynes's greatest contributions were to be to the art, or science, of statesmanship, it is interesting to ask how the young Keynes viewed the public realm.

An important clue is the way he was wont to rank vocations, or career choices. 'Is there any brother', he asked in a paper he read to the Apostles in 1909, 'who would not rather be a scientist than a business man, and an artist than a scientist?' Artists and scientists came out top because theirs were the occupations with the highest ethical value. Of the two, Keynes ranked the scientist somewhat below the artist 'not because his activity is one of use and not one of value, but first because . . . his quality is [probably] lower, and secondly, because he will spend a larger part of his time in what has no intrinsic value whatever'. Keynes's ranking criterion is plain. He distinguished between those occupations associated with intrinsically valuable states of mind, and those which were merely useful and which, in addition, were likely to lead to bad states of mind. Business was useful, but was associated with a bad state of mind – love of gain. There is much evidence from the early period of his life that Kenes ranked politics on a par with what he called 'business and bridge', or even lower. And he was no doubt already placing himself in this hierarchy – as a scientist with some of the capacities of the artist.

'Miscellanea Ethica' had as one of its proposed sections a treatise on 'the theory of and method of Politics'. Keynes never produced one himself, but in his papers there is an unpublished hundred-page essay on 'The Political Doctrines of Edmund Burke'. It was submitted for the University Members Prize for English Essay in November 1904, duly winning it.[29] Keynes's interest in Burke dates from his time at Eton. Nevertheless, he was an unusual subject for a liberal non-conformist to write about, since he was one of the founding fathers of modern conservatism. (Keynes never acquired a comparable knowledge or appreciation of John Stuart Mill.) It is interesting, therefore, in showing one type of assessment which a Mooreite might make about the value of public life.

In Moore's ethical scheme, politics is at best a means to the good. But it was an indirect means. Keynes commended Burke as the first utilitarian political philosopher – the first to espouse consistently the 'greatest happiness' principle. But he emphasises that Burke regarded this as a political, not an ethical, principle, and that he agrees with Burke on this point. Physical calm, material comfort, and intellectual freedom were the joint means to both happiness and ethical goodness, so the government 'which sets the happiness of the governed before it will serve a good purpose, whatever the ethical theory from which it draws its inspiration'. Equity, in the sense of the absence in law or policy of 'artificial discrimination in regard to individuals or classes' is treated here by Keynes as a contribution to contentment, not as an independent political or ethical principle.

Keynes thought that one important consequence of Burke's political utilitarianism was his championship of 'expediency against abstract right', most notably shown in his opposition to the coercion of the American colonies. He quotes him approvingly: 'The question with me is, not whether you have a right to render your people miserable, but whether it is not in your interest to make them happy'. This stand, Keynes thought, put Burke in the ranks of the 'very great'.

Another consequence was Burke's 'extreme timidity in introducing present evils for the sake of future benefits':

> Burke ever held, and held rightly that it can seldom be right ... to sacrifice a present benefit for a doubtful advantage in the future.... It is not wise to look too far ahead; our powers of prediction are slight, our command over results infinitesimal. It is therefore the happiness of our own contemporaries that is our main concern; we should be very chary of sacrificing large numbers of people for the sake of a contingent end, however advantageous that may appear ... We can never know enough to make the chance worth taking.... There is this further consideration that is often in need of emphasis: it is not sufficient that the state of affairs which we seek to promote should be better than the state of affairs which preceded it; it must be sufficiently better to make up for the evils of the transition.[30]

Keynes endorses this principled rejection of revolution. He also strongly supported Burke's 'timidity' in embarking on war – 'with much prudence, reverence, and calculation must it be approached', he quotes. Keynes was taking the sensible view that there was a better defence of conservatism to be made for public than for private life, as the consequences of failure in the former would affect more people.

On the other hand, he thought that Burke's hostility to rational schemes of social reform carried the principle of prudence much too far. His mistrust of rationality, Keynes thought, sprang from two sources: he felt that the masses would be more contented and the state as well as morals more secure if custom and habit were left undisturbed, and he 'suspected that the current grounds of right action were, in many cases, baseless....'. In this second, obscurely phrased, reason for Burke's conservatism, he seems to be implying that Burke would not have been so suspicious of reform had he not, like Moore, had the wrong theory of probability.

Keynes went to some lengths to argue that rationality is compatible with democracy, because, hitherto, the scope of democracy had been extremely limited, and because over time its exercise might improve the rationality of citizens. However, he had little time for Burke's now fashionable 'small platoons'. He was a Whig, not a communitarian.

If Burke's mistrust of reason pushed Keynes away from political conservatism, another set of arguments in Burke, concerning property rights, pushed him away from socialism. Burke defended property rights on two grounds. Redistribution of wealth would make no real difference to the poor, since they far outnumbered the wealthy. In addition, it would 'greatly reduce in numbers those who could *enjoy* the undoubted benefits of wealth and who would confer on the state the advantages which the presence of wealthy citizens always brings' (emphasis added). Keynes felt that this double argument 'undoubtedly carries very great weight: in certain types of community it is overwhelming, and it must always be one of the most powerful rejoinders to any scheme which has equalisation as its ultimate aim'. However, Burke carried his defence of existing property rights to the extreme. He was so concerned to defend the 'outworks' of the property system that he did not see that this might endanger the 'central system' itself. Burke's principle of expediency could be used against his own defence of sacredness of contract.

Keynes offered an ambivalent summing up of Burke's political legacy:

> His goods are all in the present – peace and quiet, friendship and affections, family life, and those small acts of charity whereby one individual may sometimes help his fellows. He does not think of the race as marching through blood and fire to some great and glorious good in the distant future; there is, for him, no great political millennium to be helped and forwarded by present effort and present sacrifice.... This may not be the right attitude of mind. But whether or not the great political ideals that have inspired men in the past are madness and delusion, they have provided a more powerful motive force than anything which Burke has to offer.... For all his passions and speechmaking, it is the academic reasoner and philosopher who offers us these carefully guarded and qualified precepts, not the leader of men. Statesmen must learn wisdom in the school of Burke; if they wish to put it to any great and difficult purpose, the essentials of leadership they must seek elsewhere.[31]

One can see why a Mooreite of Keynes's kind found Burke attractive: he provided a principled objection to pushing the claims of public life too far. Keynes could not, of course, foresee that Burke's precepts would be disparaged for most of the twentieth century, and that this would determine the course of his own life. But strong traces of Burke are to be found in his own approach to statesmanship.

7

Cambridge and London

I. THE WRECKAGE

Maynard remained at King's for a fourth year. On 16 July 1905 Neville had written in his diary, 'We have not yet decided whether Maynard shall take Part II of the Moral Sciences Tripos or the Economics Tripos.' Maynard started weekly supervisions with Alfred Marshall. But he had by no means decided to become an economist. His main intellectual preoccupation was still moral philosophy. With Strachey gone – 'The wicked dons of Trinity have failed to make me a fellow', he told Duncan Grant – Keynes had also become secretary of the Apostles. Reduced to one undergraduate member, Hobhouse, the Society badly needed fresh blood. Maynard made it his business to put it back on its feet again. Much of his postgraduate year was spent in doing so.

October opened with a visit from Swithinbank and the first inspection of 'embryos'. 'Never has a term opened with so fair a prospect,' Maynard enthused to Lytton. The dazzling vista comprised three freshmen – Henry Norton and Henry Goodhart who had come to Trinity from Eton, and Lytton's own younger brother James, who had come to Trinity from St Paul's. Maynard felt that Norton, a mathematician, had a 'very good logical kind of mind', even if his person was 'girt about by a writhing mass of aesthetic and literary appreciations, which I have – so far – discovered no means of quelling'. His appearance was 'ordinary public school'. Goodhart's presence was 'very apostolic and so is his mind'. James Strachey was never in his rooms. 'There was a wonderful interview with Swithin very late on his last evening,' Maynard told Lytton. 'We got as far as it is possible for pure friendship alone without passion.' As Swithin got into the cab taking him to the station, he leant out and smiled. 'I am leaving heaven,' he said.[1]

The trouble was, Maynard soon discovered, that whatever else it might be, Cambridge was not heaven. The party was over. He felt he was living in a world of leftovers. Fay and Furness were amusing enough companions, but neither was tuned into the Mooreite wavelength. Sheppard, who in theory was, lacked what H. O. Meredith called a 'serious bottom'. He complicated Maynard's life by never bothering to prepare papers for the Society when it was his turn to read. Worst of all was Hobhouse. Heading steadily towards his third-class honours in the natural sciences, 'Hobby' was an unbearable reminder of misplaced hopes. Even the way he ate butter caused Maynard to shiver with horror, 'and that simply because I used to be in love with him altogether and now ... hate him for what he is. ... He never *adds* anything. He lives according to rules and contorts himself trying to discover them, when of course they don't exist.'[2]

The prospects which had briefly opened out for the Society soon faded. Norton retained his embryonic status by virtue of his mental qualities. Goodhart sank quickly from sight: 'He is a strong churchman. ... Also he shows the most alarming tendency towards the most incredibly long-winded boring speeches.'[3]* James Strachey was promising, but looked incredibly young, and, like his brother, was prone to long silences. At Oxford there were at least Swithinbank and Daniel Macmillan, the latter captivating Lytton when he paid a visit early in November. 'As for the general society,' Lytton reported to Maynard, 'I was as usual struck by the extraordinary gentle politeness of it all, and by the high level of intelligence. Don't you think the Society has probably wrecked Cambridge? The Society apart, where can one find a "push" in Cambridge with an even moderate amount of sense, of cultivation, and of impropriety? It's all or nothing with us, Oxford's the glorification of the half-and-half.'[4]

The two friends often discussed Mooreism in this way. Its 'nose to nose' ideal seemed to incapacitate them for life outside the confines of the Society. There must be a 'new method, something that will bring ease, that will allow half and halfdom when there are ten, and the whole hog when there are two,' Maynard replied to Strachey.[5] The tone of Grecian suggestiveness which went down so well with the brothers could also suggest to outsiders a wickedness which Maynard at least was far from feeling. A party which he gave for his brother Geoffrey and Rupert Brooke who had come up in December for entrance scholarships (at Pembroke and King's respectively – which they got) left him feeling 'very misanthropic ... the corruption and effeteness of what is supervening; and my utter helplessness and incapacity of creating the impression I wish'. Hobhouse, Norton, Sheppard, Furness and he had floated round the Rugby schoolboys for five hours. 'It seemed to me', Maynard went on to Lytton,

> that we were trying to drag Rupert and my poor brother in and wrap them in our own filth packet; and that there was a kind of fate which completely frustrated us whenever we tried not to. I want to make a move against our methods – for I don't think we're at all corrupt within. As it is we aren't – en bloc – fit company for the youths.

Moribund though his emotional life was, Maynard eagerly responded to intellectual challenges. He found his economics for Marshall exciting. Four folders of his notes and essays have survived, on 'Pure Economics', 'Capital',

---

* Henry Goodhart-Rendel was to become Slade Professor of Fine Art at Oxford.

'Taxation' and 'Trusts and Railways'. For theory, he studied the two privately printed papers of Marshall, 'The Pure Theory of Foreign Trade' and 'The Pure Theory of Domestic Values', as well as Jevons, Cournot and Edgeworth. Marshall was impressed by Maynard's work, scrawling remarks in red ink all over his essays in his large loose writing. Although he found one paper on 'Capital' too logomachic for his taste, he thought Keynes had written a 'brilliant answer' to a question on comparative railway systems. For his part Maynard wrote to Lytton Strachey on 15 November:

> I find economics increasingly satisfactory, and I think I am rather good at it. I want to manage a railway or organise a Trust or at least swindle the investing public. It is so easy and fascinating to master the principle of these things.

And on 23 November:

> Marshall is continually pestering me to turn professional Economist and writes flattering remarks on my papers to help on the good cause. Do you think there is anything in it? I doubt it.
> I could probably get employment here if I wanted to. But prolonging my existence in this place would be, I feel sure, death. The only question is whether a government office in London is not death equally.

Strachey replied on 27 November: 'Oh no, it would surely be mad to be a Cambridge economist. Come to London, go to the Treasury, set up house with me. The parties we'd give. . . .' Maynard was attracted by the prospect of endless gossip with Strachey in London. Besides, he probably felt a need to get away from Harvey Road. A visit to London from 14 to 18 December, when he stayed with Lytton at 69 Lancaster Gate, decided him. On his return he informed his parents that he would abandon the economics tripos and concentrate on the Civil Service Examination. Marshall regretted his decision. As late as May 1906 he was still urging Maynard to take the tripos – 'merely re-reading Economics in the few days before it, you would *probably* get a first-class'.[6] But Maynard was adamant. He never did take an economics degree.

On his return from London, he was stirred briefly into political activity by the general election which the minority Liberal government of Campbell-Bannerman had called for January 1906, a few weeks after the Conservative prime minister Balfour had given up the hopeless task of trying to run the country with a party so badly split on protection. The fiscal question was the only one capable of bringing Maynard to political life, and he now spent some days on the campaign trail on behalf of Edwin Montagu in Cambridgeshire and Freddie Guest in Staffordshire. If the Liberal landslide of 12 January failed to move him to great enthusiasm it did at least stimulate him to get the Society on to a more political tack. He wrote to Strachey on 20 January:

> I tried a novel breakfast party this morning – Keeling* and Fay; and I
> think it was rather a success. We began with the labour movement and
> finished up on Ethics. They seem to know as much about productive
> cooperation as we know about unproductive copulation, and there was
> a splendid flow of conversation.

The plan to make the Society more political, which included electing Fay,
soon petered out. With free trade secure, Maynard's uninvolvement in
politics became about as complete as was possible for someone of his
temperament.

His labours for the Society took a different form: that of trying to revive
his friendship with 'Dilly' Knox. Knox had come up to King's in 1903, but
he and Maynard had seen little of each other, moving in quite different
circles. Now Knox started to come into the reckoning as a potential Apostle.
'With the least bit more sense he would be obviously superb,' Maynard had
confided to Strachey on 28 November 1905. But this was Knox's trouble. His
brilliant mind was applied to pedantry and trivia: he lacked 'serious bottom'.
Nevertheless, Maynard tried for some months to 'enter Knox's citadel and
tear down the grinning mask',[7] not just for the Society's sake but for the
sake of their old friendship. 'Arise, shine,' he wrote to him in a letter he
never sent.[8] But Knox soon faded away again. This left Keynes with his two
original embryos – the manic mathematician Henry Norton and the silent
James Strachey. Their 'births' took place on 17 February 1906.

In December 1905 Maynard had started reading psychology for the Civil
Service Examination. In January 1906 he moved to more familiar territory.
'Have you read the Ethics of that superb Aristotle?' he asked Strachey on
23 January. 'There never was such good sense talked – before or since.'
On 7 February he wrote:

> My dear, I have been deep in Greek philosophy these last few days,
> Thales and Pythagoras, Zeno and his lover Parmenides. I have been
> curiously happy reading about these strange quibblers for hours
> together; and I don't wonder Aristotle put this intellectual activity first.
> Still I don't agree with him. Love first, philosophy second, Poetics third,
> and Politics fourth. I would change with you – for he [Duncan Grant]
> seems to love you.

If metaphysics entranced him, the political science and jurisprudence on
which he now started filled him with gloom. 'I am doing hardly any work
and shall never be able to pass into that dreadful Civil Service,' he told
Strachey.

Early in March, Maynard spent a long weekend in Oxford. He attended
a meeting of the Jowett Society where he opened a 'sad discussion' after a

---

* Frederic 'Ben' Keeling had come up to Trinity College the previous autumn. He restarted
the University Fabian Society.

paper on 'Time and the Absolute', and dined at All Souls, whose pomp he found 'incredible'. But his flirtation with Daniel Macmillan made no progress. When Strachey lamented his failure to build on a 'semi-embrace' Maynard replied (on 11 March): 'My dear, I have always suffered and I suppose always will from a most unalterable obsession that I am so physically repulsive that I've no business to hurl my body on anyone else's. The idea is so fixed and constant that I don't think anything – certainly no argument – could ever shake it.'

On Monday 19 March Maynard left England for Italy. He stopped briefly in Paris to see Duncan Grant who had gone there to study painting, spent a couple of days with Lytton in Genoa, 'eating omelettes and discussing ethics and sodomy',⁹ and then joined Mary Berenson in Florence. The introduction had come through Alys Russell, Mary Berenson's sister. Mary Berenson was a vital, extravagant, flirtatious woman of forty-one. She came from a family of Philadelphia Quakers, the Logan Pearsall Smiths, who had settled in England; had married a Fabian lawyer, Frank Costelloe, by whom she had two daughters, Rachel and Karin; and had then run off to Italy with the art connoisseur Bernard Berenson, to much scandalised comment in staid circles. Clad in a fur coat, Maynard embarked with the mother, two daughters and an Oxford undergraduate, Geoffrey Scott, on a week's tour of Tuscany. He wrote to Lytton Strachey on 2 April:

Mary is just the person to travel with in a motor – for her incredible competence as a hostess; all the arrangements for one's comfort were complete. She was full of Italian and money and which hotel was best and what food they could best cook. We must have cost her pints of gold – for everything down to entrance fees to galleries was paid.

The interest I learnt to take in food was almost indecent.... One is always hungry in a motor and we ate all day. The last hour or so of each drive was spent in plotting the menu and the first act on reaching the inn was to order it. And she roars with laughter the whole time, allows you to laugh at her, and never worries one.

Mary Berenson and her daughters left Keynes and Scott at Siena where they settled down for ten days of work in a 'pension with eleven spinsters' in the Via delle belle Arte. Maynard spent six hours a week on history, repeating to Lytton that he had never come across a subject 'that is so easy and cloys so quickly'.

The Italian trip ended with a week with the Berensons at their villa I Tatti in Settignano, just outside Florence, where Maynard admired the old masters – 'there are six in my bedroom and study' he told his parents – and fell a little in love with Rachel (Ray). 'But as she isn't male I haven't had to think of any suitable steps to take', he told Lytton.

While all this was going on, dreadful things were happening in Paris. A post from Lytton brought news that Hobhouse had visited Duncan there,

Duncan had fallen in love with him, and he with Duncan. 'Great God,' Maynard wrote back. 'It's more wild and more mad than anything ever happened in the world before. Oh and we have created it. It has sprung and sprouted from the tips of our penes [sic] – from yours and mine. And it will spread and grow over the whole world.' He was careful, though, to be suitably sympathetic: 'You know – as always how much I am in love with you and Duncan as a unity – that I can't help feeling that this is only an episode.'

He left I Tatti on 18 April to join his brother Geoffrey in Germany. The visit was not a success. Maynard reported to Lytton the next day from Feldberghof:

> Here I am with my brother – a monument of physical endurance on the top of a high mountain in the midst of snow. I thought I would use this opportunity to make his acquaintance – and I dreamt how I would worm out of him all his amours, or failing them at least learn all the latest Rugby scandals.
>
> But what a blow! My dear, here he is at nineteen and ... simply uneducated. Oh what's the good of Rugby?

Maynard and Neville made their usual thorough preparations for the impending Civil Service Examination. To cover the period of the examinations, stretching from 2 to 24 August, Neville had taken a flat at 33 Coleherne Court, London, into which Maynard moved with Florence and Margaret on 1 August. The next day he took his English composition, selecting as his essay subject 'Drama, Melodrama, and Opera' on which he had already read a paper to the Apostles. To James Strachey he wrote (2 August) of his fellow examinees, 'They are rather a crew – a few of the more presentable I knew, but good God! I trembled for our Indian Empire when I saw the bulk of them.' The family celebrated the end of the ordeal on Friday 24 August with a visit to Shaw's *You Never Can Tell* at the Royal Court. Then Maynard fled to Surrey to stay the weekend with his Eton friend Humphrey Paul. 'The Maurice Macmillans have taken a house there,' he wrote to Strachey on 28 August, 'so I spent most of yesterday with Dan. His brother Harold who has just got into College is growing up in the Dan style but much more exquisite.... I played golf with him.' In mid-September he set off for ten days' holiday in the Highlands, staying with James Strachey and Henry Norton in a cottage near Inverness. Here Lytton joined them for 'terrific excursions into the mountains'. Maynard told his father that he had made a start on Probability 'and am rather hopeful. My method is quite new....' With the Civil Service Examination out of the way, he had begun working on his fellowship dissertation, just according to his father's schedule, drawn up five years previously.

After going through his papers with his father, Keynes had estimated that he would come in the first ten. This might not be quite good enough as he had determined to take only the Treasury or India Office. However, he came second, with 3498 marks out of a possible 6000. First was Otto Niemeyer, a classical scholar from Balliol College, Oxford, with 3917, who entered the Treasury, where he became a champion of the economic policy Keynes later attacked.

By 4 October Maynard was announcing to Lytton Strachey, 'Yes I am a clerk in the India Office – having passed the medical with flying colours, balls and eyesight unusually perfect they said. My marks have arrived and left me enraged. Really knowledge seems an absolute bar to success. I have done worst in the only two subjects of which I possessed solid knowledge, Mathematics and Economics.'

II. THE INDIA OFFICE

On 16 October 1906 Maynard started his civil service career as junior clerk in the Military Department of the India Office, at a salary of £200 a year, his first job being to arrange the shipment of ten young Ayrshire bulls to Bombay. The India Office consisted of six departments run by secretaries. There were six assistant secretaries, eight senior clerks, ten junior clerks and seventy-six second-division clerks. Its main function was pushing paper to and from India, about 100,000 pieces of it every year. It was hardly a job to excite Keynes's full interest. Everything had been reduced to routine – a tribute to a vanished world where problems were routine too. This antiquated machine exercised ultimate control over the British Raj. Its Secretary of State, John Morley, was almost an antique himself; the permanent under-secretary, Sir Arthur Godley, was something of a reformer, but he could make little headway against tradition.

Keynes had chosen the India Office because it was one of the two top home departments of state, not because he had any interest in India. Certainly his attitude to British rule was conventional in every sense. He believed the regime protected the poor against the rapacious money-lender, brought justice and material progress, and gave the country a sound monetary system: in short, introduced good government to places which could not develop it on their own. Unlike Leonard Woolf, who saw colonial rule from the lowly position of a district officer in Ceylon, and unlike E. M. Forster and Lowes Dickinson who travelled in Asia, Maynard always saw the Raj from Whitehall: he never considered the human and moral implications of imperial rule or whether the British were exploiting the Indians. Although he was to write and advise extensively on Indian affairs, the furthest east he ever got was Egypt; the only Indians he ever met were at Cambridge or

London; the only books he ever read on India were specialised tomes on finance. This was the tradition set by Macaulay and Mills in the nineteenth century: good government of India was a matter not of local knowledge but of applying sound utilitarian principles from London.

One advantage of this approach to policymaking was that it economised enormously on the time that needed to be spent in the office. Civil service life was adapted as far as possible to the habits of the Oxford and Cambridge graduates entering the Administrative Section. Late rising in the mornings was safeguarded by starting work at 11.00 a.m. The day ended at 5.00 p.m. with an hour's break for lunch. There were two months' holiday a year, plus bank holidays and, of course, Derby Day. Saturday hours were from 11.00 to 1.00. 'I am delighted to find that we have shorter hours and longer holidays than any other office,' Maynard informed his father on 17 October. Florence had at first thought he would have no time to work on his fellowship dissertation. She need not have worried. Keynes's speed in emptying his in-tray was always remarkable. He found plenty of time to write his thesis and do his personal correspondence in office hours. Evidently it occurred to someone that Maynard's talents were being wasted in the Military Department; or it may simply be that a vacancy occurred elsewhere. 'After a state interview of incredible pomp' with Godley[10] he was moved to the Revenue, Statistics and Commerce Department at the beginning of March 1907. It had, he informed his father, 'very little routine work ... and deals with all questions of commerce, Land Revenue, Plague, Famine, Opium Trafffic, and so forth'. Installed in a 'charming room to myself overlooking the Park',[11] he was set to work editing the annual report on the Moral and Material Progress of India. 'A special feature of this year's edition,' he gossiped to Lytton, 'is to be an illustrated appendix on Sodomy'. He wrote to him on 7 March: 'Yesterday I attended my first Committee of Council. The thing is simply government by dotardry; at least half those present showed manifest signs of senile decay, and the rest didn't speak.'

He took a service flat – 125b St James's Court, five minutes' walk from his office – on a two-year lease, at a rental of £90 a year. He was soon complaining of an 'epidemic of dinner parties – five in six days'. He saw Strachey regularly for lunch or tea. They talked about Duncan Grant, and Maynard commiserated with him on the death of Thoby Stephen, from typhoid, on 20 November 1906. At this stage, Maynard was not a member of Old Bloomsbury. He had hardly known Clive Bell and Thoby Stephen at Cambridge; he dined occasionally with Vanessa and Clive Bell in London, but was not part of the Bloomsbury At Homes. However, there were many Apostles in London apart from Lytton, of whom the Sangers were special friends. There was the Etonian set based on the two Youngs, Geoffrey and Hilton, Robin Mayor and Ralph Hawtrey. And there was Mary Berenson who had a flat in Victoria where she entertained Maynard and Geoffrey Scott –

the latter often staying overnight with Maynard at St James's Court. Cultural life included Shaw's *Man and Superman* and Wagner's *Tristan und Isolde*. March 1907 dates Maynard's first apparent interest in picture buying. He had been taken by Strachey to a show of Simon Bussy's at Leighton House, Bussy having married Strachey's sister Dorothy. 'It seems to me essential to buy one – the cheapness!' he wrote to Florence.[12]

Every weekend Maynard left London, generally staying in Cambridge with his parents, and attending meetings of the Society. Nothing much seemed to have changed. Maynard told Lytton Strachey on 5 November 1906:

> We all lost our hearts to Percy Sanger and couldn't think why we hadn't kissed him when he left.
> Bertie [Russell] was up too.
> McT[aggart]. read a paper to the Sunday Essay on Moore's Ethics. It was in the form of an attack but it was really a final capitulation. For after all, McT. is candid. Oh, his physical beauty was astounding.
> As for me and Dil – well, I don't know that there's much to tell you.

In March 1907, holiday time came round again. Maynard, James Strachey and Norton crossed over to Paris for a long weekend with Duncan Grant. On his return Maynard joined Moore's reading party assembled at North Molton in Devonshire. This was his first invitation to one of those famous gatherings, regarded as a supreme mark of Moore's favour. Others present were the two Stracheys, Norton, Ainsworth, Bob Trevelyan and Sanger.[13] The weather was 'quite inconceivable', Strachey wrote to Duncan Grant on 1 April. 'I haven't seen a cloud for the last fortnight.' Ainsworth was lying by him with 'a pair of blue spectacles to keep off the rays of the sun ... reading Plato'. Trevelyan, the poet, was 'fast asleep and dreaming of his opera on Bacchus and Ariadne, which he has just written for Tovey to set to music, and is the greatest balls you can imagine'. A few feet away under an umbrella sat Maynard reading Galsworthy, with Norton doing mathematics on the grass beside him, and Moore, 'lying full length on a rug, with an umbrella poised over him, making pencil notes in the margin of Locke's *Essay on Human Understanding*'.

In June Maynard was off on his travels again, this time to the French Pyrenees, where he and Fay, now lecturing at Christ's College, Cambridge, joined Neville and Geoffrey for a walking and climbing holiday. Maynard never had much enthusiasm for either pursuit, and stole precious hours to study probability in his bedroom and read Jane Austen in the lee of a rock. 'I should like to go on doing it here for months,' he wrote to Lytton Strachey on 5 July. 'Also it is a very long time since lust has been at so low an ebb (I suppose it is the result of so much walking)....'

Maynard and Fay left Neville and Geoffrey to walk to Biarritz, spending three days in a peasant's hut in Spain, near Torla, in 'the most wonderful

valley I have ever seen'.[14] In Biarritz, Maynard had the kind of holiday he
enjoyed most, breakfasting in bed, reading a novel for an hour or so, working
on Probability for another couple of hours, and then, as he told his mother,
'food and sun and laziness for the rest of the day'. At night, they went to the
casino, where Maynard soon lost all his money at *petits chevaux*, playing his
own special system, and was reduced to trying to win some of it back from
Fay at piquet in their hotel bedroom.

Despite being congratulated by no less a person than John Morley, the
Secretary of State, for a minute of 'admirable promise', Maynard was starting
to get bored with his job. He resented having to spend a torridly hot summer
in London. First he said there was too much to do. Then there was not
enough to do. As an antidote to depression he went on a book-buying spree,
one of his acquisitions being 'a most beautiful quarto in a quite magnificent
elaborately tooled 17th century contemporary binding' by the Jesuit Father
John Keynes.[15] It was during this summer that Maynard decided to leave the
India Office, complaining to Strachey on 13 September that he was 'bored
nine-tenths of the time and rather unreasonably irritated the other tenth
whenever I can't have my own way'.

It was not till Saturday 12 October 1907 that Maynard came back to
Cambridge for a three-week holiday. 'I have seldom been in Cambridge so
long', he wrote to Strachey on the 16th, 'and had so little to report. I dissert,
I play golf daily with Fay and Dil (in his gold rimmers) and that is all.'
Bernard Shaw 'converted us all to socialism' at the Cambridge Union, Lytton
Strachey arrived for his annual inspection of the 'embryos', and after much
labour, which continued for some months after Maynard returned to Lon-
don, Rupert Brooke was duly born as an Apostle.

Maynard's three weeks of Cambridge life had whetted his appetite for
more. His hopes of a rapid release from the India Office rested on getting a
prize fellowship at King's. He was now working almost full time on probability. On 6 December he wrote to Florence: 'I have not averaged an hour's
office work a day, so I am well up with the dissertation.' He handed it in on
12 December 1907. The examiners were W. E. Johnson and Alfred North
Whitehead.

On 3 February 1908 Neville talked to W. E. Johnson about Maynard's
chances. 'On the whole his verdict appears more favourable than Whitehead's.' Neville by no means shared Maynard's enthusiasm for quitting the
India Office. A prize fellowship was for six years only. It offered no career
prospects, but could be held concurrently with his India post. On 1 March
1908 father and son had their first and only recorded row. 'Maynard wishes
to throw up the India Office if he gets a Fellowship at King's. I have argued
with him in vain. I think he would give up the idea if I said definitely that
I desired him to do so. But I do not think that I ought to take so decided a
position as that. He will be throwing up a certainty and taking risks. That
fits in with his scheme of life, not mine.'

The next day Maynard told Pigou, one of the electors, that if elected he would come back into residence. The election took place on 17 March. There were four candidates for two places. Only after fifteen votes had been taken did it become clear that Maynard would not be filling one of them. The two new fellows were Page and Dobbs. 'We feel very much disappointed and depressed,' Neville wrote in his diary. 'I had reconciled myself to Maynard's giving up the India Office, for he seemed so thoroughly to have set his heart on returning to Cambridge and a student's life.' Maynard was not so much disappointed as furious. He was particularly annoyed when told that one reason for turning him down was that he would have another chance next year. He raged against Whitehead's incompetence as an examiner, claiming that he had not bothered to try to understand what he was saying.

Keynes's dissertation is essentially the development of ideas in his Apostles paper of January 1904 (see p. 94 above). He set out to create a 'new kind of logic' applicable to 'doubtful arguments and uncertain conclusions'[16] which may, nevertheless, be rational and objective. His argument is summed up in these passages from the first chapter:

In the ordinary course of thought and argument we are constantly asserting that the truth of one statement, while not *proving* another, is nevertheless *some ground* for believing the second. We assert that, with the evidence at our command, we *ought* to hold such and such a belief.... We recognise that *objectively* evidence can be *real* evidence and yet not *conclusive* evidence.... I do not think I am straining the use of words in speaking of this as the probability relation or the relation of probability.

The idea of a premiss's having some weight to establish a conclusion, of its lying somewhere between cogency and irrelevancy, is altogether foreign to a logic in which the premiss must either prove or not prove the alleged conclusion. This opinion is, from the nature of the case, incapable of positive proof. The notion presents itself to the mind, I feel, as something independent and unique....

Yet that 'probability' is, in the strict sense, indefinable, need not trouble us much; it is a characteristic which it shares with many of our most necessary and fundamental ideas....

One of the most striking things about the dissertation was the boldness of Keynes's claims. Implicit in his argument was the view that probability should be rightly considered as the *general theory* of logic, of which deductive logic was a special case. Similarly, he was to argue in 1936 that he was producing a 'general theory' of employment, of which the classical theory was a 'special case'.

Failure to get elected a fellow of King's in 1908 was the worst academic blow Maynard ever suffered. And even then it was merely a postponement.

The chance to resume his student's life came more quickly than he had anticipated. A fortnight after the fellowship débâcle, Maynard received a cryptic communication from Marshall. Marshall had been paying £100 a year for a lectureship in economics out of his own professorial stipend. The recipient of this bounty had just obtained a chair at Leeds University. Marshall cautiously suggested to Keynes that the sum might be made available to him. The caution is understandable. Marshall was about to retire. He could not bind his successor. But he had no doubt that if his own favoured candidate, Pigou, succeeded him, the offer would become definite. In fact, it was Pigou who suggested that Marshall write to Maynard.

On 30 May the first condition of Maynard's return to Cambridge was fulfilled when Pigou was elected to Marshall's chair, over Ashley, Cannan and Foxwell. On 3 June the Economics and Politics Board, chaired by Neville, authorised two lectureships in economics, one to be offered to Maynard, the other to Walter Layton, who had just graduated from Trinity. The understanding was that Pigou would provide them each with £100 a year. Neville immediately offered Maynard an extra £100 for as long as he needed it. On 5 June 1908, his twenty-fifth birthday, he resigned from the India Office. 'Please do not think,' he wrote tactfully to Sir Thomas Holderness, 'that I have disliked my work in the Revenue Dept. . . . But the choice has been between two quite opposed ways of life, and on the whole I think, now at any rate, that the way here is better.'

His civil service superiors, while greatly regretting his loss, had no doubt that he had made the right choice. 'I personally am one of the last to quarrel with your decision,' wrote Godley. To Holderness Maynard's letter came as a blow, but 'I have never been quite able to satisfy myself that a government office in this country is the best thing for a young man of energy and right ambitions. It is a comfortable means of life and leads by fairly sure, if slow, stages to moderate competence and old age provision. But it is rarely exciting or strenuous and does not make sufficient call on the combative and self-assertive elements of human nature.'[17] In 1914 Edwin Montagu, then Under-Secretary of State for India, wrote to Holderness, 'I have been often struck by the tedium of life of junior Departmental Officers in the Office. If . . . freedom of expression and opportunity had been allowed to Keynes, should we have ever lost him?'[18] The answer is probably yes.

Brief though Maynard's stay at the India Office had been, it had an important effect on his career. The flippant and disgusted tone of his letters to Strachey revealed only part of his attitude, though no doubt a most important one. It left out how good he was at his job, including getting on with his superiors. His secret was genuine ability of a high order, plus what Desmond MacCarthy called 'conversation calculated to impress men of forty'. He was certainly interested in the statistical aspects of his departmental work; and from Lionel Abrahams, head of the Financial Department, he learnt about India's currency arrangements. Godley, in a letter dated

30 March 1909, hoped that Maynard would 'continue to keep an eye on Indian affairs'; Francis Drake, assistant secretary of the Revenue and Statistics Department, had no doubt 'we shall find something to worry you about from time to time'.[19] These proved to be understatements. His expertise on India, supplemented by his study and teaching of economics, and his contacts with civil servants led on quite logically to his writings on India's monetary system and his membership of the Royal Commission on Indian Currency and Finance; these in turn brought further fame at Whitehall and important political contacts. Keynes was summoned to help in his country's crisis in 1914 and to the Treasury in 1915 not just as a monetary economist, but as someone who could apply theory to administration. Austin Robinson is right to say that Keynes had, at the India Office, learnt to 'see the problems of economics from the angle of the administrator'.

On 21 July 1908 Maynard returned to Harvey Road and moved into King's next day. He was happier than his parents knew. For not only had he recovered Cambridge; he had won Duncan Grant.

8

Lytton, Duncan, Maynard

Duncan James Corrowr Grant was twenty-three in 1908, eighteen months younger than Maynard. Born on 21 January 1885 in Scotland at The Doune, Inverness, family home of the Grants of Rothiemurchus, he had spent his early life in India, where his father, Major Bartle Grant, was stationed. From there he was sent to Hillbrow Preparatory School, Rugby and, in 1899, to St Paul's, which he attended as a day boy, living with his cousins the Stracheys at 69 Lancaster Gate or with his parents in Hampstead, when they were in England. At the age of seventeen he had finished his 'rather brief education at St Paul's school' and had enrolled as a student at the Westminster School of Art. Duncan inherited the beauty of his mother, Ethel McNeill, and his father's musical tastes. They loved their only son, but never quite knew what to make of him. Duncan sometimes felt that his family thought him half-witted.

Maynard had got to know him through Lytton Strachey. In fact for some years he knew more of him than he knew him, since Lytton used Maynard as an outlet for his feelings about his cousin. In turn, Lytton consoled Maynard about Hobhouse. Feeling rejected, they confided in each other – at the rate of almost a letter a day for nearly a year; Strachey's full of romantic but self-mocking passion; Keynes skipping in short, busy paragraphs from love to Cambridge gossip to work.

The affair between the cousins had run into trouble almost from the start. 'There's distinctly something of the lovee about his affection if not about his lust,' Lytton complained to Maynard on 13 October 1905; Maynard in reply commanded him not to think that every kind of disaster was in store. Soon Lytton was lamenting Duncan's indifference, 'an adamantine and irrevocable rock which no power under heaven can move'. Maynard wrote back practically that Duncan was probably tired from painting so much at the National Gallery. Keynes, it can be seen, was not entirely satisfactory as an outlet. Lytton was both a rationalist and a romantic. He wanted reassurance that his fears were groundless, and also to savour the sorrow of unrequited love – conditions which were difficult to reconcile. Keynes did his best. Later Lytton was to say that Maynard's common sense was enough to freeze a volcano. He called him 'an Apostle without tears'. Perhaps in Maynard's lame responses to his agonies are to be found the seeds of the disintegration of their intimacy. Yet Lytton's fires were partly epistolary; truth was sacrificed to style. And this Maynard knew well enough.

In February 1906 Duncan Grant got his chance to study painting in Paris when his aunt Elinor, Lady Colville, gave him £100 for his twenty-first birthday. He enrolled at La Pallette, an art school run by Jacques-Emile Blanche, living at the Hôtel de l'Univers et du Portugal near the Palais Royal. His affair with Hobhouse started up soon afterwards, and continued at intervals till the end of the year: he and Hobhouse spent a holiday together at Rothiemurchus in August. This time Duncan's feelings were fully engaged. 'My darling,' he wrote to Hobhouse on 10 July, 'if I could only be sure you *really* loved me I should be perfectly happy.... Oh my dearest angel do be able to tell me it's different than it was with Keynes.' Their previous rivalry forgotten, Lytton and Maynard united in deploring Hobhouse's conduct. 'Of all prostitutes, the spiritual ones are the worst,' Strachey declared contemptuously. Under the strain, Lytton's health collapsed – pains in his chest, pains in his balls, and 'wet dreams intolerably frequent.... I'd give anything to see you, Maynard'. By December the affair was over. 'Arthur told me he had no feelings towards me at all,' Duncan informed James Strachey on 18 December.

In October 1906 Duncan returned to Paris, which remained his base till the summer of 1907, a curiously isolated expatriate figure in the artistic capital of the world. Maynard visited him there in March 1907 in the company of Norton and James Strachey. 'It was charming,' Duncan told Lytton, 'having Keynes and Norton here. I did seem to like Keynes much more than before....' After the Hobhouse episode, Lytton's affair with his cousin had started up again in a somewhat desultory fashion. He never seems to have seen Maynard as a potential rival in love. As compared with his own capacity for the *grand amour* Keynes's feeble lechery seemed to offer no possible threat. He should have been more alerted to those eyes which, as he noted, burnt with an 'ambiguous flame'. He should have been alerted, too, by what he knew of Duncan's character. Maynard's less passionate personality would make fewer demands on Duncan than had Lytton's – demands which Duncan could not meet. Lytton's summaries of Maynard left out his capacity for cherishing those he loved – something very reassuring to Duncan, who was too proud and innocent to protect himself from the world.

Of medium height, with dark good looks, Duncan had eyes 'extraordinarily grey and liquid, very pale, with huge irises and long lashes' as well as what Strachey called 'incomparably lascivious lips'.[1] He had an original but completely untrained intelligence. Maynard would have been delighted by the fact that he had never mastered the multiplication tables. He loved music and dancing. His visual sense made him 'intensely observant and amused in everything he saw: and the things he saw were especially those to which the majority of people were blind'. The very absence of mind which made him seem half-witted to conventional people – his clothes, for example, looked, and often were, other people's cast-offs – was part of his charm for Maynard. Yet he was certain of what he wanted to do. Duncan, in short, fitted the type whom Maynard was always disposed to worship: the artist with an inner integrity but with an outward need for protection.

Early in June 1908 Lytton went to spend a month in Cambridge, leaving Duncan and Maynard in London. Their affair started as soon as Lytton left. On Sunday 28 June, Florence wrote to Neville in Switzerland: 'John has brought Duncan Grant down with him. This morning we all sat in the garden & read, & this afternoon they two have bicycled to Clayhithe for tea.' This trip to Cambridge must have taken place without Lytton's knowledge. From Fellows Road, Hampstead, Duncan wrote to Maynard on 29 June: 'I know I needn't tell you how much I enjoyed my Cambridge visit ... indeed I don't think I have ever been so completely happy, anyhow since I left school.' They continued to see each other frequently in London. Taking them, on his return to London, to lunch at Simpsons on 14 July, Lytton was alerted to new developments by a whispered aside from Keynes to Duncan, suggesting – as he wrote to his brother James – 'a liaison between Duncan and our dear Détraqué'.[2] Next day he saw Maynard and it all came out. Keynes wrote to his new lover at once:

> Dearest Duncan, Lytton has been. He begins 'I hear that you and Duncan are carrying on together'. I feel quite shattered by the interview, but I suppose it wasn't very dreadful really. He takes the cynical line – much interested as a student of human life. But it gave him, as he said, a turn. . . . Oh dear, I don't know what to think of the interview and feel ill and rather distraught. I wish there was no one else in the world but you.

Two days later, Lytton's fury exploded in a letter to his brother James:

> What was so shocking about my interview with 'him', when he made the announcement, was the incredible lack of feeling. It quite gave even me a turn. I believe I might have passed on in the conversation from that, without a visible break, to probability – he would never have noticed. Unfortunately I was too honest, and had a fit, which at least did make him begin very dimly to realise that it was perhaps rather odd and important that he was 'in love'. I think ever since the Hobber days there has been distinct deterioration. Then, there was certainly just a touch of romance; and now the hardness is complete.

Of all Strachey's amorous crises, writes his biographer, this was his 'most wretched'.[3] However, a reconciliation of a kind was patched up. Maynard made the first move, writing to Lytton on 20 July:

> I want very much to write and don't know what to say. Has your confusion died away? Do you yet know what you think and feel about us? Please don't be unsympathetic and don't, if you can help it, hate

me. Can I come and see you? This is my last minute in this office, but I
shall probably be in London until Wednesday.

'The letter seems to me to show affection,' Lytton wrote to his brother on
21 July. To Maynard he replied: 'I only know that we've been friends for
too long to stop being friends now.' When he got back to Harvey Road on
the 22nd Maynard found 'three most lovely books – a present from Lytton.
I feel that they are a token of a good deal – it is *too* good of him to behave
like this.'[4]

Maynard moved into King's on 25 July. Two days later Duncan left for
the Orkney Islands. He had been invited to stay on Hoy by the millionaire
Thomas Middlemore, a friend of his mother's, who had bought the island in
1898 for £32,000.

Although Maynard missed Duncan terribly, he adored being in Cambridge again, and regaled his friend with the familiar gossip. 'Nothing could
be more peaceful than existence here,' he wrote to Duncan on 26 July. The
next day, while Duncan was whirling through the night to Hoy, Maynard
listened to a Mr Schloss* reading a paper on 'Relationships' in Ben Keeling's
room to the 'Fabian boys':

> A dreadful, silly, maundering paper, followed by a blithering speech
> from Daddy Dalton.† In spite of the serried ranks of females, the paper
> was chiefly about sodomy which is called 'the passionate love of
> comrades'. Really James is quite right – these Fabians talk about nothing
> else.... The thing has grown with leaps and bounds in my two years of
> absence and practically everybody in Cambridge, except me, is an open
> and avowed sodomite.
>
> Shove‡ I've now seen twice. He's much the best of them – quite a
> cut above the others in my opinion. Indeed he's very charming, though
> not very clever I dare say, and quite nice to look at....
>
> Dear Duncan if I could kiss you and hold your hand I should be
> perfectly happy, and from wanting to I am discontented and almost, not
> quite, miserable. Find us a lovely cottage in the North and we will stay
> there forever....

Meanwhile, Duncan had braved a stormy three-hour sea-journey from
Stromness to Hoy, to be received with champagne on his arrival at Melsetter,
Middlemore's estate. 'I cannot describe the beauty of these islands, you are
going to see them so I won't even try,' he wrote to Maynard on 29 July. The
Middlemore house, 'a masterpiece of Celtic art' overlooking the sea, was full
of Burne-Jones cartoons, Turner watercolours and Morris tapestries. 'Old

---

* Arthur Schloss had come up to King's in 1907. He later changed his name to Waley, and
became famous for his translations of Chinese poetry.
† Hugh Dalton, the Labour politician, had come to King's from Eton in 1906.
‡ Gerald Shove, also an arrival at King's in 1907, became an economist.

Middlemore' was a 'model of true courtesy but talks slower than anyone in the world and thinks even slower'. Duncan painted and read, walked with the women, talked with the men, played cards with both, ate and drank prodigiously, and desperately missed Maynard. 'I would give my soul to the Devil if I could kiss you and be kissed,' he wrote on 29 July. 'I wish you were here to stand between me and the world.'

They were reunited at Stromness on 18 August. 'I know we will be happy,' Duncan had written. His expectation was fulfilled. Indeed, the next two months were probably the happiest in Maynard's life. They spent the first fortnight at Stromness, where they lodged in the Mason's Arms Hotel. 'The view above this town,' Maynard wrote to Lytton, 'is of the Bay of Naples and the Island of Capri. We strolled off this evening to have a better look at it and left my rug and papers and Duncan's picture in the field where we were. Imagine our horror on returning to find everything slobbered over ... by a herd of cows. But the picture was benefited and probability none the worse....' They returned to Hoy and this time persuaded the owners of a farm they had admired to let them have accommodation there. Here they settled down, Maynard told his mother, to 'fixed hours of painting and probability'. The peat fires were always lit, and the animals so strange and numerous that even Maynard started to take an interest in them. The only problem was that everyone was suspicious of German spies, so that 'they will have to get used to us before sitting for portraits'. By 13 September, Duncan had started painting Maynard, Probability's back had been broken, and Maynard had started writing a paper for the *Economic Journal*.[5] Duncan himself dated Maynard's real appreciation of painting from this time. 'Maynard with his writing board was a good subject, so while he was immersed in the "Theory of Probability" I ... was immersed in trying to figure out the shape of his face. The result of this I think was that Maynard gradually accepted the fact that painting had its difficulties too, in fact he accepted, without me having to point it out, that the painter had a serious job on hand.'[6]

It was not till 22 October that he and Duncan at last tore themselves away, Duncan to go to Rothiemurchus. Maynard arrived back in Cambridge on the evening of the 23rd, his father, as always, being there to meet him at the station. He moved into his new rooms at King's on the 24th. Lytton was his first guest. 'I am so happy to be in Cambridge that I am as cheerful as anyone could wish,' Maynard wrote to Duncan. 'When I have both you and Cambridge, I shall be the most fortunate creature in the world.'[7] Lytton, on the other hand, was far from pleased with the company of his successful rival. 'It was hardly anything but horror,' he told his brother. 'It wasn't only his indelicacy – which was complete, lasting up to the very last, but the sense that it was no good expecting any more to get anything out of that relationship. ... It was ashes and dry bones. ... In future I shall go to Trinity.'[8] The failure of this reunion was to have bitter consequences for Maynard over the next few months.

The old life re-established itself. Golf with Neville at Royston in continuous rain reduced him to taking quinine. Dickinson read a paper on
immortality. Rupert Brooke now called Keynes Maynard. There were beau-
ties to be inspected for the Society: George Mallory seemed 'perfectly lovely'.*
Duncan came up on 31 October. 'His train was 17½ minutes late. So at least
I was informed by Maynard at 1.14,' James Strachey told his brother. 'The
general appearance is *extraordinarily* married – If D. comes here to live,
however, there'll certainly be flirtations with – oh! anyone. But what I now
see is that that won't matter a bit ... the Machine will merely be amused
and exclaim "You always come back to me – to me – to me!" And he always
will.'⁹

On 10 November, Maynard went to London to superintend the removal
of his things from St James's Court, where he got influenza so badly that he
had to spend a couple of days in Hampstead Hospital. Strachey saw him
'rigged out in shetland waistcoats, with long grey arms, fairly beaming with
fatuity, for all the world like a gorilla trying to be Mary Moore. It was
incredibly shocking! And poor dear Duncan at the end of the bed, sending
out oeillades.... I fled from the place, howling.'¹⁰ Maynard returned, still
weak, to Harvey Road on 16 November, where probability occupied most of
his time, moving back into King's on the 20th.

He and Duncan, who had got back to London early in November, now
went through a miserable time – partly due to the after-effects of the
influenza they had both suffered. Duncan, who was searching for a studio
in which he could paint and which Keynes could share as a London pied-à-
terre, was by 18 November 'extremely depressed and ... almost in tears,
completely unbalanced. Simply because you are not here to right me. I have
these sudden fits of depression occasionally merely because someone makes
a remark to me which I imagine proves that they have no more idea of what
I'm like than a cabbage.' Maynard at first functioned happily in the day but
was sad in the evenings because Duncan was not there; his feelings were
like 'those of a homesick schoolboy'.¹¹ By 23 November he was 'excessively
miserable during a large part of the day and hardly know how to support
existence.... If I knew you were coming, I should feel more cheerful in the
meantime....' He tempted Duncan for a long visit by the promise of 'millions
of people to come and sit for you.... If only you come, I shall be happy in
body and mind, and really able to do work.' Nor were the freshmen inspiring,
the only one of note being a 'Mr [Dennis] Robertson of Eton and Trinity
[who] came to lunch and for a walk with me yesterday. There's a good deal
in his favour, but a little pudding headed perhaps.'¹² It's not clear whether
this was intended to refer to his appearance or his intelligence. (Robertson
was rejected as a potential Apostle, not securing election to the Society till

* George Leigh Mallory, who died in the attempt on Everest in 1924, was then in his third
year at Magdalene College. He was more Geoffrey's friend than Maynard's.

1926 at the unusually late age of thirty-six.) Duncan came on 28 November and stayed till 15 December with Maynard at King's, finishing the portrait he had begun in the Orkneys. Neville bought it for Florence – the first of many sales Duncan made through Maynard.

Duncan's visit revived Maynard's intellectual interests. The revised version of his fellowship dissertation was practically finished by 4 December.[13] A visit from Swithin provided, as always, a welcome, but worrying, experience. Swithinbank, who had gained a disappointing second class in classics at Balliol and had narrowly been dissuaded from embarking forthwith to the Fiji Islands as a sanitary inspector, had surprised everyone by coming third in the Civil Service Examination that September. This seemed to ensure a place in the home Civil Service; but, possibly because he never expected to come so high, he had put himself down for the Indian Civil Service only; and was now busy reading books on Burma, preparatory to going out there as a district commissioner. Duncan, who had just met Swithin in London at the Stracheys, found him 'the most beautiful person I've ever seen'. At King's, Maynard and Swithin had one of their usual grand conversations lasting most of the night.[14] By contrast, a conversation with another old flame, Hobhouse, left Maynard 'absolutely shattered'. 'He seemed to me awful, horrible, a thing which ought to be put out of the way; and yet I could not forget how much I had been in love with him. I'm sure he was not like this then; it is impossible.'[15] Duncan had rented a studio in St John's Wood, and Maynard spent the first fortnight in January with him. In the mornings, Pernel, one of Lytton's sisters, would sit for her portrait, and he would study finance. They prepared their own lunches and spent most of the afternoons washing up. In the evenings they went to the theatre. 'The new studio', he told his sister Margaret, 'is really a charming place – a fairly large white room with two seat windows to the ground.'[16]

Apart from physical attraction which is indefinable, the attraction between Maynard and Duncan was very much one of opposites: each admired and valued that in the other which he himself lacked. Duncan was beautiful, artistic, unworldly; Maynard was clever, practical, kind. But in this very lack of fit was obvious potential for friction. Maynard liked his life to be well arranged; Duncan's arrangements were chaotic. Maynard was thoughtful to friends; Duncan was thoughtless. Maynard began to complain about his failure to write regularly, about his habit of putting off visits. Duncan could not be tied down to a routine of letters and visits, and disappointed expectations started to prey on Maynard's mind, leading to lovers' tiffs. 'Darling Maynard, what a brute you make me out to be,' wrote Duncan on 29 December, after Maynard had complained of the misery caused by Duncan promising, but failing, to write on a certain day.[17]

'Dearest Maynard, we mustn't often behave like we did today,' wrote Duncan early in 1909. 'It is too exhausting for one's nerves. . . . You must try – no it's no use. . . . I must try to behave better, less vaguely & selfishly &

then everything ought to go more smoothly.' Maynard's way of showing affection by monetary gifts could also give rise to misunderstanding. Duncan was 'very much enraged' to receive £5 through the post for his twenty-fourth birthday (21 January 1909). 'It's too absurd of you,' Maynard wrote to him. 'The thing is good as a means and absolutely unimportant in itself.'[18]

Maynard and Duncan lived very full lives. Maynard had started lecturing, coaching and writing in Cambridge; Duncan had begun to paint professionally in London. Their social lives were also crowded. But whereas Maynard always arranged his life so as to leave room for Duncan, Duncan's arrangements tended to exclude Maynard. Much of Duncan's spare time was spent going to concerts – sometimes with Lytton. On 24 January he took tickets for Wagner's *Ring*, about which he was 'much excited'. Maynard disliked music. He dreaded Duncan drifting into 'all sorts of unnecessary engagements which will make it impossible for us ever to meet again'.[19]

By mid-February Maynard was reminding Duncan that they had met only three times in the last five weeks. But Duncan's absence was not the only cause of his low spirits at this time. Strachey, as it turned out, had not forgiven him for taking Duncan away from him even though he now found Duncan 'quite singularly unattractive'. He and his brother started a malicious campaign against 'Pozzo di Borgo', as they had taken to calling Maynard among their Cambridge friends – Apostles and embryos – and succeeded in turning opinion against him.* Maynard felt hurt and unloved. Eventually Strachey realised he was going too far. 'I've been feeling rather uneasy about the Pozzo man,' he wrote to James on 14 February. 'On Wednesday night I was at Richmond, and Moore incidentally mentioned him as appearing very depressed and silent – "Looked as if he might be feeling that people didn't like him." I do hope it's nothing definite, or possibly even that it's untrue. But I can't help feeling rather guilty.... Then I suppose there's the possibility that he's beginning to find a coolness in Duncan – or even that he's beginning to think that Duncan hasn't got much to offer him that he wants. However no doubt the most probable thing is that he's only troubled in a way that's infinitely vague. Only I don't like to imagine it; and if, après tout, il a lu ces lettres!'

Lytton's attitude is easy to understand. In his friendship with Maynard he had always been the leader. Now Maynard had become much too successful. Successful in work, while Strachey was still struggling to make ends meet churning out reviews which he hated, he had proved successful in love too – and at Lytton's expense. Nor could he help reducing love to numbers. 'His statistics make me gasp,' James had written to Lytton, as Maynard revealed the details of his sexual encounters. (He kept count of

* Contrary to what has been said, Lytton Strachey had no one in mind when he started calling Maynard Pozzo di Borgo. See his letter to James Strachey, 26 November 1908. In Italian, 'pozzo' means 'sewer'.

them in his engagement diary.) The scatological incidents with which he
enlivened his talk now seemed to Strachey to be merely disgusting – when
applied to Duncan. 'His conversation', he wrote to James a little later, 'does
appear to me inordinately filthy. I felt as if I was walking in a drain.'

Lytton's attitude to Maynard at this time helped shape Bloomsbury's
later attitude to him. His outbursts were not confined to his brother. On
5 February 1909 he wrote to Leonard Woolf in Ceylon:

> As for poor old Keynes, he's quite absolutely sunk – it's really remark-
> able, the unveiled collapse. If ever a human soul was doomed, it's he.
> And by God I think he deserves his fate. Looking back I see him,
> hideous and meaningless, at every turn and every crisis, a malignant
> goblin gibbering over destinies that are not his own.... He'll end a
> spiritual Nixon,* with a whole internal economy of metal makeshifts for
> lungs and lights and heart and genitory organs; but he'll never know;
> he'll never hear the clank.

Virginia Stephen was the recipient of similar views. Virginia hardly knew
Maynard, and Woolf had heard little but ill of him from Lytton during his
years in Ceylon. Their critical attitude to Keynes, which was lifelong, may
thus have its roots in Lytton's sexual jealousy.

That jealousy was real enough. But one must also consider these friends'
feelings about each other in the light of Strachey's epistolatory philosophy
as set out to John Sheppard on 25 March 1903: 'It is much easier to say
filthy things than charming things, which one may feel just as much if not
more.... It'd take fourteen years to say everything one thought about
anyone. So one just says the things which are the amusingest & of course
the nastiest as well.'

Once his rival was down, Lytton's own wound began to heal. He could
afford to be less venomous. On 16 March 1909 Maynard heard he had been
elected to a prize fellowship at King's, all opposition to his thesis having
collapsed. From Belsize Park Gardens, his new family home, Lytton wrote to
him on 17 March:

> Dear Maynard,
>   I was very glad to hear of the fellowship. One couldn't feel absol-
> utely sure with those devils! I suppose you're now established for the
> rest of your days, and it seems very clear that you've acted wisely....
>   I've been wanting to write to you for some time, though really I
> think it's hardly necessary – only to say that you must always think of
> me as your friend. I shall think of you in the same way. But I've been
> rather afraid that lately you may have felt that things had become

---

* J. E. Nixon (1839–1916) was an eccentric lecturer in classics, parts of whose body were
'metal makeshifts'. The legend was that two men, Nicholson and Dixon, had been so
dismembered in an accident that only enough was left to rivet together one man – Nixon.

different. I don't think it's the case. The only thing is that I'm sometimes uneasy and awkward perhaps, partly I suppose because of my nervous organisation which isn't particularly good – but I don't see how it can be helped. I can only beg that you'll attend to it as little as possible, and believe me to be a sensible decent person who remembers and knows.

Maynard was clearly pleased with this delicate apology. But he failed to find the right words in his reply, dated 21 March:

Dear Lytton,

I was *very* glad to get your letter.

Tonight I dined for the second time at their High Table. The food is excellent but, by God, one feels a don. I play the part admirably, perhaps it belongs to me, but I should like to rape an undergraduate in the Combination Room, just to make them see things a little more in their true light.... I hope to be in London sometime this week but the business of rooms for next term and so forth keeps me hanging about.

Lytton complained to his brother that his gesture of reconciliation had been met by a 'sterile letter'. He and Maynard remained friends; but the best days of their friendship were over.

PART TWO

ON THE BRINK

Then the shot was fired in Sarajevo which destroyed the civilisation ... which I had known in the first 34 years of my life.

> Leonard Woolf, *Beginning Again: An Autobiography of the Years 1911 to 1918*, p. 144

What an extraordinary episode in the economic progress of man that age was which came to an end in August 1914! The greater part of the population, it is true, worked hard and lived at a low standard of comfort, yet were, to all appearances, reasonably contented with this lot. But escape was possible, for any man of capacity or character at all exceeding the average, into the middle and upper classes, for whom life offered, at a low cost and with the least trouble, conveniences, comforts and amenities beyond the compass of the richest and most powerful monarchs of other ages. The inhabitant of London could order by telephone, sipping his morning tea in bed, the various products of the whole earth ... and reasonably expect their early delivery upon his doorstep; he could at the same moment and by the same means adventure his wealth in the natural resources and new enterprises of any quarter of the world, and share, without exertion or even trouble, in their prospective fruits and advantages; or he could decide to couple the security of his fortune with the good faith of the townspeople of any substantial municipality in any continent that fancy or information might recommend. He could secure forthwith, if he wished it, cheap and comfortable means of transit to any country or climate without passport or other formality, could despatch his servant to the neighbouring office of a bank for such supply of the precious metals as might seem convenient, and could then proceed abroad to foreign quarters, without knowledge of their religion, language, or customs.... But, most important of all, he regarded this state of affairs as normal, certain, and permanent, except in the direction of further improvement....

> J. M. Keynes, *Economic Consequences of the Peace*, pp. 6–7

9

Pre-war Economic Interests

I. ATTITUDES TO ECONOMICS

Keynes was only spasmodically interested in economics before 1914. His return to Cambridge was inspired by boredom at the India Office and a desire to be back in that city, not by love of economics. His main intellectual interests were probability theory and statistics. His earliest published papers had to do with problems of statistical measurement. He was employed, however, to lecture on monetary theory, which did eventually lead to his main work. But there was little in pre-war conditions to stimulate his interest in monetary policy – except in connection with the special monetary arrangements of India, a legacy of his spell in the India Office. For Britain it was a time of prosperity and full employment. The monetary regime of the day, the international gold standard, was unchallenged, and, largely controlled from London, seemed to work smoothly. Nor was Keynes's interest in economics much stimulated by social problems. Free trade promised automatic improvement; besides, he was too absorbed in private life.

Keynes was still very much an apprentice in his new craft. He had not taken a university degree in economics. His formal training was limited to one term's postgraduate work with Marshall. Mostly he learnt on the job. Compared with today, there was little to learn, and that little was not difficult. Most British economists before Marshall were men reared on a single book – John Stuart Mill's *Principles*. Their successors also tended to be men of a single book – Marshall's *Principles*, supplemented by oral tradition, Marshall's evidence to a couple of Royal Commissions and privately printed fragments of the Master's thought. Keynes's own copy of Marshall's book was the third edition of 1895. It was comprehensively annotated, showing that he had read it thoroughly, almost certainly in the summer of 1905. In addition, Keynes had soaked up much economics at home; and, although he had not been in the Financial Department of the India Office, he left Whitehall with a good working knowledge of India's currency and banking system. But his reading was not extensive. He started on Adam Smith only in 1910, and never became erudite in the literature. His grasp of theory came not so much from reading about it as from working out the problems for himself, and discussing them with others. In this way he acquired a firm understanding of a fairly limited range of theory.

Having embarked on economics, Keynes was no less eager than most economists to display his professional competence, seizing such opportunities as his contacts put in his way. His career as an economic journalist started almost immediately on his return to Cambridge. He had the style, lucidity and above all the quickness to do it. To Duncan Grant he wrote on 6 February 1909:

> Oh, I don't think I told you that I've taken to *Journalism*. Last Tuesday night I received a letter enclosing an article about 'Shippers, Bankers and Brokers' from the Economist ... and asking if I would write a letter on it 'suggestive and provocative' as soon as possible. I seized my pen and had despatched a reply within an hour and a half of opening the request. Today I open my Economist and find it, a column long, in the leading position, and the Editor [F. W. Hirst] writes to say that he will treat it as a contribution. So I shall get at least a guinea.

His debut as a professional economist was an article in the *Economic Journal*, 'Recent Events in India', published in March 1909, in which he attempted to correlate Indian price movements with the inflow and outflow of gold. Producing 'statistics of verification', he wrote to Duncan Grant on 18 December 1908, threw him into a 'tremendous state of excitement.... Nothing except copulation is so enthralling.'

A landmark in Keynes's professional involvement in the subject was his appointment as editor of the *Economic Journal* in October 1911 – a post which his father had turned down twenty years earlier. Reading manuscripts played an important part in his economic education. As he was thought, at twenty-eight, to be young for the job, he was given a supervisory editorial committee; but from the start he took his own decisions. His first editorial act was to turn down a contribution from the economic historian Archdeacon Cunningham. 'It was the most complete wash and had nothing to do with economics,' he told his father. Keynes made an excellent editor, imaginative in soliciting contributions, prompt in his response to them, helpful in his comments. The foundation of his editorial achievement was the speed with which he got through the work. In 1912 he was elected a member of the select Political Economy Club, founded in 1822. He travelled up to London regularly for its Wednesday evening meetings, dispatching his *Economic Journal* business on Thursdays at Adelphi Terrace.

Despite these extensions to his education, Keynes's range remained narrower than Marshall's or Pigou's. Before the war he lectured mainly on the pure and applied theory of money. He had attended Marshall's lectures on money in 1906 and remembered them as being illustrated with 'some very elegant diagrams'. Keynes did nothing before 1914 to develop monetary theory from the point where Marshall had left it. But he was fascinated by the behaviour of financial markets, as illustrating his theory of rational behaviour under uncertain conditions. In 1908 he told his father: 'I lie in bed for hours in the morning reading treatises on the philosophy of probability by members of the Stock Exchange. The soundest treatment so far is by the owner of a bucket shop.'[1] The investor, he wrote in 1910,

> will be affected, as is obvious, not by the net income which he will actually receive from his investment in the long run, but by his expectations. These will often depend upon fashion, upon advertisement, or upon purely irrational waves of optimism or depression.[2]

He was already pointing to the part played by 'expectations, ignorance and uncertainty' in decisions to invest.[3]

His other main intellectual interest was the problem of causality in economic behaviour – particularly what could and could not be inferred from statistical evidence. On balance Keynes took the view that the use of statistics was mainly descriptive. This corresponded with his rejection of statistical theories of probability. Only under very stringent conditions could the past be used to infer the future.

Keynes's interest in money fitted the needs of the Cambridge economics tripos, following Marshall's retirement and Foxwell's withdrawal. What Marshall called the 'brilliant, compact group of earnest men' whom he joined in Cambridge consisted of the Professor (Arthur Pigou), W. E. Johnson, Lowes Dickinson, John Clapham, C. R. Fay, H. O. Meredith, Walter Layton and L. Alston. Economics was still a small tripos – only six candidates took the first Part I in 1905; by 1910 there were twenty-five. Pigou and Keynes were the two main theorists – the real successors of Marshall and Foxwell.

In 1915 Keynes wrote, 'The strength of our Economics school in the last few years and its attractiveness to a very able set of men have largely depended in my opinion on a combination in the teachers of a general agreement on principles with much variety of outlook, sympathies, and methods.'[4] The principles were those of Marshall. Keynes was a loyal pupil of the old professor, though he did not share Pigou's veneration of him – he thought him 'rather a silly [man] in his private character'.[5] There was also an important difference of sympathy, for Keynes, unlike Marshall, did not regard economics as a 'handmaiden of ethics' – it was not the activity through which his ethical beliefs found expression. He was a follower of Moore, who had cut the links which for Marshall connected economics to ethics. Indeed, Keynes's social philosophy was already somewhat archaic, if measured by the progressive thought of the time. Like his mother and the Charity Organisation Society, he believed that good character produced good individual material conditions rather than the other way round: anyone of 'capacity or character at all exceeding the average' could escape from poverty, he wrote.[6] As for the economic progress of society as a whole, he believed with Marshall that it could be safely left to market forces operating in the existing framework of law and institutions. The key requirement was the maintenance of free trade. Before the First World War he was not even a monetary reformer, except in the Indian context. These attitudes amounted to the view that no important innovation in economic theory or practice was needed. Keynes was strongly influenced in his attitude by the mood of 'automatic' progress which revived in the 1900s and against which his own experiments in living were undertaken. There is no premonition in his writings of England's economic decay, such as had haunted Sidgwick and Joseph Chamberlain.

Although Keynes acknowledged Marshall as his master, in some respects he was personally closer to Foxwell, who wrote little but was immensely erudite in the history of economic thought and institutions. Keynes admired his iconoclasm, his literary style, his bibliomania, his love of fine craftsmanship and of music. Foxwell's sense of values, in short, appealed to him more than did Marshall's. For his part, Foxwell much preferred Keynes to Pigou, and not just because he had lost the professorship to the latter. 'He is such a prig,' Foxwell remarked of Pigou in 1901.

With 'the Prof', as Pigou was known, Maynard's relations were friendly but not close. They had known each other from Maynard's undergraduate years, when they had played fives and talked economics. But their temperaments and values divided them. Pigou inherited Marshall's moral authority. 'Tall and handsome as a Viking',[7] a Harrovian and son of an army officer, Pigou carried himself as if on parade. Morals in his mind were inextricably linked with physical exertion, and he was never so happy as when taking parties of handsome, athletic young men on climbs in Switzerland or the Lake District. Economics for him was a moral enterprise. In his inaugural lecture in 1908 he welcomed the man who had come to the study of economics because he had 'walked the slums of London'.

As colleagues, Keynes and Pigou had their differences. Pigou was appointed professor at the age of thirty, without experience of administration, for which he never developed much aptitude. Though a prolific writer (Pigou's way of learning about a subject was to write a book on it), he disliked lecturing and examining, at least before the First World War, and in 1911 Keynes 'had to give him rather a pi-jaw which he took very well. He said he was quite unaware that he was giving the impression of avoiding duties....'[8] His father wrote in his diary on 8 October 1911 that 'in many ways he [Maynard] seems to be taking Pigou's place as Professor of Political Economy'.

In pre-1914 Cambridge it was Pigou rather than Keynes who provided intellectual leadership in the Faculty. Keynes pursued economics because he was good at it, not because he had a mission to improve the world. He did not rank it very highly, but some parts of the subject gave him real intellectual pleasure without taking up an excessive amount of time: this was important, as his main intellectual interest remained his work on probability, the long vacations being largely occupied in turning his fellowship thesis into a book.

On Tuesday 19 January 1909 Keynes gave the first of his twice-weekly lectures on money, credit and prices 'before an enormous and cosmopolitan audience – there must have been at least 15, I think'.[9] Given that he was having to 'mug up' the subjects of his lectures, his pre-war lecturing load was quite heavy, reaching a hundred hours in his third year, or an average of four hours a week spread over three terms. At this period of his life he was an excellent lecturer, not yet having resorted to reading his lectures from the proofs of his books. His father noted competitively that his lectures were more popular than Meredith's, or even Pigou's.

Maynard did individual coaching mainly for the money. The pay was ten shillings an hour. '[It] is so good', he told Duncan Grant, 'that I could hardly resist it.'[10] By Michaelmas Term 1909 he had twenty-four pupils, bringing in almost £100 a term. He calculated that his income that year would be £700. By December 1910 he had already saved £220. Much of this coaching was hack work which he hated. He felt he was becoming 'little more than a machine for selling economics by the hour'.[11] He particularly disliked teaching women students. 'I seem to hate every movement of their minds,' he told Duncan Grant.[12] He was determined to build up an income independent of coaching as quickly as possible, and, in fact, by the end of 1909 was already cutting down on his tutorial work.

Keynes disliked individual coaching because it took up too much time, not because he disliked the company of able students. On 21 October 1909 he started a Political Economy Club. Over the years it became the most famous institution of the Cambridge Economics Faculty. It was modelled on the exclusive don–undergraduate discussion societies of King's and Trinity. It met on Monday evenings in his rooms. Membership was by invitation. Each week there would be a paper; all those present would comment on it, in an order determined by lot. Keynes would sum up the discussion. He was at his best when strenuous intellectual activity could be carried out in an intimate atmosphere. He was extremely sensitive to his surroundings. 'The shape of rooms ... seems extraordinarily important to one's calmness and the flow of ideas in work. ... It is very difficult to be at ease in a very high room or in one which is crowded with a great variety of objects.'[13]

His own club met in a long room of agreeable proportions, against a background of murals of semi-nude grape-pickers and dancers painted by Duncan Grant. Stretched out in a comfortable armchair, hands tucked up in his sleeves, Maynard gave the appearance of complete relaxation. But the mental machinery was whirring the whole time. His summings-up, interlaced, as one pre-war student put it, 'with more human and spicy remarks', as well as with flights of fancy, were eagerly awaited by the audience. He was always kind to his students, drawing them out rather than crushing their unformed thoughts. Eminent visitors, on the other hand, could be roughly treated. 'I was on several points taken unawares,' complained Norman Angell (author of *The Great Illusion*), much bruised after one session in 1912.[14]

Many of his students of this period became personal friends; some as colleagues and collaborators were to play an important part in shaping the Keynesian Revolution. Chief of these was Dennis Robertson, son of a clergyman, who went to Eton the year Keynes left, and came up to Trinity College in 1908 to read classics. Keynes became Robertson's director of studies when he switched to Part II of the economics tripos in 1910. But Robertson's early work on the trade cycle was influenced more by Pigou than by Keynes.[15] Another important collaborator of the 1920s was Hubert Henderson, a Scotsman from Aberdeen, who came to Emmanuel College in 1909. Frederick Lavington, another student, who died young, was an important name in the development of Cambridge monetary theory. Dudley Ward, an undergraduate at St John's and friend of Rupert Brooke, later joined Keynes at the Treasury in the First World War. Hugh Dalton was also taught by Keynes, but preferred Pigou. Freddie Hardman, killed in the war, and Archibald Rose were students who became close personal friends. Another pre-war student was Claude Guillebaud, Marshall's nephew.

Maynard was fiercely loyal to his students. When Pigou and Edward Cannan wrote dismissive reports on Gerald Shove's dissertation on the Rating System, submitted for a prize fellowship at King's in 1914, Maynard circulated a note of dissent to the Fellowship Electors so hostile to the referees' judgement that Clapham considered it 'insulting'.

II. MONEY, STATISTICS, TRADE

Keynes's lectures were almost entirely about money – and its role in economic life. To the layman 'money makes the world go round', but this was not the way economists saw it. Economic theory at the time regarded money as an insignificant thing – merely as an extension of barter. Its use added nothing of theoretical significance to what had become the main object of economic enquiry, which was to show how a system of free competition allocated resources most efficiently between different uses. Marshall, for example, omitted from his *Principles* (1893) possible complications to the barter theory of prices arising from 'changes in the general purchasing power of money'.[16] The 'later study' of these was postponed till volume III, *Money, Credit, and Commerce,* which did not appear till 1923. Money took on an independent existence only in times of crisis and panic – about which it was almost impossible to generalise, and which were expected to become less important as financial institutions improved. It took the Keynesian Revolution to give it a starring role in the economic drama.

Keynes's pre-war lectures expounded the then prevailing quantity theory of money. This purported to prove that a change in the money supply caused the price level to change proportionately – that is, it had no effect on the volume of trade and employment. The link between money and prices was demonstrated by the famous 'equation of exchange'. Keynes used two forms of this equation in his lectures, Irving Fisher's* 'transactions' version, first published in 1911, and Marshall's earlier (and unpublished) 'cash balances' approach, saying they came to 'practically the same thing'. Fisher's equation of exchange, $MV=PT$, states that, in any period, the quantity of money (M) times its velocity or 'rapidity' of circulation (V) – the average number of times a dollar or pound changes hands – equals the average price of transactions (P) multiplied by their total number (T). All this means is that the money value of what is spent equals the money value of what is bought, hardly a surprising conclusion. In Marshall's cash balances version, $M=kPT$, M, P, and T have the same meaning as in Fisher's equation, and k – the average fraction of the community's wealth which is held in cash accounts – is the reciprocal of V, the velocity of circulation.

The Cambridge equation emphasised the role of money as a temporary abode of purchasing power between selling and buying. This recognised that wages and other incomes are not all spent the moment they are received. But it did suggest that individual motives for holding liquid assets could be further analysed. Marshall conjectured that the individual fixed the fraction (k) of the assets he wanted to hold in money after 'balancing' the convenience of holding cash against the interest or income earned from buying investments. This implied that a reduction in interest rates following an increase in the money supply might not necessarily lead to a proportionate increase in spending but reduce the cost of holding cash in non-interest-earning form. This is the germ of Keynes's later liquidity-preference theory of the rate of interest, in which interest is a reward for parting with money.

Three conditions need to hold to convert the 'equation of exchange' into a theory of the price level: first, that the causation runs from money to prices, secondly, that the velocity of circulation or fraction of assets held as cash – is institutionally determined and changes only slowly, and thirdly, that the volume of transactions is determined by 'real' variables like productivity and thrift. If these conditions hold, M and P must vary in proportion. This is the quantity theory of money.

In his pre-war lectures Keynes treated the quantity theory of money not

---

* Irving Fisher was professor of economics at Yale.

just as a logical exercise – a statement of the conditions necessary for it to be true – but as a realistic set of assumptions about the real world. He certainly believed that the causation ran from money to prices, castigating 'businessmen' and 'popular opinion' for holding the contrary view.[17] He believed that the 'rapidity of circulation' or 'demand for money balances to hold' is institutionally determined and not subject to erratic shifts.[18] He also accepted the third proposition – that the volume of transactions, or amount of production and employment, is determined by 'real' forces.[19] At the same time he recognised that fluctuations in prices can have temporary effects on the velocity of circulation and the state of trade, though his discussion was distinctly perfunctory. The most interesting point in it was that he preferred falling to rising prices.[20]

Keynes's account of the 'transmission mechanism' from money to prices was strictly Marshallian, with a heightened emphasis, though, on the role of the banking system in creating credit: 'the supply of purchasing power depends upon banking and gold jointly'.[21] As Keynes tells it, an increase in the central bank's gold reserves leads to lower interest rates. Entrepreneurs increase their borrowing; it is the spending of their new deposits which first causes prices to rise, and this stimulus 'gradually spreads to all parts of the community, until the new gold is needed to finance a volume of real trade no larger ... than before'.[22] The important point, though, is that it takes *time* for an injection of money to have its final effect on prices, and it is while prices are adjusting to changes in the money supply that trade may be boosted or depressed.

Keynes's one pre-war discussion of the business cycle, read to the Political Economy Club (London) in December 1913, is entitled 'How Far Are Bankers Responsible for the Alternations of Crisis and Depression?' Keynes argued that bankers can lend to entrepreneurs without borrowing the equivalent amount from savers; credit creation can be an independent source of investment. However, when investment 'runs ahead' of saving there has to be a depression to enable saving to 'catch up'.[23] He was to take up these ideas again in the 1920s.

At this stage Keynes showed little of Fisher's zeal to control the business cycle by stabilising the value of money. Yet his orthodox account of the quantity theory was achieved only at the expense of numerous qualifications, round which his future work would revolve. For example: 'The fact that money is used not only for immediate purposes of exchange, but also as a store of value and for future exchanges, renders its present value dependent, not only upon its present volume, but also upon beliefs which are held respecting its future volume and the future demand for it'.[24] This qualification destroys much of the utility of the quantity theory. But Keynes had neither the need nor the interest to ponder its implications before the war.

The part of economics which interested him most at this time had to do with the use and misuse of statistics. Keynes was not hostile to statistics. His 'capacity for observing and assimilating facts was remarkable, and facts for him included numbers. He liked to get a feel of the order of magnitude of the problems with which he was dealing. . . .'[25] He championed the cause of better statistics, and it was through his efforts that the statistician Udny Yule got a lectureship in Cambridge in 1912. The misuse of statistics he thought arose from the fact that the statistician passed almost unaware from statistical description to inductive generalisation.

What particularly riled him about this slippery slope was the illusion it produced of precise knowledge of, and perfect control over, human events in the minds of those skilled in statistical and mathematical manipulations. This was an enduring obsession arising from his interest in the nature of probability. In his fellowship dissertation, Keynes had attacked the frequency theory of probability, according to which probability is a ratio (relative frequency) of the times something happens to the times it might happen. It is thus an inductive theory, using facts about the past to predict the future. Keynes's fellowship dissertation was mainly a positive statement of his own logical theory of probability. But he also saw the need to undermine the frequency theory by questioning the validity of induction as a predictive tool. In 1910 he started work on a new section of his thesis dealing with the logic and justification of inductive arguments, which he extended to include the logical basis of statistical inference. His later famous, or notorious, scepticism about econometrics – the use of observed relationships between two or more variables to estimate these relationships in the future – stems from this early work.

The hardest part of his Indian article for the *Economic Journal* had been the statistical tables. His first ecstatic reactions to having discovered a positive correlation between gold flows and price movements soon gave way to a sober reappraisal of the limits to establishing the truth by statistical methods: 'The index number of prices is not well established, the volume of currency can only be estimated, and agreement may be due to the fortuitous balance against one another of causes unconnected with the present discussion.'[26]

A better 'index number of prices' would certainly have helped. But how was it to be constructed? 'I'm busy with an abstruse treatise called "The Method of Index Numbers with Special Reference to the Measurement of General Exchange Value"', Keynes informed Lytton Strachey on 4 April 1909. He wrote at incredible speed over the Easter vacation, and on 10 May was able to tell Duncan Grant that he had won the University's Adam Smith prize, worth £60. His essay – which returns to the subject of his first papers for Marshall in 1905 – is a brilliant piece of work, showing that, as a young man, Keynes was a very competent mathematician. In it is to be found Keynes's first recorded discussion of the problems of measuring the national income. As usual his examiners' report infuriated him, particularly

Edgeworth's. 'I feel *convinced* that I'm right on almost every point he attacks and where my argument is novel, he simply hasn't attended to it. His criticisms show a *closed* mind. . . .'[27]

The problem which Keynes highlighted has not vanished, it has merely been suppressed. It is that 'there is no strictly numerical quantity corresponding to the conception of a general level of prices', and therefore no certain way of constructing a general price index – one that measures the 'average' movement of prices, up or down, over time. In any period some prices rose and others fell. If the relative importance of articles consumed never varied, the problem could be overcome by correct weighting. But in practice their relative importance in consumption was constantly changing with their prices, so that there was nothing constant to compare from one year to another. The best that could be done was to construct an index number which included as many commodities as possible both important absolutely and possessing the greatest stability of relative importance; in which the commodities were correctly 'weighted'; and with a base year which was frequently revised. He strongly attacked the alternative solution proposed by Jevons and Edgeworth, who suggested taking an unweighted geometrical mean of a random sample of prices as the required measure, on the ground that a general factor, money, affected all prices equi-proportionally, and that fluctuations in relative prices could be subject to the 'calculus of probabilities'. Real problems, he seemed to be saying, could not be disposed of by elegant mathematical theorems.[28] When Edgeworth died in 1926, Keynes wrote: 'The hope . . . of gradually bringing the moral sciences under the sway of mathematical reasoning steadily recedes.'[29]

Keynes was highly sceptical of the method of 'inductive correlation', believing that the conditions which had to be satisfied for it to be valid were rarely realised. He poured scorn on empirical efforts to prove the validity of the quantity theory of money:

> In the case of the history of gold prices . . . factors other than gold production have changed and fluctuated so hugely . . . that the use of any apparent close coincidence between the level of prices and gold production in support of the Q.T. [quantity theory] is a gross example of a *post hoc, ergo propter hoc* argument. Since other factors have *not* remained constant, the theory would only lead us to anticipate a coincidence between prices and gold production if the other factors happened to balance one another; and one cannot easily prove this without assuming the theory itself.[30]

However, Keynes's most savage attack on what he took to be the misuse of statistics was his assault, in 1910, on Karl Pearson, a leader of the statistical school of probability. Pearson's study of slum children in Edinburgh and Manchester had divided their parents into two groups, abstemious and alcoholic. He found a negative correlation between child deprivation –

in terms of health, strength, and intelligence – and parental alcoholism, but a positive one between child deprivation and parental feeble-mindedness. Keynes accused him of misusing statistics to prove his eugenic theories. The fact that children of alcoholic parents were no worse off than children of non-alcoholic ones did not prove that alcoholism and poverty were unrelated; the relevant question was whether the children of the first group would have been better off than those in the second had their parents not taken to drink. It was a very Victorian battle: behind the statistical fusillades lay the entrenched positions of the temperance reformers on one side (here represented by Keynes's mother) and the eugenicists on the other. What is striking is how strictly Keynes interpreted the 'other things being equal' condition. The fact that this condition was so rarely satisfied was, in his view, the main barrier to statistical investigation of social problems and the inductive use of econometric data.

Keynes's commitment to free trade was no less firm than his commitment to the quantity theory of money. He regarded the case for free trade as scientifically established; denial of it was evidence of incompetence in economic reasoning. The most extensive surviving record of the way he defended free trade before 1914 comes from some notes he made for a speech to the Cambridge Union on 8 November 1910, in which Keynes argued that protection could not increase employment. He emphasised the impossibility of general overproduction. Unemployment occurred only as a result of miscalculation of one sort or another. The first effect of a tariff would be to increase miscalculation. His notes ended:

I have said nothing of the positive arguments for F.T.

International Relations
Internal Corruption
Trusts
Raising of Cost of Living
Undesirable Redistribution of Wealth
Increased costs of production limiting competition in neutral markets.

Equally orthodox was an article Keynes contributed to the *New Quarterly* in February 1910 in defence of unlimited capital mobility. There were no new paths of thought here.

One must remember that ever since the 1880s 'irregularity of employment' had been increasingly recognised as a grave social evil. In his tariff-reform campaign which started in 1903 Joseph Chamberlain had specifically advanced protectionism as a remedy for unemployment. No doubt many of his arguments were bad ones; in particular he failed to deal adequately with the relationship between foreign trade and employment. Keynes's attitude now seems unduly complacent. But events provided no stimulus to rethink old orthodoxies. Between 1900 and 1914 British exports revived; free trade seemed adequate to sustain British prosperity. Given all its other advantages, as well as the fact that protectionism had become the creed – from Keynes's point of view – of the least progressive, most economically illiterate section of the Conservative Party, there was no call on him to shift from his inherited professional and political position.

10

Private Lives

I. PRIORITIES

In the years following his return to Cambridge, the pace of Keynes's life quickened. The semi-idle junior clerk at the India Office became the hard-working Cambridge economics don, journalist, editor and author. His first book, on India's monetary system, appeared in 1913. Over four successive long vacations in England, from 1909 to 1912, he worked on turning his thesis on probability into a book – a task which dragged on as he rewrote and added new chapters. But probability also accompanied him to the Pyrenees, Greece and Sicily; he took index numbers to Versailles; and Indian currency to Egypt. Unlike his father, he could combine his intellectual work with involvement in practical affairs. He started managing his college's finances; in 1913 he was appointed to the Royal Commission on Indian Currency and Finance. His hobbies blossomed. Golf was in retreat, but he went on adding to his book collection; in 1911 he bought his first important works of art; he gambled at Monte Carlo, and from 1913 on the Stock Exchange. As he was to do all his life, he still found time to pursue intellectual hobbies.

Only politics languished. If Liberal England was dying, Maynard and his friends were extraordinarily unaware of it. The Fabians had reached Cambridge, the Suffragettes marched and chained themselves to railings, Lloyd George's budget of 1909 and the House of Lords' reaction to it provoked a constitutional crisis, the class war intensified, Ireland was in uproar, one international crisis followed another. Maynard knew about these things, was marginally involved in some of them, but was basically indifferent to them, and hardly conscious of their longer-term implications. The way in which he wrote of Europe after the First World War reflected a different perspective – that of his travels, the freedom of exchange, the stability of currencies, the sense of progress, the ordered conditions of life. The 'extraordinary bitterness of political and social controversy' recalled by Esmé Wingfield-Stratford hardly found an echo in his world.

Partly this was because he was still under the spell of *Principia Ethica*. But it was genuinely possible to indulge a different kind of hope at that time, one which was cut off by the war. In his influential book *The Great Illusion*, published in 1911, Norman Angell came close to arguing that a

major war was an economic impossibility as well as an absurdity. The world
had become too interdependent; there could be no 'victors' in any rational
sense. Keynes and his friends, like Angell, were rationalists and meliorists.
They were aware of dark forces lying in wait to ambush civilisation, but
believed they would be scattered by 'automatic' economic progress. In the
years before the war Keynes and his friends were caught up in a cultural
renaissance. These things occupied the foreground of their consciousness;
the atavistic posturings of the statesmen seemed to be 'the amusements of
the daily newspaper', as Keynes later put it.

II. CAMBRIDGE CONNECTIONS

In the summer of 1909 Maynard moved into the suite of rooms over the
gatehouse leading from King's Lane to Webb's Court which he occupied
till he died. He never became a 'College' character like Oscar Browning, Sheppard or Pigou, parading his eccentricities to the delight of the
undergraduates. To all but a tiny circle he was the don 'who can quote
figures at you'.[1] That circle still consisted of the Apostles and their friends.
Here nothing much seemed to have changed. 'Even the womanisers pretend to be sods, lest they shouldn't be thought respectable,' Maynard
informed Duncan soon after his return to Cambridge.[2] The great event of
his first term as a lecturer was the 'birth' of Gerald Shove, after much
opposition from Lytton. 'An election is an awful and terrifying thing,'
Maynard told Duncan. Behaviour at King's was growing less and less
restrained. The day after Founder's Feast on 5 December 1909, Maynard
wrote to Duncan:

> Yesterday evening will always mark an epoch, I think, in the history of
> King's manners. If there was debauchery, it was private. Manners not
> morals gave way. Quite suddenly our rigid rules of convention that one
> kisses no one in public utterly collapsed – and we all kissed! The scene
> really can't be described. Alfred, Frankie [Birrell],* Gerald, Mr. Hardman,
> Sheppard – and many others ... everybody was there. What our reppers
> [reputations] will be, heaven knows.... We've never behaved like this
> before – I wonder if we ever shall again....

---

* Francis Birrell, the son of the Liberal politician Augustine Birrell. He had come to King's
from Eton to read history in 1908, and was an 'embryo'. Alfred Brooke was Rupert Brooke's
brother. 'Freddie' Hardman was one of Keynes's students.

No doubt Maynard embroidered for the benefit of Duncan in London; yet the historian of King's College, Patrick Wilkinson, records that a visitor to the college in 1908 was surprised at 'the openness of the display of affection between [male] couples'.[3]

On 7 April 1909 Maynard and Duncan left for a fortnight's holiday in Versailles. It brought about the first crisis in their relationship. Indeed, by the time they got back the affair seemed to be over, Duncan writing to James, 'I've told him that I'm no longer in love with him.'[4] Lytton noted this development with grim satisfaction. The report, however, was premature. It is clear, though, that while Maynard was as much in love with Duncan as ever ('I still reckon everything here with reference to when I shall see you again,' he wrote to him forlornly from King's on 26 April), Duncan refused to be locked into a single relationship. A reconciliation was patched up, and the relationship drifted on. As for Lytton, 'I find that I'm not at all in love with Duncan – but my rage against Pozzo only seems to have increased.'[5]

At Cambridge, the most memorable event of the summer term was staged by Geoffrey, now in his final year at Pembroke. He and two friends had invited the novelist Henry James to visit Cambridge, Henry James accepting, so Maynard informed Duncan, 'in an enormous letter even more complicated than a novel'. On Sunday 13 June 1909 Maynard gave a breakfast party for Henry James at King's. It was not a success. He had invited, among others, Harry Norton, who responded to each remark with manic laughter. Henry James was not amused. Desmond MacCarthy found him sitting disconsolately over 'a cold poached egg bleeding to death' surrounded by a respectful circle of silent undergraduates. However, the visit did produce a classic James remark. Told that the youth with fair hair who sometimes smiled was called Rupert Brooke, who also wrote poetry which was no good, Henry James replied, 'Well, I must say I am *relieved*, for with *that* appearance if he had also talent it would be too unfair.'[6]

Geoffrey followed his Henry James coup by landing a first in the natural sciences tripos. The family celebrated with a holiday in the Pyrenees, where they had been two years before. Maynard found his brother's company a great disappointment. 'Geoffrey is *hopeless*,' he complained to Duncan from Lychon on 28 June. 'I don't quite know what I am doing here.' They drove and walked in the mountains. Soon Maynard was able to report that he was doing 'a moderate amount of work with a good deal of pleasure'. But he found a 'dreadful lack of excitement'. It was to be his last Continental holiday with his parents.

He spent only four days in Cambridge – long enough to catch a glimpse of Augustus John encamped at Grantchester 'with two wives and ten naked children' – before rushing off, on 26 July, to Burford, in the Cotswolds, where he had rented a house for the summer, and where he received a succession of visitors. Swithinbank was the first to come, full of Burmese words, scandals about Eton and Dan ('inordinate wine and women'), and complaining that he had 'never copulated and so far as he can see never will'. On 31 July, James Strachey appeared; on 2 August Swithin left to coach Harold Macmillan, Dan's younger brother, now an Eton Colleger. On 3 August Sheppard turned up with Cecil Taylor (known as 'Madame'). Duncan came on 5 August and resumed his portrait of Taylor. 'How scandalous', James wrote to Lytton, 'that two people (in modern life) should live in such undetermined relations [as Maynard and Duncan]. It's evident that the reason *we* don't understand them is that *they* don't.... And poor Duncan. "I'm sorry, Duncan, but you really mustn't put that cup there." "Replace that volume, *please*, if you don't require it any longer."'[7]

Except for a brief visit from Florence and Margaret in mid-month, Maynard and Duncan spent September at Burford alone. He resumed his work on probability; Duncan painted still lives in the mornings and landscapes in the afternoons. They took long bicycle rides, recapturing the contentment and companionship they had found at Hoy. Whitehead had told Maynard to publish his dissertation right away. But Maynard was dissatisfied with it. 'It wants a good deal of alteration,' he told Lytton on 23 August. 'Part I will soon be finished.... After every retouch it seems to me more trifling and platitudinous. All that is startling is gradually cut out as untrue, and what remains is a rather obscure and pompous exposition of what no human being can ever have doubted.' 'I shall soon be laying Probability aside until the Easter vacation,' Maynard told his father on 3 October. He had finished sixteen chapters of a projected twenty-six covering the fundamental ideas and their mathematical statement. He still hoped for early publication.

III. POLITICS

On 7 November 1909 Maynard visited Rupert Brooke at Grantchester and found him wearing nothing but an embroidered sweater and sitting in the midst of admiring female Fabians. Women and politics had hit undergraduate life. Their meeting ground was the Cambridge University Fabian Society. Restarted in 1906 by 'Ben' Keeling, as the first undergraduate club open to both sexes, it claimed a hundred members a year later. Radicalism at Cambridge now meant socialism and the women's vote more than sodomy and atheism. Undoubtedly the success of the newly formed Labour Party in the 1906 election had something to do with the change. Keir Hardie and Ramsay MacDonald came to Cambridge and had their meetings wrecked. Nationally, the women's movement had taken a militant turn with the establishment of the Suffragettes. On 29 April 1909 Lloyd George infuriated the right with a 'class war' budget which proposed a modest 'supertax' and a tax on land values to help pay for Dreadnoughts and social insurance. In England, as indeed on the Continent, radicalism and reaction seemed to be shaping up for a fight, thus forcing politics on the attention of the least politically attentive.

The change in sexual atmosphere had a number of causes. Among them was the strong heterosexual lead given by Rupert Brooke, Cambridge's outstanding undergraduate of his generation. As Hilton Young noted, Brooke, despite his beauty, was 'beef and beer, not nectar and ambrosia'.[8] There were also co-educational influences from Bedales. Then there was the presence of a group of clever, attractive and rebellious women students. Three families did much to put women on the map at Cambridge, at least for the elite of undergraduates: the Costelloes, the Oliviers and the Darwins, the first two with Fabian fathers. Although Moore returned to Cambridge in 1911, his glory, according to Keynes, undimmed, he seemed less relevant to the new generation of students than Mr and Mrs Webb, Bernard Shaw, H. G. Wells and even William Morris. All-male reading parties in country inns gave way to camping, hiking and mixed bathing, as the older ideals of a simplified life, with unstuffy clothes and wholesome food, re-emerged in a heterosexual setting. 'Ka [Cox] came striding along the road in time for lunch yesterday,' Virginia Woolf wrote to her sister in 1911, 'with a knapsack on her back, a row of red beads, and daisies stuck in her coat.'[9] The 'neo-pagans', as she called the circle round Rupert Brooke, flocked to the Fabian summer schools in Wales, where they slept on the beach, and alarmed the prim Beatrice Webb with 'their anarchic ways in sexual questions'.

With the Fabians as the new centre of attraction, the Apostles lost something of their éclat. There was an overlap, of course. Rupert Brooke was the socialist crusader in the land of sods; James Strachey preached the doctrine according to Moore at the Fabian summer camps. The Society resisted the socialist onslaught with the well-tried tradition of sterility: there was one election only between 1909 and 1912, by which time the socialist tide had largely spent itself. Maynard's pattern of life was not uninfluenced by these new currents. Women younger than himself – notably Ka Cox and Daphne and Brynhild Olivier – became part of his circle of friends, though there is no evidence that his ways had become any less unflirtatious than those noticed by Ray Costelloe in 1906.

Peter Clarke has written of Maynard's political position at this time: 'There is, in short, unmistakable evidence of an earnest political commitment to the new Liberalism.'[10] The evidence is that he spoke, in February 1911, with Sidney Webb, in support of a motion at the Cambridge Union 'That the progressive reorganisation of Society along the lines of Collectivist Socialism is both inevitable and desirable'.[11] One could add that a few months later he announced to his surprised father that he was 'in favour of the confiscation of wealth', and that in 1913 he had lunch with Beatrice Webb at Newnham, which he found a 'deep spiritual experience'. As the basis for a claim of 'earnest political commitment' to anything, such evidence is extremely flimsy. Whatever Keynes's political views, his *commitment* to doing anything about them was very weak.

In his Cambridge Union speech Keynes defended the public service motive for action. Nelson was a 'servant of the State, and he was not efficient from motives of material self-interest, but because it pleased him to do his "job" as well as possible'. More generally Maynard's political views at this time were conditioned by the fiscal debate in which progressive or 'confiscatory' taxes were seen as the main alternative to protection. Keynes's support for increased direct taxation stemmed more from his commitment to free trade than from any enthusiasm for 'redistribution'. It was the threat to the 'old' not the attraction of the 'new' Liberalism which stirred him to intermittent political activity in these years. As secretary of the Cambridge University Free Trade Association he presided at a big free-trade meeting at the Cambridge Guildhall on 30 April 1909, the day after Lloyd George's budget speech. That summer he took time off from probability to write an article for the *New Quarterly*, edited by his friend Desmond MacCarthy, rebutting the protectionist charge that the budget would cause a flight of capital. After the House of Lords threw out Lloyd George's budget on 30 November, provoking a general election, Keynes wrote an article in the *Cambridge Daily News* advising his readers to vote Liberal on the ground that a Conservative victory would cause a constitutional crisis. He then trundled across to Birmingham for some electioneering on behalf of Hilton Young, who was fighting Austen Chamberlain at East Worcester. 'Life without a howling audience to address every evening will seem very dull,' he wrote to Lytton Strachey from the Queen's Hotel, Birmingham, on 14 January 1910. On 8 November 1910 he spoke once more in defence of free trade at the Cambridge Union. 'His cold, intellectual style is well suited to destructive criticism of economic fallacies and he was delightfully crushing,' noted *Granta*. He campaigned again on behalf of Edwin Montagu at Histon in the December general election. These were the high points of Keynes's pre-war political involvements.

IV. BLOOMSBURY

His interests at this stage of his life carried him not to Westminster, Whitehall or the City but to Bloomsbury. In December 1909 Duncan took the lease of a ground-floor flat at 21 Fitzroy Square. The front room was to be his studio: Maynard had a bedroom at the back. The Bloomsbury Group

– 'Old Bloomsbury' as Virginia Woolf and Vanessa Bell later called it – had already come into existence, drawing its name from a particular kind of social and cultural life which grew up among a group of friends in a couple of adjacent Georgian squares in that unfashionable part of London. The most convenient starting date is March 1905 when the Stephen children – Vanessa, Thoby, Virginia and Adrian – launched their Thursday evening At Homes at 46 Gordon Square, to which Thoby's friends, down from Cambridge, started to come: notably Saxon Sydney-Turner, Clive Bell, Lytton Strachey and Desmond MacCarthy. Thoby Stephen ('the Goth') with his Apostolic connections was the key link between the Cambridge and London worlds. But the common ground of their intercourse had already been prepared. For at almost the exact moment when the Strachey generation of Apostles was working out, under Moore's influence, a philosophy of life which scorned worldly values and conventional duties, the Stephen children had fled the stuffy respectability of their South Kensington house, with its encumbrance of smart relations, for what Virginia called the 'crude and impertinent' life of Bloomsbury – perhaps with the idea of establishing a salon for Thoby's friends already in their minds. The conversation on beauty, love, philosophy may have been liberating, but it was far from vivacious. Except when Clive Bell, an agreeable, foxhunting man with a taste for pictures, was there to add a flow of chatter it was marked by huge silences which would have done credit to McTaggart. The other essential feature of the situation was that the Bloomsbury At Homes offered an opportunity for unflirtatious contact between the sexes. Vanessa and Virginia, though both beautiful, had fled the marriage market which passed for ordinary social life. Thoby's friends were either not interested in women or sexually inhibited in their presence. There was a certain security in this situation for both sides. The men also lacked what Virginia called 'physical splendour'. As she remarked: 'The society of buggers has many advantages – if you are a woman. It is simple, it is honest, it makes one feel ... in some respects at one's ease.'[12]

In 1907, following Thoby's tragic death from typhoid – an event which linked the two sides in a common sorrow – Clive Bell married Vanessa Stephen. There were now two Bloomsbury salons – the Bells' at 46 Gordon Square, and that of Virginia and Adrian who took over 29 Fitzroy Square. Vanessa Bell, with her Pre-Raphaelite face but down-to-earth manner and bawdy tongue, was determined to make her career as a painter. Her Friday Club became a centre for the discussion of the visual arts. Virginia, socially awkward and frightened of men, had started working on her first novel, *The Voyage Out*. Their younger brother Adrian was an amiable, ineffective giant. At Cambridge he had been (in Quentin Bell's phrase) an 'evening shadow' of Thoby; but he was clever, ironic and occasionally alarmingly high-spirited. The Thursday evenings at Fitzroy Square were frequented by a new generation of Apostles and their friends – Harry Norton, James Strachey, Gerald

Shove, Francis Birrell. The characteristic Bloomsbury mode was establishing
itself – a painful honesty in conversation and personal relationships, a
passion for literature and the visual arts. Politics, together with bourgeois
sexual conventions, were damned as prime examples of cant; but there was
a profound insight into the niceties of intellectual and cultural rank, and a
constant concern with the problem of domestic servants.

What had not yet started was the debate about what Bloomsbury stood
for, who was in it, whether it was good or bad, subsequently subjects of
absorbing interest to both its admirers and detractors. Nor could it start
until the circle had attained, through the achievements of its individual
members, and their public support for each other, the status of an influential
cultural coterie. The public image of Bloomsbury was already forming just
before the First World War, as champions of the 'shocking' in modern art
and design. It was sharpened by Bloomsbury's general hostility to the First
World War. It became fixed with Lytton Strachey's disparagement of the
achievements of 'Eminent Victorians'. By the 1920s the main line of criticism
had become clear. According to Arnold Lunn, in a letter to Clive Bell dated
16 January 1957, Bloomsbury's worst fault was to dismiss all conventional
values with a 'snigger', a 'raised eye-brow'.[13]

Michael Holroyd's biography of Lytton Strachey (published in 1965)
revealed another aspect of Bloomsbury's collective life: the widespread
homosexuality and bisexuality, the sexual merry-go-round, as friends
became lovers and then went back to being friends. Today Bloomsbury
repels as much as it fascinates. Can such people ever have felt deeply about
anyone or anything? Their very vocabulary seems insipid: people and
opinions were 'charming', or 'amusing', or 'absurd'. But they were also slayers
of hypocrisy and lovers of the arts.

Once the debate is launched along these lines, it is impossible to get
away from the question of G. E. Moore and the influence of *Principia Ethica*
on Bloomsbury. This is quite distinct from the trivial question of who in
Bloomsbury actually read the book: enough did for its flavour to be common
property. For it was Moore who tried to redefine the content of ethical
discussion by insisting that the primary question was not 'what ought I to
do?' but 'what is good?' Moore drew attention, in precise philosophic form,
and for a certain group of people, to the question of what is meant by being
civilised. He did this against the background of widespread dissatisfaction
with certain ideals of conduct held up for admiration by the Victorians,
including conventional sexual morality, but also the pursuit of material
success, the exaltation of activities which were useful, and so on, as well as
with the philistine attitude to the arts which accompanied them.

Bloomsbury, it is true, was devoid of Christian belief. But in this there
was nothing distinctive, and its atheism was not derived from Moore. More
distinctive was Bloomsbury's hostility to beliefs *religiously* held. For all
beliefs, one must be able to produce arguments commanding the assent of

reason. If Christianity was not such a belief, then so much the worse for Christianity. But the same applied to Marxism and to what Keynes called the 'pseudo social service' religions. In the inter-war years, the Bloomsbury attitude of scepticism to all political dogmas came equally under attack from right and left. And there is no doubt it encouraged, though it did not entail, political passivity. Political activity could certainly be justified if there was an immediate political threat to civilised values – for example, the threat of war. Whether a life *wholly* devoted to politics was compatible with a good state of mind was far more doubtful.

None of this is to deny the existence of a tension between Cambridge rationality and Bloomsbury sensibility. Virginia Woolf was struck by the 'crippling effect' of Cambridge's *'analytical* spirit' on her father, unrelieved by any 'distracting interests – music, art, the theatre, travel'.[14] Bloomsbury's outlook represents an attempt to marry Cambridge rationalism to aesthetic and sexual emotion. The way it did so was to apply the analytical method to love and the arts. The marriage was made easier by Moore's doctrine that 'good' itself was unanalysable.

A second way to think of Bloomsbury is as a group of friends, but with the proviso that they 'found' each other because it was very easy for them to do so. Of course, one cannot ignore elements of accident and individual choice in bringing the group together. Nevertheless, the fact remains that Bloomsbury was formed out of a few pre-existing and overlapping family and cultural connections: the Cambridge Apostles on the one hand, and the two family clans of Stracheys and Stephens on the other. This goes some way to explaining Bloomsbury's exclusiveness.

Bloomsberries, as they called themselves, were curious about outsiders. They were also frightened of them, and could be chilling to them. Bloomsbury provided a retreat for people, some of whom had been scarred early in life by their contact with the outside world. Within the circle of intimacy they developed opinions, styles of conversation, behaviour, even dress, which shocked outsiders. Blasphemy was a credo going back to Cambridge days; bawdiness was almost *de rigueur*. The characters and sexual tastes of their friends, the continual rearrangement of their affairs, were topics of absorbing interest. Keynes fitted in well enough. He was unshockable; and the indelicacy to which he gave free rein with his friends was usually regarded as a social asset. 'You are rather like a Chinese Buddha as a host,' Vanessa Bell wrote to him on 16 April 1914 after one weekend house party. 'You are silent but not so silent as Saxon & manage to create an atmosphere in which all is possible. Perhaps you talk more than a Buddha would though. Anyhow the result is what I imagine it would be with a Buddha. One can talk of fucking & sodomy & sucking & bushes all without turning a hair.'[15]

A third aspect of Bloomsbury is that it was a cultural, not an academic, coterie. Maynard Keynes was one of the very few members who held an academic job. Perhaps this was the last period in English history when a group of such intellectual excellence could have assembled in London outside the university system. It was this assimilation of fine intellects into the tradition of the salon rather than the common room which made Bloomsbury such a formidable cultural force. Bloomsbury consisted of both creators *and* publicists. On balance, the achievement of the latter was greater than that of the former. By international standards the Bloomsbury painters – Vanessa Bell, Duncan Grant, Roger Fry – were not in the front rank. Likewise, in literature only Virginia Woolf is indisputably in the highest class. But in the way they set about redefining the relationship between culture and society, and in their advocacy of specific theories, the Blooms- bury publicists were first class.

That the opportunity was there for any clever and strongly motivated cultural coterie to seize is plain in retrospect. Bloomsbury was a particular expression of, and gave direction to, the 'revolt against the Victorians'. The rejection of conventional sexual morality was one facet, but only one, of the revolt against 'false values' in the name of which Victorians had sacrificed the possibility of leading a good life. Members of Bloomsbury were generally exceptional children of exceptional parents, who had seen their parents' lives being cluttered up and strangled by unnecessary duties. In place of these, Bloomsbury substituted the ideal, not of doing what one liked, but of doing what was good. Cultural enjoyments were placed at the centre of the good life. Instead of culture being an aid to good conduct, good con- duct was redefined as the means to culture. This in turn led to a change in cultural theory and practice. An attempt was made to detach the cultural object from conventional associations. Already before 1914 Roger Fry and Clive Bell, Bloomsbury's two main art publicists, were insisting that aesthetic enjoyment derived from 'significant form' in the pictures themselves rather than from associations in the viewer's mind. In Virginia Woolf's novels, too, story-telling is sacrificed to form. In his biographies Lytton Strachey deliber- ately distorted his portraits to shock his readers into seeing familiar things in new ways. As in their art, so in their lives members of Bloomsbury refused to allow feelings to be cramped by conventional associations. They were not sexual anarchists but rather creators of a new kind of sexual order inherent in a proper concept of the good life. That is why Bloomsbury was able to undertake the frequent rearrangement of its emotional affairs while remain- ing so (comparatively) free from sexual jealousy.

In these ways, Bloomsberries were cultural and sexual revolutionaries. In other ways they remained rooted in the assumptions of their times. Indeed, the particular form of their 'revolt against the Victorians' depended on other aspects of Victorian life remaining in place. Culture was not regarded as a force to reshape social relations, but to reorient the elite to 'what is good'. Bloomsbury was as hostile to any notion of 'proletarian culture' as it was to that of 'capitalist culture'. Both were symptoms of a degraded industrial system. There was little desire in Bloomsbury to make contact with the 'mass mind', little faith in the possibility of a 'common culture'. Bloomsbury's cultural artefacts were highbrow; its propaganda aimed entirely at the (highly) educated middle classes. There was always a tension between its cultural ideals and democratic sentiment: civilisation, as Clive Bell put it, rested on having someone to do the dirty work. Maynard Keynes, as we shall see, attempted to go beyond this contradiction; but it cannot be claimed he got very far. And he, like the rest of the Bloomsberries, depended completely on domestic servants to sustain their own lives. In these ways Bloomsbury was rooted in the class assumptions of the Victorians. Their revision of the Victorian scheme of life tended to take them back to the eighteenth century idea of a cultured aristocracy rather than towards the ideal of a civilised democracy; or rather they could not conceive of a civilised democracy which lacked an endowed aristocracy of talent, with all its inegalitarian implications; while their own experience seemed proof that such an aristocracy could not come out of 'nowhere'.

The cultural influence which Bloomsbury eventually acquired was based on the clarity of vision of its publicists and the mutually supporting achievements of its members. But two further ingredients must be added: its relative financial independence and its power of patronage. Bloomsberries were not rich. But they were never forced into dependence on institutions alien to their spirit. There was just enough inherited wealth to go round to enable them to lead their preferred lives until their own talents could give them an earned independence. No Bloomsbury group would have been possible had people like Strachey and Bell, Virginia and Vanessa, been dispersed round the provincial universities. Equally important, Bloomsbury over the years was able to find outlets and platforms for its work and theories in influential journals and art galleries and thus, to some extent, become an arbiter of taste. Through this position members were able to get their younger friends jobs, commissions and shows. None of this would have been possible had they not, in fact, wielded the power of the pen and the brush to great effect. But it was not enough. Financial backing was needed. Here the role of Maynard Keynes became crucial. He gave Bloomsbury financial muscle, not just by making a great deal of money himself, which he spent lavishly on Bloomsbury causes, but by his ability to organise financial backing for their enterprises. (Before 1914 he had already started managing some of his friends' money for them.) Indeed, from the First World War onwards it is almost impossible to find any enterprise, cultural or domestic, in which members of Bloomsbury were involved which did not benefit in some way from his largesse, his financial acumen or his contacts. Condemned, or selected, by aptitude and disposition to work largely in the world of means rather than ends, this was his way of promoting and paying homage to the vision of the good life which he shared with his friends.

It was in the winter of 1910–11 that the world first discovered the existence of Bloomsbury. On 5 November 1910, Roger Fry, an old Apostle, who had just resigned a lucrative job with the Metropolitan Museum of Art in New York, put on an exhibition called 'Manet and the Post-Impressionists' at the Grafton Galleries. It was an event of momentous importance in the history of British taste. Its core consisted of twenty-one Cézannes, thirty-seven Gauguins and twenty Van Goghs which Fry and Desmond MacCarthy had selected from dealers and private collectors in Paris. Although most of the paintings were twenty or thirty years old, they horrified a British public which had missed out on Impressionism itself (represented in England only by the productions of the New English Art Club) and which was therefore still habituated to what Frances Spalding has called 'story-telling in paint'. Critics dismissed the French paintings as 'the output of a lunatic asylum'. To some of them brash colour, broken brushwork and distorted shapes portended the dissolution of the social order. Roger Fry was by this time intimate with the Bells; and Bloomsbury took up the cause of Post-Impressionism with enthusiasm. Vanessa and Clive Bell, Virginia, Adrian, Roger Fry and Duncan Grant all went to the Post-Impressionist ball in March 1911, the women scandalising the press and the other guests by appearing as Gauguin-like savages, draped in African cloth. Fry put on a second Post-Impressionist exhibition, more professionally organised, in October 1912, dominated by the works of Picasso and Matisse, but in which Duncan Grant was also represented together with other modern English painters. Less revolutionary, but more dramatic, in its impact on London's artistic life was the first season of the Ballets Russes in June 1911, in which Diaghilev introduced to London audiences the fabulous Nijinsky in Schumann's *Carnaval* and Weber's *Le Spectre de la Rose*, both choreographed by Michel Fokine. In the latter, Nijinsky's leap through the open French window, light as a petal in the breeze, to alight beside the sleeping Karsavina, electrified London audiences.

Leonard Woolf, returning from seven years in Ceylon, strongly felt the exhilaration of life in 1911, when it seemed as if the world was on the brink of becoming civilised. It was a wonderfully sunny summer. In politics it looked 'as if militarism, imperialism, and antisemitism were on the run'. The revolution of the motor car and aeroplane had started; Freud, Rutherford and Einstein had begun their work. 'Equally exciting things were happening in the arts. On the stage the shattering impact of Ibsen was still belatedly powerful and we felt that Ibsen had a worthy successor in Shaw as a revolutionary.... In painting we were in the middle of the revolution of Cézanne, Matisse, and Picasso.... And to crown all, night after night we flocked to Covent Garden, entranced by a new art, a revelation to us benighted British, the Russian ballet in the greatest days of Diaghilev and Nijinsky.'[16] Bloomsbury felt no premonition of disaster, only a joyful sense of awakening after the long Victorian night.

V. THE END OF THE AFFAIR

Considering how many values and friendships he shared with Bloomsbury, Maynard's entry into the charmed circle was surprisingly delayed. Bloomsbury was not the centre of his social or intellectual set during his years at the India Office, though he saw something of the Bells. In 1909 he was still Keynes, not Maynard, to both Vanessa and Virginia. Lytton's hostility probably explains why Bloomsbury was so tardy in accepting him as a member. It was now Duncan who eased Maynard's passage into Bloomsbury, Duncan's charm winning much readier acceptance than Maynard's frightening, and occasionally gloating, brilliance.

For Duncan Grant, the move to Bloomsbury in 1909 proved as liberating as it had been for the Stephen sisters five years previously. 'Fitzrovia' was then the home of the artistic avant-garde. The fashionably dressed Walter Sickert, doyen of the New English Art Club, had his studio at 19 Fitzroy Square, where he played host to a Fitzroy Group which included painters like Spencer Gore, Augustus John, Robert Bevan and Harold Gilman. Henry Lamb had taken over Augustus John's studio at 8 Fitzroy Street. The young Slade School painters Gwen Darwin and Stanley Spencer came to Vanessa Bell's Friday Club. Here, on 21 February 1910, Duncan heard Roger Fry on 'Representation as a Means of Expression'.[17] Fry was in the throes of the life-change which would turn him from a painter of mock seventeenth-century landscapes and authority on Old Masters into an intimate of Bloomsbury and a revolutionary protagonist and theorist of modern art. Duncan's friendship with Vanessa and Clive and Roger developed rapidly in his new surroundings. 'Duncan may be going to be a great painter,' Vanessa wrote to Clive in 1910. 'There seems to me to be something remarkably fine in his work & in the grand manner. He is certainly much the most interesting of the young painters.'[18]

In February 1910, Duncan had his first dinner at 44 Bedford Square with the exotic Lady Ottoline Morrell. She found him shy, vague, elusive and bewitching; he was readily absorbed into her world of lustre and illusion, fascinated by her extraordinary face with its jutting jaw, and by her fantastic clothes. Ottoline was not part of Bloomsbury, but she provided a welcome relief from its austerities, and was a perfect foil for its malice and cultural snobbery. A generous, clever, though absurd, aristocratic groupie of the arts, she felt it her mission to inspire and promote writers and artists, which she did to great effect; without, of course, receiving the gratitude she deserved. Duncan became a regular member of her salon. In 1912 he met Nijinsky there. Maynard's first recorded dinner party at Ottoline's did not take place till Thursday 15 June 1911.

Duncan's absorption in his new life inevitably made Maynard and Cambridge seem more remote. He took to wandering into 29 Fitzroy Square, home of Virginia and Adrian, in his borrowed, oversize trousers, vague and charming. His intimacy with them was fortified by the famous 'Dreadnought Hoax' of 20 February 1910 when he was commandeered by Adrian and his friends to join in impersonating the Emperor of Abyssinia and his family. Dressed in exotic clothes and jewels as princes of the blood, he and Virginia visited the British fleet anchored at Weymouth with their 'father' and were received with royal honours on the flagship by the Admiral, Sir William Fisher, Adrian's cousin, who was completely taken in by his six-foot five-inch relative disguised as an interpreter. 'What a lunatic affair! Are you going to jail for it?' enquired Maynard anxiously, after news of the hoax, released by one of the hoaxers, was splashed across the front pages of the newspapers. (Duncan was temporarily abducted by some hearties, but all he got in the way of official reprimand was a mild ticking off from Reginald McKenna, First Lord of the Admiralty.)

On 28 February 1910, Duncan confessed to Maynard that he was falling in love with Adrian Stephen. 'Adrian', wrote David Garnett, 'had extraordinarily innocent eyes: he looked through them at the passing scene like the child in Hans Andersen's story of the Emperor's new clothes – as though he could not believe what they saw. Then, aware of the inadequacy of words, he caught one's eye and either made a most horrific comic grimace, or laughed.'[19] One can see why Duncan, with his painter's eye for the absurd and incongruous, and with his suspicion that clever people thought him little better than a half-wit, should feel at ease in Adrian's company. Maynard professed to take his infatuation lightly. 'It sounds perfect from the point of view of pleasure,' he wrote back on 3 March. This seems an inadequate response. But perhaps Maynard realised that Strachey-like outbreaks of recrimination and despair would only destroy their friendship. He adapted himself to the new situation as best as he could. Duncan did not give up Maynard; he simply added Adrian. Maynard's love for Duncan did not die. But he accepted that his place in Duncan's life would become progressively smaller. And this helped him accept, and be accepted by, Duncan's new friends.

On 17 March 1910, Maynard and Duncan left London for Marseilles, where they boarded the SS *Danube* for a seven-week holiday in Greece and Asia Minor. They shared a large cabin. By 22 March Maynard had read 'nearly half of Adam Smith. It is a wonderful book.' In Athens, they established themselves in a hotel overlooking the Parthenon; and then started on a week's tour, by horse, of the Peloponnese. To his parents Maynard extolled the 'wonderful Hermes of Praxiteles' and 'the most perfect temple' at Bassae, but the place that impressed the travellers most was Brousse, the ancient Ottoman capital, where they spent a week in a town 'crowded with mosques and baths and mausoleums'. They returned via Constantinople and Berlin, reaching England on 8 May.

That summer Maynard made a determined effort to finish probability, with a new section on the justification of inductive methods. 'No clear or satisfactory account of them is to be found anywhere,' he wrote.[20] On 7 June, Lytton, who was staying at Cambridge, found 'The Society ... incredibly stiff and metaphysical. Pozzo on Induction – so solid and bulky with Hawtrey, poor old Dickinson, Robin Mayor, Hardy and the rest *en suite.*' Maynard went on working on induction at King's over the Long Vacation term. He found the work very difficult. 'I've had to rewrite what I've been doing over and over again,' he told Duncan on 10 July, 'but I think I've really made some progress and that my final account of the nature of scientific argument is better than anyone else's. But there is still time for it to break down.' The first chapter on induction was finished on 27 July.

Probability went back with him to the Little House, Burford, which he had once again rented for the summer. Visitors came in relays. To Duncan he explained, 'I find that I don't, on the whole, like to be quite alone. I can't do any more work than usual and my mind preys on itself in the most dreadful way.'[21] James Strachey arrived on 3 September from his Fabian summer school to find Maynard and Gerald Shove discussing probability. 'I must say that I require a *touch* of the Artistic Temperament,' he told his brother Lytton. 'They weren't very sympathetic. In the evenings Pozzo plays patience nowadays.'[22] When Strachey left, Maynard took off on a solo bicycle trip in Berkshire, Hardy's *The Dynasts* in his pocket. He returned three days and twenty punctures later. Probability made better progress. On 19 August he felt that 'the end really seems to be in sight now'. By 29 August he had finished Part III comprising six chapters on induction and analogy, and was starting on Part IV, applications. By 25 September he had a complete first draft, and looked forward to delivering the book to the Cambridge University Press that autumn.

It was not till 14 September that Duncan finally arrived for a fortnight. He had stayed briefly with Maynard at Cambridge at the end of July, but the visit had not been a success. 'I only hope I did not behave so unbearably as to make it too unbearable for you,' he had written after he left. Instead of coming to Burford in August he had gone to stay with Adrian at Skegness. For consolation Maynard turned to the 'frivolous young butterfly' Frankie Birrell. 'I must try, if I can, to fall in love with someone besides you,' he wrote to Duncan.

Although he and Duncan still made love occasionally, the sand of their affair was running out. Duncan took to jogging with Adrian before breakfast; he was now frequently away for weekends with Roger Fry at his house, Durbins, near Guildford. On 17 December Maynard wrote a note from 21 Fitzroy Square:

Dearest Duncan.
It makes me miserable not to find you here – though I expected

that you would in the end stay at 29. I don't know what to do about staying in London. You're married to Adrian now, which you weren't before. So you naturally want always to be with him, when you haven't got any necessary engagements. So I shall hardly ever see you except when out of kindness you think you ought to try and make some arrangements. Thus I'm always in the position of pressing you to do what you'd rather not, and you of wondering how much your fondness for me demands of you. I can't bear such a state of affairs. It's wretched to be trading on your kindness, and I'm always in a state of uncertainty as to whether you will in the end turn up.

What do you think? It seems to me that when you're alone with me, it's all right. But when Adrian is in the next house, whenever you're with me it's being away from him, and you see me because I want it, not because you do. Please don't misunderstand this letter. It's the fault of fate and not at all of yours. But I'm feeling very wretched and don't know what I ought to do. Your ever loving,

JMK

PS. Please when you read this letter try and decide exactly what your feelings are about it.

Duncan replied next day in terms which were far from reassuring, although perhaps meant to be:

Dearest Maynard,

Please do not be so depressed. I hope most of your depression is the result of severe tiredness and overwork, because I don't honestly think things have changed as much as you think. I certainly am not always wishing to be with Adrian when I am with you. For one thing it is not always possible to be with him & when I am as certain as I am of Adrian's affection for me, I can afford to be much 'kinder' as you call it than [was] the case when I was uncertain about it. I simply mean that I have none of the anxieties that I used to have & can therefore enjoy myself in every way more than I used to including being with people I like.

To be quite practical I should probably be in the studio in any case ... for nearly all day every day. I might want to be with Adrian in the evening but there do occur occasions when I cannot. I don't know how you would like this state of affairs – but it would mean seeing you a good deal....

Yrs,

Duncan Grant

Maynard found some compensation with St George. St George (as Maynard and Duncan always called him) was a 'lovely' Cockney lad, Francis St George Nelson, seventeen years old in 1909 when Duncan first engaged him as a model. He was employed in the pantomime, and would disappear for long intervals on tours with collapsing theatrical companies, who left him stranded in a succession of seaside towns, Maynard having to organise hurried rescue operations. Maynard and Duncan were genuinely fond of St George, who was by no means averse to 'fun and games'.

Maynard and Duncan took their last pre-war foreign holiday together, to Morocco and Sicily, in March–April 1911. Once again, there was trouble over the arrangements, Duncan insisting on meeting Adrian in Italy. After spending a few days in Tunis ('The Arabs are wonderful – very beautiful and the first race of buggers I've seen,' Maynard informed Lytton) they crossed to Palermo, where they went to the opera. At Taormina, they stayed at a hotel kept by a Dr and Mrs Dashwood, where all the guests dressed for dinner as in an English country house. At Segesta they admired 'one of the finest [Greek] temples in Sicily'. At Monreale they saw the magnificent cathedral 'entirely clothed with pictures and mosaic' before going on to Syracuse. Duncan was much impressed by the Byzantine remains which soon started to influence his painting; Maynard by Duncan's Italian. The holiday ended badly. Duncan sailed from Sicily on 9 April, leaving Maynard in the company of Lytton's sister Dorothy, who had married the painter Simon Bussy. On 15 April the two friends had a painful reunion at Naples:

> I only sent you away to-night [Maynard wrote] when, being tired, my nerves and feelings had been too much strained by the course of the day. You tried to hush up the fact that I had any feelings, and I thought that alone I might get well sooner. But it hasn't been so, and I have to write a letter because in this wretched town I feel miserable and lonely. You could have made me much happier if only your feelings had allowed you to speak one kind word openly. Dearest Duncan, I came deeply needing some open sign of affection, and although I felt you had affection for me underneath, you seemed sodden and had none to give away to me.

The wound of Duncan's coldness was only partly healed by three days at I Tatti, where he discovered Geoffrey Scott, and allowed his moral fibre to be sapped by the tremendous luxury generated by Berenson's increasingly profitable art partnership with Joseph Duveen.

The months which followed were an unhappy period in Maynard's life. Duncan had given it an emotional centre, which was now crumbling. Nor could the spate of marriages going on around him fail to remind him of his own uncertain prospects. Jacques Raverat and Gwen Darwin, Oliver Strachey and Ray Costelloe, Fay: they all succumbed in the summer of 1911. Even Furness, back on leave, announced marital plans.

However, Maynard was more resilient than Lytton had feared. *Probability* remained unfinished, because as a result of his controversy with Karl Pearson (see pp. 134–5) he had decided to add yet another section, on the logical foundations of statistics.[23] He spent much of July and August 1911 at King's working on the extra chapters, although he kept having dreadful dreams about Duncan which woke him up in tears. There were the usual distractions. Rupert Brooke was visited at Grantchester, where Geoffrey appeared 'looking more like a tree or some natural object than ever'.[24] There was a mild flirtation with Justin Brooke, who reminded Maynard of a 'faun or some creature of the wood'. When statistics palled, he slipped up to London to 'view Mr Nijinsky's legs'.[25] There was a brief excursion to Court Place to stay with Mary Berenson. From there he wrote to Duncan on 29 July: 'We are going out for a picnic with the entire bunch of Oliviers. What will poor I do amongst so much female beauty?' By 22 August he was (he told Lytton) 'absolutely alone reading endless and appalling books in German and would be fairly contented if it weren't for an angry member vainly demanding a little excitement'.

The member was quelled by a few days camping at the end of August in Devon with assorted women – Virginia Stephen, Ka Cox and Daphne Olivier. To his father Maynard wrote that 'camp life suits me very well. The hard ground, a morning bathe, the absence of flesh food, and no chairs, don't make one nearly so ill as one would suppose.' But Duncan had refused to come. He had spent the earlier part of the summer at Durbins, with Roger Fry and Vanessa Bell, who had just become lovers. Now he stayed in London painting murals of bathers and footballers at the Borough Polytechnic at the Elephant and Castle, which reminded *The Times* reviewer more of 'primitive Mediterraneans in the morning of the world' than of 'Cockney bathers in the Serpentine'. Back in Cambridge, Maynard was 'all solitude and heat. It is one of my consolations to pick up each afternoon a few books from my shelves, take them to Mr Stoakley and choose a binding. Then I get shaved.'[26] A visit to Duncan in London early in September was a failure, leaving him depressed. 'I always want so much to see you that I am easily disappointed if, when I can see you only for a short time, something in your state of mind interferes between us.' In desperation, he brought a boy back to 21 Fitzroy Square. 'He told me that there are many fewer of them about this week because last week the police were active and locked two up.'[27] Despite episodes of this kind Maynard was never, as he told Duncan, 'much affected ... by *mechanical* randiness'.[28] It was affection he chiefly wanted, and he was failing to get it any more from Duncan.

On his return from London he was diverted from probability by a new adventure, involving an Indian called Bimla Sarkar ('Bridegroom of the Goddess of Purity') who had arrived in Cambridge the previous autumn to prepare himself for entry into one of the colleges. Instead he had succeeded only in accumulating debts, which his father refused to pay. How Maynard first got involved with him is unknown. At any rate he set to work to clear up the mess; by 16 March 1911 Sarkar was writing to him that 'so long as I live I shall bear the most grateful memory of your kindness to me'. He decided he wanted to read economics under Keynes. When Maynard got back to King's in September after his summer camp with the neo-pagans, he found Sarkar in attendance. 'I've spent much of to-day attending to his affairs and trying to console and divert his mind,' Maynard explained to Duncan on 7 September.

> He is a strange and charming creature. I don't know how our relation-ship is going to end. I have had all to-day the most violent sexual feelings towards him; and he on his part has paid me four or five visits on one pretext or another, finally saying that he came because he was so miserable when he was anywhere else.

Sarkar became another of Maynard's protégés. He got him into Clare College, but he soon had to withdraw, as his father refused to send money. Maynard supported him for several months, but in the end threatened to have him repatriated. Sarkar refused to go: the shame would be too great. Gradually his position improved. He found an uncle to support him in Tufnell Park, London. Maynard went on seeing him, giving him presents and bailing him out in emergencies.[29]

The final diversion of this lonely summer was provided by politics. In the middle of September Maynard set off with Gerald Shove for a fortnight's tour of Ireland with a group of fifty Liberal MPs – members of the 80 Club, of which he too was a member. The company of the politicians was a wonderful restorer of self-confidence. 'You haven't, I suppose, ever mixed with politicians at close quarters,' he wrote to Duncan on 3 October. 'They're *awful.* I think some of these must have been the dregs anyhow, but I've discovered, what previously I didn't believe possible, that politicians behave in private life and say exactly the same things as they do in public. Their stupidity is inhuman.' Maynard eventually managed to break free from his '50 pomposities' and spend a week by himself. Except for Galway, he found Ireland sadly lacking in mystery. The country round Glengariff, he felt, was exactly what a hotel keeper, having the best taste of his class, would have created. 'Although [it] is wild and almost uninhabited, I feel as if Queen Victoria and the Prince Consort must some time about 1850 have unveiled it and declared it open.' The visit, he told his mother, had converted him to Home Rule, though 'it is perfectly plain that the people are now on the whole prosperous and that the conditions and feelings of twenty years ago have gone away completely.'[30] The comment is another example of Keynes's political complacency before the First World War.

He returned to Cambridge in a much better state of mind. To Duncan he wrote on 31 October: 'To-night I feel extraordinarily happy and very much in love with you and as if whatever you did and whomever you might love didn't matter in the least. But I suppose it's a temporary madness.'

11

An Indian Summer

I. CHANGING PATTERNS

Keynes was one of those rare persons who can both think and act at the highest level. His life falls into cycles or phases, in which the emphasis shifts from one to the other. These shifts were related to what was happening in the world. At some times, particularly during the two world wars, there was a greater demand for Keynes's practical genius, and a greater satisfaction to be had from exercising it. But the cycles can also be seen in terms of action and reaction. Periods of great intellectual effort demand their release in practical activity, while practical activity prompts, sooner or later, a yearning for the cloister. Before 1914, Keynes's desire for the cloister was uppermost, partly because he was at this period most under the immediate influence of Moore's philosophy, partly because the nature of his sexual relations fitted private life better than public life – a point of considerable importance even today, but more so then, when homosexual acts were illegal, and the danger of blackmail much greater.

As he approached thirty, the practical, administrative, worldly side of his nature began to assert itself. The back of probability was finally broken in 1912. By then, too, his affair with Duncan had petered out. He needed more work, more 'amusement', to fill the empty hours. Once drawn into something, the desire to do it thoroughly, as well as his speed in the dispatch of business, would ensure that his involvement expanded.

The start of this changeover can be seen in his Cambridge life in the years leading up to the First World War. A letter he wrote to Duncan on 24 November 1910 gives a good indication of his state of mind at this time:

> I've got very little news, for I've been very busy and seem to have more and more purely business engagements – which leave me, when I've finished them, feeling dissatisfied with existence. I am going to do some electioneering. And at other times I'm apt to be playing bridge. These things amuse me at the time, but one's not, as St. George says, best pleased with oneself in the long run. And the future doesn't seem any better, for I wretchedly want, at the same time that I do not want, to do these things. The Provost sent for me the other day, and I went feeling as if the headmaster had sent for me for goodness knows what. But he

only wanted to know whether I should like before very long to become a Bursar for the College (i.e. manage the College Estates). I said I would if it did not mean so much work as to interfere with more serious occupations – for it makes my fellowship permanent and will, of course, some of it, amuse me. Also Meredith has been made a Professor at Belfast, and I shall probably succeed to the University lectureship he gives up. [Maynard was appointed to the five-year Girdler's Lectureship in Economics in December 1910.] Why is it so difficult to draw the line between doing no routine work and doing too much?

Maynard's fellowship in fact became permanent the following June, when he was appointed college lecturer in economics. But the Provost's approach indicates the area of college life in which he had started to make an impact. Anything to do with financial administration 'amused' him, and he had already begun to run a critical eye over the college accounts, having been appointed an inspector of them in 1909. In 1911 he graduated to the Estates Committee, from which position he planned a campaign against the conservative administration of the bursars, Grant and Corbett, who believed in starving college services and investments in order to maintain large cash balances. Mobilising the younger fellows – who now included Dillwyn Knox – he succeeded in getting the bursars' policy defeated at the college's annual congregation on 11 May 1912. As a successful rebel, he was naturally co-opted on to the Bursarial Committee. His ascent to the bursarship itself was now a foregone conclusion. In 1912 he became a fellowship elector, which meant that every year he had to read several enormous theses on any subject under the sun. These growing college responsibilities were added to old university chores never relinquished. He continued to serve on the committees of the Union and the Liberal Club. He kept up his attendance at most of the old societies, and in 1911 was invited by McTaggart to join a new one – the Eranus. He developed an interest in psychic phenomena, going regularly to meetings of the University's Society for Psychical Research, and joining its committee in 1911. Whether he had any psychic experiences himself is not recorded. But it was an interesting throwback to Henry Sidgwick, whose efforts to establish the immortality of the soul by empirical methods Keynes had so derided in 1906.

Keynes's 'amusements' by no means replaced the serious aspects of his Cambridge life, particularly the quest for friendship. Although he 'took wing' from the Apostles in November 1910, having read the Society twenty papers in nearly eight years, his friends were still mainly Apostles, while the inspection of 'embryos' continued to provide new, though increasingly less intense, emotional satisfactions. By 1911 his closest Cambridge friend was Gerald Shove – the 'silent Shove' as Rupert Brooke called him – a man subject to black moods but with a vehement, biting edge and a blasphemous, daredevil side which Maynard found attractive. Together they would go to inspect university athletes at sporting events, Shove being quite overcome by the beauty of Philip (later Noel) Baker,* a King's undergraduate, as he ran in the half-mile – and surmising that Pigou's fainting fits were occasioned by the same stimulus. In March 1912 he and Maynard took an 'eating and gambling' holiday in Monte Carlo, Maynard's first Easter holiday for three years without Duncan.

Maynard's romantic interests lay elsewhere. In the spring of 1912 there was a brief 'adventure' with a King's College undergraduate called Chester Purves. But that summer he fell more substantially in love with Gordon Hannington Luce of Emmanuel College (one of the exceptional undergraduates attracted to that college in that period), who had become an Apostle in January 1912. Lucy, as his friends called him, was the thirteenth son of an impecunious vicar, fair and stocky, with poetic ambitions. Maynard became very fond of him, falling into his usual protective role by advancing him money to continue his studies in English literature. Luce returned his affection, and an affair between the two men flowered briefly in the summer of 1912. But there were few prospects in England for aspiring poets without private means, and, like Swithinbank, Luce decided to go East, Maynard using his India Office connections to get him a job teaching English literature at the Government College, Rangoon. He embarked in September 1912, accompanied by Furness who was returning to Egypt, and E. M. Forster and Lowes Dickinson who were going out to India. In Burma he made contact with Swithinbank, looking gauntly beautiful, but pale, 'gentle, but administrative ... not cold, but somewhat closeted'.[1] Luce, much to Maynard's dismay, soon married a Burmese girl, Teetee Moung Tin. But their friendship survived.

A few days after Luce sailed for Burma, Maynard was off to Hungary to visit another Apostle called Ferenc Békássy, an aristocratic friend of Noel Olivier's from Bedales, who had come to King's in October 1911 to read history. He was far from being standard Apostolic Man, preferring Nietzsche to Moore, and action to contemplation, though he too had poetic leanings. Maynard spent a fortnight in September 1912 at his ancestral home, Kis Sennye, Rum, in a medieval splendour which conjured up Tolstoy's Russia, before returning via Vienna, whose 'many new buildings in the flat style' and 'astounding' Breughels greatly impressed him.[2]

It was on his return from Vienna that he met one of the most brilliant products of that brilliant culture – a slender young man of twenty-three with fair hair, blue staring eyes and a passion for philosophy, called Ludwig Wittgenstein. At the behest of his father, a millionaire industrialist, Wittgenstein had enrolled at Manchester University to study aeronautical engineering, then in its infancy. But having read Russell's *Principles of Mathematics*, he became obsessed with 'Russell's Paradox' and decided to give up trying

* Later a Labour politician, who won the Nobel Peace Prize in 1959.

to design an aeroplane and instead study philosophy under Russell at Cambridge.* Maynard, who was introduced to him by Russell on 30 October 1912, immediately recognised him as a man of genius, and a fortnight later had engineered his election to the Apostles, ignoring Russell's warning that Wittgenstein would not thank him for it. Russell was right. Wittgenstein was appalled at the thought of having to spend his Saturday evenings in the company of Békássy – whom he detested as a Hungarian aristocrat – and a King's freshman called Francis Bliss, who did not number philosophical acumen among his accomplishments. After one meeting, Wittgenstein resigned, complaining to Keynes that the brethren had not yet learnt their toilets, a process which, though necessary, was indecent to observe.[3] Lytton Strachey persuaded him to withdraw his resignation, but Wittgenstein stopped attending. Keynes thought him 'a most wonderful character.... I like enormously to be with him.'[4] Wittgenstein showed his generosity when he put up £200 a year to relieve W. E. Johnson of his teaching responsibilities. But relations were never easy with this prickly genius. The misunderstandings which marked everyone's dealings with him come out in a note he wrote to Maynard, who handled the details of Wittgenstein's gift. 'Thanks very much for the trouble you take over my business. *My* reason for not seeing you oftener last term was that I did not wish our intercourse to continue without any sign that *you* wished to continue it.'[5]

Two of Maynard's students who did not become economists but became close personal friends were Sydney Russell Cooke, later a stockbroker, and Archibald Rose, already a diplomat. Maynard had an affair with 'Cookie' which went on for some months in 1913–14; they gambled together modestly on the Stock Exchange. Archibald Rose was an advanced student with thirteen years in the consular service in China behind him – a very small, fastidious man, with a droll manner, who had learnt Mandarin and become a good amateur jockey. Maynard introduced him to economics, and he introduced Maynard to riding. He and Rose would go riding most Saturday afternoons in 1912 when Maynard was in Cambridge. Rose, who went back East again in 1913, was one of Maynard's few close friends who understood the active side of his nature, and sympathised with it. 'I want you to have a "middle-period" – somewhere out of Cambridge. It seems to me necessary if you are really to fulfil yourself,' he wrote to him from Delhi on 4 February 1914. On 24 July of that year he urged him to do 'something which would be primarily practical'. His wish was granted sooner than he expected.[6]

Cooke and Rose were friends from outside Maynard's usual world. They had no entry into his general Cambridge set of Apostles, embryos and

* Russell had found that either answer to the question 'Is the class of classes which are not members of themselves a member of itself?' implies its contrary. This is analogous to the famous paradox of the Cretan who said that all Cretans are liars. If true, false. If false, true.

neo-pagan women who still assembled at country inns for leisurely holidays, spiced with intrigue and gossip. Maynard was present at the New Year's reading party of 1912, which Rupert Brooke got together in West Lulworth, Dorset. While Maynard wrote his next term's lectures, Ka Cox flirted with the painter Henry Lamb to Rupert's fury, as did Lytton Strachey, though to less effect. This was a holiday of some importance in the cultural history of the time, since it marked the start of Brooke's estrangement from Blooms-bury, and his transformation from 'the Fabian intellectual to the chauvinistic fugleman of 1914'.[7]

Maynard himself rented the Crown Inn, Everleigh, near Marlborough in July and August 1912. This was another neo-pagan occasion, with three of the Olivier sisters turning up, as well as Ka Cox, smarting from her rejection by Rupert. Brynhild, the most beautiful, though not the cleverest, of the Olivier girls, was at this time very attracted to Maynard. He was happy enough to take her riding; but she made no progress with him, and soon married a Kingsman, A. E. Popham. Maynard still felt that women were intruders into the cloister, unless like Vanessa and Virginia they posed no threat of emotional entanglement. From the Crown Inn he wrote to Duncan on 26 July:

> I don't much care for the atmosphere these women breed and haven't liked this party nearly as much as my last week's. Noel is very nice and Daphne very innocent. But Bryn is too stupid – and I begin to take an active dislike to her. Out of the window I see Rupert making love to her ... taking her hand, sitting at her feet, gazing at her eyes. Oh these womanisers. How on earth and what for can he do it?

Maynard's relations with his family, too, were changing in the years before the war. He was becoming less dependent on his father, more on his mother. In October 1910, at the age of fifty-eight, John Neville Keynes became registrary – or administrative head – of the University, a post he filled with exemplary tact and good sense for fifteen years. Six months later he was made an honorary fellow of his old college, Pembroke. At last the iron grip of duty started to relax. His hours of work dropped from 2000 in 1910 to 1500 in 1913. By contrast Florence's energy continued to expand. Her appetite for business was voracious. In 1911 she was elected a Cam-bridge town councillor; she joined the Committee of the National Council of Women. She travelled all over England attending conferences; at Cam-bridge she became a familiar, if unsafe, figure on her bicycle, rushing from one good cause to another – now stirring up the Public Health Committee on sanitary arrangements, now agitating about juvenile unemployment. To Maynard's friends she was the 'good Mother Keynes'. It is not clear how much, if anything, Florence knew of Maynard's sexual tastes. 'I had a dreadful conversation with my mother and Margaret about marriage,' he wrote to Duncan Grant on 11 October 1910, 'and practically had to admit what I was. How much they grasped I don't know.' Whatever Florence may have suspected, she remained devoted to him, and proud of his successes. He returned her devotion. There was no break or quarrel, just development and change.

Maynard was less successful in his relations with Geoffrey. He was pleased enough when he heard that his brother had won first prize in the scholarship examination at St Bartholomew's Hospital, the first step in his career as a surgeon. 'Please give him my congratulations,' he wrote to Neville on 30 September 1910. 'We're really a wonderful family, take us all round, at examinations. Probably the finest in the kingdom, I expect. If only the examination system lasts another two or three hundred years, we shall end, I'm sure, by being the Royal Family.' Geoffrey had very much Maynard's double character, that of the scientist who valued, above all, the arts. By 1911 he had submitted his first Blake bibliography to Cambridge University Press. (It was turned down.) He collected antiquarian books, loved the ballet, was a friend of Rupert Brooke and the sculptor Eric Gill (a couple of whose sculptures Maynard bought). But he lacked poetry. Maynard required a touch of fancy in his intimates. Geoffrey was cruelly hurt by his brother's indifference, and by his parents' obvious preference for Maynard. His father's refusal to lend Geoffrey £350 to buy a Blake masterpiece was a bitter blow. 'Blake is a cult', Neville told him dismissively. By contrast, Neville showed increasing confidence in Maynard's financial judgement, transferring to him the management of Florence's dowry, worth £5000. But mainly Geoffrey kept his frustrations to himself; they emerged only by omission in his autobiography seventy years later. The surface of family life continued unruffled.

Maynard was much closer to his sister Margaret. 'Yesterday Margaret came to lunch with me and we got on very well together,' he told Duncan on 1 July 1910. 'She's charming, I think – much nicer than your horrid Geoffrey.' Margaret's competitive successes were modest by Keynes standards – 'two second prizes for her annuals and a third for beans', Maynard informed his parents the same month. However, in February 1911 he found her pamphlet on *The Problem of Boy Labour* 'extraordinarily good – so written as to be a most interesting and even moving document'.[8] The great love of Margaret's life before her marriage was Eglantyne Jebb, whose sister Dorothy had been at Newnham. The intimacy between Maynard and Margaret was deepened by his knowledge of this relationship. In February 1913, after a short courtship which involved joint committee work, Margaret became engaged to A. V. Hill, a physiologist who was fellow and Junior Dean of Trinity College, Cambridge. They were married in June 1913 and had a daughter – christened Mary Eglantyne, but always called Polly. Hill was 'frightfully puritanical – but then that suits her', Maynard told Duncan.[9]

In 1908 Maynard had left London for Cambridge; now he was drawn increasingly to London. From the autumn of 1911, when he started editing

the *Economic Journal,* he took to spending the middle of each week in term-
time in the capital – a pattern which continued until 1937. The new
regularity of his visits coincided with the general demand for the revision of
Bloomsbury's living arrangements. As Quentin Bell describes it:

> The lease of 29 Fitzroy Square was coming to an end; Virginia and
> Adrian, tired perhaps of their quarrelsome tête-à-tête, proposed a dom-
> estic revolution: they would share their home – it would have to be
> a large home – with other friends; for this purpose they considered a
> house in Bedford Square, but it was at 38 Brunswick Square that in
> October [1911] they found what they wanted.[10]

This revolution suited Maynard, who was physically cramped and emotionally frustrated in his back room at Duncan's. The lease of 38 Brunswick
Square was taken in his name. He had the ground-floor room, running the
length of the house, Adrian had the first floor, Virginia the second. A couple
of months later, Leonard Woolf, back from Ceylon, moved into the top floor;
Vanessa decided that she liked him 'very much.... He is of course very
clever & from living in the wilds seems to me to have a more interesting
point of view than most of the "set".'[11] Virginia was put in charge of the
domestic arrangements. Living was collective, but feeding was individual,
each 'inmate', as Virginia called them, picking up his tray from the hall, and
returning it when his repast was finished. Rents, which Virginia collected,
varied from 35s to £2 a week. 'The only thing that seems certain,' Virginia
wrote to Ottoline Morrell, 'is that a house is the cheapest way of living and
if you have a house you must have servants.'[12] This plan was to be the basis
of the collective living arrangements of the Bloomsbury unmarrieds for the
next ten years or so.

Maynard remained at 38 Brunswick Square for the next three years.
During that time there were changes. Leonard Woolf married Virginia
Stephen in August 1912, and they both moved out in October. Leonard's
place on the top floor was taken by Maynard's brother Geoffrey in January
1913. In his autobiography, Geoffrey made a point of emphasising that he
was never a member of the Bloomsbury Group, for some of whose members
– notably Clive Bell and Harry Norton – he developed considerable antipathy.[13] The closest he got to Virginia was when he saved her life in September
1913, after she had taken an overdose of veronal in Adrian's room. Not that
Virginia was particularly fond of Maynard: 'No: being in Spain does not
make me love him better,' she wrote to Ka Cox on her honeymoon.[14] Gerald
Shove and Henry Norton occupied Virginia's old rooms at various times.
The appearance of Maynard's room, too, changed considerably in these
years, as Duncan and Frederick Etchells painted its walls with a continuous
street scene, in a spotted style reminiscent of Signac. It was dominated by a
collision between two hansom cabs. Whether Maynard found it calmed his

nerves may be doubted. But his London life was intended for excitement, not calm.

There were hints, no more, of the more substantial London existence Maynard was to create for himself in the 1920s. There was talk of a City directorship and editorship of the *Morning Post*, both of which came to nothing.[15] He was almost made chairman of the Gilchrist Trust, but the trustees eventually decided in favour of 'past experience' rather than 'young blood'.[16] He turned down a consultancy worth £200 a year.[17] Through his membership of an economics dining club which met alternately in Cambridge and London, as well as through the Political Economy Club, he started to make contacts with financial journalists like F. W. Hirst, editor of the *Economist*, and with bankers and businessmen who would be useful to him later. He began investing on the stock market, with the proceeds of his own savings, as well as Neville's 'birthday money'. In 1914 he also started speculating with the help of a £1000 overdraft facility from his bank, Barclays, and the proceeds of a £1000 loan from Roger Fry. The picture he gave in 1919 of the pre-war 'inhabitant of London', lifting up his telephone – as he sipped his morning tea in bed – to invest his money all over the world, is already recognisably himself.

II. INDIAN CURRENCY AND FINANCE

Keynes's continuing interest in Indian finance went beyond the affairs of Bimla Sarkar. Following his retirement from the India Office he played a delicate part, acting as public defender and private critic, of India's evolving financial system. In the Lent Term of 1911 he gave six lectures at the London School of Economics and at Cambridge on 'Currency, Finance and the Level of Prices in India'. These lectures formed the basis of a paper, 'Recent Developments of the India Currency Question', which he read to the Royal Economic Society on 9 May 1911. As usual, he showed a draft to Lionel Abrahams, the financial secretary at the India Office, where Maynard was accepted as a licensed critic.

Maynard had grasped the significance of India's monetary arrangements – namely, that they represented not an imperfect or limping gold standard but 'a more scientific and economic system' in the forefront of monetary progress, which he called the gold-exchange standard. 'If the gold is only required for foreign payments and not for internal circulation,' he wrote in February 1910, 'it is cheaper to maintain a credit at one of the great financial centres of the world, which can be converted with great readiness to gold when it is required, and which earns a small rate of interest when it is not required.'[18] The vision had come long before he was ready to work out all its practical consequences. But he was convinced, as he said in his paper to the Royal Economic Society, that out of this system would evolve 'the ideal currency of the future'. Even before he delivered his LSE lectures he had had the idea of turning them into a 'small book'.[19]

The decision to break off from probability to write a book on India was taken suddenly early in November 1912. India's monetary arrangements had briefly become a matter of public interest as a result of the Indian 'silver scandal' which broke at the beginning of the month, an offshoot of the far greater Marconi scandal raging at the same time. The thread linking the two was the suggestion that public figures, some of whom were Jews, were using their political positions to enrich themselves by diverting government contracts to firms in which they had a financial interest. *The Times* ran five articles on India's financial system; questions were asked in the House of Commons.

Keynes signed a contract with Macmillan to write a book on 'The Monetary Affairs of India' on 15 December; at the same time he decided that his book on probability should also be published by Macmillan, instead of by the Cambridge University Press who had been making difficulties about setting the book up in print before he had finished writing it. Both Macmillan's contracts were on a half-profits basis. A great attraction of the new publishing connection was that he would be dealing with his old Eton friend, Daniel Macmillan.

The book (whose title was changed to *Indian Currency and Finance*) was written astonishingly quickly, mainly over the Christmas vacation. By 6 March 1913 Neville was already starting to read proofs of it, two days before Maynard left for Egypt to stay with Furness, now a high official in the Egyptian Ministry of the Interior, who had promised him 'all the attractions which made Gomorrah such a popular resort in the good old days'. While in Egypt, he accepted an invitation from his old chief, Sir Thomas Holderness, to serve on the Royal Commission on Indian Finance and Currency, which the government had decided to set up to appease its critics. This high honour had come to Maynard just two months before his thirtieth birthday.

Indian Currency and Finance began with an account of the evolution, and a parade of the virtues, of the gold-exchange standard, a system based on a paper currency maintained artificially at par with gold by means of credits abroad in sterling, as opposed to the gold standard proper, in which there was a gold currency for internal circulation and gold reserves for settling international debts. Far from being a sign of second-class status, the former system, Keynes maintained in his justly well-known second chapter, was in the 'mainstream of currency evolution', because it economised on the use of gold internally and internationally, thus allowing greater 'elasticity' of money in response to business needs. Looking beyond India, Keynes foresaw the international gold standard giving way to a more scientific system based on one or two currency reserve centres. 'A preference for a tangible reserve currency', he declared confidently, 'is ... a relic of a time when governments were less trustworthy in these matters than they are now.'[20]

In his description of the interlocking mechanisms – the purchase and sale of Council bills in London, the regulation of the note issue, and the management of the government's reserves and cash balances – by which the Secretary of State supported the exchange value of the rupee, Maynard showed his mastery of the working of financial institutions. He showed how, contrary to nationalist assertion, India benefited from holding its reserves in London.[21]

However, the absence of a central bank was a major weakness. Government reserves for maintaining the exchange were not part of bankers' reserves. This meant that the Indian money-market was starved of funds during the busy season when gold and silver had to be imported from London, raising the discount rate unduly to cover the cost of remittance. Also, part of the imported metals went into hoards. If the government's reserves could be added to the bankers' reserves, the note issue could be expanded, allowing lower interest rates and inhibiting hoarding. On the practicability of establishing a central bank, Keynes was non-committal, his caution enhanced by his foreknowledge of his appointment to the Royal Commission.

As always with Keynes, the general tone of technical mastery and *gravitas* is enlivened by passages of fancy and spiced by bantering asides at the expense of figures in authority. Quoting the words of a secretary of state who had vetoed a proposal to set up a central bank in 1867, he commented: 'no need to name him, it is the eternal secretary of state speaking, not a transient individual'. A rational project had been 'smothered in the magnificent and empty rhetoric of political wisdom'.[22] Discovering the 'shocking' fact that the Indian government's stockbroker was paid more than any other official except the viceroy, he wondered 'how long it will be found necessary to pay City men so entirely out of proportion to what other servants of society commonly receive for performing social services not less useful or difficult'.[23] It was the subversiveness of tone more than of thought which gave Maynard some of his reputation for radicalism.

By the time *Indian Currency and Finance* appeared, the Royal Commission had already been taking evidence for a month. It held its first meeting on 5 May 1913 and adjourned for the summer on 6 August. Its chairman, Austen Chamberlain, son of Joseph Chamberlain, who read Maynard's book in August for the first time, did not know 'whether to congratulate you on it or console myself', since Maynard would certainly be considered 'the author of the Commission's report'.[24] Maynard had taken a vigorous part in the cross-examination of witnesses, being especially sharp with advocates of a full gold standard for India, and with critics of the idea of a central bank.

On the central question of whether India should aim for a gold currency, it transpired that the Commission, with one exception, favoured Keynes's view that the existing gold-exchange standard should be maintained. But a split was apparent on the banking question. Lionel Abrahams of the India Office had prepared a memorandum for the Commission in June, arguing that the main advantage of having a central bank would be 'the deposit with the Bank of money now in the Reserve Treasuries which could be placed at the disposal of trade with a beneficial effect on the rate of discount and on business generally'.[25] However, the Commission refused to commit itself in favour of this proposal. Instead it asked two of its members, Keynes and Sir Ernest Cable, to draw up a scheme for a State Bank over the summer.

Maynard had been enjoying his London life. On duty he presented a picture of perfect bureaucratic respectability, appearing at the Commission 'bald and top-hatted', hobnobbing with civil servants and politicians. He met Asquith for the first time.[26] His social life was filled with another cast of characters, whom he was no doubt starting to titillate with spicy gossip from high places. Evenings at 38 Brunswick Square would often be spent playing poker with Adrian, Gerald Shove and Saxon Sydney-Turner. Sometimes Noel Olivier and Karin Costelloe would drop in; also a gauche young friend of Adrian's called David Garnett, then a biology student at the Royal College of Science, and known as Bunny because of a rabbit-skin cap he had had as a boy. Bloomsbury parties were getting wilder. Karin wrote of one, in late June 1913, to her mother Mary Berenson:

> Oliver [Strachey] and I went as Karsavina and Nijinsky (he in a red ballet costume and I in a piece of purple satin and a wreath). We enacted Spectre de la Rose with much success. We followed that by the ballet of Job, in which Keynes, as the devil, poured boils in the shape of cherries upon the writhing Roger Fry. Then came Lytton's play acted by Clive, Marjorie, Vanessa and Duncan. It was a wildly twisted take-off of the actors themselves, exquisitely finished, very witty, and not exactly proper. . . .[27]

There were more serious cultural events. That summer Diaghilev brought two 'firsts' to London: Chaliapin in *Boris Godunov* and Stravinsky's *The Rite of Spring*. On 8 July Roger Fry's Omega Workshops opened at 33 Fitzroy Square, a venture designed to turn the talents of Bloomsbury painters and their friends to decorative art. Maynard was an early customer, though not apparently a financial backer. 'The Omega stuffs look very fine on my chairs,' he told Duncan on 25 September. 'Unfortunately the upholsterer has stuck them on what is, to my thinking, upside down.'

He managed to snatch a few holidays. In July he spent some days with Sydney Russell Cooke and his family on the Isle of Wight, going on to stay with the Macmillans at Birch Grove in Sussex. (Perhaps it was on this occasion that Harold Macmillan remembers his parents being annoyed with

Keynes for appearing at breakfast in slippers.) In mid-August there was a brief interlude of camping with Duncan, Vanessa, Adrian, Roger, Gerald and Daphne Olivier in Norfolk. On 10 September he joined Clive and Vanessa and a large Bloomsbury weekend house-party at Asheham, the Woolfs' country house in Sussex, before rushing off to Birmingham for a meeting of the British Association for the Advancement of Science. All the decent hotels in Birmingham were full, so he stayed in a kind of superior pub. To Duncan he wrote on 11 September: 'I found St George last night (cured, thank God, of his [venereal?] disease) and he is living with me at this quasi-hotel, – though, in effect, only at night as I desert him all day for my scientific friends.' In addition to nights with St George, and learned daytime discussions with Fay and Meredith, Maynard went to a football match which reminded him of a Roman amphitheatre – 'The crowd makes a dull roar nearly all the time, rising to a frenzy of excitement and rage when the slightest thing happened' – and visited the Birmingham Repertory Theatre. It was, he told Duncan, 'exactly what we ought to have in Cambridge'. This thought lodged in his mind, long after St George had vanished from his life.

Indian business, meanwhile, had resumed when he went to stay with Sir Ernest Cable in Devon on 27 August. Cable, the owner of a big jute business in India, and a former member of the Bengal Chamber of Commerce, had written a skeleton memorandum dealing with the capitalisation of the proposed State Bank. He invited Maynard to stay with him to discuss it and have 'a day or so at the partridges'. Maynard went back to King's to write the final memorandum which, he said, 'ought to make any banker's mouth water'. It was circulated to the Commission over his sole signature on 6 October 1913.

The memorandum contained a number of sections dealing with the Bank's constitution, capitalisation, functions and so on. Keynes rejected the model of the Bank of England as unsuited to Indian conditions. In his scheme, tailored to meet inherited arrangements, the three existing 'Presidency Banks' at Calcutta, Bombay and Madras would form the 'head offices' of a federal system over which a central board would preside at Delhi: a model adapted from Germany, and similar to the Federal Reserve System currently being established in the United States. Perhaps of most interest to the student of Keynes's thought is the contention that certain public functions are best performed by semi-autonomous bodies rather than directly by the state – which foreshadows the argument in his well-known essay of 1925, 'Am I a Liberal?' The great advantage of an independent central bank was that it would shield the Secretary of State from political criticism.[28]

He was equally emphatic about the economic advantages. The capacity of a central bank to mobilise the reserves now scattered through the banking and treasury systems would make India much better able to meet a banking crisis.* By holding the balances of the government and as manager of the Paper Currency Reserve, the Bank would have both more resources, and more discretion, to expand credit money.[29]

More witnesses were seen from 23 October to 14 November. Then Chamberlain and Basil Blackett, the Commission's secretary, drew up a draft report, which was circulated for comments. By this time clear areas of agreement and disagreement had emerged. The gold standard was definitely rejected. There were too many doubters and vested interests for the State Bank proposal to go through. A compromise was patched up whereby Keynes's memorandum would appear as an annexe to the Report, with a recommendation that an expert committee be set up to study it. The Commission would make its proposals for giving more elasticity to the currency on the assumption that there would be no central bank. At drafting sessions Keynes was impressed by the chairman, writing to his mother: 'I must say that Austen came out of the ordeal very well, and I believe he may yet be Prime Minister. I don't suppose in the purely intellectual sense that he is any stupider than Campbell-Bannerman was.'

It was now that a row blew up over what Chamberlain was to call 'a minor point of note issue management'. The point of dispute was highly technical. Keynes was determined to establish the principle that the various reserve funds – the gold standard reserve, the paper currency reserve, and the government's cash balances in the reserve treasuries – should be treated as a single reserve from the point of view of lending. However, this was beyond the grasp of his more prosaic colleagues, who thought that the technical reforms which he and another Commissioner, R. W. Gillam, proposed were too clever by half.

The Commission broke up for Christmas without having resolved the issue. At the beginning of January 1914 Keynes left England for Roquebrune on the Riviera – although without Sydney Russell Cooke, whom he had hoped would come with him – intending to return in time for the Commission's next meeting, fixed for 12 January. But just as he was about to set off back home he was 'smitten down by a somewhat bad attack of tonsillitis – temperature 103'.[30] He was being nursed, he reported, by Dorothy Bussy's sister, Mrs Rendel. An hour after receiving a telegram that his illness had been rediagnosed as diphtheria, Florence left Cambridge, crossing the Channel on 14 January. At midnight of the 15th she reached Menton, where Maynard was now in a nursing home feeling better. He was cheered up not just by Florence's arrival, but by that of Duncan, who had come out to stay

* 'With no central reserve, no elasticity of credit currency, hardly a rediscount market, and hardly a bank rate policy, with the growth of small and daring banks, great increase of deposits and a community unhabituated to banking and ready at the least alarm to revert to hoarding ... there are to be found most elements of weakness and few elements of strength' (*CW*, xv, p. 197).

with his mother. As Maynard continued in a highly infectious state, Florence improbably took to the tables at Monte Carlo in Duncan's company. 'My companion won rather more than I lost and remonstrated at being dragged away,' she recalled many years later.[31] Maynard's departure was delayed till the end of the month; he was still being prescribed strychnine for 'paralysis of the soft palate' in March. Meanwhile his father noted (22 January 1914) that 'Maynard is afraid that in his absence the reactionary party got too much their own way on the Commission.'

In his absence the Commissioners, trying to make sense of his notes, had managed to hit on a formula which was somewhat more restrictive than their original one. Angered, Maynard fired off a letter from Menton on 23 January saying that if the new draft stood he would have to write a note of dissent to the Report. Back in England, he sent Chamberlain a cogent letter on 3 February. The basic failure of the new formula, he wrote, was its inability to think of the various funds as other than in watertight compartments. 'The Government's real capacity to make temporary loans depends on the sums in their paper currency reserve and in their balances regarded jointly. . . . In fact, the proposed scheme extends and perpetuates the multiple reserve system which is anyhow a great defect in the Indian system.'[32] He proposed new drafting amendments. Before this onslaught, Chamberlain gave way and, on his own authority, authorised the changes. Whether he understood what he was doing is doubtful. He regarded the issue as of little practical importance. Marshall, who read the Report when it came out, was 'entranced by [Keynes's State Bank memorandum] as a prodigy of constructive work. Verily we old men will have to hang ourselves, if young people can cut their way so straight and with such apparent ease through such great difficulties.'[33]

III. ON THE BRINK OF CIVILISATION

Vanished worlds always seem different in retrospect: more golden, or blacker. Joys and sufferings are never so intense as recollection or history makes them. In particular, a great foreclosure always makes the preceding prospect seem rosier than it was. So it is not surprising that Keynes and his friends looking back on the world before 1914 thought that it was on the point of coming right for them, would have come right for them had it not been for the war. They were, of course, a highly privileged group, and the golden age they looked back on was very much that of their world. Nevertheless, they were not wholly wrong, either about their prospects or about possibilities in general; and even if they were wrong this would not matter from the biographical point of view, for it was their own interpretation of past experience which influenced their subsequent lives and future efforts.

In his essay 'Before the War', dated 1917, Clive Bell wrote, 'Not, I suppose, since 1789 have days seemed more full of promise than those spring days of 1914.'[34] For Bloomsbury, promise meant chiefly culture; culture in 1914 meant to them, above all, ballet. Ballet was the art form which defined the age, just as thirty years previously it had been Wagnerian opera. It owed its ascendancy mainly to Diaghilev, the greatest of the twentieth-century impresarios. Diaghilev not only introduced to the West the genius of the singer Chaliapin and the dancers Karsavina and Nijinsky, but he was determined to make the ballet a catalyst for all that was modern and exciting in the arts. He coaxed miraculous scores out of Ravel, Stravinsky, Strauss and Debussy; the visual impact of his productions – with scenery and costumes designed by Benois and Bakst, and Nijinsky's miraculous elevation – was profound. As Richard Shone writes, 'Its influence was widespread in the theatre, in interior decoration and fashion, and painting. ... It was not simply the revelation of colour that astonished the painters but the dancers' command of space and the movement of bodies in a way never seen before.'[35]

But the effect of the Ballets Russes was not just confined to the arts. It brought Society and the arts into contact in a way which Post-Impressionism had not, and in this Bloomsbury, naïvely no doubt, saw a great hope: the governing class was becoming civilised at last. As Lydia Lopokova later put it, Diaghilev 'had the cunning ... to combine the excellent with the chic, and revolutionary art with the atmosphere of the old regime'.[36] Ottoline Morrell and Lady Cunard led the way. According to Osbert Sitwell, Margot Asquith made 10 Downing Street 'a centre of such an abundance and intensity of life as it had not seen for a hundred years and is never likely to see again'.[37] The civilising and elevating mission of the arts was taken seriously by Bloomsbury. It was bound up with their optimism about the future. There is no hint in pre-war London of aestheticism as an escape from a crumbling society, which is said to have dominated the cultural consciousness of pre-1914 Vienna. Rather the arts, with 'progressive' politics and economic improvement, seemed to be marching hand in hand towards a better future. The political vocation itself might be held in low esteem; certainly the Bloomsbury publicists had only the haziest notion of where or how the masses were to fit into this newly civilised world; but that things were getting better they had no doubt. Hence the profound shock of the events of August 1914. That these archaic, *opéra bouffe* figures in their uniforms and top hats would be able to close down civilisation was simply not a thought which had occurred to them.

Keynes was too preoccupied with the proofs of probability to take much notice of gathering war clouds. Although the Archduke Franz Ferdinand had been assassinated on 28 June, only a month later was there a first reference in Keynes's letters to the worsening international situation. Characteristically it was in the context of Stock Exchange speculation. Maynard had put in an order for Canadian Pacific and Rio Tinto, 'which is courageous of me.... The odds appear to me *slightly* against Russia and Germany joining in.'[38] On 30 July he was still gossiping to Neville by letter about his rooms which he had just had redecorated ('I can't make up my mind about the carpeting of the big room') and about his plans to go camping in Cornwall with Geoffrey and Margery and Brynhild Olivier. On 31 July Maynard wrote to his father that the war news 'interferes dreadfully with my work – I cannot keep my mind quiet enough.' Next day Germany invaded Belgium. On 4 August 1914 England declared war on Germany, and Bloomsbury's – and Maynard's – world changed forever.

PART THREE

THE END OF INNOCENCE

My Christmas thoughts are that a further prolongation of the war ... probably means the disappearance of the social order we have known hitherto. With some regrets I think I am on the whole not sorry. The abolition of the rich will be rather a comfort and serve them right anyhow. What frightens me more is the prospect of *general* impoverishment. In another year's time we shall have forfeited the claim we had staked out in the New World and in exchange this country will be mortgaged to America. Well, the only course ... is to be buoyantly bolshevik; and as I lie in bed in the morning I reflect with a good deal of satisfaction that, because our rulers are as incompetent as they are mad and wicked, one particular era of a particular kind of civilisation is very nearly over.

J. M. Keynes to Florence Keynes, 24 December 1917

Like you, I can contemplate with a considerable degree of equanimity the reduction of large incomes – even including our own.... I suppose we shall all buy our meals from communal kitchens & that we are already beginning to provide for [this]. It will be more difficult to re-construct our houses so as to reduce the demand for domestic servants....

Florence Keynes to J. M. Keynes 26 December 1917

If we aim deliberately at the impoverishment of Central Europe, vengeance, I dare predict, will not limp.

J. M. Keynes, *The Economic Consequences of the Peace*, p. 170

12

Adapting to War

I. WAITING FOR EMPLOYMENT

Keynes was not allowed to remain in distracted idleness at Cambridge. Two days before England declared war he had received a mysterious letter from Basil Blackett at the Treasury saying he urgently wanted to pick his brains, 'for the Country's benefit'. Keynes persuaded his brother-in-law A. V. Hill to drive him up to London the same day in the sidecar of his motorcycle, and went straight to work at the Treasury. On 6 August he was able to report to his father from Treasury Chambers:

> The pressure of the financial crisis ought to be over by tomorrow.
> The Bankers completely lost their heads and have been simply dazed and unable to think two consecutive thoughts.
> Specie payments by the Bank of England have now been saved – by the skin of its teeth. The points now to concentrate on are the saving of the acceptance houses (I doubt if a single Director of the Bank of England is solvent today) and the settling of the £1 note issue. I've just heard that they consider I played an important part in preventing the suspension of specie payments, as it was my memorandum [which] converted Lloyd George.

Keynes published three lengthy accounts of the crisis, which he intended to use for a short book which never materialised. Essentially it arose from the inability of foreigners to pay their debts to City firms. By a double chain reaction, this threatened to deprive the Bank of England of the gold it needed to defend the gold standard.

At the end of July 1914, £350m of bills of exchange – debts owed by foreigners to the London accepting houses – were outstanding. The inability of foreigners to remit funds to London as these bills matured threatened the solvency of the holders of this debt and, in turn, their intermediate holders, the discount houses, and their ultimate holders, the joint stock banks. A second source of strain on the banks was the inability of foreigners to pay up on settlement date to the City stockbrokers through whom they had bought shares on the stock exchange. The forced sale of securities reduced the value of another part of the banks' assets. The banks reacted by calling in their loans from the discount houses (who were forced to get their bills re-discounted by the Bank of England at rising interest rates), cashing notes for gold at the Bank of England, and refusing to pay out gold to customers even for small amounts, thus producing queues in Threadneedle Street as people flocked to the Bank of England to obtain gold coin. The 'internal run' cost the Bank of England £12m of its £27m gold reserve in a few days. To protect its reserves bank rate was put up from 3 per cent on 29 July to 10 per cent on 1 August, and August bank holiday was extended by three days. The stock exchange was closed on 31 July.

The bank chairmen went to Asquith and Lloyd George on 1 August asking to be relieved of their obligation to pay out gold on demand. Lloyd George tended to side with them. Pending a decision, the government declared a month's moratorium on debts.

In this crisis Keynes gave the advice he was to continue to give throughout the war. In a crucial memorandum of 3 August, which converted Lloyd George, he argued against suspending specie payments 'before it is *absolutely* necessary'. He took Bagehot's position that the gold reserves were there to be used, not 'hoarded'. He employed the confidence argument. The future position of the City would be jeopardised if it suspended specie payments at the first sign of emergency. This was particularly so in view of the growth of London as banker for others' reserves which is 'profitable and enormously enhances London's position as a monetary centre'. Keynes suggested that gold payments be restricted internally, but retained for international transactions.[1] This was the opinion which, more or less, carried the day. The banks' gold reserves were centralised in the Bank of England. The Treasury was empowered to issue emergency currency notes of £1 and 10s, or 'Bradburies' as they were named, since they were signed by Sir John Bradbury, joint permanent secretary of the Treasury. Gold payments for external debts were kept. The banking crisis was over.

There remained the problem of restarting the City. Keynes argued that all that was necessary was for the Bank of England to guarantee new engagements by the accepting houses, combined with a moratorium on past acceptances, leaving the banks and discount houses to hold some bad debts for the time being. (No one, it must be emphasised, expected the war to go on for long.)[2] However, the government instead instituted a package of rescue operations which Keynes considered grossly extravagant. Guaranteed against loss by the government, the Bank of England bought up £180m worth of debt itself, relieving the City and joint stock banks at the expense of the taxpayer and flooding the money-market with funds which drove down interest rates and provided the basis for the inflationary finance of the early months of the war.[3]

What emerges from Keynes's published accounts in the *Economic Journal* and elsewhere is a profound antipathy towards the joint stock bankers. He criticised them for unduly restricting loans to the stock exchange, for calling in an unnecessary amount of loans from the discount market, for drawing gold from the Bank of England and hoarding it, and for refusing to pay customers gold when requested. 'Our system', he wrote, 'was endangered, not by the public running on the banks, but by the banks running on the Bank of England.'[4] To Marshall he complained on 10 October that Sir Felix Schuster, governor of the Union Bank, was cowardly, and Sir Edward Holden, chairman of the Midland Bank, was selfish; the rest were 'timid, voiceless and leaderless'. He blamed the low calibre of directors and bank managers.[5] However, a more recent writer, Marcello de Cecco, sees the actions of the bankers, as well as of other actors, as part of an ongoing power struggle in the City, with the joint stock banks, essentially, trying to take over the control of the gold reserve from the Bank of England, and lucrative business from the merchant banks. In a letter to Keynes, dated 9 October 1914, Sir Felix Schuster, rejecting Keynes's strictures, blamed the fall in share prices and the 'internal run' largely on the discount houses. Insofar as the banks contributed to the latter, it was because the Bank of England failed to supply them with the £5 and £10 notes being demanded by customers for their summer holidays, having run out of the paper on which to print them. More importantly, it was not the bank chairmen who were urging suspension of specie payments: it was Lord Cunliffe, governor of the Bank of England. Keynes retracted some of his criticisms.

In his *Economic Journal* article of December 1914 Keynes poked fun at the idea that a gold reserve was for display only: if it were so one might just as well 'melt the reserve into a great golden image of the chief cashier and place it on a monument so high that it could never be got down again'. A more important pointer to the future is his view that the gold standard was an interference with the task of currency management, 'the intellectual and scientific part of the problem [which] is solved already'. He feared that the influx of gold, which had followed Britain's success, alone among the Allies, in preserving specie payments, would produce inflation.

> If it proves one of the after effects of the present struggle, that gold is at last deposed from its despotic control over us and reduced to the position of a constitutional monarch, a new chapter of history will be opened. Man will have made another step forward in the attainment of self-government....[6]

There was a personal side to the banking crisis. Keynes and his father had lent money to the discount market. Like others in the same position, they feared a default. In urging the government, in his memorandum of 5 August, not to guarantee the bills held by the discount houses, Keynes was giving advice directly contrary to his own interests.

Keynes's memorandum of 3 August 1914 may have helped to turn Lloyd George into a currency expert. It did not lead to a partnership between the two men. Keynes's intervention did not secure him an immediate Whitehall appointment. Instead Lloyd George appointed the financial journalist, Sir

George Parish, whom he had long consulted on economic matters, as his Special Adviser. Keynes was sent back to Cambridge.

He tried to slip back into the old routine. He resumed work on the proofs of probability. On 23 August he went camping in Cornwall for a few days with the Olivier sisters. But he was restless. He wanted an occupation connected with the war. This he found in writing. His article on 'Currency Measures Abroad' had already appeared in the *Morning Post* on 11 August. From Asheham, where he stayed from 28 August to 7 September, he conducted a correspondence in the *Economist* about the gold holdings of the joint-stock banks. He finished his account of the financial crisis for the *Economic Journal.* Short of being in the war machine itself, the best he could do was to offer his advice from the outside. One man happy to listen was Edwin Montagu, since February Financial Secretary to the Treasury. In a letter of 4 September Keynes warned Montagu of the dangers of inflation and expressed mistrust of Lloyd George. 'As one of the few people who combine special knowledge of these things with *not* having their personal future at stake, I chafe at being a purely passive observer,' he wrote.[7] He slipped across to Paris in mid-December to compile 'Notes on French Finance'. He wrote newspaper articles on the financing of Germany's war effort, condemning the censor's policy of limiting access to the German press.[8] In these ways he was staking his claim for future employment.

On 10 October 1914 he returned to a Cambridge depopulated of undergraduates, and with the Backs behind King's occupied by a military hospital. He now lectured to 'blacks and women', comforted the 'wounded Tommies. . . . Some of them look very nice,' and helped Sheppard look after Belgian refugees – 'ugly, bourgeois, and bores'.[9] London living arrangements had changed too. At the end of September, the lease on 38 Brunswick Square expired. Keynes moved into rooms in 10 Ormond Street. Bloomsbury was once again rearranging its emotional affairs. Adrian Stephen, his affair with Duncan Grant over, had just got engaged to Karin Costelloe. Meanwhile Duncan had replaced Roger Fry as the object of Vanessa's love. Duncan was not in love with her, but their painting drew them together, and when the Brunswick Square ménage broke up, he went to live at 46 Gordon Square, taking a studio at 22 Fitzroy Street. Vanessa found Maynard very gloomy at the beginning of October: '[He] seems to be fearfully lonely in his rooms. He talked a great deal about Duncan & said rather bitterly I thought that it was strange that the effect of Adrian's marriage should be to separate him from Duncan – they had lived together now for 6 years off & on.'

On the credit side was Maynard's growing friendship with Vanessa herself, which started from their time in camp together in Norfolk in 1913, and ripened in April 1914, when Vanessa had joined Maynard's house party at Asheham, which he had rented from the Woolfs. Maynard's lack of delicacy, which offended even Lytton, excited the bawdy Vanessa, who wanted to be one of the boys. By the autumn of 1914 their intimacy was cemented by their unrequited love for Duncan. Vanessa offered to take Maynard as a lodger at 46 Gordon Square but he, sensing perhaps that the situation might become too emotionally fraught, decided to stay put at Ormond Street.

One course of action Maynard never considered was enlisting. This was not just because he thought he could help the war effort more by doing something else, but because fighting lacked for him any romantic appeal. His attitude was completely different from that of bored aristocrats like Julian Grenfell who saw in war an escape from uselessness. Grenfell's attitude was shared by Maynard's friend Ferenc Békássy, and it greatly distressed him. He did his best to dissuade him from returning home to enlist in the Hungarian army. He also did his best to stop his brother Geoffrey from volunteering for the Royal Army Medical Corps, again unavailingly. He was terrified lest Duncan, pressurised by his family's military tradition, should volunteer.

On the other hand, Maynard, at first, had no great anti-war feeling. He was not a pacifist, and was not interested in the political origins of the war. For example, he had nothing to do with the Union of Democratic Control, started by left-wing Liberals and liberal-minded socialists who attributed the war to Britain's secret military commitments to France. His instinctive attitude was that of the economist and civil servant. The war was a fact of life. It should be run as efficiently as possible while it lasted, and he felt (rightly) that he had a contribution to make to that end. He also shared the common view that the war would end quickly – not because he believed that the Entente's forces would soon be in Berlin, but because he thought, like Norman Angell, that the modern world was organised for peace, and could not readily be put on a war footing. His initial attitude to the war was thus fairly cool because both its appeal and its horror lay outside the limits of his imagination.

Maynard's friends were divided in their response. Békássy returned to fight for the Central Powers. Another close friend of Maynard, F. L. ('Peter') Lucas, a Trinity classicist who had recently been elected an Apostle, also joined up. So did Rupert Brooke. Desmond MacCarthy volunteered for the Red Cross. But most of Bloomsbury and their friends resisted the call to arms. In his biographer's words, 'Lytton himself seems to have believed that all physically fit intellectuals should be prepared to defend the shores of England, but with this reservation: no intellectuals were in fact physically fit.'[10] In intervals of reading Maynard's article on the financial crisis at The Lacket, near Marlborough, which he had rented from Hilton Young, Lytton 'knit a muffler in navy blue wool for the neck of one of our sailor-lads. I don't know which but I have my visions.'[11] Basically, Bloomsbury just wanted to be left alone. Unwillingness to fight did not as yet extend to active opposition to the war. In this respect it was unlike Bertrand Russell, who from the start opposed it on political grounds. In the Russell generation of Apostles there was a considerable reserve of pro-German, anti-Russian feeling, to which Maynard himself was not immune.

It was only as reports of casualties started to come that the horror of what was happening dawned on Maynard. On 15 August, he had had a cheerful letter from Freddie Hardman: 'Is there anything particular you would like me to bring you back from Berlin – a little etching or so?' Maynard wrote back, on 25 October, a letter full of Cambridge gossip. It was returned with the word 'Killed' scrawled across it. Hardman had died leading his men in hand-to-hand fighting. 'It is too awful that such things should happen,' Maynard wrote to Duncan on 4 November. 'It makes one bitterly miserable and long that the war should stop quickly on almost any terms. I can't bear that he should have died.' On 9 November he reported that Lucas had come to say goodbye. 'It is dreadful that he should go. All my subconscious feelings about things are now deeply depressed, which they weren't before. It seems to make it hardly any better that we should be winning.'

II. TREASURY OFFICIAL

On 6 January 1915, on the recommendation of Edwin Montagu, Keynes at last got a job in Whitehall as assistant to Sir George Paish, at a salary of £600 a year. The appointment was temporary, for the duration of the war. He was given a desk in Basil Blackett's room in Treasury Chambers, Whitehall (looking out to Horse Guards at the back) and allowed to continue editing the *Economic Journal*, and writing, provided he did not use official materials. He started work on 18 January. On the 21st he wrote to his father: 'After a slack beginning I am now very busy, having become Secretary of a Secret Committee of the Cabinet presided over by the Prime Minister. First meeting this morning. So I know exactly what a cabinet meeting is like. This is of course absolutely private.'[12] (Asquith told his confidante Venetia Stanley that the secretary of the Committee was 'a clever young Cambridge don called Keynes'.) The Committee was to enquire into rising food prices. By 25 January Keynes had produced a memorandum; over the next couple of months he was active in organising government purchases of Indian wheat at below the world market price.

On 30 January his father received more news: 'I *am* going to Paris – and we start Sunday or Monday. It's a most select party: Lloyd George, Montagu, the Governor of the Bank of England [Lord Cunliffe], and me, together with a private secretary. We are to be guests of the French Govt.'[13] Keynes's chance came because Lloyd George had 'no use', he told Montagu, for his permanent secretary, Bradbury and for Malcolm Ramsay, head of the Financial Division. Montagu suggested Keynes, and so he was chosen, together with Blackett, to represent the Treasury. His friends found him 'happy and excited' at the prospect of the trip. Britain, he told them, was to lend Russia between £60m and £100m, and Italy a 'large sum which simply means bribing [it] to come in [to the war] ... fearfully immoral'.[14] In Paris Keynes met Alexandre Ribot, the French Finance Minister, and attended a reception given by President Poincaré. The newspapers registered a new arrival on the Allied scene: Professor Kains of the London School of Economics.

The conference which Keynes attended in Paris from 2 to 5 February was the first inter-Ally conference. It inaugurated the whole complex system of inter-Ally war credits. Russia, and to a lesser extent France, could no longer export enough goods or gold to pay for their purchases abroad of essential war materials. Britain, whose international financial position was much stronger, had to start financing them. Britain and France agreed to make a joint loan to Russia; Russia agreed to increase its wheat exports as soon as the Dardanelles were open. Russia and France also agreed to transfer gold to the Bank of England. Britain's first credit to France followed in April. From the decisions taken at the conference stemmed the whole post-war debt problem, since it was decided that transfers were to take the form of loans, not grants. Once Britain started to finance its allies, it was inevitable that it would seek to control their foreign spending, so as to make sure that the money was not frittered away or simply used to support the exchange value of their currencies. Financial control led, by stages, to a centralised buying system, with Allied orders abroad placed through Britain, and paid for by British credits earmarked for Allied accounts at the Bank of England. This was the system which Keynes helped to build up over the next two years, and over which he came to preside.

At this stage he was simply one junior adviser among many. But he was quick to make his mark at the Treasury, helped in this by the rapid eclipse of Sir George Paish. On the outbreak of the war, he later recalled, Paish

> was sent for by Mr. Lloyd George to go to the Treasury as his leading financial expert, and for about a day and a half in August 1914 he was very important at the Treasury. As usual, however, Mr. Lloyd George soon got bored with him and stopped reading his lengthy memoranda. He was, however, given a good salary and an exalted title ... and ... a room at a considerable distance, over at the Road Board in Caxton House.[15]

Keynes served in the Treasury in both world wars. Its atmosphere was much more congenial to him than that of the India Office. It had been placed by Gladstone at the heart of British government to enforce economy on the other Departments – chiefly in those days, the military – and inherited the Gladstonian doctrine of annually balanced budgets and Gladstone's belief that money was best left to fructify in the pockets of the people. These precepts were not obviously suitable to the conduct of a great war, nor, as Keynes was to point out much later, to the conduct of economic policy during a depression. But between 1914 and 1918 the Treasury fought a strong rearguard action against war spending without limit, and found no more redoubtable champion than Keynes. The Treasury lived up to its own economical precepts. The Department he joined was small and exclusive, and even the unprecedented demands of total war did not succeed in expanding the permanent numbers of the administrative class by more than three, from 37 to 40, though about a dozen temporaries were added. The officials were split into six divisions, which between them had charge of raising the revenue and allocating the spending of the government. Economy of numbers meant that junior and even temporary officials could exercise large responsibilities. Keynes already knew Ralph Hawtrey, the Treasury's one economist, and Basil Blackett, a first-class clerk in the Finance (1D) Division. He got to know others, like Otto Niemeyer, with whom he would clash in the 1920s, and Frederick Phillips, who would become an ally in the 1930s. It was in this 'rather select club' that Keynes gained the knowledge of government finance and the 'insider' reputation which gave unique authority to his later public pronouncements.

As Elizabeth Johnson rightly says, Keynes 'seems to have possessed a Treasury eye from the start'.[16] He was quick to relate individual spending proposals to overall principles of financial policy, and to appreciate the connection between internal and external finance. He had the indispensable civil servant's gift of producing crisp, lucid memoranda at a moment's notice. He enjoyed the atmosphere of the Treasury – 'very clever, very dry and in a certain sense very cynical; intellectually very self-confident and not subject to the whims of people who feel that they are less hidden, and are not quite sure that they know their case'. He appreciated that its aesthetic – the very form of a Treasury draft – was an indispensable ingredient of its prestige. Here was one source of his lack of rapport with Lloyd George. The Chancellor, he wrote later, 'had no aesthetic sense of the formalisms'. He also 'never had the faintest idea of the meaning of money'.[17] On his first trip to Paris, Keynes did not hesitate to tell Lloyd George to his face that his views on French finance were 'rubbish'.[18]

Maynard celebrated his appointment at the Treasury by giving a party for seventeen on 6 January 1915 at the Café Royal. Guests included the Bells, Sheppard, Cecil Taylor, Frankie Birrell, Duncan Grant, David Garnett, assorted Oliviers and Stracheys, and Desmond MacCarthy. Afterwards they went back to 46 Gordon Square for Clive and Vanessa's party. There they listened to a Mozart trio and then went upstairs for the last scene of a Racine play, performed by three puppets made by Duncan, with words spoken by the weird-voiced Stracheys. 'The evening ended with Gerald Shove enthroned in the centre of the room, crowned with roses....'[19] Bloomsbury was recovering its nerve after the initial shock of war. Ottoline Morrell had resumed her Thursday-evening dinner parties, where much drink was consumed, and dancing became wild to Philip Morrell's accompaniment on the pianola. The gaiety of those who fought and those who stayed behind had not yet been much dimmed: the ghastly slaughter was still largely in the future.

At his dinner party, Maynard had put David Garnett between Vanessa and Duncan and that, figuratively, was where he was to remain for the next four years. Duncan fell passionately, and jealously, in love with Bunny, whose own animal spirits were, as Michael Holroyd writes, 'strong and surprisingly various'.[20] (He even did Maynard a 'good turn' one night.) Vanessa, who loved Duncan, realised that the only way she could hold him was to allow Bunny to share their lives. A ménage-à-trois soon developed, conducted in a succession of rented farmhouses. In the spring of 1915 they took Eleanor, near West Wittering, Sussex, from the St John Hutchinsons. Maynard would visit them at weekends, a semi-avuncular fourth. 'Till this morning', Duncan wrote to Hilton Young from Eleanor in April 1915,

> there was a house party of sorts consisting of Lytton Strachey and Keynes. Maynard is a very grand person now.... He goes to the Treasury every day and works very hard and he told me he had saved the Government £1,000,000 in a morning.... Lytton is getting very benign and is writing I'm told a very good book consisting of short lives of eminently disagreeable Victorians....[21]

Maynard found no one to take Duncan's place in his life. Frankie Birrell slept with him 'for old time's sake', and there were pick-ups. These casual adventures were not without danger. His landlady at 10 Great Ormond Street, her interest aroused by the odd sexual goings-on, hinted at blackmail.[22] Maynard decamped in February 1915, renting 3 Gower Street. Here he let upper rooms to Gerald Shove and John Sheppard, who was working as a translator at the War Office. The attics were taken by Katherine Mansfield and Middleton Murry, who later married.

Absorption in Whitehall and Bloomsbury helped keep Keynes's mind off the fate of his fighting friends as well as the larger issues which preoccupied some of his anti-war ones. But to the latter his gaiety seemed forced, his arguments insincere. He was good at his work – tossing off elegant memoranda at twenty-four hours' notice – and enjoyed it. Moreover, pardonably identifying the public interest with his own employment, he convinced himself that the conduct of the war was at last in capable hands. 'We are bound to win – & in great style too, having at the last minute applied all our brains & all our wealth to the problem,' he told the Woolfs over oysters at Richmond on 20 January 1915. But he was uncomfortable when asked why he had allowed *his* brain to be mobilised. His standard answer was that he worked only for pleasure – and war work gave him pleasure. Bertrand

Russell and D. H. Lawrence, with whom Maynard dined in Cambridge on 7 March 1915, were not alone in finding this answer an evasion. 'Keynes', Russell wrote to Ottoline Morrell, 'was hard, intellectual, insincere, using his intellect to hide the torment in his soul.... [He] spoke as tho' he only wanted a succession of pleasant moments, which of course is not really true.' Both Russell and Lawrence attributed Keynes's frivolity to the 'sterilizing' effect of homosexuality; Lawrence went as far as to find Keynes 'corrupt and unclean'.[23] Yet there was truth in Keynes's reply, though it does not entirely reflect credit on him. He had not begun to think seriously about his own relationship to the war. He was fascinated by his work – that was justification enough. More disturbing thoughts he brushed aside with the reflection that the war was bound to end soon. 'German finance is crumbling,' he told the Woolfs in January.[24]

Yet depression was never far below the surface of his buoyancy. He wrote to Duncan on 25 April:

> This has been a horrible weekend, and I feel again, although I thought I would not, as I did after Freddie's death. Yesterday came news that two of our undergraduates were killed, both of whom I knew, though not very well, and was fond of. And to-day Rupert's death. In spite of all one has ever said I find myself crying for him. It is too horrible, a nightmare to be stopt anyhow. May no other generation live under the cloud we have to live under.

On 25 June Békássy was killed in Bukovina. Maynard reminisced about him to Duncan before adding, 'But it's no use talking about him. I think it's better to forget these things as quickly as possible.'

The change of government in May 1915 brought Keynes new responsibilities. On 19 May Asquith formed a coalition with the Conservatives. Two things brought it about. 'The dearth of munitions had become a public scandal. And Lord Fisher [the First Sea Lord], after "anxious reflection", had come to the conclusion that he could no longer continue as the colleague of Churchill at the Admiralty.'[25] In the background was the failure of the Anglo-French spring offensives on the Western Front – beaten back it was alleged because the artillery ran out of shells – and the setback at the Dardanelles. Lloyd George was made the first Minister of Munitions; Reginald McKenna went to the Treasury, 'holding the Exchequer as a seat-warmer for Lloyd George'.[26] Maynard became a member of the Treasury's Finance Division, centrally concerned with the financial direction of the war. Early in June he accompanied the new Chancellor to Nice for a day's conference with the Finance Minister of Italy, Britain's newest ally. Crossing the Channel in a battleship and returning in a destroyer filled him with childlike excitement.

No sooner had he started on his new duties than he was obliged to take an enforced rest of almost two months, afflicted first by appendicitis, which required an emergency operation, and then by pneumonia. It was not till 9 July that he returned to Cambridge, by car, with his parents. On 14 July he was able to dine at King's. A couple of days later he continued his convalescence at Garsington, near Oxford, which Ottoline Morrell had just transformed from a rather run-down Tudor manor house into a lush, perfumed oasis for her writer and painter friends. Ottoline 'liked Keynes immensely' – better than in the very first days of the war, when he had stayed overnight at Bedford Square. Then she saw him as 'that satyr Keynes, greedy for work, fame, influence, domination, admiration', with a manner which, except to a few intimate friends, 'borders on the insolent'. Under the more relaxed conditions at Garsington she started to appreciate 'the atmos-phere of his personality – a detached, meditating and yet half-caressing interest in those he is speaking to, head on one side, a kindly yet tolerant smile and very charming eyes wandering, searching and speculating, then probably a frank, intimate, and perhaps laughing home-thrust . . . '27 In the following months, Maynard frequently made up house-parties at Garsington, mingling with Bloomsbury friends and a sprinkling of Liberal politicians. On this occasion he went on for a weekend with Lord Cunliffe, the governor of the Bank of England, on the Isle of Wight, before returning to the Treasury at the beginning of August.

13

Keynes and the First World War

I. WHAT KIND OF WAR?

No sooner had Keynes returned to active duty than he found himself involved in a big row between McKenna and Lloyd George about the shape of the British war effort. The Treasury had a well-defined position, which it called 'discrimination'. There were not enough resources to go round. Therefore one had to choose where to put them – raising large armies, producing shells or producing goods for export. As Chancellor, Lloyd George had accepted this logic.[1] But a change of office brought a change of view. As Minister of Munitions Lloyd George now expected enough shells for a seventy-division field army. McKenna, however, inherited Lloyd George's previous programme of 'discrimination' – which he interpreted as discriminating against great armies and munitions in favour of the export trade. The Treasury's argument was simple. The financial structure of the Alliance depended on Britain's being able to export or borrow enough to pay for the Alliance's external spending. So the export industries had to be kept going at all costs; and Britain must maintain its creditworthiness with the United States by not allowing its exchange rate to fall. Lloyd George tended to pooh-pooh such arguments. There were more resources available, he claimed, than the Treasury believed. For example, women could be drawn into war work; and the Americans would always provide credit in their own interest.

In McKenna the Treasury had got a Chancellor after its own heart. Lloyd George and he were temperamentally poles apart. 'A mind that saw everything in pictures clashed with one that saw everything in figures; emotion was brought daily to earth by calculation.'[2] He and Lloyd George would have irritated each other at the best of times. Now they were also on opposite sides of the political argument. Lloyd George, together with most Conservative members of the Coalition, was in favour of conscription. McKenna, Grey, Runciman, Crewe and most of the old Liberals round Asquith opposed it.

It was in relation to conscription that the economic arguments became politically relevant. That there was nothing so desirable as winning the war was generally agreed. But there was room for much debate about what kind of war Britain should be fighting. The Treasury line gave comfort to all those who believed that Britain should fight a war which interfered as little as possible with 'business as usual'. This was basically the position of the Asquithians. They accepted the war as a necessary evil, but feared its consequences and tried to limit its damage. The weakness in the Asquithian position was Asquith himself. He was against conscription; but favoured the massive British military build-up which made it inevitable. Asquith did not realise this. He and his Secretary of State for War, Lord Kitchener, supported the generals' strategy of massing guns and men for a breakthrough on the Western Front in order to avoid conscription, not to promote it. But their policy depended on the generals winning the quick victories which they promised but failed to achieve. Lloyd George did not suffer from this inconsistency. He wanted Britain to fight the total war which would give scope for his organising and political genius. But his instinctive mistrust of all experts extended to the generals and their promises of military break-through in Flanders. He wanted great armies – but to use them elsewhere.

McKenna at the Treasury was clearly in a key position to influence this debate, which meant that Keynes, who soon became his favourite adviser, was drawn into it too. The two men, who came from very much the same background, got on excellently. Keynes's economics and sympathies both inclined him to the Asquithian side. He too, at this stage, was not against the war, but for limiting its effects. He was well placed to appreciate the impact of domestic policy on external finance; and to understand how the external constraint might be used to influence domestic policy. Above all, he was desperately anxious that the state should not interfere with the lives of his friends. All his instincts, therefore, favoured Britain fighting a war of subsidies, not of great armies. This was traditional British policy, and made economic sense. Its morality is questionable. It suggested that British liberals were indifferent to people being killed, provided they were foreigners. Keynes soon realised this, and from 1916 onwards he wanted to end the war by a compromise peace.

Some characteristic attitudes emerge, which were to be repeated in the Second World War. Expecting a short war, the government had decided to finance its extra expenditure by borrowing. However, its first war loan of £350m in November 1914, had been largely taken up by the banks, who counted the Treasury bonds as part of their reserves, and lent just as much as before to private customers. So inflation had taken off. As soon as he got to the Treasury Keynes started saying that government spending should be financed by taxation, not by inflationary loans. He minuted on 15 May 1915: 'The public is the only ultimate source of command over the material resources of the country; and direct application to them is the only safe way of securing command over these resources, except for temporary periods for amounts that are not too large.'[3] Keynes was against inflation because of its effects on the balance of payments, and thus on the sterling–dollar exchange rate.[4] The government must either 'conscript' wealth on a much greater scale than it was doing, or reduce the rate of increase of its war spending.

Keynes favoured the latter on political grounds. McKenna decided to pursue both strategies simultaneously. In his budget of 21 September, he increased income tax and imposed excess profits tax and also the 'McKenna duties' on certain imports. At the same time he started arguing the case for moderating Lloyd George's munitions programme.

E. V. Morgan writes that 'the dollar exchange was the crux of the problem, for upon the maintenance of an adequate supply of dollars at a reasonable price, depended the whole vast purchasing programme of food, materials and munitions for ourselves and our Allies'.[5] By the spring of 1915 the dollar exchange had turned adverse – that is, American exporters held more claims on sterling than British exporters held claims on dollars. As a result the price of obtaining dollars started to go up. In April 1915 the Bank of England began shipping gold from Ottawa to the British government's New York purchasing agent, J. P. Morgan, and buying dollar securities held by British subjects. (In July McKenna saved one desperate situation by commandeering $40m worth of Prudential Assurance's American securities to pay the advance on a munitions contract.) At the same time, Britain put pressure on its allies to centralise their gold holdings at the Bank of England, in return for British credits.

These measures could not avert an exchange crisis in August 1915. By I September, sterling was selling at a discount of 7 per cent in New York (a pound was fetching $4.47 instead of the official rate of $4.80). To restore the position the Bank shipped more gold to New York; the Treasury also opened its own account at J. P. Morgan, into which it paid the proceeds of sales of dollar securities, collateral and gold. But an American loan, negotiated in September by Lord Reading, was disappointing, only £100m being obtained instead of the hoped-for £200m, and of that only £33m was taken up by the American public. It was clear that, outside the New York financial community, and its associated munitions interests, there was little enthusiasm for lending money to the Allies.

On 23 August 1915, McKenna presented his case against Lloyd George's demands for larger armies to a new Committee on War Policy, primed by a memorandum from Keynes. His chief argument was that 'the labour forces of the United Kingdom are so fully engaged in useful occupations that any further diversion of them to military uses is *alternative* and not *additional* to the other means by which the United Kingdom is assisting the Allied cause'. It was not possible to control production, he maintained, without controlling consumption in an equally drastic manner. Hence 'without a policy for the confiscation of private income, a considerably increased army and a continuance of subsidies to allies are *alternative*'.[6]

The over-ingenuity of McKenna's arguments was not the decisive factor in his failure to win over his colleagues. An important decision in favour of the Western military strategy had already been taken. On 20 August – three days before McKenna addressed the special Cabinet Committee –

Kitchener told the Cabinet that he had been forced to agree to the French demand for a renewed autumn offensive. Joffre, the French Commander-in-Chief, was convinced he could win a great victory. For the British the result of the Battle of Loos – which opened on 25 September and was called off a fortnight later, without gaining any ground – was 60,000 casualties; the French lost 150,000. The generals' response was to plan bigger offensives for 1916.

As Zeppelins dropped bombs round him in Gower Street, Maynard wrote to his mother (8 September), 'I'm extremely busy at the Treasury, but am enjoying the work. Today I have been commissioned by the Chancellor to write an important memorandum; and, as usual, have only a day to do it.' Keynes's memorandum of 9 September, 'The Financial Prospects of this Financial Year', which was circulated to the Cabinet, formed the basis of McKenna's statement to the Cabinet on 13 September in preparation for his emergency autumn budget. McKenna said he could keep things going till 31 March 1916 with the aid of familiar expedients; but reverted to his argument that, beyond that, Britain must conserve resources to outlast Germany financially. Keynes's note took an extremely gloomy view of the financial prospect. He calculated the budget deficit for the current year at £700m and growing rapidly. About £500m of this deficiency could be met, he thought, from 'real' resources: the proceeds from taxes and loans, the sale or liquidation of capital assets, and the proceeds of loans from abroad. The balance would have to be met by 'inflationism' – by printing money. 'We ought to be able to do this without producing a catastrophe in the current financial year, provided peace puts us in a position to cancel this inflationism immediately afterwards. Otherwise the expenditure of the succeeding months will rapidly render our difficulties insupportable.' The reason was that inflation would bring about a collapse of the exchange and with it the ability to pay for imports from the USA.[7]

According to one commentator, 'McKenna's report and Keynes's memorandum marked the emergence of the Chancellor and his brilliant young aide as the Laocoön and Cassandra of the British Government.'[8] Keynes's alarmist assessment infuriated Lloyd George. In his *War Memoirs* he wrote that:

> Mr. McKenna's nerve was shaken by these vaticinations of his chief adviser Mr. J. M. Keynes. The latter was much too mercurial and impulsive a counsellor for a great emergency. He dashed at conclusions with acrobatic ease. It made things no better that he rushed into opposite conclusions with the same agility.... When the hour of impending doom struck and we still bought greater quantities than ever of food, raw material and munitions from abroad and were paying for them and our credit was still high, the date of the impending collapse was postponed until the autumn.[9]

The McKenna–Keynes line failed to sway Asquith either. Its financial pessimism encouraged him to gamble on a quick military victory as a way of
evading his growing political dilemmas. Thus, paradoxically, it encouraged
commitment to the Western strategy which, in the long run, required
conscription.

McKenna's defeat in the autumn of 1915 was a defining movement
in the war. The Treasury lost control over domestic spending. This meant
the war would be financed mainly by loans, since the tax base could not
be expanded sufficiently. And the Treasury's defeat made conscription
inevitable.

In the Treasury, preparing for the budget is always the most hectic time
of the year, and by 15 October Keynes was writing to his father that he was
'exceedingly done up ... it was a combination of work and excitement....
I've been moving in very high life most of the week ... and I am spending
the weekend with the Prime Minister.' In her diary for Saturday 16 October,
Margot Asquith wrote that she and a 'Treasury man Keynes' had won nine
pounds at bridge off Lady de Trafford and Edwin Montagu. This weekend
was the start of Maynard's friendship with the Asquiths. The Prime Minister
liked to spend the weekends away from London at his country house, The
Wharf, in Sutton Courtenay, Berkshire, relaxing with friends over a game of
bridge. He and his daughter Violet would sometimes motor over for Sunday
lunch to Ottoline at Garsington, where the mandarin liberalism of Balliol
College, Oxford, mingled warily with the subversive culture of Apostolic
Cambridge. Maynard was not a great bridge player; but he was better than
Margot, who played with ardent incompetence; and he won large sums of
money at The Wharf and at 10 Downing Street, despite the distracting
attentions of Margot's flirtatious stepdaughter, Elizabeth Asquith (later
Princess Bibesco). Margot, whose insomniac nights were spent in writing
acute character sketches of her prominent friends, left none of Maynard.
Was he still too junior to engage the full attention of a prime minister's
wife? By the time he became a great man, Margot Asquith's diary had
stopped.

In a last effort to preserve the voluntary recruitment system, Lord Derby
was made director-general of recruiting in October 1915, with the promise
that if his recruiting campaign failed, the government would introduce
compulsion. Keynes went on pointing out that 'to carry overseas each new
division of an expeditionary force is *alternative* to carrying food, munitions
or other necessary commodities to the allies or to ourselves'.[10] But these
arguments made no impression on the course of events. Asquith agreed
with them;[11] but he would not go against the advice of the generals, and by
the end of 1915 the army was firmly in the hands of the 'Westerners'. Both
Haig, the new Commander-in-Chief, and Robertson, the new Chief of the
Imperial General Staff, were 'unswerving in their belief that the war could
only be won by killing Germans in Flanders. And they were both prepared

to accept without flinching the British share of the casualties which this must involve.' On 28 December the War Cabinet approved of Robertson's plan for a vast new Allied offensive in the spring of 1916. 'In these circumstances,' wrote Roy Jenkins, 'the job of the politicians ceased to be that of looking for strategic alternatives and became concentrated upon supplying men and munitions for the slaughter.'[12] The same day, 28 December 1915, the Cabinet accepted the principle of military conscription. On 27 January 1916 the Military Service Act received the Royal Assent. The question of what kind of war Britain should fight had been settled.

II. CONSCIENTIOUS OBJECTION TO CONSCRIPTION?

Under the Military Service Act all bachelors and childless widowers between eighteen and forty-one were 'deemed ... to have been duly enlisted'. Certificates of exemption could be granted by government departments to those of their officials who were doing work of 'national importance'. Others could apply for exemption to local tribunals on grounds of (a) the national importance of their work, (b) hardship, (c) ill-health, or (d) 'a conscientious objection to the undertaking of combatant service'. A tribunal could either reject such an application outright or give an exemption on one of the four grounds. An exemption could be absolute, conditional or temporary. A conscientious objector could be given an exemption outright or 'from combatant service only or may be given [it] on condition that [he] is or will be engaged on some work which in the opinion of the Tribunal is of national importance'. The Act provided an appeals procedure from the decisions of the local tribunal.

In a volume of personal reminiscences, *Old Friends*, published in 1957, Clive Bell wrote: 'It seems not to be known ... that ... Keynes was a conscientious objector.'[13] The evidence is that, on receiving his call-up papers, he applied for exemption on grounds of conscientious objection, was summoned to appear before the Holborn Local Tribunal on 28 March 1916, wrote from the Treasury on 27 March that he was too busy to attend, and received a letter two days later, saying that his application for exemption had been dismissed because 'you have already been exempted for six months by the Treasury'.

That Keynes applied for exemption from military service on grounds of 'conscientious objection to conscription' is beyond dispute, despite the obfuscation of Keynes's first biographer, Roy Harrod. A draft of a letter, dated 28 February, intended for the Holborn Tribunal reads as follows:

> I claim complete exemption because I have a conscientious objec-
> tion to surrendering my liberty of judgment on so vital a question as
> undertaking military service. I do not say that there are not conceivable
> circumstances in which I should voluntarily offer myself for military
> service. But having regard to the actually existing circumstances, I am
> certain that it is not my duty so to offer myself, and I solemnly assert to
> the Tribunal that my objection to submit to authority in this matter is
> truly conscientious. I am not prepared on such an issue as this to
> surrender my right of decision, as to what is or is not my duty, to any
> other person, and I should think it morally wrong to do so.[14]

The Tribunal must have received a letter of this character or it would not
have summoned him to appear before it.

The ground of Keynes's objection to being called up is not quite clear.
Was he taking the classical liberal view that the state has no right to
conscript its citizens for military service under any circumstances? Or was
he arguing that if, in the actual circumstances, he did not believe it was his
duty to volunteer, the state had no right to make him fight? Keynes did not
object to conscription in the Second World War. The most reasonable
interpretation of the letter is that he was simply asserting the right of
conscientious objection. The state had no right to compel the individual to
do something he conscientiously believed to be wrong. Since Keynes was
not a pacifist on principle, the inference is that he was saying something
about the war itself – that it was not the kind of war for which he felt it was
his duty to volunteer to fight.

The question, then, is why he appealed for exemption on grounds of
conscientious objection, having already been exempted because he was at
the Treasury. The obvious explanation is that it was a statement of a
position, a gesture of solidarity with his Bloomsbury friends, many of whom
were pacifists or opposed to the war on political grounds. But there is
another explanation: Keynes's letter was intended for use. Since, when he
wrote it out, he had already been exempted by the Treasury, this must mean
that on 28 February 1916 he was thinking of *resigning.* If so, his non-
appearance at the Tribunal a month later can be explained by the fact that
he no longer intended to resign, and was therefore no longer bothered by
the verdict.

How close did Keynes come to resignation in January–February 1916?
Michael Holroyd takes the view that there was 'no chance of resignation'.[15]
However, there is important contrary evidence which needs to be set out to
give a picture of his state of mind in the circumstances in which he found
himself.

Conscription cast its shadow before it. From the autumn of 1915
Keynes's involvement in the war effort came under increasing criticism from
his friends, some of whom were beginning to suffer. In October that year,

Duncan Grant and David Garnett had left for Paris, where Duncan had been commissioned to design costumes for a play. At Folkestone, Duncan was abused by an English officer for being a pacifist and, on arrival in France, refused admittance and deported as an undesirable alien. Keynes succeeded in getting the officer reprimanded; but Bunny, who had been allowed to proceed to Paris, wrote him an angry letter on 15 November: 'What are you? Only an intelligence that they need in their extremity.... A genie taken incautiously out of King's ... by savages to serve them faithfully for their savage ends, and then – back you go into the bottle.' David Garnett felt ashamed of this letter, but to his surprise Maynard 'agreed that there was a great deal of truth in what I had said'.[16]

Throughout January 1916, Keynes's attitude fluctuated. On the 6th he told his father he wanted to resign. On the 13th he wrote to Florence that he would stay on 'until they actually begin to torture my friends'. A real split, he thought, would 'bring peace nearer'. These excerpts have to be set in context. On 29 December 1915, five of Asquith's ministers – Simon, McKenna, Runciman, Grey and Augustine Birrell – had submitted their resignations. Asquith gave the background in a letter he wrote to Edwin Montagu the previous day:

> The ground they [McKenna and Runciman] put forward is not the actual decision of the Cabinet: indeed they both say they will not oppose the proposed Bill. The ground is that the reasons given for the decision involved the raising of men for 67 Divisions, and that in their view such men are not forthcoming, without fatal injury to our other resources & obligations.

By offering a compromise setting up a Cabinet Committee to 'investigate, over a period of a month, the competing military and economic claims'[17], Asquith persuaded all but Simon to stay.

What would Keynes have done had McKenna and Runciman gone? There is important evidence on this point. On 31 December 1915 Lytton Strachey wrote to Ottoline Morrell:

> I went to see [Bertrand Russell] this morning and we had lunch with Maynard in an extraordinary underground tunnel, with city gents sitting on high stools like parrots on perches, somewhere near Trafalgar Square. Maynard ... couldn't tell us much – except that McKenna is still wobbling; but he seemed to think it not unlikely that he and Runciman would resign – in which case he would resign too, and help them fight it.[18]

When McKenna decided to stay, Maynard stayed on to help his chief fight for the Treasury position. The Treasury section of the Committee's report was drafted by Keynes in late January. The key argument was that the Chancellor attached decisive importance to the maintenance of specie payments, and that this was inconsistent with the policy of 'raising great armies'. The Committee's report was signed by Asquith, Austen Chamberlain and McKenna on 4 February 1916. It concluded that the risks of maintaining a sixty-plus-division army in the field could be contemplated for a short period, but only with the help of underspending by the Allies. It was, in effect, a gamble on a quick victory. Since McKenna signed the 4 February report, why should Keynes have still been contemplating resignation on 28 February, the date of his letter to the Holborn Tribunal? Here we must introduce another factor: the pressure on him to do so by his Bloomsbury friends, and particularly by Lytton Strachey, which reached its maximum shortly before Keynes sent off his letter.

Applications for exemption had to be in by 2 March. Practically all the male members of Bloomsbury decided to claim exemption as conscientious objectors. It is too sweeping to call them all pacifists. Gerald Shove was. But in the early days of the war it would have been hard to find any member of Bloomsbury who would not have been prepared to fight – in principle. It was the progress of the war itself that changed attitudes. By 1916 no one in Bloomsbury believed any longer that the objects and possibilities of the war justified the sacrifices being demanded in its name – sacrifices of lives and liberties. Maynard shared the political and ethical positions taken up by his friends. He had come to the conclusion that it was wrong to continue the war. He wanted a 'peace without victory'. He knew this was the view of some members of the Cabinet, notably Lord Lansdowne. He would have preferred them to resign and lead a campaign for the opening of peace negotiations.

But, as Paul Levy rightly points out,[19] the very fact that this was his position demanded some sort of response from him. How could he justify his own war work if he disagreed with the objects and methods of the war? Keynes could hardly have replied that it was his 'duty' since, as he wrote in 1938, 'we entirely repudiated a personal liability on us to obey general rules'. He had promised to resign if McKenna did; but what, in the end, did McKenna's conscience have to do with his? 'Certainly', writes Michael Holroyd, 'both Lytton and Russell felt he had "ratted", and, individually, they both pressed him to quit the Treasury, reasoning that it must be impossible to reconcile his avowed sympathy for conscientious objectors with the job of demonstrating how to kill Germans as cheaply as possible.'[20] The climax of this pressure came on 20 February 1916, when Lytton Strachey 'put the conscientious objector's equivalent to the white feather on Keynes's dinner plate'.[21] Strachey had cut out a newspaper report of a vehemently militaristic speech by Edwin Montagu ('it had every horror – not only protection but the necessity for smashing Germany etc.', he reported to his brother James) and enclosed it with a single-line letter to Keynes: 'Dear Maynard, Why are you still in the Treasury? Yours, Lytton.' Strachey's letter to his brother goes on:

I was going to post it to him, but he happened to be dining at Gordon Square where I also was. So I put the letter on his plate. He really *was* rather put out when he read the extract.... The poor fellow seemed very decent about it, and admitted that *part* of his reason for staying was the pleasure he got from his being able to do the work so well. He also seemed to think he was doing a great service to the country by saving some millions per week.... He at last admitted that there *was* a point at which he *would* think it necessary to leave – but what that point was he couldn't say.[22]

The next day Keynes sent off a cheque for £50 to the National Council against Conscription. He got the Treasury six-month certificate of exemption on 23 February. Five days later he applied for exemption on the grounds of conscientious objection to meet the 2 March deadline. Was it a gesture of appeasement or a contingency plan? The most probable answer is that he was keeping his options open. He had not decided to resign, but he might. He had indicated to his mother the circumstances in which he would: if they started 'torturing my friends'. No one knew yet how the appeal system would work out in practice. The general expectation in Bloomsbury was that many of them would go to prison. If Maynard resigned, he would refuse to volunteer or be drafted. His position would then be exactly the same as that of his Bloomsbury friends.

If Keynes was wobbling in the last week in February, by 28 March, the day fixed for the tribunal's hearing, he had clearly decided to stay put. Several factors influenced him. We must remember that throughout this period he was under great pressure from his parents not to 'throw everything up'. There were claims of affection here as strong as those which bound him to his friends. A second factor was that Keynes really hoped the war might soon be coming to an end. In January and February 1916, President Wilson's special envoy, Colonel House, had been on a tour of belligerent capitals urging a peace conference. On 6 March, the British and American governments reached an understanding that when 'the moment was opportune' the European Allies would invite Wilson to summon a peace conference.[23] Keynes would undoubtedly have heard of this agreement from his Cabinet contacts. He felt that the opportune moment could not be long delayed. Money was running out fast – he had fixed 31 March 1916 for the end of the world, though this had been postponed by a few months. He was probably the author (under the pseudonym 'Politicus') of an article in the April number of Gerald Shove's pacifist monthly *Face the Facts* which said that the stalemate on the Western Front was 'speedily making the case for immediate negotiations unanswerable'. He expressed similar views in an address to the Admiralty on 15 March. There was no point in resigning if peace was coming soon anyway.

Keynes seems to have realised, moreover, that he might use his official position to save his friends from imprisonment.[24] Naturally enough the case that concerned him most was Duncan's. Early in 1916 he advised him and David Garnett that it would strengthen their claim for exemption on conscientious grounds if they were seen to be engaged on 'work of national importance' before their cases came up. A cousin of Duncan's had recently died, leaving a neglected house and orchard in Wissett, a village in Suffolk, where Duncan and Bunny set up as fruit farmers, Vanessa looking after them. Duncan's and Bunny's applications were heard on 4 May before the local tribunal at Blymouth, Maynard coming up to give evidence on their behalf. Adrian Stephen presented their case very badly, 'as though he was addressing a Judge in Chancery'. The chairman, thinking Tolstoy was a town in Russia, was unimpressed when told that Garnett's mother Constance, a lifelong pacifist, had visited the pacifist sage there.[25] They were refused exemption. Later that month their appeal was heard at Ipswich. By this time Maynard had taken charge, arriving for the hearing full of Treasury briskness. 'Carrying a large locked bag with a Royal cipher on it, he demanded that our cases should be heard as expeditiously as possible, as he had left work of utmost national importance to attend.'[26] This time they were awarded non-combatant service (that is, in the army, but not fighting) against which Maynard immediately appealed. In mid-July 1916, both Duncan and Bunny were exempted from military service on condition that they did work of 'national importance'; but their existing work at Wissett did not qualify because they were self-employed. On 11 August Maynard put the case for their being allowed to stay on at Wissett before the Central Tribunal. But by this time they had already decided to seek employment elsewhere.

This was only one of a number of cases in which he was involved that summer. He appeared in June on behalf of Gerald Shove; he helped the appeal of an undergraduate from Pembroke; he got McKenna to write a letter on behalf of the novelist Gilbert Cannan. On 18 June 1916 he wrote to Dennis Robertson: 'The Tribunal crisis is getting over now as concessions to the COs are impending. But it has been a foul business, and I spend half of my time on the boring business of testifying to the sincerity, virtue and truthfulness of my friends.' In this activity he was able to find a moral justification for staying on at the Treasury.

14

Touch and Go

I. SOCIAL LIFE

The pattern of Maynard's wartime life was now established. He spent his days working at the Treasury. The evenings he would spend with others – either with the great and the good or with such friends as remained in London. He took as many weekends as he could in the country or with his parents at Cambridge. A noticeable change came over his social life. Put bluntly, the supply of young men had dried up. Cambridge was no longer available to replenish his friendships; existing friends were at the Front or scattered round the countryside doing agricultural work.

For the first time in his life Maynard had to console himself with female companions. Women, too, felt a dearth of eligible men. A group of them, known as the 'Cropheads' or 'Bunnies' because they wore their hair short, attached themselves to the Bloomsbury men. They included three ex-Slade students, Dorothy Brett, Dora Carrington and Barbara Hiles, and the Newnham graduates Fredegond Maitland, Faith Bagenal and Alix Sargant Florence. It was the war, in fact, which enabled Bloomsbury to catch up with heterosexuality. The 'buggers' belatedly discovered the joys of domesticity. Adrian Stephen had led the way by marrying Karin Costelloe; now Gerald Shove confessed that he wanted, above all, to be looked after – in 1915 he married Fredegond Maitland, a niece of Virginia Woolf. James Strachey capitulated in 1920, after a long siege, to Alix Sargant Florence. With Bunny Garnett away in France for much of 1915, Duncan and Vanessa became lovers. Most amazing of all, in 1916 Lytton Strachey found himself – in Clive Bell's words – 'distinctly épris of [Dora] Carrington ... he discovered suddenly that he was profoundly moved by her legs. I suppose he will soon discover that she has an amazing soul.'[1] In December 1917 he settled down with her at the Mill House, Tidmarsh, near Pangbourne, Maynard contributing twenty pounds a year to the rent.

Maynard himself was attracted to Barbara Hiles, a vivacious, doll-like creature, with red cheeks, blue eyes and curly hair. But there was, as yet, no question of his 'settling down', unlike his brother Geoffrey, who married Margaret Darwin in 1917. Maynard's life was much fuller, more exciting, than that of his Bloomsbury friends. On his Treasury income (now £700 a year) he could run a bachelor establishment. And 'home life' was provided by his parents at Cambridge, as well as by Vanessa, Duncan and Garnett at Wissett, and later at Charleston.

Not that he spent all his free weekends with these two 'families'. In 1916 his friendship with Lady Ottoline Morrell was at its height, and he was frequently at Garsington. On one occasion, Asquith's daughter Violet (now married to Maurice Bonham Carter) and Lytton Strachey had such a violent argument about conscientious objectors that all Maynard's wit and Desmond MacCarthy's anecdotage were needed to salvage the weekend.[2]

Garsington was filling up with 'honorary gardeners' – conscientious objectors employed by Phillip Morrell to do 'work of national importance'. That summer Aldous Huxley, Gerald and Fredegond Shove, Clive Bell and others took up residence in the main house or in nearby cottages, occasionally bestirring themselves to cut wood, prune hedges or mind the hens. (The supply of eggs fell off suddenly after Gerald had been put in charge of the poultry.) Ottoline's reputation never recovered from the influx of articulate, witty and alarmingly gossipy writers and intellectuals, who included D. H. Lawrence and his wife Frieda. Devoted to the encouragement of Art and Beauty, the Art she made of herself was too flawed to survive continuous exposure to the connoisseurs of human nature with whom she liked to surround herself. Her hospitality was rewarded with merciless lampoons in conversation, letters and novels. Maynard was happy to accept Ottoline's hospitality without malice, though he enjoyed the spiteful stories his friends spread about her. At Garsington, he struck Aldous Huxley as 'fascinating – he had this immense range of knowledge, and he would come out with these *curiously* elliptical remarks about things....'[3]

On 6 June 1916, Kitchener was drowned off the Orkneys when the ship taking him to Russia on a mission to discuss military and financial strategy hit a mine. Maynard had been excluded from the party only at the last moment. The thought of how nearly he had been with Kitchener was enough to give Neville headaches. Instead, Maynard stayed in London receiving deputations from the Holy Synod of Russia and the government of Serbia to whom, as he told his father, he 'doled out presents I should have liked myself'.[4] (He initialled chits for the purchase of beeswax for the Russian Church and underwear for a Grand Duchess.[5]) His memoranda continued to rile Lloyd George, who succeeded Kitchener as Secretary of State for War. In a note of May 1916, Lloyd George had called the Treasury's attempts to ration Russian buying the 'height of stupidity', suggesting that American contractors would be willing to provide credits directly to the Russians, without charge to the British Exchequer, rather than see their industries collapse for want of foreign orders. McKenna's reply of 5 July 1916, drafted by Keynes, and circulated to the Cabinet, entered into detailed criticisms of Lloyd George's logic and facts, rather in the manner of a tutor reproving the efforts of a backward student.[6] Lloyd George notched up another grievance against Keynes. July sped by in conference with the French and Italian finance ministers.

September 1916 found him with the McKennas at Munstead House, Godalming, where, Maynard informed his mother,

the C[hancellor] of [the] E[xchequer] is taking an intermittent holiday and where we mix up talk about the nation with walks over the hills. We are on very intimate terms now and I have got extremely fond of him. I'm living in extreme luxury here, in bed till lunchtime and much pampered. Before I took my holiday I was feeling more used up than I have been for a long time.

With Bloomsbury now virtually emptied of Bloomsberries, the question arose what to do about 46 Gordon Square. Clive Bell hoped Maynard would take it over. He had a personal motive, requiring a London bedroom for his fortnightly tryst with his mistress Mary Hutchinson, the wife of the lawyer St John Hutchinson and a cousin of the Stracheys. Maynard foresaw problems. The lease of Gower Street still had nine months to run. He wrote to Vanessa:

Clive whom I've just been talking to may be rather a difficulty I think. He evidently means to be in London a fair amount and also to be an inhabitant of Gordon Square; and there isn't really room for him. I feel a little in danger of becoming, by virtue of the change, instead of a householder the rather insecure tenant of two rooms.

Maynard's misgivings turned out to be justified; however, there were advantages, and he moved in at the end of September 1916, taking Sheppard with him from Gower Street. He paid the rates and the two servants, Blanche and Jessie; the Bells continued to pay the rent, keeping four rooms for their own use. Harry Norton joined them in March 1917. Dorothy Brett, Dora Carrington and Barbara Hiles moved into 3 Gower Street.

Wissett was abandoned at the same time, following the Central Tribunal's ruling that Duncan and Bunny could not remain self-employed. The first plan was for them to join the honorary gardeners at Garsington. But this would have left out Vanessa. Virginia had meanwhile discovered a farmhouse in Sussex, a mile from Firle, and four miles from Asheham, which she urged Vanessa to take. 'It has a charming garden, with a pond, and fruit trees, and vegetables, all now rather run wild, but you could make it lovely. The house is very nice, with large rooms, and one room with big windows fit for a studio.'[7] It became vacant in September 1916; Vanessa, in 'one breathlessly efficient day' at Lewes, rented it from James Stacey who held a lease from Lord Gage, the owner, and persuaded a young farmer, Mr Hecks, to employ Duncan and Bunny as labourers on his farm. Maynard paid his first visit to 'Duncan's new country house' as he called Charleston at the end of October.[8] It soon became his favourite weekend retreat.

The double rearrangement consolidated Maynard's position in the Bloomsbury Group. No. 46 Gordon Square was, in the words of Clive Bell,

Bloomsbury's *'monument historique'*, and now Maynard was left in effective possession. Most of the practical arrangements for Bloomsbury's collective London life were concentrated in his hands. The move to Charleston gave him a secure foothold in what was to become Bloomsbury's chief rural outpost. It was an ideal weekend place – only an hour by train from London. Moreover at Charleston he could relax in a way which was impossible with the more rigid Woolfs and Stracheys. Here he was accepted for what he was. He could bask in a warm glow of approval and affection, unchilled by the Cambridge habit of relentlessly dissecting character and analysing motives, from which he rarely emerged unscathed. Charleston was more a world unto itself than the other Bloomsbury establishments. The lives of Lytton Strachey, the Woolfs, even Clive Bell, for all their commitment to unworldly values, overlapped too much with Maynard's for them not to feel threatened by his successes. Jealousy tended to take the self-protecting form of disapproval. With Vanessa, Duncan and Bunny, Maynard's relationships were non-competitive. They could much more easily accept him as an authority on matters outside their range. They regarded his sorties into high society as sources of amusing gossip rather than as subjects for moral sermons. They were not always questioning his sense of values. Even Maynard's grossness, which offended Lytton Strachey, was less out of place in Charleston's earthy, bawdy atmosphere.

Charleston became Maynard's chief wartime family. He would arrive on a Friday or Saturday evening, recount his war news, and then stay in bed till lunch the following morning, by which time he would have worked through his files, leaving a wastepaper-basket full of torn-up paper. After that he was a free man. There would be gossip and walks on the Downs. He even became an honorary gardener in a small way, weeding the gravel-path methodically with his pocket-knife while kneeling on a small piece of carpet. 'It would have been easy to tell the length of his visits by the state of the path,' recalled David Garnett. Maynard infected them all with his buoyancy.[9]

II. FINANCIAL CRISIS AND CHANGE OF GOVERNMENT

As the third winter of the war approached, the crisis which the Treasury had for so long predicted seemed finally upon them. By that time Britain had become completely dependent on the United States for fighting a Continental war. The stability of the Allied exchanges, and the whole structure of inter-Ally finance, depended on Britain being able to borrow enough dollars in the United States to pay for Allied spending. On 3 October 1916, at the suggestion of a Foreign Office clerk, Richard Sperling, an inter-departmental committee was set up under Lord Eustace Percy to review the position. Keynes was the Treasury representative. In two trenchant memoranda he spelt out the details and implications of Britain's growing dependence. He estimated that over the coming six months Britain would need to spend at least $250m monthly in the United States, of which it would have to borrow at least $200m, but he doubted whether private American banks would go on lending on such a scale. Over McKenna's initials appear the ominous words, 'If things go on at present, I venture to say with certainty that by next June or earlier the President of the American Republic will be in a position, if he wishes, to dictate his own terms to us.'[10] In Cabinet, Lloyd George once more attacked this despondent conclusion. 'If victory shone on our banners,' he said, 'our difficulties would disappear. Success means credit: financiers never hesitate to lend to a prosperous concern.' The revelation of British dependence on the United States (Lord Eustace Percy wrote that 'our job is ... to keep sentiment in America so sweet that it will lend us practically unlimited money') had its impact on the review of British war aims taking place at the same time, out of which emerged Lord Lansdowne's memorandum of 13 November 1916 calling for immediate peace negotiations.

Except for bankers of German origin like Paul Warburg, the American financial establishment was pro-Ally, as was the US Treasury. American farmers and manufacturers, too, had a vested interest in maintaining a high level of Allied buying – which was on a much larger scale than Germany's. New York was also eager to take London's place as the world's financial centre. But political relations between America and Britain were bad for much of 1916. Britain's use of its naval supremacy to prevent American supplies from reaching Germany – it also started black-listing American firms which traded with the enemy – aroused great anger at a time when Germany, behaving with unusual circumspection, had reduced its submarine campaign. The execution of the leaders of the Easter Rebellion in Dublin infuriated Irish-American opinion. With the presidential election approaching, Wilson was anxious to conciliate American voters of Irish and German descent, who were anti-British, and of Polish and Jewish descent, who were anti-tsarist. Also, Wilson wanted to stop the war, and whereas Germany was proving relatively amenable to his peace moves (at least verbally), Lloyd George, in a well-publicised interview on 22 September 1916 with an American journalist, enunciated the policy of the 'knock-out blow'.[11] As if all that was not enough, Britain's reliance on J. P. Morgan as its American financial agent was also politically counterproductive, since it saddled the Allied cause with the opprobrium traditionally attaching to Wall Street bankers. In his memorandum of 10 October, Keynes drew the sensible conclusion that 'the policy of this country towards the USA should be so directed as not only to avoid any form of reprisal or active irritation but also to conciliate and please'.[12] These words fix the moment when financial hegemony passed irrevocably across the Atlantic.

On 27 November 1916 the US Federal Reserve Board brought on the worst British financial crisis in the war by telling its member banks to cut down their credit to foreign borrowers, and warning private investors against giving loans on the security of Allied Treasury bills. Its main motive was to bring financial pressure on the Allies to end the war. President Wilson strengthened the Board's warning for the same reason. There was nothing for it but to pay up. For three weeks Britain lost gold at an average of over $5m a day, 'which in those days', Keynes recalled, 'we considered simply terrific'. By mid-December the crisis had eased, with the help of underspending by the Allies, and generous overdraft facilities made available by Morgan.

Keynes's loyalties were again being cruelly torn. On the one hand he was working feverishly to get Britain through the financial crisis; on the other hand he hoped the crisis itself would bring the war to an end. His hopes rested once more on President Wilson, who had launched another peace initiative on 18 December calling on the belligerents to state their peace terms. By this time Keynes was having to carry on his work under a new, and much less welcome, political chief. On 6 December, Lloyd George replaced Asquith as Prime Minister, the Conservative Bonar Law succeeding McKenna as Chancellor of the Exchequer. Keynes's depression at this turn of events was not improved by his indifferent health. He had three bad attacks of influenza in the winter of 1916–17, and was generally run down.

On the other hand, the financial situation seemed to favour the President's call, on 22 January 1917, for a 'peace without victory'. The drain of gold still continued. On 22 February Keynes calculated that available resources would not last 'for more than four weeks from today'. The British were, in fact, saved by the Germans, who had no idea of the desperate straits to which their enemy had been reduced – something which would have been signalled had Britain suspended convertibility, against which Keynes continued to argue vigorously and successfully.[13] They launched unrestricted submarine warfare on 1 February, in order to cut off Allied supplies from the United States, not realising that finance was about to accomplish the same result. As President Wilson himself saw, the German action killed off the last hope of 'peace without victory'. On 6 April America declared war on Germany. Keynes's skill in controlling Britain's overseas spending, by helping to stave off financial collapse, had the paradoxical result of delivering the President to Lloyd George and to the policy of the knock-out blow.

This time there was no serious thought of resignation. Lloyd George cordially reciprocated Keynes's mistrust. Maynard explained to his mother on 11 February that:

> I was approved and included in the final list to get a C.B. [Companion of the Bath] this honours list. But when Lloyd George saw it he took his pen and struck my name out – an unheard of proceeding. Partly revenge

for the McKenna War Council Memorandum against him, of which he knows I was the author.

But in compensation Keynes was named head of 'A' Division, a new division carved out of the Finance Division, dealing with external finance, and reporting directly to Sir Robert Chalmers, joint permanent secretary, and the Chancellor. By the end of the war his staff numbered seventeen, mostly temporary civil servants. They included his old student Dudley Ward, a clever young man of eighteen called Rupert Trouton, who became his student after the war, and Oswald Toynbee Falk, a partner in the stockbroking firm of Buckmaster and Moore. An actuary who was passionate about ballet, Falk joined the Treasury team in October 1917, soon after Keynes had become a founder-member of a small dining club which Falk started – known as the Tuesday Club – which met at the Café Royal to discuss post-war financial problems. Andrew MacFadyean, who was transferred to Keynes's group, recalls the exhilaration felt by

> a younger man to see that razor-sharp mind dissecting a problem and stating it in terms which made it look simple, and in language which it was a joy to read. . . . Keynes would rarely – that at any rate is the impression left on my mind – reach the Treasury before midday and he would leave it about eight. He was a prodigiously fast worker, and there was never much in his in-tray at the end of the day.[14]

Keynes's promotion locked him even more closely into his Treasury work. Soon he was able to draw comfort from events in Russia. The revolution of 12 March 1917, leading to the abdication of the Tsar, had 'immensely cheered and excited him', he told Florence. 'It's the sole result of the war so far worth having.'[15] The anti-tsarist attitude of Maynard's generation died hard.

Both America's entry into and Russia's gradual retirement from the war promised to ease the financial strain of the previous few months. After July Keynes refused any more credit to the Russian government.[16] His reaction to the Bolshevik Revolution of October is unrecorded. His last official intervention in Russian affairs was to draw up a currency board scheme for the White Russian government at Archangel, which was implemented between 1918 and 1920.[17]

III. THE FINANCIAL DIPLOMACY OF WAR

At the end of May 1917 Keynes was made Companion of the Bath, Third Class, 'through the kindness of Chalmers who exerted the strongest possible pressure through the Chancellor of the Exchequer and made mine the sole name put forward by the Treasury'.[18] Unexpectedly he got on excellently with the new Chancellor, Bonar Law. Cautious and pessimistic, Law was no intellectual like McKenna, but he was extremely quick to grasp, and remember, a point put to him 'in those hurried moments which a civil servant gets with his chief before a conference'.[19] Law came to rely on Keynes's advice in all matters of external finance. Keynes became genuinely fond of Law, a sad man, whose sadness was increased by the death of two of his sons on active service. He was soon making up bridge fours at 11 Downing Street.

Once America entered the war on the Allied side, the game of international finance changed, and with it Keynes's role. Funds were now assured. The question was the terms on which they could be obtained, and the implications of the new relationship for the conduct of the war, war aims and the balance of post-war power. America would back the Alliance till it won, but with a view to playing a dominant part in the peace settlement and post-war trade and finance. Britain had to contrive to manage its affairs so as to limit the scale of its liabilities and keep the maximum room for post-war manoeuvre. As was to happen much more obviously in the Second World War, British brains were matched against US money – or that is how the British saw it. One of those brains was Keynes's.

Admittedly the plot was not clear-cut. There were internal frictions on both sides. In the United States there were four centres of financial power: the Treasury, the Federal Reserve Board, Wall Street and Congress. William Gibbes McAdoo, the Secretary of the Treasury and Wilson's son-in-law, combined, on one hand, a somewhat desperate ambition to bring the other three under his control with, on the other, considerable ignorance of finance, and considerable fear of Congress in practice. His policy in 1917 was partly governed by a determination not to allow US Treasury funds to be used to pay off British debts to the New York bankers. Benjamin Strong, the leading force in the Federal Reserve Board, wanted both to establish the Board's independence of the Treasury and to see his own bank, the Federal Reserve Bank of New York, supplant the Bank of England as manager of the world's monetary system. Leading New York bankers like the Anglophile Thomas W. Lamont saw private loans to Europe as the best way of establishing New York's financial hegemony; they disapproved of official interference in the lending business. Many Congressmen disliked the New York bankers as much as they mistrusted the British; they would have preferred America to stay out of the war.

Britain's financial policy was under better control, but there were elements of divided jurisdiction here, too. The Treasury's old hankering for limited financial commitments ran up against the insatiable demands of the war departments both of Britain and of its European allies. Such control as it was able to retain over total spending rested on the sanctity of the sterling–dollar exchange and the limitation of shipping space. But it had to share management of the exchange rate with the Bank of England, whose governor, Lord Cunliffe, resented the meddling of Treasury officials in the Bank's traditional preserve. In 1915, taking advantage of his friendship with Lloyd George, Cunliffe managed to get McKenna to agree to centralise the management of the exchange in a London Exchange Committee – a consortium of bankers, of which he was chairman. However, the Treasury, notably Sir Robert Chalmers and Keynes, chipped away at the Committee's functions, and by the summer of 1917 Cunliffe was ready for a showdown.

The third force in Britain's US financial diplomacy, the Washington Embassy, was more of a hindrance than a help. The ambassador, Sir Cecil Spring-Rice, a diplomat of the old school, and a friend of Theodore Roosevelt, was on bad terms with the Democratic administration. A man of wit, as well as of biblical turn of phrase (he wrote the hymn 'I vow to thee my country'), he did the British cause little good with his party joke that 'Wilson is the nation's shepherd and McAdoo his crook'. The Embassy was also woefully lacking in financial expertise. Until the able and diplomatic Lord Reading was appointed ambassador in January 1918, Britain had to rely on high-powered *ad hoc* missions to advance its financial interests in the United States; but these tended to create further jurisdictional and personal disputes.

Keynes's hope that America would take care of his problems was not realised; the problems just changed. In January 1917, the British Treasury, in an effort to distance itself both from J. P. Morgan and from the Bank of England, had sent out its new Financial Secretary, Sir Samuel Hardman Lever, to New York to raise money and take over the management of the Morgan account. Lever, a chartered accountant with New York connections, succeeded in swelling the British government's debt to Morgan's to $400m by the time America entered the war; but when he asked McAdoo, on 9 April, for $1500m for six months, he was met with astonishment and annoyance. McAdoo was suspicious that the money would be used to pay back Morgan's and support the sterling–dollar exchange rather than to buy American goods; also no machinery for allocating the proceeds of the $2000m Liberty Loan, authorised by Congress, among the various Allied claimants had yet been worked out. Lever, a morose man, did not help matters by his secretiveness; nor did successive missions to the United States headed by Balfour and Northcliffe (the newspaper proprietor) bring about any large-scale release of funds. McAdoo, 'a Wall Street failure with designs on the Presidency', as MacFadyean acidly described him, was content to advance the begging British money in weekly dribs and drabs, using the Allied penury to concentrate control of purchasing in US Treasury hands.[20]

In June the situation got worse as heavy British demands for wheat, coinciding with the withdrawal of US funds from London to invest in the Liberty Loan, weakened sterling. In London, Keynes masterminded the Treasury's campaign to keep the US money flowing, drafting the crucial memoranda and telegrams explaining the British government's position to the Americans, as well as the instructions Bonar Law was sending to Lever. Last-minute American advances enabled the British to scrape through June. However, on 20 July, Bonar Law transmitted to McAdoo a message drafted by Keynes that 'our resources available for payments in America are exhausted. Unless the United States government can meet in full our expenses in America, *including exchange*, the whole financial fabric of the alliance will collapse. This conclusion will be a matter not of months but of days.'[21]

On 28 July Lever was instructed, on Keynes's advice, to support the sterling–dollar exchange as long as he had any dollars left, and then suspend convertibility. The Bank's remaining gold was to be protected as the ultimate liquid reserve.[22] Kathleen Burk writes that Keynes 'grasped the nettle and suggested the heretofore unthinkable: in a choice between the rate of exchange and the remaining gold, the rate would have to give way'.[23] A telegram drafted by Keynes to McAdoo, explaining the exchange situation, brought about a further release of US funds at the eleventh hour, saving the position.[24]

The government's ability to contain the crisis was hampered throughout this period by friction between the Treasury and the Bank of England. On 3 July 1917 Cunliffe complained to Bonar Law that Chalmers and Keynes between them were reducing his Exchange Committee to a 'cypher' by withholding from it information and assets. In retaliation he gave instructions to withhold the Bank's gold at Ottawa from Sir Samuel Hardman Lever in New York. He also demanded that Chalmers and Keynes be dismissed. Bonar Law responded by forcing the resignation of the megalomaniac governor.[25] It is easy to see why his Treasury officials loved him.

The crisis – 'the worst ... I can remember since the war began'[26] – left Keynes shattered. For five weeks he had worked nine to thirteen hours a day 'of the hardest possible exertion'. Matters were made worse by German air-raids which forced him to flee to the basement of Gordon Square. His only relief had been six hours of strenuous weeding at Charleston. Florence swelled with pride at Maynard's importance. 'How exciting it must be for you to attend the Cabinet meetings. Indeed, it seems to me that you are having such experiences as will make the whole of life pale afterwards.'[27]

The effect of his holiday was 'wearing off dreadfully quickly and I must try to get some more if I am to keep well'.[28] The break came in the unexpected form of a trip to the United States with Lord Reading – a month away with almost nothing to do, he informed Vanessa from The Wharf on 3 September, the eve of his departure.

Reading was sent to America to try to resolve the impasse between Hardman Lever and the US Treasury (McAdoo was now refusing to see Lever). Keynes's voyage out, on the SS *Louis*, took a week, of which he spent three days seasick. There were daily two-hour conferences with Reading and Colonel Ernest Swinton, assistant secretary to the War Cabinet. For the rest Keynes sat on deck or played piquet, winning twenty pounds off a Polish count. In Washington he stayed in a 'small and comfortable house' with the Readings, both of whom he 'liked immensely',[29] despite Lady Reading's deafness. Reading's job, like that of all previous special commissioners, was to squeeze more money out of McAdoo. He finally succeeded in getting McAdoo's agreement for a proper schedule of monthly loans. In addition, with Keynes's help, he arranged a $50m loan for British purchase of Canadian wheat, a considerable concession, since US policy was to provide dollars only for things bought in the United States. Reading, who thought very highly of Keynes,[30] wanted him to stay an extra ten days, but Bonar Law refused. Keynes made a less favourable impression on the British ambassador. Spring-Rice wrote to his wife Florence:

> This morning we got a visit from Reading's Treasury clerk who was very Treasuriclarkacious and reduced Dicky [Sir Richard Crawford, his economic adviser] to silentious rage and Malcolm [Robertson, a counsellor] to a high treble. He was really too offensive for words and I shall have to take measures. He is also a Don and the combination is not pleasing. He is also a young man of talent and I presume the rule for such nowadays is to show his immense superiority by crushing the contemptible insignificance of the unworthy outside. He does it hard. Lord Reading himself is most agreeable and pleasant to deal with.[31]

Keynes reported back to London that the ambassador was mentally unhinged; soon afterwards he was retired.[32]

Keynes was not a success with the Americans either. 'Rude, dogmatic, and disobliging' to them in London, he made a 'terrible impression for his rudeness out here', Blackett wrote from Washington.[33] Again the feeling was reciprocated. 'The only really sympathetic and original thing in America is the niggers, who are charming,' Keynes informed Duncan Grant. He returned to Britain on the SS *Aurania*, converted into an American troopship, in a two-week zigzag across the Atlantic to avoid German submarines, docking at Liverpool on 22 October 1917.

The era of exchange crises was over. Worries about maintaining the sterling–dollar exchange – hitherto the pivot of inter-Ally finance – gave way to the worries of bargaining with Allied and American officials over the

distribution of American largesse, a process involving different rituals, skills
and techniques. Political and diplomatic factors came to the fore, technical
economic considerations retreated. Politics were now as rampant in the
sphere of external finance as they had long been in the sphere of domestic
finance. On the whole Keynes did not welcome this change, though it
lightened his burden. His whole training as an economist and Treasury
official rebelled against such blatant political interference with the allocation
of resources. Personally he lacked the emollient skills of a Lord Reading.
Intellectually he felt himself, and the tradition he represented, to be far
superior to anything the Americans could put up against him, and he
resented the change in Britain's circumstances which separated the brains
from the money.

The bulk of his time was now spent in negotiations at innumerable
inter-Ally conferences. In November 1917 he was over in Paris for one such
jamboree, sitting with Balfour, Reading and Northcliffe as part of the British
delegation. In December 1917 he wasted days on 'a newly established
monkey-house called the Inter-Ally Council for War Purchases and
Finance',[34] where he had to listen to 'vain, mendacious and interminable
French and hateful Yank twang'.[35] Set up at the insistence of the Americans
and under an American chairman, Assistant Secretary to the Treasury, Oscar
T. Crosby, an ex-director of a street-car company, to scrutinise competing
Allied claims for American money, it met monthly, alternately in London
and Paris. British estimates of what they would require in America in the
coming month were worked out by an American Board in Whitehall, of
which Austen Chamberlain was chairman and Keynes Treasury representative. They were then taken to the Inter-Ally Council. Keynes described its
second meeting in Paris at the end of January to Basil Blackett in America:
'A vast number of us sit round a table in a gilded palace to listen to the
eloquence of Crosby – equally torrential in either language.' Tiresome as
the business was, Keynes conceded it had its uses. Treasury control over
Britain's external spending could be reinforced by 'flourishing the name of
Crosby with great effect in the faces of recalcitrant departments'.[36] To his
Charleston friends he retailed more intimate gossip about his Paris jaunt. He
had dined at the Ritz with Lord Beaverbrook, 'hideously ugly and utterly
debauched'.

The last big battle he waged on behalf of the Treasury was the attempt
to get America to take over the financing of France and Italy, thus reducing
the rate of increase in Britain's debt to the United States. Under the previous
division of labour agreed with McAdoo, America was to supply dollar credits
directly to each Ally for its purchases in the American market, Britain
financing all its European Allies' other purchases. But Britain could no longer
do even this reduced job out of its own resources. Consequently it was still
having to borrow big sums in the United States on its Allies' behalf. As the
British Treasury saw it – accurately, as it turned out – Britain was accumu-

lating liabilities to the United States which it would have to pay back, in order to lend money to its Allies, much of which it would never see again. The Americans, of course, preferred to accumulate superior British obligations to inferior French and Italian ones.

In a telegram which went from Bonar Law to Lord Reading at the end of March 1918 Keynes insisted that 'the US Treasury should take over all the future obligations of France and Italy ....' Britain would continue to procure supplies for its European Allies outside America, being paid in dollars obtained from the American Treasury rather than in European IOUs.[37] Implicit in this proposal was continued British Treasury control over the non-American buying of its Allies. Keynes saw an opportunity for Britain to corner the world commodity markets.[38] The French and Italians naturally resisted this part of the British plan. They proposed that their non-American purchases be placed in the hands of an inter-ally executive committee. Keynes did not find this at all welcome. However, he reluctantly had to concede that 'if Mr McAdoo accepts our proposals for taking off our shoulders the burden of French and Italian finance ... the Americans can justly ask for an inter-ally body to pronounce on the propriety of allocations they are expected to finance'.[39] Britain's financial dependence on the United States was the rock on which Keynes's ingenious plan foundered. It was unrealistic to expect that the Americans would allow their money to be used to bolster Britain's competitive position in world markets. The Americans, Keynes exploded, in much the same language he was to use in the Second World War, seemed to take pleasure 'in reducing us to a position of complete financial helplessness and dependence'.[40]

If the management of Britain's external finance no longer gave him much intellectual or emotional satisfaction, contemplation of domestic politics induced a feeling of black despair. 'I work for a government I despise for ends I think criminal,' he told Duncan Grant on 15 December 1917. Maynard rejected Lloyd George's commitment to total victory, and feared its consequences. The Prime Minister's remarkable political skills aroused in him only aesthetic and moral repugnance. He lived in the hope that Lloyd George's deviousness would prove his undoing. He fantasised about the downfall of his class which had so spinelessly placed supreme power in the hands of an adventurer. Maynard's political understanding was not the most conspicuous of his qualities at this period of his life. He was taking too many political lessons from the Asquithians, whose failures had opened up the path for Lloyd George. He failed to give Lloyd George credit for his courage and resourcefulness in adversity, and for his determination to keep British lives out of the generals' maw. All he could see was that he was playing the part of a 'dirty scoundrel' with the generals – an ironic identification with the generals' own view.[41] He failed to realise that Asquith, McKenna and the others did not want a negotiated peace any more than Lloyd George did, and failed to explain anyway how the Germans were to be brought to a conference except on their own or on the Allied terms. Indeed, a gross overestimate of the strength of the German moderates, as well as a misunderstanding of their aims, was characteristic of the whole British middle-class peace movement.

From Charleston, where he spent the Christmas of 1917, Maynard sounded off to his mother about the prospects for the future:

> My Christmas thoughts are that a further prolongation of the war, with the turn things have now taken, probably means the disappearance of the social order we have known hitherto. With some regrets I think I am not on the whole sorry. The abolition of the rich will be rather a comfort and serve them right anyhow. What frightens me is the prospect of *general* impoverishment. In another year's time we shall have forfeited the claim we had staked out in the New World and in exchange this country will be mortgaged to America.
>
> Well, the only course open to me is to be buoyantly bolshevik; and as I lie in bed in the morning I reflect with a good deal of satisfaction that, because our rulers are as incompetent as they are mad and wicked, one particular era of a particular kind of civilisation is very nearly over.[42]

The proximate cause of this gloomy epistle was the government's announcement of food rationing. Like other less reflective members of the middle classes Keynes tended to equate social order with the continuance of his own customary standard of comfort, and to take an exaggerated view of the consequences of any diminution in it. To Florence his Christmas visions suggested communal kitchens and the drying up of the supply of domestic servants.[43] Maynard's incipient Bolshevism stopped well short of food rationing, which filled him with horror. He feared he would have to take frequent trips abroad to get a square meal. 'The proposed [rationing] rules seem to me appalling – calculated to dry up the food supply on the one side and starve me on the other.'[44] In fact, food rationing worked perfectly well in both world wars, and posed no permanent threat to the social order.

There was still the hope that the war would end before the expropriation or starvation of the rich took place. On 29 November 1917 the *Daily Telegraph* published Lord Lansdowne's Peace Letter calling for renewed efforts to end the war by negotiation. Keynes immediately perked up. His hopes of an early peace were kept alive by the proclamation of Wilson's Fourteen Points for ending the war, and Lloyd George's speech to the Trades Union Congress setting out the Allied peace terms. But soon he was reduced once more to seeking relief through a change of government. The Prime Minister was in great trouble following his dismissal of Sir William Robertson, Chief of the Imperial General Staff. But he struggled on. Maynard wrote to Florence on 22 February 1918:

The course of politics at the beginning of the week was deeply shocking. Bonar could have become prime minister if he had liked, but he funked it; and as no one else seemed inclined to take the job, the goat* struggled through.... His method of disposing of Robertson was an extraordinarily characteristic compound of humbug, chicane and straightforward lying.

Contrary to his hopes, the Goat overcame yet another – and the last – challenge to his leadership in the Maurice debate of 9 May 1918.[45] As Ludendorff launched a desperate German offensive on the Western Front Keynes reflected on the state of the nation from the congenial surroundings of The Wharf:

Politics and War are just as depressing, or even more so than they seem to be. If this Gov[t] were to beat the Germans, I should lose all faith for the future in the efficacy of intellectual processes: – but there doesn't seem to be much risk of it. Everything is always decided for some reason other than the real merits of the case, in the sphere with which I have contact. And I have no doubt that it is just the same with everything else.

Still and even more confidently I attribute our misfortunes to George. We are governed by a crook and the results are natural.[46]

IV. 'HE MUST BE TALKED TO'

If Keynes despaired about the government, his Bloomsbury friends were starting to despair about him. It was no longer primarily his war work to which they objected; but the effect of that work, and of its accompanying social life, on his character. Virginia Woolf forecast that if he remained much longer at the Treasury he would be lost to humanity, as perhaps he already was.[47] To be sure, he was still very much a part of both London and rural Bloomsbury. He was regularly to be seen at the 1917 Club, a Soho meeting place for radical and anti-war intellectuals, often in the company of Barbara Hiles. Such frolics were regarded with indulgent amusement by his friends. But the weekends at The Wharf, the dinner parties and receptions of Allied and parliamentary bigwigs, the bridge parties with Bonar Law, from all of which he would return full of self-importance and authoritative pronouncements – that was another matter.

* Lloyd George was generally called 'George' or 'the Goat' by his political opponents. He was known to dislike being called plain Mr George; the second suggested a propensity to play around – with women and truth.

Not that his connections and salary were not useful. He intervened with Max Beaverbrook, the new Minister of Information, to get commissions for Duncan and other painters under the Ministry's War Artists Scheme.[48] He provided Bunny with money for his bees at Charleston. The most stunning of his coups occurred in March 1918. Duncan had found out that the contents of Degas' studio were about to be auctioned off in Paris. Couldn't Maynard persuade the government to buy some of them for the National Gallery? Maynard, who was due to go to Paris himself for a meeting of the Inter-Ally Council, promised to approach Bonar Law. On 21 March Duncan received a telegram at Charleston: 'Money secured for pictures'. Maynard explained to Vanessa two days later. 'My picture coup was a whirlwind affair – carried through in a day and a half before anyone had time to reflect what they were doing. I have secured 550,000 francs to play with [equal to about £20,000]; Holmes [Sir Charles Holmes, the Keeper of the National Gallery] is travelling out with us; and I hope we shall be able to attend the sale together.' He added, 'Bonar Law was much amused at my wanting to buy pictures and eventually let me have my way as a sort of joke.'[49] Vanessa replied excitedly, 'We have great hopes for you & consider that your existence at the Treasury is at last justified.' David Garnett added, 'You have been given complete absolution & future crimes also forgiven.'

Maynard attended the sale with Holmes on 26–27 March. Prices were depressed as the German bombardment could be heard fifty miles away. The following evening Austen Chamberlain, who was driving back to London, dropped Keynes off at the bottom of the lane leading to Charleston. He arrived at the farmhouse just as Vanessa, Duncan and David Garnett were finishing supper, informing them that he had left a Cézanne in a haystack. While Holmes had bought a Corot, a Gauguin and several paintings and drawings by Delacroix, Ingres and Manet for the nation, Maynard had helped himself to one of the plums of the collection, Cézanne's *Apples*, for £327, as well as two pictures by Delacroix and an Ingres drawing. This was the start of his career as a serious collector. As Holmes had a prejudice against Cézanne, no conflict of interest had arisen. In fact, £5000 of Bonar Law's donation remained unspent.

Maynard's absolution was short-lived. What he called his 'experiments in High Life' continued through the spring and summer – dinners with a Rumanian prince, with the Princess of Monaco, and, to cap it all, with the Duke of Connaught, George III's great-grandson. In mid-May he was able to take a week off at Charleston, where the weather was perfect. 'I sit out or weed all my working hours and my daily bag from the Treasury doesn't mean more than one or two hours of work a day.'[50] His portrait was painted by Duncan, Vanessa and Roger Fry. Less perfect was Maynard's character, in the opinion of his friends. David Garnett described Bloomsbury's cogitations on this absorbing subject in a long diary entry dated 28 May 1918:

Maynard. There has been a general alarm that he is going rapidly to the devil. Nessa told me about a scene when she was in London. Harry, Sheppard & she were talking. Maynard came in, contradicted everyone, and refused to go into anything. The subject was whether one could have any feeling at all about England after the refusal of Emperor Karl's overtures. . . .* Maynard treated them with contempt & behaved like a public-schoolboy of the worst kind & said several times 'Go to bed, Go to bed'. Sheppard got very angry & said – 'Maynard you will find it a mistake to despise your old friends'.

Nessa . . . suggests that Maynard is now possibly so far on the downhill path that nothing will save him. Harry thinks it is not at all simple – That M. is aware of many of his habits being disgusting to other people – such as helping himself with his own spoon or fork instead of passing his plate, and persists in doing them because it flatters him that people like him so much they don't mind what he does. (This is often my own feeling but not about table manners – but in complete unreserve of all baseness with Duncan.)

Sheppard says Maynard is . . . a bit mad on the subject of his own importance. He had heard him say the other day to Jessie [the parlour-maid at No. 46] 'I'm going to dine tonight with the Duke of Connaught. Isn't that grand?' – 'Yes Sir that is grand'. Sheppard refuses to regard this as the obvious thing it would be in 99 cases out of 100 – a joke. He says Maynard really thinks it is grand – knowing he couldn't impress Harry & Sheppard with the Dk of Connaught he had to tell Jessie. 'Nonconformist snobbery. I know all about it – they're like bugs in the rug. Bugs in a rug'.

General conclusions were that Maynard has a lot of low blood in him – Sheppard . . . says from his nonconformist snobbish ancestry. That he is at a critical point in his life, that it may be fatigue [or] deterioration of his brain which is the only thing that ever made him remarkable. . . . Duncan has been asked to give him a lecture. . . .

Bunny's own attitude to Maynard was more generous and better balanced:

My own view of the whole thing is that it is one of their periodic alarms. . . . Maynard is always very tired. He works too much. He then wants something he can do with one tenth of his attention – which is to talk to the inane about the inane. Anything requiring him to think new thoughts or follow new arguments produces violent irritation in self-protection. His character is not entirely dependent on brain. He has

* Emperor Charles of Austria had approached Poincaré, the French President, on 20 March 1918 with a peace offer, accepting the return of Alsace-Lorraine to France, and all the open Allied demands. However, the Allies were tied by their secret commitments to give Constantinople to Russia and the Tyrol, Trentino and Istria to Italy, and so rejected this opportunity of shortening the war by detaching Austria-Hungary from Germany. Clemenceau made public Charles's letter in April 1918.

a great deal of *love* & capacity for love. That will keep him if not straight
at least capable of zigzagging back.

Soon Clive Bell was adding his voice to the chorus of complaints. He
had lent his room at 46 Gordon Square to a friend of his '*emballé* of a young
woman'. Unfortunately they had used Sheppard's room by mistake. 'We
were given no warning of this,' Maynard explained to Duncan on 16 June
1918, 'and it was very embarrassing to the regular inhabitants all of whom
happened to be at home: poor Sheppard was too nervous to ... go to bed
until 3.30 when the lovers disappeared. We are sending a protest to Clive
that he must restrain his good nature more narrowly.' Maynard's letter to
Clive was not well received. He 'took it upon himself to write me the sort
of letter an ill-bred millionaire might write to a defaulting office boy', he
complained to Vanessa. He decided on counter-measures. 'If Maynard can
behave like an old virgin Jewess I can behave like a British businessman.
The house is ours, stands in my name.... I say – denounce the treaty.'[51]
However, actual possession and a Treasury salary increased to £1000 a year
proved stronger than Clive's resentment. The lease of 46 Gordon Square was
renewed in September 1918 – in Maynard's name. Clive retained his two
attic rooms. But there was still friction. Maynard had commandeered Clive's
bed, substituting one that felt 'more like the seat of a third-class railway
carriage'. As the war's end approached, Clive wrote to Maynard, 'I must have
my bed back.... Nothing could be more easy for you than to get a new one
for yourself.' Since Maynard proved in no hurry to oblige, Clive had his own
bed moved upstairs. 'Dear Maynard,' he wrote from Garsington, 'I had no
notion of leaving you to sleep on the floor.' He was sending down his third-
class railway carriage. 'As you appear to fuck less than I do it may serve well
enough.'[52]

By August 1918 it was clear that Germany's last fling had failed. The
British counterattack breached the Hindenburg line on 29 September.
The same day Ludendorff insisted that the war must end to save his armies.
On 4 October the new German government of Prince Max of Baden asked
for an armistice on the basis of Wilson's Fourteen Points. 'What an astonishing fortnight this has been in the history of the world!' Maynard wrote to
his mother on 13 October. 'Six months from now expect me back at
Cambridge quite quit of the Treasury.' Twelve days later doubts had
returned. 'I still think the prospects of peace good. But I suspect a possibility
of wickedness on our part and an unwillingness to subscribe to the whole
of Wilson's fourteen commandments.'

The war ended for Maynard in an unceasing social whirl: weekends with
the Asquiths, the McKennas, Maud Cunard and Sir Thomas Beecham; dining
out every evening with politicians, diplomats and society hostesses. On top
of this Duncan and Vanessa had been staying at 46 Gordon Square decorat-
ing Maynard's drawing room, and the Diaghilev Ballet had returned to

London. Oswald Falk took Maynard to see it. 'There's no genius in it this year, but all the same it is most enjoyable,' Maynard wrote to Duncan on 17 September. 'The lady, Lupokova, is poor. But the new Nijinski – Mr [Stanislav] Idzikovski – , although no replacer and just an ordinary well trained youth, has a charm or two. At least I think so.' On 10 October Maynard met Lydia Lopokova, possibly for the first time, at a party given by the Sitwells in Chelsea. On 19 October, after having been to the ballet again with his young friend the painter Edward Wolfe, he was writing about her quite familiarly to Duncan, though his interest was clearly elsewhere:

> We went round afterwards to Lupokova who was as usual charming (making us pinch her legs to see how strong she was – which we did very shyly; Clive should have been there). But why I mention this is to lead up to Idzikovski whose acquaintance at last we've made. The Ballet had been Enchanted Princess and [Prince] Igor and Wolfe had been rapturous over Idzi's body. So on visiting Lupokova we enquired after him. 'I hear his voice in the passage outside,' cried Lydia. 'Call him in.' Which done, in stepped the most ridiculous little creature you ever saw. Very tiny (which we expected) but with white flaxen hair brushed back from his forehead, a pasty face with ridiculous little peaked features, the whole crowned by pince nez with no rims to them. . . . The others didn't seem to take him at all seriously and Mr. Baroque [Lydia's husband Randolfo Barocchi] gently ragged him, throwing his arms round him and crying out 'Good night, my love' as he went away. 'I don't like dancing with him,' said Lydia. 'It is not nice to dance with something only up to your breasts and I am always afraid he will drop me'.

Maynard's days were spent in exhausting negotiations with the French. Early in November he was 'writing a Memorandum on Indemnities at top speed for an airman to fly to Versailles with'.[53] On 21 November 1918, ten days after Germany's surrender, he wrote to his mother, 'I have been put in principal charge of financial matters for the Peace Conference.'

One nightmare was over; another was about to start. Less than a year later Maynard had quit the Treasury and was penning his passionate denunciations of the Peace Treaty. Yet it is clear that the fury which went into *The Economic Consequences of the Peace* was not the product of the Peace Conference alone but had been building up throughout the war. The attitudes he displayed in that book – mistrust of Lloyd George, contempt for the Americans, anger that politics had ousted reason, fear of general impoverishment – had all poured out in his wartime letters. The monkey-house of Versailles was merely the monkey-house of the Inter-Ally Council writ large. It is wrong to portray Keynes, as Harrod does, as having gone to Versailles with high hopes, only to feel betrayed. He suspected 'wickedness' even before the war ended; Versailles confirmed it. Another point must be borne in mind. Keynes carried to the conference a burden not just of collective guilt but of personal guilt for his part in the war. He was looking for a way of making an act of personal reparation. Versailles provided him with the issue he needed, as, in the nature of things, it was bound to do.

15

Zigzagging: Keynes at the Paris Peace Conference

I. THE COST OF THE WAR

The Paris Peace Conference opened in January 1919. Keynes's main job in the two months preceding it was to prepare the Treasury's position on the question of a German indemnity. He and the economic historian W. J. Ashley had produced a paper on the historical experience of collecting indemnities as early as 2 December 1916.[1] Basing themselves mainly on the indemnity which Germany imposed on France in 1871, they concluded that payments from losers to victors would be favourable to victors provided they took place over a period of years rather than all at once. That some payment would be required from Germany was clear from the terms of the armistice agreement.

In his Fourteen Points Wilson had talked only about Germany 'restoring' the invaded territories. But the armistice agreement which the Germans signed contained a rider, inserted by Britain and France, that by 'restoration' the Allies understood that 'compensation will be made by Germany for all damage done to the civilian population of the Allies and to their property by the aggression of Germany by land, sea, and from the air'. (The British had changed 'invasion' to 'aggression' in order to get a larger share of the spoils.) Although this formula ruled out charging Germany for the whole cost of the war it left plenty of scope for the Allies to bid up their competing claims for 'compensation'.

Treasury planning for reparations took place within the framework of Wilson's Fourteen Points as modified by the rider. In Keynes's first memorandum on the subject, dated 31 October 1918, a further point emerged: any reparation demanded of Germany for the damage it had caused must take into account its capacity to pay. It must not be so severe as to crush Germany's productive power; for, in the end, moveable property, gold and foreign securities apart, Germany could pay only by exporting goods to earn foreign currency.[2] There were thus two sets of figures involved: the damage Germany had done by its 'aggression', and the probable size of its 'capacity'. The first was actual, the second hypothetical. There was no reason why they should match.

In the main Treasury memorandum of 26 November 1918, largely based
on Keynes's 31 October draft, they did not. It was estimated that a round
figure of £4000m might be taken as representing the preliminary claim of
the Allies under the head of 'reparation'. The Treasury document emphasised that this represented damage 'done *directly*' to the civilian population –
mainly destruction of civilian life and property through enemy action. It
excluded indirect damage – for example, the Allies would not be entitled to
claim the costs of pensions paid to widows of soldiers killed in action. Britain,
it was suggested, could legitimately claim 15 per cent of the total damages.
However, the maximum Germany could pay was estimated at £3000m; and
an actual payment of £2000m would be 'a very satisfactory achievement
in all the circumstances'. The assumption was that Germany would pay
this over a number of years in the form of an annual tribute. 'If Germany
is to be "milked", she must not first of all be ruined,' the memorandum
concluded.[3]

The Treasury was not the only agency concerned with working out the
sums of German payments. A powerful lobby of business and Dominion
interests believed that Germany must be charged the 'whole costs of the
war'. Lloyd George was a 'Jekyll and Hyde', sometimes breathing fire against
Germany, at other times recognising the need for moderation and worried
by the effect which large German transfers would have on Britain's export
industries. However, he had to pay attention to the opinions of the Conservatives, who provided him with his parliamentary majority, and to the
Dominion leaders gathered in London in the Imperial War Cabinet.

The general election of 14 December 1918 provided the link between
'the mentality of war, especially economic war, and the making of peace'.[4]
The Australian Prime Minister, William Morris Hughes, was enraged by the
Wilsonian formula (which excluded reparations to Australia) and the Treasury estimates based on it. On 7 November he publicly demanded that
Germany be made to pay the costs of the war; his cry was taken up by
leading newspapers. Hughes's outburst, repeated a few days later, frightened
Lloyd George, as the Dominions were to be directly represented at the Paris
peace talks and Lloyd George had to carry them with him. On 26 November,
the day after the dissolution of Parliament, the Imperial War Cabinet decided
to appoint a Committee of its own to determine how much Germany
should and could pay. Hughes was made chairman to muzzle him, and
Lord Cunliffe was included on the Committee to add the authority of an
ex-governor of the Bank of England. Keynes and Hubert Llewellyn Smith
of 'A' Division attended the first few hearings.

The Committee's final report of 10 December put the total cost of the
war at £24,000m (which is roughly what the Treasury had estimated), and
claimed that Germany could and should pay the whole amount in annual
instalments of £1200m. The War Cabinet rejected this conclusion as a 'wild
and fantastic chimera', but not before Lloyd George had promised at Bristol

on 11 December that if re-elected he would charge Germany the whole cost of the war, an 'expert' Committee having told him Germany could pay it. In his election campaign, Lloyd George had yielded to popular clamour as well as to the pessimistic forecasts of his campaign managers. Fighting on a Coalition programme of reconstruction, he found that his speeches fell flat unless he talked about punishing Germany. Other ministers used more extreme language. At Cambridge, Sir Eric Geddes, First Lord of the Admiralty, declared on 9 December: 'The Germans are going to be squeezed as a lemon is squeezed – until the pips squeak.'

The effect of the election campaign on the peace negotiations was not confined to the election promises given by Lloyd George and others. In sweeping away the old Liberal Party (even Asquith lost his seat) the electorate saddled Lloyd George with a Jingo majority in Parliament (383 Conservatives, many of them businessmen). Furthermore, at the height of the election, Lloyd George accepted a recommendation by the Imperial War Cabinet that Hughes and Cunliffe, the chief authors of what he later called the 'wild and fantastic report', should be the British representatives – together with a judge, Lord Sumner – on the Reparations Commission at the Paris Peace Conference. Keynes and the British Treasury were thus formally excluded from the reparations side of the peace talks. This decision had baleful consequences. When, in Paris, Lloyd George eventually turned to Keynes and others to provide him with more realistic figures, he found he was saddled with the 'Heavenly Twins', as Cunliffe and Sumner were known, who prevented a coherent British position from emerging.

Keynes and the Treasury view were not without supporters. The US Treasury saw eye to eye with them. Bonar Law, the Chancellor and head of the Conservative Party, was a notable force for moderation. Jan Christian Smuts, leading the South African delegation to Paris and also a member of the British War Cabinet (his double position was one of the war's constitutional anomalies), was full of admiration for Keynes's 'masterly memorandum on Indemnities'.[5] On the other side, Leo Amery, the Colonial Secretary, wrote to Smuts on 26 December:

> Hughes's figures seem to me exaggerated. On the other hand the Treasury memorandum goes much too far the other way and is full of crude economic fallacies such as one would naturally perhaps expect from a professor like Keynes. Neither of them takes any account of what is really the most important question, which is to make sure that whatever the amount Germany does pay, we should get our fair share.[6]

In France it was accepted that no French government could survive which did not demand from Germany the whole cost of the war ('L'Allemagne paiera') since to raise taxes was considered political suicide. The political chiefs of Britain and France were united in their determination to wriggle out of their commitment to 'reparation only'. The point on which they differed was the division of the loot.

II. DR MELCHIOR

Keynes went to Paris on 10 January 1919 as the chief Treasury representative of the British delegation, assisted by Dudley Ward, Oswald Falk and Geoffrey Fry of 'A' Division. He had a room at the Hotel Majestic with the rest of the British delegation. His job was to handle the financial aspects of the transition to peace. Relief matters were in the hands of an Inter-Ally Supreme Council for Relief and Supply, of which the American Herbert Hoover was director-general, and on which Keynes served under Lord Reading. A decision to supply the Germans with 270,000 tons of food was taken by the Council on 12 January, conditional on the Germans handing over their merchant marine. But at the Armistice Commission, over which Marshal Foch presided, the French Finance Minister, Louis-Lucien Klotz, objected that 'Germany should not pay for [the food] out of assets which were available for Reparation'.[7] Keynes, left to represent the British position, protested loudly: 'as a result deadlock and the matter referred to the Supreme War Council in the afternoon [of 13 January]'. Here President Wilson held forth eloquently on the dangers of bolshevism if Germany were not fed; Hoover, desperate to unload his 'abundant stocks of low-grade pig products at high prices' on the Germans, added supporting arguments. Klotz reluctantly accepted a compromise whereby Germany should be allowed to earmark resources to pay for some of the food, subject to an investigation of the German financial position. Next day (14 January) Keynes, together with Norman Davis, Assistant Secretary to the American Treasury, and Comte de Lasteyrie and Professor Attolico, representing the French and Italian Treasuries, joined Marshal Foch's train *en route* for Trèves (or Trier), where the Marshal was due to meet President Erzberger of Germany. They had arranged to meet German financial experts to discuss means of payment. Keynes recalled that on the journey, and at Trèves itself, when not in conference, he made up an almost continuous Anglo-American bridge four.[8]

The financial discussions took place on the train. The German team was headed by Dr Kaufmann, President of the Reichsbank. But it was another German who made the deepest impression on Keynes. This was Dr Carl Melchior, a partner in the banking firm of M. M. Warburg. 'Dr Melchior: A Defeated Enemy', posthumously published in 1949, is the most intimate and accomplished of all Keynes's writings, offering a highly emotional account of a personal drama. It was first read to Bloomsbury's Memoir Club in February 1920, where it greatly impressed Virginia Woolf with its 'method of character drawing'. She thought the 'set-pieces' were very brilliantly told. Keynes wrote of 'a very small man, exquisitely clean, very well and neatly dressed, with a high stiff collar which seemed cleaner and whiter than an ordinary collar', and added:

> This was he with whom in the ensuing months I was to have one of the most curious intimacies in the world, and some very strange passages of experience – Dr Melchior.... This Jew, for such, though not by appearance, I afterwards learnt him to be, and he only, upheld the dignity of defeat.[9]

Fraternisation between victor and vanquished was forbidden, and the conference ended, as it had been conducted, with frigid formality, thawed only slightly by the natural gregariousness of the Americans, and little accomplished. But Keynes and Melchior had made an unstated contact. The suffering in Melchior's face made a more vivid impact on Keynes than did the collective sufferings of France. His French colleague de Lasteyrie, a 'genteel Catholic', represented to him the 'grasping sterility of France'; or of that part of France which, 'in spite of what Clive [Bell] and Roger [Fry] may say, *is* France'. Keynes recalled: 'I don't believe I have ever ... been so rude to anyone'.[10]

Following Trèves, Keynes collapsed with a severe attack of influenza, which called for a fortnight's convalescence with the Bussys on the Riviera. Before leaving Paris he wrote an atmospheric letter to Bradbury (25 January 1919) which shows how soon he had lost all faith in the integrity of the peace conference:

> This is a shocking place, – of muddle and physical, spiritual and intellectual hot air.... The President is a rather vulgar nonconformist surrounded exclusively by toughs. The Americans are quite devoid of idealism but their intense hatred of the French does instead. We and the Yanks are lined up together against the French on practically every occasion big and small.... The hot central heating and rich bad food so promote the circulation of bile in the head as to cause members of the delegation frequently to fall down in the hall and break their limbs.

On 19 February, back in Paris and after a second fruitless conference at Trèves, Keynes had another row with Klotz. He curtly told the French Finance Minister that Britain could no longer provide support for the French franc. The franc plummeted, followed soon afterwards by sterling, ending a hundred years of fixed exchange rates. Klotz wrote a book in 1924, blaming Keynes's 'swollen vanity' for the 'financial catastrophe which has fallen on the world'. But Keynes was acting on the authority of Austen Chamberlain, the new Chancellor of the Exchequer, who had been told by Colonel House, Wilson's special adviser, that American official aid to Britain was being cut off.[11] Continuous contact with France's garrulous Finance Minister on the Supreme Economic Council (which had replaced the Council for Supply and Relief on 8 February) did nothing to increase Keynes's already limited sympathy for French demands. 'A short, plump, heavy-moustached Jew, well-groomed, well kept, but with an unsteady, roving eye, and his shoulders a little bent with instinctive deprecation',[12] Klotz represented, to Keynes, the other face of France's grasping sterility – a view not uninfluenced by the anti-semitism which was normal to his class and generation.

On 4 March Keynes was once more negotiating with the Germans, this time at Spa, in Belgium, Germany's wartime military headquarters, where he stayed with General Haking, Britain's chief military representative on the Armistice Commission, in Ludendorff's villa, surrounded by 'the theatrical melancholy of black pinewoods'. The head of the British delegation, Admiral Hope, informed the German delegates that no foodstuffs would be allowed to enter Germany until 'substantial progress' had been made in handing over the German passenger and cargo vessels. The head of the German delegation, Braun, replied that the delivery of the German merchant fleet was contingent on firm promises from the Allies to make available enough food to feed Germany till the next harvest (in August).[13] But there was no way such promises could be given, since the French had not yet agreed to allow the Germans to pay for any food beyond a small amount. Meanwhile, Haking told Keynes that the Germans were starving and the social order was on the point of collapse.

Keynes was convinced that some way had to be found of breaking the deadlock. If the Germans would agree to give way on the ships, he and the Americans would bring pressure on their political chiefs to overrule Klotz. As Keynes tells it:

> I looked across the table at Melchior. He seemed to feel as I did. Staring, heavy-lidded, helpless, looking, as I had seen him before, like an honourable animal in pain. Couldn't we break down the empty formalities of this Conference, the three-barred gate of triple interpretations, and talk about the truth and the reality like sane and sensible persons?

He tells how they escaped from Melchior's mutinous, 'bolshevised' clerks to a small room where they were at last alone:

> I was quivering with excitement, terrified out of my wits at what I was doing, for the barriers of permitted intercourse had not then begun to crumble, and somewhat emotional. Melchior wondered what I wanted.... I tried to convey to him what I was feeling, how we believed his prognostications of pessimism, how we were impressed, not less than he, with the urgency of starting food supplies ... that they [the Germans] must make up their minds to the handing over of the ships;

and that, if only he could secure a little latitude from Weimar, we could between us concoct a formula which would allow the food supplies to move in practice and evade the obstructions of the French.

By now both Keynes and Melchior were in a highly emotional state. 'We both stood all through the interview. In a sort of way I was in love with him.' Keynes and Melchior agreed a form of words, for Admiral Hope to present to the German delegation, to the effect that if the Germans agreed to hand over their merchant marine, the Allies would agree to supply the food the Germans required, subject to the approval of the Supreme War Council as to quantities, and to the approval of the Supreme Economic Council as to arrangements for payment.[14] 'We pressed hands, and I hurried quickly into the street....'[15]

Weimar was contacted but refused to budge. Keynes left for Paris on 6 March determined to 'attract the attention of the Great Ones' who were frittering away their time debating how many votes Brazil should have on some sub-commission, and listening to endless speeches in unknown languages by Copts, Armenians, Slovaks, Arabs and Zionists.[16] This time he managed to engage Lloyd George's interest. A meeting of the Supreme War Council was called for 8 March.

The story of that dramatic meeting, in which Lloyd George turned with terrible fury on Klotz, stimulated Keynes to the most vivid piece of writing in his memoir; his account is substantially confirmed by Lord Riddell in his *Intimate Diary of the Peace Conference*. Lord Robert Cecil presented the British case. The Germans must promise to deliver the ships. The Allies must promise to start delivering the food as soon as Germany started releasing the ships. The Germans must be allowed to pay in gold. The blockade must be lifted to the extent of allowing them to start exporting some goods and buying food from neutrals. Lloyd George clothed Lord Robert's flat prose with tempestuous imagery: if the Allies refused to revictual the Germans they would be sowing the seeds of Bolshevism, of the next war. It was 'a superb farrago of sense and sentiment, of spontaneous rhetoric and calculated art'. Clemenceau gave way on the gold.

Lloyd George had another trick up his sleeve. Suddenly a secretary rushed in with a telegram. Tearing it open, the Prime Minister read out a message from General Plumer, commanding British occupation forces on the Rhine. It demanded food 'without delay'. Women and children were dying, the people were in despair and felt that an end by bullets was better than death by starvation. Despite the effect produced by this *coup de théâtre* Klotz, misjudging the atmosphere, still made difficulties.

> Never [Keynes wrote] have I seen the equal of the onslaught with which that poor man was overwhelmed.... Lloyd George had always hated and despised him; and now saw in a twinkling that he could kill him. Women and children were starving, he cried, and here was M. Klotz

prating and prating of his 'goold'. He leant forward and with a gesture
of his hands indicated to everyone the image of a hideous Jew clutch-
ing a money bag. His eyes flashed and the words came out with a
contempt so violent that he seemed almost to be spitting at him. . . .
Everyone looked at Klotz . . . the poor man was bent over his seat, visibly
cowering.

The Prime Minister had not finished. Unless Klotz ceased his obstructive
tactics, he roared, three names would go down in history as the architects
of Bolshevism: Lenin, Trotsky and. . . . 'All round the room you could see
each one grinning and whispering to his neighbour "Klotzky".'[17] This was
the moment when Maynard changed his mind about Lloyd George. He
suddenly realised that 'he can be amazing when one agrees with him. Never
have I more admired his extraordinary powers.' The seeds of Maynard's later
'betrayal' of Asquith, of his collaboration with Lloyd George in the Liberal
Industrial Enquiry of the late 1920s, were planted in that inspired half-hour.

Four days later Keynes was on his way to Brussels with the First Sea
Lord, Admiral Wemyss, who was authorised to accept the surrender of the
German ships. The admiral was worried that the Germans might demur
about handing over their ships unconditionally, which is what the Supreme
War Council had insisted on. Would Keynes make sure that everything
went smoothly? Once more he sought out Dr Melchior in his hotel room.
He told him that the leader of the German delegation would be called upon
to surrender the ships right at the start of the conference. But then, as
Melchior's face fell, Keynes added that once the German statement to that
effect had been made the Allies would immediately give their undertaking
to revictual Germany. Could Melchior make sure that the German part of
this script was followed to the letter? 'Yes,' he replied. 'There shall be no
difficulty about that.' The next day everything went according to plan.
Within days, 'the food trains started to Germany'.[18] There were to be further
meetings, near Paris, with Melchior and other German bankers to discuss
the handover of German gold and securities, but the battle had been won.

Throughout this period Keynes was living in an extreme state of nervous
excitement. To his mother he wrote on 16 March:

> I am Deputy for the Chancellor of the Exchequer on the Supreme
> Economic Council with full powers to take decisions; also one of the
> British Empire representatives on the Financial Committee of the Peace
> Conference; Chairman of the Inter-Allied Financial Delegates in Armi-
> stice Negotiations with the Germans; and principal Treasury Represent-
> ative in Paris. All of which sounds rather greater than it is; but it's a full
> day's occupation.

He rushed about in 'draughty motor cars from one overheated room to
another', eating excessively rich food and sometimes overwhelmed with
work.[19] The Hotel Majestic swarmed with Scotland Yard officers. Members

Florence Ada Keynes.

John Neville Keynes.

Maynard at the age of three.

Geoffrey (8), Maynard (12) and Margaret (10).

Sheridan's *The Rivals* at Eton: Harold Butler as Sir Lucius O'Trigger, Maynard Keynes as Bob Acres.

Maynard Keynes, Bernard Swithinbank and Gerard Mackworth Young.

The Committee of the Cambridge Union, 1905.

Duncan Grant.

Arthur Lee Hobhouse.

Maynard Keynes, portrait by Duncan Grant, painted on Hoy, 1908.

Bertrand Russell, Maynard Keynes and Lytton Strachey at Garsington, c. 1915.

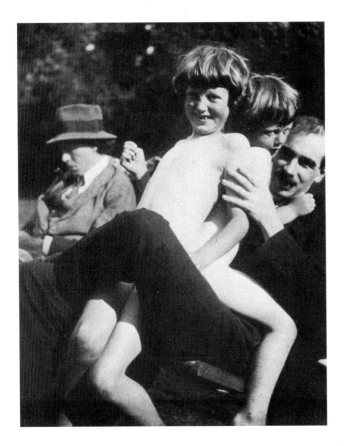

Maynard Keynes with Julian and Quentin Bell, Clive Bell in the background, West Wittering, 1915.

Sir Austen Chamberlain.

Reginald McKenna.

Clemenceau, Wilson and Lloyd George after the signing of the Treaty, 28 June 1919.

Maynard Keynes at
Charleston, where he wrote
*The Economic Consequences
of the Peace.*

Daniel Macmillan,
who published the book.

of the British delegation hurried from one committee to another. The red boxes circulated unendingly, full of unread memoranda; and the 'feverish, persistent and boring gossip of that hellish place had already developed in full measure the peculiar flavour of smallness, cynicism, self-importance and bored excitement that it was never to lose'.[20] To Vanessa Bell, Keynes wrote, 'I'm absolutely absorbed in this extraordinary but miserable game. I wish I could tell you every evening the twists and turns of the day, for you'd really be amused by the amazing complications of psychology and personality and intrigue which make such magnificent sport of the impending catastrophe of Europe.'[21]

III. THE REPARATIONS TANGLE

Keynes had, as yet, had little to do with drawing up the financial terms of the peace settlement. The detailed work of the conference was being done by the Expert Commissions, with contentious issues referred to the Supreme War Council, or Council of Ten as it was known, which became the Council of Four late in March. The Reparations Commission was divided into three sub-committees, on evaluation, capacity and guarantees. In the first sub-committee the Australian Prime Minister, Hughes, a blunt, impetuous man whose deafness was a considerable help in resisting counterarguments, joined the French in claiming the whole cost of the war, his argument being that the tax burden imposed on the Allies by the German aggression should be regarded as damage to civilians. The claim came to about \$125bn, or £25bn. The American John Foster Dulles took the line that there had been a contract with Germany, which limited its liability at most to \$25bn–\$30bn, or about £5bn–£6bn.

Faced with an American veto, the French abandoned their claim to war costs, being impressed by Dulles's argument that, having suffered the most damage, they would get the largest share of reparations. Once the percentage game started, the British discovered that their share would go up relative to the French by including in the Allied claim the costs of pensions paid to war widows, and separation allowances paid to the wives of combatants. The American Assistant Secretary to the Treasury Norman Davis 'finally agreed to include these items in the categories of damage because we thought it just, and because we thought it would not increase the amount which Germany would eventually pay, but would only change the basis of dividing what she did pay, which seemed to us more equitable'.[22] However, the French refused to set a figure on their claim, since they feared it would be too small to satisfy French public opinion.

All this was going on in February. In the second sub-committee, the chairman Lord Cunliffe thought that Germany could pay £25bn, but finally agreed to recommend £8bn if the Americans would agree. The French Minister of Reconstruction, Louis Loucheur, told Davis privately that he was satisfied that the Germans could not pay anything approaching this, but could not advocate a smaller sum than Lord Cunliffe was doing. On 1 March Keynes reported to Austen Chamberlain that the range of disagreement was between £6bn and £9bn.[23] Deadlock was reached when the banker Thomas W. Lamont, representing America, refused to go above £6bn, of which half was to be paid in German currency. In Tillman's summary, 'Direct negotiations for a fixed sum through the determination of German capacity to pay had by early March failed as completely as the attempt to fix the sum through the evaluation of damages.'[24]

On 10 March, in an effort to break the deadlock, Lloyd George, Clemenceau and Colonel House (representing Wilson who was away in the United States) appointed a secret committee consisting of Edwin Montagu, Davis and Loucheur to determine what sum could be collected from Germany, and in what proportion it should be distributed. An agreement on percentages was reached: 55 per cent to the French and 25 per cent to the British. Montagu and Loucheur also agreed with Davis that the most Germany could be expected to pay over thirty years was £3bn – the figure cited in the British Treasury memorandum of 26 November 1918 – Loucheur telling Montagu that 'Germany could not ... pay more than £2bn which would have to be supplemented by ... "monkey's money" '.[25] Lloyd George seemed to accept this on 15 March, saying to Davis that he would have 'to tell our people the facts'. But on 18 March Lloyd George decided to postpone the public enlightenment. These events marked Keynes's first involvement in the reparations question. Montagu naturally consulted him; there is a memorandum from Keynes, dated 11 March, stating that whereas Germany should be required to 'render payment for the injury she has caused up to the limit of her capacity', it was impossible at the present time to determine what her capacity was, so that the fixing of a definite liability should be postponed.[26] Since this is what the Treaty actually did, it would seem that Keynes's advice was contrary to his later view (expressed in *The Economic Consequences of the Peace*, pp. 85, 99) that the Allies should have fixed a definite sum in the Treaty. However, he was still assuming in March that the *total* of claims would not amount to more than £3bn, the political leaders not yet having agreed to the inclusion of pensions and separation allowances.

Lloyd George's strategy at this point was still to bind Cunliffe and Sumner to a 'reasonable' sum. The experts worked out a flexible plan, allowing for a minimum of $25bn (£5bn) and a maximum of $35bn (£7bn). This was the nearest they got to harmonising the views of Davis and Lamont on the one hand, and Cunliffe and Sumner on the other. There is a letter in

Keynes's hand to Lloyd George, dated 22 March, enclosing a schedule of annual payments based on the smaller sum, which he had worked out with R. H. Brand of Lazards. Keynes's touch appears in the words: 'In our opinion, long before the amounts are collected, the Allied governments may, and probably will, find that such collection is doing them as much damage as to the enemy.'[27] But Lloyd George would not accept £5bn as the total claim unless Cunliffe and Sumner accepted it, fearing that their opposition would 'crucify' him in Parliament;[28] the Heavenly Twins refused to budge. Keynes was now taking a more charitable view of the Prime Minister. He wrote to his father on 30 March: 'For the last ten days I've had the experience of working intimately with the PM and have seen a fair amount of Wilson and Clemenceau. The fact is that Ll.G. has, at least for the time being, taken a turn towards a heaven place and away from a hell place, so that my services are not quite as inappropriate to him as usual.'

After a weekend at Fontainebleau, Lloyd George returned to Paris in a liberal mood, declaring once more (26 March) that he and Clemenceau should tell the people the truth. Wilson responded enthusiastically to this suggestion. 'I cannot fail to express my admiration for the spirit which manifests itself in Mr Lloyd George's words. There is nothing more honourable than to be driven from power because one was right.' This was the last thing Lloyd George had in mind. A couple of days later, he decided to leave out of the Treaty any definite figures. A Reparations Commission was to be given until 1921 to work out what Germany owed, subject only to the proviso that it pay £1bn on account. Twisting and turning, Lloyd George had eventually found a way out of his embarrassing commitments to the Jingoes and the Heavenly Twins.

As we have seen, the idea of including pensions and separation allowances in the claim for damages dated from February. But the American President had not yet agreed to this apparent breach of the Fourteen Points. At first he had strongly resisted it. But he was converted by a 'legal opinion' prepared by Smuts on 31 March 1919, at Lloyd George's request. Smuts argued that while direct war expenses could not be legitimately claimed from the Germans, 'disablement pensions to discharged soldiers, or pensions to widows and orphans or separation allowances paid to their wives and children during the period of their military service' could.[29] Smuts's aim was to get the British Empire a larger share of reparations. He saw that it would increase the total claim against Germany; but assumed that this would anyway be scaled down to Germany's 'capacity to pay' which, like Keynes and the Americans, he estimated at between £2bn and £3bn.[30] Wilson, seeing a way of squaring British and French demands with his conscience, dismissed the legalistic objections of his advisers – 'Logic! Logic! I don't give a damn for logic. I am going to include pensions' – even though he recognised that 'it was not in the minds of those who drew up the Armistice ... to include pensions'.[31] Keynes's unflattering assessment of the President in *The Economic Consequences of the Peace* was largely based on this single episode, which he regarded as a prime example of Wilson's casuistry.[32]

The crucial defeat in the battle to limit Germany's bill came at a meeting of the Council of Four on 5 April 1919, when Lloyd George, citing Lord Sumner, agreed to extend the time-limit of annual payments beyond thirty years 'if it turns out that all cannot be paid in this period'. In Wilson's absence, it was Colonel House who sold the pass. This concession destroyed the assumption that the inclusion of pensions would make no difference to the total amount which Germany would be called on to pay.[33] As Florence Lamont wrote in her diary, 'L.G. does not want anything put in to limit the capacity of the Germans to pay.'[34]

The Americans complained that Keynes failed to stand up to Lloyd George.[35] But no one in the British delegation did. Smuts, who might have done, was away ill for most of March; he returned to write his fateful 'legal opinion' on pensions – a document which his biographer says 'did more to damage his reputation than any other document that he ever produced in his life'[36] – before being dispatched on a mission to Hungary. The Foreign Secretary, Arthur Balfour, who had the authority to do so, was so cynically detached from the proceedings that when Margot Asquith visited Paris she found that 'no one seemed to know whether he was there or not'. Keynes encountered him one night 'in a rather elevated condition in the street. He seized me warmly by the arm and marching along linked embarked on a discussion on the merits of Tiepolo.'[37] Keynes himself was no more part of Lloyd George's circle than he had been in the war. Lloyd George used him, as he used Montagu, to wriggle out of his commitments to the Heavenly Twins. But he never thought of taking his advice. Keynes later told Margot Asquith that the British were the best-equipped delegation in Paris, but that for all the use the Prime Minister made of them 'we might have been idiots'. Eventually Keynes realised that he could do no more good at the Treasury; but not before he made one further attempt to influence events in the direction of sanity and moderation.

IV. 'GRAND SCHEME FOR THE REHABILITATION OF EUROPE'

Keynes's closest political friend in Paris was the South African Defence Minister, Jan Christian Smuts. A Cambridge graduate of 1894, Smuts was an intellectual general, a politician with philosophical interests and ambitions. (He later invented a philosophy called Holism.) He shared with Keynes a high-minded approach to peacemaking, as well as an antipathy to the

French, and a marked distrust of Lloyd George. Their disillusion with events in Paris developed in parallel. After his return from Hungary, Smuts wrote to his friend Mrs Gillett on 9 April:

> This afternoon ... Keynes came to see me and I described to him the pitiful plight of Central Europe. And he (who is conversant with the finance of the matter) confessed to me his doubt whether anything could really be done. Those pitiful people have little credit left, and instead of getting indemnities from them, we may have to advance them money to live.[38]

Smuts's account of the suffering in Central Europe concentrated Keynes's attention on a scheme which had been germinating in his mind. This was to link the reparations' question with the question of inter-Ally debts. The British and French wanted to milk Germany partly for the purpose of paying back America. If the Americans could be persuaded to scale down their claims this would ease the pressure on Germany. As early as November 1918 Keynes had pointed out the advantage to Britain of an all-round debt cancellation: Britain held a lot of bad debts from its European allies, while America held a lot of good debts from Britain. If some means were not found of reducing Britain's obligations, Britain would be left open to 'future pressure by the United States of a most objectionable description' and its foreign investment potential would be crippled.[39] On 28 March 1919 he circulated a paper arguing that the attempt to collect all the debts arising from the last war (including reparations) would poison, and perhaps destroy, the capitalist system. 'I do not believe that any of these tributes will continue to be paid, at the best, for more than a very few years. They do not square with human nature or march with the spirit of the age.' The paper is notable for its sense of the fragility of capitalist civilisation. But Keynes recognised that total cancellation was not practicable. So he hinted at a scheme by which Allied governments would accept German reparation bonds 'in final discharge of the debts incurred between ourselves'.

On 12 April he returned to England. Five days later he wrote to his mother that he had been busy getting through the Cabinet a '*grand* scheme for the rehabilitation of Europe'. The plan had taken shape in discussions with Smuts, and Smuts gave it enthusiastic support, while acknowledging that the idea was Keynes's.[40] Austen Chamberlain recommended it to Lloyd George as being marked by 'all Mr. Keynes's characteristic ability and fertility of resource'.[41] Lloyd George was impressed too: scaling down demands on Germany in return for a remission of debt to the United States was something which he could sell to Parliament. He passed on the Keynes Plan to President Wilson with a warm covering letter. Keynes's scheme provided for the issue by the German government and its defeated allies of £1345m worth of bonds, on account of reparations, and 'in payment of all indebtedness between any of the allied and associated governments'. No interest was to be paid on them for five years, and they were to be jointly guaranteed by the issuing governments and by the Allied governments in certain specified proportions. Of the total, £1000m of bonds were to be paid to the European Allies, and the rest retained by the Central Powers. The bonds were 'to be acceptable as first-class collateral for loans'.[42]

Keynes was trying to kill a number of birds with one stone. All inter-Ally debts arising from the war were to be reduced and the balance discharged by means of a German debt which could be transferred without putting immediate strain on the German balance of payments. European credit would be rehabilitated; the United States would be assured of a demand for its exports; the Central Powers too would obtain funds to feed their people. Thus the plan served both the immediate purpose of providing the European countries with means of payment for imports and also the long-term purpose of greatly reducing the overhang of debt arising from the war. It was compatible with decisions already taken on reparations – which provided for an initial German payment of £1bn – while improving the prospect of getting an eventual sum within Germany's 'capacity to pay'. In an accompanying memorandum intended for Wilson and Clemenceau, Keynes wrote:

> A proposal which unfolds future prospects and shows the peoples of Europe a road by which food and employment and orderly existence can once again come their way, will be a more powerful weapon than any other for the preservation from the dangers of Bolshevism of that order of human society which we believe to be the best starting point for future improvement and greater well-being.[43]

The American reaction was disappointingly cool. Thomas Lamont, writing with all the authority of a partner in J. P. Morgan, condemned it as 'unsound in conception, and impracticable in execution'. He argued that its adoption would give the impression that the European countries were insolvent, and would diminish the Europeans' incentive to work. Furthermore, it would require Congressional approval, which would not be forthcoming. Lamont wanted American credits to be extended through 'normal commercial and banking channels'. He proposed setting up a private Finance Corporation in the United States to channel American savings to Europe in co-operation with British banking groups.[44]

At dinner with Keynes and Smuts on 3 May, Davis and Lamont revealed another objection to the Keynes Plan: 'They see that any assistance they give to Germany will enable us to extract more reparation, and they are determined they will not assist.'[45] Any hope that Wilson would forgo part of the European debt to the United States foundered on the rock of Lloyd George's reparations policy. On 3 May the President wrote to the Prime Minister:

You have suggested that we all address ourselves to the problem of helping to put Germany on her feet, but how can your experts or ours be expected to work out a *new* plan to furnish working capital to Germany when we deliberately start out by taking away all Germany's *present* capital?[46]

Keynes argued against this interpretation, but his heart was not in it. As he told Philip Kerr, Lloyd George's private secretary, 'There is a substantial truth in the President's standpoint.'[47]

Keynes's last hope that out of the horrors of Paris would at least come a plan to put Europe back on its feet had gone. By early May a draft Treaty had at last been assembled out of the labours of fifty-eight specialist commissions and the deliberations of the Council of Four, giving Keynes for the first time an overall view of the proposed settlement. He was horrified. In a letter of 4 May he declared, 'The settlement is a paper settlement which even if it is accepted cannot possibly be expected to last.' He doubted whether the Germans would sign it.[48] To Duncan Grant he wrote on 14 May:

It's weeks since I've written a letter to anyone, – but I've been utterly worn out, partly by incessant work and partly by depression at the evil round me. I've been as miserable for the last two or three weeks as a fellow could be. The Peace is outrageous and impossible and can bring nothing but misfortune....

Thank God I shall soon be out of it and I suppose it won't be many weeks before I've forgotten the nightmare. I'm writing to the Treasury to be relieved of my duties by 1 June if possible and not later than 15 June in any event.

Lloyd George himself was beginning to have doubts. In the words of André Tardieu, later French Prime Minister,

Those were atrocious days. Mr. Lloyd George, thoroughly alarmed by the consequences either of a refusal to sign or of a crisis in Germany, suggested unthinkable concessions on almost every point. He excused himself for doing it so tardily. He spoke of consulting the Commons. The work of two months was threatened with ruin. M. Clemenceau stood firm.[49]

Lloyd George 'asked for a thoroughgoing revision of the Reparations Clauses, and inclined under the influence of Mr Keynes to the lump sum proposed in March by the American experts'.[50] Keynes briefed him as well as he could. On 7 May Smuts wrote to Mrs Gillett:

Poor Keynes often sits with me at night after a good dinner and we rail against the world and the coming flood. And I tell him that this is the time for Grigua's prayer (the Lord to come himself and not to send his Son, as this is not a time for children). And then we laugh and behind the laughter is Hoover's horrible picture of thirty million people who must die unless there is some great intervention.

Mrs Gillett, referring to the Anti-Corn Law League, had reminded Smuts that economic reform had preceded franchise reform in the nineteenth century, and that 'now it seems as though in the same way the political and territorial questions won't be solved till the economic world is righted'. Smuts reported this remark to Keynes, who said 'how true it was and he had never thought of it that way'.[51] Perhaps here we have the origin of the main theme of the *Economic Consequences of the Peace.*

Keynes was still trying to do good. At the end of May he attempted, without success, to get the successor states of the Austro-Hungarian Empire relieved of their obligation to export cattle to Italy and Serbia.

Then he took to his bed 'partly out of misery for all that's happening, and partly from prolonged overwork'. He had moved out of the Majestic to a flat on the edge of the Bois 'with an excellent French cook and a soldier servant to valet for me', rising only for meetings and interviews with the Chancellor, Smuts, the Prime Minister and suchlike. But it was all too late. Quite apart from Clemenceau's intransigence, Wilson had convinced himself that the draft Treaty was in conformity with his Fourteen Points. Besides, at the last moment he did not want any change in the Treaty 'simply because it was severe ... he wanted this to be a historic lesson, so that people might know that they could not do anything of the sort the Germans attempted without suffering the severest kind of punishment'.[52] It may also be that Lloyd George had received secret information that the Germans would sign, come what may, and that German protests were for form's sake only.[53]

The Treaty of Versailles was signed on 28 June 1919. By then Keynes had already left Paris and the Treasury. 'I can do no more good here,' he wrote to Norman Davis on 5 June. 'You Americans are broken reeds.' To Lloyd George he wrote on the same day:

> I ought to let you know that on Saturday I am slipping away from the scene of nightmare. I can do no more good here. I've gone on hoping even through these last dreadful weeks that you'd find some way to make of the Treaty a just and expedient document. But now it's apparently too late. The battle is lost. I leave the twins to gloat over the devastation of Europe, and to assess to taste what remains for the British taxpayer.

16

Civilisation under Threat

I. WRITING THE BOOK

On 25 June 1919 Keynes wrote to his mother from Charleston, 'On Monday I began to write a new book ... on the economic condition of Europe as it now is, including a violent attack on the Peace Treaty and my proposals for the future.... I was stirred into it by the deep and violent shame which one couldn't help feeling for the events of Monday, and my temper may not keep up high enough to carry it through.' On Monday 23 June, the Allies had finally cut off any hope of modifying the draft proposals presented to the Germans; but the idea of making a public protest was already in Keynes's mind. He had written to Smuts on his return to London (8 June): 'I hope immensely that you may come to the conclusion that some explanation of what is really happening and a protest against it is now the right course. If so, I am at your service by pen or any other way.'[1] Smuts urged him on 10 June to start writing 'a clear, connected account of what the financial and economic clauses of the treaty actually mean, and what their probable results will be'. In the event he signed the Treaty of Versailles on 28 June, while publicly protesting its inadequacy. On 17 July, on the eve of his departure for South Africa, he wrote to Maynard once more, apparently reversing his previous advice:

> After giving the matter my closest consideration I have seen no great profit in a regular attack on the Treaty. It is past and nothing can undo it except time and the Great Mercy which works away all our human follies. Better to be constructive. My protest on signing the Peace had a great effect both here and on the Continent.... You will find many opportunities to help the world, especially when the real trouble over the Reparations and financial clauses begins with Germany.[2]

Keynes had resigned from the Treasury, he had told Smuts, in 'misery and rage' – a misery and rage which had been building up right through the war. He set to work with the urgency of despair. Virginia Woolf, who saw him at Charleston, noted in her diary of 8 July:

> He is disillusioned, he says. No more does he believe, that is, in the stability of the things he likes. Eton is doomed; the governing classes,

perhaps Cambridge too. These conclusions were forced on him by the dismal and degrading spectacle of the Peace Conference, where men played shamelessly, not for Europe, or even England, but for their own return to Parliament at the next election.

To Lord Robert Cecil Keynes wrote on 26 July, 'I find I take a not less pessimistic view as to the prospects of Europe and of European order, unless early steps are taken to make and *admit* as a dead letter many of the *economic* clauses of the treaty. Do you agree?'[3]

Other influences played their part in shaping the book. Margot Asquith wrote him a rather incoherent letter on 13 June demanding that he give her a description of the men and meetings at Paris for her diary.[4] She may well have planted in his mind the thought of supplementing his economic exposition with an account of the characters of the Allied leaders, and the atmosphere in which they worked. A remoter influence was Lytton Strachey's *Eminent Victorians* which had appeared in 1918. David Garnett feels that it tempted Keynes to be 'more indiscreet than he was by nature: to have the courage to print what he would have said in conversation'.[5]

Before he could settle down to his writing, there was practical business to attend to. Resignation from the Treasury had naturally cost him his Treasury salary of £1200 a year. Within a few weeks of his return he had turned down a new chair of currency and banking at the London School of Economics, and a professorship at Leeds. More tempting was the offer of the chairmanship of the British Bank of Northern Commerce, which promised £2000 a year for one day's work a week. He finally turned it down on the grounds that the Bank was under foreign (Scandinavian) control, but he let it be known that he was open to other offers. Meanwhile, currency speculation offered a more amusing and lucrative way of making money than selling economics by the hour. He returned to Cambridge to arrange the reduction of his college and university teaching commitments. He wrote to Duncan Grant from King's on 17 July:

> Most of the day I think about my book, and write it for about two hours, so that I get on fairly well and am now nearly half-way through the third chapter of eight. But writing is *very* difficult, and I feel more and more admiration for those who can bring it off successfully. I've finished to-day a sketch of the appearance and character of Clemenceau, and am starting to-morrow on Wilson. I think it's worthwhile to try, but it's really beyond my powers.

In London on the 29th (he told his mother),

> I gave a party at Gordon Square to round up the season which was judged a great success – I was too much preoccupied with the strenuous staff work of host to see much of it. We sat down twenty-three to supper shortly before midnight and did not rise from table until half-past one.

It is astonishing what the resources of a household are, when pushed. The next evening [30 July] was amidst much excitement the last night of the ballet, all of my various worlds being there. I also kept various business appointments, gave evidence before the Indian Currency Committee, addressed the Fight the Famine Council, opened a discussion on the Peace Terms at a City Dining Club [the Tuesday Club], and lunched and dined out every day – after which I was quite ready for the country. It's amusing to pass from Cambridge where I'm a nonentity, to London where I'm a celebrity.

From the beginning of August Keynes settled down to a regular routine at Charleston. He breakfasted at 8 a.m., and wrote till lunchtime. After lunch he read *The Times* and then gardened till tea. After tea he did his correspondence. He had his own servants, Blanche and Jessie, and Gordon Square was shut up. There were readings for his friends. 'I expect your psychological analysis of Wilson is absolutely correct. It explains everything,' wrote Leonard Woolf to him on 21 August. He added, 'I hope you're doing Lloyd George.'[6] Keynes did, in fact, write a sketch of the British Prime Minister, but was dissatisfied with it, and left it out on Asquith's advice. On 3 September he informed his mother that he had 'managed to keep up my average of 1,000 words fit for the printer every day, seven days a week; but there are still some very difficult bits to do. I hope to finish by the first week of October and have it actually published before the last day of the month.' As soon as he had finished a chapter he would send it off to Miss Pate's at Cambridge to be typed. By 23 September he had sent the first five chapters to R. & R. Clark, Macmillan's Edinburgh printer, to be set up in galleys. This was nearly four-fifths of the whole. But he had not managed to start the two remaining chapters, and so reckoned he was ten days behind schedule. 'They weigh rather heavily,' he told Florence, 'as I am getting stale and should like to take a month off. . . . But I suppose I must persevere.'[7] By the beginning of October he had started on his last chapter and was postponing his departure from Charleston.

Meanwhile in the United States President Wilson had collapsed on a speaking tour which he had undertaken to rally support for the Treaty. Lytton Strachey wrote to Keynes from Pangbourne on 4 October:

I seem to gather from the scant remarks in the newspapers, that your friend the President has gone mad. Is it possible that it should have gradually been borne in upon him what an appalling failure he was, and that when at last he fully realised it his mind collapsed? Very dramatic, if so. But won't it make some of your remarks almost too cruel?

Even when he was writing flat out, Keynes was not the person to be doing just one thing. He decided to pay for printing the book himself, leaving Macmillan with 10 per cent of the profits for distributing it, instead of the usual fifty–fifty basis. He signed a contract to this effect on 21 August, and arranged to print 5000 copies. Keynes hereafter paid for the printing of all the English editions of his books, supervised the details of their production, and reaped the profits. He never employed a literary agent. Felix Frankfurter, an American lawyer he had met in Paris, managed to get an offer of an American edition from the new firm of Harcourt, Brace, and Howe, which Keynes accepted, despite discontent at the 'low' royalty of 15 per cent.

Keynes's dealings with Macmillan in August were not confined to his own book. He arranged for the publication of a volume of Luce's poems, again at his own expense (they appeared in 1920 and, as Keynes had anticipated, did not pay). At the same time, Maynard was helping two other friends, David Garnett and Frankie Birrell, to set up a bookshop in London.[8] Finally, to relieve the tedium of country life, he had begun speculating on the foreign exchanges which 'will shock father, but out of which I hope to do very well'.[9] 'Money is a funny thing,' he wrote to Florence on 23 September. 'It seems impossible to believe that the present system will be allowed to continue much longer. As the fruit of a little extra knowledge and experience of a special kind, it simply (and undeservedly in any absolute sense) comes rolling in.' Soon he was to discover that a little extra knowledge was no guarantee against financial catastrophe. He also agreed to join the board of the National Mutual Life Assurance Society.

By 11 October Keynes had sent off chapter 6 and the greater part of chapter 7. As is common with authors, the story had grown in the telling – from an estimated 40,000 to 60,000 words. He now had to return to Cambridge to resume his lectures, though not before spending two days in Amsterdam from 13 to 15 October attending a bankers' conference called by Dr Vissering, governor of the Netherlands Bank, to discuss a scheme for an international loan. It was in the context of this proposed loan – which would have to be furnished mainly by American banks – that Keynes received an important criticism of his book. He showed a copy of the proofs to Arthur Salter, secretary-general of the Reparations Commission. Salter thought that his portrait of the President being outmanoeuvred by the cunning Europeans would jeopardise the chances of securing American money.[10] Keynes agreed to tone down certain passages but was adamant on the main point:

> The moderate people can do good and perhaps the extremist can do good; but it is no use for a member of the latter class to pretend he belongs to the former. Besides, it is such a hopeless business trying to calculate the psychological effects of one's anticipated actions; and I have come to feel that the best thing in all the circumstances is to speak the truth as bluntly as one can.[11]

To General Smuts, Keynes wrote on 27 November that 'attempts to humour or placate Americans or anyone else seem quite futile, and I personally despair of results from anything but violent and ruthless truth-telling – that will work *in the end*, even if slowly'.¹²

The Economic Consequences of the Peace was published on 12 December 1919. Shocking as it appeared to many readers, it would have been even more so, had Keynes not left out many insulting passages on the advice of his mother and his friends. By Christmas it had sold 2642 copies – satisfactory but not spectacular. On 29 December, Daniel Macmillan wrote, 'I have no doubt that you will be fully justified in printing the 5000 copies.'¹³ Neither of them sensed that it was about to become an international bestseller and, over the coming months and years, one of the most influential books of the twentieth century.

II. THE ECONOMIC CONSEQUENCES OF THE PEACE

The Economic Consequences of the Peace has a claim to be regarded as Keynes's best book. In none of his others did he succeed so well in bringing *all* his gifts to bear on the subject in hand. Although the heart of the book was a lucid account of the reparation problem, the book was no mere technical treatise. The torrid *mise-en-scène* at Paris is vividly recreated; the failings of Clemenceau, Wilson and Lloyd George are displayed with cruel precision. The writing is angry, scornful and, rarely for Keynes, passionate: never again were his denunciations of bungling and lying, or his moral indignation, to ring so loud and clear. Giving shape to the whole is a brooding sense of menace; a sense of the impending downfall of a civilisation; of the mindless mob waiting to usurp the collapsing inheritance; of the futility and frivolity of statesmanship. The result is a personal statement unique in twentieth-century literature. Keynes was staking the claim of the economist to be Prince. All other forms of rule were bankrupt. The economist's vision of welfare, conjoined to a new standard of technical excellence, were the last barriers to chaos, madness and retrogression.

Unless one keeps Keynes's perspective firmly in mind, the intensity of his denunciations may seem puzzling, even perverse. After all, the Treaty did accomplish some things of which a liberal could approve. It set up the League of Nations; it freed subject nations from autocracy; it prevented the dismemberment of Germany. Keynes does not weigh these achievements in the balance. His book was written very much from an Anglo-American point of view; and most British and American opinion was disposed to judge the Treaty on economic grounds: the Jingoes, by whether it had succeeded in making Germany 'pay' for its aggression; the liberals, by whether it had provided for the resumption of economic progress. With the war over, the security issues which dominated the French faded with extraordinary speed from the Anglo-American consciousness. Traditionalists could take comfort in the destruction of the German navy, whose existence had been the chief pre-war threat to Britain. Liberals tended to pin their hopes on the League. Hardly anyone was interested in the Treaties separately concluded with Austria and Hungary by which Eastern Europe was roughly divided up in accordance with Wilson's principle of 'self-determination'; and Keynes's book was not about them, except insofar as they impinged on his central theme. That theme was about how the war had damaged the delicate economic mechanism by which the European peoples had lived before 1914, and how the Treaty of Versailles, far from repairing this damage, had completed the destruction.

The argument is impressively set out in chapter 2. Despite the extraordinary rise of population in the nineteenth century, free trade and the capitalist ethic had kept the Malthusian peril at bay. In Europe, the 'interference of frontiers and tariffs was reduced to a minimum.... Over this great area there was an almost absolute security of property and person.'[14] Germany had been the locomotive of the Continental economic system. 'Round Germany as a central support the rest of the European economic system grouped itself, and on the prosperity and enterprise of Germany the prosperity of the Continent mainly depended.'[15] Free trade, coupled with the export of capital, had also established an equilibrium between the Old World and the New, based on the exchange of Europe's manufactures for the food and raw materials of the Americas, and the 'annual tribute' which the investment of Europe's surplus capital enabled it to draw from the New World. This global system, which sustained a growing population at an increasing standard of life, depended in turn on a shared morality, which emphasised above all the virtues of abstinence, prudence, calculation and foresight – the basis of the accumulation of capital. Throughout Europe 'all those instincts of puritanism' which in previous times had led people to withdraw from the world were redirected to the task of securing a prosperous future. A radically unequal distribution of income was sustained by a bluff or deception, by which the workers were subjected to an enforced abstinence on the tacit understanding that the capitalists 'saved' most of their profits. Thus the world's economic organisation ultimately rested on the exercise of the Victorian virtues.[16]

Even before the war, Keynes argued, this 'economic Eldorado' was being threatened by the decrease of Europe's pull on the resources of the New World, and by the instability of the 'psychological conditions' underlying the social order. What the war had done was to destroy Europe's economic organisation, largely destroy Europe's stake in the New World, and shake the social order by disclosing 'the possibility of consumption to all and the vanity of abstinence to many'.[17] As a result it had set free the 'Malthusian devil'. The first result of his rampage was seen in Russia.

The mood of menace here conjured up also overhangs chapter 6, in which Keynes discusses the condition of Europe at the war's end. The problems out of which Bolshevism grew were now being reproduced all over the Continent. As a result of the war Europe faced an 'absolute falling off' in its standard of living.[18] Moreover, all the belligerent governments had been forced by the war to embark on a ruinous course of inflation, which was potentially fatal for capitalist civilisation. Keynes invoked Lenin, who had said that 'there is no subtler, no surer means of overturning the existing basis of society than to debauch the currency'.

The 'good peace', Keynes claimed, should have addressed itself directly to these problems, which affected European victors and vanquished alike. Instead the treaty-makers produced what he called a 'Carthaginian Peace' whose effect, if not intention, would be to impoverish Europe. He attributed this result to two things – the inadequacy of the statesmen's ideas, and the inadequacy of their characters.

The second of these explanations is the famous one, enshrined in chapter 3 of the book. But the condemnation of the Treaty as a whole rests much more on the first of them. Keynes's thesis, stated simply, is that the Big Three all gave politics precedence over economics. Thus having stated the economic problem facing Europe in chapter 2, Keynes writes, at the start of chapter 4:

> The thoughts which I have expressed in the second chapter were not present to the mind of Paris. The future life of Europe was not their concern; its means of livelihood was not their anxiety. Their preoccupations, good and bad alike, related to frontiers and nationalities, to the balance of power, to imperial aggrandisement, to the future enfeeblement of a strong and dangerous enemy, to revenge, and to the shifting by the victors of their unbearable financial burdens on to the shoulders of the defeated.[19]

The lack of vision on the part of the treaty-makers would not have mattered so much, Keynes suggests, had they stuck to the framework of the Fourteen Points, which ruled out a 'Carthaginian Peace' and specifically excluded punitive damages. It is to explain how the Versailles Treaty fell so far short of the Fourteen Points that Keynes penned his character sketches of the Big Three.

Of the Allied chiefs Clemenceau comes off best. His is not only the most successful portrait – the account Keynes leaves of him 'throned, in his grey gloves, on the brocade chair, dry in soul and empty of hope, very old and tired, but surveying the scene with a cynical and almost impish air' is unforgettable – but his faults were faults of opinion not of character. He knew what he wanted – to crush Germany for a generation or more – and pursued his aim with single-minded determination, skilfully playing on the weaknesses of his colleagues. 'One could not despise Clemenceau or dislike him, but only take a different view as to the nature of civilised man, or indulge, at least, a different hope.'[20]

It is the President and Prime Minister who share the blame for the failure to make a wise peace, since together American money and British brains could have overcome French intransigence. The American and British Treasuries were largely agreed about reparations. They should have prevailed; their failure to do so was due to the temperaments of their political chiefs.

Wilson, we are led to believe, was insensitive to his surroundings and atmosphere. His neck was stiff with rectitude. He descended on Paris trailing his Fourteen Commandments ('God had only ten,' Clemenceau remarked wryly), to be defeated in a game whose rules he never mastered. Wilson's mind was packed with principles not policies. He was incompetent in council; and he had the theologian's capacity for self-deception. This last is the key point of Keynes's analysis. The President would do nothing that was contrary to his principles; but those principles

> became a document for gloss and interpretation and for all the intellectual apparatus of self-deception by which, I daresay, the President's forefathers had persuaded themselves that the course they thought it necessary to take was consistent with every syllable of the Pentateuch. . . . Then began the weaving of that web of sophistry and Jesuitical exegesis that was finally to clothe with insincerity the language and substance of the whole treaty.[21]

The spider who spun the fatal web which trapped the President was Lloyd George. Lloyd George was cast in the role of the enchantress, the Welsh witch, the *femme fatale*.

> To see the British Prime Minister watching the company, with six or seven senses not available to ordinary men, judging character, motive, and subconscious impulse, perceiving what each was thinking and even what each was going to say next, and compounding with telepathic instinct the argument or appeal best suited to the vanity, weakness, or self-interest of his immediate auditor, was to realise that the poor President would be playing blind man's buff in that party.[22]

Although Keynes's character sketch of Lloyd George is unfair, it is a pity he left it out. The key to Lloyd George, the reader would have read, was his lack of principle; he was

> rooted in nothing; he is void and without content. . . . One catches in his company that flavour of final purposelessness, inner irresponsibility, existence outside or away from our Saxon good and evil, mixed with cunning, remorselessness, love of power, that lend fascination, enthralment, and terror to the fair-seeming magicians of North European folklore.[23]

Lloyd George's objectives were plucked from the circumambient atmosphere; and at Paris he was hostage to a parliamentary majority and public opinion created by his promise to demand of Germany the full cost of the war. Since this promise was in flat contradiction to the armistice agreement and the advice of his own experts his only hope of avoiding political defeat at home was to devise formulae designed to persuade the President that his (Lloyd George's) policy conformed completely to the Fourteen Points. Thus he set to work on the Presbyterian, with a success which eventually alarmed him. As Keynes tells it:

> To his horror, Mr. Lloyd George, desiring at the last moment all the moderation he dared, discovered that he could not in five days persuade the President of error in what it had taken five months to prove to him to be just and right. After all, it was harder to de-bamboozle this old Presbyterian than it had been to bamboozle him.[24]

Keynes estimated that under the terms of the armistice agreement the Allies were legally entitled to claim between £1600m and £3000m, which it would have been 'wise and just' to compound at £2000m. This section of the book (pp. 73–85) largely recapitulates the arguments and estimates of the Treasury Memorandum of 26 November 1918. As in that memorandum, he assumes that the cost of separation allowances and pensions was excluded. Keynes condemned the inclusion of these items in the claim against Germany in the Peace Treaty as a 'breach of contract'. He wrote:

> There are few episodes in history which posterity will have less reason to condone ... a war ostensibly waged in defence of the sanctity of international engagements ending in a definite breach of one of the most sacred possible of such engagements on the part of the victorious champions of these ideals.[25]

The section on Germany's capacity to pay (pp. 106–31) contains whole paragraphs lifted verbatim from the same Treasury document. Keynes emphasised the contradiction between reducing Germany's capacity by territorial and other confiscations and increasing its liability. Apart from immediate transfers of gold and movables, Germany could pay reparations only by means of an export surplus, which would give it the foreign exchange to pay its annual 'tribute'. However in the five years before the war Germany's adverse balance of trade averaged £74m a year. By increasing its exports and reducing its imports Germany might 'in time' be able to generate an annual export surplus of £50m, equivalent to £100m at post-war prices. Discounted over thirty years this would come to a capital sum of £1700m. Adding to this £100m–£200m available from transfers of gold, property and so on, he concluded that '£2000m is a safe maximum figure of Germany's capacity to pay'.[26] Thus, by a bit of juggling with the figures, Germany's capacity could just about be squared with its 'legal' liability. Allowing £500m for ships and property already ceded, this left £1500m payable in thirty annual instalments of £50m a year.

In chapter 7, Keynes outlined his own alternative peace treaty. Revision of the territorial clauses would have to be entrusted to the League of Nations, though Keynes noted that the unanimity requirement gave it 'an almost fatal bias towards the *status quo*'.[27] Economic revisions could be made outside the League machinery. Germany's cash indemnity should be limited to £1500m, with most of it going to France, Britain waiving any claims of its own. All inter-ally debts were to be cancelled, leaving the American taxpayer with a net liability of £2000m. A European 'free trade union' should be set up to offset the economic disorganisation of 'innumerable new political frontiers'. There should be a new international loan, mainly from the United States, to finance Continental Europe's adverse trade balance and stabilise the exchanges. And communism's appeal might be lessened if Russia could be reintegrated into the Continental trading system 'through the agency of German enterprise and organisation'.

Keynes's attempt to repair the damage the war and the treaty had done to Europe's political and economic prospects stands out today in all its ingenuity, boldness, and prescience. None of his plans was adopted. The reparation and debt overhangs continued to poison international relations for years, as Keynes predicted they would. An impoverished Germany unleashed a savage war of revenge, as Keynes predicted it would. American underwriting of European reconstruction, a 'free trade union' of the European peoples – these ideas had to wait for a second world war. In Russia 'war communism' was entrenched. 'Never ... has the universal element in the soul of man burnt so dimly,' Keynes concluded. It was the epitaph for the interwar years.

III. CONTROVERSIES

On 23 December 1919 Keynes wrote to Lytton Strachey:

> The book is being smothered ... in a deluge of approval; not a complaint, not a ... line of criticism; letters from Cabinet Ministers by every post saying that they agree with every word of it, etc., etc. I expect a chit from the PM at any moment telling me how profoundly the book represents his views and how beautifully it is put. Will it be my duty to refuse the Legion of Honour at the hands of Clemenceau?

As always, Keynes exaggerated to amuse his friends. Bloomsbury was enthusiastic: *The Economic Consequences of the Peace* was Keynes's reparation to them for his war service; and for once they were generous to their old friend. Lytton Strachey wrote from Pangbourne on 10 December:

> Your book arrived yesterday and I swallowed it at a gulp. I think it is most successful. In the first place, extremely impressive; there is an air of authority about it which I think nobody could ignore. I was rather afraid at Charleston that it might appear too extreme, but I don't think this is at all the case. As to the argument it is certainly most crushing, most terrible.

On 30 January 1920, Luce wrote from Rangoon:

> I don't think anything so great on politics or so profoundly moving has appeared in English since [Burke's speech on Conciliation].... Incidentally, your style too was a revelation to me. Where did you get it from?...
>
> There are times when I long to see you back in politics, pilot of the state, and yet I would not sacrifice your happiness to the world's. What is so exhilarating is to find in your book the demonstrable proof of the rightness of my loving you as I do and have done.[28]

The earliest criticism came from Austen Chamberlain. While 'full of admiration for a brilliant piece of work', Chamberlain nevertheless wrote to him (22 December):

> Frankly I am sorry that one who occupied a position of so much trust and consequence ... should feel impelled to write in such a strain of the part his country played in the peace negotiations.... I cannot help fearing that our international course will not be made easier by such comments from a late public servant.

On 27 December the banker R. H. Brand wrote that chapter 3 would 'do harm in America, and will impair your usefulness in helping in the near future'. McKenna, who also wrote on 27 December, dismissed that suggestion: 'Fudge! It will do nothing but good anywhere. Until we get back to the truth there is no hope for the world.'[29]

The earliest reviews were by no means unanimous. The Liberal and Labour press was laudatory; but the right-wing *Sunday Chronicle* of 21 December called Keynes a representative of 'a certain ... dehumanised intellectual point of view' which failed to accept that Germany had to be punished. The charge that Keynes was pro-German became standard in such circles. One reader of the *Saturday Review* thought he should have been given an Iron Cross.

The book's sales soon started to leave Macmillan's gloomy projections far behind. Keynes had had to order an early reprint of 3000 copies following an unfortunate mishap in December, when 2000 unbound copies had been thrown into the North Sea to save the ship carrying them from

Edinburgh to London from capsising in a storm. (They were later washed ashore in Denmark, and sold as waste paper.) At the year's end he ordered a second reprint of 5000. By 21 January 1920 English sales had reached 7700, and Keynes ordered a third reprint of 5000. Handling the foreign rights himself, he arranged a French edition, which was published by *La Nouvelle Revue Française* in June. He also agreed to a cheap edition of 10,000 copies to be published by the Labour Research Department at 2s 6d per copy. By 9 February 12,300 copies had been sold out of 16,000, and Keynes ordered a fourth reprint of 5000; a fifth reprint of the same number followed a month later. The US edition was doing even better. The first printing of 20,000 sold out immediately. By 22 April, 18,500 had been sold in England, and nearly 70,000 in the United States. It was only in June that the sales started to fall off, Keynes ordering a sixth reprint of 3000 in August. By this time world sales were well over 100,000, and the book had been translated into German, Dutch, Flemish, Danish, Swedish, Italian, Spanish, Rumanian, Russian, Japanese and Chinese. Keynes had started to make a lot of money. His English profits, at three shillings a copy, came to £3000; there was £6000 from his American sales. Much of this went on his speculations; but his income rose from £1802 in the tax year 1918–19 to £5156 in the year 1919–20.

The main British criticism was not that Keynes had got his figures wrong, but his priorities. 'The revision of political frontiers was an absolutely vital preliminary to the work of building a New Europe,' wrote the historian R. W. Seton-Watson.[30] Wickham Steed, editor of *The Times*, saw the book as a misplaced revolt of economics against politics. 'If the war taught us one lesson above all others it was that the calculations of economists, bankers, and financial statesmen who preached the impossibility of war because it would not pay were perilous nonsense.... Germany went to war because she made it pay in 1870–1, and believed she could make it pay again.'[31] A notice in the *Iron and Coal Trades Review* of 9 January made the good point that it was 'the very nation which was extracting the chief profit from the machine' before 1914 that had set out to destroy it. Economic prosperity, evidently, was no guarantee of political good behaviour.

Liberals of the political, rather than the economic, kind were worried by Keynes's indifference to political aims in general and to the League of Nations in particular.[32] The 'ultimate' criticism of the book, according to a reviewer in the *Times Literary Supplement*, was that Keynes was interested 'in only one aspect of the work'.[33] Some critics also felt that Keynes had ignored the fact that politics is the art of the possible. The Treaty was the best that could have been done under the circumstances. A more robust defence of the treaty-makers, and especially Wilson, was provided by the idiosyncratic American economist Thorstein Veblen. Wilson, he argued, had shown a 'notable leniency' to Germany in the interest of combating Bolshevism. It is now accepted that Keynes's criticism of Wilson's character hinged on a mistaken assessment of the President's priorities. Wilson conceded on points which Keynes thought important, but which Wilson did not. It is also now recognised that the Treaty was much less of a triumph for French diplomacy than Keynes made out.

Keynes attempted no general reply to his critics until the end of 1921 when Macmillan published his *A Revision of the Treaty*. By this time a number of leading American and French participants had had their say. The official Wilsonian response came in March 1920 with Bernard Baruch's *The Making of the Reparation and Economic Sections of the Treaty*, largely written by John Foster Dulles. The Wilsonians did not, on balance, dispute Keynes's economic logic or conclusions, though some felt that the Treaty contained adequate safeguards for revision. What they were mainly concerned with was to salvage Wilson's reputation, and their own hopes for US international leadership, from the damage done by what McCormick called Keynes's 'vicious' book.[34] Their defence was that, given the state of public opinion, Wilson had made the best peace possible. Specifically, 'the repression and minimizing of the vengeful elements in the Treaty were due in large measure to Woodrow Wilson'.[35] If the Treaty had faults they were the faults of democracy.

Baruch's argument, together with the course of events in 1920–1, led Keynes to modify his view of Lloyd George. In *A Revision of the Treaty* he is transformed from a mere power-seeker into Faust. The defence of Lloyd George, Keynes wrote, was that he had made 'the best momentary settlement which the demands of the mob and the characters of the chief actors enjoined to permit', and 'that he had spent his skill and strength for two years in avoiding or moderating the dangers [of the settlement]'. Such a defence 'would be partly true and cannot be brushed away'. Keynes conceded that 'a preference for truth and sincerity *as a method* may be a prejudice based on some aesthetic or personal standard, inconsistent, in politics, with practical good'. But in any case 'private individuals are not under the same obligation to sacrifice veracity to the public weal'. This amounted to a considerable modification of Keynes's earlier stand. He is here conceding that intellectuals and politicians may have different obligations; that the intellectual's duty was to tell the truth in face of *necessary* political lying, with the bonus that if he did so politicians would not have to lie as much. Few intellectuals nowadays would make such a confident distinction between truth and falsehood in public affairs as was still possible for someone of Keynes's generation.

In *A Revision of the Treaty* Keynes has a chapter on the legality of the claim for reparation. In his *Economic Consequences* he had omitted all mention of Smuts's part in 'bamboozling' the President on this issue. But Baruch had published Smuts's crucial memorandum of 31 March 1919. This publication was embarrassing to both Keynes and Smuts. Keynes defended Smuts vigorously against the charge that he had *proposed* including the costs of pensions and separation allowances in the reparation bill (though he wrote to him, 'I am not sure it won't serve you right for writing that memorandum');[36] nevertheless, when he dealt with the Smuts memorandum in his second book, he was highly dismissive of its contents.[37] Keynes's view that the armistice agreement with Germany was a contract and not an unconditional surrender on Germany's part stands up quite well in retrospect. The German armies in the West were undefeated; its conquests in the East were still unchallenged; it would have been very difficult for the Allies to prolong the war for another winter. Germany – and Keynes – were entitled to feel that the peace should have had elements of a negotiation.

As was to be expected, the reception of *The Economic Consequences of the Peace* was least enthusiastic in Paris. French critics like Raphaël Georges-Lévy in his *La Juste Paix* argued that Germany could readily pay what the Allies claimed. Keynes had failed to appreciate the German power of production: 'cette omission vicie tout son travail'. Recent scholarship based on French governmental as well as American and European banking archives is kinder to France's financial motives and logic than Keynes was. French claims for reparations are now seen to be more modest and defensible than Britain's; while the important linkage is not between reparations and security but between reparations, inter-Ally debts and an American loan. Schuker argues that, in the absence of official American aid, reparations represented France's only hope for access to scarce capital and energy for reconstruction; Trachtenberg emphasises that the French object was to get access to German coal (through deliveries in kind) and American credit (by 'monetising' a fixed German debt). The inability of the peacemakers to agree on a fixed sum was a defeat, not victory, for French aims. A perverse outcome of the reparations issue was inherent in the conflicting interests of the Great Powers. Lloyd George's election promises and Wilson's 'bamboozlement' form at best a sub-plot to the main story.

Keynes himself never had to deal with the most widespread charge against his book. This is that, by discrediting the Versailles Treaty, it encouraged the 'appeasement' of the dictators in the 1930s, and thus helped cause the Second World War. This attack was spearheaded by Etienne Mantoux's book *The Carthaginian Peace or the Economic Consequences of Mr. Keynes*, published in 1946 after Keynes's death. Mantoux, who was killed fighting the Germans in 1945, had a personal interest in the Versailles Treaty. His father, Paul Mantoux, the economic historian, had acted as interpreter at the private meetings of the Council of Four, and had challenged Keynes's description of the atmosphere of these meetings on the ground that Keynes had not been present at them. Etienne Mantoux claimed that Keynes's book helped cause the United States to abandon the Treaty of Versailles legally, Britain to abandon it morally, and weakened even the French will to enforce it. America retreated into isolationism; Britain embarked on the 'appeasement' policy; France's morale was broken. As a result, Hitler was given a free hand to destroy the Treaty in the 1930s. Mantoux singled out two aspects of Keynes's pernicious influence: (1) the guilt complex produced by his accusation that the Allies had broken faith, and (2) the indifference to Germany's territorial aggrandisement in the 1930s produced by his argument that 'frontiers and sovereignties' were unimportant.

The indictment is less formidable than it appears at first sight. Keynes did not destroy the Treaty of Versailles; it destroyed itself. Too harsh to conciliate, it was not harsh enough to secure compliance. Mantoux, in fact, concedes that an enforceable treaty would have required permanent Allied occupation of the Rhine bridgeheads.[38] But Keynes can hardly be blamed for this omission. Nor is Mantoux's claim that Keynes's book helped prevent the US Senate from ratifying the Treaty tenable, though it is often repeated. It is clear that the architect of the Treaty's defeat in Congress was President Wilson himself, who refused to accept the amendments which would have ensured its passage. There is more to the charge that Keynes's picture of the President's being 'bamboozled' by the wily Europeans strengthened isolationist sentiment. But American opinion was hardly ready for a US assumption of world leadership; even the Anglophile east coast establishment was not prepared for America officially to underwrite the reconstruction of Europe.

Nor is there a much stronger case for saying that Keynes turned British opinion against the Treaty. The facts did so; Keynes merely pointed them out. Liberal opinion had already started to question the 'Carthaginian Peace' before Keynes's book appeared; no one in the British delegation, even Lloyd George, doubted that the economic clauses would have to be revised. It was the Lloyd George tactic of inserting unenforceable claims which destroyed the credibility of the Treaty. Constant revision of the schedules of German payments in the 1920s paved the way for Hitler's successful assaults on the territorial clauses in the 1930s. Overall the mood of appeasement in the 1930s was created more by the revulsion against the slaughter voiced by poets, novelists and playwrights than by rejection of punitive damages.

Mantoux attacks Keynes's 'economism'. He points out that it was the Second World War, not 'economics', that solved the German problem. Yet the Second World War came after the great depression which brought Hitler to power. The great depression in turn was brought about by the failure of economic leadership in the early 1920s. Had Keynes's 1919 programme been carried out it is unlikely that Hitler would have become German Chancellor. It is absurd to blame Keynes for events which took place because his advice was not followed.

None of this is to deny that *The Economic Consequences of the Peace* was a very influential book. Of the dozens of accounts of the Treaty which appeared in the 1920s it is the only one which has not sunk without trace. It captured a mood. It said with great authority, flashing advocacy and moral indignation what 'educated' opinion wanted said. It also had an influence at a deeper level. Wickham Steed was right: it was a revolt of economics against politics. The war had been fought in the name of nation, state, emperor. These, Keynes argued, were false gods, from whom he sought to divert allegiance towards economic tasks. It was a message calculated to appeal to the nation of Cobden and Bright, once it had recovered from its intoxication with military victories. It helped form the outlook of a new generation. The 1920s saw a new breed of economist-politician, who talked about the gold standard and the balance of trade as fluently as pre-war politicians had talked about the Two-Power standard and the balance of power. There were even economist-poets like Ezra Pound and T. S. Eliot. The idea that the creation of opulence was the main task of rulers was born in 1919, though it came of age only after the Second World War. The Keynes of the *General Theory* whom Mantoux admired cannot be separated from the Keynes of the *Economic Consequences* whom he denounced.

In the main part of his book Mantoux took the standard French view that Germany could have paid much more than Keynes said it could pay, or than it did pay. But he did not support this contention by good arguments (though such arguments are available). He claimed that the Weimar Republic could have restricted German consumption to pay reparations as Hitler did to pay for rearmament.[39] This ignores not just the fact that in the first case German sacrifices would have been demanded for a much less appealing purpose, but also the additional problem posed by having to 'transfer' the sacrifice abroad. He argued that Germany had no trouble collecting 'indemnities' from conquered countries in the Second World War.[40] But Keynes was assuming peacetime conditions, not permanent armies of occupation on Germany's soil. Finally, he argued that the United States had lent Britain and France large amounts of capital in the First World War, and its exports had increased proportionately.[41] But this ignores the fact that the loans were specifically contracted to meet additional demand for munitions; in any case, no problem of lost jobs arose, because large numbers of British and French workers had been drafted into the army. It is hard to disagree with Harrod's conclusion that Mantoux's arguments are 'feeble in the extreme'.[42]

Keynes's treatment of Germany's 'capacity' to pay reparations reveals an attitude to economic life which was to play a key part in the Keynesian revolution, namely, the notion of economies as 'sticky', not 'fluid'. The German economy would not *automatically* adjust to make possible the transfer of the resources demanded of it. It would have to be made to adjust by policy; and could be pushed only so far.

How well does Keynes's polemic stand up in the light of all the attacks made on it? He can surely be acquitted of the absurd charge of having helped cause the Second World War. His case on reparations remains unshakeable, not because all his arguments were good, but because he understood that the political will to extract large payments from Germany for thirty years or more would not be available. His ground for calling the inclusion of pensions and separation allowances in the reparations bill 'a breach of contract' is strong, though not unchallengeable. As far as the motives and characters of the principal actors are concerned, he got Clemenceau about right, Wilson more wrong than right, and failed to get Lloyd George into balance. He was right to insist that economic prosperity was a necessary condition of an enduring peace; wrong to imply that it was a sufficient condition. After 1945, Germany's reintegration into the European community was based on the destruction of its capacity to wage aggressive war.

From the biographical standpoint *The Economic Consequences of the Peace* is a key document. It established Keynes's claim to attention. Until then he had been known only to small groups. In 1919 his qualities were broadcast to the world. A book conceived in a moment of passion and despair set its author on his lifelong course. He had spoken like an angel with the knowledge of an expert. This mastery of science *and* words was to be the basis of all his achievement. But there was something else. Keynes asserted not only his own claim to attention but the claim of economic science to shape the future. The princes of the old world had left a dreadful mess; it was the task of the scientists to clean it up. This was a message with a powerful appeal to the rising generation. And it immediately raised the question with which Keynes was to wrestle for the next sixteen years of his life: was the inherited economics of the nineteenth century adequate to its new task? Or was that, too, part of the old world which had been swept away in the war? His eventual answer was given in *The General Theory of Employment, Interest and Money*.

PART FOUR

THE ECONOMIC
CONSEQUENCES OF THE WAR

MOSES: It is not the business of a Ruler to be truthful, but to be politick: he must fly even from Virtue herself, if she sit in a different Quarter from Expediency. It is his Duty to *sacrifice* the Best, which is impossible, to a *little Good*, which is close at hand.

MR LOKE: If Men were told the Truth, might not they believe in it? If the Opportunity of Virtue and Wisdom is never to be offer'd 'em, how can we be sure that they would not be willing to take it? Let Rulers be *bold* and *honest*, and it is possible that the Folly of their Peoples will disappear.

(From 'A Dialogue' 'apparently in the writing of Voltaire', published 'for the first time' in Lytton Strachey's *Books and Characters* (1922), dedicated to 'John Maynard Keynes')

17

Keynes in the 1920s

I. CAMBRIDGE

The war had brought to an end the undergraduate phase of Keynes's life. He was now a public man, and the air of publicness stayed with him for the rest of his days. He changed physically. When the war ended he was thirty-five and still slim. In the 1920s he filled out, started to look prosperous, lost his hair, developed a stoop. In 1908 he had left London to return to Cambridge. In 1915 he returned to London to serve his country. Thereafter Keynes was as much a man of Whitehall and the City as of Cambridge – connections which tethered him to public policy. Marriage and a house in the country followed almost as a matter of course.

A few intimates apart, it was Cambridge undergraduates who first heard Keynes's denunciations of the Treaty of Versailles. Having quit the Treasury, he returned to King's in October 1919 and gave his autumn lectures, 'The Economic Aspects of the Peace Treaty', from the proofs of his forthcoming book. They made a powerful impression on those who heard them. The idea that the world was being ruined by stupidity rather than by wickedness was a doctrine with obvious appeal to the clever.[1] This was to be the attraction of the Keynesian Revolution itself. Like his new American friend, the journalist Walter Lippmann, whom he had met in Paris, Keynes was moved to wrath not so much by a 'fiery passion for justice and equality', as by 'an impatience with how badly society was managed'.[2] This was the new liberal mood. The twentieth-century claim to rule would be based on competence not ideals. Ideals were too costly.

But the effect of Keynes's utterance was paradoxical. *The Economic Consequences of the Peace* made him a hero of the left, to which, as Kingsley Martin remarked, 'he never belonged'. Henceforth the intelligentsia of the left always listened with one ear to what Keynes was saying. The Labour Party emerged from the war as the Conservative Party's main challenger for power. Keynes's ability to speak to both sides of the political divide from a position in the centre was to be crucial to the making of the Keynesian Revolution.

Keynes's return to King's established a pattern for the next eighteen years of his life. Generally, he was in Cambridge in term time from Thursday evening until Tuesday lunchtime. Mid-week would be spent in London.

Vacations were divided between London, foreign travel and Sussex. Keynes did not much like Cambridge out of full term. There were no sabbaticals in those days, and he took only one term off teaching between 1919 and 1937. His writing as well as his other activities had to be fitted into the normal framework of the academic year.

What did he do in his long 'weekends'? His teaching responsibilities were much reduced from before the war, his livelihood no longer depending on 'selling economics by the hour'. Having given up his Girdler's lectureship, he confined himself to just eight lectures a year, compared to the hundred he had given in 1910–11. These took place in the autumn or summer terms, on Friday or Monday mornings. They were generally early drafts of books he was writing. After 1922 he lectured on 'The Theory of Money' for ten years, before changing to 'The Monetary Theory of Production' in 1932. His first two sets of lectures in 1919 and 1920 attracted audiences of hundreds. Many were not studying economics at all. They came simply to hear Keynes tell how to set the world to rights.

Keynes was responsible for the economics teaching at King's. He conducted his tutorials or supervisions, generally in groups of three or four, on Friday or Saturday evenings before dinner. At first there were not many economics undergraduates at King's – no more than half a dozen a year. Keynes took no first-year students; he farmed out most of his college teaching to Gerald Shove, who initially held no college or university appointment.

The Political Economy Club – or Keynes Club, as it was known – which Keynes had founded in 1909 continued to meet most Monday evenings in his drawing room overlooking Webb's Court – 'the pleasantest sitting room I have ever been in', Virginia Woolf wrote after a visit in 1923. By then Vanessa Bell and Duncan Grant had covered up Grant's pre-war murals of semi-nude dancers and grape-pickers with eight panels of allegorical figures representing the Muses. Membership of the Keynes Club was by invitation. It consisted of Keynes's closest teaching colleagues, graduate students and the best of the second- and third-year undergraduates. The senior members in 1923 were Professor Pigou and Gerald Shove (King's – though Pigou rarely came), Dennis Robertson and Frank Ramsey (Trinity), Austin Robinson (Corpus), Frederick Lavington (Emmanuel), Philip Sargant Florence (Caius) and Maurice Dobb (Clare). The brightest economics student of the early post-war period, Joan Maurice (later Robinson), who came up to Girton in 1922, was excluded from this all-male gathering.

Keynes chaired the university's Faculty Board of Economics and Politics for most of the inter-war years. As a result of his *Economic Consequences of the Peace* he had gained a reputation as the most radical of the younger economists. But partly because of the way his life was arranged – and especially because of his incessant involvement in public controversy – he made no important theoretical contribution to his discipline until the appearance of his *Treatise on Money* in 1930. His polemics of the 1920s were directed against the mistakes of the policymakers, not against the theories of his colleagues. It was not till Britain's return to the gold standard in 1925 that Keynes started to think that mistaken policy was the result of mistaken theory. After that his policy critique took on an increasingly theoretical turn. But till the early 1930s his policy proposals leapt ahead of his theory, which remained relatively conservative.

The oldest fixed point in Keynes's university life was the Saturday after-dinner meetings of the Apostles. The Society was another of the war's casualties. Discontinued between 1914 and 1918, it was revived by F. L. ('Peter') Lucas, the last of the pre-war 'births'. Lucas had returned to Cambridge in 1919 after a harrowing war, in which he had been wounded and gassed (Keynes eventually got him a job in Intelligence). In 1920 King's appointed him a fellow in classics before he had even graduated from Trinity, but he soon became a fellow in English, a Georgian survivor, who hated the post-war world. In setting out to revive the Apostles, Lucas had the support not only of Keynes, but of Keynes's oldest college intimate, John Sheppard, by now a somewhat wizened cherub. Two King's men, Alexander Penrose and 'Scanes' Spicer, were 'born' in November 1919. The two 'births' in 1920–1 were Jack (known as Sebastian) Sprott of Clare College, and Penrose's younger brother Lionel from St John's, later an eminent geneticist. Frank Ramsey, George ('Dadie') Rylands and Richard Braithwaite were added the following year. This was the immediate post-war circle of Maynard Keynes's 'young men'. The new generation of Apostles was less homoerotic than the pre-war one, and showed a tendency to early matrimony, Lucas setting the trend by marrying the novelist 'Topsy' Jones in 1921.

Cambridge for Keynes also meant family – lots of it. His parents remained solid presences at 6 Harvey Road, and most Sundays in term time Keynes would walk up there from King's, for lunch or tea and a gossip about the great world. Neville Keynes was sixty-six when the war ended, though he remained university registrary till 1925. As his duties contracted, so did his anxieties, and he moved into tranquil old age with a new hobby: collecting and listening to gramophone records. Florence, eight years his junior, was in no mood to retire. As Neville's life gratefully subsided, hers rose to a peak of activity. Both parents took immense pleasure in their son's growing fame, a pleasure unclouded by jealousy or criticism, though attended by spasms of worry. Both continued to exert moral authority over him – Florence, in particular, reminding him that he came from a line of preachers and benefactors.

Childless himself, Maynard was embedded in an extended family of Browns and Keyneses. Although he was the only one touched by genius, the overall standard of achievement was impressively high – a tribute to both heredity and family tradition. His younger brother Geoffrey and his wife Margaret gave Maynard four nephews: Richard (1919), Quentin (1921),

Milo (1924) and Stephen (1927). Maynard's sister Margaret and her husband A. V. Hill had four children: Polly (1914), David (1915), Janet (1918) and Maurice (1919). Maynard's grandparents, Dr John Brown, the 'Baptist bishop', and his wife Ada Haydon Brown, were still living in Hampstead when the war ended. He died in 1922, she in 1929, both aged ninety-two. If Keynes was oppressed by the weight of these family connections, he did not show it. He was always generous with advice and practical help, particularly to the younger generation.

King's College remained his spiritual home, increasingly so as the years went on. Keynes rarely used the word, but he thought of himself as part of the 'clerisy' – a secular priesthood, setting standards of value and behaviour, practising the arts of leadership and mutual accommodation. He played a full part in the college's corporate life. He was, of course, a member of the College Council, or governing body, which met weekly on Saturdays (and sometimes on Mondays too), often for four or five hours, interrupted by lunch. But his influence was chiefly felt on three committees: Estates, Buildings and Fellowship. The first he totally dominated, even before he became first bursar in 1924. In the early 1920s he started a revolutionary policy of switching the college's investments from land into securities, and by 1925 he calculated that his policy had made the college £235,000 richer.[3] He also dominated the Buildings Committee, planning and supervising a grandiose rebuilding programme which stuttered its way into the 1930s. Building appealed to his imagination for the reason it has appealed to all master-builders: he wanted to leave his footprint on earth. As a fellowship elector his influence was less overwhelming, but it was rare that a candidate who had Keynes's backing failed to secure an appointment at King's. Here, as in other areas of college life, much of Keynes's influence rested on his friendship with Sheppard, who became vice-provost in 1929. Keynes never became a 'university' politician, but between 1920 and 1927 he was a member of the Council of the Senate, which carried through a major centralisation – into faculty boards – of university teaching and research.

This was a not unusual busy don's life. However, Cambridge was only one of Keynes's worlds – and for much of the 1920s not his most important one.

II. BLOOMSBERRIES

With the end of the war, returning Bloomsbury grouped itself round 46 Gordon Square in such numbers that Lytton Strachey foresaw that Gordon Square would become 'a sort of College ... the *rencontres* in the garden I shudder to think of'.[4] His mother, the still vigorous Lady Strachey, and assorted daughters were installed at No. 51, where Lytton also had a pied-à-terre. His brother James and Alix Sargant Florence, married in 1920, lived at No. 41, when they were not being psychoanalysed by Freud in Vienna. Portions of this house were sub-let to a succession of younger Bloomsberries. Virginia Woolf's brother Adrian Stephen and his wife Karin set up as practising psychoanalysts at No. 50. To Virginia Woolf, who still lived in far-off Richmond, Gordon Square seemed like a 'lion's house at the Zoo. One goes from cage to cage. All the animals are dangerous, rather suspicious of each other and full of fascination and mystery.'[5] The Bloomsbury animals spread to outer cages in Tavistock and Brunswick Squares, Great Ormond, Bernard and Fitzroy Streets. Walter Sickert, still living in Whistler's old studio in Fitzroy Street, kept alive the atmosphere of the 1890s. Lady Ottoline Morrell, wrinkled and powdered, came back to Bedford Square, Garsington at last emptied of its troublesome wartime house-guests. One of the last of these had gone off with 113 of Philip Morrell's favourite hens. 'Such a difficult thing to do,' Violet Bonham Carter remarked to Keynes.

The pattern of communal London living, disrupted by the war, gradually dissolved as the Bloomsberries grew older and formed their own separate households, in the country or even abroad. They visited, of course, corresponded relentlessly and retained London bases. But the close-knit character of the pre-war group was gone, as Vanessa Bell later acknowledged. Two attempts to institutionalise themselves testify to the breakdown of the spontaneous sense of community. On 5 February 1920 Keynes gave a luncheon party at the Café Royal to which Duncan Grant's 'oldest friends' were asked to celebrate his first one-man show at the Paterson and Carfax Gallery. What a pity, Lytton Strachey said, they couldn't have such a party once a week. A month later, and perhaps as a direct result of this reunion, the Memoir Club came into existence, with Molly MacCarthy as its convener. Ostensibly formed to help her husband Desmond write his long-awaited literary masterpiece, it met regularly during the inter-war years, chiefly to listen to Old Bloomsberries talking about themselves. Keynes read it 'Dr Melchior' in 1921 and 'My Early Beliefs' in 1938. In 1924 David Garnett and Francis Birrell founded the Cranium Club, whose members dined at the Verdi Restaurant in Wardour Street on the first Thursday of every month. Cranium's membership gives the best snapshot of the world of Bloomsbury men in the 1920s. Sixteen had been in or around Bloomsbury before the First World War; eleven were wartime or post-war additions – chiefly relations, friends and lovers of the older generation. Curiously, Keynes was not asked to join till 1929. Someone must have blackballed him.

Keynes's place in this family of friends remained as complicated after the war as it had been before it. They loved him for his brilliant and restless mind; they were amused by his roving eye; but they continually criticised him for being worldly, domineering, manipulative, acerbic, wilful – flaws of character which, in their view, were not redeemed by aesthetic sensibility. Of all the Bloomsberries, with the exception of Clive Bell, his character was the most contested. By contrast, Keynes was almost pathetically loyal to his friends. They were not just his friends but his ideal. Lytton Strachey, it is said, was asked in the war why he was not fighting for civilisation. 'Madam,' he replied, 'I *am* the civilisation for which they are fighting.' Lytton's joke was Maynard's belief; his life was spent fighting for the civilisation which his Bloomsbury friends at least partially represented. His friends' criticisms of his character were often acute; but he was also being judged by rarefied standards. Bloomsbury's ideal was that of the enchanted adolescent, from which point of view all the compromises involved in growing up look like treachery. But Maynard understood better that the enchanted garden would become a wilderness unless it was defended from outside. As he mellowed, and the Bloomsberries entered middle age, their appreciation of him grew; in the end, they became, as Clive Bell called them, 'old friends'. But there was much passionate argument on the way.

Chief among his friends were his Charleston 'family'. Vanessa Bell had taken the Sussex farmhouse in 1916 to provide a home for Duncan Grant and Bunny Garnett. Garnett married Ray Marshall in 1921 to a 'universal howl of execration from Bloomsbury'. Duncan, however, decided to make his home with Vanessa. He still fell in love with young men, and needed fairly frequent interludes from domesticity. But he understood that only Vanessa could provide him with the stable background he needed to paint, which is what he cared about most. Their daughter Angelica had been born on Christmas Day 1918, Maynard agreeing to be godfather. 'Oh Lord, how guilty I shall feel if it's not a boy,' Vanessa had joked. When Angelica was born, Keynes sent a present of £200 (£4000 in today's values) from the Paris Peace Conference. His favourite Bloomsbury child was Quentin, the younger of Vanessa's two boys by Clive Bell. He took both Julian and Quentin to the ballet soon after the war, noting that while Julian (aged ten) enjoyed the juggling best, Quentin (eight) seemed 'fascinated by the ballet itself'.[6] What tied Maynard to Charleston was his love for Duncan, which never faded. He supported Duncan right through the interwar years, and in 1937 settled a substantial income on him. Keynes was the rich, generous, worldly, slightly wicked uncle to the Charleston family, which is why his marriage to someone completely outside it came as such a shock to them.

On 8 November 1919 Lytton Strachey was telling his brother James, 'I do not like [Pozzo]'. But he seems to have been won round by *The Economic Consequences of the Peace*, which he praised lavishly. The success of Lytton's own *Eminent Victorians* (1918) had mellowed him and he became notably less critical of Maynard in the last decade of his life, though no less amusing about him. He found the atmosphere 'sympathetic' when he stayed at King's in May 1920, despite the presence of Lord Chalmers, formerly of the Treasury, who made pompous, long-winded speeches. 'How Pozzo can take such obvious absurdities at all seriously quite beats me,' Strachey complained to Carrington.⁷ He reported to his brother on another visit in 1921: 'a typical incident walking back with Pozzo' over a field after they had taken tea with Sebastian Sprott. 'He suddenly said he wanted to pump [urinate], and did so, walking along all the time in the most extraordinary way with legs apart, though there were people all about. "Oh, it's alright, it's alright, one can't be seen, as long as one keeps walking." He looked like a monstrosity of a gardener with an inefficient watering-pot....'⁸

Virginia Woolf remained unreconciled. On 13 February 1920 she noted in her diary that it was to the credit of Cambridge that Keynes was unmoved by his success and had become more, rather than less, modest. But she could not resist a slighting reference to his *Economic Consequences of the Peace* – 'a book which influences the world without being in the least a work of art'.⁹ Visiting Charleston on 22 September 1920 she 'had a vivid sight of Maynard by lamplight – like a gorged seal, double chin, ledge of red lip, little eyes, sensual, brutal, unimaginative. One of those visions that come from a chance attitude, lost so soon as he turned his head. I suppose though it illustrates something I feel about him. Then he's read neither of my books.'¹⁰ What particularly depressed Virginia in 1920 was that both Lytton and Maynard were famous while she was not. Nor could Maynard have endeared himself to her when he told her to stick to non-fiction.¹¹ Not till *Jacob's Room* was published in 1921 did the critics realise a genius had flowered, and did Virginia Woolf start to feel more secure.

Bloomsbury's position between the wars is paradoxical. It seemed to wield immense cultural power; at the same time the world's springs of action were increasingly remote from its own. In a sense it triumphed. Its writers, painters and publicists all rose to the height of their success and influence in the 1920s. They became arbiters of taste, the conduit through which writers like Dostoievsky, Proust and Chekhov, painters like Cézanne, Matisse and Picasso and thinkers like Freud entered British consciousness. Apart from its translations, the Hogarth Press, started by Leonard and Virginia Woolf, specialised in publishing experimental writing and experimental thought. Together with the Sitwells, Bloomsbury championed the cause of the ballet; the products of the Omega Workshops influenced furniture design. Bloomsbury morals, too, seem to have spread everywhere.

But Vanessa Bell was right to say Bloomsbury died in 1914, and not just as a closely knit group. Its rootedness in the Edwardian era distanced it alike from the post-war avant-garde and the new Victorianism. The truth is that many of the post-war experiments in life, letters and art were fed not by hope but by despair, a despair which also lay at the heart of the Puritan revival in public life. These were all complicated reactions to the war: and old Bloomsbury had no imaginative contact with the war. Its rationalism rebelled against a heroic view of life; its individualism shuddered at the thought of collective renewals. Even its espousal of Freud – there were four

practising Bloomsbury psychoanalysts – seemed a superficial concession
to the existence of unreason, rather than a coming to terms with tragic
events: 'when reason dies, monsters are born'. Members of Bloomsbury were
Voltairean survivors, by now subversive by habit, but anxious to retain their
dividends and beautiful Georgian houses.

Lytton Strachey's irony caught a temporary mood; but the real irony
was that it was his civilisation rather than that of his *Eminent Victorians*
which had gone down to defeat – something which he recognised when he
wrote *Queen Victoria* (1921). The authentic voices of the 1920s were those
of Evelyn Waugh and T. S. Eliot. Eliot's poetry evoked a world of fragments,
left-overs. In painting the iconoclasm of Post-Impressionism gave way to the
horrors of Surrealism, reminiscent of Bosch, Breughel and Goya. Bloomsbury
had grown up in the sunlight of Asquithian liberalism, its natural habitat. Its
project – if one can call it that – was to permeate the governing class with
civilised values, just as the Fabians had tried to permeate it with collectivist
ones. From its immaculate London squares it now looked out with irony and
detachment as feeble reaction shaped up to the onslaught of revolutionary
conditions. Baldwin and MacDonald, George V and Queen Mary, were not
Edwardian uncles but Victorian grandparents. So was Sir William Joynson
Hicks, Baldwin's censorious Home Secretary, who presided over the prosecution, for obscenity, of D. H. Lawrence's *Lady Chatterley's Lover* and
Radclyffe Hall's *The Well of Loneliness*. The trade union leaders were another
lot of Victorian dinosaurs raised to prominence by the war. What did
Bloomsbury have to do with this world, or indeed the far madder world of
the 1930s which followed it? What indeed is a Voltaire to do when the
ancien régime has been abolished?

Keynes, a man of Bloomsbury, was also a man of Whitehall. His project
was to bring a new machinery of progress to the aid of Edwardian liberalism.
As he memorably expressed it at the end of his life, the important thing was
to keep alive 'the possibility of civilisation'.

III. OFFICIAL CIRCLES

The question of Keynes's relationship with the 'official mind' of the inter-
war years is highly complex. There *was* a 'Bloomsbury problem' about
Keynes. Russell Leffingwell, an American Treasury official at the Paris Peace
Conference, wrote in 1931:

> Keynes is always perverse, Puckish. He attacks anything sound or
> established or generally accepted, partly for the fun of it, partly for the

purpose of stimulating debate. In doing so he is utterly irresponsible. He doesn't care how much harm he does.... He is just a bright boy, shocking his admiring elders by questioning the existence of God, and the Ten Commandments.[12]

However, Leffingwell never made the mistake of thinking that Keynes was uninfluential. In a letter to Walter Lippmann dated 30 December 1931, he refers to 'Keynes and all his school, which means all the Treasury civil servants who to a greater or less extent follow him.... Strakosch, Blackett, Salter, Hawtrey, etc.', in his '"inflation theory"'.[13] We need to ask how this could have seemed to be the case when Keynes himself had described his writings, in the very same year, as the 'croakings of a Cassandra who could never influence the course of events in time'.[14]

The answer is complicated. Keynes's influence waxed and waned between the wars; his views and personality excited a large range of responses. Also, his theories and policies changed, and those who supported his views on 'managed money' in the 1920s by no means supported the theory of 'unbalanced budgets' in the 1930s. It is important to remember, though, that at no time was he the only actor on the stage. Keynes's scenes were always full of Top People from the interlocking worlds of banking, politics, administration, economics, journalism, not just in Britain, but in America and in Europe. Most of them no doubt were fascinated by the very qualities they mistrusted. Sound men like the American banker Bernard Baruch thought his facility with words was his undoing. But he was never booted off stage, and his voice always gave a distinct flavour to the conversation.

Keynes was certainly not cut off as a policy adviser from the moment his *Economic Consequences of the Peace* appeared. Within a couple of months of its publication in December 1919, Austen Chamberlain, the first post-war Chancellor of the Exchequer, was consulting him on monetary policy as though he had never left the Treasury. His friend and admirer Basil Blackett occupied the new key position of controller of finance at the Treasury. On reparations, as we shall see, he was (uniquely) consulted by both the British and the German governments. If Keynes received a snub at this point, it was not from 'official circles', but from the academic profession, when in July 1920 the annual general meeting of the British Academy rejected his nomination for a fellowship in the Economic Section. This most unusual step was taken at the behest of 'archaeologists and literary men' who disapproved of Keynes's book. Keynes was so incensed by this, and also by Pigou's exclusion the previous year because he had been a pacifist in the war, that he instructed his sponsor, Professor W. R. Scott of the University of Glasgow, not to put his name forward again. After Pigou was elected in 1927, he relented and was himself elected in 1929.[15]

Keynes's loss of influence at the Treasury was gradual and can be explained in two ways. In 1922 power in his old department passed from Basil Blackett to Otto Niemeyer, who succeeded him as controller of finance when Blackett took up an appointment as finance member of the Viceroy's Council in Delhi. Niemeyer was the new Puritan broom at the Treasury. Keynes's influence was at its lowest during his ascendancy, which lasted till he left for the Bank of England in 1928.

More fundamentally, as Henry Roseveare has pointed out, the Treasury's finance division had become 'thoroughly cosmopolitan' in its outlook as the result of the development of 'A' Division during the war and the Treasury's subsequent involvement in the Paris Peace Conference, the reparations issue and efforts at European reconstruction.[16] Treasury officials like Bradbury, MacFadyean and Leith-Ross served on the Reparation Commission in Paris during the first years of the peace, while Ralph Hawtrey, director of financial enquiries since 1919, was the main author of the resolution at Genoa in 1922 calling for a general resumption of the gold standard. The common position of these internationalists was that recovery from war required putting the pre-war structure of the international economy back into place, whereas Keynes increasingly took the view that each country must first balance its own economy with the least social cost to itself. He became steadily more insular in outlook, whereas the previously insular Treasury became steadily more international: a conflict he dramatised in his *Tract on Monetary Reform* (1923). Keynes's falling out with the Bank of England, and particularly its governor Montagu Norman, in 1922, has to do with the same issue. Norman championed the debt settlement with the United States; Keynes attacked it. For all his peculiarities (he was declared insane by Jung!), Montagu Norman was a visionary banker, trying to build up a government of central bankers to replace the old 'automatic' gold standard. Keynes was not against the idea; but he sensed (rightly) that countries had to solve their own problems first. International finance would prosper once domestic adjustment had been secured; it could not be the means to force it.

Of course, the Treasury and Bank of England were directly involved in the financial diplomacy of the 1920s and Keynes was not. In that sense his book did cut him off from official circles. More importantly, it made him *persona non grata* with the French, whose prime minister and policy he had so mauled, and with much liberal opinion in the United States: Bernard Baruch, for example, never forgave him for his ridicule of Woodrow Wilson.[17] That Keynes contributed importantly to American isolationism or French intransigence is far fetched. What has not been sufficiently appreciated is the extent to which Keynes was anti-American in the 1920s – partly as a result of his disillusionment with the quality of American statesmanship, partly because he resented American money-power. He never visited the United States in the 1920s, despite repeated invitations: a striking case of reverse isolationism.

In publishing *Economic Consequences of the Peace*, Keynes took a calculated gamble that he could do more good trying to persuade the public of
the iniquity of the Treaty than working from the inside to try to improve it.
In any case, he had committed himself to a line of argument which made
attendance by him at conferences of 'experts' superfluous: that nothing
good could come out of reconstruction efforts till the economic clauses of
the Versailles Treaty were scrapped and inter-ally war debts forgiven. Since
this was not practical politics, he had nothing to contribute except 'violent
and ruthless truth-telling'.

By 1929, Keynes thought he was becoming 'more fashionable again'.[18]
By this time an influential body of opinion had come to agree with him that
the return to the gold standard in 1925 had been a mistake. However, the
1930s were very different from the 1920s; on balance, Keynes was more
isolated – further from the corridors of power – in the second than in the
first decade of peace. The main reason for this was the collapse of the Liberal Party and of the intellectual nexus, which would have called itself
Liberal, through which he had tried to exert influence in the 1920s.

He could have had a political career in the Liberal Party had he wanted
one. He was on excellent terms with Asquith and McKenna, leaders of
the 'old' liberalism, and continued to spend weekends at The Wharf. Few
believed that the Liberal Party was finished. In 1920 Margot Asquith sent
Keynes a characteristic note from Paisley, where her husband was campaign-
ing (successfully) in a parliamentary by-election, warning him against
'the snob movement towards Labour ... like the snob movement towards
Ugliness in Art, Discord in Music & Sexlessness in Women. But there is
nothing eternal in chic.'

Keynes had no intention of joining Labour, but he would not come to
the rescue of the sinking Asquithian ship. He turned down three offers in
1920 to stand for Parliament, including one from Cambridge which tempted
him most; and he continued to resist further offers throughout the inter-
war years. His personal involvement in the making of Liberal policy started
only when Lloyd George took over the leadership from Asquith in 1926. He
hoped for a serious Liberal revival and a power-sharing government with
Labour, and invested a great deal of intellectual energy in providing such a
combination with a programme of action.

Until 1931, Keynes was part of a network of well-connected Liberal
mandarins who 'met each other constantly in Whitehall, in the Westminster
lobbies, in clubs, in Fleet Street, the City, and at the ancient universities'.[19]
Indeed, the powerful stream of Middle Way opinion generated by this group
helps explain the moderation of politics in the Baldwin Age, though their
influence has scarcely been recognised. Keynes expounded his own distinctive monetary theories in the columns of the *Nation* and at meetings of the
Tuesday Club. Started by Oswald Falk in 1917, its core members were Falk
himself and the four Cambridge economists, Keynes, Layton, Henderson and

Robertson. The City was represented by Charles Addis, Bob Brand, Reginald McKenna and Henry Strakosch, the Treasury by Basil Blackett and Otto Niemeyer, public service by John Anderson and Josiah Stamp; and financial journalism by A. W. Kiddy and Hartley Withers. Keynes addressed the Club on fifteen occasions and chaired many other meetings; guests who heard him included Montagu Norman. He was the dominant force, as Falk recalled, and an uncomfortable colleague. Few could keep up with him, as his ideas changed so quickly. Yet, when they were in his mind, he defended them passionately and ruthlessly, with a cutting-edge so sharp, and a command of language (as well as insult) so effortless, that even formidable intelligences were made to feel foolish in opposing them. At the same time, he was, like most of the others, an intellectual administrator. He had a civil service mind; in this kind of circle he stood out by the speed, fertility and energy with which he applied abstract ideas to the practical problems of the hour.

The Keynesian Revolution has been exclusively presented as a revolution in economic theory. It is easy to forget that it was part of a continuing revolution in government. As a result of the increasing absorption of academics into government service, political and intellectual authority started to merge. The growing use of experts in government was intended as a barrier to democracy; it also reflected the greater complexity of governing an urban, industrial society. But it was also a response to the demand of bright university men for new careers to replace the reduced attraction of the clerical and imperial callings. Recruitment to the higher civil service by competitive examination after 1870 was the key step in professionalising public administration. But it was the First World War which opened up government to university academics. They got to know their way around Whitehall running shipping or rationing schemes. Some of them stayed; others never ceased to see themselves as an extended arm of the state. The First World War experience led to a marked change in intellectual climate. There was more of a disposition to look to government to solve problems, less to look to the market or private enterprise: indeed contempt for the businessman's capacity became a fixed point with the new clerisy. From this perspective the Keynesian Revolution in economics is a key episode in the takeover of the governing function, as well as of the agenda of government, by the universities.

Not just Keynes's role, but the history of government and politics in the inter-war years thus calls for a more nuanced approach. There was no 'wilderness'. Until 1931 consensus politics and Middle Way economics marched hand in hand – much as they did in the 1950s and 1960s. Disputes over doctrine and policy (which were often fierce) belie the fact that policy was rarely intransigently applied. After 1931 there was a change. Business Conservatism was in the ascendant – much as in the 1980s – until it was discredited by appeasement. Yet the reality of much of the inter-war years is not of a right-wing orthodoxy, deeply entrenched, but of a political Middle Way looking for an economic doctrine to fit its socially appeasing inclinations. This Keynes eventually supplied.

IV. MONEY-MAKING

Unlike most of his Bloomsbury friends, Keynes had no inherited capital, so he badly needed to make money to support his expanded life-style. He had started to supplement his academic salary by investments before the war. In 1915 his gross annual income came to just over £1000 (£40,000 today) of which 30 per cent was investment income. His average annual income from 1919–20 to 1928–9 inclusive was £5068 (about £130,000 today). Of this, 'academic income' was £2372 a year, or a little under half. However, 'academic income' included income from 'lectures, Fellowship, examining, the Royal Economic Society, books and articles and his position as Bursar of King's College, Cambridge'.[20] Keynes's teaching and RES income did not exceed £700 a year in the 1920s, or about 14 per cent of the total. Income from 'books and articles' thus came to about one-third of total income over the period. This shows the importance of Keynes's writing in sustaining his life-style. This source of income was at its peak in the years 1920–3 when it provided almost 80 per cent of the total. But even in the late 1920s about 20 per cent of Keynes's income still derived from his writing. The share of investment, directorship and consultancy income in total income rose from 21 per cent between 1919–20 and 1922–3 to over 70 per cent between 1923–4 and 1928–9.

Keynes's chief business partner was Oswald Toynbee ('Foxy') Falk. Keynes brought Foxy into the Treasury in 1917 and Foxy brought Keynes into the City after the war. Their friendship was often explosive, for they both had brilliant minds, powerful personalities and the utmost confidence in their own ideas. It lasted till Keynes's death, though it cooled in the 1930s, after a series of business clashes on the boards of companies they together controlled.

Falk, a partner in the stockbroking firm of Buckmaster and Moore, was a very tall man, with a fine head, aquiline features and the broad shoulders of a golfer, a sport at which he excelled. He loved pictures and adored the ballet – he had an affair with Pavlova. Prodigiously gifted intellectually, his faults were hauteur and impetuosity: he was much better at making fortunes (for himself as well as his clients) than keeping them. His hatred of socialism, which proved permanent, dated from the First World War, when the government acquired his Picassos, which he had sent to America for safekeeping, for what he considered a grossly inadequate amount of dollars. But he was just as intolerant as was Keynes of stupidity in high places: he never spoke to his friend Montagu Norman again after the return to the gold standard.

It was Falk and Geoffrey Marks who arranged for Keynes's appointment to the Board of the National Mutual Life Assurance Company in 1919; he became its chairman in 1921, for £1000 a year. As always he knew immediately how the business should be run. 'A Life Office', he declared on the day of his appointment, 'ought to have only one investment and it should be changed every day.' Seconded by Falk, and encouraged by Marks, Keynes initiated what was called an 'Active Investment Policy', which combined investing in real assets – at that time considered revolutionary – with constant switching between short-dated and long-dated securities, based on predictions of changes in the interest rate. He and Falk became financial consultants to the chairman of the department store Debenhams, at £500 a year each. Other City directorships followed, Keynes's mid-weeks in London being largely spent on his City business.

Keynes had started gambling on currencies in the intervals of writing his *Economic Consequences of the Peace* in 1919, finding it both amusing and challenging. 'I feel absolutely confident that the right thing to do is to bull dollars and bear marks', he wrote to Falk on 1 September. 'Speculation', Nicholas Davenport wrote, 'improved his economics and economics improved his speculation'.[21] In the 1930s, as we shall see, his investment philosophy changed in line with his economic theory.

Keynes's other main way of making money was through journalism. He wanted to address the public in any case, and he proved an eloquent populariser of abstract ideas. But between 1920 and 1923 he was much more of a writer for hire than he would ever be again. This was partly because he needed the money. He wrote only four newspaper articles in 1920. There were fourteen in 1921, twenty-five in 1922 and fifty-one in 1923, his peak year, which coincided with his becoming proprietor of the *Nation and Athenaeum*. If we take worldwide syndication and special journalistic assignments into account, we are talking of income supplements of about £1500 in 1921 and over £4000 in 1922. Keynes's failure to produce a major work of theory till 1930 was the direct result of the way he spent the first few years after the war.

Keynes always insisted that wealth should not be hoarded but spent on civilised living. Practising what he preached, he earmarked some of his first profits from currency speculation for buying pictures. Although he was not much moved by visual art, he tried to live his life by aesthetic standards, and having pictures was part of being civilised. He invariably bought on the advice of Duncan Grant and Vanessa Bell, but the timing of his purchases depended on the state of his balance with Buckmaster and Moore. He acquired some of his best paintings between the autumn of 1919 and the spring of 1920 when his currency speculations prospered. In November

1919 he bought Seurat's *Promenades* for £320 from the Chelsea Book Club, London agents of the Vildrac Galleries in Paris: one of twenty-eight oil studies for his masterpiece *La Grande Jatte*. Works by Picasso, Signac, Matisse and Derain were added over the next few months. This phase of picture-buying ended with his purchase of Renoir's *Head of a Boy* in Paris in May 1920, at a cost of £300. Except for a Cézanne acquired in 1924 on his own initiative ('the worst picture Cézanne ever painted', his friends remarked cattily), Keynes bought no more works of important French painters till 1935, when he was again making large profits on the stock market, though he bought many English pictures in the interval, chiefly the work of his friends, and supported their activities in other ways.[22]

The main areas of Keynes's future life were already mapped out in 1920. No one would have predicted that his principal contribution would be to economic theory. Rather, the war had revealed him as a very unusual type of public servant, exceptional in his ability to apply economic theory incisively to the financial problems of government. Then came *The Economic Consequences of the Peace*, which showed his unique power as a persuader. In this book he put forward the revolutionary claim that economics should control the peace, not that the peace required a revolution in economics. Though he did not yet know the precise turn his life's work would take, his instinct had already told him it would lie in the sorting out of the problems created by the war and the peace.

18

The Transition to Peace

I. EUROPE'S UNFINISHED CIVIL WAR

The lives of Keynes and his generation were blighted by the failure to overcome the consequences of the First World War. That failure meant there could be no sustained economic and political recovery from the effects of the war. The shakily restored international system collapsed into world depression in 1929, and into world war in 1939. Totalitarianism gained a deadly grip over a large part of the world's population. Keynes lived to see a Soviet empire arise in eastern Europe on the ruins of the Nazi empire. Not for nearly half a century was that final consequence of the war cancelled.

A giant step in this descent was the inability of American and European statesmen to liquidate the twin and connected problems of inter-ally war debts and German reparations. The dominance of these questions unsettled everything for the first five post-war years. They absorbed the best energies of the world leaders; they produced an atmosphere of continual crisis which choked off attempts to normalise economic relations. They detached the United States from Europe, broke up the Anglo-French entente and almost destroyed the fledgling Weimar Republic. When the clouds partly lifted in the mid-1920s, it was too late to undo the damage. The expectational environment had become hopelessly soured.

Keynes's private life was played out against the background of impending catastrophe. But the summer of 1920 was an interlude, providing a last precise reminiscence of those extended pre-war house-parties when Bloomsberries and their friends assembled for their annual festivals of intellect, art and sexual intrigue, undisturbed by the political projects which were to play serpent to their paradise. At Charleston, Maynard worked on the proofs of his book on probability, Duncan Grant and Vanessa Bell painted in a new makeshift studio beyond the walled garden, Lytton Strachey read them his *Queen Victoria*, and Mary Hutchinson stopped Clive Bell from working at all. Bunny Garnett 'turned up in a motor', followed by Peter Lucas, 'perfectly charming as ever' and having a calming effect on the manic mathematician, Harry Norton. Virginia Woolf, breaking off from *Jacob's Room*, would drop in from neighbouring Rodmell for argument and gossip over lunch or supper. Maynard insisted that life be ordered on 'Charleston time' – one hour ahead of summer time – which led to inconveniently early teas, revolts in the kitchen and dark mutterings from Clive Bell. 'How mad they all are,' Lytton wrote to Carrington. 'The result is extremely Tchekhovesque. But luckily the atmosphere is entirely comic.... Everyone laughs and screams and passes on.'[1]

Maynard had hoped to have the Cambridge undergraduate Sebastian Sprott to stay for the last part of his holiday. 'We – that is Clive Bell, Duncan Grant, Norton, Lucas and I – are desolated that you can't come,' he wrote to him on 3 October. 'But families are families I know.' Instead, Maynard went up to London on 6 October and brought back Gabriel Atkin, a young painter and musician of moderate talent, who served as an occasional boyfriend to him as well as to Siegfried Sassoon. On this occasion, though, Atkin was distinctly *hors de combat*, having an abscess on the cheek and being forced to spend, as Duncan reported with some glee to Vanessa, his time 'in bed ... alone'.[2]

Unattached since the break-up of his affair with Duncan Grant in 1911, Maynard no longer hankered after a grand passion – or so he told his friends. 'The shallow waters are the attraction. Up to the middle, not head over ears at my age,' he ambiguously informed Lytton.[3] Sebastian Sprott fitted the bill perfectly, and from October 1920 Keynes was considered by Bloomsbury to be 'married' to Sprott. The product of a dominating mother and a tough boarding school (Felsted), Sprott had come up to Cambridge in 1919 to read moral sciences, in which he got a double first. He became the intimate of stars like Keynes, Strachey and Morgan Forster, but was never a star himself, despite a stagey presence modelled on Ronald Firbank. He fitted in: unambitious, presentable, clever, sympathetic – an ideal houseguest or holiday companion. Strachey once sent him a letter in an envelope addressed: 'Kind Cambridge postman, please do not / Forget, through loitering, love or talk, / To leave this letter with the Sprott / Who lives at 7 Brunswick Walk'. The letter arrived punctually.

Sprott was the type of aesthetic, middle-class homosexual mainly attracted to working-class youths. He blazed the trail to the Berlin night clubs later followed by Christopher Isherwood and W. H. Auden, and later dropped the Bloomsbury 'Sebastian' for the more proletarian 'Jack'. Keynes never shared his taste for the low life. He refused to idealise the working class, British or German. He worshipped artists, not toughs. In any event, Keynes's own sexuality was in a state of transition. He could contemplate at least the possibility of a love affair with someone of the opposite sex. His flirtation with Barbara Hiles apparently continued after she became Barbara Bagenal: there is a strange letter from Duncan Grant to Vanessa Bell in 1920, written with characteristic disregard for the existence of Mr Bagenal, in which he wonders whether 'Barbara would be a good mother for Maynard's children'.[4] More elusive was Maynard's relationship with his new secretary, Naomi Bentwich.

It was Naomi Bentwich herself who suggested, in August 1920, that she become Keynes's secretary on a part-time basis. She was then earning a precarious living on the register of Miss Pate's Cambridge secretarial agency. In that capacity she had typed chapters of Keynes's *Economic Consequences of the Peace* with growing excitement and enthusiasm, and conceived the plan of working for him. On 23 August Keynes wrote to her offering her a half-time job, at £300 p.a., combining work for him (taking his dictation, typing his articles) with compiling the decennial index of the *Economic Journal*, which he still edited. 'Is this the kind of work you had in mind?' he wrote. It was; and she took her first dictation when Keynes returned to King's in the middle of October 1920. She remained his secretary for seven months. During that time (and for several years afterwards) she experienced the most turbulent feelings towards him, and about him, which she recorded in her diary. She later used these records, together with letters she and Keynes exchanged, as the basis of an unpublished autobiography, 'Lucifer by Starlight: A Human Document'.

Naomi Bentwich came to Keynes with an unusual background for a secretary. She was a dark-haired, attractive, intelligent, idealistic young woman of twenty-nine, born into a prominent Anglo-Jewish family. After taking a secretarial course, she read moral sciences at Newnham College until 1917. She had been active in the No-Conscription Fellowship, visiting Garsington with Bertrand Russell. W. E. Johnson had been her tutor. Thinking it a shame that Johnson had never written a book, and that it was important for his logical thought to endure, she offered to take down his thoughts in short-hand, without charge. This was evidently the incentive he needed, and she spent much of her free time from 1915 to 1920 writing down Johnson's dictation, typing it out and contributing, by her comment and criticism, to the fashioning of what became the three volumes of his *Logic*. It is generally agreed that without Naomi's help Johnson could never have produced these books.[5]

But this was not all. Johnson, a fifty-seven-year-old widower in 1915, fell in love with her. Naomi Bentwich, who found the sexual emotion 'disturbing', resisted his advances, telling him that her love for him must always be that of a 'daughter to a very dear father', but offering a consolation prize of a kiss 'twice a day'. Johnson capitulated. 'You are too far above me,' he wrote to her, 'to let me feel anything but a very distantly admiring love.' This response made Naomi Bentwich 'completely happy'. But soon there were signs that Johnson's feelings were not quite as distant as he had led her to believe. Naomi told him they must fight the 'animal passion' together for the sake of his work. Eventually, in 1920, they decided to marry. But the plan was abandoned in face of ferocious resistance from Johnson's sister and housekeeper Fanny, who said she would go mad, and from Naomi's own father, who could not bear the thought of his daughter marrying a Gentile. It was thus on the rebound from the passionate Johnson that she first confronted the subtle, almost invisible, sexuality of Keynes.

I wasn't prepared [she wrote in her memoir] for that big room of his over the Queen's Lane entrance to King's College with its startling wall paintings by Duncan Grant ... where a nude negress ... alongside a cardinal in scarlet ... proclaimed the free individualism which Keynes's literary style had led me to expect.... All the same I was happier in the little inner room with its crimson curtains, his study, in which I was almost always alone with him. I usually sat there in a big armchair in front of the fireplace, and he sat at his desk by the window with his back to me. I can't remember that we shook hands at that first meeting; certainly there was no tea; his manner was abrupt.

Miss Bentwich would go to Keynes two or three times a week, sometimes of an evening. Keynes would dictate his correspondence to her, and dismiss her. Their relationship was purely formal, but she could write of one afternoon in November 1920, that 'he sat back in his desk chair and looked over his shoulder at me. I seemed to sink into deep pools of sympathy, and by the lovely look in his eyes and his smile ... knew that he understood as no one else understood.'

II. UNENDURABLE FACTS

The First World War had been followed by an inflationary boom. Wages had risen faster than prices in the last two years of the war, but rationing had prevented people from spending their increased money incomes on consumption goods. With the removal of controls the public went on a spending spree, prices rising by 50 per cent between April 1919 and April 1920. Money wages now lagged behind the rise in prices, producing what Keynes would later call a 'profit inflation'.

Once the boom got going, prices were pushed higher and higher by gambling in commodities, shares, property, while interest rates were held down. Who would not borrow at 4 per cent a year, with prices going up 4 per cent a *month*? Old companies were bought and sold, and new ones floated, as an almost daily occurrence. 'Practically every country', Keynes wrote in 1929, 'was off the gold standard, and money was the one commodity to the rapid manufacture of which there was no serious impediment.'[6] Britain itself had formally abandoned the gold standard in March 1919 because of fear of social unrest if demobilisation led straight to the dole queue. The Cabinet interpreted a general strike on the Clyde in April 1919 as a revolutionary uprising. So banking and political logic combined to keep money amazingly cheap long after the boom showed signs of getting out of hand. As in the war, the government was using inflation to solve its problems, because it could think of nothing else to do.

As Susan Howson tells it, the emergence of the 'dear money' policy in the winter of 1919–20 is really the story of how the Bank of England, aided and abetted by Sir John Bradbury of the Treasury, regained control of financial policy from the politicians who had usurped it during the war. The copper-bottomed argument put by the officials was that inflation had to be rapidly liquidated, and indeed reversed, if sterling was ever to return to the gold standard at its pre-war parity with the dollar. This objective, proclaimed by the Cunliffe Report in August 1918, had been accepted by all the political parties. Implementation of the objective required balanced budgets, the active use of interest-rate policy to stop credit expansion, and legal limitation of the note issue.[7] Lloyd George, Bonar Law and Austen Chamberlain accepted the end but shrank from the means. Yet, because they accepted the end, they ran out of arguments for opposing the means, especially once inflation had got out of control. And they might have had less depression later on had they acted sooner to curb the boom.

Keynes himself never regarded the return to the pre-war gold standard as the overriding aim of policy. But he hated inflation, as a destroyer of capitalism. Thus he found himself on the side of the Treasury and the Bank against the politicians. Consulted by Austen Chamberlain in February 1920 on what course monetary policy should take, he said bank rate should be put up to 10 per cent if necessary and held there for as long as was needed to break the boom. Chamberlain reported Keynes as saying that he did not believe that a 'dear money' policy would lead to unemployment.[8] Bank Rate was put up to 7 per cent on 15 April and held there for a year. In the same month the government imposed new taxes.

The combination of a fiscal and monetary squeeze soon brought the boom to an end; no one, least of all Keynes, expected the severity of the collapse which followed. Consumer spending fell first, followed by investment spending. Prices started to tumble in October; unemployment rose sharply in November. Output fell by 15 per cent over the next twelve months; unemployment rose to 22 per cent. In an unprecedented, and final, display of price and wage flexibility, wholesale prices were almost halved, money wages fell by one-third in the same period. Later Sir Josiah Stamp shrewdly observed that the collapse was started by 'the refusal to mature of an anticipated inflation. . . . it is just the feeling you have when you go upstairs in the dark and tread on a top step which is not there'.[9]

Keynes, too, had taken part in the gambling mania, and like the others felt he was gambling on a certainty. He had started speculating on currencies with 'Foxy' Falk in the autumn of 1919. He believed that, as British prices rose faster than American ones, sterling would go down against the dollar; whereas, with the inflation rate in France, Germany and Italy higher than in Britain, sterling could be expected to appreciate against their currencies. For a time this assumption proved correct. From March 1919, when the sterling–dollar exchange was uncoupled, till February 1920, sterling fell from $4.70 to $3.40, and by the end of 1919 Keynes's realised profits were over £6000. Encouraged by these results he decided to form a syndicate with Falk. It started operations in January 1920 with a paid-up capital of £30,000, half provided by Falk, the other half by Keynes, who invested £8000 of his own money (mainly lent by his father and his brother-in-law A. V. Hill), £4500 of Duncan Grant's and Vanessa Bell's and £2500 of his brother's. Keynes had sole control of his half of the operation. The sleeping partners handed over their money to Keynes with the most sublime confidence in his wakeful ability to multiply it for them, a confidence Keynes appeared to have shared. As he explained to his father on 11 December 1919, 'The affair is, of course, risky. But Falk and I, seeing that our reputations depend on it, intend to exercise a good deal of caution.' Given Neville Keynes's obsessive anxiety, his decision to finance his son's gambling to the tune of £5000 was almost heroic.

At first all went well. The Keynes group bought rupees and sold francs and lire, and by the week ending 27 February 1920 realised profits stood at £8643 and book profits at £18,525 on a total investment of £200,000. 'My debt of gratitude to you increases (like my capital) by geometrical progression,' wrote Geoffrey Keynes to his brother. Early in March the Syndicate took the fateful decision to go long in dollars, buying £150,000 worth at $3.68 to the pound. But sterling refused to fall. 'Dollars are certainly puzzling,' wrote Falk to Keynes on 30 March, as the pound rose to $3.89. It is plain that he and Keynes were gambling that action on the bank rate would be postponed till May.[10] In fact it was put up on 15 April, and had already been anticipated.

For the time being losses on dollars were more than compensated by profits on francs, and in mid-March Keynes swept Vanessa Bell and Duncan Grant off for a six-week Easter holiday in Italy, starting at the Hotel de Russie in Rome. The visitors were less impressed by the grim industrial and political situation than by the stunning fall in the value of the lira: 25 to the pound in 1914, it was 35 in March 1919, then 81 on 3 April 1920 and almost 100 by 16 April. Keynes informed his companions that spending was more than a pleasure, it was a duty. They went on a shopping spree, buying over £300 worth of furniture and fabric, Keynes's purchases including seventeen pairs of gloves as presents. 'Win or lose, this high stake gambling amuses me,' he wrote to his father from Rome. Neville Keynes's reaction can be imagined.

The holiday ended at the end of April with a few days at I Tatti, where Keynes had stayed before the war. Bernard Berenson had mobilised Florentine society to meet the world-famous economist. The climax of the stay was a grand dinner party given in Keynes's honour by the American collector Charles Loeser, at which Duncan Grant, mistaken for Keynes, was closely questioned about the reparation problem, while Keynes, posing as 'il pittore Grant', gave his expert opinion on his host's Cézannes. No one seems to have been amused when the prank was discovered. Keynes never went to I Tatti again.

A few weeks after returning to England Keynes was ruined. Francs, lire and marks had all started to appreciate against sterling. The movement did not last long, but long enough to clean him out. On 27 May he was forced to liquidate his positions. He lost all his group's capital, and owed his broker nearly £5000. His debts – that is, including his 'moral debts' to his family and friends – came to just under £20,000.

Keynes somehow made his remaining assets add up to £21,500, thus claiming that he was still solvent. Fortunately, most of the debts were to family and friends. His father immediately wrote off £2000 of his own loan, and made it clear that all his resources were at his son's disposal ('All we can do we will do,' he cabled on 27 May). Florence took Maynard's reverses stoically. 'It was perhaps necessary to throw something overboard to propitiate the Gods – and if they are content with money, we will not grudge it to them,' she wrote in her birthday letter of 3 June. From Bloomsbury Keynes never received a word of reproach. Critical as his friends were of his aesthetic and political judgements, they never lost faith in his financial genius. None of them seemed to doubt for a moment that they would get their money back.

Nor were they wrong. Keynes paid off his immediate debt to Falk with a £5000 loan from the financier and philanthropist Sir Ernest Cassel, a supporter of the Papworth Community for tubercular patients, which Florence Keynes had helped establish in 1919. With £1500 on account from his publisher Daniel Macmillan, and £500 from Basil Blackett,[11] Keynes was in again almost immediately, convinced, as he told Cassel on 26 May, that it must be right to 'sell marks, francs, and lire forward' if one could stand the racket for a couple of months.[12] He formed a new syndicate with his former pupil Sidney Russell Cooke, a stockbroker with Capel, Cure and Terry. This time he was right. 'My finances have been prospering pretty well lately,' he told his father on 13 September. By the end of 1920 he had repaid Cassel and Blackett and had a small profit. In 1921 he formed another syndicate with Reginald McKenna. The 'moral debts' to Duncan and the others were cleared off in 1922, by the end of which Keynes had 'something between £25,000 and £30,000' left over for himself.[13]

Keynes's gains and losses were short term. Many economists at the time believed that economies reacted to shocks like alert individuals: rapid losses followed by quick recoveries, with agents switching into new lines of business just as Keynes switched into new currencies and commodities. The great lesson of the first post-war depression was that economies are much more sluggish than individuals. Once prices started to fall after July 1920 the expectation that they would go on falling caused people to act in ways which ensured that they did go on falling. Dealers unloaded their stocks; owners sold their property and businesses as the banks called in mortgages; manufacturers stopped hiring labour; workers resisted employers' attempt to cut their wages, so real wages went up as profits fell, which added to bankruptcies, and so on. The cumulative effects of all their actions was to push economic activity down, not up. The economy, evidently, was not like a central-heating system, producing a thermostatically controlled temperature. When the temperature dropped, economists looked for the automatic adjustment and discovered there was none – or that it was much feebler than they had imagined.

Keynes's autumn lectures on 'The Present Disorders of the World's Monetary System' – 300 students turned up to the first one at twelve o'clock on Monday 18 October 1920 – reflected his own as well as his nation's experience. His style was not dramatic; it was his ability to relate economics to dramatic events which drew students to him. His theme was how monetary disorders could have serious consequences for production and employment. He started by observing that 'a change in prices and wages as measured by money is capable of transferring wealth from one class to another, and redistributing fortune in a way which baffles anticipation and upsets design. It is for that reason that we have to concentrate on what is nothing more than an intermediary [money] and not an object of consumption.' Monetary instability, he went on to say, undermines the *virtue* of the capitalist system, and 'the nature of the defence' which can be made by the businessman for his existence. The prevalence of monetary disorders after the war constituted 'an essential change in the social structure'. By monetary disorder Keynes meant inflation. Deflation, although its immediate evils were greater, was a derived phenomenon, brought about by the inevitable collapse of the inflationary boom. That is why Keynes, like all the monetary reformers of the 1920s, attached supreme importance to price stability: stable money is necessary for stable capitalism.

This new interaction of government, business and unions to keep an inflationary boom going beyond the point when it would 'naturally' collapse constituted in Keynes's view another fundamental change from the pre-war position. In his fourth lecture on public finance he noted that 'under pressure of war governments learnt a new mode of covert taxation by manufacturing money' – a discussion which foreshadows his section on the 'inflation tax' in the *Tract on Monetary Reform*. In his seventh lecture, entitled 'Do We Want Prices to Fall?', Keynes revealed the nub of his disagreement with the actual policy being pursued by the Treasury and the Bank of England. Inflation must be liquidated, and he was prepared to accept the unemployment cost of doing so. But he insisted that it should not be carried so far as to bring about a severe *actual* fall in price level. 'Having reached a level here and now – whatever that level may be – we should fix ourselves there, and not aim at getting back to what, after all, was a perfectly arbitrary pre-war level.' Devaluation should be preferred to further deflation – that is, 'we should accept a permanently diminished value for the standard coin measured in gold'.

Here Keynes felt he was restating orthodox doctrine in face of revolutionary innovations by the monetary authority. As Morgan remarks, the maintenance of a high bank rate during the long period of collapsing prices and activity was 'diametrically opposed to the established practice of reducing the rate as soon as the peak of the boom had been passed'.[14] In retrospect, Keynes felt that 'most of the troubles' which followed might have been averted had steps been taken to stabilise the situation towards the end of 1920 when the rate of inflation reached zero. (Though whether monetary policy alone could have done this is very doubtful.)

A great deal of monetary disorder, he said, 'is in essence a blind reaction against those natural forces which are inevitably tending to lower the standard of life.' Europe was overpopulated: 'The period during which the law of diminishing returns was suspended is at an end, there must now be a tendency for the level of life to fall just as inevitably as the tendency was for the level of life to rise in the nineteenth century.' The problem is: 'are we going to reduce our population or are we going to return to the lower standards of life which have existed during the greater part of Europe's history?' On this gloomily prophetic note Keynes left his 300 students, among whom were C. R. Fay, Austin Robinson, Rupert Trouton, Maurice Dobb, R. W. Procter, F. W. Paish and Arcadius Skidelsky.[15]

III. RUBBISH ABOUT MILLIARDS*

Throughout 1920 Keynes had watched in fascinated horror the experts and statesmen tramp round the holiday resorts of Europe talking what he called 'rubbish about milliards' in their efforts to determine Germany's reparation bill. Officially this was the job of the Reparation Commission in Paris, which was supposed to report in May 1921. However, the British and French recognised the inconvenience of leaving the German liability undetermined for so long, and started direct negotiations among themselves and with the Germans. The French, in particular, were keen to get their hands on German resources as quickly as possible to reconstruct their devastated regions.

The prime mover in all this activity was Lloyd George, who now emerged

---

*What were then called milliards are now called billions – thousands of millions. All reparation calculations were made in pre-war gold values, when the pound was worth twenty marks.

as Europe's great hope. He took credit for postponing the fixing of a definite sum until the 'hot passions' of 1919 had had time to cool – forgetting his part in inflaming them.[16] Free of the encumbrance of the Heavenly Twins, he now wanted to keep Germany's annual payments as small as possible, wavering between Keynes's view that Germany could not pay large annual sums and alarm at the effects on British trade if it did. However, his bid for moderation was weakened by the refusal of the United States to scale down the debts it was owed by the Allies. This left him *à deux* with the French, whose position became steadily more intransigent. Deprived of the prospect of American assistance, they now relied on Germany to pay the whole cost of restoring their invaded provinces. However, they were much more interested in payments in kind than in cash, which they hoped to achieve through direct negotiations with the Germans, backed by threats to seize German mines and forests. Nor, without American backing, could Lloyd George offer them the security guarantee for which they might have traded large reparations. Instead they pursued plans for setting up an independent Rhineland, which conflicted with their aim of securing an economic agreement with Germany. The Germans played a waiting game. They evaded the Allied proposals. They defaulted on their interim coal deliveries.

Lloyd George's policy was to get Germany to accept the appearance of a large debt and France to accept the reality of a small one. His unrivalled repertoire of blandishments and threats was directed now at his ally, now at his erstwhile enemy. With much expert adjustment of the figures the prize seemed within his grasp, but always just eluded him. Finally, his patience, though not his stamina, ran out. At the end of 1920 he told the French that they must determine a joint position forthwith. Briand, the new French prime minister, agreed. A conference was summoned to meet in Paris in January 1921.

Keynes had accepted an invitation from C. P. Scott of the *Manchester Guardian* to comment on proposals agreed at the Paris conference. His articles, which appeared on 31 January and 1 February 1921, marked the start of his highly profitable association with that newspaper. Keynes estimated that Germany would be required to pay £400m a year over forty-two years – 'double the highest figure that ... any competent person here or in the United States has ever attempted to justify'. The only conclusion to be drawn was that the proposals could not be meant seriously. Keynes wrote: 'The thought of the two Prime Ministers in Paris muddling over silly formulas, with M. Loucheur buzzing about between them ... is, for anyone who realises what it is like, a thought of gibbering nightmare.'[17] To the French economist Henry de Peyser, who objected to this image, Keynes wrote with passion, 'I will be no party to a continuation of a European blood feud, however great the past guilt. In Cambridge here, this term we are performing the Aeschylean trilogy.... I want to see the Furies turned into Eumenides, clothed in red robes, and pacifically housed in the Acropolis.' In a letter to a British correspondent, Neil Malcolm, Keynes expressed the hope that the Germans would reply to these preposterous proposals, sensibly and with dignity, and not put forward 'semi-sensible and semi-sophistical counter-proposals'.[18]

But the German counter-offer at the London Conference of 1 March 1921 gave an impression of 'evasiveness and insincerity'.[19] Lloyd George dismissed it with contempt; he and Briand, alleging German default both in delivering war criminals for trial and in making interim payments, announced a package of penalties. Allied troops marched into Duisburg and Dusseldorf on 8 March.

Keynes's comment appeared in the *Manchester Guardian* on 5 March. While criticising the German proposals as 'ill-judged', Keynes mainly condemned Allied sanctions against Germany as illegal. 'The penalties', he wrote,

> can hardly ... be intended to raise money, and are rather designed to frighten Germany into putting her name to what she cannot and does not intend to perform by threatening a serious step in the direction of the French policy of permanently detaching the Rhine provinces from the German Commonwealth. The grave feature in the Allies' communication lies partly in our lending ourselves to a furtherance of this policy, and partly in contempt for the due form and processes of law. . . .

IV. ALL IN THE MIND?

By this time, Naomi Bentwich had fallen passionately in love with Keynes, a love which she was convinced he had deliberately kindled in her. As she took his dictation that Lent term she became aware of 'personal moments'. Once their hands met as she passed him a paper and she blushed deeply. Another time he slipped some *Economic Journal* writing paper into her hands 'in such a way that his lovely long fingers fluttered gently over the backs of my hands with an electric touch'. Once he asked her to turn round so that he could look at her – she felt – in profile. On 13 March he began dictating a letter and halted suddenly, gazing intently at her for what seemed an age:

> My heart was throbbing, but, with the image of Johnson before me, I kept my eyes down. I was confronted with the love of a man I adored, and yet blindly I fought. Suddenly I was aware of tugging against him with all my might. My whole being was concentrated in resistance; and the silence endured for so long that I felt as if my will would snap. Then, to my profound relief, he stuttered, and I dared to look up imploringly

at him. His chin was resting in his hand and his brow was puckered up; he blinked rapidly, and I felt his pride making a determined stand for mastery. After what seemed 5 minutes, but may have been one, he stumbled in a quizzical embarrassed voice: 'Who can you suggest as finance minister for Albania?'

She noted in her diary, 'He is too confident; there is no *Weltschmerz* in him at all. But how attractive he is. I have never seen any man so beautiful as he looked on Friday and again to-day: his long, exquisitely graceful lines, his face pale and nervous, his eye-lashes long and black, half obscuring his liquid, lustrous eyes.'

Naomi Bentwich was now daily expecting some explicit indication of Keynes's love, or at least desire, for her. He had dictated a letter to her in which he said that he would be inaccessible to correspondence for three weeks, and she imagined that he might be about to sweep her off on a holiday. But, on going to take dictation at 46 Gordon Square for the first time on 17 March 1921, she noticed 'two passports on a small table in front of us. I choked down my disappointment as well as I could.' Two days later she came back for more dictation. Keynes was in an angry mood, told her the indexing of the *Economic Journal* was going too slowly, but then remarked amiably that he was going to Algiers for a lazy sixteen days in the desert. He left on 20 March, with Sebastian Sprott as 'companion secretary'. In the desert they went through the proofs of his book on probability, Sprott compiling the index. It was on this holiday that Keynes apparently refused to increase a tip he had given to a shoe-shine boy, remarking, 'I will not be party to debasing the currency.' They were back in London on 12 April. At home for the vacation, Naomi Bentwich analysed her feelings for Keynes. If only he had confessed his love, 'I should not have hesitated to become his wife at a day's notice. . . .' But he wasn't a good man: he reminded her of Sir Willoughby Patterne in Meredith's *The Egoist*. Her task was to make him a better man. 'It is a more difficult task than getting Johnson to write the Logic, and it needs absolutely different talents – subtlety, humour, tact, brilliance – all sorts of qualities I haven't got. . . . But I shall never despair of myself so long as I can see clearly what ought to be done. . . .'

Miss Bentwich returned to her secretarial duties at Cambridge. Everything Keynes now did seemed to confirm her suspicion that he was angry because scorned. His notes were curt; he was evil and sentimental by turns. 'If only he would have dropped the pretence of officialdom, but he would not.' She wrote in her diary for Thursday, 28 April, 'To-day I expected him to drop the veil, and was strung right up to refuse him. But he had himself well under control, tried his best to make me talk politics in a friendly way; he told me he was writing another article over the weekend, and when I asked him if it would have to be cabled he blinked.' Next day he was in a fury. He dictated his article fast. 'I can always remember how furiously he hissed: "I didn't" when I queried what seemed like a contradiction.'

This was the last dictation Miss Bentwich took from Keynes. Confident that she had a sexual hold over him, she determined to take the offensive, without waiting for the signs of amorousness which Johnson had shown.

My most dear Keynes [she wrote him that same day]

I do understand you – I'm sure I do. You see, I must not be broken by your passion, because it would only mean misery to us both later on, for I am simply not the kind of person you thought I was when you tried to win me that way. But neither am I the intriguing thing you thought me this evening. I have been playing your game simply for your sake; because I have for you the kind of love that sees the loved one's faults and wants to cure them. There is a strength in goodness that there is in nothing else in the Universe; and with that strength added to the power for good that you have in you, you would be the veritable King of Kings I love to think you.

Your great fault is your egoism. It makes you unwilling to take any risks, and that is a great practical weakness. It has put you in my power twice, for instance, in this silly game of intrigue that we've been playing together. But worse than that, it makes you terribly cruel sometimes: to protect yourself, or to get what you want, you allow yourself to do ignoble things which I know you condemn in an hour of cool judgment.

It seems to me, if I can make you love me in a self-forgetful way, it would be a way of giving you the strength you need. That is all I am trying to do.

Keynes's reply came a few hours later. Incredulously Miss Bentwich read:

Your letter just received has filled me with more surprise than I can say. The whole thing is a disastrous misunderstanding on your part. I have no feelings of any kind such as you imagine, and never have had any. I can't even remember most of the incidents on which your imagination seems to have built meanings. I thought your manner a little odd sometimes and a little abrupt – and I stupidly put it down to overwork.

I am immensely sorry to have been the unintentional cause of so much unhappiness. Clearly you can't go on being my secretary and we must bring the arrangement to an end. But I hope you will go on with the *Economic Journal* Index. If you would like to see me, I shall be here at 6 o'clock this evening. But do not come, if you think better not.

Don't think this letter unkind, but I want it to be absolutely clear.

She turned up at 6 p.m. on 30 April. Keynes had no inkling that she was on the verge of hysteria. He flung himself in his chair, stretched out to his full length with his hands in his pockets, and with a mischievous gleam in his eye said, 'Oh Miss Bentwich, that letter, how could you!' He denied he had ever tried to arouse emotions in her. If Miss Pate or others heard of these incidents they would think them figments of her imagination. 'I've been extraordinarily stupid,' he said, flinging his head back and starting to stride round the room.

Miss Bentwich tried to recover from her mistake. 'Well, if I'm mistaken I'm very glad, and let's go on as before.' But Keynes would not have it.

> 'Oh, no, impossible – quite impossible' and he went on striding about. I told him I was unconvinced and stood up to go. He opened the door, and I was slowly going down the stairs, puzzled, disappointed, half-defiant, when suddenly he darted to the top of the staircase, and resting his forehead on his raised forearm, he looked down at me with the sweetest expression on his face, and the most wonderful look in his eyes – a look which penetrated my soul. A celestial rapture seized me – a beauty overpowering all analysis; then it was that there passed between us that mysterious exchange of looks, full of meaning, in which all was true.... I saw God in his eyes – the God in us that loves.... I never looked on Keynes again.

The last article Keynes dictated to Naomi Bentwich appeared in the *Manchester Guardian* on 6 May 1921. It was a comment on the decision of the Reparation Commission, published on 27 April, to fix a total German debt of 132 billion gold marks, or £6.6bn. This turned out to be the lowest figure that was politically possible. Yet when the conjurors had done their work, it became clear that this, too, had been whittled down to no more than 50 billion marks (£2.5bn.) – 'the sum', Lloyd George wrote, 'suggested by the German negotiators at Versailles'.[20] The trick was done by requiring Germany to issue three sets of bonds, but to pay interest and sinking-fund payments only on the first two, amounting to £150m a year. As a Belgian official, Gaston Furst, put it, 'the Schedule of Payments elegantly resolved the difficulty on which all previous negotiations had foundered: the German debt was reduced in fact to a reasonable amount but this reduction was sufficiently carefully disguised to keep public opinion free from perceiving it and becoming aroused'.[21]

In his article, Keynes praised the Reparation Commission's verdict as 'a signal triumph for the spirit of justice which the German people themselves will not fail to recognise'. He urged the German government to accept the schedule of payments, though he did not believe it could be fulfilled. The Germans did accept, though only after the usual political crisis leading to the formation of a 'government of fulfilment' headed by Joseph Wirth and Walter Rathenau. Keynes 'claimed some credit for having urged the Germans to accept the Ultimatum and said that he had taken particular pains to have the article advising acceptance telegraphed in full to the German press'.[22]

Naomi Bentwich felt she knew exactly what Keynes meant. Her Keynes had always been a partly fictional character, and as time went on she found it easier to create a dream world in which his denials could be interpreted as 'denying not me but his own thwarted desire', and his writings on reparations as a secret code by which he conducted a subterranean affair with her. In November 1921 she wrote him thirty-two pages setting out her ethical beliefs. 'Here most beautiful Maynard Keynes is my soul.' He sent them back with a short note: 'Thanks for letting me see the enclosed.' On 16 November she wrote, 'Come here and carry me off.'

Keynes now contacted members of the Bentwich family: Naomi should not be left alone. But the passionate, accusing letters continued; occasionally Keynes wrote brief, perfunctory replies. In his circle she was known as the Mad Woman. Had Keynes stopped writing articles, or had she confined her newspaper reading to the religious column of *The Times*, as she vowed to, she might have come to terms with the fact of his indifference. But every public word by him, or mention of him, revived her feelings. Keynes's answers sounded like a stuck gramophone record: 'I don't reply to your letters', he wrote on 27 April 1924, 'because I fear that whatever I may say your imagination will twist it to some illusion.... The articles in the *Manchester Guardian* to which you refer are not written by me and I have nothing to do with them.'

Today there is a precise medical term for Naomi Bentwich's delusions: de Clérambault's syndrome, first identified in 1942, and defined as a 'delusional conviction of being in amorous communication with another person'. Had Naomi Bentwich never met Keynes, her 'madness' might never have occurred. In September 1926, she had a complete breakdown and was sent to Switzerland for a cure. Gradually she picked up the pieces of her life. In April 1928 she married Jonas Birnberg, a vegetarian schoolmaster of stern morals who had waited for her for ten years with the patience of Job. 'For us our union would make no heroic demands,' Miss Bentwich wrote. She survived into her nineties, a tiny woman in Blackheath, convinced that something had happened, after all, those many years ago.

19

Probability and Goodness

I. UNFINISHED BUSINESS

There was one big piece of unfinished business left over from before the war. Keynes's *A Treatise on Probability* had been set up in proof in 1913, but was published only in August 1921 after he had to make an 'enormous number of corrections' on his proof. It had been, he told his publisher Daniel Macmillan, 'a pretty constant companion' for the ten pre-war years. He paid £767 11s out of his own pocket for 2500 bound volumes.

It goes all the way back to the paper he read to the Apostles in 1904 when, still an undergraduate, he had attacked G. E. Moore's theory of how people ought to behave in the face of uncertainty. His endeavour was inspired by his determination to enlarge the scope of individual judgement and narrow that of custom as the 'guide of life'. This, in his view, required linking the concept of probability to beliefs rather than to empirical regularities. Its published form in 1921 still carries the trace of the quest by Keynes's generation of Apostles for a liberating science of morals to complement G. E. Moore's liberation of ethics from the utilitarian straitjacket of the Victorians.

Its distinctive philosophic ingredient is the appeal to reason rather than observation as the source of knowledge, coupled with the doctrine that ideas are independent objects, rather like Platonic forms, capable of being 'perceived' by the mind. Thus probability was, for Keynes, a 'real objective' relation we 'cognise', just as, for G. E. Moore, 'good' was an 'intuited' non-natural property of things. This way of doing philosophy was already old-fashioned by the 1920s. Wittgenstein asked, '*Where in* the world is a metaphysical subject to be noted?'

Keynes's book belongs to the early modern tradition of understanding probability as logical and *a priori*, the tradition of Leibniz, Bernoulli and Laplace. Given its somewhat antiquated epistemology, it is not surprising that it soon became unfashionable. Conceived as an attack on the frequency theory in which probability is a fact of nature, it was soon superseded by, or assimilated to, 'subjectivism', according to which probability is a degree of belief in some proposition, justified or not. What is more surprising, indeed scandalous, is that students of Keynesian economics for long paid it little attention, despite the fact that Keynes's economics are rooted in the problems of ignorance and uncertainty. The reason is that, until recently, standard interpretations of Keynesian economics mistakenly gave rather a small place to uncertainty. This neglect has at last been remedied by scholars like Rod O'Donnell and Anna Carabelli. It is now possible to see that Keynes's theory of probability gave a distinctive flavour to his economics. Indeed, certain characteristics of it cannot be understood without reference to it.

A Treatise on Probability can be seen as an exploration of what it means to behave rationally under varying conditions of knowledge, ranging from certainty to uncertainty. But it was not a complete theory of rational behaviour. In Keynes's philosophy, what it was rational to do was jointly controlled by probability and ethics. In deciding on a course of action, a person had to make two decisions: what were the most likely effects of one's actions? And would those effects make the world a better place? Rationality, in other words, had reference to both means and ends. This is in sharp contrast to modern economics, which takes ends as given (that is, as purely subjective) and focuses solely on the rationality of means. That Keynes's major philosophical work was in the sphere of 'practical' rather than 'speculative' ethics indicates his orientation towards the world rather than the cloister. But he never lost his sense of the ends to which economic life was directed. And for an economist, he was unusually alert to the ethical costs of social progress.

II. THE PRINCIPLES OF CONDUCT

Moore had rejected the proposition that probability could be a guide to conduct on the ground that it was impossible to know the probable effects of actions stretching into a remote future. The best we could do, in most cases, was to follow moral rules which were generally useful and generally practised, as Hume had suggested. This conclusion stuck in the young Keynes's gullet. 'Before heaven,' he recalled in 1938, 'we claimed to be our own judge in our own case.' Moore, he already said in 1904, was working with the wrong theory of probability. He was confusing knowledge of probabilities with knowledge of relative frequencies of occurrence, and claiming that if we do not have such knowledge – and particularly if we do not know that any good we can achieve in the near future will not be outweighed by harm in the far future – we have no rational basis for individual judgement. Keynes said this was wrong. All we had to have was *no reason to believe* that any immediate good we achieved would be overturned by distant consequences.[1] More generally, probabilistic knowledge was a kind of logical knowledge, concerning the 'bearing of evidence' on conclusions.[2] It was to do with beliefs, not with what actually happened. *A Treatise on Probability*, published seventeen years later, was a working out of this audacious insight.

Keynes claimed that the mind could often 'reduce' uncertainty to probability, by 'perceiving' a relation between the evidence (the premiss) and the conclusion of an argument, such as would sanction a 'degree of belief' in the conclusion. The logic he proposes, that is, is one of partial entailment, or inference. He conceived of probability as the 'general theory' of logic, of which the deductive logic of Aristotle was a special case.

Probability, it will be seen, has two sides. It is subjective, in the sense of being relative to our knowledge and reasoning power. But, given these, the probability relation is 'unique and objective': everyone similarly equipped in these respects would perceive the same probability, would draw the same conclusion and should act on the same hypothesis.

Keynes's view of probability as logical *insight* was conceived as an attack on the dominant theory of his day – the frequency theory – which said that probability was a *fact of nature*. For example, if one in ten smokers dies of cancer the probability of smokers dying of cancer is 10 per cent. The identification of probability with frequency, Keynes writes, 'is a very grave departure from the established use of words; for it clearly excludes a great number of judgements which are generally believed to deal with probability'.[3] Moreover, the frequency theory assumed the 'inductive hypothesis' which could not be proved by induction. Frequencies may be part of the evidence we use to make a probability judgement; they are not probabilities themselves.

The important implication of this is that we can and do have probabilities without numbers. We can have good grounds for preferring one conclusion to another, without having any basis for saying 'This is three times as probable as that.' (Just as we can say, 'This is greener than that', without being able to say 'This is three times as green as that'.) In fact, most probabilities in Keynes's *Treatise* are non-numerical; they permit approximate rather than exact comparison – 'more or less likely' – with the possibility of being able to assign numbers to probabilities limited to certain restricted states of knowledge. Sometimes, though, probabilities are unknown; sometimes we know them but cannot compare them. Keynes gives the following example of the difficulty of comparing probabilities based on different arguments:

> Is our expectation of rain, when we start out for a walk, always *more* likely than not, or *less* likely than not, or *as* likely as not? I am prepared to argue that on some occasions *none* of these alternatives hold, and that it will be an arbitrary matter to decide for or against the umbrella. If the barometer is high, but the clouds are black, it is not always rational that one should prevail over another in our minds, or even that

we should balance them – though it will be rational to allow caprice to determine us and to waste no time on the debate.[4]

The domain of rational belief was thus much more extensive than Hume or Moore had allowed. We can have probabilities when we don't have frequencies; and, even when we have frequencies, all we know for certain is that there is a probability of the conclusion being right: probability begins and ends with probability. Thus Keynes's theory is both optimistic about the power of human reason and pessimistic about its ability to penetrate the secrets of the universe. We have only limited insight into the 'nature of reality'. He quoted Locke to the effect that 'in the greatest part of our concernment, God has afforded only the Twilight, as I may so say, of Probability, suitable, I presume, to that state of Mediocrity and Probationership He has been pleased to place us in here'.[5]

However, we are still some way from a complete statement of Keynes's theory of rational *behaviour* under uncertainty. In deciding how we ought to act, we need to take into account two further considerations which Keynes called 'the weight of argument' and 'moral risk'. By the first Keynes means roughly the *amount* of evidence supporting the probability belief. This does not necessarily alter the probability, but can alter the amount of confidence we have in our judgement of the probability. The more facts we have the more confident we are that our belief is justified. The principle of 'moral risk' suggests that it is more rational to aim for a smaller good which seems more probable of attainment than to aim for a larger one which seems less so. Other things being equal, therefore, 'a high weight and the absence of risk increase *pro tanto* the desirability of the action to which they refer'.[6]

One important conclusion for action is that, in most cases, it is more rational to aim for an immediate good than to aim for a remote one, since the first is more likely to have behind it both a greater weight of argument and a higher probability of attainment. Considerations of this kind certainly influenced Keynes's ideas about what it is rational for a reformer to aim at. In particular, they help explain his hostility to revolutionary socialism, which prefers a greater good with a lower probability of attainment to a smaller one with a higher probability of attainment. This line of argument reflects, as we have seen, the influence of the political philosopher Edmund Burke (see pp. 96–8).

In preparing his thesis on probability for publication before the First World War, Keynes added extra sections on induction and statistical inference. Two points only need be mentioned. A thoroughgoing empiricist, he wrote, cannot make use of induction without inconsistency, for the use of the inductive method requires that a prior probability be assigned to its validity.[7] Keynes's view of induction as a logical principle influenced Russell, who acknowledged his debt to Keynes in his *Problems of Philosophy* (1912).

Keynes's hundred-odd pages on statistical inference are remarkable chiefly for their attempt to reduce the domain of its validity to those sets of cases for which *stable* as opposed to *average* frequencies are available.[8] He does not tell us, in the *Treatise*, how stable he thought social, as opposed to natural, structures were. It is characteristic of Keynes that he always wanted his data in a raw, not 'cooked' form, and much preferred tables to graphs, so that 'vigilant observation' of changing reality was not hampered by concoctions and manipulations which *assumed* that reality was unchanging. This is the root of his objection to the misuse of econometrics in social science. These additions to the *Treatise* reinforce its central message, which is that the perception of probability, 'weight' and 'risk' are all highly dependent on judgement. Whether or not there is a map in heaven, there is none on earth. Reason, at all times, controls probability, choosing and shaping the data presented to our senses to yield arguments in which one can have greater or lesser degrees of confidence. That is why Keynes thought of his theory as a branch of logic, to distinguish it from mere belief on one side and statistics on the other.

There are two main links between Keynes's theory of probability and his economics. First, any economics based on the assumption of certain knowledge was bound to give a misleading account of economic behaviour. A 'calculus of probability' which promised, through exact actuarial computation, to reduce uncertainty to the same calculable status as certainty, was inherently fraudulent. Non-numerical probabilities give a rational basis of judgment; they do not guarantee that things will turn out as we expect.

The second link, which has been less noticed, concerns the way economics should be done. Keynes always had a bias against excessive formalism, which he thought gave a spurious certainty to conclusions which were at best probable – in his sense of being more likely. In his economic writings he preferred to use ordinary language. Following Aristotle, we might call this a rhetorical logic, based on premises which are intuitively appealing and whose conclusions are established by arguments which are persuasive, not demonstrative. He was fond of saying 'An economist cannot convict his opponent of error; he can only try to convince him'.

Probability is Keynes's tool of action. But for behaviour to be fully rational requires that not just the means but the ends should be rational. Keynes jettisoned Moore's morals, but not his ethics. 'By far the most valuable things we know or can imagine', Moore had written, 'are certain states of consciousness, which may be roughly described as the pleasures of human intercourse and the enjoyment of beautiful objects'. He added that 'it is only for the sake of these things – that as much as possible may at some time exist – that anyone can be justified in performing any public or private duty; that they are the *raison d'être* of virtue; that is they ... form the rational ultimate end of human action and the sole criterion of social progress'.[9]

Moore's criterion poses obvious problems for the social reformer. Only states of mind are good. But what is the relationship between good states of mind and the usual aims of social reform: freedom, justice, peace? Is it, for example, self-evident that the gains from a more equal distribution of income will always outweigh the losses to civilised ways of living hitherto created by moneyed elites? Clive Bell, who was also a follower of Moore, did not think so. In his book, *Civilisation*, published in 1928, he argued that high culture depended on the existence of inequality. Then again, although Moore said that to maximise the amount of good states of mind was the only justification of duty, he did not say that it was everyone's duty so to act. Most members of Bloomsbury were concerned chiefly with their own states of mind, not the world's. The young Keynes had asked: should I make myself bad that the world should be better? (See pp. 93ff. above.)

Moore's answer was that states of mind are 'highly complex *organic unities*' which contain both an experiencing subject and an object of experience. What this amounted to saying was that the best states of mind could not be enjoyed in isolation; that a cruel and ugly world will have a smaller quantity of good states of mind than a humane and beautiful one. As Keynes explained, the principle of organic unity helped reconcile Moore's teaching with 'other ethical systems' and it 'permitted us, in effect, to take into account almost any kind of circumstance as modifying the sum of goodness, even if the original source of this goodness must be, in every case, the states of mind of conscious beings'.

However, Moore also drew attention to the class of 'mixed goods', in which good states of mind *depend* on the existence of evil states of affairs, imagined or real. He gave as an example the dependence of pity on suffering.[10] Moore believed that the actual existence of suffering (as opposed to the appropriate emotion to imagined suffering) could never be part of a good 'whole', the negative value of suffering outweighing the positive value of pity, but Keynes was not so sure. 'I am not certain', he wrote, 'that all tragic states of affairs are bad on the whole, when everything has been taken into account, or that the goodness of the states of mind, if it is very great, may not outweigh the badness of states of affairs.... [But] it is possible, I think, to imagine two states of affairs, one of which is tragic or unjust, and the other not, such that the states of mind in each are of exactly equal value, and to believe that the tragic state of affairs is less desirable than the other.'[11] This is from a paper Keynes read to the Apostles in 1910, and re-read in January 1921. It may have been partly re-written for its second outing. But even if not, it is hard not to believe that his choice of subject in 1921 was some sort of response, in a Mooreian framework, to the conviction of his friends Ferenc Békássy (who was killed) and 'Peter' Lucas (who survived to hear him in 1921) that the war was an ennobling experience, despite its horrors. Keynes had an optimistic, not a tragic, view of life, but he was far too intelligent not to understand the appeal of war, or to recognise that progress carried ethical costs.*

How then are certain good feelings to be kept alive when the circumstances giving rise to them have disappeared? Keynes gave an ingenious answer in a letter he wrote to Lucas, whose book on tragedy had just been published, in 1928:

> In actual life many of the feelings which we deem noblest and most worth having are apt to be associated with troubles, misfortunes, and disasters. In itself we generally judge the state of mind of the hero going into battle as good – but it is such a pity that he should be killed. Similarly, feelings of sympathy are good in themselves. In fact, the worst of real life is that feelings good in themselves are too often stimulated or occasioned or provoked by evil happenings. If, on the other hand, it were possible to sympathise with, enjoy at second hand, or admire, the noble feelings *without* the evil happenings which generally accompany them in real life, we would get the best of both worlds. Now, as it seems to me, the object of Tragedy is precisely to secure for us a conjuncture in which this comes about.... We come into contact with noble feelings and escape the bad practical consequences....
>
> All of this is connected with my favourite dilemma – the difficulty or impossibility of both being good and doing good. In Tragedy we can witness the spectacle of people being good in a realm which is completely divorced from all consequences, so that we do not have to weigh up against the excellence of being good the appalling nature of the consequences of such behaviour and the events associated with it.[12]

The cost of heroism, or pity, in other words, can be reduced to the price of a theatre ticket: a good bargain for the social reformer, but hardly likely to convince the sceptic that the states of mind of the spectator hero and the real hero are of equal value.

Keynes's conception of the good life influenced both the way he lived his own life, and his public aims. He tried to combine a personal ideal of civilised living with the championship of causes which would bring the good life – good states of mind – within reach of the many. Management of the economy was the chief of these, but he also advocated liberal moral codes and supported the arts out of his own pocket. To the extent that Mooreism influenced his social philosophy it was to restrict rather than enlarge his passion for social reform. This is because Moore's 'ideal' utilitarianism offers a weaker criterion for the social reformer than does hedonistic utilitarianism, since it calls for a judgement about the effects of material progress on states of mind whose goodness is not identified with pleasure

* This paragraph has been rewritten in the light of R. M. O'Donnell's paper 'Mixed Goods and Social Reform', *Cahiers d'économie politique*, nos. 30–31. L'Harmattan, 1998. It does not represent Professor O'Donnell's views.

or happiness. Keynes was largely immune from the main democratic passions of his day; indeed, his attitude to democracy itself was quite cool. At the same time, he enjoyed bad states of mind – what he called 'business and bridge' – more than a true disciple of Moore should have. Like most successful people, Keynes did what he was best at and enjoyed most, lived with his contradictions, and found forms of words to reconcile what he was doing with what, according to his beliefs, he ought to have been doing.

III. THE RECEPTION OF THE *TREATISE*

The earliest reviews of *A Treatise on Probability* were appreciative. C. D. Broad, a follower of Moore and Russell, and four years younger than Keynes, expressed himself in 'substantial agreement' with him. Bertrand Russell considered 'the mathematical calculus' to be 'astonishingly powerful' and 'the book as a whole one which it is impossible to praise too highly'. But he refused to accept the twin theses that probability was indefinable and that many probabilities are not numerically measurable. Russell hankered after a 'modified form' of the frequency theory.[13]

The old Apostle and statistician Charles Sanger was pleased that Keynes 'does not prefer algebra to earth', and quoted approvingly a sentence from the *Treatise* to the effect that 'sensible investigators only employ the correlation coefficient to test or confirm conclusions at which they have arrived on other grounds'. The *Spectator*'s 'S' found that 'Professor Keynes's equations demand a mental activity which does not accord well with reading.'[14]

Young Cambridge was unconvinced. Keynes wrote to Broad on 31 January 1922,

> I find that Ramsey and the other young men ... are quite obdurate, and still believe that *either* Probability is a definitely measurable entity, connected with frequency, *or* it is of merely psychological importance and is definitely non-logical. I recognise that they can raise some very damaging criticisms against me on these lines. But all the same I feel great confidence that they are wrong.[15]

Frank Ramsey had come up to Trinity from Winchester in 1920, aged seventeen. Keynes thought him 'by far and away the most brilliant undergraduate who has appeared for many years on the borderline between Philosophy and Mathematics'.[16] A theorem he wrote as a schoolboy was up to fellowship dissertation standard, in the opinion of his father, the President of Magdalene College; Frank's brother became Archbishop of Canterbury.

Ramsey was a huge, shambling bear of a man, worshipped for his intellect and loved for his sweetness of character. He became an Apostle in 1921 and was elected a fellow of King's in 1924. As a member of the Society he struck a new note. After yet another endless discussion of the value of different states of mind, Ramsey told the brethren that such discussion 'although a pleasant way of passing the time, is not discussing *anything whatever*, but simply comparing notes' (emphasis added).[17] This was the authentic philosophical voice of the post-war generation, soon to be turned on Keynes's pre-war edifice.

Ramsey had two bites at Keynes's theory. In the *Cambridge Magazine* of October 1921, he accused Keynes of muddling up the perception with the existence of probability relations, pointing out the lack of necessary correspondence between the two. His fundamental attack was launched in the paper called 'Truth and Logic' read to the Cambridge Moral Science Club in 1925. After an hour or so of beautiful demolition work little of the baroque edifice of the *Treatise* was left standing.

Probability, Ramsey said, had both an objective and a subjective side. Both statistical and epistemological interpretations of the concept had a basis in ordinary language. Probability often meant proportion. If we say the probability of recovery from smallpox is three-quarters, we mean that is the proportion of smallpox cases which recover. Probability is thus a property of nature. But we also have the authority of language for thinking of it as 'partial belief'. When someone says that three-quarters of smallpox victims will recover, we may reply, 'That is probably true.' How do we justify the second statement? Keynes says, 'We perceive it.' We proceed in other words from full belief in the evidence to partial belief in the conclusion.

Ramsey's criticism was direct. He denied that there were

> any such things as the probability relations he [Keynes] describes. He supposes that, at any rate in certain cases, they can be perceived; but speaking for myself I feel confident that this is not true. I do not perceive them, and if I am to be persuaded that they exist it must be by argument; moreover I shrewdly suspect that others do not perceive them either, because they are able to come to so very little agreement as to which of them relates any two given propositions.[18]

Ramsey's statement, once made, seemed obvious. The Emperor had no clothes. All Keynes had established was that we make judgements of probability, not that there were objective probabilities corresponding to them.

Keynes's mistake, Ramsey felt, lay in mixing up factual and logical arguments. We may infer a factual conclusion from a factual premise, but we cannot say the conclusion is logically necessary. The main requirement in logic is that arguments should be non-contradictory. But with Keynes's probability arguments 'we could accept the premisses and utterly reject the conclusions without any sort of inconsistency or contradiction'.[19] Inductive arguments are not weaker versions of deductive ones. They are to do with the acquisition of beliefs, deductive arguments with the laws of thought. Keynes's theory of probability mixed up the logic of discovery with the logic of implication.

Ramsey tackled the problem of what made beliefs rational along different lines. Agents are conceived of as adopting strategies for getting what they want, that is, they are assumed to be equipped with consistent preferences. The rationality of such strategies is to be judged by their success. People start by attaching probabilities to different possible outcomes. These probabilities are subjective – they have no necessary sanction in logic or nature. Ramsey next construes these subjective degrees of belief as betting rates: all probabilities can be reduced to numbers. The first rationality requirement is that the odds agents are willing to offer on different propositions must not be such that a clever gambler can make a 'Dutch book' or profit against them whatever happens.[20] The second requirement is that strategies should be consistent with the facts. Personal or subjective probabilities are brought closer to objective probabilities through a learning process. Full rationality is reached when, in the words of Martin Hollis, 'starting price odds reflect the merits of the horses'.[21] The learning process is inductive. Unlike Keynes, Ramsey takes a pragmatic view of induction. It is a 'mental habit'. The only way of judging mental habits is to ask whether they 'work'. Whatever its status in epistemology, induction is a useful mental habit.[22]

Ramsey's critique won the day. By the early 1930s, Ramsey's friend Richard Braithwaite was calling Keynes's theory of probability 'very puzzling indeed'. 'Does Keynes really perceive his logical relations of probability holding between two propositions? If he does not, what reason is there to suppose they exist? For they are quite unlike other logical relations.' Moore's ethical theory too was in retreat, Cambridge philosophers – Broad excepted – analysing ethical propositions in terms of subjective statements of approval and disapproval. Modern philosophy had arrived. A Chinese philosopher visiting Cambridge to learn about the nature of truth discovered he had learnt a great deal about the correct use of the English language.[23]

Although it is often said that Ramsey merely 'developed' Keynes's theory in a constructive way, the two approaches come out of different mental universes. In Keynes's world, notions of objective goodness and probability form the foundation stones of ethical and practical reason. Without such foundations thought is 'adrift'. Ramsey's world is made up of preferences and bets. It is a world in which the subjective and pragmatic character of thought is accepted. We use techniques which work. Keynes's people are thinkers, and he equips them with the tool of thought: logic. Ramsey's people are actors, and he equips them with the tool of action: calculating power.

The contrast between the two men is generational. Whereas Keynes's generation saw in metaphysics a salvation from doubt, Ramsey's generation threw it out because they felt it responsible for the First World War. Show that some statement is nonsense, they seemed to be saying, and perhaps people will stop arguing about it, and concentrate their energies on problems which can be solved. Channel reason into science, not metaphysics, and you will get a peaceful, prosperous world. Thus one illusion replaced another: the metaphysical illusion giving way to the positivist illusion that fanaticism is a kind of error rather than a need, that evil is solely due to defective thinking and that 'human behaviour is completely determined by the state of knowledge'.[24]

How far Keynes was shaken out of his pre-war beliefs by Ramsey is hard to tell. It was characteristic of him to admire the brilliance of Ramsey's performance and love him for it. Following Ramsey's death at the age of twenty-six in 1930, Richard Braithwaite edited a collection of his published and unpublished writings. Keynes must have had in mind Ramsey's critique of his *Treatise* when he wrote, in a review of the Braithwaite collection, that the essays were a 'remarkable example of how the young can take up the story at the point to which the previous generation had brought it a little out of breath, and then proceed forward without taking more than about a week thoroughly to digest everything which had been done up to date ...'

In his review, Keynes declared that the published version of Ramsey's criticism of his own theory of probability was very interesting 'both in itself and as showing in some detail how far his mind was departing ... from the formal and objective treatment of his immediate predecessors'. He acknowledged his own debt to Russell, whose early work had suggested that the field of logic could be 'enormously extended'. But the 'gradual perfection of the formal treatment' at the hands of Russell, Wittgenstein and Ramsey himself had been to 'empty it of content and to reduce it more and more to dry bones, until finally it [logic] seemed to exclude not only all experience, but most of the principles, usually reckoned logical, of reasonable thought'. Ramsey had been led to a concept of 'human logic' as distinct from 'formal logic'. He had argued

> against the view which I had put forward, that probability is concerned not with objective relations between propositions but (in some sense) with degrees of belief.... Thus the calculus of probabilities belongs to formal logic. But the basis of our degrees of belief – or the *a priori* probabilities, as they used to be called – is part of our human outfit.... So far I yield to Ramsey – I think he is right. But in attempting to distinguish 'rational' degrees of belief from belief in general he was not yet, I think, quite successful. It is not getting to the bottom of induction merely to say that it is a useful mental habit. Yet in attempting to

distinguish a 'human' logic from formal logic on the one hand and descriptive psychology on the other, Ramsey may have been pointing the way to the next field of study when formal logic has been put into good order and its highly limited scope properly defined.[25]

The implication for economics of the two different ways of thinking about probability, Keynes's and Ramsey's, would be profound. There is a strong implication in Keynes that beliefs, or expectations, about the future can be both rational and subject to disappointment, because the future is unknowable. Knowledge of past frequencies is an important element in making a probability judgement, but it cannot give rise to a mathematical prediction. That is why investment can collapse: current prices do not contain all the information needed to predict their future course. By contrast, Ramsey suggested that as knowledge accumulates – as people learn from their mistakes – the subjective probabilities they attach to possible outcomes come to equal the objective probabilities of those outcomes occurring. This points away from Keynesian economics to strong versions of modern rational expectations theory, in which people are said to hold true beliefs about future events. This is equivalent to saying there can never be undesired unemployment. In the 1970s, rational expectations theory emerged as a stick with which to beat Keynesian economics, restoring classical economics to the position from which Keynes had dislodged it.

20

Russian and German Affairs

I. CHARLESTON AND CAMBRIDGE

Keynes spent his third post-war summer holiday at Charleston writing his third post-war book – *A Revision of the Treaty* – which he describes as a 'sequel' to *The Economic Consequences of the Peace* and which was partly a history, partly a defence against critics of the earlier book, and very much a scissors-and-paste job. His mother helped him once more with newspaper cuttings. By 1921, Georges Clemenceau, the French Prime Minister, 'dry in soul and empty of hope', had left the scene for his family home in the Vendée. 'The great thing about this wood,' said Clemenceau about his pine forest, 'is that, here, there is not the slightest chance of meeting Lloyd George or President Wilson. Nothing, here, but squirrels.' In his introduction, Keynes commented wryly, 'I wish that I could claim the same advantages for this book.' But it was 'this Faustus of ours', Lloyd George, who continued to excite his theological imagination: 'The deeper and the fouler the bogs into which Mr Lloyd George leads us, the more credit is his for getting us out. He leads us in to satisfy our desires; he leads us out to save our souls. . . . Who, ever before, enjoyed the best of heaven and hell as we do?'

A Revision of the Treaty was not the only thing Keynes wrote that summer. In August and September, five articles by him on 'Europe's Economic Outlook' appeared in the *Sunday Times*. They covered much of the ground of his lectures the previous autumn. The first, published on 21 August, made the greatest impact. Keynes predicted that 'some time between February and August 1922 Germany will succumb to an inevitable default'. The Paris correspondent of the *Sunday Times* wrote, 'Rarely – probably never in the history of international politics – has a single and opinionative article had such far-reaching effects.'[1] One can see what he meant. The mark plummeted, the great German inflation started and Germany obliged by applying for a moratorium, slightly ahead of schedule, at the end of 1921. Maynard's father thought he had been 'wise' to close his mark account at Buckmaster and Moore before his article appeared.[2] This was an ethical, not an economic, judgement. Keynes was in an odd position. He was perfectly entitled to bet on his predictions; but such was his authority that his predictions, when published, were also a cause, though no doubt a minor one, of their coming true. By October he was busily selling marks again, and with increasing profit.

Keynes spent the summer of 1921 at Charleston with Vanessa Bell and Duncan Grant, visited by Cambridge friends like Sebastian Sprott, Peter Lucas and Douglas Davidson – the last having just joined his brother Angus at Magdalene College. When, in October, Vanessa, Duncan and the children left to spend the winter in St Tropez, Keynes sent them books, tinned food, advice on currency movements, and the Cambridge gossip they loved to hear.

> Last night [he reported to Vanessa on 19 October] I had to give the Princess [Elizabeth Bibesco, Asquith's daughter] her long promised dinner, theatre and tête-à-tête. She groped me in the stalls without the least concealment from the company and when the lights went up it turned out that her neighbour on the other side was my friend Mr. Cockerell of the Fitzwilliam Museum – which ought to be very good for my reputation.

Keynes saddled himself with two large extra-university commitments. He accepted an invitation from his old friend Edwin Montagu, Secretary of State for India, to go to the subcontinent early in 1922 as vice-chairman of a Royal Commission to advise on Indian fiscal policy – 'a last effort, almost certainly doomed to futility, to save India for modified Free Trade'.[3] After a visit to Manchester on 24 October he accepted an offer from C. P. Scott, editor of the *Manchester Guardian*, to edit twelve supplements for that paper's *Commercial*. He boasted to Vanessa that his income for 1922 would be £8000.[4]

All this he took in his stride, but 'what tends to break me down (and spoil my handwriting)', he wrote to Vanessa on 12 December, 'is not work, but too many parties, hospitality and drink. I've entertained enormously at Cambridge this term.' His engagement diary shows that much of his hospitality was directed at Sebastian Sprott, Douglas Davidson and 'Dadie' Rylands. Dadie was the outstanding undergraduate actor of his time, excelling in female parts. He and Maynard became close friends, drawn to each other by a mutual love of the theatre and English literature. Dadie was a pretty, naughty, high-spirited youth, who took to the intimacy and eccentricity of King's like a duck to water. Lytton Strachey, who had revisited his old haunts, wrote to his brother James on 26 November, '[Keynes's] activities seemed terrific – particularly the social ones, and he confessed he was terrifically exhausted keeping it up. I don't know whether there are other reasons for his exhaustion, but on the whole I should think so.'

II. LYDIA LOPOKOVA

Although Maynard and Sebastian spent a 'quiet and very happy Christmas with Lytton' at his country home in Tidmarsh, Maynard's personal life was about to take a turn which would astound his personal friends. The first hint of impending rearrangements came in a letter he wrote to Vanessa at St Tropez on 22 December 1921: 'Loppy came to lunch last Sunday, and I again fell very much in love with her. She seems to me perfect in every way. One of her new charms is the most knowing and judicious use of English words.' His engagement diary for Sunday 18 December records a day enigmatically poised: '1.30 Loppy.... 8.00 Gabriel [Atkin]'.

He took Lydia Lopokova to supper at the Savoy after the ballet, *The Sleeping Princess*, on Friday 23 December, where they chatted till 1 a.m. They arranged to meet again after his return from Tidmarsh. From this point on, the progress of their affair was astonishingly rapid. 'I'm entangled – a dreadful business – and barely fit to speak to,' he wrote to Lytton on 27 December. 'What is to be done about it? I am getting terrified,' he wrote to Vanessa the next day. Vanessa wrote back on 1 January 1922, 'don't marry her. Flight to India may save you. However charming she is, she'd be a very expensive wife and would give up dancing and is altogether to be preferred as a mistress.' Vanessa seems to have been jumping to conclusions. Maynard replied on 6 January, 'You needn't be afraid of marriage, but the affair is very serious and I don't know in the least what to do about it. I begin to think it's a good thing I am going to India. However, she's very adorable.' And he followed this up on 9 January: 'I'm in a terribly bad plight, almost beyond rescue. Clive simply grins with delight at seeing me so humbled.' On 21 January Keynes informed Edwin Montagu that he would not be available to go to India after all.[5]

It was more than three years since Maynard had first fallen under Lydia's spell, when she had captivated her war-weary audiences at the Coliseum. Her first letter to him, dated 29 December 1918, thanks him for a copy of *The Economic Consequences of the Peace* and wishes him a 'most happy New Year in which my husband joins me heartily'. The critic Cyril Beaumont has described the impression Lydia made on him that autumn:

> Lopokova off the stage was very much like Mariuccia on it. Under medium height, she had a compact, well formed little body which would have delighted Theophile Gautier. Her hair was very fair, fluffed out at the forehead, and gathered in a little bun at the nape of her neck. She had small blue eyes, pale plump cheeks, and a curious nose,

something like a humming-bird's beak, which gave a rare piquancy to her expression. She had a vivacious manner, alternating with moods of sadness. She spoke English well, with an attractive accent, and had a habit of making a profound remark as though it were the merest badinage. And I must not forget her silvery laugh.

Maynard was back from the Paris Peace Conference in time to see her triumph in Massine's *La Boutique Fantasque* at the Alhambra Theatre in June 1919. Frederick Ashton said her performance was 'like champagne corks popping'. Lopokova, Beaumont wrote, 'had an extraordinary resemblance to a doll, for which her rounded limbs, plump features, curved lips, and ingenuous expression were admirably suited'.[6]

But on 10 July 1919 she suddenly 'disappeared'. Beaumont had noticed a 'certain coolness between Lopokova and [her husband] Barocchi' after the production of *Boutique*. From the Savoy Hotel she wrote to Diaghilev that 'for reasons of a personal nature, I have had a nervous breakdown so serious that only with difficulty was I able to get through the performances...'. It was clear that Lydia wanted to escape from Barocchi, and this she could not do while she remained with the Diaghilev company, whose business manager he was. No one knows what caused this sudden estrangement. It may have had to do with Barocchi's philandering.[7] She went to stay with Russian friends in north London. Nothing was seen or heard of her for eighteen months. Where was she in this interval? We cannot be sure, but there is strong circumstantial evidence that she spent part of the time in Russia. Lydia never referred to the missing months. No one who knew her had any idea what she had done in that time, except presumably Maynard himself, who kept silent. She simply put the episode behind her.

By May 1921, Lydia was back in London with Diaghilev for a brilliant season at the Prince's Theatre. Among the hearts she captured on her reappearance were those of the artificial-silk manufacturer and picture collector Samuel Courtauld and his wife Elizabeth ('Lil'), who became life-long friends. But Lydia seems to have re-entered Keynes's life only after Diaghilev's *The Sleeping Princess* opened at the Alhambra in November 1921, and then not immediately. He had moved back to 46 Gordon Square after the Cambridge term ended on 5 December, but spent most of the time till Christmas finishing off his new book, *A Revision of the Treaty*. He did not mention Lydia when he wrote to Duncan in Paris on 21 December, only to Vanessa, still in St Tropez, the next day. He may have felt embarrassed about telling an old boyfriend about a new girlfriend.

Lydia Lopokova was then thirty, with an astonishingly varied life already behind her. Born Lydia Vasilievna Lopukhova, in St Petersburg, on 21 October 1891, she was the third of five children, four of whom – Evgenia, Fedor, Lydia herself and Andrei – were educated at the Imperial Ballet School, graduated to the Maryinsky Theatre and became professional dancers, Fedor eventually becoming the Maryinsky's director and chief choreographer. All except Lydia stayed in Russia and, after the Revolution, were stuck there. Lydia herself joined the *corps de ballet* of the Maryinsky in 1909. She danced in Paris with other members of the Imperial Ballet assembled by Diaghilev in 1910, her virtuosity and ingenuousness making a great impression in *Sylphides*. But instead of going back to St Petersburg, and before Diaghilev formed his permanent company in 1911, she left, with her brother Fedor and sister Evgenia, for the United States, lured by a contract to appear as a 'specialty act' in a touring vaudeville programme. She was only nineteen, and it was the first of those gambles with her career for which Lydia became famous. Together with Pavlova and Mikhail Mordkin, with whom she often danced, she put ballet on the map in America. Her charm, gaiety and naughtiness made her a favourite with audiences everywhere. By the end of 1915, after spells of straight acting, she was talking of settling permanently in the United States, and of marrying Heywood Broun, a giant of a sports writer on the *New York Herald Tribune*, who alternated his coverage of baseball matches with 'puffs' for Lydia's dramatic performances.

She might have done all this (for a time) had not Diaghilev, stranded by the war in Switzerland with a skeleton company, managed to fix up an American tour. This opened in New York in January 1916. In engaging Lydia to be his *première danseuse*, Diaghilev shrewdly realised the value to him of her American connections; she worked indefatigably on and off stage to ensure the tour's success. She danced for the first time with Nijinsky in *Spectre de la Rose* at the Metropolitan in April, earning a rare unfavourable comparison with Karsavina. In fact, she virtually saved the Ballets Russes single-handed. Diaghilev, understanding her value and realising her flightiness, sought to bind her to the company by getting her to marry Randolfo Barocchi, a wealthy backer, now his business manager – a very small Italian with well-trimmed beard and whiskers, an engaging charm and a gift for mimicry.

Although she was a performer of great virtuosity and charm, Lydia was not a classical dancer like Pavlova or Karsavina, the outstanding ballerinas of the age. She lacked the grace and lyricism of the purest classical type. She was very short and rather dumpy; her head was often likened to a plover's egg; her personality, comic and pathetic, showed through everything she did. But she was more than a 'character dancer'. 'To one's astonishment,' wrote her friend Lydia Sokolova,

> everything she attempted came off. Few dancers have performed with such assurance or flown through the air as she did. Lydia had tiny strong feet, little hands and short arms. She had no idea of hairdressing and wore very little make-up on stage – what there was was usually still there the next morning – but when she stood looking up at Big Serge

(which was what she called Diaghilev), with her screwed-up little bun of hair, the tip of her nose quivering, and an expression between laughter and tears, I defy anybody to say she wasn't worth her weight in gold.[8]

It was a bold gesture of Diaghilev to challenge post-war taste with a lavish revival of Tchaikovsky's *The Sleeping Beauty*, reeking of nineteenth-century romanticism. It was a sign, perhaps, of his lack of faith in the revival that the Alhambra's proprietor, Sir Oswald Stoll, got Diaghilev to change the name to *The Sleeping Princess*.* Diaghilev's production, which opened on 2 November 1921, was the most magnificent account of this work which has ever been staged. The budget of £10,000 put up by Stoll was soon overspent, and another £10,000 reluctantly handed over.

Lydia was one of four ballerinas who danced the leading part of Aurora, but her own special roles were those of the Lilac (or Good) Fairy and the Enchanted Princess, danced in the Bluebird *pas de deux* with Idzikovsky, which was generally reckoned to have stolen the show. However, the critics were cool; and the public preferred their Christmas pantomimes. Instead of running into the early summer, which would have enabled Diaghilev to pay back Stoll, *The Sleeping Princess* was rudely bundled off the stage on 4 February 1922.

Keynes sat it out to the end, in the half-empty stalls. On him, at least, *The Sleeping Princess* made a lifelong impression. The Perrault fairy-tale, mingled with memories of the Victorian pantomimes and melodramas he had seen with his father as a child, merged in his imagination with his love affair with Lydia, itself a most fanciful conjunction. Its symbolism permeated his thoughts. It was *The Sleeping Beauty* which he chose for the gala reopening of Covent Garden on 20 February 1946, two months before his death.

A few days before *The Sleeping Princess* closed, Diaghilev fled from his creditors to Paris, leaving his company stranded and penniless in London. Maynard quickly took control of Lydia's finances, persuading her to open a bank account rather than leave her earnings with the head porter at the Waldorf, where she was staying. With Vanessa still abroad, Maynard installed Lydia in her flat at 50 Gordon Square, where she started giving enormous tea parties for the hungry dancers. Maynard was spending most of the spring term in London anyway, working on his *Manchester Guardian Commercial* Supplements, so he was with her much of the time, 'to severe complaints from Sebastian' at Cambridge, he told Vanessa.[9]

Maynard's infatuation with Lydia was at first a source of astonishment, rather than distress, to his closest friends. Duncan wrote to Vanessa on 25

---

* Diaghilev mischievously told Lydia that he had changed the name to *The Sleeping Princess* because her nose was the wrong shape for her to be regarded as a Beauty.

January, 'As for Maynard, until I see him carrying on with L. I must give up trying to imagine what happens – it beggars my fancy.' Duncan's incredulity is understandable. It was not the fact of Maynard wanting to 'carry on' or 'settle down' with a woman which surprised him; other Bloomsbury homosexuals had taken this route, Duncan himself, even Lytton. It was his choice of woman, and the intensity of his feeling. Lydia came from right outside the circle of women whom Maynard's friends would have considered suitable or sensible for him. Had he settled down with one of the Cambridge or Slade School 'neo-pagans', few Bloomsbury eyebrows would have been raised. But what, at least partly, defined Keynes's homosexuality was his inability to enter into a loving relationship with women of this kind. His sexual and emotional fancy was seized by free spirits. The two great loves of his life, Duncan and Lydia, were both *uneducated*; their reactions were spontaneous, fresh, unexpected. Keynes was not looking for an inferior model of himself, but a complement, or balance, to his own intellectuality. One must remember, too, that there was nothing earthbound about Keynes's brain. His fancy could leap and soar over all rational obstacles. He was a gambler, and Lydia was his greatest gamble.

III. THE RECONSTRUCTION OF EUROPE

Keynes's cancellation of his trip to India meant he could devote himself to planning the Reconstruction Supplements to the *Manchester Guardian Commercial*. The first one was now brought forward to April 1922. There were to be twelve issues altogether. Keynes was to be paid £200 an issue as general editor, one shilling a word for international rights to his signed articles, and further payments for his unsigned contributions. He eventually produced a dozen signed articles, some of substantial length; so his earnings for the venture approached £4000.

Although Keynes did not come cheap, he worked obsessively hard on his new assignment. Cambridge was confined to the shortest of weekends, with Gerald Shove taking over his teaching duties for the term. This left most of the spring term of 1922 free to prepare the Supplements, including his own contributions. They were billed as an 'exhaustive survey of European conditions, financial, economic, and industrial, written by the chief authorities in Europe', to be printed in five languages and 'based on more complete knowledge than is yet anywhere available'. Keynes, like Diaghilev, was the impresario of a complex project. He had to decide the themes and topics for each issue; assemble contributors; fix scales of payment; calculate costs per issue; arrange translations. The *Manchester Guardian* provided an extensive back-up service, though its editor, C. P. Scott, developed mixed feelings about Keynes. He disapproved of his 'arid intellectualism', and wrote to the historian J. L. Hammond, 'Keynes is a brilliant and original thinker in his own subjects, but he is also about the most obstinate and self-centred man I ever encountered.'[10]

Salvation through Knowledge was the flag under which Keynes's ship sailed, and he was determined to assemble a glittering crew. He understood the importance of psychology for European reconstruction, and enlisted writers and thinkers of the stature of Maxim Gorki, Henri Barbusse, Anatole France (whose contribution, however, never arrived), Benedetto Croce and Guglielmo Ferrero. Other contributors included Carl Melchior, Hjalmar Schacht, Walter Lippmann, Luigi Einaudi, Arthur Pigou, Oswald Falk, Asquith and Sidney Webb.

The first Supplement appeared on 20 April 1922, with 30,000 copies printed of the English edition. They then continued, at intervals of about three weeks, till 4 January 1923, priced at one shilling each. The first issue dealt with the problem of the foreign exchanges. Keynes had no fewer than three signed articles in it: versions of two of them went into his *Tract on Monetary Reform*.[11] Despite its forbiddingly technical aspects, the question being discussed was simple in outline and of immediate practical import-ance. Everyone agreed on the need for the world to get back to a fixed exchange-rate system as soon as possible. The question which Keynes posed was 'Stabilisation or Deflation?' Should the disordered currencies of Europe be fixed at their existing depreciated values in terms of gold, or should an effort be made to restore them to their higher pre-war values? The monetary reformers, who now included most economists, answered, 'Stabilise' (or devalue); the 'sound money' men, who were mainly bankers, responded, 'Deflate'. Keynes was a monetary reformer. He insisted that it was 'far more important to fix the exchanges than to improve them'. This was to bring him into increasing conflict with the Bank of England and the British Treasury, who aimed to restore the pre-war gold value of the pound. The same day as his article appeared Keynes wrote to Luigi Einaudi, 'We both agree that the immediate problem is to persuade the world that a return to the pre-war parity is an absurdity....'[12]

An 'important and novel feature' of the first Supplement, which ran through all twelve issues, was the business 'barometer', based on an 'index' of business conditions. Compiled for Europe by the London School of Economics and for the United States by the Economic Research Department of Harvard University, these barometers claimed to be able to forecast changes in the economic weather. Keynes spent a great deal of time discussing with William Beveridge and A. L. Bowley at the LSE and Charles Bullock at Harvard the theory of the barometers and acquiring rights to publish them in the Supplements. He was normally quite sceptical about using inductive methods to forecast future events, but was for a while captivated by them. In fact, in a letter to Oswald Falk, dated 26 October 1921, he proposed developing special indexes to indicate 'strength of tendency' as distinct from 'tendency', which he called Accelerators or Accentuators.[13] Keynes helped start the London and Cambridge Economic Service – a regular survey of business conditions – in 1923, and produced for it for seven years an annual memorandum on stocks of commodities. The difference between Keynes and some of his fellow 'barometricians' was that he did not, in fact, believe that business conditions were like the tides – beyond human control. Rather he was looking for an adequate statistical basis for the 'scientific' control of credit which, in his view, was the key to the successful control of the business cycle.

IV. THE GENOA CONFERENCE

By the time the first Supplement came out Keynes was comfortably ensconced in the Hotel Miramare in Santa Margherita. He had arrived on 8 April to cover the Genoa Economic Conference for the *Manchester Guardian*, the third and last of his journalistic coups, which added thirteen articles to his workload, and over £1000 to his income.[14] It was a curious assignment, since Keynes must have known that the Conference, attended by twenty-nine countries, would accomplish little or nothing. It was the remnant of a far grander design by Lloyd George, the centrepiece of which was to have been a British guarantee of French security in return for French concessions on reparations, but which also included involving America and the leading European powers in an international consortium to finance the reconstruction of Soviet Russia. German participation in such a scheme would have the advantage of generating revenues for reparations without hurting British trade.

However, these larger elements had obstinately refused to fall into place. The French prime minister, Aristide Briand, had resigned after the Cannes Conference of January 1922, suspected of being under Lloyd George's thumb. His successor, Raymond Poincaré, a tenacious lawyer from Lorraine, with the mind of an accountant, came to power pledged to 'uphold firmly all France's rights under the Treaty of Versailles'. He refused to come to Genoa himself, and removed reparations from its agenda. This caused America to withdraw too, on the grounds that no real 'business' would be done.[15] All that was left was Lloyd George's hope of reviving Europe's economy (and Britain's flagging export trade) by financing the rebuilding of the Soviet Union, for which he had no money.[16] Lloyd George had clearly become a closet Keynesian, but too late. Had he been able to offer France a larger share of a smaller indemnity, as Keynes had suggested, he might have made progress. But this he was prevented from doing by his own misdeeds at Paris in 1919, and by America's insistence on full payment of the British debt. Nor could he offer France any British troops for its defence: only paper promises. Meanwhile, Germany had virtually stopped paying reparations, and the mark (par value twenty to the pound) had fallen from 250 in March 1920 to over 1000 by March 1922.

Although Keynes came to Genoa as a journalist, he would not have been Keynes had he not arrived with an ingenious plan. This was his scheme for stabilising the exchanges. Its appearance in the *Manchester Guardian* on 6 April was carefully calculated to make it the first talking point of the Conference; advance copies had also been circulated.

Keynes proposed that victors and neutrals should fix their exchange rates straightaway on the basis of their currencies' current gold values. These would be the permanent values of those currencies which had depreciated by over 20 per cent; stronger currencies like sterling would be allowed to 'crawl' up to their pre-war parities by no more than 6 per cent a year, if their prestige was thought to require it. Central banks should allow a 5 per cent difference or 'band' between the selling and buying price of gold to accommodate temporary fluctuations in the demand for their currencies. They should be allowed to borrow gold from the Federal Reserve Board of the United States at 10 per cent interest per annum up to a borrowing limit of $150m for any country, and $500m in total at any one time.[17] Keynes kept producing such plans, with technical variations, for the rest of his life: the last of them led to the setting up of the Bretton Woods system in 1944. But, until the last one, they always foundered on the unwillingness of the United States to play its allotted role as lender of the last resort. Monetary reform at Genoa proceeded along different lines, with the adoption of resolutions recommending 'means of economising the use of gold by maintaining reserves in the form of foreign balances'.[18] This proposal for setting up a gold-exchange standard was the work of Ralph Hawtrey, then at the high point of his influence at the British Treasury.

What chiefly interested Keynes at Genoa was the presence of a Russian delegation, invited, for the first time since the war, to join the high priests of Europe in their deliberations. He denied – in an article published on 10 April – that 'the issue of the near future [is] between the forces of Bolshevism and those of the bourgeois states of the nineteenth century type'. Bolshevism was a temporary delirium like Jacobinism, 'bred by the besotted idealism and intellectual error of the sufferings and peculiar temperaments of Slavs and Jews'. He expected Russia and the West to converge in time on moderate socialism. Meanwhile, 'Soldiers and diplomatists – *they* are the permanent, the immortal foe.'[19] Keynes could not believe that the Soviet Union was a new form of power state which might be even more threatening to liberal values than 'soldiers and diplomatists'.

In his hopes for convergence he was undoubtedly influenced by his liking for Chicherin, an elegant homosexual of the old school, who came to Genoa as Soviet Russia's Commissar for Foreign Affairs. Keynes invited him to dinner on 12 April, telling him, 'The question whether or not the Conference is going to be no better than a bore depends almost entirely on yourself and Mr Lloyd George between you.' In fact it was Chicherin who gave Keynes an interview in the Hotel Imperial in Santa Margherita on 13 April. Keynes developed an affinity for this 'rather amiable and agreeable snake',[20] who, however, was a mere executant of Soviet foreign policy.

Every day Keynes received an adoring letter from Lydia in London; except for two short notes, none of his to her have survived (in fact, none before September 1923). On 11 April she was 'very anxious to see your articles printed: to-day I went to three news stands, but not one ... did ... produce *Manchester Guardian'*. She added, 'I live simple working man's life, and you – do you go in the evenings to dissipated houses?' (Keynes had been gambling at the Casino in Rapallo.)

On 18 April Keynes turned again to Russia. Lloyd George, too, wanted to strike a sensible bargain with Chicherin, but was hamstrung by the French insistence that the Soviet Union should first acknowledge the Tsarist debts. To Keynes this seemed like a dreadful rerun of Versailles and its 'rubbish about milliards'.

> We are pressing Russia to repeat words without much caring whether or not they represent sincere intentions, just as we successfully pressed Germany.... We act as high priests, not as debt collectors. The heretics must repeat our creed.... Genoa, instead of trying to disentangle the endless coil of impossible debt, merely proposes to confuse it further with another heap of silly bonds. The belief that all this protects and maintains the sacredness of contract is the opposite of the truth.[21]

Britain should write off the Russian war debt to itself. Russia should be allowed to compound with its other pre-war creditors for a modest annual sum, after a five-year moratorium. Wherever possible private properties held by foreigners 'should be restored to their original owners on the basis of partnership or profit-sharing-arrangements between the owners and the Bolshevik government...' This would open the way for a return of foreign capital to the Soviet Union. Inducements could take the form of *de jure* recognition and an export credit of £50m to be spent by Russia buying British and German agricultural machinery and means of transport. 'If Russia exports food again one year earlier than she otherwise would, this may lower the price of wheat enough to save us a huge sum on our food bill alone.'[22]

None of this, of course, came to pass. The two pariahs, Russia and Germany, signed a separate treaty at Rapallo on 16 April, cancelling all claims on each other and making the debt-collectors look foolish. It did not lead to the reconstruction of Russia by German capital, because Germany had none. The question remains: could the Bolsheviks have been bribed to abandon their revolution by Western credits? The Revolution had not yet been set in Stalinist concrete. Lenin was a supreme opportunist. He had embarked on a limited return to capitalism with the New Economic Policy in March 1921, which welcomed foreign capital. Rathenau's view was: 'Let private trading corporations go in individually. When they have got a sufficient number of contracts, the Soviet system will fall.'[23] Lloyd George and Keynes felt the same. We will never know, because the bribery was never attempted.

Maynard's articles on Russia excited Lydia very much. 'I see you have sympathy for Russia,' she wrote to him on 18 April. 'When Chicherin reads it he will follow your direction....' Lydia's commentaries can hardly be called profound. But that was not their purpose. They were designed to build up Maynard's self-esteem. He never got praise like this from his Cambridge or Bloomsbury friends. A year earlier he had confided to Virginia Woolf that 'he liked praise, & always wanted to boast. He said that many men marry in order to have a wife to boast to. "I want it [praise] for the things I'm doubtful about."'[24] He was particularly doubtful about his journalism, mistrusting his own facility. Lydia swept these doubts away. 'Do not speak against your articles in jornalism [sic],' she wrote on 22 April, 'just think how many people read, understand and remember it'; and on 28 April, 'You say you don't do much good. It is not true.... Do you not see how they need you?' Lydia's praise was unstinting. 'Your articles ... *breathe* to me'; 'your plans ... are like clear compact buildings'.

But it was not just his mind that Lydia wanted. Her early letters are full of expressions of sexual, mainly oral, endearment: 'I gobble you, my dear Maynard'; 'I retain infinitely your warm wet kisses'; 'I cover you with kisses full of flame'; 'With caresses large as sea I stretch out to you'; 'I want to wrap around you and give the [abundance] of my feeling.' She often signed herself 'your faithful dog'. To inspire such sexual devotion must have done wonders for the morale of someone who was convinced that he was unattractive to both sexes. Keynes appeared to reciprocate: 'I want to be ... gobbled abundantly,' he wrote from Genoa on 24 April. Sexual relations certainly developed, and by 1924 Lydia was appreciative of Maynard's 'subtle finger'. She had a childish sense of humour which suited him. 'Last night,' she wrote on 21 April, 'I had such a laughter I thought I could not finish from it – Miassin while dancing lost halph his shirt, collar, hat; when I saw that I immediately thought to have a decidedly funny disaster is to lose his trousers.'

V. THE PROPRIETIES

Maynard returned from Genoa on 4 May to the growing complications of his affair with Lydia. He had installed her in Vanessa's flat at 50 Gordon Square. This worked perfectly well while Vanessa was away in Paris. But she returned at the same time as Maynard left for Genoa. Lydia, who had committed herself to the choreographer Léonide Massine, stayed on as her lodger. There seems to have been little friction between them at this stage. In fact Vanessa told Roger Fry that she saw very little of Lydia, then only late at night, and that she was very charming, though 'there is some truth perhaps in Clive's complaint that she has only one subject of conversation, the ballet'.[25] It was in fact Clive, Vanessa's husband, who first turned against Lydia. Clive certainly loved the idea of Lydia. In fact he dedicated an excruciating poem 'To Lydia Dancing' ('Is it true? / Are Ariel's Whims / Embodied in your artful limbs?'). He also flirted with her, as he did with all pretty women. This apparently aroused the jealousy of his mistress Mary Hutchinson. At any rate it seems to have been Mary who 'set Clive against Lydia'.[26] He suddenly suggested to Vanessa that they spend their summer holidays in France, because a whole summer of Lydia at Charleston would be too boring. Arrangements in Gordon Square would also have to be changed. Matters were complicated because Lydia disliked the idea of living with Keynes as his mistress. She thought it would be 'too scandalous'. In any case, Vanessa told Clive, 'I don't see that we can go out of our way to consider proprieties for them – nor do I think we can start on the summer holidays with Lydia as part of the establishment. I get on with her perfectly well & like her very much – but I see that the introduction of anyone – especially female, for more than a week into such an intimate society as ours is bound to end in disaster.' Vanessa (who, it seems, was left by Clive to do his dirty work) finally wrote to Maynard in blunt terms on 19 May that he and Lydia would not be welcome to spend September at Charleston.

Nothing was settled immediately. Lydia sensed that all was not right. There is a very rare note of asperity in her letter to Maynard dated Monday 12 June 1922: 'Clive gave a tea party – iced coffee was tasty; as usual great many boring people, including Ottoline, Mary, J. H. Smith and others.' For most of June and July Lydia danced at the Coliseum, while Maynard continued to work on the Supplements.

Keynes travelled to Oxford on 4 August to address the Liberal Summer School on reparations. A day later Lydia's season at the Coliseum ended. On 8 August the two lovers travelled together to Ostend to see the Diaghilev ballet and gamble with Sheppard: the proprieties could be dropped for 'abroad'. On their return, Maynard went to stay for a few days with the McKennas in Menabilly in Cornwall, while Lydia danced in Manchester. 'I float rapidly between Cornwall, Hamburg, Sussex and Wiltshire,' Keynes wrote to Sebastian Sprott from Menabilly on 19 August. On 23 August Lydia danced the can-can before the rheumatic old ladies of Harrogate; three days later Keynes revealed his latest financial plan to the rheumatic old bankers of Hamburg. On 7 September they both moved into Parsonage House, Oare, near Marlborough, Wiltshire, which Maynard had rented from Geoffrey Fry, who had served under him in the Treasury. Here they finally spent three weeks together. Their neighbours were Desmond and Molly MacCarthy, their only visitors Sheppard and Cecil Taylor. 'We are very happy here,' Maynard wrote to Vanessa on 17 September, 'and time flies by. We ride every day in most perfect country and by the end of the week the riding master thinks Lydia will be accomplished.'

In Bloomsbury the game of domestic musical chairs was finally concluded. Lydia moved from No. 50 to No. 41, Vanessa from No. 50 to No. 46, and Clive from No. 46 to No. 50. Lydia opened on 9 October with a three-week season of *divertissements* at the Coliseum. This time, with Maynard's encouragement and under his direction, she started a ballet company of her own. Stoll paid her £175 a week, out of which she paid the other dancers. 'From the artistic point of view', Cyril Beaumont wrote to her, 'your attempt is miles above the Massine show.' A new entertainment, *Mozart's Evening Music*, produced by her friend Vera Bowen, choreographed by Massine and designed by Duncan Grant, opened at the Coliseum on 19 November. On 29 October Vanessa had reported to Roger Fry, 'Maynard is in London for a few days. Then he's going to Berlin to help arrange their finances. Lydia & he seem to have settled down to married life & I'm not at all sure it won't end in real marriage as I think she's beginning to want a baby very badly & will soon insist on it. Well, if so I shall have to move once again....'

VI. THE UNLUCKY EXPERTS

Keynes's appearance in Berlin on 2 November 1922 marked the return of the experts after the collapse of Lloyd George's grand political initiatives. Lloyd George's failure at Genoa not only doomed his premiership, but also marked the effective end of the Anglo-French entente. He was convinced that, had Briand stayed in power, a 'European appeasement from the Urals to the Rhine might have been reached in 1922'.[27] This is wishful thinking: Anglo-French differences were too great. After Genoa, London came to understand that the key to a European settlement lay in Washington, not Paris. The American objective, which reflected the views of both the new Republican administration of Warren Harding and the New York bankers, was to take financial questions out of politics, treating them as purely business matters. The administration's programme linked a resumption of private US lending to Europe to payment of the Allied war debts to the USA, settlement of the reparations question by financial experts, not politicians, and currency stabilisation. Throughout the summer and autumn of 1922, experts and bankers met and produced plans: they all foundered on the rock of Poincaré's refusal to 'allow a committee of bankers to arbitrate the rights of France or influence her destiny'.[28] The Balfour Note of August 1922 announced Britain's intention of limiting its claim to reparations and the war debts it was owed to the net amount required to meet its obligations to the United States. Despite its hostile reception in both America and France, it was the opening move in the realignment of British policy.

In his speech to the Liberal Party Summer School on 4 August 1922, Keynes rejected the Balfour Note's attempt to link the reparations problem and Britain's debt to the United States. 'We must abandon the claim for pensions and bring to an end the occupation of the Rhinelands. . . . If France would agree to this, which is in her interest anyway . . . it would be right for us to forgive her (and our other Allies) all they owe us . . . regardless of what the United States may say or do.'[29] In more sombre mood, he wondered whether all these debt-collecting plans, sensible or crazy, did not misunderstand modern economic life. The analogy between governments and business firms was wrong: if a state defaulted on its debts 'there is no legal process for dealing with it . . . it is foolish, therefore, to suppose that any means exist by which one modern nation can exact from another a tribute continuing over many years'. European civilisation needed German support to defend it against the 'dark forces' of Bolshevism. All Keynes's old animosity against Lloyd George burst out: he had 'proved himself the least capable of enduring and constructive statemanship of any man who has long held power in England'. It was time, he concluded, for 'new men . . . to make the speedier progress which Europe's state imperatively now demands'.[30]

The day of the new men came at last. On 22 October 1922, Lloyd George fell from power, victim of the Chanak crisis and the 'stench of the Honours scandal'.[31] He was succeeded by Keynes's old Treasury chief Andrew Bonar Law, who, after a general election in November, formed a purely Conservative government. In Germany, Joseph Wirth was succeeded on 14 November by Wilhelm Cuno, a 'non-political' Hamburg shipowner and a friend of Melchior. A new man of a rather different kind, Benito Mussolini, seized power in Italy on 30 October.

Lord D'Abernon, the British ambassador in Berlin, had persuaded the Wirth government to invite Keynes to Berlin as a member of a commission of experts to advise on currency reform. The commission was made up of some 'very clever men' (Keynes, Cassel, Brand and Jenks, an American professor) and 'the requisite ballast of dull ones to lend respectability' (Vissering, Dubois and Kamenka). They were joined in Berlin by members of the Reparation Committee – Barthou and Bradbury – who were quarrelling about conditions for a moratorium. The arrival of so many currency doctors proved almost fatal for the currency – 'the moment they appear the mark bolts: this time it has got quite out of control, in a headlong flight towards the abyss'.

Keynes was in Berlin for a week; Melchior provided him with a flat and secretary at the Hamburg-Amerika line's headquarters in Bellevuestrasse. By 5 November, Brand was complaining about overwork – and Keynes. '[He] is rather upsetting the other members of the Ctee. He is so arbitrary & critical ... that he rather loses the effect of his extraordinary cleverness. They get distrustful of him. He always wants to rush everyone.' On the 7th the experts submitted their reports to the German government. 'One banker & 3 Professors' (Brand, Cassel, Jenks and Keynes) signed the majority report, drafted by Keynes. This called for the immediate stabilisation of the mark by Germany's own efforts, but emphasised that this required a two-year moratorium on reparations payments and a budget balanced 'by the utmost economy in government expenditure and the utmost of rigour in the collection of taxes'. A foreign loan would be useful, but not indispensable. Lord D'Abernon thought that the report was 'the most important document which has been drawn up in the recent course of the reparation controversy'; he added, 'it received not the smallest attention, either from the Allies or from Germany. Creditor and debtor – who agreed in nothing else – agreed in ignoring it.'[32]

The experts' report was not pro-German. The Germans argued that the reason for the collapse of the mark was an adverse balance of trade, so that stabilisation required, in the circumstances, a large foreign loan. Keynes completely rejected this reasoning. As he wrote in the eleventh Reconstruction Supplement on 7 December, 'If the quantity of a currency can be controlled, then sooner or later it can be stabilised. This simple truth still holds good. The quantity of a currency can be controlled unless the government is in financial difficulties.'[33] Thus the key to stabilisation, Keynes told Rudolf Havenstein, president of the Reichsbank, was to stop printing money.

This is Keynes at his most orthodox, speaking in the accents of Hume and Ricardo. It was also the French position. What he insisted on, against the French, was that the strain a social system could take before it collapsed was very limited.

With Cuno, advised by Melchior, installed as the new Chancellor in Berlin, and Bonar Law as British prime minister, Keynes now had access to policymakers in two countries. In London he found he was being consulted 'almost as in the old Treasury days'.[34] He saw Bonar Law on 19 December and offered him a scheme of his own, again designed to ensure that France got a larger share of scaled-down reparation payments.[35] The previous day he had been consulted by Stanley Baldwin, the new Chancellor of the Exchequer, about the American debt, which Baldwin was about to go to Washington to settle. At the same time he had opened up a line of communication, through Melchior, to the new German government. 'I think you will find hardly a prominent politician in England', he wrote to Melchior on 1 December, 'who is not astonished and dismayed by the extraordinary weakness of the German government ... in its perpetual attempts ... to try and find out some useless formula which will not offend.... Is there no one in Germany capable of calling out in a clear voice ...?'[36] This was probably the moment he decided that he would be the clear voice. Melchior passed his comments on to Cuno. Keynes felt that at last he was where he wanted to be: helping to shape policy in both countries from both inside and outside.

VII. KEYNES–MELCHIOR

What followed over the next few months, and especially in May–June 1923, was certainly one of the strangest episodes in Keynes's life and one of the most curious in the hidden diplomacy of the inter-war years. Essentially he and the German banker Carl Melchior turned the 'curious intimacy' they had established at Spa in 1919 to the task of securing an Anglo-German agreement. The complicity of victor and vanquished on that occasion was re-enacted in a correspondence – parts of which are unfortunately missing – in which Keynes offered constructive criticism of German tactics which Melchior passed on to Cuno, and Melchior sent Keynes 'inside' political and financial intelligence which he would use in discussion with British officials. By these means the two friends hoped to attune their own governments to each other's wavelength.

Their friendship enabled, rather than caused, them to play a game which they conceived to be in the national interests of their own countries and of Europe as a whole. For Melchior the prize was to isolate France. Keynes believed that French policy under Poincaré disguised economic and territorial ambitions which threatened Britain's commerce. The risks in this amateur diplomacy were obvious. By encouraging the Germans to believe that, sooner or later, the British would come down on their side, Keynes encouraged German resistance to French demands. Like most Englishmen he also underestimated French resolve. The results were unexpected by both. By helping to crowd out direct Franco-German negotiations, the Keynes–Melchior initiative paved the way for eventual American intervention, which resulted in the Dawes Plan.

The occasion for this private initiative was France's resort to force to overcome the German default. The statesmen and experts had assembled once more with their plans – in London on 9 December 1922, in Paris on 2 January 1923. At the first of these conferences, Bonar Law, 'clear and acute, but ultra-pessimistic',[37] presented the British Treasury proposals, which implied 'a radical rethinking of reparations'.[38] Poincaré, predictably, rejected the British ideas and prepared to act. Having persuaded a majority on the Reparation Commission to declare Germany in default on coal deliveries, he sent French engineers and troops into the Ruhr on 11 January 1923. 'France', Keynes declared, 'has chosen to tear up the Treaty and break the peace of Europe.'

While Keynes was gaining credit with the Treasury he was losing it with the Bank of England. Baldwin, the new Chancellor of the Exchequer, had sailed for Washington with Montagu Norman, the governor of the Bank, at the end of December to arrange for a settlement of the American debt. With the governor it was a matter of honour that Britain should pay back what it had borrowed. Honour coincided with the City's interests, Anglo-American co-operation to restore the gold standard, and the resumption of American lending in Europe, all of which were essential elements in Norman's grand design. Keynes had consistently advocated cancellation of inter-ally war debts. He did not consider them moral obligations since they were incurred in a common cause. He feared that Britain would feel obliged to make one-sided payments even if it received nothing from its debtors. Moreover, the war debts raised the same theoretical and practical issues as did German reparations. They had created no profitable assets out of which to repay: payment could be made only by lowering living standards. In his *Revision of the Treaty* he predicted, rightly, that 'America will not carry through to a conclusion the collection of the Allied debt any more than the Allies will carry through the collection of their present reparation demands. Neither, in the long run, is serious politics.'[39] But in the long run, as he was himself to say, we are all dead; and in the short run American lenders wanted their bond. As President Calvin Coolidge was to say, 'We hired them the money, didn't we?'

Keynes was shocked when Baldwin returned in January with his provisional settlement, stipulating annual British payments of between $161m and $184m. stretching sixty-two years ahead. He and McKenna advised Bonar Law to reject the terms: let 'America discover that they are just as completely at our mercy, as we are at France's and France at Germany's', Keynes wrote to Baldwin's private secretary, J. C. C. Davidson, on 30 January.[40] Bonar Law threatened to resign if the Cabinet agreed to them; but McKenna, who had urged him to resist, now backed down. Norman was furious with Keynes for endangering his designs. In Washington he had been much impressed with the 'newly-found desire on the part of the Americans to come into Europe again'.[41] He now dismissed Keynes as a 'clever dilettante with an even greater potential for mischief than the irresponsible Beaverbrook'.

Meanwhile, there was a diplomatic impasse in central Europe. Instead of capitulating when French troops marched into the Ruhr, as perhaps Poincaré expected, the German government called for a policy of passive resistance – non-work in the occupied areas – which was financed by an empty exchequer to the final ruin of the mark. This drove the French and Belgians to commandeer the railways and mines of the Ruhr and work them with their own labour. The British balanced in the middle, 'unwilling to break with France or to discipline Germany'.[42] (D'Abernon likened Bonar Law to Pontius Pilate.) The Americans would do nothing till the debt situation was finally resolved. The circumstances were made for 'a further series of individual initiatives, more or less detached from the position of the various governments'.[43]

It was not till 20 April that Lord Curzon, the francophile British Foreign Secretary, invited Germany to submit proposals for a settlement. The German reply of 2 May, in which Melchior collaborated, offered a little less than Bonar Law had asked for, to be paid for by means of an American loan. It did, however, offer to submit to impartial arbitration the question of German capacity to pay. The French and Belgians rejected the German offer on 6 May; the British followed suit on 13 May, but suggested that Germany 'reconsider and expand' its proposals, which at least kept open the door for further exchanges. Keynes's reaction was scathing:

> From the days of Versailles until now the Notes of the German government have lacked both passion and persuasiveness.... One might suppose her statesmen ... were nourished exclusively on potatoes.
>
> Heaven knows that propaganda is a sinful thing! But there is nothing wrong in writing a short sentence.... The peace of Europe, almost, is menaced by prose style. Who, smiling at his German governess,* could have foreseen that this national peculiarity would have turned out so important!
>
> The faults of form are not only literary ... by making her proposal appear to depend on an international loan, impracticable in size and to be contributed by others, she has contrived to make it look a deception and an evasion at the same time.[44]

But his vitriol was reserved for the French:

> The French reply, sent without consultation with her Allies, offends against more important things than tact or style. The small, malignant

_____
* Keynes had two as a child.

figure of Poincaré lacks even the grim, ingratiating quality of the old grey owl Clemenceau. One feels oneself in a black cavern, narrowing to a point through which nothing human can creep, nightmare narrowness.

Keynes's letter of 10 May to Melchior is missing. But he evidently told his friend that he intended to 'come over to Germany and lift the veil'.[45] In preparation for this visit he wrote a private letter to the German Chancellor, enclosing 'A Suggested Reply to Lord Curzon'.

It contained four short paragraphs. Germany would accept Bonar Law's 'general scheme' of January 1923, including the securities proposed in the event of a default, 'provided that the amount of the annuity commencing in 1927 (i.e. the rate of interest on the first series of new bonds) is determined in due course by an independent tribunal as proposed in her previous communication'.[46] In a follow-up letter of 24 May he urged that the German reply 'get away from the capital sum (which is bound to fall short of what people here expect) and from the loan (which is absurd), and to speak in terms of annuities'. Once more he emphasised the importance of language: *'In the long run* firmness and a proud bearing will produce more effect on opinion than conciliation and moans.'[47]

Through Melchior, he advised the Germans to delay their reply to the British Note pending government changes in Britain. Stanley Baldwin replaced Bonar Law as prime minister on 22 May; Robert Cecil was definitely in the Cabinet, and Reginald McKenna was expected to be Chancellor of the Exchequer, so 'there are now two very influential figures [in the government] who do not believe in huge figures'.[48]*

Keynes had decided to slip over to Berlin for the weekend. On 30 May he saw Baldwin and McKenna, explaining to Baldwin that he was going over to Germany to try to influence the German government into 'more fruitful paths'.[49] He arrived in Berlin on Friday 1 June, and stayed in Melchior's flat. Over the weekend the German reply was hammered out in conversations between Keynes, Cuno, Melchior and the German Foreign Minister, Rosenberg. Melchior relates that they were 'all aware that success was improbable'. Keynes returned to London on the morning of Monday 4 June, the day after his fortieth birthday, and lost no time in communicating the draft German reply to Baldwin. It was seen and approved by McKenna and Norman, and favourably received by the British Treasury. By the time it was officially delivered on 7 June, 'Cuno and von Rosenberg were aware that it was not going to be rejected by the British government.'[50]

The German Note was much admired for its conciliatory character and tautness of style. Germany agreed to submit its 'capacity to pay' as well as

* Baldwin's plan to make McKenna his Chancellor fell through, and Neville Chamberlain became Chancellor of the Exchequer.

the amount and method of payment to an impartial international body. If large-scale loans proved impracticable, it would substitute a scheme of annuities. It offered definite guarantees for payment. 'In a matter so vast and complicated', the Note concluded, 'real progress cannot be made by the exchange of written documents, but can only be achieved by word of mouth at the conference table.'[51] Keynes was in the fortunate position of being able to write an appreciative review of his own handiwork, praising the Note's 'tone and method of approach', its avoidance of 'irrelevant and controversial issues' and 'faults of manner and expression'.[52] He urged Baldwin 'to promote a settlement along the lines offered by Germany', but at the same time to 'woo France and be prepared to act by her with generosity in return for concessions to our point of view'.

The Keynes–Cuno initiative was the high point of Keynes's involvement in reparations diplomacy. It failed to thaw the diplomatic ice. Baldwin responded to the German *démarche* with a display of masterly inactivity; and events took their course as the economic collapse of Germany finally produced the diplomatic movement which Keynes had failed to secure. In September, the German mark reached 250 million to the pound. As no one would now accept its currency, the German government had to surrender. Cuno's successor, Streseman, called off passive resistance; Hjalmar Schacht, Havenstein's successor as president of the Reichsbank, introduced a new currency, the Rentenmark, in November. These developments opened the way to France's eventual acceptance of a committee of 'impartial experts', set up under the American banker Charles Gates Dawes, to work out a new reparation scheme. The experts' report, published in April 1924, managed to avoid mentioning a capital sum, suggested a year's moratorium, and thereafter proposed variable annuities related to the size of Germany's export surplus under a fixed-exchange regime. Acceptance of the Dawes report was eased by the replacement of Poincaré by Edouard Herriot in June 1924. General acceptance of the Dawes Plan in turn led to the Dawes Loan, through which private American money returned to Europe. All the stages of the nightmare, it seems, had to be gone through before the new financial hegemony of American banking could be established and central Europe brought back to economic life.

In the 1920s bankers and financial experts filled the gap between the *laissez-faire* ideology of governments and stabilisation requirements. Instead of abolishing the wartime debts, as Keynes had wanted, the Dawes Plan made private bankers responsible for a recycling mechanism built on debt. By these means the reparations question was 'solved'. Early in 1923 Keynes had started to write a new book in which he expounded his plans for a monetary remedy for Britain's unemployment problem. The fight against Britain's return to the gold standard had started.

21

Monetary Reform

I. THE BRITISH DISEASE?

What started Keynes on the road to the Keynesian Revolution was the incomplete British recovery from the depression of 1920 to 1922. Nothing like the collapse of prices, output and employment had been seen since the end of the Napoleonic Wars. When the position was finally stabilised in 1923 it was on the basis of 10 per cent unemployment, which lasted for the rest of the decade. On top of this came the great depression of 1929–32 and the incomplete recovery from that. Over the whole inter-war period Britain never experienced anything like full employment. Hitherto, large-scale unemployment had been seen as a problem of the business cycle. It now seemed that it might be endemic.

The economics of the day did nothing to illuminate such persistence. In retrospect, it seems clearer than it did at the time that between 1919 and 1922 the British economy suffered from two major 'shocks' from which it never recovered between the wars. The first was a 'real' shock – a once-and-for-all increase in British unit labour costs. In 1919–20 trade unions were able to win a 13 per cent reduction in the working week at unchanged productivity.[1] This meant a 13 per cent rise in the efficiency wage – the wage per unit of output. Superimposed on this was a 'monetary' shock – the savage deflation of prices – which left the real wage – the purchasing power of the money wage – higher at the end of the depression in 1922 than it had been in the boom of 1920. This was because money wages, though surprisingly flexible by later standards, still failed to fall as far as wholesale and retail prices. It was this deadly double-blow of a union-induced rise in unit costs and a government-induced deflation which left profit expectations in the British economy too low to provide for full employment. However, the persistence of this 'disequilibrium' remained unexplained.

As we have seen, Keynes thought that most of the ensuing trouble could have been avoided had an attempt been made to stabilise the economy at the end of 1920, on the basis of zero inflation, 6–7 per cent unemployment and an exchange rate of $3.60 to the pound. Instead deflation was allowed to continue unchecked. Real interest rates remained punitively high right through the period of falling prices, 1921–2. The authorities allowed the depression to gather force unchecked because they were determined to *improve* the sterling–dollar exchange so as to make possible the restoration of the gold standard at the pre-war sterling–dollar parity of $4.86 to the pound. The deflation was eased up only when the pound rose to $4 and above. Thus equilibrium was 'restored' by the end of 1922 on the basis of a much lower level of prices and a much higher level of unemployment than at the end of 1920. From this sequence it would appear that the British unemployment 'problem' of the 1920s was policy-induced, the crucial policy being the maintenance of 'dear money' right through the slump. The 'real' shock of the shorter working week might have been overcome had British industry been allowed to compete at a lower exchange rate.

Although Keynes was extremely critical of excessive deflation, no more than anyone else did he think it would create a permanent unemployment problem. Thus he looked forward, in September 1921, to 'trade recovery, tolerable employment, and a new equilibrium'.[2] What pulled him up short was that there was no return to 'tolerable employment' *after* prices had stopped falling in the last quarter of 1922. Unemployment in the spring of 1923 was almost as bad as it had been a year previously. It was this persistence of high unemployment which alerted him to the possibility that the costs of the deflation might be more than 'transitional'.

The appearance of this strand in his thinking, which was to become central in the development of the Keynesian Revolution, dates from a series of four lectures he gave to the Institute of Bankers from 15 November to 5 December 1922. Keynes argued that the root of the problem was that wages had not fallen as rapidly as prices. Since 'the business of forcing down ... wages into equilibrium is almost hopeless, or ... will take a long time', the only remedy for unemployment was to engineer a rise in prices and a fall in the exchange rate.[3]

We have in these lectures an important early clue to what Keynes was to say in the years ahead. Wages were 'stickier' than consumer prices. This observation was not novel. More novel was the conclusion that, as a practical matter, the price level and exchange rate should be adjusted to the going wage rate, rather than the other way round. The most novel observation of all was that it was 'almost hopeless' to try to bring about a general fall in real wages by cutting money wages. Was this just because of existing wage-fixing arrangements? Or was there a more fundamental, theoretical reason? Keynes was not yet ready to say

II. A GREATER NATION

By 1923 Keynes had acquired a journalistic platform from which to mount his assault on the policy of deflation. In March of that year he became chairman of the board of directors of the Liberal journal, the *Nation and Athenaeum*, with Hubert Henderson as editor. The *Nation*, started in 1907 with Rowntree money, had been the bastion of the high-minded liberalism which had flourished in Oxford and Hampstead before the war. By the early 1920s, both the *Nation* and the Liberal Party were in a state of collapse. It was in these circumstances that a number of Manchester-based Liberals, led by E. D. Simon, a businessman and Liberal MP, C. P. and 'Ted' Scott (father and son) of the *Manchester Guardian* and Ramsay Muir, Professor of Modern History at Manchester University, decided to start annual summer schools alternating between Oxford and Cambridge. These would work out a Liberal policy for the 1920s.

At the end of 1922 the Rowntrees decided to sell the *Nation*. This coincided with the Summer School Committee's search for a platform from which to expound modern liberalism and Keynes's own desire for a regular journalistic outlet for his ideas on monetary reform. With his usual energy he started organising financial backing for a takeover bid. Together with Arnold Rowntree, L. J. Cadbury and E. D. Simon he formed a New Nation Company to buy the old *Nation* from the Rowntree Trust. This was done in March 1923 for £12,500, Keynes becoming chairman of a board of directors consisting of himself, Simon, Layton and Rowntree. Having ruthlessly disposed of Ramsay Muir's claims to be editor, Keynes offered the job to his Cambridge colleague Hubert Henderson, then a fellow of Clare College. Henderson objected that he 'had never edited anything; he had done very little journalism. Maynard, like a prancing steed, overrode all his objections.'[4] Henderson accepted on terms (including the previous editorial salary) which Keynes had refused Muir. Layton foresaw that the journal would be dominated by the 'Cambridge School of Economics', but this could not be helped, as it was 'not our fault if all the best Liberals were trained in the Cambridge Economics School....'[5] Keynes had acquired virtually untrammelled freedom to shape the journal as he wished.

Why did he take on this huge extra chore? First, during the period of his maximum involvement – from 1923 to 1925 – he was a man with a message, or rather a double message: to stop the return to the gold standard and to get a sane settlement of reparations. He was a preacher who needed a pulpit. Secondly, though Keynes's gospel was preached to all parties, its primary purpose was to equip the Liberal Party with a philosophy of government, and he believed that the Liberal temper was more readily attuned to his message than dynastic Conservatism or class-war Labour. Thirdly, Keynes was attracted by the role of patron of Bloomsbury: Bloomsbury writers dominated the back part of the paper. Finally, the *Nation* presented a challenge to him as an entrepreneur. He actively involved himself in trying to restore its circulation and revenues. Such a degree of proprietor involvement would not have been possible without an editor as compliant as Hubert Henderson. Keynes's collaboration with Henderson in the 1920s is as remarkable in its way as his later theoretical collaboration with Dennis Robertson at Cambridge, for in temperament they were both totally unlike him. Henderson was an argumentative, parsimonious Scot, cautious, sceptical, unheroic. 'I never knew anyone so instinctively protective of his habits,' Keynes told Lydia on 15 November 1925. He entirely lacked Keynes's facility in writing. Lydia commented 'Every Wednesday Hubert comes home at 3 am preparing his appearance in Nation, with you it is one hour or 1½. Different glands, different speed, and different merits.' Henderson was more intellectually fastidious than Keynes, shunned popularity, mistrusted Keynes's flights of fancy and was adept at spotting weak points in his mentor's reasoning. His own analysis of Britain's economic ills placed much more weight on structural maladjustment than failure of monetary policy, which he regarded as an aggravating, not fundamental, factor. In the 1930s he came to mistrust Keynes's monetary panaceas as much as he had the Treasury's. The violence with which he spoke out against Keynes in the 1930s reflects something of the resentment he felt at having to subordinate his own views in the 1920s to those of his masterful proprietor.

Keynes's first choice as literary editor was T. S. Eliot, then languishing at Lloyd's Bank. But Eliot 'spun out the situation into endless complexities',[6] and Keynes approached Leonard Woolf. E. M. Forster warned Woolf of the danger of working for Keynes: 'Maynard, since I have seen him apart from the Cambridge haze that envelops one's friends, has always seemed to me a curious mixture of benevolence and school-boy selfishness.... I should work under him if you needed the money and were certain to get it – not otherwise.'[7] Woolf did need the money and took the job for £500 a year, half Henderson's salary. (This was later reduced to £400.)

If the 'Cambridge School of Economics' dominated the front of the *Nation*, Apostolic Cambridge and its close connections reigned in the back. Woolf brought in two groups of writers – members of Bloomsbury, old and young, and writers he published in the Hogarth Press. Within a few months Henderson was complaining to Woolf of the 'insolent tone' of reviews by Clive Bell, Bunny Garnett, Francis Birrell, Dadie Rylands and Raymond Mortimer, and urged him to choose reviewers more appreciative of 'the better type of non-Bloomsbury writing'. Woolf stuck to his ground; Bell protested loudly that 'the best writers of the day were not to be ruled by financiers'; Keynes patched up a truce.[8] He sympathised with both sides, for in his personality, as in his writing, Cambridge utilitarianism and aestheticism clashed and mingled.

What he could not ensure was a buoyant circulation. Although he cut the cost per issue from 9d to 6d and assiduously solicited foreign subscriptions by announcing that his communications to the press now appeared exclusively in the *Nation*, circulation fell from about 8000 to between 6000 and 7000 – well below the *Spectator* and somewhat lower than the *New Statesman*. By the end of the decade the *Nation* was just about breaking even. Nevertheless, he had had to pay out £4000 of his own money over the period to keep it afloat, and other guarantees had also been called up. The limits on the *Nation*'s success paralleled those set to the Liberal revival by the social and economic forces of the time. Keynes's decision to merge the *Nation* with the *New Statesman* in 1931 symbolised the fact that historic liberalism had run its course.

III. SECOND THOUGHTS ARE BEST

An appreciative, though discerning, reader of the *Nation* was Lydia Lopokova. 'With palpitations I demanded [it],' she wrote to Maynard on 5 May, the date of the first issue under the new management. 'The cover gives confidence of strength. The British Policy in Europe [Keynes's article] is powerful and reads with easiness.... Sarah B[ernhardt, by Lytton Strachey] is brilliant only I am confused how to take ... serious or not serious, and when?' On 26 May: 'The whole number looks alive, because it is touched by your flicker....'

In Bloomsbury parlance, Lydia and Maynard were now 'married', which simply meant they were an acknowledged couple. Lydia lived at 41 Gordon Square; Clive at No. 50; Vanessa and Maynard shared No. 46, where Lydia also took her meals. Her latest engagement, in *Togo, A Noble Savage*, a feeble Massine ballet stuck into an even feebler variety show, *You'd Be Surprised*, played to half-empty houses at Covent Garden before expiring on 24 March 1923. After that she joined the ranks of the unemployed. But even when working she was free on Sundays. With Maynard in Cambridge, she often turned to Vanessa for company. Lydia had 'today spent 3 solid hours sitting in my room gossiping', Vanessa complained to Roger Fry after one session in February. 'This now happens every Sunday which is usually my one day at home for doing odd jobs, also as you know very often at tea time.'[9]

Maynard's friends were clearly hoping that he would tire of Lydia. They couldn't understand what he saw in her. The idea of sexual passion seemed to be too far-fetched. Virginia Woolf was the most forthright opponent of marriage. There was much about Keynes she disliked; but she venerated his brain and could not bear to see him hitched to a 'parrokeet'. On 28 April she wrote to her sister, 'We're dining with Maynard on Tuesday. What about Lydia? I hope to God Maynard has been restrained – a fatal and irreparable mistake.' And a month later: 'Unfortunately, talking to Lydia, I called Maynard "your husband". I see this is not the thing to do. Poor little parrokeet – there she sits in the window in a pink kimono awaiting him, I suppose. "Maynar liked your article so much Leonar. . . ." I suppose she has to read the *Nation* now. What tragedies these parrokeets go through. . . .'

Nineteen twenty three was an awful year for Lydia. With her divorce proceedings from Barocchi deadlocked between three sets of lawyers in three countries, her marriage prospects were as uncertain as her career ones. Maynard's feelings remained mysterious. His activities gave him little time for her. He had proposed to spend his Easter holidays in North Africa – with Sebastian Sprott! Lydia kicked up such a fuss about this that he abandoned the plan; but the revelation of his continuing attempt to get the best of both worlds must have been disconcerting. Without dancing engagements, and with her 'maestro' Enrico Cecchetti retiring to Italy, her thoughts once more turned to acting. She immersed herself in *Rosmersholm*, remarking 'that it was very difficult to play Ibsen, only action in the mind'. Vanessa's reservations, on the other hand, seemed to have been growing. She resented the loss of her old intimacy with Maynard. She now saw him mainly in Lydia's company; he spoke only of the *Nation*, politics, investments, business matters. Lydia's presence seemed to her to symbolise the passing of the old order.

Throughout this difficult time, Lydia was sustained by her own circle of friends. They were rich lovers of the arts, devoted to ballet, and to Lydia in particular. They were grander and more conventional than Maynard's Bloomsbury friends, ballet linking their world of money and chic to the avant-garde in art, music and thought.

Vera Bowen was Lydia's greatest woman friend in the 1920s. Married since 1922 to Harold Bowen, a scholar of Persian, linguist and (unsuccessful) playwright, she was a clever, vivacious, quarrelsome Russian who had settled in England in 1914 and had the money and leisure to indulge her passion (and talent) for producing ballets and plays. She had joined Maynard in relaunching Lydia's career after the fiasco of *The Sleeping Princess*; he arranging the contracts, and she the productions, of the performances Lydia gave at the Coliseum and Covent Garden in 1922–3. A fastidious woman, she took in hand Lydia's 'education', trying to get her to dress elegantly, as she did herself, and taking her round the concerts and art galleries. Lydia was much more receptive to the latter than the former: off and on stage she remained a sartorial mess. Vera was the only friend Lydia could confide in about her affair with Maynard; but their friendship experienced a distinct chill in the summer of 1923 as a result of Maynard's haggling with Vera over the financial terms of the July–August production of *Masquerade* at the Coliseum.[10]

After Maynard, the most important man in Lydia's life was Samuel Courtauld, the artificial silk manufacturer and picture collector. Courtauld's hospitality was as lavish as his benefactions: Lydia and the Bowens could often be found at the weekends in his grand house at 20 Portman Square, eating and drinking too much, and complaining afterwards of the excruciating dullness of the company. The Bowens considered the Courtaulds (especially Sam's wife Elizabeth or 'Lil') to be social climbers, Vera declaring that Sam's gift of £50,000 to the Tate Gallery in 1923 to buy nineteenth-century French pictures was 'an occult scheme of social advancement' aimed at a peerage.[11] Lil's real passion was the opera: she financed the Covent Garden seasons from 1925 to 1927. They both spent part of the year in the United States, where Samuel Courtauld owned the Viscose Company. Lydia loved Sam, a shy, dour man of exacting standards and submerged passions. 'I always feel a pact of friendship to Sam (without going to bed with him) and that is why it is so nice,' Lydia wrote to Maynard on 22 November 1924. And on 7 March 1925: 'Honesty, sincerity, competence, intelligence, modesty are Sam's feathers, but he can't soar, his little feet follow him' – unlike Maynard, whose mind was 'human and divine' (27 February 1925). For his part, Sam adored Lydia, thawed in her company, flirted with her and took her for long drives in his Rolls-Royce. He also got on well with Maynard. He was the kind of visionary businessman whom Maynard admired, belying his frequent dicta about the degeneration of family firms. A little later, Maynard persuaded him to back Duncan and Vanessa and other Bloomsbury painters in the London Artists' Association.

Bloomsbury, whose snobberies were intellectual and aesthetic, feared that these rich friends of Lydia's would corrupt Maynard. They were certainly right to foresee that Maynard would escape from Bloomsbury's orbit. He moved increasingly in the company of 'thinking' or 'civilised' bankers, businessmen, politicians – people who, like him, straddled ideas and affairs, the arts and money-making. Lydia did not pull him into this world: public affairs did that. Nevertheless, Maynard and Lydia together were much more socially attractive than Maynard would have been on his own, or linked to a Bloomsbury blue-stocking. People like the Courtaulds or Grenfells, Bob Brand and Oswald Falk tended to *revere* him for his mind, but *love* Lydia for her gaiety and charm; and, in a world which prized social values, the combination became a valuable social asset. Nor should its importance in Maynard's political evolution be underestimated: if intellectually he was drawn to the left, socially he was increasingly tethered to the right.

That summer – 1923 – there was no Charleston for Maynard and Lydia. Instead Maynard took a grand house, the Knoll, at Studland, Dorset, seaside home of the Duke of Hamilton. As usual he filled it up with his friends:

Raymond Mortimer, Dadie Rylands, the Hendersons, the Woolfs. Virginia Woolf, who 'wanted to observe Lydia as a type for Rezia', a character in a novel (*Mrs Dalloway*) she was writing, has left two memorably nasty descriptions of her stay. In her diary for 11 September she wrote:

> Maynard is grown very gross & stout, especially when he wraps his leopard spotted dressing gown tight around his knees & stands in front of the fire.... He has a queer swollen eel like look, not very pleasant. But his eyes are remarkable, & as I truly said when he gave me some pages of his new book [on monetary reform] to read, the process of mind there displayed is as far ahead of me as Shakespeare's.

Lydia was another story. Ignorant 'of the most binding of all laws of female life', she had thrown her sanitary towels into the empty grate.

> Imagine the consequences [Virginia wrote to Jacques Raverat on 4 November 1923].... The cook's husband, and Duke's valet, did the room. Soon the Cook herself requested to speak with the lady. There was such a scene, it is said, as shook the rafters, – rages, tears, despair, outrage, horror, retribution, reconciliation: and – if you knew Lydia, you'll see how naturally it follows – lifelong friendship upon a basis of – well, bloody rags. Really, there is a curious feeling about that menage, as well may be with such a foundation. Lydia has the soul of a squirrel: anything nicer you can't conceive: she sits by the hour polishing the sides of her nose with her front paws. But, poor little wretch, trapped in Bloomsbury, what can she do but learn Shakespeare by heart? I assure you its tragic to see her sitting down to King Lear. Nobody can take her seriously: every nice man kisses her. Then she flies into a rage and says she is like Vanessa, like Alix Sargent Florence, or Ka Cox ... – a seerious wooman.[12]

This was the last holiday Lydia spent with Bloomsbury; it probably put paid to Maynard's lingering hopes of a commune. Shocked by her treatment, Lydia fled to Colworth, the Bowens' country pile in Bedfordshire, to pour out her troubles to Vera, a ready listener, while Maynard went off stag hunting in Devon. 'Vera in return ventured on the most outspoken criticism of Bloomsbury and its ways. Loppie looks on the end of her Maynard attachment as inevitable and not even out of sight.'[13]

It is easy to sympathise with Lydia, surrounded by all those supercilious and disapproving Bloomsberries. Cut off from family and career – Diaghilev had transferred to Monte Carlo – she was stranded in a foreign country, and tethered to a man she admired and loved, but who spoke no Russian, and for whom Russian culture was a closed book. Lydia's adjustment to her situation was much more heroic than that of Maynard, who simply added her to a busy life. He had no thought of giving her up. In the interval of writing an article on population, he wrote to Lydia: 'Shall you and I begin our works on population at the same time?' And: 'My dearest poet, I am sure that when you make your contribution to the population it will be a poet that comes out.'[14]

At 46 Gordon Square, Vanessa had taken further steps to insulate herself from Lydia by arranging a separate dining room for the Bells. By these means she gradually excluded Lydia, and hence Maynard, from her life. For Maynard too had to make a choice. And when the crunch came, he chose Lydia. His friendship with Vanessa did not end: it just subsided. Lydia's love, too, survived Bloomsbury's hostility. How near she came to giving him up can be guessed at from her inscription on the back of a photograph of them both she sent to Vera after their marriage: 'Second Thoughts Are Best'. There is no evidence, in Lydia's letters, of the hurt she suffered at Vanessa's hands. The evidence is in the way she and Maynard arranged their lives, and in how she lived after his death. Lydia reacted to her exclusion much as Vanessa had anticipated – by not wanting to see Vanessa any more. The two women spent their last years in Sussex a few hundred yards from each other, both with their memories of Maynard, almost strangers to each other.

IV. THE THREE DEVILS: DEFLATION, POPULATION, PROTECTION

On 7 July 1923, with unemployment at 1.3m, or 11.4 per cent of the insured workforce, bank rate was put up from 3 per cent to 4 per cent. In the *Nation* on 14 July Keynes denounced the rise as 'one of the most misguided movements of that indicator which has ever occurred'. The Bank, he wrote, 'thinks it more important to raise the dollar exchange a few points than to encourage flagging trade'.[15]

This attack marked his public break with official policy. The confident tone in which it was delivered reflects the influence of the new book on monetary policy he had started to write at the beginning of the year. It was the start of his campaign against the return to the gold standard at the pre-war sterling–dollar parity. In a longer perspective, it was the start of the Keynesian Revolution. From 1923 till 1937 Keynes was the leading intellectual critic of the monetary, and increasingly the fiscal, policy actually pursued.

Bank rate was put up to correct the fall in sterling against the dollar – from $4.70 in March to $4.56 in June. The rise was not universally welcomed. In the Commons on 12 June Baldwin had said that 'there is no greater necessity for this country ... than cheap money'. Sir Charles Addis, chairman of the Hongkong and Shanghai Banking Corporation, and a director of the Bank of England, had written to Montagu Norman on 4 June, 'The first consideration in determining a change in Bank Rate should be the condition of trade and industry.' So Keynes was not without allies. On the other hand, Reginald McKenna told Norman on 20 June that 'our Rates are too low & diff[erence] between 3 & 4% cd not really affect trade....'[16]

The issue Keynes was raising was of theoretical as well as practical importance. The rise in bank rate might temporarily correct the sterling–dollar exchange by bringing American money back to London. But it could bring about a 'real and lasting' improvement in the exchange only by producing 'some curtailment of credit and some fall of sterling prices'. In other words, the raising of bank rate was a signal that the government intended to 'produce a falling tendency in sterling prices', and that if a 4 per cent bank rate did not suffice to lower them they would be prepared to raise it to 5 per cent or more. 'This is the moment when the Bank of England chooses deliberately to add one more discouragement, one more warning sign to anyone who contemplates new business that he had better wait a bit and keep his hands in his pockets, even if it means that his workmen must keep their hands in their pockets, too.'[17] Even more than the actual it is the *expected* rate of interest which determines investment decisions.

Critics accused Keynes of being an inflationist. To this charge he made a robust reply:

> A policy of price stability is the very opposite of a policy of permanently cheap money. During the last boom, the present writer preached vehemently in favour of very dear money, months before the Bank of England acted. But when employment is very bad, enterprise disheartened, and prices with a falling tendency, *that* is not the moment to raise the Bank Rate.[18]

The City editor of *The Times* made a shrewd thrust. 'As prices have remained stable within the past eighteen months,' he wrote, 'it is difficult to appreciate the force of many arguments employed by those who are avowedly in favour of stabilisation.' This raised a hornets' nest of problems which was to take years to sort out. What did one mean by the 'price level'? If there were several price levels, which of them was it important to try to stabilise? What caused any of these price levels to be what they were? In the *Nation* of 28 July Keynes admitted that wholesale prices had remained fairly stable. But he insisted that actual purchasing power had been 'silently and steadily' deflated for some time, and that this partly accounted for 'the failure of trade and employment in this country to keep pace with the revival in the United States....' In support, he cited the shrinkage in bank deposits by about 10 per cent since January 1922, as well as the fall in the retail price index since that date. The Bank of England 'has been using its secret and enormous powers to *contract* credit by no less an amount than 10 per cent'. He demanded 'an authoritative enquiry into the methods of compilation of index numbers'.[19]

An important assumption underlying Keynes's criticism was that the price level depended on monetary policy. 'Expert opinion' supported him in the belief that

> it lies in the power of the Bank of England, and the Treasury, within wide limits, to determine in the long run how much credit is created. If the Bank of England had pursued a different policy, I believe that prices would stand at a different level.... the policy of the Cunliffe Committee assumes that the authorities have the power in the long run to fix the price level, just as much as the policy of price stabilisation assumes it.

He concluded that 'lack of confidence' in the price level was 'a considerable cause, and probably the only remediable one, of present unemployment'. This qualification is important. Keynes never claimed that *all* unemployment could be cured by monetary policy, only that part of it which was the result of deflation. If the Prime Minister and the governor of the Bank announced that they were determined to do 'all in their power to promote and preserve confidence in the existing level of sterling prices (letting the dollar exchange go hang, if necessary), great good would result'.[20]

Keynes's speech to the Liberal Summer School at Cambridge on 8 August 1923 gives a further insight into the thinking going into the book he was writing. Modern capitalism, he said, could not stand a violently fluctuating standard of value. Only if the value of the currency was subject to conscious control could a capitalist society be defended against the 'attacks and criticism of Socialist and Communist innovators'. Keynes explained how falling prices, and even more a 'general expectation' of falling prices, must always be bad for business. 'If they [economic agents] felt confident that the price would not fall, they would not hesitate to buy. They put off their purchases, not because they lack purchasing power, but because *their demand is capable of postponement* and may, they think, be satisfied at a lower price later on (emphasis added).' Keynes was later to identify this ability to 'postpone demand' as the distinctive feature of a 'money economy'. In his address, Keynes gave two hostages to fortune. Economists, he declared, were 'as united on the scientific theory of [how to maintain stable money] as they are about free trade'. Events were to prove otherwise in both cases. Also, he still insisted that the market system was self-correcting: 'Sooner or later a rising tendency of prices will spring up again ... partly because postponed demands cannot go on being postponed indefinitely; partly because catastrophes tend to diminish the supply of goods and to increase, rather than to diminish, the supply of money. For this reason I am not so pessimistic as the President of the Board of Trade about the prospects of employment in the long run.'[21] Later, Keynes was to abandon this view also. The economy is not self-correcting. Demand postponed, he would say, is demand destroyed.

In his early discussions of unemployment, Keynes always insisted that 'the problem of unemployment is ... in part, a problem of population'.[22] By this he meant that there was a surplus of employable population at the existing level of real wages. He attributed the emergence of this surplus to a shift in the terms of trade against industrial products: a given quantity of industrial output could buy less food and raw materials than before. This meant that real wages per worker had to come down to achieve the same level of employment as before; in the longer term, the rate of growth of the population would need to be slowed down if living standards were to rise – hence the importance of birth control.

In the autumn of 1923 Keynes found himself unexpectedly embroiled in a debate about these matters with Sir William Beveridge, the new director of the London School of Economics. In his Presidential Address to Section F of the British Association, delivered on 18 September 1923, Beveridge produced statistics showing that the terms of trade had not turned against the industrial countries. Britain's economic problem required no Malthusian explanation; it was simply a problem of structural readjustment, since 'Providence had not concentrated on these islands the coal and iron supplies of the world'. What was needed was not birth control but free trade.[23] In his reply in the *Nation* of 6 October Keynes conceded that his statistics on the terms of trade were inconclusive, but insisted that 'unemployment may be a symptom of a maladjustment very closely connected with population – namely, that which results from an attempt on the part of organised labour, or of the community as a whole, to maintain real wages at a higher level than the underlying conditions are able to support'.[24] He remained a neo-Malthusian. On several occasions in the 1920s he called for a population policy. He believed that Britain would be better off 'if we had fewer to employ and to feed' and that 'the greater part of man's achievements are already swallowed up in the support of mere numbers'.[25]

He soon had an opportunity to test his belief in free trade. Foiled of cheap money, Baldwin announced at Plymouth on 25 October 1923 that protection was the only cure for unemployment. On 12 November he decided to seek a mandate to introduce protection and imperial preference, Bonar Law having promised not to do so without a general election. Election day was fixed for 6 December.

'Good bye Baldwin – he is finished now,' was Keynes's immediate reaction to Baldwin's Plymouth speech. 'At least the days of praise from all are finished; the old struggle of the parties begins again.'[26] The election was a political watershed, though not quite as Keynes predicted. Most expert opinion predicted a Baldwin victory. Montagu Norman advised Lydia Lopokova to get more dresses at the Galeries Lafayette to beat import duties. Instead the election produced a large free-trade majority. Yet the main beneficiaries were not the Liberals, reunited under Asquith's leadership, but the Labour Party. With 191 MPs to the Liberals' 157 (the Conservatives remained the largest party with 257), Ramsay MacDonald formed the first

Labour government with Liberal support. The nervously affluent locked away their silver; some went abroad, never to return. The modern form of two-party politics had arrived.

The Cambridge Liberal Association invited Keynes to stand for Parliament, unopposed by the Conservatives. Despite Lydia's urging ('One more thing, can it matter to you?'), he refused. But he took a moderately active part in the campaign, speaking in Lancashire at Blackpool, Blackburn and Barrow. He also wrote three articles on the election for the *Nation*. His object was what would now be called a hung parliament, to prevent the 'quack remedies' of both right and left. Against the 'mystical stupidities' of Conservatism he counterposed the no less mystical belief in free trade. 'If there is one thing Protection can *not* do, it is to cure unemployment,' he wrote on 24 November. To claim otherwise 'involves the protectionist fallacy in its grossest and crudest form'. But then he contradicted himself. It might increase employment temporarily, but only by putting up prices and depressing wages. Keynes forgot to mention that his own plan involved doing just the same thing by cheap money and devaluation. To bolster up a shaky case, Keynes claimed that Britain would soon be back at full employment anyway.[27] His argument seemed to amount to this: protection could not cure unemployment if there was no unemployment to be cured.

Keynes always had mixed feelings about the hustings. His new suit not being ready, he campaigned in an old shabby one, which he thought went down better with cotton operatives. He found his Blackburn audience of 3000 'serious and intelligent – a quite different type from London working classes. The interest they take in politics is extraordinary; and the more serious a speech is, the better they seem to like it. The Election was a big education for them; and I feel like a preacher – half enjoying it. If only my voice was different, I'd be in danger of enjoying it too much.' There was the rub. 'I hate my ugly voice more than ever,' he told Lydia after speaking in Blackpool's Opera House on 4 December. On Lydia, at least, Keynes's arguments had their usual gratifying effect. 'Free Trade', she wrote to him, 'is admirable. So decisively clear. Protection as a cure for unemployment – ca n'existe pas! When you speak of our imports as incomes it seems to me a suicide not to trade free. Life without incomes is deplorable.'[28]

A lecture to the National Liberal Club on 13 December shows how far Keynes had come in his thinking over the previous twelve months. The political-economy note is sounded from the start: 'It is obvious that an individualist society left to itself does not work well or even tolerably.... The more troublous the times, the worse does a *laissez-faire* system work.' He enumerated the 'triple evils of modern society' as profiteering, precarious expectations and unemployment, all 'mainly due' to the 'instability of the standard of value'. However, he believed that as a result of one of the 'biggest jumps ever achieved in economic science', the control of the credit cycle was in sight. All that was needed was 'so to regulate the supply of

Bradburies [see p. 176 above] and of bank credit that their volume in terms of goods will be reasonably steady; i.e., that the index number of prices will never move far from a fixed point'. This could be done by the Bank of England, without the need for any legislation.

The issue was not one between collectivism and *laissez-faire* but between targeted state action and a socialism which was 'out of date and contrary to human nature'. But there was not much time to avoid the latter. Keynes declared:

> I would like to warn the gentlemen of the City and High Finance that if they do not listen in time to the voice of reason their days may be numbered. I speak to this great city as Jonah spoke to Nineveh. . . . I prophesy that unless they embrace wisdom in good time, the system upon which they live will work so very ill that they will be overwhelmed by irresistible things which they will hate much more than the mild and limited remedies offered them now.[29]

These remedies he was now ready to offer to the world.

V. IN THE LONG RUN WE ARE ALL DEAD

A Tract on Monetary Reform was published on 11 December 1923. It continued Keynes's habit of publishing his books on current affairs at the end of the year, a schedule which reflected the fact that he mainly wrote them in the university's long summer vacations. The *Tract* sums up what Keynes had been thinking and writing about the theory, practice and objects of monetary policy over the previous three years. Most of it was culled from already published, or lecture, materials. The result is the most sparkling of his economics books. In the opinion of Milton Friedman, it is his best.[30]

The central policy proposal of the *Tract* was that monetary policy should be used to stabilise the price level, not the exchange rate. Its central theoretical claim was that this could be accomplished by stabilising the 'demand for money' for business purposes, rather than the supply of money. If the demand for money can be stabilised by policy, then, according to the quantity theory of money, the price level can be whatever the monetary authority decides.

The *Tract*'s personal intellectual ancestry can be traced back to Keynes's *Indian Currency and Finance* (1913), with its concern with seasonal fluctuations in the demand for rupees, as well as to his pre-war lectures on the theory of money. What did Keynes mean, then, when he

talked about a scientific breakthrough? He meant that a greater understanding of the theory of money, in particular the role of the banking
system in creating credit, would enable the central bank to even out fluctuations in business activity. This was not a theoretical revolution, still less
one Keynes had pioneered. He drew freely not just on the monetary theory
of the Cambridge school, but on several decades of innovation in monetary
practice.

What made his book shocking was its iconoclasm of expression and its
frontal attack on the gold standard. The tone was heavily ironic. Keynes was
still very much the Cambridge Apostle blaspheming against conventional
morality. He was writing, at least partly, for the reader who shared the values
of Lytton Strachey. This made for entertaining reading, but bad advocacy.
As in *The Economic Consequences of the Peace* he could not help mocking
the 'sound men' he needed to persuade.

The *Tract on Monetary Reform* opened in a mood of scientific optimism.
'Nowhere is the need of innovation more urgent' than in questions of
currency, he declared in his preface, and he dedicated his book to the Bank
of England. 'Unemployment, the precarious life of the worker, the disappointment of expectation, the sudden loss of savings, the excessive windfalls
of individuals, the speculator, the profiteer – all these proceed, in large
measure, from the instability of the standard of value.'

Chapter 1 is about the *effect* of a change in the value of money on the
short-run distribution of wealth and level of output. Although the discussion
of the adverse effects of a changing price level was not new,[31] Keynes was
unusual in his stress on the 'stickiness of social and business arrangements'
and the need it created for completely stable prices if capitalism was to
be consistent with social stability. Inflation, he says, inflicts most injury by
altering the distribution of wealth; deflation by retarding the production of
wealth. In the first case, businessmen gain at the expense of savers and
most workers whose incomes are fixed (in the short run), while their value
falls. This is good for business, but undermines capitalism in the long run,
by turning entrepreneurs into profiteers and drying up the supply of
savings. Falling prices on the other hand injure output and employment
by imposing windfall losses on businessmen, whose major costs of production (including wage costs) remain fixed in the short run, while the selling
prices of their products fall. In the deflationary case, 'the *fact* of falling
prices injures entrepreneurs; consequently the fear of falling prices causes
them to protect themselves by curtailing their operations'. Thus 'a comparatively weak initial impulse may be adequate to produce a considerable
fluctuation'.[32]

Keynes concluded chapter I with a famous, carefully nuanced, passage:

> Thus inflation is unjust and deflation inexpedient. Of the two per-
> haps deflation is, if we rule out exaggerated inflations such as that of

Germany, the worse; because it is worse, in an impoverished world, to provoke unemployment than to disappoint the *rentier*.[33]

The important qualifying phrase 'in an impoverished world' has been ignored by those who claim this passage as evidence of Keynes's indifference to inflation. In fact, as he makes clear, 'it is not necessary that we should weigh one evil against the other. It is easier to agree that both are evils to be shunned.'

Having dealt with the effects of changes in the value of money, Keynes turned in chapter 3 to the causes. These involved the famous quantity theory of money. According to the theory, the price level varies proportionately with the quantity of cash issued by the banking system. 'This theory,' Keynes writes, 'is fundamental. Its correspondence with fact is not open to question.'[34] But, having delivered himself of this judgement, he proceeds to show that it has little correspondence with fact.

Money is the stock of bank notes issued which are at any time partly in people's 'pockets' as cash and partly in their bank accounts – what Marshall called 'cash balances' held for spending, and which Keynes called $k + k'$. Provided these balances are being spent at the same rate from one period to another, there must be a constant relationship between money and prices, since things must cost what you pay for them. In the long run, Keynes wrote, 'this relationship will hold. But this *long run* is a misleading guide to current affairs. *In the long run* we are all dead. Economists set themselves too easy, too useless a task if in tempestuous seasons they can only tell us that when the storm is long past the ocean is flat again.'[35]

What Keynes meant by this, the most famous of all his remarks, was that, in the short run, changes in the *speed* with which people spend their cash – what economists call the velocity of circulation – can change prices independently of changes in the quantity of cash. What happens according to Keynes is that they speed up their spending when prices are rising and slow it down in the reverse case. He produced figures showing that roughly the same volume of currency had supported a price level 50 per cent higher in October 1920 than in October 1922, the difference being explained by a big increase in bank desposits since the earlier date. So the task of a banking system which wants to keep prices stable is to provide more money when people are tending to spend less and less money when they are tending to spend more. As Keynes put it:

The business of stabilising the price level, not merely over long periods but so as to avoid cyclical fluctuations, consists partly in exercising a stabilising influence over k and k' [the cash balances] and insofar as this fails or is impracticable, in deliberately varying n [the supply of notes] and r [the banks' ratio of reserves to liabilities] so as to counterbalance the movements of k and k'.[36]

This was the crux of the modern 'scientific' theory of monetary policy.

By concentrating attention on variations in the 'demand for money to hold', Keynes has moved some way from the traditional quantity theory of money, in which it is the supply of cash or legal tender which controls the price level – though this departure was no novelty to students of Marshall. What caused fluctuations in velocity, apart from uncertainty about the future course of prices, is left unanalysed. The lack of attention in the *Tract* – apart from the single case of seasonal fluctuations in agricultural countries – to possible non-monetary causes of fluctuations in spending is strikingly orthodox.[37]

In chapter 5 Keynes outlines the aims and mechanisms of monetary policy. The monetary authority's aim should be 'to prevent a movement of [the price of a standard composite commodity] by more than a certain percentage in either direction from the normal'. In deciding what was 'normal', the monetary authority should take into account the 'state of employment, the volume of production, the effective demand for credit as felt by the banks, the volume of new issues, the flow of cash into circulation, the statistics of foreign trade and the level of exchanges', the interpretation of which will give scope for the 'play of judgement and discretion'.[38] Keynes had already made it clear that he wanted prices to go up and the exchange to go down before attempting to stabilise the former: normalisation should precede stabilisation.

Having achieved the 'normal' price level, the monetary authority will then maintain it, as required, by offsetting a rise or fall in the public's cash balances (or the velocity of circulation) by varying the supply of credit.

We now come to the nub of the argument. Management of domestic prices in the interests of business and social stability would be rendered impossibly difficult if Britain returned to the pre-war gold standard. Faced with a choice, price stability must come before exchange stability, since 'the contracts and business expectations which assume a stable exchange must be far fewer, even in a trading country such as England, than those which presume a stable level of internal prices'.[39] Exchange-rate policy should be subordinated to the needs of the domestic economy.

Keynes admitted that in the the nineteenth century the gold standard had 'afforded not only a stable exchange but, on the whole, a stable price level also'.[40] This was owing to 'special conditions' which had disappeared. By and large gold discoveries had kept pace with business needs, thus obviating large fluctuations in the value of gold; and the distribution of gold had reflected a state of competitive equilibrium between the main trading nations. But a quarter of a century had passed since the discovery of an important gold deposit. Moreover, most of the world's monetary gold was now locked up in America.[41] Given the existing (and prospective) distribution of gold, a restoration of the gold standard would mean that 'we surrender the regulating of our price level and the handling of the credit cycle to the hands of the Federal Reserve Board of the United States', whose interests might diverge from those of the Bank of England, and whose capacity to 'manage' money was as yet untested.[42] Keynes insisted that Britain must be free to manage its monetary standard *independently* of the United States.

Keynes acknowledged that the Federal Reserve Board had successfully managed to 'sterilise' gold inflows in the interests of domestic price stability, but feared that the eventual dishoarding of America's gold stock would lead to a worldwide inflationary movement – as did eventually happen, but not until the 1960s! Keynes described the fictions by which the American monetary authority contrived to 'manage' money without appearing to do so:

> The theory on which the Federal Reserve Board is supposed to govern its discount policy, by reference to the influx and efflux of gold and the proportion of gold to liabilities, is as dead as mutton. It perished, and perished justly, as soon as the Federal Reserve Board began to ignore its ratio and to accept gold without allowing it to exert its full influence [on the price level], merely because an expansion of credit and prices seemed at that moment undesirable. From that day gold was demonetised by almost the last country which still continued to do it lip-service, and a dollar standard was set up on the pedestal of the Golden Calf. For the past two years the United States has *pretended* to maintain a gold standard. *In fact* it has established a dollar standard; and, instead of ensuring that the value of the dollar shall conform to that of gold, it makes provision, at great expense, that the value of gold shall conform to that of the dollar. This is the way by which a rich country is able to combine new wisdom with old prejudice. It can enjoy the latest scientific improvements, devised in the economic laboratory of Harvard, whilst leaving Congress to believe that no rash departure will be permitted from the hard money consecrated by the wisdom and experience of Dungi, Darius, Constantine, Lord Liverpool, and Senator Aldrich.[43]

Keynes did not despair of reconciling the two objectives of price stability and exchange stability: a wise currency policy should aim for both. If domestic prices in the two countries could be kept stable enough for long enough the exchange rates of their currencies would eventually settle down at their 'purchasing power parities'. A policy directed to steadying prices, credit and employment would thus tend to steady the exchange rate as well. In order to combine 'stability of prices over long periods' with 'stability of exchanges over short periods', the monetary authority should 'regulate' but not 'peg' the price of gold. 'A willingness on the part of the Bank to buy and sell gold at rates fixed for the time being', Keynes wrote, 'would keep the dollar–sterling exchange steady ... so that the exchange rate would not move with every breath of wind but only when the Bank of England had come to a considered judgement that a change was required for the stability of sterling prices.' Gold reserves should be kept purely as a 'war chest' for emergencies; they should be uncoupled from the note issue, which should be geared entirely to domestic price and trading requirements.[44]

Keynes foresaw that the world would eventually move towards a centrally managed currency system, but in the meantime the best solution would be to have two managed currencies, dollars and sterling, with a 'crawling' peg between them, and close co-operation between the two monetary authorities to keep prices and exchange rates steady. Other countries should base their currencies on dollars or sterling by means of a gold exchange standard, holding gold reserves at home and dollar or sterling balances in New York or London.[45]

This is the central thread of the argument. Two technically sophisticated subsidiary discussions concern the 'inflation tax' and the 'forward market' in currencies. The first is a device by which a government can transfer resources to itself without applying to Parliament for the money. Keynes described the technique with some admiration: 'its efficacy, up to a point, must be admitted' – Ralph Hawtrey hoped he did so ironically rather than prescriptively.[46] In the last section of chapter 3 Keynes showed how traders and investors can use 'forward markets' to hedge against currency fluctuations. It was a chapter for connoisseurs. Both techniques were illuminated by his own experiences, the first as a Treasury official in the war, the second as a post-war currency speculator.

The *Tract* has the special atmosphere of all of Keynes's economic journalism – of revealing esoteric knowledge, of profaning sacred wisdom. It was full of 'blasphemies' designed to amuse Bloomsbury and provoke the complacent. He describes the gold standard as a 'barbarous relic'.[47] In an elaborate Stracheyesque joke he bewails the afflictions of the virtuous saver, wiped out by inflation – 'He who neither spent nor "speculated", who made "proper provision" for his family, who sang hymns to security and observed most straitly the morals of the edified and the respectable injunctions of the worldly wise – he, indeed, who gave fewest pledges to Fortune has yet suffered her heaviest visitations.'[48]

To those who claimed that devaluation of a currency was a 'breach of contract', Keynes gave this answer:

> Such persons, by overlooking one of the greatest of all social principles, namely the fundamental distinction between the right of the individual to repudiate contract and the right of the State to control vested interest, are the worst enemies of what they seek to preserve. For nothing can preserve the integrity of contract between individuals, except a discretionary authority in the State to revise what has become intolerable. The powers of uninterrupted usury are too great. If the accretions of

vested interest were to grow without mitigation for many generations, half the population would be no better than slaves to the other half. ... The absolutists of contract ... are the real parents of revolution.[49]

Beneath both the technical and the ironic drapery of the *Tract* were a series of connected propositions which were to inspire Keynes's economic work for the rest of his life. Economic health was too important to be left to *laissez-faire*. Economic management, which had already started, must become part of the modern science of government, not the tool of vested interests. The war had vastly increased the dangers of social upheaval. To preserve the core of an individualist society from revolutionary danger some of the outworks had to be sacrificed.

VI. REACTIONS

In contemporary reviews, the brilliance of Keynes's *Tract on Monetary Reform* was widely conceded, but its actual proposals were equally widely regarded as impracticable or mischievous. Roy Harrod wrote that the *Tract* came near to making the desirability of the gold standard a live issue.[50] There is little evidence of this in initial reactions to the book. Keynes failed to carry even his friends on this point. What most worried the sceptics was Keynes's assumption of omniscience and incorruptibility on the part of his putative managers. Josiah Stamp, a fellow mandarin, found dismaying Keynes's 'desertion of the best physical base (gold) for what may or may not be our best mental basis, the basis of day-to-day judgement. For one who often finds the living occupants of our most reputable national institutions so lacking in true qualifications for their task, he [Keynes] shows a surprising confidence in the effectiveness of human agency for giving theory a perfect touch in practice.'[51] The anonymous reviewer in *The Times Literary Supplement* expressed a common view when he wrote that the virtue of gold was that 'it prevents politicians from resorting easily to the manufacture of money'.[52]

Socialists drew opposite conclusions from Keynes's book. The reviewer in the *Manchester Guardian* asked: if collectivism is to be applied to money, why not to the elimination of 'inequality, injustice, and poverty'? H. G. Wells, a great admirer of Keynes, took it to be a sign of his 'penetrating' but 'limited' mind that he could not see the possibility of supplanting private gain by public service in a sphere wider than monetary management.[53] Between the rules of non-interference and the imperatives of socialism, Keynes's Middle Way was finding it hard to get a hearing.

Perhaps his advocacy would have seemed less shocking had it been less mocking. It would have helped with the sound men to present his proposals in the guise of a managed gold standard. As Josiah Stamp rightly noted, Keynes abhorred 'conventional façades'; but these were nevertheless required to convert the 'beta-gamma' minds. Keynes could not help himself, nor would he have wanted to. He was part of the modernist movement, dedicated to undermining 'delusion' (Bloomsbury code for Christianity and Victorian morals) which put limits on human freedom and the play of reason. The recognition that 'delusions' might be a necessary protection against moral fallibility or just plain incompetence came hard, and late in the day, and then only grudgingly.

For Keynes the *Tract* was an interim statement. The book was scarcely out before he was drawing up a plan for a 'short new book, which would be a sequel to *Monetary Reform*'.[54] On 2 May 1924, he wrote to Lydia, 'In making up my lectures, the shape of my new book begins to form in my mind.' To a German correspondent he wrote on 23 April 1925, 'I am beginning to feel that all comments on my *Tract on Monetary Reform* are dealing with the remarks of some dead person, and not of the present me. The new book on Monetary Theory which I have in preparation will, I am hopeful, throw much new light on my fundamental arguments in favour of the dogmas to which I have rashly given utterance without sufficiently substantiating them.'[55] *A Treatise on Money* would come out in two volumes seven years after the *Tract*. For the moment, there was the battle against the return to the gold standard to attend to.

PART FIVE

THE CROSS OF GOLD

By the return to the gold standard in 1925, at an unsuitable parity, the Bank had set itself a problem of adjustment so difficult as to have been well-nigh impossible. On the one hand, it was obviously impracticable to enforce by high Bank rate or by the contraction of credit a deflation sufficiently drastic to bring about a reduction in internal costs appropriate to the parity adopted. On the other hand, the maintenance of a low Bank rate, which would have rendered London unattractive to foreign short-term funds, would ... have led to a rapid loss of gold by the Bank and a much earlier collapse of the gold standard....

> J. M. Keynes, in the *Lloyds Bank Monthy Review,* April 1932

I do not think England made a mistake in restoring the pound to its pre-war value in 1925. The mistake was in permitting the trade-unions, after the general strike, to impose a rigid wage scale on British industries and subsidising the resulting unemployment by the dole.

> Thomas Lamont to Louis Wiley, 4 November 1931

22

Gold and Marriage

I. MARRIAGE PROSPECTS

On Christmas Day 1923, Maynard took Lydia for a fortnight's holiday to Monte Carlo. While he and Sheppard played the tables at the Casino, Lydia went to the rehearsals of the Ballets Russes (now established in Monte Carlo), helping Anton Dolin, Diaghilev's latest boyfriend, learn his part in *Daphnis and Chloë*. Refreshed by his gambling in modern currencies, Keynes returned in Cambridge to his study of ancient ones. Day and night he browsed, consulted and scribbled on Babylonian and Greek weights – 'absorbed in it to the point of frenzy', he wrote to Lydia on 18 January 1924. Lydia was 'in full sympathy' with his 'Babilonian madness'. 'It is a treasure of your intelectual spirit, I have such an affection for you in that forme.'[1]

His affair with Lydia seems to have moved into calmer waters. He sent her a tender poem written by a Babylonian woman 2000 years before Christ – 'Come to me my Ishtavar and show your virile strength / Push out your member and touch with it my little place' – and, in more masculine mood, an algebra problem! She deftly applied his language to her affairs: 'My inclination', she wrote to him, 'is to make order or write letters; there is also a probability of a middle course in reading a book'; and, when he sent her money, thanked him for adding to her 'purchasing power'. He called her his 'précieuse ridicule'.

Their affair had finally been revealed to Keynes's parents – nearly two years after it had started. Florence Keynes had met Lydia, by mistake, and to general embarrassment, on 15 February 1923 at Geoffrey Keynes's house in London, where she was consulting him about an inflamed toe.[2] But her first meeting with her as Maynard's betrothed took place at his sister's house in Highgate on 16 November 1923. It was a great success. 'Your mother is a nice woman,' Lydia wrote to Maynard. 'You have her eyes and searching mind. I like to look at her. I was excited so I spoke too quickly or forgot the words. . . . She kissed me before going away.' Florence was charmed by Lydia, which it was easy to be. But above all she was overjoyed that her brilliant but wayward son had found a woman with whom he could share his life. Soon Lydia and Florence were unloading 'our feelings for you and for each other in relation of your being our entire idol'.[3] Lydia and Maynard took to calling his parents 'the starychki' ('old ones' in affectionate Russian). For

Lydia, Florence and Neville would become M.i.l. and F.i.l. – mother- and father-in-law.

There was still little prospect of an early marriage. Lydia's divorce proceedings from Barocchi dragged on in the hands of her pessimistic solicitor, Kenneth Brown, Maynard's uncle. Lydia sought to have the marriage annulled on grounds of Barocchi's bigamy, since his own divorce from an American, Mary Hargreaves, had not been completed when he married Lydia. The tracking down of Mary Hargreaves took till May 1924. This completed the case. But the High Court hearing, fixed for July, was postponed till January 1925.

Unlike Maynard, Lydia was underemployed. Her first engagement in 1924 started only on 1 April – a fortnight's programme at the Coliseum with Stanislas Idzikovsky – only obtained, she thought, because Oswald Stoll wanted to keep in with Maynard.[4] Harold Bowen remarked sourly that 'Lydia was not dancing very well, though there is a becoming photograph of her in *The Times* this morning. The costumes were ludicrous. . . .'[5] The engagement over, Lydia and Maynard snatched a long weekend at Charleston from 19 to 23 April, Vanessa and Duncan having prudently decamped. They loved it so much that Maynard formed a plan to take Tilton, a neighbouring farmhouse, for the summer.

On 24 April Lydia left for Paris to start rehearsals for a six-week engagement at the Théâtre Cigale. Comte Etienne de Beaumont and Léonide Massine had arranged a ballet programme, 'Les Soirées de Paris', as the first venture of what they hoped would be a new ballet company to rival Diaghilev's. Lydia, on Maynard's advice, accepted a reduced salary of 15,000 francs (£200), in the expectation, which was not realised, that the show would transfer to London. Lydia's excitement at being in Paris was short-lived. The Boulevard Raspail was 'hell after Gordon Square' for sleeping; her room at Cayre's Hotel was too small for her exercises. Soon Lydia was having her first row with the Count. A happily married homosexual, he had choreographed a ballet called *Vogue*, full of sexual perversions, in which he wanted Lydia to appear with the 'rage of Paris', Rupert Doone. 'We lie on a beach in Lido,' Lydia informed Maynard, 'the man and the boy are "getting on" so I must produce a vexed face. . . . I cannot look jalous, not in my nature of such circumstances.'[6] Finally, she told the Count she would not appear in *Vogue*. 'Je vous déteste,' he replied, but let her off.

Cambridge had its own horrors. College meetings went on for six hours. On 20 May Maynard was making a 'speech in Senate House on the subject of pensions for old professors. Why I trouble myself on such matters I cannot imagine.' He minded Lydia's absence. 'Darkness and desolation' at Gordon Square was followed by 'five Board meetings one after another'. He complained to Vanessa Bell of 'widowhood', and she arranged an old-style Bloomsbury party for him on 13 May, at which Marjorie Strachey made 'terrible revelations about her private vices', and only he and Virginia Woolf emerged unscathed.[7] Back in Cambridge on Thursday 15 May, he 'began an article for the *Nation* ... and felt interested in it.... But I shan't be able to finish it until to-morrow's lecture is out of the way.'[8] Appearing on 24 May under the title 'Does Unemployment Need a Drastic Remedy?', it is a milestone in the development of his thought.

Lydia opened on Saturday 17 May in *Le Beau Danube*, a new ballet by Massine, in which she created the part of the Street Dancer. Massine was her hussar and, in her opinion as well as that of the Bowens, deliberately contrived to steal the limelight. Lydia received rough criticism in the French press: 'Tant mieux pour la femme, tant pis pour la danseuse.' Maynard arrived for her opening night in *Gigue* the following Saturday, by which time she had moved to a hotel mercifully free of milkmen banging pots at 6 a.m. 'Maynard', wrote Harold Bowen in his diary, 'caught us at the theatre and demanded a critique [of the Beaumont ballet] to be finished by V[era] for Monday, so that he could place it in this week's *Nation*.' When Vera complained about cuts to her article, Keynes wrote to her 'in an annoying way that it was a condition of journalism, sometimes it happened even – imagine! – to him'.

Maynard returned from his 'happy two days' in Paris to a grand reception in London for the Queen of Rumania, at which Baldwin told him, 'You look such a good dog with that colour [the Order of the Bath] round your neck,' and Lloyd George seemed suspiciously friendly. (A fortnight later, the Queen tiresomely turned up in Paris, where Lydia had to perform for her.) Feeling 'extraordinarily well in the head', he accomplished 'what I don't do above one day in the year – I wrote for five hours with full concentration and without flagging. The result is that I have almost finished a long article (replying to my critics) for next Saturday's *Nation*. If only one was always at the top point of one's cycle.'[9]

Maynard wrote to Lydia from King's College on 8 June:

> In my bath to-day I considered your virtues – how great they are. As usual I wondered how you could be so wise. You must have spent much time eating apples and talking to the serpent! But I also thought that you combined all ages, – a very old woman, matron, a debutante, a girl, a child, an infant; so that you are universal. What defence can you make against such praises?
>
> I have written quite a lot of words to-day – my pen writes faster.
>
> I *do* agree with you about the new ballet, it must escape from these ugly abstractions just as painting has from cubism; it is *no good* really, I'm sure – just dernier cri.

She replied two days later from the Hôtel San Regis:

> *Oh* Maynard what you thought of me in a bath room on Sunday is something like wooing in absence. I am flattered and shy, and flattered

again, I am not all what you say, but I shall improve with time and eat
more apples.

Keynes spent much of early June 'copying out prices' and working on
his Sidney Ball Lecture at Oxford for that November, 'The End of *Laissez-
Faire*'. Meanwhile, the Count's ballet season was not going well. He lacked
Diaghilev's vision and authority; his 'polite but feeble falsetto' failed to keep
his unruly entourage in order; audiences melted away. Lydia had her third
opening night on 15 June, appearing in *Les Roses*, as well as *L'Amour*, a
seven-minute 'sketch about a girl who dreams of dolls, I am one of the dolls'.
The Bowens thought it 'inconceivably feeble';[10] Maynard returned to Paris
on 21 June to be with Lydia for the final fortnight of her season.

He undoubtedly hoped to get on with his new book in the summer
months at Tilton. But it was not to be.

> My dearest, darling L [he had written to Lydia on 16 May]
> I have been touched this afternoon. I had news that my old master
> who made me into an economist ... could not live much longer; so I
> went to pay him a last visit. Lying in bed in his night cap he looked like
> an old sage, which is what he is, – very Chinese. His voice was very
> weak but he told he how he first came to study economics, and how
> such study was a sort of religious work for the sake of the human race.
> He was still able to laugh, but he has no memory for what happens now
> and has probably forgotten my visit already.

Alfred Marshall died on 13 July, at the age of eighty-two. With help from
his widow Mary Marshall, and the air at Tilton – 'there is no air like this for
work', he told his mother – Keynes wrote a seventy-page (20,000-word)
memorial in August, published in the September issue of the *Economic
Journal*. He steered a tactful course between the homage due to the founder
of the Cambridge School and his own lack of respect for Marshall's Victorian
'earnestness'. Marshall to him was a period piece from a period he did not
like. Pigou, who was Marshall's true successor, gave a memorial lecture on
him in October which Keynes also did not like.

Keynes's balancing act was a delightful, wholly appropriate encomium
which nevertheless skated over difficult personal questions. The essay
entranced Mrs Marshall and was adjudged by Schumpeter to be 'the most
brilliant life of a man of science I have ever read'.[11] The Bloomsbury reaction
is given by Lytton Strachey, who also judged it one of Keynes's 'best works':

> What a world it opens up! What strange people were the married monks
> of the nineteenth century! By the way you don't say – perhaps in the
> circumstances you couldn't – whether he used French letters. Or was
> he (or she?) naturally sterile? That they should have no offspring seems
> to have been an essential part of their system of existence. I am alarmed,
> horrified, impressed – almost over-awed – by such a life.

'No – I don't think he used letters,' Keynes replied, 'but became sterile soon after marriage.' With that limp explanation, Lytton had to be content.

The Charlestonians were still far from reconciled to Maynard's marriage. On 18 July 1924 there was a party in the old style at 46 Gordon Square, for which Duncan devised a transvestite ballet in which Lydia danced, and which had Angus and Douglas Davidson and Dadie Rylands as chorus girls, and Barbara Bagenal, Frances Marshall and Bea Howe (later Lubbock) as the 'male' members. But the Keyneses' presence at Tilton over the summer filled the Charlestonians with despair. Exasperated by their proximity, Vanessa Bell went to Norfolk to look for a new house: 'she is so damned uncompromising', wrote her sister to Roger Fry.

But Virginia, at neighbouring Rodmell, was just as fierce. Lydia was high-spirited, charming, altogether delightful, but – and this was fatal – had no 'head piece'. You could not 'argue solidly' when she was there, and 'as we … prefer reason to any amount of high spirits, Lydia's pranks put us all on edge'. Lydia asked Leonard to tell her about Ramsay MacDonald, and then caught a frog and put it in an apple tree, 'and that's what's so enchanting about her; but can one go through life catching frogs?'[12] With her worries about the divorce added to the scarcely disguised disapproval of Maynard's friends, and without dancing engagements, the autumn of 1924 was another unhappy time for Lydia. She wrote to him at Cambridge from London in October, 'Please, be very fond of me, otherwise I'll pour oceans of tears in the night. . . .'

II. DOES UNEMPLOYMENT NEED A DRASTIC REMEDY?

In 1924 Keynes produced a sheaf of lectures and articles, culminating in his Sidney Ball Lecture at Oxford on 6 November, which were all variations on three interrelated themes: the inadequacy of *laissez-faire* as political philosophy, the inadmissibility of a *laissez-faire* attitude to foreign investment, and the need for the state to mobilise for a programme of domestic investment savings currently going abroad. The general attack on *laissez-faire* will be considered in the next chapter, but the second and third themes form the basis of his advocacy, for the first time (in the *Nation* of 24 May 1924), of public works to cure unemployment.

In the group of lectures and articles dealing with the 'State and Foreign Investment'[13] Keynes denied that foreign investment necessarily served either rational self-interest or maximised the national income. It was, rather, the result of an institutional bias to foreign and imperial investment: the underwriters of the City found large government loans the easiest to handle, and the Trustee Acts gave an 'artificial' stimulation to colonial investment.[14] Not only had individual investors in the nineteenth century regularly lost their money in South America, but 'If a loan to improve a South American capital is lost we have nothing. If a Poplar housing loan is repudiated, we ... still have the houses.'[15] Keynes calculated that half of available savings still went abroad. Most of them could have been usefully invested at home, 'and must be if our national equipment is to grow as fast as the population'.[16]

Keynes's next step was to apply this analysis to the current British situation. As unemployment, despite the trade revival, remained obstinately stuck at 10 per cent of the insured workforce, his mind turned to 'drastic remedies'. In his two *Nation* articles of 24 May and 7 June 1924, he recognises for the first time that an economy may be 'stuck in a rut', with no 'favourable impulses' being automatically generated to get it out, though he did not explain why. In such circumstances, 'we need an impulse, a jolt, an acceleration' to generate 'cumulative prosperity'. The impulse was to hand: the diversion of British savings from foreign investment to capital construction at home. Public works make their first appearance on Keynes's agenda. The context is important. Lloyd George had written an article in the *Nation* on 12 April calling for a programme of public works. This caused considerable controversy. Keynes intervened in support of his old *bête noire*.

Keynes's starting point was that unemployment had not fallen to the level of 4 or 5 per cent he had predicted in December. He reckoned, from historical experience, that by this stage of the business cycle (the boom) 'normal' unemployment of adult males should have been down to 300,000. Instead it was 'stuck' at 770,000. The conclusion Keynes drew was that *laissez-faire* could no longer be relied on to restore full employment. Faced with structural obstacles like trade union restrictions, labour immobility and rigid wage scales, businessmen lacked the profit incentive to invest in new domestic enterprises. So savings drifted abroad. But labour should not be forced into new directions by the pressure of starvation. Rather, 'prosperity is cumulative' and 'we must seek to submerge the rocks in a rising sea' of confidence and courage. He proposed that the government should apply its Sinking Fund not to pay off dead-weight debt, but to a big, £100m a year programme of housing, road-building and electrification. He did not think the government should necessarily build the houses or roads itself, or raise the whole of the finance from taxation. 'Politico-economic evolution' pointed to 'co-operation between private initiative and the public exchequer'. Keynes wrote that the 'true socialism of the future will emerge ... from an endless variety of experiments directed towards discovering the respective appropriate spheres of the individual and the social....'[17]

The theoretical part of the argument was incomplete. What was wrong with British savings being invested abroad rather than at home? Keynes explained that 'a foreign loan does not ... automatically create a corresponding flow of exports'. An increase in the lending country's exports might require a considerable depreciation of its currency. The reduction in real wages in the 'sheltered' trades this entailed could be brought about only through industrial struggle. 'Our economic structure is far from elastic, and much time may elapse and indirect loss result from the strains set up and the breakages incurred'.[18] Investing at home rather than abroad was a much quicker route back to full employment. Keynes ignored the possibility that a transfer of buying power abroad would automatically set up an increased demand for British exports at existing prices, without requiring them to be forced out by lower prices. To his fellow-economists, his proposals seemed illiberal without promising a greater aggregate employment.

Keynes was to play variations on these ideas for the rest of the 1920s. Although the theory was undeveloped, the attitude of mind was unmistakable. Economies were sticky, not fluid. The classic price adjustment mechanisms might work in the long run, but could society stand the 'breakages' they involved in the short run? It was a question which was to have increasing resonance as Britain prepared to return to the gold standard.

III. WHY GOLD?

Even though Keynes never believed that currency depreciation was a cure-all for unemployment, neither had he come to believe that currency appreciation was the answer. To make it more expensive for foreigners to buy British goods hardly seemed the way to cure unemployment. Raising the value of the pound would have to be offset by a reduction in British costs; and that, experience showed, could be brought about only by a further rise in unemployment.

Yet this was the policy on which British governments had embarked. It was what was meant by putting the pound back on the gold standard at its pre-war parity with the dollar: £1 = $4.86. Since the suspension of convertibility of the pound into gold in 1919 sterling had floated against the dollar. However, the Cunliffe Report of 1919 proclaimed the goal of returning the pound to the gold standard 'at parity' with the dollar as soon as possible, and from the middle of 1920 onwards British monetary policy was managed to this end. This meant, as we have seen, that monetary policy could not be used to offset the economic collapse of 1920 to 1922. Between 1920 and 1925, the governor of the Bank of England, Montagu Norman, used 'moral suasion' to limit foreign lending, not to encourage home investment as Keynes wanted, but to strengthen the pound. By the beginning of 1923 the gap between British and American wholesale prices had been substantially narrowed, the pound had recovered to $4.70 and a new 'golden' age was in sight. However, while deflation had gone on in Britain and the United States, inflation continued unchecked throughout most of continental Europe, with the German mark eventually collapsing altogether, and the franc and the lira depreciating to a small fraction of their prewar values.

Putting the pound back on the gold standard meant putting sterling back into a fixed exchange-rate system in which the domestic money supply was controlled by international gold movements, sterling was freely convertible – at least by non-residents – into gold at a fixed price, and in which capital movements were unrestricted. Fixed exchange-rates were a benefit to international trade; the gold standard provided a means of international payments, and a mechanism – the convertibility of paper money into gold – to maintain the official rates of exchange between currencies and prevent any cumulative price movement in the system as a whole, up or down. In his *Tract on Monetary Reform* Keynes had attacked the gold standard for not providing *enough* price stability; and implicitly argued against a further deflation of British prices to restore the pre-war gold value of sterling. Ideally, he would have liked British prices to rise, not fall, before they were stabilised. Critics of Keynes's plans for reform argued that a commodity standard was the only safeguard against inflation.

Keynes's friend Nicholas Davenport believed that the policy of going back to gold sprang from a sadistic desire by the bankers to inflict pain on the working class. Keynes himself hinted at Freudian explanations. In *A Treatise on Money*, he gave a reference to Freud's *Collected Papers*, edited by his friend James Strachey, where Freud claimed that the baby's 'interest in faeces is transformed into the high valuation of *gold* and *money*'.[19] Bankers would have regarded this idea as fanciful. Fixed exchanges and sound money, they would have said, were necessary to economic progress. The gold standard provided the only secure basis for both.

Rational or irrational, there was a great deal of callousness in the 'hunger' for gold. The rulers of Europe had destroyed a delicate social and economic equilibrium in their pursuit of 'victory at any price'. Now they expected the workers to bear the costs of trying to restore it. Just a small sacrifice, they said – and the world would be golden again, as they remembered it in the summer of 1914.

Keynes had outlined his alternative. He favoured independently managed national monetary systems; these would be consistent with *de facto* exchange-rate stability over long periods. But he also understood that this approach was not practical politics; so he set himself the lesser aim of trying to ensure that the return to gold was brought about with the least disruption possible to the British economy. His general line in 1924 was one of 'wait and see'. He was not against fixing the pound at its pre-war parity with the dollar if circumstances justified; but he argued that it should not be an object of policy and was especially opposed to a deliberate policy of deflation to bring it about. Thus for tactical reasons he abandoned outright opposition to the return to gold and pushed the case for delay. The embargo on gold exports, started in 1920, was due to expire in 1925. It would have to be either renewed or allowed to lapse.

The resumption of gold payments might have come in 1923 or 1924 had it not been for financial uncertainty about the future political direction of both the Baldwin government and its Labour successor. These factors caused a 'flight from sterling' in mid-1923, and a low level ($4.30–$4.40) for most of 1924. Not that Labour ministers shared Keynes's doubts about the wisdom of returning the pound to the gold standard: Philip Snowden, Labour's Chancellor of the Exchequer, was a strong supporter of gold, and in April 1924 appointed a Committee on the Note Issue, headed by Austen Chamberlain, to advise him on 'when and how the final step should be taken'.[20]

Expert opinion, as revealed in the evidence to the Chamberlain Committee, was almost unanimously in favour of restoring the gold standard. Three benefits were most commonly adduced. The first was that it would anchor the value of domestic money, or prevent inflation. Secondly, the return to gold was seen as an industrial policy. It was denied, most forcibly by Sir Felix Schuster, that there could be any long-run difference of interest between the City of London and the 'trade of the country', since 'traders lose much more by variations in the Exchange than by having to pay a little more for their banking'.[21] This was not a view shared by the Federation of British Industries, which nevertheless agreed that a *'general* return to [a] gold basis ... would be greatly to our benefit'.[22] Finally, the bankers were unanimous that a return to gold was necessary to restore the City of London to its position as the world's leading banker, and sterling to its position as the world's leading currency. In the absence of a resumption of gold payments, not just the US dollar, but even the German mark would become 'a far more popular currency than the British pound'.[23]

Keynes's argument in the *Tract* that the gold standard itself was an important source of price instability weighed much less heavily than the perception that inconvertible paper standards were inherently inflationary, since it cost almost nothing to manufacture bits of paper signed by a central bank's cashier. To those who argued that the British experience of 1922–5 showed that a paper standard need not be inflationary, Montagu Norman pointed out in 1925 that, 'These three years of "managed" finance have been possible only because they have been made up of steps – deliberate steps – towards a golden summer.'[24]

Keynes was right to distinguish between fixing the exchange and the rate at which it was fixed. 'I should simply aim', he wrote, 'at something as near as possible to what we are in fact adjusted to when the change is made.'[25] He was alone of those experts regarded as reputable in being willing to contemplate the dreaded devaluation. Devaluation, wrote Pigou in his draft report for the Chamberlain Committee in September 1924, 'has only to be mentioned to be dismissed'.[26] This is the point at which irrationality infected British financial decision-making. The policy of forcing up the level of sterling assumed away the problem of forcing down domestic money wages. Keynes understood full well that British policymakers lacked the ruthlessness of Mussolini, who in 1927 simply announced that the lira was at par and ordered all wages to be cut by 20 per cent. That is why Mussolini was so admired in certain British circles in the 1920s.

IV. EFFORTS AT PERSUASION

Keynes gave his own evidence to the Chamberlain Committee on 11 July 1924. Since his turn towards insular capitalism he was no longer the Treasury's favourite son. But he still moved in the circles from which the Committee's membership – Austen Chamberlain, Otto Niemeyer, Bradbury, Pigou and Gaspar Ferrer (a banker) – and witnesses like Montagu Norman, Sir Charles Addis, Edwin Cannan, Sir Henry Goschen, Walter Leaf, Reginald McKenna, Sir George Paish and Sir Felix Schuster were drawn. He had his reputation to consider; he could not appear to favour a policy which smacked of inflation.

The discussion before the Committee has a modern, quasi-monetarist flavour. National monetary management, Keynes said, was the way to achieve price stability, not fixing sterling to gold. Could one rely on the Bank of England to manage money? Keynes had no doubt: the Bank was 'one of our Heaven-sent institutions by which through anomalistic methods we get the advantages both of a private and a public institution'. There would always be 'half a dozen persons in the City' well competent to manage a discretionary monetary policy'. On the other hand, the only way of dealing with a 'wicked' Chancellor of the Exchequer – one who persisted in running budget deficits – was to 'throw him out of office'. Keynes's practical objection to an immediate return to gold at the pre-war parity with the dollar was that it would require a 'drastic restriction' in credit, enough to bring down money wages by about 12 per cent. Deflation on this scale would be 'socially and politically impossible'. 'Is it an essential part of your views that we ought not to restore the old parity of the sovereign?' asked Austen Chamberlain. Keynes denied it: he thought this would happen automatically through a rise in American prices in the not too distant future.[27] The advice of the Committee's report report, drafted by Pigou, and submitted in September 1924 was, essentially, to wait for external events to waft sterling back to par.

A more sophisticated discussion was started by the banker Sir Charles Addis a few days after Keynes gave his evidence. Addis urged a 'pre-commitment' to return to the pre-war parity at a fixed date in order to influence wage expectations. In his reply of 25 July Keynes concentrated on business expectations, ignoring Addis's point:

> Either the government's announcement is believed and the future is discounted immediately in the rate of exchange, in which case we suffer all the elements of a violent and sudden deflation; or else the Government's announcement is disbelieved, or only half believed, in which case we have a slow movement with the expectation of a further movement in the same direction, the effect of which on trade and employment hardly bears thinking about. As soon as the business world has good reason to believe that prices are likely to fall, no course is open to it except to contract its engagements, draw in its horns and go out of business as far as may be until the *funeste* process is over.[28]

Such explicit discussion of the effects of expectations on events was rare at the time.

The general election of October 1924 found Keynes briefly on the hustings, hating his voice as much as ever. As usual, he was wildly over-optimistic about Liberal prospects: gambling on Keynes's forecasts, Vanessa and Duncan lost £70 each, which he forgave them. (His total losses came to £350.)[29] The Conservative victory under Baldwin at last opened the door to a 'golden' age. Sterling, which had been in the $4.40–$4.50 range in the summer of 1924, rose to $4.70–$4.80 from December through to April 1925. This reflected foreign speculation on a rise, but also a compelling international conjuncture. The spread in wholesale prices between the USA and Britain, which had been estimated at about 10–12 per cent in the summer of 1924, narrowed substantially in late 1924 and early 1925 with a rise in American prices, as the Federal Reserve Board, under the leadership of Benjamin Strong of the Federal Reserve Bank of New York, pursued an easy-money policy, partly to offset a domestic recession, partly to ease the return of sterling to parity. The same policy – which involved holding interest rates in New York 1 per cent below those in London – also made it profitable to borrow money in New York and lend it to London.

Under these circumstances, the British authorities came under great pressure from Strong not to let the 'golden opportunity' slip. In Strong's view stabilisation of sterling was the key to ending currency disorganisation, which had been a 'withering influence' on international trade.[30] He and Norman, who went to New York in December 1924, agreed that the failure of Britain to take the opportunity to return to gold now would have consequences 'too serious really to contemplate'. Norman assured himself of a 'cushion' of credit to defend sterling if it went back to gold in the near future. He cabled to the Bank on 6 January 1925: 'our return to gold is desired by responsible people here and opposed only by certain politicians and cranks'. March 1925 was the date he suggested.[31]

In an address to the Tuesday Club on 14 January Keynes made his accommodation to the inevitability of sterling's *de facto* return to parity, and sought to narrow the gap between 'the Monetary Reformers and the Gold Standarders' to one simple point: 'Should the removal of the embargo [on gold exports] come first or last?' Keynes proposed that it should come at the end of the process of adjustment and not in order to force it: 'We must take steps to be at par first and *say* we are there after we are there.' He pointed out that the present value of sterling was the result of heavy speculation of the pound and of an American boom. To link the pound to the dollar at near the top of the boom would be to bear the brunt of the ensuing American deflation, plus the 8 per cent by which sterling was below par when the boom started. Keynes proposed to begin the 'necessary adjustments to parity' by a 'firm monetary policy here'. He would let the sterling–dollar exchange go to $4.86 and then keep it there by a tight monetary policy. When all internal adjustments seemed complete and there was no special boom in America or bull speculation in sterling, he would remove the embargo, but keep gold out of domestic circulation and restrict the right of mintage to the Bank of England. The alternative of removing the embargo immediately 'seems to me to involve wishing the end, but not the means. I think it is all the more dangerous because in the early stages it is perfectly feasible.'[32] Keynes evidently preferred a clear-cut policy, even if it was wrong, to a policy of half-measures.

In the Bank of England, Sir Charles Addis, perhaps persuaded by Keynes, now fought for delay. The final meeting of the Chamberlain (now Bradbury) Committee took place on 28 January 1925. The governor brought along Addis, so the Committee could hear both points of view. Norman argued that the 'rise in the Dollar exchange' was the decisive argument for an early return. Addis countered that it was not just a question of 'capacity to return to the gold standard which nobody doubts, but of your capacity to maintain it after you have reached it'. He argued for a delay of six months at least.

It was Pigou who put the knife into Addis's testimony. How was Addis's view that the exchange should remain stable 'for some time before committing oneself' consistent with his view that the government should commit itself to return to gold later? Would not that announcement itself keep the exchange stable? Would it not 'have destroyed the value of the test, the stability of the exchange as a test?'[33] The Committee agreed with Norman that the time had come, and reported accordingly. Niemeyer, one of the signatories of its report, immediately began the task of persuading the Chancellor of the Exchequer, Winston Churchill.

Churchill understood modern no better than old-fashioned economics, but he was worried about the domestic, and particularly the deflationary, implications of returning sterling to par. On 29 January, with the Bradbury Committee's report fresh in his hands, he produced an 'Exercise', setting out objections to a quick return to gold, which led Bradbury to think that 'he appears to have his spiritual home in the Keynes–McKenna sanctuary'.[34] Churchill was certainly familiar with Keynes's arguments, from the *Nation*.

For a brief moment Keynes might have felt that his persuasion was starting to work. In reply to the 'Exercise', Charles Goodenough, chairman of Barclays Bank, had told Churchill 'not only that the pound ought to achieve parity by natural processes before the decision was taken, but that it should be maintained at par for several months without our being finally committed' – which was also Addis's position.[35] More importantly, Churchill himself was inspired by reading a new Keynes article in the *Nation* of 21 February to fire off a Sunday morning salvo to Niemeyer, dictated from his bed, which contains perhaps the most savage indictment of the Treasury and Bank ever penned by a Chancellor of the Exchequer. The relevant passage starts, 'The Treasury have never, it seems to me, faced the profound significance of what Mr Keynes calls "the paradox of unemployment amidst dearth". The Governor allows himself to be perfectly happy in the spectacle of Britain possessing the finest credit in the world simultaneously with a million and a quarter unemployed,' and ends, 'I would rather see Finance less proud and Industry more content.'[36]

The Treasury and the Bank used two main arguments to convince Churchill. The first was the negligible divergence between British and American prices. Niemeyer argued early in February that they were 'within 4.5 per cent of each other, if not nearer', so that the 'extra sacrifice' to regain parity was hardly worth considering. Bradbury thought the price differential was not more than 2 to 2.5 per cent. These estimates were important in countering the critics' argument that the rise in sterling was largely capital-induced.[37] Opinion, though, was still divided about whether the remaining gap would be closed by American inflation or needed to be closed by British deflation. The Treasury's other main argument was that the return to gold was an *employment* policy. British unemployment would only be mopped up by a worldwide trade recovery, for which stabilisation of the exchanges was a necessary condition. Thus there could be no contradiction between the interests of finance and industry, as Churchill had implied. 'The real antithesis', Niemeyer pointed out, 'is between the long view and the short view.'[38]

One may wonder whether, in these months, Keynes did not regret having resigned from the Treasury in 1919. Would the decision have gone the other way had he stayed? Or would he himself have been singing a different tune? As it was, it was not till 17 March that he got his chance to confront the Treasury's arguments directly, by which time it was almost too late. His engagement diary for that day has a note: '8.30. Winston'. Churchill had arranged for the subject to be thrashed out one more time at a dinner party at 11 Downing Street, to which he had invited, as well as Keynes, Niemeyer, Bradbury and McKenna. The only record of what was said is contained in the memoirs of his private secretary, P. J. Grigg, who was present and who recalled that 'the Symposium lasted till midnight or after'. The argument finally ended when Churchill asked McKenna, 'Given the situation as it is, what decision would you make?' McKenna, an ex-Chancellor himself, replied, 'There is no escape; you have to go back; but it will be hell.'[39] This is what Keynes meant about McKenna 'always letting one down in the end'.

It was the last argument. On 20 March Churchill decided to lift the gold embargo in his budget statement. In announcing Britain's return to the gold standard at the pre-war parity on 28 April, the Chancellor declared, 'If we had not taken this action the whole of the rest of the British Empire would have taken it without us, and it would have come to a gold standard, not on the basis of the pound sterling, but a gold standard of the dollar.'

V. THE ECONOMIC CONSEQUENCES OF MR CHURCHILL

In the weeks following the return to gold, Keynes developed three lines of attack on the decision.[40]

First, he pointed to the double-edged consequence of using bank rate to maintain the restored parity. A bank rate high enough to attract foreign funds to London but not high enough to enforce a 'deflation of credit' would secure the worst of both worlds: Britain could maintain the overvaluation of its currency, 'paying its way by borrowing instead of exporting', and leaving the economy locked into permanent unemployment. It was a prescient prediction of how policy actually worked in the gold-standard years.[41]

Secondly, he attempted a more precise way of analysing the extent of sterling's overvaluation. He distinguished for the first time between the price levels of 'unsheltered' and 'sheltered' goods. The prices of unsheltered – or internationally traded – goods had to conform to world conditions of supply and demand. The prices of sheltered goods and services – those sold mainly at home, like houses and transport – had no automatic tendency to adjust to the prices of unsheltered goods. To put the matter concretely: if the sterling proceeds from the sale abroad of a ton of coal were suddenly reduced by 10 per cent, there was no assurance that the sterling cost of producing that ton – which would include freight charges and interest payments – would also fall by 10 per cent. A comparison between British and US cost-of-living indices in January 1925 showed a disparity of 18 per cent. This gave a more accurate indication of the extent of deflation required than a comparison of wholesale prices.[42]

The third point Keynes made was that labour was the main non-traded good. In assuming that domestic prices 'automatically' adjust to any given exchange rate, policymakers were assuming perfectly competitive wage rates. This ignored the 'deplorably inelastic conditions of industrial organisation today'. In his evidence, on 9 July 1925, to the Balfour Committee on Trade and Industry Keynes pointed to the 'power of trade unions in preventing the cutting of rates [of pay] by competition from unemployed labour', to the effect of the dole in reducing 'the extreme pressure to find employment elsewhere', to the lack of a proper housing market. Keynes told the Committee that 'we are in something much more like the medieval conditions, in which it was so difficult to change the internal value of money that when you were in disequilibrium with the external value you had to have what was called a debasement of the currency. . . .' More important than the growing inflexibility of supply was the change in demand conditions: in the nineteenth century 'everything was on a general crescendo'; the economy was never faced with the problem of reducing average costs by 10 per cent.[43]

Before he appeared before the Balfour Committee Keynes had offered Geoffrey Dawson of *The Times* a series of articles on the effects of the return to the gold standard. When Dawson saw them, he turned them down: 'They are extraordinarily clever and very amusing; but I really feel that, published in *The Times* at this particular moment, they would do harm and not good.'[44] Beaverbrook was more receptive, and they appeared in the *Evening Standard* on 22, 23 and 24 July. A week later an expanded version was published by the Hogarth Press, ed *The Economic Consequences of Mr Churchill*. Seven thousand copies were printed, priced at 1s a copy. They sold out immediately; several more editions were printed over the summer. But the pamphlet flopped in the United States, with only 210 sold after six months, and 216 copies given away.

The Economic Consequences of Mr Churchill was more than the echo of a name. Like its best-selling predecessor, Keynes's pamphlet combined a scorching analysis of policy with a passionate denunciation of injustice. He can be criticised, as at Versailles, for seeing the matter more clearly in retrospect than before the fateful decisions were taken. It needed the decision itself to crystallise the indictment.

'Our troubles' arose from the fact that sterling's value had gone up by 10 per cent in the previous year. The policy of improving the exchange by 10 per cent meant reducing average wages by 2s [10p] in the pound. This could only be achieved by restricting credit. How can credit restriction reduce money wages?

> *In no other way* [Keynes stated] *than by the deliberate intensification of unemployment.* The object of credit restriction, in such a case, is to withdraw from employers the financial means to employ labour at the existing level of prices and wages. The policy can only attain its end by intensifying unemployment without limit, until the workers are ready to accept the necessary reduction of money wages under the pressure of hard facts. . . . Deflation does not reduce wages 'automatically'. It

reduces them by causing unemployment. The proper object of dear money is to check an incipient boom. Woe to those whose faith leads them to use it to aggravate a depression![45]

Keynes never blamed Winston Churchill personally for the return to gold. Nor did Churchill take Keynes's attack personally: in 1927 Keynes was elected to the Other Club, the society started by Churchill and F. E. Smith in 1911 for 'dining and wagering'.*

Keynes understood that the Bank and government would shrink from applying the measures their decision entailed. They would try to borrow rather than deflate. Politics would cause them to do things which would defeat their economic objective. This in fact happened the very day Keynes's pamphlet appeared. In June the coal owners had demanded a new agreement with the Miners' Federation which implied a substantial wage reduction. The miners, backed by the TUC, prepared for a general strike. The Prime Minister, Baldwin, declared bluntly that 'all the workers of this country have got to take a reduction of wages to help put industry on its feet', but on 31 July he agreed to give the coal industry a subsidy of £10m to pay wages at the existing rate for nine months.

Keynes was too astute a publicist to ignore this early confirmation of his argument, and he inserted an extra chapter into the Hogarth pamphlet dealing with the coal industry. Churchill had unwisely said that the return to gold had no more connection with the troubles of the coal industry than did the Gulf Stream. Keynes showed that if British collieries were to compete with American and European coal they would have to lower their sterling prices by 1s 9d a ton. To achieve this the coal owners proposed to lower the standard of living of the coal miners. Warming to his theme, Keynes went on:

> It is a grave criticism of our way of managing our economic affairs, that this should seem to anyone to be a reasonable proposal. . . . If miners were free to transfer themselves to other industries, if a collier out of work . . . could offer himself as a baker, a bricklayer, or a railway porter at a lower wage than is now current in these industries, it would be another matter. But notoriously they are not so free. Like other victims of economic transition in past times, the miners are to be offered a choice between starvation and submission, the fruits of their submission to accrue to the benefit of other classes.[46]

Even at his most bitter Keynes was always ready with a policy. His remedy (within the new constraints of the gold standard) was typically resourceful. Lower bank rate, cheapen credit and encourage an exodus of gold to the United States, in order to stimulate a rise in prices there. (Hawtrey

---

* Rule 12 of the Club stated: 'Nothing in the rules of the Club shall interfere with the rancour or asperity of party politics.'

at the Treasury was urging the same policy.) At the same time, try for a 'social contract' by which all wage-earners would be asked to accept a 5 per cent reduction in money wages and all dividend-holders a 1s increase in income tax. Only by a simultaneous reduction in all the main elements of cost could prices be brought down without without disturbance of relativities and without outrage to the sense of fairness.[47]

> We stand [Keynes wrote] mid-way between two theories of economic society. The one theory maintains that wages should be fixed by reference to what is 'fair' and 'reasonable' as between classes. The other theory – the theory of the economic juggernaut – is that wages should be settled by economic pressure, otherwise called 'hard facts', and that our vast machine should crash along, with regard only to its equilibrium as a whole, and without attention to the chance consequences of the journey to individual groups.
>
> The gold standard, with its dependence on pure chance, its faith in 'automatic adjustments', and its general regardlessness of social detail, is an essential emblem and idol of those who sit in the top tier of the machine. I think that they are immensely rash ... in their comfortable belief that nothing really serious ever happens. Nine times out of ten, nothing really serious does happen – merely a little distress to individuals or to groups. But we run a risk of the tenth time (and are stupid into the bargain), if we continue to apply the principles of an economics, which was worked out on the hypothesis of *laissez-faire* and free competition, to a society which is rapidly abandoning these hypotheses.[48]

VI. WAS KEYNES RIGHT?

Keynes's opposition to the restoration of the gold standard in 1925 can be summed up as follows. The decision to go back at the pre-war parity committed Britain to a reduction in the money costs of production. It was difficult to secure a reduction proportionate to an increase in the international value of sterling because of the 'stickiness' of money-wage rates and other costs. Under the circumstances, it would have been better to adjust the international value of sterling to domestic costs of production.

History's verdict has been on Keynes's side. Few economists now deny that sterling was overvalued between 1925 and 1931. Subsequent defenders of the decision blamed its failure on events which could not have been foreseen: the 'stickiness' of wages (in contrast to the experience of 1921–2), the subsequent French and Belgian currency stabilisations at a small fraction of their par values. They do not defend the results. Nor do critics now claim that a lower exchange rate would itself have solved all Britain's economic problems. Rather it would have created a more buoyant climate for solving them.

In Moggridge's view, the overvaluation of sterling was much more striking in relation to the devalued European currencies than to the dollar.[49] Before the return, Keynes was as much America-centred in his calculations of purchasing-power parity as the others: a universal mindset stemming from the fact that in the war the sterling–dollar rate was the only one which mattered. By concentrating on the sterling–dollar rate Keynes ignored the strongest argument for not rushing the return to gold, which was to wait and see how other European currencies, particularly the franc, settled down. In retrospect, the strongest criticism of the return to gold in 1925 is that it was not part of a concerted move back to a fixed exchange-rate system, with the parities and 'rules of the game' agreed in advance. The inattention to *detail* which marked Britain's actual return was to cost it – and the world monetary system – dear in the years ahead.

VII. MR AND MRS J. M. KEYNES

On 4 August 1925, at the St Pancras Registry Office, Lydia Lopokova became Mrs J. M. Keynes. What she called her 'degree nisi' had been pronounced in January and made absolute in July. The wedding ceremony was 'the simplest imaginable'. Vera Bowen and Duncan Grant were the witnesses; otherwise it was mainly family. Keynes's maternal grandmother, aged eighty-eight, was there, but not his father, aged seventy-three. Lydia, in a fawn-coloured outfit, 'looked like a little ghost – as scared of the newspaper people and photographers as if she had never faced the public before', wrote Florence to Neville. Maynard's old friend Gordon Luce opened his newspapers in Rangoon a fortnight later to 'gruesome pictures' of the famous couple: Maynard, at thirteen stone, had visibly entered prosperous middle age. Duncan described the nuptials to the absent friends at Charleston. 'My future prospects are blighted,' he told them without emotion. He had, hitherto, been Maynard's heir. Clive Bell bet Duncan a champagne dinner that Maynard and Lydia would not have children within a given period. 'Maynard is too fast on the trigger,' he announced.

Maynard and Lydia had planned to spend the first month of married life at Tilton, but the house was already let to tenants, who refused to budge. So they rented another house, Oaklands, in nearby Iford, just south of Lewes, where the usual stream of visitors arrived. A disturbing guest was the philosopher Ludwig Wittgenstein, who landed from the Newhaven ferry on

20 August for a six-day stay. He had given up philosophy to teach in a village school in Austria because, he explained to Keynes, the pain it gave him overcame the pain of doing philosophy, as a hot-water bottle pressed against the cheek takes away the pain of a toothache.[50] He had also given up his huge inheritance, so Keynes had to send him £10 for the journey. Wittgenstein's conversational method was like a punch in the face. 'What a beautiful tree,' Lydia remarked, no doubt brightly. Wittgenstein glared at her: 'What do you mean?' Lydia burst into tears.[51] Keynes too was driven frantic by Wittgenstein's obsessive monologues. He had struggled to understand Wittgenstein's *Tractatus Logico-Philosophicus*, published in 1922, but his mind was 'now so far from fundamental questions that it is impossible for me to get clear about such matters'.[52] When he tried to explain Wittgenstein's philosophy to the Apostles in Cambridge in November, he found that 'it escapes the mind – I could only half remember it'.[53]

On 3 September, Maynard and Lydia left for a fortnight's visit to the Soviet Union. Maynard adored train journeys: to be conveyed, reading masses of books and newspapers, in a travelling armchair, with no duties or responsibilities, was his idea of a perfect break. He went to meet Lydia's family in Leningrad, and also as the official representative of Cambridge University at the bicentennial celebrations of the Russian Academy of Sciences. They stayed a week in Leningrad and then went on to Moscow. There is no record of what Keynes made of Lydia's family, or they of him, beyond a brief 'I have got to love him already' from Lydia's mother Karlusha to Florence Keynes, dated 17 September.

In Moscow it was business as usual – meetings with GOSPLAN (the Soviet planning authority) and the State Bank, concerts, *Hamlet* (presumably in Russian) at the Moscow Art Theatre, banquets. Maurice Dobb, who was also in Moscow, remembered Keynes 'instructing' the GOSPLAN economists 'in the virtues of financial rectitude and "Treasury control"'.[54] Keynes also met Preobrazhensky, who introduced himself as a 'professional revolutionary'. In between these surreal encounters, he gave two lectures on 'The Economic Position of England' and 'The Economic Transition in England' before audiences of Russian academics, the second based on the speech he had just given to the Liberal Summer School, 'Am I a Liberal?' His suggestion that a liberalism remodelled on collectivist lines was the true alternative to both anarchical capitalism and Marxist communism predictably failed to win the assent of the Soviet economists.[55]

On their return to Iford, Maynard and Lydia walked over to neighbouring Rodmell to see the Woolfs – 'M. in Tolstoi's blouse & Russian cap of black astrachan – A fair sight, both of them, to meet on the high road', Virginia commented, continuing:

An immense goodwill & vigour pervades him. She hums in his wake, the great man's wife. But though one could carp, one can also find them

very good company, & my heart, in this the autumn of my age, slightly
warms to him, whom I've known all these years, so truculently pugna-
ciously & unintimately. We had very brisk talk of Russia: such a hotchpotch, such a mad jumble, M. says, of good and bad, & the most extreme
things that he can make no composition of it – can't see yet how it
goes.[56]

Keynes spent the rest of the summer vacation at Iford, turning the
jumble into a composition: three articles under the title 'Soviet Russia'
appeared in the *Nation* on 10, 17 and 24 October. They were published by
the Hogarth Press in December as *A Short View of Russia*, one of his most
eloquent productions. Lytton Strachey came to observe the new ménage and
was not impressed. 'The Keynes visit was rather lugubrious, somehow or
other,' he informed Carrington. 'For one thing the house was so hideous.
Then Lydia is a pathetic figure, to my mind – and so plain. Maynard is
engrossed as usual in his own concerns. He was very interesting on Russia
and Wittgenstein; but there is a difficulty of some kind in one's intercourse
with him – he seems rather far-off. . . .'[57]

The merits of Maynard's marriage continued to be sharply disputed by
his friends. They saw only a conflict in his character between worldliness
and unworldliness, with his marriage to Lydia as a capitulation to the
former. They did not see that a revolution in economic statesmanship could
not be launched from fortress Bloomsbury. It required a different attitude
to the world and its concerns, a different location in that world. Perhaps
his marriage made Maynard more worldly, in the sense of being more at
ease in the world; but that was no bad thing, if his mission was to save the
world. Marriage softened his asperity, widened his sympathies, made him
more 'human', less relentlessly brilliant.[58] It also gave him the physical and
emotional security to build for the future. He acquired a stronger sense of
direction. In 1921 he had told Daniel Macmillan that he would 'never
attempt anything again on so large a scale' as the *Treatise on Probability*. In
the eleven years following his marriage to Lydia, he produced two books
which rivalled it in scale and exceeded it in importance. In 1921 he had
addressed the Apostles on the dilemmas of the brilliant but uncreative
mind, suggesting that money-making was the only suitable sphere for its
employment. After 1925 he seems to have understood that it might be
possible to be creative in economics. It would be wrong to say that Lydia,
or marriage to Lydia, planted the thought in him. But she certainly
understood, and tirelessly pointed out, that he had the stuff of creation
in him. 'The truth', she told him, 'lies in your eyes'; he came to understand how life with Lydia might give the truth he saw space and time to
grow.

A great part of Lydia's charm for Maynard, as we have seen, was her
extremely individual use of the English language, or what Keynes called

'Lydiaspeak'. Her emphases, pronunciation and unerring choice of words and phrases were a constant joy. After attending a wedding party she spoke of 'Jesus fomenting wine out of water at Cannes'. Having seen a hostess's famous collection of birds, she reported, 'I had tea with Lady Grey. She has an ovary which she likes to show every one.' Her words, she told Maynard, were designed to 'enigmatise you', and, certainly to him, she remained an adorable enigma, a bubbling brook of surprises.

Marriage to Lydia also brought out Maynard's protectiveness. He understood that she was defenceless in the world of refined intellectual feelings on which his Bloomsbury friends prided themselves. A lesser man might have tried to mute her often embarrassing style. But Maynard accepted Lydia for what she was, and never indicated – in public at least – that he found her conversation foolish. When Clive Bell snubbed her for a remark she made about Proust, he was furious in her defence.[59] He regarded her utterance as privileged, beyond rational criticism. He made her know that, whatever Bloomsbury might think, she was his 'miele' or 'beloved', his 'dearest beautiful one', his 'dearest darling Lydochka', his 'dearest pupsik' – or 'little navel'. (She called him, less romantically, 'lanky', 'my dear long tree' or 'you dear musky one'.) Lydia felt keenly her lack of intellectual power. When she wrote to him, 'Is it not sad for you that I am not a learned woman and never will be?', he immediately wrote back, 'Do not be sad and especially do not be a learned woman. Your Maynarochka.'[60] Clive Bell used to say that her spiritual home was Woolworth's. She was full of prejudices against Jews and Negroes which the English educated classes no longer expressed so crudely. Maynard did not seem to mind.

Lydia's domestic concerns extended to Maynard's wardrobe. She opened his tallboy and was shocked to find what she called his 'pantalets' full of holes, hardly any socks, and masses of dress shirts; when she upbraided him for coming to bed looking like 'Christ in the last stages', he collapsed into helpless giggles.[61] Her attention to his underwear was closely allied with concern for his health. She constantly urged him to wear vests to protect him from the icy Cambridge blasts, though it was her firm belief that vests, unlike 'pantalets', must have 'little holes' to 'air' him properly. Maynard was, in fact, quite prone to colds. He frequently referred to his 'cycles', the low points of which, he playfully suggested, coincided with her monthly periods – 'guests' in Lydiaspeak. 'I bleed exactly to suit your prediction,' Lydia wrote to him on one occasion, suggesting that her menstrual movements attracted his barometric interest. But his concern was more than statistical. When she complained of being unwell, he bombarded her with letters, telegrams and telephone calls from Cambridge.[62] Behind his fascination with the working of her body there was a practical object: they planned to have children when Lydia gave up dancing.

Although she never claimed to be an intellectual, Lydia could occasionally astonish critical Bloomsberries with her sureness of artistic judgement.

'How does her mind work?' Virginia Woolf once asked herself. 'Like a lark soaring ... & direction at Maynard's hands,' she concluded.[63]

The biggest change which marriage made was to their living arrangements. Lydia moved out of 41 Gordon Square into No. 46; Vanessa moved out of No. 46 into No. 37. The break-up of the old ménage was not without friction. There were rows over rates and rents. Maynard claimed a picture of Duncan's and screwed it to the wall: Vanessa arrived with a screwdriver and took it off triumphantly to No. 37.[64] Vanessa seemed to be saying: by marrying Lydia, you have given up your right to a share in Duncan. Soon Keynes was building a library and extra bathrooms in No. 46: the installation of bidets marked one break with the old order. The whitewashing of Duncan's and Vanessa's murals was another. Lydia was determined to create her own ambience. Her favourite occasions were Russian-style Sunday lunches, which went on for most of the day. Ballet dancers like Frederick Ashton would mingle with young men from Cambridge like Dadie Rylands and Douglas Davidson, who were renting rooms from Vanessa, friends like the Bowens, Frank Dobson and Boris Anrep, and the occasional highbrow, and high-born, 'Bolshie' from Russia. This was how Lydia liked to entertain. In her own circle, she was quick-witted, uninhibited and fun to be with. Like many people in the theatre, she was both conventional and unshockable; with her ballet background, she effortlessly straddled the chic and the camp. On the other hand, arranging or attending the more frozen variety of banking/political dinner party in mid-week, when Maynard was in town, filled her with dread. He would carefully instruct her in the social art of extending, accepting and refusing invitations, but she hated doing it: 'All my "lingo" stops for those occasions, the pen droops out, I become illiterate and illegitimate.'[65]

Lydia knew all about Maynard's sexual past, though she did not necessarily want to be reminded of it. Though she brought out Maynard's heterosexuality, she did not abolish his homosexuality. Indeed, in the late 1920s she became a bridge between the heavily homosexual or bisexual world of London ballet society, based on the studios of Marie Rambert and Ninette de Valois, and the literary and theatrical young men circling round the yellow-haired Dadie Rylands when he returned to King's College, Cambridge, in 1927. However, Maynard was by now an avuncular rather than active presence on this extended gay scene, rendered so by both growing age and his love for Lydia. The only recorded episode of him 'straying' was when, at an evening party, he gave Fred Ashton and his friend William Chappell 'terrible great smacking kisses' on the balcony at 46 Gordon Square. Lydia, showing perfect understanding and mastery of the situation, said 'Maynar', dear, have some more *Bols*' when he returned to the drawing room.[66]

On 3 March 1926 Keynes took possession of Tilton, in East Sussex, on a twenty-one-year lease after complicated negotiations with the Gage estate.

It was only a couple of years later that he discovered that '1000 years ago Tilton was called Teliton ... and that the tenant was called de Cahagnes – which is the same name as Keynes'. There he spent the happiest, and most productive, months of the rest of his life. Tilton was a plain but surprisingly roomy two-storey farmhouse, beautifully situated in several acres of lawn, orchard and woodland, on the north edge of the South Downs. As he told his mother, it was an ideal place for work, and his main early improvement was the construction of a library and 'loggia' from a group of outhouses at the end of the courtyard at the south of the house. They looked out on to an orchard, with the Downs rising up beyond, from the top of which could be seen Newhaven and the Channel.

Keynes's architect, George Kennedy, a fellow Old Etonian and fringe Bloomsberry, gave Keynes a spacious, formal library and an Italianate terrace with a vaulted ceiling, opening out to the orchard. It was in this rather damp annexe, approached from the main house by a covered pathway, that he wrote much of *A Treatise on Money* and most of *The General Theory*.

Tilton was never a grand house. Unlike Charleston it boasted a telephone and electric lights. But, despite the additional bathrooms, the water pipes burst, the boiler was often out of action and members of the household went for days without washing. A primitive central-heating system pumped hot air into the hall through a grille; elsewhere coal fires belched smoke profusely from the chimneys; there were large patches of damp, and the books in the library curled. Lydia was convinced that the English did not understand about chimneys. At Christmas, she and Maynard would huddle round the smoking fire with watering eyes and layers of extra woollens.

The modest staff of six would be considered astonishingly ample by today's standards. Tilton was looked after the year round by Ruby and Edgar Weller, installed in a cottage in the grounds, she as housekeeper, he as chauffeur/gardener. Edgar created the gardens and kept them impeccably. By 1926 Tilton could boast blackcurrants 'dropping from every corner', and a kitchen garden 'proliferating' with beans and carrots.[67] With Maynard's encouragement, Edgar started a serious vegetable and fruit garden, which was soon producing for market. Pig farming was added, and Maynard and Lydia would take squealing pigs to the market in Lewes in the back of their Morris Cowley. When the Keyneses came down to Tilton they would bring the Harlands from Gordon Square, he as butler, she to cook. Then there was Edgar's aunt, Penny ('Auntie'), Lydia's seamstress and dressmaker, as well as a succession of unidentified maids.

Tilton was what would now be called a holiday home. Until Maynard's heart attack in 1937 and the outbreak of war in 1939 modified the routine, he and Lydia were in residence over part of the Christmas and Easter holidays and for about two and a half months in the summer. Like the Charlestonians, the Tiltonians were not integrated into the local community. They were friendly enough with their landlord, Lord Gage, who liked having artists and writers as tenants; but county society was anathema to them. Their company was the guests they asked down. The Tiltonians saw little of the Charlestonians, who in any case were spending an increasing part of the year at Cassis, in the South of France. In the summer of 1927, Vanessa had 'for the most part managed to forget the Keynes' existence';[68] this is typical of a mountain of dismissive comment. Vanessa's constant maliciousness about 'the Keynes' has to be set against Maynard's 'doglike affection' for his old friend, which 'almost brought the tears' to Virginia's eyes,[69] and also against the financial backing he was providing Vanessa and Duncan. Duncan did not share Vanessa's malice – he was entirely without it – but he played up to it. It seemed to be the price he was willing to pay for his own freedom to have affairs; but perhaps he too found it hard to understand, or accept, Maynard's newly-discovered heterosexuality. The Keyneses and the Woolfs visited each other regularly at Christmas, mainly, it seems, because they got into the habit of doing so. The visits do not seem to have given the Woolfs much pleasure. On 30 December 1929, Virginia wrote to her sister:

> What should we find at the gate, coming to tea Saturday in the rain, but a seedy grey Rolls [Maynard had bought it from the Courtaulds]; with the detestable Edgar and the Keynes. I don't see that one's friends have any right to mutilate one's life in this way. There I was forced to rake the cinders of Bloomsbury gossip with Lydia – it was an insult – a murderous act and one has no remedy. They had a bag of crumpets, which Maynard steeped in butter and made Lydia toast. It is this kind of tallow grease grossness in him that one dislikes. But of course I admit they were amiable in the extreme. But then, curse them, we have to lunch at Tilton tomorrow.

'It was the common opinion of Bloomsbury', writes Nigel Nicolson, 'that the Keynes' were remarkably economical in their hospitality.' Virginia gossiped to Lytton on 3 September 1927 about 'a night at Tilton, when we picked the bones of Maynard's grouse of which there were three to eleven people. This stinginess is a constant source of delight to Nessa – her eyes gleamed as the bones went round.' Russians are well known for their hospitality, so the stinting seems to have been Maynard's. Wine did not agree with him, and he drank it sparingly. He gobbled his food down without much attention. Perhaps the truth is that neither of them cared enough about food or drink – or more generally about domestic style – to give them much thought or time

Despite their friends' apparent lack of pleasure in their company, Maynard and Lydia were wonderfully happy in their country house. They were far from heroic walkers, but would regularly tramp across the Downs or through the woodlands for a couple of miles with their dogs Patsy, Pushkin and Ross. The scents and noises of the countryside enchanted them. 'What a melody of a morning,' Lydia wrote one early March, 'music in the air, smells of strength and softness, one squeaks, stretches and blinks in perfect bliss.' Although, as she remarked, 'the elements' were often 'atrocious', there were the long summers when she could sunbathe naked in the courtyard or loggia reading Tolstoy's *War and Peace*, while Maynard scribbled away happily on the theory of the bank rate in his library.

23

Keynes's Middle Way

I. VICTORIAN PRESUPPOSITIONS

Victorian governments believed that an economy prospers best when left to the free play of market forces. From this followed the golden rule of 'non-interference' or *laissez-faire*. The idea that the economy should be 'managed' to secure 'objectives' like full employment or stable prices would have struck the Victorians as incomprehensible or merely fanciful. In chapter 2 of *The Economic Consequences of the Peace* Keynes challenged this perspective. He denied that it was *laissez-faire* which had brought the British economy prosperity; rather circumstances had made possible a degree of indifference by governments to economic outcomes which was now unthinkable. Peace and security had underwritten a worldwide system of free trade and capital mobility; a social and moral equipoise which rendered the duty of saving 'nine-tenths of virtue' had kept the class war at bay. This whole 'complicated and artificial' system depended on precarious balances which were already endangered before the war, and which the war had shattered: the class balance between capital and labour, the psychological or moral balance between saving and consumption, and the balance of trade and capital transfers between Europe and America.

It was his sense of the precariousness of capitalist civilisation which drew Keynes to monetary policy. Instability in the value of money was undermining the social contract on which capitalism was based. Workers' acquiescence in a modest reward depended on capitalists doing their duty of investing. Inflation and deflation cut the moral link between effort and reward, leading to the unjustified enrichment of some and the unjustified impoverishment of others. Keynes also pointed to the increasing unwillingness of modern societies – Britain being the society he knew best – to adjust their internal structures to the ebb and flow of money. Hence stability of prices was the essential requirement of social stability.

Keynes was well aware that if capitalism failed to fulfil its promise there was another economic system, communism, which appealed to worthier motives than money-making, waiting to take over. Nineteenth-century economists had looked to liberal politics to underwrite economic prosperity. Keynes was the first economist to argue that economic prosperity was the only secure guarantee of liberal politics.

II. THE LIBERAL CONTEXT

Keynes's understanding of the diseases of modern capitalism, and the remedies for them, was not developed in isolation. He and Hubert Henderson both saw that new theories about controlling the business cycle might provide liberalism with an alternative to the protectionism of the right and the redistributionism of the left, especially if dramatised as an unemployment policy. Lloyd George seemed to grasp this, Asquith did not. That is why the man of ideas was drawn, despite the past, to the man of action.

Keynes's active involvement in the politics of the Liberal Party between 1924 and 1929 raises the question of the relationship between Keynes's liberalism and that body of ideas known as the 'new' or 'social' liberalism which flourished before 1914 and is distinguished from the classical or individualistic liberalism which preceded it. 'From 1906 to 1914', wrote Henderson, 'a common economic policy united the parties of the Left – the development of the social services involving public expenditure, and the raising of the money by stiffer taxes on wealth.'[1] There were similarities as well as differences between this tradition and Keynes's liberalism. First, and most obviously, Keynes added macroeconomic stabilisation to the pre-war Liberal agenda and, in fact, gave it priority. The short-run instability of capitalism was a greater threat to the social order than any long-run inequity in the distribution of wealth and income. The greatest economic evils, Keynes proclaimed, were the fruits of 'risk, uncertainty, and ignorance'. The state's main economic duty was to offset the effects of these by monetary policy and capital spending. What Keynes did, in essence, was to transfer the problem of social justice from the microeconomy to the macroeconomy. Injustice becomes a matter of uncertainty, justice a matter of contractual predictability. Redistribution plays a minor part in his social philosophy, and then only as an adjunct to the machinery of macroeconomic stabilisation, not as a means to an ideal end.

Secondly, it was Keynes's statism and elitism which distanced him above all from the pre-war New Liberals. The New Liberals valued democracy as an end in itself and wanted to extend it to control private and public concentrations of power. Keynes's purposes required a managerial state.

A final point to note is the difference in intellectual style between Oxford and Cambridge. 'What a home of diseased thought Oxford is,' Keynes had written to his father in 1906 after reading a book on logic by the philosopher Horace Joseph. Oxford was the centre of the new liberalism of the pre-war era. Not only was Oxford (by Cambridge standards) ignorant of economics, but the Oxford-based attack on *laissez-faire* was couched in a mixture of Hegelian and biological language which Keynes and his generation at Cambridge found repellent. Yet one must be aware of the connections as well as the differences. There was a large trace of Hegelianism in Moore's doctrine of 'organic unities'; and by the 1920s Keynes was willing to acknowledge that many processes of production and consumption were 'organic' rather than atomistic.

It would be wrong to see Keynes's Middle Way as a compromise between right and left. It involved new ideas, unfamiliar to either tradition. It is best thought of as a New Way. Today we might call it a Third Way.

III. THE END OF *LAISSEZ-FAIRE*

Keynes's 1924 Sidney Ball lecture, 'The End of *Laissez-Faire*', delivered at Oxford on 6 November 1924 and published in 1926, provides the framework within which his arguments developed over the next five years. Like all his best work, it is full of sparkling prose and arresting ideas. He seems to have read, or at least delved, quite widely in the history of economic and political thought: the essay version is sprinkled with references to Locke, Hume, Rousseau, Paley, Bentham, Godwin, Burke and Coleridge, as well as to the nineteenth-century political economists. An important source was Leslie Stephen's *English Thought in the Eighteenth Century*. But no less characteristically its superb style hides a deal of hasty argument. As Schumpeter remarks, Keynes never gave himself the extra fortnight needed to perfect his occasional pieces.

Keynes traced the origins of *laissez-faire* thinking to the eighteenth-century view that social well-being resulted from individual calculations of self-interest, a synthesis powerfully reinforced by Darwin's theory of natural selection. 'The principle of the survival of the fittest could be regarded as a vast generalisation of the Ricardian economics. Socialist interferences became, in the light of this grander synthesis, not merely inexpedient but impious, as calculated to retard the onward movement of the mighty process by which we ourselves had risen like Aphrodite from the primeval slime.'[2] The other buttress of *laissez-faire* is the 'efficacy, and indeed the necessity, of the opportunity for unlimited private money-making as an *incentive* to maximum effort'. 'Love of money' activates the machinery of *laissez-faire* in the same way as 'sexual love' activates the mechanism of natural selection. However, the beauty of the theory is purchased at the expense of the facts: the conclusion 'that individuals acting independently for their own advantages will produce the greatest aggregate of wealth, depends on a variety of unreal assumptions to the effect that the processs of production and exchange are in no way organic, that there exists a sufficient foreknowledge of conditions and requirements, and that there are adequate opportunities of obtaining this knowledge'.[3]

Rather than pursuing these questions, Keynes explains the continued resilience of *laissez-faire* ideas by the 'poor quality of its opponent proposals – protectionism on the one hand, and Marxian socialism on the other' and its roots in nineteenth-century business sentiment. The conclusion Keynes draws from all this is that the question of the proper sphere of individual and state action cannot be settled on abstract grounds. Each age, he implies, needs to distinguish for itself between what the state ought to do and what can be left to the individual; or, in Bentham's terms, between the Agenda and Non-Agenda of government.[4]

Keynes then develops what looks like a public-goods argument for state intervention. 'We must aim', he wrote, 'at separating those services which are technically social from those which are technically individual.' The most important items on the Agenda relate 'not to those activities which private individuals are already fulfilling, but to those functions which fall outside the sphere of the individual, to those decisions which are made by no one if the State does not make them'. Remedy for the evils arising from 'risk, uncertainty and ignorance' required 'deliberate control of the currency and of credit by a central institution, and ... the collection and dissemination of ... business facts'. He proposed in addition a 'coordinated act of intelligent judgement' concerning the aggregate volume of savings and their distribution between domestic and foreign investment, and a population policy 'which pays attention to innate quality as well as to ... numbers'.[5] Keynes does not explain why the last two goods are *technically* social – that is, why private individuals cannot provide savings and children in the amounts they desire. We have here a good example of the difficulty of trying to build collectivist conclusions on individualistic premises.

Keynes's public goods are to be provided by the state. Rut when he talks about the state the private–public distinction breaks down because of the existence of intermediate institutions. He points to the growth of 'semi-autonomous bodies within the State' like the 'universities, the Bank of England, the Port of London Authority, even perhaps the railway companies', as well as to mixed forms of industrial organisation, such as joint-stock institutions, 'which when they have reached a certain age and size [tend] to approximate to the status of public corporations rather than that of individualistic private enterprise'.[6] What is striking is not Keynes's recognition that the growth of private power posed new questions for the relationship between the state and the economy – this recognition was widespread in the political thought of the time – but his way of resolving the issue. Old-fashioned liberals still aimed to break up concentrations of private power; social liberals wanted to subject it to 'democracy' – whether by decision-sharing, profit-sharing or wider share ownership. Socialists saw it as furnishing a justification for nationalisation. These were all efforts to secure accountability, whether to consumers, workers or electors. Keynes had no real interest in them. He was no pluralist. He welcomed the 'aggregation of production' as tending to stabilise the economy; he accepted uncritically the view that captains of industry were constrained, by the size of their undertakings, to serve the public interest; and he assumed, without further argument, that an interconnected elite of business managers, bankers, civil servants, economists and scientists, all educated at Oxford and Cambridge and imbued with a public service ethic, would come to run these organs of state, whether private or public, and make them hum to the same tune. He wanted to decentralise and devolve only down to the level of Top People.

Keynes's anti-market, anti-democratic bias was driven by a belief in scientific expertise and personal disinterestedness which now seems alarmingly naive. This runs through his work and is *the* important assumption of his political philosophy.

'The End of *Laissez-Faire*' is a flawed production; but it remains the most impressive short attempt to define a social and economic philosophy fit for the time of troubles framed by the two world wars. Nearly eighty years after it was written its spaciousness, humanity and sheer linguistic vivacity still shine brightly. Its faults are shortness and hastiness. Every proposition cries out for development, criticism, refinement. Had he lived longer, Keynes would surely have been tempted to embed his economic theory (which came later) in a culminating work of political and social philosophy to rival and confront Hayek's *Constitution of Liberty*. For the argument is not over. Capitalism may have vanquished socialism, but the debate between *laissez-faire* and Keynes's philosophy of the Middle Way is still fiercely joined.

Over the next five years Keynes extended the analysis of 'The End of *Laissez-Faire*' in various directions. Three discussions are worth following: his account of the 'stages of capitalist development', his attitude to the politcal parties, and his view of the relationship between economic development and the good life.

In 'The End of *Laissez-Faire*' Keynes had talked about the growth of semi-autonomous bodies between the individual and the state. In two talks he delivered in the summer of 1925 – 'Am I a Liberal?' in Cambridge on 1 August, and 'The Economic Transition in England' in Moscow on 15 September – he tried to set this development in a historical framework, producing a non-Marxist theory of 'stages of economic development' suggested by the American John Rogers Commons. Commons, an institutional economist who taught at Wisconsin University, is an important, if unacknowledged, influence on Keynes at this time. Indeed, Keynes wrote to him in 1927 that 'there seems to me to be no other economist with whose general way of thinking I feel myself in such general accord'.[7]

Commons distinguished three epochs, which he called the ages of scarcity, abundance and stabilisation. The second was associated with the triumphs of individualism. England, Keynes claimed, was:

> now entering on a third era, which Professor Commons calls the period of stabilisation, and truly characterises as 'the actual alternative to Marx's communism'. In this period, he says, 'there is a diminution of individual liberty, enforced in part by governmental sanctions, but mainly by economic sanctions through concerted action, whether secret, semi-open, open, or arbitrational, of associations, corporations, unions, and other collective movements of manufacturers, merchants, labourers, farmers, and bankers.'
>
> The abuses of this epoch in the realms of government are Fascism on the one side and Bolshevism on the other. Socialism offers no middle course, because it also is sprung from the presuppositions of the era of abundance. . . . The transition from economic anarchy to a regime which deliberately aims at controlling and directing economic forces in the interests of social justice and social stability, will present enormous difficulties both technical and political. I suggest, nevertheless, that the true destiny of New Liberalism is to seek their solution.[8]

The capitalist system had become rigid, but the authorities still acted on the assumption that it was flexible.

> The idea of the old-world party that you can, for example, alter the value of money and then leave the consequential adjustments to be brought about by the forces of supply and demand, belongs to the days of fifty or a hundred years ago when trade unions were powerless, and when the economic juggernaut was allowed to crash along the highways of progress without obstruction and even with applause.
>
> Half the copybook wisdom of our statesmen is based on assumptions which were at one time true, or partly true, but are now less and less true by the day. We have to invent new wisdom for a new age. And in the meantime we must, if we are to do any good, appear unorthodox, troublesome, dangerous, disobedient to them that begat us.[9]

Keynes was describing what Mancur Olson in the 1980s called the 'sclerotic society':[10] one in which the accretion of powerful vested interests has robbed the economy of vitality. His own stylisation of this process is important for understanding the spirit of his economics. The great art of economics, he always believed, was to choose models relevant to the contemporary world. Organised producer groups were now in a position to resist large changes damaging to themselves. Hence the importance of stabilising prices: 'For the most violent interferences with stability and with justice, to which the nineteenth century submitted . . . were precisely those which were brought about by changes in the price level.'[11] So 'the first and most important step . . . is to establish a new monetary system . . . which will not ask from the principle of diffusion more than it can perform'.[12] But, in addition, a new partnership had to be established between the government and the private sector to match the growing corporatism of industry. 'Our task must be to decentralise and devolve wherever we can, and in particular to establish semi-independent corporations and organs of administration to which duties of government, new and old, will be entrusted – without, however, impairing the democratic principle or the ultimate sovereignty of Parliament.'[13]

Although Keynes intended his 'new wisdom' to transcend party politics, there remained the question of which of the main political parties was most likely to apply his conception of modern statesmanship. The historic Liberal Party was clearly on its way out: Keynes believed it might well end up 'supplying Conservative governments with cabinets and Labour govern-ments with ideas'.[14] 'How could I bring myself to be a Conservative?' Keynes asked himself in 'Am I a Liberal?' 'They offer me neither food nor drink – neither intellectual nor spiritual consolation. I should not be amused or excited or edified.'[15] For a Liberal of Keynes's generation, the Conservative Party was the historic enemy, and remained so throughout the inter-war years, despite the 'decency' of Stanley Baldwin. It was the party of stupidity, superstition and prejudice. It was also the party of protectionism and jingoism. The other problem with the Conservatives was that they were guardians of the reactionary codes of morals against which Keynes's gener-ation had rebelled. He attributed the stupidity of Conservatism to its attach-ment to the hereditary principle. This also explained the inefficiency of British industry. British capitalism was dominated by third-generation men.[16] His initial respect for Baldwin rapidly waned – 'There was an attraction at first that Mr Baldwin should not be clever. But when he forever sentimental-ises about his own stupidity, the charm is broken.'[17] Yet it is easy to imagine Keynes at home, or as at home as he would ever be, in the Conservative Party of Macmillan and Butler – both of whom became personal friends. He admired Conservatism's elitism: 'the inner ring of the party can almost dictate the details and technique of policy', he remarked admiringly.[18] It was only to stupid elitism that he objected.

In the circumstances he faced, Keynes undoubtedly saw the Labour Party as more likely to execute the policies of the Middle Way. If the Conservatives were the stupid party, Labour was the silly party. But at least much of its heart was in the right place. What was needed, he suggested, was Labour's head of steam yoked to the programme of liberalism. In most of his political commentary Keynes is engaged in a dialogue with the Labour movement. This sometimes involved him in very ambiguous use of language as he tried, at one and the same time, to distinguish his position from that of socialism and also to stress the compatibility of a range of liberal and socialist aspirations. This is true of his utopianism. He insisted that 'the Republic of my imagination lies on the extreme left of celestial space'.[19] But the ideal he sometimes chose to call socialist has much more to do with ends such as leisure, beauty, grace, excitement or variety, which, as Anthony Crosland rightly observed, are 'not to be subsumed under any defensible definition of socialism',[20] than with equality, fraternity, democracy.

Keynes emphatically rejected socialism as an *economic* remedy for the ills of *laissez-faire*. Its doctrines were ideological, obsolete, irrelevant, inimical to wealth-creation, and likely to involve gross interference with individual liberty. The inefficiency, as well as irrelevance, of socialism as an economic technique had been vividly brought home to him in Soviet Russia. Secondly, Keynes objected to the revolutionary strain in socialism. He gave two reasons. He did not regard the existing order of society as so bad that it could not be reformed; and it was doubly wrong to have a revolution to establish a system worse than the one being overthrown.

Keynes also rejected the class basis of socialist ideology and politics. 'It [the Labour Party] is a class party, and the class is not my class. If I am going to pursue sectional interests at all, I shall pursue my own.... I can be influenced by what seems to me to be justice and good sense; but the *class* war will find me on the side of the educated *bourgeoisie*.'[21] Keynes's attitude was, of course, influenced by his social background and milieu, which, in Cambridge and London, were not anti-working class but non-working class: Eton Scholars, civilised bankers and industrialists, upper-middle-class writers and painters. Keynes did not hesitate to describe himself as a 'leveller': 'I want to mould a society in which most of the existing inequalities and causes of inequality are removed.' But he went on, 'I do not want to level individuals. I want to give encouragement to all exceptional effort, ability, courage, character. I do not want to antagonise the successful, the exceptional. I believe that man for man the middle class and even the upper class is very much superior to the working class.'[22]

Finally, and significantly, Keynes objected to Labour's anti-elitism. He felt that 'the intellectual elements in the Labour Party will [n]ever exercise adequate control; too much will always be decided by those who do not know *at all* what they are talking about'.[23]

Keynes admired three things about socialism: its passion for social justice (even though he distanced himself from it);[24] the Fabian ideal of public service; and its utopianism, based on the elimination of the 'money motive' and 'love of money'. It was his utopianism which linked up his work as an economist with his commitment to the good life.

The most eloquent expression of his utopianism is found in his essay 'Economic Possibilities for Our Grandchildren', first delivered as a talk to the Essay Society at Winchester College on 17 March 1928, and repeated and revised on a number of occasions before its publication in 1930. Its context is important. His visit to Soviet Russia in the late summer of 1925 had triggered or, more accurately, reactivated reflections on the moral value of capitalism, and he told Lydia on 6 November that he had written 'some philosophical pages about Love of Money'. Another important influence at this time was Freud. In June of that year, James Strachey had reported Keynes 'engrossed in the Case Histories [of Freud]'.[25] Keynes was fascinated by Freud's reflections on the pathology of money, particularly its association with the anal sadistic character, and by the Freudian mechanism of sublimation. Freud enabled him to build on his insight into the sacrificial nature of capitalism, first expressed in *The Economic Consequences of the Peace.* Here the price of economic progress is seen as the cultural deformation of the 'rentier bourgeoisie', who have sacrificed the 'arts of enjoyment' to 'compound interest'.[26] Was there any escape from the dilemma that economic progress seemed to depend on motives condemned as immoral by religion and neurotic by psychology?

For a brief moment Keynes toyed with the idea that the Soviet Union might have discovered at least the beginning of an answer. Admittedly, he produced, in *A Short View of Russia,* published in December 1925, one of the most searing attacks on Soviet communism ever penned:

> For me, brought up in a free air undarkened by the horrors of religion, with nothing to be afraid of, Red Russia holds too much which is detestable. Comfort and habits let us be ready to forgo, but I am not ready for a creed which does not care how much it destroys the liberty and security of daily life, which uses deliberately the weapons of persecution, destruction, and international strife. How can I admire a policy which finds a characteristic expression in spending millions to suborn spies in every family and group at home, and to stir up trouble abroad? ... How can I accept a doctrine which sets up as its bible, above and beyond criticism, an obsolete economic textbook which I know to be not only scientifically erroneous but without interest or application for the modern world? How can I adopt a creed which, preferring the mud to the fish, exalts the boorish proletariat above the bourgeois and intelligentsia who, with whatever faults, are the quality of life and surely carry the seeds of all human advancement? Even if we need a religion, how can we find it in the turbid rubbish of the Red bookshops? It is hard for an educated, decent, intelligent son of western Europe to find his ideals here, unless he has first suffered some strange and horrid process of conversion which has changed all his values.[27]

Yet, although he found the system in many ways detestable, Keynes thought it just possible that Soviet communism might 'represent the first confused stirrings of a great religion', that beneath its cruelty and stupidity 'some speck of the ideal may lie hid'.[28] The significance of Bolshevism, he thought, lay not in its economics but in its attempt to construct a social system which condemned personal enrichment as an end and made it impossible for anyone to pursue it seriously. It was this, he thought, which gave communism the moral edge over capitalism.

After a further visit to Russia in April 1928, Keynes reluctantly concluded that the price for the creed was too high. 'It is impossible to remember, until one gets in the country, how mad they are and that they care about their experiment more than about making things work.'[29] The romance was clearly over. One could not enjoy good states of mind unless things worked. What Keynes's mild flirtation with Soviet communism shows is the need he had, in common with others of the non-believing generation, for a cause, a vision of the good life, to which he could hitch his worldly activities. It was to show how capitalism, despite its faults, might be evolving the conditions of the good life that Keynes wrote 'Economic Possibilities for Our Grandchildren'.[30]

Keynes's thesis was that the engine of capitalism was driven by a neurosis which he calls 'love of money'; but this neurosis is also the means to the good, because it is the means to the abundance which will make capitalism unnecessary. Keynes calculated that if capital increased at 2 per cent per annum, population growth levelled off and productivity rose at I per cent per annum, in one hundred years the prospective population of the 'civilised' world would have a standard of living between four and eight times as high as in the 1920s, obtainable at a small fraction of the effort currently being expended.[31]

With most wants satiated, the 'love of money' would be recognised as 'a somewhat disgusting morbidity, one of the semi-criminal, semi-pathological propensities which one hands over with a shudder to specialists in mental disease'.[32] People would be free to adopt once more the 'sure and certain principles of religion and traditional virtue', valuing today over tomorrow, ends over means, the good over the useful.

'Economic Possibilities for Our Grandchildren' is typical, in its ratio of fancy to hard argument, of Keynes's table talk. These were the lines on which his mind instinctively, and habitually, ran, when not reined in by the requirements of formal treatment. It gives a better idea than his more academic or specialised pieces of what went on in his own mind. In his disapproval of business pursuits he was a typical son of England's 'educated bourgeoisie': they despised money-making as a career or vocation, though they were not averse to a bit of it on the side. His utopia suggests an enlarged Bloomsbury at the top and bread and circuses for the masses. It is a paradise of leisure. But what will most people do? It is also typically parochial, in being confined to the 'civilised' world.[33]

In the essay Keynes remarked, 'Perhaps it is not an accident that the race which did most to bring the promise of immortality into the heart and essence of our religions has also done most for the principle of compound interest and particularly loves this most purposive of human institutions.'[34] There are a few other references to Jews in Keynes's writings which would now be construed as anti-semitic. In *A Short View of Russia* he had doubted whether communism 'makes Jews less avaricious'. After a visit to Berlin in

June 1926, he depicted Germany as under the 'ugly thumbs' of its 'impure Jews', who had 'sublimated immortality into compound interest'. This was for a talk to the Memoir Club, published only posthumously; it was his most prejudiced utterance on the subject, but it falls a long way short of the murderously flip remarks which even someone like Dennis Robertson was capable of making.[35]

Stereotyping of Jews was common in Keynes's circle, and the stereotypes were usually unfavourable. Keynes's letters are mercifully free from personal abuse – not so Lydia's, or those of some Bloomsberries. Individual Jews were exempted by the devices of exceptionalism or non-recognition of their Jewishness. Thus was decency reconciled to prejudice. But the occasion for decency did not often arise. Although Virginia Woolf married a Jew, and Sraffa and Wittgenstein were half-Jewish, there were very few Jews in Keynes's world in the 1920s. That came later – with the exodus from central Europe. Meanwhile, stereotyping could flourish, and there was no need to mind manners.

Keynes's own stereotyping took place on the philosophical, not vulgar, plane. Much like Weber's disciple Sombart, he thought of Jews as embodying the 'spirit' of capitalism, which to him was an abstract 'love of money'. His fancy was seized by the idea of a nexus between immortality and compound interest – in the individual psyche, in the history of the Jews and in the history of capitalism. 'Compound interest' is the 'impure' form of immortal longing. And so Keynes distinguished between the 'pure' or religious or intellectual Jews like Einstein, or Melchior, or his favourite pupil Richard Kahn, and the money-loving Jews like Clemenceau's Finance Minister, Klotz. His first cousin, Neville Brown, remembers Keynes wondering whether he had a Jewish forebear, because, he said, he could do certain mathematical calculations in his head which only Jews could also do.[36] When 'Economic Possibilities for Our Grandchildren' was published, Professor Radin of the University of California pointed out the lack of congruence between Keynes's hypothesis and the facts. He told Keynes that 'the hope of immortality played an extremely unimportant part in Jewish theology' and that the Jews were 'not especially distinguished by their concern with compound interest or the accumulation of money' – rather the reverse: civic insecurity had made many Jews 'extremely extravagant' and prone to 'reckless gambling rather than painful accumulation'. In his reply, Keynes apologised for having been thinking along 'purely conventional lines'. But he was reluctant to give up his fancy: 'I still think that the race has shown itself, not merely for accidental reasons, more than normally interested in the accumulation of usury.'[37] This correspondence took place in the autumn of 1933. It has to be balanced by Keynes's condemnation of the 'barbarism' taking place in Germany at the time. (See p. 504.) Keynes's anti-semitism, if such it was, was little more than a theological fancy: the expression, perhaps, of some unresolved conflict about his own

Nonconformist roots. There is no evidence that it influenced his personal conduct.

IV. CONCLUSION

Keynes's politics of the Middle Way in the 1920s can be interpreted in two senses. It can be seen as an expression of an Aristotelian sense of balance, with both nineteenth-century individualism and twentieth-century communism being viewed as excesses of their virtues. Or Keynes can be seen as a prophet of individualism on the defensive. The institutions of society had become like rocks which required the most skilful circumnavigation if the ship of state were not to be smashed up. There was no margin left for stupidity, silliness or obsolete ideas in government. Only the most generous and disinterested spirit, equipped with high intelligence and scientific policies, could save the social order from shipwreck.

Both perspectives are valid, the first reflecting Keynes's education, the second his experience. In 1926 there seemed little evidence of his spirit in high places. Baldwin's government and the trade unions were set on a collision course.

24

Working with Lloyd George

I. RUN-UP TO THE GENERAL STRIKE

'"All the workers of this country have got to face a reduction of wages" murmurs Mr Baldwin between a sermon and a subsidy.' This comment by Oswald Mosley, a rising Labour politician, neatly captures the state of mind of the Baldwin government following Britain's return to the gold standard. Commitment to the pre-war parity logically required an all-round reduction in industrial costs. But, stranded between *laissez-faire* and fear of social revolution, the government could neither impose an industrial policy of its own, nor afford to stand aside to let employers fight it out with the trade unions. It was in the coal industry that irresistible logic first came up against immovable force. When the coal owners had demanded a 10 per cent wage cut from their workforce and the TUC had warned this would mean a general strike, Baldwin stepped in with a compromise: a temporary subsidy to the coal industry plus a Royal Commission, headed by Sir Herbert Samuel, to tell it how to reorganise itself. The subsidy was due to expire on 30 April 1926. The unions prepared their resistance; the government prepared for a general strike; men of goodwill hoped that the Samuel Commission would come up with a magic formula.

While this time-bomb was ticking away, there was nothing Keynes could do. He had made clear his opposition to a policy of 'intensifying unemployment' to bring down wages. In a speech to the Manchester branch of the Federation of British Industries on 13 October 1925 he suggested an escape from the policy of cutting wages. A policy aiming at 'production up to capacity and full-time employment may enable us at the same time to pay present real wages and, nevertheless, reduce our costs'.[1] This seemed to put the problem in a new light. Might not a fuller utilisation of idle plant pay for itself by cheapening the cost to the employer of each worker employed? This was one of Keynes's thoughts that flickered and died. What remained was the idea that prosperity is 'cumulative', that what British industry needed was fattening up, not dieting.

The autumn of 1925 found Keynes, as usual, complaining of overwork ('too much to do, no leisure, no peace, too much to think about....'). A substantial commitment was organising the London Artists' Association, in homage to both art and friendship. The idea was to give the leading

Bloomsbury painters and their protégés – a group headed by Duncan Grant, Vanessa Bell and Roger Fry – a guaranteed income, so they could paint without worrying about money. Perhaps Keynes saw it as a way of compensating Duncan for the loss of his inheritance. He persuaded Sam Courtauld and two other businessmen to join him in guaranteeing the members an income of £150 a year. The Association held their first London show, at the Leicester Galleries, in April 1926. It was hailed by their relentless publicist Clive Bell as 'an event of capital importance ... no less than the reassertion of an English school'. By 1929, 700 works of art, worth £22,000, had been sold.[2]

From the start tensions dogged the Association's life, which reflected those between Tilton and Charleston. Keynes wanted to bring in non-Bloomsbury painters like Matthew Smith and Paul Nash, partly to strengthen the financial basis; Duncan, Vanessa and Roger Fry objected to his interference. Keynes was right, for many reasons, not least because he foresaw that Duncan and Vanessa would get tired of subsidising the non-earners. But it was a fixed idea at Charleston that Keynes had no artistic judgement: his role should be to pay up and leave artistic policy to them. 'If one wants to make him do something,' Vanessa wrote to Roger Fry, '[the only way] is not to listen to a word he says, to let him talk, keeping one's attention firmly fixed to one's own ideas, & then repeat them regardless of what he's said.'[3]

Maynard's friends assumed that, when she married, Lydia would give up dancing. With only one three-week engagement in the year preceding her marriage (in a slight comedy called *The Postman*, in which she fell off her bicycle), this seemed a reasonable assumption. But in October 1925 Diaghilev offered her an engagement for his four-week autumn season at the Coliseum, with a chance to star in her favourite roles, *Boutique, Good-Humoured Ladies, Carnaval* and *Petrushka*. She was not in full training and found the Coliseum season hard work for her toes. Nevertheless, it was a great success, and Lydia was recalled again for the summer season in 1926.

Early in 1926 the issue of the future of the Liberal Party came up. Following the electoral débâcle of 1924, Asquith (now the Earl of Oxford and Asquith) retained the party leadership, with Lloyd George chairman of the Liberal rump of forty-two MPs in the House of Commons and controlling a vast fund dubiously accumulated in Coalition days. The party was starting to shed MPs to both right and left. There were rumours that Lloyd George had been trying to work out a deal with Ramsay MacDonald; in the *Nation*, Hubert Henderson ran the idea of a progressive alliance between the Labour and Liberal parties.[4]

Keynes intervened in the discussion in a 'frank speech' on Labour–Liberal relations at the presidential dinner of the Manchester Reform Club on 9 February, an occasion sufficiently august for him to get his hair cut. It was published in the *Nation* on 20 February as 'Liberalism and Labour'. His argument was that sensible Liberals should start talking to sensible socialists.

His defeatist mood annoyed Lloyd George, but the real trouble with his argument, as Keynes no doubt recognised, was that the 'sensible' people on both sides had no ideas. Ramsay MacDonald had nothing to offer between utopia and Treasury finance; Philip Snowden was a socialist of the old Henry George type, sharing Lloyd George's passion for land reform, but in all other respects an orthodox Gladstonian. Similarly, the 'sensible', or Asquithian, Liberals by no means agreed with Keynes. They had all supported the return to the gold standard. Lloyd George had both ideas and energy, but sensible people regarded him as the devil incarnate.

Neither would the most important Labour convert to Keynes's ideas, Oswald Mosley, have been widely regarded as a sensible socialist. 'Tom' Mosley's reputation at this time was that of a rakish young man about town, a seducer of both crowds and women. (Lydia one night dreamt she was kissing him.)[5] Yet his pamphlet, *Revolution by Reason*, published in 1925, was the first political attempt to apply Keynes's ideas to economic policy. Mosley squarely blamed unemployment on the lack of 'effective demand'. Keynes had met Mosley at dinner parties in London; there is no evidence that he read, or discussed, his pamphlet with him. He did read an enlarged, and more muddled, version of it, written by Mosley's friend John Strachey, and, he told Strachey on 5 January 1926, 'liked it very much'. But he could not appreciate Mosley's flash of intuition about a 'lack of effective demand', mainly because it *was* a flash of intuition. Had Mosley been able to explain properly how it could occur, he, and not Keynes, would have been the author of the new economics.

Keynes also responded sympathetically to the Independent Labour Party's pamphlet, *The Living Wage*, published in 1926. Heavily influenced by J. A. Hobson's 'underconsumptionist' theory, it aimed to increase working-class purchasing power through redistributive taxation and credit expansion. In a letter to Brailsford, one of its authors, dated 27 October 1926, Keynes wrote:

> I don't think I quite subscribe to Hobson's doctrine of underconsump-
> tion. But I do agree with a notion, which is perhaps kindred to his, to
> the effect that prosperity is cumulative. If in existing circumstances we
> could do something, orthodox or unorthodox, to stimulate demand,
> from whatever quarter, that demand would call forth an increased
> supply, which in turn would maintain and intensify the demand, and so
> on. But all the same it is not quite what Hobson has in mind I think.[6]

At this stage in his own development, Keynes could see a leakage of demand occurring only through foreign lending unrequited by exports. He did not yet see thriftiness as such as a potential subtraction from demand.

Labour's leadership presented a depressing spectacle, but Keynes was discovering a new sympathy for the Fabians of the older generation. Beatrice Webb had written him a warm letter of appreciation when 'Liberalism and

Labour' appeared in the *Nation* on 20 February 1926. She particularly liked the echo of the old Fabian idea of permeation.[7] Before the war Keynes had mocked her. But, after lunching with her and Bernard Shaw on 19 March, he took her *My Apprenticeship* (sent to him for a review which he never wrote) to Andalucia, where he and Lydia spent their Easter holiday. He was much moved by her account of her struggle to replace her lost Christian faith by a new 'religion of humanity'. On their return on 18 April, Duncan Grant reported, 'Maynard almost became a Socialist owing to his reading Mrs. Webb on the train in Spain.' He added cattily, 'I see Socialism is going to become for them a moral excuse for meanness.'[8] Maynard and Beatrice now embarked on an improbable friendship based on mutual fascination, much incomprehension, but a shared belief in social science and public service.

Another friend from the mid-1920s was H. G. Wells. Maynard gave his novel *The World of William Clissold* an enthusiastic review in the *Nation* on 22 January 1927. His sense of elitism was attracted by Wells's idea that the motive force for change had to come from the men of power and knowledge – the business tycoons and the scientists – rather than from socialist intellectuals or workers. 'Clissold's direction is to the Left – far, far to the Left; but he seeks to summon from the Right the creative force and the constructive will which is to carry him there.' Similar themes impregnated the work of Bernard Shaw, another old Fabian whom Maynard and Lydia were starting to see in London. The men of power, represented in *Major Barbara* by the arms manufacturer Undershaft, lack ideals; the men of knowledge are impotent because they have no faith; the masses are potentially destructive because they have no knowledge. 'What a debt every intelligent being owes to Bernard Shaw!' Keynes wrote. 'What a debt also to H. G. Wells. . . .'[9]

Keynes returned from his Easter holiday in Spain to a Cambridge crisis. The Provost of King's College, Walter Durnford, grandson of the flogging Dr Keate of Eton, had died on 9 April. Should Keynes offer himself for election? Most of the younger fellows wanted him to; most of the older ones favoured Clapham, the economic historian, who represented Nonconformity, mountaineering and convention. On 23 April Keynes told his 'dearest darling Provostess' that he was 'weakening', but that he felt it was a 'wrong inclination'. Virginia Woolf reported him to Vanessa, on 29 April, 'torn between the Provostry of King's and respectability; and Gordon Sqre and scalliwags'. In a letter to C. J. Gray, who represented the younger fellows, Keynes put his doubts in different language which perhaps amounted to the same thing: 'I am much afraid . . . that the position of Provost may be in some ways unsuitable to a person of my activities and temperament.' By this time, it had become clear that, if Keynes stood, the college would be bitterly split. To avoid this, he threw his weight behind a compromise candidate, A. E. Brooke, an elderly divinity professor and uncle of Rupert Brooke, who was duly elected. The mixture of motives which led Maynard to withdraw is nicely, though unkindly, captured by Virginia Woolf: 'Maynard has decided not to stand.... He says he would always be called Provost and not Keynes; he would become respectable; he would sink and disappear.... So he is *not* lost to Bloomsbury. But as everyone agrees he would almost certainly have failed, the arguments do not convince me. Leonard said he seemed greatly depressed.'[10]

Maynard was out of humour for much of the summer term of 1926. The feasting and drinking which followed Brooke's election left him exhausted and with a 'bad complexion'. He was with Leonard Woolf and Gordon Luce for Lydia's first-night appearance on 17 June in *Pulcinella* at Her Majesty's Theatre, spoiling the evening for Leonard with his nervousness. The sensation of the Diaghilev summer season was Stravinsky's *Les Noces* – 'musically it is a wonderful orgy, but as a ballet it is more like mathematics', Lydia wrote to him on 30 May. Lydia saw that her dancing days were coming to an end: she felt 'mentally shaky after my 6 months absence of legs', feared she was becoming a 'second hand dancer', and felt she would 'like to retire for ever after London season'. On 20 June she and Maynard left London for Berlin, where he was to give a lecture at the University.

II. THE BREAK WITH ASQUITH

The cause of Maynard's depression and irritability had less to do with his failure to get the Provostship of King's than with the General Strike and the painful personal circumstances accompanying it. Throughout his life he complained that disturbing public events were bad for his nerves: this was one reason for the supreme importance he attached to peace and contentment as goals of statesmanship. But there was a further factor. The General Strike produced another upheaval in the Liberal Party, and this time Keynes backed Lloyd George against Asquith. His breach with old friends was not only distressing to him; it made many rub their eyes. The scourge of the Welsh Wizard now emerged as his champion. It was no good Keynes saying 'I support Mr Lloyd George when he is right, and oppose him when he is wrong.' The Asquithians – Simon, Runciman, Phillips, Maclean, Pringle, Grey, Gladstone – who were bound together by personal loyalty and historic memory rather than by ideas, viewed his abandonment of their old leader as a betrayal. The mistrust which Keynes's policies inspired in sound quarters was now compounded by his cohabitation with sin.

The occasion of the break was the General Strike. The coal industry had finally run out of time. The Samuel Commission, reporting in March 1926, had recommended wage reductions now and reorganisation later. The Miners' Federation rejected the cuts, and the owners the reorganisation; the TUC promised to support the miners. Over-optimistic as ever, Keynes was convinced a bargain would be struck; and, with his usual confidence, told the *Nation*'s readers on 24 April what it should be. The coal-mining industry had to raise its net proceeds by 3s a ton. This could come only from lower wages, economies of production and higher prices to domestic consumers. Keynes suggested 1s from each of the three sources, with a temporary subsidy to help the second. If only life were so reasonable! Keynes thought that the miners would prefer a modest wage reduction to 'widespread unemployment'. He assumed that the government accepted the need for a further subsidy. He believed that the owners accepted the need for some concentration of production on the most efficient pits. All three suppositions were wrong.[11]

The government's temporary subsidy ran out on Friday, 30 April. Baldwin, displaying a lethargy remarkable even for him, bestirred himself to seek a compromise only in the week it was due to expire. When the Cabinet rejected his proposal to extend it for a fortnight, he broke off negotiations with the TUC on a flimsy pretext: when the TUC delegation arrived at 10 Downing Street on Sunday evening, the Prime Minister had gone to bed.

The General Strike which started on 1 May was called off by the General Council of the TUC, which had never wanted it, on 12 May, after it had received a meaningless assurance from Baldwin that the government would 'consider' certain suggestions put forward by Sir Herbert Samuel. This fig leaf barely disguised an unconditional surrender. The miners held out till the autumn, when starvation forced them back on the owners' terms. The government's strategy was vindicated. But in the longer run Keynes's analysis was the more percipient. His view was: one can run a modern industrial society either by conciliating the major interests or by exercising class power. He stood for the former; the government had adopted the latter, and won. But it did not know what to do with its victory. Significantly, Baldwin rejected the package of measures proposed by Lord Birkenhead for permanently weakening the trade unions. Of his proposals to end immunity for trade union funds, to require secret ballots on strike action, to impose restrictions on picketing, and changes in the political levy, only the last was enacted.[12] The unions remained unappeased and unbowed. The industrial heartlands of northern England, Scotland and Wales, already distressed and soon to be crippled by the great depression, were alienated from the Westminster system. The whirlwind was reaped only in the 1970s when, strengthened by decades of full employment and pro-union legislation, the trade unions paid back the government and the middle classes for the wrongs inflicted between the wars. In 1984 the miners rose again, in a conscious, but much more vicious, echo of 1926 and were crushed again.

But by this time Keynes's Middle Way of class conciliation and full employment had been abandoned.

Only one politician, Keynes thought, rose to the occasion. Before the General Strike started Lloyd George had urged the government to keep negotiating until a settlement was reached. After it had been called, he declared support for the government, but flayed it for its dilatoriness in starting negotiations, its precipitancy in breaking them off, its insistence on unconditional surrender and its refusal to print the appeal of the two Archbishops for a negotiated settlement in its strike newspaper, the *British Gazette*. His tone was in marked contrast to that of Asquith and Simon, who laid weight on the illegal and unconstitutional character of the strike.

Keynes's relations with Lloyd George had been thawing for some time. It was now seven years since he had declared, desperately, to Margot Asquith in Paris that he could not bear working for such a man for another day, another hour. Even then, though, his loathing was pierced by flashes of admiration. 'He can be amazing when one agrees with him,' he had told Bloomsbury's Memoir Club in 1920.[13] Now he was finding that he was agreeing with him more and more. Lloyd George might know nothing about economics and finance. But his expansionist instincts were now much more in tune with Keynes's views than the dreary negatives of the Treasury and the Bank of England. As early as 1920 he had declared, 'we must have more output'. He had favoured public works in 1924; in 1925 he had condemned Churchill's 'egregious recklessness' in returning Britain to the gold standard. Out of power, with his natural radicalism reasserting itself, with his energy unimpaired, and in the market for bold ideas, he was a much more attractive proposition than in his days of glory.

Lloyd George showed his disapproval of the Asquithian line on the strike by refusing to attend a meeting of the Liberal Shadow Cabinet on 10 May. Asquith, goaded, it is said, by his wife Margot and his daughter Violet Bonham Carter, chose to make an issue of Lloyd George's non-attendance; after letters from both men to each other appeared in the national press on 26 May, Asquith, supported by the Old Guard, declared that Lloyd George had 'expelled himself' from the Shadow Cabinet, said he would not remain leader of the Party if Lloyd George returned, and called on his friends to support him.

Those friends were too few; and Keynes was no longer one of them. Like most Liberals he thought Lloyd George had shown the true Liberal temper during the strike, and was appalled that Asquith had handed the game to the Labour Party. On 22 May, the *Nation* had seen in the collapse of the strike a new chance for liberalism to discredit Labour's 'class war' approach to industry and politics; now the opportunities opened up by Lloyd George's display of statesmanship had been lost. 'Who would have believed', Hubert Henderson wrote in the *Nation* of 29 May, 'that in a controversy between these two statesmen Mr Lloyd George would be triumphantly and unmistakably in the right?' Lord Oxford, he said, had 'blundered'.

Letters attacking the *Nation*'s position now started flooding its correspondence columns; Asquith's family mounted its private bombardment. Margot Asquith's assault on Maynard started on 22 May. A passionate lioness, she turned with desperate loyalty on those who hounded her wounded mate:

Dearest Maynard,
Nothing has so amazed me as yr. praising LL.G.'s conduct in the Strike & saying it means 'Liberalism'. Poor LL.G.! his incapacity to see an inch before his *own* nose & his Press, his lack of all public conscience, as well as his private treachery to his leader & colleagues have *finished* him. . . . *No* one has ever been so generously patiently & humanely dealt with by a Chief as LL.G. but . . . he is a natural cheat & liar & wd blackmail his mother. The Gen. Strike has shown the difference between politicians & statesmen & was stopped by Liberalism and Liberals.

And on 28 May: 'Is this the man who represents Liberalism better than the blundering Oxford? . . . I wd rather be a tiny Party straight than a straggling Party crooked. I may be a fool but I prefer the Truth.' Keynes sent a reply on 30 May:

My dear Margot,
I have been wretched over this business since I heard last Tuesday what was going on. I know what LL.G. is like and so do most of those who feel as I do over this affair – we are under no illusions. But the split has come in such a way that any radical, who is not ready to subordinate his political ideas entirely to personalities, has absolutely no choice.
I see nothing satisfactory in the outlook. But at least my feelings are unchanged. 'The Blundering Oxford' remains the one I should *like* to follow and whom I love and respect.

Margot Asquith returned on 31 May with 'It comes to this: LL.G. or H.? – those who prefer the former will not want to retain us as a friend.'[14]

Lloyd George was not slow to cement promising political alliances. On 6–7 June, Maynard and Lydia spent their first weekend at Churt, his country house. 'It can't do any harm,' Maynard thought, and 'why not?' They returned to Gordon Square with the gift of a fresh trout caught by a passionate Liberal land reformer. On Monday, Maynard wrote to Lydia, 'LL.G. doesn't taste very nice in the mouth when one smacks the tongue in retrospect. What do you think? However, it's life.' He attended a meeting called by Lloyd George in London on 29 June to discuss setting up a Radical League outside the Liberal Party.[15]

The painful switch of loyalties was made no easier by the fact that on 12 June Asquith had a stroke, which incapacitated him for three months. A

letter by Keynes appeared in the *Nation* on the same day. Lloyd George's
conduct during the strike had been admirable. If he left it, the Liberal Party
would die of inanition. 'Lord Oxford is a whig. Mr Lloyd George is a radical.
The Liberal Party is strongest when these two elements in it, which have
always existed side by side, can work together.'[16] This conciliatory letter
brought a sad, but less angry, one from Margot, dated 20 June and written,
as was her wont, at 4 a.m.:

> I can see you have *no* idea how ill Henry is.... I open all his letters but
> he only sees the ones I think will cheer him up so I cd not show him
> yours. When he read the 'Blunder of Ld O' before he was ill he said to
> me: 'This isnt Maynard, its Henderson; Maynard wd never approve of a
> Gen. Strike; he's far too clever! but I'm surprised he put it in his paper.'
> I cd see it hurt him.... Remember he is *very* unceltic ... He is really
> dying of a broken heart & he is not at *all* sentimental.

Keynes never saw Asquith again. He died on 15 February 1928. Maynard's obituary notice in the *Nation* was warm, respectful and just: 'He was
the perfect Whig for carrying into execution those Radical projects of his
generation which were well judged'. Margot Asquith wrote to him, 'I know
dear Maynard that you liked him *very* much once, & that you like me very
much now....'

III. THE LIBERAL INDUSTRIAL INQUIRY

Maynard made two weekend excursions from Tilton in the summer of 1926.
On Saturday, 7 August he and Lydia went to stay with the Webbs at Passfield
Corner in Hampshire, Maynard going on to Easton Lodge to address the
Independent Labour Party Summer School on 'The Future Balance of British
Industry'. Beatrice Webb wrote down her impressions of him:

> Hitherto he has not attracted me – brilliant, supercilious, and not
> sufficiently patient for sociological discovery even if he had the heart
> for it, I should have said. But then I had barely seen him; also I think
> his love marriage with the fascinating little Russian dancer has awak-
> ened his emotional sympathies with poverty and suffering. For when I
> look around I see no other man who might discover how to control the
> wealth of nations in the public interest. He is not merely brilliant in
> expression and provocative in thought; he is a realist: he faces facts and
> he has persistency and courage in thought and action. By taste an
> administrator, by talent a man of science, with a remarkable literary gift,
> he has not the make-up of a political leader. Not that he lacks 'person-

ality' – he is impressive and attractive, he could impose himself on an audience and gather round him a group of followers and disciples; if he could tolerate a political party as God makes it, he could lead it. But he is contemptuous of common men, especially when gathered together in herds. Hence his antipathy to trade unions, to proletarian culture, to nationalism and patriotism as distinguished from public spirit. The common interests and vulgar prejudices of aristocracies and plutocracies are equally displeasing to him – in fact he dislikes all the common-or-garden thoughts and emotions that bind men together in bundles. What Keynes might achieve is a big scheme of social engineering; he might even be called in to carry it out, but as an expert and not as a representative.[17]

On 25 September, Keynes was one of '14 professors' summoned to Churt. 'The occasion', Keynes reported to H. G. Wells, 'was a gathering of a few trying to lay the foundations of a new radicalism; and for the first time for years I felt a political thrill and the chance of something interesting being possible in the political world. But I have no trust yet. Ll.G. was as good as gold – it is scarcely conceivable that anyone could be so good. But how long it will last I don't know.'[18] Earlier in the year, the Liberal Summer School Committee (which included Keynes) had decided to set up an industrial inquiry. Lloyd George had promised to back it with £10,000 from his fund and the services of a secretariat. The events of the early summer cast doubt on the commitment. But on 15 October Asquith resigned the Party leadership, leaving Lloyd George in control. For the next three years he poured out his heart, energy, brains and money in an effort to revive a party dying at its roots. It was a glorious but forlorn battle. None of the top Liberal politicians – all, except Sir Herbert Samuel, Asquithian leftovers – really believed in him or his plans; they were, anyway, a colourless lot. The Liberal revival depended on one man's force and another man's brains. Lloyd George was the political tycoon; Keynes the thinker.

On the inquiry, Keynes served on an executive committee of a dozen, headed by Walter Layton. There were initially five specialist committees: state and industry (Ramsay Muir), labour and the trade unions (E. D. Simon), unemployment (Lloyd George), pay and status (E. H. Gilpin), industrial and financial organisation (Keynes), staffed by twenty-five supporting experts and politicians. Keynes's committee was responsible for covering 'the organisation of business' and 'national finance'. These reflected the interest of the author of the *Tract on Monetary Reform* and 'The End of *Laissez-Faire*' in stabilising a 'sticky' economy. Keynes was not given (or did not choose) the unemployment problem. One wonders what the result would have been had he and his fellow economists on the inquiry – Layton, Henderson, Robertson, Stamp – had the unemployment brief.

While the industrial inquiry got down to business, Keynes was educating himself, for the first and last time, in the practical problems faced by a declining British industry. Unlike Marshall, he had little respect for the business vocation but under the influence of Shaw and Wells he began to take a more favourable attitude to the tycoon as a type of social reformer; and to see the evolution of big business as providing a motivational Middle Way between profit-maximisation and public service. But these speculations remained essentially abstract. What chiefly impressed Keynes about British businessmen was their stupidity and laziness. He was a firm believer in the three-generation cycle: the man of energy and imagination creates the business: the son coasts along; the grandson goes bankrupt. In 'Am I a Liberal?' he wrote, 'I believe that the seeds of the intellectual decay of Individualistic Capitalism are to be found in ... the hereditary principle.'

Despite his strictures on business competence, Keynes took with surprising levity the problem of training people for a business career. He rejected the notion of courses for business studies. It was a mistake for a university, he said in a radio discussion in 1927, to 'attempt vocational training. Their business is to develop a man's intelligence and character in such a way that he can pick up relatively quickly the special details of that business he turns to subsequently.'[19] He was about to apply the theory to himself.

Keynes was drawn into the problems of coal and textiles – Britain's two chief decaying industries – by the return to the gold standard and the General Strike. In *The Economic Consequences of Mr Churchill* he had argued that going back to gold at the pre-war parity had put two shillings on each ton of coal, logically entailing a 10 per cent wage reduction. A year later, however, his emphasis had switched to reducing surplus capacity. The main need was 'to transfer men out of the industry, to curtail production and to raise export prices'. He suggested that the owners form a cartel to restrict output. In an article published in the *Nation* on 13 November 1926, Keynes contrasted the situation in two decaying industries, coal and cotton. Coal had ruined itself by uncontrolled overproduction, cotton by 'organised short-time extending over five years'. He calculated that half of Lancashire's business in coarser cottons had gone permanently to Japan. But instead of concentrating production on its most efficient units – mainly those producing finer cottons – Lancashire had kept its capacity and workforce through short-time working which raised its costs of production above competitive levels by adding additional overhead costs to wage levels which were too high. Reduced sales, countered by short-time working, leading to higher costs was a 'cumulative road to perdition only limited by the rate at which other countries can erect new spindles'. The termination of short-time working was urgently needed through 'amalgamation, grouping, or elimination of mills'.

This was explosive stuff: here was a mere theoretician telling practical men how to run their affairs! However, there were some who were willing to listen. On 16 November 1926, the Short-Time Committee of the Federation of Master Cotton Spinners invited Keynes to Manchester to discuss the points raised in his article. Keynes came to Manchester on 22 November. His meeting with the Committee was followed by a communiqué in which he advocated a cartel to fix minimum selling prices and assign quotas.[20] This rapid shift in Keynes's position is typical of his flexibility. The idea of permanently shutting down productive capacity was still too shocking to contemplate. So Keynes put his weight behind a more flexible and efficient scheme for market-sharing, with a provision for quotas to be transferred from weaker to stronger firms. This was the basis on which the Cotton Yarn Association was set up on 18 February 1927, headed by John Ryan. When free-riding caused it to fail, Keynes backed a proposal to form a combine of mills to rationalise production and buy up surplus capacity. Partly as a result of these efforts the Lancashire Cotton Corporation was formed, with Bank of England backing, early in 1929; much of the management came from the Cotton Yarn Association. Keynes commented, 'One is disposed to murmur with Galileo – It moves all the same.'

Keynes used to come away from Manchester with feelings of 'intense pessimism'. All his prejudices against third-generation men were confirmed. Late in the Second World War he lamented that Hitler's bombers had not been able to destroy every factory in Lancashire 'at an hour when the directors were sitting there and no one else'. Immediately, Keynes's involvement with cotton reinforced his pessimism about curing unemployment by tackling the supply-side problems of British industry. The rocks could not be shifted; they had to be submerged in a rising tide of prosperity.

Keynes's education in the realities of British business life fertilised his contributions to the Liberal industrial inquiry. Specifically, they strengthened his conviction that the era of the individual family firm was over, and the day of the combine had arrived.

Little of the work of the inquiry has survived in Keynes's papers. According to his engagement diary, his committee met at his house in London several times in the winter of 1926–7. At a plenary session at Churt from 8 to 11 April 1927, two committees, Keynes's and Ramsay Muir's, were entrusted with preparing a complete draft of the Report by 17 June, and 'readjusting and readorning' the 'Liberal blather' went on all through 1927. There were four more weekends at Churt – 24–26 June, 17–19 September, 28–30 October and 9–11 December – to hammer the report into final shape, Lloyd George providing a fleet of Daimlers to ferry members of the inquiry to and from his house. Finally it was done. *Britain's Industrial Future* was published, in yellow covers, at the beginning of February 1928. '[It] has had rather a bad press,' Keynes wrote to Lydia on 5 February, 'but I daresay it deserves it. Long-winded, speaking when it has nothing to say, as well as when it has, droning at intervals "Liberals, Liberals all are we, gallant-hearted Liberals." It would have been so much better at half the length splashing only what is new and interesting and important.'

Keynes was right: the report is heavy reading. 'How many people', it asks on p. 78, 'have any clear idea of the constitution of the Metropolitan Water Board?' and then goes on to expound it. The report inhabits the world of means, not of ends. Nevertheless it addressed the central political problems of the day: the role of the state in the economy (though, of course, without reference to the later Keynesian theory of demand management), and class conciliation in industry. On both these issues it tried to carve out a Middle Way between individualism and state socialism.

At the end of April 1927, Keynes had prepared a draft on 'The Financial and Industrial Structure of the State', based on a talk to Liberal candidates in January, which was intended to provide a general framework for the whole report. Little of it survives in the final version. But it is the most compact expression of his general approach at this time, though doubtless tailored to the needs of his Party. Its main theme is the contrast between the nineteenth-century world of small private firms operating in a continually expanding economy and the twentieth-century world of joint-stock companies, run by salaried managers under the nominal control of anonymous, ignorant shareholders, faced with large-scale structural adjustment. The tendency towards cartel, merger and monopoly was driven not only by the technical conditions of production and the financial advantages of large-scale industry in raising money from the Stock Exchange, but by the menace of surplus capacity. Adaptation had become both more necessary and more difficult. Thus the picture of society painted by the theoretical individualist no longer 'fits the facts as a whole'. Great businesses of vast scale, salaried management and diffused ownership had to be accepted as naturally evolved, containing elements of efficiency and inefficiency. Law and central organisation needed to be adjusted 'to the actual state of affairs'.

Keynes went on to give a list of 'the various types of socialised, semi-socialised, and other State-regulated enterprises'; claimed that they controlled two-thirds of the total capital of the country; suggested that 'evolution' was tending to convert private companies into public or semi-official boards, with capital in the form of fixed-interest bonds rather than shares; and argued that such boards would take over increasing parts of industry, that there was no reason to suppose that they would be less efficient than the boards of large private companies and that 'the choice between a Public Board and a Private Company' would 'resolve itself into little more than a question of the appointment of the Directors'.[21]

This draft brought strong criticism from the banker Robert Brand, whose Liberalism was distinctly more right-wing than Keynes's. (He had written a pamphlet *Why I Am Not a Socialist* in 1925, in which he had defended profit as a reward for risk and argued that state enterprises would involve the community in vast losses because they were sheltered from the failure which private enterprise visits on the incompetent.) Brand argued that the idea that two-thirds of large-scale industry was no longer administered by private enterprise was definitely misleading. Apart from public utility enterprises, not a single manufacturing or commercial enterprise appeared on Keynes's list.

> I certainly hold strongly to the opinion that the world is essentially a 'chancy' and risky place, and will always remain so.... I would prefer the losses resulting from the risks inherent in almost every sphere of life coming out into the open ... rather than being hidden and concealed as they are where public or semi-public corporations can cover them up by a recourse to rates and taxes....[22]

The issues here split liberalism straight down the middle. Keynes was much less willing to take *social* risks than was Brand. This was connected with a different judgement on the link between efficiency and profit. Brand came to industrial problems from the side of business, or money-making. 'Knowledge of real life', he wrote in *Why I Am Not a Socialist*, showed that courts of efficiency, audit and professional honour, such as the Webbs proposed, were no substitute for the court of profit. Keynes came to the same problems from the side of academic life, administration, public service. The necessity of profit as a spur to effort, he wrote in his report, was greatly exaggerated. 'It has never been even supposed to be true ... of the soldier, the statesman, the civil servant, the teacher, the scientist, the technical expert.' And what was true of this group was true of most people: 'a certain salary, plus the hope of promotion or of a bonus, is what the generality of mankind prefers'.[23] Thus the trade-off between stability and efficiency could be made more favourable than Brand supposed. Perhaps Keynes was already starting to idealise his youthful period in the India Office: at the time he had complained of 'government by dotardry'.

Brand's objections proved decisive. Most of Keynes's evolutionary speculations were omitted from Book II; a strong section on the virtues of individualism was inserted;[24] the suggestion that the public concern might become the typical unit of industrial organisation was dropped; and proposals for reorganising business structure largely limited to making the various existing forms of public concern more 'lively and efficient'.[25]

However, there is a further typical theme in Keynes's section of the report. *Britain's Industrial Future* proposed that the investment funds of the public concerns, whether borrowed or (as with the road fund) raised by taxation, should be pooled, and segregated into a capital budget, to be spent under the direction of a national investment board. Keynes estimated that the board would influence or control the spending of £100m p.a., or one-fifth of annual national savings, using it to finance 'new capital expenditure by all central, local, or *ad hoc* offficial bodies . . .' as well as to make advances for new capital improvements to railways, or even to private companies, on the lines of the Trade Facilities Acts.[26] In addition, the state should issue national investment bonds for capital development, thus slowly replacing dead-weight debt by productive debt.

A few typical Keynes touches enliven Books II and V for which he was mainly responsible. Ignorance, chapter XI proclaimed, is the root of the 'chief political and social evils of the day'. 'How can economic science become a true science, capable, perhaps, of benefiting the human lot as much as all the other sciences put together, so long as the economist, unlike other scientists, has to grope for and guess at the relevant data of experience?' It concluded, 'The nationalising of knowledge is the one case for nationalisation which is overwhelmingly right.'[27] In a striking phrase, the process of revaluing the currency was likened to the 'once fashionable medical policy of "bleeding" ... [it] is infallibly accompanied, whenever taken, by severe trade depression'.[28] The Bank of England should be more accountable and less secretive in its operations;[29] the national accounts should be reformed to distinguish between the capital and current account, and between national and local taxes and expenditure. There was an interesting suggestion for a separate, or earmarked, social services budget.[30] Keynes's summary of the report is prescient: 'It may ... have a good deal of influence on future political programmes, whether or not there is a Liberal Party to push the matter through.'[31]

25

The Riddle of Savings

I. HATCHING DENNIS'S EGG

In politics and economic policy Keynes worked most closely with Hubert Henderson; in economic theory his main partner was Dennis Holme Robertson. From 1913 to 1930 it is almost impossible to say which ideas were Keynes's and which Robertson's. They started sparking each other off when Robertson was writing his dissertation on business cycles in 1912 and 1913. Their open divergence started only in 1931. It is a tribute to Cambridge's 'passion for truth' that they worked together harmoniously for so long, despite the great difference in their methods and characters; and even though they fell out in the 1930s, there was a partial reconciliation during the Second World War.

Keynes's great respect for Robertson's ability was reinforced by personal affection. Also much in their background and training was the same: both were scholars at Eton, though Robertson was a classical scholar and had no mathematics; both were pupils of Marshall and Pigou at Cambridge; both had artistic leanings; both were excellent stylists; and both had a Victorian sense of duty. But Keynes was much more of a gambler, in private life and in ideas – and, at the highest level, more creative.

Robertson had had a brilliant undergraduate career at Cambridge before the war, to which was added a fine war record which included the award of the Military Cross. His books, *A Study of Industrial Fluctuation* (1915), *Money* (1922), and *The Control of Industry* (1923) – the last two written at Keynes's behest as part of the Cambridge Economics Handbook series – had established him by the early 1920s as one of Cambridge's leading economists. However, beneath the glittering successes was a lonely, vulnerable, self-torturing man, whose fastidious mind and sense of piety fitted him more to be a critic of other people's ideas than an innovator of his own. He craved the love of young men, especially of the Kingsman Dadie Rylands, but could not command it. Although only thirty-five in 1925, he already looked older than his age, with a domed, bald head which 'poked in and out of his shoulders like a tortoise'.[1] He was a fine amateur actor, with particular success in the roles of sly or foolish old men: his Justice Swallow was a triumph. He had a feline playfulness. Each chapter of *Money* was headed by a quotation from Alice in Wonderland; the question of what money is was discussed by a 'Bradbury' and its interlocutor; Robertson called a person's bank deposit his 'chequery', 'because it is both a breeding ground and homing-place for cheques, as a rookery is for rooks'. But Robertson's humour could turn waspish. Wrapped up in literary allusions, subtleties, and neo-logisms his economics was rather like a secret garden – inviting but impen-etrable. As John Vaizey put it, he was 'easy to like, but hard to persevere with'.[2]

Robertson's mind seems so odd and eccentric, his personality so but-toned up, that it is tempting to draw a connection between his own character and the character of his economics. Gordon Fletcher has made a brave stab at doing so. In Fletcher's view the tension in Robertson's character between his 'desired self' and 'duteous self' gave his economics a 'curious half-way house appearance', both 'innovative and fettered'. The former was a product of his leaping intellect, the latter of 'a temperamentally determined need for unbroken links with his origins . . .'.[3] The thought here is that Robertson's personal insecurities made him unwilling to let go of classical economics, which abstracted from the complexities of real life, and provided for him a substitute religion. That is why he could add to classical foundations to the point of logical absurdity, but shrank from demolishing them.

Although Keynes and Robertson stimulated each other intellectually, one can already see a difference in approach between the two men, which was to widen over the years. From his first book onwards, Robertson had set short-term stabilisation problems in the context of securing long-run econ-omic growth, in contrast to Keynes's indifference to the long-run, summed up in his famous remark: 'In the long run we are all dead.' Robertson thought that industrial fluctuations were inseparable from the use of fixed capital, in turn inseperable from economic progress: 'out of the welter of industrial dislocation the great permanent riches of the future are gener-ated'.[4] Keynes did not agree: he aimed to avoid fluctuations, Robertson to limit them. Robertson was better disposed than was Keynes to the *ethics* of capitalist accumulation, being impressed, as was Marshall, by its sacrificial – and therefore altruistic – nature, whereas Keynes, as we have seen, despised and mocked what he called 'love of money'. Though before the war Robert-son had worried that people unthinkingly sacrificed too much for economic growth, in the changed conditions after the war, he worried that people would not *save* enough to keep investment going. Keynes, by contrast, came to worry that they would not *invest* enough to use up what a life-denying Puritan psychology had habituated them to save.

Robertson's *A Study of Industrial Fluctuation* was a 'real' (as opposed to monetary) theory of the business cycle. The upward phase is started by new investment opportunities, such as those provided by inventions. However, competition between entrepreneurs and the long gestation period of fixed capital outlay multiply the chances of miscalculation and lead to more investment being undertaken than is profitable, producing an inevitable collapse. By over-investment, then, Robertson simply meant that in the upswing of a cycle more investment is made than would pay all the investors, leading to a decline in the demand for capital goods: it is the downward revision in the marginal utility of capital goods relative to consumer goods which brings about the collapse

Keynes rejected Robertson's main conclusion that more investment could normally occur than was profitable. He was much more interested in Robertson's *secondary* thesis that over-investment might occur in relation to available saving, and it was this particular tangled thread that they followed together in the 1920s. The stimulus had been given by the Frenchman Marcel Labordère, a brilliant amateur economist whom Keynes had met in 1911. Labordère had been led to philosophise about the causes of financial crises by his own ruin in the great stock exchange crash of 1907. The result was three brilliantly suggestive parables in the style of Xenophon. His conclusion was that the business cycle results from over-investment relative to saving. Introducing money into his more realistic third parable, Labordère divides the investment fund into 'capitaux réels' and 'capitaux apparents' – the latter being bank credit. This extra source of funds can keep investment running ahead of 'real' saving for a time, until interest rates rise and bring about a collapse.[5] Keynes passed these thoughts on to Robertson, whose dissertation supervisor he was, and Robertson incorporated the idea of 'overinvestment in relation to saving' as a possible cause of crisis into his thesis on industrial fluctuations. The ideas of Labordère, in turn, formed the basis of Keynes's talk of December 1913 to the Political Economy Club, entitled 'How Far Are Bankers Responsible for the Alternations of Crisis and Depression?' (see above p. 132). It was his first attempt to integrate monetary theory and the saving–investment relationship into the explanation of business fluctuations. But it was not developed, and he did not return to it till after he had finished his *Tract on Monetary Reform.*

In his textbook *Money* (1922), Robertson, following the Keynes of 1913, clearly identified bank credit as a source of loanable funds for investment. Credit creation forces up consumer prices. All those who could not increase their money incomes in line with inflation (to some extent wage-earners but particularly bondholders or 'old widows') were 'forced', by having to reduce their consumption, to 'pay' for the increased spending of entrepreneurs or governments. The concept of 'forced saving' – which goes back to Joplin and Bentham   had re entered the economic literature, put there by reflection on how governments had financed their war-time spending. Keynes's chapter on the 'inflation tax' in his *Tract on Monetary Reform* discusses how inflation enables a government to spend what private households have to forgo. To obviate 'the inflation tax' Keynes wanted the Bank of England to keep prices stable. He denied that inflation as such could create additional resources for investment: it could only redistribute resources between different sections of the community. Robertson, on the other hand, believed that inflation provided an important source of loanable funds to businessmen, enabling them to create new capital assets. His *Banking Policy and the Price Level* (1926) was conceived as a critique of Keynes's stress on preventing any fluctuations in the price level. 'I do not feel confident,' Robertson wrote, 'that a policy which, in the pursuit of stability of prices, output, and employment, had nipped in the bud the English railway boom of the forties, or the American railway boom of 1869–71, or the German electrical boom of the nineties, would have been on balance beneficial to the populations concerned.'[6]

For over a year in 1924–5, Keynes was heavily involved in what he called 'the hatching of Dennis's egg', and their debates largely revolved round the question of whether inflation could be an additional source of saving. Keynes denied that inflation *automatically* generated more saving, or 'lacking' as Robertson called it. Inflation could produce new 'lacking' only by *inducing* the community as a whole to save a higher proportion than formerly out of its money income. He later concluded that any 'induced lacking' (forced saving) was 'too precarious a source of additional savings to deserve separate notice'.[7] In his book, Robertson thanked Keynes for having alerted him to the existence of 'induced lacking', while denying that it was the only source of additional investment funds created by inflation.[8]

Nevertheless, Keynes's engagement with Robertson at this point in his life was crucial in the development of his own ideas. As compared to the *Tract on Monetary Reform*, Keynes's explanation for fluctuations in prices and output had shifted from changes in the quantity of money to disturbances to the saving–investment relationship. But the hardest part of the work was still to come. Later he was to tell Robertson that 'I certainly date all my emancipation from the discussions between us which preceded your *Banking Policy and the Price Level*.'[9] In retrospect, Keynes's rejection of Robertson's 'forced saving' doctrine was a vital negative decision. As he explained to Robertson in 1931:

> When you were working on your *Banking Policy and the Price Level*, and we were discussing it, we both believed that inequalities between saving and investment – using those terms with the degree of vagueness with which we used them at that date – only arose as a result of what one might call an act of inflation or deflation on the part of the banking system. I worked on this basis for quite a time, but in the end I came to the conclusion that this would not do. As a result of getting what were, in my opinion, more clear definitions of saving and investment, I found that the salient phenomena could come about without any overt act on the part of the banking system.[10]

II. WRITING THE *TREATISE*

Keynes had written to Lydia from Cambridge on Sunday, 30 November 1924, 'I have begun the new book! – today, and have written one page. This is the first sentence: – "I begin this book, not in the logical order, but so as to bring before the reader's mind, as soon as possible, what is most significant in what I have to say."' If only he had stuck to this intention! Early drafts of the tables of contents show that Keynes's intention was to study the theory of money in relation to the 'credit cycle' for the practical purpose of devising an optimum banking policy. If fluctuations in bank lending round the available volume of 'real credit' caused both inflation and deflation and boom and slump, a policy of credit stabilisation by the central bank would simultaneously avoid both phenomena. We can see here why Keynes was so reluctant to abandon the quantity theory: it could be used both to explain and to cure the diseases of the macro-economy.

The train thus set going in 1924 did not change direction much over the next three years: it simply became longer and filled up with passengers. Unlike the *General Theory*, *A Treatise on Money* was composed in solitude and was not circulated for comment until it was too late to change. Robertson was away for almost a year from 1926–7 – partly to escape from Keynes's suffocating embrace. Ralph Hawtrey was at Harvard in 1928–9. The criticisms he made on his return were fundamental, but were too late for Keynes to use. The 'Prof' (Pigou) was no help. He hated discussing economics anyway, and by 1928 was seriously unwell with heart trouble. Keynes found his book on *Industrial Fluctuations* (1927) 'rather miserable – perhaps Mrs. Marshall is right that he should have married, his mind is dead, he just arranges in a logical order all the things he knew before'.[11] Most important of all, although Keynes gave lectures from successive drafts of his book, he had no graduate students able or willing to engage with him on points of theory. This was in strong contrast to the powerful support group which would assist in the birth of the *General Theory*.

Keynes started on the second chapter in February 1925, and worked on it intermittently till April. However, little more was done in 1925, and it was not till April 1926 that he was back at work in his new study at Tilton. By the end of August he had drafted about 55,000 words of Book I entitled 'The Theory of Money'. This now included a 'fundamental equation of price', together with the 'variability of its elements' (though the drafts suggest this was still the old Fisher quantity equation). By 31 August 'the plurality of price levels' and the problem of index numbers (which he had dealt with in his Adam Smith Prize Essay in 1909) had appeared; as well as the chapter on 'the *modus operandi* of bank rate'. By 12 September he had evidently started work on Book II, 'The Theory of Credit'. He had made sufficient progress to write to Daniel Macmillan on 22 September, 'I am now at work on a serious treatise to be entitled "The Theory of Money and Credit", for publication about a year hence or a little later.' At this stage, all that Keynes contemplated was the two sections – Money and Credit – running to between 100,000 and 120,000 words, and nineteen chapters.[12] A ledger entry at R. and R. Clark, his Edinburgh printer, dated 28 September 1926, reads: 'On the basis of 120,000 words, with 300 to the page, the extent will be about 400 pp....'

Keynes got back to writing again at Cambridge on 21 January 1927. On Friday, 28 January he looked forward to three peaceful writing days – 'A happy country has no history' – and had redrafted one of the chapters. He went down to Tilton to collect some others, and forgot to bring them back. By 27 May he was 'rewriting successfully one of the bits I was troubled about at Tilton'. Work went on through the summer of 1927, Keynes resisting an invitation from the Courtaulds to join them in Greece. (Lydia said she had told Sam that 'if you were searing about your book, no one could sway you the other way'.) Three tables of contents from this period show an alarming tendency for the book (now renamed *A Treatise on Money*) to expand. There were now five books (or sections) and twenty-six chapters. Keynes seemed to be aiming at a completeness appropriate to a full-blown Treatise rather than splashing what was new and important. In retrospect, this decision to expand the book into a treatise can be seen as a mistake. Too much of his intellectual capital was being locked into a fixed investment, at a time when circumstances and his own ideas were exceptionally fluid.

On 18 January 1928 Keynes reported the arrival of a large packet of proofs from Clark's in Edinburgh. But now there was a major derailment. Dennis Robertson had returned from a trip to Asia in April 1927, looking 'only moderate – rather older, *very* bald, with the bones of his skull showing more than they did ... very Chinese'.[13] The major impact of Robertson's return was to cause Keynes to abandon his notion that the sole aim of monetary policy should be to stabilise the price level. For a rise in the price level might be required to reverse a previous 'profit deflation'. An important additional impetus to this line of thought came from Reginald McKenna. Keynes reviewed a collection of his annual speeches to shareholders as chairman of the Midland Bank on 2 November 1928.[14] McKenna's central contention was that a policy of credit restriction to avoid inflation *when there were large unemployed resources* was tantamount to policy of 'continuous deflation'.[15] A correct criterion for banking policy would, in other words, need to have regard to appropriate credit policy for different phases of the cycle, and not just to the situation of full employment.

Keynes's new line of thinking is contained in a draft of the *Treatise* which seems to date from the autumn–winter of 1928:

> Nevertheless, it must be admitted that the advocates of price stability, amongst whom I number myself, have erred in the past when their words have seemed to indicate price stability as the sole objective of monetary policy to the exclusion of the right adjustment of the supply of bank credit to the business world's demands for it – or at least as an objective which, if reached, would necessarily involve the simultaneous attainment of all associated objectives. To speak or write in this way is unduly to simplify the problem by overlooking the dual character of the functions of the banking system [to achieve price stability and equilibrium between saving and investment].... Mr D. H. Robertson's acute and profound criticisms (in his *Banking Policy and the Price Level*), emphasising the other side of the problem, have therefore been calculated to exert a most salutary influence on contemporary thought (and have done so on mine). On the other hand, Mr. Robertson ... seems to me, in that book, not to state the problem clearly enough as a problem of reconciliation of purposes – and, if necessary, of compromise.[16]

To his American publisher, Alfred Harcourt, Keynes wrote on 26 September 1928: 'I have devoted the whole of this summer to my Treatise on Money, thus completing four years' work on it.... I should say that four-fifths is now completely finished. I am hopeful that I shall have finished it before Easter [1929], and that it may be published in this country about May.'[17]

On 10 December 1928 Keynes still thought that there was a reasonable chance of the *Treatise* appearing in 'the first half of 1929' in its single volume, five-book form.[18] By 18 February 1929, he was postponing publication till 1 October. But the autumn publication plan was abandoned too. The book had been derailed once more by the intellectual controversies surrounding the general election of May 1929. 'I am ashamed to say', Keynes wrote to Daniel Macmillan on 20 August, 'that after I had got more than 440 pages into paged revise I had to come to the conclusion that certain chapters must be drastically rewritten, and the whole very considerably rearranged.' January 1930 was to be the new publication date, and there were now to be two volumes.

III. ASPECTS OF KEYNES

Like most authors, Keynes complained endlessly about interruptions to his
work of his own devising. Apart from his fixed commitments in Cambridge
and London, there were what the edition of his *Collected Writings* calls his
'Activities' – hundreds of pages of them for this period. Gold and Russia
took up his time and energy in 1925. Much of 1926 and 1927 was taken up
with his Liberal Party and cotton work. There was an endless succession of
one-off events. Despite his efficient work habits, it is small wonder that he
lost the thread of his ideas, left chapters mouldering for months unread at
Tilton. By the end of 1928 the complaints of tiredness grow more insistent.
These circumstances, quite as much as the changing tack of his own ideas,
explain why the different parts, or phases, of the *Treatise* fit so ill together.

In February 1927, Keynes finally resigned from the 'Chinese torture' of
the University Council, but he was as heavily involved as ever in the college
building programme. The Annual Audit dinner of 1927 provided him, as
first bursar, with a chance to test one of his favourite theories:

> The most interesting part [he wrote to Lydia on 18 November 1927] was
> the negotiation with a farmer who has been in a state of violent quarrel
> with the College for 7 years. I had never seen him before but had been
> led to believe he was an impossible character. But he came up for the
> dinner last night, and as soon as I cast eyes on his *hands* I knew that all
> this was a complete mistake – that he was very nice, absolutely honest
> and capable, and that the only thing wrong with him was a violent
> temper which we had managed somehow to arouse. So I proceeded to
> ... behave to him as though he were perfectly sensible and nice with
> the result that we came to a complete settlement.... Hands! Hands!
> Hands! Nothing else is worth looking at. In 10 seconds I had completely
> revised my idea of his character.

While the *Treatise* meandered on its rather solitary way, Cambridge
economics was coming to life. These were the days before the great Cambridge schism of the 1930s. A younger cohort of economists, which was to
play a central part in Keynes's story, was moving into position. Of the
coming stars, Joan Maurice and Austin Robinson, married in 1926, returned
to Cambridge at the end of 1928, after a spell in India, he to a lectureship in
economics. Austin Robinson was more an academic politician and administrator than a theorist, but his wife Joan, who joined the faculty in 1931, was
a woman of outstanding brains, personality and looks, to whom the word
'blue-stocking' applies in its best sense. Photographs show a serious young

woman with intense, questioning eyes, and hair plaited into two buns, rather like ear muffs. She brought to economics 'the extraordinary ability to zero in on the heart of the matter and in a few well-chosen words to convey its essence. She had an irritating penchant to dismiss as nonsense ideas with which she did not agree.' In the 1930s she was to be intimately involved in the Keynesian Revolution, which she later tried to generalise into a long-period theory of employment.[19]

Keynes had had good economics students before, but Richard Ferdinand Kahn was the first who was able and willing to help him in his own work. Kahn was taught by Gerald Shove, and, once a fortnight on Saturday, with three others, was supervised by Keynes. 'I actually trembled as I was about to enter Keynes's rooms in College for my first supervision ...', Kahn recalled. On 29 April 1928, Keynes wrote to Lydia, 'Yesterday my favourite pupil Kahn wrote me one of the best answers I have ever had from a pupil – he must get a first-class.'

When Kahn first met Keynes at the age of twenty-two he was a slight, serious, rather beautiful young man, with masses of thick, black hair. He spoke with an air of quiet authority, which contrasted oddly with extreme nervousness about his health – a lifelong obsession. Of German ancestry, he remained an orthodox Jew all his life, more faithful to the letter than the spirit: he would get his gyp (college servant) to open his letters on the sabbath, even though he wasn't allowed to himself. Keynes, who could never resist classification, took to referring to him as 'the little Rabbi'. To friends of his own age he was Ferdinand, which somehow seemed more appropriate than Richard. He was a much better mathematician than most of those in Keynes's circle; he recalled Keynes himself as being a poor mathematician by 1927; his ability to think mathematically was to be of crucial help to Keynes in the early 1930s. His mind was remarkably meticulous and he took great pains to help his friends. His relationship with Keynes was a prototype of the other important relationships of his life, particularly that with Joan Robinson. He was the self-effacing backroom boy rather than the star of the show; an excellent listener, with a hard core of analytic power.

Kahn duly got his first, and stayed on at King's to compete for a college fellowship, immersing himself in an examination of Marshall's theory of the short period. This led him into another area of criticism of Marshall then opening up at Cambridge under the influence of Piero Sraffa. It was Sraffa who gave Cambridge economics its shot in the arm in the late 1920s. Robertson's *Banking Policy and the Price Level* was considered largely incomprehensible by the young. Keynes's *Treatise on Money* had not yet appeared. Sraffa's ideas filled the gap. 'Sraffa is established here and in a terror of nerves over his lecture,' Keynes reported to Lydia on 9 October 1927. 'He asked me yesterday whether he could not suddenly become ill and run away.'

Sraffa had first introduced himself to Keynes in London in December

1921, when doing some research at the London School of Economics. He was then twenty-three, a tall, erect law graduate of Turin University, who had written a thesis on Italian monetary management during the war. Although he was to become professor of economics at the University of Cagliari in 1926, his well-known socialist sympathies and his friendship with the communist leader Antonio Gramsci made life difficult for him in fascist Italy. At this time, his intellectual interests overlapped with Keynes's, and he produced the Italian translation of *A Tract on Monetary Reform*. But Sraffa had already started to work on problems of classical value theory bequeathed by Ricardo – a lifetime obsession which led him away from the short-run monetary problems which preoccupied Keynes.

After 1924, Sraffa started coming over to England regularly. It was his article, 'The Laws of Return under Competitive Conditions', appearing in the *Economic Journal* of December 1926, which caused so much excitement in Cambridge. The question which Sraffa posed was: how is equilibrium reached under conditions of falling cost curves and 'imperfect competition'?

If Sraffa's ideas gave Cambridge its second (that is, post-Marshallian) wind,[20] it was not a wind which filled Keynes's sails. Although he found Sraffa's work 'very interesting and original'[21] – and indeed got him his University lectureship and rooms and high-table rights at King's – he was too absorbed in his own project to see its relevance to his concerns. Sraffa never himself seems to have considered the possible bearing of 'increasing returns' on the unemployment problem. Moreover, Keynes did not think the theoretical problems for value theory raised by Sraffa of serious practical importance – an attitude he was to take to the whole of Sraffa's work. Any tendency towards monopoly, he thought, would be offset by the well-known tendency of long-established firms to decay. More helpful, he felt, was a two-hour discussion he had with Sraffa on the Pure Theory of the Credit Cycle on 2 March 1928, leading to the correction of a few 'small mistakes' in his book. Still, it remains a puzzle that the two escape routes from Marshallian orthodoxy – the one associated with Sraffa and imperfect competition, the other with Keynes and effective demand – never converged in Keynes's lifetime, though leading Keynesians like Kahn and Joan Robinson were heavily involved in both 'revolutions'.

Sraffa gradually took root in Cambridge and became one of Keynes's best friends. 'Pottering with Piero' round the antiquarian bookshops on Saturday afternoons became his substitute for riding with Sebastian Sprott, or buying indifferent furniture. Sraffa was someone Keynes liked to worry about. He was negligent about his clothes, had a horror of lecturing and took drastic action to evade it: 'Piero *was* ... to have given his lecture tomorrow,' Keynes wrote to Lydia on 16 January 1929. 'He sat next to me in hall talking in high spirits and came to the combination room afterwards, then he rose from the table, delivered the whole of his dinner on the mat, lay on the ground almost fainting with no pulse at all, was doped with brandy – and so won't lecture to-morrow after all! I am having (once more) to make the necessary announcement.' His aversion to teaching became so profound that Keynes had to invent a number of jobs to keep him in Cambridge – including the editorship of the Royal Economic Society's edition of Ricardo's papers. Sraffa was addicted to Sherlock Holmes stories, and he now followed every clue to new caches of Ricardo papers with a persistence which the great detective would have envied. But he took much longer to solve his cases. In 1933 Keynes puffed the 'forthcoming complete and definitive edition of the works of David Ricardo … to be published in the course of the present year'. In fact the first four volumes of the eleven-volume edition appeared in 1951. By 1928 Sraffa had already prepared a manuscript of a slim theoretical volume. It appeared only in 1960, under the title *Production of Commodities by Commodities*, and fuelled a famous debate on capital theory.

Someone who took thirty-two years to publish an eighty-seven-page 'prelude to a critique' was clearly not inspired by any great sense of urgency. Sraffa felt much the same about public writing as Keynes did about public speaking: 'I confess that always, when I read something which I have written, I feel such a deep disgust that I cannot resist the temptation to destroy it, unless I have a definite engagement to deliver it.'[22] This neurotic fastidiousness, as well as his great subtlety of mind, endeared him to Keynes. Passionately devoted to his mother, Sraffa was a lame eagle, to be protected from an unkind world.

A year after Sraffa's arrival, the Divine Fool started knocking at the gate. 'A letter from Ludwig', wrote Keynes to Lydia on 28 November 1928. 'He … wants to come and stay with me here for a fortnight. Am I strong enough? Perhaps if I do no work between now and then, I shall be.' Wittgenstein had given up teaching in his Austrian village in 1926, returning to Vienna to build an obsessively functionalist house for his sister. Now the house was finished, and Wittgenstein turned again to philosophy to cure his intellectual and emotional headaches. On 17 January 1929 Keynes wrote, 'Ludwig … arrives to-morrow.… Pray for me!' And the next day: 'Well, God has arrived. I met him on the 5.15 train. He has a plan to stay in Cambridge permanently.' While God whistled Bach in the drawing room, Keynes crept to his study to write his letter to Lydia. 'I see that the fatigue is going to be crushing. But I must not let him talk to me for more than two or three hours a day.' Keynes fled to London a day earlier than usual. He returned to find God in very good spirits, because the authorities had agreed to let him become a research student under Frank Ramsey. (In June 1929 he successfully submitted the *Tractatus* for a doctorate of philosophy.) Complaining that he 'was not born to live permanently with a clergyman', Keynes gave Wittgenstein notice to quit on 2 February; Wittgenstein moved in with Ramsey and his wife, then with Maurice Dobb, though not before Keynes had caught a savage cold from him which required ten days' absence from University.

What did they talk about for two or three hours a day – or rather, what did Wittgenstein talk about, for he disliked interruptions to his monologues? Much of the conversation must have been philosophical. Keynes's interest in philosophy had been kept alive by Ramsey, a seventeen-stone presence at King's, still, incredibly, only twenty-five, as well as by Richard Braithwaite. Ramsey, Braithwaite and Wittgenstein had rejected the central contention of Keynes's *Treatise on Probability*, that probability is a logical relation. The intellectual current of the time – and one must add here the overwhelming influence of Freud – was running strongly against the pre-war rationalism of Keynes's generation. Ramsey himself had been psychoanalysed in Vienna, to cure him of his unsettling passion for married women; what is rational, he said, is what works. For Wittgenstein, philosophy was a kind of inspired madness. There is talk of a lunch at which Ramsey, Wittgenstein and Sraffa discussed probability with Keynes. It is hard not to believe that Keynes's intercourse with the most powerful philosophical minds of the day shook him out of his comfortable pre-war certainties, which, of course, were bound up with the belief in 'automatic' progress. Who could now credibly assume that people behaved rationally? Or that, even if they tried to, logical intuition could tell them what was rational to do or believe?

The research leading to nuclear fission had already started in Cambridge's Cavendish Laboratory, highlighting the contrast between the weakness of philosophy and the power of experimental science. Keynes knew the brilliant young Russian atomic physicist Peter Kapitsa, though not well, shrewdly predicting that he would go back to the Soviet Union, 'because he is a wild, disinterested, vain, and absolutely uncivilised creature, perfectly suited by nature to be a Bolshie'.[23] The obsession with the power of science had, by the late 1920s, produced the first communist 'cell' at Cambridge. They were mainly young scientists, who knew nothing about politics, but saw Marxism as the first true 'science of society' and Stalin's Russia as the first experimental laboratory for testing out its theories.[24] The main link between Keynes's circle and the Marxist scientists round Kapitsa and the crystallographer J. D. Bernal was Alister Watson, 'a very clever mathematician', later physicist, who came up to Trinity College from Winchester in 1926.[25] Watson became the leading Apostle of the late 1920s; Anthony Blunt, also at Trinity, learnt his Marxism from Watson and was 'born' into the Society in May 1928. Both stayed on at Cambridge in the 1930s.

Keynes was never in the least influenced by Marx, but he too was infected with a spirit of boldness, a new willingness to experiment in social and economic policy. The switch in allegiance from Asquith to Lloyd George was symbolic of this: from the man of balance to the man of power. Everything had to be questioned, nothing deserved to be taken on trust. If something seemed likely to do good – try it out, even though Ricardo and Mill and Gladstone had proved it to be nonsense; for to where did their 'proofs' point except to the grave? Thus was Keynes's ingrained Edwardianism undermined by the facts and spirit of the age. But, even as he accommodated to them, he never surrendered to them. His ultimate aim was to control the new forces at the behest of the Edwardian ideal of rational, civilised living.

Largely through his continuing connection with the Apostles, Keynes's life remained balanced between the pre-war and post-war generations: a mixture which enabled him to be both *enfant terrible* and authority figure. Disconcertingly, the young now included the children of his best friends: Julian Bell and Molly MacCarthy's nephew Francis Warre Cornish both arrived at King's in 1927, Julian a 'great lumbering lion-like creature, with thick tawny curls, a ridiculous nose and eyes ... a big babyish joyful aesthete'.[26] At forty-five, Keynes was finding contact with the young increasingly difficult. He was always kind to them. He loved talking to them, in the way students enjoy talking about everything, but found that his reputation intimidated them. Lunch in January 1928 for Julian and four of his friends which went on till 4 p.m. was 'hard work', with himself having to introduce all the topics of conversation.[27] On 25 November 1928, his 'party of young boys' ('rather hard work') included Michael Redgrave, Anthony Blunt, Julian Bell and Charles Gifford: the last, a mathematician, had just come up to Trinity from Winchester, having asked Keynes down to the school to give his talk on 'Economic Possibilities for Our Grandchildren' earlier in the year. A more relaxed occasion was the mingling, a month earlier, of the Bloomsbury generations at a party in Dadie Rylands's rooms: Vanessa Bell up to see Julian, Virginia Woolf to read her paper ('A Room of One's Own') to the young ladies of Girton, Lytton Strachey, the wicked uncle, Julian and his half-sister Angelica. In December Julian, a talented poet, succeeded where his father had failed by being elected an Apostle.

Young Cambridge in the late 1920s was poetical and theatrical rather than political. Keynes had got the theatre-going habit from his father. His education, love of language and natural sense of style had given him a discriminating appreciation of drama, both classical and Elizabethan. For someone of his tastes, King's was a congenial place to be. Not only were the classics and literature taught as 'part of life' – and Greek drama translated with a view to live performance – but, with its reputation for eccentricity and homosexuality, King's attracted young men who loved dressing up. Sheppard, Dadie Rylands – after his return to King's as a fellow in 1927 – Frank Birch (a history don) and Donald Beves, all King's men, were the pillars of the college's theatrical life. Keynes reported to Vanessa early in 1929 that the (bisexual) Julian was 'hopelessly infatuated with [Anthony Blunt]. . . .'

It was Keynes's links with the theatre which brought Cambridge into Lydia's orbit. Lydia was thirty-five in 1927. She had steered clear of any further ballet engagements in order to have a child. The letters she and Maynard exchanged give only vague hints of what happened. There is some suggestion that she miscarried in May 1927, Keynes assuring her that 'we shall have in the end what we so much long for'.[28] In June Lydia went butterflying with Neville Keynes in Switzerland; she put in a guest appearance with Diaghilev's company at the Prince's Theatre in July 1927, at a gala performance of the *Polovtsian Dances* before King Alfonso of Spain, who had especially asked for her. Then apparently she became pregnant again. On Monday, 10 October 1927, Keynes wrote, 'Dearest Lydochka, Well, I have had the telegram – the sad deed is done and my dear little bun has had its throat cut. No more to be said until I see it [you?], except a tender touch where the sweet bun was.' It is hard to know exactly what these words mean, since there was no external scar on Lydia's body. At any rate, there seem to have been no further plans to have a child. Family folklore is that Lydia's pelvis was too narrow to have a baby.

Deprived of baby and career, Lydia pottered around rather aimlessly in the winter of 1927–8. But Maynard had a plan. In October 1928 we find him coaching her by letter: 'Sorrow, borrowed, owed. Can you hear me pronouncing them?' Lydia's o's, pronounced 'oah' in the Russian style, were always a problem for her. A triple bill had been arranged at the ADC Theatre, in which Lydia was to dance in Stravinsky's narrative ballet *The Soldier's Tale*, and also to appear in Shakespeare's *A Lover's Complaint*, as the rustic maiden bewailing her seduction by the young Michael Redgrave. Duncan Grant was commissioned to do the sets and costumes, and Maynard undertook to guarantee the occasion against loss. It was the first staging of Shakespeare's poem, and Lydia's public debut in England as a straight actress. Keynes, of course, knew all about her acting in America. 'Out of the charades and other nonsense at the parties at Gordon Square'[29] the thought had come to him that her piquant charm in dance might transfer to speech; and early ambitions regained take the place of lost motherhood.

Lydia charmed everyone at rehearsals, the box office was sold out, the performances in early November went well, and Frankie Birrell loyally praised her in the *Nation*. Keynes had launched her on a new career. She did not become a continuous part of his Cambridge life till much later. She still 'visited', staying with his parents in Harvey Road; he continued to live in his bachelor rooms. But she had established a presence in Cambridge which was to grow with the years. More improbably, her willingness to extend her range was to make her a central figure in forging a new English style out of the traditions of the Elizabethan masque and the Russian classical ballet, leading to the birth of the Camargo Society in 1930. In setting much of this machinery in motion Keynes was not only bringing his different worlds together, but guilefully fertilising his marriage.

IV. THE ECONOMICS OF INERTIA

Peter Clarke has compellingly argued that the final derailment of the *Treatise on Money* came about as a by-product of Keynes's involvement with Lloyd George, and his resulting confrontation with the Treasury view.[30] A general election was due in 1929. Lloyd George was planning his political come-back on the basis of a great programme of public works to mop up 'abnormal' unemployment. This policy received Keynes's enthusiastic endorsement. On 31 July 1928 he flew Lloyd George's kite in an *Evening Standard* article, 'How to Organise a Wave of Prosperity'. This started a discussion, both within the Treasury and within the government, which also had its eye on the coming election. As the debate became public in the run-up to the election in early 1929, Keynes was forced to sharpen his analytical tools in order to meet objections, crystallised in what became known as the Treasury view. As a result of this debate, Keynes felt he had to restructure his book and 'drastically rewrite' certain chapters. This is what held up its publication till the autumn of 1930.

The 1928 article, in itself, said little new. Keynes pointed to the depressed condition of much of industry, with unemployment 200,000 higher than the previous spring. This was because 'we have deflated prices by raising the exchange value of sterling and by controlling the volume of credit; *but we have not deflated costs*'. There was a way to break the deadlock: a programme of national development to start a 'cumulative' upward movement; working plant to full capacity, which would itself reduce costs; and some rise in prices to reduce the cost-price gap. Keynes wrote, 'When we have unemployed men and unemployed plant . . . it is utterly imbecile to say that we cannot *afford* these things. *For it is with the unemployed men and the unemployed plant, and with nothing else, that these things are done.*' The whole subsequent history of the Keynesian Revolution was not able to improve substantially on this rationale for state action to get an economy out of depression.[31]

It was the emergence of a political challenge to the prevailing economic consensus that forced both the Treasury *and* Keynes to sharpen their analytic tools. The old debate about whether Britain should or should not go back to the gold standard was over. The exchange rate had been fixed, and unemployment had not gone away. Given that the interest rate could not be lowered while Britain remained on the gold standard, the problem as it presented itself to the Liberals was how to get more investment at the ruling interest rate. Lloyd George, prompted by Keynes, said the government must borrow the money itself. But this raised, or rather highlighted, the issue of where the money was to come from. If the government borrowed private savings, this would surely 'crowd out' private investment. Keynes himself had advocated mobilising savings 'going abroad', but had not explained why this would increase employment. Either, it seemed, there must be some cache of unused savings, or the banks would have to create 'new' money, which it was then thought would be inflationary.

It was along these lines that the Treasury developed its response to the Liberal initiative. Following the publication of Keynes's article, Churchill asked Richard Hopkins, Frederick Leith-Ross and Hawtrey to comment on it. Sir Richard Hopkins had just succeeded Otto Niemeyer as controller of finance, Niemeyer having gone to the Bank of England; Leith-Ross ('Leithers') was his deputy. But it was Hawtrey, director of financial enquiries, and the Treasury's sole professional economist, who put his finger on the weak spot in Keynes's argument. Basing himself on an article he had published in *Economica* in 1925, he simply said that with a fixed money supply, any loan raised by the government for public works would be at the expense of existing 'consumer outlay'.* This became the basis of the Treasury view that any additional expenditure must be at the expense of something already being done, unless it was inflationary.[32] Leith-Ross commented, 'What Keynes is after, of course, is a definite inflation of credit.' Hawtrey's abstruse formulation was simplified for Baldwin's speeches: 'We must *either* take existing money *or* create new money',[33] and, of course, 'new money' meant the dreaded inflation.

The Treasury View assumed that all savings were being invested – that is being used to buy new capital equipment. But was this true? Robertson had talked about savings being 'hoarded' (kept idle). Keynes suggested two other possibilites. Savings might be used to buy existing assets, simply bidding up their prices, as in a stock market bubble.[34] Alternatively, savings exported abroad would not add to investment if they caused the capital-lending country to lose gold and raise domestic interest rates.[35] In all three cases, a country's savings could be said to be 'running ahead of' (not being used for) current investment.†

Keynes refused yet another invitation to stand as Liberal candidate for

---

* In his article in *Economica*, March 1925, p. 40, Hawtrey wrote that 'The money borrowed is genuine savings. In other words, it must come out of consumers' income. The effect of this diversion of a part of the consumers' outlay into the hands of the government is to diminish by that amount the effective demand for products.' Hawtrey's view that only an expansion of credit will increase the demand for unemployed labour led him to condemn public works as a 'piece of ritual'.

† The last possibility was strongly suggested to Keynes by his involvement, early in 1929, in a debate with the Swedish economist Bertil Ohlin on German reparations. Keynes argued that the transfer abroad of an additional capital sum – whether it be a loan or an indemnity – required an increase in a country's competitiveness; Ohlin denied that any such 'transfer problem' existed.

Cambridge University. However, he was a member of a special committee, chaired by Seebohm Rowntree, charged with turning the report of the Liberal industrial inquiry into the campaign document, *We Can Conquer Unemployment*, and he endorsed Lloyd George's decision to issue his famous pledge, of 1 March 1929, 'to reduce the terrible figures of the workless in the course of a single year to normal proportions' by means of a large scheme of national development.[36]

The Liberals proposed to finance their public works programme by activating 'idle balances' – a Robertsonian idea. McKenna calculated that between 1919 and 1928 the ratio of 'time deposits' to 'demand deposits' had risen from 28.6 per cent to 44.7 per cent; although the total volume of money had risen, the proportion 'actively engaged in trade' had shrunk.[37] This was the old 'velocity of circulation' approach: money had become arthritic, like Robertson's old lady; it was being hoarded, not being invested. J. A. Hobson took up the same line in the *Nation* of 30 March, when he talked of the Liberal road-loan policy as a way of 'melting . . . frozen savings'. The Treasury's riposte, published by Stanley Baldwin's government on 13 May in one of six *Memoranda on Certain Proposals Relating to Unemployment*, denied that demand deposits were 'idle'. They were regarded by industry as an essential liquid reserve, and were employed in loans to the short-term money market.

Keynes's own justification for a public works programme, entitled 'Can Lloyd George Do It?', published on 10 May, and co-authored with Hubert Henderson, did not rely on any theory of idle or hoarded savings. To the Treasury argument that no savings were available to finance *additional* investment Keynes and Henderson replied that this assumed full employment of all resources. The unemployed resources included savings which had not 'materialised' owing to the want of prosperity.[38] This was an odd way of putting it. But the thought Keynes was expressing was that any policy (including a loan-financed public works' programme) which succeeded in restoring a 'normal' level of income would create the saving needed to finance the investment.

Corresponding to this, the employment-creating effects of additional government spending would not be limited to those directly employed on government projects. For every man put to work building a road or a house, at least one other would find a job supplying the inputs required. Furthermore, the additional purchasing power thus created would exert a 'cumulative force' on trade activity, making the employment effects of a given capital expenditure far larger than the direct and indirect effects indicated above, though 'it is not possible to measure effects of this character with any sort of precision'.[39] The 'employment multiplier', worked out by Richard Kahn in 1931, was an attempt to measure these 'cumulative' effects.

The pamphlet concludes with Keynes's familiar contrast between the forces of life and death:

Negation, restriction, inactivity – these are the government's watch-words. Under their leadership we have been forced to button up our waistcoats and compress our lungs. Fears and doubts and hypochondriac precautions are keeping us muffled up indoors. But we are not tottering to our graves. We are healthy children. We need the breath of life. There is nothing to be afraid of. On the contrary. The future holds in store for us far more wealth and economic freedom and possibilities of personal life than the past has ever offered.

There is no reason why we should not feel ourselves free to be bold, to be open, to experiment, to take action, to try the possibilities of things. And over against us, standing in the path, there is nothing but a few old gentlemen tightly buttoned-up in their frock coats, who only need to be treated with a little friendly disrespect and bowled over like ninepins.

Quite likely they will enjoy it themselves, when once they have got over the shock.[40]

It was exhilarating stuff.

Lifted up by his own rhetoric, Keynes was extremely optimistic about the electoral prospects of the party he supported. He was convinced that Hubert Henderson – whom he had persuaded to stand in his place – would get in at Cambridge, and that the Liberal Party nationally would get over 100 seats. In fact, the general election of 30 May 1929 produced 287 Labour MPs, 260 Conservatives and 59 Liberals. Henderson was not one of them, and Keynes lost £160 on his bets, though he won £10 from Winston Churchill. Although the Liberals got 23 per cent of the vote (as against 38 per cent for the Conservatives and 37 per cent for Labour) they obtained only 10 per cent of the parliamentary seats. Lloyd George's last fling had failed. MacDonald formed his second Labour government, with the Liberals holding the balance of power. 'I can't see that anything satisfactory can possibly result from it,' Keynes wrote gloomily to Lydia on 3 June.

V. *A TREATISE ON MONEY*

The more direct approach to the analysis of output and employment opened up by Keynes's confrontation with the Treasury in 1929 had, in a sense, made much of the *Treatise on Money* redundant, from his point of view, when it was finally published in October 1930. It had started with the attempt to use the quantity theory of money to explain fluctuations in output. When he finished it, he realised that this theory was no longer needed to explain the salient facts; indeed, it was a distraction, focusing attention on price levels rather than on actual production. So we see an embryonic theory of output trying to escape from the straitjacket of the theory of money. But there is another reason for the failure of the *Treatise*. In aiming for the comprehensive coverage appropriate to a full-blown academic study, Keynes allowed his distinctive ideas to get submerged. Perhaps he wanted to establish his credentials as a serious economist by writing an unreadable book. Whatever the case, the *Treatise* exaggerated his weakness and failed to exploit his strengths. The kind of treatment he attempted was much more likely to reveal his limitations as a theorist than his strengths as a creative thinker. It had a dreadfully dampening effect on his style.

In fact, the *Treatise*'s ideas are really quite simple. A country in which interest rates were forced upwards by the need to defend the currency and in which wages could not be forced downwards to restore profits was quite likely to find itself in a low-employment trap. This is Keynes's stylised explanation for Britain's 'special problem' of the 1920s. But behind this explanation is a theory of how a modern economy works.

Keynes's central proposition is that there is no automatic mechanism *in a credit money economy* to keep saving and investment equal. This is because banks create money. As we have seen, this idea of Keynes goes back to 1913. There is a rate of profit on capital (which Keynes, following Wicksell, called the 'natural' rate) and there is a rate of interest on loans – the 'market' rate. But the market rate as determined by the credit policy of the banks might be higher or lower than the 'natural rate'. Thus the 'credit cycle' is characterised by an oscillation of the market rate of interest round the natural rate.

The practical import of all this is that the only short-run balancer a credit-money economy has is banking *policy*. Under the restored gold standard the Bank of England was prevented from setting bank rate low enough to allow a level of investment equal to what the community wanted to save: hence mass unemployment. Crucial to this demonstration is Keynes's switch in emphasis from the stock of money to the flow of spending. It was insufficiency of spending on investment relative to the rate of saving which caused both the price level to fall *and* people to be unemployed.

Fundamental in terms of economic psychology is Keynes's break from the classical view of saving as providing an automatic fund for investment. He dismissed the 'abstinence' theory of economic progress in a couple of superb paragraphs:

> It has been usual to think of the accumulated wealth of the world as having been painfully built up out of that voluntary abstinence of individuals from the immediate enjoyment of consumption which we call thrift. But it should be obvious that mere abstinence is not enough

by itself to build cities or drain fens.... It is enterprise which builds and improves the world's possessions.... If enterprise is afoot, wealth accumulates whatever may be happening to thrift; and if enterprise is asleep, wealth decays whatever thrift may be doing.

Thus, thrift may be the handmaid and nurse of enterprise. But equally she may not. And, perhaps, even usually she is not. For enterprise is connected with thrift not directly but at one remove; and the link which should join them is frequently missing. For the engine which drives enterprise is not thrift, but profit.[41]

Unfortunately, Keynes tried to formalise these pathbreaking ideas in 'Fundamental Equations' – introduced at the start of chapter 10 in pages of dismal algebra – whose origins lie in the quantity theory of money. The quantity theory states that changes in the quantity of money affect prices only. (More precisely, that prices will change in proportion to changes in the quantity of money). Therefore the quantity theory cannot explain change in output: it is a theory of prices only. However, it is valid only if all prices in the economy change instantly and equiportionally: when the money supply is increased by 10 per cent all prices instantly have to go up by 10 per cent. This is an impossibly stringent condition. Keynes's strategy was to use quantity theory algebra to show how changes in money expenditure could give rise to *disequilibrium* prices, whose liquidation required temporary changes in output and employment. However, this strategy had severe drawbacks. It committed him to special (and eccentric) definitions of income, profit, and saving. It also committed him to an idea which was inconsistent with what he was already wanting to say: that changes in flows of expenditure were in some sense derived from changes in price levels. Keynes had come to think that changes in money expenditure could come about independently of changes in the supply of money or credit, and he was groping for a more direct way of expressing the connection between spending and output.

The three awkward definitions are: (*a*) the community's money income (otherwise the 'normal' or equilibrium earnings of the factors of production, or costs of production); (*b*) profits, which are defined as the difference between costs of production and selling prices, and exclude entrepreneurs' 'normal' earnings; and (*c*) saving, defined as that part of the community's 'normal' income withheld from consumption. The purpose of excluding profits and losses (which Keynes also calls 'windfalls') from income is to segregate the variable causing output to expand or contract. But the attempt results in non-operational definitions of income and saving which caused much misunderstanding. The idea that aggregate saving can 'run ahead of' or 'fall behind' investment depends entirely on the way income and saving are defined.

Formally, the *Treatise* is an attempt to capture, in a set of equations, the dynamics of an economy in transition from one (consumer) price level to another. We are presented, on the one side, with the flow of money earned by workers and businessmen in producing consumption and investment goods, and, on the other, its division into the parts which are spent on buying consumption goods and which are saved. The economy is in equilibrium if the proportions of money earned in producing consumption and investment goods are the same as the proportions spent on current consumption and being saved.

In this situation costs of production equal the selling prices of consumption goods; profits are zero; saving equals investment: all true by definition. If, on the other hand, people spend less on buying consumption goods than they have earned producing them, that is, decide to save more out of their 'normal' income, consumer prices fall. In this situation, by definition, the costs of consumer goods exceed their prices; profits are negative by the same amount; and saving 'runs ahead' of investment.

This torturous approach was designed to emphasise one key point. If what people want to save exceeds the cost of investment the economy as a whole becomes depressed unless something is happening simultaneously to raise the *value* or profitability of investment. The required investment does not happen automatically. Whether it happens depends on 'a different set of considerations'[42]: whether the anticipated profitability of investment is going up, or the rate of interest falling, or a mixture of both, at the same time.

Depression arises if the incentive to buy *new* pieces of capital equipment is insufficient to absorb the rate of saving out of 'normal' income – in other words if the expected rate of profit falls below the market rate of interest set by the banking system. Keynes applies the uncertainty analysis started in the *Tract* to a specific set of prices – those of capital goods. It is the oscillation of the 'natural' rate of interest, driven by volatile expectations, around the market rate set by the banking system which explains the business cycle.

The *Treatise* contains the first of Keynes's two famous discussions of the psychology of the stock exchange, much influenced by the collapse of the long 'bull' market on Wall Street in 1929. The key idea is that part of savings is 'held' for speculative purposes, because of uncertainty about the future value of capital assets. If the price of shares on the stock-market is expected to go up, savings will be redistributed from 'hoards' to 'securities', and vice versa if the price of shares is expected to fall. When most investors are 'bulls' you get a stock market boom; when most of them are 'bears' you have a stock-market slump. Thus a 'speculative' motive for money balances to hold is identified in the *Treatise*, but it does not become Keynes's liquidity-preference theory of the rate of interest till *The General Theory*.

Keynes does not doubt that any 'gap' between investment and saving can be closed by manipulating the market rate of interest. But in an open economy under a fixed exchange-rate system, the rate of interest has two jobs to do which may be incompatible: to regulate the volume of investment and to manage the balance of payments. If a community's desire to lend savings abroad exceeded its net export surplus, gold would be exported, which the monetary authority would have to offset by raising the rate of interest, thus increasing the cost of capital at home. The ultimate effect of a high bank rate would be a decline in 'efficiency wages' (money income), making possible an enlargement of the export surplus. This restates the inconsistency of policy thesis expounded in the *Tract*. Keynes's exposition of the *modus operandi* of bank rate remains a classic of its kind; but it is a price-level, rather than output, adjustment model that he has in mind.

Did Keynes see flexible wages as a complete cure for any shift in the saving or investment function? One part of the *Treatise* suggests he did. In Book IV, we get a classical credit-cycle story depending on lagged wage adjustment. In the upswing there is a sequence of commodity (price) inflation, profit inflation, and income inflation, which then reverses itself in the downswing: prices fall, profits fall, and finally money wages fall as the final act in the adjustment process.[43] Yet in Book III, Keynes tells the famous 'banana parable', in which flexible wages do not cure the initial disturbance because, if saving goes up in response to a thrift campaign, while employers reduce wages, 'the spending power of the public will be reduced by just as much as the aggregate costs of production'.[44] There will be no position of equilibrium until either all production ceases and the community starves to death, or until growing impoverishment causes the community to save less, or unless 'investment is stimulated by some means or another', for example by loan-financed public works. If both interest-rate adjustment and public works are ruled out, then the only realistic adjustment mechanism left is impoverishment. Keynes called this 'nature's cure'. Thus there are two inconsistent stories in the *Treatise*. The first is the story of a deep cycle, in which relative price adjustments come into play, however slowly, to restore equilibrium at unchanged levels of aggregate output and employment. In the second story, the adjustment to a new position of equilibrium takes place through the reduction in output, with a stable point reached when the community is too poor to save. The second story points to the *General Theory*, but Keynes cannot yet say whether, barring government intervention, a stable position is possible short of mass starvation – obviously an unsatisfactory conclusion.

The main object of national monetary policy should be to maintain a rate of interest consistent with full employment at a price level given, in the long run, by the behaviour of 'efficiency wages'. Such interest-rate autonomy could only be guaranteed by periodic adjustment of the exchange rate. The existence of downward wage rigidity, Keynes argued, was incompatible with a '*laissez-faire* attitude to foreign lending'. Hence he doubted whether 'it is wise to have a currency system with a much wider ambit than our banking system, our tariff system and our wage system'.[45] This somewhat extreme statement of monetary nationalism was not entirely inconsistent with the idea of a more flexible international currency system. If changes to the gold standard were ruled out, the government itself must start a programme of public works.

A Treatise on Money turns out to be mis-named. The disturbances Keynes is describing are not necessarily caused by acts of inflation or deflation by the banking system. They can be triggered by non-monetary forces – a thrift campaign, a wage push, a collapse of business confidence. However, he still expected the monetary authority to be able to neutralise the effect of those forces by supplying an appropriate quantity of money. 'Those who attribute sovereign power to the monetary authority in the governance of prices', he wrote,

> do not, of course, claim that the terms on which money is supplied is the *only* influence affecting the price-level. To maintain that the supplies in a reservoir can be maintained at any required level by pouring enough money into it is not inconsistent with admitting that the level of the reservoir depends on many other factors besides how much water is poured in.[46]

26

The Slump

No one in the summer of 1929 suspected that the world economy was about to collapse. With shares on Wall Street rising ever more dizzily, Americans believed they had discovered the secret of permanent prosperity. As long as the United States boomed, the rest of the world felt secure. There was little hint of trouble in international politics either. Under Stalin Soviet Russia had turned from exporting revolution to terrorising its own people. The Locarno Treaty of 1925 had lulled French fears and seemingly tamed German ambitions: Hitler, wrote Lord D'Abernon in 1929, had 'fad[ed] into oblivion'.[1] Mussolini appeared to have settled down too; in 1928 he delighted sound finance by overvaluing the lira. There were, of course, disturbing signs for the augurs to read: the diversion of US savings into the Stock Exchange boom from 1928 onwards made it more difficult for primary producers to finance their debt, for Germany to pay reparations, for Britain to maintain the gold standard. In retrospect one can see that demand was being switched from production to speculation. But the worry of a few was drowned by the chorus of optimism.

After the excitements of electioneering, Keynes's life reverted to its normal routine. Most of the summer of 1929 was spent rewriting the *Treatise* at Tilton. It was interrupted by a ten-day Continental outing, from 19 to 29 July, during which he had to 'transit his mental faculties' to two days of lectures in Geneva at the invitation of the Financial Section of the League of Nations, followed by a holiday with Lydia in Burgundy. 'This sort of trip in spite of its positive qualities', Lydia wrote to Florence, 'one could only perform once a year, as one's liver reserves cannot survive.'[2]

The returning travellers plunged into ballet rehearsals at Tilton and in London. Lydia had agreed to dance with Anton Dolin and George Balanchine in a five-minute ballet inserted into one of the first British 'talkies', *Dark Red Roses*, the idea being that, as in *Hamlet*, the 'play within the play' would mime the main story and have a great effect on one of the characters. Keynes, of course, was in charge of all the practical arrangements. Balanchine arrived at Tilton on 9 August to practise the score, taken from Moussorgsky's *Khovanshina*, on a grand piano specially bought from the Courtaulds. 'With Keynes', writes Balanchine's biographer, 'he got on beautifully, for Keynes loved to talk about ballet, and Balanchine loved to talk about economics . . . .'³

While the filming took place at Wembley on 19 and 20 August, news came through of Diaghilev's death in Venice. 'The dancers crouched on the floor in a little group,' Maynard wrote to his mother, 'talking memories of him hour after hour. It was an extraordinary scene – with masses of machinery all round, the crowds of supers in dress clothes with jaundiced made up faces (supposed to be watching the ballet) and they in their central Asian costumes.' While Diaghilev lived he *was* ballet. With his death, the struggle for the inheritance started. Later that year Lydia, with Maynard's backing, would assist Ninette de Valois in starting the Camargo Society, forerunner of the English National Ballet.

Dark Red Roses had bad luck. In the ballet the music was slightly out of synchronisation with the dance. Soon after the first showing in October, a fire destroyed the film studio and almost all the copies of the film. It was the only time Lydia danced before the cameras.⁴

Filming and a weekend with the McKennas out of the way, Maynard got down to his book again, taking the odd afternoon off to beat Lydia at tennis. Friends and relations came and went: the Hendersons, Sebastian Sprott, Peter Lucas, Sheppard, his mother Florence (approaching seventy and just about to become Mayor of Cambridge) and his brother Geoffrey (now an established and increasingly eminent surgeon). Frances Marshall, down to stay at Charleston, found that 'the feud with Tilton' was still going strong. Lydia spent all day 'bowling for the pig' at the Firle fair, and 'horrified the village by bursting into tears' when she failed to win it. However, all was 'honey' when she dropped into Charleston one morning in white trousers, a red shirt and a large straw hat trimmed with poppies to borrow some eggs.⁵ The feud was absent from Cambridge, where Julian Bell – 'a very lovable old bear' – was often in Maynard's company, though he found his girl-friend, Helen Souter, 'too plain'. Sam and Lil Courtauld came to lunch on 29 September, Sam being shocked, but 'inwardly pleased' when Maynard argued for Protection. There was a BBC broadcast, a night at Churt with Lloyd George and a meeting in London with the new Chancellor of the Duchy of Lancaster, Oswald Mosley, who had been appointed to ginger up the Labour government's public works programme.

A fortnight after Maynard's return to Cambridge, the painfully con-structed edifices of the post-war world started to collapse. 'Wall Street did have a go yesterday. Did you read about it?' he wrote to Lydia on 25 October. 'The biggest crash ever recorded. Falk's voice on the telephone this morning rather worried and uneasy, I thought.' The *New York Evening Post* had asked him for a short message, and he had spent half an hour writing it and twenty-five minutes dictating it down the telephone, which gave him a headache. 'Thus I've been in a thoroughly financial and disgusting state of mind all day.'

Keynes's telephoned prophecy about the consequences of the Wall Street crash proved spectacularly wrong. There would be a 'bad winter of unemployment in Britain' as the result of the 'dear money' which had recently prevailed; but he looked forward to 'an epoch of cheap money ahead [which] will be in the real interests of business all over the world'. With low interest rates, 'enterprise throughout the world can get going again ... commodity prices will recover and farmers will find themselves in better shape'.[6]

As we know, the Wall Street crash triggered the greatest world depression of all time. The collapse of wholesale prices in 1930 completely swamped any effect of cheap money: real interest rates rose sharply even as nominal interest rates fell. These events were to shake Keynes's belief in the efficacy of monetary policy during a severe slump. However, till well into 1930 few believed that anything worse was happening than a cyclical downturn, which would soon correct itself. Indeed there was some recovery of both share prices and activity in the spring of 1930.

Keynes has been accused of not predicting the depression. 'There will be no further crash in our lifetime,' he is reported as saying in 1926.[7] Also, if the value of an economist's theory is judged by the state of his portfolio, Keynes comes off badly: by the end of 1929 he was almost wiped out, for the second time in his investing career.

The truth is more complicated. Keynes's analysis of US business prospects was coloured by his admiration for the stabilisation policies of the Federal Reserve Board. He assumed that the Fed would be able and willing to prevent a serious slump from developing. However, he never succumbed to the widespread belief that the US had 'learnt the secret of perpetual prosperity',[8] and by 1928 he felt he had good reason for worry.

That year, his business partner Oswald Falk came to the conclusion that credit conditions in the USA were 'unsound', and that the National Mutual, the Independent Investment Company and other companies which he and Keynes controlled should get out of Wall Street in particular and equities in general. This was also the position of Keynes's Harvard correspondent Charles Bullock, and most 'sound' banking opinion in the United States, alarmed by the great rise in collateral loans following the cut in the discount rate to 3.5 per cent in August 1927.

These apprehensions in 1927–8 became the basis of the subsequent orthodox explanation of the US slump. In his book *Sailors, Statesmen and Others*, published in 1935, the Labour MP Commander Kenworthy recalled that Oliver Sprague, the financial expert, had told Labour MPs in 1931 that 'the Federal Reserve Board had desired to break the American boom in 1927, but that the wicked politicians had brought pressure to bear against this plan, because of the forthcoming presidential election campaign of Mr Hoover'.[9] Writing in 1934, Lionel Robbins likewise argued that the slump originated in the credit expansion started by the Federal Reserve Board in

1927, partly to offset a mild recession in the United States, mainly to help Britain stay on the gold standard. This unleashed an orgy of speculation which could not be checked by the dear money imposed subsequently.[10] The slump was the punishment, as well as the cure, for the reckless extravagance of the previous years. The boom was the fantasy, the slump the reappearance of reality.

Keynes never took the view he attributed to 'some austere and puritanical souls' that slumps were an 'inevitable and desirable nemesis on ... man's speculative spirit', that it would be 'a victory for the mammon of unrighteousness if so much prosperity was not subsequently balanced by universal bankruptcy'.[11] Nor did he agree that America was on the booze in 1927. The test of inflation, he repeatedly said, was the 'test of prices'. Judged by the commodity price index, there was no danger of inflation in 1927. Hence by raising the discount rate from 3.5 per cent in January 1928 to 5 per cent by July 1928 in order to choke off speculation, the Federal Reserve Board was imposing an act of deflation on a thriving US economy. This was the basis of Keynes's commentary on the American situation in 1928. In July and September he argued that the danger facing the US was not inflation, but deflation.[12] 'The difficulty will be', Keynes wrote in September 1928, 'to find an outlet for the vast investment funds coming forward – particularly if central banks resist the tendency of the rate of interest to fall.' 'Why is the Federal Reserve Board so disturbed about what appears to be a reasonably healthy situation?' he asked the American economist Allyn Young on 15 August 1928,[13] and in reply to Professor Bullock he wrote on 4 October 1928, 'I cannot help feeling that the risk just now is all on the side of a business depression.... If too prolonged an attempt is made to check the speculative position by dear money, it may very well be that the dear money, by checking new investments, will bring about a general business depression.'[14] So by 1928 Keynes thought a slump was likely if policy was not changed.

Both sides accused the other of looking in the wrong place. Orthodox banking opinion saw in the speculative boom a clear indication of unsound credit conditions; Keynes, on the other hand, believed that the inflated share prices on Wall Street were an inaccurate indicator of the total position. 'Thus I attribute the slump ... primarily to the effects on investment of the long period of dear money which preceded the stock-market collapse, and only secondarily to the collapse itself.'[15]

Keynes's expectations in 1928 were influenced by his own business dealings. He was not wiped out on Wall Street, since he owned no shares there. The origin of his difficulties lay in the commodity markets, in which he had been speculating with mixed success for six years. By the end of 1927 his net assets totalled £44,000. But in 1928 he was long on rubber, corn, cotton and tin, when the markets suddenly turned against his position. His losses on commodities forced him to sell securities to cover his position, by the end of 1929 on a falling market. This left a securities portfolio dominated by 10,000 shares in the Austin Motor Company, whose value fell from 21s in January 1928 to 5s by the end of 1929. By that date his net worth had slumped from £44,000 to £7815.[16]

Keynes's picture of what was happening in the United States is thus in part a generalisation of his own speculative experience in 1928. Plentiful savings, as he saw it, were combined with an underlying tendency to under-investment, offset by the pumping up of credit by the Federal Reserve System. When the pumping slowed down, the economic balloon shrivelled up. Keynes was to build on this analysis in explaining the deepening depression. The second of his personal financial setbacks also ended the speculative phase of his financial operations. Thereafter he adopted what he called a policy of 'faithfulness' – investing in a few favoured shares and sticking to them through thick and thin. A decade spent in trying to 'beat the market' had convinced him that this new strategy was the only rational response to uncertainty.

The intimate phase of Keynes's collaboration with Oswald Falk now came to an end. There was not just the dispute over the future course of US prices, but also Falk's increasingly dictatorial behaviour on the companies which he and Keynes ran. On the PR ('All is flux') Finance Company, which engaged mainly in commodity speculation, Keynes and Falk agreed to split responsibility following the losses of 1928, Keynes handling the capital subscribed by his family and friends (Walter Langdon Brown, Geoffrey Keynes, Neville Keynes, A. V. Hill, Clive Bell, David Garnett, Roger Fry and Lytton Strachey), and Falk the rest. After one year of the new arrangement – during which Wall Street had collapsed – the Keynes-controlled share of the capital had gone down from £28,000 to £24,000, the Falk share from £56,000 to £20,000.[17] Falk's poor showing was due to his impetuous decision, reversing his 1928 arguments, to 'bull' New York in the summer of 1929. The same decision, taken against Keynes's advice, involved the Independent Investment Company in heavy losses in 1929–30, as a result of which Falk had to agree 'to pay attention to the opinion' of members of an enlarged board.[18] Early in 1930 Lydia noted, with a rare touch of malice, that Falk had been obliged to put his country house, Stockton, up for sale. Keynes's falling out with Falk was the first of a number of close friendships which cooled as the depression hotted up – those with Sam Courtauld, Hubert Henderson and Dennis Robertson being similarly affected. Worst of all, his former pupil, and, later, co-director of the National Mutual Assurance Society, Sidney Russell Cooke, shot himself dead on 3 July 1930, victim of the financial reversals he and his firm, Rowe and Pitman, suffered in the long bear market which started with the Wall Street crash.

II. THE MACMILLAN COMMITTEE

'As you said, I am becoming more fashionable again,' Keynes wrote to Lydia on 25 November 1929, following his appointment as a member of the Macmillan Committee on Finance and Industry. A wide-ranging inquiry into how the working of the banking system affected the economy, it was not intended to influence immediate policy. This was to be the job of the Economic Advisory Council, a brainchild of the Prime Minister, Ramsay MacDonald, to which Keynes was also appointed, after attending three luncheon parties hosted by MacDonald in November and December. Keynes's inclusion on these committees was designed to give the appearance, not the reality, of radical movement. In fact, as the depression deepened, the movement was all the other way: back to orthodoxy. Policy which started off as open, and reasonably flexible, gradually narrowed to a single point: defence of confidence, which included defence of the pound. Nevertheless, between 1929 and 1931 Keynes directed his persuasive efforts at MacDonald, rather than Lloyd George, and in fact dropped out of Liberal Party politics altogether.

The Macmillan Committee and the EAC gave Keynes the direct access to 'inside opinion' which he had been denied since the early 1920s. Specifically, he was given a chance to confront the Treasury and the Bank of England; and to argue his case before leading businessmen, bankers, civil servants and economists. The result was a two-way flow of ideas. Keynes won considerable ground, but he was forced to retreat on specific issues. Moreover, the differences which opened up on the EAC's Committee of Economists in the autumn of 1930 determined him to write another major book of theory 'to bring to an issue the deep divergences of opinion between fellow economists which have for the time being almost destroyed the practical influence of economic theory'.

'Keynes dominated the proceedings of the [Macmillan] Committee, both in examining witnesses and shaping the report'[19] in over forty-nine days of taking evidence and over a hundred meetings. In addition, he spent five sessions in February and March 1930 outlining his own thoughts on monetary theory and policy, and a further three days in November. His exposition enthralled the Committee. It was a masterpiece of sustained logical thinking, which also shows him fully in command of both language and mood. The chairman, Lord Macmillan, a judge, who was ignorant of finance but open-minded and sympathetic, said that he lost track of time when Keynes was speaking. Keynes's two main allies were McKenna and Ernest Bevin. McKenna was sharp, cocky and well informed throughout. Keynes went out of his way to woo Bevin, the powerful general secretary of the Transport and General Workers' Union, taking him as a guest to a meeting of the Political Economy Club in London early in December 1929. Bevin, besides being a quick learner, spotted Keynes as an economist sympathetic to the working class. His exposure to Keynes's ideas at this point helped lay the industrial foundations of the wartime and post-1945 'consensus'.

Keynes's exposition to the Macmillan Committee, based on his *Treatise on Money*, reflected the experience of the 1920s, not the 1930s. It was an analysis, not of a world in deep depression, but of the problems of an arthritic economy in an otherwise moderately prosperous world.

It started on 20 February 1930, with an account of the *modus operandi* of bank rate under the gold standard. The great virtue of the bank rate was that it acted simultaneously to correct both a country's external and domestic imbalances.[20] But there was an implication which was not so well understood. Domestic costs can be reduced only by paying factors 'less for their efforts' – by lowering profits or wages. Bank rate's only direct power was to reduce profits by increasing the cost of borrowing.[21] Thus 'there is no other way by which bank rate brings down prices except through the increase of unemployment'.[22] It is the increase in unemployment which brings down wages, makes exports more competitive and increases our ability to invest abroad, enabling bank rate to be lowered, 'having done its work' – with foreign lending equal to the export surplus, and full employment restored.[23]

However, the working of this equilibrating mechanism depended 'on the assumption that money wages are not fixed, that they are reasonably fluid and responsive to unemployment'. But if, as a matter of fact, selling prices are flexible, and wage costs fixed, all raising bank rate does is to increase unemployment. The adjustment process jams at this point. 'Since 1924 money wages have remained for all practical purposes fixed.'[24] The question of why British wages were, or had become, so 'sticky' provoked some of the most interesting exchanges on the Committee. It was a puzzle to Keynes; it has remained a puzzle to this day. In his Ludwig Mond Lecture at Manchester University on 7 November 1929, Keynes had given a reason: wage rates were fixed by 'social and historical forces', not by the marginal productivity of labour.[25] Before the Macmillan Committee, Keynes denied that money wages had ever been downwardly flexible. Thus the return to gold in 1925 set bank rate 'a task it had never been asked to do before in the economic history of this country'.[26] He would not accept that unemployment benefit had caused this wage-stickiness, though he conceded that the dole had a reinforcing effect.

Keynes ended the first part of his testimony:

> I conclude, for these various reasons, that bank rate policy, whilst theoretically intact, has broken down as a practical instrument for

restoring true equilibrium. It leaves us in a chronic position of spurious equilibrium, and in that spurious equilibrium the brunt falls on profits. As long as we have a form of society in which profit is the driving force of enterprise you will have a gradual decay if you have a situation in which it is impossible to earn profit.

The heart of Keynes's exposition, which occupied most of the second session, Friday 21 February, was his saving-investment analysis. He reported to Lydia on 23 February, 'On Friday they found my speech much more perplexing, as I thought they would. I think I did it all right. But it was unfamiliar and paradoxical, and whilst they couldn't confute me, they did not know whether or not to believe. . . . I got back to Cambridge very tired.'

What Keynes provided was a summary of the *Treatise* theory, replete with banana parable. If saving exceeds investment, the remaining income for consumption is not sufficient to buy consumption goods at prices which cover their costs: hence unemployment. The rate of investment is governed by the interest rate. If this was higher than the expected yield of domestic investment, savings would be lent abroad. But net foreign investment could not be greater than the surplus of exports over imports, which could be increased only by lowering British money (and to a lesser extent real) wages. So there was no guarantee that total investment would be equal to total saving under the gold standard. 'If you had complete fluidity there would always be a point where our wage system would allow our foreign invest- ment to be equal to the surplus of our savings over home investment; but if our wage system is rigid the amount of our foreign investment is rigid also.'[27] In that case, saving is 'spilled on the ground, and becomes business men's losses'.[28] Keynes added that in a closed system this problem would not arise.

CHAIRMAN: In a self-contained state bank rate would function perfectly?
J.M.K.: Yes, because in a self-contained state you could keep wages fixed; you could reconcile yourself to that fact and keep your investments always equal to the savings, and let the price level adjust itself to the level of income.[29]

Keynes summed up the logical relationship between his bank-rate exposition and his saving–investment analysis in the following taut sequence:

The way prices are forced down is this. You put the bank rate at a level at which savings are in excess of investments. Business men make losses, prices fall, and then at long last the business man forces down the remuneration of the factors of production and prices [wages?] are then lower. But if you jam the machine halfway through so you have a chronic condition in which business men make losses, you also have a chronic condition of unemployment, a chronic condition of waste; and the excess savings are spilled on the ground.[30]

His listeners were bemused. 'What happens to my savings?' asked Brand. Keynes elucidated: 'Thus ... the savings which are spilt on the ground are the savings which ... he [the businessman] *would* have had if his business income [from profits and shares] had been normal. So you will see that the spilling of savings on the ground is ... practically the same as business losses.'[31] As long as Keynes persisted (as a result of his *Treatise* definitions) in calling non-existent savings 'excess savings' he was bound to confuse his audience. However, he chose his *Treatise* definitions to illustrate the process by which savings are destroyed or created, rather than the outcome of the process. As he put it, 'I want to study what happens during the process of disequilibrium [not what happens in a position of equilibrium].'[32]

Of course, Keynes did understand that the fall in income would itself reduce saving:

> In actual fact ... we do get some relief ... insofar as the growing impoverishment of the community is leading to diminished savings; it is the route by which in the long run you would – failing any other – bring about equilibrium. The continuation of the present state of affairs would in the end so impoverish the community that they would not have a sufficient margin of income to save, and when that had gone far enough we should find unemployment disappear ... in fact, if there were not some reduction of savings going on I think the position would be very much worse than it is from the point of view of employment.[33]

There is a clear hint here of the idea that the process of depression itself eventually rebalances saving and investment at a lower level of income. His idea was that as the machinery of production shrinks the unemployed find low-paid service jobs outside the industrial system – as 'gardeners and chauffeurs'.[34] However, this kind of rebalancing of the economy, as well as being retrogressive, would clearly take a long time, so not unsurprisingly he put it 'very low' on the list of remedies he started advocating to the Committee on his third day of testimony, 28 February.

He started by ruling out devaluation, except as a last resort.[35] A second type of remedy was 'an agreed reduction of the level of money incomes in this country', as he had recommended in 1925. The sacrifice would apply to *all* 'wages, salaries, and emoluments of every kind', and would be balanced 'to a considerable extent' by the resulting fall in the cost of living. Bevin was quick to point out the difficulty: 'What guarantee of that is there?'[36] This has plagued all subsequent attempts to develop 'incomes policies'. Trade unions have some control over the wage bargain: they have none over the price level. Keynes next discussed relief of particular taxes on employers. Fourthly, costs of production could be lowered by 'rationalisation', leading to a long-run increase in efficiency.[37]

The remedies so far were all directed towards lowering production costs. A fifth remedy, protection, could give direct relief to the business community by raising prices at unchanged costs of production.[38] The virtue of protection is that 'it does the trick, whereas in present conditions free trade does not'.[39] Free-trade policy was part of 'the bank-rate policy argument'. It presupposed a 'fluid' system in which employment would always be distributed in line with comparative advantage. However, 'as soon as that link in the chain is broken the whole of the free-trade argument breaks down'. It was better for Britain to produce motor cars inefficiently under protection than to produce nothing at all. Keynes was not yet ready to endorse protection publicly. He disappointed the Committee's tariff reformer, Sir Walter Raine, by saying that he was 'frightfully afraid of protection as a long-term policy'. It was like 'drug-taking': once tariffs were put on 'you will never get them off again'.[40] He would prefer his sixth remedy, which he postponed till the fourth session on 6 March.

This was the Liberal policy of loan-financed public investment. The 'Treasury view' that additional investment would be at the expense of existing investment was 'pure logical delusion'. It ignored the distinction between saving and investment; it 'only demonstrates that home investment is not a cure for unemployment, by first of all assuming . . . that there is no unemployment to cure'.[41]

Against the Treasury view, that the loan-financed public expenditure would draw on savings already being invested, Keynes argued that the new expenditure would itself create the saving to repay the loans: half from saving on the dole, another half from restoring 'normal profits'.[42] He next disposed of the Treasury objection that it was difficult to find sufficiently attractive new investment opportunities. If the rate of interest is fixed by bank-rate policy at 5 per cent, it is true that investments which bring 4 per cent are unproductive. But that is not the real choice: the choice may be between investing £100 at 4 per cent and losing £100; so 'new investment yielding four per cent or in special cases three per cent would be nationally preferable to unemployment and business losses'.[43]

Keynes's seventh remedy, introduced on 7 March, was for 'concerted policy between the leading central banks of the world not only to prevent a further fall in international prices, but . . . also to raise prices to a parity with the international level of money incomes and with the international level of money costs of production'[44] Deflation, in other words, was a world problem, caused, as he had said earlier, by 'the return to the gold standard in many other countries which caused them to behave just as we have'.[45] The problem of the sagging commodity price index was a problem of under-demand rather than over-investment; 'world-wide encouragement of investment and of capital development generally would help'.[46] Standing in the way were the 'gold hoarding propensities' of the Bank of France – it was hardly an exaggeration to say that economic science was 'non-existent' there

– and the tendency of the Federal Reserve System to be dominated by domestic considerations. In his concluding remarks, Keynes registered, for the first time, the onset of the world depression:

> it is now fairly obvious that we are on the downward slope of an international credit cycle.... The intensity of our own problem today is due to the fact that we now have the influence of this international depression superimposed on our own pre-existing domestic troubles. ... A year or two ago our troubles were primarily domestic; now the international problem is at least equally important.[47]

In the coming months he would deploy these suggestions in different combinations, in his successive plans to counter the slump.

Keynes's nine-hour 'private' testimony to the Macmillan Committee was a magnificent performance, intellectual and stylistic. It not only greatly influenced its hearers. It was immediately recognised as of first-rate importance by Bank of England and Treasury officials: the confident simplicities of their reasoning were shattered, never to be revived. But this does not mean that Keynes had 'won' the argument. The Bank and Treasury were reserving their fire. When it came, Keynes did not emerge unscathed. He was forced to reconsider his position in two crucial respects.

First in the field was the Bank of England. The Bank went into the hearings in confident mood: after giving his testimony in November 1929, Sir Ernest Harvey, the deputy governor, had received a 'charming letter' from Keynes which led him to believe that 'we at any rate have nothing to fear' from the Macmillan Committee.[48] This confidence was shattered after the cross-examination of the governor. Montagu Norman's testimony, on 26 March 1930, was a disaster for the Bank. He was ill at ease, ill-informed, vague, contradictory, resentful and unforthcoming. He hated the game of consequences which Keynes, McKenna, Bevin and others forced him to play, being forced back, time and again, on such phrases as 'I do not know', 'I would not like to say', 'I am not sure' or 'I don't remember'. He eventually remarked to Bevin, 'It is a curious thing, the extent to which many who inhabit the City of London find difficulty in stating the reasons for the faith that is in them....' Keynes remembered him as 'an elf; an artist, sitting with his cloak round him hunched up, saying "I can't remember – " thus evading all questions, & triumphing – going away disguised – going mad'.[49] His deputy, Harvey, was given the unenviable task of 'doctoring' his evidence for the printed record, 'so threadbare and deliberately negative had been the Governor's contribution'.[50]

Nevertheless, Norman's strategy was perfectly clear. He wanted to shift responsibility for unemployment from the Bank's shoulders to others. First, he denied that the level of employment was the Bank's responsibility. The Bank was responsible for maintaining the gold standard. This it had done, despite the unanticipated difficulty of the subsequent undervaluation of the

French franc. It was up to industry to make itself competitive. 'I have never been able to see myself why for the last few years it should have been impossible for industry starting from within to have readjusted its own position.'[51] More importantly, he denied that the Bank had the power over credit conditions which Keynes claimed for it. Bank rate affected only 'short money', leaving the 'whole mass of credit' little changed.[52] Primed by its three resident economists, Henry Clay, Walter Stewart and Oliver Sprague,[53] the Bank developed these two interconnected points. In doing so it revived the Real Bills doctrine of the nineteenth century: the view that the banking system responded to the needs of trade; it did not cause the needs of trade to be what they were.

The Bank of England's evidence raised a crucial theoretical point. Clay was asserting that the supply of credit was endogenous not exogenous. The banks cannot create credit in excess of the demand for it. 'The truer view', wrote Clay, 'seems to me to be, that while the conditions of sound banking impose a limit on the extension of credit, the *origin* of credit is to be found in the action of the businessman, who approaches his bank for assistance with a business transaction, and the *basis* of credit in the probability that the transaction can be done at a profit.'[54] This amounted to a denial of the agenda of the monetary reformers. As Keynes put it in his cross-examination of Stewart: 'what you are saying is that there is always the right quantity of credit?'[55] Stewart doubted whether 'the expansion of bank credit in quantity was a determining factor in prices and trade activity';[56] 'there are a great many things that people can do with money besides buying commodities. They can hold it.'[57] All that meant, Keynes rejoined, was that you 'would have to dose the system with money', 'feed the hoarder' in order to bring down money rates.[58] Keynes's belief in monetary manipulation was shaken, but not shattered. He still believed that when interest rates were lowered investment projects became profitable at the margin which were not profitable before. But he admitted that bank rate was a weaker instrument than he had believed. For the first time, he acknowledged that what is important for recovery is falling *real* interest rates. Moreover, 'cheap money does very little by itself to mend matters. In the main it creates an environment in which enterprise is more likely to lift its head again.'[59] However, there was another controllable element in the situation, the volume of investment. If businessmen would not invest, the government always could. At this point, the Treasury view came into Keynes's sights, in the person of Sir Richard Hopkins.

Keynes thought he knew what the Treasury view was and that he was in a position to refute it. The Treasury had claimed that additional loan-financed public spending could not add to investment and employment, only divert them from existing uses. This was true, Keynes was prepared to say, only on the assumption of a fixed money supply and full employment. But Hopkins had foreseen this. He too had a political motive. He did not want to make it seem that the Treasury was against action to help the unemployed, especially as there had been a change of political masters. An argument designed for use by Churchill and Baldwin in defending the Conservative government's record needed to be modified for the use of Labour ministers committed, however haltingly, to public works schemes.

The Treasury was not opposed to government spending in principle, Hopkins declared at the outset of his evidence. Its objection was to a particular plan, that put forward by Lloyd George in 1929. This plan, far from 'setting up a cycle of prosperity' as Keynes had hoped, would much more probably produce a crisis of confidence in the business community, leading to capital flight and rising interest rates. The more distrusted the plan was, the higher the rate of interest would have to go.[60] This new version of the Treasury doctrine would later be labelled 'psychological crowding out'. It showed how, even with less than full employment, loan-financed government expenditure might make no difference to the level of employment. Further, Keynes had consistently argued that 'cheap money' was the main requirement for recovery. He had advocated public works as an alternative to it. Following the Wall Street collapse, interest rates were starting to tumble. Was not Keynes's advocacy of new public expenditure likely to retard the fall in interest rates?

The reformulation of the Treasury view as a confidence argument took Keynes by surprise. He threw question after question at Hopkins. Eventually the chairman concluded: 'I think we may characterise it as a drawn battle.'[61] Keynes wrote to his wife (18 May 1930): 'I had a rather exciting cross-examination. . . . Sir R. Hopkins . . . was very clever; but he did not understand the technique of what we were discussing; – so the combination made for good hunting. But it proved that the Treasury don't know any more than the Bank of England what it is all about – enough to make tears roll down the eyes of a patriot.'

The question posed by Hopkins was: could Lloyd George's policy have worked if the market judged it unsound? Or to put it more generally: was the aggregate amount of investment in a free society any more 'controllable' than was the rate of interest? Keynes was not shaken in his conviction that the state could and should maintain employment at a high level. But for the first time he started to pay explicit attention to the role of 'confidence' in influencing the 'dynamics' of an expansionary policy. As we shall see, this led him to place increasing emphasis on protection in the coming months.

Keynes's appearance before the Macmillan Committee marks the start of the Keynesian Revolution in policymaking. No policymaker after 1930 made the mistake of assuming that all prices were flexible and that, by fixing the exchange at any level one wanted, one secured an automatic adjustment of costs. When the gold standard was abandoned in 1931, it was abandoned for good: 'cheap money' was the slogan of the 1930s. This was Keynes's victory. But the influence did not flow all one way. The Bank was not shaken out of its belief that monetary policy was less powerful than Keynes was suggesting. This was Clay's victory. The Treasury had brought the confidence issue to the forefront of the public works discussion. This was Hopkins's victory. Keynes was influenced by both arguments. The main conclusion he drew from all this is that his theory had to go back to the drawing board before it could hope to overcome the 'model' of the economy lodged in the minds of the 'practical men'. The *General Theory* was, in part, a response to the objections of the Bank and the Treasury to his proposals.

Keynes's own policy agenda had not changed since 1922 when he first noticed that it was 'almost hopeless' to try to force down wages in line with prices, and suggested the alternative aim of forcing up prices to the level of the 'going' wage rate. Less clearly, Keynes was coming to see that public spending was needed as a complement to cheap money in order to raise prices and thus restore 'normal' profits. The question of 'confidence' might be met by a policy of protection. Finally, Keynes was looking to a 'social contract' to prevent British 'efficiency wages' from rising faster than elsewhere in the long run. This was the drift of his thinking on policy by the autumn of 1930.

III. THE COMMITTEE OF ECONOMISTS

On the Macmillan Committee, Keynes tried to get bankers, civil servants and economists to rethink their principles. As a member of the Economic Advisory Council he had a chance to persuade the government to do something. The EAC met once a month: MacDonald presided, Philip Snowden, Chancellor of the Exchequer, and J. H. Thomas, Lord Privy Seal, also attended. Keynes soon realised he was back in the 'monkey house', as he liked to call committee meetings at which no business could be done. The EAC was further weakened by Snowden's success in blocking various lines of inquiry, for example into monetary policy, and by his favouring of the views of businessmen above those of economists. As a means of silencing the businessmen, Keynes urged MacDonald to appoint a small committee of economists 'to closet themselves together and try to produce, say by the end of October, an agreed diagnosis of our present problems and a reasoned list of possible remedies'.[62] MacDonald set up the Committee on 24 July 1930 with Keynes as chairman and Pigou, Henderson, Stamp and Lionel Robbins as the other members. The secretaries were A. F. Hemming, joint secretary with Henderson (who had relinquished his editorship of the *Nation*) of the EAC, and Keynes's pupil, Richard Kahn, now a fellow at King's. The Committee met for the first time on 10 September.

This 'small but significant victory for the economists' point of view'[63] was made possible by the damage the government had suffered through Oswald Mosley's resignation on 19 May. In a powerful resignation speech on 28 May Mosley had attacked not only the policy of inaction but also the institutional machinery for dealing with unemployment. Mosley's resignation strengthened MacDonald's position against Snowden. He now took over the chairmanship of a panel of ministers to deal with unemployment, shifting the discredited J. H. Thomas to the Dominions Office. Over the Treasury's objections, more money was made available for local authority spending on public works. The advice MacDonald now sought from the EAC Committee of Economists was a further direct challenge to Treasury control. It gave Keynes his best chance since the war to change the direction of economic policy – if he could carry his fellow economists with him.

Keynes produced a short list of questions for the second meeting of the Committee on 11 September. He asked his colleagues to estimate the effects on unemployment, prices and real wages of an increase in investment (at home and abroad), or a tariff, or a reduction in British money wages. In the second part of his questionnaire, he asked them to estimate 'how much too high (in order of magnitude are) (a) real wages, (b) money wages at the existing level of world prices?', continuing, 'If your estimate of the excess of real wages is greater than your estimate of the increase of real wages per unit of productivity [since 1910–14], how do you explain this?' When the doctors assembled at Stamp's house, Shortlands, on 26–28 September, to compare their diagnoses of the sickly British economy, they soon found themselves at loggerheads.

In theory the Keynes–Henderson axis, as expressed in their 1929 pamphlet *Can Lloyd George Do It?*, should have been the pivot on which everything turned; but, as Dalton noted, Henderson's 'positive side' had wilted since his appointment as joint secretary to the Economic Advisory Council. It was Henderson, not Keynes, who had become MacDonald's favourite economist. MacDonald liked to needle Snowden by setting up committees, but was happy to accept excuses for inaction delivered in a Scottish accent. Henderson's reports to the EAC had been getting steadily more gloomy and alarmist. He was increasingly worried about the effects of a budget deficit on business confidence. The change in his views was partly the result of a change in position: Henderson was now inside the government machine, Keynes outside it. But Henderson also thought the slump had drastically curtailed the field for national manoeuvre. Unorthodox experiments carried a higher economic and political risk. Henderson's shift is symptomatic of a wider movement of opinion. Historians have exaggerated the support which existed for radical solutions to unemployment.[64] The fair-weather radicalism of the 1920s, unbacked by intellectual conviction, was the first casualty of the slump. Everywhere hard times were met by retrenchment.

Henderson's defection from the joint position of *Can Lloyd George Do It?* was signalled in a letter to Keynes of 30 May 1930. The gist of it was that, with the slump gathering force, nothing should be advocated, or done, which would lead businessmen to expect heavier taxation. Given the world depression, the budgetary cost of public works schemes was bound to shoot up, as the projects financed became progressively less remunerative ('parks and playing grounds'). Business would expect higher taxes, and:

> the alarm might quite easily serve to counteract fully the employment benefits of the programme, and you would then be in the vicious circle of requiring a still bigger programme, still more unremunerative in character, with an increasing hole in the Budget, and increasing apprehension, until you were faced with either abandoning the whole policy or facing a real panic – flight from the pound and all the rest.[65]

In his reply to Keynes's questionnaire of 11 September, Henderson stressed that, it would be 'utterly wrong under present circumstances to embark on anything in the nature of a gamble.... [In] view of the present state of business confidence, I am very doubtful whether anything which is clearly calculated to make things worse a little later on would yield any immediate advantages on balance.' He favoured tariffs for revenue, balance-of-payments and protective purposes, but they were no alternative to lower money wages, though they might make the reduction needed less. Unemployment benefit should be examined: it was an 'essentially new phenomenon', affecting both labour mobility and the budgetary balance, 'thus creating a new vicious circle in the history of the trade cycle'.[66]

At fifty-three, Arthur Pigou, Professor of Political Economy at Cambridge, was the senior economist on the Committee. His fellow member Lionel Robbins described him as a 'recluse', who 'hated oral discussion of technical subjects'.[67] Partly because of these habits, he was also by this time a fairly isolated figure at Cambridge. Heart trouble in the late 1920s had given him a shambling, unkempt appearance. He wrote to Keynes in 1929, 'My heart is nearly as good as new; I plan to renovate my head next.' But both Keynes and Kahn feared the Prof might have gone 'gaga'. Keynes was fond of Pigou, and they agreed about policy more often than not; it was to Pigou's way of doing economics that Keynes chiefly objected. 'My main hesitation', he wrote to him on 5 January 1930, '... arises out of a doubt as to whether the method of abstraction by which you first of all deal with the problems in terms of a barter economy, and then at a later stage bring in monetary considerations, is a legitimate means of approach in dealing with a short-period problem of this kind, the characteristics of which are, or may be, hopelessly entangled with features arising out of monetary factors.'[68]

Inasmuch as the *General Theory* was a methodological revolution, it was chiefly directed against Pigou's method of economic analysis.

In reply to Keynes's questionnaire, Pigou explained the unemployment problem in terms of shifts in demand unaccompanied by shifts in people, leaving real rewards to sections of labour wrongly distributed. In addition, the decline in prices following the return to gold, uncompensated by reductions in money wages, had left real wages ahead of the real aggregate demand for labour. Money-wage rigidity in face of shifts in demand and falling prices had been promoted by the dole. Pigou's analysis suggested that if money wages were completely flexible there would be no unemployment problem. Like Keynes, Pigou assumed that wages were fixed in the short run, and therefore that 'unsound devices' might be psychologically useful. Thus public investment might increase employment if 'it bamboozles wage earners into not claiming money-wage increases equivalent to price increases'; a tariff would increase employment 'insofar as it removed errors of pessimism or created errors of optimism in businessmen's minds'. Keynes commented, 'Must they always be errors?' Monetary cures, Pigou implied, could affect real events only if workers and businessmen were subject to 'money illusion'. The debate on this question goes on to this day.

Keynes's most intransigent opponent was the thirty-two-year-old Lionel Robbins, who had just been made Professor of Economics at the London School of Economics. He was jealous of Cambridge's prestige and was determined to build up the LSE as a rival centre of power and influence. A powerful and passionate man, anti-collectivist, pro-free trade, with a temper as quick as Keynes's, he alone had the intellectual conviction to resist Keynes's consensual embrace. Perhaps Keynes did not realise the strength of Robbins's *laissez-faire* convictions when he suggested him for the Committee; or perhaps he simply overestimated his own powers of persuasion. Two years after his experience with Robbins on the Committee of Economists he refused to debate unemployment with him on the wireless: 'He is so difficult and queer! Also his reasons for differing are so eccentric and so totally different from the ordinary man's, that it may be difficult to bring out the real points which are perplexing the public.'[69]

What made their disagreements non-negotiable was that they had diametrically opposite *theories* of the causes of the slump. Robbins's derived from Austrian economics. For Robbins the slump was not the disease which needed cure: it *was* the cure for the previous disease of over-expansion of credit. The wasting away of the patient was simply the removal of layers of blubber caused by years of riotous living. If this might seem an odd way of describing Britain's experience in the 1920s, Robbins had an ingenious answer: Britain was suffering from the effects of having consumed its capital during the war without having adjusted its standard of living to its reduced circumstances. The cure would be rendered far less painful if wage flexibility were restored. Here Robbins agreed with Pigou. Unlike Pigou, though,

Robbins was fundamentally opposed to Keynes's 'remedies', which, he thought, could only retard the healing forces of the slump. In the *General Theory*, Keynes would write ironically, 'It is the distinction of Prof Robbins that he, almost alone, continues to maintain a consistent scheme of thought, his practical recommendations belonging to the same system as his theory.'[70] Robbins later regretted his quarrel with Keynes. He conceded that, whatever the validity of his explanation of the origins of the slump, in terms of overinvestment, its '*sequelae* ... were completely swamped by vast deflationary forces'; his cure was 'as unsuitable as denying blankets and stimulants to a drunk who has fallen into an icy pond, on the ground that his original trouble was overheating.'[71]

Josiah Stamp, the most respected public servant of his day, was indifferent to theory, but most of his instincts were 'Keynesian'. Although a director of the Bank of England, he found Norman 'impulsive, rigid, and depressing'.[72] He testified to the Macmillan Committee that the return to gold had depressed British industry, and argued that deficit finance could lift the economy from a low- to high-employment equilibrium.[73] In a notably relaxed broadcast conversation with Keynes in February 1930 – 'he slightly towards the "right" and you slightly towards the "left"'[74] – and marked by friendly exchanges starting 'My dear Stamp', and 'Hush, Maynard', Stamp had worried that Keynes went too far in his attack on foreign lending, but conceded graciously, 'I never can answer you when you are theorising.' His role on the Committee was to keep the peace.

Keynes's answer to his own questionnaire, dated 21 September, was so congested, and the terms so complicated, that he had to plead for the charity of his fellow economists. Nevertheless his 'prolegomena', derived from the disequilibrium model of the *Treatise*, provided a framework for analysing the link between unemployment and the level of real wages which his foremost critic, Robbins, conceded to be of 'great aesthetic beauty'.

Real wages are in equilibrium, Keynes wrote, when profits are 'normal'. Disequilibrium real wages might arise either because of a change in labour productivity or because of a change in the terms of trade, since movements in either will affect the real value of output to firms. Keynes denied that British real wages had been increasing ahead of British productivity. Only one-ninth of 'abnormal' unemployment could be attributed to this cause. Most unemployment was due to the rise of sterling in 1924–5 having turned the terms of trade against Britain 'without this being compensated by a reduction of money wages to correspond to the new equilibrium terms of trade'.[75] Sterling's overvaluation thus narrowed the export surplus available for foreign investment while imposing a high bank rate which forced British savings abroad. As Keynes put it, 'the foreign balance is tending to decline at a time when foreign lending is trying to increase'.[76] Thus investment was falling short of savings – whence business losses and unemployment.

Beneath Keynes's technical drapery a fundamental question was being asked. How much could workers *do* about their unemployment? Keynes admitted that excessive real wages were correlated with unemployment, but he denied that the causation ran from wages to employment, as the analytical method of the other economists forced them to argue. It was not that excessive real wages caused 'abnormal' unemployment: rather, 'abnormal' unemployment and excessive real wages were joint effects of the fall in prices and loss of export markets due to sterling's overvaluation. It was the fall in output which caused the employed workers' share of output to rise, not workers' efforts to encroach on profits. Thus, 'Real wages seem to me to come in as a by-product of the remedies which we adopt to restore equilibrium. They come in at the end of the argument rather than at the beginning.'[77] Keynes accused economists like Pigou of treating the wages question solely as 'part of the long-period theory of distribution' in a closed system, while keeping the 'short-period theory of money and international trade' in a separate compartment of their minds.[78]

The policy alternatives suggested by Keynes's analysis were to *meet* the worsened equilibrium terms of trade by cutting money wages or *improve* them by reducing the pressure to lend abroad or enlarging the foreign balance at the given terms of trade. Of the latter, the first pointed to the stimulation of home investment, the second to protection. All three remedies implied some fall in the 'real wage' – employed workers' standards of living – since they all involved a decline in money wages relatively to cost of living. But in the case of the second and third remedies the real wage reduction comes about as a 'by-product' of an exogenous stimulus to demand. He wrote, 'It is better, if possible, to raise prices than to reduce money wages,' for three reasons: (1) 'Because there is less social resistance to keeping money wages unchanged when cost of living rises x per cent, than to reduce money wages x per cent with prices unchanged.' (2) 'Because, although a reduction of x per cent in money wages will mean a smaller reduction in real wages, this will not be believed.' (3) 'Because the method of raising prices throws the burden over a much wider area. In particular, it throws a due share on the *rentier* class and other recipients of fixed money incomes. Thus, from the point of view both of justice and of self-interest, the trade union leaders are right in preferring a rise of prices to a reduction of money wages as a means of restoring equilibrium.'[79] This is what Keynes had believed since 1922.

In developing his familiar case for increased home investment Keynes made use of a 'primitive draft' of the 'employment multiplier' worked out by Richard Kahn, joint secretary to the Committee, helped by the young statistician Colin Clark. In *Can Lloyd George Do It?*, Keynes had suggested that an initial expenditure on public works sets up a 'cumulative effect' through an 'increase in effective purchasing power'. Kahn had worked out a formula for calculating the net addition to employment produced by the consumption of the newly employed. Following Kahn, Keynes assumed that 'a given amount of primary employment gives rise to an approximately equal amount of secondary employment'. He emphasised that 'the amount of secondary employment ... does not depend on how the primary employment has been brought about' – thus brushing aside the Treasury's warning about possible repercussions of the initial expenditure on the state of business confidence. He reckoned that £150m of extra investment (enough to employ 750,000 for a year) would 'substantially' cure the unemployment problem through its repercussions on consumer spending. Keynes denied that the additional spending would be inflationary; but he failed to grasp the real significance of Kahn's work, which was that the investment programme would create the saving required to finance it.[80]

The most contentious feature of Keynes's paper was his espousal of protection. Tariff protection was put forward as a way of improving the balance of payments, thus satisfying 'the pressure to lend abroad at existing relative rates of interest'.[81] Beyond this Keynes stressed its effects on increasing capital wealth, business confidence and home investment, and enabling real wages to be reduced by raising prices rather than cutting money wages. A more fundamental attack on the free-trade case comes with the argument that 'any manufacturing country is probably just about as well fitted as any other to manufacture the great majority of articles'. Further, he would preserve 'essential industries' like British agriculture, even at the expense of some inefficiency, rather than have the rural population 'driven to live in Birmingham making screws'. This marshalling of the arguments for a tariff shows that Keynes had come to regard it as the only policy option, short of the unthinkable devaluation, left open to a British government, to protect the people from the full severity of the slump. This was a correct political judgement, but one that stuck in Robbins's gullet.

What would happen if the slump were allowed to run its course? Keynes admitted that 'certain mitigations' might come to the rescue:

> The gradually increasing impoverishment of the country will diminish saving, and the lower money wages will make us steadily more independent of imports; – a point may come, for example, if we stick to *laissez-faire* long enough, when we shall grow our own vines. Provided there is a residue of British exports (e.g., peers and old masters) which America is glad to have, and we can reduce our necessary imports *plus* our surplus savings to equality with this residue, equilibrium will be restored.[82]

The economists dispersed on 28 September, to meet again in London on 7–8 October. For this meeting, Keynes circulated a draft report which is perhaps the most balanced statement to come from his pen of what a Keynesian unemployment policy at the time might have looked like, both in terms of the modesty of what could be achieved by demand expansion and because of its attention to supply-side factors. It gives an excellent, though incomplete, insight into the conditions of effectiveness of Keynesian measures to reduce unemployment. The balance was forced on Keynes by the need to accommodate the differing analyses of his fellow economists. But this strengthened rather than weakened it, by forcing him to take into account the psychological repercussions set up by government action.

He rejected a policy of cutting money wages on the grounds set forth in his first paper, but to satisfy Henderson, Pigou and Robbins, he urged a number of labour-market reforms including the reform of restrictive practices, removal of obstacles to labour mobility and a 'drastic amendment of the conditions of eligibility of unemployment benefit' which 'immobilises' labour in declining industries 'in a state of subsidised unemployment'.[83] Of price-raising measures, those were to be preferred which 'are likely to have a large effect on employment and a relatively small effect on real wages'. He also made more effective use of Kahn's multiplier to define the conditions under which additional primary employment could give rise to 'secondary' employment. How much 'reflation' would be needed to restore full employment depended 'on the responsiveness of the volume of output to the stimulus of a small change in price', but he thought it a reasonable hope, 'having regard to the surplus capacity which now exists for the production of almost every class of goods – that a fairly large increase of output could be obtained to a fairly small improvement in prices'.[84]

The next matter to consider was 'how, in practice, increased investment can be brought about'. The task was to restore business confidence. Keynes took on board Hubert Henderson's suggestions for confidence-raising measures like balancing the budget and drastic reform of the dole, but in 'the long run we do not see how business confidence is likely to be maintained otherwise than by an actual recovery of business profits'. A tariff on manufactured imports emerges as the residual 'emergency' solution: the only measure which could raise output, employment and profits, without damaging business confidence, thus bypassing the Treasury objection to public works.[85]

In the event, discussions of Keynes's draft occupied the meetings of 7–8 and 15–16 October, both in London. By the second of these meetings, Henderson and Robbins were in open revolt. Henderson accused Keynes in his draft of running away 'by complex sophistication' from the 'plain moral of the situation, as plain as a pikestaff ... [which is] the disagreeable reactionary necessity of cutting costs (including wages) in industry and cutting expenditure in public affairs'. He accused his former mentor of not minding 'if there was a flight from the pound and a real dégringolade of British currency and credit'. However, he threw out a lifeline to Keynes: 'I can see no adequate reason for depriving ourselves, at a very critical time, of the great relief which a moderate general tariff would afford in many ways – relief to the Budget position, relief to the exchange position, some slight direct assistance to employment, and a much-needed stimulus to business confidence.'[86]

Henderson's outburst coincided with Robbins's rebellion. Robbins was passionately opposed to any version of a tariff. It was incredible, he burst out, that the finest minds in England were joining company with Beaverbrook and Rothermere in an 'Eldorado banal de tous les vieux garçons'. He presented an alternative draft report, which he said he would issue on his own rather than accept Keynes's draft.

By this time Keynes was 'so tired and in such a bad cycle that I hardly know what to do with myself'.[87] Strain from overwork no doubt partly explains what Robbins called his 'ungovernable rage' at the weekend meeting in Cambridge when Robbins demanded the right to a separate report. 'He denounced me before the others and laid it down that, as a minority of one, I was not entitled to a separate report.'[88] Henderson would not, of course, support Robbins on free trade. Pigou and Stamp wanted a consensual report. Pigou, representing the Cambridge establishment, told the young LSE upstart, 'One ... tries to reach the greatest possible measure of agreement and then, if necessary, adds a minute of dissent on particular points.'[89] Precedents were hunted down to show that what Robbins proposed was inadmissible. Keynes read out a letter from Hemming, the Committee's joint secretary, commenting 'very adversely' on Robbins's emotional condition. The row continued at a further final meeting in London on 22–23 October. Eventually, on Hemming's advice, Keynes allowed Robbins a separate report, at the end of the main report, but before the statistical appendices.[90] Dalton, who had had a blow-by-blow account from Robbins, a former student, noted in his diary, 'The tariff stuff is pitiable. I was taught to despise Protectionists at Cambridge. I do still.'[91] The economists' report was initialled on 24 October.

Redrafted and reshaped within Keynes's original framework by Pigou, Henderson and Robbins, it was 'a surprisingly coherent document'.[92] Keynes conceded on diagnosis to maximise support for protection. The diagnostic section follows the Pigou–Henderson–Robbins line on the genesis of British unemployment: adjustment to war and post-war shocks had been impeded by labour-market rigidities. Kahn's multiplier argument for public works did not survive. Keynes secured majority support for protection, he, Henderson and Stamp advocating a temporary 10 per cent tariff on imports for revenue purposes, plus a protective tariff on iron and steel, on condition 'that the industry should rationalise itself in accordance with an approved plan'. Pigou admitted the theoretical case, for tariffs but dissented from the actual proposals. These objections to protection were voiced much more strongly by Robbins and formed the core of his dissenting report. While he later saw his quarrel with Keynes on public spending as 'the greatest mistake of my professional life', he believed he was right on the tariff question. When he argued that it was easier to put on tariffs than get them removed, Keynes

apparently replied, 'How can you say the public will show reluctance? I have
not yet spoken on the problem.'[93]

The economists' report – and more so the discussion which preceded it
– is important biographically and intellectually, but left no immediate mark
on policy. After reading it, Snowden spoke 'with withering scorn of Keynes
and Stamp'; he found Robbins's dissent 'a most trenchant reply', Robbins
having meanwhile 'alerted Labour ministers to the intensity of expert opposition to Keynes'.[94] Mosley tried to rally the Labour Party behind a policy of
protection and imperial 'insulation', but though this gained him the support
of some young Tories (and encouraged him a little later to start the New
Party) it got little response from the predominantly free-trade Labour Party.
The report's five-month discussion by the Economic Advisory Council
'cannot be regarded as a success'.[95] The Cabinet Committee set up to
consider it dismissed it as a 'disappointing document', lacking unanimity
and too general to be of use.[96] With these words it was buried. But the
political economy case for protection was too compelling to disappear,
though it needed a change of government for it to be accepted. In deciding
to drop public works and go all out for a tariff Keynes once more showed
his uncanny ability to anticipate what would soon be politically acceptable.
His own public conversion to protection in March 1931 helped create the
political climate for the Import Duties Act six months later.

While the politicians, businessmen, bankers and economists talked, the
slump had been getting steadily worse. 'Stimulated by the sense of impoverishment resulting from Stock Exchange losses, the "vicious circle" of
reactions which characterises the typical trade depression is now in full
play. . . .. The fall in the prices of primary products during the last few months
. . . is a movement of the first order of magnitude comparable with the
fluctuations which have ushered in the most severe depressions in economic
history.' This was how Henderson presented the gathering world depression
to the Economic Advisory Council in May 1930. He was still hopeful that
trade depression, 'though for some time cumulative in its operation, sets
forces in motion which ultimately effect a cure; notably cheap money'.[97]
However, the cumulative forces continued to gather strength. After noting
the 'catastrophic fall' in prices since September 1929, the economists' report
declared that 'there is no recorded case in recent economic history of so
violent and rapid a collapse in the prices of staple commodities'.[98] After a
temporary recovery, Wall Street broke again in May and again in October
1930. Keynes was still expecting a recovery of prices in September and
advised John Ryan, secretary of the Lancashire Cotton Federation, to buy
large supplies of Indian and American cotton as a speculation on a rise.[99]
By 10 October he was writing to Lydia, 'Very bad smash on Wall Street,
revolution in Brazil, coming collapse in Germany – means that nothing is
safe.' Unemployment surged relentlessly ahead. 'The Great Depression',
as Henderson presciently predicted it would be known to posterity, 'has

engulfed almost every country, whether free trade or protectionist, agricultural or manufacturing, backward or forward. . . .'[100] It formed the crucial background to the generalisation of Keynes's theory from the 'open' to the 'closed' economy, as well as his radical re-evaluation of the prospects of unmanaged capitalism.

Throughout 1930 Keynes had expended a huge amount of energy to no avail. Under the impact of the depression, the government's hopeful inquiries were wound up. A decisive moment, as A. J. P. Taylor writes, was Labour's rejection of Mosley's New Deal in May 1930: 'the moment when the British people resolved unwittingly to stand on the ancient ways'.[101] At the Labour Party's Conference in October, MacDonald shuffled off responsibility for the slump on capitalism. 'So, my friends,' he cried in his melodious Scottish baritone, 'we are not on trial; it is the system under which we live. It has broken down, not only in this little island; it has broken down in Europe, in Asia, in America; it has broken down everywhere *as it was bound to break down* . . .' (emphasis added).[102]

IV. MAYNARD'S CHEERFULNESS

Keynes's analysis of the slump is remarkable for its buoyancy. He utterly rejected the idea of Lydia's 'Bolshie' friend Dmitri Mirsky that this was the final crisis of capitalism. But equally he rejected the orthodox view, with its powerful moral overtones, that the slump, being the cure for previous excess, had to be allowed to run its course. Partly this was a matter of natural optimism, partly it was the result of his conviction, rooted in analysis, that capitalism was not sick but unstable. Keynes's activism, which drew him so strongly to short-term problems, made him utterly opposed to the doctrine of nature's cure – whether it came from Marx or Hayek. That is why he was so resistant to structural analyses of the slump. For such analyses pointed to the need for vast, and possibly catastrophic, changes in the 'structure of production', whereas his own analysis suggested that the cure lay in a revival of cheerfulness or, as he was to call them, 'animal spirits' To be sure, Keynes was not simply applying the doctrine of Coué to economics. Businessmen's sagging spirits would not revive spontaneously, though he did believe the slump would level out – 'the mere lapse of time tends to bring about some degree of recovery'.[103] Things had to happen which would cause businessmen to see the world in a more confident way. But, before the right things could be made to happen, the slump had to be seen as a man-made catastrophe, not as a visitation from God or nature. It had to be seen as *manageable*, robbed of its cosmic significance, presented in a frame that made technical solutions seem feasible. Keynes's paradox, which few could grasp and which many would find unacceptable today if expressed in ordinary language, is that horrendous events may have trivial causes, and easy remedies. When our world collapses, we want to believe that something is greatly wrong; and we mistrust someone who says it was all the result of avoidable policy mistakes.

Keynes's cheerfulness comes out in his choice of 'Economic Possibilities for Our Grandchildren', which he had first given to the Winchester Essay Society in 1928, for a public lecture in Madrid on 9 June 1930. He had been invited over by the Anglo-Spanish Friendship Society. 'The prevailing world depression,' he declared,

> the enormous anomaly of unemployment in a world full of wants, the disastrous mistakes we have made, blind us to ... the true interpretation of the trend of things. For I predict that both of the two opposed errors of pessimism which now makes so much noise in the world will be proved wrong in our own time – the pessimism of the revolutionaries who think that things are so bad that nothing can save us but violent change, and the pessimism of the reactionaries who consider the balance of our economic and social life so precarious that we must risk no experiments.[104]

The ten days he and Lydia spent in Spain were a particularly welcome break for both of them. Maynard was exhausted by the Macmillan Committee hearings, the EAC and trying to finish his book. A shattering blow was the death, on 19 January, of Frank Ramsey, at Guy's Hospital, following an operation for jaundice. He was only twenty-six, 'in a way the greatest genius in College and such a dear creature besides', Maynard wrote to Lydia. 'Poor Lettice and the two babies.' Ramsey's death not only impoverished economics – to which he had started to make notable contributions – but broke up the powerful intellectual circle, formed when Sraffa and Wittgenstein arrived in Cambridge, which had rekindled Keynes's love of philosophy. Spain provided a rest and a tonic. Following numbing entertainments given by the British Ambassador and Spanish grandees in Madrid, the visitors slowly wended their way home through the Romanesque cities of Old Castile.

That summer at Tilton, country life, Bloomsbury-style, continued as inharmonious as ever:

> Duncan [Clive Bell reported to Lytton Strachey on 6 September] seems to have been pressing on his affair with George Bergen, an Eastside Jew boy from New York.... Vanessa is rather unhappy I'm afraid....
>   Also the Keyneses have fallen into the deepest disgrace.... Virginia, suffering a good deal from the heat, having entertained Vita [Sackville-West] and her children to breakfast, & Ethel Smythe in the forenoon, received a visit from the Keyneses at tea-time; and showing them over

the hot-house fell down in a swoon. The Woolves, either on principle or from economy, were without a servant, so Maynard and his chauffeur [Edgar Weller] helped to carry her into the house and lay her down on the floor. Whereupon the Keyneses and chauffeur made off. As Virginia had a second and worse attack a few minutes later this conduct was generally condemned, although Maynard says that he could tell by her colour that it was not a swoon but a touch of the sun. She is getting better but is not yet perfectly recovered.

Cheerfulness, or some would say foolhardiness, was very much to the fore in Keynes's enthusiastic backing of Lydia's plans for a new ballet venture. Lydia had started on her career as a straight actress at the ADC Theatre in Cambridge in November 1929. But she eagerly seized the chance of a second ballet career offered by a scheme to produce ballets in London and provide work for ballet dancers and choreographers living there. In the autumn of 1929 she began taking lessons with Madame Zanfretta – 'good old Italian School, more strict than Checchetti' – and joined Arnold Haskell, Philip Richardson, Edwin Evans and Ninette de Valois in founding the Camargo Society at the end of 1929, named after the stage name of the eighteenth-century Belgian dancer Anne Cuppi. The idea was to put on original and classical ballets four times a year before subscription audiences in the West End, using the dancers of the Mercury Theatre Club and the Vic-Wells School. Lydia joined its Committee as 'choreographic adviser'.

Ninette de Valois, Frederick Ashton and Constant Lambert now became regular guests at Lydia's all-day Sunday lunches, discussing their projects with much consumption of Russian food and Maynard's excellent claret. 'My Lankiest, it is extraordinary how much human beings talk,' Lydia told Maynard on 13 October 1929, after Ninette had stayed five hours. She had to tell Ashton, then a competent young dancer in Marie Rambert's Mercury Theatre Club, that his future lay in choreography, not dancing, and that he could not expect leading roles in Camargo's productions. 'So you see, it is all delicate, but we are facing frank grounds,' she explained to Maynard.[105] Ashton recalls that 'she could be extremely nice at first, but then extremely outspoken and frank'.[106] Karsavina, living in London, was also recruited to help the new venture. 'She would love to talk to you about home industries,' Lydia wrote to Maynard.

The Camargo Society was another addition to Maynard's role as patron of the arts. He had backed the London Artists' Association out of friendship for Duncan and Vanessa; he backed Camargo, as he was later to build the Arts Theatre at Cambridge, to give his beloved Lydia an appropriate stage for her genius. 'Using my tongue more than my legs', Lydia appeared at the Arts Theatre Club from 10–16 December 1930 in a masque of poetry and music, *Beauty, Truth, and Rarity*, produced by Dadie Rylands, with a cast of

Cambridge undergraduates. She repeated her 1928 performance as the Afflicted Fancy in *A Lover's Complaint*, acted the Lady in *Comus* for the first time in public, and danced a pavane by Dowland with Fred Ashton. She danced in Camargo Society productions of *Cephalus and Procris* in January 1931; William Walton's *Façade*, with Ashton, in April; Constant Lambert's *Rio Grande* as the Queen of the Whores in November; *The Origin of Design* in 1932; and *Coppélia* in 1933. Arnold Haskell thought Lydia 'wonderful both in her acting and dancing' in the masque,[107] but in his more considered judgement her career in the English ballet – which ended in 1933 – fell short of her Diaghilev days 'for a very understandable reason: the choreography assigned to her was insufficient in complexity to extend a dancer of such wide experience. She forced her effect and earned applause through over-acting, where before she had been subtle and restrained.... This mixture of an old tradition with a new development can never succeed.'[108] Maynard's family connection with Camargo extended to Geoffrey Keynes, whose adaptation of William Blake's designs for his poem *Job*, set to music by Vaughan Williams, choreographed by de Valois and with décor by his sister-in-law Gwen Raverat, became the Society's most important original work.

Patronage mingled in Maynard's mind with larger purposes. The attempt to start an English ballet company in the depth of a depression was a considerable act of faith, Maynard's support for it a conspicuous symbol of the cheerfulness he was advocating. The depression was a time to be doing things, not closing them down. 'The patient does not need rest. He needs exercise,' he declared in a radio broadcast in January 1931. Of course, they soon ran out of money. Lydia appealed to Maynard for help on 29 January 1931: 'Oh Lank! Committee for ever, one could run "Camargo" without a committee, only with cash, instead we all meet, and we are all different like Liberals.' Maynard agreed to become treasurer. Their attempts to raise money from the Courtaulds brought what Lydia called a 'frigidaire' in her relations with Sam, who had subscribed a mere £25 to the Society. Lydia was not the only one to come away empty-handed. Mosley had been to solicit funds for his New Party. Sam 'liked Mosley very much, he does not think him big enough to rule the country'.[109] To Lydia Sam wrote with dignity that 'we should be able to differ amicably on artistic matters'.[110] The reason for the Courtaulds' coolness towards the Camargo Society was not just artistic: Maynard noted in January 1931 that shares in Sam's company were worth £54m less than they had been eighteen months before.[111] After a 'shocking' meeting with Lil and Sam in May, he seems to have got a promise of support.[112]

Maynard continued to press for action in his public pronouncements. On 13 December 1930 he was praising Oswald Mosley's Manifesto, signed by seventeen Labour MPs, for 'offering a starting point for thought and action'.[113] In a radio broadcast on 15 January 1931 Keynes told the British housewife to spend, not save. He urged the same attitude on the local authorities:

> I read a few days ago of a proposal to drive a great new road, a broad boulevard, parallel to the Strand, on the south side of the Thames, as a new thoroughfare joining Westminster to the City. That is the right sort of notion. But I should like to see something bigger still. For example, why not pull down the whole of South London from Westminster to Greenwich, and make a good job of it – housing on that convenient area near to their work a much greater population than at present, in far better buildings with all the conveniences of modern life, yet at the same time providing hundreds of acres of squares and avenues, parks and public spaces, having, when it was finished, something magnificent to the eye, yet useful and convenient to human life as a monument to our age. Would that employ men? Why, of course it would! Is it better that the men should stand idle and miserable, drawing the dole? Of course it is not.[114]

The forty leading articles, the cartoons and the sheaves of letters which followed this broadcast made Keynes feel very 'prima donnish'. 'Never such publicity in my life,' he told Lydia. Yet in fact he had never been so isolated. The clamour for retrenchment, particularly on the dole, was reaching a crescendo. On 29 January 1931, the Treasury memorandum to the Royal Commission on Unemployment Insurance – prepared by Hopkins – had declared that 'continued state borrowing on the present scale without adequate provision for repayment ... would quickly call in question the stability of the British financial system'. On 11 February, Snowden agreed to set up an Economy Committee (headed by an actuary, Sir George May), remarking in the House of Commons that expenditure which may be 'easy and tolerable' in good times, 'becomes intolerable in a time of grave industrial depression'.

Henderson thought Keynes had gone mad:

> My complaint against the tenor of all your public writings or utterances ... [he wrote on 14 February] is that in not a single one of them has there been a trace of a suggestion that the Budget situation is one which is really very serious and must be treated seriously. On the contrary, over and over again you have implied that it doesn't matter a bit, that expenditure is a thing you want to press on with, whether by the Government or by anybody else, and that the question of whether it involves a Budget charge is a minor matter which is hardly worth considering.... The effect is to convey the impression to all people, however intelligent and open-minded, that you have gone completely crazy, and impairing all the influence you have with them, while pleasing and encouraging only those who say that you mustn't lay a finger on the dole.[115]

No reply by Keynes is recorded. But in a letter to the New York banker Walter Case, of Case, Pomeroy & Co., Keynes refused to join the 'bears' on sterling. 'My own view', he wrote on 21 February, 'is that all this pessimistic prognosis is complete moonshine.... The introduction of a tariff which is a resource for both the Budget and for general business confidence which we still have up our sleeves ... may quite suddenly reverse sentiment when it will be discovered that the market is completely bare of stock.... I may perhaps add that it is not by any means off the map for the present Labour Government to have recourse to a revenue tariff.'[116]

Once more, Keynes seems to have been relying on his powers of persuasion. His public response to the looming financial crisis was given on 7 March, seven weeks before the budget, when his 'Proposals for a Revenue Tariff' were published in the newly merged *New Statesman and Nation*. It was one of Keynes's most powerful pieces. 'As the recantation of an avowed free trader, it caused a sensation.'[117] At Lord Rothermere's request he provided a more popular version for the *Daily Mail*. 'What do you think? Is it loss of virtue – to write for Lord R. in exchange for 10 eiderdowns?'[118] (Keynes was paid £100.) In the columns of the *New Statesman*, free traders sprang to the defence of their cherished dogma. In a passionate and vituperative reply, Lionel Robbins said Keynes had overestimated the yield of his tariff by £20m to £30m. There were 'half a dozen ways of meeting [the budget problem] each better both administratively and economically than this stale and dreary expedient of a tariff'. The only solution was to reduce costs; tariffs never came down, they simply grew.[119] Beveridge and E. D. Simon also weighed in on the free-trade side. Keynes replied realistically, 'Now free trade, combined with great mobility of wage-rates, is a tenable intellectual proposition.... The practical reason against it, which must suffice for the moment, whether we like it or not, is that it is *not* one of the alternatives between which we are in a position to choose. We are not offered it. It does not exist outside the field of pure hypothesis. The actual alternative is the policy of Negation.'

The controversy raged for several weeks and was taken up by other journals. Politically, Keynes's new departure had little effect in the quarters where it mattered most. Conservatives welcomed his conversion and added his arguments, somewhat inconsistently, to their own proposals for protection. The Liberals regretted his new stand and recalled his brilliant articles in defence of free trade in 1923. Copies sent in advance to MacDonald, Snowden and Lloyd George produced no result. Snowden's budget of 27 April had no revenue tariff: Keynes called it in the *Evening Standard*, 'The Budget That Wastes Time'.

Maynard was again working flat out in the winter of 1930 and spring of 1931, in mainly atrocious weather. To his writing, broadcasting, corresponding, teaching, bursarial work, committee work, City work, ballet work, drafting the Macmillan Report, 'arguing out the Treatise' with Hawtrey,

Robertson, Kahn and the 'Circus' (see pp. 481–2 below) was added the chore of winding up the *Nation* and transferring its titles to a new company, of which he remained chairman. The *Nation's* death was not due to financial problems. Losses were reduced to £250 a year in the last three years of its life, following ruthless cost-cutting and a large increase in advertising revenue. What caused Keynes to call it a day was the departure of Hubert Henderson to government service in 1930, the impending loss of Leonard Woolf and the failure of the Liberal Party to break through in the 1929 general election. The political balance of the left-centre had shifted decisively to the Labour Party. The *New Statesman* board, for its part, was determined to get rid of its long-standing editor Clifford Sharp, by now an alcoholic. Keynes had first proposed a merger in the summer of 1929, the two papers combining to form a 'Liberal' journal. This was turned down. In the autumn of 1930 he put together a new merger package. What decided him to try again was that he knew Kingsley Martin was available to take over the editorship of the *New Statesman*. Keynes had known Martin at Cambridge and, though he failed to get a fellowship at King's College, was so impressed by his thesis on Lord Palmerston that he got him a reviewing job in the *Nation*. When Martin, languishing at the *Manchester Guardian*, told Keynes that he was in the job market, Keynes suggested him to Arnold Bennett, chairman of the *New Statesman* board, as a possible editor of the magazine.

The first issue of the *New Statesman and Nation* appeared on 28 February 1931. It styled itself as an independent organ of the left, without special affiliation to a political party. Many of the *Nation's* contributors continued to write for it, including Keynes, who, as we have seen, produced one of his most notable articles for its second issue. Keynes continued to interfere in editorial policy, objecting particularly to the paper's growing sympathy for Soviet communism; but whereas the *Nation* bore the stamp of Keynes, the *New Statesman* was unmistakably Kingsley Martin's.

With hindsight one can see that from this period of intense strain date the first signs of the breakdown of Keynes's health. He complained of a bad toothache at the end of January, and spent over an hour with the dentist, who dragged out a tiny fragment of nerve. Lydia kissed his 'corrected teeth', but by the end of February he was ill with tonsillitis and influenza. After taking a week off (during which he presumably wrote his article on protection), he was back in time for a six-hour College Council on 7 March: 'like being with lunatics each of whom sees very small rats and mice running in every direction, but no two of them see the *same* rats and mice'. On top of this there were servant problems. In January, the Harlands suddenly left the Keyneses' service after ten years, Alice Brown replacing Mrs Harland as cook. Lydia acquired a maid, '14 years of age, small, one crossed eye, glasses, no man would snatch her, only disadvantage Roman Catholic', who had to be dismissed in May. Something of Maynard's lassitude emerges from his letter to Lydia of 4 May: 'Last night an evening squash at Dadie's, but such a party

needs too much surface vitality. I was sleepy and inactive. Sat down next to
Lettice [Ramsey] and could find nothing to say to her. Was introduced to a
Siamese Prince, half Russian, and could find nothing to say to him. Found
myself next to Michael Redgrave, and had nothing to say to him. So I must
come back to my dearest Countess of Talkie.'

On 30 May, Maynard and his Countess embarked at Southampton for
New York on the SS *Adriatic*, his first visit since 1917. He had been invited
by Quincy Wright, an economist at Chicago University, to take part in a
symposium on unemployment organised by the Harris Memorial Foundation. It was an opportunity to study American conditions first-hand. They
spent two weeks in New York at the Ambassador's Hotel, Maynard seeing
columnists, Federal Reserve Bank officials and other bankers, to whom he
was introduced by Walter Case, whose firm Case, Pomeroy & Co, employed
him as a consultant. On 20 June, President Hoover announced his plan for
a one-year moratorium (that is, suspension, not remission) of all inter-
governmental payments, including reparations, arising from the war. For a
week there was a boom on the world stock markets. It collapsed once it
became clear that France was making difficulties. Keynes praised the Hoover
initiative as 'a first step of the greatest practical value'. It was the effective
end of the miserable reparations saga. But it came too late to save the
financial system. Keynes reported to Falk that he had not realised how
insolvent the banks were: 'They have purchased great quantities of second-
grade bonds which have depreciated in value and their advances to farmers
and against real estate are inadequately secured.' So nervous were depositors
that safe deposit boxes were no longer obtainable: there must have been
$400m–$500m actually hoarded in boxes.[120] To Henderson he wrote; 'At any
moment bank runs are liable to break out almost anywhere in the country.
All this tends towards a mania for liquidity by anyone who can achieve it.'
'Barmy' opposition from some New York banks was inhibiting the Federal
Reserve Board from open-market operations to push up bond prices.

In Chicago, Keynes gave three lectures, on 22 and 26 June and on 2
July, as well as a talk to the Chicago Council on Foreign Relations on the
Hoover moratorium. The lectures are his most complete explanation on
record of the causes of the great depression. They are also the last occasion when he deployed an unmodified *Treatise* model to explain what was
going on.

The leading characteristic of the 1925–8 boom, he explained, was an
'extraordinary willingness to borrow for purposes of new real investment at
very high rates of interest'. The resulting prosperity, based on 'building, the
electrification of the world, and the associated enterprises of roads and
motor cars', spread from the United States to the rest of the world, except
Britain. The part played by inflation was 'surprisingly small'. The slump
which followed was due to 'extraordinary imbecility', not overinvestment
producing an inevitable reaction. Business conditions required interest rates

to fall; but instead the Federal Reserve System pushed up interest rates to check Wall Street. Very dear money in the United States had contractionary effects elsewhere. Also speculation was attracted to Wall Street away from foreign bonds. Once the decline started it gathered cumulative force. This was 'the whole of the explanation for the slump'.

Keynes also took part in a number of round-table discussions with the economists to whom he had lectured. The main point of interest is that the Chicago economists were much keener than he was on public works as a remedy for American unemployment; indeed, American economists had been discussing fiscal stabilisation from the early 1920s onwards. Keynes remained true to his *Treatise* analysis that in a closed system (to which America approximated more than Britain) a reduction in the rate of interest would do the trick.[121] Although the Chicago economists seemed more Keynesian than Keynes on this point, the truth is that none of them had the confidence to carry out a theory-based policy of public works, because bits of the theory were missing. Specifically, the multiplier was unknown in Chicago.

The visitors spent their last weekend in the United States staying with the Walter Cases at Bald Peak Country Club in New Hampshire. Lydia reported it heaven after Chicago, 'where we were boiled in the day time and fried at night, when I walked like Eve without garments into the passages of the hotel to get the draft, and could have been arrested, [while] Maynard with better manners lied in bed and sweated quietly...' In New Hampshire Maynard played golf in the day and bridge in the evenings, with equal lack of proficiency.

V. *DEGRINGOLADE*

They arrived back in Southampton on 18 July to the onset of the British financial crisis. While they were on the high seas, Montagu Norman received a cable from Harrison, governor of the Federal Reserve Bank of New York: 'We are concerned and surprised at the sudden drop in sterling exchange today. Can you throw any light on this?' Norman could not. The Macmillan Report had been published on 13 July. Most of it was a sophisticated account of the technique of monetary control, with a long-term recommendation that monetary policy should be directed much more to the control of domestic prices than to the exchange rate. It marked belated acceptance of Keynes's position in the *Tract on Monetary Reform*. On the question of immediate remedies for the slump, the Committee predictably divided into warring groups. The largest group of those who published addenda attached themselves to Keynes's advocacy of capital development under cover of a tariff. Ernest Bevin added a separate addendum advocating devaluation, which the Keynes group rejected 'in the special circumstances of Great Britain'. The report was generally regarded as a triumph for Keynes. However, this mattered less than a small section of figures showing that in March 1931 London had a net short-term debtor position of £254m. Everyone knew that the City had been borrowing short and lending long. But with London's short-term assets being immobilised by foreign moratoria – Germany defaulted on 15 July – the question of the City's solvency was posed. This was shortly followed by doubts about the government's solvency. The May Report of 31 July forecast a budget deficit of £120m and demanded economies of £97m, including a 20 per cent cut in the standard rate of unemployment benefit. (The projected deficit turned out to be £170m.) Thus the *dégringolade* which Henderson had long foreseen came to pass. Britain was regarded by investors as an unsafe place in which to hold money. Within a month the Labour government had been swept away, to be followed shortly by the gold standard itself.

Unlike in the financial crisis of 1914, when he was summoned to London, Keynes passed the 1931 crisis fretting at Tilton. True enough, MacDonald wrote to him on 2 August from Lossiemouth asking for his reactions to the May Report. Keynes replied on the 5th that they were not fit to be published. But he strongly urged MacDonald not to attempt to carry out the Report, for reasons he had long given but more especially because 'it is now clearly *certain* that we shall go off the existing parity at no distant date ... when doubts, as to the prosperity of a currency, such as now exist about sterling, have come into existence, the game's up ...' As always, he was ready with a plan for converting disaster into success. 'I should seek forthwith to win the hegemony of a new Currency Union' embracing the Empire, but including 'anyone who felt inclined to come in', and based on a gold currency, devalued by at least 25 per cent.[122] He soon changed his mind about making public his view on the May Report, writing in the *New Statesman* of its authors: 'I suppose that they are such very plain men that the advantages of not spending money seem obvious to them. They may even be so plain as to be unaware of the existence of the problem which I am now discussing.' The problem was that the reduction in purchasing power which would follow the recommended economies would add 250,000–400,000 to the unemployed and diminish tax receipts, thus reducing the budget 'saving' from £120m to £50m. 'At the present time,' Keynes continued, 'all governments have large deficits. [They are] nature's remedy, so to speak, for preventing business losses from being ... so great as to bring production altogether to a standstill.' His policy would be to 'suspend the Sinking Fund, to continue to borrow for the Unemployment Fund, and to impose a revenue tariff'. Nevertheless, the report was valuable because 'it invites us to decide whether it is our intention to make the deflation effective by transmitting the reduction of international prices to British salaries and wages'.[123]

There was no reference in his published article to the 'certainty' of devaluation. Indeed, in another letter to MacDonald, enclosing the final version of his article, he backtracked by saying that 'it probably still lies within our power' to keep on the gold standard, and that he personally 'would support for the time being whichever policy was made, provided the decision was accompanied by action sufficiently drastic to make it effective'. Keynes's hesitations were seen by MacDonald as reinforcing the Bank's advice to carry out the May Report's recommendations.[124] Perhaps Keynes was held back by an ingrained patriotism from actually urging, or even positively wanting, devaluation. When Falk suggested that the Independent Investment Trust, of which they were both directors, should sell sterling and buy dollars, he wrote back, 'What you suggest amounts in the present circumstances to a frank bear speculation against sterling. I admit that I am not clear that this would be against the national interest. . . . All the same I am clear that an institution has no business to do such a thing at the present time.'[125] But another attitude emerges which contradicts his general bias to moderation: his demand that whatever action is taken should be 'made effective'. This reaction is understandable, but once more, at the critical moment, his counsel was clouded. This was a great pity. When the gold standard was abandoned a month later, one of the former Labour ministers, Thomas Johnston, said, 'No one ever told us we could do that.'

The Bank of England having obtained temporary credits from the Bank of France and the Federal Reserve Bank of New York, the Labour Cabinet tried to agree an economy package as a condition for a further loan to be arranged by its New York broker, J. P. Morgan. The New York requirement was a programme to balance the budget which would be supported by 'all three parties'. The Conservative and Liberal leaders (minus Lloyd George, recovering from a prostate operation) told MacDonald that they would support him only if he carried out the May Report. The political advantage of having 'unpalatable measures' implemented by the Labour government had not of course escaped them.[126] The Cabinet supported – by fifteen votes to five – Keynes's suggestion that a revenue tariff be used to help balance the budget. Had the government adopted this strategy, the Conservatives would have been hard pressed to withhold their support. But Snowden's veto left the government with no counter-play. When MacDonald could not persuade a large minority of his Cabinet to go beyond £56m of economies, with the balance met by taxation, and leaving the dole largely untouched, he went to Buckingham Palace, on 24 August, to resign, only to emerge as head of a 'national government' to 'defend the pound'. It contained three (later four) of his Labour colleagues, including Snowden, but, with the bulk of the Labour Party now in opposition, it relied on Conservative and Liberal support in the House of Commons. Failing to saddle a Labour government with unpopular measures, the Opposition had achieved the next best thing – to detach MacDonald from the party he led. The new Cabinet agreed a programme of cuts on 27 August. Two days later it raised loans totalling £85m in New York and Paris.

Keynes hated what was happening, but took comfort from the fact that at least the issue between deflation and reflation had finally been joined.[127] In the *Evening Standard* of 10 September, he continued to urge import controls, though he personally believed that devaluation was now desirable.[128] Two days later he was writing in the *New Statesman* that 'the "economy" policy can only delay, it cannot prevent, a recurrence of another crisis similar to that through which we have just passed'. If the new government was serious about preserving the gold-standard system it should immediately summon an international conference 'to reverse the whole trend of deflation'. Meanwhile, Britain should impose controls on the export of capital.[129] 'The budget and the Economy Bill [introduced on 8 and 10 September] are replete with folly and injustice,' he wrote in the *New Statesman.*[130] He explained to Walter Case on 14 September that 'every person in this country of super asinine propensities, everyone who hates social progress and loves deflation, feels that his hour has come and triumphantly announces how, by refraining from every form of economic activity, we can all become prosperous again'.[131] On 16 September, at the invitation of a small group of politicians including Mosley, he addressed a meeting of MPs in the House. His notes are remarkable for the passion which he generally expunged from his public utterances:

> I speak from a full heart. The course of policy pursued so far has reduced us to a point of humiliation one could not have conceived. During the last 12 years I have had very little influence, if any, on policy. But in the role of a Cassandra, I have had considerable success as a prophet. I declare to you, and I will stake on it any reputation I have, that we have been making in the last few weeks as dreadful errors of policy as deluded statesmen have ever been guilty of.[132]

The only person in the House of Commons who understood and supported Keynes was Oswald Mosley, soon to be cast into the political wilderness. In a powerful speech on the reassembly of Parliament on 8 September, he had said:

> Perhaps my views can be briefly summarised if I say that I believe it is vastly more important to deal, and deal quickly, with the industrial situation than it is to deal with the Budget. And for this reason: the continual decline and collapse of the industries of this country makes completely illusory any attempt to balance the Budget. You may balance the Budget on the present basis of revenue, but there is no one in the House who can say with any confidence that this basis of revenue will be long maintained. ... Suppose that we adopted the view that it is far

more important to have industrial recovery than to balance our Budget.... We should then adopt the method of balancing our Budget advocated by Mr. Keynes and other economists which is simply to continue to borrow – I know that it shocks Hon. Members – to continue to borrow to provide for the Unemployment Insurance Fund, or I would prefer to say, borrow to provide constructive works to give employment in place of it, to suspend the Sinking Fund, and to raise the remainder by a revenue tariff or, as I should say, a protective tariff.[133]

The crisis Keynes had predicted came much sooner than he had foreseen. A mutiny of naval ratings at Invergordon on 16 September, suggesting that the Empire itself was crumbling, led to another run on the pound. On 18 September, the Bank of England told the government it could not hold the exchange beyond the weekend. On Monday, 21 September, Philip Snowden reversed Winston Churchill's decision of six years before and suspended convertibility. The cross of gold had been lifted, this time for good. 'At one stroke, Britain had resumed the financial hegemony of the world,' Keynes announced. Graham Hutton remembered him 'chuckling like a boy who has just exploded a firework under someone he doesn't like'.[134]

The restored international gold standard had collapsed, never to be revived. Why had it failed the second time round?

Keynes's answer, given in an article he wrote in April 1932, was that Britain's return to gold in 1925 at an over-valued exchange rate had set monetary policy an impossible task. It was impossible to enforce a bank rate high enough to reduce wages; a lower rate, on the other hand, would have caused Britain to go off gold much sooner. So a middle course of continuous borrowing was adopted. But the price was the accumulation of short-term debt: 'sooner or later ... the insecure structure had to crumble'.[135] The New York financial community took a different view. In the opinion of Thomas Lamont, England had not made a mistake in going back to gold in 1925. 'The mistake was in permitting the trade unions, after the general strike, to impose a rigid wage scale on British industries and subsidising the resulting unemployment by the dole.'[136] His friend Russell Leffingwell saw the malign influence of Keynes in all this. 'The Treasury civil servants who to a greater or less extent follow him, have not the judgment of practical men. They are mathematical tripos men. They are civil servants. They are professors.... They are not bankers and they are not business men. The one thing that bankers and business men in England know is that confidence is based on keeping one's promises. That is something Keynes will never know.'[137]

VI. THE END OF CHAMPAGNE

The day the pound went off gold, Beatrice and Sidney Webb came to spend the night with Maynard and Lydia in what Beatrice called 'their ramshackle old farmhouse under Firle Beacon'. 'What frightens me about the future', Beatrice had written to Keynes on 3 September, 'is the emergence of class war in its most insidious form; the sabotage of the standard of living ... by an organised Capitalist Party, and, on the other hand, unintended sabotage of Capitalist enterprise by a Trade Union Labour Party.... But what is the moral of the sorrowful tale ... a Creed Dictatorship?'[138] Keynes, accompanied by the general secretary of the TUC, Walter Citrine, joined them before dinner 'in a great state of inward satisfaction at the fulfilment of his policy of ... inflation.... He had lunched with Winston, who said he had never been in favour of the return to the gold standard.' Lydia noticed that:

> Beatrice was very much alive with Royal Commissions and Labour party conversations, she drank wine, smoked cigarettes and altogether till 12 o'clock, kept the termometre of society going. The husband was nice too, but much older, rather sad to be out of office.... Then we had Mr. Citrine ... flirting with Maynard. However all night long I heard the steps and the banging of the doors. Mr. Citrine was ill with indigestion and Beatrice as usual was making tea at 4 o'clock in the morning, dragging Sidney out of bed to provide the company. At 8 o'clock everyone was dressed, before the water was given, although I was careful not to encourage them about the bathroom, as our boiler refuses to boil this summer.

Beatrice had lunch next day with Beveridge, 'who heartily dislikes Keynes and regards him as a quack in economics'.[139] Keynes and Lydia returned to London on 27 September. There was 'too much going on now for me to stay away any longer'.

The gold standard, and therefore the occasion for the National government, having gone, the Conservatives were eager for a general election to give them a mandate for protection, which was now no longer necessary. Keynes did his best to stiffen MacDonald against the clamour, urging that the National government should stay in office for six months to deal with 'the currency question, the Indian Conference, and the Disarmament Conference' before leaving the parties to return to their normal alignments.[140] On 5 October he lunched with the Prime Minister at Chequers, before going on to Lloyd George, now recovered, at Churt.

Whatever Keynes said to MacDonald, the die was cast. On 6 October

Parliament was dissolved. Cambridge is 'democratic more than fascist, but chiefly perplexed', Maynard wrote to Lydia on 11 October. 'We discuss whether we ought to give Feasts and if so should wine be consumed. The decision is to give Feasts but without ostentation substituting beer and cheaper claret for champagne! So you see that we too are patriots. . . .' Lydia told Sam and Lil that she would vote Labour. 'I have rolled my eyes on the manifestoes of Ramsay and Stanley, but they close instantaneously with dreariness.' On 27 October the National government, appealing for a 'doctor's mandate' and aided by a vitriolic broadcast from Snowden denouncing Labour's programme as 'Bolshevism run mad', swept to the greatest electoral victory in British history, winning 552 seats to Labour's 46.

PART SIX

THE ECONOMIST
TO THE RESCUE

He had one foot on the threshold of a new heaven, but the
other foot ... in the Benthamite calculus.

J. M. Keynes on G. E. Moore

You certainly have an amazing gift for making your discontent
with the traditional ideas 'get you somewhere' instead of landing
you in a maze of general carping and dissatisfaction.

H. O. Meredith to J. M. Keynes, 15 May 1936

27

Portrait of an Unusual Economist

I. THE *ZEITGEIST*

Keynes was an applied economist who turned to inventing theory because the theory he had inherited could not properly explain what was happening. Like the other Cambridge economists of his day, he was drawn to economics chiefly by the prospect it held out of making the world better. They were interested in what Pigou called 'fruit', or results. The 'light', or illumination, which guided their steps, had been supplied by Marshall. Marshall, in their view, had left an '*organum* of thought', powerful, comprehensive and flexible enough to explain how modern economies behaved. They believed it to be much superior to that to be found anywhere else: a view partly based on ignorance, partly on the belief that Marshall had mined, sifted, restated and synthesised all that was valuable and true in economic thought up to his day. The Cambridge economists were improvers, not scholars. Their belief that the theory they needed for action was 'all in Marshall' survived into the 1920s. In 1922 Keynes wrote that 'important improvements' to the 'existing method of thinking' were becoming rare, and the main task of economists was to exercise 'skill in the application' of existing principles to the facts. By 1928 he acknowledged that 'controversy and doubt are increased', but thought that further research should clear it up. Most Cambridge economics in the 1920s is accurately described as 'glosses on Marshalliana'.[1]

From the start 'scientific' economics had been strongly normative. By increasing understanding of 'economic laws' it hoped to shift actual economic arrangements towards the competitive ideal which would maximise the creation of wealth; hence the strong association between nineteenth-century economics and the policy of *laissez-faire*. Adam Smith and his followers were chiefly preoccupied with the failures of government. Their idea was that government should keep law and order, and get out of economic life.

By the last quarter of the nineteenth century the mood had changed. The failures of *laissez-faire* were palpable; the competence and integrity of governments were much improved; the growth of democracy had increased pressure on the state to 'solve' or at least alleviate social problems. What Dicey called 'the age of collectivism' dawned. Feeding the growth of collectivism was the growth of the social sciences, and the parallel emergence of an activist intelligentsia, claiming a right of direction, vacated by the aristocracy and the clergy, by virtue of superior intellectual ability and expert knowledge of society. The central claim which emerged from the confluence of these two tendencies was that society was a machine whose working could be improved by deliberate action, with unintended side-effects being equally amenable to correction and control, much as a mechanic fine-tunes an engine.[2] It was the vision of a Corbusier, applied to society as a whole. Indeed, there are parallel movements in the arts and in politics. Noel Annan talks of modernism and collectivism as the two movements in whose shadow his generation grew up.[3] In their different spheres, usually in conflict with each other, they boldly proclaimed that we can make of our lives and the world what we wish.

Keynes's relationship to the twin movements of modernism and collectivism is extraordinarily important in understanding his work. He was linked to modernism through his membership of Bloomsbury; and to collectivism through his philosophy and economics. Bloomsbury's aesthetic theory – insofar as it was expressed in the writings of Roger Fry and Clive Bell – located beauty not in the subject matter or 'narrative' of a work of art, but in its formal structure, intuitively apprehended; the shift from flow of narrative to flow of thought is the distinguishing mark of Virginia Woolf's novels. A parallel shift towards formalisation, or model-building, was taking place in economics. The general effect of the move to abstraction was to place the mind of the economist rather than the narrative of the market at the heart of economic reasoning. Modernism in the arts and collectivism in politics and economics thus came together in the assertion that the interpretation of reality is a creative act. The claim to direction on behalf of those gifted with a special insight into the nature of reality becomes indistinguishable in practice from the claim that reality can and should be constructed by powerful minds.

Keynes's confidence was also cultural. His was the last generation which claimed to direct human affairs in the name of culture rather than expertise. He addressed the world as a priest, not as a technician. And though he rearranged its theology, economics spoke, through him, as a church, not as a branch of the differential calculus. After the First World War, culture, as the nineteenth century had known it, disintegrated. The disciplines turned inwards; their practitioners talked to each other, not to the world. This had less to do with the explosion of knowledge than with the breakdown of the larger frameworks of thought which had proportioned knowledge to the purposes of human life. Indeed, with the breakdown of – for want of a better word – religion, what obstacle was there to the cancerous growth of academic pedantry on the one side, and what Keynes called 'love of money' on the other?

Keynes's doctrine of means was always far more cautious than his doctrine of ends. Ends were taken to be self-evidently good or bad. Judgement of means took place in the 'twilight of Probability'. Rational action was constrained by two further principles, the 'weight of argument' and the doctrine of 'least risk'. Here Moore's influence was crucial, though Keynes found the same message in Burke.[4] Probability might be the 'guide of life'; but the guide had to make his way through the fog of uncertainty.

Monetary theory provided an ideal vehicle for the kinds of limited, compact projects of amelioration and reform which appealed to Keynes's temperament and understanding. The theory of money, in the modern, 'Cambridge' form bequeathed by Marshall and developed by Pigou, might be applied to controlling price fluctuations which Keynes, together with Wicksell and Fisher, regarded as the chief cause of business fluctuations. Keynes used the theory of money before the war to suggest measures to stabilise the seasonal purchasing power of the rupee; after the First World War, he saw the management of money as the way to stabilise the British price level. For Keynes, the key breakthrough to a 'scientific' theory of money was the realisation that its quantity, in a credit-money economy, was controlled by the banking system, while the demand for it, in the short period, was unstable. Both of these propositions were stated in his *Tract on Monetary Reform*. When we add to this that the duty of the monetary authority was so to regulate the stock of money as to keep saving equal to investment, we have the *Treatise on Money*. In the interval between these two books Keynes came to the conclusion that there was nothing except banking policy itself to keep economies stable. Order has to be created; it is not natural. This was part of the modernist/collectivist mindset. However, Keynes did not deny that much of economic life was non-chaotic and self-regulating. State intervention was eventually – after a refinement of theory in the 1930s – limited to one point only: ensuring a level of demand consistent with full employment.

The charge, therefore, that Keynes substituted an economics of power and will for the self-regulatory mechanisms of civil society, including the market system, is greatly exaggerated. Uncertainty pervades both private and public calculations of means to achieve given ends. The uncertainty which imposed mediocre performance on unmanaged market economies applied equally to the effects of government policy. Keynes's disciples, the policymakers of the 1960s and 1970s, actually did start to act as though they believed that the power of economists over economies was virtually unlimited. This is because they had inherited Keynes's machinery, but not the philosophy which sets limits to the scope and effectiveness of that machinery. Their hubris was inevitably overtaken by nemesis.

II. THE PERSONALITY OF AN ECONOMIST

Like many who aspire to it, Keynes thought a lot about greatness – how it came about, what it consisted of. As an admirer of Galton, he believed in the importance of hereditary connections; but he also understood how tradition shapes achievement, and discovered (or perhaps invented) a Cambridge tradition of economics, stretching back to Malthus, 'the first Cambridge economist'. Keynes used his biographical essays to ponder and delineate the character of economic and scientific genius. (He never felt confident enough to attempt a biographical sketch of an artist.) 'An easy subject, at which few excel!' he wrote of economics in his essay on Marshall. 'The paradox finds its explanation, perhaps, in that the master economist must possess a rare combination of gifts ... He must be mathematician, historian, statesman, philosopher – in some degree ... as aloof and incorruptible as an artist, yet sometimes as near the earth as a politician.' In a striking phrase, he tells of Marshall's ambition to observe business life 'with the eyes of a highly intelligent angel'.[5] Keynes claimed for Malthus 'a profound economic intuition and an unusual combination of keeping an open mind to the shifting picture of experience and of constantly applying to its interpretation the principles of formal thought': an ideal combination, in his view, of the necessary intellectual qualities of a great economist.[6] What he picked out from Jevons was his 'unceasing fertility and originality of mind', his 'divine intuition', his 'inductive curiosity' and delight in statistics, closely linked to his antiquarianism, his electrifying style of exposition, his showmanship, his single-mindedness. He noted of Jevons what Schumpeter was to notice about him: that he left no perfect work, that he always attempted 'what he could not quite succeed in doing', that he was 'a man of parts – parts which he could not put together as a whole'.[7] And in Keynes's essay on Isaac Newton we have that extraordinary characterisation of the first modern scientist as 'the last of the magicians'. Keynes wrote of Newton, 'I fancy his pre-eminence is due to his muscles of intuition being the strongest and most enduring with which a man has ever been gifted,' and quoted de Morgan's verdict: 'so happy in his conjectures as to seem to know more than he could possibly have any means of proving'.[8]

The qualities which Keynes repeatedly singles out – 'divine intuition', 'unusual powers of continuous concentrated introspection', logical capacity, a feel for the salient facts, style, many-sidedness, theoretical and practical gifts in combination – are the qualities he most admired, aspired to and thought were required for great achievement in economics. All these qualities describe, to some extent, Keynes himself – as he certainly knew.

In 1912 Keynes first made a crucial distinction between Jevons and Marshall which was equally self-referring: 'Jevons, perceiving some one part of the theory with penetrating clearness and illuminating to the utmost possible extent; Marshall, exhaustively aware of the whole theory and its interconnections, but discarding, in his attempt to take in the whole stage at once, the limelight which, presenting some parts in a more brilliant aspect, must necessarily leave others in a greater obscurity.'[9] (The comparison was less kind to Marshall after Marshall's death: Jevons 'chisels in stone, where Marshall knits in wool'.) In this respect, Keynes was like Jevons. Jevons was in the tradition of the pamphleteer: he wanted to 'spill his ideas, to flick them at the world'; Keynes, too, urged his fellow economists to 'leave to Adam Smith alone the glory of the quarto ... pluck the day, fling pamphlets into the wind, write always *sub specie temporis*, and achieve immortality by accident, if at all'; to this, Marshall had already replied that 'if the economist reasons rapidly and with a light heart' his economics is likely to suffer from 'bad connections'.[10]

Robertson's criticism of Keynes for exactly these faults was precisely anticipated by Marshall's criticism of Jevons: 'His success was aided even by his faults ... he led many to think he was correcting great errors; whereas he was really only adding important explanations.'[11] Keynes, however, went one better than Jevons: the pamphlets are the 'ghosts in the machine' of his treatises; and his distinctive ideas come out better in his shorter pieces written for a purpose. The battle between the splashers and the synthesisers continues unabated in economics, as it always has. In the next generation, Kaldor is the great example of the first, Hicks of the second. The splashers are more intuitive than logical, the synthesisers more logical than intuitive, though elements of both must be present in any scientific achievement. In modern economics, scientific breakthroughs have been frequent, scientific revolutions almost non-existent. Keynes came closest to the latter; but even he was absorbed, as we shall see.

In another respect, Keynes was closer to Marshall, even more so to Foxwell, the two outstanding Cambridge economists of his youth. Comparing Marshall to Edgeworth, Keynes wrote, 'Edgeworth wished to establish *theorems* of intellectual and aesthetic interest, Marshall to establish *maxims* of practical and moral importance.' He perceptively noticed that Marshall was good at mathematics, but Edgeworth thought mathematically.[12] Like Marshall, Keynes believed that mathematics were useful as a check on one's thoughts; he did not think his thoughts mathematically. He allowed his mathematics to rust away because, unlike Edgeworth, he was not interested in 'mathematicising' the social sciences. He believed with Foxwell that 'economics ... belongs to the art of managing public affairs by the application of sound reasoning to the whole *corpus* of experience', though he would never have claimed, as Foxwell did, that it was not a branch of logic.[13] Good economic performance, he thought, required an amalgam of intuition and logic applied to a wide range of facts, not to simplified and artificial hypotheses. But he was great and perceptive enough to appreciate types of mind utterly unlike his own, and he leaves Edgeworth seated, as a boy, aloft in a heron's nest reading Homer. 'So, as it were, he dwelt always, not too much concerned with the earth.'

Keynes's scepticism about the use of mathematics in economics grew rather than diminished with age, though it was present from the start. It has to do with his growing understanding of the complexity, and reflexive nature, of social life. A fundamental statement is in his essay on Edgeworth:

> Mathematical Psychics has not, as a science or study, fulfilled its early promise. In the 'seventies and 'eighties of the last century, it was reasonable, I think, to suppose that it held great prospects. When the young Edgeworth chose it, he may have looked to find secrets as wonderful as those which the physicists have found since those days. But ... this has not happened ... quite the opposite. The atomic hypothesis which has worked so splendidly in physics breaks down in psychics. We are faced at every turn with the problems of organic unity, of discreteness, of discontinuity – the whole is not equal to the sum of the parts, comparisons of quantity fail us, small changes produce large effects, the assumptions of a uniform and homogeneous continuum are not satisfied. ... Edgeworth knew that he was skating on thin ice; and as life went on his love of skating and his distrust of the ice increased, by a malicious fate, *pari passu*.[14]

Keynes, however, did not retreat from the attempt to capture important elements of this complexity in models – the hallmark of economic procedure since Ricardo's time. On the contrary: the greater the complexity and uncertainty of human life, the more important it was to build lean, spare models suitable for the explanatory purpose in hand. In the deductive–inductive debate, he was on the side of the deductive school, unlike Beveridge, who believed that 'laws' could be discovered by accumulating facts. He criticised both Marshall and Malthus for trying, later in life, to make their theories more realistic by burdening them with historical detail. The approach to realism should be achieved by choosing a type of abstraction which can explain the salient characteristics of the epoch or problem to be investigated. Thus Keynes would criticise the classical economists of his day for using models which assumed full employment instead of constructing models which tried to explain why persisting unemployment could occur. The counterpart of this was Keynes's own willingness to change his model or – in popular perception – his mind, when the facts or problem changed.

The fluctuating nature of the data requires that economists not only 'think in models' (which is fairly easy) but be imaginative and creative (which is very difficult). Progress in economics consists of theory invention.

Good economists, Keynes told Roy Harrod in 1938, are scarce because 'the gift of using "vigilant observation" to choose good models ... appears to be a very rare one'. Intuition thus controls both the deductive and inductive sides of the economic inquiry. From the almost limitless data of experience, the economist has to discern those facts which constitute the important causes of the phenomenon he is trying to explain. The good economist's crucial gifts are the power of introspection and a 'sense of magnitudes'. Keynes consistently championed the cause of better economic statistics, but his purpose was not to provide material for proof or disproof of theories, still less for prediction, but to limit the play of intuition and fancy. He told Austin Robinson that his best ideas came to him from 'messing about with figures and seeing what they must mean'.

Keynes's insistence that successful economic reasoning is based on intuition and argument does not mean that he thought himself any less of a scientist. He believed that the scientist's intuitions deserved the same respect as the artist's. They were a privileged form of knowledge, reached by 'direct acquaintance' with reality. They must not be shrivelled prematurely by devastating criticisms on points of fact or logic, such as academics are too wont to dish out. This attitude, when carried into practice, made Keynes a wonderful teacher: his habit of claiming the same latitude for himself as he accorded his students annoyed his critics. What he has to say about Freudian theory is extremely interesting in this context:

> Professor Freud seems to me to be endowed, to the degree of genius, with the scientific imagination which can body forth an abundance of innovating ideas, shattering possibilities, working hypotheses, which have sufficient foundation in intuition and common experience to deserve the most patient and unprejudiced examination.... But when it comes to the empirical or inductive proof of his theories, it is obvious that what we are offered in print is hopelessly inadequate to the case....
>
> I venture to say that at the present stage the argument in favour of Freudian theories would be very little weakened if it were to be admitted that every case published hitherto had been wholly invented by Professor Freud in order to illustrate his ideas and to make them more vivid to the minds of his readers. That is to say, the case for considering them seriously mainly depends at present on the appeal which they make to our own intuitions as containing something new and true about the way in which human psychology works, and very little indeed upon the so-called inductive verifications....[15]

Today we are much more reluctant to give intuitions such privileged epistemic status.

By now we will not be surprised to learn that Keynes attached high value to eccentricity and what he often called 'crankiness'. By a crank Keynes meant someone whose curiosity, obsession, flair or intuition is, in varying degrees, stronger than his logic or intellect, or runs ahead of it. The founder of eugenics, Francis Galton, with his habit of counting the number of fidgets in his audience as he lectured, was clearly a borderline case. 'His original genius', Keynes wrote, 'was superior to his intellect, but his intellect was always just sufficient to keep him on the right side of eccentricity.'[16] As Keynes's respect for orthodox economics waned, his respect for 'economic heretics' increased. They appear in the *Treatise*; they stalk chapter 22 of the *General Theory*: 'the army of heretics and cranks, whose numbers and enthusiasm are extraordinary', with a 'fierce discontent ... far preferable to the complacency of the bankers'.[17] Although Keynes tended to use the word 'crank' indiscriminately in conversation, he distinguished between the 'great Trinity of crankdom', consisting of John Taylor Peddie, A. W. Kitson and Major Douglas, for whom he had little time (though he made amends to Douglas in the *General Theory*), and people who got in touch with him like P. Larranaga, a Basque mining engineer, who struck Keynes as a brilliant amateur, but not a crank, M. C. Rorty, an American engineer with a plan to raise investment, A. G. MacGregor, also an engineer, who wanted to raise wages in the slump and lower them in the boom, and Ian Sutherland, an Australian, whose pamphlet, *The Monetary Puzzle*, he thought had a 'touch of genius'.[18] As Keynes himself got more heretical, he became more interested in heretics of the past, as he tried to establish an anti-Ricardian lineage for his own ideas. Reading a book by Werner Stark, a Czech refugee, on *The Histories and Historians of Political Economy*, he wrote that '[Thomas] Hodgskin is a lot more interesting than I had realised. Here again a man who perceives ideas of the future very obscurely and imperfectly is much more interesting to posterity than to his contemporaries. The former, in the light of subsequent knowledge, can interpret the significance of his thought, whilst to the latter it would be no more than a hopeless and boring muddle.'[19]

Keynes's favourite economist of all was undoubtedly Thomas Malthus. In the final version of Keynes's essay on Malthus, written in 1932, we are treated to the two faces of Malthus – the Malthus of Population and the Malthus of Effective Demand. These are astonishingly like the two faces of Keynes. Keynes never wrote a treatise on population. Yet putting the economic problem in a historical setting meant, for much of Keynes's life, putting it in a Malthusian setting.

Malthus interested Keynes for a number of reasons. There is more than a trace of ancestor worship in his frequent tributes to the 'first Cambridge economist'. Malthus's father Daniel, a man of intellectual distinction and notable friendships who nevertheless allowed 'diffidence to overcome ambition', reminded Keynes of his own father; and his account of a delightful father–son relationship mirrors his view of his own relationship with Neville Keynes. With part of his mind at least Keynes was attracted by what he saw as Malthus's peculiarly English combination of adventurous thinking and conventional living. As he told the Malthusian League in 1927: 'It is not necessary in England to lead a bold life in order to have bold ideas.' Keynes never sympathised much with the radical intelligentsia of the Continent whose intellectual iconoclasm had to express itself existentially. Though his own private life was far from conventional he kept up appearances and valued them. Of the first edition of Malthus's *Essay on the Principle of Population*, Keynes wrote, 'It is profoundly in the English tradition of human science ... a tradition marked by love of truth and a most noble lucidity, by a prosaic sanity free from sentiment and metaphysic, and by an immense disinterestedness and public spirit.'[20] That this was a tradition Keynes admired is clear from this passage. But he only fitfully managed to attach himself to it. His temperament was only partially suited to it, and in any case the tradition itself had been fractured by the collapse of belief in a divine order.

Keynes increasingly saw Malthus as the founder of the 'true' tradition in British economics, derailed by the abstractions of Ricardo. In a 1935 tribute he praised Malthus's attempt to 'penetrate ... events ... by a mixture of intuitive selection and formal principle'. Keynes's own identification with Malthus is even clearer when he writes in the same essay:

> In the closing years of the eighteenth century the misery of the labouring class presented itself to Malthus as chiefly consisting in their low standard of life. In the years after Waterloo ... it presented itself to him as chiefly a problem of unemployment. To these two problems his work as an economist was successively directed. As the solution of the first he had offered his principle of population. ... In the second half of his life, he was pre-occupied with the post-war unemployment, and he found the explanation in what he called insufficiency of effective demand: – to cure which he called for a spirit of free expenditure, public works and a policy of expansionism.[21]

As Keynes's own interest shifted from the problem of insufficient resources to that of their under-use, so the emphasis in his often reworked essay (dating from 1922) on Malthus shifted from the Malthus of Population to the Malthus of Effective Demand. As early as 1924 he was quoting Malthus's letter of 9 October 1814 to David Ricardo in which Malthus denied that 'consumption and accumulation equally promote demand'.[22] In the autumn of 1932, while re-working his essay on Malthus for publication, he read, for the first time, the Malthus–Ricardo correspondence, which had been recently unearthed by Piero Sraffa. 'If only Malthus', he wrote in this essay, 'instead of Ricardo, had been the parent stem from which nineteenth-century economics proceeded, what a much wiser and richer place the world would be today!'[23] There must at least be a possibility that Keynes was himself influenced by the Malthus of Effective Demand, rather than, as has hitherto been supposed, discovering him after he had developed the principle independently himself.

Keynes and his fellow Cambridge economists were men brought up on a single book, Marshall's *Principles*, published in 1890, supplemented by a few other published fragments and 'oral tradition', mainly about his theory of money. When Keynes published his *General Theory* in 1936, the strongest reproaches of his fellow Cambridge economists, notably Pigou and Robertson, were directed against his alleged disloyalty to the 'Old Master'. The house that Marshall built, they implied, was sufficiently capacious to accommodate the extra furniture Keynes wanted to bring into it. This is partly true; it is also true that Keynes remained unmistakably a Marshallian. He wholly endorsed Marshall's view of economics as 'not a body of concrete truth, but an engine for the discovery of concrete truth', a view based on Marshall's perception that the 'habits and institutions of industry' do not stay constant.[24] The theory of money he taught at Cambridge till the early 1930s was Marshall's. He never abandoned it, but came to restrict its applicability to conditions of full employment. Moreover, he developed it creatively with Dennis Robertson. The great advantage, from Cambridge's point of view, of Marshall's quantity-theory equation over Fisher's was that it concentrated attention on people's motives for holding money. As Kahn has put it, Fisher and his successors thought of money 'as a means of effecting transactions', Marshall and his successors as 'a form of holding wealth necessary for effecting the ordinary transactions of life without trouble'.[25] Marshall left tools, here, for integrating the theory of money with the theory of value, though he did not use them. Finally, Keynes was permanently influenced by Marshall's technique for dealing with time.

There is a famous Cambridge joke. In the 1960s a group of Cambridge economists were discussing Bergson's aphorism that time is a device to stop everything happening at once when one of them, Dharma Kumar, quipped, 'And I suppose space is a device to stop everything happening in Cambridge.'[26] The idea that things don't all happen simultaneously and that economic theorising has to take account of this is the hallmark of the Cambridge way of doing economics. In the preface to the first edition of his *Principles*, Marshall wrote that 'the element of Time . . . is at the centre of the chief difficulty of almost every economic problem'; on p. 30 of the eighth edition comes the sentence, 'the condition that time must be allowed for causes to produce their effects is a source of great difficulty in economics'. Marshall felt passionately that the major disagreements in economics arose from not specifying the time-period in which the causes in dispute were supposed to determine outcomes. He introduced the idea of time, therefore, as a way of making theorising more able to take account of complex and shifting reality. One of his favourite devices was to allot different outcomes to different time-periods. Thus he reconciled the Jevonian and Ricardian value theories by asserting that utility governed value in the short period, but cost of production determined it in the long period.[27] In the period being considered, the non-dominant forces are 'segregated into a pound called *caeteris paribus*. Their activity is not denied, Marshall says, 'but their disturbing effect is neglected for a time'.

As Keynes himself pointed out, the problem of time lay at the heart of the quarrel between Malthus and Ricardo. Ricardo wrote to his friend on 24 January 1817:

> It appears to me that one great cause of our difference in opinion on the subjects we have so often discussed [Ricardo was thinking especially of the possibility of the failure of 'effectual demand'] is that you have always in your mind the immediate and temporary effects of particular changes, whereas I put these immediate and temporary effects quite aside, and fix my whole attention on the permanent state of things which will result from them.

To this, Malthus replied 'with considerable effect' on 26 January:

> I certainly am disposed to refer frequently to things as they are, as the only way of making one's writing practically useful to society, and I think also the only way of being secure from falling into the errors of the taylors of Laputa, and by a slight mistake at the outset arrive at conclusions the most distant from the truth. Besides I really think that the progress of society consists of irregular movements, and that to omit the consideration of causes which for eight or ten years will give a great *stimulus* to production and population or a great *check* to them, is to omit the causes of the wealth and poverty of nations – the grand object of all enquiries in Political Economy.[28]

Keynes sided wholeheartedly with Malthus. He never admired Ricardo's cast of mind, and by 1933 could write that 'the obliteration of Malthus's line of approach and the complete domination of Ricardo's for a period of a hundred years has been a disaster to the progress of economics'.[29]

One of the chief debates about Keynes's theory of employment would concern the question: in what kind of 'period' is it meant to be true? Economists would accuse Keynes of breaking off his analysis prematurely. His short-period method, they said, ignored forces tending to restore full employment. He was guilty of treating as non-existent in fact influences on employment which he excluded on purely methodological grounds. The debate has gone on interminably ever since. Keynes could no doubt have invoked the principle of indifference which justifies the theorist in sterilising the influence of those things about which nothing certain can be said.

III. THE MASTER-ECONOMIST?

How did Keynes measure up to his ideal of the 'master-economist'? He was not interested in being anything but a 'great' economist. Why should he be? He knew himself to be a member of the intellectual aristocracy. His own intellectual career had been an almost unbroken success story. He was one of Marshall's anointed successors. (Was there a feeling here that he had to make up for his father's failure to satisfy Marshall's hopes?) But he had also been a member of Pop at Eton, president of the Cambridge Union, a member of the Apostles. In four years he had risen to control of a key department of the Treasury, created, it almost seemed, for the exercise of his particular talents. His *Economic Consequences of the Peace* was a bestseller and the most influential book to come out of the war. Keynes's life as it unfolded was continuing confirmation to him of his supreme talent in a variety of fields. He had every reason to be colossally self-confident, and so he was. The only obvious areas of diffidence had to do with his physical appearance and his speaking voice. He did his best to turn himself into a normal-looking member of the Establishment, with military moustache, and City suits which he wore even in the country. In the 1930s he enjoyed the role of squire of Tilton. About his voice he could do nothing. It was the voice of a scholar, a man of taste and erudition, slightly precious, without much resonance or range, deficient in rhetorical quality. He made music with his pen. But where an argument had to be put, he was a brilliant advocate, as his testimony to the Macmillan Committee shows.

Much in Keynes's life was coded, hidden from the prying outsider. His extreme reluctance to give interviews testifies to his self-protectiveness. He was not as he seemed, in appearance, habits or thought. In thought, the tension arises at precisely the points where heart and head failed to fuse. This poses a problem for the interpretation of both his philosophy and his economics. He left a huge corpus of guarded utterances, which includes three treatises. He chose to play the academic game, because he enjoyed it, and because he knew that his influence depended on his playing it. He accepted the conventions of economics, especially the convention of rationality. Yet scattered through his writings are clues to the fact that he regarded the intellectual technique he practised as a surface technique only, and public life as a world of appearance; that he realised that beneath the knowledge in which he publicly dealt there lay an esoteric knowledge open only to a few initiates, the pursuit of which fascinated him as it did Newton. His writings, like those of Ibsen, are full of 'overtones' which may be 'felt and heard by the sensitive', but 'which will be out of proportion and almost vulgar if . . . sufficiently emphasised to be obvious and inescapable'.[30] But he knew perfectly well what he was about, for the stability of the public sphere was necessary to protect the secret places where disguises are not needed, and things can be assessed at their true worth.

The thought that he was saying something new seems to have been with him from the start, coupled with the conviction that his elders were too stupid or conventional to understand it: for example, his comments on his examiners at Eton and later. Throughout his life, though decreasingly as he got older, he seemed to Hubert Henderson to be an *enfant terrible*, anxious above all to avoid stating a conventional opinion. This was not just the arrogance of an individual, but the arrogance of a place, Cambridge. Keynes proclaimed himself a rebel against Marshallian orthodoxy. But for most of his life Cambridge economics, like Cambridge philosophy, saw itself as far in advance of anything being done elsewhere. Marshallians in the 1900s, even in the 1920s, saw themselves as pioneers, blazing new intellectual trails. It was also the arrogance of a group, Bloomsbury. Both combined to give Keynes that sense of 'colossal superiority' of which he wrote to Strachey in 1905.

Keynes displayed an awesome array of talents, without being preeminent in any. He was not a genius in the sense of being a Divine Fool as was Mozart or Wittgenstein – extraordinary at one thing, babyish in everything else. He was a wonderful all-rounder, with a superbly efficient thinking machine. At Eton he had excelled at mathematics *and* classics, and throughout his life he effortlessly bridged the two cultures. He was not a remarkable mathematician. Nor was he a great philosopher. As a historian he was an inspired amateur. He had a theory of politics, but it never saved him from the charge of being politically naive. Keynes was great in the combination of his gifts. His achievement was to align economics with changes taking place in ethics, in culture, in politics and in society – in a word, with the twentieth-century spirit. But, like Jevons, his qualities never quite jelled. That, rather than too great a haste, is why he failed to produce a work of art, although his writings are full of artistry. His best stylistic achievements were in his shorter pieces – notably his biographical essays. In his big books he was the pamphleteer trying to rein in his imagination, school himself to the demands of a formal treatise. He had powerful intuitions of logical and historical relationships, but was not at his happiest in sustained argument. Like Marshall, his concentration came in short bursts. His temperament was too restless, his mind too constantly active, and bursting out with ideas and plans, for thinking in solitude.

It is commonly agreed that Keynes was 'the most intuitive of men',[31] using intuitive as people talk, or used to talk, of 'feminine' intuition – as something apart from rationality. More interesting is the privileged epistemological status Keynes claimed for intuition in general, and his intuitions in particular. This does tell us something about the way he worked with colleagues and critics. His view of how knowledge in economics was obtained had profound implications for his strategy of argument and persuasion. He regarded an economic argument as, in the first instance, a way of engaging the 'intuitions' of those taking part. At this stage, Keynes always pleaded for 'charity' towards factual or logical mistakes or obscurities, since much the most important thing was to get the drift of the argument, to consider whether it had value. Keynes's most acid controversies after the publication of his *Treatise on Money* were with critics like Hayek who, he felt, missed what he was driving at in order to trip him up on logical points. But it followed that argument or conversation could not be fruitful once opposing intuitions came to light, unless or until a conversion took place from one camp to another. Good conversation, in economics as in other subjects, started from shared sympathies and could not survive a falling out of sympathy. In the 1920s Keynes's good conversations in economics were with Robertson, Hawtrey, Henderson, Gerald Shove, less frequently with Pigou: all Cambridge men, within the Marshallian tradition. These good conversations (except with Shove) came to an end in the 1930s, to Keynes's regret, because his intuitions had started to diverge too seriously from theirs. In the 1930s his good conversations were with disciples like Richard Kahn, Joan and Austin Robinson, though he continued to have bad ones with his older colleagues.

As with all original minds, Keynes's intuitions were never fully captured by his analytical system. His books are full of historical generalisations which are not 'modelled' at all. And his theory of liquidity preference hardly captures the richness and passion of his informal speculations concerning the psychology of hoarding or his view that 'love of money' was the cancer of economies.

Arthur Smithies has written that Keynes's 'analytical achievement was always in response to the practical situation that confronted him'.[32] Moggridge has noted Keynes's 'immense practicality and almost complete absorption in questions of policy', adding that 'he used traditional methods of analysis for policy problems until they broke down and then proceeded to fashion new tools to fill in the gaps'.[33] To this we may add that the key to Keynes's effectiveness as a policy adviser, both inside and outside the government machine, was his speed and skill in drafting. His wont was to come to meetings with completely formulated drafts while the others 'blathered'. These drafts inevitably became the basis of discussion. Throughout his life Keynes had a plan ready for any occasion or problem. It was part of his colossal self-confidence; it was also a sign of the quality of his mind.

All this is true, but incomplete. Although it is clear that a practical challenge was the spur, Keynes always had intellectual ambitions, or tastes, surplus to the requirements of the problem. The 'tool-maker' view of Keynes is the view of those who have been mainly interested in expounding or using the tools. The idea that he was basically an extraordinarily clever civil servant can be overdone. After all, he had spent ten years working on and off on his *Treatise on Probability*. The truth is that a problem got Keynes interested in a subject, but that very soon he became fascinated in developing it for its own sake. Many of the chapters in the *General Theory* are not needed for the tool-box. They are there because he wanted to say something about the nature of economic life.

Keynes's achievement as an economist is inseparable from his style. He was the greatest persuader in twentieth-century economics. In his best work, style and content are fused to electrifying effect. Unlike Ralph Hawtrey (boring) and Dennis Robertson (over-subtle), Keynes wrote in a way that compelled attention from both economists and laymen. What was his secret? Four qualities stand out. First, there was his desire and ability to connect economics with commonsense. It was indeed his consistent aim to overcome the cleavage 'between the conclusion of economic theory and those of commonsense'.[34] When he came to argue that employment depends on aggregate demand, he was simply generalising the intuition of the automobile worker who remarked: 'When no one's buying cars there's no point in making them'. Keynes's purposes required the artful use of ordinary language, in contrast to the practice of most economists of stating counter-intuitive theories in incomprehensible language. Secondly, Keynes's writings struck a note of urgency. At a time when most economists reacted to the collapse of the old order with excuses for inaction, he always addressed the public with a plan to make things better. Thirdly, he spoke with moral conviction: the conviction that the world could, and should, be made better by purposeful government action. Finally, he spoke with authority: not just the authority of Alfred Marshall and Cambridge economics, but that of the author of *The Economic Consequences of the Peace*, who had seemingly sacrificed a position at the heart of government to tell the truth. John Coates rightly sees him as using a particular kind of discourse, characterised by 'clear prose and compelling argumentation', as contrasted with the formal precision of mathematical models.[35] Keynes thoughts of economics much as he thought of probability theory: as a logic of non-conclusive arguments. In the history of public language this comes closest to the Aristotelian notion of the *enthymeme* – a 'rhetorical logic', appropriate to reasoning about 'things which are variable', and taking its premises from the audience's stock of social knowledge.

A detailed analysis of Keynes's use of language would be well worth doing. Here only a few hints can be given. As one would expect, the more technical his audience, the more technical his language: he used styles of argument, calculated to persuade the particular audience he was addressing. But in all his writing, he tried to uncover and express a common core of intuitive feeling. Thus while he explicitly addressed the *General Theory* to his 'fellow economists', he insisted that 'the ideas which are here expressed so laboriously are extremely simple and should be obvious'.[36] His economic writings drew on a wide, if not extravagant, range of cultural references, much of it what one would expect of a grandchild of the manse, a classical scholar, and a lover of the dramatic arts. He was a striking phrase-maker in his own right. In most of his writing he was both trying to persuade people that orthodox views – whether practical or theoretical – were wrong and that his own alternatives were right. So his arguments typically had both a 'destructive' and 'constructive' side. In handling opposing arguments he could be unscrupulous. He was not afraid to use emotive language (the gold standard was a 'barbarous relic', high interest rates were 'usury'); and he made good use of the Aunt Sally. Another technique was to point out the paradoxical quality of opponent beliefs, two of his favourites being the paradox of thrift and the paradox of prudence. The former lent itself effortlessly to the *reductio ad absurdum*: 'For take the extreme case,' Keynes says in a broadcast of 1931. 'Suppose we were to stop spending our incomes, and were to save the lot. Why ... in the end ... we should all starve to death.'[37] By the paradox of prudence Keynes meant that what was prudent for a household might be imprudent for a government, and vice versa. These paradoxical consequences of orthodox reasoning he traced back to the 'fallacy of composition': the belief that what was virtuous for an individual was bound to be beneficial for the community. Of course, the fallacy of composition can no more be proved than the atomic hypothesis which comes more naturally to economists. Perhaps Keynes's way of thinking was the result of much youthful discussion of Moore's principle of organic unities.

In developing his positive alternatives, Keynes relied more heavily on persuasive arguments than on demonstrative proofs; or rather he made a great effort to develop his proofs from premises rooted in the general perception of what was happening. A big blow to him was the failure of the fundamental equations of the *Treatise on Money* to capture what he wanted to say. He resolved to leave to other economists the task of reducing the theory of his new book to equational form. To bolster his arguments Keynes used a number of familiar persuasive ploys. One was the invention of tradition: his new theories would not seem so shocking if he could claim a reputable lineage for them. He also relied heavily on ambiguity, the chief rhetorical use of which was to create the widest possible agreement, by leaving room for alternative interpretations of the same words. People have been arguing about some of Keynes's ambiguities ever since. What did he mean by 'general theory'? What did he mean by the 'socialisation of investment'? What did he mean by 'social justice'? What did he mean by the 'state'? Much of this is a far cry from what passes as the 'scientific method'. But then Keynes did not believe that economics was a natural science.

In his attitude to his fellow humans, Keynes was a mixture of benevolence and intolerance. He had a great capacity for affection, and was always loyal to his friends. For example, affection led him to keep on Hugh Durnford as Second Bursar of King's till 1935, although everyone knew he was not really up to the job. Keynes's loyalty to his students was also conspicuous; in many cases his support for them continued long after they left the university. There was no trace of malice in him, or jealousy. He was appreciative of mental quirks, oddities, obsessions, which he often saw as containing interesting possibilities. He revered genius, a word which he used in its original sense of a 'free spirit', and which he used generously. He loved his French friend, Marcel Labordère, whom he hardly ever saw, for the sheer poetry of his mind, and addressed him as 'My dear Alchemist'; Labordère saw the same quality in him. Like many intellectuals, he had immense respect for practical expertise, even of the humblest. He was quick to excuse the faults of youth and inexperience. His social sympathies were not as highly developed as his personal ones, but as he grew older these expanded too; and at all times he could be angered by specific acts of injustice, whether to individuals or to groups. In general, he was not a patient man, but he could take enormous trouble with the affairs of his friends, and those he thought deserving of it.

At the same time, he could be devastatingly rude – especially to those he thought ought to know better. Stories of his rudeness are legion. On one occasion at a board meeting of the National Mutual, he broke out at Francis Curzon, brother of the marquess, 'Really, Curzon, you have all the pompos-ity of your brother and none of his intelligence.' Keynes was by no means easy company for the slower-witted. He was almost invariably the cleverest person in any gathering, knew it and showed it. Kenneth Clark, who served with him on CEMA (the Council for the Encouragement of Music and the Arts) during the Second World War, complained that he used his brilliance 'too unsparingly . . . he never dimmed his headlights'.

Keynes admired artists above all others and had well-developed aes-thetic tastes of his own, especially for poetry, Shakespeare in particular. His own ability to find fit words for themes and occasions was incomparable. He loved the dramatic arts best of all, and might have been a keener opera-goer had he been exposed to opera earlier. But music in all its forms came late to him, though often on a Sunday evening he would slip into a concert in the college chapel. How much he really enjoyed pictures, as opposed to the idea of having them, and supporting those who painted them, is dis-putable. Although he built a fine collection, he often bought dross – out of loyalty to his friends. He had little taste in furniture, though he spoke, as a young man, of the need to work in beautiful rooms. As he grew older, the coarseness which comes out in his letters to Lytton Strachey, and the comments of his Bloomsbury friends, vanished; those who knew him only in later life would have been amazed to learn that his 'mind was like a sewer'. He was not a fastidious man, but he had fastidious sides to him. He had his collars specially made for him at Cambridge, until his tailor stopped making them. He always wore silk underwear, though sometimes until it was in tatters. He liked well-kept hands and fingernails, and used these as a test of character. A great hoarder of letters, he threw away Goldie Lowes Dickinson's, because he could not stand their messiness. His personal, as well as work, habits were as orderly as the processes of his mind. He was as economical in his use of time as he was in his entertainments. He composed his essays and books in long-hand, often in pencil, on a writing board, sitting in an armchair, before sending off drafts to be typed. He rarely rewrote his short pieces; his big books, though, went through many drafts, and he left none of them completely satisfied. Whether he worked so hard from a sense of duty, a sense of pleasure or an incapacity to relax is difficult to say. He dominated any committee he was on, and did most of the work.

He had his full share of the foibles, some amiable, others less so, which he so admired in his biographical subjects. His fanciful mind made him a great 'sounder off'. He tended to lecture people on their own expertise, taking up some point, playing with it, developing it into a fantastic theory. A typical *obiter dictum* was his assertion before the Lottery Commission in 1932 that stock-market gambling was so prevalent in the United States because not enough grass grew to encourage horse-racing.[38] Some people thought there was a touch of charlatanry about him. He could be as credulous as any alchemist, and in the same way, investing money in 1930 in a process which guaranteed to turn base metal into gold, and speculating that the discovery might solve the world's unemployment problem.[39] He had the utmost confidence in his predictions of specific events, which was rarely justified by the outcome, though he was excellent at spotting general trends. He consistently lost money (his own and his friends') on the results of general elections. Quentin Bell tells the story of how he assured his friends in Sussex that a neighbouring, and highly polluting, cement factory would soon go bust, because its finances were wrongly constructed. It went on polluting long after he died. He almost invariably refused to sign circulars, write introductions to other people's books and allow his speeches to be printed, having decided views on why these things should not be. He had a profound mistrust of solicitors and accountants, and thought of their employment as a disagreeable necessity, to be avoided wherever possible. He had a great capacity for fussing, bombarding ministers with letters, not just about great failings in national policy, but about tiny lapses in the running of their departments. Almost any matter, however small, was capable of arousing his indignation – as when he fulminated for several months to the Lewes Borough Council over a small mistake he alleged them to have made in charging him a tiny sum for summoning the fire brigade to Tilton.

Keynes was a man of endless fascination, not altogether lovable. That he mellowed as much as he did was due, in no small measure, to the influence of Lydia, the enduring love of his life. He was, in his own sense, a great genius and a great thinker. His supreme effort of imagination and intellect was yet to come.

28

The Practical Visionary

I. PATTERNS OF PERSUASION

Early in October 1931, Vanessa and Duncan went to the cinema in London, when:

> suddenly Maynard appeared on the screen enormously big, in a well-appointed library blinking at the lights & speaking rather nervously & told the world that everything was now going to be all right, England had been rescued by fate from an almost hopeless situation, the pound would not collapse, prices would not rise very much, trade would recover, no one need fear anything. In this weather one can almost believe it. . . .[1]

Keynes was clearly in an upbeat mood. On 16 October 1931, he sent off the manuscript of his 'Essays in Prophecy' to Daniel Macmillan. They were published a month later under the title *Essays in Persuasion*. In the preface he wrote:

> We are standing at a point of transition. It is called a national crisis. But that is not correct – for Great Britain the main crisis is over. There is a lull in our affairs. We are, in the autumn of 1931, resting ourselves in a quiet pool between two waterfalls. Scarcely any one in England now believes in the Treaty of Versailles or in the pre-war gold standard or in the policy of deflation. These battles have been won – mainly by the irresistible pressure of events and only secondarily by the slow under-mining of old prejudices. But most of us have, as yet, only a vague idea of what we are going to do next, of how we are going to use our regained freedom of choice.[2]

The essays were a collection of his chief non-theoretical writings of the previous decade – 'the croakings of a Cassandra', he called them, 'who could never influence the course of events in time'. In saying that his prophecy had been more successful than his persuasion, Keynes was selling himself short. The drip of his pen had played its part in undermining old prejudices. That there was no serious attempt to revive the gold standard is a tribute to Keynes's persuasion in the 1920s. *The Times*, champion of monetary orthodoxy, wrote *finis* on that episode by saying that in 1925 'honour was at stake and worth an effort', but that 'British industry failed to make the necessary adjustment.'[3] From now on Keynes found *The Times* open to him, and his most important policy suggestions in the 1930s appeared in its columns.

On 21 January 1932, Lytton Strachey died of cancer. Keynes had not seen much of his old friend of late, although they had continued writing to each other and sending each other their books. Lydia had refused to go to Ham Spray, apparently because she disapproved of Carrington's immorality.[4] On Carrington, Lytton's death had a devastating effect. 'Nothing seems to me worth anything in comparison with that perfection of jokes and intelligence,' she wrote to Sebastian Sprott in March, a few days before shooting herself. The letter Maynard must have written to Carrington on Lytton's death has not survived, destroyed perhaps in one of the bonfires Carrington made of their possessions before she died. Lytton was part of Maynard's life which Lydia could not, and did not want to, share – the friend who had had a decisive influence over his style and sense of values. The memorial of their friendship is their letters, nearly a thousand of them, mostly dating from before the First World War, when they had openly discussed their feelings, joked about their friends and fought each other for the love of Duncan Grant. 'The letters? – for God's sake, lock them up for years yet,' Maynard told Lytton's brother James after Lytton's death.[5] Death started taking its toll of other pre-war friends: Goldie Lowes Dickinson in 1932, Roger Fry in 1934, Frankie Birrell and Brynhild Popham (née Olivier) in 1935. 'I am an idealist', Maynard told Virginia Woolf, '& therefore on the whole I suppose I think that something may continue. Clearly the brain is the only exciting thing – matter does not exist. It follows therefore ... but one is very vague.'[6]

Keynes's own health collapsed in the autumn of 1931, for the second time that year. 'I *am* after all having my days in bed and in horrid circumstances,' he scribbled to Lydia on 25 October 1931. 'I woke up yesterday with the most dreadful pains in my chest, so bad that I telephoned at once for a doctor. It turns out to be a sort of rheumatism, and inflammation of the sheaths of the small muscles which encircle the lungs (intercostal). Not at all dangerous or serious but horribly painful.' He was nursed by Richard Kahn and his bedmaker, Mrs Taylor, his bed being moved from his bedroom, where icicles had formed, to his study. Lydia (rightly) suspected pleurisy. That winter and early spring Keynes complained repeatedly of bronchitis, of lumbago, of rheumatic pains 'flying about the body'. He underwent periods of daily massage and treatment from Lydia's sun-ray lamp. Keynes had never looked robust; he had started to look unwell. He had put on a lot of weight. Vanessa Bell found him 'incredibly white and fat' in Lewes in the summer of 1930.[7] A portrait painted by William Roberts in the winter of 1931 shows a portly-looking Keynes, cigarette clutched in spatula-like fingers, with a no-longer birdlike Lydia beside him.

In the 1930s, Keynes was never as active in public life as he had been up to 1931. Partly, and certainly at first, this was because economic policy had caught up with his prescriptions. The deflationary constraint of the gold standard had ended, the decade of cheap money was at hand. The Keynesian agenda of the 1920s, applied in the 1930s, enabled Britain to escape the worst of the world depression. He endorsed, and partly inspired, the cheap-money policy and its corollary, managing sterling at a low rate of exchange with the dollar (initially at about $3.50), which followed the end of the gold-standard era.[8] He applauded Chamberlain's conversion of £2bn of 5 per cent war loan to 3.5 per cent as 'a constructive measure of the very first importance', not on budgetary-saving grounds, but for its effect on the long-term interest rate.[9] All this had its expected results. The balance of payments improved. Cheap money (bank rate stayed at 2 per cent from June 1932 to 1939) facilitated a boom in private house building, which helped revive economic activity. But recovery was slow in coming and it was seriously incomplete. Unemployment did not fall below 20 per cent till the middle of 1933.

Keynes found other things to applaud. Reparations were finally cancelled at the Lausanne Conference in July 1932. Keynes congratulated MacDonald, who presided: 'It is a long time since June 1919 when I resigned from the British delegation in Paris in an enraged and tormented state of mind. The waste over the intervening years has been prodigious. But it is a comfortable feeling that at last it is cleaned up. For whatever America may do, this is necessarily the end so far as Germany is concerned.'[10] Britain made a last token payment of its war debt to America in December 1933, and after that paid no more. After the Second World War, the victorious Allies declined to repeat their mistakes of 1919. Keynes's persuasion prevailed.

Keynes did not so much oppose the government's tariff and imperial-preference policy as regard it as a distraction from the more important task of general currency realignment. Free traders like Lionel Robbins argued that 'exchange-rate flexibility provided a complete solution to Britain's problem of external balance'.[11] Keynes agreed that the case for a tariff had lost its urgency, and that anything a tariff could do 'currency depreciation is doing and ... better'.[12] However, he believed in a managed, not floating, currency, and he did not recover his free-trade faith. In fact he developed a case for combining tariffs with limited currency depreciation.

Keynes had always tried to balance price and exchange stability. He applauded the devaluation of sterling not on narrow nationalistic grounds, but as providing a non-deflationary standard of value for the sterling bloc – the group of over twenty nations, mainly primary producers, who had devalued their own currencies in line with sterling in order to preserve their entry to the British market. This collective devaluation had also freed the debtor group of nations from the thrall of the creditor nations, led by the United States and France, which remained on the gold standard. The spontaneous emergence of a sterling bloc, or club as Keynes called it, suggested to him 'a reputable sterling system for the Empire . . . managed by the Bank of England and pivoted on London', with sterling stabilised in terms of a basket of commodities, and the Bank of England keeping its exchange as steady as possible with the dollar.[13] Eventually equilibrium would be reached between the two clubs – largely through the destruction of the creditor position of the USA and France – which would allow the restoration of a single international monetary system. He hoped such ideas might be pursued at the Imperial Conference held at Ottawa in July 1932, with Britain being prepared to bargain the value of sterling against the level of Dominion tariffs.[14] But he rightly suspected that the 'ultra-conservative' Neville Chamberlain and Montagu Norman would 'nip anything construc-tive in the bud'.[15] Chamberlain duly obliged by stopping any discussion of currency questions.[16]

Meanwhile, the departure of some countries from the gold standard had only tightened the grip of deflation on those countries which remained on it, hindering global recovery. Nearly half the banks in the United States failed in the depression, depriving their depositors of spending power. Keynes, like Milton Friedman subsequently, blamed the Federal Reserve Board for its failure to prevent a collapse of the US money stock. It did not start to buy securities on any scale till 1932. By then it was too late. The banks which survived became safety-deposit institutions, refusing to lend. This was the context in which Keynes was to develop his proposals for international public works to raise the price level in 1933.

Keynes appreciated that 'sound finance' was necessary at a time of financial crisis, to boost confidence and to make possible the transition to easy money; but no policy which did not aim directly at increasing total expenditure was likely to bring recovery. With the conversion operation over, he started fretting for an expansionary fiscal policy. To Harold Macmil-lan he wrote on 6 June 1932: 'There are enormous psychological advantages in the *appearance* of economy. It prepares the way for the conversion of the Debt and it tends to lower the long-term rate of interest. The opposite would also be bad for business sentiment. But that does not prevent economy from being deflationary and probably injurious to business profits.'[17] The debate was a repeat of his tussles with Hubert Henderson and Sir Richard Hopkins in 1930. They stressed the adverse effects on confidence and therefore interest rates of unbalancing the budget, Keynes the beneficial effects on activity.

The relative meagreness of Keynes's public activities in the early 1930s is also explained by the collapse of his networks of persuasion. Politically he was homeless. The Liberal Party virtually ceased to exist in October 1931, the ageing Lloyd George heading a family group of four MPs. The parliamentary Labour Party was reduced to a rump. Its leading Keynesian, Mosley, was out of Parliament and had started the British Union of Fascists.

Keynes's intellectual networks had also collapsed. Kingsley Martin's *New Statesman* could not give him the platform he had had in the *Nation* under Hubert Henderson. Its politics was too left-wing for his liking, and it was not interested in economics. The old liberal-minded world of clubs and committees, of civil servants and of bankers, politicians, economists and do-gooders, on which Keynes had cast magic spells till 1931, had also lost influence, as business Conservatism, headed by Neville Chamberlain, seized power from the nerveless grasp of MacDonald and Baldwin. The Tuesday Club, which Keynes had used to such effect as a sounding board in the 1920s, met less and less frequently: Keynes did not address it once between 1930 and 1934. He still had access to MacDonald, both privately and as a member of a number of expert advisory committees which the Prime Minister appointed to strengthen him politically. Keynes thought that Mac-Donald had 'given up thinking nonsense'.[18] But, whatever he thought, the ex-Labour Prime Minister was a prisoner of his huge 'national' majority of right-wing Conservative MPs. The depression had anyway caused rifts in the old mandarin circle – over free trade, over unbalanced budgets and, increasingly, over economic theory. It would regroup at the end of the 1930s. Meanwhile, Keynes fell back on a new support group of Cambridge disciples headed by his 'favourite student' Richard Kahn. He appears a more isolated figure in the 1930s than in the 1920s, but his very isolation gave him the breathing space to write his great book.

The depression radicalised Keynes intellectually, but not politically or socially. Politically, he still thought of himself as a liberal, a believer in individual freedom and its corollary of limited government. He never embraced socialism. In the 1930s, he insisted as he had in the 1920s that the state should not try to take over the functions of private enterprise, merely fill its gaps. His political economy thus shows great continuity with his Middle Way notions of the 1920s. Socially, indeed, he was growing more conservative. He 'is the most crusted tory of my acquaintance', Sam Court-auld remarked in September 1932 after spending a 'happy' weekend at Tilton, during which Keynes had told him that 'the age of institutions is the best criterion of their worth, & progress is only admissible if it is so slow as to be imperceptible. . . .'[19] This was, as we shall see, at the precise moment when his economic theory was being radicalised. The paradox is apparent rather than actual, for ever since 1919 he had preached that radical thought was the only antidote to radical change.

While privately conceding that 'one could not possibly have wished the Labour Government to be returned' in October 1931,[20] Keynes continued his dialogue with the Labour Party. Addressing a socialist group on 13 December 1931 on the 'Dilemmas of Modern Socialism', he delivered his retrospective judgement on Labour's two years in office. The problem with the Labour Party was that it lacked a viable philosophy of government. Committed to a socialist utopia it failed to interest itself in the problem of running capitalism. As a result it combined redistributionary threats which depressed businessmen with slavish adherence to financial orthodoxy which depressed the economy. It had been 'totally out of sympathy', Keynes said, 'with those who have had new notions of what is economically sound ... such as Mr Lloyd George or Sir Oswald Mosley or Mr Bevin or myself'. Yet starting, Keynes suggested, from a different intellectual perspective – that of a general deficiency of purchasing power – his own policies could be shown to be consistent with a range of socialist policies, notably central controls on investment and measures of income redistribution not to knock capitalism out but to raise purchasing power.[21]

When he reviewed the Labour Party's policy on banking, in the *New Statesman* of 17 and 24 September 1932, he supported nationalisation of the Bank of England, but attacked the Party's demand for 'democratic interference' in its working. It was the policy, not the structure, of the Bank which was at fault, and care should be taken to protect its 'autonomy' and 'independence and prestige' which were national assets. He accepted Labour's proposal for a national investment board, but rejected the idea of 'qualitative control' over investment. The task of such a board should be to maintain the aggregate rate of investment high enough 'to ensure the optimum level of employment', not to choose between investment projects. Keynes emphasised the 'smallness of the part [in investment] which purely private enterprise now plays'. If the state could determine 'the rate of aggregate investment' of 'public and semi-public bodies', it could 'safely leave industry to raise what funds it needs as and when it chooses'.[22]

The left was by no means receptive to Keynes's way of analysing the economic problem. After 1931, its favoured remedy was the physical planning of production, in the belief that 'socialist' planning and public ownership would themselves be sufficient to restore full employment. The main intellectual input into Labour's economic theory, apart from Marxism, came from the London School of Economics. Hugh Dalton upheld Cannan's old-fashioned quantity theory of money on Labour's Finance and Trade Committee; younger socialist economists from the LSE like Evan Durbin and Hugh Gaitskell were much influenced by Lionel Robbins's and Hayek's pessimistic 'Austrian' analysis, which seemed to reinforce the view that slumps were inevitable under capitalism. In addition, 'the Labour Party was highly suspicious of Keynes' both because of his association with Lloyd George and Mosley and 'for his unfortunate manner'.[23] Keynes himself steered well clear of such Labour Party think tanks as the New Fabian Research Bureau or the XYZ Club, the latter started in 1932 by his friend Nicholas Davenport. The historian A. L. Rowse wanted Keynes to join the Labour Party. His ideas, Rowse argued, could succeed only if they were in the 'right relation' with the organised working class.[24] But Keynes remained suspicious of Labour. 'I should officially join that party', he wrote to Rowse in 1936, 'if it did not seem to be divided between enthusiasts who turn against anything if there seems a chance that it could possibly happen, and leaders so conservative that there is more to hope from Mr. Baldwin.'[25]

Keynes had already started to feel that practical persuasion had to be based on a new theory. 'I have begun again quietly in my chair writing about monetary theory,' he told Lydia on 22 November 1931. The passionate rows between the economists in 1930 had shocked him, and, as he later put it in the preface to the *General Theory*, 'almost destroyed the practical influence of economic theory'. When the *Treatise* was published in October 1930, he recognised that it was an artistic failure. He did not immediately see it as an intellectual failure. The adverse comment it got, as well as changes in the total situation since it was conceived, persuaded him otherwise. Perhaps the two failures are connected. A new explanation of prolonged depression was needed, which the formal apparatus of the *Treatise* could not supply.

II. INFLUENCES

Keynes's return to theory was inherent in his analysis of the slump. He refused to think of it as the final crisis of capitalism. In his preface to his *Essays in Persuasion* he emphasised his 'central thesis throughout – the profound conviction that the economic problem ... is nothing but a frightful muddle, a transitory and *unnecessary* muddle'. The obstacles to recovery, he told an audience in Hamburg in January 1932, were not material but 'reside in the state of knowledge, judgement and opinion of those who sit in the seats of authority'.[26]

Peter Clarke has argued that, unlike the composition of the *Treatise*, the development of the *General Theory* 'must ... be understood in "internalist" terms. It was the outcome of a process of intellectual discovery rather than of political invention.'[27] The *General Theory* was certainly not tied to a political campaign, as the revised *Treatise* partly was. But Clarke's alternatives ignore the impact on Keynes's theorising of the changing economic and political environment.[28] A theory designed to save the world can never be wholly 'internalist' in inspiration.

The *General Theory* was projected against the background not just of the world depression, but of its political and social repercussions: specifically, the spread of communism and fascism. The flight of the intelligentsia from democracy had started. 'Stephen [Spender] is going bolshy like most of my friends,' noted Harold Nicolson in his diary of 24 September 1931. In January 1933, Adolf Hitler became Chancellor of Germany.

The *Treatise* was constructed with the British problem very much in mind. The *General Theory* was designed to supply a theory for a world in depression. This is one of the many ways in which the new theory is more 'general' than the old. But there was a special reason for the shift. Keynes was particularly impressed by the scale of the American collapse. Here was no sclerotic economy like Britain, but one which still bore many of the traces of nineteenth-century 'fluidity'. The US collapse spurred Keynes to think more generally about the predicament of modern economies. The older emphasis on 'rigidities' gives way to a new attention to 'uncertainty', as America replaces Britain as the example *par excellence* of the distressed economy.

Formally, the switch is from a model of an 'open' to that of a 'closed' economy. Here again, the American example may have been influential, as foreign trade was far less important for America than for Britain. But, in addition, analysis of unemployment in terms of maladjustments between different countries seemed to make much less sense when unemployment was truly 'general'. As Keynes noted in the *New Statesman* of 24 December 1932, 'The course of exchange, as we all know, moves round a closed circle. When we transmit the tension, which is beyond our own endurance, to our neighbour, it is only a question of a little time before it reaches ourselves again travelling round the circle.'[29] By 'closing' the economy Keynes is in effect saying there is no solution within the system; it has to come from outside. The government becomes the last frontier. Another effect of the depression can be seen in the switch from dynamic to static analysis. What needed to be explained was not the business cycle, but the persistence of a low level of business activity.

The generality and depth of the depression damaged Keynes's never very robust faith in the classic price adjustment mechanisms. He had proposed a national treaty to reduce British money incomes in 1925, and supported a similar scheme implemented in Australia in 1931. Now, in June 1932, he told the Australian economist Giblin, 'if wages are reduced prices are sure to go down too. . .'.[30] This is a 'closed economy' idea: wage reductions applied all-round simply destroy purchasing power.

Experience of the great depression also reinforced Keynes's doubt about the efficacy of cheap money. 'It may still be the case', he said in his Halley-Stewart Lecture of 4 February 1932, 'that the lender, with his confidence shattered by his experience, will continue to ask for new enterprise rates of interest which the borrower cannot expect to earn. . . . If this proves to be the case there will be no means of escape from prolonged and perhaps interminable depression except by direct state intervention to promote and subsidise new investment.' The notion of a 'liquidity trap' had its origins in the severity of the depression.

The world slump was the indispensable background; its existence penetrated every thought Keynes had. Yet at the same time the new theory emerged through a process of intellectual argument, marked by a sense of high responsibility from all concerned to get the logic of the argument right. This argument is extremely well documented. In the period 1931–2 Keynes engaged in intermittent, but intense, correspondence on points of theory with Hawtrey, Robertson and Hayek. There are the 'pooled memories' of the so-called Cambridge Circus. There is the evidence of early drafts of the new book and Keynes's other writings, as well as fragments of lectures, and complete sets of the lecture notes of some of his students, which run from 1932 to 1935.

III. WHAT WAS WRONG WITH THE *TREATISE*?

The birth of Keynes's new model of the economy started with the demolition of his old one. The Fundamental Equations of the *Treatise* are static price-level equations, which Keynes had tried to dynamise by adding terms for business profits and losses. Changes in output and employment are incidents, however painful and protracted, in the divergence and eventual reconvergence of prices and costs. The banana parable tells a different, and partly contradictory, story: how when businessmen make losses (or saving 'runs ahead' of investment) the economy runs down to a low point and gets stuck there. But the working out of this story is confused and implausible, and as Keynes admitted before the Macmillan Committee, the trouble could easily be cured by lowering the rate of interest. This suggests it was designed to illustrate Britain's peculiar problem under the gold standard, not offer a theoretical explanation of persisting mass unemployment. Keynes was still a long way from having a theory of 'output as a whole'.

Even before the *Treatise* was published, Ralph Hawtrey at the Treasury pointed Keynes in the direction he wanted to go. 'If anything occurs to affect the demand for goods', Hawtrey wrote to Keynes in the summer of 1930, 'the first result is an increase or decrease in sales at *existing prices*. . . . There is always some interval of time before prices are adjusted, and the interval may be considerable'. Moreover, 'we have here a disturbance of equilibrium *before* any change in prices, and therefore independent of the existence of windfall gain or loss or of any difference between investment and saving. . . . Thus the changes of prices when it does occur is not by itself an adequate measure of the departure from equilibrium.'[31] On 28 November Keynes conceded that 'it will probably be difficult in future to prevent monetary theory and the theory of short-period supply from running together'.[32] In Keynes's mind the direct effect of a fall in spending on quantities was starting to overshadow its effects on costs and prices.

Hawtrey's comments were complemented by those Keynes got from the

'Cambridge Circus', the name retrospectively given to a group of his younger colleagues who started meeting after the *Treatise* was published in October 1930. They were Richard Kahn, Piero Sraffa, Austin and Joan Robinson, and James Meade. The first four were teachers at Cambridge; Meade was spending a postgraduate year at Cambridge before taking up a fellowship in Oxford. Informal discussions started in Richard Kahn's rooms at King's College in November 1930 and went on sporadically for some months. Keynes did not attend these meetings, Richard Kahn acting as go-between.

The Circus soon spotted that the Fundamental Equations assumed a fixed output – the so-called 'widow's cruse' fallacy.[33] As Austin Robinson put it: if an entrepreneur loaded with profits decided on his way home to have a shoe-shine, was the effect solely to raise the price of shoe-shines rather than affect the numbers of shoes shone?[34] Keynes was hurt. 'I think you are a little hard on me', he wrote to Joan Robinson on 14 April 1932, 'as regards the assumption of constant output.... Surely one must be allowed at a particular stage of one's argument to make simplifying assumptions of this kind'. He admitted though that his theory had 'not followed out the consequences of changes in output....'[35]

The most important effect of the Circus discussions was to reinforce the impetus Hawtrey gave Keynes to working out an equation for output. A model which assumed fixed output could not be used to explain what caused output to be what it was.

In his review of the *Treatise* in the *Economic Journal* of September 1931 Dennis Robertson criticised the non-operational definitions of 'saving' and 'income'. 'Excess of saving over investment' was defined as equal to 'business losses'. This meant that as long as businessmen continued to make losses, saving would always 'run ahead' of investment, i.e. no position of equilibrium was possible. Robertson asked: 'How many of those ... who have taken up the cry that a slump is due to an excess of Saving over Investment realise that the savings which are so deplorably abundant during a slump consist largely of entrepreneurs' incomes which are not being spent, for the simple reason that they have not been earned?'[36] If business profits and losses were counted as additions to, or deductions from, incomes, the inequality between saving and investment automatically disappeared. But this meant scrapping the whole idea of the 'normal', or equilibrium, level of income. The level of the community's income (or output) becomes the variable to be explained, not departures from a 'normal' income. This is the entry point of the *General Theory*.

Whereas Cambridge, young and old, offered constructive criticism of the *Treatise*, Friedrich Hayek's was, and was meant to be, destructive. Brought to the London School of Economics by Lionel Robbins as part of a power play against Cambridge, Hayek, then aged thirty-two, came from Vienna equipped with an 'Austrian' theory whose intellectual defences against government interference with market forces were both more sophisticated and much more intransigent than any on offer in Britain or the United States. At its heart was an inter-temporal theory of value – an application of marginal utility theory to capital formation. On the one hand are consumers with 'time-preferences' (demands) as between consumption and capital goods. These time-preferences govern their decisions as to how much of their incomes to spend on consumption and how much to save. On the other side are producers who adjust their production plans in the light of the (shifting) demands for the two types of good. If people decide to save more, demand for consumer goods falls, but this is offset by an increase in demand for capital good, and vice versa. (The Austrian theory was pro-saving, since the Austrians believed, unlike Keynes that it was out of the savings of individuals that the wealth of nations was built up.) The price which co-ordinates the inter-temporal plans of consumers and producers is the rate of interest. However, interest rates can do this job efficiently only if money is kept 'neutral' – that is, in the absence of inflation or deflation by the monetary authority.

This is the crucial point in Hayek's theory of the business cycle. A fall in interest rates produced by credit expansion sends a false signal to producers to increase the production of capital goods. The crisis which produces the slump is a crisis of over-investment – over-investment in relation to the amount of consumption individuals want to postpone – financed by credit-creation by the banking system. The slump was merely the process of eliminating those investments not financed by genuine savings. If govern-ment, in reaction to a slump, manufactured more money it would only prolong the agony; the quickest cure was for people to save more, so as to bring down the rate of interest, and thus enable a recovery in investment. Keynes was familiar with this over-investment theory: he had said much the same thing in his lecture of 1913. In his *Treatise on Money* he had gone some way in escaping from it.

Hayek's explanations for the slump were received with raptures at the LSE when he lectured there in the spring of 1931; less enthusiastically at Cambridge. A one-lecture version of his theory to the Marshall Society in January 1931 was greeted with complete silence. Richard Kahn, who was in the audience, felt he had to break the ice. 'Is it your view', he asked Hayek, 'that if I went out tomorrow and bought a new overcoat, that would increase unemployment?' 'Yes', replied Hayek, pointing to a blackboard full of triangles, 'but it would take a very long mathematical argument to explain why.'[37] For three or four years afterwards, Hayek's theories vied with Keynes's for the succession to classical economics. Many famous later Keynesians like Nicholas Kaldor and A. P. Lerner started off as Hayekians.

In his review of the *Treatise* for the LSE-based journal *Economica*, Hayek accused Keynes of lacking a theory of capital. Keynes's account of a change in the direction of money flows (between consumption and saving) impinged on a rigid structure of production. An analysis of the reasons which made different stages of production more or less attractive would have shown that changes in savings habits could never of themselves give rise to total profits or losses, or a divergence between saving and investment. Only a change in the 'effective' quantity of money could do that. If this 'mistake' were eliminated, Keynes's theory was simply a version of a 'forced saving' theory.

Keynes was enraged by Hayek's review, scribbling on his copy: 'Hayek has not read my book with that measure of "good will" which an author is entitled to expect of a reader. Until he can do so, he will not see what I mean or whether I am right.' His own rejoinder to Hayek's attack in the *Economica* of November 1931 soon 'drifted' into a critique of Hayek's own book, *Prices and Production*, published in September 1931, which he called 'one of the most frightful muddles I have ever read.... It is an extraordinary example of how, starting with a mistake, a remorseless logician can end in Bedlam.'[38] The mistake Keynes identified was the belief that decisions to save are simultaneously demands for investment goods. However, he conceded that his own book lacked 'any satisfactory theory of capital and interest' and promised to remedy this. The two men exchanged an inconclusive series of letters on definitions in the winter of 1931–2. Keynes then broke off: 'I am trying to reshape and improve my central position, and that is probably a better way to spend one's time than in controversy.'[39]

Keynes and Hayek remained on friendly terms. Keynes got on 'very well' with him in private life. Hayek recalled the 'the magnetism of the brilliant conversationalist with his wide range of interests and bewitching voice'.[40] But there was, and could be, no meeting of minds. This was largely because of the different way they did their economics. Whereas Hayek started from premises which could not lead to perverse outcomes, Keynes started from perverse outcomes and tried to construct premises consistent with them. What he had not yet explained, in terms of fundamental theory, was how the perverse outcomes were possible.

IV. TOWARDS *THE GENERAL THEORY*

Keynes started work on his new book early in 1932 with most of the criticisms of the *Treatise* to hand. On 22 March 1932 he 'bowed the knee' to Hawtrey and Robertson by acknowledging that 'excess savings' came from incomes which had not been earned. He proposed a definition of 'total income' to include 'abnormal' profits and losses, so that 'savings and investment are, necessarily, and at all times, equal – being indeed the same concept looked at from opposite points of view'. Further 'S[aving out of total income] always and necessarily accommodates itself to I[nvestment].... [it] is no longer the dog ... but the tail'.[41] By this formula Keynes disposed of the Fundamental Equations, equilibrium and disequilibrium prices and the Robertsonian mix of voluntary and forced saving. Output (real income) changes in line with investment; savings are always voluntary and are generated by the flows of income. At Tilton that summer Keynes wrote 'nearly a third of my new book on monetary theory' as well as piecing together some 'Essays in Biography' as a complement to his *Essays in Persuasion*. A Swedish visitor, Per Jacobsson, head of the monetary department of the newly formed Bank for International Settlements at Geneva, records him as wrestling with 'some difficult theoretical problems on the rate of interest....'[42]

We can follow the evolution of his ideas in the two sets of eight lectures he delivered in Cambridge in the autumn of 1932 and 1933. An edited version of his students' notes has been transcribed and published by the Canadian economist T. K. Rymes.

'Gentlemen, the change in title of these lectures' – from 'The Pure Theory of Money' to 'The Monetary Theory of Production' – 'is significant'. With these words on 10 October 1932, recalled Lorie Tarshis, 'Keynes began the first of his eight lectures and in effect announced the beginning of the Keynesian Revolution'. The subject of Keynes's inquiry was: what determines the volume of output in a monetary economy? The question is *The General Theory*'s, but much of the answer is still wrapped up in the language and concepts of the *Treatise on Money*. Nevertheless, many of the familiar building-blocks of *The General Theory* are in view. They are even clearer in the repeat set of lectures he delivered in the autumn of 1933.

The volume of output is determined by aggregate 'disbursement', or expenditure. If spending falls short of current income then income has to fall to the level of expenditure, via a reduction in employment. In explaining why the costs of production or current income can be reduced only by cutting employment rather than by cutting money-wages, Keynes offers a first sketch of chapter 2 of *The General Theory*. The argument is sharpened in 1933 by the proposition that the real wage depends on the level of aggregate spending, now called 'effective demand,' not on the money-wage bargain ('there may be no escape for labour from high real wages in a slump'), and by the corresponding concept of 'involuntary unemployment'.

Expenditure is determined, in a *laissez-faire* economy, by the 'factors of market psychology': the state of time preference (later the consumption function) relating saving to income; expected 'quasi-rents' or the expected profitability of investment (later the marginal efficiency of capital); and the state of liquidity preference, which, together with the quantity of money, determines the rate of interest. These 'parameters' of a monetary economy, together with the aggregate supply schedule and 'earnings response' (of costs to prices) tells us 'what state of output would ensue ... and how the parameters would have to be influenced to get the desired output'. This is put more sharply in 1933: 'the fundamental forces determining the volume of employment are the state of confidence, the propensity to consume, liquidity preference and the quantity of money. We may call this the General Law of Employment.'[43] The roles of expectations and uncertainty are now much more prominently highlighted.

That the amount of aggregate disbursement determined by the 'factors of psychology' may be insufficient to maintain full employment is clear to Keynes but the reason is not precisely stated in 1932. Keynes has already decided that the rate of interest is determined by the demand for money, rather than by the demand for loans. So determined, the interest rate 'fixes the present value of the prospective quasi-rents'.[44] The duty of the monetary authority is to 'maintain a rate of interest which leads to an optimum level of investment'.[45] The proposition that the 'speculative' motive for holding money may set a floor to the fall in the interest rate is not clearly stated till 1933.[46]

Keynes asks: what, in the absence of stabilisation policy, is to stop income and output running down 'until production was at a total stand-still?' The short answer is that, following a shock to investment, expenditure on consumption falls less than income. It is this which makes possible 'stable equilibrium'.[47] This, too, is said more sharply in 1933: 'Saving must equal Investment, income will adjust itself to meet this condition'.[48] This is the root of the idea that stable equilibrium is possible short of full employment.

One reason for the relative imprecision of the 1932 lectures is that Keynes made no use of Kahn's multiplier theory. Like Kahn himself, he failed to see its logical connection with monetary equilibrium analysis.

Richard Kahn's article, 'The Relation of Home Investment to Unemployment', published in the *Economic Journal* in June 1931, was designed to combat the British Treasury's objections to loan-financed public works programmes as a remedy for unemployment. These were based on the meagreness of the employment afforded by a given expenditure of money, the budgetary burden entailed, and the 'crowding out' of private investment. In their pamphlet of 1929, *Can Lloyd George Do It?* Keynes and Henderson had asserted that a public works programme would provide, in addition to a calculable amount of primary employment, 'secondary' employment resulting from the newly employed spending their wages, but that these secondary effects were incalculable. The question Kahn asked was: what was to stop an extra £1 of income in one person's hands from raising the community's income to infinity? The intuitive answer is that some fraction of the extra income will be 'saved' each time it is spent until the stimulus exhausts itself. Provided this fraction is known, the total of increased income or secondary employment can be added up to a finite number, which can be expressed as a ratio or multiple either of the initial investment or of primary employment. Moreover, additional investment would, by raising aggregate incomes, create an equivalent amount of saving, thus exemplifying Keynes's assertion that 'investment always drags saving along with it at an equal pace', and countering the Treasury argument that loan-financed public investment would take savings from existing uses. This in essence is the multiplier theory.

It was not how Kahn set it out. He achieved his 'leakages' from the enlarged expenditure stream by deducting unemployment benefit (what the unemployed were already spending) and extra spending on imports (which did not directly increase domestic employment); and he failed to realise that his formula had established the necessary equality between saving and investment. (In an 'open' economy the necessary equality is not between saving and investment but between saving and imports and investment and exports.) The *personal saving* leakage first entered the multiplier literature with an article by the Danish statistician Jens Warming in the *Economic Journal* of June 1932. Warming 'combined an exclusively income-related personal saving function with Kahn's own multiplier algebra to render neatly the income adjustment mechanism by which saving is equilibrated with an initating change in investment'. Keynes almost certainly saw Warming's article when it was first submitted to the *Economic Journal.* So the theoretical influence may have run more directly from Warming to Keynes than from Kahn to Keynes at this point. Kahn, influenced in turn by Warming, presented a multiplier derived from the marginal propensities to save and import in a paper in Cincinatti, Ohio, in December 1932. Keynes's *The Means to Prosperity*, published in three months later, presented this revised version of Kahn's theory in support of his argument for a loan-financed public works programme.[49]

Much ink has been spilt over the question of when exactly Keynes came to understand his new theory of effective demand. That it was some time between 1932 and 1933 is indisputable. The answer depends on the test of understanding being used. Perhaps Keynes himself should have the last word. Original thinking, he remarked in his lecture of 6 November 1933, starts as a 'grey, fuzzy, woolly monster' in one's head. 'The precise use of language comes at a late stage in the development of one's thoughts. You can think accurately and effectively long before you can, so to speak, photograph your thought.'[50] Keynes knew more than he could say in the autumn of 1932, but he was more confident about what he knew a year later, and therefore could say it better.

In a letter Keynes wrote to Harrod in August 1936, he looked back on this period:

> You don't mention *effective demand*, or, more precisely, the demand schedule for output as a whole.... To me, the most extraordinary thing, regarded historically, is the complete disappearance of the theory of the

demand and supply for output as a whole, i.e. the theory of employment, *after* it had been for a quarter of a century the most discussed
thing in economics. One of the most important transitions for me, after
my *Treatise on Money* had been published, was suddenly realising this.
It only came after I had enunciated to myself the psychological law that,
when income increases, the gap between income and consumption will
increase – a conclusion of vast importance to my own thinking but not
apparently, expressed just like this, to anyone's else's. Then, appreciably
later, came the notion of interest as being the meaning [measure?] of
liquidity-preference, which became quite clear in my mind the moment
I thought of it. And last of all, after an immense lot of muddling and
many drafts, the proper definition of the marginal efficiency of capital
linked up one thing with another.[51]

It must have been an exciting time for good economics students at
Cambridge. One of them, Antony G. Gilpin, supervised by Keynes in his final
year 1933/4 wrote to his parents: 'Economics lectures this year seem mainly
to consist of elaborations or refutations of theories taught us last year. Shove
dissects Marshall; Keynes attacks Pigou; Robertson disagrees with Keynes,
and leaves it to his audience to decide who is right; an intense lady, Mrs
Joan Robinson, tries to explain why they disagree. It is interesting but
confusing.'[52]

V. THE MEANS TO PROSPERITY

With increasing confidence in his analysis, Keynes started to propound his
policies for the 1930s. By the autumn of 1932 the brief British recovery had
fizzled out. Real interest rates had come down dramatically, but, following a
flurry of activity after devaluation, output fell to its lowest point in August/
September 1932 (though the fall was nothing like as severe as in 1921) and
unemployment remained above 20 per cent of the insured labour force from
January 1931 to May 1933. This was despite the 'confidence' generated by
the National government with its balanced budget and huge Conservative
majority. Here was Keynes's unemployment equilibrium in real life. He now
had a much firmer theoretical basis for arguing that increased government
spending was the only way to full employment: for, with private spending
so depressed by the fall in national income, where were the spontaneous
forces to bring recovery?

Keynes posed the important question at the end of 1932: 'Will it be
apparent by the middle of 1933 that this slump is the same in kind as past

slumps though more violent in degree, and is gradually working itself off by the operation of natural forces and the economic system's own resiliency? Or shall we find ourselves after a modest upward reaction and dubious hopes of recovery, plunged back again into the slough?'[53] He had little doubt of the answer. His policy advice from this time onwards is dominated by the belief that there was no way out of the slump unless governments took action to raise world demand. He did not, of course, discount the possibility of 'some accidental event' turning up to 'put speculators in funds and spirits'.[54] But this was not the 'internal efficacious mechanism' which classical economists relied on. Yet the verdict on the 1930s remains open. The depression in Britain reached its trough in the last quarter of 1932. There *was* a predominantly market-led recovery in Britain and some other countries which was deeper and longer than Keynes expected (it did not collapse till 1937). It is at least an open question whether Keynesian policies in Britain could have achieved much more, given the pre-Keynesian climate of expectations and the decentralised character of economic decision-making. The American recovery under the New Deal was rather less successful than Britain's. Hitler's Germany alone provided triumphant vindication of Keynesian economics, but only in semi-war conditions, backed by terror.

Keynes's main insider influence was exerted through the Committee on Economic Information, effective residuary of the Economic Advisory Council. Stamp was its chairman, and its members, apart from Keynes, were Citrine, Cole, Sir Alfred Lewis (of the National Provincial Bank), Hubert Henderson, Sir Arthur Salter (who had just retired as director of the Economic and Finance Section of the League of Nations) and Sir Ernest Simon. Two Treasury officials attended: Sir Frederick Leith-Ross from 1932 and Sir Frederick Phillips from 1935. The first of its regular 'Surveys of the Economic Situation' appeared in March 1932. Arthur Salter recalled that:

> Some twenty reports (almost all unanimous), each of about twenty pages, were laboriously discussed and drafted ... Of the policy urged on the Government I will only ... say that it bore the impress of Keynes, that it was basically different from the official policy actually being pursued on the joint advice of the Treasury and the Bank of England, and that there would now [1967], I believe, be a general consensus that, where they differed, the committee was right and the official policy wrong.[55]

Keynes's influence was soon felt. The first of his Committee's surveys on the internal situation in November 1932 criticised the balanced-budget policy, curtailment of the public works programme and cuts in wages and unemployment benefit as deflationary, and said that, while they might have been necessary to get over the financial crisis, the time had come 'to back up the cheap money policy with a more liberal budgetary policy'.[56] Keynes had also begun his public campaign. He felt intuitively that the psychological moment had come to strike. A correspondence in *The Times* in October shows the economic profession lining up into two camps based on Cambridge and the LSE. Pigou, D. H. McGregor, Keynes, Layton, Salter and Stamp signed a letter on 17 October which said that economising on consumption led to unemployment. Saving did not automatically flow into investment when confidence was low but led to a reduction in national income. So public investment should be encouraged. Of the critical letters which followed, the chief one came from the LSE under the signatures of T. E. Gregory, Hayek, Arnold Plant and Lionel Robbins, supporting the balanced-budget policy. Keynes and his co-signatories replied on 21 October that it was an illusion to think that money saved today represents money available to be spent tomorrow when confidence returns. 'Insofar as labour and capital are idle, the resources available for paying income to their owners are not conserved; they simply do not come into existence.'[57] The influence of Keynes's ideas on these collective statements is palpable.

In a broadcast conversation with Stamp on 11 January he delivered two good *mots* – 'Look after unemployment, and the Budget will look after itself' and 'We must save if spending is to be healthy, and we must spend if saving is to be healthy'.

Early in 1933 he sensed it was time to go on the offensive. On 22 February he wrote to Geoffrey Dawson, 'I have felt very strongly moved in the last day or two to write two or three articles on the present situation, which I would offer you for *The Times* and then perhaps expand shortly afterwards into a pamphlet.' His purpose in writing was to influence the budget in April and the World Economic Conference due to assemble in London in June. Dawson offered £60 for four articles, double the standard rate of payment (though Keynes got paid £100 per article from the *Daily Mail*). On 27 February the Reichstag in Berlin went up in flames. Newspaper attention being concentrated on this outrage, the publication of Keynes's articles, designed to suggest a 'means to prosperity' which did not involve burning down parliaments, was delayed till 13–16 March. But, even before this, an advanced set of the articles had reached the new American president, Franklin Roosevelt. Keynes's pamphlet, *The Means to Prosperity*, was published later that month. An American edition, published in April, incorporated additional material on 'The Multiplier' which had appeared in the *New Station* (Cambridge's nickname for the recently merged *New Statesman and Nation*) on April Fool's Day.

Keynes's articles had a sensational impact, despite being more sombre in mood, more solid in style than similar productions in the 1920s. Gone was the linguistic vivacity, the delight in paradox, which had marked *The Economic Consequences of Mr. Churchill* or *Can Lloyd George Do It?* Bloomsbury wit, digs at stupid bankers, mad politicians and so on were put aside in favour of a wholly serious, unadorned development of his case; perhaps he felt, too, that the world depression was too serious a disease to be treated by wit. At fifty, the *enfant terrible* was acquiring *gravitas*. From now on he would display his iconoclasm much more sparingly, at least in public. Macmillan, not the Hogarth Press, published the pamphlet, symbolising the shift in desired audience. *The Means to Prosperity* was also much less parochial than the two earlier series, as befitted a *world* in depression. Remedies for Britain were explicitly linked to the recovery of world demand, and the argument culminated in a plan for world reflation. The articles marked, that is, the emergence of Keynes as a world statesman; or rather, the re-emergence of a much more mature Keynes than that of 1919 when he had first tried to legislate the world back to prosperity. There was also a new search for consensus. Although the multiplier theory was his own special contribution, his international plan built on the work of Henderson and others and was close to becoming the Treasury view. Keynes had also emerged from the tunnel of the *Treatise*. Theory was kept in the background, but the work he had done over the previous year enabled him to put simple ideas directly.

The start of the pamphlet was, however, characteristic. The world's troubles were due not to material destruction, but to 'failure in the immaterial devices of the mind' – more plainly, 'clear thinking'. What was needed to cure them 'was a blend of economic theory with the art of statesmanship.... political economy'.[58] He then applied the multiplier theory (which was for the first time labelled as such) to confute the two main arguments against 'loan expenditure' by government: 'the meagreness of the employment created' and the 'strain on national and local budgets'.[59] To obtain the magnitude of the multiplier 'we have simply to estimate ... what proportion of typical expenditure becomes someone's income and what proportion of this income is spent. For these two proportions, multiplied together, give us the ratio of the first repercussion to the primary effect.... we can then sum the whole series of repercussions....'[60] Keynes calculated a British multiplier of 2; the American multiplier would be more than 2, for reasons which Kahn had given.[61] Keynes added a number of refinements to Kahn's article. The exposition is worked out in terms of changes in national income as well as employment, the two coming to 'much the same thing'.[62] He emphasised favourable international repercussions: Britain's beneficent action would be 'twice blessed' since out of an increased national income it would be able to buy more foreign goods, setting up a foreign-trade multiplier for other countries.[63] He simplified the calculation by ignoring repercussions on prices until 'our remedy was becoming very successful'.[64] As in the Liberal industrial inquiry, he suggested dividing the budget into capital and income accounts.[65] He argued that the same principle which multiplies an initial reduction of expenditure multiplies any increase. 'Just as an initial impulse of modest dimensions has been capable of producing such devastating repercussions, so also a moderate impulse in the opposite direction will effect a surprising recovery. There is no magic here, no mystery; but a reliable scientific prediction.'[66] On the other hand, Keynes had come to feel curiously insecure in doing even simple arithmetic calculations. 'I hope I don't make any bloomers,' he wrote to Kahn, who was in America lecturing on the same subject. 'I wish you were here to look over my shoulder.'

The second and third articles introduce and expound his plan to raise world prices. This aspect of the plan was put forward mainly for relieving debt burdens, something of particular importance to primary producers: in much of the world, recovery of profits had to lead recovery of demand. His international recovery plan was worked out with Hubert Henderson and Basil Blackett on one of MacDonald's endless advisory committees.[67] He had been plugging variants of it for a couple of months and managed to express its rationale more vividly in the *New Statesman* of 24 December 1932 than in his *Times* articles:

> What is the charm [he wrote] to awaken the Sleeping Beauty, to scale the mountain of glass without slipping back? If every Treasury were to discover in its vaults a large *cache* of gold proportioned in size to the scale of its economic life, would not that work the charm? Why should not that *cache* be devised? We have long printed gold nationally. Why should we not print it internationally? No reason in the world, unless our hands are palsied and our wits dull.[68]

Conceding to orthodoxy, Keynes proposed to revive a modified gold standard. To relieve the anxiety of central banks an international authority should create additional world reserves by a fiduciary issue of gold certificates up to $5bn which all participating countries would accept as a means of international payment. They would receive a quota equal to their gold reserves in 1928. In return for their *caches* of gold certificates they would be required to agree to return to the gold standard, though within wider bands (Keynes suggested 5 per cent) and at adjustable parities; they would have to renounce exchange restrictions, reduce their tariffs, eliminate import quotas and embargoes on foreign lending, write down their debts. Keynes was relaxed about having described the gold standard as a 'barbarous relic'. He now wrote, 'A barbarous relic, to which a vast body of tradition and prestige attaches, may have a symbolic or conventional value if it can be fitted into the framework of a managed system of the new pattern. Such transformations are a regular feature of those constitutional changes which are effected without revolution.'[69] Keynes already had a vision of a permanent system: 'there should be an elasticity in the quantity of the additional reserves outstanding, so that they would operate, not as a net addition to the world's monetary supply, but as a balancing factor to be released when prices are abnormally low as at present, and to be withdrawn again if prices were rising too much.'[70]

The pamphlet ended with the final, now habitual, warning: if measures like this were rejected, 'we must expect the progressive breakdown of the existing structure of contract and instruments of indebtedness, accompanied by the utter discredit of orthodox leadership in finance and government, with what ultimate outcome we cannot predict'.[71]

Keynes's articles marked the start of public understanding of the Keynesian Revolution. They begat an enormous debate which went on in several countries. Economists and politicians started to bandy the concept of 'repercussions' around as though they had known about it all their lives. Sharp divisions emerged between the Expansionists and Those Who Wanted to Sit it Out. An editorial in *The Times* of 13 March was cautiously supportive; masses of letters appeared in the following days, mainly in favour of Keynes, including one drafted by Roy Harrod and signed by thirty-seven university teachers of economics. There was no signatory from the LSE. Sir Josiah Stamp threw his weight behind unbalancing the budget. Cassel in Sweden supported him. Sir Arthur Salter, in the *Manchester Guardian* of 21 March, wrote that Keynes 'has expressed the strong, and now almost overwhelming, mass of opinion, lay and expert alike, that the time has come for expanding public investment. . . .'

Keynes's articles as usual received close scrutiny by the Treasury and the Bank of England. The new generation of Treasury officials – particularly Sir Richard Hopkins and Sir Frederick Phillips – were much more sympathetic to Keynes than Sir Otto Niemeyer had been in the 1920s, but they still felt bound to reject his suggestions. 'The one gilt-edged argument', minuted Phillips, who orchestrated the scrutiny, 'is *delay*. Keynes's whole point is the urgency of immediate action, whereas we know perfectly well that public works don't get started in a year and don't get in full working order for three years.'[72] In his reply to critics in *The Times* of 5 April, Keynes tried to meet this line of attack by switching the emphasis in his proposals from increasing government spending to remitting taxes. This would have the great advantage of avoiding delay, and also energising expenditure through 'numberless normal channels'. Phillips queried Keynes's budgetary calculations. 'Perhaps the process he intends would be better described as a speculative balancing of the Budget over a long term of future years without regard to the deficit produced in the early years of the period.' Phillips also revived the Treasury's earlier objection that Keynes's argument was only right 'if there were large unused savings and if they can be attracted into investment by issuing gilt-edged stock without raising the long-term rate of interest'.[73] It was Henderson who finally scotched this line of criticism, pointing out correctly that Keynes's proposal did not assume idle bank deposits. The main objection to Keynes's plan, Henderson said, was 'that any substantial increase of internal trade activity in England, unless accompanied quickly by a corresponding movement elsewhere, would tend to increase imports and to render the balance of trade adverse. . . .'[74]

You often say [Henderson wrote to Keynes on 28 February] 'It's nonsense to talk about confidence; confidence depends on orders.' Very

likely. But I maintain that if you were to announce that you were going
in for a large £200 million programme, you would not get a single order
under that programme for at least a year, whereas the effects on the
gilt-edged market and the like of the announcement of your intention
would be immediate. You might thus easily get a vicious circle wound
up before your virtuous circle had begun to operate at all. Speaking
generally, therefore, I am very much off the idea of public works as a
major constructive remedy for our present troubles.[75]

Scrutiny of Keynes's proposals went hand in hand with preparations for
the budget. Chamberlain asked to see Keynes on 17 March: 'Could it be that
the Walls of Jericho are flickering?' Keynes asked Richard Kahn. He tried
hard to give them a final push. Resuscitate the national income, he advised
Chamberlain on 5 April, and the revenue will flow in; allow it to fall and
there will always be a budgetary problem. 'Unfortunately, the more pessimistic the Chancellor's policy, the more likely it is that pessimistic anticipations will be realised and vice versa. Whatever the Chancellor dreams, will
come true.'[76] Chamberlain still dreamt of economy. In his budget speech of
25 April, he condemned 'those speaking as having authority' who proclaimed that unbalancing the budget leads to salvation. The proposal to aim
for a budget balance over time involved a great optimism that tax cuts
would bring increased revenues. But what would happen to private spending
'if the public realised, as they certainly would do, that what was spent today, had presently to be paid for?' Britain had stood the strain better than
any other country because its budget was balanced. It was now being asked
to throw away the advantage gained just when the benefits were about to
be reaped and other governments were following suit. 'No Finance Minister',
Chamberlain declared bleakly, 'ever deliberately unbalanced his Budget.'
The Bank of England's reaction focused on international repercussions:
'There is a rather marked absence of comment by Keynes on the probable
effects of his proposals on the sterling exchange.'[77] Predictably the Bank
objected to vesting management of a restored gold standard in an international board.

   The Means to Prosperity is a key document in the history of the Keynesian Revolution. At this level, the level of practical policy, grounded for the
first time in the multiplier analysis, the Keynesian Revolution was on the
way to being won. As indeed it was won during and after the war. The
abstract argument whether the economy possessed long-run self-stabilising
properties was relegated to academic discussion. The substantial remaining
doubts concerned practicability and psychological repercussions.

   These are the points that have been taken up by later historians. They
estimate the multiplier in the early 1930s as much lower than 2 – nearer 1
– and argue that the kinds of fiscal deficits and adverse trade flows needed
to make any substantial impact on the employment figures would rapidly

have brought on a major financial and political crisis requiring either the reversal of the policy or the move to a completely state-controlled economy like that of Nazi Germany.[78]

VI. LET GOODS BE HOMESPUN

On 17 April 1933 Keynes arrived in Dublin on a two-day visit, his first since 1911, to deliver the first Finlay Lecture at University College. He chose as his subject 'National Self-Sufficiency'. Composed almost immediately after his *Times* articles, it seemed to swing the full circle from Adam Smith to Friedrich List, German founder of economic nationalism; or, for the contemporary-minded, to Dr Schacht, Nazi Germany's economic overlord. Keynes had in fact been pursuing both lines of thought – internationalism and nationalism – for some time past without bringing them together. In his Dublin lecture he adduced four main arguments for a greater degree of national self-sufficiency. First, he was 'not persuaded that the economic advantages of the international division of labour to-day are at all comparable with what they were.... Experience accumulates to prove that most modern mass-production processes can be performed in most countries and climates with almost equal efficiency.... Moreover, as wealth increases, both primary and manufactured products play a smaller relative part in the national economy compared with houses, personal services and local amenities which are not the subject of international exchange....'[79]

Secondly, he stated bluntly that free trade, combined with international mobility of capital, was more likely to provoke war than keep peace. In times of stress, particularly, the ownership of national assets by foreigners was likely to 'set up strains and enmities' which, he implied, had led to war in 1914. So: 'I sympathise ... with those who would minimise rather than with those who would maximise economic entanglement between nations. Ideas, knowledge, art, hospitality, travel – these are the things which should of their nature be international. But let goods be homespun whenever it is reasonably and conveniently possible; and, above all, let finance be primarily national.'[80]

Thirdly, Keynes urged the case for 'politico-economic' experiment: 'We each have our own fancy. Not believing we are saved already, we each would like to have a try at working out our salvation. We do not wish, therefore, to be at the mercy of world forces working out, or trying to work out, some uniform equilibrium according to the ideal principles of *laissez-faire* capitalism.'[81]

Finally, the system of economic calculation which made 'the whole conduct of life ... into a sort of parody of an accountant's nightmare' is seen to have failed in its own terms. In a High Victorian outburst Keynes declared:

> We have to remain poor because it does not 'pay' to be rich. We have to live in hovels, not because we cannot build palaces, but because we cannot 'afford' them.... We destroy the beauty of the countryside because the unappropriated splendours of nature have no economic value. We are capable of shutting off the sun and the stars because they do not pay a dividend. London is one of the richest cities in the history of civilisation, but it cannot 'afford' the highest standards of achievement of which its own living citizens are capable, because they do not 'pay'.
>
> If I had the power today I should surely set out to endow our capital cities with all the appurtenances of art and civilisation on the highest standards ... convinced that what I could create, I could afford – and believing that money thus spent would not only be better than any dole, but would make unnecessary any dole. For with what we have spent on the dole in England since the War we could have made our cities the greatest works of man in the world.
>
> ...Today we suffer disillusion, not because we are poorer ... but because other values seem to have been sacrificed ... and sacrificed unnecessarily. For our economic system is not, in fact, enabling us to exploit to the utmost the possibilities for economic wealth afforded by the progress of our technique ... leading us to feel we might as well have used up the margin in more satisfying ways.
>
> But once we allow ourselves to be disobedient to the test of an accountant's profit, we have begun to change our civilisation.[82]

Having delivered this Ruskinian denunciation of capitalist civilisation, Keynes ended with some words of caution against silliness, haste and intolerance. But the balance was not well held. Perhaps defending himself, he wrote, 'Words ought to be a little wild, for they are the assault of thoughts upon the unthinking. But when the seats of power and authority have been attained there should be no more poetic licence.' Like a gazelle, Keynes leapt from one mode to another. Did he not see that duller spirits might not be able to make the transition? Or did he think the gazelles would always be in power? It was the nearest he ever came to endorsing communist, or fascist, economics. The fascist leader Oswald Mosley congratulated him on his conversion. Keynes replied that he wrote as he did 'not to embrace you, but to save the country from you'.[83]

A vivid account of Keynes's lecture has been left by James Meehan in his biography of George O'Brien, who had invited him:

> Keynes gave the first Finlay lecture, on 'National Self-Sufficiency', in the Physics Theatre in Earlscourt Terrace.... Finlay lectures have usually been well attended but this first one surpassed them all. Almost all the

Maynard Keynes and Lydia Lopokova, c. 1922.

Maynard Keynes
with Virginia Woolf,
Studland, Dorset, 1923.

Peter Lucas, Dadie Rylands and Sebastian Sprott, Cambridge, 1922.

'Second Thoughts
Are Best . . .',
Lydia and Maynard
Keynes.

Maynard Keynes in
Russia, 1925.

Above, left. Samuel Courtauld stepping out of the Rolls-Royce he sold to Maynard Keynes.

Above. Robert Brand.

Left. Vera Bowen.

Below, left. Maynard Keynes and Lydia in Berlin, 1928.

Below. Piero Sraffa, Maynard Keynes and Dennis Robertson at Tilton, 1927. Maynard Keynes is sitting on the bird bath.

Cartoon by Vanessa Bell, 1927, of Lydia and Maynard dancing a version of the cancan from *Boutique-Fantasque* (the 'Keynes-Keynes').

'An Extra One', the resignation of Sir Oswald Mosley, 19 April 1930.

Punch, February 1931.

Richard Kahn and Lydia sitting on
the bird bath at Tilton, c. 1931.

Hubert Henderson.

F. Hayek, 1931.

Oswald Falk.

Maynard Keynes,
Beatrice and Sidney Webb at
Passfield Corner, c. 1928.

George Bernard Shaw
and Maynard Keynes,
Fitzwilliam Museum,
Cambridge, 1936.

members of the new government were present. Headed by Mr de Valera, they sat on one side of the theatre as far removed as possible from the members of the government they had replaced. It was assumed, for some reason which is lost to memory, that the lecturer would denounce the pursuit of protection by high tariffs which had contributed to the Great Depression. The smiles and self-confidence were therefore much more obvious on one side of the theatre than on the other. But as Keynes proceeded to show himself unexpectedly friendly to the erection of economic defences, above all when he declared that 'were I an Irishman, I should find much to attract me in the economic outlook of your present Government towards greater self-sufficiency', the smiles faded from one side and appeared on the other.

As Meehan implies, Keynes's Dublin lecture, indeed the Irish visit, was a political event. He had arrived in the middle of the so-called trade war between Britain and Ireland. When de Valera replaced Cosgrave in 1932, he renounced the oath of allegiance and packed off the Governor-General to a suburban villa, shorn of powers and dignity; he also withheld payment of land annuities owed to the British government. Britain retaliated by imposing economic sanctions in the form of agricultural duties; Ireland countered with duties on British coal and manufactures. For Keynes to appear in Dublin as an economic nationalist pleased the Irish government, but annoyed the British. Naturally enough Keynes saw himself as a peacemaker. He wrote to Stamp on 29 April:

the general tenor of my remarks was in the main an apology for contemporary movements to greater self-sufficiency. Since, however, de Valera has been considering doing some foolish things, I feared that this might be taken as giving him undue encouragement. I therefore interpolated a passage of warning relating to Irish conditions.

Keynes had a long private talk with de Valera, 'who impressed me distinctly favourably.... I was very glad to find that his mind was moving from his insane wheat schemes to peat proposals which are at any rate harmless and might quite conceivably turn out well.' Cosgrave, on the other hand, was 'such a nineteenth century liberal!'[84]

Keynes had the usual round of exhausting engagements: lunch with the Lieutenant Governor; press conference; dinner with the Governor of the Bank of Ireland, and so on. He had time to see his friend George Thomson of King's. His lecture on 19 April was followed by a dinner given by O'Brien to which he had 'invited', on Keynes's prompting, some of the best wits of Dublin. It was, by O'Brien's account, a total failure. There were too many wits and Gogarty* talked too much. Worse still, Keynes was called to the

* Oliver Joseph St John Gogarty, Irish poet and notorious bore; the inspiration of 'stately, plump Buck Mulligan' in Joyce's *Ulysses*.

telephone in the middle of the meal. When he came back, he said, 'You may be interested to know that the United States has just left gold.' The short silence that was felt to be appropriate was broken by Gogarty: 'Does that matter?'

VII. FAREWELL TO THE CONFERENCE

On 29 June 1933 Lydia Lopokova graced the dismal obsequies of the World Economic Conference with her final appearance on the ballet stage. It was a gala performance of *Coppélia* at Covent Garden, organised by her husband Maynard Keynes. At forty, Lydia had decided it was time to hang up her shoes. The gala performance was also the last event staged by the Camargo Society. The Society had not only prolonged Lydia's dancing career, but had given a focus to her life after her failure to have a child in 1927. She loved her 'Russian lunches' at 46 Gordon Square, at which ballet gossip, plotting new productions and political chatter, stimulated by Maynard's wine, went on all day. On these occasions she sometimes acted as an eccentric conduit for Maynard's ideas, repeating parrot-like that 'higher prices create more employment' but 'I do not know why.'[85] Vera Bowen had largely dropped out of her life; Sam Courtauld, whose wife Lil had died of cancer at the end of 1931, remained a dogged admirer. But her constant companions of this period were Camargo's mainstays Ninette de Valois, Fred Ashton and Constant Lambert. With her ballet career finally over, she and Maynard prepared for her next gamble, her appearance as Olivia in Shakespeare's *Twelfth Night.*

The gala, on which Maynard netted £314, was more profitable than the conference, the most futile gathering of the inter-war years. The delegates from sixty-six countries who had assembled at the South Kensington Geological Museum on 12 June, and now thronged the grand tier boxes at Covent Garden, had done their mechanical dances like the wound-up dolls in Coppélius' workshop, but there was no force to kick them into life. In his opening address MacDonald talked vaguely about reducing war debts, which they had all agreed not to discuss. This was attributed to senility rather than bad faith. The British had a plan, a watered-down version of the Keynes–Henderson proposals called the Kisch Plan, to redistribute gold from America and France to the rest of the world so they could trade. Not surprisingly the Americans and French objected, and it was never produced. The French, who headed a gold bloc in western Europe, wanted to restore the international gold standard, which not surprisingly the British, and now the Americans, who had just left it, rejected. The Americans supported a scheme for international public works, which the British rejected. The Conference was left with no agenda. Its programme had expired.

Keynes tried to give it the kiss of life with a plan of his own. America's decision to leave the gold standard had taken him by surprise. 'My little proposals are too modest and moderate for this lunatic world,' he told his mother on 23 April. 'There seems to be nothing between a Government which does nothing whatever and one which goes right off the deep end.' But he was ever resourceful. He was covering the Conference for the *Daily Mail*, and he published his new plan in the issue of 27 June, sending copies to Neville Chamberlain and Montagu Norman. It involved an all-round devaluation in terms of gold of the world's leading currencies of between 20 and 33 per cent, as a prelude to *de facto* stabilisation. The Treasuries of the participating countries would appropriate the windfalls accruing to the banks and put them into circulation by public works or immediate relief of taxation. Owing to the increase in effective gold reserves, exchange and import restrictions would be abolished. Five per cent of the profit of countries with large gold holdings would be put into a pool to help debtor countries. These revamped ideas were designed to give Britain and America a common basis for action, but had something to offer the gold bloc and the debtor nations too.[86] Meanwhile, President Roosevelt had been on a fishing trip and was having ideas of his own. On 3 July the appalled delegates, who included his own, received his 'bombshell', rejecting attempts to stabilise currencies as 'the fetishes of so-called international bankers'. Despite the fact that Roosevelt's message scuppered his own plan, Keynes proclaimed that 'President Roosevelt is Magnificently Right' in choosing the path of national currency management, though he hoped he would not reject reasonable cooperation between the Federal Reserve Bank of New York and the Bank of England. Britain should ignore the threats of the gold bloc to leave the conference, and throw in its lot with the United States in a 'sterling–dollar bloc committed to economic progress and the restoration of economic health'. For the United States:

> invites us to see whether without uprooting the order of society which we have inherited we cannot, by the employment of common sense in alliance with scientific thought, achieve something better than the miserable confusion and unutterable waste of opportunity in which an obstinate adherence to ancient rules of thumb has engulfed us. Nor is the prescription alarming. We are to put men to work by all means at our disposal until prices have risen to a level appropriate to the existing debts and other obligations fixed in terms of money; and thereafter we are to see to it that the purchasing power of our money shall be kept stable. . . . We are offered, indeed, the only possible means by which the structure of contract can be preserved and confidence in a monetary economy restored.[87]

Ever optimistic, Keynes was inventing Roosevelt's programme for him. He was soon to say, quite accurately, that Roosevelt had about as much idea of where he would land as a pre-war pilot.

The Conference lingered on in a coma for the best part of a month. Keynes dined with the Prime Minister on 4 July and helped concoct an American statement designed to keep it alive. But, unlike the world economy, it was beyond resuscitation. On 27 July it adjourned *sine die*. There was, after all, 'no cat in the bag, no rabbits in the hat – no brains in the head'. In his last article, Keynes pointed out that a pow-wow of sixty-six nations would never agree. Only 'a single power or a like-minded group of powers' could force through a plan. It was not a lesson he would forget.[88]

29

New Deals

I. SOCIAL EXPERIMENTS

The rhythms of the 1920s and 1930s are curiously similar. Both decades were bounded by catastrophe; their middle years promised well only to deceive. In both decades, the world seemed to be recovering from war and depression respectively, only to collapse back into depression and war respectively. Such disasters discredited the cosmopolitan, non-interfering principles which had governed economic affairs in the nineteenth century: the idea that capitalist market economies, left to themselves, would deliver jobs for all who wanted to work and increasing prosperity for all – the latter removing at the same time the main causes of war. As Keynes noted in his 'National Self-Sufficiency' articles, social experiments were in fashion; all of them, whatever their political provenance, envisaged a much enlarged role for government, and a greatly restricted role for free commerce.

These social experiments were influenced more by morals, geopolitics and political ideology than by new economic thinking. The economic crisis of the twentieth century was met by nineteenth-century ideas funnelled through the experience of the First World War. It was the critics of the nineteenth century – all those who rejected *laissez-faire* capitalism on religious or moral or strategic or social or aesthetic or tribal grounds – who got their chance between the wars. The war itself was plausibly attributed to the worldwide 'struggle for markets'; it had shown what governments could achieve by mobilising the resources of their communities. If they could do this for war purposes, why not for peace purposes?

Keynes has often been placed in the tradition of these nineteenth-century critics of capitalism. Thus Mini locates him in the romantic, anti-Benthamite movement, represented by Coleridge, Carlyle, Arnold, Ruskin and other opponents of Victorian capitalism.[1] Some have seen him as heir to the socialist revolt against intolerable industrial conditions. There have been persistent attempts to reconcile him to Marx. The 'National Self-Sufficiency' articles seem to hark back to Friedrich List. Keynes has been identified with the machinery of central control – planning, corporatism, rule by techno-crats – arising out of the war. All these readings have their place, if only because any critic of the nineteenth century was bound to sound, in some respects, like any other critic. Keynes did not disdain the support of the older traditions in his campaign of persuasion, because persuasion, to be effective, has to link up to something already in people's minds. At the same time, it is important to understand that he felt himself to be saying something completely new about the behaviour of economies, something which had never been said or thought before – except possibly by Malthus; and which, if accepted, would make most of these other traditions redundant, or at least remove them from centre stage.

None of the critics of nineteenth-century capitalism had been able to mount an effective challenge to the central *economic* theory of *laissez-faire*, namely that, left to itself, a competitive exchange economy tends to produce more output and allocate it more efficiently than any alternative system. Critics lacked the intellectual tools to challenge the internal logic of this argument. They attacked the market system from outside as being inconsistent with tradition, morals, social health or the security of the nation. Marx produced the most sustained economic critique of capitalism. But even he could not show convincingly why the 'robbery' of working-class 'holdings' by a capitalist class – even if this could be demonstrated – should impede either wealth-creation or optimal employment.

All these critics, Keynes said, lacked a theory of effective demand. The fatal flaw in the system, he pointed out, lay in the variability of spending relative to earnings; and this was rooted in the use, and purposes, of money. The result was that the market system was liable to prolonged collapses. If communities could be induced by policy to spend what they can produce, the existing system could be saved. Thus Keynes was radical in his economics, 'moderately conservative' in his social aims. The points of contact between Keynes and the nineteenth-century critics lay in the very restricted area opened up by Keynes's theory of deficient aggregate demand. But the kind of intervention required to fill this gap in *laissez-faire* fell very far short of the social revolutions on offer in Europe and elsewhere; its purpose was to make the capitalist market system work better, not destroy it.

This then is the standpoint from which to understand Keynes's reactions to the various contemporary attempts to overcome the inter-war crisis of capitalism. In Europe the characteristic form of such attempts was fascism, the root idea behind which was geopolitical, not economic. Europe, it was claimed, was being dwarfed by the rise of America and Russia. Spengler's *Decline of the West* (1917) was an obituary of old Europe's culture of competing city, later nation, states. The future seemed to lie with continental-scale empires. Europe must be united, by force if necessary, to preserve both its way of life and its means to life. The economic reasoning behind this, if it can be so called, was that to allow the means of life to be traded across political frontiers was to put yourself at the mercy of more powerful states. Only a very large state could be securely self-sufficient. If you did not have enough territory you must grab it. Hence the fascist drive for empire, which in the case of Germany meant Continental empire. It is easy to understand how such ideas got their chance with the breakdown of the world economy. But they were by no means a rational response to such a breakdown, since they were held independently of whether the world economy was working well or not.[2]

In Britain, European unification, political or economic, voluntary or forcible, was seen as a threat rather than a promise. Britain's own Empire was fading but still intact; imperial economics, in Britain, meant regrouping British trade on the British Empire. Keynes was not interested in this, but he no more felt part of Europe than did most of his fellow countrymen. His French was always poor; his German had rusted away to dust; he never spoke or wrote either language and soon stopped trying to follow any serious argument in them. 'England still stands outside Europe,' he had written in 1919. 'Europe's voiceless tremors do not reach her. Europe is apart and England is not of her flesh and body. But Europe is solid with herself.'[3] In the 1930s, Europe acquired a dreadfully raucous voice, but this increased Keynes's alienation from the Continent.

Keynes, of course, had good liberal friends in Europe, dating from his Treasury and Peace Conference days. The trouble was that European liberals were against social experiments, while those who favoured them were anti-liberal. Economics might have tried to bridge this divide. But, although the main European countries had economists, they lacked an economics profession organised for theoretical research in the Anglo-Saxon sense. The exceptions were the Swedes and the Austrians, who, however, were largely cut off from the dominant Continental traditions, though not from each other. Keynes regarded French economists as antediluvian.[4] In Germany, there was no professional opinion he could get in touch with. He had admirers outside the economics profession, like Wladimir Woytinsky, adviser to the German trade union movement, who sent him a copy of his proposals to raise prices in December 1931. Keynes replied with what John Garraty describes as 'polite indifference'.[5] At this time, Melchior and the economist Bonn advised him to turn down an invitation to address a group of economists and industrialists in Berlin, as these were 'not quite the right people' for Keynes to be talking to.[6] But there were no 'right' people with the 'right' ideas. Nevertheless, by October 1934 three million workers had been re-employed in Germany over two years, half the previous total of unemployed, and Keynes's silence on Hitler's New Deal was deafening.

The reason is that Hitler's recovery programme was too mixed up with imperialist aims and terroristic methods for it to hold any attraction for him. Keynes was trying to save liberal society, not destroy it. He would give no comfort to its enemies. 'Germany is at the mercy of unchained irresponsibles,' he wrote on 15 July 1933. And on 19 September: 'Broken in body and spirit, [they] seek escape in a return backwards to the modes and manners of the Middle Ages, if not of Odin.'[7] Anti-semitic though Keynes occasionally seems by the standards of our day, he was outraged by the state-sponsored outbreaks of Jew-baiting in Nazi Germany. On 25 August 1933, he wrote to Professor Spiethoff, who was arranging the publication of a German translation of 'National Self-Sufficiency':

> Forgive me for my words about barbarism. But that word rightly indicates the effect of recent events in Germany on all of us here.... It is many generations in our judgement since such disgraceful events have occurred in any country pretending to call itself civilised.... If you tell me that these events have taken place, not by force, but as an expression of the general will ... that in our view would make some of the persecutions and outrages of which we hear ... ten times more horrible.[8]

When Germany withdrew from the World Disarmament Conference on 14 October, he wrote to Lydia, 'Everyone must soon be faced with the alternative of simply allowing Germany to rearm when she likes, or of attacking her as soon as she begins to do so. Hideous!' Keynes never went to look at the 'new' Germany. Carl Melchior, subjected to anti-semitic attack, died in December 1933. When the Mayor of Hamburg visited King's College in 1934 and invited Keynes over, he replied, 'After the death of my friend ... there is nothing left that could attract me to Hamburg.'[9] He served on the Academic Assistance Council set up to help German scholars fleeing the persecution, and contributed to its fund.

In the early 1930s what would now be called Keynesian methods of fighting the depression were tried out in Japan and Sweden. It is unlikely that Takahashi, the Japanese Finance Minister, drew much inspiration from Keynes; but Ernst Wigforss, Sweden's Finance Minister, did; more so perhaps than from the younger Swedish school of Lindahl, Myrdal and Ohlin, who were themselves in touch with Keynes, but who never made the transition from the monetary disequilibrium approach of Wicksell (or indeed the Keynes of the *Treatise*) to the *General Theory* position. Keynes kept a watching brief on Swedish developments, but Sweden was too small to be a centre of attraction. In a letter to Markus Wallenberg of Stockholm's Enskilda Bank, he advised going slow on public works and urged a conservative budget 'if ... this would be helpful as a transitional measure towards much lower interest rates'. For 'in the long run ... nothing on earth will save the capitalist regime except the steady lowering of long-term rates of interest to a level at which in contemporary conditions current savings can still be profitably absorbed along normal lines'.[10]

Britain's intellectual class was more susceptible to the appeal of Soviet Russia, especially in the 1930s, when capitalism seemed on the verge of collapse. *Soviet Communism: a New Civilisation?* asked the Webbs in their last massive tome, published in 1935. (The second edition dropped the question mark.) Reformist hopes had depended on the success of capitalism in creating wealth. Its failure in the early 1930s convinced many on the left that it could be kept going only by methods of barbarism; that progress had come to depend on its abolition; that the Soviet experiment of central planning of a publicly owned economy pointed the way forward for all. Keynes had flirted with Soviet communism as a 'new religion', but, unlike the Webbs, he could never think of Soviet Russia as a serious intellectual resource for Western civilisation. In the 1920s he had said that Marxism and communism had nothing of scientific interest to offer the modern mind. The depression did not alter his view. Russia 'exhibits the worst example which the world, perhaps, has ever seen of administrative incompetence and of the sacrifice of almost everything that makes life worth living . . .'; it was a 'fearful example of the evils of insane and unnecessary haste'; 'Let Stalin be a terrifying example to all who seek to make experiments.'[11] He found Kingsley Martin too 'pro-Bolshie' in the *New Statesman*.[12]

These strictures were probably influenced by Lydia's report of her visit to her family in Leningrad at the end of 1932 in the company of her friend Lady Muriel Paget. She was depressed to find her mother and sister sharing a tiny flat with her sister's ex-husband, forcing her mother into '7 years of waiting in a chair at night' for the ex-husband to leave.[13] Fedor Lopukhov, now chief teacher of character dancing at the Maryinsky Theatre, wrote Keynes fulsome letters of thanks, on what appeared to be rolls of lavatory paper, for the money and clothes regularly sent from London. To poverty and incompetence, terror had been added as Stalin's dictatorship took hold. Lydia was advised to keep both private and public comments on Russia circumspect for fear of reprisals on her family. Both she and Maynard cultivated the Russian ambassador to London, Ivan Maisky, partly in an effort to get Fedor and Andrei out (on the pretext of ballet engagements), but Maisky was unable to arrange it.

This left the United States. Keynes was not notably pro-American. He shared all the usual cultural prejudices of his class against American materialism; he also resented the passing of British power and influence to the United States. But he was more intellectually at home with Americans than with any other group of foreigners. The Americans at least were making attempts to tame, manage and regulate the rampant individualism of their system. In the 1920s Keynes had found much to admire in the way the Federal Reserve Board set out to stabilise the purchasing power of the dollar; in the 1930s it was the New Deal which excited his interest. Disillusion with *laissez-faire* at home thus led Keynes not to Berlin or Moscow but to Washington. From the 1930s onwards his efforts at persuasion were increasingly directed towards the United States. For Keynes remained convinced that in economic thinking, if no longer in business life, the British still enjoyed a comparative advantage over everyone else. But equally he understood that America, not Britain, held the key to the survival of capitalist civilisation.

II. THE ECONOMIC LABORATORY OF THE WORLD

Herbert Hoover's departure from the White House on 4 March 1933 ended the paralysis at the centre of American government. His successor Franklin Delano Roosevelt, likening the depression to war, claimed emergency war powers to fight it; he promised to expel the money-lenders from the temple. His inaugural speech sent waves of hope throughout the world.

America certainly needed action. 'Even I would hardly think that I could know what to do if I were President,' Keynes wrote to Lydia, 'though I expect I should when it came to it.'[14] As Arthur Schlesinger tells it: 'The national income was less than half of what it had been four short years before. Nearly thirteen million Americans – about one-quarter of the labour force – were desperately seeking jobs.' Roosevelt responded with his 'Hundred Days', 'a presidential barrage of ideas and programmes unlike anything known to American history'. Eager young lawyers, college professors, economists, sociologists flooded into Washington as the New Deal gathered pace.[15] Congress enacted a hotchpotch of recovery measures, culled from different strands of America's political tradition, inspired by no coherent plan, certainly not one of Keynesian provenance, but by the conviction that 'something had to be done' to stave off collapse and start the wheels of industry rolling. The immediate result of this frenetic activism was a tremendous upsurge in confidence. Wall Street started booming, much to Keynes's benefit. Industrial production almost doubled between March and July. Government was in charge again, not events.

Keynes followed Roosevelt's experiments with genuine, but baffled, admiration. 'Your President has persuaded Congress to provide him with some lovely blank sheets of writing paper and some beautifully sharp pencils, but what part of his powers he really means to rely on, we, over here, simply don't know,' he told the *Herald Tribune*'s columnist Walter Lippmann in a transatlantic broadcast conversation on 11 June.[16] Particularly mysterious was the almost immediate revival of business activity, long before the expansionary measures in the President's programme could have had time to work. Keynes feared that Roosevelt was 'depending far too much on psychological as distinct from real factors'. Lippmann, primed by Keynes on his trip to London that summer, was one of the first to warn Roosevelt against the danger of muddling up spending with planning, recovery with social reform.[17]

This was the theme taken up by Keynes himself at the end of 1933. He had not yet tried to intervene in the New Deal. Now he was urged to do so by Felix Frankfurter, Professor of Administrative Law at Harvard University, future Supreme Court justice and an unofficial member of Roosevelt's 'brains trust', who was spending the academic year 1933–4 at All Souls College, Oxford, and who dined with Keynes at King's College on 6 December. Frankfurther invited Keynes to address the President directly. He wanted Keynes to tell Roosevelt what to do – and what not to do. As a trust-buster in the Progressive tradition (he had voted for La Follette in 1924), he wanted to wean the President from the corporatist National Recovery Administration (NRA) codes, which exempted industry from the anti-trust laws. Those who wanted to restore the free market increasingly looked to Keynes's spending theories to support their aims.

Keynes's 'Open Letter to the President' was published in the *New York Times* on 31 December, after Roosevelt had received a private copy. Keynes did not pull his punches. The NRA should be put into cold storage. It was a programme of reform, disguised as recovery, which probably impeded recovery. What Roosevelt should aim to do was to keep the dollar–sterling exchange as stable as was consistent with an accelerating programme of loan-financed public expenditure and open-market operations to reduce the long-term rate of interest. 'The United States is ready to roll toward prosperity, if a good hard shove can be given in the next six months.'[18] Herbert Stein complains that Keynes's letter was ill-timed and badly argued. There was 'no hint of the multiplier, no consideration of popular concerns about where the money was coming from....' But all this was in *The Means to Prosperity*, which Keynes had sent the President earlier in the year. Stein says it 'sounded like a letter from a school teacher to the very rich father of a very dull pupil'.[19] This is a matter of taste, but there is no doubt that Keynes's intellectual style, then and later, antagonised many Americans. It is unlikely that it made any difference to his persuasiveness. He could not hope to run the New Deal by surface mail.

The Roosevelt programme certainly needed intellectual stiffening. Although in 1931 Keynes had found considerable support in Chicago for countercyclical public works policy, the New Deal was undertaken in defiance of the professional views of most American economists.[20] Keynes is nowadays credited with having had little influence on the New Deal – except right at the end of the 1930s. And this is true in the sense that Roosevelt refused to come down decisively in favour of Keynes's ideas. He preferred to keep all balls in play, with a disregard for logic 'which drove logical men to despondency'.[21] But Keynes had considerable influence on specific policies, Lippmann writing to him on 17 April 1934:

> I don't know whether you realize how great an effect that letter had, but I am told that it was chiefly responsible for the policy which the Treasury is now quietly but effectively pursuing of purchasing long-term government bonds....[22]

By the time he got Lippmann's letter, Keynes had decided to go to the United States to see for himself what was happening.

Maynard and Lydia sailed for New York on 9 May 1934. Shortly before they docked on 15 May, their ship, the SS *Olympic*, rammed and sank a lightship in the fog, killing seven people.[23] The occasion of Maynard's visit was to receive an honorary degree from Columbia University, New York, on 5 June 1934; its motive was 'inquisitiveness'. He cut down his speech-making and social life to a minimum. He wanted to find out what was happening, and exercise private persuasion in the quarters which mattered.

They stayed nine days in New York at the Ambassador's Hotel. Walter Case fixed up appointments for him with leading bankers, businessmen and banking economists from whom he learnt firsthand the depth of business hatred of the New Deal. Keynes went on to Washington on 24 May, where he stayed at the Mayflower, 'Washington's finest hotel', leaving Lydia to spend the weekend of 26–28 May with the Walter Cases in New Hampshire. Felix Frankfurter stage-managed the Washington part of Keynes's trip, supplying him with a sheaf of introductions. 'I am sure a lot of his Wall Street friends will pump him full of poison,' he wrote to Tom Corcoran at the Reconstruction Finance Corporation. 'He is as keen as a lynx, but even he doesn't know the stuff that's buried in the tomes of the Senate Committee [on Banking and Currency], and so even he has hardly an idea of the piracies and greed of American finance or of the huggermuggery and abuses of the Stock Exchange.'[24]

On 25 May there were ten hours of conferences, and Maynard found 'life too strenuous for comfort'. In the morning he saw Roosevelt's Secretary of Labor, Frances Perkins. According to Perkins's own account, Keynes gave a simple exposition of the multiplier in terms of grocery purchases, which left her baffled.[25] He lunched with Rexford Tugwell, leader of the planning group in Roosevelt's brains trust and 'Walter [Case]'s bête-noire'. There was a meeting with William Phillips, Assistant Secretary of State, 'to discuss War Debts, German debts etc.', followed by tea with Supreme Court Justice Brandeis 'to talk legal side of Securities Act, Utilities etc.'. Brandeis and Tugwell were at opposite poles of the New Deal – trust-busting versus central planning – and significantly Keynes had more sympathy with the former, not least because he regarded planning as a distraction from recovery. The day finished with a dinner given by Herbert Feis, an old friend from Treasury days and economic adviser to the State Department. It was 'awful hard work trying to be at the top of one's form, to put oneself over the blighters, *all* day', Maynard told Lydia. On 26 May, 'feeling most lonely', he had lunch with Bewley, of the British Embassy, tea with Henry Morgenthau, Secretary of the Treasury, and dinner with Calvin Hoover, agricultural economist and minor brains-truster, for whose book on Russia he had found an English publisher. (Hoover had also written on Hitler's New Deal, Lydia remarking that 'he always gets into an upheavaled country and scribbles its effects'.) Using Keynes's bathroom to wash his hands, Hoover was careful to take a clean towel from the pile, without disturbing the others. Entering the bathroom after him, Keynes swept the whole pile to the floor in lordly fashion, explaining, as he crumpled them up, that his methods of using towels would do more to stimulate employment than Hoover's.

Keynes finally saw Roosevelt for an hour on Monday, 28 May. No one knows what they talked about. Keynes found the tête-à-tête 'fascinating and illuminating'; Roosevelt told Frankfurter that he had had a 'grand talk with Keynes and liked him immensely'.[26] As always, Keynes paid particular attention to Roosevelt's hands – 'Rather disappointing. Firm and fairly strong, but not clever or with finesse.'[27] On Tuesday, his last full day in Washington, he addressed a luncheon meeting of nine leading senators on his recovery plan, and a dinner meeting at the Commerce Department of over fifty NRA organisers; he also saw Lewis Bean of the Agricultural Adjustment Administration. He wrote to Lydia, 'I've had enough I can tell you, and must come away as I'm incapable for the time of absorbing any more information or impressions.'

In many of these meetings, Keynes was 'more of an admiring observer than ... an instructor',[28] but he was also quoted as saying on several occasions 'that if federal recovery expenditures, then running around $300 million a month, were raised to $400 million a month, the United States would have a satisfactory recovery'.[29] He told Frankfurter, 'Here, not in Moscow, is the economic laboratory of the world. The young men who are running it are splendid. I am astonished at their competence, intelligence and wisdom. One meets a classical economist here and there who ought to be thrown out of [the] window – but they mostly have been.'[30]

Back in New York, Keynes was again subjected to conservative influences, at a weekend session of the National Industrial Conference Board, an employers' organisation. But he refused to be shaken from his belief in the New Deal. At the Commencement Day luncheon, given in his honour by Columbia University on 5 June, he said that the New Deal had aroused his 'deepest sympathy' because it represented an attempt to make the economic system work without destroying the 'free play of individual initiative' and the 'inestimable liberty of thought and speech'. The 'experimental and empirical method' was inevitable because there was 'no one to whom the President could look for infallible advice'. He concluded with his familiar warning that 'If the ... problem is not solved, the existing order of society will become so discredited that wild and foolish and destructive changes will become inevitable.'[31]

In his last major engagement, a speech to the American Political Economy Club the next day, Keynes gave a précis of his 'theory of effective demand' to an audience of economists. This had been the basis of his discussions with officials in Washington. America thus received Keynesian economics ahead of England, because there was more to hope for in America than in England.

'In a given situation,' Keynes said, 'output and employment cannot increase unless entrepreneurs anticipate an increased effective demand and prepare to meet it.' In American conditions this anticipation depended on the scale of government loan expenditure. He said a number of other interesting things. All government loan expenditure, including spending on relief, should be treated as equivalent to investment 'at least when ... considering short-run effects'. This was to prove a dangerous doctrine when applied mechanically after the Second World War. He explained that a part of the increased expenditure would be taken up by increased production, a part would go to raising prices. The price effect would become greater as recovery proceeded and bottlenecks were encountered. Anticipating chapter 19 of *The General Theory* he argued that 'true' inflation was not possible till full employment occurred. 'When a point has been reached at which the whole of the labour and capital equipment of the community are employed, further increases in effective demand would have no effect whatever except to raise prices without limit.' At this point the precepts of sound finance would apply again.[32] Having delivered himself of these pronouncements, Keynes sailed back to England on 8 June. He was once more credited with magical powers over the New Deal. Opponents attributed the continuing deficit in the federal budget (a modest $4bn a year!) to 'the advice that Mr John Maynard Keynes the English economist gave the President in June'.[33] On 9 January 1935, Lippmann reported Roosevelt's policy to be 'far more in accord with what you advised last spring' than with the NRA phase.[34] But Roosevelt, incensed by business and judicial opposition to the NRA, and with his re-election prospects threatened by populists like Huey Long and Father Coughlin, was about to swing the New Deal off into a radical, non-Keynesian orbit.

Keynes, like Roosevelt, left different people with different impressions. Some thought he regarded loan-financed public spending as mere pump-priming to get out of a deep slump; others as a permanent part of the machinery for maintaining demand. Keynes explained to Victor von Szeliski, chief statistician of the Research Planning Division of the NRA, that 'My *theory* is the same whether the expenditure is by government or by private capitalism. ... Only in the event of a transition into Socialism would anyone expect government expenditure to play a predominant part year in year out.' But people did not so easily separate theory from political intention.

Szeliski asked another pertinent question. Why was Keynes advocating increased government loan expenditure in the United States when Britain was recovering from the depression with a balanced budget? Keynes wrote back:

In the case of England our progress has been much slower and on a smaller scale than it would have been if there had been more government loan expenditure. Such improvement as we have, however, is almost entirely attributable, in my judgement, to increased private loan expenditure due to the great fall in the rate of interest. We are in fact in this country in the middle of a building boom. In the case of the United States I see no likelihood of private investment developing on an adequate scale for some considerable time to come.[35]

III. STILL WORKING

Keynes returned from the United States in June 1934 with a violent toothache. He had to have his wisdom teeth out – 'a wise routine at my time of life' – chafing at the verbose attentions of the matron in his nursing home. But Virginia Woolf found him 'very fertile' at Tilton in August, speculating about the effects of the American climate on work, the effect of Jewish emigration on the German balance of payments, and other such topics. It was 'that queer imaginative ardour about history, humanity' which Virginia found so attractive about him: 'able to explain flints & the age of man from some book he has read', but 'amused too by little scenes. . . .' He complained that 'great men, Shaw & Wells, are not serious; they do their stunt. Why can't they be simple, & do no stunt? He said Shaw never said anything new, but Charlotte [Mrs Shaw] does. He has a ranging adventurous mind, which I enjoy.'[36]

In the spring of 1934 Keynes's new theory of employment had taken final shape. He had worked at it in his greatest effort of concentrated energy since his dissertation on probability in 1906–7. He felt he was racing against time. Hitler had become German Chancellor, Mosley had started the British Union of Fascists, communism had captured student politics at Cambridge. Keynes was convinced that another great depression was due in three or four years' time. Could the new system of thought be in place by then?

As always, when Keynes was fired up he worked at a tremendous pace. On Friday 20 October 1933 he had reported to Lydia from Cambridge a '*tremendous* burst of activity at writing my book this morning – scribble, scribble, scribble for 3½ hours, which, of course, left me as weak as a rag'. With the writing went the arguments. Hawtrey, he told Lydia, on 30 October, was:

very sweet to the last but quite mad. One can argue with him a long time on a perfectly sane and interesting basis and then, suddenly, one

is in a madhouse. Are all the economists mad except Alexander [Kahn]*
and me? It seems so, yet it can't be true. I have just been having a
hopeless debate with Dennis. His mind, though frightfully ingenious,
seems to me to be maliciously perverse. Again it is like arguing with a
madman. But when I talk with Alexander, it's all so quite different.

Two events on Armistice Day, 11 November 1933, crystallised the
problem of the 1930s as Keynes saw it. Sheppard was elected Provost of
King's, the subversive old Apostle looking 'very ecclesiastical as he came
into chapel to accept office, with silk gown, white hair and reverently bowed
head!'[37] Keynes was genuinely, and increasingly, moved by such ceremonies,
which reminded him of his own initiation into the brotherhood of 'research,
religion, and education' in 1909, of the vows he had then made to preserve
'the laws and traditions' of his College.[38] On the same day young Cambridge
erupted in a great anti-war demonstration which marked the start of communism's capture of student politics. Two Apostles, Julian Bell and Guy
Burgess, used Julian's beaten-up Morris as a battering ram to break through
a barricade outside Peterhouse.[39] The juxtaposition of the two happen-
ings, the first symbolising what Keynes meant by civilisation, the second
the destructive forces ranged against it, could only have strengthened his
resolve to save the heritage of the past from its wreckers.

Keynes had a ruthless power of concentration. He kept his activities in
separate compartments of time, but his feelings pointed them to the same
end, which he would have called 'the good life'. It is not surprising therefore
that, as pressure of theoretical work lifted, a new, or rather very old, dream
should have come into his mind. The idea of a repertory theatre for
Cambridge had occurred to him as early as 1913. Now he became obsessed
by the thought of creating a stage for Lydia. On 18 September 1933 she had
made her professional acting debut at the Old Vic as Olivia in Shakespeare's
Twelfth Night. Over the summer Keynes had carefully gone through her part
with her, but, as she herself recognised, 'I do not always pronounce ideally.'
The performance was a critical disaster. *The Times* cruelly mocked her
'Illyrian accent'; the *Daily Telegraph* critic (W. A. Darlington) called her 'the
most humourless female in literature'; Virginia Woolf thought it (privately)
a 'dismal farce', though her notice in the *New Statesman*, written at Lydia's
request, was relatively kind.[40] As the three-week run ended, Keynes wrote to
her (on 15 October), 'Don't be too sad about the acting. I swear we will have
another go. Dadie to whom I talked about it again presses Nora [in Ibsen's
A Doll's House]. He says it is the perfect part for you. . . .'

Lydia never tried to act Shakespeare again. While she consoled herself
with her 'Russian lunches' at Gordon Square, Maynard plotted his theatre
for her at Cambridge. On 18 February 1934 he reported terrible exhaustion

---

* Lydia's nickname for Kahn, to distinguish him from the other Richard – Braithwaite.

after 'fighting through the Building Scheme [to reconstruct the Provost's Lodge] and the first stages of the theatre scheme' through College Council. 'I made eight speeches altogether, one lasting nearly half an hour and another three-quarters of an hour.... But the scheme went through.' Lydia was determined to succeed as an actress. On 4 March 1934, she appeared as Nora in an Arts Theatre Club production in London, Maynard putting up a £125 guarantee. This time the critics were much more friendly; 'Dear Old Maynard was – and this is true – streaming tears,' wrote Virginia Woolf to her nephew Quentin Bell, 'and I kissed him in the stalls between the acts; really she was a marvel, not only a light leaf in the wind, but edged, profound, and her English was exactly what Ibsen meant – it gave the right aroma.'[41]

In the autumn of 1934 Keynes lectured from the proofs of his book, now entitled *The General Theory of Employment, Interest and Money*. Michael Straight, in his first year at Trinity College, remembers the excitement they aroused. 'The largest lecture hall in Cambridge was crowded.... It was as if we were listening to Charles Darwin or Isaac Newton. The audience sat in hushed silence as Keynes spoke. Then, in small circles, he was passionately defended and furiously attacked.'[42] Keynes disliked lecturing, and Lydia, as always, bolstered his confidence. 'To-morrow is your ordeal, My Lank,' she wrote to him on 18 November. 'I know you will do it as ever interestingly, as you always give a new twist to everything you say.'

Keynes's lectures were delivered in a not untypical term of activity. Bursarial work, culminating in the College's annual audit, dominated the first half of term. The theatre project groaned along slowly. There was an article to write for the *New Statesman*, heavy lunches, dinners, Feasts – all of which left him 'rather chippy' and signing his letters to Lydia 'Your weary lank'. On Thursday, 15 November he wrote to her:

> Conferences all day [about the theatre]. Lots of little improvements thought out, and now George [Kennedy] has been finally instructed to prepare finished plans for the builders. So you can count the nights until your first night....
>
> Duncan has done a record even for him! It appears that he is coming to the Feast here tonight as the guest of George Barnes. A few minutes ago I heard D's voice on the telephone. He was at Peterborough, having got into the wrong train! and would not arrive here until 9.30. All right, I said, have dinner in the train, for by that time there will be nothing but drink here, no food. I can't, came the voice back, for I lost all my money at King's Cross and have only fivepence in my pocket – I had to borrow from the stationmaster to telephone to you.

On Monday, 3 December:

> My last lecture was nearly a disaster. My watch stopt just before I was due to start, and I didnt discover the right time until ten minutes after

I ought to have begun. So I rushed down the street and began so breathless that I could hardly speak.... I am frightfully tired this evening. But this, I think, is my last heavy day for a long time.

On the 4th:

I was thoroughly overtired yesterday and didn't sleep well. So to-day I am very chippy and in a cycle. However life is peaceful. I worked all day in my office, except for an hour's stagger with Piero in the afternoon; and there Alexander sits too, trying to understand everything more clearly than is possible.

IV. KEYNES VERSUS MARX

Keynes's conviction that Washington, not Moscow, was the economic laboratory of the world was not widely shared in Cambridge. Anthony Blunt, returning in October 1934 from a year in Rome to a fellowship at Trinity College, found that 'all my friends ... almost all the intellectual and bright young undergraduates who had come up to Cambridge ... had suddenly become Marxists under the impact of Hitler coming to power'. Marxism was embraced by the 'brightest and the best' as the cure for war, fascism and unemployment. Membership of the University's Socialist Society and Labour Club, both Marxist-dominated, rose to about 1000 – a fifth of the undergraduate total – by the time of the Spanish Civil War.

Marxism invaded and captured the Apostles, the citadel of Keynes's Cambridge. According to Noel Annan, who came up to King's College in 1935, fifteen of the thirty-one Apostles elected between 1927 and 1939 were 'communist or *marxisant*'. By contrast, only five of the forty-four inter-war elections could be called 'lifelong homosexuals': a question-begging phrase.[43] 'We talk endlessly in the Society about Communism, which is dull,' reported Keynes's new friend Victor Rothschild;

Guy [Burgess], Alister [Watson] and Richard [Llewellyn] Davies speak with shiny eyes and sweaty foreheads ... vehemently but somewhat illogically it seems to me.... Hugh Sykes Davies prates endlessly about Sadism and Swinburne, while Guy, [William Grey] Walter and I content ourselves with obscene jokes about electric currents. In fact an atmosphere of decadence is appearing and we need your presence.[44]

The Society was, in fact, peripheral to the student politics of the 1930s; its notoriety stems from the fact that four of the eight Cambridge men known to have been recruited to spy for the Soviet Union – Anthony Blunt,

Guy Burgess, Leo Long and Michael Straight – were Apostles. Blunt and Burgess were part of Keynes's Cambridge circle – he sat next to Burgess at a College Feast on 24 February 1934 – but what he thought of them is not recorded. The cold-eyed aesthete and the dissolute cherub were no doubt attractive, clever and amusing enough to pass the time with.

Keynes had his own way of analysing and combating the Marxism that gripped the young. He could never take it seriously as a science. But he did take it seriously as a sickness of the soul, for which his generation was partly responsible. For had not Marx – as well as Freud – invaded the spaces left vacant by his own generation's demolition of Christianity? Virginia Woolf has left a fascinating account of having Keynes and T. S. Eliot to dinner in April 1934. Eliot had just published some lectures, *After Strange Gods: A Primer of Modern Heresies*, greatly admired by Keynes, in which he attacked the absence of moral and religious judgements in literary criticism. Keynes had followed Eliot's tortured road back to Christianity with sympathy, starting with a note of appreciation of his *Fragment of an Agon* in 1927. At dinner Keynes said to Eliot, 'You have brought up again one of the primal questions, & nobody has even tried to consider it.' No, replied Eliot, looking, according to Virginia, 'much like a great toad with jewelled eyes'. Keynes told Eliot that 'he would be inclined not to demolish Xty [Christianity] if it were proved that without it morality is impossible'. He said to Virginia, 'I begin to see that our generation – yours & mine ... owed a great deal to our fathers' religion. And the young, like Julian, who are brought up without it, will never get so much out of life. Theyre trivial: like dogs in their lusts. We had the best of both worlds. We destroyed Xty & yet had its benefits.' Then Julian Bell came in and Keynes turned to 'the economic question: the religion of Communism'. Marxism was 'the worst of all & founded on a silly mistake of old Mr Ricardo's which M[aynard] given time will put right. And then there will be no more economic stress, & then – ? How will you live, Julian, you who have no moral strictness?' Julian replied that the absence of the old morality had landed his generation in psychoanalysis, but that 'I prefer my life in many ways.'[45]

If morals depend on religion, the question is: which religion? Keynes could never follow Eliot all the way back to Christianity. His own religion of sweetness and light and optimism, based on Moore's *Principia Ethica*, had inoculated him and his Cambridge friends from that experience of moral chaos which fuelled Eliot's quest for moral authority. Keynes never needed a Jehovah, because he had never experienced despair. It was not his atheism, but his faithfulness to Moore's revelation, embedded in the life of a secular religious order, which kept him out of the Christian camp, just as it immunised him against the appeal of communism. The question of the 'leap of faith' which troubled so many would-be believers did not worry him unduly: for Keynes's religion, too, depended on a direct judgement of what was good, and could no more be proved or disproved than could the existence of God. But he could see that the religion of Bloomsbury and King's had no appeal to someone like Julian Bell when the world was ablaze. Putting out the fire was a necessary condition for a return to the paths of true religion. Thus far he agreed with Julian. But he could not stomach Marxism as an analysis, or communism as a method. Thus he could both love the communist generation for their idealism, and attack them for their muddle-headedness.

Keynes's assault on the scientific pretensions of Marxism and the horrors of the Soviet system was unremitting, and needed no revelation of mass murder. He insisted on the supreme importance of 'preserving as a matter of principle every jot and tittle of the civil and political liberties which former generations painfully secured....' He was outraged when London University tried to silence the loquacious Harold Laski of the LSE, writing in the *New Statesman* to defend the professor, but adding, 'Too many of the younger members of the Left have toyed with Marxist ideas to have a clear conscience in repelling reactionary assaults on freedom.'[46]* In November 1934 he wrote an article for the *New Statesman* in which he developed his critique of Marxism in the wonderfully good-natured way he had acquired in dealing with sages of the older generation. Its occasion was the publication of an interview H. G. Wells had had with Stalin, on which both Shaw and Keynes were asked to comment. Wells had suggested that in the West the planned economy would be brought about by an intermediate class of technicians and engineers, not by the class struggle between capitalists and workers. Stalin, at his suavest, replied it was impossible to plan the economy without getting rid of private property; the technical intelligentsia could not play an 'independent historical role'. Shaw dismissed Wells's observations as 'Clissoldism', and accused him of instructing Stalin, not listening to what Stalin had to say. Shaw had evidently not felt himself to be under any such limitation in his own two-and-a-half-hour conversation with Stalin in 1931, reducing the monster to silence except for simulated laughter at Shaw's jokes. Stalin thought Shaw a buffoon.

Keynes performed a delicate balancing act between the two socialist gurus. He tried to defend Wells, though he could hardly have enjoyed his feeble performance. 'Wells', he told Virginia Woolf, 'is a little squit.... Shaw feels it. Shaw wd. never write of anyone he respected as he wrote of Wells.'[47] But he did not say this in public. As against Stalin and Shaw, Keynes accepted the Wells doctrine of the intermediate class, as he had when he first reviewed Wells's *The World of William Clissold* in 1927. The trouble was that Wells had no instruction to give. This was Keynes's summary of the whole 'planning' movement. It was all machinery; no ideas to animate it. On the other hand, Shaw was as much a slave to obsolete economics as were

---

* Laski tried to have it both ways, one side of him deeply rooted in the constitutional legalism of Brandeis and Frankfurter, the other playing with revolutionary violence.

Asquith and Dean Inge. 'Th[at] system bred two families – those who thought it true and inevitable, and those who thought it true and intolerable. There was no third school of thought in the nineteenth century. Nevertheless, there is a third possibility – that it is not true'; and this will allow us to escape without revolution or socialism.

Had Shaw kept up with the newspapers since the death of Queen Victoria, he would have known that capitalists were no longer the self-assured Titans of the nineteenth century. 'Their office-boys (on salaries) rule in their mausoleums.... Time and the Joint Stock Company and the Civil Service have silently brought the salaried class into power.' Communism as an economic system is 'an insult to our intelligence'. Its 'subtle, almost irresistible, attraction' is that it promises to make the situation *worse*. It is a protest against the 'emptiness of economic welfare, an appeal to the ascetic in us....' It was the curate in Wells which drew him to Moscow. 'When Cambridge undergraduates take their inevitable trip to Bolshiedom, are they disillusioned when they find it all dreadfully uncomfortable? Of course not. That is what they are looking for.'

Dora Russell – Bertie's third wife – asked what was intended as the killer question: Why hadn't the world adopted Keynes's plans if nobody was exerting power to prevent it? Keynes was modest, but consistent, in his reply: 'Because I have not yet succeeded in convincing either the expert or the ordinary man that I am right. If I am wrong, this will prove to have been fortunate. If, however, I am right, it is, I feel certain, only a matter of time, before I convince both; and when both are convinced, economic policy will, with the usual time-lag, follow suit.'[48]

Shaw wrote Keynes two spry Shavian letters, putting him right on Marx, the Koran, Ricardian economics, Jevonian economics, Fabian economics, Shaw's own contributions to economics, the horrors of academic life, and much more, before calling Maynard 'a bright and promising youth, frightfully handicapped by the Cambridge nullification process, with some inextinguishable sparks of culture in you which make you interesting'. Keynes read the second one out delightedly to Virginia Woolf. His reply to Shaw's first letter is dated 2 December:

> My feelings about *Das Kapital* are the same as my feelings about the *Koran*. I know that it is historically important and I know that many people, not all of whom are idiots, find it a sort of Rock of Ages and containing inspiration. Yet when I look into it, it is to me inexplicable that it can have this effect. Its dreary, out-of-date, academic controversialising seems so extraordinarily unsuitable as material for the purpose. But then, as I have said, I feel just the same about the *Koran*. How could either of these books carry fire and sword round half the world? It beats me. Clearly there is some defect in my understanding.... But whatever the sociological value of [*Das Kapital*] I am sure that its contemporary *economic* value (apart from occasional but inconstructive [sic] and

discontinuous flashes of insight) is *nil*. Will you promise to read it again, if I do?

Keynes's second letter is dated 1 January 1935:

> I will try to take your words to heart. There must be *something* in what you say, because there generally is. But I've made another shot at old K.M. last week, reading the Marx-Engels correspondence just published, without making much progress. I prefer Engels of the two. I can see that they invented a certain method of carrying on and a vile manner of writing, both of which their successors have maintained with fidelity. But if you tell me that they discovered a clue to the economic riddle, still I am beaten – I can discover nothing but out-of-date controversialising.
>
> To understand my state of mind, however, you have to know that I believe myself to be writing a book on economic theory, which will largely revolutionise – not, I suppose, at once but in the course of the next ten years – the way the world thinks about economic problems. When my new theory has been duly assimilated and mixed with politics and feelings and passions, I can't predict what the upshot will be in its effects on actions and affairs. But there will be a great change, and, in particular, the Ricardian foundations of Marxism will be knocked away.
>
> I can't expect you, or anyone else, to believe this at the present stage. But for myself I don't merely hope what I say, – in my own mind I'm quite sure.[49]

Keynes's Political Economy Club of dons, postgraduates and the best Part II students continued to meet weekly in his rooms on Monday evenings. One of those who attended was the handsome but troubled Michael Straight, son of a Standard Oil heiress whose second husband Leonard Elmhirst had started a utopian community art Dartington Hall in Devon. Straight has left two impressions of Keynes in action in the autumn of 1935. The first, in a letter to his mother dating from mid-October, describes a meeting of Keynes's club addressed by an Italian postgraduate, Zampart Lambardi, on 'The Price Level and Stabilisation', at which he was drawn to speak ninth, before Keynes. 'I felt my stomach contracting continually, in fact almost shrinking through my back. I couldn't understand one word of his wretched paper.' Three other second-year students had to speak before him.

> [Peter] Bauer, the Austrian, spoke so fast that no one could understand what he said, so that he got away with it. Stamp, the son of Josiah Stamp, made a long and intricate analogy about a traveller and a map in which he never mentioned economics – so he got away with it; and [Alexander] Henderson trotted out some phrase from Joan Robinson which he'd obviously just learnt beforehand and sat down before anyone could ask him what he meant – so he got away with it.
>
> I tried to say something about the price level and stabilisation and

didn't get away with it. After I had finished a halting pointless speech I turned to Lambardi and put in a form of a question. But he looked up with a perplexed face and said quite justifiably that he couldn't see the point of what I'd said.

I turned round and asked in a despairing strangled voice if *anybody* could see the point in what I'd said.

But needless to say none of them could and Keynes nobly rescued me by saying 'I think I know what you mean...' and then explaining a long and difficult theory which of course had never entered my mind but with which I fervently agreed.

Then he wound up brilliantly and I sneaked out before anyone had a chance to pin me down....

In his published recollection of this event, Straight says that after Keynes had finished speaking he glanced at him without even a smile, so as not to lay claim on his gratitude. The occasion is a good example of his winning way with the young.[50]

A fortnight later, on 28 October, there was a discussion on Marx. Straight, then a fervent Marxist who, characteristically, had opened *Das Kapital* for the first time only the evening before, had just spoken, when Keynes got up.

He stood like a great bear in front of his fireplace. He rocked back and forth. Marxism, he said, was even lower than social credit as an economic concept. It was complicated hocus-pocus, the only value of which was its muddleheadedness. He had read Marx, he said, as if it were a detective story, trying to find some clue to an idea in it and never succeeding.

It was the first time, Straight recalls, that a leading Cambridge intellectual challenged the 'new orthodoxy that had fastened itself upon the minds of the undergraduates'.[51]

V. MODEST PREPARATIONS FOR THE GOOD LIFE

The depressed condition of capitalism in the 1930s did not stop Keynes from becoming 'horribly prosperous'. In 1929 he had lost practically all his money; in 1931 he even tried to sell two of his best pictures, his Matisse *Déshabillé* and his Seurat *Study*, but found no buyers at his minimum price. By 1936 his net worth came to over £500,000, or about £16m in today's values. His capital had appreciated by twenty-three times, in a period when Wall Street's stock prices had only trebled, and London's had hardly moved at all. Most of Keynes's gains came from New York. He re-entered Wall Street in 1932, and dollar shares made up 40 per cent of his portfolio by 1936. Over his life Keynes was a spectacularly successful investor, though he suffered three major setbacks – in 1920–1, 1928–9 and 1937–8. Practically all his durable gains came after 1932. Keynes's annual income was large, but not stupendously so. Between 1930 and 1936 it averaged just over £6000 a year (gross) – the equivalent of about £150,000 today. In the two tax years 1936–7 and 1937–8 it shot up to over £16,000 a year (now £500,000) but never got as high again. His academic income came to about a third of the total from 1930–6; the rest was from dividends and fees. He and Lydia lived very comfortably, but not extravagantly.

Keynes was also partly responsible for the investment policies of a number of companies, and of King's College, Cambridge. The PR Investment Trust for friends of Keynes and Falk was wound up in 1935. The Independent Investment Trust also suffered in the depression. Falk and Keynes again fell out, Keynes playing little part in the 1930s. This left the National Mutual and the Provincial Insurance Companies (the latter a family trust managed by Francis Scott). The more directly under Keynes's control the investments were, the better they performed. The outstanding example is his management of the College Chest. Unlike the other college funds, it was his sole responsibility. Its capital increased sevenfold from 1920 to 1936 – from £30,000 to £200,000 – again mostly in the 1930s. The National Mutual and the Provincial, whose investment decisions were decided by boards on which Keynes sat, did less well, but still 'gave a good thrashing' to the indexes.[52]

Keynes's personal investment philosophy changed with his economic theory, the symbiotic connection between the two being most apparent in chapter 12 of the *General Theory*, when he sharply distinguishes between investment and speculation. In the 1920s Keynes saw himself as a scientific gambler. He speculated on currencies and commodities. His aim was to play the cycle. This was the height of his 'barometric' enthusiasm, shared with Falk, when he believed it was possible, by forecasting short-term rhythms, to beat the market. The gambling instinct was never quite extinguished. There is a famous occasion in 1936 when he was forced to take delivery of a month's supply of wheat for England from Argentina on a falling market. He planned to store the wheat in King's College Chapel, but was told it was too small. Ever resourceful, he proposed to object to its quality: the cleaning took a month, by which time its price had risen sufficiently for him to escape without loss. There were loud complaints that some 'infernal speculator' had cornered the market![53]

By the 1930s he was prone to dismiss this kind of activity as a mug's game. His new philosophy can be summed up as fidelity to a few carefully chosen stocks: his 'pets', as he called them. The investor should buy, not sell, on a falling market; the expectation of picking up bargains was more rational than yielding to the panic psychology of the crowd. Thus his personal investment philosophy came into line with his increasing theoretical emphasis on the need to stabilise investment. The investor, like the government, should fight the mania for liquidity. The realisation that, as he put it in his 1938 Memoir Club paper, 'My Early Beliefs', civilisation was a 'thin and precarious crust' also pointed to the investor's rational interest in social stability. A new form of the equation between long-run self-interest and the public good had formed in Keynes's mind.

As an investor Keynes thought of himself as a 'contrarian'.

It is the one sphere of life and activity [he told Labordère on 28 September 1937] where victory, security and success is always to the minority and never to the majority. When you find any one agreeing with you, change your mind. When I can persuade the Board of my Insurance Company to buy a share, that, I am learning from experience, is the right moment for selling it.

A sign of Keynes's growing social conservatism was his commitment to the countryside. To the young Keynes, as to any bourgeois of his time and place, rural life (though not owning a country house) was synonymous with prejudice and superstition. In the 1920s he had pooh-poohed land as an investment, and had liquidated many of the College's land holdings. This attitude started to change when the agricultural depression at the end of the 1920s faced King's with the choice of selling a large estate, Elsham, in north Lincolnshire, which it had bought in 1925, or farming it itself. Keynes emerged as the unlikely champion of the second course. 'There was something expiatory in this,' wrote Hugh Durnford, the domus bursar at the time. Keynes, whose attitude to farming had been that of a hard-headed accountant, now succumbed to the romanticism of the soil. Nor was this an abstract fancy. He took his duties as an improving landlord seriously, visiting the estate frequently, and learnedly discussing points of stock and the dietary habits of pigs with the labourers. This, his first serious contact with an admittedly untypical segment of the English working class, humanised rather than radicalised him. It also brought out a latent paternalism. In 1930 he started a piggery with Edgar Weller at Tilton, contracting to deliver pigs of a certain quality to a local bacon factory. They acquired a huge boar, Tilton Beau; Keynes congratulated Weller on his white sow's 'huge progeny'. He began to see himself as the Squire of Tilton. In 1934 he acquired shooting rights over Tilton Wood. At the end of 1935, he took out a new twenty-one-year lease on the house and the whole farm – about 300 acres in all – and appointed a bailiff, Logan Thompson, to manage it. Lydia started distributing presents to the farm workers at Christmas. At the same time, as we have seen, he began lauding national self-sufficiency, and talking about the dignity of manual labour. All this was part of an evolution in his character, and outlook, for which his economics provided a sophisticated rationale.

Critics would say that the *General Theory* marked an intellectual retrogression. More justly it can be seen as a spiritual and moral adaptation to the realities of the 1930s.

Keynes was not one of those who averaged out his consumption over his life-time. He was not extravagant, but when he had money he spent it, not on good living, but on the good life. Thus the scale of his benefactions rose in the 1930s with increasing wealth, this despite the fact that two of his good causes succumbed to the depression. The Camargo Society, as we have seen, was wound up in 1933, after putting on two seasons of ballet in the depth of the slump. The London Artists' Association came to an end the same year. There had been fierce quarrels with Duncan, Vanessa and Roger Fry about enlarging the Association in 1930, with Keynes championing the claims of the younger painters; Duncan and Vanessa resigned from it in 1931 after receiving an offer from Thos. Agnew & Sons 'too good to be refused'. Their defection doomed the Association, since they were its best-selling painters. For a few years after the rupture with the LAA, relations between Tilton and Charleston became distinctly chilly. Leaving the Association proved a false move for both Duncan and Vanessa. They lost touch with the younger painters, and their own individuality was not strong enough to impose itself on contemporary taste. Their reputations went into rapid decline.

Keynes used his wealth to buy both pictures and books. He added two Cézannes and two Delacroix to his collection in 1935–7. He also bought his first painting from Ivon Hitchens, another young English artist who became a favourite in the late 1930s. The picture which escaped him was the finished painting of Seurat's *la Grande Jatte*, of which he owned one of the three studies. He had a chance to buy it from the family in 1935: it is now the jewel of Chicago's Art Institute. The mid-1930s also saw the start of large book and manuscript purchases. He had 'evolved the plan of forming a really comprehensive collection to illustrate the history of thought'. Starting with the purchase of thirty-six titles from Gibbon's Lausanne Library auction in December 1934 he systematically pursued it for the rest of his life. His book and manuscript collecting increasingly absorbed energies earlier devoted to the stock market, but it was governed by the same principle of buying stock which he thought underpriced relative to its intrinsic worth.[54] From this time, too, he started making substantial donations to charities, settling annuities on Bunny Garnett, Duncan Grant and younger relations, and giving lavish presents, mainly of rare books, to his friends.

Keynes's main capital spending in these years went on his building programme. Having secured his new lease at the end of 1935, he commissioned George Kennedy to rebuild Tilton, with a new wing and a big new main staircase. Kennedy had also submitted plans, costing £42,000, for a new theatre and hostel for King's College students at Cambridge, on a site facing Peas Hill and St Edward's Passage, but the College Council refused to finance the theatrical part. Keynes submitted a memorandum on 25 July 1934, in which he undertook to accept financial responsibility for building and running the theatre, on a long lease of part of the site. This broke the deadlock. 'I believe', he wrote,

> that a good small theatre, equipt with all the contrivances of modern stagecraft, is as necessary to our understanding of the dramatic arts, with their complicated dependence on literature, music and design, as a laboratory is to experimental science. It is the outstanding characteristic of our own generation that we have gone far to restoring the theatre ... to the place in the serious interests of the University which it held at the beginning of the seventeenth century.[55]

Kennedy submitted a new plan for a theatre costing £15,000. In October 1934, Keynes appointed Norman Oppenshaw Higgins, who ran the 'excruciatingly uncomfortable' Cosmopolitan Cinema, as secretary, at £400 a year, of a company of which he would be chairman, to build 'The Cambridge Arts Theatre'. The other members of the Board were Dadie Rylands and Miss J. M. Harvey, who had been secretary of the Camargo Society and now ran the London Film Society. Higgins would manage the theatre, which would also show films. When Higgins protested that he knew nothing of theatrical management, Keynes assured him that 'we shall learn by experience unencumbered by notions which may prove inappropriate to the present venture'.

The plan was for a theatre to seat 500–600. Soon a restaurant was added to the plan, Keynes insisting that a civilised theatre-goer 'must be able to dine within the building'. Building started in March 1935. Since few preference shares were taken up, Keynes ended up paying £20,000 himself to build the theatre, half in the form of an interest-free loan to the company, his sister Margaret and Miss Harvey putting up much smaller sums. 'The greatest comfort of all, I think, from having some money,' he wrote to Lydia on 17 January 1935, 'is that one does not need to badger other people for it.'

As he was providing most of the money, Keynes naturally kept a tight control over costs. But, being Keynes, he developed an insatiable interest in every aspect of the work. 'You can't imagine the details which have to be attended to,' he told Lydia on 10 February 1935. Keynes himself corresponded with Professor Inglis of the Engineering Laboratory on lighting and electrical problems. He fussed about the position of the wind and string instruments in the orchestra pit, and weighed the acoustical effects of separating the under-stage from the orchestra by curtains or 'some sort of wooden contraption'. He approved the design and positioning of the seats. He worried about the colour of the panelling. Influenced by his experience of Lydia's backstage conditions, he worked with Higgins to get the dressing rooms 'as large and convenient as possible'. Finding the right people to run the restaurant proved a nightmare without end. An offer to a Mrs Burton had to be hurriedly withdrawn when her own restaurant went bust. Dadie produced a 'rich young baronet with social connections'. Kahn offered a lady with the right 'nuance'. Higgins proposed a butler married to a Hungarian cook. Eventually a Mrs Hooper and a Mrs Travers were appointed at £3 a week. More satisfying was the decision of the Board that 'the Chairman and Mr Rylands should proceed with the purchase of wines at their discretion'. But the restaurant never did work properly. To Keynes also fell the task of organising the programme for the first season. He wrote to playwrights to send him plays, to theatre managers to exchange productions; he tried to link up with pre-London runs. The Irish dramatist Sean O'Casey was highly sceptical of the whole idea. 'Is it out of his mind he [Keynes] is?' he asked David Garnett, whom Keynes had used as an intermediary. 'Better by far to build a convalescent Home for the English Dramatic Critics.'[56] An opening season was cobbled together, its highlights being a gala opening by the Vic-Wells ballet, and an Ibsen cycle of four plays, featuring Lydia as Nora in *A Doll's House* and Hilda Wangel in *The Master Builder*. The original plan was to open in October. But this had to be postponed as the building took longer to finish than anticipated.

Early in January 1936 he was still inspecting the 'designs for matchboxes, uniforms for the page boys, cork floors for dressing rooms, etc., etc.'. Men worked all through the night to get everything ready for the opening. At last, on 17 January, Keynes could tell Lydia that the 'fundamentals are finished'. He was well satisfied with the theatre's final appearance, except that 'its curious pentagonal shape [which symbolised the five arts of drama, opera, ballet, music and cinema] makes it look to my eye a little lopsided'. The theatre, which has no frontage of its own, being approached from under the student hostel, is still in use. It illustrates Kennedy's particular skill in conjuring spacious interiors out of nothing, and in adapting his designs to other buildings already there.[57]

Maynard's book was also in a 'retouching' state.[58] This meant some fairly drastic rewriting, mainly shortening and simplifying. 'What I have to say is not really so terribly complicated,' he wrote to Harrod, 'but there is some evil genius which sits at the elbow of every economist, forcing him into all sorts of contorted and unnecessary complications.'[59] He took his new theory to Oxford in February 1935; the result was a notable duel with Hubert Henderson, now a fellow of All Souls. Galley proofs went out to Harrod, Hawtrey, Kahn and Joan Robinson in mid-June. The exchanges with Robertson were not resumed, by mutual agreement. Keynes had found Dennis's commentary earlier in the year 'most painful'; his state of mind 'pathological'. Neither Henderson nor Pigou received proofs. Thus, of his own generation, Keynes thought only Hawtrey was sufficiently sympathetic to help him in his last stage. The battle-lines were forming up.

Harrod's criticism had the greatest effect; Keynes wrote to him on 10 September that he had 'gained a great deal from your hard knocks, and would like some more'. Harrod was by then teaching economics at Christ Church, Oxford. Though he had not been involved in the Circus, he and Meade were the chief Keynesians at Oxford. This had not stopped Harrod from calling Pigou's *Theory of Unemployment* a 'supreme intellectual achievement' when he reviewed it in the *Economic Journal* in 1934. Harrod's chief aim was to get Keynes to tone down his criticism of the classical school. He wrote to him on 30 August 1935:

> Your really important and effective criticism of the classical view occurs in Book I. It is implicit in the classical view that any given level of output is uniquely correlated with a given level of *real* wages.... Once you knock that on the head, as you do most effectively, the level of output is either indeterminate, or has to be determined by some new equation not provided for in the classical system. Thus the way is clear for a radical reconstruction. Your new equation is the liquidity preference schedule.... No further criticism of the classical system is required. All your subsequent criticism is fussy, irrelevant, dubious, hair-splitting and hair-raising.[60]

Harrod criticised Keynes's assault on the classical theory of the rate of interest partly on grounds of controversial manners, but also because he thought Keynes had misunderstood the classical theory. On the first point, he urged Keynes to 'minimise and not maximise the amount of generally accepted doctrine that your views entail the scrapping of. A general holocaust is more exciting. But ... you no longer require these artificial stimulants to secure attention.'[61]

Keynes replied on 27 August:

> But the general effect of your reaction ... is to make me feel that my assault on the classical school ought to be intensified rather than abated. My motive is, of course, not in order to get read. But it may be needed in order to get understood. I am frightfully afraid of the tendency, of which I see some signs in you, to appear to accept my constructive part and to find some accommodation between this and deeply cherished views which would in fact only be possible if my constructive part has been partially misunderstood. That is to say, I expect a great deal of what I write to be water off a duck's back. I am certain that it will be water off a duck's back unless I am sufficiently strong in my criticism to force the classicals to make a rejoinder. I *want*, so to speak, to raise a dust....[62]

Harrod's substantive criticism was stated as follows on 12 August 1935:

> I hold there is sense in saying that interest equates the demand for investment to the supply of saving. And I also hold that the fact that S must be equal to I does not itself invalidate the proposition that interest

is the price which makes them equal. I further hold that if there was some other mechanism for securing constancy of income, which the *old* classical doctrine assumes (i.e. it implicitly assumes constancy of income and does not envisage the rate of interest as the mechanism for keeping incomes constant) then the classical doctrine that it is the rate of interest which equates the propensity to invest to the propensity to save would not only make sense but also be true.

The essence of your point I feel to be that the *cet*[*eris*] *par*[*ibus*] clause of the supply and demand analysis, which in this case includes the level of income, is *invalid*. The classical theory [therefore] is invalid but not nonsense.[63]

Harrod's criticism amounted to saying that, if real wages were flexible, the classical theory of interest would be true. However, Keynes insisted that the classical theory of the rate of interest made no sense on any assumption at all. 'It has to be discarded in toto, and is incapable of rehabilitation in any shape or form.'

The fault of the classical theory [he wrote on 10 September] lies, not in its limiting its terrain by assuming constant income, but in its failing to see that, if either of its own variables (namely propensity to save and schedule of marginal efficiency of capital) change, income must also *cet. par.* change; so that its tool breaks in its hand and it doesn't know and can't tell us what will happen to the rate of interest, when either of its own variables changes.

I say, therefore, that it is *nonsense* to assume at the same time that income is constant and that the propensity to save and the schedule of the marginal efficiency of capital are variable.[64]

Keynes did not shift from his position that the classical rate of interest theory was a 'nonsense theory',[65] though he did drop the argument that what made it nonsense was the identity of saving and investment. He also used a suggestion by Harrod to draw a diagram – which became the only diagram in the *General Theory* – of intersecting curves, the first showing how much investment will take place at each rate of interest, the second showing how much will be saved out of income at each rate of interest. Keynes accepted the diagram suggestion because it showed 'most elegantly' the relation 'between the rate of interest and the level of income, given the schedule of the marginal efficiency of capital and the propensity to consume', not because he believed, as Harrod did, that saving is *simultaneously* determined by the rate of interest and the level of income; the interest rate, he insisted, has 'nothing whatever to do with saving'.[66]

In his historical chapter, Keynes was determined to make amends for the savage review he had written of one of J. A. Hobson's books in 1913.[67] Kahn did a lot of the mugging up; but Keynes himself had been in correspondence with Hobson in 1935, and he took advantage of this both to apologise to him and to restate his own theory succinctly:

> The essence of my argument is that no more savings can come into existence than is provided for by the outlet in current investment. If the inducement is weak relative to the propensity to save, the result is a deficiency of effective demand which leads to diminished employment; and the unemployment is increased by whatever figure is necessary so to impoverish the community as to reduce the amount people desire to save to equality with the amount they are willing to invest.[68]

Apart from a short visit to Antwerp with Lydia in July 1935 to discuss exchange stabilisation, Maynard spent the summer and early autumn at Tilton working on his revisions. Once more, he was not in the best of health. Influenza in June was followed by a 'furious bilious attack' in August. Florence and Neville Keynes came to stay, Neville miraculously recovered from a serious illness. In August Kahn stayed, and also Maynard's niece Polly Hill, reading economics at Newnham, and longing to be supervised by her uncle. Kingsley Martin was another visitor. Maynard had recently persuaded him to stay on at the *New Statesman* and not take the chair in Aberystwyth which tempted him; he had also had to sort out the vexed matter of literary editorship (claimed by both Raymond Mortimer and Bunny Garnett); he had been much taxed, too, in fixing up a job to enable Piero Sraffa to stay at Cambridge. But it was his fate, and desire, to solve other people's problems. On 15 September Lydia reported to Florence that she had been reading a book on Abyssinia: 'What a country to live ... no one has w.c. except for the King of Kings....' The Abyssinian crisis was about to erupt, shortly followed by the general election in which Maynard, for the first and only time in his life, voted Labour, though he still looked forward to evolutionary progress under 'good King Baldwin'.

On Christmas morning Lydia carried 'sacks of merchandise' to the villagers. She and Maynard looked over their 'black-pink piglets' from the 'most handsome and expensive sow in England ... with such gloss on them that any film star would envy'. Duncan Grant, Duncan's mother and Kahn were guests at their lunch of turkey, ham, cheese and celery, and they all chatted so long they missed the King's Christmas speech, the last before he died. Maynard, Lydia reported to Florence, was 'quite well'. Every day they would be conveyed by Edgar to the top of the Downs, 'then we descend, droop into chairs, drink tea, and drop our senses into somnambula'.[69]

The General Theory of Employment, Interest, and Money was published on 4 February 1936. The Arts Theatre had opened the previous day: two projects, linked by a common feeling, converging at a single moment in time.

30

Firing at the Moon

I. VISION AND METHOD

The General Theory of Employment, Interest and Money is a work of enduring fascination. It is simple and subtle, obscure and profound. It offered a systematic way of thinking not just about the behaviour of contemporary economies, but about the pitfalls in the quest for greater wealth at all times. It combined a vision of the future with a rigorous demonstration of the possibility of underemployment equilibrium. Although young economists of speculative bent were drawn to it as a storehouse of suggestive ideas, it was its practical usefulness which chiefly attracted them in a world poised between decaying democracy and rampaging dictatorship.

At its core is a 'theory of output and employment as a whole', to distinguish it from the orthodox theory of what causes 'the rewards and distribution between different uses of a given quantity of resources' to be what they are.[1] Keynes was the first economist to visualise the economy as an aggregate quantity of output resulting from an aggregate stream of expenditure. This new way of seeing the architecture of an economy is the *General Theory*'s most enduring legacy.

Output and employment depend on the amount of the community's spending. If workers and machines stand idle it is because the community is not spending enough to buy the output they can jointly produce. If we can measure in money what the community is buying and how much extra output the unemployed would add if they worked, we can calculate how much extra 'demand' or spending power needs to be 'injected' into an economy to close the 'output gap'. Thus Keynes's aggregate concepts led directly to the development of national income accounts and to the policies of 'demand management' with which his name is associated. The dependence of employment on spending is driven home by one of the best-known – and extremist – passages in the *General Theory*:

> If the Treasury were to fill old bottles with bank-notes, bury them at suitable depths in disused coal-mines which are then filled up to the surface with town rubbish, and leave it to private enterprise on well tried principles of *laissez-faire* to dig the notes up again ... there need be no more unemployment.[2]

However, this 'model' of the economy is embedded in a moral drama which constitutes Keynes's vision of the economic process. As he tells it, it is the 'psychology of society' as fashioned by the need to act in the face of an uncertain future which sets mankind its permanent economic problem. Because the future is unknown, and often thereby feared, the 'good life' which is the only rational object of economic striving is postponed by systematic economic underperformance. Actual output is normally below 'potential' output; in depressions disastrously so. It is only in moments of 'excitement' that the economic machine works at full blast. This helps explain why economic progress has been so slow and fitful.

It is in his explicit recognition of the effect of uncertainty on human behaviour that Keynes's break with the vision of classical economics arises. Classical economics was concerned with the logic of choice under conditions of scarcity; Keynes's economics with the logic of choice under conditions of uncertainty. This shift in perspective leads to a radically different interpretation of the psychology of action. What Keynes calls the 'propensity to save' is associated less with the urge for a better tomorrow than with anxiety about tomorrow. Investment, too, is less a matter of rational calculation than of 'animal spirits'. Uncertainty, therefore, imposes a kind of permanent fearfulness about the future which puts a damper on economic progress. Economic activity can be lifted out its normal rut only by the stimulus of exciting events. Typical is Keynes's speculation – in his *Treatise on Money* – that the treasure seized by Drake from the Spanish in the 1570s and 1580s was not just the 'fountain and origin of British foreign investment', but more generally the foundation of its economic growth.[3]

Emphasis on uncertainty leads Keynes to a different perspective on the origins and use of money. As Keynes sees it, money was invented not just (or mainly) to improve on barter but to provide a 'store of value'. Holding cash reduces exposure to the unknown and thus alleviates anxiety. People always face a choice between spending money one way or another or *not spending it at all*. Liquidity provides a retreat from activity. People's freedom not to spend in a monetary economy is the logical crux of Keynes's denial of Say's Law that 'supply creates its own demand'. Instead, he told students in 1933, 'expenditure creates its own income.'[4]

Keynes's view of the role of 'love of money' changed with his theory. He always thought of it as a kind of perversion of life's true aims, which arrived with Puritanism. But in the 1920s he regarded it as at least functional: the non-consumption of the cake provides the fund for the capital investment which leads to the era of abundance. In the *General Theory*, 'love of money' has come to explain why the cake is not larger than it is. In Keynes's new morality play, its role is not to build a better tomorrow, but to deprive entrepreneurs of capital by maintaining a usurious rate of interest. The government's job is to encourage enterprise by lowering the cost of capital and, if that is not enough, to supply the missing investment itself. That way the rate of growth can be speeded up and the day of abundance, leisure, and enjoyment of life come sooner.

The *General Theory* may be interpreted as a moral drama, but it is not a historical or sociological one. The social landscape visible from Keynes's earlier writings has vanished: the Puritan *rentier* class, the business class, the workers, are represented only disembodied 'propensities'. There is no mention of the Great War and political and currency disorders, the changing balance between capital and labour, all of which might be called *causes* of the great depression. The question of whether the great depression of the 1930s was *sui generis* or an ever-possible outcome of the normal working of a market economy is a historical-cum-sociological one which cannot be answered by economics alone.

In terms of formal theory, Keynes's revolutionary achievement was the demonstration of the possibility of under-employment equilibrium. A decentralised capitalist economy lacks any automatic tendency to the full employment of its resources. In place of the classical story of adjustments in relative prices which maintain (or soon restore) 'optimum' equilibrium, Keynes posited many possible levels of equilibrium, each corresponding to a set of expectations about the future. John Hicks was the first to notice the revolutionary character of Keynes's 'method of expectations'. He wrote, 'The point of the method is that it reintroduces determinedness into the process of change. The output of goods and services and the employment of labour, together with the whole price system, are determined over any short-period, once the stock of goods (... including capital goods) existing at the beginning of the period is given and *once people's expectations of future market conditions are given too*' (emphasis added).[5]

The idea that a market which had excess supplies of workers and plant could be 'in equilibrium' is not in itself new. It had its roots in Marshall's concept of a 'short-period' or 'temporary' equilibrium, an analytic device Marshall used to distinguish between the initial adjustment of the quantity of employment to a given capital stock (factories, machines) and the contraction or expansion of the capital stock itself which economic forces tend to bring about in the long run. His aim was to show that a full supply response to a demand shock takes time, and that in this interval labour supply is elastic. What Keynes did was to take over Marshall's method for dealing with the influence of time in a single market and apply it to a whole economy. His under-employment equilibrium is one in which an economy-wide surplus of labour has developed in relation to the existing economy-wide stock of plant. By using the 'method of expectations' to freeze the frame of a moving picture he suggests that this 'short period' may last a long time. This seemed a reasonable analytical device in the circumstances of the great depression; it also enabled Keynes to posit stable mathematical functions for variables 'which can be deliberately controlled or managed by central authority....'⁶ Whether the 'freeze' can be regarded as a genuine 'equilibrium' is more doubtful, precisely because it excludes changes in the 'structure of production' which the Austrian and Swedish economists regarded as central to the full 'classical' adjustment process. Keynes acknowledges that slower-moving recovery forces some into play, but he denies that they tend towards full employment. Long-period employment may be fuller than employment at any one time; but it is not normally full.

The *General Theory* consists both of Keynes's positive theory and an attack on something he calls 'the classical theory'. Stalking his book is what Dennis Robertson called 'a composite Aunt Sally of uncertain age' and what Keynes called the Classical Economist. Keynes's method of attack on this mythical figure was annoying, but highly effective. It was to tease out the 'implicit assumptions' underpinning his opponents' belief in a self-regulating market, essentially by showing what they must assume to believe the things they did. The *General Theory* involved a triple act of creativity: Keynes not only invented his own theory, but also classical theory, *and* a dissenting tradition of economists to which he claimed to be heir.

The difficulties Keynes encountered in forcing his vision into the straitjacket of his model makes the *General Theory* very difficult to digest. Much of Book II dealing with definitions is as much a nightmare to read as it must have been for Keynes to write. The uncertainty about whether his 'unemployment equilibrium' was temporary or persisting makes it hard to relate it to classical discussions which assumed a tendency to full employment. Once the *General Theory* was published Keynes repeatedly warned against premature formalisation of his theory. But its reduction to a mechanical model was inseparable from its triumph as a tool of policy.

All of which makes it easier to understand why the 'simple' ideas of the *General Theory* are apt to get lost in a maze of puzzles and paradoxes. Pigou wrote of it: 'We have watched an artist firing at the moon. Whatever be thought of his markmanship, we can all admire his virtuosity.' Once the *General Theory* was mastered, glimpses of the moon disappeared, as inappropriate matter for an economics textbook.

II. *THE GENERAL THEORY*

An economy's output depends on two streams of demand – consumption demand and investment demand: in Keynes's notation, $Y = C + I$. All this means is that the value of current output must be the same as the income spent on buying it. Gone are the special definitions of the *Treatise*, which can make saving unequal to investment. S[Saving] = Y[Income] – C[on-sumption]. So I = S. Saving and Investment are yoked together like Siamese twins: they both rise and fall with output (income). Since employment depends on output, Keynes has a theory of employment. He can say that employment depends on 'effective demand' – what people spend on buying consumption and investment goods. This is the 'simple and obvious' idea underlying the *General Theory*.

Chapter 3 is a preliminary statement of the 'theory of effective demand'. Effective demand is defined as entrepreneurs' expected sales proceeds (incomes) from the amount of employment they decide to give. Employment will be in equilibrium – with no tendency for its amount to change – when the proceeds entrepreneurs expect from selling a quantity of output equal the expected costs of producing that output. Keynes contends that the economy can be in equilibrium, with expected sales proceeds equal to expected costs, at less than full employment. The rest of the book shows how this can come about.

Books III and IV dealing with consumption demand, investment demand, and the rate of interest are the analytical kernel, because these variables determine the volume of output and employment. In the short run the 'propensity to consume' is a 'fairly stable' proportion of current income. According to Keynes's 'psychological law', when income increases consumption rises less than income, and when it decreases it falls less.[7] The fact that consumption is more stable than income gives the system a certain measure of stability. More importantly, if the propensity to consume is known one can show that expansions and contractions of income converge to a fixed position in which saving and investment are equal. If, in the language of the *Treatise*, saving is 'running ahead' of investment, a fall in income automatically eliminates the 'excess saving' by making the community poorer; if investment is 'running ahead' of saving, a rise in income automatically produces the extra saving by making the community richer. As Austin Robinson put it 'in equilibrium ... saving must equal investment ... if these two tend to be unequal, the level of activity will be changed until they are restored to equality'.[8]

The famous income multiplier, derived from Kahn's employment multiplier, shows by *how much* income has to fall or rise to eliminate any gap between intended saving and actual investment. It also establishes income/output adjustment as the main mechanism by which an economy reaches a new position of equilibrium: hence the popular Keynesian slogan 'quantities adjust, not prices'. According to one leading student, this double demonstration is the 'major novel feature' of the *General Theory*.[9] It is also the part of the *General Theory* most useful for policy, for it tells a government how much extra spending is needed to eliminate unemployment, or how much spending has to be curtailed to eliminate inflation. This second was of no concern to anyone in the early 1930s, but was the way in which the

Keynesian aggregate arithmetic proved most useful to governments in the Second World War.

What the consumption function brings out is that a society which saves part of its income may quite possibly find itself in a situation of 'under-employment equilibrium'. Keynes's famous 'paradox of thrift' was that unless the expected profitability of investment was going up, any increase in the desire to save was liable to lead to a reduction in actual savings, via a fall in income. But an increased propensity to save was liable to have a malign effect on the inducement to invest by reducing entrepreneurs' expectations of future consumption on which the expected profitability of investment depends. Keynes put it like this: a decision to save depresses the business of preparing today's dinner, without stimulating the business of preparing tomorrow's; in fact 'since the expectation of future consumption is so largely based on current experience of present consumption', it depresses the business of preparing for tomorrow's business too.[10] So the more 'thrifty' a society is, the more liable to stagnation it is. Moreover, insofar as recoveries generate an excess of income over consumption, saving and investment may be equalised before full employment is reached. This was the basis of Keynes's view that under *laissez-faire* recoveries are liable to peter out before full employment is attained; or to put it another way, full employment was a 'special case', not the general case.

Given a community's 'propensity to consume', the amount of employment depends on its rate of investment, or the rate at which it is adding to its capital stock. There is an 'inducement to invest' whenever the expected rate of return on the investment is higher than the cost of borrowing money; when what Keynes calls the 'marginal efficiency of capital' is positive. In chapter 12, 'The State of Long-Term Expectations', the instability of investment demand emerges as the crucial cause of fluctuations in employment. The reason is the volatility attaching to expectations of the future yield of capital goods.

Keynes's starting point is the 'extreme precariousness of the basis of knowledge on which our estimates of prospective yield have to be made'.[11] The stock exchange reduces the riskiness of investments by making them 'liquid' for individuals, but this makes investment as a whole much more volatile, since investors can buy and sell at a moment's notice. Share prices depend not on real investment prospects, but on prevailing sentiment, which can fluctuate violently with the day's news. It is the flimsiness of knowledge supporting conventional share valuations which makes the investment function peculiarly dependent on 'animal spirits', defined as a 'spontaneous urge to action rather than inaction'.[12]

Many Keynesians have seen chapter 12 as containing the 'vision' of the *General Theory*, and indeed the core of the Keynesian Revolution, both in its attack on the ethics of capitalism – 'when the capital development of a country becomes a by-product of the activities of a casino, the job is likely to be ill-done' – and in its rejection of calculability in human affairs. Keynes muses that 'the only radical cure for the crises of confidence which afflict the economic life of the modern world would be to allow the individual no choice between consuming his income and ordering the production of [a]specific capital asset....'[13] But the discussion leads more soberly to the conclusion that the state should take 'an ever greater responsibility for directly organising investment ... on long views'.[14]

Thus far Keynes's theory may be summarised as follows. Aggregate output or real income is determined by consumption and investment demand. Given the propensity to consume, real income changes with investment demand. This is equivalent to saying that real income adjusts to maintain saving equal to investment. But the theory is not complete: the interest rate is needed to establish a 'determinate' level of income because of its influence on the rate of investment. What then determines the interest rate?

'The rate of interest', Keynes writes, 'is the "price" which equilibrates the desire to hold wealth in the form of cash with the available quantity of cash'.[15] The greater people's preference for holding their savings in money, the higher the rate of interest they will demand for parting with money. A collapse in the expected profitability of investment tends to lead to an increase in liquidity-preference, thus pushing interest rates up when they need to come down. The chain of logic of the *General Theory* is thus completed by showing that the rate of interest can remain above the 'rate of return to capital' necessary to secure full employment.

Why should people choose to hold their wealth in cash? The 'necessary condition', indeed the 'sole intelligible explanation' for what Keynes somewhat awkwardly calls the 'speculative' motive for holding cash, is the 'existence of *uncertainty* as to the future of the rate of interest'.[16] Keynes reasons that, if this were not so, investors who wanted to get out of equities would buy government debt. This would drive up the price of bonds and lower their yield, making it more profitable for businessmen to borrow for investment. But if 'speculators' think the interest rate is 'too low' – has fallen below its 'conventional' or expected level – they will sell bonds for cash, thus aborting, or reversing, the fall in the rate. Keynes does not inquire into what causes the expected rate of interest to be what it is – a point picked up by Dennis Robertson.

The monetary authority can step in by buying bonds itself (open-market operations). But this can generate offsetting bond sales by the private sector if monetary policy is regarded as 'unsound'. One can then get a 'liquidity trap', a situation when monetary policy cannot push the interest rate beneath a floor set by the fear of inflation or default. The lower the rate of interest the smaller the 'earnings from illiquidity' available to insure against the risk of loss on capital account. This, says, Keynes is the main obstacle to the fall of the interest rate to a very low figure. A long-term rate of 2 per cent 'leaves more to fear than to hope, and offers, at the same time, a running yield which is only sufficient to offset a very small measure of fear'. Liquidity preference may then become 'virtually absolute' in the sense that almost everyone prefers holding cash to holding a debt. However, the flight to cash may occur at a higher rate of interest, as happened in the United States in 1931–2. In this event, the monetary authority will have lost effective control over the long rate. However, a monetary policy in which the public has confidence may succeed, whereas one judged 'experimental in character or easily liable to change' will fail.[17]

The theory of the rate of interest rounds off Keynes's story. Itself determined in the market for money, it helps fix, through its effect on the inducement to invest, the level of the community's income at any point in time; through its effect on the propensity to save out of a given income, it helps determine the size of the multiplier.

Keynes's 'general theory' brought together two ideas: (a) that the inducement to invest is normally too weak and the propensity to hoard too strong to provide for full employment of resources in normal times; and (b) that it was changes in output and employment, not in wages and interest rates, which adjusted the economy to any 'shock' to investment demand. The two propositions in combination suggest that a capitalist economy oscillates round levels of output and employment which are normally appreciably less than 'full'.

The second proposition is the essence of Keynes's 'short-period' theory. To convince his fellow-economists that it was the correct, or relevant, theory, Keynes had to show what was wrong with the orthodox story: he had to destroy 'classical' attempts to explain persisting unemployment, since the *fact* of it could not be denied. Classical economists argued that if money wages were flexible, employment would be preserved, whatever happened to money demand. The fact that wages were 'sticky' was then a sufficient explanation for how unemployment could develop and persist – at least till wage-adjustment came into play. This is what Keynes used to believe: he wrote as much in the *Economic Consequences of Mr. Churchill* (see above pp. 352–4). But this is *not* in the *General Theory*. Here the argument, in chapter 2, is that a reduction in money wages will not necessarily preserve employment, because the volume of employment depends on real wages, not money wages, and to the extent that a money wage reduction destroys purchasing power and thus lowers selling prices, it will do nothing to restore employers' profits: hence Keynes's pregnant remark in 1933: 'there may be no escape for labour from high real wages in a slump'. In his *Theory of Unemployment* (1933), Pigou had arged that with perfect wage flexibility, wages would fall more than employers' income (profits) – costs more than prices – thus preserving employment by reducing workers' real wages. Keynes finessed the argument by putting 'expected' in front of income. In chapter 19, he argued that the effect on employment of a fall in money wages would depend on what it did for profit *expectations*, that is to say, for the components of aggregate demand: consumption, investment, and interest rates. He concluded that an all-round reduction in money wages could improve employment on two conditions: (a) if it improved business confidence, and (b) by leading to a reduction in the demand for transactions balances (or payments for wages) relative to the stock of money. This would allow interest rates to fall. But (a) was highly uncertain, and a surer policy for achieving (b) would be to increase the stock of money: 'Only ... a foolish person ... would prefer a flexible wage policy to a flexible monetary policy.'[18] In short, the required reduction in the average real wage should be brought about by a policy of expanding aggregate demand, the result of which would be to raise prices. Involuntary unemployment exists, Keynes wrote, whenever a rise in prices relative to existing money wages would increase the quantity of employment.

Keynes's theory of employment does not, therefore, depend on money wages and prices being fixed. Nor did Keynes believe that wages and prices remained the same as aggregate demand was expanded: in fact it was part of his theory that prices as well as output rose when demand was stimulated in conditions of involuntary unemployment. In chapter 21, 'The Theory of Prices', Keynes acknowledges that rising employment will be accompanied by moderately rising prices, apart from any change in average wages rates, because labour is not all of one type, because there are likely to be supply 'bottlenecks' and because the cost of capital might rise faster than the cost of labour. Indeed, such a rise in the price level relative to wages was accepted by Keynes as a condition of recovery. But, in addition, recovery was likely to put upward pressure on money wage rates. Thus there are likely to be positions of 'semi-inflation' short of full employment. At full employment, the quantity theory of money comes into its own, with any further expansion in money demand going wholly in raising prices. This leaves indeterminate how any increase (or for that matter decrease) in money demand is divided between prices and output, though Keynes thought it reasonable to assume that 'a moderate [increase] in effective demand, coming on a situation in which there is widespread unemployment, may spend itself very little in raising prices and mainly in increasing employment'.[19] In 1939 he was half-persuaded by J. G. Dunlop and L. Tarshis that increasing returns to scale and imperfect competition would lower average unit costs as employment increased, obviating the need for prices to rise and real wages to fall.[20] Many post-war Keynesians thought that this factor would be sufficient to rob full-employment policies of any inflationary sting.

The upshot of Keynes's discussion of the wages problem was to knock on the head the 'classical' contention that, with money wage rates perfectly flexible, there is no obstacle to full employment at any level of money income. Rather Keynes showed that only one level of money income (or aggregate demand) will bring about a real wage consistent with full employment.

The other classical adjustment mechanism was the rate of interest. Keynes confessed that he found it 'difficult to state ... precisely' what the classical theory of the rate of interest was, but thought it was seen 'as the factor which brings the demand for investment and the willingness to save into equilibrium with one another'.[21] He dismissed this as a 'nonsense' theory, because it ignored the effect of a shift in the demand curve for capital on the income out of which savings are made. The received theory of interest only made sense on the assumption that income stayed constant as investment changed. 'The mistake originates', Keynes writes, 'from regarding interest as the reward for waiting as such, instead of as the reward for not-hoarding.... Only in the event of money being used solely for transactions and never as a store of value would [the classical] theory become appropriate.'[22]

Most of the rest of the *General Theory* is intended to be suggestive rather than conclusive. It contains a theory of economic history in which the weakness of the 'inducement to invest', owing to uncertainty, is presented as a permanent problem, and in which the nineteenth century is seen as a 'special case' in which the psychological propensities are in such a relation as to establish 'a reasonably satisfactory average level of employment'.[23] Keynes's conviction that 'the economic system in which we live' is characterised by fluctuations round a 'chronic condition of subnormal activity' is expressed in a number of places,[24] leading to the paradoxical conclusion that 'the remedy for the boom is not a higher rate of interest but a lower rate of interest! For that may enable the so-called boom to last.'[25] There are 'Notes on Mercantilism' in chapter 23 in which Keynes establishes a historical lineage for his concern with effective demand, and includes a defence of the medieval usury laws, much to the disgust of Roy Harrod. There are what Pigou called his 'Day of Judgment' reflections on the fate of mature capitalist economies if the state is not brought in to supplement failing private investment demand. One version of this 'secular stagnation' thesis, in chapter 17, 'The Essential Properties of Interest and Money', has particularly fascinated ecnomists of speculative bent. In this superb crystallisation of his deflationary vision Keynes suggests that the desire to accumulate money can knock out all other forms of production, so that wealthy societies, like King Midas, starve in cities of gold. The only remedy, Keynes suggests, is to make money go bad, like green cheese, so that people lose the desire to hold on to it.[26] After the Second World War, governments adopted his advice, bringing about a situation which Keynes – in another frame of mind – predicted in 1933: 'an entrepreneurial system which would be as prone to excessive demand and over-employment, as our actual system is to deficient demand and under-employment'.[27]

Keynes's last chapter, 'Concluding Notes on Social Philosophy', may be seen as an updating of his Middle Way ideas of the 1920s, suggested by his new theory. Excessive thriftiness could be tackled by redistributing spending

power to those with a high propensity to consume (the workers). The
rewards to hoarding could be lowered by fixing a low interest rate. This
would remove the scope for savers to exploit the scarcity value of capital:
'the euthanasia of the *rentier'* would be the consequence. Because monetary
policy was unlikely to be able to maintain an 'optimum rate of interest',
Keynes advocated a 'somewhat comprehensive socialisation of investment',
an ambiguous phrase which has to be interpreted in the light of his
endorsement ten years previously of the growth of the public utility sector
of the economy. With these central controls establishing a full-employment
volume of demand, there would be 'no more reason to socialise economic
life than there was before' – an endorsement of the private enterprise system
which fell some way short of full-blooded.[28] With demand-deficiency
removed, communism and fascism would lose their appeal. In a much-
quoted peroration, Keynes anticipated his own triumph by writing that 'the
power of vested interests is vastly exaggerated compared with the gradual
encroachment of ideas'.[29]

III. KEYNES AND THE CLASSICS

The publication of the *General Theory* was followed by a war of opinion
among economists. It was immediately perceived to be an immensely disturbing work. It was extensively reviewed in the leading journals as well as
the popular press all over the world. Although reactions to it were sharply
divided, there was no case of outright dismissal. Even the most hostile critics
recognised that Keynes had a case to be answered. It is impossible here to
do justice to the dust it kicked up. Essentially, though, there were two issues.
The first had to do with the relationship between Keynes's theory and
classical theory. This was mainly of interest to the older economists, who
almost unanimously rejected the new doctrine. The second was the internal
discussion between those – mainly younger economists – who accepted
the *General Theory* in some form or other. The question here was: was it to
be thought of as a policy machine, applicable to certain conditions which
happened to be the relevant ones, or the foundation of a genuinely new
economics? Keynes took an active, even heroic, part in both arguments. He
had, as he told Lydia, 'such a dreadfully controversial temperament'. However, he was more actively engaged in the first discussion than in the
second. This was a shame, because he made little progress in convincing
the older generation, while losing control over the interpretation of his
'revolution' by the young.

Keynes had severely mauled Pigou in his book, and Pigou struck back in a 'most dreadful' and 'profoundly frivolous' review in the *Economica* of May 1936. Keynes read it not without a touch of sadness: 'I wish all the same, that I had succeeded in conveying to him what my argument is; for I should be intensely interested to know what he thinks of it. But it is no use whistling a new tune to an organ grinder, when the organ builder and the musician one knew once are no longer alive.'[30]

Like other senior Cambridge economists, Pigou deplored Keynes's sarcastic sallies at the totems of his profession, especially Marshall – a technique, he suggested, he had learnt with *The Economic Consequences of the Peace*. 'Einstein actually did for Physics what Mr Keynes believes himself to have done for Economics. He developed a far-reaching generalisation, under which Newton's results can be subsumed as a special case. But he did not, in announcing his discovery, insinuate, through carefully barbed sentences, that Newton and those who had hitherto followed his lead were a gang of incompetent bunglers.'[31] Pigou deplored Keynes's habit of lumping together all economists who disagreed with him as 'classical' and attributing to them conclusions inconsistent with their theories. Keynes had accused Marshall and Pigou of abstracting from monetary disturbances: but this was simply part of the well-recognised technique of starting with simplifying assumptions. Keynes's own abandonment of it in order to 'reach a stage of generality so high that everything must be discussed at the same time', led to loose and inconsistent use of terms and the muddling up of stationary and moving states.

On the substance of the theory, Pigou rejected Keynes's view that the rate of interest is independent of the supply of saving or the demand for capital. If the demand for real capital increases, the rate of interest is bound to rise, unless kept artificially low by monetary policy.

> A decision to have one's teeth extracted is not in itself a decision to buy false ones. But few people in fact make the first decision without also making the second. Since false teeth are only wanted some months after the extraction, an increase in the number of extractions does not at once entail an addition to the capital stock of false teeth. But, none the less, a low propensity to retain one's natural teeth is 'conducive to the growth' of that capital stock.

Pigou rejected Keynes's stagnationist thesis, or what he called the Day of Judgement: 'An era that has witnessed the development of electrical apparatus, motor cars, aircraft, gramophone and wireless, to say nothing of tanks and other engines of war, is not one in which we can reasonably forecast a total disappearance of openings for new investment.' Pigou agreed that employment could and should be much fuller than it had recently been, but warned that, as employment improved, wage-earners would regain control over their own level of employment – that is, their own real wage. Any attempt by banking policy to force a higher level of employment than was desired, Pigou implied, would simply lead to inflation.[32]

Pigou's irritation is obvious, as is its cause. He had tried to refute the *General Theory* before it appeared, and thought he had: Keynes had simply ignored his argument. Pigou thought he had proved that when money wages fell, prices fell, but not in the same proportion, since nothing had happened to change non-wage-earners' income. This leads to an 'automatic' increase in employment because with the old volume of employment there would be a disequilibrium, prices being above marginal costs.[33] Keynes had not countered this directly, merely asserting that changes in money wages can affect employment only through their influence on cash balances and expectations. When Pigou restated his position in an article in the *Economic Journal* in 1937, it was denounced by Keynes and his disciples as 'outrageous rubbish', the product of incipient senility, and Pigou retracted. But Pigou went on gnawing at the problem and finally came up in 1941 with the 'Pigou effect', which *was* a theoretical answer to Keynes. An all-round deflation of money wages would restore full employment, not by directly pricing workers back into jobs, but by increasing the real value of money and thus the real wealth of bondholders, whose extra spending would offset the decline in spending elsewhere. By this time Keynes's theory had taken hold and no one was listening to Pigou. In fact, no one was really listening to Pigou in 1936. Attempts to salvage the old doctrines by adding arguments which no one had thought of before fell on deaf ears. Keynes's devastating charge that the old doctrine was *no use* in the circumstances fitted the intellectual and popular mood of the day.

Keynes had little correspondence with Pigou, since Pigou preferred to work out his ideas in isolation – unlike Hawtrey, who loved nothing better than to write huge nit-picking memoranda. As he had done with the *Treatise on Money*, Hawtrey began preparing a commentary on the *General Theory* for internal circulation in the Treasury as soon as he got proofs from Keynes in 1935; as he and Keynes discussed it, it grew longer and longer and was eventually published as a chapter in his book, *Capital and Employment*, in 1938. It was as dry and critical as a civil service paper can be, and Keynes was saintly to put up with it after his book was published, since Hawtrey made few positive statements of his own. However, Hawtrey made one point which was to crop up time and again in the disputes which followed. 'So far as the essentials of your argument are concerned,' he wrote to Keynes on 1 February 1936, 'your criticisms of the classical theory might have been confined to the single point that the theory assumes the effects of the speculative motive on cash balances to be negligible.' 'My dear Ralph,' Keynes wrote to him on 15 April, 'I find your [last] letter ... rather shattering. For, after reading it, I am now convinced that nothing that I can say will open your eyes – I do not say to the truth of my argument – but to what the essence of my argument, true or false, actually is. I doubt if we ought, either of us, to continue this correspondence any longer.'³⁴ But they did.

The breach between Keynes and Hubert Henderson, opened up over public works in 1930–1, was widened by the *General Theory*. Henderson had resigned as secretary of the Economic Advisory Council in 1934 to take up a research fellowship at All Souls' College, Oxford. He had written a short review of Keynes's book for the *Spectator* of 4 February 1936, but he reserved his main attack for a meeting of the Marshall Society at Cambridge on 2 May. Following this meeting, Keynes wrote to Lydia:

> Hubert came to the Marshall Society yesterday, with Dennis in the chair, to read his paper against my book. I was astonished at the violence of his emotion against it; he thinks it a poisonous book; yet when it came to the debate there was very little of the argument he was really prepared to oppose. He came off badly in the debate with Joan and Alexander and myself barking round him. The undergraduates enjoyed the cock fight outrageously. One got the impression that he was not much interested in pure economic theory, but much dislikes for emotional or political reasons some of the practical conclusions to which my arguments seemed to point. As a theoretical attack there was almost nothing to answer.³⁵

Keynes's view was not shared by the chairman, Dennis Robertson. 'Of course, I think you have much the best of it,' he wrote to Henderson after reading his summary of the argument at the meeting, prepared immediately after.³⁶ The strength of Henderson's feeling can be gauged by a letter he wrote to Harrod on 2 April 1936:

> I have allowed myself to be inhibited for many years from publishing many things by a desire not to quarrel in public with Maynard ... but it is impossible to accept the position that Maynard is to be allowed to deliver the most extravagant attacks upon the main body of orthodox economic theory, conveying the impression that everything that has been said hitherto is nonsense and that here is a great new light to which the heathen must be converted, and that others must abstain from effective reply to avoid the impression of economists quarrelling. You see, I don't believe there is a great new light at all. I regard Maynard's book, as I say in my paper, as a farrago of confused sophistication, and I find intensely exasperating the tacit assumption that prevails in certain circles that those who do not accept its general doctrine are to be regarded as intellectually inferior beings.³⁷

Henderson's attack was directed against what he saw as the two main fallacies of the *General Theory*: its theory of employment and its theory of interest. His method was largely historical and institutional, which is perhaps why Keynes and his supporters felt that 'as a theoretical attack there was almost nothing to answer'. Henderson upheld Marshall's short-period/

long-period distinction. Natural forces worked clumsily and in the long run, and *laissez-faire* was therefore unviable. But that was no reason for dismissing the classical theory as nonsense. Specifically, he denied that 'in the ordinary working of the economic system there is a chronic and general deficiency of effective demand, and that in this is to be found the main explanation of unemployment'. He said there was a 'minimum' (what would later be called 'natural') rate of unemployment (which he estimated at 6 per cent) on which was superimposed structural and cyclical unemployment. Keynes's attempt to create boom conditions 'stronger and more prolonged than almost any of which we have experience' would lead to inflation followed by an inevitable reaction.[38]

Secondly, Henderson denied that the rate of interest was unaffected by the propensity to consume or the demand for capital, citing the fact that interest rates fall in depressions and rise in booms. Conversely, even large changes in the quantity of money had had no lasting effects on interest rates. This suggested that interest-rate behaviour was adequately explained by the 'classical' forces of productivity and thrift; it also cast doubt on Keynes's contention that 'the rate of interest can be brought down to as low a level as is desired and kept down by increasing the quantity of money sufficiently'. Henderson summed up the orthodox theory as follows: 'The actual movements of the rate of interest are determined by the relations of demand and supply in what is sometimes called the capital market. Orthodox economic theory asserts that the fundamental factors that lie behind supply and demand in the capital market are savings and investment.'[39]

The Cambridge meeting was followed by a painful exchange of letters between the two economists, which Keynes broke off. Henderson wrote to Keynes, much as Ricardo had written to Malthus, 'Your mood nowadays seems to be one of saying "I am not interested in the long run: it never happens." Whereas it seems to me essential to any clearness of economic thought to distinguish between the immediate and the ultimate consequences of any change.' Keynes's real crime, in Henderson's eyes, was to have destroyed the defences which classical theory, in separating out monetary from real factors, had built up against inflation. He seemed curiously unworried about the huge scale of unemployment.[40] Of the four senior economists, Henderson most explicitly upheld what Friedman was to preach in the 1960s: that monetary forces have no (long-run) real effects.

Robertson, too, was brooding about how to respond to the *General Theory*. On 19 February 1936, he informed Henderson that he had 'cravenly' refused to review it for the *Economist* (Austin Robinson did it instead), but might write 'one or two articles later on the points of substance, eschewing the need to assess the thing as a whole'. Robertson's draft article was criticised by both Sraffa and Henderson. As a result he had decided to rewrite it from the start. 'It's a disaster', he told Henderson, 'that the case for relative sanity here should be in such stale & incompetent hands.'

The intermittent bouts of correspondence between Keynes and Robertson in 1936–8, in turn reproachful and joking, reveal the wreckage of their friendship. On his way to America in September 1936 Robertson wrote to Keynes, 'it's no use pretending I like it [the *General Theory*] much better, or that I don't agree more or less with most of the Prof.'s review....' He was preparing some notes which he hoped would be published. 'Whether afterwards you will feel that the sort of tabu which has arisen between us can profitably be removed, I don't know.... perhaps we could meet rather oftener than we have done this year, and talk about drama and foreign policy ... and even ephemeral economic situations?'[41]

Keynes wrote:

It's awfully difficult to keep off Economics but *I* don't, dear Dennis, feel differently, and we must try to come to closer touch again. But indeed it is easy for *me*! For whilst, putting it at its worst, I only think you very obstinate, you and Hubert think me very wicked! – for being so cocksure and putting all the driving force I know how behind arguments which for me are of painfully practical importance.[42]

They had a long talk at King's on 11 October, Dennis 'very sweet and charming and rather well, I think, though also dotty'.

Since his debates with Keynes in the 1920s, Robertson had developed his own theory of the rate of interest in an attempt to reconcile the 'classical' view of interest as being determined by the forces of productivity and thrift and the insight of his *Banking Policy and the Price Level* that the power of the banks to create credit can cause saving to diverge from investment. In 1934 he recast the distinction between the 'natural' and the 'market' rate of interest. This was the 'loanable funds' theory of the rate of interest with which Robertson 'confronted Keynes', a 'composite made up of savings and ... bank money ...'[43]

Robertson's 'Some Notes on Mr Keynes's General Theory of Employment', published in the November 1936 issue of the *Quarterly Journal of Economics*, expresses his two main criticisms of it, from which he never subsequently deviated: the static nature of Keynes's analysis, and Keynes's ignoring of any influence on the rate of interest of the forces of productivity and thrift.

The publication of Robertson's 'Notes' prompted Keynes to write to him on 13 December: 'there is not a great deal that is fundamental which divides us'. However, he vehemently denied that his interest-rate theory was simply a 'backdoor' statement of the classical theory. By accepting that the rate of interest is determined by 'the demand for cash relative to its supply', it was Robertson, rather, who had 'come right over to the liquidity theory of the rate of interest'.[44] Keynes ended his letter on a note of playful reproach. 'The last thing I should accuse you of is being classical or orthodox. But you won't slough your skins, like a good snake! You walk about with the whole lot on from the earliest until the latest, until you can scarcely breathe, saying that, because your greatcoat was once your vest, your present vest and your greatcoat are the same.'[45]

Robertson's reply to Keynes on 29 December reveals the depth of his dissatisfaction with Keynes's controversial *method*:

> I do venture to think that with each new skin you are apt to put on a pair of blinkers, which makes it hard for you to see what other people, especially Pigou, are at.... Both over the *Treatise* and this book I have gone through real intellectual torment trying to make up my mind whether, as you often seem to claim, there is some new piece on the board or rather a rearrangement, which seems to you superior, of existing pieces....
>
> To begin with, may we not, for purposes of serious discussion, abandon the (journalistic) practice of labelling *authors* as 'classical' or the reverse, and use the word 'classical', if at all, to signify an analysis which assumes the rewards, real and money, of factors to be plastic and consequently all resources to be employed.

Robertson went on to say that the abandonment of these assumptions in the study of dynamic situations did not require the abandonment of 'the concept of the rate of interest as the *price* of the use of a certain factor of production per unit of time, that factor being what Marshall calls "free or floating capital" [and] what I call "loanable funds".' When income is stationary 'the supply of loanable funds is, on my definitions, identical with the supply of savings; when income changes they diverge by the amount of bank money, or hoarding or dishoarding'. In both types of situation 'the rate of interest *is* the price at which the quantity of loanable funds demanded is equal to the quantity supplied', though the disposition to hoard must be taken into account as an influence on it.[46]

After conceding to Robertson (and also to Ohlin) in June 1937 that 'planned investment ... may have to secure its "financial provision" *before* the investment takes place'[47] (for the context of this concession see pp. 569–70), Keynes now had reason to feel that 'the strictly intellectual differences between us are probably very small indeed at bottom'.

This proved too optimistic. Articles and rejoinders flowed continuously in the *Economic Journal*. The correspondence between Keynes and Robertson, and their private comments on each other, grew increasingly testy. Robertson accused Keynes of 'successive over-emphasis', of casting a 'fatally distorting beam on one object after another in succession'.[48] The last thing Keynes wanted was to be caught up once more in the weed and tangle of 'forced savings' from which he had so painfully extricated himself. He found Robertson's restatement of his loanable funds theory, which appeared in the *Economic Journal* of June 1938 'completely worthless and, what is more, intolerably boring'.[49] On 25 July 1938 he wrote to Robertson: 'Our forebears believed that ... the rate of interest depends on the supply of saving. My theory is that it depends on the supply of inactive money. There is no possible reconciliation between these views'. Finally, Pigou, as the professor at Cambridge, decreed that the controversy must cease and that Robertson must get on with 'constructive work of his own', rather than spend all his time criticising 'Mr Keynes on this and that'.[50] Robertson was starting to feel a 'back number' at Cambridge. Research students, he told Hubert Henderson, wanted to work with Kahn and Joan Robinson, not him. In 1935, Keynes reported Robertson 'dangerously near trying to prevent [Joan Robinson] from lecturing'; quarrels with Keynes and Keynes's young Turks, especially Joan Robinson, brought him close to psychological breakdown.[51] In 1938 he left Cambridge to take up a chair at London University, driven out by the increasing hostility of Keynes's disciples.

The leading American reviewers, Alvin Hansen, F. W. Taussig, Joseph Schumpeter, Frank Knight and Jacob Viner, the last two from Chicago, echoed the main themes of the senior British economists: Keynes's liquidity-preference theory was a modification of, not an alternative to, the classical theory of interest, capable perhaps of explaining the emergence of mass unemployment, not of determining a position of 'under-employment equilibrium'; he had misrepresented classical theory; policies based on his doctrines would lead to inflation. Viner, the most sympathetic of the senior American economists, wrote: 'In a world organized in accordance with Keynes's specifications there would be a constant race between the printing press and the business agents of the trade unions, with the problem of unemployment largely solved if the printing press could maintain a constant lead....'[52] Knight argued that socialising investment meant 'taking it out of business and putting it into politics'.[53] For Schumpeter, Keynes's book marked a 'scientific regression' in its mixing up of science and politics. His 'under-employment equilibrium' assumed 'fixed production functions'. His advice expressed the 'attitude of a decaying civilization'.[54] Viner's was the only American criticism to which Keynes made a public reply. Privately he wrote: 'Indeed with Professor Knight's two main conclusions, namely, that my book has caused him intense irritation, and that he had great difficulty understanding it, I am in agreement'.[55]

The only other set of reactions worth noticing comes from Sweden. Keynes gave a 'wonderful talk' on his theory to the Economic Club in Stockholm in September 1936 *en route* with Lydia to Leningrad to visit her family; in turn, Bertil Ohlin used the Marshall Lectures at Cambridge in November 1936 to give an account of the Swedish disequilibrium method, derived from Knut Wicksell, which Keynes had briefly espoused in the *Treatise*. The Swedish economists were particularly concerned to show adjustment as a *process* which reconciles inconsistent plans; their method more naturally brings out the role of both output and prices in adjusting economies to shocks, without implying a sharp cleavage between them.[56]

Keynes failed to persuade them to give up their own style of theorising. Gunnar Myrdal later wrote that 'the Keynesian revolution ... was mainly an Anglo-American occurrence. In Sweden ... Keynes' works were read as interesting and important contributions ... but not in any sense as a revolutionary breakthrough'.[57]

In Britain and America, the Keynes versus Classics debate kept coming back to the role of the rate of interest in adjusting the economy to 'shocks'. The senior economists wanted to preserve some adjustment role for 'natural' forces in order to limit government intervention and block off inflation. They clung to the notion of the self-adjusting economy because they mistrusted Keynes's theory of the self-adjusting politician.

IV. WHOSE *GENERAL THEORY*?

More important than the passionate, expiring cries of the older generation in deciding the fate of the *General Theory* was the way in which it was received, and interpreted, by the young economists. On both sides of the Atlantic it was primarily viewed as an engine of policy, capable, as Keynes's student Lorie Tarshis put it, of restoring and maintaining prosperity 'without the support of prison camps [and] executions'.[58] It was less important to have an interminable debate about the causes of unemployment, than to know that mass unemployment could occur and persist, and that something could be done about it. Theoretical requirements could be met by means of *ad hoc* assumptions. As Paul Samuelson later put it, 'Had Keynes begun his first few chapters with the simple statement that he found it realistic to assume that modern capitalist societies had money wage rates that were sticky and resistant to downward movements, most of his insights would have remained just as valid....'[59] This became the standard form in which the Keynesian Revolution took root in the pragmatic American soil – a soil already prepared, to some extent, for its reception by home-grown discussion of stabilisation policy, in Chicago and elsewhere. The key moment was the conversion of Alvin Hansen, a respected economics professor of fifty, to the new doctrines. His seminar at Harvard became the focal point for the study and dissemination of Keynes's ideas. The recruitment of the young Harvard activists to Washington gave a boost to Roosevelt's languishing New Deal. John Kenneth Galbraith has written: 'By the end of the 1930s [Lauchlin] Currie [Roosevelt's main economic adviser] had established an informal network of converts extending into all the fiscally significant agencies'.[60]

Among the younger British economists the theoretical issues raised by the *General Theory* were not disposed of in such a cavalier way, but the thrust of interpretation was the same. The architects of the policy-oriented approach were John Hicks, Roy Harrod, James Meade and Nicholas Kaldor, who moved quickly from reconciling Keynes's theory with classical doctrines to developing a model of the *General Theory* which could be taught, assimilated, and used for policy.

Keynes's own attitude to the management of his revolution was ambiguous. He had aimed to capture economic reality in all its richness and complexity *and* to provide a tool for policy. Both were elements in his persuasive strategy. From this set of aims which he held in balance in his own thought, two types of theory eventually emerged, both children of the *General Theory*. The first is what George Shackle called an 'economics of disorder', dominated by unruly, uncertain and fluctuating expectations and relationships. The second is an economics of given expectations and mathematical functions fit for policy manipulation. Keynes acquiesced in the second for pedagogical and and policy purposes, while at the same time warning that 'as soon as one is dealing with the influence of expectations and of transitory experience, one is ... outside the realm of the formally exact'.[61]

Ironically, it was Hicks, who had played no part in the making of the *General Theory*, who was chiefly responsible for the form in which it was disseminated. His two-curve diagram – IS-LM – was first published in his famous paper 'Mr Keynes and the Classics: A Suggested Reinterpretation' in *Econometrica* in April 1937. But as Warren Young shows in his fascinating book, *Interpreting Mr. Keynes*, Hicks was building on mathematical (but non-diagrammatic) models of the *General Theory* presented by Harrod and Meade at the Econometric Conference held at Oxford in September 1936. (Other young economists had also been quick to convert Keynes's model into equational form.) What Hicks did was to convert Keynes's theory into a special case of a generalised theory of employment, which could be presented as a set of simultaneous equations, devoid of causal significance, but whose solution could include any number of equilibria, depending on the behavioural assumptions adopted.

The Oxford meeting, which Young claims to be 'perhaps the most important meeting in the history of economics',[62] crystallised what he calls a split in the 'General Theory Group' over 'whether the approach they were developing was a determinate system which could be expressed in the form of simultaneous equations or a system fraught with uncertainty and animal spirits'. Kahn and Joan Robinson (who did not attend the Oxford meeting) saw the *General Theory* as a revolutionary break with orthodoxy, the Oxford economists 'as not unreconcilable with the orthodox mainstream. ...' The triumph of the 'mathematically elegant' approach was due to the fact that working economists did not know how to digest the *General Theory* until Hicks's diagram told them how to see it, and also that Hicks's model 'was the conceptual manifestation of the quest for continuity and certainty. ...'[63]

Hicks, or perhaps ultimately Keynes, reconciled revolution and orthodoxy in a double sense: in terms of the discipline of economics, and in terms of the continuity of political and social institutions. The determinate system in which the 'authority' could act on the multiplier by fiscal policy also gave economists a potentially key position at the centre of government.

After the Oxford meeting, Kahn and Joan Robinson, who had played such a large part in the genesis of the *General Theory*, were edged out of the development of the Keynesian Revolution. Kahn later regarded the reduction of the *General Theory* to 'diagrams and bits of algebra' as a great tragedy. Keynes's 'insistence on the overwhelming importance of expectations, highly subject to risk and uncertainty, was one of his biggest contributions. This completely undermines the prevalent idea – for which Keynes's attempt at simplification is responsible – that [his] schedules can be regarded as stable relationships handed down from heaven.'[64] However, it has to be said that there is no evidence that Kahn and Joan Robinson protested *at the time* against the reduction of the *General Theory* to 'diagrams and bits of algebra', or to the apparent 'capture' of the revolution by Hicks, Harrod and Meade. Kahn's lack of public involvement in these discussions is striking. Perhaps he felt inhibited by the Master's own position.

When Harrod sent him a copy of his own paper in advance of the Oxford meeting, Keynes seemed to accept Harrod's implicit case for pursuing a different strategy from his own in developing his doctrine:

> You don't feel the weight of the past as I do. One cannot shake off a pack one has never properly worn. And probably your ignoring all this is a better plan than mine. For experience seems to show that people are divided between the old ones whom nothing will shift ... and the young ones who have not been properly brought up and believe nothing in particular. The particles of light seen in escaping from a tunnel are interesting neither to those who mean to stay there nor to those who have never been there! I have no companions, it seems, in my own generation, either of earliest teachers or of earliest pupils; I cannot in thought help being somewhat bound to them....[65]

It is as though he was saying: if this is where the young wanted to take his ideas, so be it. If he resented Harrod not sharing some of his deepest intuitions, he did not show it.

A copy of Hicks's paper reached Keynes in October 1936. He replied on 31 March 1937 – *six months* later, a rather astonishing lapse of time for such a punctilious correspondent: 'I found it very interesting and really have next to nothing to say by way of criticism.'[66]

What he did was to go on fighting for his own vision. For example, in the published version of his Stockholm address of September 1936, he wrote: 'For the rate of interest and the marginal efficiency of capital are particlarly concerned with the *indefinite* character of actual expectations....

They belong, that is, to a stage of our theory *when we are no longer assuming a definite and calculable future'* (emphasis added).⁶⁷ In February 1937 he restated his theory in a way which brought out better than his book had its epistemological assumptions. This article in the *Quarterly Journal of Economics*, entitled 'The General Theory of Employment', is of particular importance because it was Keynes's first published piece of post-*General Theory* theoretical writing. In it he attempted to answer not just the criticisms of the older generation, particularly those of Robertson and Viner, but also implicitly the attempts of his younger followers to bury his vision in algebra. For fundamentalist Keynesians it remains the canonical statement of the Master's position.

Keynes's restatement of the 'essence' of the *General Theory* is concerned particularly with the effects of uncertainty on investment and the rate of interest. His objection to the classical theory rests on its assumption of a calculable future in which 'risks were capable of an exact actuarial computation'. Actually, he says, 'we have, as a rule, only the vaguest idea of any but the most direct consequences of our acts'. This makes wealth 'a peculiarly unsuitable subject for the methods of classical economic theory'. It is uncertainty which explains why liquidity, or money, carries a premium. Why else, he asks, should anyone 'outside a lunatic asylum wish to use money as a store of wealth?' To be sure, economic agents use varied 'techniques' or 'conventions' to save their faces as rational people, the chief of which is that the future will be like the present. But being so flimsily based on knowledge, they are liable to be swept away at any turn in the news. Keynes then goes on to say that were 'our knowledge of the future calculable', there would be no need 'to work out a theory of the demand and supply of output *as a whole'*, because demand would never be a problem. His remedies were 'on a different plane from the diagnosis.... They are ... subject to all kinds of special assumptions and are necessarily related to the particular conditions of the time'.⁶⁸

Finally, there is Keynes's debate in 1938 with the Dutch statistician Jan Tinbergen on the value of econometrics. The League of Nations had sponsored a book by Tinbergen to test various hypotheses about the trade cycle. Keynes attacked Tinbergen's efforts with an astonishingly fierce barrage of arguments (and some excellent jokes) on statistical philosophy. His main point is that economics, because of the nature of its material, is a 'moral science', requiring the constant exercise of judgement by the economist in choosing and applying models. He queried Tinbergen's logic in applying the 'method of multiple correlation' to non-homogeneous material and his assumption of fixed coefficients for long series.

> Is it claimed that there is a likelihood that the equations will work approximately *next* time?... One can always cook a formula to fit moderately well a limited range of past facts. But what does this

prove?... What place is left for expectations and the state of confidence relating to the future? What place is allowed for non-numerical factors, such as inventions, politics, labour troubles, wars, earthquakes, financial crises?[69]

He warned against the danger of filling in real numbers for the variable functions 'which one can be sure will not apply next time'. As he explained to Harrod on 16 July:

It is as though the fall of the apple to the ground depended on the apple's motives, on whether it is worth while falling to the ground, and whether the ground wanted the apple to fall, and on mistaken calculations on the part of the apple as to how far it was from the centre of the earth.[70]

Harrod defended Tinbergen by saying that he did not neglect unmeasureable variables but brought them in as random shocks. Keynes was not persuaded. In his published review of Tinbergen's book he repeated that Tinbergen's method left out any causal role for psychology, expectations, and unexpected events; that it depended on inadequate statistics, ignored the need for judgment in specifying the variables, and neglected the possible mutual reactions among the variables themselves. He concluded with the 'strange reflection' that Tinbergen's work was likely to be 'the principal activity and *raison d'être* of the League of Nations' in 1939.[71]

The nature of Keynes's attempt to reconcile the two divergent strands of his *General Theory* is a strange story in itself. The book is, on the one hand, an attempt to explain why output and employment are subject to large fluctuations. For this Keynes needs uncertain expectations. As he says, with a calculable future there would be no problem of demand. On the other hand, he attempts to provide a model suitable for policy-makers to act on. For this he needs a model which assumes a 'definite and calculable future'. But the two requirements are logically inconsistent. The short-period is not a determinate state of affairs but an analytic fiction. Policy is projected into an actual world of fluctuating events and uncertain expectations which are 'frozen' by assumption. What then becomes of the theory of the determinate multiplier? Keynes's continual warnings against the 'blind, mechanical' manipulation of his theory for policy purposes was certainly needed. But its very formalisation at the hands of Hicks and others, of which he approved, and in which expectations are taken as given, was bound to invest it with a 'spurious precision'.

These were problems for the future. By the end of the 1930s, the Keynesian Revolution was on the offensive, the classical system in retreat. Some theoretical honours had been salvaged, but there was a growing conviction that the world was more like that of Keynes than that of the Classics. The collapse of the boom in 1937–8 long before full employment had been regained in either Britain or the United States seemed to vindicate Keynes's view that unmanaged capitalism could not even secure a reasonably satisfactory average of employment over the cycle. However, Keynes's successes had been achieved at great personal cost. He was an affectionate man, and his quarrels with his Cambridge friends and colleagues, especially Dennis Robertson, wounded him, as indeed they did Robertson. G. E. Moore had taught him to value friendship above almost all else. Was his attack on what these friends held dear, in an effort to save the world from further misery, an example of what he called his 'favourite dilemma – the difficulty or impossibility of both being good and doing good'?

PART SEVEN

PAYING FOR THE WAR

Well here am I, like a recurring decimal, doing very similar work in the same place for a similar emergency.

J. M. Keynes to Russell Leffingwell, 1 July 1942

31

Curing Invalidism

I. WONKY BREATHING MUSCLES

It was not in Keynes's nature to take life more easily. He loved nothing better than to sit in his study scribbling. But the structure of his life was built on activity, and his activities had a momentum of their own. The publication of the *General Theory* had coincided with the completion of the Cambridge Arts Theatre. On Monday 3 February 1936, he and Lydia were in their box with the Vice-Chancellor for the opening. In the Ibsen cycle which started on 17 February, Lydia played Nora Helmer in *A Doll's House* and Hilda Wangel in *The Master Builder*. These were the best of Lydia's stage performances, the critics favourable, even Bloomsbury enthusiastic. Here was another of Keynes's dreams come true, another achievement to be ticked off. For the next year he spent most of his time managing his two creations, his mind switching from 'controversialising' with his fellow-economists to promoting Lydia's stage career and getting decent food and service in the theatre restaurant. Nor did his building work stop with the Arts Theatre. With Wall Street continuing to boom Keynes had money to spare. Tilton was rebuilt by George Kennedy 'on a magnificent scale', with a new wing, a spacious new hall and landing and a bathroom for each guest. On 13/14 July he bought forty lots at a sale of Isaac Newton's papers at Sotheby's and started preparing notes for a biographical study.

By the autumn the food at the Arts Theatre restaurant was no better: there was no tinge, Keynes informed Lydia, 'of French cooking from the alleged elderly French chef'. Kahn was doing 'wonders' with the college accounts, but he still had to do one horrid table of figures for himself: after three hours he was 'so exhausted that I cooked it and made it come right by cheating. I simply couldn't go on any longer looking for the mistake.'[1] His forgetfulness was becoming a problem. He left his glasses in London; he forgot his cigarettes when he went to dine with Victor and Barbara Roths-child. 'I was convinced that I had stuck them in my pocket – I was so looking forward to smoking after B[arbara]'s beautiful coffee out of Venetian cups – and then nothing! I was so disappointed that I searched in my pockets for ten minutes in vain.' There were other signs of time passing. His Cambridge tailor, 'The Bodger', no longer made his special socks; the Avoca collars he had worn since childhood were extinct. 'It is dreadful to be so antediluvian.' On the other hand, he was sleeping well, feeling much less tired, and 'full of bright ideas, scribbling away and having at last made a beginning on my Foxwell' – a biographical essay he had undertaken following Foxwell's death.[2] He sat next to W. H. Auden at dinner in hall:

> He was most charming, intelligent, straightforward, youthful, a sort of senior undergraduate; altogether delightful, but but but – his finger nails are eaten to the bones with dirt and wet, one of the worst cases ever, like a preparatory schoolboy. So the infantilism is not altgether put on. It was most disconcerting. For all other impressions so favourable. But those horrid fingers cannot lie. They must be believed. I talked to him about F.6 [*The Ascent of F.6*, the play he had written with Christopher Isherwood]. He has re-written the last part and would like us to look at it again.

Auden's fingernails, Keynes thought, explained 'something unsatisfactory in his work'.[3]

Maynard's mind may have been as bright as ever, but his body had started to fail. For some years he had suffered from what he called his 'intercostal' pains, which shot all round his chest. He interpreted them as rheumatic, and connected them with his attack of pleurisy in October 1931. There was a history of tooth and gum trouble. He started to complain of breathlessness, not only after exertion, but when lying in bed, as he had experienced as a boy when winded at football, though not so acute. He had a severe attack of influenza with fever at Tilton over the Christmas vacation. 'Maynard is better,' wrote a worried Lydia to Florence on 5 January 1937. 'To-day he walked beautifully in the morning, slept for ¾ of an hour afterwards – lately he seems like his old self, perhaps he works a little less.' From Cambridge, he wrote to Lydia on 22 January, 'My health is progressing, though I feel very tired about six o'clock and my breath is terribly short and painful if I run upstairs or walk fast (which probably means that rheumatism in the chest is not far below the surface).' These were tell-tale signs of coronary artery insufficiency. 'My beloved girl,' he wrote two days later,

> My breathing muscles were so wonky to-day that I only just managed to walk to Harvey Rd. So Fil in a loud voice, strong with power, and a most tyrannical manner insisted on sending for his favourite doctor to see me. He has given me two kinds of tablets to swallow and an ointment and recommends the lamp. I am perfectly well so long as I sit in a warm room, and the weakness only comes on when I walk in the cold East wind. So don't worry. The complaint is exactly what I thought it was – rheumatism in the little muscles of the chest *plus* post-influenza. . . . My head is in good form.

Keynes went on working hard, writing articles for *The Times* on 'How to Avoid a Slump', preparing a lecture for the Eugenics Society on 'Some

Consequences of a Declining Population'. Delivered on 16 February 1937, this latter is one of his most sizzling concoctions, in which he examines the implications of a declining population for economies faced with a chronic problem of deficient demand. Hitherto he had believed with Malthus that increasing population kept societies poor. Now he saw population growth as a major cause of their prosperity. Keynes's lecture anticipated Harrod's 1939 essay on dynamic theory.[4] Lydia was also on stage, in Cambridge and London, as Célimène in Molière's *The Misanthrope*, Raymond Mortimer in the *New Statesman* noticing that her voice had 'improved enormously, both in power and variety'. Once more, Keynes had involved himself in all the details.

Keynes had been taking Florence's advice and eating less. He didn't feel the 'intercostals' until he walked, but still couldn't walk more than a quarter of a mile without pain. Maynard 'only needs a little rest and a little gambling at the Casino', Lydia told Florence as they left for Cannes on 13 March, Maynard, of course, with a briefcase full of work, including his Stockholm lecture, which he was preparing for publication. But his chest was no better, and he could not walk more than a few hundred yards. There were spasms of two or three minutes, and two days after arrival he had an attack lasting three-quarters of an hour. As soon as they returned, Maynard wrote to Uncle Walrus (Florence's brother, Sir Walter Langdon-Brown) with a detailed account of his symptoms and their history:

> Mother wants me to consult you about my chest. . . . Some four years ago [it was five and a half years] I had an acute attack of intercostal rheumatism with a slight temperature, and remained in bed for some time, being attended by L. B. Cole of Cambridge.* At that time I had a good deal of pain from time to time simply lying in bed. After I had recovered from that, I had no noticeable trouble before, say, six months ago. At the end of the summer, however, and during the winter I was rather liable to an attack of breathlessness and discomfort in the chest on starting a walk. If, however, I rested a little and persevered, this would pass off. . . . The pain, however, such as it was, was exactly the same in quality as that which I now have more acutely.

Uncle Walrus examined him on 31 March and had an X-ray of his chest taken next day. He reported on 8 April that Maynard's recent influenza 'has had a slightly poisonous effect on certain muscles in the heart or on the chest wall, but there is no evidence of any organic change'. Every precaution must be taken not to overtax the heart muscle 'while it is being given time to recover from the infection'. He prescribed daily doses of 'an improvement on luminal ... in conjunction with a heart tonic ... called protheonal'. A few days later Maynard complained to Langdon-Brown that

---

* Dr Leslie Cole was a physician at Addenbrooke's Hospital, Cambridge.

the medicine was making him drowsy and unfit for work. What Uncle Walrus failed to discover were the streptococcal bacteria swarming around in Maynard's mouth.

Keynes returned to Cambridge, where, after lunch on 4 May, he had five spasms of a different character. But he carried on until he collapsed, apparently at Harvey Road, on Whit Sunday, 16 May. On 20 May, Langdon-Brown reported to Florence that 'his heart muscle is somewhat damaged and it is vital that he should have a complete investigation and a long rest however difficult it may appear to be'. But he still had no idea of the extent of the problem. Keynes, he wrote, had suffered a 'pseudo angina'; the 'prognosis is a good one, sudden death not occurring'. Maynard stayed in bed in Harvey Road for over a month, nursed by Florence and Lydia: he still managed to write a letter to *The Times* on the gold problem. Friends commiserated, Virginia Woolf writing to Lydia on 6 June, 'I hope he won't get stronger *mentally* as his normal strength is quite enough for me.' On 18 June he was driven to Ruthin Castle in north Wales, a private sanatorium for the sickly rich. F. C. Scott, his co-director of the Provincial, had recommended it as 'supreme in diagnosis' if rather primitive in its methods of treatment.

II. TYPES OF INVALIDISM

Started at Duff House, Banff, in Scotland, the sanatorium had moved to more accessible premises in 1923, and now advertised itself as a 'clinic or private hospital for the scientific investigation and treatment of illness, and for the maintenance of health ... the first institution of its kind in the United Kingdom'. It comprised three groups of buildings set in 475 acres, including the old castle ruins, with sixty-four patient rooms, as well as a grand reception room, library, dining room, consulting rooms, laboratories, kitchens, larders, staff rooms, offices, diet rooms, an X-ray department and medical baths. The Vale of Clwyd enjoyed what the brochure called 'a mild and equable but not relaxing climate', being buffeted by mountain and moorland air, supplemented by breezes from the Irish Sea. But 'the friends and relations of patients', it promised, 'will find abundant interest in the neighbourhood. The town has a nine hole golf course....' The weekly charge, inclusive of meals, nursing and 'ordinary X-ray examinations', was a minimum of 15 guineas. Keynes stayed in the superior Castle Wing, in a huge, red-carpeted room with views on to the Clwydian hills and with a private bathroom. He would have paid 30 guineas a week. He spent over three months at Ruthin altogether, from 18 June to 25 September. He then went back to Tilton, where he was based for a further eighteen months in a twilight between sickness and health.

What exactly was wrong with him? The enquiry was conducted by the magnificent Sir Edmund Spriggs, KCVO, who had been consulting physician to King Edward VII and was now consulting senior physician at Ruthin; he was assisted by the resident physician, Sydney Wentworth Patterson, a bacteriologist. The official diagnosis was 'coronary disease, large heart and aorta; septic tonsils ... The condition is due to coronary and myocardial trouble probably associated with the tonsils.' The doctors discovered, Maynard told his brother Geoffrey, that his tonsils were in a 'shocking condition, covered with pus to the naked eye and creeping apparently with animals called fusillaria.... I gather he [Patterson] took the view that there was enough poison distilling in the system here to account for all the other symptoms. They have been tackling this by painting the tonsils ... with a preparation of organic arsenic.' The Ruthin doctors, that is, had diagnosed subacute bacterial endocarditis, caused by streptococcus viridans, green bacteria which lodge in and attack the valves of the heart, or, in Lydia's phrase, 'dripped poison into the systeme'. This diagnosis suggests that Keynes had been in trouble since the bouts of intercostal rheumatism he had been experiencing since 1931. Unfortunately, no known treatment of it was effective. Antibiotics had not yet been invented. Neither treating the throat with arsenic (more familiar in treating syphilis), nor applying Mandl's paint, a compound of iodine, which succeeded Keynes's arsenic preparation, would have cleared up the bacterial infection. So the Ruthin diagnosticians fell back on the two most ancient of remedies: rest and hope.

Keynes spent his first six weeks at Ruthin in bed, Lydia lodging in the town of Ruthin in a 'mousy room' in the Castle Hotel, with a 'hen party of Castle widows'. Except for a couple of short visits, Florence Keynes tactfully left Lydia in charge. Lydia sent her reports on Maynard's condition, in her own inimitable style. On 19 July she told Florence that 'the throat does not smell any more for the last three days, it shows the grubs are cornered and destroyed'. Once Maynard was allowed up, and when the unrelaxing weather allowed, they went for drives, interspersed by walks. By 13 September he was sleeping 'without a dope', but fretting to leave. 'The change will be welcome for both of us, because my nerves are getting very ragged, and sometimes I simply break up in torrents of tears.'

Keynes could not remain quiet. 'I fancy the embargo on movements of the mind may be removed before the embargo on movements of the body', he scribbled to Lydia on 29 June. 'At least I hope so! For my mind is terribly active. They can take away drink from patients who drink too much. But they can't take my thoughts away from me. When the Great White Chief comes round this afternoon, I shall have to confess that I have written a letter this morning to the Chancellor of the Exchequer.'

'Lying in bed, I think a good deal about foreign policy,' he wrote to

Kingsley Martin on 1 July. News had reached him that Vanessa's son Julian had been killed in Spain. Keynes wrote to her:

> My dearest Nessa,
>
> A line of sympathy and love from us both on the loss of your dear and beautiful boy with his pure and honourable feelings. It was fated that he should make his protest, as he was entitled to do, with his life, and one can say nothing.
>
> With love and affection,
>   Maynard

Soon Maynard's secretary, Mrs Stephens, arrived with vast piles of correspondence. He bombarded Norman Higgins, manager of the Arts Theatre, with programming instructions and Richard Kahn, now assistant bursar at King's, with investment instructions.

Illness made him no less combative. 'It seems to me the work of a sick man,' the far-from-sprightly Keynes commented after reading an attempted refutation of his theory by Arthur Pigou, his Cambridge colleague. Pigou, too, had heart trouble. 'Why is there such obstinacy and wilfulness in error?' he asked about Gottfried Haberler's *Prosperity and Depression*, which he got Kahn to attack in the *Economic Journal*.

In her final report to Florence from Ruthin on 22 September Lydia wrote that 'The dilated muscle is diminishing, but the complete recovery is still to come for a long time, and Maynard is to go on with the same regime. . . . he still has pains in the chest (not what they were). . . .' Dr Patterson left written instructions for his convalescence. Apart from a diet which looks surprisingly ample, Keynes was to take breakfast in bed, have a good rest after lunch, retire to bed before dinner, stay in bed one day a week. Keynes returned to Tilton on 30 September, after a stopover in London. In retrospect, he and Lydia agreed that the Ruthin regime had been a 'strange mixture of first-class medicine and first-class humbug'.

He left Ruthin in an upbeat mood, with the doctors promising him recovery within six months.[5] He would take the autumn off from Cambridge, but would spend most of it in London, gradually picking up the threads of 'real life'.[6] In fact, he stayed at Tilton till February 1938. There was a three-week visit to London and Cambridge in February–March and another of the same length to Cambridge in May–June, with mixed results. After that he did not leave Tilton again till October. The reason is that his recovery turned out to be much slower than he expected. He remained an invalid, subject to almost daily fluctuations in health, and serious setbacks whenever he came under any strain.

Lydia now became his heroic, devoted nurse. Love certainly, but also basic peasant instinct, dictated that she tend her sick mate. Keynes's debility redressed the internal balance of their marriage. Lydia had been his responsibility; for the rest of his life he became hers. She had been necessary for the completion of his ego; now he depended on her for his survival. Without being asked, she took control. To her caring she brought the discipline she had shown as a *prima ballerina*. For three years, she recorded every fluctuation in his health, mood, appearance; enforced his regime; kept at bay unnecessary business or visitors. For the first time, she found herself useful, in fact indispensable, to Maynard. Maynard was now her whole life. She gave up acting, though she still did occasional broadcasts for the BBC; she had no children; her family was far away in Russia. Maynard understood and accepted the rearrangement. He never went far without Lydia again. He increasingly invoked her authority to protect him against irksome or tiring demands. He hated being an invalid; at the same time, as Dadie Rylands shrewdly noticed, he 'enjoys the atmosphere of the nursery'. This was the first of Keynes's illnesses when he had not been nursed by his mother. It says a great deal for her understanding of the situation that Florence Keynes willingly surrendered the care of her adored, famous son to a Russian ballerina, dismissed by Bloomsbury as canary-brained.

Lydia set out to enforce the programme of rest prescribed by the Ruthin doctors. Since Keynes could barely crawl up the stairs, his bedroom at Tilton was moved to the ground-floor 'boot room' to the right of the front door as one entered, a Cézanne hung on the wall, and Lydia installed next door in the wing Keynes had built for servants. He spent half the day in bed. He was allowed to work for two or three hours in the mornings, propped up in bed or on a couch with his writing board. In the afternoons, taking advantage of the exceptional sunshine that October, he and Lydia were driven to nearby places like Glynde, Firle, Lewes or Eastbourne, so that he might be 'aired', as Lydia put it in a letter to Samuel Courtauld, 'in harmonious foliage'. Tea would be followed by rest. After an early supper, Keynes would be back in bed again, relaxing with a book, a play or the wireless. He often took what Lydia called 'dope' to fall asleep. Mrs Stephens (known as 'Missie') came once a week for his correspondence, but if these sessions continued too long they were liable to leave him 'aggressive' and 'chippy'. Visitors were discouraged, as talk made him too excited, leaving him flat and depressed. If she thought they had stayed too long, Lydia would abruptly throw them out, as the doctor had told her to: 'Now you must go.' She saw at once when Maynard was tired, and told him to lie down and stop talking – 'the only cure for the heart pain'.

His long convalescence and growing involvement in the affairs of his small estate made Tilton increasingly important to Keynes in the last years of his life. It had an ample if fluctuating staff. Penny Weller, otherwise 'Auntie', Lydia's old dresser, together with her nephew Edgar Weller and his wife Ruby, still formed the core. Edgar Weller was now confined to the garden, his erratic place at the wheel of Keynes's Rolls having been taken by Fred Woollard, Auntie's nephew-in-law and apparently a great mechanical genius, whom Lydia adored and who combined the improbable duties of 'librarian–chauffeur–masseur'. Beatty, an attractive twenty-six-year-old, cooked 'delicious' meals. Her mind, though, was 'beyond belief'. There were two housemaids, Roma, who was Swiss, and a Norwegian girl (unnamed). The household was completed by Patsy, the survivor of the Keyneses' three dogs, a 'squat, yapping brown-and-white mongrel'[7] with evil breath. 'It is rumoured that Patsy has caught a rat with his breath,' Maynard scribbled on one of Lydia's letters to Richard Kahn.

Lydia kept a tight control on visitors. The Woolfs came to tea early in October. Virginia found Maynard looking much better, 'not so white and heavy', and transformed into a medical expert. 'All London specialists were wrong about him. The only cure for all diseases is at Ruthin's.'[8] Their first non-local visitors were Auden and Isherwood, who came down from London on 11 November with Rupert Doone (director of the Group Theatre) to discuss their new 'morality play' *On the Frontier*, which Keynes wanted to put on at the Arts Theatre. He and Lydia walked with 'the boys' down from Firle Beacon, and found them 'very stimulating and interesting'. Keynes was disturbed to discover that the Group Theatre had no funds, but agreed to put up the money for a production at Cambridge and act as agent for the play. As the two authors were about to go to China, the Cambridge performances had to be postponed for a year.

With his fifty-year lease on Tilton Farm and Tilton Wood, signed in 1936, Keynes was also a farmer; and he now had the leisure to play the rural squire on an estate of about 300 acres. Tilton Farm was run by his farm manager Logan Thomson, a Yorkshireman with a taste for novels, while the gamekeeper, Mr Churchill, reared pheasants and partridges in Tilton Wood. Thomson's heart, Lydia said, was broken by the Norwegian maid who came in 1938; 'she and Logan used to drive round the farm together and seemed ... all through the summer of 1938, to be inseparable'. The convalescent Keynes loved to potter round his farm, watching the corn being threshed, the sheep being sheared, checking the quality of the milk and the condition of the pigs. He gave a big bonfire party on Guy Fawkes Day: Quentin Bell made the mask for the guy, there were sausages and beer for the farm labourers, a little speech from Maynard. Lydia attended dressed as a pig. The Saturday shoots, in which Clive Bell and members of the Keynes family sometimes took part – Keynes himself very rarely shot – had decidedly unbucolic accompaniments. The farmers would gather in Keynes's spacious new hall, whose walls were hung with Post-Impressionist paintings, and be directed by Lydia to a lavatory leading off, where a Matisse hung, with the words, 'Now you boys will want to do your little water in here'. On Christmas Day Lydia made her own contribution to the feudal system by distributing presents to the 'forty-five people in the little community'. The locals thought it was all a bit of a pretence, one of the farm workers remarking, 'Lord Gage [Maynard's landlord] is a lord and knows how the thing should be done.'

Keynes continued to scribble away on his writing board. Among his autumn productions was a memoir of Julian Bell. Virginia Woolf's appreciative letter was touched with envy. 'I wish you'd go on to do a whole portrait gallery, reluctant as I am to recognise your gift in that line when it seems obvious that nature gave me none for mathematics. Is portrait writing hard work compared with economics?'[9] Keynes would have said no: it was 'writing arguments' which was really difficult. Not that there was as much falling-off in that department as his doctors would have liked, as his arguments with Pigou on flexible wages and Robertson on interest rates testify. From this period dates the introduction he wrote (with Piero Sraffa) to the reprint of an anonymous *Abstract* of David Hume's *A Treatise on Human Nature*, the original of which he owned, which was published by Cambridge University Press in March 1938.

Keynes kept in touch with public events. On 14 November 1937 he summarised his views on the world situation to the American banker Walter Stewart: 'I do not expect a war, and I do not expect a major recession. On the other hand, international politics will interfere with the development of full business confidence, and some sort of recession seems obviously to be in progress on your side.'[10] That Britain, too, was in recession was apparent by December 1937. On this occasion, there was no Keynes Plan. The deepening recession in the United States did, though, prompt him to write another of his letters to the American President, Franklin Roosevelt, on 1 February 1938, this time private.

The slump in Maynard's health was accompanied, and aggravated, by the slump in his wealth. Wall Street's decline started about the time of Keynes's heart attack, with London following more gently. Most of Keynes's investments were in equities in the two markets; he was also highly leveraged. True to his philosophy of 'faithfulness' he hung on, but with growing anxiety. 'I don't want to have a big loan, even though the cover position is perfectly good,' he wrote to Richard Kahn from Ruthin on 2 September. 'I've not got to the point of being a bear, but I am *much* more disinclined to be bull on borrowed money. And to bring loans down sufficiently is a necessarily tedious and difficult process.'

Nevertheless, it was the course he now embarked on. His brokers, Buckmaster and Moore, demanded an increase in cover. The only way Keynes could reduce his liability was by selling on a falling market. The increasingly steep decline in share prices slowed down his own recovery, while the alternation of brief recoveries with deeper collapses produced fluctuations in his heart. 'Specs are awful,' he wrote to his mother on 10 October. 'But ... my hunch is that prices must now be somewhere near bottom.' In fact, Wall Street took another plunge nine days later. The following month Lydia noted in her medical diary, 'Slump fatal for health.' On 16 November 1937, Maynard wrote to G. H. Recknell of the National Mutual, 'Of course the right time to sell was in the spring but that was *very* difficult to detect.'[11]

Keynes had recovered enough to have dinner with Clive, Duncan and Vanessa at Charleston and lunch with the Woolfs at Rodmell over Christmas, his first evening engagements for nine months. 'We put Maynard to bed on 2 chairs,' wrote Virginia to her niece Angelica, 'and talked and talked until he worked himself into such a fury about politics, that Lydia called the car and off they drove.'¹² With Keynes on the mend, Lydia felt able to take on some engagements herself, appearing on television on 23 December reading the Hans Christian Andersen story 'Little Red Shoes'. In the spring she broadcast a series of programmes, 'Studies of Childhood and Adolescence from the Russian Masters'. Their producer was Guy Burgess.

Keynes returned to Ruthin on 11 February 1938 for a check-up. He was worried by a new localized heart pain, which usually appeared after a day of exertion just as he was about to go to sleep. The report from Ruthin was encouraging. His heart was still enlarged, but the quality of its pumping had improved. The throat swabs, Lydia explained, 'refused to grow vegetables, whilst the last time we were here, they grew at once into an orchard'. His blood pressure was still too low. The doctors would allow a 'mild return to public appearances in the near future, provided it is followed by a long summer's rest'.

On their return from Wales, Maynard and Lydia spent three weeks in London. They now occupied two houses, Keynes having acquired the lease of 47 Gordon Square shortly before his illness. The drawing room at No. 47, connected by a door to the one in No. 46, now housed his library. While they walked in the parks, took drives in the countryside, saw old friends, political tension mounted. Hitler was piling pressure on Austria; Chamberlain was trying to get Mussolini to stand up for Austrian independence; on 21 February Eden resigned as Foreign Secretary. Maynard wrote to Virginia Woolf: '[The] state of foreign politics is nearly giving me a heart attack. I always knew that Neville [Chamberlain] was the lowest (I can't spell it) flatest-footed [sic] creature that creeps. But will the country follow him [in his appeasement policy]?' Leonard and Virginia came to tea at 46 Gordon Square and found 'M. recumbent, but with a stock of ideas. Bentham the origin of evil. Lydia like a peasant woman, wringing her hands, on a stool.'¹³ On 23 February 1938, Keynes made his annual chairman's speech to the National Mutual, his first public appearance since his illness; the following day he chaired a meeting of the Royal Economic Society. He carried both off with aplomb, but the controversy in the press following his speech left him exhausted.

Maynard and Lydia spent the weekend of 10–14 March in Cambridge for the Fellowship Elections, his first visit since being taken to Ruthin. While they were there, German troops crossed the Austrian frontier, and Hitler declared the Anschluss. Keynes thought the government was 'almost wholly out of touch with the swiftly growing anti-dictator emotions of the public'.¹⁴ They got back to Tilton on 18 March.

More bad news, this time from Wall Street in late March, brought another slump in health for Maynard, who still had 'a huge American position'. Lydia took it philosophically: 'it is quite natural after so much work, change of weather, the world situation, Wall Street and life in general'. In the last fortnight in March he sold £40,000 to £50,000 worth of securities, steadily reducing his debt to Buckmaster and Moore, while preserving most of his liquid resources. In the year of 'terrific decline' which had started in the spring of 1937 he lost nearly two-thirds of his money. His net assets fell from £506,222 at the end of 1936 to £181,244 by the end of 1938, with his gross income cut by two-thirds, from £18,801 in 1937–8 to £6192 in 1938–9. The institutions whose investment policy he largely dictated – his college, the Provincial Insurance Company, the National Mutual – had also suffered heavy losses, and Keynes was driven to justifying his philosophy of 'hanging on for a rise' in lengthy letters and memoranda. To Francis Curzon, who chaired the weekly meetings of the board of the National Mutual in his absence, he wrote on 18 March: 'I feel no shame at being found still owning a share when the bottom of the market comes.... I would go much further than that. I should say that it is from time to time the duty of a serious investor to accept the depreciation of his holdings with equanimity and without reproaching himself. Any other policy is anti-social, destructive of confidence, and incompatible with the working of the economic system. An investor ... should be aiming primarily at long-period results, and should be solely judged by these.'[15] Curzon and the board were not convinced, and Keynes resigned his chairmanship in October 1938, explaining to Falk, 'One naturally chooses [to give up] that part of one's activities in which one finds the least satisfaction.'[16]

With spring turning into summer, and Wall Street at last recovering, Keynes's health slowly improved. On 29 April Lydia wrote to Kahn: 'Yesterday Maynard walked very well for a whole hour, we saw butterflies out of their cocoons tangled to their husbands, resting on the branches from time to time.' In the middle of May he risked three weeks in Cambridge, living with Lydia in their new flat at 17a St Edward's Passage. Lydia's medical diary tells the story of energetic occasions ('carried the Congregation brilliantly') interspersed with fatigue, pain, bad nights ('entered the room like a corpse ... took dope, very tired'). Still, he got by without severe damage. Sam Courtauld found him looking 'much better' at Tilton on 26 June, 'but he has to be very careful not to strain his heart, and must not talk too long. We went on a slow walk about an hour in the afternoon. Lydia seemed happier....'[17] On 28 June Keynes felt well enough to tell Spriggs that he was not coming back to Ruthin.

Maynard and Lydia remained at Tilton for four months. 'What a relief to settle with one's bags & pillows in one place....' Lydia wrote to Florence. The lanky, stooped economist in his serge jacket and straw hat and his tiny, birdlike wife with her Russian accent and exotic headscarfs must have made a strange impression on the rustics as they puffed their way slowly round their little estate. Maynard loved to think of himself as a benevolent landlord, but the performance was not wholly convincing. It was the idea of the role, not the role itself, which appealed to him. He was no countryman. He talked about his labourers as fantastical, two-dimensional creatures, comic but not sympathetic. They in turn were disconcerted by his calculations, his inquisitiveness, his ferocious intelligence. On one of their potters round the farm, when Lydia had been trying to get Maynard not to overtax his strength, he turned to his shepherd and said: 'What would you do if an old sheep looked at you as Lydia is looking at me now?' – a question, Quentin Bell remarks, 'which anyone might have found it difficult to answer'.[18]

Keynes's one major production over the summer of 1938 was a paper on buffer stocks, which he discussed with Walter Layton and Arthur Salter at Tilton, and which was read for him by his King's College colleague Gerald Shove at a meeting of Section F of the British Association in Cambridge on 19 August. Isherwood, back from China, paid a return visit to Tilton with Rupert Doone and Benjamin Britten, to finalise plans for staging *On the Frontier* in Cambridge. They agreed it should be done in November, with Lydia in the female starring role. On 23 August Keynes gave an upbeat report on his health to Richard Kahn. He had made more progress in the previous month than at any other time since his illness: 'my off days and bad moments are nothing like so bad as they used to be either in duration or intensity ... serious pain has almost entirely disappeared and I recover rapidly from fatigue'. Alas, his calm and health were to be shattered by the Czech crisis in September which led to Munich. 'I get on awfully slowly,' he gloomily wrote to his old Cambridge friend Bob Trevelyan on 27 September. 'We had a meeting of the Memoir Club last month and I read a paper on the effect of Principia Ethica on me when I was an undergraduate; and writing about Moore brought back to me vivid memories of you in those days.'[19] In fact the meeting took place at Tilton on 11 September. Virginia Woolf recorded that Keynes read 'a very packed profound & impressive paper' to a collection of Bloomsberries, old and young, then had to be 'slowly conveyed' to his ground-floor bedroom for a rest, while Lydia chirpily fed them ham sandwiches and hot cakes.[20] This was his paper 'My Early Beliefs', published posthumously, in which he partly confirmed and partly repudiated them. He and Lydia were driven up to Cambridge from London on 16 October 1938 – 'dinner with Kahn, a bit tired, looks pale, went to bed early, no pain, but might be lurking around the heart'.

III. IMPRESARIO OF THE KEYNESIAN REVOLUTION

It was in the twilight years between peace and war that the Keynesian Revolution started to take hold. The reconciliation between Keynes and the anti-Keynesians began in 1937. Its setting was the worsening international situation, which brought about massive British rearmament. But the architect of the reconciliation was Keynes himself. Bypassing contentious theoretical issues, he showed how the aggregative approach of the *General Theory* could be applied not just to the unemployment problem but to the problem of inflationary pressure at full employment, and the management of a war economy. The *General Theory*, cunningly so called, had the potential so to be applied. But Keynes's exploitation of this potential was an astonishing performance, a captivating mixture of assurance, style, intellectual flexibility and administrative fertility. Admittedly, the circle of the captivated was quite small. The Conservative MP for Lewes, Admiral Tufton Beamish, denounced his 'hoary proposal for vast schemes of public works'. John Buchan painted an unflattering portrait of Keynes as the 'half-adventurer, half-squire' and wholly amoral financier Barralty in his novel *The Island of Sheep* (1936). This reflected the standard right-wing Tory opinion of Keynes as a man of first-class brains but second-class character. The left still preferred socialism to managed capitalism, although it was starting to see how capitalism might be managed to further socialism's cause. It was the clever centre, always susceptible to Keynes's intellectual charm, which was reconciled. But that was enough.

From 1937 onwards, Keynes started applying the *General Theory* framework to the problems which would occur as Britain neared full employment and started preparing for the war. Of particular concern to the Treasury was the need to create room for rearmament without running into inflationary or balance of payments pressures. It was above all Keynes's anti-inflationary perspective which reconciled Keynesian economics to Treasury orthodoxy. Keynes's *How to Pay for the War*, and the wartime budgetary policy it inspired, were crystallisations of these pre-war discussions.

In February 1937 the Chancellor of the Exchequer, Neville Chamberlain, announced an addition to the rearmament programme, in the form of a £400m defence loan, to be spent over five years. Those schooled in the old views asked the old questions. Where would the extra resources come from? Would they not be diverted from other uses, like the export trade, which the Treasury regarded as the 'fourth arm of defence'? Would not the borrowing raise interest rates? Would it be inflationary? But times had changed. The Treasury was now committed to borrowing increasing sums for rearmament. The only theory on offer which promised both guns *and* butter and the low interest rates the Treasury wanted for its borrowing was Keynes's. At the same time, the approach of full employment gave Keynes the chance to establish his anti-inflationary credentials.

Five strands in these polemics are worth following. The first is Keynes's sketch of stabilisation technique, in three articles he wrote for *The Times* on 12–14 January 1937 – a topic absent from the *General Theory*. In a section headed 'Boom Control' Keynes suggested what would now be called a 'cyclically balanced budget' policy: governments should incur debt in the downswing and repay debt in the upswing of the business cycle. 'The boom, not the slump,' he declared, 'is the right time for austerity at the Treasury.' This fiscal theory of demand management had a powerful influence on orthodox Keynesianism after the war.[21]

Secondly, Keynes repeatedly emphasised that there was no overall shortage of resources in the British economy, but that the 'unfortunate rigidity' of Britain's industrial structure meant that heavy surpluses of labour in the 'distressed areas' co-existed with shortages in some industries and localities, so that 'we are in more need today of a rightly distributed demand than of a greater aggregate demand'.[22] This implied cutting back public spending in the booming south and increasing it in the depressed north and Celtic fringe. This had special relevance to the rearmament programme. In *The Times* of 11 March 1937 Keynes argued that defence orders should be placed, as far as possible, in the special areas of heavy unemployment.

> It is a mistake [he wrote] to suppose that this is merely a form of charity to a distressed part of the country. On the contrary, it is in the general interest. Whether demand is or is not inflationary depends on whether it is directed towards trades and localities which have no surplus capacity. To organise output in the Special Areas is a means of obtaining rearmament without inflation.[23]

Thirdly, Keynes stressed the need for a board of public investment to plan investment demand, so that a stock of new investment projects was ready to be activated as the profits from other types started to fall.[24] This became even more imperative in the twilight zone between peace and war through which Britain started to move in 1938 and 1939. He wrote to Oswald Falk on 5 September 1938: 'The trouble is that we are governed by utter boobies. Instead of devoting themselves to the none too easy task of ensuring the preparedness of this country, senior civil servants seem to devote themselves in almost every sphere of activity to providing their ministers with more or less plausible excuses for doing nothing.'[25]

Fourthly, national income statistics were needed to manage demand. At what levels of unemployment would serious inflationary pressures arise? Would it be 10 per cent, 5 per cent? No one knew. In his *Times* article of 11 March 1937 Keynes used some back-of-envelope arithmetic to calculate the size of the 'output gap'. This led him to conclude that 'the Chancellor's loan expenditure *need* not be inflationary'. But he complained that lack of adequate statistics had reduced his calculations to 'bold guesses'.[26]

The final strand of Keynes's argument was his advocacy of permanently cheap money. Short-term interest rates should be kept continuously low, in order to avoid uncertainty about the future of long-term rates. 'We must avoid [dear money] ... as we would hell-fire,' he wrote in *The Times* of 12 January 1937. This doctrine would determine monetary policy till 1951.

Cheap money was not specifically Keynesian. It was the classical response to – and it was presumed the natural result of – depression. Bank rate was set at 2 per cent in 1932. The Treasury's massive conversion operation of 1932, whereby £2bn of the 5 per cent War Loan of 1917, about a quarter of the National Debt, was converted to 3.5 per cent, was designed both to relieve the budget and to support lower short-term interest rates. The Treasury, though, did not doubt that interest rates would have to rise in boom conditions.

In the traditional view, a rise in interest rates signalled a 'shortage of saving' – a sign that demand was pressing against the limit of resources. Thus any increased government borrowing, four years into recovery, was bound to push up interest rates. This prospect alarmed the Treasury, which wanted to borrow the money to finance rearmament as cheaply as possible. It was in these circumstances that Keynes's 'monetary' theory of the rate of interest started bells ringing in the Treasury and Bank of England. According to this theory, a rise in interest rates signalled a shortage not of saving but of liquidity.

Here was the nub of the theoretical debate which followed the publication of Keynes's *General Theory*. The older school's theory of the self-regulating economy rested heavily on its view of the rate of interest as the price which balanced saving and investment. Keynes denied this. Saving rose and fell with income; the rate of interest was the price of giving up liquidity. A loan-financed rearmament programme which raised the level of national income would generate the savings to pay for it, *without requiring interest rates to rise*. But this did not explain the rise in short-term rates in early 1937 – which is exactly what the classical school would have predicted as the economy started booming. This happening in the 'real world' stimulated Keynes's last burst of theory-building. In an article published in the *Economic Journal* of July 1937, written from his sickbed in Cambridge, he argued that an investment decision may involve 'a temporary demand for money ... before the corresponding saving has taken place'. Normally this 'finance' is supplied by the banking system from a 'revolving fund' as the loans for projected investments are paid out of repayments to the banks for completed ones. But if investment demand rises unexpectedly the 'pressure to secure more finance than usual may easily affect the rate of interest through its influence on the demand for money'. Thus, although extra investment (private or public) could not be limited by a 'shortage of saving', it could exceed the supply of financial facilities 'if the banking system is unwilling to increase the supply of money and the supply from existing holders [of inactive balances] is inelastic'. The monetary authority could always create the 'finance' for additional investment by printing more money, 'a potent, though sometimes dangerous, method'.[27] This is the origin of the famous 'finance' demand for money, which Keynes had not mentioned in the *General Theory* and which he now offered as a 'bridge' between his liquidity preference theory of interest and Dennis Robertson's savings-derived loanable fund theory. It is a classic example of what Professor Clarke called 'making up theory on the hoof' to meet objections to his proposals. In his chairman's speech to the National Mutual on 23 February 1938 Keynes invented an ingenious argument based on his new theory. The rise in interest rates in 1937 had resulted not from the raising of the rearmament loan, but from the fact that it had been raised before it was spent. 'Borrowing in advance of expenditure amounts to a sort of hoarding which may cause a grave credit stringency.' The rise in interest rates could have been prevented had the government, instead of issuing defence bonds well in advance of requirements, started its investment programme 'a little before the borrowing, or at any rate ... *pari passu*'.[28] Keynes was enraged by the comments in the financial press which greeted his speech. 'Practically all City Editors (like Civil Servants and others who are in touch with money making and not themselves money-makers and so dislike the nasty thing) are congenital deflationists,' he wrote to Richard Kahn on 5 March 1938.

Keynes's other technique for avoiding high interest rates was for the Treasury to satisfy the public's desire for liquidity by borrowing more at the short end of the market, avoiding premature funding. The use of this technique by the US Treasury allowed it to borrow 'at a materially lower average rate' than the British Treasury was able to do, since the rate of interest rose with the length of maturity.[29]

The reception of Keynes's doctrine in the Treasury was cordial. The Treasury's countercyclical approach to interest rate policy was coming to be overshadowed by its concern to keep down the cost of borrowing for rearmament. Keynes's liquidity preference theory of the rate of interest suggested the technique by which this might be done. It implied that monetary policy could fix interest rates at whatever level the government wished, provided the money supply was deliberately expanded to 'feed the hoarder', and the terms of maturity arranged to suit the tastes of the investor. Keynes continued to plug this theme over the coming year.

These sketches of Keynesian policy reveal not just his capacity for theoretical invention, but his flair in applying theory, new and old, to the problems of administration. They were devised in the shadow of war, which gave them a *dirigiste* flavour that was by no means an ineluctable conclusion of his 'general theory'.

Keynes's promotion of his theory was starting to shift the Treasury out of its Chamberlainite orthodoxy. Susan Howson and Donald Winch show that 'by 1937 the macro-economic position which we associate with Keynes's *General Theory* had altered the thinking of the most important policy-making civil servants in the Treasury'.[30] They cite, in particular, the argument for countercyclical public works put forward in the Twenty-Second Report (19 February 1937) of the Economic Advisory Council's Committee on Economic Information, chaired by Sir Josiah Stamp, on which Keynes and two senior Treasury officials, Sir Frederick Phillips and Sir Frederick Leith-Ross, served.[31] This was virtually identical to the case Keynes put forward in his *Times* articles in January 1937. More important was Keynes's influence on monetary thinking. The last report of the Committee on Economic Information in July 1939, and the Treasury Committee on the Control of Savings and Investment, set up on 30 June 1939, under Sir Frederick Phillips, echoed the arguments and proposals of Keynes's *Times* articles of that year. When a 3 per cent maximum borrowing rate was decided on in October 1939 'the methods subsequently used to maintain this level were the same as those favoured by Keynes....'[32] Keynes's ideas became central to the policy discussion in the 1937–9 period, not because most of those concerned 'bought' his *General Theory*, but because they fitted the preoccupations of the policymaking elite. There was still widespread mistrust of his over-cleverness. As Schumpeter – a jaundiced witness – wrote, 'Most people who admire Keynes accept the stimulus, take from him what is congenial to them and leave the rest.'[33]

IV. PRUDENCE VERSUS APPEASEMENT

In his *Economic Consequences of the Peace*, Keynes had written: 'If we aim at the impoverishment of Central Europe, vengeance, I dare predict, will not limp.' His impassioned outburst against the Treaty of Versailles has been subject to much brutal criticism, most of it misplaced. Much less has been written about his reaction to the coming of the vengeance, in the shape of Adolf Hitler. In an unpublished chapter of autobiography, Kingsley Martin, editor of the *New Statesman*, of whose board Keynes was chairman, wrote: '[Keynes] usually, with some lapses, supported Baldwin and even Chamberlain, and even put up a half-hearted support, though an angry one, for Munich. He found it almost impossible, as I did, to "start a war" in defence of Eastern Europe when some sort of peace was offered to us and we were not necessarily engaged.'[34] That most perceptive of contemporary Keynes-watchers, Oswald Falk, wrote about 'the conflicts in his mind between his undoubted pacifism and his wish, at times at any rate, to fight evil and aggression'.[35] Most recently, Donald Markwell argues that the view of Keynes as an appeaser was, 'at best, simplistic'.[36]

The truth is that Keynes was *not* an appeaser in the technical sense, to be defined below, but the point of distinction sometimes seemed recondite. Nor were his writings on foreign policy of the same quality as his economic pronouncements. Keynes's genius as an economist owed a great deal to his intimate knowledge of the workings of Whitehall and the City of London. In foreign policy he had no such comparative advantage. He had no particular expertise to offer and no contacts at the heart of the policymaking machine; his knowledge of the United States and the Soviet Union was sketchy. So his approach was often amateurish. He ruminated from a distance; his writing was untypically vague; his influence on policy was virtually nil.

Let us try to recreate Keynes's state of mind as he contemplated the gathering war clouds. We can readily agree that 'the effects of *The Economic Consequences of the Peace* were irrelevant to Keynes's own views of how to deal with Hitler':[37] he had no personal reason to feel guilty about the 'harsh' peace at Versailles, since he had opposed it. Furthermore, since he had never supported the Wilsonian principle of 'national self-determination' – that multiplication of frontiers and sovereignties which he thought had disrupted the pre-war economic unity of Europe – he never felt the need to urge territorial concessions to Germany on ethnic or linguistic grounds. Finally, the Germany whose cause he had supported in 1919 was not the Germany of the 1930s. He loathed the Nazi regime, never visited Germany after 1933, and never drew attention to the successes of Hitler's economic policies – a commendable feat of self-denial in the circumstances.

Secondly, Keynes, was 90 per cent pacifist. Like most liberals, he regarded peace as an almost overriding good – one which should be sacrificed only in extremity, for the defence of vital interests. In this he reflected the pacificism of the democracies. His overwhelming bias in favour of peace comes out in his disinclination to underwrite the European or global status quo; his excessive faith in economic sanctions as an alternative to war; and his genuine puzzlement about how to deal with people like Hitler and Mussolini who were willing to risk war to secure their aims. The appeal of war or warlikeness lay beyond his imaginative understanding – a defect or virtue he shared with most British liberals.

Thirdly, it was an extension of Keynes's pacifism to believe that governments had no right to risk war for a principle without popular support. On 24 July 1937, he wrote to Richard Kahn on Julian Bell's death in Spain: 'He had a personal right to make his protest with his life. I feel that, though I feel ever more strongly that the NS and N [*New Statesman and Nation*] and the Labour Party are *not* entitled to urge the Govt. to make protest with the lives of the community at large when it would be entirely against feelings of the great majority of them.'

Fourthly, Keynes's foreign policy convictions in the 1930s were highly influenced by his conception of prudence. This was a set philosophical attitude, which goes back to his undergraduate essay on Burke and his distinctive theory of probability. One passage from his 1904 paper on Burke is worth recalling: 'Burke ever held, and held rightly, that it can seldom be right ... to sacrifice a present benefit for a doubtful advantage in the future.... [Moreover] it is not sufficient that the state of affairs which we seek to promote should be better than the state of affairs which preceded it; it must be sufficiently better to make up for the evils of the transition.'[38] Applied to the 1930s, the logic is very simple. At any moment in time peace is better than war. Therefore we should not risk war unless we know that it will make peace more secure; and we should not fight a war unless we know that it will make a future peace sufficiently better than the existing peace to offset the costs of war. But this kind of knowledge is rarely available. Therefore we should 'prolong peace, hour by hour, day by day, for as long as we can'. This is not an ineluctable deduction from the existence of uncertainty. One could say: if one cannot calculate the probability of an outcome, one should simply do what history and honour teaches is right. This was Churchill's view.

Fifthly, Keynes attached an enormous significance to the use of language as an element of power, especially since armaments were in short supply. As a masterly user of language himself, he understood the power of words, and particularly admired Churchill for his quality of utterance. It was not the language of moral indignation he demanded, but the language of moral eloquence. In the years leading up to the war he repeatedly accused the government of neglecting 'the power of courageous bearing', 'the capacity to appear formidable'. Such neglect would not lessen the risk of war, only ensure that we would fight it 'with no friends and no common cause'.[39] Keynes believed that a prouder bearing by Britain would have brought the United States much sooner into the moral – and eventually military – balance against the dictators.

Finally, we must distinguish Keynes's policy from Neville Chamberlain's. Personal antipathy played a part. Keynes genuinely liked Baldwin; he hardly knew his successor, and had no reason to love him, or hope for much from him. Chamberlain had one of those unmalleable personalities, peculiarly resistant to Keynes's charms and spells. Keynes's only published personal comment on him, dating from 1939, sees him as the main obstacle to all his hopes: 'In the Prime Minister's case this blindness [to the most obvious aspects of the contemporary world] is an essential element in his strength. If he could see even a little, if he became even faintly cognisant of the turmoil of ideas and projects and schemes to save the country which are tormenting the rest of us, his superbly brazen self-confidence would be fatally impaired.'[40]

As Chancellor, Chamberlain rigidly pursued the policy of balanced budgets and believed they had brought prosperity. He was appalled by the drift and lethargy of Baldwin's foreign policy, and when he became Prime Minister in May 1937 he determined to apply equally clear-cut principles to his dealings with the dictators. His policy has been aptly called 'armed appeasement'. His hope was, as he put it in a letter to his sister Hilda on 1 August 1937, that 'a double policy of rearmament and better relations with Germany and Italy would carry us safely through the danger period'.

The difference between Chamberlain and Keynes was that Keynes rejected the policy of actively seeking an agreement with what he called the 'brigand powers'. Intuitively he knew one could not do business with the Nazis on any terms acceptable to British public opinion. But that did not commit him to the defence of the European, or extra-European, status quo. The line he most consistently favoured was strong armaments, no clear-cut commitments, building up a defensive alliance of peaceful powers including the USA and the Soviet Union, and adopting a vaguely menacing posture. It was closest to the view of Anthony Eden, Baldwin's Minister for League of Nations Affairs and subsequently Chamberlain's first Foreign Secretary. Eden's policy was to keep the dictators 'guessing' while getting on to 'better terms' with the USA and Soviet Russia – the exact opposite of Chamberlain's aim of getting on 'better relations' with the dictators. The trouble was that two could play the game of bluff, so that brinkmanship offered alarmingly easy victories to the player with the stronger nerve; while, given US isolationism and Stalin's bestiality, the putative alliance for peace with the Soviet Union and the United States was never plausible. The real logic of Keynes's peace policy was British isolationism behind the defensive shield of the Channel and the Royal Navy – a logic he never accepted.

Keynes's polemics on foreign affairs, starting with Italy's invasion of Abyssinia in 1935, were at first much more directed against the left than against the government, particularly against the *New Statesman*'s line of demanding civil resistance to rearmament, while calling for military sanctions against Italy and 'Arms for Spain'. Since Keynes was chairman of the *New Statesman*'s board, and its editor, Kingsley Martin, was a personal friend, he felt this illogicality almost as a personal affront, and castigated its folly not just in contributions to that journal but in angry letters to Martin himself. The nub of his position was that 'it is better to have strong forces and no clear-cut foreign policy than to advocate no armaments one week and warlike alliances the next'.[41] The policy of the government, he argued, reflected not its pro-fascist sympathies, but the people's aversion to war. Britain should head a bloc of peaceful nations, including France, Russia and the United States, and make it so formidable that 'only a madman will confront it'. From his sickbed at Ruthin he wrote 'Since Fabius Maximus there has scarcely been a stronger case for cunctation than there is today.... Britain should build up its naval strength and wait for the dictators *to make mistakes'*.⁴²

Even Keynes's optimism was dented by the revelation of Stalin's purges. 'In truth', he wrote to Martin on 25 July, 'there are only two [ideologies]: the totalitarian states and the liberal states'. He correctly predicted a Nazi–Soviet pact.⁴³ But he still hoped to wean the United States from its isolation.

Keynes never appreciated the extent of Anglophobia in the United States. This was the real force behind isolationism. Throughout the 1930s, dislike of the fascist 'villains' was balanced by dislike of British imperialism. Bruce Bliven, who had taken Keynes's articles for the *New Republic*, was not untypical of American 'liberals' in seeing a moral equivalence between British and Japanese colonialist methods in China – much to Keynes's disgust. Americans particularly resented Britain's repudiation of its war debt in 1933. This led directly to the Johnson Act, which banned private loans to countries which had defaulted on their loans. H. C. Engelbrecht and F. C. Hanighen's bestselling book *Merchants of Death* (1934) argued that arms manufacturers and international bankers had combined with British interests to inveigle America into the First World War. It led to the setting up of the Nye Senatorial Committee, whose findings 'included a veritable laundry list of British sins during the war' and led to the passage of the two Neutrality Acts of 1935 and 1936. Where Keynes was right was in thinking that appeasement as practised by Baldwin and Chamberlain reduced Britain's prestige in America. Americans don't like to back losers. But it is highly unlikely that a 'prouder bearing' by Britain would have helped forge an anti-fascist alliance ahead of war.⁴⁴

Nineteen-thirty-eight was Hitler's *annus mirabilis*. In two bloodless coups, he annexed Austria and the German-speaking areas of Czecho-slovakia. The Czech crisis hotted up in August. The three million Sudeten Germans started clamouring for 'national self-determination'; Hitler screwed up the tension, hoping the Czech state would disintegrate of its own accord; Chamberlain sent Lord Runciman to Prague to 'mediate'. Keynes thought Hitler was bluffing. Czechoslovakia was guaranteed by both France and Russia. 'In a world war', Keynes wrote to Kingsley Martin on 26 August, 'Hitler will be beaten and he knows it.' But he added: 'I agree with you that we should bluff to the hilt; and if the bluff is called, back out. I prefer, meanwhile, meiosis and bogus optimism in public.' Keynes, that is, was no more willing to fight for Czechoslovakia than was Chamberlain, but was against telling Hitler so. That is why he was furious with Martin for raising the issue of frontier changes in the *New Statesman* of 27 August. Keynes's main proposal was to call Hitler's bluff by asking him to state his intentions. Chamberlain did not believe Hitler was bluffing. On 15 September he flew to meet Hitler at Berchtesgaden and conceded the principle of separating the Sudeten Germans from Czechoslovakia before Hitler had even suggested it. Delighted that Chamberlain was doing his work for him, Hitler raised his demands: German troops must occupy the ceded territory at once, he told Chamberlain at Godesberg on 22 September. Chamberlain rejected this 'ultimatum'. The French called up reservists; the British mobilised the Fleet. Chamberlain broadcast to the British nation: 'If I were convinced that a nation had made up its mind to dominate the world by fear of its force, I should feel that it must be resisted.' For a few days it seemed that war was inevitable. Hitler then backed down. He agreed to a new conference, with Mussolini as 'mediator'. On the afternoon of 28 September, Chamberlain announced that he was flying to Munich the next day in a last effort to save world peace. The House of Commons broke into hysterical cheering.

Glued to his wireless at Tilton, Keynes had followed these twists and turns with mounting anxiety. Lydia had reported him 'worried over the world war' on 23 September, 'very worried, upset' on the 26th. On the 27th he was 'much more cheerful, thinks there won't be a war, in spite of everything....' On the 29th his 'health improved with news and weather'. As Chamberlain winged his way to Germany, Keynes wrote to his mother:

> it was a tremendous relief to get last night's news – though my reasoning self has never wavered from the conclusion that H[itler] was totally against war. Hitler has never had much to gain from calling off his bluff until the very last possible moment; and he needed the Fleet Mobilisation and ARP precautions in London to convince him that we should really act. Given the latter, I have always believed that the former must follow. The Prime Minister has shown extraordinary character and courage and good motives. But his sympathies are distasteful. If he gets us out of the hole, it was he (and *The Times*) who got us into it by leading the Nazis into the belief that at bottom the sympathies of the English ruling class were with them.... We are not out of the trouble yet – but we *shall* be, if only the PM can bring himself to be just a little harsh to the Fuhrer.[45]

At Munich Mussolini suggested that the German-speaking areas should be occupied by German troops in ten days rather than one. Hitler agreed at once, not surprisingly, since the German Foreign Ministry had drafted Mussolini's proposal. The settlement was announced on 30 September, with Chamberlain returning to London, to an outburst of rejoicing, waving a bit of paper and proclaiming 'peace with honour ... peace in our time'. That night Keynes slept well: '*no war*, feels basically tired after the war-strain, but health is not bad at all, directed himself at a sale of sheep, bought 140, slept in the afternoon'. But on 1 October Lydia reported him 'angry at PM's cheating the nation'. His immediate reaction, conveyed in a letter to Kingsley Martin written that day, was 'painful in the way in which only a *mixed* state can be. Intense relief and satisfied cowardice join with rage and indignation, *plus* that special emotion appropriate to the state of having been *swindled* ... the whole nation *swindled* as never before in its history.'

He called for a union of progressive forces to oppose the goverment in the election he expected Chamberlain to call.[46]

Despite these fulminations, the rational difference between Keynes and Chamberlain was wafer-thin. It boiled down to thinking that Chamberlain could have got a better deal for the Czechs (what sort of deal?) had he gone on bluffing a bit longer; and disgust at the way he had clothed his surrender in fraudulent phrases. Keynes's view that Hitler was bluffing is shared by A. J. P. Taylor, but not by all historians. Like many others Keynes was convinced that both sides had been play-acting, the purpose of the play being to clear Hitler's path to the east. He now assumed that Chamberlain had given Hitler the nod to seize the Ukraine, ignoring the fact that by guaranteeing the rump of the Czech state, Britain had implicitly guaranteed the existing territorial order in eastern Europe. More presciently Keynes suggested that 'who knows [but] that in the end Herr Hitler will be the second dictator to retreat from Moscow'.[47]

V. RECOVERY

Maynard and Lydia spent most of the autumn of 1938 in Cambridge. Keynes's resignation from the chairmanship of the National Mutual Life Assurance Company spared him his old mid-week trips to London. He did no teaching, concentrating on the Arts Theatre, college business, and writing. The big event in the autumn term was the long-delayed production of the Auden–Isherwood play *On the Frontier*, which opened at the Arts Theatre on 14 November for six performances. Rehearsals soon revealed it as an amazingly feeble Marxist pastiche on anti-war themes, structured as an operatic melodrama, with a nonsensical fascist 'Leader' manipulated by a sinister arms manufacturer, Valerian, and two young lovers (one of whom, Anna Vrodny, was played by Lydia). Keynes himself realised it was out of touch with the post-Munich mood. 'Do you think you can go ahead with it in precisely its present form without feeling at all silly?' he asked Christopher Isherwood. Interestingly, a number of passages, considered offensive to Hitler and Nazism, were censored by the Lord Chamberlain's office. Despite a glittering production – Rupert Doone directed, Robin Medley did the scenery and sets, Benjamin Britten wrote the music and played the piano – and a warm send-off from Keynes, who, allowing himself a rare evening out, hosted a post-performance dinner party – the play flopped with the critics and never got a West End run. T. S. Eliot wrote to Keynes grimly: 'I'm afraid that Hitler is not the simpleton the authors make him out to be.'[48]

Keynes's continuing presence so close at hand unnerved the theatre manager, Norman Higgins. Keynes treated him, as he did all his subordinates, with a mixture of kindness and wilfulness. Even in sickness, he drove himself harder than anyone, but in return he expected Higgins to be at his beck and call, and could be unsparing in his criticisms. Higgins, for his part, adored Keynes, tried to please him in every way, but became terrified of making mistakes. Keynes now also had more time for the fussing which he so enjoyed. He convinced himself that the restaurant's pricing policy was all wrong. The existence of a high elasticity of demand for wine would justify reducing the price to Cambridge's champagne drinkers of 1929 Cliquot and 1928 Krug to fifteen shillings (about £20 today) a bottle. Dadie Rylands insisted that Cambridge was far too 'priggish and Left Book Club' to drink good wine, even at reduced prices. But Keynes persisted with his reductions, and then tried to prove his hypothesis by examining the restaurant's wine accounts. These showed that the sales of wine were 14 per cent higher after the reductions than before. After a few months of this Higgins had a nervous breakdown and had to be sent off on a convalescent cruise, which Keynes, characteristically, paid for out of his own pocket.

On 18 January 1939 Keynes had dinner in London with Kingsley Martin. They ate woodcock and talked about 'Democracy and Efficiency'. This 'conversation' was published in the *New Statesman* ten days later. It is the starkest statement of Keynes's view that the 'war economy' which was slowly taking shape might serve as some sort of model for the peacetime regulation of economic life. On the one hand, there was the need for planning and organisation. On the other hand, he urged the 'profound connection between personal and political liberty and the rights of private property and private enterprise'. He argued that the threat to liberty from the measures of planning he proposed was 'so remote from the first and the next and the next things that want doing, that it is not now, and is a long way from being, a practical issue'.[49]

On 28 February Keynes went from Cambridge to London and caught influenza. Lydia's entry on 1 March is terse: 'Bad. Called Plesch. Bad.' That was the end of the Cambridge term for him. He did not leave 46 Gordon Square till the end of March, returning with Lydia to Tilton on 6 April. How Keynes got to hear of Plesch is unrecorded, possibly from Margot Asquith, one of Plesch's patients. But Plesch's entry into his life was a decisive turning point in his illness. For 'undoubtedly it was he, and he alone, who brought me back into active life'.[50]

Keynes came to regard Janos Plesch as 'something between a genius and a quack', an impression confirmed by Plesch's memoirs, in which he sounds off about every subject under the sun. It says much for Keynes's intuition that he was willing to entrust himself to this very un-English medical practitioner – also for his desperation at the slow pace of his recovery. Janos Plesch, then aged sixty, was a self-made Hungarian Jew, who had established a fashionable medical practice in Berlin in 1910. He was a versatile linguist, connoisseur of the arts and a more than competent painter. He was consulted by Pope Pius X and the Kaiser's wife; in fact he seems to have known and/or treated every important person in central Europe, including Albert Einstein, to whom he dedicated his book *The Physiology and Pathology of the Heart and Blood Vessels*. In 1933 he left Germany (on a Hungarian passport), settled in England and, having passed the necessary examinations, started a private practice at Hereford House, off Park Lane. As his son Peter Plesch tells it, he did not try to join Harley Street, heart of the English medical establishment, as such a move would have been blocked by its leaders, Lord Horder and Lord Dawson of Penn (of whom it was said he 'killed many men'), but he did join the much more congenial Peckham Health Centre. There a patient would be seen by a group of like-minded doctors from different disciplines, all in one place.

The requirements of a 'great doctor', as listed by Plesch, were evidently tailored to fit his own qualities: 'He must be of good and agreeable appearance, he must be well educated, he must be cultured, he must be clever, he must have good manners, and, of course, he must know a thing or two about his job. But if a doctor has real personality he can do without almost all the rest.' Plesch brought some decided opinions to his treatment of his patients, which were not unlike Keynes's ministrations for sick economies. Good diagnosis was a mixture of science and imagination. The doctor must study the patient, not the symptom, letting his 'imaginative intuition' play on the evidence. Secondly, Plesch had a strong belief in assisted self-healing, declaring that 'a satisfactorily compensated sickness is very similar to health'. Thirdly, he was utterly opposed to invalidism. The instinct for life was more powerful than any other. It was fatal to tell old people to 'take it easy'; it was best 'to die in harness, and in that event death will probably be postponed to the very last minute'. Finally, Plesch rejected 'the medieval tradition of secrecy and mystification' in medical matters. Medical knowledge should be communicated in ordinary language.[51] Keynes was quick to recognise a kindred spirit. He noticed that Plesch said something with great assurance one week and exactly the opposite the next week. 'His treatments', he said, either revived his patients or 'failed completely'. Keynes collected stories of his 'peculiar and amusing cures'. Einstein, having read some chapters from Plesch's memoirs, summed up the good doctor thus in 1944: 'Talented to your fingertips, keen of hearing and sensitive, but slovenly and lacking a sense of responsibility. A true angel, but already "fallen" at birth....'

It was on this fallen angel that Keynes's hopes for better health now rested. Plesch certainly had a Keynesian approach to healing. On 28 May 1939, Keynes wrote to Bob Brand of Lazard Brothers, who had just become a Plesch patient:

> With English doctors one goes on for two or three years incapacitated from active work and exercise, and is given no definite treatment

whatsoever, merely being advised to 'rest'. This is never Plesch's method. Successfully or unsuccessfully, too drastically perhaps sometimes, he begins at once with every kind of active treatment, very fertile and ingenious in ideas, trying on every sort of thing imaginable until he finds something useful.[52]

Plesch set out not just to treat Keynes for his influenza, but to get him off his couch. He started him off on a saltless diet to reduce body fluids, ordered an icebag to be placed on his heart for three hours a day, prescribed opium pills, and even jumped on him as he lay in bed. A bacteriological examination showed Keynes's throat swarming with streptococci. Plesch told his patient that, until the streptococcus had been defeated, recovery was a 'Sisyphus task'. He decided on drastic measures. He gave him an elaborate and stringent treatment of a new drug, Prontosil, a brilliant red dye product, discovered in 1935 by Gerhard Domagk, director of research at the Bayer company, one of the firms from which the I. G. Farben combine had been formed, which was found to have powerful anti-bacterial properties. Domagk found that when this red dye extract was injected into mice which had been given lethal injections of haemolytic streptococci, they recovered. A year later, a French husband-and-wife team, the Trefouels, working at the Pasteur Institute, showed that chemicals in the body broke down the Prontosil compound into two different components, and it was one of these, sulphanilamide, which attacked the bacteria. Patterson's failure to try Prontosil on Keynes at Ruthin in mid-1937 suggests either ignorance of Germany's anti-bacterial therapy or a closed mind.

The sulpha drugs, as they came to be called, were the precursors of penicillin. The Prontosil injections made Keynes feel iller than he had ever been before, and he could scarcely stand. But Plesch assured him that once the streptococci were eliminated, he would make a full recovery, as his heart muscle was not fundamentally injured. He and Lydia returned to Tilton on 6 April; the following night he 'slept well, feels drowsy, foggy with all the poisons inside of him, but the heart has no sensations'. By 13 April he was telling Plesch that he was completely free from all heart symptoms, 'so very many thanks indeed'. He had even run after a train, for which indulgence his doctor sternly rebuked him from Monte Carlo. By this time he had taken to addressing Plesch as 'My dear Rabbi'. Lydia called him 'The Ogre'.

There is no reason to doubt Keynes's own view that it was Prontosil which had brought about his dramatic improvement. Unfortunately, it was subsequently discovered that Prontosil was effective against the streptococci lodged in the throat but not against those already firmly established in the valves of the heart.[53] So Keynes would almost certainly not live into old age. Whether, or how soon, this ever became clear to Plesch or Keynes cannot now be discovered.

Keynes now started to work at more like his old pace. At Cambridge he examined for the tripos. With war finance on his mind he wrote two articles for *The Times* on 17 and 18 April 1939, arguing for low interest rates, control of capital exports and a Department of Co-ordination with an economic general staff. Tactfully, he suggested this should be attached to the Treasury. He broadcast on the effect of rearmament on employment conditions, helped draft the Twenty-Seventh (and last) Report of the Committee on Economic Information, and wrote two more articles in *The Times* on 24 and 25 July developing his arguments for a low-interest policy. In his broadcast, he asserted that rearmament expenditure was about to bring to an end the years of 'abnormal' unemployment, and predicted accurately that 'we shall never go back all the way to the old state of affairs'.[54] In his last pre-war article he wrote: 'The key to sound public finance in the present emergency is a rigid refusal to fund short-term debt at high interest rates and a stern stiffening of taxation when we have reached the full employment of our productive resources.'[55]

By 12 July he was back at Tilton. He and Lydia went to Verdi's *Macbeth* at Glyndebourne; on 13 August he walked to the top of Firle Beacon for the first time since his illness, without ill effects. He was clearly in a buoyant, active mood. He had installed an electric fence to keep out marauders from his estate; he had ordered covered cattleyards for the winter; he had bought his manager Logan Thomson a 'very smart new car, which makes Fred [his chauffeur], to whom I have just refused a new one, very jealous'. He told his mother that he considered himself 'two thirds back to normal'. On 15 August he and Lydia flew off to Paris for a holiday in France, to take the refreshing baths at Royat, near Vichy, and get away from the latest war scare over Poland. When Clive Bell told him that another 'hullabaloo' (their name for the Munich Agreement) was unlikely, Keynes rebuked him for being a pessimist. 'I shall be most surprised if it ends in war,' he wrote to Kahn the day before they left. By 22 August Keynes was getting worried that 'Hitler does not seem to be keeping open much of an emergency exit. He seems to show in high degree what Scotland Yard says is particularly characteristic of nearly all criminals, namely an inability to vary his methods.'

On 25 August he wrote to Kahn that 'it still looks to me much more like politics than war'. He assumed, that is, that Hitler was waiting for the British to make him an offer, which would lead to another Munich. But no offer came. The British had had enough, and anyway they could not control the Poles as they could the Czechs. On 27 August Maynard decided to come home, not because he expected 'serious developments just yet', but because the hotel was closing down as the result of French mobilisation. 'First our waiter went, then the violinist, then the cellist, then both the pastry cooks, and the culmination was the departure of Monsieur Jacques, the nice and clever ... concierge, round whom all the goings on in the hotel revolved.'

They got back to Tilton on 29 August. Maynard still hoped war might be averted, but he was much less nervous than at the time of Munich.

On 1 September German troops invaded Poland. Britain declared war on Germany two days later. Maynard and Lydia took the news calmly. Some sort of die had been cast. It was not one he would have cast. Britain had gone to war for an object he did not think worth fighting for – and without the United States. But he accepted the conflict as inevitable. The British people had forced the hand of their rulers. Keynes's most important condition for going to war had been met.

32

The Middle Way in War

I. OLD DOGS

The politicians and generals occupied themselves with how to fight the war – or whether, at first, to fight it at all. For the first two years of it, Maynard Keynes was chiefly concerned with how to pay for it. The finance of war has two aspects, domestic and foreign. A government may draw resources from its own people, or from abroad – from its allies, dependents and trading partners. At first Keynes was mainly concerned with the first – how to mobilise available domestic resources for the war effort most efficiently and fairly and, on a long view, with least damage to the practices of peace. Once the war hotted up in the summer of 1940, he became increasingly involved in the second – how to pay for the imports which Britain needed to keep its war effort going full blast.

He started his efforts without any official position, nor indeed expecting one. With the outbreak of war, the government began to assemble an administrative machine to run a war economy. Although certain contingency plans had been made, the first steps were tiny. Sir Josiah, now Lord, Stamp, chairman of the London, Midland and Scottish Railway, was made a part-time adviser on economic co-ordination. Stamp's job was to prepare a 'survey' of departmental war plans, reporting to a Cabinet committee chaired by the Chancellor of the Exchequer, Sir John Simon. He was given a room in the offices of the War Cabinet at Gwydr House, a secretary, Francis Hemming, and two economists, Hubert Henderson and Henry Clay, the latter seconded from the Bank of England. Henderson was given a room at the Treasury and told to divide his time between the Stamp survey and ill-defined advisory duties. Dennis Robertson was made 'temporary administrative officer' at the Treasury to Sir Frederick Phillips, head of the Finance Division. In December 1939 a start was made to setting up a Central Economic Information Service under the direction of Henderson and Clay. This lackadaisical transition to wartime administration was much attacked in Parliament.

Keynes was not one of the chosen. He was fifty-six and sickly. Apart from the question of his health, there was no obvious slot for him. He was too eminent to be made an ordinary civil servant, and too stimulating to be let loose in Whitehall. He did not expect a government job. His first thought was to get Richard Kahn into the Treasury to do 'the sort of thing I used to do last time', while he would take over Kahn's bursarial and teaching duties at King's, and draft memoranda quietly in his room, with only occasional visits to London. This, he implied, was all he was fit for.[1] The Treasury quickly scotched the idea of letting Keynes in through the back door: Kahn was eventually appointed assistant secretary at the Board of Trade, on condition that he steered clear of currency questions. However, the thought that Keynes would be confined to King's was never quite plausible. His health, he told his friends, was 80 per cent of what it had been; and the Ogre had promised him full health eighteen months after his treatment started – that is, by September 1940. His usefulness was bound to suck him into Whitehall in the end, if the war became serious. This was by no means certain. Chamberlain was still Prime Minister, though he brought Churchill back into the government as First Lord of the Admiralty. Appeasement had not turned out as he had expected, since Hitler had taken to seizing countries without waiting for Chamberlain to offer them to him. But as Britain and France were in no position to stop Germany conquering Poland, and had no offensive plans of their own, it was not clear where the war would go.

The war opened with a flurry of controls over imports, transport, prices and assembly – and a stream of letters and memoranda from Keynes protesting against them. 'It might be sounder in every way to make motoring expensive than to make it the subject of wangling [to get additional petrol coupons]; – it might even save more petrol,' he observed acidly in his first note to the Treasury, written on 14 September. He looked to free prices to stimulate domestic production of essentials, not unmindful that the prices of Tilton's breeding sows had collapsed disastrously because the farmers could not afford to sell bacon at the tariff fixed by the Ministry of Agriculture.[2] In a note on exchange regulations, which he supplied on 24 September at the Treasury's request, he argued against 'complete exchange control on the German model' and in favour of allowing a modest 'black exchange'.[3] Rationing money was Keynes's alternative to rationing supplies, and he held fast to the distinction even when the claims of war became more clamant.

Keynes's quietist inclinations were soon overcome by the pull of events. He started coming to London regularly in mid-week, plugging himself back into his old circuits of influence and persuasion. On Wednesday 20 September he hosted the first of a number of weekly meetings at 46 Gordon Square for William Beveridge, Walter Layton, Arthur Salter and Hubert Henderson: the Conservative MP Robert Boothby formed a link between this group and an all-party parliamentary committee headed by the Liberal MP Clement Davies, who was to be useful a little later in arranging meetings with MPs. The 'Old Dogs', as the Keynes group called themselves, had served government in the last war; except for Henderson, they were reluctantly unemployed in this one. They growled away, as Old Dogs tend to, at the chaotic state of administration – 'fifty times worse than anything we had in the last war', Keynes told Henderson.[4] Of Sir Horace Wilson (Head of the Treasury), who had thought up a scheme for dispersing departments in the event of bombing, he remarked that 'it is rather terrifying that a brain that could think of such a mad plan should be in charge of so many of our affairs'.[5] Keynes had a horror of what he called the 'empty minded busybodyness' which war always caused to luxuriate. The Old Dogs put bright ideas to the departments, from where they received polite, non-committal responses. Keynes realised that his memoranda were not having much effect: 'you must either be right in or right out', he told Brand.

For the first time since his illness Keynes started going to his two dining clubs – the Other Club and the Tuesday Club. The first brought him into regular contact with its founder, Winston Churchill. The second kept him in touch with Whitehall. He wrote to Oswald Falk: 'The departments are at sixes and sevens, the home front is a real mess. There is more need even than there was last time of a method such as the Tuesday Club presents of conveying constructive criticism.'[6] He used these intimate gatherings of the great, the good and the almost good to put forward his own ideas and pick up gossip.

On 27 September German troops entered Warsaw; the next day Germany and Russia settled their zones of occupation. Bernard Shaw wrote to Nancy Astor: 'Everyone who can see three moves in front of his or her nose knows that the war is over.'[7] Some members of the Cabinet agreed. There was much defeatist talk at dinner parties and beyond: in the House of Commons on 3 October, the seventy-six-year-old Lloyd George urged a negotiated settlement. Keynes was worried about Kingsley Martin. 'His mind', he wrote to Edward Whitley, a fellow *New Statesman* board member, on 3 October, 'is ... subject from time to time to moods of extreme defeatism. I cannot feel perfectly sure that he might not suddenly come out in the paper with a leader demanding immediate peace on almost any terms.'[8]

Martin came to see him in London on the evening of 4 October with the proof of an article by Bernard Shaw called 'Uncommon Sense about the War'. Uncommon sense, according to Shaw, demanded that '[we] make peace with [Hitler] and with all the world instead of making more mischief and ruining our people in the process'. Martin's decision to publish Shaw's article gave Keynes a sleepless night. The next morning Martin found a note from Keynes on his desk, denouncing Shaw's views as 'mischievous' and advising Martin to reject his contribution, but in any case to submit it to the Censor. Keynes and Shaw then had a row on the telephone, marred by Shaw's inability to hear almost anything Keynes said to him: as Shaw later explained, he was 'too old and deaf for normal treatment on that instrument: only an oratorical performance reaches me effectively'. Keynes agreed: 'Even the one phrase you caught was wrong. To your question, whether I was crazy, I replied merely that I thought the article was a very bad one. On which there came from you a cheerful laugh, which seemed the appropriate response. . . .' Keynes was so upset by this episode – he had a 'heart attack' according to Virginia Woolf – that he applied to Plesch for a sedative. To his surprise, the Foreign Office recommended publication. Shaw was not in the least surprised. He wrote irrepressibly to Keynes after their telephone conversation: 'I was sure they would rise up and call me blessed for saying what they all wanted to say, but dared not,' attributing to his Irish extraction his insight into the true nature of the war. He added more gently, 'you must bear with me. I am sometimes useful.'[9]

Keynes did not regard Shaw's article, published on 7 October, as at all useful, though he thought that, with the deletions Shaw accepted, it was now 'harmless'. His own reply to Shaw, published on 14 October, harked back to his polemics of the mid-1930s: 'The intelligentsia of the Left were the loudest in demanding that the Nazi aggression be resisted at all costs. When it comes to a showdown, scarce four weeks have passed before they remember that they are pacifists, and write defeatist letters to your columns, leaving the defence of freedom and of civilisation to Colonel Blimp and the Old School Tie, for whom Three Cheers.'[10]

Like Churchill, and unlike Chamberlain, Keynes attached the greatest importance to drawing America into the Allied net. His reading of American opinion was filtered through the articles Walter Lippmann and Dorothy Thompson were writing for the *New York Herald Tribune*, which he thought were the 'best anti-Nazi propaganda' appearing anywhere. When Lord Macmillan at the Ministry of Information refused to distribute them in neutral and Empire countries on grounds of expense, Keynes wrote to him: 'Alas, your letter confirms the prevailing opinion that money is only available for what is useless.'[11] He drafted some 'Notes on the War for the President' on 7 November, which he correctly decided inadvisable to send. Perhaps word had got through to him that Roosevelt had not welcomed his previous attempts to advise him on how to run his administration.

Keynes was testing out his capacity for the active life. He stood the strain well, often getting tired, but rapidly recovering. He was convinced that a special course of injections, devised by the Ogre, kept him free of colds all winter. Lydia reported exhausting meetings (including one with an 'Australian magnet'), visits to the Cambridge Arts Theatre, late nights. Keynes's care for the Arts Theatre and the well-being of artists did not cease with the war. He persuaded Norman Higgins not to volunteer for the RAF. He interceded with R. A. Butler at the Foreign Office to get ballet dancers exempted from military service; both Germany and Russia had let off ballet dancers in the last war, 'and we ought not to be less civilised than they were then'. Although Butler tried, Ernest Brown, the Minister of Labour, refused. 'I am afraid he is a savage,' Keynes reported to Raymond Mortimer.[12]

One commitment he did manage to evade was an invitation from

A. B. Ramsey, Master of Magdalene College, and chairman of the University Conservative Committee, to stand for Parliament for Cambridge University as an unopposed Independent. Rather to his surprise, Plesch declared him fit for the job; but after some hesitation Keynes declined, explaining that 'the active political life is not my right and true activity'.[13] His brother-in-law A. V. Hill took his place and was Independent MP for Cambridge from 1940 to 1945. Hubert Henderson, one of many whom Keynes consulted, hoped his refusal would not preclude him 'doing something Ministerial later on, if your health is completely restored'.[14]

II. COMPULSORY SAVINGS

When not fussing about petrol coupons, Bernard Shaw and such like, Keynes was germinating his grand plan on 'how to pay for the war' – a project which kept him occupied until the partial triumph of his ideas in April 1941. The 'Keynes Plan', as it was soon known, was triggered by Sir John Simon's first war budget of 27 September 1939, but it was the crystallisation of much of what Keynes had been writing and saying in the previous two years. In the proto-war period from 1937 to 1939 the Treasury had relied heavily on borrowing for rearmament, fearing the depressing effect of increased taxes on employment and the tax yield. Simon's emergency budget of September 1939 continued this policy. He imposed additional taxes of £107m for the financial year 1939–40, but defence spending was set to rise by £600m. Since he had already projected a deficit of £500m in his March 1939 budget, this left a new projected deficit of £1000m – or 25 per cent of GDP – to be met by borrowing. This was deficit finance with a vengeance. The Treasury had evidently absorbed the lesson that no great danger of inflation threatened while the proportion of insured workers unemployed still stood at over 9 per cent. But if it thereby congratulated itself on its up-to-date 'Keynesian' approach, it was quickly disabused. Keynes had hopped over the unemployment problem to new ground. As he explained in *The Times* on 28 September, the problem was, or would soon be, one not of inadequate, but of excess, demand. The need was to limit civilian consumption of the products of a fully employed war economy, and to this the budget made hardly any contribution: the new taxes, 'appalling as [they] may seem to individuals, [are] chicken-feed to the dragons of war'.[15]

From the start he was clear about one point. The government must find some way of stopping the public consuming the extra resources which government spending would create, otherwise they would be lost to the war effort. The main technique used in the last war – stumbled into rather than deliberate – was inflation. The government printed the money to pay for its domestic war spending; increased government spending caused prices to rise; workers whose wages lagged behind the rise in prices were forced to consume less; the 'windfall' profits of entrepreneurs were commandeered by the government in the form of loans and taxes. As a result of this, the price level doubled in the four years of war. Technically, the First World War was financed by an 'inflation tax' levied on the workers, which accrued to the government in the form of taxes on, or loans from, businessmen.[16]

Keynes's 'big' idea was first revealed in what Lydia called a 'brilliant lecture' on 'War Potential and War Finance' to Cambridge's Marshall Society on 20 October, which left him 'healthily tired' but with no chest pains. He worked up this lecture into an article for *The Times*, 'Paying for the War', which he submitted to its editor Geoffrey Dawson on 26 October, calling it 'the most important proposal I have ever sent you'. At the same time he circulated copies for comment.[17] Cut in two, it appeared in *The Times* on 14 and 15 November. Keynes's solution to the expected increase in working-class purchasing power was to impose compulsory savings. A graduated percentage of all incomes above a stipulated minimum would be paid over to the government, partly as direct taxes, partly as compulsory savings. This would subsume the existing system of direct taxation. Part of the levy would be used to discharge income tax and surtax obligations, if any. The rest would be credited to interest-bearing individual accounts in the Post Office Savings Bank, and be collected (for most wage earners) through the National Insurance machinery, and would be repayable after the war in instalments to help the first post-war slump. The yield of the levy might amount to £400m more than existing direct taxation.[18]

The central point in 'Paying for the War' was the rejection of inflation-cum-rationing as a way of reducing working-class consumption. This automatically excluded reliance on traditional debt finance, which depended in large part on borrowing from the inflated incomes of the business class. Compulsory saving was the alternative. This killed several birds with one stone: it restricted working-class consumption without robbing workers of the rewards of greater effort; it drastically restricted the consumption of the wealthy without imposing penal, disincentive tax rates; surcharging post-tax or non-taxable incomes rather than increasing taxes would ensure that peace started with a more modest burden of taxation; and it avoided the need for comprehensive rationing and price controls. As explained to the Tuesday Club on 6 December, 'You will see that my object is to maintain a system of natural prices to the utmost possible extent.'

The Keynes Plan received wide press coverage, confirming Dawson's belief that 'an important article in *The Times* gets publicity everywhere else'.[19] Keynes hoped that his scheme might form the basis for the next budget, and over the ensuing months he canvassed it tirelessly in Whitehall, Parliament and press, his persuasive efforts climaxing with the publication of his booklet *How to Pay for the War* in February 1940. Keynes was an heroic controversialist. As well as taking on his critics in public, and explaining his Plan to private gatherings of politicians, businessmen and trade unionists, he replied mainly courteously, and often at length, to most letters he received. He made it plain that he was more committed to the logic of his approach than to the details of his proposals, which he modified in response to criticism and suggestions.

What was the character of the response? From the start, the economics profession was unanimously in favour of Keynes's logic. This is not particularly surprising, since Keynes had moved the discussion on to a terrain where non-Keynesian and Keynesian economics agreed. A particularly significant endorsement came from his self-styled 'scientific antipode' Friedrich Hayek, who publicly praised the Keynes Plan in the *Spectator* of 24 November. As Hayek put it to Keynes: 'It is reassuring to know that we agree so completely on the economics of scarcity, even if we differ on when it applies.'[20] The eager embrace by all economists of the 'economics of scarcity' suggests that the 'economics of plenty' which was the real subject of the *General Theory* still had only a very limited appeal. Of the inner core of Keynesians, only Richard Kahn had doubts about Keynes's anti-inflationary emphasis. Interestingly, the feature of the Keynes Plan which got least support from the economics profession was the proposal to release the blocked credits to counteract the post-war slump. Hayek did not believe in increased spending as a cure for slumps; in any case, the immediate post-war prospect was not for a slump but for an inflationary boom. Like Hicks, he favoured a capital levy to reduce effective demand after the war.

The economist–administrators in Whitehall, men like Stamp, Henderson and Clay, were also firmly behind Keynes's logic, though critical of the details of his Plan. Keynes rejected Henderson's amendment to tax only overtime pay. 'Under your plan,' he wrote to Henderson, 'everyone would have as large an income as before, and even the overtimer would have a considerably larger one,' leaving aggregate consumption 'appreciably higher than pre-war'.[21]

Another old friend, Bob Brand of Lazard Brothers, feared the effect of compulsory savings on voluntary savings – a view influenced by his close association with Sir Robert Kindersley, chairman of both Lazards and the National Savings Committee. He also thought that rationing of essentials at fixed prices was an essential *quid pro quo* for trade union wage restraint.[22] Keynes was unconvinced. When Brand supplied him with details of the German rationing scheme, he wrote back scathingly: 'The policy of fixed prices plus having nothing in the shops to buy – an expedient pursued for many years by the Russian authorities – is undoubtedly one of the very best ways of preventing inflation!'[23] When Arthur Salter, Brand, and John and Ursula Hicks publicly suggested a Treasury subsidy for an 'iron ration' of necessaries, Keynes initially resisted on cost grounds – 'As an old Treasury

man I am scared of it' – but was eventually persuaded that it was politically
necessary. It had to, however, be conditional on acceptance of compulsory
saving.[24]

Keynes thought that Kindersley's optimism concerning voluntary savings was 'obviously clouded by emotional disturbance'. He accepted that
'there will be some leakages through the withdrawals of existing savings.
But this seems to me to apply to any drastic remedy whatever.... It is true
of high surtax.' Keynes was right. The National Savings Movement campaigned vigorously to mobilise small savings throughout the war, but it
seems that 'the switching of assets was the main source of the "savings"
totals achieved'.[25]

Keynes was astounded by the hostile reaction to his proposals outside
the magic circle of economists, experts and insiders. The horror of 'compulsion' united the chairman of the National Savings Committee, the Beaverbrook press and the Labour Party in defence of voluntary saving and free
trade unionism. The *Daily Express* of 16 November 1939 rubbished his Plan
in terms which would not discredit the *Sun* today:

> Another enemy attacks the liberty of the people! Mr Keynes, the
> economist. He takes out his textbooks, he flourishes his fountain pen,
> and he rushes out of his study to demand that compulsory saving
> should be imposed. The Government, he says, should take away part of
> the workers' wages, force the public to lend them money. What an
> insult to the patriotism of our people! What a slander on their eagerness
> for voluntary sacrifice to suggest that they will not freely lend every
> pound and penny they are asked for!

What made Keynes's 'propaganda' so attractive to the 'insiders' was that
it drove home the point that, as Stamp put it, 'the war can only be paid for
by annexing a large part of the increased purchasing power of the wage
earning class and also encroaching on the pre-war standard of living'.[26] But
it was precisely this feature that made it so hard to sell to the leaders of the
Labour Party (including the trade union movement), whose support was
absolutely essential. Keynes made great efforts with the Labour Party –
indeed most of his persuasive efforts were directed at them. He had carefully
sent the manuscript of his *Times* articles to Clement Attlee on 24 October,
with a personal letter which said that his plan offered 'the only way of
handling the financial end of the war that is at the same time just and
advantageous to the working class'. Attlee's reply devastated him: the leader
of the Labour Party wrote back that Keynes's proposals would impose a
'crushing' burden on Attlee himself! Keynes sent him a testy four-page letter:
'The question is, do you prefer to be mulcted in alternative ways?... There
is not the slightest good your saying that you cannot afford any of them.
You have got to suffer the reduction one way or another.' The great
advantage of compulsory saving over orthodox taxation or inflation was that

workers would not lose the benefit of their higher wages, only be obliged to defer their spending.[27]

Even worse was Labour's public response. Arthur Greenwood, Labour's deputy leader, wrote in the *Daily Express* that the Keynes Plan smacked of Hitlerism.[28] Ernest Bevin, leader of the Transport and General Workers Union and the dominant figure in the trade union movement, said it was the government's duty to control prices, and, if it failed to do so, he would use collective bargaining to prevent any erosion of workers' real wages.[29] Keynes was particularly upset by Bevin's attitude – 'almost the worst thing I have read since the beginning of the war'[30] – as he had formed a high opinion of him when they had served together on the Macmillan Committee in 1930–1. He made repeated efforts to see Bevin, using the Liberal MP Clement Davies as his intermediary, but without success. Trade union opposition to increased burdens on their members was a key factor in stopping the government imposing heavier taxes on the working class, even in the Keynesian form of deferred pay, the Treasury's expectation being that it would stimulate equivalent claims for wage increases.[31]

Had Keynes bothered to read Labour's own booklet, also called *How to Pay for the War*, published that autumn, he would have been less surprised at the Party's frosty response. Drawn up by the economists Evan Durbin, Hugh Gaitskell and Douglas Jay of Labour's War Finance Group, it argued that, with a limited tax base and lack of direct controls on industry, large-scale borrowing was inevitable. This would be inflationary, but a 'moderate and controlled' inflation, accompanied by rationing and other restrictions on consumption, was desirable, as it would increase the profits and hence output of the war industries, increase saving when consumption was restricted, and reduce the real burden of debt. The burden of post-war debt could be further reduced by a capital levy after the end of the war.[32] Keynes greatly weakened his persuasive effort by not engaging directly with Labour's argument. Also, as in the First World War,[33] he grossly underestimated the appeal of rationing. Oliver Lyttelton, Controller of Non-ferrous Metals, made a brutal political point: 'Nobody cares a damn about justice: equality is what matters.'[34]

It was a relief to Lydia when they finally got back to Tilton on 14 December. At least he could work away quietly, without being sucked into endless meetings and dinners. Richard Kahn was their only house-guest. They took Christmas Day off, drank Sam Courtauld's champagne and retired to bed early. On Boxing Day, Keynes was back at work, going over to Charleston for tea with Duncan Grant, Clive and Vanessa Bell, and the Bells' son Quentin, whom Maynard was employing as a farm labourer. There had been a sortie to Rodmell for tea with the Woolfs on 23 December, and they returned the visit on 27 December. Such reunions, with their opportunities for reminiscence, gossip and exploration of personal standards, were now rare for Keynes – not just on account of the war, his busyness and Lydia's inaptness for the Bloomsbury style of cerebration, but because his attitude of omniscience on all topics had become too overwhelming for intimacy. Virginia Woolf described the scene at Rodmell, with Maynard 'lying extended on the sofa ... with the two fog lamps burning, & Lydia a sort of fairy elf in her fur cap.... He is now supreme, mounted on his sick throne, a successful man – farmer, bursar, a man of business, he called himself, applying for petrol. A heavy man with a thick moustache. A moralist. As interested in Patsy the[ir] black dog with the bald patch as in Europe. He was saying – odd how hard it is to remember – he was telling us about salt; water; heat and cold & their effect on the urine.'[35]

III. EFFORTS AT PERSUASION

With so many comments coming in, Keynes had suggested to Harold Macmillan on 27 November that the material of his articles be turned into a short book, initially to be called 'The Economic Consequences of the War'. On Macmillan's agreement, he set to work on revisions. These were specifically aimed at winning over Labour support. He now proposed to offer family allowances as a *quid pro quo* for wage moderation. Keynes preferred this method of reducing wage pressure to that of subsidising the sale of necessaries at fixed prices.

His concession of a capital levy after the war was a less happy compromise with his critics, for it enabled anti-Keynesians to claim, much later, that he was hostile to private enterprise.[36] The public and private discussion about 'what to do' with the deferred pay after the war offers a fascinating counterfactual perspective on the history of the welfare state. The most interesting suggestion, which came from several of Keynes's correspondents, was that compulsory savings be turned into life assurance policies. This would not just guard against the danger of premature release but give all earners a security against post-war hazards. This foreshadows the later fashionable Singapore model of social insurance. Keynes was interested, but pointed out that for such security to be achieved compulsory saving would need to be made permanent, not just temporary.[37] Hayek's suggestion of repayment in the form of shares in British industry rather than cash was another idea ahead of its time.[38] Continuing compulsory savings into peacetime to endow wage-earners with personal assets was a neglected alternative to the 'social insurance' route to social protection mapped out in the Beveridge Report of 1942. Keynes was diverted from this line of thought by his conviction that the post-war world would need more consumption, not more saving.

Through the efforts of Pethick-Lawrence and Walter Citrine, meetings with the Labour Party front bench and the Economic Committee of the General Council of the TUC were arranged on the morning and afternoon respectively of 24 January 1940. The revised proposals Keynes now presented included administration of deferred pay by trade union and friendly societies, family allowances, and a capital levy after the war. He estimated that his new proposals would maintain the pre-war consumption standard of all earning less than £250 a year, while reducing by a third the consumption of those earning over £250 a year. As he explained to Stamp on 29 January, his plan was 'not now merely a piece of technique, but aims at actually using the opportunity of war finance for constructive social reforms, and a bigger move towards equality than any we have made for a long time'.[39] However, the Labour leaders were unmoved. For all his verbal eloquence, Keynes was finding the job of persuasion incredibly frustrating. 'The trouble is not with public opinion,' he exploded to his First World War Treasury chief Reginald McKenna, 'but [with] the bloody politicians whose bloody minds have not been sufficiently prepared for anything unfamiliar to their ancestors. If the things were to be sponsored and put across with reponsible leadership, there would be practically no opposition at all.'[40]

Keynes went on trying, addressing a group of MPs on 20 February and the Fabian Society the next day. He told the Fabians that from the start of the war he had been 'obsessed with the task of finding the right solution' to the problem of reducing consumption in a way which satisfied popular psychology and social justice. He disliked the 'old-fashioned laissez-faire' solution of inflation, the 'new fashioned totalitarian' method of comprehensive rationing which would reduce Britain to a slave state, and the compromise between them of 'a totalitarian solution for a narrow range of necessaries and inflation over the remaining field of consumption'. The right solution was to fix purchasing power and allow freedom to spend the balance; to make sure that the National Debt was owned by everyone who had earned it; and to arrange the details so as to make the fiscal system an engine of social reform.[41]

How to Pay for the War was published by Macmillan on 27 February. Keynes had done his best to make his Plan more widely acceptable: to the working class by incorporating extra protections for the lowest paid in the form of family allowances and (a concession which ran counter to his liberal instincts) 'iron rations' at subsidised prices,[42] and to the financially orthodox by adding a capital levy to discharge the liability created by deferred pay.[43] He now conceded that the subsidy might be a useful *quid pro quo* for the promise of wage moderation.[44] The extra protections required offsetting reductions in children's allowances under the income tax system and increased progression in repayable tax;[45] the capital levy might be the prelude to an annual wealth tax.[46]

Keynes's private publicity machine had gone into action with 380 presentation copies, and he puffed his pamphlet tirelessly in the precincts of Whitehall. On 28 February he spoke to 250 MPs from all parties in the Commons without fatigue; on 6 March he addressed the Trade Union Club, with the octogenarian Ben Tillett in the chair; the same day Lord Balfour of Burleigh initiated a debate in the House of Lords, Keynes briefing Lord Hankey, who replied for the government. Difficult meetings at the Treasury and with the Chancellor of the Exchequer followed the next day, with Keynes having dinner in bed to recover from the strain. On 8 March he came back to Cambridge, after seeing the governor of the Bank of England Montagu Norman, 'fresh as a button [and] in the evening went to the theatre'. On Saturday there were 'sausages and Troilus' at the Cambridge Arts Theatre, with noisy undergraduates making sleep at St Edward's Passage impossible. On 11 March he did a broadcast interview with Donald Tyerman for the BBC, for which he was paid thirty guineas. There was a meeting with the Parliamentary Monetary Committee on 19 March, at which he concentrated mainly on foreign exchange matters, but also answered questions on his deferred pay proposals.

Keynes gave detailed accounts of the reactions to his pamphlet, largely based on public comment and private correspondence, to Geoffrey Dawson, editor of *The Times*. The trade union leaders were sympathetic, though Bevin was unapproachable. The economic advisers of the Labour Party – G.D.H. Cole, Harold Laski, Richard Crossman and Barbara Wootton – were 'strongly in favour'. Among academic economists there was 'almost universal agreement on principle, though some differences on points of detail'. The only outspoken opposition, 'apart from the dark questionings by the Labour Front Bench', came from Kindersley, Beaverbrook, 'who says frankly that he prefers inflation', and the communist *Daily Worker*.

Lydia and Maynard were back at Tilton on 22 March for Easter. His health had stood the strain of war work pretty well. 'I have certainly been taking in the last few weeks a burden of intellectual and nervous activities which I had scarcely expected to be able to support,' he reported to Sir Edmund Spriggs at Ruthin Castle on 13 March.[47] On 18 March he had gone to Plesch complaining of a 'feeling of distress in the aorta' from time to time. Plesch prescribed a porous plaster to be worn constantly under his left armpit. At Tilton, he had his first setback for some months, Lydia reporting him looking 'old and worn out' after a potter round the farm with Logan Thomson on 31 March. Next day, Sunday, he was discussing details of the forthcoming Cambridge Arts Theatre productions with the actor-manager Donald Wolfit. Ford's play *'Tis Pity She's a Whore* must be done, he told Wolfit in the authoritative tone he now brought to all topics, 'with gusto and in the Italian manner'. (Dadie Rylands thought no one would come 'unless the title stimulates the curiosity of the RAF'.) On Sunday 7 April, they entertained the Woolfs, Maynard telling Virginia that the war was practically won.[48] Two days later, the Germans invaded Norway – 'the first main clinch of the war', as Churchill put it. At Charleston, Lydia had a fierce argument with Clive Bell, who had made the mistake of saying he thought the Germans were winning.[49]

No appraisal of Keynes's political legacy can leave out *How to Pay for the War*. After the war ended, Lionel Robbins wrote that there were two views about how to run a war economy – the fiscal theory and the planning theory. According to the fiscal theory the government should withdraw as much purchasing power as was necessary to avoid inflation, and allow the price system to allocate resources. Since Keynes is so often unthinkingly placed in the *dirigiste* camp, it is important to insist that he favoured the fiscal theory of war control. More importantly, he *invented* the fiscal theory, precisely in order to avoid 'totalitarian' planning. He did not see demand management as a useful adjunct to planning, price fixing, rationing, bureaucratic controls and so on, but as an alternative to them, in war as in peace.

A case can be made out for *How to Pay for the War* as the quintessence of Keynes's achievement. It engaged all the qualities of his complex nature. The union of theory and practice, the linking of economic doctrine to political philosophy here achieved its most compelling artistic expression. At the core of his vision was his understanding that modern society would no longer stand 'Nature's cures' of inflation and unemployment for the malfunctioning of the market system. His answer was a permanent scheme of regulating spending to avoid booms and slumps, of which his war Plan was a first instalment, politically easier to start off as an anti-inflationary policy. This logic was still resisted by politicians and economists of the right, wedded to *laissez-faire*. But there was a sting in the tail for the left as well. For most socialists, the war offered a chance to introduce physical planning not just for war but as a permanent system. Against these temptations Keynes steadfastly defended the price system and consumer choice. He wrote: 'I am seizing the opportunity to introduce a principle of policy which may be thought of as marking the line of division between the totalitarian and the free economy.' It was an expression of his philosophy of the Middle Way.[50]

IV. THE TREASURY SAYS NO

The fate of the Keynes Plan depended on the Treasury. Keynes was heartened by the interest of the Chancellor of the Exchequer, Sir John Simon who did not raise any insuperable objections. The government had no real alternative to his Plan, he told Dawson, but 'they are extremely reluctant to adopt any drastic remedy until the necessity of it is obvious, and more than obvious, to the densest member of the public'. But with such a weight of 'authoritative support' they need not feel so scared of public opinion, if only they would 'grasp the nettle'.[51]

This was greatly to oversimplify the Treasury's problem. The general Treasury attitude to Keynes's policy proposals, going back to the 1920s, was that they were invariably stimulating but that, as one Treasury official commented on his *Means to Prosperity* in 1933, 'he has never allowed questions of time-lag or of practical feasibility to interfere with the even flow of his argument....'[52] On one point there was no disagreement: Keynes's resistance to the use of high interest rates to check a boom coincided with the Treasury's desire to borrow large sums for war as cheaply as possible, as well as 'an appreciation that the social and political climate would not permit a repeat of the *rentier*-friendly policy of the First World War'.[53] This put the burden of anti-inflationary policy on the budget. Here there was as yet no meeting of minds. The pre-Keynesian orthodoxy was that the use of borrowed money to supplement taxes was not inflationary if matched by the flow of voluntary saving. 'Chancellors imposed tax increases as sharp as they thought that the public would stomach and then hoped that the amounts they would have to squeeze out of the capital markets would not exceed the supply of voluntary saving.'[54] That is why they were so keen to encourage the National Savings Movement. Officials were only dimly aware that borrowing could be inflationary if the savings being borrowed were themselves being created by increased government spending. Keynes was the first to put clearly into circulation two propositions: (a) that 'paying for the war' meant reducing civilian consumption to the extent required by the war effort and (b) that the required reduction would not be brought about without inflation simply by the government meeting its expenditure by taxes and loans.

There was also an overwhelming practical objection to the Keynes Plan. Any *deliberate* withdrawal of spending power from the public required information about how much the 'aggregate of purchasing power' exceeded the 'available supply of goods'. This knowledge was not available to the Treasury early in 1940. The Inland Revenue knew the total amount of incomes it was taxing, but in 1939 income tax was far from being a mass tax, since about three-fifths of wage-earners did not pay it. Squeezing more money out of existing taxpayers would do nothing to stop the majority of wage-earners spending their increased earnings in the shops. An anti-inflationary budgetary policy required national or 'social' accounts. Keynes had been calling in vain for official national income statistics since 1937. In making his calculations in 1939, he had to rely on pioneering work by Colin Clark in 1938, updated by a young émigré economist, Erwin Rothbarth, working as an assistant in statistical research at the Cambridge Economics and Politics faculty.

A 'budget of national resources' was published as an appendix to his pamphlet *How to Pay for the War*. It was based on his *General Theory* concepts of aggregate demand and aggregate supply, measured in prices, and subdivided into components, to which he applied the golden rule of double-entry book-keeping, that the sums on both sides of the ledger must balance. Both conceptual and statistical problems had to be finessed on the way. There was no agreement about definitions of national income and national output – a matter which Keynes debated with both Rothbarth and Nicholas Kaldor.[55] Working-class saving behaviour had only recently started to be studied by the Cambridge graduate Charles Madge, co-founder with Tom Harrisson of 'Mass Observation', for whose work Keynes obtained a grant. Rothbarth marvelled at 'what one can do with such imperfect information'. Keynes was characteristically forthright: 'When statistics do not make sense I find it generally wiser to prefer sense to statistics.'[56]

In what were little more than back-of-envelope calculations, Keynes estimated that government spending in 1939–40 was set to rise by £1.8bn. The problem then was to stop the public from spending their increased incomes. He worked out that the government would get £900m by selling capital assets and that the full-year yield of Simon's taxes and other fiscal devices would bring in about £500m. This left a 'gap' of between £400m and £500m to be filled by extra taxes or compulsory saving if inflation was to be avoided.[57]

The logic of all this was serviceable, if crude; but the bold and fluctuating 'guesstimates' about magnitudes seemed to the Treasury too flimsy a basis for fiscal policy. The Treasury was influenced not just by public opposition to Keynes's proposals, but also by workload and administrative objections to his specific Plan raised by the Inland Revenue. It agreed that Britain could not expect both more guns and more butter. But its feeling was that temporary inflation was the least bad option, especially as the war might not last or explode into full action. In the meantime, Keynes's agitation would help prepare public opinion for higher taxes if and when they became necessary.[58] There was no need for his 'ingenious devices'.[59] The one concrete result of Keynes's agitation was that the Stamp Committee authorised the start of work on compiling national income statistics.

In these circumstances the Chancellor's interest was deceptive. In his budget of 23 April, Sir John Simon proclaimed that 'voluntarism is on trial', imposed minor indirect tax increases, raised Excess Profits Tax to 100 per cent, projected a deficit of almost £1500m and produced 'absurdly optimistic estimates' of voluntary lending. Specifically, he rejected compulsory savings, saying that they would 'kill' voluntary savings. In a letter to *The Times* on 25 April Keynes remarked tartly that it was only the government's failure to increase war output which was protecting it from the financial problem. 'Sir John Simon may claim that this is his fortune and not his fault. For the rest of us it is our misfortune and far from our intention ... how little the country understands what sacrifices victory will require.'[60]

The military and political calculations underpinning this relaxed financial strategy were soon to be shattered, and with it Keynes's own semi-detached role. On 10 May the Third Reich sprang its military might on Belgium, Holland and France; the same day the Chamberlain government fell. Winston Churchill became Prime Minister and formed a coalition with the Labour and Liberal parties. On Monday evening, 13 May, Keynes saw 'Tis Pity She's a Whore at Cambridge, gave a party for Wolfit, and early the next morning had a 'heart attack' in St Edward's Passage. He 'seems very weak, bad under the eyes, blue lips, lies in pyjamas and rests with the lovely sun from the windows', Lydia wrote in her diary. 'It is sad after 4 years of illness.' There was a further attack on Friday. Lydia wrote: 'I cried. I cannot stand the strain of illness and war.'

33

The Dragons of War

I. MAD DOGS AND ENGLISHMEN

Maynard Keynes's setback in May was a warning that his health might never fully recover. Throughout May and June he continued lecturing in Cambridge, icebags on his heart whenever he lay down. The increasingly dreadful war news so affected him that he had to have the wireless turned off. On 24 May he saw the Ogre, who prescribed fasting. For five days he lived on coffee, tea, raw cabbage and sour oranges. A regime of cold baths followed. Not till France capitulated on 17 June, with the British army safely evacuated from Dunkirk, did Keynes recover. It was a relief that Britain was now on its own, 'where, speaking for myself, I do not feel the least anxiety as to the eventual outcome'.[1]

Keynes's confidence in victory was shared by the British people. In Keynes's case, it seems to have rested on little more than the conviction that Britain was invulnerable to invasion, that Hitler would start making blunders, and that sooner or later the United States was bound to come in. He was not alone in thinking that the Nazi–Soviet Pact was a loveless union which would soon collapse. At a lunch he had with Maisky, the Soviet ambassador, on 12 June, he predicted that 'Hitler would meet his Waterloo a long way East of Berlin and that we should be there'.[2] The Grand Alliance had thus formed in Keynes's mind long before it came about in fact. It was a flimsy enough basis on which to continue the struggle.

Hitler thought the British were mad, and in the Reichstag on 16 July appealed to their 'common sense' to make peace. The appeal fell on deaf ears. Britain's moment of total isolation from the Continent was to be its 'finest hour'. The British had never trusted the French, and the Germans were now beyond the pale. At that moment, in June 1940, history lived up to the British people's conception of themselves – and their relationship with the Continent of Europe. It was to be an enduring image.

II. BACK TO THE TREASURY

Parallel with his public campaign on the budget Keynes had been conducting a guerilla campaign with the Treasury on exchange control. Any 'budget
of national resources' had to include not just domestic resources but those
which could be attracted from abroad – through export of goods or gold,
the sale of foreign securities owned by British nationals, and foreign loans.
Early in 1940 Keynes had become convinced that foreign exchange vital to
importing war supplies was leaking out through gaps in the exchange
control system the Treasury had set up on the outbreak of war. This had
aimed to channel the flow of all foreign exchange transactions involving
'hard currencies' – mainly dollars – through the Treasury's Exchange Equalisation Account. British exporters were required to sell their 'hard currency'
receipts to designated clearing banks for sterling at a fixed exchange rate
($4.03 to the pound), the banks making available the foreign exchange
needed to buy approved imports from the designated-currency countries;
and British residents were forbidden to sell securities marketable outside
the United Kingdom. Free payment in sterling was allowed within all the
countries of the British Empire except Canada, on the understanding that
their governments imposed similar exchange restrictions to those in Britain,
and sold their excess hard-currency receipts to the Bank of England in
return for sterling. This was the start of the 'fortified' sterling area. However,
the Treasury continued to allow non-residents to sell their sterling securities
for dollars in an unsupported currency market, believing that this freedom
was essential to attract and retain foreign balances (or loans) in London.[3]
This was one source of the 'dollar' drain. Another was the chaotic licensing
system, which allowed precious dollars to be squandered on non-essential
imports.
  Keynes's interest in the problem was triggered in February 1940 when
the Treasury, having requisitioned £30m worth of British-owned American
securities – which left Keynes himself with £1m to invest in replacement
shares for himself, King's College and the Provincial Insurance Company –
tried to sell large blocks of British Imperial Tobacco shares in the United
States. American holders of sterling bought shares in Imperial Tobacco by
selling their sterling securities for dollars, thus nullifying the intention of
the policy: the dollars earned by the Treasury from the sale of American
securities were those it was losing through the free exchange in London.
This episode disposed Keynes to 'go on the warpath'; he would 'follow
in Dr. Schacht's footsteps and block foreign balances as a whole'.[4] On 20
March Keynes told the Parliamentary Monetary Committee: 'It is a major

scandal that what easily may be tens of millions of resources which would be available otherwise to finance our adverse balance of trade should be allowed to escape in this way'; the drain could be stopped with 'a stroke of the pen'.[5] Keynes primed two Conservative members of the Monetary Committee, Robert Boothby and P. C. Loftus, to ask the Chancellor in Parliament whether he proposed to stop foreign nationals taking money out of the country. Simon replied dourly that freedom to sell sterling for foreign currencies was the only way of keeping non-Empire balances in London.[6]

Keynes was not ready to put pen to paper till 10 April. It proved almost impossible to get useful statistics: the Treasury, he scornfully informed Boothby, had not the 'foggiest' idea of how much they had lost in the last six months.[7] In his fact-gathering he was helped by Thomas Balogh, a young Hungarian economist at the National Institute for Economic and Social Research, Richard Kahn, Austin Robinson and his stockbroker, Ian McPherson. He was soon able to estimate losses of £100m since the war started through the various leakages. He sent a first draft of a memorandum to Henry Clay at the Bank of England on 29 April and discussed it with him and Henry Siepmann on 8 May. The Bank was the Treasury's agent in operating the system of exchange control, and Keynes found it much more eager than the Treasury to make exchange control effective. It was a most heartening experience, he told Clay, to 'discover for once people in executive positions who were in a drastic state of mind, seemed completely competent and equal to their job and were *not* enjoying living in a perpetual twilight, dim and incomplete'. On Keynes's letter, Montagu Norman scribbled the 'once ... unimaginable' words: 'He must come again'.[8] Keynes's rapprochement with the Bank was based on a misconception. The Bank came to see itself as manager of an imperial currency bloc, fortified by permanent exchange controls; Keynes viewed these controls as a necessary wartime measure, to be discontinued once the emergency was over. The Bank would later lead the opposition to his Clearing Union Plan and, even more emphatically, to the Bretton Woods Agreement and the American loan.

With the German attack on France and the Low Countries, events took control of Keynes's drafting. The Treasury blocked all sales of sterling securities owned by non-residents and negotiated bilateral payment agreements between the sterling area and neutral countries. However it did not proceed with Keynes's proposal to pool the foreign financial resources of the four Allied empires (Britain, France, Belgium and Holland), and exploit their combined bargaining strength to negotiate credits with the United States.[9] The collapsing empires managed to get their gold reserves abroad (in France's case to Canada), but Britain never regarded them as part of its own reserve, treating them as obligations to be repaid. This was a costly mistake.

On 11 June, after seeing Emmanuel Monick, the French financial attaché in London, Keynes drafted a proclamation, for use by Churchill or the

Chancellor, promising that all aid to France should 'freely be given for the common cause'. He took this round to the new Chancellor, Kingsley Wood, that afternoon, explaining that its two objects were to encourage the French and to create a good precedent for the terms of impending United States aid to Britain. Even at this desperate moment of the war, Keynes was determined that it should not end with a debt problem. On 13 June, Wood issued a statement proposing that France and Britain should 'shar[e] together the burden of repairing the ravages of war', which nevertheless fell short of the pledge Keynes wanted. 'Were it not for this desperate battle in France, I should get my Master to pump some oxygen into Kingsley Wood,' explained Brendan Bracken, Churchill's Parliamentary Private Secretary. Churchill was thinking in even more grandiose terms. On 16 June, he authorised the offer of an indissoluble Franco-British Union. But it was too late. France surrendered the next day.

Keynes was still spending his weekends in Cambridge, keeping up a semblance of normal term-time activity. From the Prof – Arthur Pigou, also one of Plesch's patients – he received a reminder of more parochial concerns:

> The chief bad thing [about the tripos results] we [Sraffa and Pigou were examiners] found was that a very large number of people had been stuffed like sausages with bits of your stuff in such a way that (1) they were quite incapable of applying their own intelligence to it, and (2) they perpetually dragged it in regardless of its relevance to the question.... My own guess ... is that the parrot-like treatment of your stuff is due to the lectures and supervision of the beautiful Mrs [Joan] Robinson – a magpie breeding innumerable parrots. I gather that she puts in the Truth, with an enormous T, with such Prussian efficiency, that the wretched men become identical sausages without minds of their own.

Keynes replied that 'if there can be a few of reasonable merit at the top, I do not so much mind what happens at the bottom'.[10]

The universities, hitherto a sanctuary for refugees from fascism, were now required to offer up sacrificial victims to the dragons of war. In June Piero Sraffa was interned as an 'enemy alien', together with Erwin Rothbarth – who had helped Keynes on How to Pay for the War – and two other economists, Hans Singer and Edward Rosenbaum at Manchester University. Keynes petitioned tirelessly for their release, to the Home Secretary downwards. His own work on bringing his national income statistics up to date had been held up because of Rothbarth's internment. He called their treatment – and that of other refugees – 'the most disgraceful and humiliating thing which has happened for a long time.... If there are any Nazi sympathisers at large in this country look for them in the War Office and our secret service....'[11] He obtained an order for Rothbarth's release in

August, and the others were freed soon afterwards. But a year later he was still trying to get Kurt Jooss, who had brought his ballet to Cambridge in December 1939, out of internment in the Isle of Wight.

On 28 June Kingsley Wood offered Keynes membership of a Consultative Council to advise on special problems facing the Treasury. Explaining his appointment to a 'new super-dud Committee'[12] to his parents, Keynes wrote, 'I have, as you know, a strong prejudice against advisory as compared with executive jobs. But I think it is wise to start with something minor like this, and it will have the great advantage of giving me direct access to the Chancellor ... with any bright ideas I may have. ...' The bright ideas soon started to flow. Three memoranda followed a brief to the Consultative Committee to investigate the issue of compensation for war damage. There was a series of notes to the Chancellor before the supplementary budget introduced on 23 July, a memorandum arguing against the closing down of the Stock Exchange, and a further note on exchange controls and payments agreements – eight meaty documents, totalling fifty-two printed pages, in one month.[13] After Kingsley Wood's supplementary budget of 23 July, which put a shilling on the standard rate and imposed a miscellany of indirect taxes, had been widely criticised for being inadequate, Keynes comforted him by pointing out that accruing revenues from the current taxes had been greatly underestimated by the press.[14]

For almost a year Keynes had been knocking at the Treasury's door. At last he was let in. On 12 August, without being assigned official duties, he was given 'a sort of roving commission'; put on several 'high up committees' with access to secret information – including the Exchange Control Conference – and, at the behest of Sir Richard Hopkins, second secretary, given an office and a part-time secretary in Treasury Chambers in Great George Street. His office was next to that of Lord Catto, who resigned as director of the Bank of England to take up, like Keynes, an unpaid Treasury job. They soon became friends, and, as 'Catto and Doggo', worked in the greatest harmony for three years before Catto became governor of the Bank of England. Fortified by a 'drastically improved' report on his heart, Keynes immediately started putting in five hours a day. But, as he told his mother on 24 August, 'like Polly [Hill – his niece and a temporary civil servant at the Board of Trade] I am only just able to occupy my time, and have not *really* enough work to do. You know how Keyneses hate that.'

The Battle of Britain started on 10 July, with the German air force concentrating its attacks on the Channel ports, before switching to London on 18 August. 'We hear all day bombs and anti-aircraft guns, feel while it lasts a bit restless, but English air men are wonderful and protect us,' Lydia wrote to Florence Keynes from Tilton on 16 August. 'It is a strange war, we walk in the fields, and yet the war rages right in the midst of it.' They had Bunny and Angelica Garnett for the weekend, with a 'skeleton' meeting of the Memoir Club at Charleston, where Virginia Woolf found Maynard 'severe, snubbing, truculent'.[15] At 46 Gordon Square, Maynard and Polly Hill slept in bunks in the basement during the weeks of nightly air-raids, 'rather like life on board ship'. Keynes was amazed at how little damage the Germans were doing in London, 'nothing that the building industry could not put right in a couple of days'. The problem was not the damage but lack of transport. 'I have not walked so much for years,' he told his mother, 'and what with perpetually running up and down the stairs to the deep Treasury basement – much more than meets with Lydia's approval – I am thoroughly exercised. . . .' Even when much heavier air-raids on London and industrial centres started in the autumn, he thought the estimates of the damage much exaggerated, especially to machine tools which were immune to blast.

> Last night [he wrote to Florence Keynes on 6 September] I went to my Other Club and was put next to Winston, so I had some two or three hours conversation with him and listening to him. I found him in absolutely perfect condition, extremely well, serene, full of normal human feelings and completely un-inflated. Perhaps this moment is the height of his power and glory, but I have never seen anyone less infected with dictatorial airs or hubris. There was not the faintest trace of the insolence which LL.G, for example, so quickly acquired. As perhaps you saw, he placed my new war damage scheme in his speech in the afternoon, so that I am now hopeful that that will really get through.

On 18 September he, Polly, Fred Woollard (their chauffeur), Mrs Stephens and Mary (their maid) were eating a duck from Fortnum and Mason for supper when a landmine burst opposite their house. The shutters saved them from injury, but all the windows were broken and the front door unhinged. Maynard was 'wonderfully calm'. Bloomsbury, he said, was evidently receiving the Luftwaffe's near misses on nearby Euston Station and the Ministry of Information tower. Repairs on No. 46 could not start till another bomb was defused, so for three weeks Keynes commuted between Tilton and London every weekday, this time by car as trains in the south-east were disrupted, the dusky evening journey made more mysterious because all roadsigns had been removed as a precaution against the expected German invasion. He now got up at 7 a.m., left Tilton at 8 a.m., and got back by 8.30 p.m. 'I never thought I should again be able to put in such a long day. I get tired, but am extremely well,' he wrote to his mother on 27 September. The only drawback was that Lydia still subjected him to nightly icebags. But it was worth even the icebags to sleep at Tilton.

III. KINGSLEY WOOD'S BUDGET

Between 21 September and 6 October 1940 Keynes produced four 'Notes on the Budget' designed to change the Treasury's approach to war finance. Their main purpose was not to argue for his own specific of deferred pay but to win Treasury acceptance for his theoretical approach to making the 'budget judgement'.

At the beginning of 1940 Keynes had estimated a 'financing gap' of about £400m–£500m, which he had proposed to plug by compulsory saving. In practice, it had been largely met by increased voluntary saving from increased output, with negligible 'budgetary inflation'. However, by the autumn of 1940 full employment had been achieved, and government spending was expected to rise further, leaving a 'prospective Budget problem ... of the order of £400 million'. The reduction in the standard of life through inflation, Keynes repeated, would necessarily be *just as great* as through taxation. 'So it would be a mug's game *not* to solve the Budget problem'. Working-class assent for higher taxes should be sought by guaranteeing to stabilise the cost of living.

Keynes recommended a modified version of his deferred pay scheme. An extra £450m of revenue should be raised by a graduated war *surcharge*, superimposed on the existing income tax and surtax. For presentational reasons he attached 'great importance' to expressing the new impost as a percentage of net – that is, post-tax – rather than gross income, since simply to slap on extra taxes (by raising the rate of income tax and reducing personal allowances) would seem to leave the poor worse off and the rich better off than would really be the case: the reverse of the psychological effect being aimed at. But only the first £50 or £100 of this surcharge on individual incomes should take the form of deferred pay, the rest being outright tax. This would deprive the rich of the incentive to sell capital assets against their prospective deferred income, while retaining the attraction of deferred pay for the poor.[16]

Keynes's 'Notes' caused a considerable stir in the higher reaches of the Treasury and he was put on the Treasury's Budget Committee. At this point there were a number of competing proposals for increasing revenue: Keynes's for a graduated surcharge on net incomes, coupled with deferred pay; Catto's for a flat-rate surcharge on incomes; Stamp's proposal – first made by Hubert Henderson – for an excess earnings tax, analogous to the Excess Profits Tax; and straightforward increases in direct taxes, championed by the Inland Revenue. Kingsley Wood ordered all four to be thoroughly examined. Over the next three months Keynes fought vigorously for the logic, psychology and arithmetic of his approach. He felt strongly that the administrative obstructiveness of Sir Gerald Canny, head of Inland Revenue, would maximise discontent with the increased taxes. At one point he minuted testily: 'A tinkering with the existing income tax, however drastic, will have no popular or political appeal.'[17] According to Sayers, Keynes's 'frequent impatience with the Inland Revenue Department's memoranda perhaps reduced the effectiveness of his presentation'.[18] He produced evidence which showed that, although most people preferred rationing to deferred pay, a large majority favoured deferred pay to higher taxes and prices.[19] He wrote to his mother, 'I spend my time trying to make them face up to the possible alternatives and choose wisely between them.'

Early in January 1941 the Treasury moved out of its bomb-damaged quarters into 'hideous' new government offices at the top of Whitehall, where, Keynes told his mother, he was 'deep into all the big questions and sit in the huddle (as we call it) with the Chancellor and the permanent secretaries'. In his summing up for the Chancellor on 10 January, Sir Horace Wilson threw out the Catto and Stamp proposals. This left Keynes's surcharge and increases in income tax as the only runners.[20] Kingsley Wood was in the mood for a bold stroke. He was 'most attracted by the War Surcharge suggested by Mr Keynes' and called for its further study 'as a matter of urgency'. He also asked for the 'considered views of the Treasury on the suggestion that as part and parcel of a severe Budget I should agree to stabilise the Cost of Living Index'.[21] Canny at the Inland Revenue once more unrolled his objections to a surcharge in a nine-page memorandum; he did, however, concede (on 15 January) that a 'withholding tax' would be feasible provided the repayable portion was 'confined to an increase in the reduced rate or to a reduction of the earned income and personal allowances'. The way was clear for a compromise. Keynes would drop the surcharge, accepting that additional revenue had to be raised through income tax; Canny would accept that part of the increased income tax would be repayable.[22] Responding to a request from Hopkins, Keynes worked out an income tax formula which would give the same yield as his surcharge.[23]

Kingsley Wood came to his decision on 1 February. Keynes's surcharge was 'impracticable' because 'its presentation to the House of Commons and the country seems bound to sound like a rehash of the Income Tax and Surtax'; it let off the surtax payer too lightly; it made life too difficult for the Inland Revenue; and it brought in only 750,000 new taxpayers. The novelty in Keynes's proposal was the 'deferred pay' part and this could be preserved by treating as deferred income 'some (indeed the greater part) of the possible increase based on income tax arrangements'. Kingsley Wood was attracted by the thought of being able to present deferred pay as part of 'saving' rather than taxes. He also accepted Keynes's plan for subsidising the cost of living.[24]

There still remained the question of how much purchasing power needed to be withdrawn. In July 1940, Hopkins had doubted whether Keynes's 'guesstimates' of the 'inflationary gap' were 'as useful as might appear'.[25] Confidence was not increased by the fact that the numbers fluctuated from month to month. In July it was £200m. In September it was £400m. By December it was £500m, the problem of excess purchasing power having been 'significantly' increased by a growing shortage of goods.[26]

By the time the notion of an 'inflationary gap' started to appear in Treasury memoranda in the winter of 1940, much more authoritative national income estimates, commissioned by the Stamp survey earlier in the year, were becoming available. On his appointment to the Central Economic Information Service in June 1940, James Meade had evolved a 'complicated system of balancing tables', based on Colin Clark's 1937 estimates and independently of the Keynes–Rothbarth effort. At the end of August he was joined by Richard Stone, a twenty-seven-year-old Cambridge economist–statistician. There was some initial Treasury resistance to Meade's enterprise, based on jealousy and what Robbins called 'prescriptive right'.[27] By 6 January 1941 they had prepared the first draft of their paper 'National Income, Saving and Consumption', which Keynes circulated to the Chancellor and Treasury Budget Committee. On 1 February, the *Economist* alarmed the Treasury by suggesting that the national income had almost doubled since before the war, which implied that inflation was spinning out of control. 'I really think', Hopkins wrote to Keynes, 'that something must be done both about the national income and about the gap. Perhaps we should talk.' Richard Stone, on whom this account is based, believes that the furore aroused by the *Economist* article was crucial in persuading the Chancellor to base the budget judgement explicitly on the new national arithmetic, and to publish the Meade–Stone document, redrafted by Keynes, as a White Paper accompanying the budget.[28]

This is not very plausible. The figure of £250m–£300m as the amount which needed to be raised in new taxation had been around for some time, based on Keynes's educated guesses and estimated yields of the politically acceptable levels of taxation. The truth seems to be that the Treasury accepted the Keynes–Meade–Stone method of analysing the budgetary problem because it gave roughly the same results as its own traditional method, which was to estimate government revenue and expenditure and adjust taxes to close any difference. But the new method seemed to provide a more accurate basis for making policy. The problem with what Keynes called the 'budget method' was that it did not give enough information. For example, how much of the extra incomes produced by the additional government spending would be saved? This depended on information about the saving propensities of different classes. The national income–expenditure approach was therefore more useful for both anti-inflationary and social policy. It told policymakers how much to take in taxes and how much to leave to saving, and how to distribute the burden of sacrifice. 'What was new in 1941', Sayers concludes, 'was the universal acceptance of the Keynesian formulation and the existence of Keynesian arithmetic as one weighty element – but only one element – in the emergence of the "decisive" hunches'.[29]

In the weeks leading up to the budget Keynes was working up to thirteen hours a day, but was in such good health that the Ogre released him from his icebags. Suddenly it was all over, 'with no more work to do than occupies the mornings'. Kingsley Wood's budget of 7 April 1941 was the first budget which Keynes had helped shape and (astonishingly) the first he had heard delivered in person. Characteristically he thought the MPs sitting below him on the floor of the chamber 'a truly sub-human collection'.

In his budget speech Kingsley Wood projected an 'inflationary gap' of around £500m. He decided to assume that personal savings would increase by £200m to £300m – mainly because there were fewer things to buy – and therefore that he should aim for £250m only in new taxation. He decided to raise the standard rate of income tax to 50 per cent, with a top marginal rate of 97.5 per cent, raise the reduced rate which applied to the first £165 of taxable income, and lower earned income and personal allowances, bringing 3.25 million new taxpayers into the income tax net. The extra tax paid by an individual resulting from the reduction in personal and earned income allowances would be 'offset after the war by a credit which will be given in his favour in the Post Office Savings Bank' which would provide 'an additional fund of post-war savings for himself and his dependents'. The credits would amount to £125m or half the increased tax yield. An analogous concession was made in respect of the 100 per cent Excess Profits Tax. The Chancellor also undertook to stabilise the price index at its existing level, about 25 to 30 per cent above pre-war, by subsidising the cost of necessaries, particularly food, warning that, if wage rates rose, the government would have to increase taxes further.

The framework set up in the 1941 budget continued through the war. Although Keynes remained on the Budget Committee, his own contributions to subsequent fiscal policy tailed off. In his 'Budget Notes' of 3 November 1941, he advocated universal family allowances, his original *quid pro quo* for higher taxes.[30] This was postponed till after the war. Keynes advised on the Pay-As-You-Earn Scheme – compulsory taxation at source assessed on current earnings – introduced in 1943 for all incomes under £600 a year.[31] In 1944 and 1945 he devoted his efforts to trying to get rebates on the Excess Profits Tax made unconditional, and taxes on small businesses reduced. 'If we ... want to remain a private enterprise country we must not kill the goose (which is what our tax system is doing), even though it is such a goose as not to be able to explain its sufferings in an intelligible human voice.'[32] On the borrowing side, he inspired the Tax Reserve Certificate scheme, announced in December 1941. This was a two-year Treasury bond, carrying 1 per cent interest, and tax-free, designed to tap bank deposits set aside for paying tax liabilities accrued but not yet collected.[33] More generally, he continued to argue, with limited success, that with cheap borrowing assured the government should 'cater to the needs of the market' in its maturities policy, issuing much more short-dated stock.[34]

Keynes's budget triumph coincided with a dreadful personal blow. At the Keyneses' traditional Christmas tea with the Woolfs, Virginia had found Maynard pugnacious, puritanical and disapproving, melting a little only when she kissed him.[35] It was the last time they saw each other. On 28 March 1941, Virginia Woolf drowned herself in the River Ouse. Maynard, who had never felt despair, and could not understand it, reported the news to his mother in his usual factual style:

> We have been much upset this week-end by the sad fate of our dear friend Virginia Woolf. Her old troubles came back on her, and she drowned herself last Friday. She had seemed so very well and normal last time we saw her. We rang up on Saturday to ask her over to tea and got this answer. It is nearly 30 years now since she poisoned herself in Brunswick Square and Geoffrey raced to Barts for a stomach pump and brought her round. I thought she had safely steered through all that as the result of the devoted care of . . . Leonard. The two of them were our dearest friends.

IV. KEYNES'S INFLUENCE

Kingsley Wood's budget was far from being a copy of *How to Pay for the War*. In his pamphlet, Keynes had recommended that about 15 per cent of domestic government spending be financed by compulsory saving; in the upshot it was under 3 per cent. This reflects both the delay in implementing his scheme – with the 'gap' being filled by higher 'straight' taxes, shortages, rationing and inflation, all of which *How to Pay for the War* was designed to obviate – and the agitation to minimise the amount of repayable taxes, whether from fear of post-war inflation or from fear that the rich would be enabled to 'live off capital'.

The social contract struck in Kingsley Wood's budget was different from the one Keynes had sought. In the original *Times* articles the reward for increased effort was simply to be postponed. There was no explicit attention to the wages problem. In the revised and expanded pamphlet, *How to Pay for the War*, wage moderation was to be secured by family allowances and an 'iron ration' of subsidised necessities. With deferred pay marginalised, and family allowances postponed, the 1941 budget sought to win consent for taxing working-class earnings by punitive taxation of the wealthy (including a 100 per cent Excess Profits Tax), price fixing and universal rationing. The Chancellor bought Keynes's technique, but the philosophy of the budget was socialist rather than Keynesian.

Total domestic government spending from 1940 to 1945 came to £19.4bn. Had 15 rather than 3 per cent of this spending been covered by deferred pay, the total of 'blocked balances' by the end of the war would have been nearer £3bn than £600m. What would the consequences have been? Social policy might have taken a different turn: Beveridge, for example, could scarcely have avoided the possibilities opened up by such a huge increase and wide distribution of personal savings for the post-war financing of social insurance. On the other hand, premature adoption of the Keynes Plan might well have made government policy too deflationary in the first period of war. What would have happened had £400m–£500m of private demand, almost 10 per cent of GNP, been withdrawn from the economy early in 1940, with unemployment still at 9 per cent? Would it have hastened the absorption of civilian manpower into the war industries? Or would it simply have led to higher unemployment, given the inescapable time-lags in converting to war production? Perhaps it was good for Keynes's reputation that the experiment was not made when he proposed it.

It is now generally agreed that the Treasury's acceptance of Keynes's logic to deal with inflation did not imply acceptance of that logic to deal with unemployment. The idea of using the budget to 'balance the accounts' of the nation did not extend to *augmenting* purchasing power when an 'output gap' developed. For the inflation problem, the orthodox and Keynesian logics coincided: for the unemployment problem, they diverged.

Keynes's influence on domestic war finance was five-fold. First, his theoretically based advocacy emboldened the Treasury and the Bank to go for cheap money. The government's maximum borrowing rate was 3 per cent, and most of its war debt was borrowed at cheaper cost than this. Even though inflation was controlled, it got most of its money at negative real interest rates.

Secondly, Keynes turned the budget into an effective weapon against inflation, by clarifying what was meant by inflationary finance. He never tired of pointing out that government spending would automatically be financed 'to the nearest ½d'. The only question was about the means by which excess private purchasing power was liquidated. One could still have what Keynes called 'budgetary inflation', even when the government was 'balancing its books', if the extra taxes and loans were being pulled in by rising money incomes. However, the 'revolution in public finance' of which Keynes talked was partial. As we have seen it was the *coincidence* between the 'budget method' and the 'purchasing power' method for calculating the inflationary gap which produced Kingsley Wood's 'budget judgement' of

1941. This double approach governed all the subsequent war budgets. As a result, the government covered 54 per cent of its spending by taxation in the five years 1940–5, as opposed to 32 per cent only in the four years 1914–18, and the price level in 1945 was only 30 per cent higher than in 1939, as compared to a doubling of prices in the 1914–18 war, virtually the whole of the rise having occurred before the 1941 budget.[36]*

Thirdly, the new budgetary arithmetic brought out clearly the fact that that part of total government expenditure being financed from abroad was irrelevant to the domestic fiscal balance. From 1941 wartime demand management was pursued without reference to the balance of payments. But to the extent that the external deficit was being financed by *ad hoc* methods, the budgetary problem was not being solved, only postponed till after the war.

Fourthly, R. S. Sayers credits Keynes with having established in Kingsley Wood's mind the 'vital link' between taxes and subsidies. 'Failure to stabilise the cost of living would render the taxation proposals inadequate, and failure to absorb extra purchasing power would make it difficult to hold the cost of living down.'[37] The problem of cost-push inflation at full employment was identified clearly for the first time.

Finally, Keynes put the social function of the budget centre stage. 'The importance of a war Budget', he wrote, 'is ... *social*: to prevent the social evils of inflation now and later; to do this in a way which satisfies the popular sense of social justice; whilst maintaining adequate incentives to work and economy.'[38] That a major function of the budget was to achieve social objectives was accepted till the advent of Thatcherism in the 1980s, but fiscal policy was only intermittently inspired by Keynes's own social philosophy.

It is the fate of all philosophies of the Middle Way to be attacked by both left and right, and so it was with the Keynes Plan, then and later. It is alleged that Keynes was too protective of the interests of capital. It is true that he greatly underestimated the buoyancy of the existing tax base. Far from the limits of taxation having been reached in late 1939, as he alleged, the budgets of April and July 1940 and April 1941 imposed large tax increases on the better-off. However, it is not evident that top marginal tax rates of 97.5 per cent and an Excess Profits Tax of 100 per cent – both of which he opposed – were the best way to preserve incentives and promote efficiency even in war. Michal Kalecki, a Polish émigré, attacked the view that the inflationary gap could or should be closed by financial

---

* As Professor Peden points out, the policy of price stabilisation was founded on a cost-of-living index based on Edwardian working-class patterns of spending. The more complete consumer price index rose by 17 per cent between 1941 and 1945, giving a total inflation over the war of about 50 per cent. This was still half of what it had been in the First World War.

measures. He concluded that 'the only fair and efficient way to stop the inflationary tendencies is some type of comprehensive rationing'.[39] This showed that the Keynesian logic could be used for regimentation by those who did not share Keynes's political values.

Two American economists, Thomas Cooley and Lee Ohanian, have argued that the huge tax increases by which Britain financed the war – which they say Keynes inspired – made Britain a stagnant post-war economy. Britain should have financed its domestic war spending by borrowing as it had done in previous wars. The argument is both fatuous (Britain stagnated after both the Napoleonic and the First World Wars) and misses its target. Essentially the American economists allege two things: that high British wartime taxes, continued into peace, lowered investment after the war, reducing Britain's growth rate relative to that of the United States, whose wartime taxes were much lower; and that Keynes was the author and inspirer of this punitive tax philosophy.[40] The first charge may or may not be true, though the two economists overlook the extent to which Britain was more heavily mobilised for war than the United States; the second is patently false. It ignores the fact that the Keynes Plan called for a *temporary* war surcharge on top of tax rates only modestly raised from their pre-war levels. It was not his doing that the tax burden was more than doubled, with punitive top marginal rates persisting into the 1980s.

The general proposition that Britain was seriously weakened by the war is incontestable. This was the price of survival. Britain's leaders, from Churchill downwards, mortgaged their country's economic future with open eyes, Keynes playing his part. Any critique of his wartime legacy needs to start here. The critics have to face honestly the question: was there a better choice? Should Britain have tried to negotiate a peace with Nazi Germany? Should it have fought a different, less expensive, kind of war? Could it have survived if it had? They set themselves too easy a task if they point out the bad consequences of the policies actually pursued and ignore the opportunity costs of the alternatives. These considerations come dramatically to the fore when the subject switches to external finance, and Keynes's part in Anglo-American relations.

34

Envoy Extraordinary

I. ENGAGING THE UNITED STATES

The British and French governments went to war with Germany in the belief that the Roosevelt administration would not risk the defeat of its fellow democracies. Keynes, too, regarded the United States as Britain's natural, and necessary, ally in the defence of freedom against the 'brigand' powers. In his 'Notes on the War for the President', written in November 1939, but never sent, he urged the United States to join Britain in a religious crusade against fascism, initially by advancing credits to the Allied governments, to be repayable to a fund to reconstruct Europe after the war and save it from communism – 'the indemnity ... paid by the victor to the vanquished'.

Like most liberal Englishmen, Keynes over-estimated support for Britain in the United States. British expectations of assistance concentrated on the President, ignored Congress and assumed that the (largely Republican) east-coast WASP elite represented US public opinion. Keynes was a great supporter of the New Deal and his comments on Roosevelt were generally laudatory, and, when not laudatory, at least optimistic. He was right not to doubt Roosevelt's democratic sympathies, his loathing of fascism. But he seriously over-estimated the extent to which Roosevelt – and the New Dealers as a whole – saw Britain as a satisfactory defender of these values. To the American left, Britain was the arch-imperialist power. The United States had won its independence fighting Britain's armies. When the European war broke out, Britain still held India and much of the Middle East and Africa by force. It was also the centre of the bankers' capitalism against which the New Deal was directed. Roosevelt himself hated the British Empire, mistrusted England's aristocracy, and suspected the Foreign Office of pro-fascist tendencies. He also thought the British were very foxy, and was determined to prevent the United States becoming a 'tail to the British kite' – that is, being trapped into defending purely British interests. It was a common interpretation that America had been dragged into the First World War on British coat-tails, and the Neutrality Acts were designed to prevent this happening again. Roosevelt's famed relationship with Churchill was also less cordial than it later became. FDR's first question about Churchill to his defeated Republican opponent, Wendell Wilkie, when the latter returned from a visit to England in February 1941, was: 'Is he a drunk?'[1] Anti-British sentiment was bolstered by the large numbers of Irish immigrants who dominated the big-city Democratic machines.

Republicans were not so much anti-British as anti-Roosevelt. They wanted America to keep out of the war, because war spelt government interventionism and extension of the hated New Deal. One Republican Congressman was to tell the British ambassador that Roosevelt was more dangerous than Hitler, Mussolini or Stalin.[2] But anglophobia was also rife in an important segment of the Republican electorate made up of the German-descended communities of the midwest.

After the fall of France, isolationists had a new argument: anglo-pessimism. Joseph Kennedy, Roosevelt's ambassador in London, returned to America in the summer of 1940 saying that Britain was finished. America should not bind itself to a 'loser'. Anne Morrow, wife of the aviator Charles Lindbergh, published a bestselling book called *The Wave of the Future*. Britain was not part of it. This was the setting for the isolationist, largely conservative 'America First' movement formed in September 1940. Throughout 1940, and well into 1941, American public opinion was strongly against American intervention in the European war.

A powerful new context for anglophobia was the economic rivalry between the two countries in the 1930s. This was the souring background to all the wartime Anglo-American economic negotiations in which Keynes was involved. Unless it is kept in mind, it is impossible to understand the conditions which the United States was determined to attach to any help it gave Britain in the war. The two main issues were currency and trade.

Britain's first offence in American eyes was the abandonment of the gold standard in September 1931. This was seen not as a forced decision, but as a deliberate attempt to undervalue the pound and thus secure a competitive advantage for British goods in international markets. It led directly to a currency war between the two countries. Briefly, the United States refused to accept the British devaluation. Between 1933 and 1934, the US administration, with Secretary of the Treasury Henry Morgenthau to the fore, forced down the value of the US dollar in order to wipe out the British advantage and regain what Roosevelt called the '$5.00 pound'. This policy was successful; there was nothing the British could do about it. Monetary peace was restored only with the Tripartite Monetary Agreement of 1936, which provided for a temporary stabilisation of the dollar, pound, and French franc, 'the gold standard on a 24 hour basis' as it was described. It was only in the run up to the war, that the United States finally acquiesced in a depreciation of sterling down to $4.02 to the pound, at which rate it was fixed on the war's outbreak.

An even touchier matter was trade relations. Britain retaliated against the US Hawley-Smoot tariff of 1931 by the Ottawa Agreement of 1932 which established imperial preference. Even free-trading Americans refused to accept that the retaliation was proportionate to the offence, because it involved not just barriers to entry but positive *discrimination* against US goods. US Secretary of State Cordell Hull considered the Ottawa Agreement the 'greatest injury, in a commerical way' to the United States during his long career.[3] Hull, a preacher by temperament, who believed that the attempt to close off markets was the single most important cause of war, made it a major objective of US foreign policy to destroy the Ottawa Agreement. Disappointed with the results of Ottawa, and needing to conciliate the United States, Britain signed an Anglo-American Trade Agreement on 17 November 1938, which according to Hull 'made major breaches in the preferential tariff wall erected around the British Empire in 1932'.[4]

The outbreak of the military war against Germany did not end the Anglo-American economic war; it intensified it, as Britain now added currency discriminaton to trade discrimination. When Britain went off gold in 1931, twenty-five countries joined it in a downward float against the dollar to protect their position in the British market and to prevent a rise in the cost of sterling debt. This was the spontaneous start of the sterling area. At its heart was a group of a dozen countries and dependencies of the British Empire which used sterling, not gold, to settle their accounts with each other, and held their reserves ('sterling balances') in London. However, sterling was freely convertible into other currencies. In 1939 and 1940 the British Treasury, as we have seen, was able to fortify the sterling area with exchange controls to prevent a loss of precious dollars for non-military purchases, while centralising the area's dollar reserves in a 'dollar pool' in London. This was a blow to US exporters. The British also launched a major export offensive in Latin America. The fact that Britain was fighting for its life did not appreciably curb American resentment at these economic measures.

Underlying the two countries' responses to the great depression was a major shift in the balance of power between Britain and the United States. In the old system, Britain had been the internationalist nation *par excellence*, the United States heavily protectionist. As Britain's international position and competitive power waned it became defensive and protectionist. It was now the United States, its hitherto protected 'infant industries' grown into vigorous adults, which clamoured for the 'Open Door'. Standing in its way was the British Empire at the head of which was a country which now desperately needed American help. The nature of the *quid pro quo* the United States would demand in return for giving help was written in this history. The American reluctance to separate the business of business from the business of war was to become Britain's chief grievance against its wartime ally.

As it happened the Allied cause received an early and, as it turned out, crucial boost. The 'cash and carry' legislation of November 1939, devised by Bernard Baruch, amended the Neutrality Acts by allowing belligerents to buy arms which they could pay for and carry in their own ships. This favoured Britain, which had both reserves and ships, but to Keynes it seemed as if the United States were placing the democracies and dictatorships on the same footing. 'Cash and carry' furnished the sole legal basis for British war imports from the United States in the first year and a half of the war. As Britain's exporting capacity declined, it was forced to cover its imports of food, raw materials and war materials from the United States by shipping gold and selling American securities. This could continue only as long as there remained gold to ship, securities to sell – and, of course, ships to carry the gold and goods. At the end of February 1940, Sir Frederick Phillips of the British Treasury estimated that Britain's gold and dollar reserves, which stood at £545m in December 1939, were running down at a rate of £200m a year.

The assumptions underlying US 'benevolent neutrality' were shattered by Hitler's rapid conquest of continental Western Europe in the spring of 1940. For the first time a British defeat, and consequent German control of the Atlantic, seemed possible. Britain's supply problem was compounded by the loss of its army's equipment at Dunkirk. Moreover, as war mobilisation accelerated, Britain's exporting capacity declined even further. In June 1940, the British government dropped its decision, taken at the outbreak of the war, to husband its gold and dollar reserves for a three-year war: its Purchasing Mission, headed by a brilliant Scottish-Canadian businessman, Arthur Purvis, started ordering in the United States and Canada as much war material as the Chiefs of Staff needed, leaving future financial problems, as Churchill put it, 'on the lap of the Eternal Gods'. Keynes himself never seems to have doubted that America would continue supplying Britain, even if Britain could no longer pay.

This hope was only partly fulfilled. Sir Frederick Phillips was summoned to Washington in July to discuss Britain's financial needs. He projected a net balance of payments deficit of $1.6bn (£400m) for the year ending June 1941, against which Britain held reserves of $1.5bn (£375m). The drain would have been even larger but for the overdraft Britain was running up with Canada for Canadian purchases in the United States on Britain's behalf. But these were draining Canada of its reserves as well. 'How about selling some of those securities you have in Argentina?' Roosevelt asked Phillips.[5] Morgenthau advised him to arrange for the sale of large British-owned American companies. Fixed assets were to be included in the balance sheet. The Americans expected the British to pay to the utmost out of their – and the Empire's – capacity.

The drain on British reserves was compounded by the lack of an American defence industry. Keynes later claimed that before Lend–Lease Britain spent about $2bn on capital construction in the United States. A particularly heavy burden was the $880m Britain paid for building aircraft factories in July 1940. These orders, of course, required payments well in advance of delivery of the goods. British-owned factories were later 'sold' to the Americans without payment. Keynes certainly regarded these capital expenditures in the United States as moral debts to Britain. As American arms production grew, so did the debate about whether the USA should concentrate on hemispheric defence or ship arms to Britain. In the month following Dunkirk, 95 per cent of Americans expected the British to lose the war. This made it seem foolhardy to sell the British scarce weapons. A further complication was that it was Presidential election year. Both Roosevelt and his Republican opponent Wendell Wilkie vied in their promises to keep 'our boys' out of the fighting. At Buffalo, on 2 November 1940, Roosevelt gave this pledge: 'Your President says this country is not going to war.'

Alerted by the British ambassador, Philip Kerr, Marquess of Lothian, to the danger of a British defeat and surrender of the Royal Navy, Roosevelt decided to act. In June 1940, he authorised the sale of a large stock of old rifles to Britain at knock-down prices. (He got round the neutrality legislation forbidding government-to-government weapons sales by selling the rifles to the US Steel Corporation, which resold them the same day to the Anglo-French Purchasing Commission.) In September, he agreed the transfer to Britain of fifty ancient destroyers, in return for Britain leasing naval bases to the United States in Newfoundland and the Caribbean, and British promises to transfer the Royal Navy to the United States in the event of a successful German invasion. By these means Roosevelt moved his country from neutrality to non-belligerence. These measures were defensive, and were presented as such. The British hoped they would lead to America's entry into the war on their side – the sooner the better.

Britain was well served by its ambassador, Philip Lothian. As a leading supporter of appeasement in the 1930s – confusing German grievances with Hitler's motives – he was not obviously destined for success in his new post. But Lothian had a chameleon-like ability to adapt himself to changed circumstances. He also had a deep underlying belief in Anglo-American partnership as the basis of future world order. As a long-serving secretary of the Rhodes Trust he was very much at home in the United States. From the moment he arrived in 1939, he argued from every platform available to him that American and British security was indivisible. As military disasters rained down in 1940, Lothian expounded one simple idea: the best way to keep America out of the war was to keep Britain in it. The message sank in. As Henry Morgenthau put it on 23 July 1940, 'the longer we keep them going, that much longer we stay out of this war'.[6] This was a decision for prioritising arms shipments to Britain; it represented no softening of the view that the British must pay for them. Morgenthau was the key link between the US administration and the British Purchasing Mission. If the British mobilised their foreign assets, he would do his best to ensure a continuing flow of war supplies.

By November 1940 the British cause in America had been strengthened by the defeat of the Luftwaffe in the Battle of Britain, so removing the immediate threat of an invasion of Britain, and by Roosevelt's re-election as President (on 4 November) for an unprecedented third term. However, Britain's financial position had deteriorated. It lost $668m (£167m) in the third quarter of 1940. At this rate it would be virtually out of gold and dollars by the end of the year. On 13 October, Lothian warned Morgenthau that Britain's reserves were nearing exhaustion. This produced another summons to Sir Frederick Phillips to come to Washington as soon as the Presidential election was over. On 23 November, alighting from his plane at La Guardia after a trip to London, Lothian told the waiting reporters: 'Well, boys, Britain's broke; it's your money we want.' The Treasury in London was furious. Lothian explained that it was necessary once and for all to disabuse Washington of the view that Britain had 'vast resources available which we have not yet disclosed'.

Lothian's bombshell 'forced the Roosevelt Administration publicly to face up to the question of the British dollar shortage'.[7] The drain had slowed down in the fourth quarter, largely owing to delays in delivery, but in December the reserves stood at just over £100m or $400m against payments owed of $1bn. If the haemorrhage continued, Britain would have to default. The US authorities were alive to Britain's problem, but did not know how to address it, technically or politically, and anyway believed it was not as urgent as the British claimed. They were still mesmerised by the 'opulence' of the British Empire. Above all, they had not made up their mind on what Lothian called 'the fundamental question ... whether [US] policy is to ... help Britain within the limits of the Neutrality Act but acquiesce in [its] defeat if these half measures do not suffice, or to adopt the policy in America's own interests that it is going to see Great Britain is not defeated whatever it may cost....'[8]

Although Phillips and David Waley controlled Overseas Finance at the Treasury, Keynes from the first interpreted his Treasury role as a licence to encamp in his First World War bailiwick. So he helped draw up the Treasury brief for Phillips's forthcoming American trip. His memorandum, dated 27 October, proposed that the US Treasury should take over the financing of all approved British military purchases in the United States from 1 January 1941. (If legislative sanction had not been secured by that date, any gold spent after 1 January should be refunded.) That way, the American government and people would know 'exactly what they were paying for'. Britain, and more generally the sterling area, could pay its way with the rest of the world, with the help of a gradual mobilisation of Britain's overseas assets. Keynes's strategy of partial self-reliance depended crucially on Britain getting help from the USA *before* its 'cupboard was stripped bare'. He pointed out not only that Britain would run out of ready cash before its assets could be sold, but that the 'stripping' policy would have the 'exceedingly inconvenient' consequence for the United States of saddling it with Britain's overseas liabilities. He argued against selling off Britain's direct investments in the United States. These were part of Britain's exporting capacity. If they were lost to Britain, Britain would be forced to restrict imports from the United States after the war. Another crucial point in his memorandum was that American assistance should be by way of grant, not loan. There must be no repetition of the debt problem which so soured relations between the two countries between the wars. The British would not for a second time 'accept the dishonour and the reproaches of default whilst allowing to the US all the consequent conveniences to their trade. This time if we are asked to pay, we shall pay' – by means of 'revolutionary changes in the commercial relations' between the two countries. What Keynes was implying was that the British would, if forced to do so, close all the markets they controlled to American goods after the war.[9]

Keynes's memorandum made the questionable assumption that Britain and America were already allies, despite the inconvenient fact that America was not actually at war. His aim was to ensure that the terms under which aid was given should not reduce Britain to satellite status during the war, or destroy its independence after it. In a typical flash of anger he minuted: 'America must not be allowed to pick out the eyes of the British Empire.'

There was no disagreement in the Treasury with these propositions, though no one expressed them as vehemently as did Keynes. On Sir Frederick Phillips fell the daunting task of persuading the Americans of their validity. Phillips went to Washington hoping to obtain a grant (not loan) from the US government to cover all payments due on Purchasing Commission contracts, both outstanding and future, from 1 January 1941. This would allow Britain to restore its minimum required reserve of $600m from the Empire's gold and dollar surpluses, while taking care of the rest of its deficits, including the adverse balance with Canada. The question of the disposal of Britain's North American assets was left open.[10]

Phillips's most urgent task was to convince Morgenthau. London had not got Morgenthau properly into focus. He was known as a loyal executant of Roosevelt's policies, and was suspected of being rather anti-British. In fact, he was passionately anti-Nazi. With America neutral, Britain was the reed that had to be supported, *faute de mieux*, despite the inaptness of imperial Britain as a champion of freedom. Morgenthau also shared the New Deal suspicion of international finance. His aim was to shift financial power from New York and London to Washington. The dollar would become the instrument of a global 'New Deal'. At the same time, his lack of financial expertise made him dependent on a small group of trusted technicians. Gradually, Feis writes, Morgenthau became 'more and more influenced by the viciously assertive staff assembled around him, led by Harry White. They used him, and he used them. . . .'[11] He would support Britain in the war against Germany, but not to preserve Britain's world position.

In 1940 he started putting pressure on the British to sell off their big American companies – Shell Oil, Lever Brothers and Brown & Williamson Tobacco. The Secretary, writes his biographer John Morton Blum, 'recognised that the loss of [Britain's overseas] investments would cripple the British economy after the war, but he maintained that England could not afford to worry about this in 1940'.[12] For the first time in its history, Britain found itself a suppliant for means-tested benefits, with Morgenthau running the benefit office. Little wonder he was cast as the villain in Keynes's, and London's, eyes.

II. LEND–LEASE

'Suave, balding Sir Frederick Phillips', as *Time* magazine called him, finally reached Washington early in December. He found his talks with Morgenthau 'heavy going'. The Secretary of the Treasury insisted that the British should turn their pockets 'inside out' and give him full details of their assets in the United States and Latin America, and what they were willing to take for them. But rescue was to hand. On 8 December, prompted by Lothian, Churchill had dispatched a desperate but dignified letter to Roosevelt which the President received while recuperating from the election on board the cruiser *Tuscaloosa* in the Caribbean. Churchill told Roosevelt that Britain was running out of the money to pay for the supplies of ships, aircraft, munitions and machine tools it needed from the United States to win the Battle of the Atlantic, carry the air war to the Continent, and maintain a military presence in the Far East. Cleverly phrased to suggest that Britain was America's forward line of defence against the Axis offensive in both the Atlantic and Pacific, Churchill's letter, 'one of the most important I ever wrote', was read and re-read by 'our great friend' as he sat alone in his deck chair.[13] After two days' brooding, Roosevelt came to his decision. Britain was to be kept in the war at any price. Lawyers found the means.

At a press conference in Washington on 17 December the President announced a programme of 'lend–lease', in the homely image of lending a neighbour a hose to put out a fire. The best security for the United States, Roosevelt said, was the defence of Britain; British orders were galvanising the American defence industry. The United States would be willing to lend or lease Britain equipment for 'fire-fighting' which would be returned after the war. This method would get rid of 'the foolish, silly old dollar sign'. In a fireside radio chat on 29 December, the night German bombers destroyed much of the City of London, Roosevelt called America 'the arsenal of democracy'.

Roosevelt followed up his words with deeds. He sent a Bill, symbolically entitled HR [House of Representatives] 1776, to Congress on 11 January 1941, authorising the President to make available to belligerents any materials necessary, in the President's judgement, 'for the defence of the United States', subject to an undisclosed non-cash 'benefit'. Britain could go on buying what it could pay for in cash and carry in its ships, and nothing more. But the American War Departments would ask for extra appropriations for supplies to 'lend' or 'lease' to the British. They would remain American property; their return after the fire was put out was, of course, purely fictional. So strong was anti-British sentiment, in the opinion of Sir Frederick Phillips, that only the President's 'brilliant handling' of the situation had made aid practical politics.[14]

Lend–Lease was the most adventurous political coup of Roosevelt's presidency. It was the one occasion in the war when he led decisively from the front on Britain's behalf. Lend–Lease not only bypassed the Neutrality and Johnson Acts, isolating the isolationists; it broke with the whole American tradition of making loans on business terms. It set the precedent for post-war Marshall Aid. Devastated by the stickiness of the American loan negotiations in Washington in 1945 after Roosevelt's death, Keynes pined for the 'gay, generous and brilliant spirit' which had conjured up this solution to Britain's problems in the hour of its need. That this British view of Roosevelt survived unscathed through all the subsequent torment of Anglo-American financial dealings testifies to the supreme psychological importance of that moment.

Getting Churchill to write as he did to Roosevelt was Lothian's last public service. Nancy Astor had converted him to Christian Science, which proscribed the use of doctors; and he died on 12 December from a liver complaint which orthodox medicine could have treated. In his last speech, read for him on the day before his death, he said, 'If you back us, you won't be backing a quitter.' On 7 January 1941 Roosevelt sent Harry Hopkins to London as his envoy, to find out Britain's needs first-hand. To impress him, Churchill took him up to Scapa Flow in the Orkneys to see off Lothian's successor, Lord Halifax, to Washington in Britain's newest battleship, *King George V*. Churchill's seduction had the required effect. 'This island needs our help now, Mr President, with everything we can give them,' he cabled on 14 January.[15] On the 31st Hopkins saw Keynes, who told him that the Lend–Lease Bill would meet Britain's requirements if the President interpreted it as covering both direct and indirect war purchases in USA, *and* reimbursed Britain in cash for advance payment on orders in the pipeline, so that it could rebuild its working balances.[16]

The announcement of Lend–Lease guaranteed Britain that it would eventually get the supplies it needed. However, it did not solve the immediate problem of assuring supplies before lend–leased goods came on stream. The enabling legislation would take some months to enact; the British claimed they could not pay for the orders already placed, much less order new goods. Churchill weighed in with a further message to the President on 2 January: 'What would be the effect upon the world situation if we had to default on payments to your contractors? ... Substantial advance payments on these ... orders have already denuded our resources.'[17] American officials simply did not believe him. Sir Frederick Phillips was giving little away. Asked by Cordell Hull why Britain could not put up collateral as security for orders, 'Sir Frederick was reticent as to most of the figures I desired.' Further enquiries produced 'similar scant results'.[18] The British believed that the USA was trying to 'strip them bare', the Americans that the British were distinctly understating their opulence.

Much of the dispute hinged on what counted as disposable assets. Were the stocks of gold deposited in London or Ottawa for safekeeping by Britain's defeated allies, as well as all Britain's overseas assets, to count as 'disposable'? Could Britain simply requisition South Africa's gold production? Most of these misunderstandings were cleared up by an improved flow of information. But the disputed definitions of wealth also hid different priorities and clashing interests. The British overstated their poverty because they wanted to lock the Americans into the war *and* maintain some independence of action; the Americans demanded payment 'up front' because they doubted the British could win it, and because they wanted to control British policy.

On 18 December Morgenthau told Phillips that Britain should go ahead and place as many contracts as it wanted. When Phillips asked who would pay, Morgenthau said, 'the President had said it was all right to place the orders now'.[19] The British Treasury interpreted this as a moral commitment to pay for all new orders. However, Morgenthau interpreted his remark as giving Phillips permission to place orders 'for anything they wanted if they said they had the money to pay for it'[20] – in other words, simply as reasserting that priority would be given to British orders for American defence goods. As Kimball puts it, 'Roosevelt gave the green light to Great Britain to make commitments they could not meet.'[21] Before Congress, Morgenthau argued the case on the ground that the British would soon run out of means of payment, not that they had already done so. He told the Senate Foreign Relations Committee on 28 January: 'If Lord and Lady Astor own real estate in New York their assets will be on the auction block with the rest.'[22] On 1 February Morgenthau authorised payment for $35m of new orders a week; but he was infuriated when spectacular sales of British securities failed to materialise.

Morgenthau's political problems got little sympathy in London. Keynes's explosion of 11 March 1941 is typical: '[Morgenthau] has been aiming, partly perhaps ... to placate opposition in Congress, and partly ... connected with his future power to impose his will on us, at stripping us of our liquid assets to the greatest extent possible *before* the Lend Lease Bill comes into operation, so as to leave us with the minimum in hand to meet during the rest of the war the numerous obligations which will not be covered by the Lend Lease Bill.' He was aiming to reduce Britain's gold reserves to nil, 'treat[ing] us worse than we have ever ourselves thought it proper to treat the humblest and least responsible Balkan country'. The main British objective must be '*the retention by us of enough assets to leave us capable of independent action*' (emphasis added).[23]

The Lend–Lease Act became law on 11 March 1941, but Congress still had to approve the Appropriation Bill of $7bn. Any hopes that it would allow some of it to be used to take over either Britain's 'old commitments' or the 'interim' (post-January 1941) orders were dashed when, on 16 March, Harold Smith, Director of the Bureau of the Budget, assured the House Appropriations Committee that none of the $7bn would be used for materials ordered before 11 March. To smooth the Bill's passage the President demanded the quick sale of a major British asset. On 15 March, Lord Halifax, the new ambassador, and Sir Edward Peacock of the Bank of England agreed to sell Courtauld's Viscose Corporation to an American banking group for $54m, about half its real value.

In an effort to prevent further sales of British assets, Keynes took up Purvis's suggestion that the Reconstruction Finance Corporation, one of Roosevelt's New Deal agencies headed by the Texan businessman Jesse Jones, the Secretary of Commerce, might lend Britain $900m against the collateral of all Britain's direct US investments. He put this to Benjamin Cohen, adviser to John Winant, US ambassador in London, on 19 March. This plan, which had the advantage that it would 'not interfere with the future export organisation of Great Britain', would, Keynes thought, 'carry the discussion onto a new terrain'.[24] Cohen was attracted by the technique of what came to be known as the 'Jesse Jones Loan', but warned Keynes about the politics: Morgenthau would interpret any approach to Jesse Jones as going behind his back. On 19 March, Morgenthau told Phillips that the President, Hopkins and himself 'had agreed that the Army and Reconstruction Finance Corporation should take over $300–$400 million' of outstanding British orders.[25] Thereafter the British always included this 'Morgenthau pledge' in their calculations of promised relief.

The new American ambassador to London, John Gilbert Winant, was much more helpful than his anti-British predecessor, Joseph Kennedy. A patrician New Englander and former Governor of New Hampshire, Winant was an ardent anglophile and though a Republican was a supporter of the New Deal and a friend of Roosevelt. He and Keynes met soon after his arrival in London in March, and from the start got on famously. He was captivated by Keynes's intellectual fizz and by Lydia's vivacity. As the war went on the Winants and Keyneses often dined together round the kitchen table at 46 Gordon Square. Keynes also established a rapport with the ambassador's more intellectually formidable economic adviser, E. F.

Penrose. Keynes's personal line to Winant reinforced his authority in the Treasury.

Winant agreed with Keynes that they should try and get away from 'the business side of things'. He even welcomed Keynes's suggestion that Americans should go without cheese one day a week to secure a better psychological bonding between the two peoples.[26] Keynes poured out his frustration at the lack of official bonding. Why not go to Washington to put the British Treasury position in person, Winant suggested? It was soon arranged that Keynes should go over as the Chancellor's personal representative to try to clear up the financing of Britain's pre-Lend–Lease orders. 'It might be useful and would certainly be exciting,' Keynes wrote to his mother of his prospective trip on 14 April, 'but the task would be difficult and unrepaying, the climate awful and the fatigue severe.' He had taken a series of vows: (a) not to talk too much, (b) never once to speak his mind or tell the truth, (c) not to drink cocktails, (d) to obey Lydia in all things. Keynes went without specific instructions, but with a general mandate to replenish Britain's reserves up to the golden minimum of $600m.

This was to be the first of Keynes's six Treasury missions to the United States, four of them during the war. By sending Lothian, then Halifax, then Keynes to Washington, Churchill's government hoped to overcome the weakness of Britain's bargaining position by the distinction of its representatives. It was a gamble both for the government and for Keynes, for without official position he was expected to succeed, by sheer personal authority, where Phillips had failed.

Keynes was in reasonable health when he set out on this arduous trip, by air across the Atlantic, via Lisbon, the Azores and Bermuda. He and Lydia and Lucius Thompson-McCausland, a Bank of England official and former scholar of King's College, Cambridge, finally reached New York at 7 a.m. on Thursay 8 May, where the press was waiting. The next day Maynard and Lydia travelled to Washington by train, booked into the Mayflower Hotel, familiar from their stay in 1934, and dined that evening with Sir Frederick Phillips and Edward Playfair. The latter, whom Maynard had known at King's College in the late 1920s, was attached to the British Supply Council (successor to the Purchasing Commission). Gerald Pinsent, Treasury adviser to the British Embassy, joined them on Saturday morning. Phillips, who was 'extremely genial and easy', was eager to hear London and purvey Washington gossip. He confirmed the great improvement in atmosphere brought about by the Viscose sale, for which Britain was receiving value well above its sale price. Keynes outlined his strategy for negotiations with Morgenthau. Because Britain's reserves had unexpectedly stabilised (albeit at a low level) there was no longer any need to try to squeeze every last dollar out of Lend–Lease. Phillips and Playfair expressed relief at not having to face a 're-casting' of the Lend–Lease negotiations, but this was, in fact, exactly what Keynes was proposing. The question of the 'consideration' for Lend–Lease cropped up. The US Treasury had previously urged that bits of the British Empire be surrendered in return, but the State Department had quashed them. They all favoured postponing the issue for six months. By then, Keynes said, they would know whether America would be in the war. Playfair and Pinsent independently confirmed that Harry Dexter White, the US Treasury's statistician, was 'deeply suspicious of us'. It was clear, though, that 'the rooted general suspicions of the Americans are encouraged by the fact that we have told then we shall be bankrupt by such and such a date ... and then that date has come and we continue perfectly solvent'.[27] 'Maynard sees people continually,' Lydia wrote to Florence on 12 May, 'talks a lot, but in good health. Often we go out together to dine ... tomorrow with Morgenthaus.'

III. ENCOUNTERS WITH MORGENTHAU

This was Keynes's first visit to the United States since 1934, and he had to discover the feel of Washington all over again. He understood no better than most Englishmen how the American political system worked, Roosevelt's predilection, like Hitler's, for governing through competing agencies, or the relative indifference in Washington to Britain's financial problems. British and American soulmates were few, suspicion and misunderstanding rife, liaison between the two sides – in economics, strategy, intelligence – virtually non-existent.

Keynes arrived with a mixed reputation, dating from the First World War, and reinforced by his controversial economic theories and his intellectual arrogance. His attack on Woodrow Wilson in *The Economic Consequences of the Peace* had not been forgotten or forgiven. To conservative bankers like Thomas Lamont and Russell Leffingwell he was the evil genius behind the destruction of the gold standard and the unsound experiments of the New Deal. Nor was he especially popular with the senior New Dealers. Morgenthau regarded Keynesian economics as a dangerous heresy and was instinctively suspicious of their author, whom he had briefly met in 1934. On the other hand, there was now a fervent band of 'Young Keynesians' among economists working in Roosevelt's New Deal agencies. Lauchlin Currie was administrative assistant to the President: his influential Memorandum on Full Employment, dated 18 March 1940, was explicitly based on 'the analysis ... of J. M. Keynes'. Anti-British as he was, Harry Dexter White at the Treasury 'revered Keynes as the greatest living economist'.[28] Admiration for Keynes as an economist did not, of course, extend to personal liking, nor support for all the demands he made on Britain's behalf. But it gave some of the officials he would have to work with an initial respect for him, and lent him a greater authority than that of an ordinary British emissary.

Keynes's personality was a source of friction. He was not a patient man, and was prone to exasperated outbursts. He sometimes picked unnecessary, and wearing, fights on small matters. His great intelligence often led him to over-complicate an argument, when a simple, down-to-earth approach would have served better. This was to prove a handicap in dealing with Morgenthau, whose understanding of technicalities was zero. Even so, Keynes's mixture of gifts made him a powerful plenipotentiary. He had a unique capacity to translate visions into plans; his language was eloquent, yet precise; and he was good at figures. Lionel Robbins, who accompanied him on three of his North American missions, wrote after his death: 'He was not always a good *negotiator*. . . . But as an *envoy* he was supreme. Not even Mr Churchill could state more magnificently the case for this country than Keynes at his eloquent best.'[29]

Beyond the personal, Keynes's relations with Americans reflected tensions between Britain and the United States generally in an era when power, but not reputation, had shifted across the Atlantic. The gap between the two was a fundamental factor in the wartime relationships between the two Allies. Although the United States held most of the trumps, American officials felt culturally unconfident and inexperienced in dealing with the British. They felt the British would 'pull a fast one' over them unless they were always on guard. There was a strong feeling that British wiles had inveigled them into the First World War; to add insult to injury, the British had got out of paying their debts. To many Americans Keynes, with his subtle intelligence, epitomised the traps which a declining civilisation could set for a rising one. They were determined not to be 'bamboozled' again, as Lloyd George, on Keynes's own testimony, had bamboozled President Wilson. Once America entered the war, Soviet Russia seemed to some American officials the more convincing, and certainly the more powerful, partner in war and peace. Thus the stage was set for Anglo-American relations till Keynes's death.

Keynes's first encounter with Morgenthau, on Tuesday 13 May, crystallised these personal as well as political tensions. It was a disaster. Keynes outlined at length his strategy of limiting Britain's use of Lend–Lease. This bewildered Morgenthau. Surely Britain would be best served by a generous interpretation of Lend–Lease? Keynes replied that Britain needed to replenish its cash balances. Morgenthau insisted that Phillips attend their next meeting. When Keynes called in at the office of Merle Cochran, Morgenthau's special adviser, to collect his hat afterwards, Cochran warned him – ominously – of US concern that Britain should build up excessive 'cash balances' under cover of Lend–Lease. He advised Keynes to keep his remarks in future short and snappy 'since [they] were accustomed to dealing that way'.[30]

The evident failure of his first meeting with the Treasury Secretary left

Keynes baffled and depressed. 'I have seldom struck anything stickier than my first interview,' he reported to London. 'One seemed to be able to get no human reaction whatever, which is, I suppose, his method of protection until he is quite sure what you are after.'[31] Lydia cheered him up. The evening of the disastrous encounter, she sat next to Morgenthau at dinner. With a quick flash of perception, she told Maynard that the Secretary was 'a good man and will do you no harm *on purpose*', a phrase he was so pleased with that he cabled it back to London. Keynes's mistake is obvious. He had used a courtesy visit to plunge into unfamiliar substance, at considerable length, in the course of it seeming to pour cold water over the efforts of both Morgenthau and Phillips, and implying that he, Keynes, had come to Washington to sort the whole matter out. The marked difference between Keynes's and Morgenthau's ways of doing business was to hamper all their subsequent dealings. Morgenthau was prickly and insecure; Keynes lacked the common touch. It is impossible to imagine the two men ruminating together, and striking deals over brandy and cigars.

But even without this awkwardness Keynes's intervention could never have been palatable. Keynes wanted to reduce Britain's dependence on Lend–Lease, and thus American control over its balance of payments. Morgenthau was aiming to maximise Britain's dependence on Lend–Lease, partly to maximise Britain's mobilisation, partly to minimise Britain's ability to rebuild its reserves. Both sides were jockeying for post-war position.

On 16 May, Keynes sent Morgenthau a memorandum offering a 'clean-cut arrangement'. Britain would undertake not to press for certain politically, administratively or legally 'difficult' purchases to be lend-leased, saving an estimated $650m from the projected Lend–Lease budget over two years, if in return the US Treasury would apply these – hypothetical – savings to 'taking over existing British commitments'. His memorandum did not mention the loan the British were negotiating with Jesse Jones.[32] The idea was for Britain to retain larger reserves and, therefore, more discretion in purchasing. But his plan, which had seemed so clear-cut and rational in London, was not practical politics in Washington. Its subtlety alone – with its suggestion of a trap – would have ruled it out. In practical terms, it fell foul of the administration's undertaking to Congress not to pay for pre-Lend–Lease orders – as Harry Hopkins pointed out when Keynes visited the ailing Lend–Lease tsar on 19 May. It also fell foul of Morgenthau's conception of himself as a sugar-daddy, keeping Britain dangling on the string of his generosity. It was worth a try, but its rejection was inevitable. Keynes's attempt to get on to human terms with the Secretary was equally unsuccessful. His 'brilliant' covering letter to Morgenthau dwelling on the 'anxieties and preoccupations' faced by the British 'moved me [Eddie Playfair] to tears & I thought would move Henry to tears, but Henry read passages out to F[rederick]P[hillips] in derisive tones (Maynard does not *know* this). Henry also believes that the sole purpose [of his visit] is to sabotage the Viscose deal.'

As Playfair perceptively noted, Morgenthau would have responded better to a begging letter. But this was never Keynes's style. 'Maynard thinks we are a great & independent nation, which on the financial side is patently not true.... I think he is inclined to ask as of right what they are only prepared to give as a favour.'[33]

Britain's greatness and independence were under jeopardy from military events as well. The war was going disastrously: the British had been driven out of Greece and Crete, Rommel was on the offensive in North Africa, German air-raids were continuing; worst of all, one-third of the supplies coming from the United States were not getting through because of the U-boat campaign. Britain's one military success while Keynes was in Washington was the sinking of the *Bismarck* on 27 May. Not till Hitler invaded Russia on 21 June 1941 was some of the pressure taken off Britain. Keynes had a dreadful hand to play; and he was too proud to beg.

IV. A WASHINGTON SUMMER

After he got back from America Keynes wrote to a friend: 'I always regard a visit [to the USA] as in the nature of a serious illness to be followed by convalescence.'[34] He was in Washington for eleven weeks. Most of his waking hours were devoted to government business. He kept up a flow of letters and telegrams to the Treasury in London which record not only the progress of his negotiations, but his reflections on the institutions and personalities of American government. Certain themes were already starting to appear: the lack of orderly business procedures, the incoherence of government organs, the infestation of lawyers, the power and calumnies of the press, the timidity of the administration, and the consequences of the division of power between the executive and legislature.

Keynes was taken by Halifax for two meetings with Roosevelt. The first was on 28 May, the day after Roosevelt's broadcast proclaiming an unlimited state of national emergency. They had gone to discuss a draft on post-war economic aims (prepared for Britain's Foreign Secretary, Anthony Eden, by Keynes). If Roosevelt had resented Keynes's letters of advice in the 1930s, he showed no sign of it. The conversation ranged widely as Roosevelt, sitting at his desk 'without ever moving or getting up', handed his visitors, sitting on either side of him without much room for their long legs (both were over six foot), morsels of food to convey from their napkins to their mouths. Keynes believed the President's strategy was to get into the war step by step. Roosevelt said that after the war Continental Europe should be disarmed, with Germany and perhaps Europe as a whole federalised, but Britain and the USA alone retaining offensive weapons. 'What about Russia?' Keynes asked pertinently. 'Now you are making things difficult,' Roosevelt smiled.

The second time, on 7 July, Keynes ruminated on the President's health: 'He is not a sick man, but he is not exactly a fit one. I thought he was fundamentally weak and tired and using his courage and willpower to keep going. . . .' Halifax disagreed. 'The President was in good form, though Keynes thought he was tired. I don't think I had that impression. The truth I think was that he was not greatly interested in the detail of Keynes's subject.'

Keynes's comments on Roosevelt – he saw him once more in 1944 – while admiring, were by no means wholly uncritical. In particular he was sceptical of what he ironically called his 'famous political instinct', which to him simply meant appeasing rather than leading Congress and American public opinion. This analysis was simplistic. Roosevelt may have been over-sensitive to political dangers. But brandishing Congress before the British was also a political tactic – an excuse for not doing what the British wanted or a lever to get the British to do what he wanted. Keynes could never understand that American and British interests were not identical, attributing differences to deficiencies in the American political system, and thus over-relying on logic and eloquence to overcome them.

Keynes found a country ruled by newspapers and lawyers. Nothing was secret: everyone and every department leaked like mad. He suggested to Roosevelt that the American method of deceiving the Germans was to publish so much vital information that they would not have the time to read it. The President laughed heartily. 'Almost before you are out of the door of [Morgenthau's office or the Oval Office] you are assaulted by the reporters for a full account of what has passed inside,' he wrote home. Keynes never completely learnt to repress his talent for the witty or caustic phrase which, speeding round Washington, sometimes undermined the relationships he was trying to build up.

From the start Keynes was exposed to American legalism. The first time he saw Morgenthau, Morgenthau's officials asked Thompson-McCausland, who accompanied him, 'Where is your lawyer?' When Thompson-McCausland explained there was none, they said, 'Who does your thinking for you?' It became one of Keynes's *mots* that when the *Mayflower* sailed from Plymouth, it must have been filled with lawyers. Americans refused to write down any oral agreement until it had been turned into a legal contract, whereas Keynes regarded legal precision as inappropriate to international agreements. Too often lawyers busied themselves to make common sense illegal.[35] His favourite expression for legalese was 'Cherokee'.

Keynes built up good working relations with other members of the British mission, after a rocky start. 'Maynard's visit', wrote Playfair on 22 May 'has been & is a great joy. He is a fine gadfly to us & to the Americans. . . . I am certain his visit will do nothing but good.' Halifax took to Lydia: 'an odder little person I never saw,' the ambassador wrote in his diary. 'I believe she used to be in the Russian Ballet – very fresh and sprightly, and after an initial shock, I rather liked her.' Thereafter he and Keynes saw each other fairly frequently. Halifax and Keynes had overlapped at Eton, but this did not make for perfect sympathy, Halifax having the traditional Oppidan's mistrust for the over-clever Colleger. He summed up his impression in his diary on 14 July: 'He [Keynes] has got a very acute but obstinate mind. He is a good fellow to do business with, and in spite of one or two tiresome qualities, I like him.'

When the Keyneses arrived in Washington, it was already hot and humid and grew progressively more so. Their suite at the Mayflower was not air-conditioned, and Maynard had to buy a tropical suit. Lydia reported to the doting Florence that it made him look 'as slim as a dragon fly ... most elegant, distinguished and really nice looking'. Her attempts to control his diet were undermined by the quantity of working and social meals. After five weeks, Maynard reported to his mother with statistical precision that he had lunched and dined out forty-seven times, 'which really is service at the front and certainly much more dangerous than the blitz'. The main social event of his fourth week was a big birthday party given in his honour by T. V. Soong, China's Finance Minister, consisting of sixteen courses, and a birthday song sung by Soong's daughter. In his last month the 'entertainments' became 'much more reasonable', and he and Lydia were often able to eat out on their own, in a little French restaurant across from the Mayflower. Despite the work and the meals, his health stood up well. The hot weather, he told his brother Geoffrey, was very good for his heart and his digestion was perfect.

There was time for a few trips out of Washington. On their first weekend, he and Lydia took their nephew Quentin Keynes, working at the British Embassy, on a picnic in Shenandoah Park, driving out on the 'wonderful road ... built by the unemployed'. On 17 June they gave him a birthday party, the guests including John Sparrow (with whom Quentin was rooming) and Michael Straight, Dorothy Elmhirst's son, whom Maynard had taught economics at Cambridge. Two weekends later they were in Princeton, Keynes talking to 'the economists', while Lydia stayed with Mary Case, Walter's widow, in the country. At Princeton, Keynes renewed his acquaintance with Einstein. They found him, Lydia wrote, 'in bed with the curly hair and the big toe out'. Keynes also talked to Walter Stewart and Joseph Willits about Rockefeller Foundation funding for what was to become the Cambridge Department of Applied Economics. At the end of June, they managed to escape Washington's tropical weather for a weekend in Virginia, at the foot of the Appalachians, Quentin driving them in a 'smart Buick'.

Keynes came to America not just as the envoy of the Chancellor of the Exchequer, but as the most famous, and controversial, economist in the world. Naturally enough his views on what US domestic policy should be were eagerly sought by the younger Keynesians working in the administration. The most important discussions – confrontations might be a better word – were held at Lauchlin Currie's house on 22 May and at a dinner meeting of officials of the Office of Price Administration at the National Press Club on 10 June. The American Keynesians had all read his *How to Pay for the War*, but were more worried about stagnation than inflation. Higher taxes and price controls were to be postponed until full employment was reached. To their amazement Keynes accused them of being inflationists. Taylor Ostrander, a US Treasury official, remembers that at one of these dinners Keynes said to Walker Salant, 'Well, I have to tell you that you are more Keynesian than I am.'

V. THE OLD COMMITMENTS

Keynes's opening gambit having failed, he had to change tack. If Britain's reserves were to be replenished, there was now no alternative to off-loading as many current imports from the United States as possible on to Lend–Lease, while averting the distress sale of Britain's remaining American assets by means of the Jesse Jones Loan. The second part of the operation, unsurprisingly, proved the easier. The Reconstruction Finance Corporation became an enthusiastic convert to lending the British government money at high interest rates, with the juiciest British investments put up as collateral. 'There is ... very strong reason to hope and believe', Keynes wrote home on 8 June, 'that, if we can get a substantial Jesse Jones loan with the earnings of the more obvious direct and market investments ear-marked to its repayment, we shall hear no more of the disposal of the equities of any of them. ... So the horrible Viscose business may after all bear fruit.'[36] Legal authorisation for a loan of $425m against collateral of $700m was given by a Congressional amendment to the Neutrality legislation, passed on 10 June, and a provisional agreement signed a few days later.

On 17 June Keynes fired off to Harry Hopkins a new scheme for extending Lend–Lease to cover additional items. This recognised that the amount available 'for relieving us of existing commitments ... will not go far to satisfying the needs which I outlined in my memorandum [of 16 May]'.[37] Hopkins did not appreciate Keynes's letter; nor did Morgenthau, to whom he sent a copy. Had Keynes heard their telephone conversation, he might have thought he had wandered into a bad B movie. Harry Hopkins plays the heavy, with Morgenthau as his more or less incoherent stooge:

> HH: Because I've got a long letter from Keynes – a long-winded letter from Keynes. ... I don't like his style and approach. My own opinion

HM: is that except from the point of view of the British Treasury, he'd be just as well off at home.

HM: You and me, both.

HH: You see, he says he's been sent here on a mission, and his mission has got to be complete.

HM: Yeah.

HH: Well, God Almighty, seems to me you might well say, 'Well, what the hell has Phillips been doing here all the time?'

HM: That's right.

. . .

HH: Here's the point about Keynes. If he hangs around here until we get mixed up in a new Lend–Lease bill, he's apt to pull something and he'll be telling us how to write a Lend–Lease bill and people will get madder than hell here about it.[38]

Whatever Morgenthau thought, Keynes's logic of trading old for new commitments was appreciated by US Treasury officials Harry White, Daniel Bell and Jacob Viner.[39] They persuaded Morgenthau to set up a Treasury committee, which would meet to decide which British orders should be lend-leased against daily reports of the Bank of England's reserve position. Starting on 19 June, Keynes, Phillips (followed by his temporary replacement Kenneth Bewley) and Purvis met a shifting collection of American officials most weekdays for the next month to approve British purchases. At meetings of the 'Committee' Keynes found Morgenthau 'all smiles and helpfulness' in his efforts to 'replenish our dollars'. It was Keynes's first continuous contact with Harry Dexter White, the 'suspicious' director of monetary research at the US Treasury.

The threads were coming together. The extension of Lend–Lease to cover additional products and orders for the Dominions might save $250m of reserves a year. Morgenthau had renewed his pledge to Phillips to find $400m for the old commitments. The Jesse Jones Loan would bring in $425m. The US Treasury now accepted the principle of allowing Britain to build up a 'free reserve' of about $600m. Lunching with the Secretary on 25 June, Keynes said he felt his original mission had been successfully accomplished. Suspicious to the last, Morgenthau asked him to put it in writing, which Keynes graciously did, using a phrase he had picked up from Morgenthau. 'Everything depends, of course, on what you call the McCoy ... going through – that is certain tanks and aeroplane engines contracted by us being taken over by your War Department and certain shipping contracts being replaced by deferred contracts for a later date.'[40] At a press conference at the British Embassy on 14 July he denied Congressional and newspaper charges that Britain was using lend-leased goods to undercut American exporters in Latin America. This problem would cause bitter mutual recrimination in the months and years ahead.[41]

How successful had Keynes been? In terms of his original logic he, and the British Treasury, had been defeated. The settlement left Britain more, not less, dependent on Lend–Lease, and therefore on the United States. Phillips had argued against allowing the USA to exercise control over the British balance of payments.[42] Yet this, in effect, is what Morgenthau's committee had been set up to do. Given the impossibility of getting the US administration officially to accept responsibility for Britain's pre-Lend–Lease orders, this was an inevitable conclusion. It set a precedent for the Office of Lend–Lease Administration to police Britain's export policy – and thus level of reserves – throughout the war. The one clear success for the original strategy was the Jesse Jones Loan, which ended the danger of further asset stripping. After a dour start, Keynes had got on to reasonable terms with most Washington officials. He had spotted White as 'one of the few constructive brains in the Treasury'.[43] He had even started to appreciate Morgenthau, 'despite that dreadful, leery smirk of his'.[44]

The mystery is how the British went on paying for the pre-Lend–Lease orders through till April 1941, after which Lend–Lease started taking some of the strain.* Official figures show that British reserves had sunk to £12m in April before picking up slightly. (For changes in the reserve position during the war see Appendix at the end of this chapter.) The answer almost certainly is that deliveries (and therefore payments) were held up by supply and shipping shortages. Playfair was suitably cynical: 'I am rather impressed by the unreality of it all: all our figures are false, & we always have just enough money, to our own surprise.'[45] In fact, what with delays and the onset of Lend–Lease, the extreme crisis had already passed by the time Keynes got to the United States.

It is worth stepping back for a moment to consider the effects of the way Britain 'paid' the external cost of the war. Of total wartime British imports of £17bn ($68bn), only £7bn ($28bn) or 40 per cent were paid for by exports and reserves. Of Britain's external deficit of £10bn (or $40bn) over the six years of war, $22bn was covered by Mutual Aid, $14bn by accumulating sterling balances in London, and $4bn by disinvestment in overseas securities. As Alec Cairncross has written, and as Keynes repeatedly pointed out to the Americans, 'the extreme to which it [Lend–Lease] allowed Britain to push her military effort enhanced the risk of economic collapse when peace returned'.[46] Had Britain fought the war entirely from its own resources it would have had $36bn less to spend. It might have survived. A massive proportion of its war effort went into defending the Empire against Germany and Italy in the Middle East and against Japan in the Far East. It could have surrendered these positions and concentrated on the defence of the Atlantic sea routes, but only at the cost of greatly strengthening Germany's

---

* Lend–Lease came to be known formally as Mutual Aid after Britain agreed to supply the United States with war materials on a somewhat different basis. These terms were used interchangeably.

strategic position. The Empire's contribution to Britain's war effort was vital. But it was very different from America's contribution, and this, too, was to cause great problems. Both Lend–Lease and the accumulation of sterling balances were at the expense of British exports. But whereas the former was a gift, the latter was a debt. So Britain would start the peace not just with an export trade 30 per cent of pre-war, but with approximately £3.5bn ($14bn) of external debt – the largest in its history. The build-up of debt and the growing size of Britain's prospective balance of payments deficit were constant worries to Keynes, and indeed to the Treasury, right through the war; but there seemed no remedy, given the policy of victory at any price.

VI. THE CONSIDERATION

Keynes remained in Washington through July to deal with the 'consideration'. Although Britain was to get its goods free of the 'dollar sign', they were not to come without strings. Section 3(b) of the Lend–Lease Act had authorised aid to Britain on 'terms and conditions' designed to 'benefit' the United States, the benefit being 'payment or repayment in kind or property or any other direct or indirect benefit which the President deems satisfactory'. The first two conditions made possible not just the return of 'leased' material, but also the transfer of assets in the Empire; the third was inserted with future benefits to US commerce in mind. Roosevelt, who had only the vaguest idea of what he wanted, might have been content with general promises. But in America an agreement is a contract, and a contract requires terms.

The US Treasury and State Department had different ideas about what should go in the contract, and fought for the right to draw it up. The Treasury's aim was to keep Britain in the war, but to render it financially dependent on the United States. By contrast, the State Department was keen to dismantle Britain's imperial preference system. The two aims were contradictory: a post-war Britain left with exiguous reserves would be more, not less, inclined to maintain imperial preference as the only basis of commercial survival. In a key move, Roosevelt, on 16 May, handed responsibility for negotiating the 'consideration' to the State Department. This gave Secretary of State Cordell Hull, backed by his Assistant Secretary, Harry Hawkins, the chance to commit the British to a free-trade agenda. For the British, the only 'consideration' which seemed just was that 'we should go on fighting'.[47] Although the consideration was now a State Department (and therefore, on the British side, a Foreign Office) matter, Keynes soon got involved, partly because he was Keynes, partly because the consideration was bound to have economic implications, partly because Halifax, whose understanding of economics was limited, chose to involve him.

From the first Keynes got on splendidly with Assistant Secretary of State Dean Acheson, the man charged by Hull with drafting the consideration. With his imposing height, clipped moustache and tweeds, Acheson looked the picture of an English gentleman. A product of Groton, Yale and the Harvard Law School, and a protégé of Felix Frankfurter, Acheson shared many of Keynes's friends, values and cultural interests. Although he supported the State Department line, he was, like Keynes, a pragmatic, rather than ideological, free trader. The two men matched each other in both intellect and arrogance. Acheson, unlike Morgenthau, was a genuine anglophile.

On 18 June Keynes was still confident that 'the background [to the consideration] is extraordinarily favourable and friendly, and I see no reason to expect that any terms to which we much object will be forced on us'. He felt sure that he and Acheson could easily draft something worth while 'with a few general directives' from the President.[48] On 21 June Keynes sent Kingsley Wood a 'skeleton draft' of an agreement he had prepared 'for my own purposes'. The President would be entitled to ask as part of the 'benefit' that Britain furnish the United States with bases and secret information; allow British-owned stocks to be used for post-war relief and reconstruction; and join the USA in promoting the 'free and healthy' flow of trade by granting free access to all purchasers of raw materials under their joint control, by participating in commodity and price regulation schemes, by reducing trade barriers and trade discrimination, and by maintaining, through 'an appropriate exchange and currency organisation', balance of payments equilibrium between national systems.[49] Keynes was warned to 'avoid making far-reaching suggestions' in his talks with the Americans.[50] In a graciously phrased rebuke, the Chancellor cabled from London that the heads of agreement which Keynes had sketched out 'raise fundamental issues.... In these circumstances we felt it unwise for you, as my representative, to cast a fly, however lightly.'[51]

At this point Keynes stumbled into a set of parallel trade negotiations. John Stirling of the British Board of Trade had arrived in Washington in December 1940 to push British exports, offering as a *quid pro quo* for a reduction of US duties a wartime abatement of imperial preferences. Harry Hawkins, head of the State Department's Division of Commercial Policy, and, like Hull, a fervent free trader, suggested, in return for immediate trade concessions by the United States, Britain commit itself to reducing imperial preference and exchange controls and quantitative restrictions *after the war*.[52] Meeting Hawkins and Stirling on 25 June Keynes rejected the idea so vigorously that he deadlocked the negotiations. Keynes sent London a spirited defence of his stand in a telegram (suppressed by Phillips and

Stirling) in which he condemned as a 'lunatic proposition' any agreement 'which presumes the abolition of all controls whatever immediately after the war' when no one knew what the trading and monetary system in Europe or Latin America would be.[53] Keynes's outburst, in sharp contrast to the usual British style of gentle remonstrance, infuriated the State Department. Hawkins minuted that Keynes 'wholly fails to see that after the sacrifices the American people are called upon to make to help Great Britain in the present emergency (even though we are thereby helping ourselves), our public opinion simply would not tolerate discrimination against our products in Great Britain and, at Great Britain's insistence, in other countries'.[54] However, the Chancellor, Foreign Secretary and President of the Board of Trade cabled the British Embassy backing Keynes's demand for 'full liberty of action at least during the transitional period'.[55]

A State Department draft of the 'consideration', consisting of seven substantive articles was finally handed to Keynes on 28 July. Acheson recalled that it was 'simple and amazingly liberal'. Basically, it affirmed the principle of a reciprocal exchange of gifts between Britain and the United States. The crucial Article VII may have been liberal, but its simplicity was deceptive. Gone was the notion of trading British reductions in imperial preference for American tariff cuts. Instead the Article proscribed 'discrimination in either the United States of America or the United Kingdom against the importation of any produce originating in the other country'. Reading this brought on Keynes's second explosion. It was impossible, he raged, for the British to make such a commitment in good faith. He then explained why. One must imagine the torrent of words pouring out very fast, as they did when Keynes got excited.

As coldly as he could – 'which I have been told is fairly cold' – Acheson told Keynes that all the Americans were asking from the British was that, in return for receiving vast quantities of aid, they would not regard themselves as free to take any measures they chose against US trade but work out with America steps which would make them unnecessary. This was Acheson's gloss, and it may have been what he believed. But it was a strained interpretation of what Article VII actually said.

Keynes was not an imperialist *per se*. But he was not prepared to dismantle imperial economics without something better put in its place; and he was very much alive to the gravity of Britain's prospective post-war economic position. Having heard Acheson out, he 'cooled off and spoke wisely about a postwar problem that he foresaw far more clearly than I did – our great capacity to export, the world's need for our goods, and the problems of payment'. 'At the end of our talk,' Acheson wrote, 'he seemed more reconciled to the Article, but by no means wholly so.'[56] Keynes felt guilty about his outburst, and before heading back for England the next day he wrote Acheson an apology.

VII. MISUNDERSTANDINGS

As soon as Keynes got back to London the understandings he thought he had achieved in Washington started to unravel. There had been a foretaste of what was to come in the unexpected hitches to the Jesse Jones Loan. Peacock returned to London on 21 June, with its broad principles seemingly settled. However, this 'unusually favourable atmosphere' was succeeded by an attitude of 'ungenerous bargaining' by the Commerce Department's lawyers. The US administration insisted on inserting a 'War Disaster Clause' allowing the Reconstruction Finance Corporation to take over the pledged assets in the event of a British default – a euphemism for a British defeat. 'The Chancellor of the Exchequer reluctantly swallowed the [modified] disaster clause ... and the agreement was signed in Washington on 21 July.'[57]

After Keynes left, Congress cut down the ordinary budget of the War Department, making it doubtful whether Morgenthau could meet his promise to take care of the 'old commitments'. On his return to Washington in August, Phillips doggedly went on reminding Morgenthau of his pledge. It was not till May 1942 that the War Department agreed to pay a total of $295m, partly in cash, partly in relief from contracts falling due.[58]

Much more important in the long run were the steps Congress took to prevent Britain exporting goods which contained lend–leased components. Keynes had tried to forestall this line of attack, but without success. General Burns, the executive officer of the Lend–Lease Administration, proposed that Britain's exports be limited to 'traditional' specialities like whisky and Harris tweed, to which Keynes ironically added haggis. A bitter three months' row followed between the two governments, but London made no ground. The British government's Export White Paper of September 1941 pledged that Britain would not export goods which incorporated Lend–Lease materials, contained materials 'similar' to those being lend–leased, or contained materials in 'short supply' in the United States. Although this was a unilateral undertaking, Lend–Lease could be be 'policed' from the supply end so as to prevent Britain's gold and dollar reserves rising above the agreed maximum by cutting down on supplies whenever reserves rose.

Britain failed to secure a revision of these arrangements when the United States entered the war. America had agreed to finance most of Britain's purchases of war materials in the United States, but had left Britain to pay for the local expenditure of its armies in the Middle and Far East out of its own resources. This led directly to the growth of the 'sterling balances' – the huge debts Britain started to pile up to Egypt and India. Despite much pressure from the British side, the Americans steadfastly resisted the principle of 'pooling' the financial resources of both countries.

The wrangle over the exact wording of Article VII also continued for several months. The Mutual Aid Agreement was not finally signed till 23 February 1942, after Roosevelt had given Churchill a written assurance that 'it is the furthest thing from my mind that we are attempting in any way to ask you to trade the principle of imperial preference as a consideration for lend–lease'.

These developments left Keynes deeply depressed. On 28 April 1942 he concluded that the various Lend–Lease imbroglios had all resulted from 'the failure to revise Anglo-American relations ... in any field outside the military and supply fields'.[59] This failure was never to be remedied.

APPENDIX

Britain's Gold and Dollar Reserves 1939–1945
(£ = US$4.03)

On last day of	Exchange Equalisation Account holdings of gold, US and Canadian $	Change	
	£ million	£ million	
September 1939–December 1940			
August 1939	503		− 395
September 1939	519	+ 16	
December 1939	545	+ 26	
March 1940	491	− 54	
June 1940	390	− 101	
September 1940	223	− 167	
December 1940	108	− 115	
1941			+ 33
March	70	− 38	
June	65	− 5	
September	69	+ 4	
December	141	+ 72	
1942			− 113
March	163	+ 22	
June	205	+ 42	
September	238	+ 33	
December	254	+ 16	
1943			+ 203
March	296	+ 42	
June	352	+ 56	
September	401	+ 49	
December	457	+ 56	
1944			+ 144
March	504	+ 47	
June	571	+ 67	
September	589	+ 18	
December	601	+ 12	
1945			+ 9
March	603	+ 2	
June	624	+ 21	
September	603	− 21	
December	610	+ 7	

Source: R. S. Sayers, *Financial Policy 1939–1945*, 496.

35

Keynes in Wartime

I. MORE THE MASTER THAN THE SERVANT

'Well here am I, like a recurring decimal, doing very similar work in the same place for a similar emergency,' Keynes wrote to Russell Leffingwell on 1 July 1942. What sort of work was it, what position did he occupy? In one of his letters from Washington in 1941 Keynes described the director of the Bureau of the Budget, Harold Smith, as a 'peculiar animal, a real chimaera, half way between an official and a minister'.[1] Probably he was not thinking of himself, but the description fits his wartime role like a glove. Keynes retained his anomalous position at the Treasury from August 1940 till he died in 1946. He was enormously influential. This influence was based on personal authority rather than official position. Officially he remained an unpaid, part-time adviser to the Chancellor of the Exchequer. He was 'in the Treasury, but not of it'.[2] Despite this, he '*was* the Treasury', according to one of his colleagues, who cited in support of this contention 'the masterly wartime Budgets, the conception of Bretton Woods, and the gradual domination of overseas financial policy'.[3] Keynes's eye ranged over the whole field of economic policy, lighting on whatever interested him.

Most of Keynes's wartime activities and efforts eluded Churchill's grand geopolitical sweep. Keynes rates a single mention in his five-volume history of the Second World War. Churchill's interest in finance was limited to its not being an impediment to deploying British power on a global scale. The terms on which the finance was obtained were of little interest to the War Leader, except when it led to rows in Cabinet. Churchill would grumble occasionally about taxes being too high. His tirades against Indian 'money lenders' grew longer as the war went on and Britain's sterling debts to India accrued. Nor was Churchill interested in post-war social and economic problems: sufficient unto the day, was his motto. So the main spheres of Keynes's activity largely escaped his notice. Churchill did attach supreme importance to Anglo-American relations, and prized and cultivated his relationship with the President. His main concern here, which did impinge on Keynes's work, was to agree to nothing which would threaten the post-war position of the British Empire. Non-agreement took the form of refusing to discuss the matter with Roosevelt; and, when forced to do so, agreeing to pious declarations like the Atlantic Charter. Churchill preferred not to think about the implications of Article VII of the Lend–Lease Agreement. As for Keynes's Clearing Union Plan, the Bretton Woods Agreement, these were at the far periphery of his vision.

Churchill's indifference to the economic and financial aspects – and consequences – of the war was shared by most of his party's high command, as well as by his Labour colleagues. This indifference gave great latitude to the economic technicians to develop their own initiatives at the sub-political or 'expert' level. Keynes took full advantage of this opportunity, crossing the boundary between administration and policymaking. So in a very different way did Beveridge. But, unlike in the United States, the experts' post-war plans never became the policies of the government. No decisions were taken to endorse Beveridge's social security scheme, the Bretton Woods Agreement or the International Trade Organisation while the war lasted. The failure of Churchill's coalition government to define its attitude to the post-war world is one reason the coalition broke up, and the Conservative section of it was so heavily defeated in the general election of 1945. As for Keynes, he found himself, for much of the war, in the anomalous position of negotiating post-war arrangements with the American, the Dominion and the European Allied governments on behalf of the British government, but without the authority of the British government.

Keynes never became a member of Churchill's government. But his authority to speak on its behalf was boosted when he was made a peer in the King's Birthday Honours List on 11 June 1942. Bloomsbury was predictably scathing. 'O-ah!' said Lydia, 'we come to be mocked,' as the newly ennobled couple braved the scorn of Charleston. 'No doubt they were,' Frances Partridge wrote in her diary, 'for Charleston cherishes what seems to me a totally irrational prejudice against titles earned by merit.'[4] More profound was the reaction from Keynes's old and now gloomy friend Foxy Falk. Voltaire, he felt, had mistaken himself for Turgot, the thinker for the statesman. 'I won't say farewell, but I can't think of you within the walls of the B. of E. and the H. of L.' The trouble was, Keynes wrote back, that he was getting too old to have any fresh ideas well in advance of the times. 'I have run as fast as I could and am now out of breath. If practical forces catch up, what can one do about it? Certainly no help to transfer into monkish rumination.' That was the point: for the first time Keynes was in a position to shape policy according to his ideas. The 'capture' would not be all one way, but that too did not displease him. His radicalism had been on a limited front, on which he felt he was victorious. Just as when he had been at Eton, he enjoyed the honours which attested recognition of worth. His mocking tone, like the later Lytton Strachey's, was now maintained from habit rather than conviction. To be an intellectual in England is not easy, so great is the mistrust of ideas. The mountain and Mahomet met halfway: if Keynes was now 'respectable', he was respectable on his own terms, not theirs, the most satisfying kind of acceptance.

Keynes plied his delighted parents with the ancestral and ceremonial detail they loved. There would be a meeting with the Garter King of Arms, Sir Gerald Wollaston, to choose his title. His first idea was to call himself Lord Keynes of Tilton, but 'I am going to try Lord Keynes of Keynes on the Garter King – Keynes being Cahagnes (spelt like that if he insists) in Normandy.' Perhaps the Garter King objected, or Keynes thought further about it. Viscount Gage agreed that he could take his territorial designation from the hamlet which belonged to him, and Lord Keynes of Tilton it was. Although it would have been natural for him to become a cross-bencher, he wrote to Herbert Samuel, the Liberal leader in the Lords, 'In truth, I am still a Liberal, and, if you will agree, I should like to indicate that by sitting on your benches.'

He was introduced on 8 July, with Lord Bradbury, permanent secretary of the Treasury when Keynes had first joined in 1915, and Lord Catto as his sponsors and was 'placed at the lower end of the Barons' Bench'. He evaded early requests to intervene in debates, on the ground that he would not speak on matters on which he had inside information without being able to use it. Life in the Lords would not be devoid of comic incidents, typical of that dotty assembly. Lord Keynes and Lord Keyes – the distinguished admiral – tended to get each other's post. The admiral, 'who never thinks twice before he acts', proved to be an affable guest at a lunch to which Keynes had been invited. He concocted 'a very polite and plausible reply' to a furious letter from Sir George Pirie, president of the Royal Society of Arts, addressed to the chairman of the Council for the Encouragement of Music and the Arts. 'I was very much puzzled as to why Sir George Pirie wrote to me,' Lord Keyes explained to Lord Keynes.

Outside the kitchen at Tilton, on a raised bed, grew a small fig-tree. It had never produced any fruit. Edgar Weller remembered Keynes standing beside it and saying ruefully, 'Barren fig-tree, Baron Keynes.'

II. THE TREASURY IN WARTIME

Keynes's wartime position needs to be set in the context of the Treasury's own partial eclipse. When Keynes re-entered his old department in 1940 its reputation was low. Churchill had a fixed antipathy to the 'Treasury view', which he believed had misled him as Chancellor in the 1920s and postponed rearmament in the 1930s; like Lloyd George in the First World War, he was determined to fight the war regardless of cost, and this initially kept his first Chancellor of the Exchequer, Kingsley Wood, outside the War Cabinet. Churchill set up a system of government which subordinated the traditional departments (including the Treasury) to a number of super-committees, whose work was co-ordinated by the Lord President's Committee, chaired by Sir John Anderson. This soon came to dominate 'the whole field of home and economic policy'.[5] On the other hand, Churchill had considerable respect for Keynes, whom he judged to have been right over the gold standard, and with whom he dined regularly at the Other Club. Keynes used these occasions to alert Churchill to his particular concerns – like the accumulation of sterling debt – which the Prime Minister occasionally took on board. The Treasury's incorporation of Keynes can be seen as a shrewd move in its longer-term effort to regain control over economic policy. Keynes's presence undoubtedly enhanced the prestige and influence of the Treasury, even though he disrupted its internal routines.

The Treasury's eclipse was due more to the pressure of war than to Churchill's antipathy. Its traditional job was to manage the government's finances. Keynes wanted it to manage the national economy through the budget. His *How to Pay for the War* was based on this philosophy. It was taken up by the Treasury partly because it was presented as an explicit alternative to physical planning. Once total war was forced on Britain by Germany, financial planning, being too slow and uncertain in its effect, necessarily gave way to the allocation of resources, especially manpower, by physical planning. The Lord President's Committee became the hub of the planning effort, co-ordinating the departmental plans through its powerful sectoral committees. The Treasury was left with three main tasks: to borrow the money the government needed as cheaply as possible; to keep the domestic price level stable, by means of a taxation scheme regarded as socially fair; and to arrange for the financing of Britain's overseas expenditure on the best possible terms.

The emergence of an economic secretariat at the heart of government happened by necessity rather than design. The planning system needed technicians, not administrators. Following the change of government in May 1940, the Central Economic Information Service, originally attached to the Stamp Survey (see p. 583) was greatly enlarged to serve the new super-committees; in January 1941 it was split into an Economic Section and a Central Statistical Office, both based in the War Cabinet Offices, the former under the direct control of the Lord President of the Council. Known as 'Anderson's Circus', the Economic Section had between nine and twelve economists, the Central Statistical Office another seven or eight. Together with the Prime Minister's Statistical – 'S' – Branch under the monumentally self-assured Lord Cherwell they formed the economic and statistical 'brain' of the centrally planned war economy. The Economic Section's historians describe it as 'the first group of professional economists to operate full-time as government economic advisers in this country – perhaps in any country'.[6] Keynes called it 'the nucleus of that economic general staff which we have so long talked about'.[7] But, in English administrative style, it serviced rather

than commanded the departments, briefing the Lord President on the items
appearing on his Committee's agenda, ensuring economic consistency
between departmental plans, servicing the sectoral committees, and studying subjects not covered by any department. Once the planning system was
set up and running, members of the Economic Section like James Meade
were left free to think about post-war problems.

Keynes served as the main bridge between the Treasury and the economists recruited into the Economic Section, the Central Statistical Office and
the Departments. They were his professional colleagues, many of them
former students for whom he was a natural leader and ally. Keynes himself
was suggested as first head of the CSO, in December 1940,[8] but refused,
preferring to remain footloose in the Treasury. The Economic Section was
immediately seen as a dangerous rival by the Treasury, which tried to curtail
its scope and functions.[9] Keynes played an important part in arranging a
modus vivendi, and he and Lionel Robbins, director of the Economic Section
from September 1941 to November 1945, 'worked together in great harmony', despite their pre-war quarrels.[10]

Close linkage between the networks of economists and career civil
servants was facilitated by Whitehall's structure and geography. Unlike
Washington's sprawling, leaky and incoherent bureaucracy, Whitehall, in
Keynes's day, was a lean, self-enclosed world, reflecting the British tradition
of centralised government and administration. In his six years at the Treasury
Keynes would have been in regular contact with no more than fifty people;
and in close and continuous contact with no more than a dozen. All the great
offices of state were bunched together. Treasury Chambers in Whitehall was
embedded in a complex of government buildings. Following a direct hit in
the autumn of 1940, the Treasury was relocated in nearby Great George
Street with St James's Park on one side and the Palace of Westminster on the
other, its dingy interior symbolising the Treasury's traditional role as the
guardian of the public purse.* Keynes was strategically located. His second-
floor office, overlooking Parliament Square, with a painting by Duncan Grant
as the sole concession to higher values, was immediately on the left of the
Chancellor's; on the right was Thomas Catto, the Treasury's other economic
adviser; across the corridor from Keynes was the permanent secretary (after
1942 Sir Richard Hopkins). The War Cabinet Offices, including the Economic
Section, were in the same complex of buildings. During air-raids, the government, headed by the Prime Minister, transferred to the basement, where a
duplicate complex of offices had been constructed. For Keynes, all this meant
that he rarely had to leave the Treasury to conduct his business, the vast
majority of meetings, including meetings of inter-departmental committees,
taking place in his or adjoining rooms.

Geographical propinquity did not, however, produce an oral culture.

* It has recently been moved again, to No. 1, Horse Guards Road.

There was no Whitehall equivalent of Morgenthau's daily 'brainstorming' sessions with his senior officials. The British system of administration was formal and hierarchical. Decision-making proceeded by an upward shuffle of paper, not by means of deals in smoke-filled rooms. Keynes's major initiatives started as memoranda injected into the policymaking machine. They were then subjected to a searching process of scrutiny and criticism by the relevant officials within the Treasury and departments on which they impacted. In monetary and external financial policy, this involved the Bank of England. Before the days of photocopiers and personal computers, this scrutiny was a laborious and time-consuming business, involving the production and circulation of carbon-copied or stencilled documents, with comments from all the relevant officials received, discussed, incorporated or rejected at each stage in a hierarchical ascent to a final product for the Chancellor's consideration. The process was predominantly literary.

Once the domestic fiscal framework had been settled, it was inevitable that an increasing amount of Keynes's attention would be taken up by overseas finance. There were many reasons for this, including his own Treasury background as first head of 'A' Division in the First World War. Here it is only important to notice that the arena of Keynes's dominance was also the arena of his greatest single failure – his inability to get Britain's rulers to understand the relationship between the economics of war and the economics of post-war survival. Once victory over Germany became certain, Keynes started to attack the 'Lady Bountiful' approach to waging war: the unfortunate Sir Frederick Leith-Ross at the Office of Economic Warfare was the frequent recipient of acerbic comment for his over-eagerness to commit Britain to expensive relief schemes which it could not afford. Keynes advocated cutting down on foreign military spending in order to halt the build-up of sterling debt, restarting the export trade and reaching agreement with Britain's creditors to 'fund' the 'abnormal' sterling balances. From 1944 onwards, he urged a policy of retrenchment for the remainder of the war in order to start the peace without having to borrow large sums from the United States. It was the defeat of this policy which forced Keynes – and Britain – to accept the humiliating terms of the American loan in 1945.

No account of Keynes's time in Whitehall should overlook the terrific strain under which he and everyone else worked – and not just from the continuous air-raids. The great advantage of private enterprise, Keynes used to say, was that it decentralised economic responsibility to the maximum possible degree. In the war it was centralised to an unprecedented extent. This meant much more work for government, with only a grudging increase in manpower to do it: quality was supposed to make up for lack of quantity. This was most vividly true in the negotiations with the Americans, but it was also true over the whole range of governmental activity. As the war went on, everyone became more and more exhausted; it was generally the case that few of those who worked in Whitehall had much idea about how to look after themselves. They did not live like athletes in training. Most smoked heavily; they took no exercise; they ate unwisely. Of Keynes's own circle, Frederick Phillips died of cancer, Richard Hopkins and Hubert Henderson suffered coronary thromboses, Dennis Robertson had gall bladder trouble, James Meade suffered from stomach ulcers. For much of the war the sickly Keynes – who drank alcohol sparingly and, at Lydia's insistence, went early to bed – stood forth as a paragon of good health.

III. KEYNES'S NETWORKS

Keynes served under three Chancellors – Kingsley Wood, John Anderson and Hugh Dalton. Kingsley Wood had replaced the indecisive and increasingly detached Sir John Simon in May 1940, Simon becoming Lord Chancellor. Wood was a solicitor by training. Despite a thin, reedy voice, he was an effective, hard-working politician, who had been in government throughout the 1930s. Keynes's attitude to him was affectionate and appreciative, without being overly admiring. He found drafting Wood's budget speeches 'a heart-breaking job ... for I know well by experience that the better I make it the less likely it is to be used!' Sir Richard Hopkins put it more politely: 'The Chancellor proceeds *from* the pedestrian.'[11] When news of Wood's unexpected death reached Washington in September 1943, Keynes, who was there on a mission, rather shocked the Americans by getting up at lunch and saying: 'No matter how ... apparently incomprehensible an economic proposition seemed to him to be, he ... had the gift of converting it ... into a platitude intelligible to the merest child. This is a great political gift, not to be despised. ...'[12]

Sir John Anderson, his successor, was a civil servant, and former chairman of the Board of Inland Revenue. Succeeding the dying Neville Chamberlain as Lord President of the Council in October 1940, he was judged by Robbins to have been 'the greatest public administrator of the age'.[13] He was also tremendously pompous – people called him 'Pompous John' – though not without a pawky, Presbyterian humour. Keynes did not, in truth, have much to do with him. By the time Anderson became Chancellor, the war economy was working on automatic pilot; all the major financial decisions had been taken, at home and abroad.

After the end of the German war, Keynes was chief economic adviser, for eight months, to Hugh Dalton, Labour's first Chancellor. Their pre-1914 Cambridge background (Dalton had attended Keynes's lectures) linked the two together; mutual antipathy kept them apart: Keynes used to call Dalton 'the Dirty Doctor'. Dalton had imbibed the earliest of Keynes's doctrines, cheap money, and stopped there. Keynes's relations with Dalton foundered during the American loan negotiations of 1945, and when he died he was on the point of quitting Dalton's Treasury.

Keynes's first Treasury permanent secretary was Sir Horace Wilson, an unusual appointment from outside the department or Inland Revenue, made at the behest of Prime Minister Neville Chamberlain, whose close friend and confidant he was. But he was too publicly identified with the policy of appeasement to thrive in the new regime. He was allowed to stay on till he reached sixty in 1942, the earliest retiring age. He was succeeded by Sir Richard Hopkins, the second secretary, who was in turn followed by Sir Edward Bridges in 1945.

At that time, the Treasury was organised into three main divisions – Finance, Supply and Establishments. Finance was split up into Home Finance and Overseas Finance. Home Finance dealt with government borrowing and debt management; Overseas Finance with the balance of payments. In charge of finance was Sir Frederick Phillips, who began the war as third secretary and in 1942 became joint second secretary with Sir Alan Barlow, who was in charge of Supply. Between 1940 and 1943 Phillips spent most of his time as British Treasury representative in Washington. Sir Wilfrid Eady took Phillips's place as head of Finance in London in 1942, David ('Sigi') Waley, promoted to under-secretary in 1943, taking charge of Overseas Finance. In 1944, the banker Robert Brand assumed Phillips's role as Treasury representative in Washington.

Keynes used to say that the Treasury was at its peak when Hopkins was in charge, with Sir Frederick Phillips as his lieutenant.[14] He thought of them as fine examples of the Treasury mind at its best – cautious but rigorous, and ultimately receptive. They did not accept, perhaps even understand, his characteristic doctrines. Sir Richard Hopkins read the *General Theory* only in 1945, after he had retired as permanent secretary. He aimed to use Keynes's brains, not his theories. But, of course, his theories, or rather his way of analysing problems, rubbed off on both men. In turn, their support for him, as well as his respect for them, was the bedrock of his institutional strength. He must have struck them at times like a spanner in the works. But they refused to allow themselves to be put off by his restless interference, and knew how to use his ideas to enhance the Treasury's prestige.

'Diminutive in stature, with a general appearance rather like that of an extremely intelligent monkey, on the subject of government finance [Hopkins] was an intellectual match for anyone of his generation.'[15] He had overlapped with Keynes at Cambridge, though there is no evidence that they knew each other then. Hopkins was quiet, shy, reserved, with a powerful mind and a dry sense of humour. He had a small circle of intimate friends. One of them was 'Monty' Norman, governor of the Bank. His son, Alan Hopkins, remembers an evening when Norman came to supper. The two men dined in almost complete silence. On leaving, Montagu Norman thanked Hopkins for a 'most interesting evening'. Alan protested: 'But you never said anything.' 'Ah, but our minds were moving along parallel lines,' his father replied. Keynes treated him with affectionate, sometimes exasperated, respect, which Hopkins reciprocated. 'Dear Hoppy ... how fearfully and dangerously rash you cautious people are,' he wrote to him on one occasion.[16] Like many cautious men, Hopkins could be fired by others' visions. He generated the Treasury consensus behind Keynes's approach to budgetary arithmetic and his Clearing Union Plan, and helped Meade's memorandum on post-war employment policy on its way to White Paper status.

Keynes got on equally well with Phillips, another reserved official susceptible to his intellectual charm. As we have seen, their ability to work together in Washington in 1941, under very trying circumstances, was key to the success of Keynes's mission. After Keynes's return, they kept up a fairly continuous correspondence, Phillips dry and factual, Keynes expansive, lively, gossipy. In 1943 Brand wrote from Washington: 'Phillips, I am sure, has valuable ideas on both schemes [Clearing Union, Stabilization Fund] and I have had more than one monosyllabic conversation with him. But, as you know, a free discussion with him, either on this or on any other subject, is practically impossible – certainly not through any ill-will on his part, but because I think the habit has now become second nature to him.'[17] When Phillips died later that year, Keynes wrote of him in *The Times*: 'His laconic manner, or, more exactly, his grunts of assent or dispute, were as well known and as well understood in Washington or Ottawa as in Whitehall; at Geneva he could be silent in several languages.'[18]

Keynes's Treasury ramified beyond Whitehall. Keynes himself spent approximately one year of the war – or 20 per cent of his time – in Washington, where a parallel British administration, which came to number several hundreds, worked out of the Willard Hotel and the Embassy's Chancellery, with Halifax presiding as a constitutional, but not entirely powerless, monarch. Apart from Phillips, Keynes was most continuously in touch with Redvers Opie, an Oxford economist who was counsellor and economic adviser to the British Embassy, and, after Phillips's death, with Bob Brand. Brand became chief Treasury representative in Washington in 1944. His friendship with Keynes dates from the Paris Peace Conference in 1919, though they started calling each other 'Bob' and 'Maynard' only in 1944. A fellow of All Souls and a merchant banker, Brand was known, at least by his friends, as the 'wisest man in the Empire' before the First World War. An extremely intelligent, shrewd and accomplished financial diplomat, bald, bespectacled and diffident in manner, he was another official dazzled by Keynes's intelligence and lightning celerity. He said that with Keynes he always felt like the bottom boy in the class. But he was not afraid to argue with him, and Keynes greatly respected both his mind and his judgement. As we shall see, Brand was one of the few who faulted Keynes's judgement in the run-up to the American loan negotiations of 1945, but he lacked the confidence to make his views prevail.

The banker Thomas Catto – who had been ennobled in 1936 – was another important ally in Keynes's first four years at the Treasury. A short, self-made Scotsman, partner in Morgan Grenfell, and since 1940 a director of the Bank of England, he had been made unpaid adviser to the Chancellor shortly before Keynes. He had the office next to Keynes's at the Treasury. 'From the first time I walked into his room with some papers in my hand to discuss with him, we seemed to take to each other,' Catto recalled. 'I came to have considerable influence with him, partly because he liked me, and partly, I think, because he found that the quickness of his mind and his sometimes startling theories did not frighten me; for I applied to them in the friendliest spirit the test of long practical experience.' Catto and Keynes worked closely together on the 1941 budget as well as on the intractable problem of the sterling balances. Catto protected the Bank's interests in the Treasury; and protected Keynes's Clearing Union Plan from the full force of Bank hostility.

With the death of Phillips in 1943 and the decline of Hopkins's health at the end of the same year, the Treasury lost its cohesion. Keynes never established the same rapport with Sir Wilfrid Eady, the new head of finance. Eady, who had been appointed to the Treasury from the Board of Customs and Excise, was a pugnacious and effective negotiator. He was dazzled and awed by Keynes, and felt a 'deep affection' for him,[19] but he lacked Hopkins's intellectual grasp of complex problems. Keynes once said to him, after some argument, 'If I had taken you very young and had limitless patience, I might have taught you the elements of economics. As it is, I must assume that you understand your own art of administration.' One could not imagine Keynes teasing Hopkins like that; it is to Eady's credit that he took no offence and tells the story against himself.[20] Eady, unlike Hopkins, had a nationalist, imperialist agenda which cut across Keynes's internationalist one. Because, however, he lacked authority, he could annoy Keynes, but not thwart him. At the end, only Richard ('Otto') Clarke, another outsider, could stand up to Keynes in the Treasury. But he was a much younger man and, like everyone else, in awe of him. Keynes was left as a solitary mountain towering over the foothills.

Keynes dominated the Treasury physically as well as intellectually. By coincidence, the men with whom he worked closest – Wood, Hopkins, Catto, Eady – were all short, whereas Keynes was over six foot.

The majesty of his appearance was notable. For three years he had been gravely ill, and he had to guard and save his strength. Tall and big-framed, he walked through the Treasury in slow processional dignity. Above his dark clothes, the ivory pallor of his face and the fine dark-blue eyes, steady and reflective, or filling with amusement, had often the effect of a light moving. Others, in Washington, noted this luminous aspect. His hands, also, were distinctive. He used them rarely in gesture,

except to gather an argument together, or, ominously, to remove his
glasses, which he placed before him, deliberately folded, with his hands
cupped over them. This was the hoisting of a storm-cone. The slight
stammer would reappear for a moment, the even, restful voice would
darken, and all those who had been fishing in troubled waters would
make for harbour. But the sky would clear with equal suddenness.[21]

His stature, as well as his isolation, became more obvious with the
departure of Dennis Robertson and Hubert Henderson in 1944, to take up
chairs in economics at Cambridge and Oxford respectively. The two men
were economists of Keynes's generation, easily able to stand up to him –
and each other – in debate. Robertson's 'first class brains' – temporarily
transferred to Washington in 1943–4 – proved invaluable in the negotiations leading up to the Bretton Woods Agreement. Keynes's relationship
with Henderson was far more stormy. Henderson's duties were as vague as
Keynes's, and he made it his special concern to pour cold water over what
he considered post-war projects for utopias, most of them inspired by his
former mentor. Hopkins's Treasury was wont to balance Keynes's optimism
with Henderson's pessimism and split the difference.

The collapse of Keynes's Treasury networks drew him closer to two
economists in the Economic Section, James Meade and Lionel Robbins.
Meade, a future Nobel Prize Winner, was the most powerful economic
thinker in the Section, as well as its main visionary. Early in the war, he was
chiefly involved, with Richard Stone at the Central Statistical Office, in
setting up the system of national accounts. Later he concentrated on post-
war employment and commercial policy. Meade was a liberal socialist, who
grafted the Keynesian analysis of unemployment on to the classical free-
trade and redistribution framework. His deceptive mildness of manner hid a
steely persistence in theoretical controversy and the pursuit of his plans.
'His interest lay in issues of principle; and, if ministerial decisions seemed
to him mistaken in principle, he thought it his duty to contest them....'[22]
This is a polite way of saying that Meade rarely took political realities
into account. The Treasury official 'Otto' Clarke called him 'ridiculously
academic and perfectionist'. Meade worshipped Keynes, without being over-
awed by him.

Robbins was less of a Keynesian and more of a politician than was
Meade. He had a powerful mind and personality, with 'a measured, eighteenth-century style that matched his Johnsonian figure and, if at times a
little ponderous, he also achieved elegance and wit'. Robbins was Pompous
John's favourite official, and their relationship, together with Anderson's
own standing in the War Cabinet, was the key to the Economic Section's
influence.[23] One of Robbins's main achievements was to secure points
rationing for foodstuffs, against the strong opposition of the Ministry of
Food. Robbins had been chastened by the theoretical defeats he had suffered

at Keynes's hands in the 1930s. The Keynes–Robbins axis became crucial in the years 1943–5, with Robbins strong in support of the Bretton Woods compromise and Keynes's positions on the loan negotiations.

By contrast, those most closely implicated in the Keynesian Revolution of the 1930s were not part of Keynes's Whitehall circuit. Joan Robinson stayed at Cambridge. Harrod desperately wanted a Treasury job. Keynes recommended him for one, but without success. Instead Harrod found a precarious perch in Cherwell's 'S' Section, from where he resigned to return to Oxford in 1942. In 'S' Section, he felt undervalued and under-used. He was a man of ideas, not of multi-coloured diagrams. After quitting Cherwell's mini-empire, he tried hard to get suitable war work, but no one would have him. Despite his powerful intellect, he was said to 'lack judgement'. The truth seems to be that he was too donnish and self-regarding to be fitted happily into a team. He was a brilliant economist; his subsequent life was to be embittered by his wartime career failure.

Keynes also tried, without success, to get Richard Kahn into the Treasury. Instead Kahn went to the Board of Trade. In October 1941 he was sent to Egypt as economic adviser to Oliver Lyttelton, Minister of State. His work involved trying to save shipping space by encouraging local food production. He became Keynes's main source of information on the Middle East. In 1942, Keynes sponsored an ingenious initiative, transmitted by Kahn, to sell Egypt and Persia gold. Gold would provide an alternative to foodstuffs as a store of value, thus reducing their rate of inflation and slowing down their accumulation of sterling balances.[24] Kahn loved Keynes, and could only function properly in his shadow. Deprived of Keynes's constant stimulus – and peremptory demands – he languished. He languished in Egypt, complaining to Keynes on 16 August 1942 that he had 'ceased to be allowed any responsibility'. Keynes supported his desperate request to return, but it was delayed because Treasury Establishment couldn't discover who paid him. In January 1943 he came back to a job in the Ministry of Supply. From there he moved on to the Ministry of Production, and then back to the Board of Trade when the two departments merged after the war. Master and disciple continued to correspond, but, being out of the loop, Kahn played no real part in Keynes's two great wartime achievements – the Kingsley Wood budget of 1941 and the Clearing Union Plan. After the war, Keynes supported his department's request that he be allowed a further leave of absence from King's to work on British tariff policy in preparation for the International Trade Conference. As he explained to Sheppard on 20 February 1946, 'he is for the first time in the war [sic] thoroughly happy and contented in his work....' But he advised Sheppard to 'order' Kahn to leave the Board of Trade on Friday night and not return till Monday morning, and spend three nights quietly at King's so he could help Dadie Rylands out with bursarial matters.

To conclude: Keynes was much less happy in Whitehall in his last

sixteen months there. He talked increasingly of resigning. It was the passing
of the inter-war generation he minded most, and its replacement by men of
inferior or as yet untested calibre. In 1945, he was unchallengeable, but
isolated. As Donald Moggridge says, 'he could be in a minority, not be
believed ... and still get most of his way'.[25]

IV. THE KEYNESIAN TEMPERAMENT

What qualities brought Keynes to the fore at the Treasury? There was, first
of all, his temperamental activism. As one Treasury official, Dennis Proctor,
recalls, 'His instinctive attitude to any problem was, first, to assume that
nobody was doing anything about it and, secondly, that, if they were, they
were doing the wrong thing.' From his office, he would let fly a swarm of
minutes, dictated to Mrs Stephens, which 'would turn up in somebody's in-
tray the next morning – or probably several people's in-trays, since he liked
to loose these missiles in a spray of carbon copies directed at several targets
at once'.[26]

Within the Treasury, as within Whitehall as a whole, Keynes was a
continuous stimulator of action, a great stirrer up. 'He accepted a description
of his functions as those of the pike put into the Roman carp-ponds, to
chase the carp around and keep them from getting lousy.'[27] He had a
seemingly insatiable curiosity about anything touching war finance, however remote from the centre of his concerns; and for most of the war he had
enough energy and speed of mind to sustain a huge scatter of interventions.
By 10.30 in the morning he had already done an amount of dictating which
would occupy another most of his day. His eye was a roving searchlight,
illuminating examples of defective reasoning or action in dark quarters.
He had no respect for administrative hierarchies or demarcations, would
go to junior officials for facts or opinions, and would not scruple to use
their testimony against obstructive superiors. This made him an unsettling
colleague.

Keynes's hunches usually ran well ahead of his knowledge of the facts.
This was almost inevitable: he was not a specialist, and he was not part of
the administrative machine. But ignorance was no barrier to his forming
decided opinions on what should be done, which he would propound and
defend passionately, and with every device of argument, rhetoric and repartee at hastily assembled meetings of officials. His initial assumption of
omniscience was, however, tempered by a marked respect for specialist
knowledge, and once a plan or pet scheme had been declared unworkable
or unsound, he would rapidly modify it or start on another tack. He could

be devastatingly rude to those who, in his view, were lazy, incompetent or obtuse. Stories of his put-downs are legion. He once told a Colonial Office official, Gerald Clauson, who had submitted a critical memorandum on buffer stocks: 'I agree with everything in this if *not* is put in front of every statement.'[28] But, as Catto recalled after his death, 'among those whom he liked, he could differ with a curious and delightful gentleness'. There is ample testimony to the kick which people got out of working with him, even though it was they who sometimes got kicked.

Most important Treasury papers came to him for comment. He felt it his duty to enquire into any matter where he suspected action was lacking or inadequate. At times a passion for detail seized him, and he would burrow into 'low level' committees to find out how the matter was really being handled. Sometimes the Chancellor of the Exchequer wanted a word with him, and he would be discovered in the Board of Trade attending a committee no one had heard of. Keynes had more contacts than other high-ranking officials, with those both above and below him.

His interventions would often be triggered by a fragment of information which had come his way from outside. Soon after his arrival at the Treasury he got interested in Bolivian tin. The 'attached correspondence', he informed Waley ominously on 3 October 1940, showed that the Bolivians had 'ratted' on their tin agreement with Britain and it was 'merely a question of time before all the Bolivian tin goes to the USA to be smelted'. In Washington, Playfair wrote to Waley on 3 April 1941: 'Are we right in thinking that [Maynard] has recently become interested in Bolivian tin? Recent instructions to deliver a rather cock-eyed ultimatum on the subject to most of the American Cabinet, nine months late & based on false premises, we assume to be one of his wilder moments. Even Hermes nods.'[29]

In the autumn of 1941, Keynes took advantage of Richard Kahn's presence in Cairo to send him a five-page plan for reorganising the Middle East's transport system.[30] Early in 1942 we find him eloquent in resisting a British loan to China – the so-called Niemeyer loan – demanded by the army to help repel the Japanese advance in South-East Asia. In a caustic note he told the story of Huxley looking up the word 'intelligence' in the *Encyclopaedia Britannica* and finding 'Intelligence, human. Intelligence, animal. Intelligence, military'.[31] There is a file in his Treasury papers marked 'Italy: Ancient Monuments and Art Treasures (Protection)'. In 1945, 'the question of the finance of reconstruction in Burma ... is a completely new subject to me. Perhaps it is lack of background that makes me find this paper almost unintelligible. Any possibility of re-writing it so that one can see what it really amounts to?'[32] Even Keynes had his limits. He resisted attemps to involve him in currency reform in Ethiopia and the tangled affairs of the British Institute in Madrid. 'After all, one must be allowed some moderate specialisation of functions,' he wrote, in a rare tone of plaintiveness.[33]

In the last analysis, what made Keynes an extraordinary civil servant was the same mixture of qualities which made him an extraordinary economist. There was, to start with, his life-enhancing vitality and optimism, like Churchill's; his conviction that to every problem there was a solution. As Austin Robinson notes, 'around Keynes something was always happening'.[34] To be with Keynes, on paper or in person, was the greatest possible *fun* – even if his rudeness could sometimes reduce grown men to tears. 'The extraordinary thing about him', wrote one of his Treasury colleagues, 'was his intellectual sex appeal and zing, always fresh and interesting and original and provocative....'[35] The Canadian official Douglas LePan pictured his Treasury office as a 'miraculous smithy', constantly sparking off fresh ideas.[36] His brain, thought Robert Brand, was different from that of even his brainiest colleagues: 'it was like something constantly throwing off sparks. "Flashing" is the only epithet I can think of.'[37] Over a lifetime of friendship, Virginia Woolf singled out the same qualities: 'that queer imaginative ardour about history, humanity', his mind 'working always', but equally amused by small incidents, his ideas overflowing 'vigorously into byepaths'.[38] He was often much too optimistic, so great was his belief in the power of thought and persuasion, especially his own. But this was a fault on the right side in the darkest days of the war, and there was no lack of counterbalancing scepticism.

But he was not all fizz. As Austin Robinson writes, doing something about a problem presented itself to Keynes in three stages: analysis, administrative technique, persuasion. His mind moved without break from theory to plan, the whole movement expressed in prose of compelling power. The war gave Keynes the chance to live up to his ideal of the 'master economist', who must touch 'abstract and concrete in the same flight of thought'. If this diluted the pure quality of his cerebration, it made him an outstanding policy adviser.

Keynes was not just a powerful theoretician. He always had a strong sense of what events required of theory. He aimed to supply serviceable theory, constantly adapting his theoretical approach to the preoccupations of government. The *General Theory* was a theory of employment, built for the situation of the early 1930s. We have already seen the way he manoeuvred it to meet the inflationary concerns of the Treasury (and economic orthodoxy) in the proto-war years and in *How to Pay for the War*. We shall see the same process at work in his Clearing Union Plan, where he used his liquidity preference theory as the intellectual pivot for a scheme of workable internationalism. A crucial element in his practical success was his feel for figures, or as he liked to put it, for 'magnitudes'. Although he was not a trained statistician, he was way ahead of most of his colleagues in his willingness to use figures or estimates to underpin his proposals.

A less noted aspect of Keynes's administrative style was his willingness to compromise. Students of Keynes have been misled by the confrontational technique which, consciously or unconsciously, he used to probe the weak-nesses of his own position as much as opposing ones. Keynes's first reaction to others' suggestions was frequently one of scorn. The words 'barmy', 'lunatic', 'nuts', tripped easily, much too easily, off his tongue. Kingsley Martin noticed that he was prone to dismiss people at first meeting as fools, 'often because he did not realise the paralysing effect of his own personality upon them'.[39] But his first reactions were not necessarily his second or his third. He could demolish any argument, including good ones, and pulverise people into accepting bad ones of his own. However, he had the saving grace of self-correction. Many noticed his habit of expounding opposite ideas with equal confidence.

The charge of inconsistency can be overdone. Keynes customarily distinguished logic from tactics. He understood the difference between the central fortifications which had to be defended, and the outposts which could be conceded. Certainty of general principles, and great flexibility and guile in applying them, was Keynes's recipe for political success. In some respects he had the mentality of a civil servant: unlike Meade, he was quick to understand political constraints, and adept at manoeuvring his forces within them.

Some said that he compromised too much, that under cover of tactical retreats he abandoned central positions, or even that there were no prin-ciples for which he would fight in the last ditch. He prized intelligence, ingenuity, flexibility over soundness, and gave the impression that one could usually have the best of all worlds – if one was Keynes or like Keynes; that is, sufficiently intelligent. We have already seen this rationalising tendency in his conduct of the Lend–Lease negotiations in 1941; we will see it again in the Bretton Woods compromise and in his acceptance of an American loan agreement which failed to meet any of his initial require-ments. Keynes was not a politician, but it sometimes looks as though he carried the principled pursuit of pragmatism to excessive lengths.

Keynes's persuasive power was enormously heightened by his use of language. His memoranda to the Chancellor were famous for their elo-quence and irony. And he had the readiest of wits. 'This is not an anthology, but an encyclopaedia, of truisms,' he once minuted, after reading a particu-larly laborious presentation. He was addicted to punning, describing Meade's proposal for a capital levy as 'capital levity', or remarking of the actor Sir Donald Wolfit, 'He will always be a lone Wolfit.' Keynes's phrase-making burnt incandescently in the humdrum world of affairs in which he moved. And it powerfully affected the prosaic practitioners of that world, who felt themselves in the presence of a divine visitor, who could speak their language, yet had another up his sleeve. It was his poetry as much as his logic which paralysed criticism. It was a sometimes unproductive gift. Those who did not adore Keynes were baffled and often enraged by his ability to slaughter them on both planes. Morgenthau was initially unreceptive to

Keynes's linguistic charm, though he thawed to it over long exposure. Furthermore, Keynes used his gifts to win arguments he should not have.

A final, and again underemphasised, element in Keynes's wartime influence was his loyalty. However many kites he flew internally, he won the respect of his Treasury colleagues by showing himself to be a team player. Once he was on the 'inside' Keynes played by insider rules. Unlike the publicity-seeking William Beveridge, he made no attempt to use insider knowledge to influence policy from the outside, confining his public pronouncements to agreed texts. A defining moment was when, having been made a peer, he decided not to make his maiden speech in the Lords on the Beveridge Report, whose proposals the Treasury judged to be unaffordable. He explained to his mother: 'I value too highly my present relations with everyone in the Treasury to want to run the risk of disobliging them.'[40]

Intellectual sparkle, analytic power, mental and physical vitality, a capacity to shape theory to events, administrative flair, an instinct for compromise, mastery of persuasive language, loyalty to his department: these were the pillars on which Keynes's wartime influence rested. 'The truth about Maynard', Lydia once told Bob Brand, 'is that he has abnormal will-power. There is nothing to be done about it. I suppose one is born like that.' Only towards the end are there signs of a decline. Brilliant phrases still abounded in his memoranda and conversation but they were embedded in increasingly wordy productions. At the end of his life Keynes started to lose his gift of concise expression; or, to put it another way, the habit of dictation, combined with great tiredness, finally took its toll.

From the autumn of 1943 his health started to fail at an increasing rate. Remarkably, in the light of modern conceptions, he still continued to smoke – mild Turkish cigarettes – though only moderately. But the major breakdown of his health was caused by his five difficult missions to the United States between 1943 and 1946. It was not work that was bad for Keynes's heart, but worry and anxiety. He was never happier than when drafting. Face-to-face meetings with the Americans, the constant moving around Washington, the crippling workload imposed by over-ambitious schedules, the small size of the British delegations, the fact that he doubled the roles of expert and plenipotentiary, his constant need to refer back to London – all tended to leave him exhausted, baffled, angry and frustrated. Almost till the end, he had remarkable powers of recuperation. On his returns, he would retreat to his beloved Tilton for ten days or so of rest and relaxation. The Treasury was worried by his absences, but even more worried by his returns, full of new, disturbing ideas to unleash on his wary colleagues.

V. EXTRA-CURRICULAR ACTIVITIES

Keynes added the Treasury job to the rest of his life, rather than cutting down on the latter. Telling Keynes to slow down would have had as much effect as telling a clock to lose time. His doctor, Plesch, understood this, and adopted the opposite strategy: when Keynes boasted of working ten hours a day, he told him to work twelve. Keynes could easily have got leave of absence from Cambridge – as he did in the First World War. Instead he continued to spend most weekends in term time 'in residence', usually with Lydia, with whom he shared the flat at 17a St Edward's Passage. His weekends followed a set pattern. On Friday evening a car would take him from the Treasury to King's Cross for the train to Cambridge, picking up Lydia from Gordon Square on the way. On Saturday morning there would be a meeting of the College Council, followed by lunch in Hall, and possibly the Estates Committee in the afternoon. On Saturday (occasionally Friday) evening he and Lydia would go to a play, opera or ballet at the Arts Theatre, entertaining guests to dinner at the theatre's restaurant before the perform-ance. Sundays would be reserved for lunch with his parents and possibly a concert in Chapel. They would return to London on Monday morning.

He remained first bursar of King's till he died, though the detailed work of preparing the annual accounts fell to Dadie Rylands and the clerks. Richard Kahn's suggestion that he take over Keynes's bursarial duties was indignantly rejected: 'There is much of the College business which I actually enjoy and would miss, if I were without it. It does not put on me any burden which is unduly heavy....'[41] On the other hand, he refused all thought of becoming the next Cambridge professor of economics on Pigou's retirement in 1943. He explained to Joan Robinson, who urged him to apply, that he couldn't go back to the grind of lecturing after the war. Richard Kahn declined to apply too; Dennis Robertson got the chair, with Keynes's blessing.[42]

Keynes was far from a sleeping member of his own Governing Body. An outburst to Provost Sheppard near the end of his life showed he had lost little of his elitism in the war, though its occasion – a report of College Council which glossed over the reasons for the dismissal of a steward – hardly merited his letter's bad temper. Keynes railed to Sheppard against soppy humanitarianism, demanded a return of 'the honest plain speaking of our predecessors', insisted that the denial of differences in ability was 'sapping this country in every direction', and concluded that 'if we go down to perdition, it will ... be in a foam of slop and soap'.[43]

The main pleasures of his Cambridge life were his parents and the

Cambridge Arts Theatre. Sunday lunches with the 'starychki' at 6 Harvey Road remained fixed points in his Cambridge weekends, occasions enhanced by his parents' wholehearted acceptance of Lydia and joy in her company. Despite the inevitable alarms, Neville and Florence remained in tolerable health. Extreme old age had finally brought John Neville Keynes complete relief from the anxieties connected with his work and the state of the world which had clouded his more active years. His retirement routine of stamp collecting, listening to opera, playing bridge and drinking his best wines was hardly disturbed by the fluctuating course of the military struggle.

Keynes's short speech, on the occasion of a luncheon at King's on 30 August 1942 to mark his father's ninetieth birthday, summed up, with typical grace and tact, the promise, disappointments and consolations of Neville Keynes's long life:

> I should like to imagine him as he was *before* I knew him ... elegant, mid-Victorian high-brow, reading Swinburne, Meredith, Ibsen, buying William Morris wall-paper, whiskered, modest and industrious, but rather rich, rather pleasure-loving, rather extravagant within carefully set limits, most generous, very sociable; loving entertaining, wine, games, novels, theatre, travel; but the shadow of work gradually growing, as migraine headaches set a readiness to look on the more gloomy or depressing side of any prospect. And then his withdrawal, gradual, very gradual, to his dear wife and the bosom of his family.... He became a perfect, lovable, dependable parent, generous, reserved and shy, leaving you always to your own will and judgement but not concealing his own counsel.
>
> For thirty-three years he was one of the best administrators there ever was, and during those years the University was a better place in my judgement than it has ever been before or since.

Neville's withdrawn serenity contrasted sharply with the still active, restless intelligence of his wife Florence, nine years his junior. After she gave up most of her public activities in the mid-1930s, she took up research into Cambridge and family history, having two books on these topics published after Maynard's death. As her contribution to war work, she took in unmarried mothers at 6 Harvey Road. She was especially delighted when Maynard succeeded Lord Eltisley as High Steward of the Borough of Cambridge, noting proudly that he united in his parentage 'University and Borough, his father having been Registrary of the University and his mother Mayor of the Borough'. His installation, on 6 March 1943, was almost a family affair, with both parents and many relatives in attendance.

Maynard's attitude towards his parents remained – as one feels it had always been – affectionate and attentive, without being overtly emotional. They were proud of him, and interested in his doings, without being inquisitive. So he plied them with what they, and especially his mother, wanted to hear: the facts about his life, news of his appointments, his opinions on matters great and small. His wartime letters to them, written from Tilton and on his foreign trips, are informative and chatty. He lists his public efforts, achievements, honours with an ironic detachment, a kind of amused wonder appropriate to a true son of Cambridge University, one whose real vocation lies in contemplation rather than in action. They contain hardly a clue to the 'inner' Keynes – a Keynes capable of torment or self-doubt. Or had such a Keynes ceased to exist?

Nor were other family members neglected. He corresponded with his brother Geoffrey, now an air commodore, about family matters and their purchases of antiquarian books – Berkeley, Spinoza, Locke. He discussed military strategy with his brother-in-law A. V. Hill, who had become Independent MP for Cambridge – the job which Keynes refused. He advised Aunt Jessie Lloyd, one of Florence's sisters, who planned to leave money to Newnham College, in memory of her daughter Muriel Lloyd, to put it into a new building with 'a very good flat for the Principal'.

Maynard's benevolence and interest extended to his nephews and nieces, though the benevolence often seemed more apparent than the interest, as he showered covenants and annuities on them. He was too intimidating to get on easily with the children of his relations or friends, but he tried to be a good uncle. He arranged for Richard Keynes and his new bride Anne Adrian to spend their honeymoon at Tilton early in 1945; he invited the nephews down to Tilton for the Christmas shoots. He dealt seriously with their questions. When Quentin Keynes wrote to him from Washington in 1943, disapproving of the exchange-control provisions of the Clearing Union Plan, because 'bringing it down to the simplest terms, this would mean that no one would be allowed to take out £10 for a week-end in Paris without applying to the Exchange Control for permission', Keynes took trouble with his reply. 'It is quite impossible to allow foreign investment ... by individuals irrespective of our collective capacity to finance it,' he wrote to Quentin. 'Unfortunately, that does have the consequence that, in order to enforce it, tourists and travellers will have to get permission to take money out of the country. I only hope that this will be interpreted with proper liberality.'[44]

Keynes attended the centenary celebration of the birth of his old teacher Alfred Marshall in Cambridge on 7 November 1942.

> Everyone was there [he wrote to Richard Kahn on 13 November] and it was one of the pleasantest tea parties given for some time. The Prof [Pigou] appeared in an apparently new suit, which he was accused of having hired, but declared that he had it laid by in tissue paper since the last war.... Mrs Marshall spoke without a note for fully ten minutes. Piero [Sraffa] was hiding his abashed head for fear of any reference to his Ricardo fiasco, when he failed at the last moment to give the

lecture.... Meanwhile [he] has been asked to join the Political Warfare
Department to promote a revolution in Italy. But even that he seems to
shilly-shally about and may be going to back out.

Keynes found time to write a substantial obituary of Mary Paley Marshall,
who died on 7 March 1944. The death of Dillwyn Knox on 27 February
1943 was a painful reminder of the first love of his life. 'It is a sad thought
to his old intimates of Eton and King's that we shall never see our beloved
Dilly again,' Keynes wrote in *The Times* on 10 March. In June 1943 he read
an essay on 'Newton the Man' at Trinity College, Cambridge – a fragment of
a much longer projected study for Newton's 300th birthday which he lacked
the leisure to complete. Studying Newton's life prompted him into a statement of a biographical credo. 'We suffer from the habit', he wrote to Eustace
Tillyard, 'of interpreting the great men of the past by reference to what came
after ... instead of ... what came before and what they were imbibing in
their youth. Tradition treats [Newton] as a pure eighteenth century figure of
almost Voltairean rationalism. In fact, the whole of his thought and temperament were rooted in what preceded him. He was, as I put it, the last of the
magicians, and not the first of the rationalists'.[45] Close attention to context,
that is, is crucial for understanding a thinker's ideas. This approach to
writing intellectual history has now become commonplace, but Keynes's
essay was then very much a pioneering effort. Did he also have in mind how
he wished to be understood by later generations?

In December 1940 Keynes finally relinquished personal control over the
bookings at the Arts Theatre. In future, he said, he would confine himself to
general principles. But of course he did not. In 1942 he was active in getting
the producer Norman Marshall to form a resident company at the Arts
Theatre, which in the spring of 1943 put on twelve weeks of Ibsen and
Chekhov – 'just the sort of thing', Keynes told the manager Norman Higgins,
'we have dreamt of having for a long time past'. He advised Marshall,
though, to do something 'to raise the average cheerfulness of the plays! In
these times one can put up with only a moderate ration of gloom and
perplexity.' Marshall proved something of a disappointment – 'idle and ...
unimaginative, rather a coward and incompetent over detail'; Higgins, by
contrast, was 'energetic, loyal, intelligent ... everything one could wish and
a great deal more'.[46] The war years were a halcyon time, the theatre, full
from the influx into Cambridge of evacuees and government and military
personnel, including the American air force. Keynes himself paid for three
thousand schoolchildren to see *Toy Princess*, a poetry and music entertainment devised by Dadie Rylands.

In addition to Cambridge activities, Keynes managed to devote an
extraordinary amount of attention to farming operations at Tilton which
now, heavily subsidised, were part of the wartime drive for agricultural self-
sufficiency. They were also much expanded, for in 1941 Keynes and his

farm manager, Logan Thomson, jointly took over Charleston farm – 'to stop its buildings falling into decay', writes Frances Spalding – Keynes lending Thomson the money to set up as an independent farmer, and giving him the profits of Charleston from which to pay it back. They now had 600 acres, and Keynes was in a position to sow 100 acres of wheat annually. Fred Woollard, his chauffeur, took charge of a magnificent new tractor costing £600. The detailed correspondence between Keynes and Logan Thomson in the war occupies a fat folder in Keynes's papers at King's College. As was his wont, he wanted to know and understand everything. He gave detailed instructions to Thomson on what to plant in the kitchen garden; he wanted to know exactly why the wheat crop at Charleston had been so bad in 1944. In October 1941 there were twelve labourers altogether, including Quentin Bell, who was paid £2 1s 0d a week to look after the pigs. Quentin was not noted for his rural skills. When organising a pheasant shoot in December 1943, Logan Thomson wrote to Keynes: 'You can probably leave out Quentin . . . from the point of view of killing anything.'

Keynes was a canny employer. On one occasion, he announced a wage increase, but eliminated the free milk allowance, which was costing him more. In 1942 he applied to the Wages Board to reduce the wages of elderly labourers: 'The main reason . . . is not so much a lack of skill as the slow pace at which they perform.' On hearing that 'Old Horace' had finally been carried off to the workhouse, Keynes commented: 'Sorry to hear that Old Horace has . . . been taken to his last home but one.'

In February 1941 he had to ward off a request from a Captain Wills to requisition Tilton as a small headquarters. Keynes – justifiably – went through the roof. 'Quite out of the question,' he thundered back. He, his wife, his 'aged housekeeper', cook and cook's daughter were in continuous residence. Although he had a resident bailiff, he was in active control of Tilton farm and had to be there frequently to take part in the management. After being seriously ill for three years, he had returned to full duty at the Treasury, but still needed to care for his health, with the country as his place for recuperation. 'I am afraid it would seriously interfere with my physical capacity to undertake my duties at the Treasury, which are of an important character, if I were deprived of my house and home,' he wrote back. No more was heard of requisition.

Keynes kept in touch with his old Bloomsbury friends as much as his duties would allow, and did his best to help them in dealing with wartime difficulties: meetings of the Memoir Club, convened by Molly MacCarthy, continued to be the focal point of old and new Bloomsbury, Maynard attending as many as he could. Duncan Grant and Vanessa Bell sat out the war at Charleston, living a 'relatively quiet life, composed of painting, gardening, keeping chickens and seeing few people'.[47] During his recuperative holidays at Tilton, Maynard saw more of Duncan than he had done in the 1930s, and the Charlestonians would come to Tilton over the Christmas holidays, with Lydia and Duncan leading the 'entertainments'. Keynes helped finance the religious murals Duncan, Vanessa and Quentin painted in Berwick Church in 1942–3, and gave money, as well as lent pictures, to a remarkable art gallery opened in Lewes by 'the ladies of Miller', two eccentric sisters, Mrs Frances Byng Stamper and Miss Caroline Byng Lucas.

Keynes's own picture buying was in abeyance, though he added the occasional Ivon Hitchens to his collection. He joined with Duncan and Vanessa in disapproving of Bunny Garnett's marriage to their daughter Angelica in 1942. The thought of Duncan's former lover marrying Duncan's daughter was too bizarre even for Keynes's relaxed morals.

Keynes did not give up the editorship of the *Economic Journal* till February 1945. His main motive was to keep abreast of economic theory. *EJ* material went with him on all his wartime American journeys. It was at the end of a speech at the dinner marking his retirement from the editorship that he offered a toast 'to economists, who are the trustees, not of civilisation, but of the possibility of civilisation'. Harrod is quite right to emphasise Keynes's careful choice of words: 'He said what he wanted to say.'[48] Keynes remained chairman of the board of the *New Statesman* till his death, though he found its journalism increasingly distasteful. In 1945 he objected to an article by Aylmer Vallance 'full of the slants, snides, sneers, and smears which Communists and Fellow Travellers habitually employ as a means for building a perfect society'.[49]

In January 1943, he resigned as vice-president of the Malthusian League in protest against the decision of its Council to urge the government to take steps to restrict the fecundity of the poor – a policy of which he had approved as a young man, but which now struck him as grossly insensitive in the light of Hitler's eugenic experiments. By contrast, the Trusteeship of the National Gallery, which Keynes accepted in October 1941, was a 'very pleasant and honourable mild job'. His appointment led Simon Courtauld to remark that 'all our most respectable institutions are being revolutionised'.

Throughout the war, Keynes kept up his reading, and commented, often extensively, on books which interested him. His letter to Friedrich Hayek on the latter's *Road to Serfdom* was a key statement of his political and economic philosophy. (See pp. 722–3.) He was 'so fascinated' by Ivor Brown's book on slang, *A Word in your Ear*, that he felt moved 'to send [him] one or two footnotes on it'.[50] A profile of Keynes by Brown appeared in the *Observer* in 1943. He managed a reader's report on a manuscript by the statistician Udny Yule, entitled 'Statistics of Literary Vocabulary', in which Yule had counted up authors' choice of nouns. 'This is far too narrow a front on which to advance with such large forces,' Keynes declared.[51] The summer of 1942 found him reading the galleys of volume one of J. H. Clapham's history of the Bank of England, supplying eight pages of comment on a 'fascinating' work, and wondering how the Bank protected its reserve in its first hundred years.[52] He promoted the efforts of a Czech refugee, Werner Stark, to rediscover and rehabilitate Bentham, got him a job lecturing at Cambridge, and paid various grants to him out of his own pocket.[53]

In May 1943 Maisky, the Soviet ambassador, sent him an article by Academician M. Mitin on 'Twenty-Five Years of Philosophy in the USSR' which he hoped Keynes would be able to get published in a respectable English journal to 'strengthen the cultural ties between our two peoples'. Keynes passed on 'this interesting but rather pathetic document' which had 'nothing whatever to do with philosophy but is a sociological document of genuine interest' to Leonard Woolf, who was editing the *Political Quarterly*. 'I wish I knew what dialectical materialism is. But I know from long experience and many efforts that this is doomed to be a sealed book to me. I shall never know.' Woolf rejected the article as total rubbish. Keynes persevered with Sydney Hooper, editor of *Philosophy*, who also rejected it. Keynes urged him to reconsider, if only to show 'how barmy the human race is'.[54] Keynes's 'blind spot' about Marxism remained. A few days' holiday gave him time to read Joan Robinson's short book *An Essay on Marxian Economics*. 'I found it most fascinating,' he wrote to her. 'This is in spite of the fact that there is something intrinsically boring in an attempt to make sense of what is in fact not sense.... I am left with the feeling ... that he [Marx] had a penetrating and original flair but was a very poor thinker indeed....'[55]

In the last years of his life, Keynes's book buying turned increasingly towards early editions of Elizabethan and Stuart drama and poetry, partly because he thought they were good bargains, partly because they 'seem to me to be silly and neurotic in just the way I fancy'.[56] He bought fine editions at auction and through the catalogues of Maggs, Quaritch and other specialist booksellers. He would browse through them in the loggia on sunny afternoons at Tilton, particularly when bouts of ill-health gave him enforced leisure, and would correspond about their contents and market value with experts, in letters full of excitement and amateurish but learned assertion.

VI. BACK AT SCHOOL

In addition to his Treasury job Keynes took on two substantial extra responsibilities in the war. On 17 December 1941, Samuel Courtauld's son-in-law R. A. Butler, President of the Board of Education, asked him to become chairman of the Council for the Encouragement of Music and the Arts (CEMA). His work for this body can be more conveniently considered later (see pp. 724–9). But it scarcely exceeded in volume his labours for his old school. In July 1940, accepting an invitation from R. C. Martineau, he was elected to represent the eighty masters on the Governing Body (called Fellows) of Eton. He was admitted as a Fellow on 5 October and at the same meeting was made a member of the General Purposes Committee. Being Keynes, he interpreted his brief in the broadest terms. At his very first meeting of the GPC 'he drew attention to various points as regards the claims [for war damage to houses owned by Eton in London]' and was soon advising on Eton's investment policies and tax affairs, the management of trust funds and properties, and future relations with the state system. This was in addition to sorting out staff grievances. Keynes loved being back at school. Meetings of the General Purposes Committee took place once every two months, meetings of the Governing Body three times a year. He would generally arrive on Friday evening, stay overnight with the headmaster, Claude Elliott, and continue on Saturday to Cambridge by train. Between the meetings there were often heavy bouts of correspondence; when other duties kept him from attending, he would communicate his views in writing, often at considerable length.

Keynes took on this extra chore not just because he enjoyed the work, but because he was passionately committed to Eton's survival. This was an aspect of his traditionalism, reinforced by his conspicuously happy memories of his schooldays. Once engaged, there was no controlling his restless probing. Even before his formal election as Fellow he had spied out inefficiencies in the system – lack of adequate pension rights for the Dames, 'barmy' retirement ages for the beaks.[57] Having denounced the school's investment and pension policies as supremely tax inefficient, he started an Investment Committee, and sketched out a new pension scheme in a letter of several pages.[58] He took his duties as masters' representative seriously, adjudicating in many disputes, often involving a mountain of correspondence. To these contentious battles, Keynes brought remarkable tact and good sense. After a famous running battle between two housemasters, Tait and Assheton, about who should get the larger House (boys' boarding houses then being run by the housemasters for profit), he came down firmly in favour of paying housemasters salaries, a reform introduced in 1945. Sometimes even his patience ran out. On 23 January 1943 he wrote to the bursar: 'Here is a copy of the letter which I have written to Colquhoun about his blasted gas-cooker.... I cannot see that this is the kind of case where there is justifiable ground for carrying the appeal to the House of Lords.'

Many of Keynes's interventions belong to a history of Eton, but some of them are revealing of his attitudes. Students of Keynesian economics will be amused by the following note to him from the headmaster: 'I am going into your suggestions for balancing the budget.'[59] His closest ally on the Governing Body was the banker Jasper Ridley, but when Ridley refused to support his proposal to buy Australian dollar bonds, Keynes was provoked into a frustrated statement of his investment philosophy: 'My central principle ...

is to go contrary to general opinion, on the ground that, if everyone agreed about its merits, the investment is inevitably too dear and therefore unattractive. Now obviously I can't have it both ways – the whole point of the investment is that most people disagree with it. So, if others concerned don't feel enough confidence to give me a run, then it is in the nature of the case that I must retire from unequal combat.'[60]

Not least of Keynes's delights, though also irritations, was Eton's magnificently eccentric resident Provost, 'Linky' Quickswood, formerly Lord Hugh Cecil, a forensically ferocious High Church Tory of traditional habits – he went on wearing knee-breeches to dinner – and even more traditional views. He regarded the war as a vulgar interruption of time-hallowed routine, and resisted the provision of air-raid shelters, on the ground that the statutes did not provide for them. 'The relentless habits of a medieval schoolman to which he subjected human problems was not always appreciated,' writes Kenneth Rose.[61] Keynes arrived in the middle of a terrific row between Quickswood and the headmaster, who was trying to get control over the election of scholars, traditionally the prerogative of the Provost and Fellows. Linky accused Claude Elliott, a man of 'brilliant administrative ability', but 'ambitious for power', of trying to reduce the Provost to even greater 'Merovingian' status. The scent of battle in his nostrils, the Provost combed ancient statutes in support of his position. 'A prize example of misdirected intellectual powers' was Keynes's verdict on a six-page letter he received from Quickswood on the subject of who was to chair the examiners' meeting. Exhaustion eventually brought a compromise. 'You will see on what statesmanlike lines [the dispute] has been conducted,' an amused Keynes told the scholars' examiner, Francis Cruso. 'His training in theology and mine in metaphysics enabled the Provost and me to reach a concordat, which I hope you will think satisfactory. The examiners are not to draw up an order of merit, but there will be no objection to their communicating to the electors the sort of list which they would have been inclined to draw up were they permitted to do so.'[62]

By 1944, Linky Quickswood was ready to go. Before the war, he had attacked bishops for refusing to retire before the onset of senility. On 14 October, having reached the age of seventy-five, he suddenly announced his own retirement. 'And so I go to Bournemouth in lieu of Paradise,' he told the assembled school. He was succeeded by the Vice-Provost, Henry Marten, who had taught Keynes history, and was now teaching Princess Elizabeth the same subject at neighbouring Windsor Castle.

Keynes himself sometimes thought of retiring from government service, particularly after 1943 – a course often urged on him in the interests of public enlightenment. His official position led him to refuse some tempting offers, including an invitation to deliver the Romanes Lectures for 1942, and, less demandingly, the Stamp Memorial Lecture at the London School of Economics. The key question was: should Keynes continue his Treasury work or try to prepare public opinion for post-war realities? In reply to one of these retiring suggestions, from Sir George Schuster, Keynes wrote on 7 February 1943: 'I think the time may well come when one can be more useful trying to affect public opinion. . . . But it does not seem to me that the time for that has yet come. . . . Whitehall . . . is in a very constructive and enterprising mood, – at least the Treasury is. So far we are all acting rather successfully as a team. So long as this is the case, I believe that team work can do more towards getting things actually done, than the baying of a lone dog.'[63] The constructive enterprise on which he and the Treasury were jointly engaged was the plan for an international clearing union.

PART EIGHT

BETTER THAN LAST TIME

The day is not far off when the economic problem will take the back seat where it belongs, and ... the arena of the heart and head will be occupied where it belongs, or reoccupied by our real problems – the problems of life and of human relations, of creation and behaviour and religion.

J. M. Keynes, *Essays in Persuasion*

36

Keynes's 'New Order'

I. SETTING THE SCENE

All those who thought about the future, even in the darkest days of the Second World War, shared one overriding aim: to do better than last time. To be sure, the First World War also hatched improving plans. But the Wilsonian programme – national self-determination, open covenants openly arrived at, the League of Nations – was primarily constitutional and political. In economics, though less so in social life, the cry was 'back to 1913'. In the Second World War, no one wanted to 'get back' to the 1930s. The problem of Germany, of peace-keeping, remained. But what distinguished the reformist efforts of the Second World War from those of the First was the much greater attention paid to economic and social policy. Most of those who pondered on such matters believed that it was defective economic arrangements which had made such a 'hash', as Keynes put it, of the inter-war years. Hitler himself could be seen as an extreme reaction to the extreme effect of the great depression on Germany. Full employment, social security, international partnership were to be the conscious goals of peace, not just the aberrant achievements of war.

The great unknown was the United States. Among policymakers in Britain and America, there was a widespread, though not universal, feeling that the isolation of the United States had been a major factor in the breakdown of both the economic and security systems of the inter-war years. Britain, as Keynes put it, had conducted the nineteenth-century international orchestra. After the First World War, it was palpably disabled from doing so. As a result, the orchestra had broken up into discordant sections. Was the United States willing to pick up the baton? This was far from clear. In 1941 it was not even in the war. But it had a post-war agenda – non-discrimination in trade – and in Lend–Lease a powerful lever to force Britain to sign up to it. To Keynes these were the 'lunatic proposals of Mr Hull'. They were lunatic, because apparently unqualified and religiously inspired. But Keynes was a pragmatist. So it might be possible to accept the American agenda, if the US administration could be made to see that it had to be underpinned by other policies and institutions, involving American money and leadership.

Qualifying all Keynes's battles with the Americans was the underlying belief that the New World had to be yoked, and kept yoked, to the Old World, if the latter were to enjoy durable peace and prosperity. It was in Britain's long-term interest to arrange for this, even if it meant having to swallow humble pie on the way. This was far from being the consensus view of Britain's elites, but it was probably the majority view. It goes far to explain what otherwise might seem inexplicable, namely the deference Britain paid to American wishes, both during and after the war.

Keynes had been handed the State Department draft of Article VII of the Lend–Lease Agreement before he left Washington in July 1941. As a 'consideration' for Lend–Lease, Britain would pledge itself not to 'discriminate' against American goods after the war. Between August 1941 and February 1942, British strategy for dealing with the draft Article VII followed two parallel courses. The first was to secure such amendments as to free Britain from any specific obligations in return for receiving American supplies. The second was to develop proposals for meeting, or seeming to meet, American requirements. Keynes wrote to Acheson on 17 October: 'When I got back here I found that Whitehall was very much more prepared to take a serious interest in post-war problems than before I left with various high up committees being established to think about this.'[1]

On 7 December 1941, the whole context of the Lend–Lease negotiations seemed altered by the Japanese attack on Pearl Harbor, and US entry into the European war. The British now hoped that talk of a consideration owing for Lend–Lease would be drowned out by the rhetoric of mutual sacrifice for a common cause. They were alarmed by the pile-up of sterling balances which would ensue from the Pacific war. Montagu Norman wanted the British to urge on the Americans 'the policy of pooling resources without any talk of consideration now or hereafter'.[2] Halifax hoped to postpone final discussion of the consideration till after the war. There was neither pooling nor postponement. The United States insisted that a 'debt' had already been incurred; and made it clear that all future supplies to Britain would be lend–leased on the same conditions as before. Churchill, conscious of disunity in his Cabinet,[3] crossed out the words 'without discrimination' from the Atlantic Charter when he met Roosevelt at Placentia Bay, Newfoundland in August 1941, and managed to avoid discussion of Article VII altogether when he visited Washington in December that year to cement the Grand Alliance.

Keynes's more serious preoccupation was to find some way by which it might be safe for Britain to accept the obligations of Article VII of the Lend–Lease Agreement. He was clear from the start that a return to the gold standard and free trade was out of the question. But might it not be possible, by a major reform of the currency system, to restore the system of multilateral payments which had underpinned trade expansion in the nineteenth century? Provided all countries were guaranteed sufficient quantities of reserves – something the old gold standard had been unable to do – it might be possible to dismantle most of the trade barriers which had grown up in the 1930s and during the war and restore that single world which had vanished in 1914. It was in this mood that Keynes started thinking about 'future currency arrangements' at Tilton in August 1941.[4] These thoughts were to occupy him for most of the rest of the war. In Washington, Harry Dexter White of the US Treasury was also thinking about 'future currency arrangements'. The compromise between the plans which the two men produced would be known as the Bretton Woods System.

It might seem odd that planning for economic disarmament started on the monetary rather than on the trade side, and made faster progress. After all, Article VII was about trade, not money. But it made sense logically and politically. World trade had broken down in the 1930s because the gold standard had disintegrated. So the way to start unblocking the channels of trade was to unblock the flow of money by which traded goods were paid for. This required an improvement on the old gold standard. It also seemed a lot easier for Britain and America to reach agreement about money. Money was too esoteric and boring to engage the attention of most politicians, whereas trade issues instantly aroused interests, passions, and prejudices. So technicians had a chance to make much more progress on money before their plans attracted political attention.

It must not be supposed that the technicians, as they were somewhat contemptuously called, operated in a historical or political vacuum. They brought to their work different understandings of what had gone wrong with the old gold standard; and different national experiences and interests. Above all the British and American plans came from two countries which expected to be very differently situated in the post-war world. The British expected to emerge from the war stripped of trade and assets and burdened with debts, the Americans in the opposite position. Keynes's, therefore, was a debtor's, White's a creditor's, perspective. The British wanted a scheme which would enable them to borrow without strings, the Americans one which would lend with strings. This difference was reinforced by another. The British plan came from a banking tradition, the American one from a legal tradition. The British wanted a scheme based on prudential maxims, the Americans one based on legal rules.

The technical debates were not merely a cover for national self-interest. Keynes and White were both interested in theory, and in finding technical solutions to technical problems. Economics often enables political conflicts which seem intractable if carried on in the language of politics to be bypassed by assuming (or the cynic would say pretending) that they can be reduced to the technical, and imposing a language of debate consistent with that assumption. As the technicians from both sides got to know each other better, a genuine camaraderie developed *contra mundis* – against the politicians, bankers, vested interests on both sides waiting in the wings to sabotage both the Keynes and White Plans. The fact that 'technicians' handled all the stages leading to the Bretton Woods Agreement ensured only that there was an agreement; it did not ensure that the politicians on either side signed up to it in good faith.

The challenge with which Article VII faced Keynes was to devise a plan to lock the USA into a system which would maintain balance of payments equilibrium between all countries without trade discrimination but also without forcing deflation, unemployment or debt-bondage on the deficit countries. He began drafting it in September 1941, soon after his return from the United States.

II. DR SCHACHT

Keynes had been giving intermittent thought to post-war arrangements even before Lend–Lease was signed. On 19 November 1940 a dossier arrived on his desk with details of something called the Funk Plan. This was a blueprint for Hitler's European 'New Order', announced by his Economics Minister, Walther Funk, at a press conference in Berlin on 25 July 1940. It was, not surprisingly, the first post-war plan to emerge from the war. It came with a note from Harold Nicolson at the Ministry of Information suggesting that Keynes make a broadcast to the Americans and Dominions to discredit it. Much to Nicolson's surprise, Keynes wrote back that it was 'excellent and just what we ourselves ought to be thinking of doing'.[5] What was going on?

The main feature of the Funk Plan was a European clearing union to be managed from Berlin. It built on the system of bilateral barter developed by Hitler's previous Economics Minister, Hjalmar Schacht, to protect the German balance of payments as Germany's economy regained full employment. Bilateral agreements were designed to balance the trade of each pair of countries without the need for gold movements, or indeed any foreign exchange transactions. In its simplest form, the two trading partners open accounts for each other in their central banks, into which each pays for its imports from the other in its local currency. Exporters could thus receive payments in their own currencies, without one currency having to be converted into another, as long as the value of the pair's exports and imports balanced. By 1938 Germany had made such agreements with twenty-seven countries, covering about half its foreign trade. In theory, the system was symmetrical; in practice, Germany was able to run up mark balances (representing import surpluses) in the accounts of its east European neighbours which depended on the German market for their exports of foodstuffs and raw materials. Bilateral clearing removed the need for both tariffs and currency depreciation. Fixed exchange rates could be maintained since, as

Paul Einzig noted, 'any currency can be kept stable by preventing transfers which tend to cause its depreciation'.[6] The Funk Plan proposed to extend Schacht's bilateral clearings into a system of multilateral clearing within German-controlled Europe, with bilateral clearing between the Union and the United States and others.

Keynes explained that:

> [though Schacht and Funk] have used their new system to the detriment of their neighbours ... the underlying idea is sound and good. In the last six months the Treasury and the Bank of England have been building up for this country an exchange system which has borrowed from the German experience all that was good in it. If we are to meet our obligations and avoid chaos in international trade after the war, we shall have to retain this system. But this same system will serve to protect the impoverished European countries and is an essential safeguard against a repetition of what happened last time.[7]

In a letter he wrote to Frank Ashton-Gwatkin of the Foreign Office on 25 April 1941, Keynes expanded on these initial observations, producing a first, very uncertain bash at his own Clearing Union Plan, which he would draft that autumn. It is essentially what his Clearing Union might have looked like *without the United States in it*. The crucial point was the priority given to achieving trade balance. If trade between the sterling area and the United States was to be on a barter (bilateral clearing) basis, monetary issues like the sterling–dollar exchange rate and creditor versus debtor adjustment became secondary. Unlike Funk, though, Keynes did recognise the need for 'credit arrangements' to deal with short-run payments imbalances: Britain, unlike Germany, was in no position to plan the trade of its Empire.[8]

Keynes never thought of the Schachtian system merely as a *pis aller*. That is to say, he did not put it on a par with what he would call 'failed experiments' like currency manipulation. In Lionel Robbins's view currency floating offered 'a complete solution to Britain's problem of external balance'.[9] But in Keynes's reading of inter-war history it was a weapon in the 'blind struggle' of countries to escape from the shackles of the gold standard, with a tendency to produce war.[10] By ensuring that 'goods exchanged for goods' the Schachtian system made possible trade which might not take place at all under *laissez-faire*. The doctrine that exchange controls were superior to currency depreciation became a permanent part of Keynes's thinking. It also became Treasury and Bank of England orthodoxy. Schachtianism might not be the best possible system, but it might easily be the best system possible.

III. THE CLEARING UNION

One of the committees set up to consider post-war issues was an inter-departmental committee on post-war financial problems under Sir George Chrystal, permanent secretary at the Ministry of Health, and a bit of a wag: he had written a book before the First World War called *Memoirs of Prince Chlodwig of Hohenlohe Schillingsfuerst*. Like most such committees, it rarely met. The work was done by the Treasury and the Bank of England. A composite document on 'Post-War Monetary, Financial and Trade Policy' – known as the 'Treasury sandwich' and later the 'Treasury Bible' – started to wend its portentous way through Whitehall in August 1941, gathering drafters and paragraphs on its journey. The British still hoped to avoid any definite commitments to 'Hullism'. This heavily influenced the approach of early drafts of the Treasury document, largely inspired by Hubert Henderson, Keynes's erstwhile ally, then resentful antagonist, now, like Keynes, at the Treasury. Henderson was a Schachtian. Commitment to Article VII, he argued, could not be reconciled with the prospective weakness of Britain's balance of payments; it was inconsistent with a system of national planning, of which exchange controls, centralised purchases of food and raw materials, and quantitative regulations of imports were an integral part. Such measures were not just for war; they represented 'an advance in the direction of a more ordered life'.[11]

Keynes would have read Henderson's gloomy memoranda as he gathered his own thoughts on 'future currency arrangements' early in September. Unlike Henderson, Keynes preferred internationalism. To the extent that he was a Schachtian, it was much more for practical reasons, to do with the situation Britain would find itself in when the war ended, and his scepticism concerning America's ability or willingness to step into Britain's shoes. This basic difference of outlook runs through their debates on both international and domestic policy. His internationalism, therefore, was contingent on getting the United States to do its duty as a creditor – by spending its surpluses, as Britain had done in the nineteenth century, and not hoarding them. He tried to work out a scheme for ensuring that it did so: this was his Clearing Union. If that failed he was ready to fall back on bilateralism.

Keynes returned to Tilton on Wednesday 3 September 1941 to spend, as he told his mother, 'several days in peace writing a heavy memorandum on post-war international currency plans'. Peace was the most elusive of his prizes. On Friday he was back in London for a meeting with Montagu Norman. The bomb explosion which killed Lord Stamp on 17 April had created a vacancy on the Court (board of directors) of the Bank of England.

George Booth, a director, and son of Charles Booth the social reformer, had suggested Keynes to fill it, as being the most qualified person acceptable to Labour. Now Norman invited him to do so. As a director, he would have to buy £2000 of Bank of England stock for £7300. Having been assured that 'unofficially' he could continue to be at the disposal of the Chancellor and Treasury – that is continue exactly as he was – he decided to accept. The appointment was announced on 18 September.

Keynes wrote jokingly to Florence: 'Rather appalling, I feel, such respect-ability! Coming after a fellowship at Eton I feel it is only a matter of time before I become a Bishop or Dean of York. . . . My election to the Court may cause a bit of a stir . . . as . . . suggesting (more probably than is the truth) that my characteristic policies are becoming orthodox.' The appointment was largely honorific – the most important function of the Court being to appoint the governor – but it was also a seal of approval from the bastion of sound money. What did it signify? 'What rejoices all your friends', gushed Felix Frankfurter, 'is that the mountain has come to Mohammed and not the other way round.' The governor had a more detached view. 'Keynes on a committee', he told Clapham, 'is rather like yeast.' Keynes was not sure who had captured whom. 'It remains to be seen', he wrote to Richard Kahn, 'which party is being made an honest woman of.'[12] Keynes now added Thursday-morning meetings of the Court to his other duties. After one, he remarked to Booth, 'I do enjoy these lunches at the Bank: Montagu Norman, always absolutely charming, always absolutely wrong.'[13] The reconciliation was superficial. Shortly after Keynes's death, Norman wrote grudgingly, 'he must have been a great economist but was a bad banker'.[14]

After the excitement of his appointment, Keynes continued his drafting on Saturday. His memorandum was finished by Tuesday 9 September. He did it, he told Kahn, in an effort 'to make my ideas concrete' and 'to press others who have different ideas to do the same'. Keynes's method, as always, was to lead from the front and force others to make clear the nature of their disagreement.

The fruit of his weekend labour was two papers, 'Post War Currency Policy' and 'Proposals for an International Currency Union'. The two ques-tions Keynes set out to answer in his first paper were: what was wrong with the gold standard, and what were the special problems Britain would face after the war?

He started off by dismissing the classical theory of the gold standard. The flow of gold never did preserve equilibrium in the balance of payments. Instead, Keynes claimed, provocatively, in the previous 500 years there had been only two periods, each of about fifty years, when the use of commodity money in international trade had 'worked' – the silver inflation period of the sixteenth century and the gold standard of the late nineteenth century, when 'the system of international investment pivoting on London trans-ferred the *onus* of adjustment from the debtor to the creditor position'.

Experience showed, he went on, that loans do not bring about a balanced position unless they create new sources of payments. Neither deflation nor depreciation necessarily produces a redistribution of trade. Tariffs, preferences and subsidies all had noxious side-effects. In the 1930s Schacht had 'stumbled in desperation on something new which had in it the germs of a good technical idea', namely, to cut the knot by substituting barter for the international use of money. Keynes quoted from Henderson's 'Nineteen Thirties' paper: 'If Germany had wished for butter instead of guns and aeroplanes, there is no reason to doubt that Dr. Schacht's expedients would have enabled her to obtain the butter instead of the metal from overseas.'

The gold standard had failed because it forced adjustment on the debtor. Adjustment, he wrote, was '*compulsory* for the debtor and *voluntary* for the creditor'. By this he meant that countries running deficits had to deflate their economies, whereas surplus countries could *hoard* their surpluses – as, in British perception, the United States and France had done for much of the 1920s. During the great depression, creditor hoarding had been aggravated by capital flight from deficit to surplus countries. 'The flow of refugee and speculative funds, superimposed on [the favourable trade balance of the United States] brought the whole system to ruin.' There was no guarantee against a repetition of hot-money flows after the war, when the position of wealth-owners would be threatened everywhere, and the 'whereabouts of "the better 'ole" will shift with the speed of a magic carpet'. Keynes echoed Henderson: 'Nothing is more certain than that the movement of capital funds must be regulated.'

After the war, Britain would need to re-establish equilibrium before it could maintain it. It would have no alternative but to refine and improve 'the Schachtian device'. It would end the war with 'a well-developed' payments and clearing system which might evolve into a permanent peacetime system, mitigating the objectionable features of bilateralism. It could stabilise and balance its trade at a high volume by continuing to buy foodstuffs and raw materials in bulk from countries willing to take its exports.

So far it had been Schacht all the way. But now Keynes suddenly changed tack. He would prefer to challenge the Americans with an 'ideal' scheme, which would enable Britain to sign up honestly to the 'blessed word [non]-discrimination'; a scheme that was 'Utopian', not in the sense that it was impracticable, but 'in ... that it assumes a higher degree of understanding, of the spirit of bold innovation, and of international co-operation and trust than it is safe or reasonable to assume'. None of this suggests any exaggerated hope that anyone would adopt this 'ideal' system. One can imagine him in his study at Tilton dusting down a copy of his *Treatise on Money* and looking up its pages on a 'supernational bank' issuing 'supernational bank money'.

The chief purpose of his International Currency Union (as he called it) was to secure creditor adjustment without renouncing debtor discipline. Its method was to marry the Schacht–Funk 'clearing' approach with the banking principle. All residual international transactions – those giving rise to surpluses and deficits in balance of payments positions – were to be settled through 'clearing accounts' held by member central banks in an International Clearing Bank (ICB). Member central banks would buy and sell their own currencies against debits and credits to their accounts at the Clearing Bank. These balances would be held in 'bank money' (later called 'bancor'). Each member bank would have the right to an amount of bank money (called its 'index quota') equal to half the average value of its country's total trade for the five last pre-war years. This was its overdraft facility. The ICB's total overdraft facilities came, therefore, to half the value of pre-war international trade – about $25bn. Each national currency would have a fixed but adjustable relation to a unit of ICB's bank money, which itself was expressed in terms of a unit of gold. But this link with the gold standard was a fiction. Whereas bank money could be bought with gold, it could not be sold for gold. Keynes called this 'one-way convertibility'. 'A gold stock which can never be paid out to *anyone* (except probably to the International Bank of Mars)' was an odd idea to Dennis Robertson.[15] Keynes's long-run purpose was to de-monetise gold, so that central banks would lose any incentive to hoard it. Bank money would be the ultimate reserve asset of the system.

The object of the ICB was to maintain balance of payments equilibrium between each member country and the rest of the world. Deposits of bank money (credits and debits) would be created by surpluses and deficits and extinguished by their liquidation. Keynes sought to bring a simultaneous pressure on both surplus and deficit countries to 'clear' their accounts. A bank whose annual 'overdraft' averaged more than a quarter of its index quota would be designated a 'deficiency bank' and *allowed* to depreciate its currency by not more than 5 per cent at the end of that year; if its average overdraft over the year was more than half its quota it would be designated a 'supervised bank', and might be *required* to reduce the value of its currency by up to 5 per cent, to sell the ICB any free gold and to prohibit capital exports. Interest would be charged on overdrafts, rising in line with the debt–quota ratio. A persistently profligate member could be expelled from the Union. There were similar provisions to liquidate persisting surpluses: any member bank in persistent credit would be allowed or required to revalue its currency (in steps of 5 per cent), be required to unblock any foreign-owned balances and investments, and be required to pay 5 or 10 per cent interest on credits running above a quarter and a half of its quota respectively to the Reserve Fund. Credit balances exceeding quotas at the end of the year would be confiscated and transferred to the Reserve Fund. If all countries were in perfect balance at the end of the year the sum of bancor balances would be exactly zero.

Attached to Keynes's Bank were a number of ancillary organisations:

a supranational police force, a reconstruction and relief organisation, and buffer stocks. These would be financed by additional overdraft facilities, transfers from the ICB's Reserve Fund and direct contributions from surplus countries. The ICB would be managed by a board of eight governors and a chairman. Britain, the Empire, the USA and the USSR would have one governor each, there would be two from Europe, one from Latin America, and one other. That Britain and its Empire could outvote the United States, which would be financing most of the overdrafts, was a felicitous touch.[16]

The choice Keynes presented in this paper was stark: either Schachtianism or the 'ideal' scheme. There was no Middle Way. But for Keynes there was always a middle way, once the action moved from theory to practice. Later he would abjure Schachtianism without the 'ideal' scheme, having persuaded himself that the American replacements – World Bank and International Monetary Fund – were almost as good. To his left-wing disciples, this was a betrayal based on self-delusion; to disciples like Harrod and Meade, it showed that Keynes's heart was always on the internationalist side. To the historian it seems as if Keynes (and Britain) had little choice.

The central idea underlying the Clearing Union plan was of a piece with the theories of economic malfunction which Keynes had been developing since the 1920s and which crystallised in his *General Theory*. Money was a medium of exchange but also a store of value. It improved on barter, but also gave people freedom not to spend at all. The pre-war gold standard system had been characterised by a widespread propensity to hoard by some countries, particularly the United States. By raising world interest rates, this propensity had spread deflation and unemployment round the system. The only escape from the vicious deflationary circle had been through policies of national self-help, which, however, had led to currency and trade wars. If the great benefit of the gold standard – multilateral clearing – was to be regained, hoarding by surplus countries must be prevented. If surplus countries refused to spend their surpluses, they would be transferred, through the overdraft facilities of the Clearing Union, to deficit countries.

To say, as Professor Moggridge does, that the 'heart' of Keynes's plan was 'to encourage balance of payments adjustment',[17] is to anaesthetise Keynes's main theoretical insight. It suggests that Keynes envisaged an equal responsibility for adjustment between creditors and debtors. In fact, this equality is purely formal. The size of the overdraft facilities – equal to half the pre-war value of world trade – points clearly to Keynes's view that the main responsibility for adjustment lies with creditors. The real 'heart of the matter' – in global as well as in domestic policy – was to prevent unemployment by reducing the attractions of holding money.

IV. RUNNING THE WHITEHALL GAUNTLET

The Keynes Plan, as it was soon called, was contributed to the Treasury's planning exercise for dealing with Article VII of the Lend–Lease Agreement. This involved not just the core of financial experts from the Treasury, the Bank of England, and the Economic Section of the War Cabinet, but officials from the Board of Trade and the Colonial Office. Keynes had his own unofficial channels of consultation. His favourite 'first class critic' Richard Kahn left for the Middle East in October. His place was taken by Roy Harrod from the Prime Minister's Statistical Office. Though he was vain, petulant and tiresome, Harrod was also brilliant and imaginative, and has a strong claim to be regarded as joint author of the Clearing Union scheme in its final form.

The focal point of the early discussions was not the Keynes Plan but the thickening Treasury 'sandwich'. The Treasury approach sought to distinguish between the 'interim system' based on bilateralism and 'what we hope to come to as soon as may be'. The latter involved vague promises of co-operation with the Americans.[18] This approach was criticised both by the Schachtians and by the liberals.

Both Hubert Henderson and the Bank of England disliked the idea of making any promises for the future, however vague. The view which they represented in their memoranda was that countries, or groups of countries, should aim to balance their post-war trade by the wartime mixture of exchange controls and state trading agreements. This would enable them to maintain stable exchange rates with each other. Article VII, with its ban on discriminatory trading arrangements – those which favoured the exports of one country over another – struck at the heart of this philosophy. The Bank's hope of preserving London as a financial centre rested on maintaining the sterling area and using exchange controls to prevent gold and dollars from draining out of it.[19]

These memoranda reached Keynes, who was part of the consultative process. His criticisms of the Bank's strategy were polite, as befitted a newly appointed director, but devastating. Did the Bank really believe, he wrote on 22 October 1941, that it could maintain the sterling area as a trading fortress after the war? Why should South Africa, able to pay in gold for American motor cars, want to restrict its imports of them? How did the Bank propose to prevent sterling area countries from using their sterling balances in London to pay for American goods? Whether Britain could afford to maintain the sterling area depended on the rest of the sterling area having a favourable balance with the United States 'in conditions of comparative freedom'.[20]

Waley of the Treasury summed up against Henderson and the Bank on 8 November:

> The doctrine that exchange control and trade controls are good in themselves is one to which we shall never get everyone on this side and still less the Americans to agree, and it seems a pity to put it forward as a doctrine. The alternative doctrine that exchange control and trade controls are bad in themselves, but that we shall have to retain them unless and until we can get rid of them because the alternatives of exchange depreciation and deflation are worse, is one which we are much more likely to get general agreement for on both sides of the Atlantic.[21]

The Treasury 'sandwich' was also criticised by the free traders, on both political and economic grounds. Dennis Robertson at the Treasury found early drafts of the document 'very gloomy [and] fraught with the seeds of future international strife and (probably) wars'. He criticised Henderson for trying to maintain 'a value for our monetary unit which doesn't reflect our diminished power of export, and then trying to make up for that by driving clever bargains with people who will probably out-Schacht us in the end'.[22] Frederick Leith-Ross worried that calling something 'interim' might be an excuse for perpetuating bad practices for years.[23] Sir Horace Wilson, the Treasury's permanent secretary, dreaded a long period during which 'we shall only allow a ship to enter Liverpool Docks if we are quite certain that she will at once re-load there with manufactured goods and will go straight back to the port whence she sailed'.[24] Sir Arnold Overton, permanent secretary at the Board of Trade and a strong free trader, rejected the claims for the Schachtian system. He pointed out that Germany got advantage from Schachtian devices only by abusing them, for example, by reselling for cash goods it got on credit.[25] Waley also found it difficult to share Keynes's faith in barter, which 'having been in abeyance from the Stone Age till 1939, was then re-discovered by Dr. Schacht'.[26]

A powerful liberalising influence came from the Economic Section of the War Cabinet, headed by that redoubtable free trader Lionel Robbins. Its 'Note on Post-War Anglo-American Economic Relations', dated 18 August 1941, had pointed out the many flaws of bilateralism and discrimination: its tendency to diminish wealth creation, the threat of retaliation, the danger to Anglo-American relations, the inducement to political and economic frictions, the disruption of imperial relations, the entrenchment of vested interests. Robbins's assistant, James Meade, urged the insertion into the Treasury draft of these balancing arguments, together with a 'precise but conditional' commitment to take part in a 'non-discriminatory trading system'.[27] Sir Sydney Caine at the Colonial Office also took up a strongly free trade position.

In mid-November, Sir Richard Hopkins produced and circulated his own

note on the Treasury 'sandwich'. He was highly sceptical about the possibility of an early return to internationalism. Roy Harrod, at the Prime
Minister's Statistical Branch of the War Cabinet, rejected Hopkins's 'ink-
black pessimism'. Britain's external balance would be found not to have
deteriorated by more than £100m a year. He remarked pointedly that the
Atlantic Charter – agreed by Churchill and Roosevelt in Newfoundland in
August 1941 – was not signed to set up 'a system of a Schachtian kind run
from London instead of Berlin. Yet how otherwise can one describe a widely
ramifying system of payments agreements and bilateral arrangements?'
Harrod then outlined his own scheme for creditor adjustment and buffer
stocks.[28] Henderson reported sourly to Hopkins: '[Harrod's] general line was
that as we could not afford to quarrel with the Americans after the war,
we must agree to scrap everything in our economic arrangements that is
objectionable to them, and repose our entire faith in Roosevelt. . . .'[29]

By mid-November 1941 the Henderson–Bank of England recipe for
Britain's future had been undermined from various sides: barter bilateralism
was economically inferior to multilateralism, it would not in fact solve
Britain's post-war balance of payments problem, it would not preserve the
sterling area, it would cause friction in the Empire, and it could not be sold
to the United States. On the other hand, the free traders were equally
opposed to the deflationary bias of the gold standard system which, in their
understanding, had made free trade impossible. So they favoured new
currency arrangements which would make the world safe for free trade. It
was these considerations which brought Keynes's utopia into the foreground. Once again, getting in early with a worked-out scheme paid off. The
Keynes Plan might be 'teased and nagged', as Harrod put it, but it was the
only document on the table which went beyond the continuation of wartime
arrangements, suggested a way of escaping from the gold standard trap, and
offered a hope of enlisting US support.

Keynes tried to disarm the Bank's suspicions. His scheme, he told
Siepmann and Bolton in mid-November, was

> primarily a contribution to the tactics of diplomacy in Whitehall and
> Washington. As regards Washington, the scheme caters for the pro-
> fessed devotion of Americans to progressive (idealist, liberal, expansion-
> ist) internationalism, and so diverts discussion from their own (entirely
> self-regarding) concrete demands. As regards Whitehall, it is meant to
> rally some of the supporters of appeasement or laissez-faire, who would
> otherwise join forces in opposition to the policies (e.g. bilateralism)
> which would suit our own interests better but which America would
> dislike. . . . The principles of the sterling area, offensive to America in an
> Imperial context, become acceptable, if they are universalised. . . . It is
> expected that while America would never agree to transfer her surplus
> to us, she would agree to transfer it to a country x (being us).[30]

The Treasury also needed to be won over. Ralph Hawtrey, still in the Treasury, with time on his hands, subjected the Keynes Plan to several of his exhausting memoranda. Hawtrey, who remained what he had always been, an eclectic monetary economist, saw no real point in Keynes's super-bank, which provided no 'adequate safeguard against the abuse of the overdraft facility by a weak, reckless, misguided or corrupt country'. The business cycle, Hawtrey insisted, as he had done ever since 1908, was a monetary phenomenon. Inflation led to deflation. If all countries maintained internal price stability, both economies and exchange rates would be stable without the need for 'contractual' transfers. Post-war reconstruction should be financed on an *ad hoc* basis and not through the 'automatic credit facilities' provided by the ICB. Temporary shocks could be dealt with by inter-bank credits. More persistent disequilibria would have to be corrected by exchange rate changes. Hawtrey shrewdly noted that 'to limit the change [in exchange rates] to 5 per cent [as the Keynes Plan did] when the restoration of equilibrium calls for a bigger sum, is to shut the way of escape from the danger of [financial] panic'. As to policy, it would be better in the first instance to aim for an Anglo-American partnership, with the under-standing that each country would maintain domestic price stability, and support each other's exchanges when required.[31] Through several redrafts of the Keynes Plan, Hawtrey persisted in his view that it had 'no stabilising principle at all.... [It] not merely acquiesces in a general resort to exchange controls and import restrictions by all countries that cannot stand the deflationary pressure, but it is only too likely, by obstructing the devaluation of their currency units, to drive them to these expedients. Even the overdraft facilities may well be an aggravation.'[32] By this time Hawtrey's views were considered rather old-fashioned, and his memoranda were too lengthy and turgid to command much attention, but he made some shrewd points.

Brand sent Keynes pertinent criticisms from Washington. While 'entirely in agreement' with the 'general object' of Keynes's scheme, he foresaw a 'good many difficulties'. These centred on the problem of reconciling inter-national co-operation with national sovereignty. Brand urged Keynes to drop any reference to an international police force, which involved a 'suprana-tional government'. Finally, he questioned whether Keynes's scheme would meet Britain's particular problem, which was that it would be faced with a large balance of payments deficit after the war. Did Keynes think that an initial depreciation of sterling would be the way to tackle this?[33]

Keynes's second draft of his Plan, dated 18 November, retained the charter and rules of the Bank virtually intact in an appendix (he now called ICB money 'grammor') but substituted for his previous first paper a glowing affirmation of the attractions of his scheme, which he had started to feel more intensely, and a robust reply to critics, actual and anticipated. Any plan put forward by Britain, Keynes explained, had to be of a general character, not a plea for special assistance, if it was to capture the 'interest and enthusiasm of the Americans'. The dismissal of the Henderson–Bank of England approach was restrained but unmistakable. The Schachtian devices, which he himself had lauded only a few weeks earlier, were now described as a 'patched up contrivance, mainly based on abnormal war experience'. Keynes's love affair with Dr Schacht was over.

Keynes also rejected the Treasury's favourite distinction between interim and long-term arrangements. His Clearing Union was intended to secure both immediate (post-war) and permanent equilibrium in members' balance of payments. 'The plan aims', he wrote, 'at the substitution of an expansionist, in place of a contractionist, pressure on world trade, *especially in the first years'* (emphasis added). This might be achieved by voluntary United States help for European reconstruction. But 'particular arrangements' were likely to be influenced by 'extraneous, political reasons' and to put specific countries into a position of 'particular obligation'. In any case, Britain, as one of the war's victors, would be a poor claimant for American help. It would be better to persuade the United States to enter into a 'general and collective responsibility, applying to all countries alike, that a country finding itself in a creditor position *against the rest of the world as a whole* should enter into an obligation to dispose of this credit balance'.

Keynes next tried to meet actual and possible criticisms and misunderstandings. The main technical idea underlying his proposal 'was to generalise the essential principle of banking as it is exhibited within any closed system ... [namely] the necessary equality between credits and debits'. Any increase in the Bank's liabilities (credits) would be exactly matched by an increase in its assets (debits). As a result, 'the Bank *itself* can never be in difficulties'. This implied that there was no limit to the amount of money Keynes's Bank could create.

Keynes did not expect that credit balances would ever have to be confiscated. 'The main point is that the creditor should not be allowed to remain passive.' Rules about exchange rate adjustments guarded against competitive currency depreciations. The discipline against persistent debtors was inadequate, but now there was no discipline at all, and 'a small expenditure of faith and a readiness to allow actual experience to decide are not too much to ask'. Keynes also emphasised the importance of transparency: the ICB would provide 'an automatic register of the size and whereabouts of the aggregate debtor and creditor positions respectively. The danger signal is shown to all concerned. . . .' On the question of national sovereignty, Keynes claimed that the surrender required by his scheme would be no greater than that presupposed by any commercial or military treaty, and that in any case a better world required a measure of 'financial disarmament'. If the ICB succeeded in maintaining balance of payments equilibrium between its members, there would be no need for discriminatory trade practices, exchange restrictions or impediments to private capital flows. The explicit repudiation of high tariffs, export subsidies, import quotas, barter agreements and blocked accounts would, he thought, 'enable us to give complete satisfaction to Mr Cordell Hull'. The satisfaction was less than it seemed. Imperial preference of up to 25 per cent could be retained under a formula allowing preferences between 'members of political and geographical groups'. Moreover the taboos against 'protective expedients' were not to apply for the first three to five years after the war.

James Meade had wanted Keynes to make clear that currency convertibility was to be the norm.[34] Keynes held fast to his conviction that member countries would need to establish and maintain the *machinery* of exchange controls as part of the monetary management of an adjustable peg system. But this need not preclude freedom of remittance for current transactions, and 'open general licences of indefinite duration' for capital transactions.[35]

Keynes bowed to the general feeling in Whitehall that the post-war order, whatever form it took, should start off with an Anglo-American agreement. The ICB was now to be founded as an Anglo-American club, which other countries would be invited to join. He nodded to the Bank of England's view that the post-war order should, evolve from, rather than supersede, existing economic blocs. Members of the ICB should, 'in some cases, be groups of countries rather than separate [national] units', bound together by customs, preference and currency unions. He even suggested eleven such economic groupings, including North America and four in Europe: the Germanic countries, the Scandinavian countries, the Latin Union, and eastern Europe. Britain, centre of the sterling area, was, of course, 'outside' Europe. Part of Keynes's allure was his ability to seize a fleeting thought and invest it with his own fancy:

> A view of the post-war world which I find sympathetic and attractive and fruitful of good consequences is that we should encourage *small* political and cultural units, combined into larger, and more or less closely knit, economic units. It would be a fine thing to have thirty or forty capital cities in Europe, each the centre of a self-governing country entirely free from national minorities (who would be dealt with by migrations where necessary) and the seat of a government and parliament and university centre, each with their own pride and glory and their own characteristics and excellent gifts. But it would be ruinous to have thirty or forty entirely independent economic and currency unions.

This picture of a provincialised Europe did not survive in later drafts.

On 1 November two American economists, Alvin Hansen and Luther Gulick, had proposed a Joint Economic Declaration by which the US and British governments would pledge themselves to set up an International Development Corporation and International Economic Board to advise governments on how to co-ordinate full employment policies. Keynes had met them in London in September, and he now incorporated their proposals into his scheme. According to Penrose they were important in convincing Keynes that the US administration accepted that full employment was a requirement of free trade.[36] Keynes explained that the 'Investment Board' he now proposed would be part of the mechanism for 'shifting the whole system of clearing credits and debits nearer to equilibrium'.[37] The idea was taken up enthusiastically by Roy Harrod, who promised to work out a plan for it.

Keynes's careful balancing act worked its political magic in Whitehall. For Meade it represented the only 'real hope of a generous and spacious economic collaboration after the war'. Robbins saw it as 'a real release of fresh air in this surcharged and stale atmosphere'.[38] 'I sat up last night reading your revised "proposal" with great excitement,' Dennis Robertson wrote to Keynes on 27 November, 'and a growing hope that the spirit of Burke and Adam Smith is on earth again.'[39] Robertson's coupling of Burke and Smith is a typically subtle tribute to Keynes's Middle Way. The Treasury started to see the Plan as the basis for a consensus position to present to ministers.

The month between the second draft of 18 November and the third draft of 15 December was one of the busiest of Keynes's life. He put in sixty hours a week at the Treasury. He was involved in budget preparations, the end-play of the Lend–Lease negotiations and relief issues. But he mainly concentrated on remodelling his Plan in response to the intensive scrutiny it was receiving.

The debate was now captured by those who accepted the fundamental postulates of the Keynes Plan, but wanted to simplify, voluntarise and liberalise it. Catto, Waley and the indefatigable Hawtrey urged Keynes to place less emphasis on rules and leave more to the discretion of member countries, creditors and debtors. (Waley presciently remarked that the American New Dealers, with their suspicion of 'money lenders', would be much more likely to accept a 'stabilisation fund' than a bank; Catto asked: why give the Bank teeth it would not be able to use?) These officials saw the ICB more like an informational and moral forum, establishing and spreading norms of good-neighbourliness.[40]

Much the most ambitious attempt to reshape the Plan came from Roy Harrod. Harrod was Schachtianism's foremost critic in Whitehall. He dubbed it a form of 'helotage' which could never be sustained in peace. It 'rivets trade to politics and turns every new commercial development into an act of economic warfare. . . . By being too obdurate in defence of Imperial Preference we might lose an Empire.'[41] Harrod's reshaping took the form of producing a plan of his own. The most important requirement was to get the United States committed to creditor adjustment. Everything else was secondary. Creditor adjustment could be secured most simply by an agreement that creditor countries would always accept cheques from deficit countries in full discharge of their debts. No pressure need be put on them to liquidate their balances with the Bank. 'So long as their credit position cannot cause pressure elsewhere, there is no harm in allowing a further accumulation.' The Americans could either spend their cheques or tear them up. Harrod did not mind very much which they did, as long as they continued to accept them. Nor need deficit countries be put under equivalent pressure, since 'debits would be automatically liquidated if and when the creditor countries took the necessary measures', though Harrod admitted that some sanction was needed against 'ultra debtors' – those countries whose deficits persistently exceeded the average of deficits. The Harrod Plan left everything else as before. Countries were free to adhere to the gold standard. There would be no need for exchange controls because countries would never need to change their exchange-rates.

Harrod combined extreme liberalism with extreme pessimism about the sufficiency of global aggregate demand – an unusual, but not necessarily illogical, pairing. He was concerned with the 'central problem' of global over-saving relative to investment. He wanted to convert Keynes's Bank into an international investment engine, with the power to create money as its main characteristic. In fact, he objected to the title 'Clearing Union', since it suggested a 'mere channel', whereas a bank could 'make advances'. As his ideas developed he came to see in Keynes's Bank a potential agent of an Anglo-American 'Condominium' or 'Service' through which the greater part of world investment would be provided, with its short-run adjustment functions as ancillary to this: a reversal of Keynes's own priorities. This perspective made Harrod much more of a free trader than Keynes, for with world full employment and growth guaranteed by his 'Service' there would be no need for any form of economic nationalism.[42] Harrod's political calculation was that the Americans would swallow the pill of his ambitious 'Service' if it was sugared with free trade.

Keynes was swayed by Harrod's arguments, but not bowled over by them. He discounted the possibility that the US would accept such a supranational agenda as Harrod's. Despite Hull, he did not think that the US administration was nearly as committed to free trade as Harrod supposed. There was a wild unreality about Harrod's ardent conjectures from which he instinctively shrank.

On 1 December Keynes attended an inter-departmental meeting at the Treasury to discuss his Plan. Arnold Overton of the Board of Trade was 'much in favour' of Keynes's scheme 'if it were practicable'. Nigel Ronald, for the Foreign Office, said they would welcome anything constructive to put to the Americans in the Article VII conversations. Robbins and Meade agreed with Harrod that the USA should not be asked to set up the full machinery of exchange control. But, in contrast to Harrod, Meade wanted to maintain provision for the appreciation of surplus country currencies. Harrod insisted that any monetary plan should be be put into the Anglo-American negotiations as part of a broader package, including trade issues, customs unions, the Hansen and Gulick investment board proposals, and so on. Keynes stated the decisive objection to Harrod's own amendments: his (Keynes's) system would break down if overdrafts became unlimited at the USA's expense. He himself might have gone too far in disciplining deficit countries, but he would not go as far as Harrod in removing any discipline at all. In the upshot, the Harrod Plan did not displace the Keynes Plan from the centre of the stage. It was too liberal for the *dirigistes*, too inflationary for the orthodox, and was thought to carry the principle of 'unlimited liability' much too far for the Americans to accept. Keynes also continued to resist Harrod's argument that Clearing Union facilities made capital controls unnecessary.[43]

On 15 December Keynes sent Harrod a carbon copy of his third draft, calling him his 'most important critic'; he wrote to Catto, Hawtrey and Waley saying he had tried to deal with their points. On 19 December he sent a copy to Montagu Norman. He had, he said, received more encouragement for his Plan in Whitehall 'than for anything I have ever suggested'. He addressed the Bank's chief concern:

> In particular, I believe that a multilateral plan is a necessary condition of the maintenance of the sterling area and the financial position of London.... From what Lord Catto tells me, I think you may have got the wrong impression of my proposals in this respect. So far from their endangering the sterling area, I claim it as one of their chief merits that they offer us the best chance of maintaining it in its traditional sense – i.e. that the British Commonwealth make London their financial head-quarters.... A multilateral system, by giving us something similar to the gold standard in its best nineteenth-century days, allows international banking (apart from capital controls) to go on just as before. A series of bilateral agreements, to which all the members of the sterling area would have to be parties, seems to me quite impracticable – and very dangerous.[44]

The executive governor, Cameron Cobbold, assured Norman that Keynes's third draft was 'fairly innocuous, so long as it is regarded as a possible framework, given certain conditions.... Let it percolate where it will.'

Keynes put forward the third draft of his Plan not as a 'cut and dried scheme' but as 'one variant of a central idea which is capable of being worked out in many ways'. He explained the central idea as 'the establishment of a Currency Union, based on international money, called (let us say) bancor, fixed (but not unalterable) in terms of gold and accepted as the equivalent of gold by ... all members of the Union for the purpose of settling international balances'. (Keynes decided on 'bancor' after Hawtrey had rejected 'grammor'.)

In his previous drafts Keynes had felt the need to prescribe definite rules governing the maximum permitted balances and the sanctions for exceeding them. Now he wrote that 'the most difficult question to determine is how much to decide by rule and how much by discretion'. He opted for discretion. He weakened and postponed the interventions designed to deter or eliminate the excess balances of both creditors and debtors. In an important concession to Harrod he now allowed credit balances to pile up without limit. Instead, persistent creditors would 'discuss' with the Governing Board, retaining the final decision themselves, whether to expand their domestic economies, appreciate their currencies, reduce their tariffs or make foreign loans. For debtors no corrective measures would be started until their deficits reached half their quotas, and these were now limited to currency depreciation. Excess credit and debit balances would still be charged interest, though this was 'not essential to the scheme'. The effect of these changes was to give the Bank a greater expansionist, but also inflationary, potential. However, the concessions were not all one way. Under pressure from the Board of Trade, Keynes made his prohibition of protective expedients more tentative. He now felt able to give Cordell Hull only 'substantial' rather than 'complete' satisfaction.

The third draft argued much more sharply than did the second that the Bank of England's proposals would break up, not preserve, the sterling area. Keynes also paid untypical homage to the gold standard – something he sometimes did to stress his conservative credentials – and made another concession to Harrod by not insisting on capital controls for all members of the Union. His praise of customs unions was much reduced, in length and enthusiasm, in deference to Hawtrey. After repeating his suggestions for ancillary institutions, and the joint management of the ICB by Britain and the United States, Keynes summarised the 'special merits' of his proposal. Britain would not be able to solve its prospective balance of payments problem or preserve the sterling area except through a scheme which provided for multilateral clearing and global market expansion. For the United States and others it offered a general framework for stable exchange rates and free trade, and attached institutions to promote post-war reconstruction, control of the trade cycle and the maintenance of active employment everywhere. Above all, it 'is capable of arousing enthusiasm because it makes a beginning at the construction of the future government of the world'.[45]

Keynes did not suffer from any undue pride in authorship. He tried to accommodate every possible point of view in an effort to maximise consent. It was a considerable feat to reshape the scheme in such a way as to preserve its central structure in the face of so many contradictory pressures.

Buoyed up by some glorious winter weather, Keynes arranged his usual shoot at Tilton over Christmas. The 'bag' was twenty-eight pheasants, four rabbits, one hare, two woodcocks and a sparrowhawk. He followed it by a dinner for thirty-five, 'Lydia delivering from her hands beef of great antiquity'. His international currency plan, he reported to his mother on

21 December 1941, 'goes as well as I could hope – indeed in Whitehall amazingly well, but there are many hurdles yet'.

The main immediate one was the Treasury, which meant Sir Richard Hopkins, the second secretary. Harrod now became an enthusiastic advocate of the liberalised Keynes Plan, insisting that it should be presented to ministers as a 'thoroughly workable and practical plan supported by the full weight of Treasury judgment'. He shrewdly surmised that ministers would be much less willing to criticise a scheme put forward by 'the collective brains of the Treasury' than one emanating from the single brain of J. M. Keynes. Harrod insisted that the Keynes Plan be put to the Americans as an interlocking set of institutions including an international investment board, a buffer stock control, a nutritional standards board and a commercial union, or else the Americans would think it was designed solely to help Britain.[46] Hopkins replied on 24 December: 'I think the Keynes Plan is now in about as good a shape as it can be put and I don't believe there is any better alternative. . . .'[47]

After Christmas, Hopkins prepared to incorporate the Keynes Plan into the Treasury 'sandwich'. Keynes wrote to Kahn on 12 January 1942:

> The difficulties come from the Bank. But how serious they are going to be remains to be seen. My expectation is that the plan will at least be set up as cock-shy for the Americans, but with what ardour and conviction it will be advocated officially is less certain. On the whole, I am pretty well satisfied with the general tenor of the post-war discussions. My advocacy of multilateralism has brought concord and harmony again with your chaps at the Board of Trade. . . .[48]

On the weekend of 24–25 January, Keynes undertook a final redraft. The scheme, now rechristened the 'International Clearing Union', which became its approved designation, provided a revised formula which would boost the total overdraft facilities from $26bn to $40bn.

On 27 January 1942 Keynes could report to Phillips in Washington that 'Hoppy has now completed the draft of a general report on the whole business which we are to discuss in a few days'.[49] The Treasury had not, in fact, done what Harrod wanted, which was to put the Keynes scheme forward as its considered view. It was 'wrapped', as L. S. Pressnell writes, in the 'sombre swaddling clothes' of an eighty-four-page Treasury 'Memorandum on External Monetary and Economic Problems' whose pessimism threatened to smother the squeals of the lively infant.[50] Keynes thought the Treasury document 'very fine', but Robbins objected to its relentlessly pro and con approach. 'I think I can detect a slight sway of the argument in favour of the Keynes–Harrod–Hansen projects', but only a slight one.[51]

Much of the original 'sandwich' was rendered beside the point by Britain's signature of the Mutual Aid (Lend–Lease) Agreement on 23 February 1942. Much heated to-ing and fro-ing between London and Washington had secured a form of words acceptable to the British. A commitment by both countries to eliminate discrimination and reduce tariffs was coupled with a commitment to expand production and employment. This could be taken to mean that moves to freer trade were predicated on measures to expand output and employment. The agreement called for an early conference between the two governments and 'other like-minded ones' to decide ways of implementing the commitment.

By the New Year, news was filtering through to London that the US administration was having some ideas of its own on the post-war order. The expected imminence of Anglo-American conversations meant that the British government had to take a decision. The Treasury coalesced behind the Keynes scheme because of fears that the American plan would be too rigid and that the British had to come up with something other than opposition.[52] But unity on the British side had been achieved only at the expense of three considerable fudges. The Bank of England, while willing for the Keynes Plan to be thrown into the negotiating pot, was not committed to it. A second gap in perception was between those like Keynes who thought that the ancillary institutions were 'in no way a necessary part' of the Clearing Union, and those like Harrod who wanted to promote the 'Keynes group of ideas' as a whole. The third area of unclarity was about whether the Clearing Union was expected both to tide countries over the transition to peace and to maintain equilibrium on a permanent basis. Overdraft facilities required for the first might be too ample for the second. But this was the only way Keynes could hope to square the need to appease America with resistance to dismantling Britain's imperial preference/sterling area system.

The Treasury Memorandum went to the War Cabinet Committee on Reconstruction Problems on 31 March 1942. Ernest Bevin, the Minister of Labour, was the last hurdle. 'Bevin comes in late,' Hugh Dalton, President of the Board of Trade, wrote in his diary, 'gives the appearance of being rather flushed, and proceeds to denounce the whole paper, saying it is an Anglo-American bankers' conspiracy against the working-class: it would doom us to two million unemployed.... And so on!' Dalton suggested they send for Hopkins and Keynes, who 'dealt cleverly' with Bevin's criticisms, which amounted to the assertion that the Keynes Plan represented a new gold standard. Keynes tried to allay Bevin's fears. The supply of bancor, he said, was 'absolutely elastic'. Gold could not in future limit the amount of money available for trade. After having heard them the Reconstruction Committee agreed to recommend to Cabinet that the Treasury paper 'might be put before the Americans' as the basis for Article VII discussions.

Bevin still needed to be squared. Keynes saw him privately on 22 April, and again reassured him that the International Clearing Bank could not possibly become an instrument of deflation and unemployment. Bevin said if this was made clear he would feel 'much happier about it'. Keynes redrafted once more to emphasise that the measures for debtor adjustment contemplated by his Plan 'do *not* include a deflationary policy, enforced by dear money ... having the effect of causing unemployment'.

With the stipulation that the USSR become a founder member of the Union, the Treasury Memorandum – in effect the Keynes Plan – was approved by the War Cabinet on 7 May 1942 as the basis for Article VII conversations with the United States.[53] What had kept it alive, Keynes told Richard Kahn, was the unattractiveness of the alternatives. 'Now it is a question of capturing American sympathy.'[54]

37

The Strange Case of Harry Dexter White

I. THE AMERICAN BIAS

Although the United States was now in the war, its 'sympathy' proved harder to capture. It was to be almost a year before British and American troops went into action together, in North Africa. In the first few months of 1942 the centre of the war shifted to the Far East, where the British suffered a string of military defeats at the hands of the Japanese. These not only damaged Britain's military reputation, but drew unwelcome attention to the existence of the British Empire. British imperialism made victory over Japan 'more difficult', in Walter Lippmann's view, 'because the United Nations are inhibited from appealing to the native populations as liberators'. This was the context in which post-war economic planning by both sides got under way. Each Ally proceeded in isolation from the other. They were also at cross-purposes. The State Department was eager to get the trade talks, so rudely broken off by Keynes in Washington in July 1941, going again. The British wanted to start with the monetary talks. However, the US Treasury was not ready to start monetary talks; and the British Board of Trade was in no position to resume trade talks, in view of the Cabinet's refusal to contemplate any changes in the imperial preference system. As a result there were no official negotiations for eighteen months on either money or trade.

Keynes's International Clearing Union was conceived as a set of inter-locking regimes governing money, investment, commodities and trade. However, only the monetary scheme – the International Clearing Bank with its overdraft facilities – had been worked out in any detail. On Keynes's suggestion, Harrod had drawn up a scheme for an International Investment Bank 'in a few free evenings' at the end of 1941 and sent it to him.[1] A summary found its way into the 'Treasury Bible'. Little more was heard of it till the Americans themselves took it up. This was a great disappointment to Harrod. The reason is that Keynes himself did not press it. He saw no particular benefit to Britain.

However, at Roy Harrod's prodding Keynes did, on 20 January 1942, draft a memorandum on buffer stocks. Keynes's Buffer Stock Plan was the British attempt to meet the requirements of American agricultural producers, represented by Vice-President Henry Wallace, which, in some respects, cut across the State Department's free-trade perspective. With typical ingenuity he worked out a plan which aimed to secure for producers stable prices without involving the creation of a producers' cartel. The policy he advocated was typical: to take a 'middle course between unfettered competition under *laissez-faire* conditions and planned controls which try to freeze commerce into a fixed mould'.[2] The centrepiece of the new Keynes scheme was a set of buffer stocks – or reserves – for the main internationally traded commodities. Each reserve would be managed by its own 'Control' capped by a General Council for Commodity Controls to ensure that individual schemes conformed to general principles. Each Control would set an initial 'basic' price for its 'commod', equal to its estimate of 'the long-period equilibrium costs of the most efficient producers', which it would vary from time to time 'by a process of trial and error based on the observed tendency of stocks to increase or decrease'. It would buy its 'commod' whenever prices fell 10 per cent below, and sell when they rose 10 per cent above, the 'basic' price. Its long-period pricing policy would aim to maintain a constant reserve, or what US Vice President Henry Wallace had called an 'ever normal granary'.[3]

The Buffer Stock Plan never won the same degree of support in Whitehall as had his Clearing Union Plan. This time his Middle Way pleased neither the planners nor the free traders. Once more Keynes was extraordinarily open-minded in drafting. But by the autumn of 1942 he had had enough. His Plan had been subjected to 'tens of thousands of minor or major criticisms from different Departments', he complained to Phillips.[4]

It was James Meade of the Economic Section who initiated the British response to Article VII's trade requirements. His Plan for an 'International Commercial Union', dating from 4 August 1942, redrafted by Hugh Gaitskell, went to the Overton Committee, which was set up by Hugh Dalton, President of the Board of Trade, to consider it in November. Meade proposed that all members of the Union would grant most-favoured-nation treatment to each other, with tariff preferences limited to 10 per cent; that quantitative import controls be outlawed except in emergencies; that export subsidies be limited to 10 per cent below domestic prices.[5] His Plan was enthusiastically endorsed by the majority of the Overton Committee in December, but furiously attacked by Hubert Henderson. For once Keynes sympathised with Henderson's 'magnificent' critique, in contrast to Dennis Robertson, who emitted a 'squeak of consternation' at the gale of protectionism blowing though the Treasury. He probably noticed that this reinforced the gale of protectionism blowing through the Cabinet and the Bank of England.

The war had had a double-edged effect on British thinking about postwar commerce. On the one hand, it was forcing Britain to live off American largesse, thereby locking it into America's Article VII agenda. On the other hand it seemed to make possible what Joseph Chamberlain and his successors had only dreamt of: the organisation of the British Empire and its

satellites as an economic unit. It was the simultaneous dwarfing of the
British economy and the strengthening of imperial organisation which made
the nationalists and imperialists in the government look to the Empire as a
guarantee of Britain's post-war independence – an independence which had
now come to include the freedom to pursue full employment policies. The
battle between the 'American' and the 'imperial' tendencies in British official
thinking came to centre on the elastic concept of the 'transition'. That a
transitional period was needed before any new post-war regime was put in
place was common ground, if only because Britain would face a large
prospective balance of payments deficit. However, a transition sufficiently
prolonged might prove to be permanent. Nationalists like Hubert Henderson
wanted important elements of the transitional arrangements built into the
permanent system. Liberals like Lionel Robbins, James Meade, Roy Harrod
and Dennis Robertson favoured a free-trade regime, but one underpinned
by global government, and modified by escape clauses. Keynes stood somewhere in the middle, with an inclination to the 'American bias'.

In correspondence with Treasury and Board of Trade officials and Meade
himself in the winter of 1942–3, Keynes sprayed the Overton Report with
criticisms. Announcing that he stood 'half way between Sir Hubert Henderson and the [Overton] Committee', he suggested approaching the United
States with a bland statement of general principles, not a specific charter. 'If
we were to take the initiative on the lines of the Overton Report,' he wrote
on 15 January 1943,

> all the other parties concerned would then seek to modify the proposals
> to their own advantage. We should have already gone to the limit. We
> should have shot our bolt, leaving the rest of the world with its
> ammunition in hand. No-one will look after us if we do not look after
> ourselves. The solution of our balance of trade problem is the clue to
> our post-war economic prospects all along the line. It is not a thing
> to be handled so light-heartedly. Without a more robust – if you like,
> a more selfish – policy, we are sunk.[6]

Keynes's failure to endorse the Commercial Union delighted Henderson and
disappointed Meade. His real reason was stated in the same paper: 'I am
fearful of prejudicing our other post-war plans by associating them too
closely with something as full of dangerous political dynamite as this.'[7]
Without Keynes's support, the Overton Committee's proposals remained
stuck in the corridors of Whitehall; and the trade talks with the Americans
remained stalled.

A fifth draft of the Buffer Stock scheme was endorsed on 14 April 1943
as an official Treasury paper. 'What's this about Butter Scotch?' Churchill
growled when it came before the Cabinet. The Cabinet agreed that both the
Buffer Stock and Commercial Union Plans might be shown to the Dominions
and 'mentioned' to the Americans in general terms. But unlike the Clearing

Union they were never published as White Papers or put forward as British negotiating positions. The Keynes Plan shrank back to what it had been at the start: a Clearing Union with optional extras.

II. THE WHITE PLAN

What the British did not know was that on 14 December 1941, a week after Pearl Harbor had brought America into the war against both Japan and Germany, Morgenthau had instructed his director of monetary research, Harry Dexter White, to prepare a memorandum on an inter-Allied stabilisation fund which would 'provide the basis for post-war monetary stabilization arrangements; and ... provide a post-war "international currency"'. In giving him the status, though not title, of Assistant Secretary of the Treasury Morgenthau said: 'He will be in charge of all foreign affairs for me. . . . I want it in one brain and I want it in Harry White's brain.'[8] White would become the central figure in all Keynes's subsequent dealings with Washington. The battle between the two would become one of the grand political duels of the Second World War, though it was largely buried in financial minutiae. This did not exclude a wary comradeship developing between the two 'technicians'. Keynes also partly misunderstood the nature of the duel.

The speed of White's reaction to Morgenthau's request suggests he already knew what he wanted to do. Indeed an initial outline of his proposals seems to have been prepared in the summer or early autumn of 1941.[9] On 30 December 1941 White handed a twelve-page memorandum to Morgenthau headed 'Suggestions for Inter-Allied Monetary and Banking Action'. This proposed two new institutions, an International Stabilization Fund and an International Bank. Morgenthau's idea for a single international currency had been dropped, White convincing him that universal currency convertibility would be 'more realistic and just as effective'.[10]

In thinking about the post-war financial architecture, White, like Keynes, drew on the experience of the inter-war years, but as seen through American eyes. There was widespread agreement in Washington that any post-war regime should provide for fixed exchange rates, trade expansion and the end of discrimination. These were identified as necessary underpinnings for American and world prosperity and the prevention of war. The institutional innovations which White proposed had also been prefigured in American initiatives: the Exchange Stabilization Fund of 1934, the Tripartite Agreement of 1936, the proposal for an Inter-American Bank of 1940.[11] If the Keynes Plan can be read as an attempt to 'universalise' the sterling area, so White's was an effort to project American power and responsibility beyond the two Americas. However, White's economic plans were mixed up with political aims which Keynes did not share. Partly these simply reflected the fact that the Americans held all the trumps and could design post-war arrangements to suit themselves. Partly they reflected a personal agenda which remains to this day a matter of controversy.

Keynes had first met White in 1935 when he toured European capitals and more substantially in Washington in 1941, when he had suggested a way through the Lend–Lease imbroglio. He would have encountered a short, stocky man in his early forties, with trim moustache, rimless spectacles and a rasping voice. No doubt he identified him as one of those 'gritty' Jewish types in Morgenthau's entourage.

In fact, he had only recently joined the Treasury after a brief academic career at a minor American college, following a doctorate at Harvard. His promotion at the Treasury was rapid. In 1938 he became director of its newly established division of monetary research, and in December 1941 Morgenthau gave him responsibility for the Treasury's foreign relations. This gave him a key role in developing America's post-war economic foreign policy. In Washington, White had the reputation of being one of the pushiest, least agreeable men in town – and also for being anti-British. Keynes would surely have reinforced White's instinctive prejudices against the ruling class of a decaying empire. Keynes might have the style which he lacked, but White had the power, and he knew it. Above all, Keynes's subtle intelligence was as much to be resisted as admired, because it could set all kinds of traps into which the unwary could fall. The fear of 'bamboozlement' was never far from the minds of those Americans who had read, as White would doubtless have read, Keynes's *Economic Consequences of the Peace*.

What Keynes never knew was that White was associated, politically and socially, with the American communist underground, and was passing confidential information to it which was being transmitted to Soviet intelligence; and that some of the Treasury people – including White's appointees – were also underground communists or agents or both. White did not believe that Soviet interests conflicted with American interests. The only matter in serious dispute is whether he knew, prior to 1944, that the information he was providing was being handed to the Russians.

White was not a member of the American Communist Party – he was too independent to take orders from anyone – but like other fellow travellers of the 1930s he greatly admired Soviet planning and readily accepted the communist view that a powerful Soviet Union was the only reliable bulwark against Nazi anti-semitism and fascist expansionism. There was thus no conflict in White's mind between his hopes for a social democratic United States, a planned international economy and a US–Soviet condominium to guarantee the peace. That is why he could declare before the House of Representatives Committee on Un-American Activities in 1948 that he could not 'do a disloyal act or anything against the interests of our country'. In all this there was an astonishing naivety about the nature of Stalinism. But this was far from unusual on the left. Except for his clandestine activities, White's beliefs were not much different from those of Harry Hopkins or Vice-President Henry Wallace, who 'saw in the march of history a coming together of the Soviet experiment in Russia with the New Deal programmes of the United States' for the greater good of mankind.[12] Roosevelt also believed that US–Soviet co-operation offered the best hope of a peaceful and progressive world. Left-wingers in the New Deal much preferred the idea of an American partnership with 'progressive' Soviet Russia to one with reactionary, imperialist Britain.

Despite White's technical interest in stabilisation plans, the main aim of his personal policymaking was to secure a political and economic alliance with the Soviet Union through the instrument of large American loans. The thread of the large loan to Russia runs from White's first proposal in March 1939 to his last efforts in 1944–5 which envisaged a huge Marshall Aid programme for the Soviet Union.[13] This must be contrasted with his niggardly attitude to British requests for financial help. Lauchlin Currie, who was for two years *de facto* manager of the Lend–Lease programme, shared White's antipathy towards British imperialism.[14] Britain's importunities were inconvenient facts which had to be dealt with. But Britain was not part of the big picture, and White was scornful, though apprehensive, of Britain's Great Power pretensions. One must bear in mind that, for White and others in both Treasury and State, Britain was still considered an economic rival to the United States, whereas the Soviet Union, with its separate system, was not. The US Treasury official Ostrander remembers Redvers Opie telling him that White was 'even more strongly anti-British than pro-Soviet'. White's Stabilization Fund was one fragment of a much larger design at whose centre lay an American–Soviet condominium, not Anglo-American co-operation. The British examined and criticised White's schemes from the point of view of how they would help them. They never understood the particular nature of White's focus, with one eye on Washington while the other swivelled on Moscow. Keynes, by contrast, rarely thought about Russia, and when he did it was usually disparagingly.

In March 1942, White revised and expanded his December 1941 draft with the help of his assistant Edward Bernstein. When Keynes first saw it in July 1942 it had become a very bulky document, with a short preamble followed by eighty pages of text.

White called for the establishment of two institutions, an International Stabilization Fund and a Bank for Reconstruction. He described their objects as (a) to prevent the disruption of foreign exchanges and the collapse of the monetary and credit system, (b) to assure restoration of foreign trade, and (c) to supply relief and reconstruction capital.[15] The Bank was a much more ambitious project than the Fund, its main purpose being 'to supply the huge volume of capital that will be needed virtually throughout the world for reconstruction, for relief, and for economic recovery'. It was to have a capital of $10bn and could also issue its own notes. Broadly speaking, it encompassed most of the work the ancillary institutions were designed to do in the Keynes Plan. Not surprisingly it was this aspect of White's Grand Design which most excited Harrod, then and subsequently, for it came closest to his own enthusiasms.[16] However, there was much more opposition in Washington and New York to White's Bank than to his Fund. This caused the Fund to replace the Bank as the centrepiece of the American plan; and so it was treated by the British for the purpose of comparing the White Plan to the Keynes Plan.

The Stabilization Fund was to be made up of levies of gold, domestic currency and interest-bearing securities totalling $5bn, each member's contribution based on a complex formula, in which gold holdings and gold production were heavily weighted. Suggested initial contributions were $3.2bn from the USA and $635m from Britain. (Foreign currencies would be supplied to members in temporary balance of payments difficulties in exchange for their own currencies up to the limit of their contributions or 'quotas'.) The Fund would fix the par values of currencies in terms of gold, which could be altered only to correct a 'fundamental disequilibrium', and would require a four-fifths majority of the votes wielded by the Fund's directors. Access to a foreign currency in excess of a member's gold contribution was subject to increasingly stringent conditions, which included correction of domestic policies. Membership of the Fund would be open to all countries which agreed to alter their exchange rates only with the Fund's approval, to abandon all exchange controls on current transactions within one year of joining or the end of hostilities, and to reduce tariffs; which agreed not to make any bilateral clearing agreements or establish 'geographically preferential exchange rates', not to allow gold to circulate domestically, and not to inflate or deflate their currencies or default on foreign obligations without Fund approval. Freedom to move capital was qualified by a member having the right to refuse inward investment, and by the country exporting capital having the right to commandeer the foreign investments of its own nationals. White also proposed an ingenious method of freeing blocked wartime balances.[17] Rigid in its insistence on exchange rate stability and elimination of exchange restrictions and discriminatory payments practices, the White Plan was distinctly frugal in providing balance of payments assistance. On the other hand, White agreed with Keynes on the need for permanent controls on private capital movements.

The Keynes and White Plans were based on different logics, which reflected different historical perspectives. Both sought to avoid the currency and trade wars of the 1930s – they wanted, that is, to recreate a liberal world economy in which stable exchange rates and free trade were the norm. For Keynes the main condition of this was that surplus countries be forced to liquidate (that is, spend) their surpluses. White's condition for his ISF was much less stringent: deficit countries should be given a breathing space to put their houses in order by the short-term loan of extra reserves. The resources behind the two schemes reflected these different priorities: $26bn for Keynes's CU, $5bn for White's ISF. The example from which Keynes's plan evolved was Britain's role in maintaining the pre-1914 gold standard: Keynes's Clearing Bank was to be the heir of the City of London. The historical precedent for the White Plan was the growing practice of inter-governmental co-operation which had grown up in the last days of the gold standard. Keynes's plan carried an implicit criticism of the United States for failing to follow London's nineteenth-century lead. White's ideas reflect a general New Deal suspicion of 'high finance', whether British or American.

However, to leave the comparison there would be to leave out White's Bank for Reconstruction ('Development' was added to the title only later). The functions of White's Bank – to recapitalise war-ravaged countries, to stabilise commodity prices, and to engage in contracyclical lending – were broadly similar to those of the institutions which Keynes suggested might be attached to, and in part financed by, the Clearing Union: a body 'charged with post-war relief and reconstruction', an Investment Board, a Commodity Control, and a contracyclical Economic Board. Keynes's Clearing Union, which pivoted on the single requirement for creditors to spend their surpluses, was conceptually more elegant than White's separation of lending functions into two institutions; on the other hand the distinction between short-term and long-term lending was easier to grasp. The combined resources of White's Fund and Bank came to $15bn, which is appreciably closer to Keynes's $26bn than the $5bn reserved for White's Stabilization Fund alone. However, it remains true that much more of Keynes's $26bn would have been available to Britain than of White's $15bn, since the bulk of the resources of White's Bank would have been applied to reconstructing Russia, whereas in theory almost the whole of the $26bn of the Clearing Union's resources could have been claimed by deficit countries, of which Britain expected to be the largest immediately after the war. Had the Keynes Plan been accepted there would have been no need for an American loan in 1945.*

On 8 May 1942, White gave Morgenthau his draft. He suggested a conference of finance ministers of all the United Nations, including Russia and China, to consider it. Morgenthau agreed to hit Roosevelt and Hull with this idea 'at the same time', promoting the scheme to his President as a 'New Deal in international economics'. Roosevelt rejected the proposed conference as premature, ordering the White Plan to be discussed more extensively with the State Department and other agencies first. Morgenthau now saw the Plan as his 'own pet' and suspected that the State Department would

---

* This is the real answer to Professor Bradford Delong who argues that the Keynes Plan and the *combined* White Plan were much more like each other than implied here.

want to kill it because they hadn't thought of it first. Inter-departmental meetings started on 25 May, with White chairing a technical committee. On 9 July, White, who was not on close terms with Phillips, handed Leith-Ross, who was in Washington to discuss inter-Allied relief matters, a copy of his Plan, which Phillips immediately transmitted to the Treasury in London. (Presumably Morgenthau had authorised White to do this.) At the same time, Phillips urged London to give the Americans a copy of the Keynes Plan as the only means of starting a dialogue. Kingsley Wood agreed in mid-July. Each side finally found out what the other was hatching.

III. MUTUAL REACTIONS

Keynes took a copy of the 'leaked' White Plan down to Tilton on 24 July. He returned to London on 3 August with notes on the American proposal. 'It obviously won't work,' he told Hopkins. To Phillips he wrote: 'Seldom have I been simultaneously so much bored and so much interested.'[18] However, he found it 'striking and encouraging' that he and White had been working on parallel lines.

His main criticism was that the Stabilization Fund 'makes no attempt to use the banking principle and one-way gold convertibility and is in fact not much more than a version of the gold standard, which simply aims at multiplying the effective volume of the gold base'. It would do little to help countries which started with only a little gold. On the other hand, he approved 'the extremely generous proposal for dealing with wholly or partly blocked balances at the end of the war' and discovered other helpful or suggestive proposals.[19] He redrafted of his own Plan, which he now understood would be the version handed to the Americans, to reduce some of the differences with the White Plan.

Richard Law, Under-Secretary of State at the Foreign Office, took copies of the revised Keynes draft to Washington in August, and Phillips gave White a copy on the 28th. 'Everybody is now supporting it,' Keynes reported to Kahn, 'and (with the exception of the Bank of England) are really enthusiastic.'[20] In his covering note to White, Phillips wrote that the British proposals were drawn up specially to 'meet the threat of another world-wide post-war depression'.

The Keynes Plan was now intensively scrutinised in Washington. The State Department took the lead, Hull's assistant Adolph Berle asking Phillips a lot of questions, which he communicated to Keynes. The politically charged ones concerned the total of quotas, the potential liability of the United States, creditors' voting rights, discipline on debtors, and the inflationary potential of bancor creation.[21] The nub of the matter, Phillips wrote, was the American fear that 'the Union would have a Bank of Issue function which would have an adverse reaction on the position of the dollar, and that the plan might involve the United States in lending an indefinite amount to the rest of the world. . . .'[22]

The desultory nature of the long-distance contacts between Washington and London was briefly interrupted by the visit of Morgenthau and White to London in October 1942 to inspect armament factories and to discuss the currency arrangements to be implemented in North Africa following the impending, and, they presumed, successful, Allied invasion. Winant, with Morgenthau's agreement, arranged a private meeting between Keynes and White. They met at the ambassador's residence on 23 October, with both American and British officials in attendance. Ernest Penrose, Winant's economic adviser, who was present, remembers a 'lively and at times somewhat acrimonious but exceedingly fruitful' discussion, dominated by Keynes and White. Keynes said the Fund wouldn't be large enough; White said it would be impossible to get more out of Congress. They discussed whether the capital of the new institution should be subscribed (White) or created (Keynes). Keynes vigorously attacked the idea of subscribed capital, but White said it was the only thing Congress would accept. He also said it would be politically impossible to use the Clearing Union for relief and reconstruction. Keynes said that the requirement for a four-fifths majority for changes in exchange rates was unacceptable to Britain, which would have to be free to act unilaterally if necessary. He argued 'heatedly' for direct talks with the United States in advance of an international conference. White replied that this would give an impression of an Anglo-Saxon 'gang up'. With this barely tactful reminder of Britain's modest place in the big picture, the meeting ended. Both men agreed to modify their schemes on a number of points. Winant presided 'with his usual charm and skill'.[23]

Denied direct Anglo-American negotiations, Britain started to organise support for the Keynes Plan. Between 23 October and 9 November its various elements were discussed at the Treasury with representatives of the Dominions and India. Keynes judged the meetings to be 'an outstanding success – really a model of what sensible, constructive international discussion should be'.[24] He could not help noticing, though, that the Buffer Stock Plan and Commercial Union were less acceptable to them than the Clearing Bank. In the light of these encounters and his meeting with White, Keynes produced a sixth draft of the Clearing Union on 9 November. This time quotas were scaled down, and there was a provision for an agreed reduction of their total in inflationary conditions. The Bank might require collateral on debit balances in excess of 50 per cent of quotas. The Governing Body could reduce or remit interest rate charges on excess balances. Exchange rate changes became more difficult, the maximum allowed being 5 per cent rather than 5 per cent a year; however there was to be a long (five-year) transitional period before this took effect. The process of adapting the Keynes Plan to American requirements without abandoning the crucial 'banking principle' was under way.

Although nothing seemed to be going on in Washington, White was busy redrafting the Stabilization Fund Plan, partly in response to Keynes's criticisms voiced at their London meeting. On 1 February 1943, without any further discussion of the Clearing Union or consultation with the British, the State Department sent the eighth draft of the White proposals – minus the Reconstruction Bank – to the British, Russians and Chinese as a 'basis of discussion'. The United States proposed to invite thirty-seven experts of the United Nations to Washington individually and separately to discuss monetary co-operation on White's 'or any other lines they may wish to suggest'.[25] The British Embassy in Washington arranged for the Latin American ministers invited to Washington to receive copies of the Clearing Union proposal.

In the game of tit-for-tat, the British government now sent copies of the Keynes Plan to Russia and China and opened discussions in London with the finance ministers of its west European allies on 26 February 1943. The Americans sent a representative but refused the British suggestion that the Stabilization Fund proposal should also be circulated so that the two schemes might be compared. They wanted discussion of the White Plan to be stage-managed in Washington, not London. Keynes presented the British scheme as having four connected parts: monetary union, stabilisation of primary product prices, commercial policy and an international investment authority. He explained his Plan's novel feature – the application of the banking principle to a closed global system. Domestic banking had evolved from the Middle Ages (always a vague period for Keynes), but banking between countries was still medieval – that is, gold reserves were 'dead', like earlier deposits of coins. Keynes attacked the principle behind the White Plan:

> We have not adopted another possible feature of banking by which you have capital, subscribed capital, which you can lend out. . . . It is perplexing to some people at first that that should not be necessary. In the first days of banking great stress was laid on the possession of capital but we have learned as time goes on that that is of insignificant importance. You need the capital if you are not in a closed system and have to meet liabilities for credit outside your system, but in a closed system you can reach your conclusion simply by offsetting the deposits of some members against the overdrafts of others. . . . As there is no liability to pay outside the system it involves no risk and therefore requires no capital.[26]

Keynes argued that centralising all foreign exchange transactions through central banks, leaving only final clearing by the Clearing Bank, would 'get rid of the whole element of exchange speculation which caused so much trouble after the last war'. He explained that quotas (overdraft facilities) would vary with the amount of foreign trade, so that – unlike under the gold standard – 'you are not fixing the quantity of international [money] irrespective of the amount of work which the international money has to do in the shape of financing trade; the two are connected together'.

At a party in London Keynes begged the Russian ambassador Maisky to send Russian experts to London. Maisky 'as usual grinned and said that all would be much easier if a second front was going on'.[27] Unlike White, Keynes thought it was not essential that Russia became a member of the Clearing Union, though it would be disappointing if it stayed out. The European Allies gave general support to the Clearing Union, but rejected any suggestion that the British and Americans should take all the main decisions. Keynes thought this lessened the need for prior Anglo-American agreement. 'With the Europeans and Dominions in sympathy with us, our position would be much stronger in a general than in a bilateral discussion.'[28]

He had meanwhile undertaken a further study of White's Stabilization Plan. On 18 February 1943 he produced a first set of notes, complaining about the obscurity of the technical details, and said the only innovations compared to pre-war practice were provisions for controlling capital movements and for liquidating blocked balances.[29]

Two clauses in White's redrafts caused the British much trouble. The accounts of the Fund and the value of the currency of each member were expressed in 'unitas' (units of account). White saw unitas as a receipt for gold deposits, not as a tradeable instrument. The Fund itself would buy and sell currencies so as to keep them in a fixed relationship with each other. Keynes saw that if unitas could be made into international 'money' it would have the double advantage of being a bridge between the subscription principle of the Fund and the banking principle of the Clearing Union and of promoting multilateral clearing. In the early months of 1943 the 'monetisation' of unitas emerged as the main British requirement for accepting a 'Fund' framework for monetary co-operation.

White's draft dated 16 December 1942 also introduced a 'scarce currency' clause, by which the Fund was empowered to 'ration' a currency for which there was an excess demand. This was designed to guard against the expected scarcity of dollars.[30] In effect, member states, deprived of dollars, would have to restrict their purchases of American goods. The scarce-currency provision can be seen as White's attempt to supply the missing discipline on creditors. Keynes wrote dismissively that it 'seems unworkable'.

This is not how it struck Roy Harrod. Reading the revised White draft and Keynes's notes on the train to Oxford late at night, Harrod felt an 'exhilaration such as only comes once or twice in a lifetime' when he came to the scarce-currency clause. The Americans, he enthused, 'were admitting the principle of joint responsibility for disequilibrium....' He wrote to Keynes at two in the morning of 4 March: 'The Americans offer us ... what we could never have asked of them in the negotiations ... that we (and other countries) should be allowed to discriminate against American goods if dollars are running short.' Two days later he added:

> I suggest that the line we ought to take is that we assumed the rationing of scarce currency to be indissolubly linked to the limited credit quota proposal. We can point out that the latter is quite unworkable without the safety valve of rationing.... Then if they are determined to wriggle out of rationing, they would be thrown back onto the unlimited credit of the Clearing Union.

Keynes concluded (8 March) that 'from the tactical point of view [there is] a lot to be said for what you put forward.... I am sending Phillips a copy of our correspondence.' To Phillips, Keynes confided, 'There are those (e.g. Roy Harrod) who argue that this is a splendid, comprehending gesture by the USA to throw the whole burden on the shoulder of the creditor.... I find it difficult to take up so buoyant an attitude. It seems to me that at the most Harry White has put a quick one across the State Department and that the real significance of this provision has escaped notice.'[31] This time Harrod had a better grasp than did Keynes of what the Americans would find acceptable.

As copies of the two Plans had now been circulated to so many other countries, official publication could hardly be delayed. The British government suggested to the US administration that both Plans be published to stop garbled accounts of them appearing in the press. Morgenthau urged that publication be delayed till experts from the two sides had met in Washington, to avoid the risk of the British and American Plans being put forward as rivals. In March the British decided to go ahead anyway and issue the Clearing Union proposals as a White Paper whatever the Americans did. The administration's hand was forced when an accurate account of the White Plan was leaked by Paul Einzig in the *Financial Times*. The two Plans were published by their respective governments on 7 April 1943. Deprived of joint Anglo-American discussions, Keynes took comfort from the extensive circulation of the American proposals. The real risk was always that the USA would 'run away from their own plan, let alone ours'.[32] This had now become much more difficult. The US Treasury Plan 'represents a big advance, and if it turns out that this is the sort of set-up which appeals to people, it will not be too difficult to make something of it. But it is a long time too soon even to breathe a suggestion of compromise.'[33]

The proposals of the two groups of experts were widely discussed in the newspapers of the two Allies, as well as in the German press. Naturally enough, 'press comment tended to take a stand on patriotic grounds rather than on the intrinsic merit of each plan'.[34] However, there was an undertow of criticism in both countries against setting up global institutions at all. The British Embassy reported New York banking and financial opinion 'unanimous against the White Plan and expressed with much bitterness. This does not mean that they favour the British plan. . . . What moved them is intense resentment at the idea of Latin American, Asiatic and other debtors becoming by right members of Governing Boards and presuming to lay down financial policies which may decide the economic welfare of all. . . .'[35] The influential Republican Senator Robert Taft accused White of wanting to pour money 'down a rat-hole'.[36] In a widely publicised address delivered to the Los Angeles Chamber of Commerce on 11 May, Benjamin Anderson, a conservative professor of economics at California University, declared that 'both plans set up a super-national Brains Trust which is to think for the world and plan for the world, and to tell the governments of the world what to do'. They were both British plans, the professor thought, in that they both reflected trends in Keynesian thinking and British monetary policy. They both attacked symptoms, not causes. Exchange instability was a symptom of monetary instability which went back to unsound fundamentals – loose fiscal and monetary policy. The Keynes–Morgenthau Plans would encourage rather than check these tendencies. The conditions for exchange rate stability were sound domestic policies, assured peace and reduction of tariffs. If these conditions were met, Europe would get the loans it needed from private investors.

In a letter to Thomas Lamont, Russell Leffingwell attacked the capital controls envisaged by the Plans: 'One naturally thinks of stable exchanges as desirable not as an end in themselves but as a means to a freer movement of goods and services. It is disappointing to find that these experts intend merely to peg the exchange by policing them and preventing remittances not approved by the policeman.'[37] What the New York bankers would have preferred was close monetary co-operation between Britain and the United States, based on an agreement on exchange rates and credit facilities to re-establish sterling as a leading currency. This was crystallised in the so-called 'key currency' plan put forward by John Williams, a professor of economics at Harvard and vice-president of the Federal Reserve Bank of New York. It seemed to Williams inescapable that 'in a world practically all of whose trading is done in one or another of these currencies [dollars and pounds], the central fact must be the establishment between them of exchange rate stability around which other national currencies can be grouped'.[38]

Both Plans received unexpectedly conscientious coverage in the German press, a sign that intellectual independence was allowed in matters which did not directly interest the Nazi hierarchy. Not surprisingly, the Germans much preferred the Keynes Plan to the White Plan, seeing it as an extension of the Funk Plan. Indeed 'the Germans maintain that the Keynes plan reaffirms what they have practised for more than a decade, namely that national economic policy should have priority over external currency policy and that the "external" value of a currency should be subordinate to the stability of its "internal" value'. The 'real daring of Keynes lies in the fact that he conceives of a clearing system as an international institution. But this may also be its weakness,' observed the *Frankfurter Zeitung* of 4 July 1943, since the establishment of economic stability within a region or *Grossraum* was more practical than a worldwide Clearing Union.[39]

Over the Easter holidays Keynes drafted a list of questions about the White Plan which he sent over to Phillips. 'The great majority of the difficulties', he wrote to Phillips on 4 May, 'arise from not making unitas an effective international unit in the sense that bancor is. If the Fund dealt only in terms of unitas, instead of dealing in dozens of different currencies, many of these difficulties would be resolved.'[40] To Dennis Robertson, Keynes complained about its lack of multilateralism:

> The fact that the adverse balance has to be calculated with each country separately and does not relate to a net adverse balance with the world as a whole makes it even more unworkable and absurd. The result is that, even a country which has a favourable balance with the world as a whole cannot use the Fund for the purpose of multilateral clearing with any individual country with which, taken separately, it is out of balance.... [T]his is outrageous rubbish and does not deserve even half-hearted defence.[41]

On 19 April 1943 Keynes wrote to his mother: 'My health is surprising – I do not know what has come over me. I have not been so steadily well for many years. This week I put my liver through its paces, lunching out every day and dining out several times on the richest and most indigestible food – without the slightest results.'

In his maiden speech in the House of Lords on 18 May 1943 Keynes mobilised the arguments in favour of his Plan in a language which he hoped that the 'educated public' to which he had always appealed would understand. Multilateral clearing – 'in English', Keynes said, 'a universal currency valid for all trade transactions in all the world' – was especially important for Britain, since 'the best markets for our goods are often different from our best sources of supply'. But if it was to be restored there must be a new money proportional to the trade it must carry and every country must have a supply of it proportional to its needs. Under his Plan every country would be allotted an additional reserve of bancor as a 'once for all endowment'. This was intended not to enable a country to live regularly beyond its means, but 'solely as a reserve with which to meet temporary emergencies'. The problems of the past had not always been caused by improvident debtors but by creditors 'hoarding beyond the reasonable requirements of caution'. The British proposals avoided the rigidity of the gold standard. There would be absolute freedom of remittance for current transactions, but 'unless the aggregate of the new investments which individuals are free to make overseas is kept within the amount which our favourable trade balance is capable of looking after, we lose control over the domestic rate of interest'. There was no intention to make the United States 'the milch cow of the world in general and of this country in particular'. His Plan did not require the United States or any other country to put up a single dollar which it would prefer to employ another way. Foreshadowing his very last academic article (see pp. 825–6), Keynes hinted that the American surplus was a product of low world employment and would disappear in due course. He emphasised the 'significant [theoretical] difference ... between a liquid bank deposit which can be withdrawn at any time and a subscription to an institution's permanent capital'. Yet in practice this difference was not great, since the security demanded by the Americans was only to a small extent gold, and largely 'an IOU engraved on superior notepaper', so that a 'synthesis of the two schemes should be possible'.[42]

In Keynes's exposition it emerged that the only freedom which any member of his Union would have to give up was the *freedom not to spend*. What could be more reasonable! Yet who was to say what level of hoarding was prudent?

Keynes received many compliments on his speech. 'Of course the standard [in the Lords] is so fearfully low', he wrote to his mother, 'that any human utterance provokes special attention.' He was not as busy as he had been, but had 'more than enough to keep me amused'. He had received forty to fifty letters suggesting a name for the new international coin, 'most of them hopeless'. On 5 June Keynes celebrated his sixtieth birthday in Cambridge – 'I have the worst of both worlds, too old to be compos mentis, and too young to be venerable.' Had he been a paid civil servant, he would have been compulsorily pensioned off.

38

Building a Better Britain

I. BEVERIDGE

Keynes was wont to say, ironically, that he used the calm of war to reflect on the turmoil of the coming peace. From 1942 an increasing part of his activity looked to beyond the war's end. His Clearing Union Plan had placed him at the centre of the search for an Anglo-American agreement on the post-war economic order. But he was also involved, though more tangentially, in the preparations for a domestic 'New Jerusalem', based on the Beveridge Plan for 'cradle to grave' social security and a full employment policy. Early in 1942 he became, too, chairman of the Council for the Encouragement of Music and the Arts (CEMA), a wartime innovation which pointed to permanent state patronage of the arts. Keynes was never a passionate social reformer. But even he was caught up in the swing to the left which took place between Dunkirk and the British victory at El Alamein in November 1942. He endorsed the demand of William Temple, Archbishop of York, for a Christianised post-war capitalism, inviting the Archbishop to the Tuesday Club, helping him with his book *Christianity and the Social Order*, and pointing out that most early economists were churchmen and 'along the line of origin at least, economics – more properly called political economy – is a side of ethics'.[1] Thus far had Keynes travelled since the assertive atheism of his youth.

During the lull in the Anglo-American negotiations, Keynes had the leisure to consider the Beveridge Plan for recasting Britain's social security system. His interest in it, both personally and as a Treasury man, centred on its affordability. This depended partly on what post-war national income and unemployment were expected to be. That in turn led on to the question of what role policy might play in maintaining high aggregate demand after the war – a matter on which Whitehall was far from decided. An Economic Section paper on post-war employment policy, from the fertile brain of James Meade, was coming under Treasury scrutiny at the same time as the 'affordability' of Beveridge's ambitious schemes was becoming an issue. On the one hand there was a natural Treasury reluctance to sanction expensive social services when Britain's post-war external position was likely to be so shaky. On the other side, the process of wartime radicalisation, impressively documented in Paul Addison's *The Road to 1945*, made some 'New Jerusalem' promises a political necessity. Keynes was drawn into these discussions as an intermediary between Beveridge, Meade and the Treasury. He had no influence on the structure of the Beveridge Report, published in December 1942, but a decisive influence on the scale of finance the Treasury were willing to make available to start off Beveridge's Plan.

William Beveridge was an implausible people's hero. A rigid, monumentally self-assured social scientist, he was always a one-man band who nevertheless craved vast responsibilities and was convinced that his talents were much under-appreciated by his political masters. His famous Report came about by the accident that no one in government could stand him. The Minister of Labour, Ernest Bevin, therefore shunted him aside to a project where it was thought he could do no harm. He was told to produce a plan for rationalising the social security system. Beveridge accepted his appointment, and departure from Bevin's Ministry, with tears in his eyes. However, he soon decided to interpret his social security brief far more ambitiously than Bevin had intended – indeed to lay down a new direction for social policy, with himself as the 'prophet pointing the way to the Promised Land'.[2] His first two papers were ready in December 1941 and January 1942. Faced with their messianic tone and contentious political and financial implications, the Chancellor of the Exchequer insisted that Beveridge alone should take responsibility for them, with the committee of civil servants of which he had been made chairman, and which included a Treasury watchdog, Edward Hales, reduced to 'advisers and assessors'. This left him free to publish a report under his own name. Beveridge and his main idea, 'National Insurance', have labelled the British social security system to this day.

Building on three basic assumptions, a National Health Service, universal family allowances and full employment, Beveridge proposed a system of national insurance for all citizens against retirement, unemployment and disability, centrally administered, and financed by equal contributions from employers, employees and the state, with equal benefits set at a physical subsistence level. This would replace the patchwork quilt of voluntary and compulsory insurance and charity, which, badly sewn and full of holes, made up Britain's social security arrangements. In March 1942 Beveridge sent Keynes copies of his two memoranda asking for his help in dealing with the financial implications of his proposals. They left Keynes in a state of 'wild enthusiasm for your general scheme. I think it is a vast constructive reform of real importance and am relieved to find it is so financially possible'. His chief concern was to limit start-up costs for the Exchequer. He was not committed to universality; and thought Beveridge's pension proposals the 'least interesting and least essential part' of his Plan.[3] This last comment is unsurprising. Keynes was not interested in pensions, but in unemployment insurance and family allowances and how they fitted into his general scheme of business-cycle management. Beveridge and Keynes met for lunch on 23

March, on the first of what Beveridge's biographer José Harris calls many convivial occasions in the Athenaeum and Gargoyle Club, though conviviality is not a word automatically conjured up by Beveridge's buttoned-up presence. Perhaps their conversations ranged more widely than the affordable scales of benefits.

With the cost of Beveridge's proposals causing alarm in the Treasury, Keynes assumed the role of Beveridge's Treasury defender. It seems that at lunch on 1 July 1942, the two men concocted the plan of appointing a small committee to consider the finance of Beveridge's scheme. Keynes got Hopkins to agree, and a committee of three consisting of Keynes, Lionel Robbins and the government actuary, Sir George Epps, met Beveridge three times in August 1942, with a final meeting in October. Keynes envisaged a 'bedrock' scheme to lower the initial cost of the plan from £700m a year to £450m, which would be only moderately above the existing cost (£315m) of social security. At the first meeting, on 10 August, they saved £100m, a good day's work in Keynes's view. Beveridge accepted Keynes's suggestion to limit family allowances to second and subsequent children, though Keynes himself backtracked from this, judging it to be 'politically unstable'.[4] Pensions caused the most trouble, as they have done ever since. Keynes suggested that the full Beveridge subsistence pension be phased in gradually.[5] Beveridge accepted this, and by 24 August, following a further meeting with the Committee, Keynes reported that Beveridge's proposals were no longer open to serious financial criticism.

The Report was published on 1 December 1942. The previous month the Allies had landed in Africa; in January 1943 the German Sixth Army surrendered at Stalingrad. The race for post-war votes was on, and in the next few weeks the Conservatives lost it, with Churchill and the Chancellor, Sir Kingsley Wood, lukewarm in their response to the People's William. The public bought 650,000 copies of the Beveridge Report, and swallowed with enthusiasm the doctrine of 'cradle to grave' security. The Treasury continued to fear that the additional taxes called for by Beveridge would inhibit post-war recovery. Keynes wanted to make his maiden speech in the Lords on the Report. He proposed to say, 'But there is nothing, my Lords, in what we are discussing today which need frighten a mouse.' In view of his colleagues' apprehensions, however, he felt this was not tactful and stayed silent.

Keynes's largely technical response to Beveridge may be contrasted with the reactions, enthusiastic or splenetic, of his friends and associates. Into the enthusiastic camp fell the Economic Section, which argued that the disincentives to work of expanded unemployment and sickness benefits would be more than balanced by the positive effects on productivity of a 'better fed, better housed, better clothed and better educated population'. Hubert Henderson was predictably scathing. He warned that universal benefits would be much more expensive than targeted ones, that redistribution on this scale would reduce economic efficiency, and condemned the 'insidious' suggestion in the Report that 'a good time can be had by all when the last shot is fired'.[6] Into the splenetic category came Keynes's old friend Foxy Falk, who wrote in *The Times* on 3 December 1942 that the Beveridge Report was the 'road to the moral ruin of the Nation ... not a symptom of the vitality of our civilisation but of its approaching end'. The battle lines on social policy were being drawn up which have raged ever since. Keynes's incuriosity about this battle is itself curious. The truth seems to be that he was not interested in social policy as such, and never attended to it. The sole question in his mind was whether the Exchequer could 'afford' Beveridge.

II. FISCAL PHILOSOPHY AND EMPLOYMENT POLICY

Beveridge had started all sorts of hares, which gave intellectual entrepreneurs like Keynes and James Meade some meaty trails to follow. He had assumed a post-war unemployment average of about 8 per cent (which he thought of as 'full employment') as the actuarial basis of his National Insurance Fund. How plausible was this? Could it be improved on? This was related to the size of the immediate post-war national income: the higher it was the more generous the start-up benefits could afford to be. These questions were thrashed out at the Inter-Departmental Committee on Post-War Internal Economic Problems, set up in October 1941, where they merged insensibly with the question of what steps could be taken to maintain high employment after the war. James Meade's paper 'Internal Measures for the Prevention of General Unemployment', dated 8 July 1941, reached this Committee in November, and it never quite lost its place as front runner in the development of post-war employment policy. Meade was a Keynesian, and his paper focused on contracyclical demand management, though it dealt briefly with the frictional and structural elements in unemployment, and the measures to be taken to deal with them.[7] The Treasury response, 'The Post-War Relation between Purchasing Power and Consumer Goods', came before the Committee in May 1942. It was mainly written by Sir Hubert Henderson, and was therefore suitably pessimistic. Drawing analogies with the period 1919–24, Henderson did not see how 'internal' measures could prevent a decline in employment in the exporting industries; since these were the source of Britain's problems, he took a gloomy view of the level of long-run demand. Keynes wrote scathingly of a preliminary draft of this paper, 'the author [seems to be] scared to death lest there might be some date at which the figure of unemployment would fall below three million'.[8] Henderson's views on this and other matters strongly influenced the Treasury's new joint second secretary, Sir Wilfrid Eady. Apart from this, the Treasury had administrative and confidence objections to public works and unbalanced budgets going back to the 1920s.

Meade wanted Keynes to produce a Keynes Plan on post-war employment policy to complement the Beveridge Plan on post-war social policy. But Keynes resisted: yet another Keynes Plan might be one too many.[9] This is a great pity, because there never was a comprehensive Keynes Plan for maintaining full employment after the war. Keynes's contribution to the famous White Paper on Employment Policy, issued in May 1944, was mainly by way of encouragement, commentary and criticism, even though parts of it clearly reflected his theories. However, the Whitehall debates stimulated by the Beveridge and Meade proposals provided Keynes with opportunities for his usual scatter of interventions, starting in 1942 and running through to his membership of the National Debt Enquiry of 1945. These point to a more or less coherent employment philosophy which is very different from what, after the war, passed for Keynesianism. They also strikingly bring out the *political* meaning which Keynes gave key terms like 'full employment', 'public sector' and 'capital budgeting', technical terms for politically slippery concepts.

A good starting point is to ask what Keynes meant by full employment. He certainly did not mean by this zero or near zero unemployment; on the other hand he did not accept the 10 per cent unemployment average of the inter-war years as the best that could be achieved. Like Henderson, and indeed Meade, he distinguished between structural unemployment and demand-deficient unemployment. However, unlike Henderson, he believed that demand-deficient unemployment could persist – the *General Theory* had been written to explain why this was so – and also that improved demand conditions might improve the supply structure of the economy by increasing labour mobility. This was the basis for his optimism. He believed that governments now had the knowledge, experience and will to prevent a recurrence of the conditions of the 1930s.

In the wartime Treasury, Keynes and Henderson resumed the debates on employment they had been having in the 1930s. Basically, Keynes attributed the 'abnormal' levels of inter-war unemployment to demand-deficiency, with structural-adjustment problems as secondary. Henderson took exactly the opposite view. Keynes also looked back to the unemployment situation before 1914, whereas Henderson concentrated on what had happened to Britain's export industries in the 1920s. From his more extended backward glance Keynes came up with 5 per cent as the 'normal' rate of British unemployment, which had been disturbed by the excessively deflationary policies adopted to restore the gold standard.[10]

It is tempting to see this 5 per cent norm as a crude precursor of the 'natural rate' hypothesis developed much later by Milton Friedman. There is a similarity, in the sense that the pre-1914 'norm' had reference to a cyclically adjusted price level. The difference is that Friedman thought of the 'natural' rate as the 'equilibrium' rate, whereas for Keynes, as we have seen, there was no unique point of equilibrium.

The background to the optimistic scenario was the war itself. By 1942, unemployment was down to under 100,000, or less than 1 per cent. Between 1941 and 1945, the official price index rose at about 2 per cent a year. But this was not of course a normal peacetime performance, nor did Keynes regard it as such. The problem of unemployment was solved, Soviet-style, by a mixture of abnormally high government spending and a battery of controls, including price controls and labour conscription, but also compulsory arbitration, rationing and subsidies – and by Lend–Lease and the accumulation of sterling debts taking care of the balance of payments.

It was natural, therefore, that when Keynes started thinking about post-war employment prospects, his mind should revert to the pre-1914 5 per cent. On 28 May 1942 he circulated estimates of post-war national income which he had prepared with the statistician Richard Stone. This *assumed* a post-war unemployment total of between 800,000 and 900,000, or between 5 and 6 per cent of the workforce. Together with other assumptions, Keynes and Stone calculated a 'standard' post-war national income of £6.5bn, or about 15 per cent higher, in real terms, than pre-war. Keynes himself thought this a bit conservative; but it was nothing like as bleak as Henderson, who, in his rejoinder to the Keynes–Stone exercise, assumed two million unemployed (12.5 per cent), which implied a correspondingly lower (£5.7bn) national income.[11] An 'agreed' figure of 7.5 per cent was eventually settled in 1943 as the actuarial basis for Beveridge, which Keynes thought too high, and Henderson too low. As it turned out, Henderson was right about national income, but wrong about unemployment.[12]

Keynes did not, of course, say that unemployment would be 5 per cent after the war because it had been 5 per cent before 1914. In a note of 3 June 1942 he explained that he and Stone had arrived at their percentage 'chiefly on the grounds that it seemed to us that this was about the highest the public would stand in post-war conditions without demanding something very drastic to be done about it, coupled with the fact that it did not seem to us impracticable to take steps which would bring down the figure to this total'.[13]

Full employment for Keynes is thus a politically determined variable. It is an estimate of the maximum unemployment the community will stand and the minimum that can be achieved without imposing on it an unwanted cost. The idea that a free society in peacetime might not be willing to pay the cost – in terms of either liberty or inflation – of a very high level of full employment escaped the hubristic Keynesians of the 1960s, who insisted that 'demand management' needed to be buttressed with 'additional instruments', like wage and price controls. Would Keynes have agreed? There is nothing, in either his pre-war or wartime writings, which suggests he would ever have gone beyond the attempt at a voluntary agreement on wage restraint. In 1940 he had drawn his own line between a 'free' and a 'totalitarian' society (see p. 595) and there is no reason to suppose that he would not have stuck to it.

Keynes never subsequently changed his mind about how much full employment was feasible. When Beveridge's *Full Employment in a Free Society* appeared in December 1944, with a much lower unemployment assumption than in the Beveridge Report itself, Keynes wrote to Beveridge: 'No harm in aiming at 3 per cent unemployment, but I shall be surprised if we succeed.'[14] Three months later he 'thought Beveridge went too far in setting an inviolable object of 3 per cent for unemployment'.[15]

After the war Keynesians had a simple answer to the question of how governments might maintain full employment, however defined. They would use national income statistics to calculate the prospective balance between aggregate supply and demand, and use fiscal policy to close any gap. If prospective demand exceeded prospective supply, threatening inflation, the government should run a budget surplus; in the opposite case, where unemployment was the danger, it should run a deficit. In either case, the state's budget was the balancing factor. Money was to be kept cheap under all circumstances.

When one looks at what Keynes said, both before and during the war, this neat fiscal schematism starts to dissolve. Keynes turns out to be as strong a believer in balanced budgets as Gladstone was! How did this square with using fiscal policy to 'balance the economy' at full employment? The answer to the riddle is that Keynes regarded public *investment* as the balancing factor, and treated the state's investment programmes as 'off-budget'. This view of things rested on his own peculiar definitions of 'public' and 'private' and on accounting conventions which drew a sharp distinction between 'current' and 'capital' spending. They both derive from the 1920s, and, in particular, from his contributions to the Liberal Yellow Book of 1928. Whether they make much sense is another matter; Meade never thought they did.

In a contribution to the Treasury's budget inquiry, which Hopkins had started in May 1942, Keynes wrote (20 July) that the 'ordinary' budget, that of the government proper, 'should be balanced at all times. It is the capital budget which should fluctuate with the demand for employment.'[16] In fact, like the Victorians, Keynes favoured running a regular surplus on the 'ordinary' budget, which would be used to reduce debt in normal times, or be transferred to the capital budget in a downturn and used to replace dead-weight debt by productive or semi-productive debt. 'Deficit finance', in this concept, would mean 'reducing the normal sinking fund to zero' rather than budgeting for an actual deficit[17] – much as Churchill had done in his budgets of the 1920s. Keynes confusingly used the term 'capital budget' in several different senses. It was not till 1945 that he sorted them out.[18] He now claimed that the term stood for three distinct concepts: (a) 'capital expenditure for the economy as a whole'; (b) '*all* capital expenditure under *public* control, including local authorities and public boards'; and (c) capital items 'paid for out of, and received into, the Exchequer': all estimated for the coming year. He called these the Investment, Public Capital and the Exchequer Capital budgets respectively. Keynes's belief that government could control the aggregate level of investment rested on his conviction that (b) came to two-thirds or more of (a).

Keynes criticised his Treasury colleagues for mixing up capital budgeting with 'deficit finance'. The technique he was suggesting, whereby the Public Capital budget would correct any projected imbalance between aggregate saving and investment, had nothing to do with 'deficit finance'. Capital budgeting was a method of maintaining equilibrium, deficit budgeting a way of curing disequilibrium.[19]

Keynes related this way of treating the budget accounts to his general thesis of creeping 'socialisation':

> We need to extend, rather than curtail [Keynes wrote to Hopkins on 20 July 1942], the theory and practice of extra-budgetary funds for state operated or state supported functions, whether it is the transport system, the Electricity Board, War Damage or Social Security. The more socialised we become, the more important it is to associate as closely as possible the cost of particular services with the sources out of which they are provided. . . . This is the only way by which to preserve sound accounting, to measure efficiency, to maintain economy and to keep the public aware of what things cost.

For Hopkins's benefit, Keynes sketched out a reform of the tax system, with contributions to a self-supporting social security fund replacing income tax. This strained the patience of even Sir Richard Hopkins. He tartly commented on 21 July 1942: 'I do not feel equal to settling between now and the 15th August Lord Keynes' suggestions for a complete remodelling of the system of direct taxation in this country. . . .'[20]

Bifurcating 'public' finance in this way enabled Keynes to divide the economic role of the state into two parts. The 'ordinary' budget would be concerned with issues of efficiency and equity; the capital budget with demand management. Critics, including most of Keynes's Treasury colleagues, saw it as a deliberate attempt at obfuscation. The public accounts were to be window-dressed to disguise budgeting for a deficit. Keynes himself would have claimed exactly the opposite: his aim was to introduce clarity into a confused discussion. The current/capital account distinction was also well understood in private business. However, there was bound to be an element of fiction in applying it to the public accounts. In the private sector, capital spending is spending which produces a cash return sufficient to service debt interest and repayment charges. Most of Keynes's 'public capital' spending does not qualify, though he thought it 'would, at least partially, if not wholly, pay for itself'.[21] Keynes was always conscious that new ideas had be 'dressed up' in familiar clothes to make them politically acceptable, especially to the business community. He contrasted theories and policies. 'Economists have to be very careful, I think, to distinguish between the two.'[22]

What turned out to be the decisive practical objection to Keynes's 'capital budgeting' was the notion that investment programmes could, or should, be manipulated to meet the needs of countercyclical policy. As Professor Thomas Wilson writes: 'Unfortunately Keynes was sometimes inclined to treat investment as though its purpose was simply to act as a conduit for the transmission of purchasing power into the economy.'[23] For these reasons, post-war Keynesian governments (especially after 1951) came to discard 'investment budgeting' in favour of efforts to influence aggregate consumption by varying taxes and hire-purchase conditions.[24] With the reaction against discretionary fiscal policy in the 1980s and 1990s, the current/capital account distinction came back into fashion, though how useful it will prove to be is still open to doubt.

There is very little in Keynes's writings about a topic which was to become of central interest in the 1970s and 1980s, namely, the effect of taxes on incentives. He fiercely opposed the 100 per cent excess profits tax, and tried hard to get it reduced. More interesting is his agreement with his former student Colin Clark that '25 per cent taxation is about the limit of what is easily borne....', though he doubted that Clark's statistics (drawn from inter-war data) proved, or could prove, his point. He arranged for the publication of Clark's findings in the *Economic Journal*.[25]

Many of Keynes's most characteristic fiscal attitudes come out in his correspondence with James Meade. This occurred in two bursts – the first in 1942 while the Beveridge Report was germinating, the second in 1943 after it had been published – both triggered by Keynes's responses to Meade's employment-maintaining proposals. The Economic Section's evidence to the Beveridge Enquiry included Meade's suggestion for contracyclical variations in national insurance contributions. When unemployment rose, contributions would be lowered; when it fell, they would be raised. After initial scepticism, Keynes was 'converted to the idea', though he stressed its limited role in offsetting fluctuations in investment demand.[26] A more substantial correspondence started in 1943. Soon after the Beveridge Report was published, the Ministerial Reconstruction Priorities Committee, chaired by Sir John Anderson, asked the Economic Section for a study of measures which might be taken to realise Beveridge's full employment assumption. The Section produced Meade's much revised paper, 'The Maintenance of Employment', which Keynes found so indigestible that he thought only 'Pompous John' would be able to read it attentively. Keynes now pressed on Meade his suggestion for dividing the budget into a current and a capital account.

Meade did not agree. Controls on domestic investment would not be prompt enough, or in some circumstances sufficient. So consumption stabilisers were needed: variations in social security contributions linked to an unemployment index which act as an 'instantaneous automatic stabiliser', and planned tax reductions, leading to unbalanced budgets, to prevent unemployment from developing.[27] In both proposals, but especially the second, there is a naive belief, which Meade never shed, that statistics would tell economists – and politicians – what they needed to do.

In his reply, Keynes restated his preference for using investment as a stabiliser, though he supported the case for 'automatic' variations in social security contributions. Against the tax variation scheme, he argued that, as people had established standards of living, a remission of taxation which they could rely on only for an 'indefinitely short period' might not stimulate their consumption by much – an early statement of Milton Friedman's permanent income hypothesis. Moreover, it would be extraordinarily difficult to reimpose the tax again when employment had improved. Varying national insurance contributions avoided this objection, 'partly because it could be associated with a formula', and partly because it would be pumping purchasing power into the hands of a class which did not save much. (Technically, the 'multiplier' effect would be larger.) However, he insisted that the insurance contribution variations be applied only to employee contributions not to those of employers or the state. The state's contribution, from its own budget, should be held constant; reductions in employers' contributions would not lead to increased employment if they were seen as merely temporary.[28] Keynes deprecated trying to superimpose on the scheme to vary insurance contributions proposals 'to reduce taxation on drink and tobacco with a view to making people drink and smoke more when they were tending to be out of work'. He thought the 'huge time-lags' involved made the effect of 'short-run changes' in taxes uncertain. Next, the idea of borrowing for capital spending in a slump would be understood much better by the 'common man' than encouraging consumption. The latter was 'a much more violent version of deficit budgeting' than the former. The fact that capital spending was 'capable of paying for itself' was much better in budgetary terms, since it did not involve a progressive increase in the National Debt. Finally, it was better to expedite investment spending whenever it was 'deficient' until the economy was saturated with capital goods.[29]

What emerges from this scatter of comments is a distinct bias against fiscal fine-tuning. The emphasis should be placed on prevention, not cure; on maintaining a steady stream of investment, not offsetting fluctuations. If – and here Keynes reverts to his ideas of the 1920s – 'two-thirds or three-quarters of total investment is carried out or can be influenced by public or semi-public bodies, a long-term programme of a stable character should be capable of reducing the range of fluctuation to much narrower limits than formerly.... If this is successful it should not be too difficult to offset small fluctuations by expediting or retarding some items in this long-term programme.'[30] This is far removed from the method of anxious interference, based on small fluctuations in spuriously precise forecasts, which became the hallmark of British Keynesian management.

In a memorandum of 25 May 1943 entitled 'The Long-Term Problem of Full Employment' Keynes, unusually for him, set his fiscal philosophy in a developmental perspective. The stimulus for this production was another monumentally gloomy paper by Hubert Henderson, who foresaw large-scale unemployment developing in the transition from wartime to peacetime production.[31] Keynes envisaged three phases after the war. In Phase I, which he thought might last five years, investment demand would exceed full employment saving, leading to inflation in the absence of rationing and other controls. In this phase, the emphasis should be on restricting consumption in order to reconstruct the war-damaged economy. In Phase II, which he thought might last between five and ten years, he foresaw a rough equilibrium between full employment saving and investment 'in conditions of freedom', with the state active in varying the pace of investment projects. In Phase III investment demand would be so saturated that it could not match full employment saving without the state having to embark on wasteful and unnecessary programmes. In this phase the aim of policy should be to encourage consumption and discourage saving, and so absorb some of the unwanted surplus by increasing leisure, with shorter hours and more frequent holidays. This would mark the entrance to the 'golden age', the age of capital saturation. Eventually, Keynes thought, 'depreciation funds should be almost sufficient to provide all the gross investment that is required'.[32] It is the age, foreshadowed in the *General Theory*, of the 'euthanasia of the *rentier*', since there will be no demand for new capital.

This is the Keynes of the 'Economic Possibilities for Our Grandchildren', that remarkable, but misguided, essay in prophecy, published in 1930, which claimed that at root the economic problem was due to a *fear of consumption*. To achieve 'capital saturation' as quickly as possible, so that mankind could confront its permanent problem – 'how to live wisely and agreeably and well' – was the overriding aim of his economic statesmanship. Once societies were over the 'hump' of scarcity, all the economic 'dentistry' in which Keynes was so heavily involved could become redundant, and the heaven opened up by G. E. Moore's *Principia Ethica*, the bible of his youth, would be established on earth.[33] Little though Keynes dwelt on ultimate questions, it is characteristic of the man that he should have reverted to this optimistic vision of plenty during the most stringent period of scarcity. On 5 April 1945 he wrote to T. S. Eliot that the 'full employment policy by means of investment' was 'only one particular application of an intellectual theorem. You can produce the result just as well by consuming more or working less.'[34]

In July 1943, discussion of post-war employment policy moved into a higher gear. On the Reconstruction Priorities Committee, Kingsley Wood wanted to postpone discussion; the Labour members, Dalton and Morrison, wanted a government commitment on the lines sketched out by Meade. Sir John Anderson, Lord President of the Council, set up an inter-departmental Steering Committee on Post-War Employment to draft a report. Its terms of reference – to study means of controlling aggregate demand – leant in Meade's direction; its heavy Treasury membership, with Hopkins in the chair, flanked by Eady and Gilbert, and with Lionel Robbins, caught between supporting his Section's collective view and his own more conservative instincts, pointed the other way.[35] The Steering Committee's Report became the Employment White Paper, published on 26 May 1944. Not being on the Steering Committee himself, Keynes was not importantly involved in its preparation. Nor did he have time for continuous scrutiny of its work. When the Committee started business in September 1943, he was in the United States. Early in 1944 his time was taken up fighting for his currency plan in Whitehall; in March he fell ill. Hopkins, too, had a heart attack at a critical stage in the drafting. The absence of Keynes and Henderson had an anaesthetising effect on the White Paper's prose. It also made its compromise position possible.

Keynes shared some of the Treasury's objections to Meade's approach. As we have seen, he disliked Meade's emphasis on fine-tuning consumption and thought that the Economic Section underestimated structural problems. But he was even more worried by Eady's ignorance of even 'undergraduate' economics,[36] dismissed one of his papers as 'not much more than Neville Chamberlain disguised in a little modern dress',[37] and tried to reduce the influence of Henderson's destructive memoranda. Caught between two fires, Hopkins steered a middle course by dividing the unemployment problem into 'demand-deficient' and 'structural', the second being more important in the transitional period. He set out to ensure that the Steering Committee's Report contained the 'essential qualifications to the aggregate demand theory'.[38] 'It is important to maintain demand,' he wrote. 'But it is also important that the obstacles to mobility should be few.'[39] In the autumn, the Steering Committee pressed ahead with a draft in order to 'scoop' Beveridge, who, advised – or instructed – by Nicholas Kaldor, was writing his own report on employment policy.[40]

The Steering Committee's report, dated 11 January 1944, nodded skilfully in all directions. It endorsed the demand-management approach but did not sanction budget deficits and also emphasised the need for 'supply side' policies to secure a balanced distribution of labour. A full employment target, it believed, would become a 'political football'. It took account of external factors. Back from the United States, Keynes commended it, on 14 February 1944, as an 'outstanding State paper', representing a 'revolution in official opinion'. Economic analysis, he declared, 'has now reached the

point where it is fit to be applied'. Unusually for him, he succumbed to
an attack of arithmetical euphoria, proclaiming the dawn of an era of 'Joy
through Statistics' when everything 'will all be obvious, and as clear as
daylight with no room for argument'.[41] He had two criticisms. The first was
the Report's cautious approach to fiscal policy. It ignored his proposals for
a capital budget. By neglecting to consider the 'multiplier' effects of injecting additional demand into the system, it was led to treat budget deficits
as the price to be paid for maintaining employment, whereas 'measures
to stabilise the national income are *ipso facto* measures to stabilise the
national budget'. 'Is it supposed', he demanded, 'that slumps increase
the national wealth?' Scornfully, yet wittily, he relived his pre-war battles
with Sir Richard Hopkins:

> How slow dies the inbred fallacy that it is an act of financial imprudence
> to put men to work! If the Minister of Labour were found praising
> periods of cyclical unemployment on the ground that they gave the
> workers a much-needed rest and improved the nation's proficiency in
> the matter of darts, it should be for the Chancellor of the Exchequer to
> protest against such idling and to demand the present proposals for
> providing employment on the ground that they were essential to the
> solvency and stability of the Budget. This section has the air of having
> been written some years before the rest of the report.[42]

Secondly, there was the Report's hesitant approach to structural problems. Keynes regarded them as secondary – he was convinced that Britain
had caught up substantially with American productivity levels during the
war, by limiting restrictive practices and imitating mass-production methods[43] – but he was never mealy-mouthed about urging that they be vigorously tackled, accusing the Treasury of defeatism.[44] In his February 1944
comment, he strongly agreed with Lionel Robbins's 'Note of Dissent' on
restrictive practices. Robbins had implied that policies of demand expansion
would fail without sufficient labour mobility and wage restraint – a view
also held by Meade.

The final skirmishes came in March 1944. Enraged by Keynes's endorsement of the Steering Committee's Report, Henderson attacked it with a
volley of papers, mocking Keynes's views and calling the Report 'a disgrace'.
Any rise in unemployment, he insisted, would be associated with an adverse
balance of payments. The policy of increasing domestic demand would
worsen the balance of payments by leading to an increase in imports and a
rise in costs. A depreciation of sterling would not correct the external deficit,
because it would lead straight to compensating wage demands. The main
effects of the Keynes–Meade policy of 'internal spending' would be a
collapsing exchange, a flight from sterling and rising inflation. He was
particularly scathing about Meade's 'automatic' variations in social security
payments based on the movement of an unemployment index. This ignored

the fact that there were many different types of unemployment (which Henderson spent much time classifying), which had different causes and required different remedies. 'The whole "automatic" approach', he wrote, 'is based on a *laissez-faire*-inspired distrust of governments ... not that I trust governments much more, but ... I trust indices much less.'[45]

Keynes attempted a last rebuttal. Starting from the same premiss ('I share his pessimistic view about our prospective external financial position'), he drew four opposite conclusions. First, since exporting 'is going to be a matter of life and death to us', the primary impulse to unemployment 'will not, and simply cannot be allowed to, come from that source'. (Eady's pertinent comment was that a categorical imperative would not itself increase exports.) Secondly, he agreed that import restrictions might be unavoidable, but this would increase the value of the 'multiplier'. Thirdly:

> the view, to which he [Henderson] obviously attaches a good deal of importance, that it will be good for our external credit if we allow large-scale unemployment to develop ... seems to me to be a plain delusion. There may have been a time when that sort of policy attracted the approval of foreign financiers. ... But the world changes. It will improve our external credit if we are seen tackling the problem of internal unemployment vigorously. ...

Finally, Henderson was oblivious to 'the social and political consequences of deliberately using domestic unemployment as a remedy for external disequilibrium', a policy which 'might easily mean the downfall of our present system of democratic government'. So 'we must discover some other way out'.[46]

The White Paper on Employment Policy (Cmd 6257) was published on 26 May 1944. Hopkins's final rewriting owed more to Henderson and Eady than to Keynes. There was nothing 'Keynesian' in the first three chapters, which dealt with the need to maintain export efficiency, transitional problems, and a 'balanced distribution of industry and labour'. How to deal with 'general unemployment', which it was emphasised would not arise for some time after the end of the war, was the subject of Chapter IV. Three co-equal conditions for success were stated: 'total expenditure on goods and services must be prevented from falling to a level where general unemployment occurs', 'the level of prices and wages must be kept reasonably stable', and 'there must be sufficient mobility of workers between occupations and localities'. The government's employment intentions would be 'frustrated' and 'fruitless' unless the second and third conditions held. In addition, the White Paper stated – three times – that those elements in general expenditure most likely to fluctuate – private investment and exports – were 'the most difficult to control', and also that 'an increase in one part of total expenditure can only within limits offset a decrease in another'.

It rejected 'deliberate planning for a deficit in the National Budget in years of sub-normal trade'. It more or less endorsed Keynes's own proposals for capital budgeting, without using the phrase. Overall its prose was so carefully balanced, that almost anything could be read into it. Contrary to much myth, there was not even a commitment to full employment. The Foreword's famous opening sentence read: 'The Government accept as one of their primary aims and responsibilities the maintenance of a high and stable level of employment after the war.'

Keynes gave the White Paper a qualified benediction. He wrote to Austin Robinson 'My own feeling is that the first sentence is more valuable than the whole of the rest.'[47]

Keynes knew that there were loose ends. On 5 June 1945 he wrote to an Australian correspondent, S. G. McFarlane: 'I expect that both of our countries incline to under-estimate the difficulty of stabilising incomes where exports play so large a part. One is also, simply because one knows no solution, inclined to turn a blind eye to the wages problem in a full employment economy.'[48] How far would he have been willing to go down the road of planned incomes in order to maintain full employment?

This question is of particular interest in light of his comments on Hayek's *Road to Serfdom*, that seminal anti-planning polemic, which was published almost simultaneously with the White Paper on Employment Policy, and which Keynes read on his sea voyage to Bretton Woods in June 1944. Hayek's was a classic 'thin end of the wedge' argument, with Keynes at the thin end of an interventionist wedge which, if not checked, would lead to totalitarianism. Hayek rejected the political stability of any 'Middle Way' between *laissez-faire* and coercive central planning. In a passage which might have been aimed directly at the 'Keynesian' parts of the White Paper he wrote:

> Many economists hope indeed that the ultimate remedy [for general fluctuations in economic activity and recurrent waves of large-scale unemployment] may be found in the field of monetary policy, which would involve nothing incompatible even with nineteenth century liberalism. Others, it is true, believe that real success can be expected only from the skilful timing of public works undertaken on a very large scale. This might lead to much more serious restrictions on the competitive sphere, and in experimenting in this direction we shall have carefully to watch our step if we are to avoid making all economic activity progressively more dependent on the direction and volume of government expenditure.[49]

Those who already saw themselves in the Keynesian camp gave Hayek's book a very bad reception.[50] Keynes's response is unexpected. Hayek's was a 'grand book', he wrote, and 'we all have the greatest reason to be grateful to you for saying so well what needs so much to be said. . . . Morally and philosophically I find myself in agreement with virtually the whole of it; and not only in agreement, but in a deeply moved agreement.'

But – here is the weakness of the book and Keynes was on to it in a flash –

> You admit ... that it is a question of knowing where to draw the line. You agree that the line has to be drawn somewhere, and that the logical extreme is not possible. But you give us no guidance whatever as to where to draw it. It is true that you and I would probably draw it in different places. I should guess that according to my ideas you greatly under-estimate the practicability of the middle course. But as soon as you admit that the extreme is not possible ... you are, on your own argument, done for, since you are trying to persuade us that so soon as one moves an inch in the planned direction you are necessarily launched on the slippery path which will lead you in due course over the precipice.

Sure of his intellectual ground, Keynes went on to say, 'I accuse you of perhaps confusing a little bit the moral and the material issues. Dangerous acts can be done safely in a community which thinks and feels rightly which would be the way to hell if they were executed by those who think and feel wrongly.'[51]

On the first point, it is game, set and match to Keynes. Hayek never could draw the line between freedom and planning satisfactorily and had to rely on his own intuition and sympathies in judging where it should be drawn, as Keynes did. His distinction between general abstract laws and laws designed to benefit particular groups does not quite do the work he wants it to. Later in his life he tried to place constitutional obstacles in the way of majorities coercing minorities. Nor was Keynes much more successful in 'drawing the line'. In 1940 he had averred that prices were 'the indispensable elements of freedom' in an economic system. But an economy in which most investment is 'socialised', the capital market controlled and imports channelled through state trading agreements is free only in a somewhat peculiar sense.

The practical conclusions Keynes drew from Hayek's failure to draw the line are far from conclusive. His dictum that 'dangerous acts can be safely done in a community which thinks and feels rightly' is obviously correct. It was *safer* to have a Churchill running the war than a Hitler, even though the wartime organisation of the two countries was totalitarian. One can multiply examples: it is safer that immigration laws be passed by liberals than by racists, that regulations be imposed by people who hate them than by people who love them. But this is a static argument. What the dictum ignores is Hayek's claim that the stock of 'right feeling' can be depleted by continuous governmental intervention: it is not, so to speak, independent of the acts being done. A society in which 'dangerous acts' by governments become continuous will lose its understanding of why they are dangerous – that is, its sense of what it is to be free. A good example is the way the extension of the social security system has eroded personal responsibility and charitable giving. It then becomes a matter of judgement as to which set of economic and social practices is most likely to preserve the moral values which Hayek and Keynes shared.

Much can be said on both sides, and Keynes was right to point out that policies which took no precautions against slumps were likely to produce 'disillusion' or, worse, hellish revolts against liberal values. On the other hand, no one who lived through the 1970s can fail to see a great pathos in Keynes's so English response to Hayek's warning – 'Don't worry, things will be perfectly all right here in England, because we're English and not crazy like the Continentals.' On this matter, at least, Keynes and Hayek fought each other to an honourable draw. The game is not over.

III. MODEST PREPARATIONS FOR THE GOOD LIFE

On 1 April 1942, Keynes became chairman of the Council for the Encouragement of Music and the Arts (CEMA). He had been talked into taking it on by R. A. Butler, President of the Board of Education; his name may well have been suggested by his old friend Samuel Courtauld, Butler's father-in-law. Butler gilded his offer by suggesting that CEMA might evolve into 'something that might occupy a more permanent place in our social organisation'.[52] It had been set up in January 1940, on an initiative from Earl De La Warr, then President of the Board of Education, to help musicians, actors and artists whom air-raid precautions and bombing were likely to render unemployed, and to bring the 'solace' of music and the arts to the bored, bombed out and evacuated. (According to David Webster it was formed 'very largely to meet the need for entertainment in air-raid shelters in London'.) With a matching grant from The Pilgrim Trust, the Board of Education supplied funds, an office, and Mary Glasgow, the Council's secretary; there was an *ad hoc* committee. By the time the Pilgrim Trust withdrew and Keynes took over, CEMA was already 'an established national institution', having organised 8000 concerts, mainly in factories, 'Art for the People' exhibitions, and plays. Keynes warned Butler (on 24 December 1941) that he had been in 'only limited sympathy with the principles on which it [CEMA] has been carried on hitherto'. There was a wealth of meaning in this warning. CEMA had brought to its new tasks the tradition of the Pilgrim Trust's pre-war adult education work among the unemployed and also a policy of directly financing drama tours itself. Both were anathema to

Keynes, the first on artistic grounds, the second on financial grounds. In the summer of 1940 he had summoned Mary Glasgow to Gordon Square. 'He wanted to know why the Council was wasting so much money on amateur effort.... It was standards that mattered, and the preservation of serious professional enterprise, not obscure concerts in village halls.'[53]

Arts policy in Keynes's time at CEMA was closely bound up with his own personal philosophy. He brought to his new job a worshipful attitude to the arts, decided views on how they should be financed, and a strong but limited range of sympathies. The homage went back a long way: philosophically to G. E. Moore's *Principia Ethica*, which he had imbibed as an undergraduate, personally to his friendship with Duncan Grant and membership of the Bloomsbury group.

Keynes, Clive Bell noted, was one of that class of benefactors 'who have devoted great powers of organisation to good purposes'. He had a complex attitude to patronage. Between the wars he himself dispensed and organised largesse for the arts, not just by buying pictures himself, but by organising the London Artists' Association and by building the Arts Theatre in Cambridge. But he never believed in an open-ended purse. It was impossible, he thought, to go on getting support for something which presented itself as a 'bottomless sink' for originally enthusiastic backers. The purpose of patronage was to enable non-profit-making activities to take place – by way of capital endowment or loan, or guarantee against loss, not to provide permanent subsidies for loss-making enterprises. He once said that if a patronage body were 100 per cent successful it would end up by spending nothing except on its own administration. 'It would choose so well and back such uniformly certain winners that all its loans would be repaid in full and none of its guarantees ever called.'[54] His own ideal was a mix of private and public patronage, but he gradually became convinced that state patronage would be the only way of saving arts from extinction when private patronage had been destroyed by high taxes.

In his own various artistic enterprises, Keynes's part was never just to raise the cash. He was keenly interested in artistic policy, relying in part on advice from his wife and his painter and writer friends, but also on his own judgement, especially in drama. His tastes and sympathies, however, were not wide. He had no innate feeling for the visual arts. 'Had he never met Duncan Grant he would never have taken much interest in painting,' says Clive Bell, who found his judgement of painters and works of art lamentable. He had only a moderate liking for music. He was unable to see foreign cultures from the inside: 'France, Italy, America even, he saw them all from the white cliffs of Dover, or, to be more exact, from Whitehall or King's combination room.'[55] His own appreciation centred on literature, the dramatic arts (including ballet) and architecture; he was a fine and discriminating user of words. His homage was to the civilising mission of the arts, and he enjoyed the company of artists.

Keynes brought to his chairmanship qualities familiar to the Treasury: the drive to translate visions into plans, the urge to get to the bottom of things, a scatter of lively interventions, prodigious hard work, impatience with muddle and sloppiness. Mary Glasgow wrote: 'Supremely intelligent himself, he was impatient of anything less than clear thinking and well-defined aims. He knew what he wanted, and he liked to have his own way. He could be very rude on occasion, and he did antagonise a number of people. Faced with an issue on which he felt deeply – and there were many such – he never hesitated to declare war.'[56] At the same time, he gave CEMA an electrifying sense of direction:

> At a time when he was probably busier than at any other period of his life, often engaged in financial conferences in America and Canada, he wrote to me, the secretary, practically every day, sometimes several times a day, as dictated missives flew into our headquarters, in Belgrave Square and later St James's Square, from the Treasury or across the Atlantic. And they *were* missives, long discourses, lists of questions, detailed comments on all that was happening in the theatre, concert halls and picture galleries. They were full of colourful, indiscreet talk about individuals and organisations.... It may well have been that he found relief in this way from the demands of his financial responsibilities. He said he gave about a twentieth part of his time to us at the Council ... [but] that in order to run things properly a chairman ought to be devoting at least a quarter.... His praise was as heart-warming as his blame was cutting.

Keynes wanted people to stand up to him, but he inspired such alarm in them that few took the chance. Mary Glasgow said that it took her three years to get over her 'paralysing awe of him', then suddenly it evaporated.[57]

Keynes's own positions were as clear-cut as any positions on arts policy can be. His first allegiance was to high professional standards; the question of whether a play or piece of music was high-brow or middle-brow was secondary. As his deputy chairman, the art historian Kenneth Clark, put it, Keynes was not 'the man for wandering minstrels and amateur theatricals'. He steered CEMA towards the excellent, in the belief that the people deserved the best, and in the hope that they would enjoy it when they got it. His principles of finance were equally clear-cut: CEMA money was to be used not to subsidise performances but to guarantee them against loss. Under his chairmanship CEMA encouraged commercial companies to form non-profit-distributing subsidiaries, operating under Council guarantee, to avoid Entertainments Tax. At first, CEMA failed to obtain automatic exemption from tax for the productions it sponsored, and much of Keynes's time was spent in exasperated correspondence with the 'illiterate' Plays Committee of Customs and Excise, trying to prove that Euripides and Ibsen were educational rather than entertaining.[58] In 1943, CEMA started supporting opera and ballet. Keynes saw his funding formula as a model for the way in which commercial companies after the war might be emboldened to woo audiences with a more demanding repertoire. There were grumblings that 'the commercial theatre was feathering its nest at the taxpayer's expense'; in fact, 'not a penny of CEMA money was spent on the ... non-profit-sharing ventures. The managements took the risk, CEMA sponsored them, and the system of guarantee against loss came into its own.'[59]

Keynes was equally clear that it was CEMA's task to equip urban centres with what he called the 'material frame for the arts of civilisation and delight'. This boiled down to buildings. As a theatre-builder himself, Keynes's imagination was fired by the noble vision of each town having its own 'art centre'; less happily, he would have attached to each of these centres a 'British restaurant'. Throughout the war, he followed a trail of derelict warehouses or damaged buildings which might be turned into theatres. Most of these schemes foundered; the plan to rebuild the burnt-out Crystal Palace 'as a vast place of entertainment where the British citizen of the future can spend a whole day'[60] came to naught. But CEMA did save the bombed-out Theatre Royal at Bristol from being turned into a warehouse by its owners.

Keynes went to Bristol for its re-opening, on 11 May 1943 and was at his most playful and paradoxical in his pre-performance speech. He described how CEMA, possessed of an 'undefined independence, an anomalous constitution and no fixed rules' and therefore 'able to do by inadvertence what obviously no one in his official senses would do on purpose,' had 'accidentally slipped into getting mixed up with a theatre building'. He hoped that 'the precedent, having been once created ... will ... be officially improper not to repeat....'[61]

Keynes's programme was not carried out without considerable internal dissension. By late 1942, CEMA had spawned a structure of expert panels for Music, Drama, Art, each with its own director, as well as Scottish and Welsh Committees, all full of prima donnas. Keynes expected to preside at quarterly meetings of the panels, whose decisions would be binding. But this proved one chore too many, and he soon handed the panels over to his deputy chairmen – Stanley Marchant for Music, Ivor Brown for Drama, Kenneth Clark for Art – with their decisions having to be ratified by the full Council. Mary Glasgow remembers frequent dinners at Gordon Square, where the directors of the panels would discuss their plans in the basement dining room, with Lydia Keynes, dressed in woollens and high, fleece-lined boots, distributing carrots to help their vision in the black-out.[62]

The Drama Panel was especially tiresome, and Keynes was driven to write to one of its panellists, Ashley Dukes: 'What can I reply to your crazy letter, except that you would do better justice to yourself and be a worthier inhabitant of the planet if you would discover the facts before circulating such a document....'[63]

CEMA's exhibitions policy ran into predictable flak from the Royal Academy. It had been sending out collections of Sickert, Wilson Steer and the Tate Gallery's wartime acquisitions on provincial tour. The Academicians complained about the lack of Old Masters in these exhibitions, and accused CEMA's Art Panel of dangerously 'modernist' tendencies. Keynes had put Henry Moore and Duncan Grant on the Panel. Why not balance them with Sir Edwin Lutyens, Butler suggested. 'I do not think he will do any harm.' 'Certainly old Lutyens [the famous architect was seventy-four] would do no harm,' Keynes responded warmly. 'But he would do no good. Is it wise to start so early in our life on the vicious practice of filling up with respectable dead heads?' Lutyens was successfully fought off, but Keynes returned from holiday in April 1943 to find that Butler had appointed a painter called Thomas Monnington, subsequently president of the Royal Academy, to balance the modernists. 'As I have never heard of Monnington, I cannot reasonably object to him,' Keynes told Butler. 'It will, I think, be of some assistance to be able to tell members of my Panel that I was not consulted.'[64]

Keynes's own ideas about the future of CEMA were slowly taking shape. 'Cema is a dreadful name,' he told Butler on 15 February 1943. '[The initials] convey nothing to anyone who does not know about it already and suggest something too much like Ensa [the organisation for entertaining troops] for our taste.... My own idea would be something like "The Royal Council for the Arts".' Butler agreed: 'Organisations which exist on their initials, I have repeatedly pointed out, end up by being second-rate.'[65] On 23 June 1943, Butler suggested setting up a small *ad hoc* committee to discuss CEMA's post-war future.

Nothing much happened, and early in 1944 Butler pressed Keynes to produce his thoughts. By this time, Keynes was so busy (and unwell) that he contemplated resigning. It was not till September 1944, in the interval between the Bretton Woods conference and the Stage II negotiations in Washington, that he managed to send Butler his memorandum on the future of CEMA, which was based on an earlier draft by a Council member, Ifor Evans. This proposed setting up a permanent Royal Council of the Arts of eleven members, five of whom would form an executive committee. This committee would chair the panels of outside experts. There would be a director-general and a small staff to service the panels. The Council would have two aims: to increase the accessibility of the arts to the public, and to improve standards of execution. It would receive an annual grant of £500,000 from the Ministry of Education rather than directly from the Treasury, because 'to have a Minister to speak on our behalf who has not a direct responsibility for maximum economy may in future conditions be an advantage'.[66]

On 30 January 1945 CEMA's Council rejected Keynes's proposed title – it decided it wanted to call itself the Arts Council of Great Britain – but accepted the rest of his proposals. The first meeting of the new executive took place in Keynes's office in the Treasury on 14 February. Keynes now pressed for a royal charter to set up the new body as quickly as possible. In one of its last decisions, Churchill's coalition government agreed to continue CEMA, just as the European war was ending. On 12 June, the 'caretaker' Chancellor, Sir John Anderson, announced that the government intended to incorporate it as the Arts Council of Great Britain, with an initial annual grant of £320,000. 'Well it does look as if the Arts Council is now fairly launched,' Keynes wrote to Butler, now Minister of Labour, on 14 June, 'and we all owe you a great debt of gratitude for having carried this through to its conclusion just before we parted company. . . .'

Keynes's last broadcast as CEMA's chairman, on 12 July 1945, traced the transformation of CEMA into the Arts Council of Great Britain. His cultured, upper-class voice, preserved in the BBC archive, with its narrow range of modulation, drawling stresses ('Exchek*ar*'), slight hesitations ('initi-a-tive', 'Bee-Bee-See'), quick irony ('half-baked') and rather distant benevolence ('I hope you will call us the Arts Council for short. . . . We have carefully selected initials which we hope are unpronounceable') recalls that era of wise and good governors planning, with high seriousness, the future happiness of their peoples. Having started with the idea of replacing what the war had taken away, 'we soon found', Keynes said, 'that we were providing what had never existed even in peacetime'.

Keynes's thoughts were by this time centred on his old dream of making London the artistic capital of Europe. The chance came when the lease of the Royal Opera House, Covent Garden, came up for renewal. During the war it had been used as a dance hall, but in April 1944 the music publishers Boosey and Hawkes were granted a five-year lease to restore it as a 'centre of opera and ballet'. Keynes became chairman of a Covent Garden Committee, set up to manage the theatre on a sub-lease from the music publishers. A single letter to his Treasury colleague, Sir Alan Barlow, in January 1945, secured the necessary funds.[67] He then acquired for the Royal Opera House Ninette de Valois' resident ballet company based at the time at Sadler's Wells, the carrot being the annual subsidy he was able to offer Sadler's Wells as chairman of CEMA. David Webster, the new managing director of the Royal Opera House, recalled that when negotiations with the Sadler's Wells trustees 'seemed almost at a standstill, he [Keynes] snatched a few minutes in the assembled House of Lords while waiting for the arrival of the King [in August 1945 to open the New Parliament] to secure the co-operation of Lord Lytton [chairman of the Sadler's Wells Board of Governors], followed the conversation with a brilliant memorandum and the transfer of the Ballet to Covent Garden came soon afterwards'. If Keynes thought that there might be a conflict of interest between his Treasury, CEMA and Covent Garden positions he gave no sign of it. He took advantage of his official positions to make his contribution to the 'good life'.

39

The Great Compromise

I. ANGLO-AMERICAN SKIRMISHING

Maynard Keynes once told James Meade that whenever he read anything about nutritional issues 'my attention wanders'. In March 1943 Roosevelt suddenly proposed a United Nations conference on food and agriculture. When Penrose explained the President's nebulous ideas to Keynes, the great economist remarked glumly: 'What you are saying is that your President with his great political insight has decided that the best strategy for post-war reconstruction is to start with vitamins and then by a circuitous route work round to the international balance of payments!'[1] Delegates of the Allied and associated nations gathered at Hot Springs, Virginia in May and emitted a suitable blast of hot air. Lionel Robbins, a member of the British team, wrote in his diary: 'It is very easy to be friendly in a luxury hotel with all expenses paid and no binding commitments on the agenda.'[2]

More important from the British point of view were the informal conversations which had been taking place in Washington between the two Treasuries on the Keynes and White Plans. Each side used the question-and-answer method to probe the technical merits and political acceptability of the other's scheme. Berle had drawn up a list of questions about the Clearing Union the previous year. In May 1943, Keynes submitted his own questions about the Stabilization Fund. Dennis Robertson, temporarily attached to the Washington Embassy, dubbed them (after Browning on Galatians) the 'twenty-six distinct damnations / One sure if another fails'.

The insertion of Robertson into the financial negotiations added considerable intellectual firepower to the British team. If Keynes was the Impressionist of the new world order, Robertson was its pointillist, reducing Keynes's lyrical brushwork to exact relationships – much as Edward Bernstein did for White. What Keynes considered a defect when directed against his own theories was an invaluable asset when deployed against the 'Cherokee' of American draftsmen. Over the coming months Robertson and Bernstein would supply much of the detail by which the principles agreed by Keynes and White were made workable.

The one clear result of the summer discussions was to show that the Clearing Union was a non-starter in Washington. The United States would not budge on subscriptions and limited dollar liability. The European Allies who had enthused about the Clearing Union in London deserted to the Stabilization Fund in Washington, influenced less by what Robertson called 'White's individual tuition hours' than by their realisation that Washington, not London, paid the piper and would therefore call the tune. A Canadian plan, dubbed 'off White' in London, tried to work out a compromise between the British and American Plans.

Robertson thought that the British had three options: to fight to the last for the Clearing Union principle; to accept the Fund principle, and concentrate on enlarging its resources and entrenching the scarce-currency clause; or, while accepting the Fund, to preserve some of the elegance of the Clearing Union by turning 'unitas' into a real medium of exchange instead of a mere unit of account. Robertson believed that the tide of events was carrying them strongly towards the second, though it might be possible to deflect it towards the third. The first option would at some time be seen 'to have vanished quietly from the map'.[3]

Keynes in London could not disagree with this. He had told Harrod in April that the British would probably have to accept the American 'dress', but he insisted to Robertson that they should be 'as difficult and obstinate as possible' to gain real value for later concessions.[4] For Keynes the most important thing was to get the Americans committed to a scheme. If they preferred a Stabilization Fund, the superior technical merits of the Clearing Union should not be allowed to stand in the way.

The bilateral discussions in Washington concluded on 24 June in a 'friendly and extremely frank' atmosphere. In London, Keynes received yet another redraft of the White Plan, dated 10 July. While he thought it 'more logical and self-consistent' than previous drafts, it showed 'no increase in political wisdom and not much in technical capacity', while some provisions were drafted 'with great selfishness in the interests of a country possessing unlimited gold'. White had told Phillips that Congress had to be satisfied on four points: that the sterling–dollar peg be maintained at $4 to the pound, that America's liability be limited to $3bn, that Congress keep control over the gold value of the dollar, and that the monetary framework should be that of a fund, not a bank. Keynes recommended that Britain accept the 'substance of White's essential conditions', subject to three British requirements: that members should have more control over their exchange rates, that the Fund should not deal in a 'mixed bag of currencies', but only in international money (unitas), and that gold subscriptions should be no more than 12.5 per cent of quotas, the balance in non-negotiable government securities.[5] Unitas still lurked in the White Plan as a unit of account. Keynes regarded making it 'a true medium of international exchange' the 'most fundamental condition of a satisfactory compromise'.[6] To Jacob Viner he explained: 'If members of the Fund were to acquire a holding of unitas in exchange for their initial contributions and then, as a result of clearing operations, exchange these holdings of unitas between one another, there would be very much less difference between the basic structures of the two schemes than there is at present.'[7] In addition, Keynes hoped that unitas would enable the Fund at some future date 'to become a credit-creating agency'.[8] His insistence on preserving unitas became an obsession, and for many months proved the main stumbling block to an agreement.

The problem of the transition to peace was starting to cast its long shadow over the Article VII negotiations. Britain's debts to the sterling area were mounting up alarmingly, while the US administration, in British eyes, was managing Lend–Lease so as to prevent the British from building up an adequate post-war reserve. Given the niggardliness of adjustment finance offered by White's Fund, how soon would Britain be able to meet its Article VII commitment to abandon its discriminatory trade and payments system? Early in August Halifax suggested to Secretary of State Hull that Britain send a strong delegation to Washington in September to initiate informal discussions on the whole field covered by Article VII. He emphasised the importance of Britain and the United States reaching prior agreement before these matters were negotiated internationally. White agreed. Having got most countries to agree to his Plan, he was at last prepared to confront the British. Keynes was delighted. Shortly before his departure for Washington, he told Winant that 'he believed that in a weekend of conversations Dr. White and he could reach agreement on most basic points of the currency proposals'.[9]

Keynes spent as much of August as he could at Tilton, relaxing over his mother's history of the High Stewardship of Cambridge, which he found 'most fascinating and interesting'. His health was no longer as perfect as it had been in June, but by the end of the month he had benefited greatly from his rest and the course of frictional tepid baths which the Ogre, Dr Plesch, was giving him in London.

II. MERGING THE TWO PLANS

On 3 September Maynard sailed from Glasgow with Lydia on the *Queen Mary*, bound for 'preliminary, informal, non-committal, purely unofficial' discussions with the Americans on Article VII. He was part of a strong British delegation headed by Richard Law, now Minister of State at the Foreign Office. It included David Waley and Frank Lee of the Treasury, Lionel Robbins of the Economic Section of the War Cabinet, Nigel Ronald of the Foreign Office, Gerald Clauson of the Colonial Office, Percivale Liesching, James Meade and Robert Shackle representing the Board of Trade, and P. W. Martin from the Ministry of Food. Lucius Thompson-McCausland came along as Keynes's personal assistant with a watching brief for the Bank of

England. In Washington they would be joined by Dennis Robertson and Redvers Opie from the Embassy. Sir Frederick Phillips would not be there. His unstinting labours for Britain's cause were over. In July he had returned to London for consultation. Already mortally ill with cancer, he died on 14 August. His passing was universally mourned. In June, Berle had told Robbins, 'Phillips is worth his weight in gold to the British Empire. If you recalled Phillips, Morgie would almost call off the war. They sit and talk to one another, about ten sentences to the hour; and everything is grand.'[10] Phillips's silences would no longer be available to soothe Anglo-American relations.

The instructions from the War Cabinet, drafted by Hugh Dalton, President of the Board of Trade, were based on Keynes's minimum requirements, with the significant addition that sterling balances should not be included in any monetary scheme. As late as 22 June Keynes had approved White's suggestion that these balances should be funded – that is, blocked by Britain, and paid back over a long period through the Fund. In effect, White was offering to put US dollars – though not very many – behind Britain's wartime liabilities. In the Bank of England's view, the blocking of sterling balances would spell the end of the sterling area, which may also have been White's motive in putting forward his proposal.[11]

Before boarding the *Queen Mary*, 'the whole party took breakfast at a large table in a private room at the Central Hotel, Glasgow, Keynes making the unseemly witticism that "it looks more like the last supper than the first breakfast"'. On the launch carrying them out to the ship, James Meade encountered Lydia 'ordering her distinguished husband to lie down and rest'. Once on board, the captain, a 'bluff and hearty sadist', threatened to clap them in irons if they broke any of the rules. One of the rules was to wear life-belts continuously. 'To have seen them [Maynard and Lydia] thus was a precious and unforgettable memory,' gushes Roy Harrod.

The experts hoped that the two sides would be able to hammer out agreed proposals on the main elements of the Grand Design – money, investment, trade, buffer stocks, employment. These could then be put to the two governments, and, if they agreed, an international conference would follow to endorse the rules and set up the institutions of the post-war system. But there was a large snag. Only the two monetary Plans had reached a relatively advanced stage of technical development, possible compromise and political support. All the rest were ideas floating around departments in the two governments. They were all Article VII matters; to Meade they were all interdependent. But, if they were all expected to go forward together, the risk was that the monetary Plan would fall by the wayside.

The British had with them not just White's revised proposal for the Stabilization Fund, dated 10 July, but also a revised version of a plan for his 'Reconstruction and Development Bank', which Redvers Opie had forwarded from Washington just before they sailed. This now aimed, in addition to reconstructing the war-shattered economies, to provide or guarantee capital for industrial development at low interest rates. Attached to it would be an Essential Raw Materials Development Corporation and an International Commodity Stabilization Corporation. But the crucial money-creating powers which had so excited Roy Harrod had been omitted; and the US administration was split on the merits of what remained of the plan, though Morgenthau favoured it.[12] On the voyage over, Keynes approved its spirit, but savaged its mechanics as 'Bedlam' and its drafting as 'positively Sumerian'. He objected strongly to two features – that debtor countries should contribute as much as creditor countries to the Bank's capital, and the severity of sanctions on defaulters. He 'gave us by way of a digression a marvellous proof of the fact that international investment always had been and always would be defaulted'.[13] The British delegates agreed not to bring up discussion of the Bank until the Americans did.

Keynes noted that White's 10 July draft of the Stabilization Fund had already been circulated to Congress. The increased Fund resources and greater flexibility for exchange rate adjustment apparently agreed with the British in June had been cancelled and the gold element in the subscription upped to between 25 and 50 per cent, depending on size of reserves, 'although they are aware that this provision is not acceptable to anyone'. All this would reduce the American team's negotiating flexibility.[14] Fighting off seasickness, the delegation met frequently during the voyage to concert its negotiating strategy. Meade was much encouraged by the line Keynes took: 'He enthusiastically supported the view that we should press for a consideration of all these projects as forming a single whole. I had feared that he might consider it his ... job to fight with the Americans toughly on the details of the monetary arrangement, and disassociate himself and the Treasury ... from other parts such as the Commercial Union.'[15] In fact, this is exactly what Keynes did.

Meade's awe-struck diary continues to give glimpses of Keynes in action. On the train journey from New York to Washington on Saturday 11 September, 'Keynes was in first-class form. The first part he spent reading the newspapers and periodicals at a fantastic rate. His great enjoyment was Hitler's speech on the defection of Italy which he continually asserted he was enjoying so much because Hitler was enjoying it all so much' – a somewhat obscure remark. 'There was a flow of acid comment on the American country-side, their air-raid precautions, lack of birds and the sterility of the land! He and Lydia and (Nigel) Ronald indulged in a tremendous discussion on modern painting; and the whole journey was rounded off by Lydia singing the Casse-Noisette music at the top of her voice and dancing it with her hands.'[16]

This time Maynard and Lydia checked in at the Statler Hotel. They preferred it to the Mayflower, because it had a coffee shop, where Keynes could take light meals. They did not expect to stay long. Keynes, as already noted, thought that he and White could settle all outstanding issues in a weekend's discussion; White thought it might take 'a week or so'. In fact, Keynes remained in America for six weeks, and the joint statement of experts was not finalised and published till April 1944.

Both sides agreed to set up groups to discuss the different elements of the Grand Design – money, investment, buffer stocks and commercial policy – with plenary sessions to 'stress the interdependence of all the subjects'. The first of these plenaries took place on 20 September, with Law leading off for the British 'in a most moving speech'. Keynes wound up for Britain when it continued a day later. 'I have never heard him better,' wrote Meade enthusiastically, 'more brilliant, more persuasive, more witty or more truly moving in his appeal ... that we should treat the whole economic problem as a unity and be prepared to present to the public a total solution of the problems of unemployment and of raising standards of living.'[17] Keynes had indulged in one of those flights of fancy which so endeared him to the technicians. Recalling the main theme of his essay 'The Economic Possibilities for Our Grandchildren', he claimed the world was in transition 'from an era of scarcity to an era of abundance', which would require a change in 'all our habits and traditions'. The problem would be one of maintaining sufficient demand; the difficulty of agreeing a global plan was that 'different countries were moving through the period of transition at different speeds'. The rich countries would need to invest in the poor ones, but the notion that they could expect full repayment of their investments was out of date, hence the need for new investment institutions.[18] All this was music to the idealistic James Meade. He was soon to discover an alarming gap between Keynes's rhetoric and his negotiating style.

Keynes naturally led for Britain on the Monetary Group, where he was normally flanked by Robbins, Robertson, Waley, Opie and Thompson-McCausland. (Meade joined the group later.) Keynes had started the monetary discussions privately with White on 13 September in a 'friendly and uncontroversial' way. He was soon able to report that they were 'going very well'.[19] White readily agreed that the Fund's resources should be increased: he was much more concerned that US liability should be limited. They circled round the problem of the transition to peace. Keynes said that the Stabilization Fund could not meet Britain's 'immediate post-war adverse balance', and that Britain might have to continue with its wartime controls. White apparently made no objection. Britain, he said, would be free to keep its sterling area arrangements for an indefinite period. He thought that Lend–Lease would continue till after the end of the Japanese war, now expected to last longer than the European one. They both thought that an international conference of ministers to approve their handiwork might be held in December or January. Keynes was impressed by White's willingness to take 'a high intellectual interest in all these questions and approach ... them on that plane and not on official or bureaucratic lines'.[20] The impression that all would be sweetness and light was soon, however, dispelled.

On 15 September, the Anglo-American monetary group held the first of eight meetings. Detailed minutes were kept by both sides. Supplemented by James Meade's diary and Thompson-McCausland's reports to the Bank of England they give a full, and sometimes vivid, account of the experts at work. The matter was often forbiddingly technical. Fifty years later there would have been overhead projectors, computer print-outs, graphs. As it was the meetings were dominated by verbal duels between Keynes and White – the rapier versus the blunderbuss. Richard Gardner says 'they were not unlike two vain and rather jealous economics professors striving to impress a university seminar'. Keynes was the intellectual superior, but White held the better cards.[21] Meade wrote: 'Ten years ago at Oxford I should never have dreamed that an economist could live in such a heaven of practical application of *real* economic analysis!'[22] The willingness to engage in argument on the merits of the case was what distinguished this seminar from the normal political pow-wow. But Keynes, White and the others were also Britons and Americans, representatives of their countries, negotiating under the authority of their governments, and therefore spokesmen for their countries' national interests. Both sides were prepared to say, when it suited them, that the other's proposals would be unacceptable to their governments – or, in the American case, to Congress and the 'American people'.

The seminars tended to follow a set pattern: the British proposed, the Americans disposed. This was the inevitable consequence of the asymmetry of power. The British were seeking to modify an American plan to their advantage. They punched: the Americans counter-punched. Both Keynes and White found the confrontations nervously exhausting. Keynes was 'sorely tried by White's rasping truculence', White, terrified by open debate with Keynes, 'tended to over-react, to the point that it affected his health'.[23] White used to get sick arguing with Keynes, because he was outgunned, sending, whenever possible, Bernstein in his place.[24]

Keynes's hope of settling the outstanding disagreements over a weekend of discussions proved wildly over-optimistic, because the technical questions masked large political differences. The British position was that the smaller the resources of the Fund, the larger must be the latitude given to members to do what they wanted; the Americans countered that the larger their liability, the more discipline the fund needed to exert over potential debtors.

White had set the Fund's aggregate resources at $5bn, in contrast to the Clearing Union's $26bn. He wanted the US liability limited to $2bn. Before the monetary conversations opened, he agreed to increase the capital of the Fund from $5bn to $8bn–$10bn (depending on how many nations joined), with a US contribution limited to $3bn rather than $2bn. This was to be balanced, though, by increased gold subscriptions.

These issues were argued out in the meetings of 17, 24 and 28 September. Keynes insisted that no member be 'required' to subscribe more than 12.5 per cent of its quota in gold. The US formula of 25 to 50 per cent gave a 'gold complexion to the scheme which we should find it hard to accept'. He suggested instead that countries with growing gold stocks might be requested to increase the gold fraction of their subscriptions. This would gradually equip the Fund with the 'ample gold reserves' the Americans wanted. Bernstein explained that the White formula should be understood to mean that a member's minimum gold subscription to the Fund should be 25 per cent of its quota or 10 per cent of its gold and foreign exchange reserves, whichever was smaller. Keynes was eventually convinced – though not till he got back to London – that this would actually reduce the amount of gold Britain would be required to pay in.

In the White draft, contributed quotas and borrowing quotas were the same. If a country paid in $100m in gold and $400m in securities, its borrowing quota would be $500m. It was obvious that the total borrowings could not exceed the Fund's total holdings. But there was no reason why an individual country's maximum borrowing quota should be exactly the same as its contribution. At the 24 September meeting, Keynes proposed that a country should be allowed to borrow up to 150 per cent of its quota. This meant that with $8bn of subscriptions, aggregate borrowing powers would amount to $12bn, 'though it was not possible that everyone should be using their full powers at once'. Bernstein replied that the Stabilization Fund scheme did not insist on precise equality between contributed and borrowing quotas, but the inequality should not be too great, or the Fund would run out of available currencies. When the discussion was resumed on 28 September, White pointed out that subscribed quotas were not the limiting factor in borrowing, since the Fund would be able to supply small countries with foreign currencies up to three or four times their quotas. This was more flexible than the British proposal, which, in order to provide for exceptional needs of individual members, would increase facilities available to all members. However, the Americans made important concessions to the British view. The Fund would be allowed to borrow additional currency from a member; and it would be allowed to increase its holdings of a (deficit) member's currency to up to 200 per cent of its quota. This represented a sizeable increase in the Fund's lending facilities over and above its subscribed capital.

But the Americans insisted that any money the Fund lent to a member in excess of its gold subscription would be at its own discretion. As they saw it, the only way to reconcile limited liability to supply currencies with exceptional demands for currencies was to police the supply. In White's 10 July draft, a member's unconditional right to borrow a currency was limited to the amount of its gold subscription. Above this, credit would be conditional on 'satisfactory measures' by the borrowing country to 'correct the disequilibrium in the country's balance of payments'. The British rejected the view that a country's unconditional borrowing right should be no greater than its gold subscription. As Keynes had put it to Viner, the issue was 'at what stage in the rake's progress' conditionality would start to apply. It dominated the meeting of 17 September and debate was resumed on 24 September and 4 October. It was never satisfactorily resolved.

At the 17 September meeting Keynes insisted that 'discretionary policing' should not apply to the quotas themselves, only to borrowings which exceeded the quotas. Otherwise drawing rights could never be established as a central bank reserve in competition with gold. The British argued that the Fund should be a 'passive transfer agent' not an 'active discretionary authority'. Keynes remarked, further, that any discretionary rights of the Fund should be framed so as to distinguish between a 'developed country managing its affairs prudently' and an 'irresponsible country anxious to exploit a new source of borrowing'. White replied that it would be foolhardy to expose the Fund to abuse. He explained that his aim was to prevent the Fund's facilities being used to finance capital flight or foreign loans by a country which couldn't afford to issue them.

At the meeting of 24 September, Berle was in the chair, White was away ill and Bernstein took the US Treasury part. Bernstein insisted that, beyond the drawing right guaranteed by the gold subscription, the Fund would supply foreign currencies at its discretion, having the power to refuse supply 'if its resources were being abused'. Keynes retorted that Bernstein's proposals would cut at the root of confidence. Emmanuel Goldenweiser of the Federal Reserve Board agreed that large countries would find Bernstein's procedure 'intolerable'.

The Americans were prepared to soften the wording, but not the substance. In the 4 October meeting White restated his view that the Fund's facilities were a privilege not a right, and were therefore rightly subject to a behaviour test. Keynes replied that the US proposals 'did not get over the objection that a member's actions would be subject to scrutiny the moment its currency in the Fund equalled its [gold] quota' and that he thought there was only a remote chance that the British government would accept it.

Keynes summarised his views to Jacob Viner on 17 October:

> Our view has been very strongly that if countries are to be given sufficient confidence they must be able to rely in all normal circumstances on drawing a substantial part of their quota without policing or facing unforeseen obstacles.... [The] Clearing Union may have been too strict on this, though this was actually balanced ... by the much greater size of the quotas.... No doubt it is a difficult issue. But I am sure that it would be very unwise to try to make an untried institution too grandmotherly.[25]

The debate over the 'nuances of uncertainty'[26] attached to drawing rights continued beyond Washington.

An equally contentious issue was exchange rates. The White draft erected barriers against unilateral changes in exchange rates. For the first 'uncertain' three years after the war members would be allowed to change their initial rates by 10 per cent without Fund approval, and by more than that with majority approval. Thereafter, rates could be altered only to correct a 'fundamental disequilibrium' and with the approval of three-quarters of the member votes.

The Clearing Union had also envisaged fixed exchange rates, but it made a difference to the British that the monetary scheme would be White's and not Keynes's. In the Keynes Plan the United States was liable, in theory, to accept up to $23bn in other countries' paper; in the White Plan, this was whittled down to $3bn. The British thus placed increasing weight on a country's freedom to devalue its currency or refuse to accept a surplus country's goods.

In its instructions to the British team the Cabinet had insisted on retaining national sovereignty over exchange rates with the possibility of an 'objective test' for exchange rate changes. Meade had been advocating 'some objective statistical test' for allowing quantitative import restrictions in his Commercial Union scheme.[27] Keynes claimed that the only suitable test was if the production costs of one country were inflating faster than those of another. Meade thought that this 'won't do' and worked out an 'objective test' of his own, based on trends in a country's balance of payments and reserve position.*

Keynes was unconvinced. But he commissioned, and endorsed, a note by Meade on 'The Problem of Securing Sufficient Elasticity for Changing the Exchange Rates',[28] which steered a tortuous path between the American demand for fixed rates and the British demand for flexibility. Exchange rates should be changed only to correct a 'fundamental disequilibrium'. Approval of a 10 per cent change over a ten-year period would be automatic. Larger changes would require Fund approval. In deciding whether to give such approval, the Fund should take into account changes in relative costs and changes in the balance of payments (combining the Keynes and Meade 'tests'), but not the social or political policies which had led to the disequilibrium. If Fund approval was withheld, the member could leave the Fund.

* Meade's test was that 'a country would be permitted to depreciate its currency by x per cent in any year if during the preceding year the fall in its net holding of International Currency, of Gold and of quick assets in the currencies of countries which were members of the Monetary Union (after deducting corresponding quick liabilities) was more than y per cent of its total international trade'. Slightly modified, this would also give a test for quantitative import restrictions.

White was sceptical about the possibility of an objective test. 'Would not reliance on the Fund's discretion be more satisfactory in a matter so full of politics?' Objecting to the procedure of the American proposal, Keynes said that discussing exchange rate changes in 'mixed company' would give rise to speculation; a devaluation must come about as a sudden act on a certain date after secret discussions. White thought that a unilateral emergency change would not be needed if there was continual contact between the three or four major Treasuries, and that speculation would be held in check by exchange controls.

Keynes's negotiating position was undermined by the British Treasury's refusal of his proposal. It would not accept surrender by treaty of its 'right to protect employment by exchange adjustment', and wanted a general promise to consult about exchange rate changes substituted for the Keynes–Meade formula. Keynes cabled back that 'it would be a very drastic change to propose that every country should be free to make unlimited unilateral alterations in its exchange merely after consultation. All of us here think that [our] proposals give sufficient elasticity and independence. We would be sorry to have to go back so completely on the idea of having some definite rules to preserve exchange stability.' Dalton in London surmised that 'while the cats are away, the mice, led by the rump of the Treasury and the bloody Bank of England', were seizing the chance to sabotage agreement with the United States. He persuaded the War Cabinet to tone down the instructions.[29]

At the joint monetary meeting of 4 October discussion turned on 'whether an undertaking to consult the Fund before changing the exchange rate should replace an obligation to obtain the Fund's approval for changes'. The Americans conceded Keynes's proposal that a country's domestic policies should not be a ground for refusing a devaluation. But there remained a gap between the two sides about how much discretion countries were to be allowed.

The British also extracted concessions on 'scarce currencies'. The White draft of 10 July only provided for the 'rationing' of scarce currencies by the Fund, but without indicating how this would work. Kyriakos Varvaressos, the governor of the Greek Central Bank, had pointed to the lack of Fund discipline on persistent creditors. At the 28 September meeting Keynes took up this argument: if, when a country's currency was declared scarce, other members were expected to maintain their exchange rates against the scarce currency, they must be allowed to restrict payments in that currency. On 4 October the United States group accepted this, but hoped that it would lead to import, not exchange, controls.[30] Meade, who was simultaneously engaged in the trade negotiations, could not believe that 'Hawkins and the other people in the State Department realise what their Treasury people are suggesting'.[31] Keynes reported to the Chancellor of the Exchequer that the new scarce-currency clause 'puts the creditor country on the spot so acutely that in the view of us all, the creditor country simply cannot afford to let such a situation arise'.[32]

Keynes's main effort to get the Stabilization Fund to put on the clothes of the Clearing Union was his proposal to monetise unitas. The crucial structural difference between the Clearing Bank and the Stabilization Fund set-ups was that in the Keynes Plan member central banks banked with the Clearing Bank, whereas in the White Plan the Fund banked with member central banks. Member central banks would subscribe their quotas to the Fund's account with them, from which the Fund could make payments to any other central bank, whenever that country's currency 'cannot be disposed of in the foreign exchange markets within the [exchange rate] range established by the Fund'. In Keynes's view, this had the overriding defect that multilateral clearing was not assured, since the Fund, at its discretion, could refuse to buy (say) sterling with its francs, even though sterling was not, in general, in over-supply. The Fund's prospective hyper-activism was also anathema to the Bank of England, which feared it could use its discretion to undermine the sterling area. The Bank instructed Thompson-McCausland that on 'no account' must the Fund be allowed to 'buy or sell currencies or gold'.[33]

Keynes's proposal for a unitas-based Stabilization Fund, designed to overcome these defects, was sent to White on 21 September. Subscriptions would be sterilised – the Fund could not transfer them to other members. In return for their deposits, member banks would receive 'credits' of unitas which they could trade with each other. This achieved two main purposes. It ensured that inter-Fund settlements were multilateral: 'a monetised unitas [would] express a generalised ... claim on the world at large' rather than a claim on a particular currency. And it assured the prized British goal of Fund 'passivity'.[34]

In a 'brilliant speech' to the joint monetary group on 24 September, Keynes 'expounded the case for making Unitas into a real transferable money'. The bluntness of Bernstein's rejection of the idea is apparent even in the bland language of the minutes: the United States, he said, would want an assurance that 'a share in their production was not claimable by tender of a new "trick" currency, and that the economic power represented by the United States gold reserves would not be substantially diminished'. More pertinently, he stressed that 'no magic could disguise the fact that the Fund might be short or long in particular currencies even in unitas terms'.

The meeting on 28 September was largely 'a duet between White and Keynes'. White rejected Keynes's proposal because it would give every country a claim on dollars, leading to the possibility that the US would have to supply the Fund with dollars equal to the total drawing rights of all the other members. 'It would, he felt, be bringing in the clearing-union principle by the back door.' White, however, made important concessions to the British position. The Fund's accounts were to be inter-convertible, and dealings in currencies take place only 'on the member's initiative'. Most of the British monetary delegates thought these concessions were enough, but not Keynes, who continued to fight for his pet. Meade was horrified. It would be 'criminally foolish' to break on this matter. If Keynes persisted 'we must organise a revolt'. Meade went through the roof when he heard that the Bank of England from London was insisting on the monetisation of unitas: 'all the other elements in these talks – our Commercial Union, the Commodity proposals, Investment, Full Employment, Cartels – all hang upon a successful outcome of the monetary talks; in the monetary talks we look like obtaining every point of substance – and there is talk of the Bank of England making agreement impossible on something which doesn't matter a tinker's cuss. Who governs England?'[35]

Keynes was much more alive than was Meade to the power of the Bank of England to sabotage an international currency scheme if it joined opponents of it in the government. So Keynes reserved Britain's position. Ironically, it was the British insistence on multilateral clearing which led the United States to make currency convertibility on current account a condition of receiving Fund assistance, which in turn led the British to the concept of an indefinite transition period.

Throughout the negotiations Whitehall had wobbled between supporting Keynes's efforts to make the Fund more like the Clearing Union and preserving Britain's freedom on the assumption that it would not be. One particularly unfortunate consequence of this uncertainty of aim was the deletion of that section of the White draft dealing with the funding of 'abnormal' wartime balances. The idea was that the Fund would gradually buy the temporarily 'blocked' sterling balances from Britain, Britain repaying the Fund 40 per cent of their value over a period of twenty years. Bound by his instructions, Keynes told White that Britain was anxious to postpone any serious discussion on 'abnormal' (sterling) balances. This momentous decision ensured that sterling debts remained unfunded for thirty years, the disproportion between reserves and liabilities leading to a succession of sterling crises in the post-war era.

By early October, the technicians had got as far as they could, and the atmosphere was not improving. The carefully calculated British strategy to reduce the areas of disagreement had clearly expired by the time of the following entry in Meade's diary, dated 4 October:

> What absolute Bedlam these discussions are! Keynes and White sit next each other, each flanked by a long row of his own supporters. Without any agenda or any prepared idea of what is going to be discussed they go for each other in a strident duet of discord which after a crescendo of abuse on either side leads up to a chaotic adjournment.... Today we first discussed the problem of policing the use of the fund, on which some compromise may be found. Incidentally it became crystal clear

that White believes that discriminatory exchange or import restrictions should be imposed against scarce currency countries rather than that exchange rates should be allowed to go. . . . We then discussed flexibility of exchange rates. The Americans insist on great stability, and we oppose with a demand for almost unilateral freedom to depreciate. Everyone seems to have forgotten the possibility of an objective test . . . which should logically provide the solution of allowing the Americans to say to *their* public that unnecessary competitive exchange depreciation had been ruled out and us to say to *our* public that we could not be prevented from depreciating if and when it became really necessary.[36]

When discussion turned to procedure, there were more explosions. Morgenthau himself had put White's plan for a Reconstruction and Development Bank officially on the conference agenda at a lunch he gave for Keynes on 14 September.[37] At the final meeting of the Plenary Conference on 30 September, from which Keynes was absent, White suddenly anounced that his scheme – minus the Commodity Stabilization Corporation – having received the President's approval, was about to be presented to Congress and published, without any consultation with the British or, apparently, the State Department. The next day Keynes got White round to see him and told him 'frankly and crudely' what they thought of him. This wigging, according to Keynes, entirely restored White's good humour and he promised to postpone publication. The document itself, Keynes thought, was 'extremely odd'. There were some 'very genuine motives' behind it, but these were 'so wrapped up and camouflaged' that it looked like the work of a 'near lunatic'.[38] Meade was sunk in despair. 'Keynes is now calling White's investment plan loony,' he wrote in his diary. 'That man is a menace in international negotiations.'[39]

Keynes's ill temper did not end there. At the meeting of the joint monetary group on 6 October, both sides agreed to prepare a directive for the Drafting Committee, which would be charged with fleshing out the principles which the experts wanted their governments to accept, as a prelude to an international monetary conference. The final meeting on Saturday 9 October, called to consider drafts of the directive prepared separately by British and American teams, was explosive:

Keynes [wrote Meade, who was not there] has been storming and saying (when Bernstein in place of a short note . . . produced yet another typically Bernstein document), 'This is intolerable. It is yet another Talmud. We had better simply break off negotiations.' Harry White has replied: 'We will try to produce something which Your Highness *can* understand.' Negotiations *were* apparently broken off at lunch time. Then the Americans produced a more reasonable draft. . . . This was discussed at 4.30 and the scene ended with love, kisses and compliments all round. But it augurs ill for the future unless these negotiations can somehow or another be got out of the hands of two such prima donnas as White and Keynes.

Keynes believed his 'explosion' had led to the 'breakthrough'. Bernstein had tried to get the British to sign an interpretation of the Stabilization Fund 'which the Talmudist wrote many months ago and has never been willing to alter, if he could help it, by one iota'. The other members of the Group 'thought I had overdone it, but after we had left the meeting a telephone message came along ... that the paper was withdrawn. ... It is one example, in my judgment, of how important it is in this country to react strenuously.'[40]

Harry White's summary of what had been achieved in Washington is just: 'It is a part compromise, but much more like the American plan.'[41] The two sides managed to produce an 'Anglo-American Draft Statement of Principles' calling for the setting up of 'an international stabilisation fund'. The US was given a quota 'not to exceed' $3bn, and Britain one of about $1.3bn. The essential feature of the Anglo-American compromise was that, in return for accepting the US principle of limited liability, Britain won a small increase in Fund resources, a greater freedom to devalue without reference to 'the domestic social or political policies which may have led to the application', a promise of passivity in currency dealings and the right 'temporarily to restrict the freedom of exchange operations' in a currency which the Fund had declared 'scarce'. Remaining disagreements were covered by rival statements. The two sides continued to dispute the proportion of gold subscriptions, the conditionality attached to drawings, the latitude for exchange rate depreciation, provisions for repaying borrowings, and the degree to which the Fund might finance capital transactions. There was a general British reservation about a non-unitas Stabilization Fund and Keynes – or rather Thompson-McCausland – produced a unitas version of the Joint Statement.[42] There was no clear acknowledgement of a transition period before the Fund would come into operation. One clear gain, soon to be lost, was the translation of the Principles from 'Cherokee' into English.

It was typical, Keynes thought, of the American way of doing business that White refused to sign the agreed document, which therefore bore Keynes's signature alone. 'During the war', he later wrote in some exasperation to the Chancellor, 'I have altogether spent five months in close negotiations with the United States Treasury and on no single occasion have they answered any communication of mine in writing, or confirmed in writing anything which has passed in conversation.'

Keynes continued to be baffled by how public business *was* done in America. He always tended to believe that the administration was guarding against phantom dangers; or, if they were real dangers, this was only because of poor presentation. Morgenthau had spent ten years at the US Treasury trying to appease a 'non existent public sentiment'. After Morgenthau had shown the experts' schemes to Congress, he mused: 'The difficulty is, of course, that these plans are presented to Congress in just about the most unattractive manner and with just about the most unattractive faces and unattractive voices that human nature can compass.' (The Senators' confusion had been compounded by the fact that 'Harry has chosen to call his Bank a fund and his fund a Bank.') He deplored the absence of the 'arts of government as we understand them. It may be that some other art, which we have difficulty in apprehending, is being employed.'[43] Keynes could never quite accept that manner of presentation, so important in a parliamentary regime, mattered little in the American system; the black arts were those of jaw-boning, arm-twisting and cutting deals.

Keynes gave his usual upbeat report on the performance of the British delegation. 'We have been a very happy party, with great concord all round.' This is not borne out by Meade's diary. Keynes started very well, eloquent, lucid, witty and enthusiastic, but got steadily more bad-tempered the further the negotiations progressed and the tireder he got. Meade was eventually made distraught by the way his 'ill-manners' in the monetary seminars jeopardised the progress he, Meade, was making with the Americans on commercial policy. Keynes, as Meade rightly surmised, had no 'fire in his belly' for free trade. He talked of the need to 'unleash and unshackle' monetary from commercial policy – a pun on the names of Liesching and Shackle who, together with Meade, were the Board of Trade officials conducting the negotiations on the latter. 'As you know', he wrote to Liesching on 8 October, 'I am ... a hopeless sceptic about this return to nineteenth century *laissez-faire*, for which you and the State Department seem to have such a nostalgia. I believe that the future lies with – (i) State trading for commodities; (ii) International cartels for necessary manufactures; and (iii) Quantitative import restrictions for non-essential manufactures. Yet all these ... instrumentalities for orderly economic life in the future you seek to outlaw.' Harrod, who quotes this letter, writes that it was 'partly meant to tease'.[44] There was more to it than that. First, Keynes was determined to get a monetary agreement accepted by the British government; hence his determination to 'unleash and unshackle' it from imperial preference, to which the Cabinet was firmly committed. Secondly, to the extent that White's Stabilization Fund fell short of his own much more grandiose Clearing Union – with no compensation for Britain in the Reconstruction and Development Bank – Keynes became more protective of national sovereignty and the right to indulge in what Robertson called 'Forbidden Tricks'. Thirdly, he doubted whether there was much enthusiasm in America, outside the State Department, for 'Hullism'. On this matter he was influenced by the bitter disputes which had been taking place in Washington that summer between British and American officials over the administration of Lend–Lease, and what these showed about America's post-war intentions.

Keynes was by now thoroughly alarmed at the prospect that Britain

would lack the means to pay its way after the war. Limiting Britain's gold
and dollar reserves to $600m had become official US policy at the end of
1942. This, together with the limitations on its exports which Britain had
accepted in September 1941 in return for Lend–Lease, meant that Britain
would start the peace with a massively adverse balance of payments deficit,
and reserves which fell far short of its rapidly accumulating debts to sterling-
area countries. Keynes's persistent attempts to slow down the rate of growth
of India's sterling balances foundered on the opposition of the India Office,
whose Secretary of State, Leopold Amery, he called a 'dangerous lunatic'.
Without some alleviation, it would be in no early position either to honour
a commitment to currency convertibility or to scrap its imperial preference
system and wartime controls on imports. Dean Acheson of the State Department understood most clearly that a policy of restricting British exports and
reserves during the war was inconsistent with the Article VII agenda. He
therefore pressed for policies which would allow Britain to build up its
reserves. He was defeated, however, by an alliance between Harry Dexter
White of the US Treasury and Leo Crowley, who had been appointed
head of the Foreign Economic Administration (successor of the Office of
Lend–Lease Administration (OLLA)) in July 1943. Crowley was an anti-British
American of Irish extraction, close to business interests in Congress. But
Harry White was the real author of the policy of manipulating the Lend–
Lease Agreement to limit the growth of British reserves. Keynes was only
peripherally involved in the Lend–Lease battles, but he left the Americans in
no doubt about his attitude. At a lunch he gave for officials of the Foreign
Economic Administration at the Statler on 24 September 1943 he asserted
Britain's determination to launch a 'frontal attack on the existing policy of
limitation [of reserves]'. His remarks had no effect. At a US Treasury meeting
on 29 September, White stated that 'the time had come to take a strong line
to reduce the lend–leasing of non-military goods'.

    Despite these undercurrents, Keynes found the post-Pearl Harbor atmos-
phere in Washington more congenial than when he had last been there
in 1941. He did not notice people as a novelist does, and his judgement
of them was based on pseudo-scientific clues (like the shape or condition of
their hands) rather than on close observation. Nevertheless, within these
limitations, he recorded some acute impressions of the Washington scene.
Adolph Berle was 'a queer attractive, unattractive figure in disequilibrium
with himself and the world'. Keynes's keen sense of the Jewishness of both
White and Bernstein did not blind him to distinctions between the two. His
depiction of Bernstein as a 'regular little rabbi, a reader out of the Talmud,
to Harry's political high rabbidom' is astute. Out of his rows, and progress,
with White, a wary admiration had developed:

    With Harry White, as you may suppose, we have been spending a
    vast amount of time. Any reserves we may have about him are a pale

reflection of what his colleagues feel. He is over-bearing, a bad colleague, always trying to bounce you, with a harsh rasping voice,
aesthetically oppressive in mind and manner; he has not the faintest
conception how to behave or observe the rules of civilised intercourse.
At the same time, I have a very great respect and even liking for him.
A very able and devoted public servant, carrying an immense burden
of responsibility and initiative, of high integrity and of clear sighted
idealistic international purpose, genuinely intending to do his best for
the world. Moreover, his over-powering will combined with the fact that
he has constructive ideas mean that he does get things done, which few
else here do. The way to reach him is to respect his purpose, arouse his
intellectual interest (it is a great softener to intercourse that it is easy to
arouse his genuine interest in the merits of any issue) and to tell him
off very frankly and firmly without finesse when he has gone off the
rails of relevant argument or appropriate behaviour.[45]

A little later Harry White told Roosevelt that Keynes was 'an extremely able
and tough negotiator with, of course, a thorough understanding of the
problems that confronted us, but when not negotiating or discussing points
of difference ... he was quite friendly'.[46]

Before he left Washington Keynes wrote to his parents 'We all really are
trying to make good economic bricks for the world after the war – however
hopelessly difficult the political problems may be.'

Maynard and Lydia spent a few days in New York, he using his 'best arts
of persuasion on the more obdurate bankers' and arranging for a show of
American pictures for CEMA, she seeing old ballet friends like Léonide
Massine. Her mother had died in Leningrad, still under German siege, while
she was in America. After returning to Washington for further Lend–Lease
discussions, they flew back by Clipper, arriving in London on 28 October.

Christmas at Tilton followed its now usual pattern. There was a shoot.
On Christmas Day, thirty-five sat down to lunch, for which 'Roma' had
prepared six rabbit pies. For the Charlestonians, Vanessa Bell and Duncan
Grant, Keynes had written out his forecasts for 1944. The European war, he
thought, would end between August and October, after a crushing Allied
offensive on both fronts. This date 'will suit President Roosevelt and he has
not overlooked this'. The last stages of the Japanese war 'may be long or
short but will remain as boring as they are now'. With Germany's capitulation 'new and harassing anxieties will arise. The fact that no-one has a
good solution will make it difficult to resist bad ones.' This time it was not
just Maynard's usual over-optimism. Few doubted that Germany would be
beaten in 1944. Safeguarding Britain's economic survival in the post-Lend–
Lease world had become a matter of urgency.

III. CONVINCING WHITEHALL

Two steps were now required to clinch the Washington agreement. The experts themselves had to resolve their remaining differences, and the two governments had to endorse their work. The first was more easily done than the second; and the second more easily done in Washington than in London. White, having got most of what he wanted from Britain – and the rest of the Allies – was now the pursuer rather than the pursued. He was supported by Morgenthau, and Morgenthau was supported by the President. Washington politics dictated speed, not delay. There was a Presidential election due in November 1944. An international treaty setting up Fund and Bank, signed, sealed and delivered and, if possible approved by Congress, would form part of Roosevelt's re-election campaign, enabling him to brand the Republicans as isolationists.

White got into action first, sending Keynes a letter with a revised draft statement of principles on 19 November. Keynes took a month to reply. He had been working through the text trying to rub away outstanding differences. The trivial issues were quickly disposed of, in exchanges between Keynes and White, and in discussions between White and Opie in Washington. Keynes accepted the American formula for gold subscriptions, and abandoned his insistence on gold sterilisation. On his suggestion, the International Stabilization Fund now started to be called the 'International Monetary Fund'.[47] On 17 December Keynes inserted a new section on transitional arrangements giving countries the right to maintain exchange controls for an indefinite period after the war.

Morgenthau and White could not understand the reason for the British delay in agreeing to publication of the experts' report, since they did not think it would commit the British government. They failed to appreciate that a government White Paper in Britain was more than an invitation to negotiate with Parliament. The British government was far from ready to make any commitments on the range of topics negotiated by the experts in Washington. Keynes noted that there were those who, having been foiled in their hope that 'these plans would die a natural death', now saw no need 'officiously to keep alive any international currency scheme at all'.

Keynes had to fight for the survival of the Joint Statement in the Treasury itself. The Chancellor, Sir Kingsley Wood, had died suddenly on 21 September, Sir John Anderson succeeding him. Anderson carried more weight in the Cabinet than Wood had done. But Keynes hardly knew him, and Anderson immediately came under other influences, notably that of Sir Wilfrid Eady. Eady had taken charge of overseas finance in the summer of

1943. While Keynes was abroad, Eady had teamed up with Henderson and the Bank of England to try to block the monetary deal. Dalton, with his acute political antennae, sniffed 'a high-powered intrigue to lessen [Keynes's] influence'.[48]

The alliance of a section of the Treasury with the Bank of England gave opponents of the Article VII agenda in the Cabinet their chance. Early in 1944, 'Hudson, Amery and Beaverbrook, with widespread Labour support, [sent] a spate of papers to the Cabinet and to Churchill opposing British entry into commercial talks with the State Department of the kind which had been envisaged by the Law Mission talks of September and October 1943'.[49] Prominent in the campaign was Churchill's court favourite Lord Beaverbrook, now Lord Privy Seal, a Canadian by birth, who had long espoused imperial economic union as a counterweight to American power. A Canadian observer wrote of an 'extraordinary harlequinade of colours', made up of 'old-fashioned Imperialists and old-fashioned protectionists, of doctrinaire socialists wedded in principle to planning and opposed in principle to gold and to international bankers, and finally of new-fangled economists (many of them at the Oxford Institute of Statistics) who favoured bilateralism on theoretical grounds'.[50] Churchill let the battle rage. Like Bevin he hated any suggestion of a gold standard, but was an instinctive free trader. However, on economic matters, he now spoke from memory. Addressing a meeting of the Party faithful in April 1943, he declared in ringing tones: 'It's all about dear food; we beat you on that before and we'll beat you again' – forgetting that he was now the leader of the Conservative Party, not the Liberal free trader of 1906.[51]

Having received Law's Report on the Washington conversations, the War Cabinet asked Law, on 21 December, to prepare a report on the matters on which ministers would have to decide. These covered the whole field of the Article VII negotiations. Keynes and other members of the Treasury and the Economic Section drafted the monetary section of Law's Report, and tried to answer questions put by ministers. The most hostile were by Bevin, Leo Amery and Robert Hudson, the Minister of Agriculture. The monetary section of Law's Report outlined two options, the first drafted by Keynes recommending acceptance of the Joint Statement, the second by Henderson recommending rejection. Once again, Keynes marshalled his arguments. Multilateral clearing was enormously to Britain's advantage, since 'our best sources of supply are not always our best markets'. The Washington Plan enabled countries to resume multilateral clearing by correcting the maldistribution of gold; the Plan was likely to 'double our resources to meet contingencies . . . not to be lightly rejected'.

Keynes argued that the compromise on exchange rates combined 'an orderly procedure for change with retaining a sufficient ultimate freedom of action to individual members'. Although monetisation of unitas was greatly to be preferred from the technical point of view, the Americans had objected that it could not pass Congress, and the experts thought the British should defer to the Americans on this point. On the transitional arrangements, the Treasury had sent a new clause to Washington, reserving for Britain full freedom in the transitional period. Britain should tell the United States frankly that it could not enter the proposed scheme unless America helped Britain after the end of Lend–Lease. The balance of advantage lay, not in postponing the scheme, but in clinching the deal as quickly as possible, because even in the interim period, when its provisions would be suspended, 'an authoritative organ of international discussion and consultation can play a specially significant part in finding the way out of the transition, where we would sit as equals, instead of waiting on the mat outside the US Treasury'.[52]

The Law Report was discussed in the War Cabinet on 9 February 1944, with Law in attendance strongly supporting the monetary compromise. A decision on what to do was needed, since Dominion representatives were coming to London to be briefed on the outcome of the Washington talks. The majority favoured the monetary proposals, despite 'a ludicrous paper' from Beaverbrook saying they meant a new gold standard, but the Cabinet did not know what to do about the other parts of the Grand Design. So it decided to set up a Committee on External Economic Policy to consider the Report further, consisting of the Chancellor, Oliver Lyttelton, Beaverbrook, Dalton, Law and Cherwell.

In this, and the subsequent Cabinet discussions, Churchill refused to give a lead. He complained that he did not understand complex economic issues, and anyway was too busy to study the papers. He was indifferent to anything except winning the war. Naturally enough, his mind was concentrated on the planned D-Day landings in Normandy. Still, with the war now more or less won, this attitude of detachment from post-war problems made less and less sense. It was to contribute greatly to the heavy Conservative defeat in 1945.

The Cabinet Committee met six times between 14 and 17 February, with Keynes attending the meeting on the 15th. Briefed by Cherwell about its goings-on, he reported to Waley at the Treasury on 17 February that it 'has been complete bedlam, which only Hoppy's hand keeps in any sort of order. Ministers are in perpetual session, driving one another crazy with their mutual ravings, the Beaver being mainly responsible, his approach being nothing short of criminal. All the same, a certain amount of progress is being made, not all of it in the wrong direction. . . .'[53]

The Bank of England put up a last-ditch fight against the experts' plan. Public acceptance of Fund principles would mean that 'we say publicly that we are working towards a system where sterling will be less useful. This can only make our transitional arrangements, where we are largely dependent on the credit of sterling, more difficult.'

Although he was a director of the Bank, Keynes's dismissal of the Bank's stand, in a letter to the Chancellor dated 23 February, was scathing:

The Bank is not facing any of the realities. They do not allow for the fact that our post-war domestic policies are impossible without further American assistance. They do not allow for the fact that the Americans are strong enough to offer inducements to many or most of our friends to walk out on us, if we ostentatiously set out to start up an independent shop. They do not allow for the fact that vast debts and exiguous reserves are not, by themselves, the best qualification for renewing old-time international banking.

He accused the Bank of wanting to lead the country down the road which led to disaster in 1931 – 'reckless gambling in the shape of assuming banking undertakings beyond what we have any means to support as soon as anything goes wrong, coupled with a policy which ... pays no regard to the inescapable requirements of domestic policies'.[54] Keynes's relentless exposure of the Bank's pretensions did eventually have an effect. 'It is sheer madness to think the Empire can create a cave where we take in one another's washing and ignore the rest of the world! ... The countries we sell to are not necessarily the countries from which we buy, and if we begin unilateral trading we return to *barter, the survival of the fittest* and *more war*.' The words were Catto's, but the thought is Keynes's.[55]

On 18 February, the Cabinet Committee recommended that discussions with Dominion experts on the monetary plan should proceed 'on the basis that, while no commitment will be entered into, our expectation is that at the appropriate time we shall find it to our advantage to participate in these schemes....' At the Cabinet six days later, Anderson expounded the case for a monetary agreement 'with heavy over-emphasised lucidity'. Beaverbrook railed against it, supported by Brendan Bracken and 'dull, deaf, boring' Hudson. Pandemonium broke out with everyone shouting at the same time. 'The PM ... deliberately allows the thing to get out of hand, explaining he hasn't had time to read the papers ... and why anyway should we be hustled, "just because a few officials from the Dominions are here; they can be entertained for a few days, and given drinks, and taken round to see the bomb craters".' After three hours, 'the PM said that it was clear we could reach no decision that night but he saw no harm in this Cabinet paper being given to their officials on the clear understanding that the Cabinet had reached no decision on it'. Churchill's understanding of what *had* been decided was that there should be no return to the gold standard, no abolition or reduction of imperial preferences except in return for tariff reductions elsewhere, and no taxation of food.[56] This was about the limit of his, and the Cabinet's, understanding of the three topics – monetary arrangements, commercial policy and buffer stocks – which had dominated the technicians' discussion of post-war economic problems over the previous year.

The politics of the battle only partially overlapped with the economic issues. Although the monetary plan could be attacked as a 'new gold standard', Keynes realised that the main political hostility to the Article VII programme was to its free-trade flavour. Specifically, the banning of 'discrimination' might bring together imperialists who wanted to strengthen commercial ties with the Empire and socialists who wanted state trading, particularly with the Soviet Union. So the only way to save the monetary plan was to detach it from the rest of the Grand Design. His line became that 'whilst the commercial scheme would find it difficult to function without the monetary scheme, the monetary scheme in no way needs the commercial proposals as an aid or support'. Beaverbrook, on the other hand, emphasised the interdependence of all the objectionable features. His tactic was to convince Churchill that the International Monetary Fund stood for the gold standard, hoping to discredit, 'by association in the PM's mind, the proposals that might affect Imperial Preference'.[57] 'The monetary plan', the Beaver wrote to Keynes, 'leads us on to the commercial plan which, in turn, is linked to the commodity scheme. This is an expression of praise for the project as a logical, self-consistent entity. But it will explain to you why I find myself in disagreement with each portion of it. I am at variance with the underlying doctrine because it is essentially international and free-trade, and because my own beliefs are neither the one nor the other.'[58]

The British were coming under increasing pressure from the US Treasury to get cracking. Early in April, Hopkins, prodded by Keynes, persuaded the Chancellor that the Fund should be allowed 'to go on alone.'[59] At a typically confused meeting of the Cabinet on 14 April, Anderson proposed that the government publish the revised Joint Statement without official commitment, and with several riders: the principles of the Fund would not apply to the transitional period, it would come into operation in stages, it would need supplementing by provisions for reconstruction, and Britain would not agree to join until it had solved its transitional balance of payments problems. They then discussed whether they should say they were in favour of the 'broad objective'. Churchill suggested some broad objectives of an innocuous kind, which Dalton pointed out applied to commercial, not monetary, policy. Beaverbrook 'keeps on shouting that he wants the Commercial Plan published as well', Bevin remarking, 'You want to strangle the one plan at birth and do an abortion on the other.' Everyone thought this was very funny.[60] In essence, the Cabinet ordered a stop to all economic planning talks with the United States except for those to do with the Fund. Churchill told the Commons in April that Article VII no more committed Britain to abandoning imperial preference than the USA to scrapping its tariffs.[61]

There were last-minute hitches, but the deed was done. On 22 April, the Joint Statement was published simultaneously in Washington, London, Moscow and Chungking. The London version had an explanatory preface by Keynes saying that the Stabilization Fund's purposes were the same as those set forth in the Clearing Union; when it was published, Keynes briefed the financial press and Members of Parliament.

He had returned to the Treasury only four days before, after recovering from a severe collapse of health. He had been working in the government for almost four years without any significant health problems under the kind of strain which caused his colleagues to drop like ninepins – a monument to the strength of his constitution, Plesch's ministrations and Lydia's *ukases*. On 17 February he explained to Margot Asquith why he could not come to see her at the Savoy:

> Although extremely recovered and being able, apparently to the outside world, to do a full day's work, this is not quite the full truth of the position. I am only able to get through the overwhelming work which I have by spending in bed practically the whole time when I am not in the office, and cutting off practically all social engagements. . . .

Winter and early spring were always bad periods for weather and work, made worse by the battle to save the Fund, and on 6 March Maynard experienced the premonitory 'heart flutters' which had preceded his collapse in 1937. He regarded them as 'primarily nervous and due to cumulative overwork and requiring nothing but rest'. He struggled on part-time at the Treasury for another few days, but they intensified, and on 17 March the Ogre prescribed complete bed rest for a month. Florence hoped that after it her son's engine 'will be like that of a car which has been de-carbonised'. He wrote to Dadie Rylands on 19 April: 'I have really been rather a long time in my ogre's hands, but at least for the last three weeks I should say that I have been suffering more from excess of drugs and all kinds of medicine than from anything else. I am now trying to get clear of these lowering intakes, and am going back to the Treasury to-day.' He added: 'What very good reviews Noël Annan has been writing in the New Statesman. Don't you think we might find some way of electing him a Fellow?' His health was now on a declining curve.

The tenth of May found Keynes in the Peers' Gallery of the House of Commons 'lacerated in mind and body' as speaker after speaker denounced the monetary plan for no other reason than that the Americans had agreed with it.[62] Some had been briefed, or had their speeches written, by the Hungarian economists Thomas Balogh and Nicholas Kaldor.[63] Keynes likened currency debates in the House to 'a loonies' picnic or an idiots' day out, where lunatic Members who on other occasions would be doomed to a decent restraint have a chance, for once, of catching the Speaker's eye'.[64]

Balogh's letter in *The Times* denouncing the experts' plan as 'highly dangerous' had appeared earlier that day. It concentrated on the insufficiency of the Fund's liquid resources, the unjustified hopes attached to devaluation, and the damage to the sterling area of the convertibility requirement. The spirit of the monetary plan was hostile to the imperial preference system and to trade agreements 'between countries desiring a planned production'. The scarce-currency clause would be inoperative so long as 'the United States is willing to purchase capital assets in the British Empire and the United Kingdom and thus provide Britain with dollars'. In a reply to Balogh, Keynes wrote that 'Schachtian minds ill consort with great Empires.'[65] He readily forgot his own past heresies when he had moved on. To an American correspondent he attributed the anti-American mood to the 'great anxiety that we should not be cutting ourselves off from conceivable expedients before we really know what expedients we are likely to need', to irritation at the 'completely untruthful charges that we are trying to take improper advantage' of Lend–Lease, and to annoyance at the apparently 'concerted effort' by America 'to prevent us doing anything at all to improve our export prospects after the war' – all of which, he did not add, he shared.[66]

Keynes himself took part in the debate in the Lords on 23 May. As a piece of rhetoric his speech reads wonderfully well. He adduced five main advantages of the monetary plan. First, it gave Britain complete freedom during a transitional period of 'uncertain duration' to retain its wartime system. Secondly, it offered currency convertibility. Without this, London would lose its pre-eminence and the sterling area would fall to pieces. 'To suppose', he said, 'that a system of bilateral and barter agreements, with no one who owns sterling knowing what he can do with it – to suppose that this is the best way of encouraging the Dominions to concentrate their financial system on London seems to me pretty near frenzy.' On the contrary, 'with our own resources so greatly impaired and encumbered, it is only if sterling is firmly placed in an international setting that the necessary confidence in it can be sustained'. Thirdly, it offered 'a great addition to the world's stock of monetary reserves' – in Britain's case worth about £325m. Fourthly, the scarce-currency clause would prevent 'the draining of reserves out of the rest of the world to pay a country which was obstinately borrowing and exporting on a scale immensely greater than it was lending and importing'. Finally, the plan set up international rules to provide orderly changes in exchange rates.

Keynes vehemently rejected the suggestion that the scheme represented a return to the gold standard – or a repudiation of his own theories. How could someone, he asked their lordships, who had attacked the gold standard as a 'barbarous relic' be accused of forging 'new chains to hold us fast to the old dungeon'?[67]

A critic of Keynes's exposition might well wonder what obligations Britain had in fact assumed in return for the benefits so enticingly displayed. He seemed to advocate the monetary plan as a way of maintaining the sterling area and imperial preference system, whereas the Americans all too clearly wanted to dismantle both. He claimed Britain's right to determine its own exchange rate, when the Americans wanted a fixed exchange-rate system. When told in Washington a little later that his line of defence had greatly embarrassed White and others, Keynes replied that it had been the only way to save the Fund from political extinction at Westminster.[68]

In the first five months of 1944 Keynes had fought virtually single-handed to protect the Joint Statement agreed in Washington from Treasury scepticism, Bank of England opposition and widespread political hostility. If ambiguous language was the price of success, then it was a price he was willing to pay, so great was the importance he attached to keeping America constructively involved in Europe's post-war life. In this judgement he was right, although he could not foresee what precise form that involvement would eventually take. Had America and Britain fallen out on the whole range of Article VII issues, had the relations between the two closest wartime Allies been seriously soured in 1944–5, who knows what the balance of forces would have been in the US administration, or what opportunities the Soviet Union would have had to exploit Anglo-American quarrels?

40

The American Way of Business

I. PREPARING FOR BRETTON WOODS

As the European war entered what it was hoped would be its final year, the United States stepped up pressure on Britain to honour Article VII of the Lend–Lease Agreement. This called on it to negotiate a liberal international trading order with the United States. The Americans expected the monetary agreement to be followed by a commercial agreement. But the British were stalling. The Morgenthau–Crowley policy of using Lend–Lease to control Britain's reserves cut across the State Department's aim of getting it to promise to liberalise its trade. A country whose 'quick assets' were about a tenth of the size of its 'quick debts' and whose export trade had been reduced to under 30 per cent of its pre-war level was an unlikely early candidate for Cordell Hull's free-trade world.

Like everyone else in Whitehall, Keynes deeply resented the way the administration of Lend–Lease seemed designed to weaken Britain's ability to survive without it. When Edward Stettinius's book, *Lend Lease: Weapon for Victory* was published in 1944 Keynes revealed his frustration at being in the trap which 'the most unsordid' act had sprung:

> You do not emphasise the point that the US Administration was very careful to take every possible precaution to see that the British were as near as possible bankrupt before any assistance was given. Nor do you refer at the end of the volume to the recent recrudescence of these same standards, according to which lend lease ought to be appropriately abated whenever there seems the slightest prospect that leaving things as they are might possibly result in leaving the British at the end of the war otherwise than hopelessly insolvent.[1]

Keynes did not interpret American policy as a deliberate attempt to destroy Britain's independence. He remained convinced of America's fundamental goodwill. Rather he looked on it as an ineluctable consequence of legal and business habits of mind unsuitable to the moral partnership in which the two countries were jointly engaged. His view, universally shared in Whitehall, was that the British had made much greater sacrifices for the common cause than had the United States, and that this asymmetry should be rectified as a *matter of justice*. This conviction was to determine his approach to Anglo-American negotiations for the rest of his life. Keynes's persistent aim, pursued whenever opportunity offered, was 'the retention by us of enough assets to leave us capable of independent action'. This thread runs from his attempt in 1941 to narrow the scope of Lend–Lease through to his continuing efforts to economise on war expenses so as to minimise Britain's external debt and hence its need for US aid after the war. His efforts to keep down sterling debts to India and the Middle East were vigorous but largely unavailing.[2] Early in 1944 he started to prepare a strategy for breaking the American embargo on increased reserves and exports. This was to feed into the Treasury's strategy for securing a continuation of Lend–Lease in Stage II, as it was now called – the period between the defeat of Germany and the defeat of Japan.

The state of the Article VII negotiations had been left as follows. The 'Joint Statement by Experts' on 21 April 1944 had finalised the principles on which an International Monetary Fund would be set up. The International Bank for Reconstruction had not been through a comparable process of bilateral or multilateral scrutiny, and remained, at this stage, merely a US Treasury proposal. Keynes had made a number of cogent and constructive criticisms in a memorandum of 21 February, redrafted early in March. Since Britain could not expect to receive much 'reconstruction' money, his main purpose was to minimise the British contribution, ensure that the Bank operated mainly by way of guaranteeing rather than making loans, and see to it that borrowers could spend the proceeds of a loan anywhere – that is, they were not to be tied to buying the lending country's goods. These comments were communicated to Washington. Keynes was starting to become an advocate of White's Bank in London. Frank Lee of the British Treasury had gone to Washington in September 1943 prepared to discuss 'Commod', as Keynes's Buffer Stock Plan was known. Robbins thought it was worth pursuing for the 'purchasing power which it distributes in times of depression and mops up in times of inflation'. But the Americans dismissed the Plan as a speculators' paradise, and it dropped out of the Article VII picture.

As already mentioned, the British had stalled on the trade talks. Harry Hawkins of the US State Department and James Meade of the Economic Section had made progress in Washington the previous autumn. The US proposal for a 'multilateral convention' on commercial policy was in close harmony with Meade's proposal for a Commercial Union. The British placed more emphasis on maintaining high levels of employment as a condition for trade liberalisation; the Americans looked to trade liberalisation to create high levels of employment. The Americans' main goal was the elimination of imperial preference; the British were after reductions in the US tariff. An obvious opportunity to trade preferences for tariffs existed. However, little attempt had been made to dovetail the principles of the IMF with those of the proposed commercial treaty. Within weeks of the Washington conversations, protectionists and subsidisers on both sides had raised a barrage of objections. A British Cabinet Committee on Commercial Policy was finally set up in July 1944. It was soon locked in battle with the Ministry of Agriculture. All this left the main matter of the Article VII agenda unresolved. But the State Department had not given up on it.

Morgenthau had hoped to have an inter-governmental conference in Washington at the end of May to ratify the Joint Statement of Experts. He wanted to offer a treaty setting up the Fund as his present to Roosevelt at the Democratic convention scheduled to start on 19 July. But with the British government still uncommitted, the most Anderson would agree to was to send experts to an international monetary conference as soon as they got an invitation. Keynes begged Harry White not to 'take us to Washington in July, which should surely be a most unfriendly act'. Morgenthau told White: 'Have it in Maine or New Hampshire, some place up in the mountains there.' On 25 May, Secretary of State Cordell Hull invited forty-four nations to attend a conference in early July at Bretton Woods, New Hampshire, 'for formulating definite proposals for an International Monetary Fund and possibly a Bank for Reconstruction and Development'. Before the conference, a smaller drafting committee would meet in Atlantic City, New Jersey.

These decisions took place against the background of the impending Allied invasion of Normandy. This for the first time concentrated the government's mind on the economic implications of the transition to peace. With the war against Germany expected to end a year or so before the war against Japan, semi-peace (Stage II) might start quite soon, and with it the problem of reconverting the British economy to peacetime production. When Stage II became Stage III (the end of the Japanese war) Britain would come face to face with the stark economic realities from which Lend–Lease had shielded it: a huge import surplus, lavish overseas cash spending, and a mountain of unfunded sterling debt. The need was so to manage Stage II that Britain started Stage III as little dependent on American help as possible.

Early in January 1944, Keynes had drafted some mildly alarmist 'Notes on External Finance in the Post-Japanese Armistice Transitional Period.[3] Now, alarmed by an American hint that Lend–Lease might be replaced by a loan for Stage II, Keynes wrote a memorandum in mid-May on 'The Problem of Our External Finance in the Transition', a final version of which was dated 12 June. Eady called it 'one of the most readable 10,000 official words of recent times'. Certainly, it was Keynes's last major state paper written at the full height of his powers – well balanced, urgent, scornful and much tauter than most of his late productions. His main point was that, without a change of policy, Britain could expect a financial disaster once Lend–Lease stopped. The government's assumption that after the war Britain could import all it needed to provide full employment and improved standards of living was 'blind faith'. He 'aimed to support faith with works'.

Keynes estimated a deficit on the balance of payments of between £1.5bn ($6bn) and £2.25bn ($9bn) over the first three post-war years. His solution was fourfold. First, Britain should fund the abnormal sterling balances at zero interest and over a long repayment period, though tied exports of capital goods might mean that some creditors got paid off more quickly; further, during the transition it should limit access to sterling area reserves to members' current dollar earnings. Secondly, Keynes aimed to raise Britain's *net* end-war reserves to £500m by stopping the United States 'chiselling at lend lease either currently or at the end of the German war', and by getting it to finance more of Britain's Middle and Far Eastern war spending. Thirdly, Britain should end its 'Lady Bountiful' attitude to the West Europeans and Russia. They should pay Britain gold, not IOUs, for reconstruction goods. Fourthly, Britain should prepare vigorously for an export drive, even if it meant stinting the consumer. Restrictions on British exports should be dropped in Stage II, without abatement of Lend–Lease. Reliance on American aid should be kept to a minimum – not more than $2bn to $3bn – and Britain should be prepared to 'do without it altogether'. The scale of the residual help needed depended entirely on the vigour with which Britain pursued the main objectives. Unfortunately:

> Our own habits are the greatest obstacle in the way of carrying out almost every one of the above recommendations. All our reflex actions are those of a rich man, so we promise others too much. Our longings for relaxation from the war are so intense that we promise ourselves too much. As a proud and great Power, we disdain to chaffer with others smaller and more exorbitant than ourselves. Having been so recently in dire extremity, our financial policy is rooted in appeasement. Above all, the financial problems of the war have been surmounted so easily and so silently that the average man sees no reason to suppose that the financial problems of the peace will be any more difficult.[4]

The success of Keynes's strategy depended crucially on Stage II arrangements. Britain must ensure the continuation of Lend–Lease, but in such a manner that it was allowed to build up its reserves and start reconverting its economy for exports. This demanded a break with the 'marginal principle' – that Lend–Lease would supply only what Britain's fully mobilised war economy could not produce for itself.

Anderson circulated this explosively alarmist brief to selected colleagues. It was a sign of Keynes's authority that it was immediately regarded as the definitive statement of the problem. Its implication, Waley argued, was that 'we shall have to practise a much greater degree of austerity than anyone has yet dreamed of'. Admiring and disturbed comments flowed in. The Chancellor held a meeting with the relevant ministers on 14 June, with Keynes, Hopkins and Eady in attendance. Keynes dominated the discussion, repeating the main points of his memorandum. In July the Cabinet authorised early Stage II negotiations with the Americans and immediate steps to prepare an export drive.

The British line in the forthcoming monetary discussions was thrashed out at two meetings between Anderson and Keynes on 8 and 16 June. The first agreed that the British should press on the Americans the 'Catto' formula on exchange rate rules. Catto had succeeded Montagu Norman as governor of the Bank of England in April. The Bank's aim was to preserve the sovereign right of nations to fix their own exchange rates; Catto's formula provided that members should have to consult the Fund, but not obtain its permission, before devaluing their currencies, reserving to the Fund simply the *ex post* sanction of cutting off the offending member from the use of its facilities. Further, it was agreed that British membership of the Fund should be conditional on a financial solution to its transitional problems outside the Fund; that the convertibility obligation would be limited to sterling required for current transitions, i.e. exclude wartime sterling balances; that the Fund would start only when Britain and America both agreed it should; and that, in any event, no agreement reached at the conference of experts would bind the British government and Parliament. Britain's negotiating position on White's Bank Plan followed Keynes's redraft in March: loans should be untied, the Bank should concentrate on guaranteeing loans, not making them, and British liabilities should be small.

II. AN INTERLUDE IN NEW HAMPSHIRE

On the evening of 16 June, Maynard and Lydia sailed on the *Queen Mary* from Southampton, accompanied by Eady, Robbins, Robertson and Ronald plus George Bolton (adviser to the Bank of England). This time the delegation included a lawyer, William Beckett, from the Foreign Office. Brand, Lee, Opie and Austin Robinson, already in Washington, would join them. Travelling with the British team were 'experts' from Holland, Belgium, Greece, Norway, Czechoslovakia, India and China, most of whom were on the Drafting Committee. Heavy work on board produced two 'boat drafts' covering the Fund and the Bank.

The experts were met by Brand and Frank Lee in New York on 23 June, then whisked off by train to Atlantic City, where they booked into the Claridge Hotel. This was a 'wretched skyscraper' of twenty storeys, which they were to share for the next week with the annual convention of the Homeopathic Institute. At the first joint session with the Americans, on Saturday 24 June, Keynes waxed eloquent on the subject of the Bank. Robbins wrote:

This went very well indeed. Keynes was in his most lucid and persuasive mood; and the effect was irresistible. At such moments, I often find myself thinking that Keynes must be one of the most remarkable men that have ever lived – the quick logic, the birdlike swoop of intuition, the vivid fancy, the wide vision, above all the incomparable sense of the fitness of words, all combine to make something several degrees beyond the limit of ordinary human achievement.... The Americans sat entranced as the God-like visitor sang and the golden light played around.[5]

Keynes had developed keen enthusiasm for the Bank, which he saw as a more rational investment engine than the 'ill-conceived racket' which had followed the last war, and one that would relieve Britain from the 'pressure ... to make advances ... far beyond what we can reasonably afford'. He still saw it, though, as an agency more for post-war European reconstruction than for long-term development.[6] However, there was no response from the US Treasury. The Bank was barely discussed. It was left to Emilio Collado to take up the Bank's cause at the State Department for a somewhat different motive – as a way of binding Latin American countries into supporting American positions on the Fund and elsewhere.

Keynes's tactics in Atlantic City were straightforward. White, he explained in a letter to Hopkins on 25 June, was anxious to avoid any appearance of a stitch-up between the British and American Treasuries. So he and White would try to agree a text behind the scenes, but present alternatives to the forthcoming 'monkey-house' at Bretton Woods, having agreed which alternatives they would drop or press. 'Harry White', he reported to 'Hoppy', is 'wreathed in smiles and amiability, hospitable, benevolent and complacent. I doubt if Sigi [Waley] would recognise him.'[7] White's attitude had changed markedly as a result of the Washington conversations the previous autumn. He realised that, without British support, nothing would get through, and Britain meant Keynes. So White set out to conciliate Keynes, to the extent that his abrasive nature allowed. They were also starting to click as human beings.

White agreed that members of the IMF should be allowed to devalue without getting the Fund's permission, and that they could decide the lengths of their own transitional periods. Questions to do with 'policing', size of quotas, and management and location of the Fund and Bank were left over to the main conference.

Keynes himself rarely attended the plenary sessions, which White controlled in masterly fashion from the chair. Nor did he see, or approve, the set of documents which would go forward to Bretton Woods. Ensconced with Lydia on the tenth floor of the Claridge, overlooking the Atlantic, he had found the conditions 'most comfortable and endurable'. However, exhaustion was setting in. After one day spent in meetings without rest, his system gave 'ominous signs of conking out'. He recovered quickly, but incessant work, meetings and nervous excitement were once more starting to affect his damaged heart muscle. Apart from one conversation with Pasvolsky, special assistant to the US Secretary of State, Keynes did not raise with the Americans the issue of financial help after the end of the German war.

On 30 June Maynard and Lydia travelled by overnight train from Atlantic City to Bretton Woods, New Hampshire, 'a wide basin of woods and meadows, surrounded by low mountains',[8] set in the White Mountain National Forest, a nature reserve of one million acres. Lydia described it as 'a cross between Switzerland and Scotland', temperate in climate, with trout in the river, 'an ideal place for a holiday, alas it is not so for Jemkins [JMK]'. Today one drives up Highway No. 93 from Boston, but in 1944 the 730 delegates and clerical staff from forty-four countries and numerous inter-national organisations – far more than expected – had arrived at the Bretton Woods railway station on special trains, their multilingual chatter producing a 'tower of Babel on wheels'. The delegates booked into the Mount Washing-ton Hotel, which had been less than fully prepared for its reopening. It was the mixture of luxury, chaos and inefficiency which impressed Lydia: 'the taps run all day, the windows do not close or open, the pipes mend and unmend and no one can get anywhere'. Despite its beauty, Bretton Woods was a 'madhouse', Lydia wrote on 12 July, 'with most people ... working more than humanly possible'. It must have reminded Maynard of the Majestic Hotel in Paris at the Peace Conference – that other grand monkey-house which had left him exhausted and ill in 1919. The difference was that this time he was one of the masters of ceremony, victimised at innumerable cocktail parties and photo-sessions.

The Normandy landings had just started, and from western Europe ghostly allies, their nations about to recover independence, were clamouring for a share in the spoils of peace. In the circumstances, it was just as well that the Americans and British had stitched things up beforehand. The main unfinished business was the allocation of quotas which White had cleverly reserved for the conference itself, in the correct expectation that this would be the only matter of interest to most delegations.

White had planned two main commissions, Commission I on the Fund, which he would chair, and Commission II on the Bank, which Keynes would head. (There was also a 'residual rag-bag,' Commission III, called 'Other Means of International Cooperation'.) Commission I would consider the composite draft prepared in Atlantic City, which included all the amend-ments left over from that meeting; Commission II, it was hoped, would knock the constitution of the Bank into shape. White was determined to maintain control of the outcome, while creating the impression of partici-pation in the process. As decisions came through they were to be turned into 'Articles of Agreement' by lawyers on a Drafting Committee, headed by the Canadian Treasury official Louis Rasminsky.

White's aim in making Keynes chairman of the Bank Commission was to neutralise him. He was well aware of Keynes's failing stamina. If he could keep him occupied on Bank business, he would have no energy or time left over for Fund business. This strategy worked. Keynes was head of the British delegation, and unofficial leader of the much larger Commonwealth group. Although the Commonwealth teams looked to Britain for leadership, they did not always follow it. In particular, the Indians and Egyptians tried hard, but unsuccessfully, to secure Fund involvement in making the sterling balances, of which they held by far the largest amount, convertible. Keynes had to intervene on Commission I on 10 July to state that, while Britain would settle the debts 'honourably', 'the settlement ... must be ... a matter between those directly concerned'.[9] This commitment, known as the 'Keynes pledge', ruled out unilateral repudiation.

Britain's conference organisation was far from ideal. Its team, while of the highest quality, was too lean – technically, legally and administratively understaffed and therefore overworked. At one point, Keynes complained that he had had barely five minutes with his 'technicians' in three days; by the end he was writing to the Chancellor, 'all of us from the top to the bottom ... are all in'. Keynes doubted – not for the first time – whether he had 'ever worked so continuously hard' in his life. Apart from presiding at his Commission and sitting at committees, he looked through a thousand documents, composed nearly a hundred long telegrams to the Treasury describing progress and asking for instructions, and as leader of the delegation had to 'make the full dress speeches and proceed to the attack with all guns blazing whenever there was trouble'. But he had a less gruelling time than the others, because Lydia, with rare exceptions, refused to allow him to attend committees after dinner, whereas the others, night after night, sat on committees till 3.30 a.m. and then started up again at 9.30 a.m.

Because of Keynes's need to rest, Robbins and Robertson were given virtually a free hand on the Fund Commission to uphold British government instructions on such matters as exchange rate adjustment, convertibility obligations, conditions attached to drawing rights, and so on. Reporting back to Keynes was done by Sir Wilfrid Eady, who sometimes floundered in the technicalities. The Bernstein–Robertson axis proved crucial in getting Commission I business done, and Keynes was fulsome in his praise of Robertson. 'Dennis ... has been absolutely indispensable. He alone had the intellectual subtlety and patience of mind and tenacity of character to hold on to all details and fight them through Bernstein (who adores Dennis), so that I ... could feel completely happy about the situation.'[10] He wrote to his mother, 'Absolutely first-class brains do help.'

Despite this encomium a bitter row blew up between the two men after the conference over the precise nature of the convertibility obligations of the Agreement. In essence, Keynes thought Robertson had agreed to a wording in Clause 8 which seemed to deprive Britain of the right to maintain exchange controls in circumstances when it might want to exercise that right. Keynes thought Britain might, as a consequence, be forced to repudiate what had been agreed. Though the point turned out to have no practical significance, its passage into oblivion took up an inordinate amount of time. It not only delayed British ratification of the Agreement, but soured relations between Keynes and Robertson. Robertson accepted responsibility for the 'blunder', but 'carried the wound with him to the grave'.[11]

White had stage-managed other aspects of the conference. He arranged for a conference journal to be produced every day to keep everyone informed of the main decisions. He also arranged daily press briefings, at which he displayed an efficient charm. Keynes appeared at only one of these, on 6 July, somewhat dampening the cheerful effect White was trying to create by saying that the Fund could be easily criticised, but all the alternatives were worse. Goldenweiser's record brings out the atmosphere of the madding crowd: the mass of stenographers working day and night, the Boy Scouts acting as pages and distributors of papers, the legal language which made everything difficult to understand, the great many varieties of unintelligible tongues, the Russians 'struggling between the firing squad ... and the English language'.[12] A controlled Bedlam was what White wanted. It would make easier the imposition of the *fait accompli*.

What the delegates did understand was that there was a cache of American dollars available, of which they wanted as many as possible for themselves. Raymond Mikesell, who served under White in the US Treasury, had worked out a complicated formula for allocating 90 per cent of the available money, leaving $800m 'to be added to any place we wanted to'. White had told him that the formula should yield a quota of $2.5bn for the USA, about half that for Britain and its colonies, with the Soviet Union and China assured third and fourth places. To 'cook' the results White wanted, Mikesell had to introduce data for national income. 'These last had to be approximated, and their uncertainty afforded opportunities for making minor adjustments to the suggested quotas when these did not conform to political realities.'[13] The quotas were made public for the first time at Bretton Woods, but the basis of their calculation remained secret. When the figures became known, there were explosions of affronted pride. White responded by setting up a Quota Committee, chaired by Judge Frederick Vinson, vice-chairman of the US delegation, to which countries could bring their complaints. When Stepanov, the Russian, was told that Soviet national income statistics did not justify a quota of $1.2bn, he replied cheerfully that he would produce new statistics. He got his way. Morgenthau, White and Vinson agreed a final distribution of their spare millions on 14 July. 'See, Fred, that is why I am Secretary of the Treasury,' Morgenthau told Judge Vinson waggishly after doing some back-of-envelope calculations. 'I can add and subtract.'[14] The largest quota holders, the USA, Britain, the USSR, China and France, became permanent members of the Security Council of the

United Nations a year later, affirming the world's political as well as financial pecking order.

Anglo-American agreement on exchange rate rules was confirmed on 8 July. The Fund was bound to accept a change in a member currency's exchange rate up to 10 per cent; and changes above this if satisfied they were necessary to correct a 'fundamental disequilibrium', the Fund being barred from objecting on the ground of the proposing member's 'domestic social or political policies'. However, no definition of what constituted 'fundamental disequilibrium' was ever agreed. If changes of above 10 per cent were unauthorised, the country concerned could still remain a member, though without use of the Fund's facilities. A little-noticed amendment allowed member countries to fix their currencies either to gold or to the dollar. This made the dollar, the only gold-convertible currency, the key currency of the new system.

The British also got their way on the transitional period, the only obligation on members being to consult the Fund if they wanted to continue payments restrictions after five years. They still hoped to have the Fund offices in London, not America. Keynes wrote Morgenthau a 'long-winded letter' asking for the decision to be postponed, which the Treasury Secretary read out at an American group meeting on 13 July. White commented, 'We are putting in twice as much money as anybody else ... it is preposterous that the head office should be any place else. We can vote it any place we want ... that is why they don't want it to come to a vote.' White correctly surmised that the British would not break off negotiations because 'they don't like where the head office is.... If they don't like it, it is too bad.... New York has become the financial center of the world. These British are just fighting up-hill.'[15] Keynes reserved the right to reopen both this question and the issue of whether the Fund should have full-time or part-time executive directors.

Goldenweiser wrote that Keynes was the 'outstanding personality.... He shone in two respects – in the fact that he is, of course, one of the brightest lights of mankind ... and also by being the world's worst chairman.' Soon Morgenthau was declaring that he had 'never had so many complaints in my life' about Keynes's chairmanship of the Bank Commission. On 13 July Dean Acheson, America's representative, told the Treasury Secretary that Keynes was rushing it 'in a perfectly impossible and outrageous way.... He knows this thing inside out so that when anybody says Section 15-C he knows what it is. Nobody else in the room knows. So before you have an opportunity to turn to Section 15-C and see what he is talking about, he says, "I hear no objection to that", and it is passed. Well, everybody is trying to find Section 15-C. He then says, we are talking about Section 26-D. Then they begin fiddling around with their papers, and before you find that, it is passed.'[16]

Keynes's haste was partly dictated by a determination to escape as soon as possible. He was growing steadily more exhausted. 'He is not the easiest of men to control, and the eagerness of his mind is such that it is intolerable for him to go slow,' Robbins wrote on 6 July. He had hoped to get away on Wednesday 19 July. In any case, the hotel had only been booked till the 21st. On 17 July Morgenthau summoned a meeting of the Steering Committee to discuss the 'Extension of the Conference'. He gave the floor to Keynes, who said he had reluctantly concluded that the conference should go on till Saturday or Sunday to give the technicians time to clear up the loose ends, the lawyers to draft the the Final Act, and all the delegations a bit of time to scrutinise it. But as 'some of my people ... are quite breaking up under the strain' he urged that from now on there should be no official committees or commissions after dinner, and that Morgenthau as 'headmaster' should declare that day to be a 'whole holiday'. The whole holiday was duly proclaimed.

The proclamation was of limited value to Keynes himself. Exhausted by a last-minute battle to save the Bank for International Settlements – which, located in Basle, was accused of having collaborated with the Nazis* – he became ill. Late in the evening of 19 July word spread that he had had a heart attack. Following an item to that effect in the newspapers, telegrams flowed in wishing him a speedy recovery; the German press published suitably adulatory obituaries. Keynes made light of it. Forgetfully he had run up the stairs to keep an engagement, had been 'knocked out' for a quarter of an hour, a distressed Lydia had blurted out the news to a lady who had a son working for Reuters. 'In fact', he wrote to Catto, 'I have been exceptionally well. ...' The last remark was certainly not true. 'As regards Keynes's health,' Robbins noted in his diary on 20 July, 'we were on the edge of a precipice. There was one evening of prostration at Atlantic City, two the first week here, three last week; and I now feel that it is a race between the exhaustion of his powers and the termination of the conference.'

The conference ended with a grand banquet on the evening of Saturday 22 July. Keynes came in a little late 'and as he moved slowly towards the high table, stooping a little more than usual, white with tiredness, but not unpleased at what had been done, the whole meeting spontaneously stood up and waited, silent, until he had taken his place. Someone of more than ordinary stature had entered the room.'[17]

As the dinner ended, Keynes moved to accept the Final Act, clothing his address with a mixture of literary and theological language, expressive of the way his mind worked and of the civilisation from which he sprang. Forty-four nations had been learning to work together. 'If we can so continue, this nightmare, in which most of us present have spent too much of

---

* The BIS had been set up in 1930, on the initiative of Montagu Norman, as a club of central bankers. Initially its main business was to handle the transfer of German reparations. It had maintained contact with both sides during the war.

our lives, will be over. The brotherhood of man will have become more than a phrase.' The delegates applauded wildly. 'The Star Spangled Banner' was played. As Keynes left the dinner some of the delegates – presumably those from the Anglo-Saxon world – started singing 'For He's a Jolly Good Fellow'. The Soviet reaction to these strange rites is not recorded.

Keynes gave the Bretton Woods Agreement its distinction, not its substance. The Agreement reflected the views of the American, not the British, Treasury; of White, not Keynes. The British contribution tended, finally, towards the negotiation of derogations, postponements and escape clauses. The Agreement was shaped not by Keynes's *General Theory*, but by the US desire for an updated gold standard as a means of liberalising trade. If there was an underlying ideology, it was Morgenthau's determination to concentrate financial power in Washington. As the *Commercial and Financial Chronicle* pointed out, 'The delegates did not reach an "agreement". They merely signed a paper which looked like an agreement.'

That agreement still had to be ratified by the US Congress and approved by the House of Commons. In Britain, the Whitehall and Parliamentary 'Schachtians' were unreconciled. They had gone along with the Clearing Union because they were convinced the Americans would turn it down. They had not banked on Britain signing up to multilateralism with far less financial protection than the Clearing Union offered. A year later, Henry Siepmann of the Bank of England told Emmanuel Goldenweiser, who was visiting London, that Bretton Woods was 'a swindle.... Keynes started the swindle by proposing to shift all the burden on the United States. He did not get away with it – and all kinds of compromises were made – but the whole thing still is dishonest....' Henry Clay, also from the Bank, called Bretton Woods 'the greatest blow to Britain next to the war'. Their argument was that convertibility of sterling into gold and dollars would remove the incentive for sterling area countries to buy British goods and hold balances in London. 'What seems to worry them – and quite understandably –', Goldenweiser shrewdly noted, 'is that Bretton Woods is an acknowledgment of the fact that London has lost its position as the financial center of the world. I think that's the emotional basis of their reaction.'[18]

After Bretton Woods, Keynes and Eady went to Ottawa to negotiate an increase in Canadian Mutual Aid. For Keynes the Canadian trip was a relaxing break. Not having to work more than half a day, it was the nearest he had had to a holiday since the war started. He and Lydia were driven from Bretton Woods to Canada in a car provided by the High Commissioner, Malcolm MacDonald, dawdling in brilliant summer weather. At the Château Laurier Hotel the Keyneses were given the Moorish suite of nine rooms. Lydia's performance captivated the High Commissioner. MacDonald and his advisers called on Keynes to hold a preliminary talk about the financial negotiations. Keynes had misplaced the key to his official red box, and he and Lydia hunted about for it in their luggage. Eventually, the conference began in a private study with Keynes, MacDonald and his officials sitting round a table. There was a knock on the door, and Lydia slipped in.

> She wore nothing but a short white chemise (presumably with a pair of brief drawers below) which hung flimsily round her otherwise bare body. In that state of near nudity she stood in apologetic manner casting a half-guilty, half-mischievous look at Keynes as she said, 'Oh Maynard darling, I am so sorry. You did give me ze key; and I forgot zat I hid it for safety between my little bosoms.' At that she clutched in her hands a ribbon hanging round her neck, and as she lifted it over her head raised from between her breasts – which so far as we could detect were not quite so small as she suggested – the lost article. … She blew him a kiss, turned in a ballerina's pirouette on her toes, glided through the door, and closed it behind her.[19]

Their visit was adjudged highly successful. In a fortnight's negotiations Keynes and Eady succeeded in extracting another $655m from the Canadians. Keynes made or cemented important political friendships – notably with Graham Towers, governor of the Bank of Canada, and Clifford Clark, the Deputy Finance Minister – as well as renewing contact with his former students Bob Bryce and Wynne Plumptre. He reported that 'Malcolm MacDonald (Ramsay's son) looks after us like a brother and arranges picnics for us in the hills, forests and lakes such as we had forgotten could exist.' The contrast between North American affluence and British penury could not have been greater. 'On this continent,' Keynes noted, 'the war is a time of immense prosperity for everyone.' They often ate beefsteaks, and Lydia went on a shopping spree, buying 'deersucker' dresses and shoes every day, presumably out of their foreign exchange allowance. Keynes was struck by the unfairness of it. Britain would end the war bankrupt, North America flush. Surely some retrospective rebalancing of the sacrifice was only just? Keynes loved Canada: 'if one ever had to emigrate, this should be the destination, not the USA'.[20] After a few days in Washington, he and Lydia flew back to England with Eady by Clipper on 20 August. It was the last time his state of health allowed him to fly across the Atlantic.

III. MORGENTHAU TO THE RESCUE

Just over a month later Keynes was on the *Ile de France* bound for Halifax, Nova Scotia, to negotiate an extension of Lend–Lease into Stage II. He saw it as 'the most important (and perhaps the most difficult) of all my missions. … I am substituting for the Chancellor of the Exchequer for a job which, on a

Janos Plesch, the doctor who brought Maynard Keynes 'back to life', and whom he called the 'Ogre'.

Maynard Keynes dictating letters on his daybed in Gordon Square, March 1940.

Maynard Keynes and Lydia arriving in New York on the 'Clipper', at 7a.m.,
8 May 1941. He had not had a chance to shave.

Sir Richard Hopkins. He reminded
Lionel Robbins of an 'extremely
intelligent monkey'.

Lionel Robbins: increasingly
Johnsonian in manner and
appearance.

Harry Dexter White, as
Maynard Keynes would have
seen him in 1944.

Sir Wilfrid Eady. Maynard Keynes
thought that, caught young, he might have
understood the 'elements of economics'.

"DO I UNDERSTAND YOU WISH TO OMIT THE WORD 'OBEY'?"

Maynard Keynes congratulated Low on capturing Morgenthau's 'dreadful smirk'.

Maynard Keynes and Harry White at the Claridge Hotel, Atlantic City, June 1944.

The start of the Loan Negotiations: Maynard Keynes and Halifax at Press Conference, Washington, 12 September 1945.

Signing the Loan Agreement, 6 December 1945 (from left to right): Maynard Keynes, Halifax, Byrnes (US Secretary of State), and 'Judge' Vinson.

Maynard Keynes, with Lydia, 'rushes from Southampton to the House of Lords', 17 December 1945.

Maynard Keynes and
Bob Brand at Savannah,
March 1946.

Maynard Keynes
speaking at Savannah.
He hoped no 'malicious
fairy' would spoil the
christening of the IMF.
Vinson was heard to
say 'I don't mind being
called malicious, but
I do mind being
called a fairy'.

point of form, is his.' On the voyage over, Keynes prepared some notes on the 'financial position in Stages II and III'. There were only two ways, he argued, for Britain to start Stage III without being 'financially at the mercy' of the United States. The first was to cut down on all overseas military commitments in Stage II not strictly necessary for the war against Japan. 'We cannot police half the world at our expense, when we have already gone in pawn to the other half.' The second was to secure the removal of 'White Paper strings on exports' before the end of 1944 as part of the re-negotiation of Lend–Lease.[21] His strategy was to ensure that Britain's imports continued to be covered by Lend–Lease, while its exports should be allowed to expand.

The parameters of the negotiation had been set by the 'Octagon' Conference between Roosevelt and Churchill at Quebec from 13 to 16 September. The war against Japan was then expected to continue for at least a year after the defeat of Germany; Churchill was determined that Britain should take part in the final assault on Japan. Both prestige and finance were involved in this decision. The prestige of the British Empire in the Far East needed restoring after earlier disastrous defeats. Furthermore, if Britain dropped out of the war Lend–Lease would stop. The Treasury saw in this double imperative an opportunity to scale down Britain's war production by more than the reduction in Lend–Lease supplies, creating a margin to increase exports and rebuild its reserves.

The State Department also saw its opportunity: in return for an extension of Lend–Lease to Stage II, Britain should pledge itself to end 'discrimination' against American goods and resume commercial negotiations.

Roosevelt, for reasons still obscure, decided to exclude the State Department from the Quebec meeting. Churchill then excluded the Foreign Office, but insisted on bringing over Lord Cherwell, and asked for Morgenthau's presence. The British shrewdly surmised that they would get what they wanted from Morgenthau without commercial strings attached. Morgenthau was in a benevolent mood. The British had co-operated at Bretton Woods. They had appealed to him for help. And he needed their help for a scheme of his own. The famous Morgenthau Plan for the conversion of Germany into a purely agricultural country had been hatched, as one might have expected, by Harry White. It would replace German by Russian hegemony on the Continent, leading to the Soviet–American condominium of which he dreamed.[22] White reported Keynes 'wholly in our corner' after a meeting in Washington on 20 August. White was wrong. Keynes, while 'much tempted' by the proposal for a temporary break-up of Germany, was never in favour of its de-industrialisation.[23] He thought that Germany should be prohibited from producing armaments of any kind, but in lieu of defence expenditures it should make a long-term financial contribution to peace-keeping, from a levy on export earnings.[24]

Roosevelt brought the Morgenthau Plan (and Morgenthau himself) to Quebec, against strong opposition from his own State Department, which opposed not just the substance of the Plan but Morgenthau's attempt to take over US foreign policy. When Morgenthau expounded his scheme on 12 September, he received from Churchill, slumped in his chair, 'a verbal lashing' such as he had never had in his life; Churchill's condemnation of it as 'un-Christian' was 'one of the less sensitive of the epithets he used'.[25] However, next day Morgenthau won over Cherwell; Cherwell then sold it to Churchill by parading the benefits it would bestow on Britain's export trade. Churchill dictated the final draft of the Plan, which he and Roosevelt then signed. This committed the leaders to the 'closing down' of German heavy industry, and envisaged 'a country primarily agricultural and pastoral in character'.[26] Here was another grand design. Germany would be de-industrialised; Britain would take over Germany's export business; Morgenthau would secure a generous Lend–Lease settlement for Britain in Stage II.[27]

On 14 September, a directive on Lend–Lease was agreed almost perfunctorily. A Joint Committee, chaired by Morgenthau, would be set up to determine Britain's Lend–Lease requirements in the light of an 'agreed record of a conversation between the Prime Minister and the President'. This confirmed that Lend–Lease supplies in amounts to be determined (the record suggested $3.5bn for munitions and $3bn for civilian expenditure) would continue after Germany's defeat and that Britain would be allowed greater latitude to export straightaway. The record, of course, omits the fact that at one point in the 'conversation' Churchill was driven to expostulate: 'What do you want me to do ... stand up and beg like Fala [the President's dog]?'

The Quebec conference was a triumph for Churchill. He had got what the Treasury had asked for. It also seemed a triumph for Morgenthau. He had got the leaders to endorse his Plan and had been restored to his favourite role as Britain's sugar-daddy. But Roosevelt was left exposed. Cordell Hull was furious that no commercial *quid pro quo* had been obtained from the British; the US military, who wanted to finish off the Japanese war on their own, were angry at having to divert supplies to Britain. Within a few weeks, Roosevelt started to retreat from the Quebec spirit. On 3 October, he told Secretary of War Stimson that Morgenthau had 'pulled a boner' on Germany. Quebec turned out to be the high-water mark of the Morgenthau Plan – and indeed of the Morgenthau–White axis. After it, Morgenthau's influence waned, and White's with it. The British Foreign Office, too, lobbied successfully against the Plan. Churchill, with an economy of truth, notes briefly in his memoirs that 'with my full accord, the idea of "pastoralising" Germany did not survive'.[28]

The Cabinet in London nominated Keynes and Sir Robert Sinclair to serve on Morgenthau's Joint Committee, Keynes representing the Chancellor and Sinclair Oliver Lyttelton, Minister of Production. But Churchill had already asked Cherwell to start off the implementation negotiations in Washington.[29] Morgenthau expressed himself 'delighted to have Lord Keynes over', but insisted 'the thing got down to Lord Cherwell and myself. That is what the President and Mr Churchill wanted.' But Morgenthau wanted details which Cherwell could not supply. On 22 September Cherwell was told to delay the presentation of the British case till Keynes came.

Maynard and Lydia arrived in Washington on 2 October. They had travelled from Ottawa in a private railway car provided by the president of the Canadian Railway 'with bedrooms, drawing room, dining room [and] a special chef ... called Romeo [who] cooked in a heavenly fashion'. They had an air-conditioned suite on the top (fourteenth) floor of the Statler, 'with windows as big as the walls, so you never get sad or bored, the whole of Washington is at your feet'. Keynes was given a room in the British Delegation offices at the Willard Hotel on Pennsylvania Avenue, next door to the Treasury.

Work on preparing the British requirements had been held up by Cherwell's 'delusion' that 'if only Mr Morgenthau and he could be left in a room together for about five minutes ... he (Lord Cherwell) would emerge with a definite promise of $5–$6 billion and no questions asked'. As a result, 'until [Keynes] came we were little better than a disorganised rabble'.[30] Keynes rejected the Cherwell approach. He knew, from his 1941 experience, that Morgenthau was likely to promise more than he could deliver, and that 'all the decisions will have to be implemented by *other* Departments [the Military and Supply Departments, the State Department and the Foreign Economic Administration] and none by the Treasury'.[31] Realistically he argued that if, as he expected, the Morgenthau Plan for Germany was defeated by the State Department 'an agreement between M[orgenthau] and Cherwell ... may not assist elsewhere as much as one might have hoped'. Cherwell should stay long enough to get the proceedings properly launched and then find 'some good excuse for going home....'[32]

For Stage II, Keynes was instructed to obtain Lend–Lease supplies equal to 75 per cent of Britain's existing Lend–Lease requirements. He was also to negotiate a drastic easing of restrictions on Britain's export trade. When he called in on Morgenthau and White for a preliminary talk, he found they were considerably more interested in their 'mad' plan for de-industrialising Germany than in the details of Lend–Lease. Fearful of getting involved in Washington in-fighting, Keynes was driven to preserve an 'unwonted and uncomfortable silence'. He did ask White how the inhabitants of the Ruhr were to be kept from starving. White replied that there would have to be bread lines. When Keynes asked whether the British would be expected to provide the bread in their zone of occupation, White said the US Treasury would pay for it, provided it was on 'a very low level of subsistence'. 'So whilst the hills are being turned into a sheep run, the valleys will be filled ... with a closely packed bread line.... How I am to keep a straight face ... I cannot imagine.'[33]

While Morgenthau went off electioneering, and Cherwell went off on a scientific tour (that is, to learn about the atomic bomb), Keynes and his colleagues prepared their 'book of words', otherwise 'British Requirements for the First Year of Stage II'. This took ten days to compile. After receiving a cable from London, indicating a prospective drop in gold and dollar reserves in 1945, Keynes added a 'Chapter 3' of additional requirements to the tune of $500m. These were to be met by a combination of additional shipments of tobacco and sugar, and money which the British claimed the Americans owed them from pre-Lend–Lease contracts, dubbed 'half-dead cats' by British officials. On 17 October, Keynes sent six copies of the 'book of words' to the US Treasury. He and Cherwell followed this up with a visit, to find Morgenthau, worn out from West Coast electioneering, uneasily fingering what he thought was a three-volume document, three copies having been left on his desk.

Formal negotiations started on 19 October in a Main Committee in Morgenthau's office, over which the Secretary presided, with two subordinate committees on munitions and non-munitions. Keynes soon realised it would be impossible to make any oral presentation at these chaotic gatherings. Morgenthau himself had only the vaguest idea of what was going on. 'At the Main Committee', Keynes noted, 'any continuous argument or indeed more than a dozen simple sentences were always out of place.' After a week, Morgenthau was reluctantly persuaded to set up a joint sub-committee under White. This helped, but only to some extent. Although White proved an efficient chairman, the Americans found it hard to field the same team for more than ten minutes at a stretch, since members were always running out to take telephone calls. Its secretary, Frank Coe, who took the minutes, kept falling asleep.[34]

In Washington, the British always had to adapt themselves to the American habits of business, with small teams facing seemingly anarchic battalions of lawyers, academics, researchers, statisticians, pressmen, photographers. When it was all over, Keynes wrote that if there was one thing he had learnt after spending almost one year out of the last four 'stepping like a cat over the hot tiles of Washington' it was that the situation was 'fluid up to almost the last moment'. 'I liken them to bees who for weeks will fly round in all directions ... providing both the menace of stings and the hope of honey; and at last, perhaps because the queen in the White Hive has emitted some faint, indistinguishable odour, suddenly swarm to a single spot....'[35] Keynes saw the Queen Bee only once during that visit, for tea on 26 November. Lydia bought herself a new dress for the occasion. Keynes reported the re-elected Roosevelt to be in 'grand form'.

The British found the Americans amazingly cordial. Morgenthau was keen to shovel his billions into Britain's empty purse. The munitions programme was agreed 'with remarkable ease and celerity', despite objections from the War Departments, who saw no need for a British 'Blücher' in the

Pacific. The civilian programme took longer to agree, but eventually the British got most of what they wanted on this as well. Keynes was less interested in the details of the programmes than in their impact on Britain's prospects for Stage III. This depended on how far Britain would be allowed to increase its reserves and expand its exports during the Japanese war. Roosevelt had accepted the case for increased exports at Quebec. But reserves had not been mentioned, and the Americans were reluctant to yield control over them. Indeed, 'White gave Keynes his own personal opinion – completely off the record – that it would be better for us to run down our gold and dollar reserves to a dangerously low level in Stage II, since this would make it easier for the Americans to give us very generous assistance in Stage III. Keynes very properly resisted this suggestion since it would put us at the mercy of the Americans in Stage III.'[36]

To augment Britain's reserves of gold and dollars, Keynes had suggested retrospective US cash payments for aircraft which Britain had ordered and paid for itself but handed over to the Americans before reciprocal aid had been formalised in September 1942. These were the 'half-dead cats'. Their revival made Morgenthau 'hopping mad', and his reaction made Keynes nervous. Lydia intervened. She went to see the reserved Secretary in his office and told him: 'Mr Morgenthau, *Maynar* cannot sleep at night. He says he wants sixpence from you: only sixpence more. Why, Mr Morgenthau, why cannot you give *Maynar* sixpence?' At which, according to her own account, Morgenthau promised her the sixpence and congratulated her on being one of the ablest and most skilful negotiators he had ever met.[37] He told Keynes he would find 'a large lump sum of new money'. 'We are agreeing with him', Keynes reported to Anderson, 'that it would be vastly better to replace half-dead cats with a new live dog. But in what kennel is he to be found?'[38]

Keynes and Halifax were getting on well. Keynes often came to see him on what the ambassador called 'Keynes's business', Halifax's understanding but detached charm providing a calming influence in moments of stress. More stimulating to Halifax was the gossip they had on the Eton Provostship. 'Linky' Quickswood had resigned. 'He [Keynes] wants me to accept the Provostship,' Halifax noted on 2 November, 'but I do not think it is quite my cup of tea. . . . He was depressed about getting decisions on post-war stuff in England and about the immersion of Ministers in day to day work. He evidently hopes that John Anderson will be Prime Minister rather than Anthony if and when Winston goes.' On the night of the Presidential election Maynard and Lydia joined the Halifaxes, the David Bowes Lyons and Isaiah Berlin for dinner in the Embassy. Bored with the election results coming in over the radio, Lydia suddenly said to Berlin: 'Do you like Lord Halifax?' Halifax was sitting a few chairs away. Berlin emitted a neighing sound. Keynes did not stop her. She went on, 'He is quite popular, but it was not always so. Do you remember appeasement? It was terrible. Munich. . . .'

Nothing from Maynard. Halifax looked embarrassed and got up and patted his dog. 'Now Frankie enough of this politics.' After telephoning Harry Hopkins, Halifax came back and announced the election was 'in the bag'.[39] Keynes was thrilled with Roosevelt's victory, writing with unnecessary asperity that his Republican opponent Thomas E. Dewey 'is one of the most miserable rats ever brought to birth'.[40]

The Russians have a word for Lydia's behaviour – *stoochki*, roughly, 'tricks'. 'Naughtiness', recalled Berlin, 'Keynes rather liked, especially against the pompous.' Lydia's remarks, like Keynes's, started on the rounds of Washington. At a dinner given by Cordell Hull, she was heard, in a lull in the conversation, to say to a neighbour, 'Two men – yes – I can see they've got something to take hold of. But two women – that's impossible. You can't have two insides having an affair.'[41] Lydia was both unselfconscious and contrived; and part of what people took to be her lack of self-consciousness was simply an exploitation of her most endearing feature.

Despite the incessant work, Keynes remained in good form and good health for the whole of his two months on North American soil. On 31 October he gave an informal talk in the State Department on the sterling area, trying to disabuse American officials that it was a nefarious conspiracy to deprive US exporters of markets. 'I guess it would have done some good', noted the ambassador. Austin Robinson remembered a drive to Mount Vernon, George Washington's house in Virginia. 'For three or four hours, [Keynes] forgot everything except the exquisite perfection of that lovely house, and the shock of beauty of the view from its terrace, while he engaged in light-hearted and completely preposterous arguments about George Washington and modern America.'

Morgenthau did his best to find an extra $400m–$500m for the British, but the President was unpersuaded, and 'Mr Morgenthau', Keynes shrewdly noted, 'has easier access to [the President's] presence than to his mind.' The new dog turned out to be a scrawny animal, worth only about $250m. Leo Crowley of the Foreign Economic Adminstration refused to put tobacco and sugar back on to the civilian Lend–Lease list, whence he had removed them in 1943. In place of cigarettes, the British were offered prefabricated houses, better for health, although worse for the reserves.

However, the nub of the matter, and the point on which the British failed to get real satisfaction, was freedom to resume exporting. They had been led to believe that the Export White Paper's restrictions on exporting would be scrapped on 1 January 1945. But at the wind-up meeting of Morgenthau's Committee on 22 November Crowley declared that they must stand till the end of the German war, whenever that was, and reserved administrative discretion even after that. Keynes was infuriated, calling Crowley a 'Tammany Polonius' whose 'ear [was] so close to the ground that he was out of range of persons speaking from an erect position'.[42] The best Keynes could secure was a promise of some administrative easement from

1 January 1945, and complete export freedom when the German war was finished. Putting the best face on it, he told Dalton on his return that this had given Britain 'all the export freedom we can use'.[43]

What were the results? On the military side of Lend–Lease the British got $2.838bn having asked for $3bn, and on the non-military side $2.569bn having requested $3bn. Morgenthau had promised to find another $250m–$300m of miscellaneous items to help the reserves. Amazingly, all this turned out to be more, not less, Lend–Lease than the British had been getting before, even though (after Germany's defeat) it would support a smaller war effort.

In fact, the agreement proved much more shaky than it seemed. Morgenthau had done his best, but American opinion had turned anti-British again, partly in response to British military intervention to put down a communist uprising in Greece. The American press screamed that Lend–Lease should not be used to shore up British imperialism. Roosevelt reneged on his Quebec commitments. Britain would get no right to export goods 'similar' to those being lend–leased till the victory over Germany. It failed to secure a promise that Lend–Lease would continue after VE Day. Above all, on Roosevelt's orders, nothing agreed in Washington was signed. This meant that there was no assurance that the $5.5bn would actually be forthcoming, or that Britain's reserves would not continue to be used as a criterion of Lend–Lease management. In his press announcement on 30 November, Crowley said that 'the amount and types of supplies would continue to be subject, as always, to adjustment from time to time....' As Dobson comments, 'It was as if the Quebec conversations had never been.'[44]

On 27 November Maynard and Lydia flew to Ottawa in a private aeroplane with Stage II proposals to put to Canadian ministers. Alighting from the aeroplane, Lydia rushed towards the waiting MacDonald, flung her arms round him, and exclaimed in a loud voice: 'Oh, my dear High Commissioner, how are you? I dreamed zat I was lying in bed, and zat you were lying in my arms.' The rest of the visit was rather an anti-climax. A conscription crisis deprived Keynes of the attention of the Canadian officials, further talks were scheduled for 1945, and on 6 December he and Lydia sailed back to England from New York on the *Nieuw Amsterdam*.

On board, he drafted a huge letter to the Chancellor summarising his achievements. On the whole it was upbeat. Keynes comforted himself with the thought that the United States was now wholly committed to Britain's restoration as a Great Power. American illusions about all its other allies had faded or were fading. 'There is nothing to be found reliable or homely in the habitable globe outside Britain and the British Commonwealth. This, today, is America's deepest, least alterable conviction – a sure rock upon which, whatever may appear on the surface, we can build with safety.' However, there were sombre lessons to be learnt for Stage III. The chief of these was to avoid 'inconvenient strings' being attached to further American help after the Japanese war had ended. He urged 'with vehemence' that 'financial independence of the United States at the earliest possible opportunity should be a major aim of British policy.... A mighty Empire in financial leading strings to others will not be mighty at all....' Britain 'must stand unpropped, or be laid low'.[45]

Maynard and Lydia landed at Southampton on 12 December. They had been away for eight days short of three months.

PART NINE

THE LAST BATTLE

There can be no Greater Error than to Expect or Calculate Upon Real Favors from Nation to Nation.

George Washington

41

Temptation

I. USURY

From the point of view of the British Treasury it would have been ideal if Germany had surrendered at the end of 1944 and Japan had fought on till the end of 1945. This would have given Britain a year to demobilise its war economy and restart its export trade under cover of Lend–Lease; this, in turn, would have made it less dependent on American help when peace finally broke out. But it was not to be. On 16 December 1944 Hitler launched his last counterattack in the Ardennes. It was soon contained but, together with Russian inaction in the east, it delayed the end of the European war by several months. The second factor, of which Keynes had no inkling, was that the atomic bomb was on the point of becoming operational. Keynes hoped that 'the Japanese would not let us down by surrendering too soon'. In the event, the use of atomic weapons abruptly terminated the Pacific war in August 1945. The Stage II arrangements, on which rested Britain's hopes of recovering a measure of financial independence before the war ended, were thus not only postponed till May 1945, but were then compressed into three months. Britain's last hope of avoiding a 'financial Dunkirk' was scuppered after Japan's surrender when Lend–Lease was suddenly cancelled instead of being tapered off. Peace started, therefore, with a balance of payments deficit of wartime proportions. This meant that Britain would have to go back to Washington cap in hand – exactly the situation Keynes had hoped to avoid.

While the Allied armies prepared for their final assault on Germany, Keynes's energies were temporarily absorbed by the less pressing problem of post-war domestic finance. Sir Richard Hopkins had set up the National Debt Enquiry the previous autumn, and Keynes was put on its Committee, together with officials from the Treasury, the Inland Revenue Department and the Economic Section. Evidently the National Debt would be hugely enlarged by the war, and the Treasury was looking for an authoritative financing doctrine, consonant with modern thought. Keynes expounded his views on savings and investment, interest rates and capital budgeting at three meetings, on 8, 22 and 27 March 1945. According to Meade's diary, he was in erratic form – 'perverse, brilliant and wayward': extreme in the statement of his liquidity-preference theory, incredibly rude to a senior

Treasury official Sir Herbert Brittain (he called him 'intellectually contempt-ible'), cautious and sensible in his policy suggestions.[1]

Keynes's view that low interest rates should be maintained after the war made a good deal of sense in light of the actual situation which faced the Treasury. But the extremism of the theoretical position from which it was argued illustrates the perverse streak in his make-up. Dennis Robertson had tried to rid Keynes of the idea that the rate of interest had *no* connection with productivity and thrift, that to set a rate of interest permanently below the profit rate was bound to produce an inflationary boom. In certain moods, Keynes seemed to accept this; but when Robertson was not there to argue with him he reverted to his extreme views. His hatred of the *rentier* was proof against economic arguments, because at bottom it was theological, not scientific. The bondholder was, in his mind, nothing but the medieval usurer, or Shylock, someone who sought to make a profit out of lending money. To Sir Cornelius Gregg, chairman of the Board of Inland Revenue, Keynes wrote on 9 April: 'In other words, it is usury to extract from the borrower some amount additional to the true sacrifice of the lender which the weakness of the borrower's bargaining position or his extremity of need ... make[s] ... feasible.... I find it interesting to put it this way because it really amounts to exactly the same thing as my theory of liquidity preference.'[2]

It is important to notice that these thoughts were in Keynes's mind as he plotted his appeal to the Americans for a grant or interest-free loan to carry Britain into Stage III. To charge interest to Britain in its 'extremity of need' would be *usury*, especially after Britain's disproportionate sacrifice for the Allied cause.[3]

II. PREPARING FOR STAGE III

On 4 January 1945, informal commercial talks between Britain and the United States had started up again in London, involving Liesching, Robbins and Eady on the British side and Harry Hawkins and Ernest Penrose of the US Embassy on the American side. The American draft of a 'multilateral convention' covered such topics as tariffs, imperial preferences, cartels, agricultural subsidies, blocked balances and procedure. The British said they favoured the American aims, but wanted to liberalise trade more cautiously; by June they had only got so far as to give the Americans a 'specimen draft of a possible statement of principles'. Keynes personally thought that it might be better for the United States and the British Empire to form a customs union 'with whatever other countries might care to join' rather than to start with a 'multilateral convention'.[4]

The British lacked a defining document for a post-Lend–Lease world. Keynes had his own ideas. A new Roosevelt 'brainwave', he told Brand on 15 February 1945, should provide for a 'reconsideration of the sharing of the costs of the war'.[5] What this boiled down to was a post-war grant from the United States to repay part of the costs of the war. This thought had been in Keynes's mind during the Stage II negotiations the previous autumn. Keynes aired it to two of Roosevelt's advisers, Judge Rosenman and Laughlin Currie when they visited London in March and April respectively.[6] Unfortunately, Roosevelt died before Keynes's ideas could reach his brain. It is unlikely that they would have lodged there.

It was the Canadians who prodded the British into more positive action. Alarmed by remarks made by the visiting British Minister of Agriculture, Robert Hudson, to the effect that the British would stand no 'multilateral nonsense', Graham Towers, the governor of the Bank of Canada, prepared a policy statement, dated 8 January 1945, called 'Post-war Commercial Policy Prospect: A Proposal for Averting a Breakdown in International Trade Relationships'. The Canadian government accepted Towers's suggestions and, in a telegram to London on 23 February, offered to replace Mutual Aid – the Canadian version of Lend–Lease – with a loan of $1.2bn at 2 per cent for three years after the war, repayment not to start for ten years, and with a waiver clause on balance of payments grounds. With a corresponding line of credit from the United States, Britain, it suggested, should be able to drop restrictive and discriminatory commercial policies. The Canadians also proposed that the US and Canada should assume some of the sterling debts, with remaining balances being scaled down. They wanted to come to London to discuss these ideas. Churchill accepted the proposal for a Canadian visit. The visit was fixed for early summer.[7] With hindsight, it seems odd that the Canadian plan failed to suggest to the British the likely form in which assistance from the United States would be offered. What it did do was to elicit a response from Keynes. In an effort to give the British officials something to discuss with the Canadians, Keynes took ten days' 'rest' in Cambridge in the second week in March to produce a memorandum entitled 'Overseas Financial Arrangements in Stage III'. Initialled on 18 March 1945, it was extensively discussed and revised before going to the Cabinet on 15 May. It provided the intellectual and mythical foundation of the American loan negotiations later in the year.

What Keynes proposed was that Britain should offer two post-war financial 'trades': to the Americans, a return to the convertibility of currently earned sterling in return for a gift of $5bn; and, to sterling area countries, immediate convertibility of part of their wartime balances, in return for cancellation and funding agreements covering the rest. Underlying these trades was the concept of a retrospective redistribution of the costs of the war he had mentioned to Brand. If the USA and sterling area countries would compensate Britain for disproportionate war sacrifices, Britain, with

higher reserves and fewer debts, could agree to enter a multilateral trade
and payments system. A 'just' accounting of the war would thus make
possible a liberal resumption of the peace. There was a beautiful moral
balance in this design, as well as a blend of morality and self-interest, which
made Keynes's argument intuitively attractive to all those who read it.

Another typical Keynesian feature was the tripartite division of possible
remedies for Britain's prospective balance of payments problem into ideal,
worst-case and intermediate solutions, which he labelled Justice, Austerity,
and Temptation. This was not just Keynes being a good civil servant, setting
out the options. It was his way of providing a framework for discussion
which could be accepted by the two main warring Whitehall factions, the
internationalists and the Schachtians. He had done roughly the same thing
in his very first paper on the Clearing Union. The words, once announced,
stuck. Everyone involved, thereafter, discussed the question of American
financial assistance in Keynes's intellectual framework. This was not the
only possible framework, and it is far from clear that it was the best. But it
was undeniably seductive, and Keynes was Whitehall's greatest intellectual
charmer. The new memorandum was nonetheless wordier, more self-indul-
gent than the Keynes of old. It suggests a certain slackening of the intellectual coil which was Keynes's brain, perhaps due to the merging of fatigue
with his long-established habit of self-confident pontification.

Without a change of policy, Britain would enter the post-war period
(Stage III) with a prospective annual balance of payments deficit of £1.4bn
or $5.6bn.A cumulative deficit of £2bn or $8bn was likely over three to five
years. This deficit had to be financed somehow. Austerity (subsequently
labelled Starvation Corner) would be the consequence of rejecting any
American help. It was Keynes's name for the policy of bilateralism advocated
by Hubert Henderson, the imperialists, the Bank of England and left-wing
socialists – those he now indiscriminately labelled 'Schachtians'. It would
require the continuation and intensification of rationing and wartime controls, national planning and the direction of foreign trade on Soviet lines, the
postponement of social projects at home and colonial reconstruction and
development abroad, and the virtual abandonment by Britain of any overseas activity, military or diplomatic, that cost money. It would risk 'serious
political and social disruption and our withdrawal, for the time being, from
the position of a first-class Power'. The more Keynes thought about Austerity
the less he liked it. In economic terms bilateralism made no sense, since
Britain bought too much from countries it did not sell to. The attempt to
negotiate bilateral agreements would break up the sterling area, which
required sterling to be 'freely convertible'. However, its chief objection was
that it would encounter the active hostility of the United States, thus
disrupting the liberal front. The US could also offer much more attractive
inducements to sterling area countries than could Britain. 'In short, the
moment at which we have for the time being lost our financial strength and

owe vast sums all round the world is scarcely the bright and brilliant occasion for asking all our creditors to join up with us against where the financial power now lies, not for the purpose of getting paid, but for the purpose of obliging us with a little more.'[8]

Keynes saw this 'disastrous' option as a 'bluff' to elicit American help. America, he thought, would be willing, even eager, to lend Britain $8bn as a commercial loan, with interest as low as 2 per cent, easy terms of repayment postponed for ten years, with provisions for deferral of repayment, and on condition that Britain made sterling area earnings convertible and signed up fully to the Article VII agenda. This was the policy of Temptation. The objection to it was not just, or mainly, because it would force Britain into possibly unsupportable debt bondage, but because it would be 'an outrageous crown and conclusion of all that has happened'. It was particularly intolerable that Britain should start the peace owing over $20bn (sterling debts plus American loan) – roughly what the Allies proposed to exact in reparation from Germany. Keynes fulminated: 'The fundamental reasons for rejection are incommensurable in cash terms.' Temptation might be transformed into something approaching Justice, the ideal alternative, if the United States lightened the annual service and repayment conditions on the loan, allowed the release of sterling balances to be deferred and desisted from financial pressure in commercial negotiations. But these mitigations would not be enough. 'The sweet breath of Justice between partners ... would have been sacrificed to some false analogy of "business".' Justice required a 'general re-consideration of the proper burden of the costs of the war'.[9]

The just solution was for the USA to reimburse Britain the $3bn it had spent in the United States before Lend–Lease started, and open a credit line of up to $5bn for ten years, at a token interest rate and on easy repayment terms. Canada would write off $500m of debt and advance $500m at nominal interest. In return Britain would accept '*de facto* convertibility of sterling' within a year of the end of the war.[10] This deal was the cornerstone of Keynes's plan from the start.

Keynes had something to say about tactics. Britain could hope to reach such an outcome only by 'robust and unyielding negotiation'. He thought there might well be a breakdown at the end of the first round. Britain should present its case to the US in the form of an appeal to Justice, pointing out that never again would it 'have a better chance of a wise act at so modest a cost'.[11] Negotiations should start at the earliest in September – after the end of the German war, the last Congressional appropriation for Lend–Lease and the ratification of the Bretton Woods Agreement by Congress. This timetable reflected the expectation that the war against Japan would still be going on.

Experience in Washington should have taught Keynes that the Americans had never accepted that they owed Britain a moral debt, and it was unlikely that the Empire would recognise one. There was an ivory-tower quality to the argument, which made parts of it remote from practical possibilities. But it was remote in another sense. Keynes's 'feel' for Washington politics was unduly influenced by his double triumph of 1944 in getting the Bretton Woods Agreement through and negotiating an exceptionally favourable Lend–Lease settlement for Stage II. His expectations for Stage III were based on the continuation in power of the duumvirate of Roosevelt and Morgenthau, and, on the British side, of Winston Churchill, with his unparalleled prestige. All these figures toppled in 1945 – through death, resignation or electoral defeat. Yet by the time all this came to pass, Keynes's Grand Design had taken root in Whitehall and could not be dislodged. When he eventually got to Washington in September his plan was unchanged, but he found that everything else had altered.

III. PERSUADING WHITEHALL

Before they could become British policy, Keynes's ideas had to be accepted by Whitehall. This time he got no input from his previous 'first class critics': Henderson, Robertson, Kahn and Harrod were not on the scene. Treasury consideration of Keynes's draft was led by Sir Wilfrid Eady, the joint second secretary. Eady was a Schachtian. In the drama which followed he was the leading opponent of a settlement with the United States on anything but Britain's terms. Keynes had written in his memorandum: 'Most of us would, when we are up against it, prefer ... Temptation to Starvation Corner....'[12] Not Sir Wilfrid Eady. In his first comment on the Keynes Plan, he wrote that it had to be 'an all or nothing business' – that is, Justice or Austerity. He thought Keynes's suggestion of a credit-line of $5bn additional to the $3bn of retrospective Lend–Lease 'plain Temptation and ... dangerous Temptation'. A loan would only sour Anglo-American relations. Apart from this, Eady injected three notable dollops of realism. He doubted whether Britain should offer '*de facto* convertibility' one year after the end of the war, since he did not foresee exports expanding sufficiently to make this a proper risk. He urged the elimination of the formula 'redistribution of the costs of the war', which he foresaw would antagonise Britain's sterling area creditors. Furthermore, he warned that Keynes's 'extraordinarily difficult financial diplomacy' would make no progress unless Britain was prepared to take 'a definitely forthcoming attitude on Article VII' of the Lend–Lease Agreement.

In effect, he accused Keynes of eliding the choice between Justice and Temptation, and making both seem too rosy and easily attainable. His alternative was to borrow on commercial terms for necessary purchases from the United States, while redirecting the flow of trade to sterling area and 'payments agreement' countries.[13]

Both the Treasury and the Bank of England raised objections which were to cause trouble later. The first concerned the treatment of sterling balances. Keynes had suggested that if sterling area countries refused his plan for a tripartite 'settlement' of their debt (a third to be made convertible, a third to be frozen, a third to be cancelled) Britain should simply freeze the lot. The Treasury official Ernest Rowe-Dutton pointed out the weakness of this so-called sanction: blocking all the balances would break up the sterling area. The second problem had to do with the riskiness of making sterling convertible into dollars on current account, Keynes's *quid pro quo* for American help. Waley, the deputy head of the Treasury's Overseas Finance Division, rejected the possibility of 'full convertibility' at 'any foreseeable future' date. The third problem, as Rowe-Dutton put it, was to find an alternative to 'unconditional surrender' if Justice were refused. The Bank of England's position was forcefully stated by Cobbold and Bolton in July: a loan was no solution, but a grant looked like charity. This might be acceptable. But the Bank, like Eady, would prefer to borrow dollars commercially to buy necessary American goods, and keep the 'dollar pool' intact. Cobbold felt confident that with British spending in America covered, Britain could finance its deficits elsewhere by continuing to run up balances with the sterling area.[14]

Stringent criticism of Keynes's approach came, as one might have expected, from the British financial team in Washington, headed by Brand and Lee, whose ears were much closer to the American ground. Brand scotched any hope of getting a free gift: it would require an 'atmosphere totally different from anything like the present one'.[15] Nor did he recommend any appeal for a gift on grounds of restitution. 'What we cannot put to the American people is that it is justice that they should give us a free grant on the ground that they should have entered the war before they did and therefore they owe us the $3 billion we spent here.'[16] The British should appeal for a free gift on grounds not of justice but of generosity: Britain needed help, but could not repay. To disguise the fact of bankruptcy, Brand would like a free gift 'dressed up' as far as possible to look unlike a free gift.[17] Brand also foresaw that the US would insist on linking any aid to a settlement of sterling debts. Keynes's proposal, he thought, was like 'the drastic reconstruction of a company and the putting in of new money'. The USA would need to know how Britain intended to deal with its other creditors.[18] This business analogy came naturally to a banker: Keynes would hate it when Marriner Eccles, chairman of the Federal Reserve Board, used the same argument in Washington in the autumn. Brand also suggested that it might be best to patch up 'some temporary interim arrangement to carry us on for a year or more after lend–lease', pending a campaign of education, and the crystallisation of anti-Russian feeling.[19]

This last point suggested an alternative strategy which should have merited serious consideration. Keynes never apparently considered the geopolitical context in which aid from the United States might be solicited. Churchill understood the politics, but failed to link it to finance. Using the phrase the 'iron curtain' for the first time, he cabled Truman on 12 May 1945, 'Anyone can see that in a very short space of time our armed power on the Continent will have vanished ... [leaving it] open to the Russians ... to advance if they chose to the waters of the North Sea and the Atlantic.' He countermanded the running down of British forces on the Continent.[20] But the connection between Churchill's fear of the Soviet threat and Keynes's hope for a gift was never made. It would have required a political context for the financial negotiation. Perhaps in 1945 this was premature: a good reason for Brand's 'interim' arrangement. The financial and political trains moved along separate tracks. They came together only with the announcement of Marshall Aid in June 1947 – which *was* the post-war version of Lend–Lease. But by then it was too late.

In wanting to explore the potential of Austerity, Eady found a powerful ally in Richard ('Otto') Clarke, who had joined the Overseas Finance Division in 1944 after a career in financial journalism. On 11 May, Clarke produced the first of a number of memoranda arguing for a serious fall-back position should Justice fail. Clarke started from a Hendersonian export pessimism, projecting an annual payments deficit in 1950 still running at between $500m and $600m a year, even in the unlikely event of a world boom. The main reason, he thought, lay in a lack of 'will to export', though an overvalued pound was a subsidiary factor. To get itself back into balance, Britain should reduce its imports and export capital equipment to its colonies to develop their agriculture, transport and electrity, using the funded portion of sterling balances to pay for such 'development plans'. (The Tanzania groundnuts scheme of 1948 was a bizarre offshoot of this approach.) Clarke favoured a 'just' settlement with the United States, but warned against being a permanent borrower or pensioner, and insisted that 'we should maintain the power and apparatus to enable us to be bilateral if events prove this to be necessary'. By bilateralism he meant 'having a UK-based multilateral group of less than world size'. This required 'currency and import discrimination' until Britain got back into balance.[21]

After some criticism from Keynes, Clarke developed what he called a Plan II. His crucial move was to reject Temptation, on the ground that a loan (with likely accompanying conditions) carried too many risks. Shorn of its complications, Plan II envisaged enlarging the 'dollar pool' to include the countries of western Europe, together with their colonial empires. In a gloss, Eady suggested that 'an expanded non-Dollar block' (which he called an 'Association'), based on sterling and managed by London, could earn enough dollars to puchase all it required from the United States. He wanted this developed as something 'to which events may force us to' and not just put forward as a 'bluff'.[22]

Keynes dismissed Clarke's paper as fantasy. He minuted: 'What these figures show is that if a tidal wave were to overwhelm North and South America ... nothing worse than starvation would supervene.' There would still be a residual deficit of 25–30 per cent with the United States, which Britain could not meet by borrowing from an enlarged sterling area, since 'they also will have a large adverse balance with the Americas'. These dismissive phrases ended the first semi-serious discussion in Whitehall of a European economic policy.[23] Keynes's hostile reaction was based not just on technical considerations. To him the Channel had become wider than the Atlantic; perhaps it always had been.

At a meeting with officials in the Treasury on 29 May, Keynes was still confident that Lend–Lease would be allowed to taper off gradually, though the others doubted this. Frank Lee, who had just flown in from Washington, thought that Keynes's Starvation Corner alternative would 'prove effective with the State Department, but not with Congress' and he doubted 'the possibility of Justice as a solution to Britain's problem'.

There the matter rested. It was assumed that Stage III negotiations with the Americans would start some time in September. But no decision on Keynes's Plan was taken by Churchill's government. Clarke has left as acute an account as one is likely to get of Keynes's over-optimism – and sense of urgency. The explanation of both, he suggests,

> is that Keynes regarded this agreement with the United States as the capstone of the great constructive effort on which he embarked in 1941 to create a world-wide multilateral financial system. To see sterling convertible at an early date was a major objective – perhaps, apart from getting the money, his most important objective. He could not tolerate that after he had overcome for three years all these obstacles which were intrinsic in the task, the edifice would collapse – and because the British had not played their part. So of course he had to believe that the Americans would help him to complete this masterpiece of his public service. He may well have felt that his health would not stand a negotiation in 1946 or 1947; and he had more mistrust than he probably should have had of the ability and willingness of Ministers, Treasury and Bank to carry the project along.[24]

IV. AMERICAN PRESSURE

On 7 May 1945, Germany surrendered, and Britain entered Stage II. No reflection by Keynes, profound or trivial, on the end or meaning of this catastrophic episode in world history has survived. If he made any to his Bloomsbury friends, Virginia Woolf was no longer alive to record it. Maynard and Lydia reopened the dining room at 46 Gordon Square. Two days after VE Day, a young official at the Canadian High Commission, Douglas LePan, caught a glimpse of Keynes at the reopening of the National Gallery, of which he was a Trustee, by King George VI and Queen Elizabeth. Keynes was standing between E. M. Forster and Henry Moore. 'I was surprised that Keynes seemed to have such bulk and mass. Formally but unobtrusively dressed in a double-breasted dark suit, he loomed benignly above his two friends, large and protective, almost avuncular.'[25]

The highlight of Keynes's May was a colloquium at King's College, Cambridge with the Canadians. It was the impending Canadian visit that had prompted Keynes to write his memorandum on Stage III and it was on the Canadian delegation which arrived in May that he first tried out his ideas outside Whitehall, even though the Cabinet had not seen, much less approved, them. The occasion was a Whitsun weekend at King's College on 19 and 20 May 1945. An account of Keynes in action on this occasion has been left by LePan, who came to Cambridge to take notes. A poet and novelist, LePan was highly sensitive to the atmosphere of the occasion, as well as recording the substance. He depicts Keynes 'displaying all his marvellous gifts – intellectual, forensic, social, cultural, personal – outspread like a spangled train'.

Although Keynes's homosexuality had long been just sentimental, he could still exert a formidable charm on the young when stimulated to do so. At dinner on Friday evening, he took LePan, then in his twenties, 'slim and almost handsome' with golden hair, by the arm and guided him to sit on his right. He seemed to sense that LePan – secretly at that time – shared his tastes. Realising that he knew little economics, Keynes tactfully shifted the conversation to ballet. The impression of weight and gravity which LePan had noticed at the National Gallery persisted; 'but as he turned and lifted his head to look down the Hall, I was also conscious of fun and sweetness and of an amused and wayward and playful spirit'.

The plenary meetings took place in the Audit Room at King's. Keynes presided, flanked on his left by Hopkins and Eady from the Treasury, Cobbold the executive director of the Bank of England, Gordon Munro from the UK High Commission in Ottawa, Alec Clutterbuck from the Dominions Office and Freddie Harmer, a junior Treasury official whom Keynes had taught economics at King's in the late 1920s. On the right sat three senior Canadian officials, Bill Mackintosh, acting Deputy Minister of Finance in his chief's absence through illness, Graham Towers, governor of the Bank of Canada, and Hector Mackinnon, chairman of the Canadian Tariff Board.

Keynes opened the meeting like 'a great conductor' taking over an orchestra. He had before him a Treasury brief containing not just his own revised memorandum on the choices facing the UK but much supporting material. 'This was his score for the meeting, but he very rarely consulted it.' He spoke for almost a day and a half. LePan said he had 'never listened to such a fine forensic performance', it 'often soared and fluttered and hovered, was bright with fancy, was variously inflected'. Like Dr Johnson, Keynes did not practise the art of accommodating himself to different sorts of people. So his personality either attracted or repelled. 'Towers ... felt deep and fundamental sympathy towards him'; Mackintosh thought he was a 'spoilt brat'.

Saturday lunch was given by Keynes and Lydia in the Combination Room. It was attended by Provost Sheppard, the heads of many colleges and colleagues like John Clapham, Dennis Robertson and Austin and Joan Robinson. LePan met Lydia for the first time. 'Lively, vivacious, amusing, with eyes that readily turned to mischief, with lips that were now pert, now prim, with an idiom that was always unpredictable but always piquant, she was the perfect hostess for a lunch that otherwise might have been rather heavy in spite of all her husband's gifts. It was obvious that she was fascinated by Maynard and that he was fascinated by her.' For all their independence, their marriage, LePan thought, was old-fashioned – and good. Similarly LePan noticed that for all Keynes's 'speculative daring, for all his scepticism, for all his willingness to follow the argument wherever it might lead', he was 'deeply attached to many of the ancient sanctities, and wanted us to share in an intimate, almost family, way his pride in Cambridge and in its traditions'. In the seating plan, the host was described as 'High Steward of the Borough of Cambridge', and other eminent guests given their full pedigrees. 'It was a *very* Cambridge occasion.' Lionel Robbins had noticed the same contrast between Keynes's speculative intellect and his reverence for tradition.

The Cambridge interlude included a play and a concert at the Arts Theatre. LePan's last recollection of that weekend was walking down the Backs to the river. Bill Mackintosh said, 'How beautiful it is.' Keynes, a step or two behind, hesitated for only a moment. 'Yes, it is beautiful, isn't it? And we want to keep it, you know. That's why you're here.' On the young Canadian official Keynes made an undying impression: 'I am spellbound. This is the most extraordinary creature I have ever listened to. Does he belong to our species? Or is he from some other order? There is something mythic and fabulous about him. I sense in him something massive and sphinx-like, and yet also a hint of wings. One of the later and more elegant Greek sphinxes, then, it must be.'[26]

Scrutiny of Keynes's proposals took place against a dissolving political background. Labour ministers had resigned from the coalition government on 20 May. Churchill formed a 'caretaker' administration. Parliament was dissolved on 15 June, the general election took place on 5 July. But the results were not to be announced for three weeks till all the servicemen's votes were in. In the interim the Big Three of Churchill, Truman and Stalin were scheduled to meet at Potsdam to settle the future of Germany and Poland. Keynes concluded that this timetable would give the Cabinet no time to consider his memorandum till 1 August. Like most 'insiders', Keynes expected a Conservative victory.

Meanwhile, President Truman's new administration was working out its own response to the expected British request for post-war aid. The agreed American position was summed up in a letter of 25 June 1945 from William Clayton, the new Assistant Secretary of State, to Frederick Vinson, about to succeed Morgenthau as Secretary of the Treasury: 'It would be quite unwise ... to consider making Britain an outright gift.... It would be unwise even to supply the funds as credit without laying down conditions that would insure a sound advance towards our post-war objectives.' Clayton had in mind a credit of 'as much as $2 billion or $3 billion', at low interest rates, repayable over thirty years and with a 'waiver' in the event of a world slump. The conditions would be: elimination of the 'Sterling Area dollar pool', funding and probable write-down of sterling balances, and elimination (or at least 'substantial reduction') of empire preferences.[27]

Keynes's bad luck with electoral predictions continued. The result of the general election, announced on 26 July, was a landslide swing to Labour, which secured an overall majority of 140. Attlee became Prime Minister, with Ernest Bevin as Foreign Secretary and Hugh Dalton of the booming voice and Keynes's none-too-friendly Cambridge ex-student, as Chancellor of the Exchequer. Dalton promptly reappointed Keynes as his chief economic adviser, but was wary of him. His principal private secretary, Burke Trend, told Dalton's biographer Ben Pimlott that 'Dalton realised that he wasn't one of his buddies out hunting in the jungle; but he also realised that you didn't offend that sort of animal unnecessarily.'[28] Hunting in the jungle, though, is just what the two wary Kingsmen were about to embark on.

Keynes initialled a further revision of his March memorandum on 23 July, after comments from the Bank of England. As always he had tried to incorporate all the suggestions he had received in order to make possible an agreed position. The main change was to leave out Temptation. There were now only two alternatives. The 'austere' one, rechristened an 'essay in cunctation', was to go on borrowing from the sterling area and make a bilateral payments agreement between the sterling area and the United States. In deference to Eady and Cobbold this was now portrayed in somewhat more winning colours. But Keynes's preferred alternative was to settle the sterling balances problem on the basis of cancellation and funding, the USA providing a 'grant-in-aid' of $5bn over three years. (The $3bn credit line had vanished.) In return Britain would make post-war sterling area earnings immediately convertible into dollars, and release the blocked balances by instalments. Britain should not be prepared to borrow 'new money' from the USA, whose repayment came ahead of debts owed to its sterling creditors, nor could it contemplate using a dollar loan to pay off sterling debt. These were 'final decisions'. The main argument Britain should put to the United

States was that only with a grant of this size could it commit itself to the Article VII agenda. It was on the basis of this document that the final Treasury approach to the Stage III discussions was thrashed out at meetings on 20, 23 and 30 July. Keynes reluctantly accepted Brand's suggestion that it be left to the Americans to propose a grant after hearing the British case. However, the idea of a grant might be tried out on them in 'absolute privacy' if the occasion offered.[29]

The chance to do so arose when Clayton came to London for a meeting of the United Nations Relief and Rehabilitation Association (UNRRA) Council at which Britain, still playing the role of 'Lady Bountiful', agreed to contribute $320m to the reconstruction of Europe. The American Assistant Secretary of State and his team had two days of financial conversations, on 3 and 14 August, with Keynes, Eady and Brand (back from Washington), and also a couple of meetings at the Board of Trade. Except for details of the sterling balances settlement, Keynes exposed the complete case he would put in Washington the following month, and got the American response. Clayton indicated that a $3bn credit would be possible, on condition that Britain dismantled the dollar pool which was 'anathema' to US exporters, agreed a 'satisfactory' (that is, non-discriminatory) commercial policy, and scaled down and funded the sterling balances. Keynes commented that he would prefer a 'more meaningless phrase' than 'credits', and that $3bn might not be enough to give confidence: if Britain was left 'but a shilling better than bust, we shall be bust'.[30]

On 11 and 15 August Keynes attended two meetings with the Americans at the Board of Trade on commercial policy, at which Clayton made it clear that the financial and commercial negotiations would have to be linked, since 'the collectibility of international credits depended on ... liberal and multilateral measures' to expand trade.[31]

According to Clayton's note of the discussions of 14 August:

[Keynes] said that the *realistic* mind is an awful thing, and to work out an *inspired* solution to the problems which face the world requires a person with a *crazy* mind. To this Clayton made reply that the view that bankers' solutions were impracticable had his considerable sympathy but that he (and he believed the American people) was essentially *realistic* and that in saying that the British should not expect to get financial assistance in the form of free grants, he would be only frank with Keynes.

Clayton summarised the meeting as follows:

Of course, we realize that the British attitude is being presented by Keynes in his usual extreme manner. My personal opinion is that to cover a basically very weak financial position with a very serious outlook the British are putting up a very determined front. Under these circumstances it would be easy for the British to go the route of bilateral trade. It is my belief that the British will press for types of financial assistance which we may not find it desirable or possible to offer and that our discussion with them will be very difficult.[32]

Both sides knew what to expect. The British would ask for a gift of $5bn, offering a *quid pro quo* of sterling convertibility on current account, and nothing else. If they did not get it, or something like it, they would be 'forced' to choose 'Schachtianism'. The Americans would offer them a credit of $3bn conditional on clearing up the sterling debt position, 'liberalising' Empire trade, and making sterling convertible into dollars. But these could be regarded as opening shots in a prolonged bargaining game.

Keynes's request for urgent financial conversations was precipitated by the military resolution of the Pacific war. On 6 August the Americans dropped their first atomic bomb on Hiroshima, followed by another on Nagasaki three days later. On 10 August Emperor Hirohito broadcast the Japanese offer of surrender. With the imminent arrival of Stage III, everything speeded up. Keynes now had to persuade the government to send him to Washington straight away. On 15 August, he saw the Foreign Secretary, Ernest Bevin. Bevin told him that he would prefer to postpone financial or commercial arrangements 'until we could see our way more clearly'.[33] Dalton was more amenable. He had received Keynes's alarmist paper 'Our Overseas Financial Prospects' the previous day, in which Keynes predicted a 'financial Dunkirk' unless Britain got immediate help. Clayton, too, urged Washington to receive the British.

On 17 August President Truman decided to terminate Lend–Lease immediately, on the advice of Crowley and after Vinson had advised a taper. On the 20th Crowley informed Brand of the President's decision. No new goods would be supplied; all goods already ordered would have to be paid for. This news sent the Whitehall machine into overdrive. On 20 August Dalton told Bevin that 'we should open discussions [with the Americans] at once'. The next day Bevin and Dalton saw Clayton, for the first time. Clayton confirmed that there was no hope of the British getting anything but 'credit on very liberal terms', but said that he would try to 'continue the flow of supplies for the present without prejudice to the terms of the settlement'. Bob Dixon of the Foreign Office telephoned Halifax at Garrowby in Yorkshire, telling him that he would have to cut short his holiday, as Bevin wanted him to lead the British delegation in Washington. 'This is an awful bore, and completely wrecks my plans,' grumbled the ambassador.

42

Averting a Financial Dunkirk

I. MAYNARD'S OPTIMISM

At 10.15 p.m. on Thursday 23 August 1945 an emergency meeting was held in the Cabinet Room at 10 Downing Street. It was chaired by the Prime Minister, Clement Attlee, flanked by the senior ministers of his government: the Lord President of the Council Herbert Morrison, the Chancellor of the Exchequer Hugh Dalton, the Foreign Secretary Ernest Bevin, and the President of the Board of Trade Sir Stafford Cripps. On the opposite side of the table were Halifax, Keynes, Bridges, Eady, Brand, Sinclair and Edward Hall-Patch of the Foreign Office. There was one item only on the agenda: how to avert the 'financial Dunkirk' which Keynes had predicted in his paper 'Our Overseas Financial Prospects', circulated a few days previously. Lend–Lease and borrowing from the sterling area had been plugging a gap in the balance of payments, which was now estimated at £2.1bn or just over $8bn. Lend–Lease running at £1.35bn would stop forthwith; borrowing from the sterling area might continue, but on a greatly reduced scale. By increasing exports, eliminating imports of munitions, and cutting down overseas expenditure the deficit for 1946 could be reduced to just under £1bn or $4bn. In 1947 it might fall to £550m and in 1948 to £200m, leaving Britain in balance by 1949. Over these three years, though, it would have to finance a total deficit of £1.7bn or about $7bn. 'Where is all this money to come from?' Keynes asked. Gold and dollar reserves, which in 1945 stood at £500m, might be run down by £250m. Britain might be able to borrow £150m net from the sterling area in 1947 and 1948. This would reduce the cumulative deficit over the three years to £1.3bn (Keynes wrote £1.25bn) or $5bn. 'The conclusion is inescapable', Keynes wrote, 'that aid of the order of $5bn is required from the United States' if Britain was to 'spend on the scale we contemplate'. The United States would probably make available between $3bn and $5bn, but the British would have to bargain hard on terms and conditions. Britain must refuse a loan. But if 'the term *credit* is no more than a camouflage for what would be in effect a grant-in-aid, that is another matter'. In return for this, Britain should 'not seek to escape our obligations under Article VII of the Mutual Aid Agreement'. Keynes warned that 'no arrangement which we can properly accept is yet in sight; and that, until such an arrangement is in sight, we are ... virtually bankrupt and the economic basis for the hopes of the public non-existent'. He ended: 'In practice, of course, we shall in the end accept the best terms we can get.'[1]

The main difficulties of the subsequent negotiations are encapsulated in this contradictory document. Britain should refuse a loan, but not a grant 'dressed up' as a loan. What did this mean? Some conditions would apparently be unacceptable; but in the end Britain would accept any conditions. No wonder Eady had referred to Keynes's 'extraordinarily difficult financial diplomacy'.

Halifax wrote in his diary of 23 August: 'Keynes gave a good exposition of the business, ending on a rather optimistic note, and we all said our say, Ministers agreeing to turn Keynes loose but without authority to settle except on reference home. This Keynes himself wanted, to strengthen his hand.'

The official record of the Cabinet discussion does not suggest that Keynes was unduly optimistic. He told ministers that the 'terms offered might vary from an out and out grant in aid to a commercial credit'. His insistence that 'he should not be authorised to agree to anything except an out and out grant', that help 'on any less favourable terms should not be accepted except after very long thought on the part of Ministers in London', that the 'financial terms ... would constitute the greatest stumbling block', do not suggest undue confidence in the outcome. Nor did Keynes promise $6bn, as Dalton later alleged. He told ministers that the Americans were thinking in terms of $3bn, 'rising possibly to 5'. The only *quid pro quo* Keynes asked for authorisation to offer was a promise 'to go to the sterling area and ask them to cancel part of our indebtedness to them and agree that the remainder should be made fully convertible by instalments'. He thought 'this was the only constructive proposal which he should put forward at the outset'. The next step was more ambiguous. Keynes thought that Britain 'could undertake the obligations' contained in the Bretton Woods Agreement, provided they were not coupled with 'dangerous concessions on commercial policy'. By this he meant chiefly making sterling convertible on current account. How much money would Britain need to accept this obligation? This was not made clear, though the implication was that it would have to be $5bn. On only one point did Keynes mislead ministers. This was in de-emphasising the linkage between financial help and a commercial agreement. On the contrary, 'Lord Keynes emphasised that there was no question of our being asked to agree to a detailed commercial treaty at this stage.' True enough: but the Americans were certainly expecting something more than a 'joint invitation to 15 other countries to attend an international conference next year'. Even worse, Keynes discussed the two countries' differences on commercial policy without pointing out that the outcome of the financial negotiations would depend on their resolution.

The Cabinet Committee accepted Brand's suggestion that the British should not ask outright for a grant-in-aid, but allow the case for it to develop irresistibly from their presentation, leaving it to the Americans to propose it. Attlee summed up that the negotiations be left to 'Lord Keynes and his colleagues on the basis that he had outlined ... and that negotiations should be *ad referendum,* reports being made to Ministers in London as and when necessary'.[2]

The nub of the matter is that Keynes's presentation of the alternatives had been seriously undermined by the Treasury–Bank refusal to have anything to do with Temptation. This middle way between Austerity and Justice was therefore unexplored before Keynes set out for Washington. He left, that is, without an agreed fall-back position. Since he disliked Austerity so much, he probably exaggerated the chances of getting Justice. Eady and the Bank of England were willing to see Keynes's mission fail, leaving Austerity as the sole alternative. The Labour ministers were caught in this cross-fire. They therefore pinned their hopes on Justice, and persuaded themselves that Keynes had promised it.

Keynes's mission to the United States was announced in the House of Commons on 24 August. The news that no Board of Trade officials would go out dismayed the Americans, since it implied that the British were not prepared for serious commercial discussions. Under pressure from Clayton and Hawkins, ministers agreed, on 31 August, that Lionel Helmore of the Board of Trade should accompany the Mission as an 'observer', with a separate Board of Trade mission to be sent out 'as soon as practicable'.[3] Robbins was soon to comment, 'If ... anybody had told me that it would have been possible for high personages in Whitehall to believe blithely ... that we could get away with a financial settlement ... with no commitments on commercial policy, I just would not have believed him.'[4]

The announcement of the Keynes Mission produced disconcerted reactions from across the Atlantic. The conservative banker Leffingwell, Keynes's old sparring partner from Paris Peace Conference days, thought that the dispatch of Keynes to America was a bad move: 'There is nothing more disturbing, I think, than the sending of Lord Keynes here. Brilliant man that he is, he is too brilliant to be persuasive with us Americans. Many Americans admire him.... But, rightly or wrongly, how many trust him? How many will accept his sales talk? No one.'[5]

Leffingwell thought that the British should make their post-war economic plans on the assumption of no help from abroad whatever, just as Churchill had made his war plans in 1940. This would do more to elicit a spontaneous American offer of help than 'a thousand Keyneses'. In other words, a 'financial Dunkirk' was needed to loosen America's purse-strings just as the actual Dunkirk had. This was psychologically shrewd.

II. OPENING MOVES IN WASHINGTON

Maynard and Lydia Keynes left Southampton on the Canadian troopship
Pasteur on 27 August bound for Quebec City. Accompanying them were
Frederic Harmer of the Treasury, Edward Hall-Patch of the Foreign Office
and Lionel Helmore of the Board of Trade. Halifax and Brand had already
returned to Washington. Even by British standards it was an extraordinarily
lean mission, to be headed by a man who was not only frail, but had started
to look old. Keynes's hair and moustache had turned white, the whiteness
emphasising his now habitual pallor. His medically ordered loss of weight
had benefited his heart but left his tall frame looking curiously under-
supported. He now needed thick glasses to read. Only when they were taken
off could one see that his eyes still burnt with brightness and amusement.
As the negotiations were to show, he had lost none of his powers of wit and
rudeness.

From Quebec, Maynard and Lydia flew to Ottawa, the pilot keeping the
plane low to avoid straining Keynes's heart. In Ottawa, he and Lydia
reoccupied the Moorish suite at the Château Laurier they had stayed in in
1944. Negotiations on the Mutual Aid wind-up were arduous 'but they are
all so friendly that there is no pain or grief'. The upshot was that the British
got $300m more than they expected.[6] On 6 September Maynard and Lydia
took the train for Washington, where they booked again into the Statler
Hotel. He was in fine fettle. Asked by British officials what conditions
were like back home, he quipped that they were not too bad – 'but don't
let on here in Washington; we must fill our mouths with false teeth and
yell as each one is pulled out'. Paul Bareau, the delegation's scribe, noted
'that infectious, that dangerously infectious optimism' with which Keynes
approached his negotiations.

At the first formal meeting of the Anglo-American Top Committee on
11 September, it was agreed to set up sub-committees covering Finance, the
Lend–Lease wind-up, Surplus Property Disposal (mainly military) and Commercial Policy. The British would be led by Halifax and Keynes on Finance
opposite Vinson and Clayton, and Keynes would lead for the British on the
Lend–Lease wind-up or clean-up negotiations, as they were known, opposite
Crowley, with Sir Henry Self, deputy chairman of the British Supply Council,
representing Britain on Surplus Property.

The State Department's insistence on setting up a parallel Commercial
Policy Committee came as a nasty surprise to Keynes – and to London. It
was the first defeat for the British negotiating strategy. However, Keynes
took comfort from Clayton's apparent willingness to keep the discussions

general, and proposed that he and Halifax lead for Britain on commercial policy. Meade was dismayed at the thought of Keynes in action without the 'commercial policy boys', and gripped by 'crazy, lunatic and self-contradictory' ideas on commercial policy.[7] Keynes was instructed to postpone the first meeting, scheduled for 17 September, till the arrival of Board of Trade reinforcements from London. Though both he and Halifax protested, the decision was confirmed.[8]

The key players on the American side were William Clayton, acting as chairman in place of Byrnes, the Secretary of State away in London, and Fred Vinson, who had succeeded Morgenthau as Secretary of the Treasury. This was an advantage, for both were pro-British. Clayton, a six-foot-six self-made cotton manufacturer from Texas, with a soft southern drawl, was an ardent internationalist. Vinson, a former professional baseball player and conservative Democrat Congressman from Kentucky, was a genial lawyer of provincial outlook, much addicted to the humbugging school of public oratory and, it is now generally agreed, somewhat over-promoted. Keynes liked Vinson, but Vinson did not like Keynes: he was too often on the receiving end of slashing remarks. The other Americans had little influence. Marriner Eccles, chairman of the Federal Reserve Board, had one idea, which he would expound in a stentorian bellow at inordinate length: that Britain was a bankrupt company, and America must get paid back ahead of any other creditors. Henry Wallace, now Secretary of Commerce, struck Keynes as 'completely gaga. He seems to pass out within five minutes of the beginning of any meeting.' Leo Crowley, the unfriendly Lend–Lease tsar, was on his way to political oblivion. His facial characteristics made him the butt of some of Keynes's unkindest jokes. They reminded him, Keynes said, of the 'buttocks of a baboon'. The nickname stuck, inspiring the 'BABOON' code name for British telegrams from the Treasury during the Loan negotiations, whose counterparts from Washington were code-named 'NABOB'. Keynes was quick to renew his friendship with Harry White, who advised him 'not to lose his temper except at the right moments'. However, with Morgenthau's departure from the Treasury, White was plainly in eclipse, though Keynes was not to know that Elizabeth Bentley had, on 21 August 1945, denounced him to the FBI as a Soviet agent. White himself was convinced that he would soon be dismissed from the Treasury, and was looking for a new job at the IMF or World Bank.[9] Keynes retained some illusions not only about White's influence with the new Secretary, but also about White's support for the British position.

The Halifax–Keynes axis was central to the British negotiating effort. Keynes quickly re-established close relations with the languid charmer and he later wrote that they worked together 'like brothers'. The ambassador's part in the loan negotiations has been seriously underplayed. He greatly preferred tennis, hunting and gossiping with old friends (Lady 'Baba' Metcalfe was staying at the Embassy for much of the autumn) to financial work, or indeed to most forms of work. He did not pretend to understand technicalities. His main role was to calm the increasingly frayed nerves of the Mission, and relate their concerns to the big picture of Anglo-American relations. When Keynes was abrasive Halifax was emollient. Late at night he would tone down Keynes's increasingly angry telegrams to London, and talk him out of resignation. He was constantly entertained by Lydia, and developed almost unstinted admiration for Keynes.

On 12 September Keynes and Halifax held a press conference at the Embassy. In his prepared statement, which he delivered on his feet, Keynes started spinning the web in which he hoped to entangle the Americans, expatiating on Britain's war-weariness, the way that Lend–Lease, while essential to Britain's full mobilisation, had led it to sacrifice two-thirds of its export trade, the transitional balance of payments deficit, the problem of the sterling balances, the advantages of a liberal trading world. He emphasised the disadvantages of a commercial loan, and said that, rather than accept it, Britain would try to 'do what we can to get on as best we can on any other lines which are open to us'. One must try to imagine that tall, stooped, by now bespectacled and rather ill-looking figure, glancing up from time to time from his hand-held text to deliver his statement in his refined voice to a room full of tough, hard-bitten and surprisingly well-informed American reporters. Harmer thought that he contrived to make it sound 'both dramatic and spontaneous'. Bareau was less impressed. 'It did not appear to create any great enthusiasm and typically Keynesian phrases like "Our pains, ours and yours, are more likely to be due to our stomachs being fuller than our heads and our appetite weaker than our opportunity" caused no amusement at all.' After an hour and a quarter, Halifax suggested drinks. He thought that 'Keynes got himself pressed a bit more than was wise when it came to questions.' Bareau, however, thought he dealt with them 'in a masterly fashion'.

At three long opening sessions of the Top Committee, on 13, 14 and 17 September, held in the board room of the Federal Reserve Building, Keynes gave a revised version of the allocution LePan had heard in Cambridge in May. 'I thought he did this quite well,' wrote the ambassador after the first lecture, which lasted about two hours.

On Monday 17 September, recalls Bareau, Keynes worked up his presentation with a magnificent development of the theme that though the Germans had invented the concept of Total War it was the British who had applied it most thoroughly in their everyday lives. It was reflected in the reckless profligacy with which Britain had thrown its overseas assets and export trade away in the common cause. 'Was not that recklessness the factor that tipped the scale and brought victory? The exposition ended with this question – and without any specific mention of that massive American grant which Keynes hoped to obtain. Keynes expected the offer to come from the other side. It never came.'[10] When the negotiations were done, an

American gossip columnist, Paul Edison, wrote: 'Lord Keynes opened the conversations ... and he talked for three days in a row. That was to explain the British position. It must have been bad.'[11]

The British had made a tactical mistake by circulating a document comparing the British and American war efforts, to the latter's disadvantage. Keynes later admitted that 'showing our medals' had been an error. It was leaked by the Americans, John Crider publishing an account of it in the *New York Times*.

On 19 and 20 September Keynes expounded further to the Joint Finance Committee. He put forward the two alternative solutions to Britain's problem – what he had called Starvation Corner and Justice – being careful to say that they were extremes within the range of which many compromises were possible. He clearly indicated that he disapproved of the austere alternative, which would inevitably lead to bilateralism and a contraction of trade. His second alternative was one which envisaged 'liquidating as far as possible the financial consequences of the war'. As to the *quid pro quo* the British could offer Keynes outlined his tripartite scheme for dealing with the abnormal sterling balances, involving cancellation, funding and release, without attaching figures. Britain would also be able to bring into force the 'major part' of the permanent Bretton Woods Agreement by the end of 1946. That is, it would be able to make sterling convertible into other currencies for current transactions – as it had been before the war. What did the Americans think? asked Keynes, fishing for an offer. Paul Bareau described the reaction:

> Vinson expressed the deepest disappointment in Keynes's statement which he said had not crystallised the situation in any way.... Keynes, said Vinson, had left so many blanks in his description of the second alternative that it was more or less meaningless to the Americans. What Vinson clearly had in mind was that the second alternative demanded American help and he was disappointed that Keynes had not mentioned that fact and had not specified the magnitude of the aid which would be required....

Under further prompting from Clayton, Keynes said that, while the British wanted the sterling debts reduced, it could not be done on a uniform basis, or by unilateral action, but would require individual settlements with Britain's creditors, according to the circumstances of each case. At this point, Henry Wallace, who had fallen asleep, woke up to ask why Britain could not trade Indian independence for a write-down of Indian debt – a suggestion which horrified both Keynes and Halifax. Marriner Eccles bellowed above the noise that all former ideas of honour and financial rectitude must be readjusted to the cataclysm which the war had caused. Britain was like a bankrupt company which had to be reconstructed, and the creditors must take the rap. This was one business analogy too far. The suggestion that countries like India and Egypt should be thought of as part of a consortium of creditors to refinance Britain's busted imperial enterprise was too dramatic a reversal of the normal order of things to be contemplated. 'These people will never be able to run an Empire,' Frank Lee remarked icily as they left the room.[12]

Keynes was being forced out into the open. At the 20 September meeting he said that Britain might cancel $4bn of the estimated $12bn of sterling debt, fund $7.2bn and release $800m over the transitional period. It would need at least $5bn, plus a Lend–Lease wind-up, from the US over three to five years to cover its adverse balance of trade, finance sterling withdrawals and pay back a number of smaller non-sterling debts. 'The Americans did not bat an eyelid and accepted the figure [of $5bn] without any demur.' In return, Britain would remove the 'discriminatory aspects of the sterling system' by the end of 1946. Vinson said that the American officials would go off and study the matter. Meetings were then suspended for a few days.[13]

Sensing that the British team's inability to disclose their hand on the sterling balances had irritated the Americans, Keynes asked London for permission to discuss debt cancellation in more detail. Worried by the prospect of leaks to sterling area countries, London refused. Keynes should try to get the Americans to make proposals. It would help if the Americans could state 'in a form which could be used' that help from them was conditional on 'an adjustment of our sterling indebtedness'.[14] Appalled at the thought of unilateral default, London clearly wanted to use the Americans to put pressure on its sterling creditors.

To conduct the trade negotiations, eight officials headed by Sir Percivale Liesching and Lionel Robbins sailed out on 21 September and arrived on the 27th. Keynes, who had been 'very angry' at the thought of their coming, greeted Robbins cordially and invited him onto the Financial Committee. As he had anticipated, the commercial negotiations, starting on 1 October, went smoothly after all the preparatory work in London. The two sides worked to an American draft constitution – known as Com/Trade 1 – of an International Trade Organization, laying down rules on preferences, subsidies, state trading, export taxes, exchange controls and cartels. Differences surfaced between the American and British approaches to eliminating 'Forbidden Tricks', the Americans favouring outright prohibitions, the British preferring a case-by-case approach. Keynes made his own typical contribution. At one point when they were discussing the control of cartels, he interjected: 'Isn't our scheme intended to get things done, whereas yours will merely provide a living for a large number of lawyers?' Vinson exploded, 'That is just the kind of statement you would make' – which makes one wonder how well Keynes would have done had he been left in sole charge of the negotiations. After eleven days the only substantial obstacle which remained was imperial preferences. The Americans insisted, from the outset, that a unilateral elimination of preferences must be a condition of financial aid. The British were prepared to trade reduction in preferences for all-round tariff reductions, and resisted any explicit link between commercial concessions and financial assistance. However, two precious weeks had been lost – one of them at sea. Keynes came to believe that this delay dissipated the atmosphere he had created in his oral presentations, prejudicing the eventual outcome.

Robbins soon sniffed out what was happening on the financial side. 'It is clear', he wrote in his diary on 29 September,

> that a pure grant-in-aid is right out of the picture. It is clear, too, that Maynard accepts this completely and is beginning to be inclined to think it is absurd to believe otherwise. I had no difficulty in refraining from saying I told you so. But I perceive that we shall have great difficulty in dehypnotising London; and I think that Maynard will have to be told that, having himself made the magic passes that now hold the King's Treasurers entranced in rapturous contemplation of ideal 'justice', it will be up to him ... to reverse the process.[15]

III. RETREAT TO TEMPTATION

Two informal meetings between Halifax and Keynes and Clayton and Vinson at Blair Lee House on 25 and 27 September made the position clear. Both sides 'understood that some amount in the neighbourhood of $5bn was in their minds as well as ours'. So far so good. But, wrote the ambassador in his diary, just 'when I thought it had been going well, we ran into trouble'. The Americans made it plain that they could not contemplate either a grant or an interest-free loan. 'We said we could not contemplate paying interest because we could not see our way to do it. And so there we were.'[16] At the second meeting, the American pair did not 'recoil too violently' from Keynes's suggestion of a combined grant-in-aid and low-interest loan, but doubted that they could get it through Congress. Halifax and Keynes left it that they would report to London and meet the following week.

On 26 September Keynes asked for London's permission to discuss 'the acceptability of a loan without interest', with annual payments limited to $100m. Reversing his previous arguments, he told Dalton that he could think of no 'plausible reason' for any gift at all, since 'retrospective lend lease corresponding to what we spent here is, most certainly, not a good starter' – as Brand had told him all along. He had, in Bareau's words, 'consigned his earlier concepts of Justice to a limbo amid the ghosts and skeletons of which only fools and dullards would roam and search'.[17] An interest-free loan might well be attainable. Harry White was apparently advising Vinson to offer one. Keynes now urged that Britain could afford to accept a $5bn loan, repayable in fifty instalments, with the first instalment postponed for five or ten years. 'Release' of accumulated sterling balances, would cost another $150m. The total would come to less than 5 per cent of the 'break even' export target of $6500m. 'Either we can manage this or we are sunk anyway.' As part of this approach, Britain should accept an escape clause based 'not on our ability to pay but on the willingness of the creditor country to receive [British goods]'.[18]

This was Keynes's personal fall-back position – the version of Temptation he had always been willing to accept. 'My advice would be to accept a settlement on these terms' if nothing 'better' was available, he cabled Dalton on 1 October, and he requested 'discretion' – though rather obliquely – to negotiate a deal. But he had not yet completely given up hope that something 'better' might turn up.[19] Not surprisingly, Dalton refused. His biographer writes that 'Keynes's steady retreat from optimism was regarded ... with incomprehension' by the ministerial team of Dalton, Bevin and Cripps which was handling the London end of the negotiations.[20] A gap had started to open up between the expectations Keynes had aroused in London and the realities of Washington. Keynes's efforts to scale down London's hopes coincided with a hardening of Labour's attitude towards the negotiations. Eady warned him on 28 September that the new government would be much less frightened by austerity than its predecessor, indeed might positively welcome it 'partly as a more noble way of life, partly as a psychological sublimation of disappointment'.

During the first bout of sitting around Keynes gave a talk to the Overseas Writers' Club, briefed both British and Dominion journalists, and tried his persuasive arts on the first of the dinner groups of American Senators and Congressmen Halifax had arranged for him. Halifax thought that Keynes handled these occasions 'admirably well', though they were 'pretty gruelling'. The American politicians, worried about Harold Laski's influence on the British government, feared that American help would be used to 'finance socialism', and wondered what benefits the Americans would gain from 'getting us up on our feet and liberalising the sterling area' and whether 'we could ... make ourselves efficient'.[21] Harmer, who attended a couple of these occasions, made a shrewd comment in his diary of 9 October:

> The pro-British line always needs defending in this country; the anti-British never. This is psychological, and need not be taken too seriously: but it is a fact which always needs remembering in handling any important issue here. It isn't that there is underlying hostility to Britain: on the contrary, there is very great friendliness. But their history starts

with the War of Independence and that colours all their thinking. They must always be able to show that they haven't been outsmarted.

On Saturday 6 October the ambassador had 'Keynes to dinner with Roger Makins [of the Foreign Office] and his wife. Lady Keynes was in grand form and kept us all vastly entertained. We got Keynes going on the subject of Monty Norman, whom he liked very much, but who he said on some sides of life was a somewhat dangerous mixture of imp and charlatan. The high moment of his power he judged to have been Snowden as Chancellor who was completely mesmerised by him.'

The first fortnight in October was the happiest part of Keynes's last Washington trip. The negotiations had not yet got too tense, Washington had cooled down from the semi-tropical summer heat, with clear blue skies and fresh breezes every day.

> We get up early [Lydia wrote to Florence Keynes on 13 October]. I ring for our breakfast, the Lord sips tea with a bun and jelly. I inhale coffee, but before I drink it I cover it with an angora scarf to keep it very hot: sometimes we get a wrong paper, I walk in the passage and steal the right paper from someone who is still asleep, but on the whole the Americans get up early – by 8 o'clock the lift is full of businessmen with a cigar.

Keynes at last received new instructions from the Chancellor on 8 October. 'If best offer is large loan at 2 per cent interest we would not accept it,' Dalton cabled. 'We remain firm that we will not accept obligations which we do not see reasonable certainty of discharging. Also such a commercial settlement would be regarded as an inequitable conclusion to our mutual effort.' Dalton was lobbing back Keynes's poetry to him. What sort of settlement would be acceptable? Dalton allowed two alternatives. London would accept a grant of $2bn 'as partial repayment of what we had to spend in America during cash and carry period', plus a credit of $3bn to $4bn on which they would pay 1 per cent interest on the drawings made. If this failed, it would accept an interest-free $5bn loan repayable over fifty years, provided the 'background conditions' were right. Dalton emphasised two requirements: (a) an 'undisputed right to restrict Britain's total imports' and (b) a waiver clause of the kind Keynes had suggested. But Keynes himself was to make no offer along these lines for the time being, leaving the Americans to take the initiative.[22]

Keynes could now feel that London had accepted his version of Temptation, and what remained to be done was to put forward Dalton's first alternative in the hope of eliciting his second. When Keynes and Halifax saw Vinson and Clayton again on 9 October, Keynes urged that $2bn of American help should come in the form of a grant, but failed to shift the American view that this was politically impossible. Vinson and Clayton also repeated

that an interest-free loan was politically unfeasible. What the British negotiators did get from Clayton was a suggestion that the Americans might
provide a loan of $5bn, repayable in fifty annual instalments starting in five
years, with an additional annuity of $50m a year to cover interest at 2 per
cent. Interest might be 'finally waived (repeat waived) and not deferred' if in
any year Britain could not pay, Clayton inviting Keynes to draft a waiver
clause. At his press conference the same day Clayton 'actually mentioned
$5bn as the agreed figure'.[23]

This was the best offer the British got, though it was not entirely firm.
Keynes clearly thought it offered the basis for a settlement. But he now
made a crucial tactical mistake. Instead of sending London a short telegram
outlining the American offer and asking for authority to accept, subject to
satisfactory background conditions, he got diverted into an overcomplicated
discussion of possible waiver formulae.[24] In short, he took his eye off the
ball. Nevertheless, Halifax thought that 'it does look as if we are moving to
a settlement with a bit of luck', and Harmer talked of trying 'to force the
whole thing to a settlement in a couple of weeks or so'.[25]

The let-down was swift and brutal. Dalton cabled him bluntly on 13
October that 'we do not find a loan on these terms acceptable'. It failed 'two
tests of principle'. First, it lacked the 'sweet breath of justice'. Secondly, there
was no 'reasonable certainty' that Britain would be able to discharge the
debt. To Clayton and Vinson, the difference between $100m and $150m
might be 'peanuts', but 'unfortunately it cannot be so to us'. To add to this
annual liability, repayments to the sterling area as part of the deal were 'the
last straw'. Dalton instructed the British negotiators to continue to seek 'a
complete or partial interest-free grant, and to resist annual payments exceeding $100 million'.[26]

The lack of an agreed fall-back position now started to have a deadly
effect. Keynes had insisted in London on not being allowed to accept
anything but a grant. Now when he asked for flexibility to negotiate a loan,
it was being denied him.

IV. DESCENT INTO HORROR

Keynes and Halifax dutifully tried out Dalton's now exploded formula on
Clayton and Vinson on 15 and 16 October. They asked for a grant-in-aid of
$2bn and a credit line of up to $3bn at 2 per cent interest, capital repayment
and interest starting in five years' time. But they 'made no progress whatsoever', with the atmosphere 'gloomy and unconstructive'. Moreover, Clayton's
mind also seemed to be moving in the 'unpleasant direction of proposing a

reduction in the credit below 5 billion whilst keeping the annual service charge at $100 million'.[27]

On Wednesday 17 October, Keynes drafted NABOB 177 to London, dispatched at 1 a.m. the following morning. 'I thought it was quite brilliantly done,' the ambassador wrote in his diary that day, 'with pleasant touches of wit redeeming the atmosphere of official telegrams.' The telegram sent 'after consultation with the Ambassador, Brand, Self, Liesching, Robbins and Hall-Patch' and 'representing our collective opinion' was a plea to London to authorise Keynes to accept the Clayton offer. Keynes admitted that the British had failed to achieve any of their objectives. 'In this business country', Keynes wrote ironically, 'where it is a moral duty ... to make ... money ... some imitation of a normal banking transaction is necessary if the moral principles of the country are not to be affronted.' On the other hand, some settlement with the United States was essential. He wanted authority to negotiate a settlement on the basis of a loan of $5bn at 2 per cent interest, payable over fifty years, in which the interest portion would be waived whenever 'home-produced exports' were insufficient to finance the pre-war volume of imports.[28]

What he did not realise when he dispatched this telegram was that the Clayton offer had been withdrawn. Keynes's 'friend' Harry White had stabbed him in the back, and he never knew it. A US Treasury committee headed by White concluded that Britain's prospective balance of payments difficulties had been exaggerated and that Britain would not need as much as $5bn to get it through the transition.*

At the meeting of 18 October, Vinson told Keynes, Halifax and Brand that the 'best offer' they could make was a loan of $3.5bn at 2 per cent, repayable over fifty years, plus whatever was needed to 'clean up' Lend–Lease at 2⅜ per cent, repayable over thirty years. The total in the round figures then being bandied around came to about $4bn altogether. Asked how they had arrived at the lower figure, Clayton said that it assumed that Britain would run down its gold and dollar reserves to $1bn at the end of the transition – a replay, it seemed, of the previous American management of Lend–Lease. Britain's commitment to liberalising sterling area payments would remain unchanged.

Keynes treated the American proposals 'very roughly', wrote Halifax, 'and at one time the argument became strained. I thought of interrupting Keynes in one of his explosions. On second thoughts I was not sure that the explosion was not doing good and so let it run.' Keynes said that their proposal would certainly be quite unacceptable to London, and therefore he would like their advice as to whether it would not really be better for him to break off and to go back to London, with 'dangerous and even tragic

* White was flying a complicated kite of his own, which involved the United States buying part of Britain's sterling debt from its holders. It came to nothing.

consequences'. Vinson demurred: 'In Kentucky we never ask our guests to leave.'[29]

Too late, Keynes now returned to Clayton's proposal of a $5bn loan. It seemed that the Americans might, after all, agree to go up to $4bn plus the Lend–Lease clean-up. They then started talking about waiver conditions, Clayton insisting that 'the criterion of our external income must include our net invisible income'.

To his mother Keynes wrote on 21 October, 'We have reached a point in our negotiations where we can get no further without instructions from London.... On the face of it things don't look too good. But it is almost essential for them as for us to reach an acceptable conclusion. So I remain fairly optimistic and, with the onset of senility, don't worry anything like as much as I used to....' Dalton was due to present his budget on 23 October, so another period of waiting began.

In the previous seven weeks, the attitudes of the principals in London and their agents in Washington had grown distressingly apart. To put it simply, Britain's negotiators in Washington were instinctively pro-American; their masters in London were instinctively anti-American. Conservative (or in Keynes's case Liberal) envoys were negotiating on behalf of a Labour government committed to large-scale nationalisation. Keynes's preference for the 'American' to the 'Russian' bias had hardened with the advent of a Labour government in Britain and the first rumblings of the Cold War. The very reasons which were making the Labour Cabinet hesitant to tie Britain to America's coat-tails were, for Keynes, increasingly important arguments for doing so.

As in the negotiations leading up to the Bretton Woods Agreement, Keynes often railed against the United States, and sometimes talked of breaking off negotiations. But he would never have done so unless he had been convinced that America positively meant Britain harm. As it was, there was always enough 'give' in the American position to reassure him of America's underlying goodwill. So it was easy for him to fall back on such second-order explanations of Anglo-American conflicts as misunderstandings arising from the different British and American ways of doing business, and, above all, from the need for the administration to pacify Congress.

Keynes was also conscious of the timetable. The Bretton Woods Agreement had to be ratified by Parliament by the end of the year. A financial agreement had to be in the bag by then, or it could well lapse. This was, for Keynes, a decisive argument against breaking off: the whole edifice of post-war reconstruction was at stake. Vinson and Clayton also had a tight timetable. They wanted Congress to ratify the loan before it adjourned in mid-December, fearing a build-up of opposition. The Americans, Keynes was convinced, would never force the British to break off. This gave him what little leverage he had.

A further factor which made Keynes increasingly anxious to force the pace of agreement was the precarious state of his health. In letters home, he insisted that he felt 'pretty well and equal to one more push'. Lydia was exercising 'iron discipline about diet, ice-bags, rests and sleeping'. As often as they could they had supper alone in their suite in the Statler, and retired early, with Lydia removing the ice crystals from below their salads to put into the icebag on Keynes's chest. However, Keynes had already had a 'slight heart attack' on 7 October, 'due to over-eating on top of over-working'.[30] As the negotiations lengthened, his heart pains returned, and he started taking sodium amytal capsules to relieve them. A fully fit man might have flown back to London to obtain more flexible instructions. But Keynes was trapped in Washington by his infirmities. He could not risk air travel. Instead, he begged Sir Edward Bridges, the Cabinet secretary, to come out, so that he could confirm the Mission's account of the Washington atmosphere. But this was vetoed by Attlee, who didn't want 'crossed wires on finance'.[31] So, as Robbins put it, Keynes would 'spend hours late at night drafting telegrams, superb in literary style and wit, which had better been left to small fry, both because of the labour saved and because of the palpable unsuitability of many of his flourishes for the persuasion of bewildered ministers who felt they had once already been taken in by his eloquence'.[32] This last point is important. Keynes was eloquent, not terse. He needed to create an atmosphere for his persuasion. Today, one can enjoy the atmospherics of his NABOBs, but also understand why hard-pressed ministers and officials back in London found them rather confusing.

While worsening American terms made Keynes more, rather than less, eager to finish off the negotiations quickly, this had the opposite effect in London. Some still clung to the hope of ideal Justice. Others worried about Britain's capacity to repay debt. Ministers also foresaw another trap: that Britain would be forced to commit itself to making sterling convertible before it had recovered its solvency.

The Bank of England's position was the most intransigent – and politically hopeless. Determined to maintain the sterling area, it opposed debt cancellation, premature convertibility, and borrowing from America. If it had a policy, it was to enforce Starvation Corner on Britain and use the sterling debts as a lever to impose British exports on sterling area countries. This raised the question of commercial policy. Here imperialists and state-trading socialists united in demanding an escape from the Article VII commitment. Eady at the Treasury and Cobbold at the Bank were against any agreement that tied Britain's hands in any way. This struck a responsive chord in the Labour Cabinet, which feared that an American loan, with all its strings, would limit the possibility of insular socialism.

Exponents of *Realpolitik* will say that Keynes was blind to the real conflicts of interest between the two powers. But his London critics failed to offer a plausible alternative. In the last resort, no one was really ready for Starvation Corner. England was a democratic, not Soviet, state. Instead, as

Freddie Harmer noted, London clung to the 'lunatic idea that we could break with the Americans on anything they really care about and still get enough finance on some terms or other to get us through'.[33]

The divided counsels in London were reflected in the BABOONs Dalton sent on 27 October in reply to Keynes's NABOBs of 19 and 20 October. Meade thought these were 'the lowest point of Eady's and Cobbold's efforts'.[34] They were based on the idea – logical in itself – of a trade-off between assistance and obligations. Britain would either accept $4.5bn, of which $2.5bn would carry interest of 1 per cent, undertaking to ratify the Bretton Woods Agreement, sponsor an international trade conference, and settle with its sterling area creditors; or it would seek to borrow $2.5bn on commercial terms, plus whatever was needed to settle the Lend–Lease account, without undertaking any obligations whatsoever.

Dalton's BABOONs left Keynes 'white with rage and talking about resigning'. But by the next day, Harmer noted, 'M. had thought it out very well and after writing and destroying one or two vitriolic drafts produced a very good one'. Alternative B, he told Dalton, was a non-starter: the commercial rate of borrowing was 3 per cent and would involve immediate repayment of capital. If it were raised the Americans would assume that Britain was bent on creating a separate economic bloc. Alternative A just might run, with interest at 2 per cent, not 1. London agreed to 2 per cent.

Keynes's parallel efforts to clear up the question of the sterling balances also ran into trouble. The Americans wanted the sterling balances dealt with because their existence affected British ability to service any American debt. When Keynes's proposals for scaling down, funding and releasing the debts reached London, 'Cobbold and Eady threw a fit, saying we could in effect give the Americans no assurances about getting our sterling creditors to scale down their balances or about the amount to which we could release sterling balances for conversion into dollars.'[35] A heated exchange followed. Eventually Keynes was moved to a jibe at the Bank's expense: 'Some fig leaves which may pass muster with old ladies in London wilt in a harsher climate.'[36] Keynes received permission to pass on his suggestions for scaling down balances to Harry White, but minus quantities, commitments or dates. In his BABOON 156, Dalton explained that, had American aid taken the form of a grant, the 'moral impetus' created would have enabled Britain to secure a 'large cancellation' of sterling balances. Without this 'moral impetus' no results at all could be guaranteed, and if the Americans made any attempt to tie down the British to figures 'the whole negotiations must break down'.[37]

With the commercial negotiations also threatening to founder on the rock of Dominion objections to the elimination of trade preferences, Robbins and Hall-Patch flew back to London on 28 October 'ostensibly to discuss Anglo-American differences over Imperial Preference'[38] but also to remove misunderstandings about the financial negotiations. Robbins carried a letter from Keynes to Dalton, complaining that 'dangerous and, indeed, demented advice is abroad', and warning that the government was risking a financial débâcle as in 1931. 'There is no way out remotely compatible with the present domestic policy of the Government except on the basis of substantial American aid.'[39] Keynes and Halifax decided to put off trying even Dalton's Alternative A on the Americans until Robbins had returned.

Robbins and Hall-Patch returned from London on 7 November. They reported ministers in a frightful muddle. They spent all their time discussing the theory of nationalisation; most of the senior officials were working to the verge of collapse. Stafford Cripps understood what was going on and Bevin was starting to; but Dalton was quite unable to read any of the papers and had not even consulted the Prime Minister. Keynes commented, 'When I first knew Dalton as an undergraduate at King's he was a passionate supporter of Joe Chamberlain and his room was plastered with placards about Imperial Preference. Then one night when he was drunk he was converted to Fabianism by Rupert Brooke. Hence all our present troubles.' The Robbins–Hall-Patch visit to London had its effect. The dispute over imperial preference was resolved – or at least shelved – making it possible for the Cabinet to accept a 'United States Proposal to Establish an International Trade Organization' on 6 November.* And Dalton's Alternative B was scrapped, the Mission being told to press on with Alternative A. If that failed, the negotiators could accept a new Alternative B – $4bn at 2 per cent interest, repayable over fifty years, with an option for a further $1bn on the same terms.[40] Little by little London was giving ground.

The ambassador's diary of 6 November takes up the story:

From the State Department I went on to the Treasury, where Keynes, Bob Brand and I tried the first of the two London alternatives on the Americans. They did not like it too much, as I expected.... They are to think about it.... It looks to me more and more as if Vinson was the sticking point rather than Clayton. We did our business in a very much over-heated room with all the Venetian blinds down, although the sun was shining brightly outside. That the Americans should like living this way is a constant puzzle to me.

The new British plan – presented as a draft agreement – which the American Top Committee went off to consider envisaged an American credit in two parts: $2bn plus an amount (which the British still hoped could be limited to $500m) for cleaning up Lend–Lease, and a further sum up to $2bn for making currently accruing sterling 'available without discrimination' for non-sterling transactions and for partial release of accumulated sterling

* The Cabinet finally accepted a formula, presented by the Americans, but actually drafted by the British negotiators, the gist of which was that preferences rates were not to be reduced until general tariff rates had been reduced to the preferential rate.

balances. The $2.5bn would carry 2 per cent interest and would be repayable in fifty equal instalments starting in 1951. The remaining credit facilities, also repayable in fifty instalments starting in 1951, would be interest free. In any year in which British visible and invisible exports fell short of the $7bn needed to finance the pre-war volume of imports, interest would be waived. Capital repayment could be deferred in the event of a breakdown in multilateral clearing ('less than 75 per cent of British exports being sold to countries of which the currencies are freely convertible into dollars'), an international depression, or the dollar having been declared a 'scarce currency' by the IMF.[41]

After considering Alternative A for three days, Vinson and Clayton rejected it on Friday 9 November. Keynes then activated the fall-back position. Talks proceeded 'on the assumption that the loan will be increased to 4½ billion inclusive of lend–lease clean-up', the whole at 2 per cent interest. But this concession on amount was accompanied by an avalanche of new and old demands. The Americans knew they had the British on the rack. Interest might be postponed, but not waived; the test for activating the deferment should include the state of Britain's reserves; currently earned sterling should be made convertible not just for sterling area countries but for the non-sterling area countries with which Britain had payments agreements; and repaying the American loan should have priority over other debts.

Keynes couldn't stand it any longer. Bareau's semi-official note – he was not present – cannot altogether hide the drama of the occasion:

> Lord Keynes ... appeared to lose both patience and interest in further conduct of the negotiations, and wished to settle with the Americans roughly on their terms and using the wide discretionary powers which London had given the Delegation. On Saturday morning he was talking of settling the deal and seeing the press in the course of the afternoon. He was, however, dissuaded from following this plan.[42]

The meeting which followed on Saturday 10 November was 'tense and painful'. The Americans turned the screw tighter, by demanding a scrapping of the Anglo-American Petroleum Agreements, signed as recently as 24 September, which reserved Britain's right, under Article XIV(2) of the Bretton Woods Agreement, to discriminate against foreign imports. 'We had a great deal of trouble particularly over this oil question,' Harmer noted, 'and only a good deal of firmness and tact (with Lionel R. preeminent) got [Maynard] to face it properly and not side-step.' The American demand that, in return for a loan, Britain give up its transitional right to continue wartime exchange controls under Article XIV of the Bretton Woods Agreement, was destined to become London's last sticking point.

On Monday 12 November, the technicians from the two sides argued technically, while Keynes and the ambassador had another meeting with

Vinson and Clayton, which went no better. At one moment, Keynes burst out: 'Why do you persecute us like this?' Clayton was at his most doctrinaire, haranguing them on the theme that Britain's greatness had been built on free trade and convertibility. Coming out of the explosive confrontation, Keynes remarked: 'At one time I had come to believe that the *Mayflower* came over to this country filled with lawyers. I am now inclined to go back to my original belief that it was filled with theologians.' Harmer reported 'M. . . . nervy and difficult to deal with. He is quite exhausted and the effects are not easy for the rest of us ... everything is rather a nightmare.' The Americans promised a counter-draft by 15 November. 'I am becoming steadily more worried,' wrote Hall-Patch. 'The "smoke-filled" room technique with no witnesses and no record is a form of negotiation which is only possible if you are supremely confident that the people with whom you are dealing are powerful enough to put through what they agree with you is reasonable. With the rabbits with whom we are dealing I am not sure it is the right technique. . . .'[43]

Nevertheless, Keynes was 'moderately hopeful' that the revised American draft agreement would take into account the comments of the British experts, and that he could sail home on the *Queen Mary* on 30 November. The new American text arrived at the Statler Hotel at 9 a.m. on Thursday 15 November. Freddie Harmer 'went up [to Maynard's room] and found M. in bed looking very shaken and white; and all he could say was that we had better pack up and go home'. The American technicians, Harmer felt, 'had been at work and every kind of silly and insulting technicality had been written into the draft: together with several major new points which would have caused an explosion of fury if sent home'. At ten o'clock they all met at the Embassy. Halifax 'took charge very firmly of the position. It was decided that we should refuse to discuss the draft and merely offer to send it to London for instructions, warning them of possible consequences. M. very nervy and finding it difficult to control his feelings. (The personal aspect of all this to him is obvious.)' When Harry White rang up offering to see Keynes for technical discussions, 'M was appallingly rude to him on the telephone – just what we wanted to avoid.'

The 'most momentous' meeting of the Joint Finance Committee took place that afternoon at three o'clock, with Halifax, Keynes, Brand, Robbins, Hall-Patch, Lee and Harmer representing Britain, and Vinson, Clayton, Eccles, McCabe, Thomas, White and Collado for the Americans.

Halifax opened 'in plain language of rather melancholy menace' that the American proposals had brought them to the precipice of failure. The American draft included suggestions which would be quite unacceptable to London. If these suggestions represented the Americans' last word, the British delegation would have no choice but to go home. Perhaps after a year or so they might be able to resume with better hope of success. Meanwhile, there could be no question of Britain ratifying the Bretton

Woods Agreement or taking part in the International Trade Organization discussions.[44]

> This statement [wrote Bareau, who was present] caused very visible shock to the Americans. Vinson immediately began to urge how completely at a loss he was to understand the Ambassador's contention that parts of the American document did not even offer a basis for discussion. While Eccles was droning on ... Vinson and Clayton had a whispered conversation at the end of which Vinson said that nothing which the Ambassador had indicated suggested that we must face breakdown. This document and the clauses which gave offence to us must be discussed over again. We must not remit the document to London.... The Ambassador picked up the ball admirably. 'We are all friends in this room,' he said, 'and we all want to serve the same cause.'

Keynes then went through the American memorandum clause by clause, in his most mocking style. No waiver, the Americans had said, could be given if Britain's gold and foreign exchange reserves were above 15 per cent of its imports. The effect of this, Keynes retorted, would be 'to keep Britain on the breadline'. It may well have been on this occasion that he was provoked into one of his famous pieces of repartee. He was arguing that Britain's gold reserve was already far too low, when an official of the Federal Reserve Board chipped in: 'Your gold reserves must be an essential criterion. You might find a great deal of gold hidden in a cave.' Keynes immediately turned to Frank Lee: 'Gold in a cave, Frank, put that down in the Agreement. We accept that.'* He tore into the clause deferring rather than cancelling interest payments. 'The Americans accepted that for 55 years we should not pay if we could not pay, but after that period we should pay even if we could not do so.' Finally, Keynes rejected prioritising the American debt. Eccles argued that, if America was asked to refinance a bankrupt concern, it had a right to insist on an upper limit on repayments to previous creditors. Keynes exploded: 'You cannot treat a great nation as if it were a bankrupt company.'[45] Harmer thought 'M. not at all in good form – far too worked up, and the whole atmosphere was very trying. But as a result they decided to have a further meeting immediately, with a view to technical discussion of the less important points in the morning.'

The first of these took place on Friday 16 November with Keynes and White as the principals. 'Some very trying discussions ensued with M. almost uncontrollable,' noted Harmer. The Saturday meeting was a replica of the first, only worse. Harmer wrote: 'We were all thoroughly worried by now. M.'s health cannot stand this strain.... One of the first essentials is to give him somehow or other a rest next week, and we must hope that after

---

* The story was told to me by the late Paul Bareau, in this form. There have been several variants.

Monday's meeting there will be a lull while we wait to hear from London. Meanwhile we must somehow or other get through Monday without explosions.'

Keynes and the others spent Sunday drafting a batch of telegrams to London setting out the points at issue. The Mission prefaced this series with the statement: 'We should warn you that ... we are having heavy going and there may be further troubles ahead.' The ambassador's journal on Sunday 18 November for the first time mentioned 'internal friction' in the British ranks. 'Keynes, who has a good many of the defects of genius, is not an easy member of a team. I get on very well with him and I think everybody has immense admiration for his qualities. But most people whose minds do not work as quickly as he does are a bit apprehensive of his ingenuity in producing new suggestions they have not had time fully to consider. Bob Brand is very sane and I rely greatly on his judgment.' Bareau confirms that a 'Mutiny on the Bounty' took place that day. In preparation for Monday's meeting, the British team decided that as much of the talking as possible was to be left to the ambassador and kept 'away from the Lord'. Technical matters were to be referred to Brand, the cautious banker.

The British were expecting the Americans to table formal proposals at the Finance Committee on Monday 19 November, which they could transmit to London. But instead 'they offered for discussion a provisional text which still included our amendments and proposed omissions in square brackets'.[46] Vinson 'brusquely' proposed that they go through them. Since the matter was highly technical, and the ambassador and Brand could not cope, the British had no choice, in Bareau's words, but to 'pass the ball to Lord Keynes'. There then began a 'long and at times very tedious discussion of the various points of difference in the draft scheme'. After the meeting, Keynes, who according to Harmer was 'much more himself', remarked that he and Harry White had agreed that Bretton Woods and $4bn were too high a price to pay for having to listen to Marriner Eccles. Keynes added, 'No wonder that man is a Mormon. No single woman could stand him.' Such moments of levity were getting fewer.

Little though it looked like it at the time, the three meetings of 16, 17 and 19 November once more brought the two sides to the brink of an agreement. The subsequent nightmares were the result of London's attempt to impose vetoes on what Keynes had negotiated.

The points of dispute had been narrowed to the following. On the amount of the loan, the British wanted to borrow $4bn plus $500m to pay for Lend–Lease supplies 'in the pipe-line' when Lend–Lease was cancelled, both at 2 per cent. The Americans offered $3.75bn at 2 per cent, and calculated Britain's Lend–Lease debt at $750m to be serviced at 2⅜ per cent. The British wanted to make the amount of net, rather than gross, reserves a criterion for activating the waiver. The Americans insisted that the waiver could not be claimed unless repayments to holders of sterling balances were simultaneously reduced, and that accelerated repayments to sterling area debtors should be accompanied by accelerated repayment of the American loan. The British wanted to limit the repayment reductions to loans incurred after the American loan, and exclude colonies from the accelerated repayment restriction. They also wanted to restrict currency convertibility to sterling accruing to sterling area countries only, whereas the Americans wanted to make sterling earned by countries outside the sterling area convertible as well. Keynes might have been forgiven for thinking that another day would wrap things up.

While London pondered, Keynes wrote several 'atmospheric' letters. To Eady, 21 November:

> As you may have surmised, life here for the past three weeks or longer has been absolute hell; though I doubt if you can have guessed quite how bad it has been.
>
> Everything that we think we have settled with the Top Committee is then transmitted by them inaccurately to experts and lawyers, who have not been present at the discussion. The latter work without consultation with us and produce to their own top lads something which bears not the slightest resemblance to what we have agreed. This is then adopted by the American Top Committee and hurled at us in what looks very like an ultimatum. We then in a series of exasperated meetings have to throw out as much as possible to bring the text, not completely, but as nearly back as we can. This sort of thing does not happen just once but time after time after time.[47]

To Florence Keynes, 21 November:

> They mean us no harm – but their minds are so small, their prospect so restricted, their knowledge so inadequate, their obstinacy so boundless and their legal pedantries so infuriating. May it never fall to my lot to have to *persuade* anyone to do what I want, with so few cards in my hand.
>
> As you may suppose I am beginning to use up my physical reserves....

After his return from Washington, Keynes gave the Ogre a detailed account of the collapse of his health:

> For the first eight or nine weeks I was extremely well, – provided I did not walk anywhere, scarcely conscious of physical deficiencies.... In the last few weeks, however, when I was conducting a war on two fronts and suffering the greatest responsibilities and irritations, I began to give way. Every two or three days, when there was something particularly annoying or tiring, symptoms would appear which made Lydia very cross. Whenever my emotions caused a discharge of adrenalin, it was more than the old heart could comfortably manage. So, in addition to

the ice-bag, I took to spending as many hours out of the twenty-four as practicable in a horizontal position. What really got me through, however, was the marvellous effect of the sodium amytal. . . .[48]

London did not like the American draft at all. Following a tense Cabinet meeting on 23 November, notable for Herbert Morrison's attack on the Treasury for not giving Keynes enough elbow room, the Mission received, this time from the Prime Minister, new instructions. The government would be willing to accept a credit 'of not less than $4bn including Lend/Lease at 2 per cent, to be repaid over 50 years beginning after 5 years'. In return, it would be willing to 'liberalise' sterling area arrangements, recommend Parliament to accept the Bretton Woods Agreement and endorse the 'principles of commercial policy' agreed on 6 November. But it would not – 'repeat not' – agree to complete the negotiations with creditor countries over the accumulated sterling balances before the end of 1946, rank the American debt above others, accept a reserve criterion for the waiver, or abrogate Britain's rights to maintain exchange controls with non-sterling area countries. Keynes was slow to see the danger. A meeting with Vinson on 26 November went well, Vinson agreeing to charge Britain only 2 per cent interest on the Lend–Lease debt. Keynes drafted a series of compromise clauses covering the disputed matters which he thought the Americans would accept, and sent them to London.[49] To Dalton he pleaded on 27 November: 'A quick OK . . . and we may be home in both senses of the word'. The result, according to Harmer was 'swift and disturbing'. London objected 'to our having maintained a fixed date . . . for the liberalisation of the sterling area'. Keynes was 'profoundly upset . . . because he was committed, it was an integral part of the whole plan as he saw it, and he did not see how he could retract. Some very troubled days followed. M. . . . on the verge of physical collapse; Lydia in floods of tears. . . . Telegrams passed to and fro: M's getting more desperate. . . . London getting more and more curt, and completely uninformative.'

Keynes believed that Dalton had gone back on 'the most attractive offer we were in a position to make'. He pointed out that Dalton had completely misunderstood the difference between sterling accruing from post-war exports and the sterling debts which Britain had accumulated during the war. Only convertibility of the former was being proposed.[50] Dalton now replied disingenuously that he did 'not know of any long-standing undertaking' to release current earnings in advance of negotiations over the blocked balances.[51] Keynes (rightly) saw the hand of Eady in his new discomfiture. 'The trouble about these telegrams', he fumed, 'is that they are all drafted either by Sir Wilfrid Eady or by the Treasury messenger boys. . . .'[52] The crucial Cabinet discussion took place on Thursday morning 29 November. Two ministers, Shinwell and Bevan, attacked Keynes's proposed terms. The agreed Cabinet draft, sent to Washington at 4.40 p.m., and arriving on the morning of the 29th, Washington time, insisted that Britain must reserve the right to continue exchange controls, disallowed by the Bretton Woods Agreement, and refused to put a date on making sterling convertible for sterling area countries. Furthermore, the government wanted to be able to postpone repayment of principal as well as to waive interest, and refused to accept any linkage between its obligations to the Americans and those to other creditors.[53]

On receipt, the Mission went into a huddle. NABOB 419, sent at 3.17 a.m. on 30 November, declared its 'unanimous conviction that the course we are told to take must be disastrous'.[54] Attlee and Dalton sent a curt note back to Halifax: 'It is now our firm opinion that you should put [our] text to the Americans as soon as possible with the supporting arguments which we have supplied to you.'[55] Faced with the Mission's mutiny, Dalton decided to send Edward Bridges – together with another Treasury official, A. T. K. Grant – to Washington immediately to carry out the Cabinet's instructions. Robbins's terse note for that morning reads: 'Complete slap in face. Arrival Bridges telegram. Meeting Ambassador. Dramatic moment – Maynard threatens to resign. Lunch Ambassador.'[56] Bridges arrived at lunchtime on Saturday 1 December and immediately went into conference with the Mission. Bareau writes:

> Although Bridges handled the situation *vis-à-vis* his colleagues here extremely tactful [sic] it very soon became evident from the tone of London messages that he was intended to supersede Keynes as the effective operational head in the financial negotiations. All the telegrams started to come in addressed 'personally' to him. It became quite evident from this behaviour ... and remarks of AG[rant] that Keynes in effect had lost the confidence of his ministers in London some time ago, and that they had all been surprised in London not to have had his resignation before now. It had certainly not been for want of trying on their part.[57]

What Bridges discovered on that Saturday was that the Mission were united behind their sick and embattled chief. On Sunday 2 December, the British and Americans went into all-day discussions at the Joint Finance Committee. Vinson, realising what had happened, generously went out of his way to praise Keynes's conduct of the negotiations. By the end of the day, a number of British officials were near collapse; so was Clayton, who had got up from his sickbed to be there.

The predictable result, as Robbins put it, was 'exactly as anticipated, humiliation'.[58] The British submitted their Cabinet draft which the 'Americans plainly did not view ... with any favour'. The Americans produced their draft, and the British team spent most of the day trying to modify it as London wanted. They had a few successes. The American offer of $3.75bn of 'new money', coupled with $650m for the Lend–Lease clean-up, made a total of $4.4bn, more than London had been willing to accept. On the waiver, the Americans rejected the proposal that the principal might be postponed, but accepted a modification of their claim to priority. There was a small American concession on the timing of the release of the sterling area's current earnings, now postponed till a year after Congress ratified the Agreement (that is, till mid-1947). However, the Americans insisted that Britain give up its right, under Article XIV of the Bretton Woods Agreement, to retain exchange controls on sterling earned by countries outside the sterling area. Bridges's conclusion was that 'there is not much left to argue about', and he asked for discretion to settle 'without further reference back'. In other words, having sniffed out the Washington atmosphere, he was telling London politely to back off. He did so with decisive brevity. When told that a new BABOON had arrived, he said, 'Let them Baboon away. If the buggers give the right answers they will save the timetable.' The conversion of Bridges, noted Bareau, had been complete.

London did continue to baboon away on Britain's transitional rights under Bretton Woods without effect. The government came close to breaking off the negotiations on this 'clear and limited issue'. Dalton wrote in his diary: 'They [the Americans] would almost certainly, we thought, have to come back to the negotiations in a month or two.'[59] More wishful thinking! There was a bizarre final touch. The British officials assembled at the Willard after dinner on Tuesday 4 December to await a message 'at the very highest level' from the Prime Minister to the President, who was duly informed that a telegram was on its way. When it arrived it turned out to be from Attlee to Bridges, demanding a last stand on transitional protection. Halifax rang up Truman and told him he could go to bed. Keynes proposed that they all go to bed. But Bridges said they had to find Vinson and put to him the formula suggested by London. But where was Vinson? After much telephoning, he was tracked down to a nightclub – at the Willard Hotel itself. He eventually arrived in Brand's room, 'well primed with liquor', but sufficiently sober to reject the remaining British demand, that convertibility of sterling be limited to sterling area countries. He then telephoned Dean Acheson, whose reaction was even more unfavourable. NABOB 463 from Bridges to the Prime Minister went out at 5.41 a.m. the next morning: 'We fear that you must take it that there is no chance of getting the decision reversed and that no appeal to the President would affect this. If we are to reach agreement we believe we must accept the American formula.... This telegram has been seen by and has the full agreement of the Ambassador, Brand and Keynes.'[60] At ten o'clock that morning London's capitulation was received. 'They told us to have another go but not to make ourselves a bore by pressing it,' wrote the ambassador. 'So after a chat among ourselves we went off, as Keynes said, "to fire a blank cartridge at Vinson".'

Thus it was done. The Anglo-American Financial Agreement was signed by Halifax and Clayton at the State Department on Thursday morning 6

December. In the group photograph taken at the signing, Keynes sits on
Halifax's right at the glass table, detached and lifeless, no spark of animation
lighting up his features. He is desperately tired, but the day has only begun.
There is a press conference for British and Commonwealth journalists,
memoranda and letters to write, then a cocktail party for American commen-
tators and editorial writers. Finally, there is his own dinner party for the
whole delegation at the Statler Hotel 'in honour of a job finished by a team'.
He nibbles at his food, then is up on his feet with a tongue-in-cheek tribute
to Vinson and Clayton, warning the guests never to think of Americans as
peculiar kinds of Englishmen. The ambassador is suitably light and amusing.
He feels sure that, with Lydia's departure, Washington's retail stores will
suffer a trade recession. Brand repeats his familiar tale that working with
Keynes always makes him feel like the class dunce. Frank Lee wittily pulls
Maynard's leg. Robbins, full of eloquence, talks of an escape from the dark
ages. Lydia bubbles with delight at Maynard still being alive.

On Friday 7 December, Keynes called on President Truman to say
goodbye. Then he and Lydia went to New York, saw some banking friends,
collected a silver tankard bequeathed by J. P. Morgan to the Bank of England,
and caught the *Queen Elizabeth* on 11 December, leaving a Mission, as Frank
Lee wrote, '"lapsed in time and passion" without your inspiration and fire'.[61]

V. KEYNES'S DEFENCE

While Keynes was still at sea, the government whipped both the Loan and
Bretton Woods Agreements through the House of Commons with a large
majority (343–100), but a lame defence. Twenty-nine Labour MPs voted
against; so did seventy Conservatives, mainly imperialists, although they
had been told to abstain. Even supporters of the loan thought it was a bad
business. The *Economist* summed up the general reaction: 'We are not
compelled to say we like it.... Our present needs are the direct consequences of the fact that we fought earlier, that we fought longest and that
we fought hardest.'[62]

Robbins recalls that, 'grey with anxiety, Keynes sat in his cabin receiving,
with growing anger and contempt, the misrepresentations, as they came
from the wireless operators, of *his* efforts and *his* loan, and polishing the
periods of the defence which he was gathering all his remaining forces to
make'.[63] He got back to England on 17 December. With the briefest stopover
at Gordon Square, he went straight from Southampton to the House of
Lords, where the peers' debate on Bretton Woods and the loan had started,
and sat through five hours of it.

Keynes himself opened the second day's debate. His aim was to dispel the ignorance and mistrust which had enveloped the speeches in both Houses. Even supporters of the loan treated it as a humiliating imposition, and directed their wrath at its source – the United States. Keynes's defence of the loan rested on the proposition that the deals with the Americans, embracing the Loan and Bretton Woods Agreements and Commercial Policy, were interlinked parts of a coherent design, each of which, and the whole together, represented not an assertion of American power but a reasonable compromise between two great nations with the same goal: to restore a liberal world economy. Far from being humiliated, Britain stood to gain substantially. Moreover it had received unique loan terms – 2 per cent – in recognition of its unique contribution to the Allied victory. Thus were the desperate wrangles in Washington glossed over and polished for public consumption.

Keynes finessed the issue of unequal bargaining power and clashing national interests. America and Britain were pursuing the same goals by different methods, born from different national characteristics. It was in terms of the 'complex politics of Congress', the 'remoteness' of public opinion, the contractual and commercial basis of American life that Keynes explained the characteristic American approach to negotiating with the British. The Americans wanted everything cut and dried, the British preferred things left 'vaguer'; the package of deals represented a 'workable compromise between the certainty they wanted and the measure of elasticity we wanted'. But basically they both wanted the same thing.

As we can see, Keynes was engaged in a delicate balancing act between what Britain had a right to expect and what America could reasonably be expected to give. Only in regard to one particular did his benevolence break down, and a hint of passion show through: 'On the matter of interest, I shall never so long as I live cease to regret that this is not an interest-free loan. The charging of interest is out of tune with the underlying realities. It is based on a false analogy.' It was inconsistent with the unique character of Britain's contribution. But even on the question of interest the Americans had offered substantial mitigations. 'The balm and sweet simplicity of no per cent is not admitted, but we are not asked to pay interest except in conditions where we can reasonably afford to do so, and the capital instalments are so spread that our minimum obligation in the early years is actually less than it would be with a loan free of interest repayable by equal instalments.'

By this route Keynes approached his peroration:

> The separate economic blocs and all the friction and loss of friendship they must bring with them are expedients to which one may be driven in a hostile world.... But it is surely crazy to prefer that. Above all, this determination to make trade truly international and to avoid the establishment of economic blocs ... is plainly an essential condition of the world's best hope, an Anglo-American understanding.... Some of us, in

the tasks of war and more lately in those of peace, have learnt by experience that our two countries can work together. Yet it would be only too easy for us to walk apart. I beg those who look askance at these plans to ponder deeply and responsibly where it is they think they want to go.

After five more hours of discussion, the House approved the the financial resolution by 90 votes to 8, about 100 peers abstaining. The Bretton Woods Agreement was approved without a division.[64]

There was much myth-making in Keynes's speech. But against the background of a hostile public opinion and his own extreme exhaustion, Keynes's defence of his handiwork ranks as the most courageous and skilful public speech of his life. He knew the case he wanted to present and he found fit music for his vision. The prose of Washington had – almost – been turned back into poetry. Perhaps it is in the realm of rhetoric that his true greatness lies, using that word in its classic sense of the 'art of persuasion'. 'How much easier', James Meade lamented, 'affairs of state would be if rational men having agreed on a rational course of action were then permitted to give a rational account of it!'[65] Keynes sometimes talked in this way, but his sense and use of language – the words and phrases which came into his mind naturally, because of the kind of person he was and the culture which he breathed – demanded and commanded assent at some different level. The magic of Keynes's words is still potent more than half a century later, yet with the distance of time, we must ask the question: was his vision fit for the circumstances? Or was it 'demented advice abroad'?

Much has been said about Keynes's negotiating style. On this, his penultimate mission to the United States, he was engaged in two sets of negotiations – with Americans in Washington and British in London. How are we to judge his performance? On the Washington side, his crucial failure was to get on terms with Vinson. The Kentucky lawyer and the waspish Bloomsbury intellectual were like chalk and cheese. Keynes's old Washington network was broken, and he was too tired and ill to build a new one. He was not the ideal negotiator for the long grind which developed in Washington. Bareau's summary stands for many: 'He was too brilliant, too crushing and, towards the end, too exhausted.'

But none of this is to say that he failed as a negotiator. Although he succumbed to moods of despair, he was extremely resilient and – as the ambassador rightly discerned – both tenacious and fertile. He had the quality of waking up every morning full of fight. No other British representative in Washington in the autumn of 1945 had the technical competence and confidence to handle a complex financial negotiation. Vinson and Clayton were no match for Keynes in argument. But they always held the whip-hand. It was a case of brains pitted against power. No doubt Keynes frequently bewildered them. But many of the technical complications which developed in November – and particularly the frequent backsliding of the two top Americans – were not his fault, but a consequence of their ignorance, and saying things which their 'technicians' – off stage in the informal sessions – then made them withdraw.

It is also misleading to see Keynes in isolation from the rest of the Mission. Halifax, Brand, Robbins and Liesching all played key roles in moving things along – on some occasions when Keynes might have broken down under the strain. The most warming revelation of the Washington negotiations is the support which these men and their juniors gave Keynes. They respected, admired and in some cases loved him for his genius, his wit, his resilience, his buoyancy, his gaiety of spirit and his sheer persistence, and became increasingly protective of him as his health declined.

Keynes was rather less successful with London. He himself must be held mainly responsible for the overestimation of what was possible, and Whitehall's corollary reliance on his 'magic' to achieve unrealisable goals. Contemporary opinion is unanimous that Keynes hypnotised Whitehall into believing what, of course, it wanted to believe – that it could get the best of all possible worlds. It is not enough to point to qualifications and doubts in his pre-Washington advice; to say that he did not hide from ministers the probability of having to slide down the slippery slope of Temptation. The hypnotism lay not in the arguments, but in the choice of language. The phrase 'sweet breath of Justice' set the standard by which the outcome of the negotiation would be judged, and 'Starvation Corner', 'financial Dunkirk', the penalties of failure. All the decisions were taken within the emotional framework Keynes established.

Having bamboozled Whitehall before he left, he had to de-bamboozle it when he got to Washington. But his arts of communication were not attuned to the medium of the telegram. He needed room to develop spacious, subtle arguments, when what harassed ministers required were terse statements of pros and cons, with clear-cut recommendations. These Bridges was able to provide in the last week of the negotiation. Keynes was right to want him over earlier, though his eventual arrival was humiliating. Not till 17 October did Keynes clearly state that only a loan of 2 per cent was available, and even then held out hopes that better might be forthcoming. Almost nowhere in the long series of NABOBs and other messages did Keynes flatly say that this or that was all that was on offer. Ministers were thus left in a continual state of surprise, which eventually turned to loss of confidence in Keynes's negotiating skills. In the final stages they deprived him of virtually all negotiating discretion.

But the problems were not just of Keynes's making. The death of Sir Frederick Phillips and the illness, and then semi-retirement, of Sir Richard Hopkins had seriously undermined his position at the Treasury. The new triumvirate of Eady, Clarke and Grant at Overseas Finance never approved of the loan, and would not have been sorry to see the negotiations fail.

Although Dalton wrote Keynes a gracious note after the Cabinet's last concession – 'My dear Maynard, Thank you from the bottom of my heart for all you have accomplished in this long, hard fight – against great odds.... You have got us the dollars....' – he did not really trust Keynes, and had a different agenda. What also coloured Dalton's attitude was an antipathy to Halifax – the man of Munich – a leftover from Churchill's machinations, and, like Keynes, with no place in the new 'galère'.

Had Churchill and Roosevelt still been in power, or even Churchill alone, it is possible that Britain might have got at least an interest-free loan, with fewer strings. Vinson and Clayton repeatedly pointed out that domestic politics would not allow it. It must never be forgotten that Keynes negotiated in the autumn of 1945 with people who were highly suspicious of giving money to a socialist government, with a Congress behind them which was even more suspicious. A Churchill in power would not only have made this irrelevant, but would have been able – and probably willing – to play the Soviet card. Whether this would have worked in the autumn of 1945 is doubtful. The Soviet decision not to ratify the Bretton Woods Agreement, which Harold James has called the real start of the Cold War, came on 29 December 1945. George Kennan's famous long telegram, sent from Moscow on 22 February 1946, was the first major analysis which identified the Soviet Union as an enemy of the United States.[66] But these developments came too late to influence the outcome of the Keynes Mission.

All of this raises the question of whether Keynes had set out the alternatives rightly in his memorandum of 18 March 1945. The Austerity option, with its unpleasant combination of stinting and Schachtianism, left out two choices for Britain involving neither starvation nor anti-Americanism.

The first was devaluation. Britain was driven to this in 1949. But it was not unthinkable in 1945. Expectation of a British devaluation was one reason Harry White gave to the Senate Banking Committee in the summer of 1945 for denying that Britain would need extensive transitional assistance. Keynes had a long-standing objection to this line of thought. He feared that currency depreciation would drive Britain further from equilibrium by producing a fall in export prices larger than an increase in export volume. To this was added a pessimistic appraisal of the speed of reconversion. Both strands were present in Keynes's reply to a question at his Washington press conference on 12 September 1945:

> There are certain conditions in which it [devaluation] certainly helps a country. The right level [of the exchange rate] depends on the real wages in the respective countries, and if wages are on a real competitive basis, as I believe ours are, I think countries can very easily make their positions worse, and not better, by altering their exchange. You see, it simply means paying more for your imports and [receiving] less for your exports. Now, if you are in great difficulty about markets, you may be

driven to that. That is not our position today.... We can sell anything we can produce. Our problem is to reconvert our industry quick enough ... to have the exports, and in those circumstances you can't imagine anything more foolish than to be trying to sell those exports at quite unnecessarily low prices.

Thus in 1945 Keynes thought that Britain was competitive on price, and that the export problem was due to lack of supply. Meade of the Economic Section had pooh-poohed this argument when Keynes produced it at the National Debt Enquiry earlier that year, pointing out that 'as we produced manufactured goods in competition with many other exporting countries and in competition with the home industries of many of our customers it seemed to me highly improbable that a decline in our export prices relatively to others would not cause a very substantial expansion of our exports'. Meade might have added that the main impact of a decline in sterling would have been to increase the *profitability* of exporting, thus producing a supply response. But Keynes would not be budged.[67]

The second omitted choice was simply to wait till the post-war position had become clearer, borrowing short-term to cover necessary imports. Keynes was right to believe that a breakdown in negotiations for the loan after they had started would have been very damaging to Anglo-American relations. But this would not have been the case had they never been started – or at least not on such a grand scale. It is hard not to agree with Clarke's (retrospective) judgement on the whole affair:

The simplest plan ... for which [sic] nobody could have persuaded Keynes ... was to abandon the concept of a 'Grand Design' negotiation in autumn 1945.... We could easily have said 'We are willing to sign the Bretton Woods Agreement and participate in the International Commercial Policy conference; but we are not willing to accept any prior commitments at all until we see how the new world develops: we would be willing to negotiate in 1947.' We would have borrowed, say $1,000 millions ... and would have undertaken to accept a loan for the residue of Lend–Lease at the rate of any ultimate major loan. After the abrupt end of the war and the cessation of Lend–Lease, the Americans could not have refused or tried to impose strings. In fact events by 1947 showed that the multilateral theologians' concepts of the course of events had been utterly wrong, and that the doctrines of the 1945 negotiations had fallen into the background of US policy, and that the combination of the Communist threat to Europe together with the world dollar shortage had persuaded the Americans to grant billions of dollars in pursuit of European discrimination against the USA! So the idea of postponing the 'Grand Design' negotiation, and borrowing relatively small amounts, if necessarily expensively, would have been well justified by events.[68]

This is not just hindsight: Brand, Bevin, Eady, the Bank of England suggested it at the time, though often in passing. Had Keynes advocated it, there wouldn't have been much opposition. In retrospect, one can see why it was ruled out. It was a combination of Keynes's eagerness to launch his internationalist ship before he died and Labour's 'New Jerusalem' hopes which conspired to get an unworkable agreement. Hopes triumphed over reality.

43

The Light is Gone

When he got back from America Keynes was half dead with fatigue. At a dinner given by Dalton for the loan delegation at the Savoy, he had been 'forced to lie on a sofa and rest throughout most of the evening'.[1] For the last time his amazing powers of recuperation saved him. By the time Leonard Woolf came for his usual Christmas dinner at Tilton, he had already started to feel better, though Lydia was exhausted. They talked about Virginia Woolf: Keynes suggested to Leonard that he read excerpts from her diaries at the next meeting of the Memoir Club, which he duly did at 46 Gordon Square in February. On Boxing Day, Lydia distributed her 'Washington booty on a lavish scale' at a party for the farm labourers and their families, with 'the usual sketches and songs and beer and refreshments, with the children of the hamlet exceptionally attractive and well-behaved. The Charlestonians joined us. We feel that we have our own little rural civilisation down here.'[2] Charleston's contribution to civilisation was a skit on the popular radio programme *The Brains Trust*, with Duncan Grant taking the part of a bishop. On 28 December, Maynard's nephews, Richard and Stephen Keynes and Maurice Hill, came for the shoot. Maynard 'very much enjoyed having the boys' and Stephen shot his first pheasant.

On 1 January 1946 Mrs Stephens arrived 'and work begins again'. But it was work he enjoyed – 'free from worry'. Much of it had to do with plans for the reopening of the Royal Opera House. There was a minute to Dennis Proctor of the Treasury warning against inflationary wage settlements.[3] He also resumed work on a paper 'Will the Dollar be Scarce?' which he had sketched out with Freddie Harmer of the Treasury and David McCurrach of the Bank of England during a lull in the Washington loan negotiations. By 5 January, a couple of days before his return to London and Treasury work, the 'perfect weather' had made him feel 'wonderfully well' again. An American Treasury official who saw him in his Treasury room on 18 January found him looking 'remarkably well and rested'.

Keynes read a version of his 'Will the Dollar be Scarce?' paper at the Political Economy Club on 2 February 1946, now taken over by Dennis Robertson, and meeting on Thursday evenings in his chilly drawing room at Trinity College. Keynes's thesis was that America's dollar surpluses would disappear sooner than they all thought, owing to the operation of the 'invisible hand'.[4] The late Harry Johnson remembers Keynes in an armchair by a fire which glowed but gave out little heat, with his legs 'slumped out in front of him'. Barely glancing at the notes beside him, he gave a 'a very elegant talk, beautifully constructed, every sentence a piece of good English prose and every paragraph cadenced – just a wonderful performance'. Its theme was rather 'anti-Keynesian', his negative answer to the question he asked depending very heavily on the 'long-run classical mechanism, basically the influence of balance-of-payments surpluses on money, wages, and so forth'. Afterwards Johnson told Dennis Robertson how much he had enjoyed the paper. Robertson replied, 'Ah, but you missed something that used to be there – the impishness of his mind.'[5]

Dadie Rylands hoped that in 1946 Keynes would not be entirely sacrificed to the welfare of his country and would find time to 'turn over the leaves of Jacobean play-books with a decanter of claret by your side'.[6] It was certainly Keynes's intention to cut down his Treasury work, both for health reasons and because he was out of sympathy with the new regime. He did not click with Dalton; he mistrusted Labour's *dirigiste* tendencies. Socially, he got on much better with left-leaning Conservatives than with right-leaning socialists. But set against his inclination to resign was the continuing opportunity to 'avert evils', which 'is as much as one can plausibly hope for in this world'.[7] The financial problems of peace, while not so dire, seemed no less urgent than those Keynes had confronted in the war. Also, like all those who have had a commanding influence on affairs, Keynes felt that the work he had started would be ill done if he were not there to continue it.

Above all, there was the task of making a success of the loan. He had no doubt that it could be done. The great obstacle, he told the columnist Walter Lippmann, was 'the inner reluctance [in England] to accept a situation so utterly reversed from what she is used to and to find herself asking for financial aid instead of giving it'.[8] Making the loan work meant cutting out extravagance at home and abroad, and settling the sterling balances problem. Although, as a member of the Budget Committee, Keynes took part, as usual, in the pre-budget discussions, most of his Whitehall time was taken up with loan-related matters.

To Brand he wrote on 29 January: 'The mixed chauvinism and universal benevolence of the FO and other departments and the weakness of the Chancellor in these matters are slopping away on everything and everybody in the world except the poor Englishman the fruits of our American loan.'[9] A 'hair-raising' paper[10] on Britain's overseas financial commitments was rushed to the Cabinet in February. Britain, Keynes warned, stood ready to squander the loan 'to cut a dash in the world'.[11] The cost of keeping an army of Poles in Italy should be weighed against the cost of the bacon ration. Britain should cease all political loans. It should drastically reduce its overseas military forces in Greece, Egypt and elsewhere: 'We simply cannot afford to make our plans on the basis of being half and half-heartedly ready for war with Russia. . . . We are spending twice too much for solvency, and twice (or four times) too little for safety. . . .' The policy, by which Britain would be left alone responsible for feeding a de-industrialised and bankrupt Germany, was 'the craziest ever – if one did not remember last time'.[12]

Keynes was also preparing for the inaugural meeting of the International Monetary Fund and World Bank. His appointment as British governor of both institutions was announced on 19 February. After some negotiations, the meeting was fixed early in March at Savannah, in Georgia. 'I remain dreadfully in two minds about going,' Keynes wrote to Bridges on 12 February. But he longed to be in at the birth, there were still issues to settle about the location of the Fund and the Bank and the role of the executive directors, and Plesch and Lydia thought a break in warm weather, without too much work, would be good for him. What turned the decision in favour may well have been his love of sea travel. 'It is in fact a holiday jaunt,' he told Sheppard.[13]

Keynes's good health did not last. Covent Garden was due to reopen on 20 February with a gala performance of *The Sleeping Beauty*. It would be danced by Sadler's Wells Ballet, with new sets by Oliver Messel, conducted by Constant Lambert, and with Margot Fonteyn as Aurora – one of the parts Lydia had danced when Keynes was courting her during the run of Diaghilev's magnificent but ill-fated production at the Alhambra in 1921 – and Robert Helpmann doubling as Prince Florimund and the evil fairy Carabosse. As chairman of the Covent Garden Trustees it would be Keynes's duty to greet the King and Queen, and lead them to the Royal Box. He was thrilled to have engineered the reopening. There was much work to be done to transform the wartime dance hall to its former grandeur. The wooden floors were taken up, the bandstands removed, the red seats brought out of store, and the whole theatre repainted. In the two or three weeks before the gala performance Keynes nervously visited Covent Garden several times. A particular pleasure was arranging for his ninety-four-year-old father to attend a matinée performance in the directors' box later in the month.

Keynes told his mother that the opening night went off 'in great glory'. The Royal Family and Cabinet attended. Unluckily, Keynes had had 'a rather severe day at the Treasury, and the weather was cold, so that I was rather shaky by the evening and could not perform all my duties'. This was an understatement. He rushed to the theatre after a difficult three-hour pre-budget meeting with Dalton, and a few minutes before the royal party arrived he had a minor heart attack. Lydia received King George VI, Queen Elizabeth and the other royals on his behalf. He forced himself to entertain a party of people in the first interval and to make presentations to the King and Queen in the second. Queen Mary, the Queen Mother, well briefed or with a prodigious memory, told Keynes she remembered with great pleasure meeting his mother, Florence Keynes, at Papworth some years previously. Keynes received many letters afterwards saying how emotionally the occasion had struck them. 'The explanation, I think, is that many people had come to fear in their hearts . . . that all the grace and elegant things from the

old world had passed permanently away, and it caused an extraordinary
feeling of uplift when it was suddenly appreciated that perhaps they had not
entirely vanished.'[14]

Once again there was that miraculous power of recovery. The next day
he felt perfectly all right, and Plesch renewed his permission to travel. On
24 February Maynard and Lydia sailed to America for the last time on the
Queen Mary, accompanied by Rowe-Dutton from the Treasury and Roy
Bridge and George Bolton from the Bank of England. They arrived in New
York on 1 March. Despite a rough crossing he had not missed a single meal.
Their week in New York was crowded with ballet activities, as well as
Keynes's discussions with officials of the Federal Reserve Bank. He and Lydia
concocted a letter of ballet gossip to Ninette de Valois, who ran the Sadler's
Wells Ballet Company. They had tea with Balanchine and Danilova, whose
Ballet Russe de Monte Carlo 'was the only serious artistic enterprise in the
country'.

By 5 March they were back at the Statler Hotel in Washington. Keynes
saw both Morgenthau and his successor, Vinson. He told Morgenthau that
Bevin was 'a great guy', but answered with his usual brusqueness when
Morgenthau asked him what Britain would do if America imposed economic
sanctions on 'fáscist' Argentina: 'Nothing. We just can't be bothered with
that sort of thing. We are too dependent on the Argentine for beef.' He told
Morgenthau that Winston Churchill was in Washington to head off Bernard
Baruch's opposition to the Anglo-American loan.[15] Churchill did better than
that. Three days before the Savannah conference opened he made his
famous speech at Fulton, Missouri, Truman's home state, warning of the
'iron curtain' which had descended across Europe, and linking it to centrally
directed communist expansionism working through fifth columnists. One of
those agents, Harry Dexter White, noted that the future of the world would
depend much more on friendly relations between the USA and the Soviet
Union than between the USA and Britain.[16]

Keynes's meeting with 'Judge' Vinson suggested that Savannah would
not be quite the holiday he was expecting. He was told bluntly that the
Fund and Bank would both be located in Washington, rather than New
York as the British wanted. This decision was to keep them free from the
taint of 'international finance'. Keynes, by his own account, reacted 'very
vehemently'. They also talked about Harry Dexter White. White had been
approved by the Senate as executive director of the Fund, and Keynes hoped
he would be made its managing director. But Vinson told him the latter idea
had been dropped. The Americans wanted an American as head of the Bank,
and therefore a European would have to head the Fund.[17] Keynes did not
know that White's nomination as managing director had been dropped as a
result of an FBI report on him received by Truman on 4 February. The
administration decided that the best way to ease White, who was under FBI
surveillance, out of the Treasury without alerting the Soviets to the fact that

he had been rumbled was to allow him to take up the low-security-risk job of Fund executive director. Savannah was the last time he and Keynes met, and clashed, on the international stage.

In Savannah, 750 miles south of New York, Maynard and Lydia stayed at the General Oglethorpe Hotel on Wilmington Island, where the meetings were held. The usual huge collection of bodies had assembled – nominated governors, their alternates, observers, secretaries and reporters. Keynes fell in love with this gracious nineteenth-century city on to which had been superimposed a busy twentieth-century port. On arrival he issued a press statement in which he called Savannah 'a beautiful woman ... whose face was concealed behind a veil of delicate lace'. To Halifax he wrote of the American South, 'It is quite a different nation here, and in many ways a preferable one.'[18]

Unfortunately the cast of American negotiators assembled at Savannah, headed by Vinson and Clayton, was the same Keynes had recently encountered in Washington. At the inaugural meeting of governors on Saturday 9 March, 'Vinson', wrote Bareau, 'made a long and turgid speech full of emotional and fundamentally insincere expressions of hope. He was followed very much in the same strain by the Chinese, Czechoslovakian, French and the Mexicans. A breath of fresh air was introduced into the proceedings by Keynes' speech with its fairy tale metaphors....'[19] In Keynes's mind, and language, the birth of the twins 'Master Fund and Miss Bank' – whose names, he wished, had been reversed – fused with the great first-act christening party in *The Sleeping Beauty* which he had just seen danced, when the fairy godmothers showered their gifts on the newly born Princess Aurora. The gifts bestowed by Keynes's godmothers were to be Universalism, Courage and Wisdom. Having playfully embroidered this theme, Keynes expressed the hope that there was 'no malicious fairy, no Carabosse' whom the organisers had forgotten to ask to the financial christening. 'For if so', he went on, 'the curses which that bad fairy will pronounce will, I feel sure, run as follows: – "You two brats shall grow up politicians; your every thought and act shall have an *arrière-pensée*; everything you determine shall be not for its own sake or on its own merits but because of something else."' If the twins ever became political, their best fate would be to fall into 'eternal slumber'.[20] Whether the delegates quite followed the thread Keynes was so expertly spinning may be doubted. Vinson sensed that Keynes's barbed words might be directed against him. 'I don't mind being called malicious, but I do mind being called a fairy,' he growled.[21]

Two main issues divided the British and Americans: the location of the Fund and Bank and the Fund's *modus operandi*. The British wanted the two institutions to be apolitical, deciding matters on technical criteria. To this end they wanted them located outside Washington; and wanted the Fund, in particular, to be under the unencumbered control of the managing director and his staff, with the twelve executive directors and their alternates representing their countries or regions on a part-time basis, and at part-time salaries. The Americans wanted the Fund and Bank to be located in Washington; they wanted the executive directors to be full time, and lavishly reimbursed. They also envisaged a staff of 300 technicians, whereas Keynes thought thirty would be 'more than adequate to handle the business of the Fund'.

The two questions were thrashed out on 13 and 14 March. Paul Bareau's note runs: 'The Committee on the Site met in the afternoon and all opposition to Washington was brushed aside with complete brutality by the Americans.' Keynes decided to concede graciously, but felt a grave mistake was being made. The decision, he said, was *nem. con.* – nobody opposing, but by no means all supporting. On the second day, Clayton offered a compromise on the second issue which Keynes reluctantly accepted: though both executive directors and their alternates would be full-time, only one of them would need to be 'continually available'.[22] But Keynes balked at the tax-free salaries proposed for both of them, and other staff, set at American standards, arguing that it would be wrong 'to load the budgets of these bodies with such high emoluments for such a large body of officials'. Had the British foreseen the problem, they would have insisted on salaries being paid by the member governments.[23] On Dalton's instructions, Keynes voted against 'life in Washington with no defined or onerous duties and a grand, tax-free salary'.[24] Not surprisingly, he was the sole critic of this rosy prospect: and his was the only negative vote recorded at the conference.

Although Keynes said afterwards that 'I went to Savannah to meet the world and all I met was a tyrant,' the acrimony of the Savannah meeting has been exaggerated. Keynes kept himself well in hand, and in truth did not have much to do. Nevertheless, the strain was still too much. On the morning of 19 March, he started off for breakfast down the interminably long corridor of the swaying special train taking them from Savannah to Washington. Walking, by his own account too fast, he ran out of breath. He struggled to the dining car, feeling completely 'knocked out' and 'winded', as if at the end of a long race.[25] After an hour he seemed better, and started on the long walk back to his compartment. He never made it. Fighting for breath and life, he was carried back to the dining car and laid on a table. Lydia was by his side, Bob Brand and Harry White hovered anxiously. After two hours he had recovered. He managed to get to the taxi taking them to the Statler. After a good night's rest, he felt 'completely as usual'. He and Lydia booked into the Waldorf Astoria in New York next day, and sailed for Southampton on the *Queen Mary* early on 21 March.

Keynes's final reflections on his last American trip were contained in a note he wrote for Dalton in London on 4 April. He was confident that the American loan would get through Congress owing to the 'changed situation in relation to Russia'. He now advised a policy of 'drift' for six months on the sterling balances, since it paid Britain to go on accumulating them. This was surely Temptation with knobs on. He repeated his conviction that the United States was now a high-cost country, whose competitive advantage – and with it, by implication, the dollar-shortage – would drain away.[26]

Eady was shocked by Keynes's appearance on his return to the Treasury on 27 March: 'he was not only very white, but he slumped in his chair, and very gentle as though he found it very difficult to revive interest in all the many daily things on which he guided us'.[27] But he was soon back to form, reducing James Meade to tears with 'the whole battery of ... wit, petulance, rudeness and quick unscrupulousness in argument' directed against Meade's economic forecasts. Meade had worked out a plan to bring the national income and expenditure estimates into the same financial year as the budget estimates of revenue, so that planning policy and fiscal policy could operate with the same set of figures. Keynes was furious. He wanted wartime planning to die away, and thought it would if it was kept as far away from budgetary preparations as possible. It was Meade's last encounter with him, which did not affect his judgement that he was 'the greatest genius I have ever met'. He would always refer to him as 'My God'.[28]

Keynes managed to snatch two weekends at Tilton before the start of his Easter holiday. On one of them, he wrote a 3000-word essay on 'Bernard Shaw and Isaac Newton'. 'Pitiably old' at ninety, GBS had written to Keynes in January, following his speech on the loan, commenting on the 'tragic spectacle' of their Lordships 'talking vociferously – and oh! how earnestly – without understanding a single one of the substantives they were throwing about. And the strange figure of Maynard Keynes rising and chilling them with a cold blast of knowledge and reality.'[29] Keynes had been asked to contribute to a volume of tributes to GBS on the occasion of his ninetieth birthday. He spent Sunday 7 April writing it, apologising to the editor for 'such a poor and perfunctory thing'. His essay twitted Shaw on minor errors and anachronisms in his play *In Good King Charles's Golden Days*, which was set in Newton's non-existent Cambridge house. It ends: 'Wishing not to be absent from this volume of tribute but still deprived of leisure of mind and pen by vain pre-occupation with the perplexed business of the world, I write in haste these scanty lines. They do little justice to the love and honour in which I hold GBS.'[30]

On Thursday 11 April he had lunch at the Bank after the regular meeting of the Court. He told Henry Clay that he relied on Adam Smith's 'invisible hand' to get Britain out of the mess it was in, and went on: 'I find myself more and more relying for a solution of our problems on the invisible hand which I tried to eject from economic thinking twenty years ago.' 'An interesting confession for our arch-planner,' Henry Clay noted. The now-retired Montagu Norman, the recipient of Clay's letter, wrote back: 'About Keynes ... I think he relied on intellect, which perhaps means that he ignored the "invisible hand", and I guess he was led astray by Harry White. But surely it is easy to arrange a loan if you ignore its repayment, and is there any hope of that, unless there is to be such an inflation across the Atlantic as will affect their claims and provide an easy way out?'[31]

Keynes's Easter holiday started the next day, on 12 April. It was a glorious spring – 'definitely not the old England.... Is it sunspots?'[32] He did a couple of hours' Treasury work each morning. He sat in the garden reading his latest purchases of Elizabethan and Jacobean authors. His mother had come to stay and they wandered round the farm together. One morning clad in straw hat and light-blue jacket bought in America, he took her to see veal being carved into joints for the Easter feast for the families on the estate.

Keynes was exhausted, but he was not ready to die. On Thursday 18 April he had tea with Clive and Vanessa Bell and Duncan Grant at Charleston. He went without Lydia and stayed almost till dinner. It was like old times.

> I have seldom known him in better spirits [wrote Clive Bell to Mary Hutchinson]. He was extremely gay and full of projects. We talked of Roger [Fry] – about whom I happened to have written something for the Americans – and the fine show at the Tate, and plans for future shows of French painting. He was delighted with Kingsley Martin's misadventures in the Russian zone, abused the government, and took more than half seriously a wild project of Duncan's for a gala performance at Covent Garden in honour of Shaw's ninetieth birthday, to end with a laurel crowning by a pretty young actress (not Dame Sybil Thorndike) in the manner of Voltaire. Probably he would have realised it triumphantly. I have some reason to think he had been given, and was much pleased to have been given, an OM [He had].... The last thing he said to me was that he had something in mind to write about Lytton [Strachey], and that if he could get it done he would read it at the next meeting of the Memoir Club.[33]

On Saturday 20 April he made his third ascent of the week – by car – to Firle Beacon, with Lydia and his mother. He decided to return with Lydia by the footpath. He had not walked down the path for years, not since his illness. He felt quite fit to do it again. 'I watched the two of them,' Florence wrote later, 'as they disappeared gradually below the brow of the hill – he, bending down to her in animated talk, she looking up in eager response.' He had been describing a poem by Thomas Parnell, a friend of Pope and Swift, the first edition of which had just reached him. He had ended his explanation with the words: 'And the meaning of it all is: don't worry, there is always divine justice.'[34]

Keynes died in his bed on the morning of Easter Sunday, 21 April. There is some dispute about the details. Roy Harrod writes: 'Early next morning his mother heard a sound of coughing in his room. She went to seek Lydia, who was with him in a flash. An attack, such as he had often endured before, had just come on, but this time there could be no recovery. In a few minutes it was all over. His features assumed an expression of beautiful peacefulness.'

Clive Bell's account (written two days later fom Charleston) is different: 'Maynard died as suddenly as possible. Lydia had brought him a cup of tea at ten o'clock in the morning: he made a grimace and collapsed....' Moggridge writes: 'But next morning there was another attack. This time there was no recovery: in Lydia's presence, he died within three minutes.'[35] Lydia was present at his death, and so was Florence. Clive's account is to be preferred as being the most immediately recorded: Logan Thomson brought Charleston the news the same morning. Were there any last words? If so, they were not recorded.

This time there was no weeping and wailing from Lydia. When Vanessa and Duncan dined with Lydia, at her request, that evening, she was calm and collected. Dozens of letters of condolence arrived, from the eminent, from former students, from economists and from old friends. Most of them were beautifully, even arrestingly, phrased. 'He taught us', Hugh Dalton wrote, 'to unite Reason with Hope.' A common theme was that Keynes was unique and irreplaceable. Lionel Robbins said that 'he has given his life for his country, as surely as if he had fallen on the field of battle'; his most intransigent intellectual opponent, Friedrich Hayek, wrote that 'he was the one really great man I ever knew, and for whom I had unbounded admiration. The world will be a very much poorer place without him.' The historian Charles Webster, whom Keynes scarcely knew, offered the best succinct summary: 'He was the greatest intellectual force of our generation and one of the greatest of its men of action.' His brother Geoffrey had glimpsed another truth, no less important: that Maynard and Lydia were an inseparable team: 'I always enjoyed enormously seeing [them] together. They were both so vital, and each so continuously amused by the other's company. There was never a trace of staleness in their married life.'[36]

The Times obituary of 22 April wrote: 'To find an economist of comparable influence one would have to go back to Adam Smith.... And finally there is the man himself – radiant, brilliant, effervescent, gay, full of impish jokes.... He was a humane man genuinely devoted to the cause of the common good.' Catto, for four years his Treasury neighbour, wrote: 'More and more I came to admire his brilliant intellectual gifts, his vivid and exhilarating imagination, amounting to genius; and that facility of expression in speech and in writing that was so fascinating.... He was tenacious in his beliefs, yet, among those whom he liked, he could differ with a curious and delightful gentleness and, contrary to the general idea of him, he could readily accept constructive criticism.' His Treasury colleague David Waley singled him out for 'foresight, breadth of vision and courage'. Keynes, he wrote, 'always saw many moves ahead in the game'. Also, he never wrote a dull paragraph. 'It was impossible for him to be boring because

it was impossible for him to be bored. Everything interested him because
everything in his mind fitted instantaneously into its place in the conflict
between Wisdom and Folly.... He had in Whitehall no enemies. Those who
knew him best loved him most deeply.' Eady wrote: 'When we came back to
the Treasury after Maynard's death, the drab corridors were grey and silent,
the files were strangely heavy and lifeless. The kindly light had gone out.'

Keynes was cremated in Brighton on 24 April. He had wanted the urn
containing his ashes to be deposited in the vault of the chapel of King's
College. His brother Geoffrey forgot all about this clause in Keynes's will
and scattered his ashes from the point halfway up the Downs above Tilton
which Maynard had loved so well. Memorial services were held in the
Bethlehem Chapel of Washington Cathedral on 25 April, attended by Vinson
and Clayton, and with the lesson read by Bob Brand, at Westminster Abbey
on 2 May, and at King's College Chapel on 4 May.

The memorial service in Westminster Abbey was an extraordinary
occasion in which all the many lives of Keynes were represented. The
mourners were led by his widow, parents and family. Most of the senior
members of the Cabinet, led by the Prime Minister, were present, though
Winston Churchill was unavoidably absent in the United States. The Court
of the Bank of England were there, minus Catto, also abroad, but plus
Montagu Norman. The surviving members of the wartime Treasury turned
out in force, as well as the American ambassador John Winant, the Australian
Prime Minister and the High Commissioners of the Commonwealth. The
Provost and fellows of King's College, the Provost and Vice-Provost of Eton,
the leading British economists, his colleagues on the Arts Council and a
generous sprinkling of peers turned out to pay him their last tribute. Duncan
Grant, Vanessa Bell, Clive Bell and Leonard Woolf, survivors from Old
Bloomsbury, were there, as were many former students and artists, including
Margot Fonteyn and Robert Helpmann, who had so recently danced in *The
Sleeping Beauty.*

That Maynard Keynes should be mourned in death by a governing class
he had often derided, and enfolded by a religion whose tenets he had
dismissed as 'hocus-pocus', was not inappropriate. Keynes's world had been
that of the British Establishment, at no time more than in the last six years
of his life. He was tethered to it by upbringing, inclination, aptitude,
language and, above all, by his Englishness. By Establishment I mean here
not a closed order or corporation but an elastic governing class with an
instinctive sense of self-preservation, and therefore an exceptional capacity
for self-renewal. This expressed itself in the meritocratic selection of its elite,
and the authority and honour given to exceptional ability. In England it was
not necessary for rebels to become revolutionaries in order to 'get on'. They
were absorbed by the established order and used to strengthen its defences.
A harsher Continental tradition is apt to understand this process of absorption as one of betrayal and co-option. This was certainly how some of the

intransigent Keynesians interpreted the Master's shift back to economic liberalism in the last years of his life. Keynes of course never saw it in this way: Mahomet may have gone to the hill, but the hill had also come to Mahomet. In the world of economics and finance Keynes had come to occupy the same position as Churchill in the world of politics: he *was*, in fact, the Churchill of his domain. Both had been called on by their country in its hour of need, previous sins forgiven.

The elasticity of this order depended on a shared sense of Englishness, which in turn expressed itself in a rather uncomplicated patriotism: the complications in the use of these terms came later. Virtually anything could be forgiven provided one's patriotism was not in doubt. Schumpeter was penetrating when he wrote that Keynes's advice was in the first instance 'always English advice, born of English problems even when being addressed to other nations', that 'barring some of his artistic tastes, he was surprisingly insular, even in philosophy, but nowhere so much as in economics', and that his 'patriotism ... was so genuine as to be subconscious and therefore all the more powerful to impart a bias to his thought and to exclude full understanding of foreign (also American) viewpoints, conditions, interests, and especially creeds'.[37] There is one caveat to this view. Schumpeter left out the imaginative quality of Keynes's utterance. It gave Keynes a universal appeal; his words still have the power to provoke and move the economist and layman the world over.

That Keynes should be honoured at Westminster Abbey and in an Anglican ceremony was also fitting. It was not just that the proximity of Westminster Abbey to Parliament and Whitehall symbolised the Erastian character of the British state; it was also that Keynes was steeped in the culture of Christianity. Moore's *Principia Ethica*, which remained his 'religion under the surface', was a secularised version of monasticism, whose unworldliness, Keynes once said, made the New Testament, by comparison, a 'handbook for politicians'. As his worldly concerns multiplied – for Maynard Keynes was not by nature destined for the cloister – he came to realise that it was not Christianity which was the enemy, but the 'Benthamite calculus' or, more mundanely, materialism. As he became older, the atheism of his youth – the rejection of Christian dogma – ceased to define his attitude to Christianity. He had come to value it for social and moral reasons.

Like Odysseus, Keynes was a successful, not a tragic, hero. He heard the beautiful singing of the Sirens, but took precautions against being shipwrecked, keeping to the course for which his talents and the state of the world predestined him. Artfully, he strove for the best of all worlds, in his life and his work, and, miraculously, came close to achieving it.

So Keynes went to his eternal rest. Lydia wrote: 'And now I am so utterly alone without him. The light is gone. I grieve and weep.'

Epilogue

Keynes's Legacy

I. MAYNARD'S BEQUESTS

Maynard Keynes cared most for his family and friends, the arts, his College and his country. He died in the knowledge, or expectation, that he had left them all well provided for. 'In the long run', he famously wrote, 'we are all dead.' But Keynes cast such a long shadow that it would be a bold author, even now, who would want to apply this dictum to him. In the nearest reaches of that shadow were his testamentary dispositions, and their effect on his widow, his family and friends, and his College. Beyond that stretched the influence of his life, achievements and ideas. The modern world cannot do without Keynes, any more than it can do without Marx – though both have been repeatedly declared dead and buried. Both men expressed permanent truths about the human condition, even though these were not necessarily central to what they thought would happen or wanted to happen.

Keynes's will was probated on 19 September 1946. He left £479,529, roughly equivalent to £12m or $19m today. Of this just over £400,000 was in securities, most of the rest in pictures and rare books and manuscripts. The two executors of his will and trustees of his estate were his brother Geoffrey Keynes and his 'favourite student' Richard Kahn. After bequests of £40,000 (which included £4000 to each of his eight nephews and nieces, and smaller sums to Duncan Grant, Logan Thomson, Norman Higgins, Frederick Woollard, farmhands and servants), Keynes directed that a trust fund be set up, the income of which (apart from annuities to Duncan Grant and his secretary, Mrs Stephens) was to go to his widow Lydia during her lifetime, with the stipulation that her post-tax income should never fall below £1500, a curiously pessimistic assessment of her financial prospects. After her death, the capital sum would revert to King's College, Cambridge, together with his pictures, books and manuscript collections, notably the Newton MSS.

Keynes divided his private papers into two. His personal papers and contributions to the Memoir Club, which he left to Geoffrey Keynes, were to become the property of King's College after Lydia's death; his economic papers were left to Richard Kahn and were to be deposited in the Marshall Library, at Cambridge.

Typically, Keynes left his trustees and ultimate legatee, King's College, a wide discretion. The trustees were to invest the capital as they saw fit. He nevertheless hoped 'without imposing any obligation to that effect', that his College would apply the money it would eventually receive 'for buildings of greater amenity and beauty' on sites it owned and to make grants or advances to the Cambridge Arts Theatre. Interestingly, he 'requested' (rather than 'directed') his brother to 'destroy the greater part' of his personal papers, and Richard Kahn to do the same to his economic papers; he wanted none of his papers published except his two talks to Bloomsbury's Memoir Club.

When Roy Harrod had finished writing his biography, he returned Keynes's wartime papers to the Treasury, much to Kahn's annoyance. The rest of the economic papers were preserved. Possibly some of the personal papers were destroyed by Geoffrey Keynes. The personal papers have, of course, been extensively used by biographers, but the only part to have been published so far are the *Two Memoirs* – 'Dr Melchior' and 'My Early Beliefs' – in 1949, and three years of Keynes's correspondence with Lydia Lopokova before they were married.[1] About one-third of Keynes's economic papers have been published as part of the Royal Economic Society's edition of the *Collected Writings of John Maynard Keynes* in thirty volumes (1971–89). This was successively edited by Elizabeth Johnson and Donald Moggridge.

Then there was Keynes's public legacy. His chief gifts to the arts were the Cambridge Arts Theatre, paid for out of his own pocket, the Arts Council of Great Britain, which started its official life in August 1946 under Sir Ernest Pooley, and with an annual Treasury grant of £320,000, and the reborn Royal Opera House, Covent Garden. All three institutions survive, though none has quite fulfilled Keynes's hopes.

His economic bequests were more controversial. Most tangible was the American loan of $3.75bn he had negotiated in 1945 to see Britain through the immediate post-war years. This proved the least durable of his legacies, quickly dissipated in the convertibility crisis of mid 1947 – though, without its false promise, the British welfare state might never have taken root. The Bretton Woods Agreement was partly his invention, Britain's acceptance of it largely the result of his untiring advocacy. The International Monetary Fund and World Bank – the 'twins' he christened at Savannah a month before he died – are still with us, though other elements of that Agreement, notably fixed exchange rates and capital controls, are gone. Beyond all this stretched the 'Keynesian Revolution' – the logic and practice of managing economies so as to maintain full employment and avoid depressions like that of 1929–33. In the form Keynes left it, his Revolution was never wholly accepted; and the debate about its value and relevance, and its author's place in the pantheon of thought and statesmanship, continues. We still live in the shadow of Keynes, not because his legacy has been assimilated, but because it is still disputed.

II. LYDIA'S WORLD

Lydia Keynes was fifty-three when Maynard died, and lived another thirty-six years.[2] A week after his death, his nephew Richard Keynes reported her 'wonderfully cheerful; and quite in her old form most of the time' at Sunday lunch at 6 Harvey Road, Cambridge, 'and then she remembers, and bursts into tears for a moment. But it is soon over.' Lydia was not one to mope. 'I used to think of [Maynard] every day, but now I don't think about him at all,' she told Fred Ashton a few years later. The truth was that, while she and Maynard had been extraordinarily happy together, a huge part of his life had been beyond her reach, interest and understanding. As for the rest, she kept her silence. No one could coax her into revealing reminiscence. This is surprising only to those who live by the pen. She was not a gossip or a writer. Her significant memories were, in any case, too intimate for circulation. She had done her duty by Maynard, and was now entitled to her privacy. When journalists rang for comments, she would pick up the telephone, pretend to be her own secretary, and say in a thick Russian accent, 'No, Madam does not give interviews.'

Above all, she no longer had Maynard to protect her. So she withdrew into the world of ballet, where she had been a star in her own right, and on which subject she could speak as an expert. Even here, though, she needed support on public occasions. In 1947 she asked Provost Sheppard of King's College, Cambridge, for help in making a speech to honour Ninette de Valois. 'Please do scribble something to me in typewriting, put yourself in my shoes and spread your general wits across my nervous system.' She signed herself 'your uneconomic geisha'.

At the same time, she inherited Maynard's income (managed by two trustees, his brother Geoffrey and Richard Kahn), his homes, his staff, his pictures, his family and many of his friends, his routines. She kept up, and expanded, that part of their married life which had been most closely connected with the stage. She was a member of the Arts Council Drama Panel and Trustee of the Cambridge Arts Theatre, though she soon resigned from the former. She divided her time, as they had both done, between Tilton, Gordon Square and St Edward's Passage. For ten years after his death she remained an enthusiastic theatregoer in Brighton, London and Cambridge.

She continued to come up to Cambridge to see her 'dear old characters', whom she also had to stay at Tilton. These included Jack Sheppard, Provost of King's, 'Dedy' as she called Dadie Rylands, a new friend, Noel Annan, who succeeded Sheppard as Provost in 1956 at the early age of thirty-nine, and, of course, Maynard's parents, the *starychki*. Neville Keynes died in 1949, aged ninety-seven, but Lydia's bond with Florence ('M.i.l.') continued unbroken till Florence's death in 1958, at the age of ninety-six. Florence's lucid and loving letters to her 'Lyddy' continued till the end. Two years before her death she wrote: 'I always think of you & the happiness you gave him.' In Cambridge, Lydia usually took her meals at the Theatre Restaurant, opposite her flat, attended by the head waiter, Mr Schurch. She had a natural affinity with the more theatrical King's College dons, her quick wit and mastery of the *double entendre* perfectly fitting their camp style. She once told Noel Annan that Englishmen were either 'boys or old boys'; it was less of a complaint than a typically sharp observation. Lydia's visits to Cambridge tailed off in the later 1950s. The flat in St Edward's Passage, having been largely unoccupied for some years, was given up in 1965. In 1967, by which time she was seventy-five, she declined to come up for the opening of the new Keynes Building.

In London, Lady Keynes was still invited to some of the official receptions she and her husband might have graced. She refused most of them, but, exceptionally, turned up in 1950 at a party at the American Embassy for the Achesons: she thought the Foreign Secretary, Ernest Bevin, looked far from well. Mostly, though, she stuck to her own world. Her 'boyfriends' were homosexuals like Richard Buckle, Fred Ashton, Cecil Beaton, Raymond Mortimer, Eddie Sackville-West. These men, particularly the ballet critic 'Dicky' Buckle, had the advantage of being available as escorts. Lydia was also 'thick', as she put it, with Laurence Olivier and Vivien Leigh. No. 47 Gordon Square was sub-let. At No. 46, Lydia herself occupied less and less space, driven from most of the house by the cold as well as by the expense. The basement was let out to a caretaker; the upper floors to a society for Christian aid. She liked them as tenants because they were clean. Lydia herself often answered the doorbell. 'Are you Christian?' she would teasingly ask a likely looking stranger. She now camped out in the ground-floor front room – their old dining room – which had her bed, a large mirror and barre; she entertained in a small, high back room at a table covered with oilcloth, 'where among the piles of books and tins of food, one was surprised', Buckle wrote, 'to find a Cubist Picasso and Delacroix's sketch for the mural of "Jacob Wrestling with the Angel" in the church of Saint-Sulpice'. She took daily meals at Antoine's in Charlotte Street.

Asked by *Newsweek* in 1955 to compare contemporary dancing with that of her youth, Lydia answered sensibly: 'Why confuse the standards of to-day with those of 30 years ago? To-day is to-day and yesterday is history. The great thing is that Ballet flourishes.' History reappeared when Pablo Picasso visited London in November 1950. She asked him for the drawing of her with Massine dancing the can-can from *La Boutique Fantasque* in the early 1920s. He promised to send it, could not find it, and sent her the photograph inscribed 'pour Lydia en attendant l'original'. The original never did arrive. On 13 April 1949 she took Maynard's old friends Duncan Grant and Vanessa, Clive and Quentin Bell to Fred Ashton's new production of *Cinderella*. It was 'glorious', she reported. 'Fred has achieved "magnum opus". I laughed and cried. . . .' By the early 1950s, she felt Ashton was 'stale', and needed to get away from Sadler's Wells. She was out of sympathy with modern ballet, feeling that it had become purely technical and acrobatic. The glory days of Covent Garden in the 1960s, made memorable by the partnership of Margot Fonteyn and Rudolf Nureyev and by the superb ballets of a revived Fred Ashton and Kenneth Macmillan, largely passed Lydia by. In 1965 she gave up Gordon Square as well. By then she had started to live in contented seclusion in her beloved Tilton.

Lydia once told Ninette de Valois that whenever she and Maynard returned to Tilton after their travels 'we were like two children setting out on a long, long holiday'. As she grew older she became increasingly reluctant to leave what had been their joint refuge from the world. After Maynard's death she never went abroad, not even to Russia, though she maintained a correspondence with her brother, Fedor Lopukhov, the choreographer at the Maryinsky Theatre in Leningrad. 'Tilton community suits me,' she told Richard Kahn, 'no diplomacy, "gentleman's agreements" or prima donnas.' She was remarkably self-contained, she never suffered from loneliness or boredom. 'The world is full of nightmares, but Tilton woods are full of beauty,' she wrote. And when the summer sun came to turn her into a 'Red Indian', '24 hours is just not enough to be happy. I wish for 48.' Her enjoyment of country life, especially in summer, was rhapsodic: surrounded by 'broad beans, green peas and weeds', her skin 'rattled' from the sun, 'so rewarding and sudorous'; she became 'like a plant with two arms'; life was a 'melody, away from Oxford Street'. On top of the Downs with her farmers' boots, she became 'celestial . . . gliding through the ridges and sweating out my fibrositis'. But winter, too, had its special quality, with the apples in her orchard 'who still hang like a hangover' in December.

Once Lydia no longer had to play the great man's wife, her natural bohemianism asserted itself. Her clothes had always been eccentric; now they became bizarre. She relied on woolly hats and brightly coloured boots to adorn – and protect – the extremities, and was not much interested in anything in between, provided it kept her warm. She treated the English climate as an extension of Russia's, arctic for most of the year, but interspersed with precious intervals of sunshine. She dressed accordingly. For much of the year she would be heavily bundled up against the cold, both inside and outside the house. When the sun shone, she would strip almost naked, to thaw out her body under its health-giving rays. Tilton saw her in both aspects – trundling up the flinty private lane wrapped up in old scarves and Maynard's pullovers, or flitting half naked among the broad beans and cabbages in the garden, or sunbathing quite naked in the redcurrant bushes within a few yards of a footpath. Once asked if this habit might not cause embarrassment, Maynard replied, 'No – passers-by simply can't believe their eyes.'

Lydia accepted the coming of old age without fuss, and preferred to be comfortable rather than smart. On being asked for a photograph by the choreographer Walter Gore in the mid-1950s she replied, 'Would you like me as I am or as I was? There is quite a difference.' When Cecil Beaton visited her in July 1951, she greeted him 'wearing a mercerized silk skirt of cream leaf pattern, cocoa-coloured stockings, woollen socks, straw boots, an apron, and about three different sweaters over a silk blouse. Her head was tied in a maize-coloured handkerchief: a pale grey, shiny face without make-up, but freckled and sunburnt at back of neck.'

At Tilton, she bustled round the house, with headscarf round her hair, a cigarette dangling from her mouth, looking like a charlady, though she never did much cleaning. Nor did she bother much with cleaning herself. When she arrived to stay with the Oliviers without her toothbrush, and Vivien Leigh offered to lend her one, she said: 'Oh my dear, do not worry. What's the point of cleaning your teeth? You have to lose them some time.' In 1965 she told Jack Peters, the bursar's clerk at King's – an unusual recipient for such news – that 'I have now removed my few remaining teeth, all very painless and successful. I am now relieved of the task of cleaning my teeth with a toothbrush, it is all done scientifically by a special detergent, supplied by the dentist.' What she enjoyed most was relaxing with the newspapers and magazines that Maynard had loved to read, and which continued, uncancelled, to be delivered; being driven, by the farm manager Logan Thomson, to Lewes or Eastbourne for lunch and a shopping expedition, or to a theatre in Brighton; and wandering on the Downs, learning poetry and taking in the 'melodies' of the countryside.

Most of Tilton, like 46 Gordon Square, was abandoned, as Lydia concentrated her living in a small space on the ground floor, like a bird making its nest. She never cooked, and kept clear of the kitchen at the rear of the house. She took her meals in the small dining room on the left of the front door. Logan Thomson would often join her, as she liked a 'man at the table'. To the right of the front door was the 'boot room', where Maynard had died, and in which Lydia now slept, with a bathroom beyond in the 'wing' which Maynard had built. Behind the dining room was the large apple-green drawing room, with its overstuffed grey sofas and armchairs in the 1930s style, with two hexagonal tables with shelves for books, an old upright piano from a junk shop, and windows hung with thick beige curtains. This was used mainly in the evenings, or when she had guests to stay. As the years went by, Lydia lived increasingly in the front part of the entrance hall, separated from the panelled rear by an arched entrance which could be closed off. Here she would sit surrounded by her impedimenta: tins of food and powdered milk, originally bought to survive the wartime blockade, and still not removed from their shelves, perhaps for fear of future poverty;

and rows of tiny boots, shoes and ballet slippers on the floor. At the back of the enclosed courtyard behind the main house, Maynard's old study stood dank and abandoned. The garden, so expertly created by Edgar Weller, was increasingly unkempt, the flowerbeds and lawn tennis court reverting to rough grass, the vegetable gardens, their fencing broken, overrun by rabbits.

The dilapidated house was still thickly hung with pictures, the best ones – the Seurat, the two Cézannes, the Picassos – in the drawing room. Lydia said, 'Cézanne painted hundreds of apples and I have five of them.' Maynard's pictures were so valuable that a huge burglar alarm was attached to an outer garden wall of the house to protect them. Lord Gage contributed to the defence by leaving the private road off the main road so full of holes as to deter the most intrepid burglar. Every so often the bell would start ringing loudly when a branch fell on the telephone line, or when someone touched a picture accidentally. The police would then roar up the drive. The pictures came to be hung higher and higher to avoid setting off the alarm accidentally. Eventually Lydia could stand it no longer and insisted that they be removed. After a year of nagging at Richard Kahn (who excused himself from action on the ground that he was 'terribly tied up in Important Government Business') she managed, in 1967, to get them transferred to King's, and then to the Fitzwilliam, where they are on permanent loan. 'Now I can once again live in the drawing room without disturbance....' she told her laggard trustee. 'I have filled all the empty spaces with Duncan, Vanessa, Matthew Smith, Gore and Quentin Bell and the effect is most pleasing, in fact one or two I prefer to the old ones.'

As time went on, and 'staff problems' mounted, she became less inclined to have guests to stay at all, and put them up, at her expense, at the White Hart Hotel in Lewes. 'I do hope you will not think this very rude of me,' she wrote to Richard Kahn in 1967, 'but nowadays I enjoy people for a few hours during the day, but hate to have them sitting on my doorstep. Forgive me.' She was just as decided with Geoffrey Keynes: 'I love you and long to see you but not, my dear, at breakfast.'

Lydia had inherited a staff reduced by wartime labour shortages, and it never recovered to its former amplitude. At Gordon Square, Mrs Turtle came in to clean, and Mrs Beaumont cooked. At Tilton, the chauffeur Fred Woollard went when the Rolls was sold. Edgar Weller now had a full-time job, but he and Ruby stayed on at Tilton Cottage (Ruby as cleaner). There were the Carters to cook and garden. Servant problems were not long in coming. In 1949, Mrs Beaumont said she wanted to sleep out and have Fridays to Mondays off, at which Lydia told her 'the sooner we part company the better'. Mrs Carter (Rosie) had to go to hospital to be 'de-warted, inside of a nostril'. Then in 1956 the Carters left her with one week's notice after twelve years. 'It's all the full employment,' Kahn commiserated, 'Maynard is to blame.' Their place was taken by the Taylors. Mrs Taylor had a part-time job in a lunatic asylum in Eastbourne, and did not much differentiate between Lydia and her other customers. Lydia disliked Mrs Taylor intensely, but it never occurred to her to sack her. Instead she had the doorways connecting the servants' quarters to the main house bricked up, so she would not be driven mad by the cook's chattering proximity. Traffic between the two parts of the house had to pass through the front door, except for meals, which came through a hatch. On the cook's days off, Lydia and Logan took lunch at the White Hart Hotel.

Her third 'cooking couple', the Lessiters, stayed from 1962 to 1966. Mavis Lessiter, now Hicks, remembers Lydia as a lady of routine. Every morning she made her breakfast, washed some dishes in the pantry, fed the cat and took a walk down the lane. Ruby would arrive to clean. Logan would come to lunch and often to dinner before going off for a pint at Berwick. By this time Lydia rarely went to London. The Lessiters had two sons, of whom Lydia was very fond. 'She treated us like family,' Mavis Hicks said, and was hurt and upset when the family emigrated to New Zealand. There was then a year's interregnum before the Whiters arrived. Jean Whiter found everything in an advanced state of decay. She restored the first-floor bedrooms, so that the Keynes family could come to stay. She found the bedclothes and sheets full of burns and had to confiscate Lydia's cigarettes when she went to bed. She and Ruby bickered endlessly.

Relations with Charleston thawed, though Lydia was too hurt by earlier snubs, and by now too self-contained, to pass much time with the ageing Bloomsberries. She still had to summon up courage to see the forbidding deep-voiced Vanessa Bell, though she found Leonard Woolf 'sweet and noble'. The Charlestonians were sometimes asked to help entertain Maynard's nephews when they came to stay. But Angelica Garnett's daughter, Henrietta, remembers relations between the two houses as distant, if no longer frosty. One summer afternoon, when she was ten – this was in 1955 – Henrietta went boldly up to the front door of Tilton, knocked and was greeted affectionately by a tiny lady, much muffled up with pullovers and headscarves, looking 'rather like an old tea-cosy, except for her feet, which were delicate and beautiful, and for her hands, which were very graceful'. She sat Henrietta down in the drawing room, offered her a glass of sweet Sauternes, and talked about the ballet in St Petersburg before the First World War. After a number of such visits over the years, Henrietta thought 'how queer it was that, at tea with Lydia, there was never any tea'. Lydia outlived all the original Bloomsberries, Vanessa Bell dying in 1961, Clive Bell in 1964, Leonard Woolf in 1969, and finally Duncan Grant in 1978.

It was Logan Thomson who replaced Maynard as the man in the house, possibly as the man in Lydia's life, though there is no evidence that she was sexually involved with him. Logan still ran the Tilton and Charleston Farms, whose profits he shared with Lydia; he did less and less work. His parents had died; he lived in the pink bailiff's house at Tilton with his aunt. Logan was devoted to Lydia, and she came to depend increasingly on him – to write her letters, to handle her money, to keep her company, to take her out. He tried to keep the house and grounds in order. When the aunt died and Logan gave up the farms in 1966, he moved into Tilton. He was a man of few words, but he and Lydia enjoyed their silences together, as Morgenthau and Sir Frederick Phillips had done in the war.

Lydia's relations with Logan, and also with Ruby Weller, were a strange mixture of democracy and formality. They would all go to plays in Brighton, eating fish and chips before the shows. But Ruby always called her 'Your Ladyship' and Logan called her 'Madam'. Ruby, too, stayed with Lydia till the end of her days at Tilton. They quarrelled endlessly, but 'You can't help being fond of her, can you?' Ruby said.

To Richard Kahn fell the unpromising job of controlling Lydia's overdraft. The income she inherited was not far short of what she and Maynard had jointly enjoyed in their last years. But she also inherited the punitive tax rates imposed to pay for the war, and which now served to finance Labour's 'New Jerusalem'. She also had personal securities of her own, which came to £24,000 by 1956. Had he not sold 'a considerable part' of her original holding of Hawker Siddeley, they would have been worth much more, her trustee informed her gloomily.

Lydia was not extravagant with money, she was careless. Whenever she needed cash, she wrote out cheques, and never kept the stubs, or looked at her statements. Often she just signed the cheques, leaving it up to Logan and others to fill in the amounts. She was a mixture of generosity and peasant habits. She always responded to appeals from ex-dancers in need like Karsavina, Baranova, Larionov and Goncharova, and in 1950 set up a charitable trust fund to help them. 'I know Maynard would have done something immediately to relieve their worries,' she told Richard Kahn. She financed a play by Richard Buckle. But she cut up newspapers for lavatory paper.

Lydia wrote to Kahn guiltily about her purchases, and slyly about her need for cash to make more. On 18 March 1949: 'I bought a new hat, a scarf and pair of shoes. I wanted to refurbish myself.' On 14 September 1950: 'If I don't buy [my coat] now the price of wool will be unsupportable later.' On 27 May 1951 she informed her trustee that 'I am going to London, must buy something, otherwise there will be unemployment.' She justified her habits by her late husband's theories: 'Maynard always said "Money's for spending, it goes round and round".'

Kahn ponderously rebutted Lydia's economic dicta:

It seems to me [he wrote on 26 June 1952] that you are being somewhat premature in applying the ideas associated with the name of the late Lord Keynes to the hints dropped by the Chancellor of the Exchequer, that the country is in for a touch of unemployment. We paid £500 into your account in March and another £500 as recently as the middle of

May, on each occasion the account having become overdrawn. By the 21st June it had become overdrawn again and another £500 has been paid in. This means that in the past quarter you have been spending at more than twice the proper rate. I am afraid it is my duty to warn you that this cannot go on.

It's not quite clear why Lydia was going through so much money at this time. She thanked Kahn for his 'innumerable scriptures', which seemed 'Chinese' to her. In 1959 she wrote him: 'Dear Richard, It appears that I ought to be redecorated. I look in the mirror and think it's long overdue. I should be glad of your opinion.' After Lydia gave up her properties, her cash position improved and by the late 1960s she was underspending her income.

Richard Kahn was devoted to Lydia, not just for her own sake, but because of the part she had played in the life of his hero. But he was not an entirely satisfactory trustee. He lacked Maynard's speed in transacting business; he also suffered from bouts of depression during which he was incapable of conducting business at all. So in good peasant fashion Lydia would sell her furniture and other personal possessions to meet her expenses. In 1956 she needed to get the roof at Tilton repaired, but Kahn was too busy to reply to her letters. So she sold for £5000 a cast of a Degas ballerina given to her by Samuel Courtauld. In 1958, she wrote to Dadie Rylands, 'no letter from Kahn, constipation'.

Kahn generally came down to Tilton after each Christmas to discuss farm accounts with Logan Thomson. Lydia dreaded these bursarial visitations, though she kept up a cheerful front, promising him 'Tilton's speciality, well prepared electric blankets', and assuring him that with '80 degrees hot water', there would be 'not a dull moment in the bathroom'. Once she wrote: 'How would you feel about endowing your bed with a couple of pairs of sheets (and perhaps some pillow slips if you are feeling generous)?' She was fiercely protective of Logan, though: 'Logan is a farmer, not a bursar or civil servant who writes memorandums all day long. . . .' She mocked her trustee for his forgetfulness ('We screamed with laughter, especially when you signed [yourself] Logan'), for his illegible handwriting ('It is a dream to read your typed letter'), and for his bureaucratic habits: 'Yesterday we went to see a film which was your cup of tea, a life story of a civil servant in the Treasury. . . .' She accused him of addressing her as though she were a 'chart or a trade cycle', and handed his article on tariffs to Logan, unread. She forwarded to him enquiries from Japan, saying that 'I really [am] incapable of dealing with Oriental economics.' After receiving a further batch of technical papers, she asked him: 'Would it cause unemployment if I sent a circular letter to the effect that Maynard is no more alive for 5 years?'

But Lydia was tied to Kahn, not just by Maynard's will, but by his love for Maynard. She tried to thaw out his frozen feelings: 'You sound so tired and hurried in your letter; if only you pick broad beans you'd forget all about index of prices....' And having once scolded him for acting like 'Oliver Cromwell', she concluded, 'Still, all in all, you are noble and good, and I am very fond of you.'

Kahn struggled on doggedly to fulfil his Master's trust, despite increasing deafness and oddness. In 1959, he converted her life interest into an annuity to release capital for a new 'Keynes Building' at King's College. He assured her that her position would be fully safeguarded. Lydia was (rightly) worried by the thought of a fixed annuity. 'What happens to me if I live to one hundred and you economists let inflation run away again?' In 1970, Lydia informed her trustee that she was eighty. Kahn disagreed (10 April 1970):

> You will remember that when Jack Peters and I negotiated your annuity with the insurance company we had to try to estimate your age. The evidence before us were various passports, a marriage certificate, a statement from your brother and, for what it was worth, a statement from you.... It became apparent that in your young days you were seriously understating your age and that as you got less and less young you began more and more to overstate it.
>
> We did our best to arrive at a fair estimate and the insurance company accepted it. According to this estimate your age at present is 78½.

III. A MAN FOR ALL SEASONS?

In the thirty years following his death, Keynes's reputation soared and then crashed. The magic seemed to work, then suddenly it faded. The years of success were the so-called 'golden age' lasting roughly from 1950 to the early 1970s, when the 'mixed economies' of Western nations achieved a stability and rates of economic growth unequalled in economic history. Then came the time of troubles, when the economic machine stuttered and stalled, and familiar patterns of boom and slump reasserted themselves. The Keynesian age – as the golden age is often known – ended in 'stagflation' – a combination of rising inflation *and* rising unemployment. New magicians appeared who talked about the need to return to 'market disciplines' and 'Victorian values' and who said that the government was the problem, not the solution. In the golden age most economists would have called themselves Keynesian; by the early 1990s, only a minority. How much had Keynes to do both with the golden age and with its collapse?

There were four important elements in the post-war Keynesian mindset.

The first was that, for various different, and largely unexplained, reasons, economies were sticky, not fluid. They would adjust only sluggishly, if at all, to 'shocks'. So, Keynes said, governments must intervene to stop unemployment developing; because, if they did not, unemployment might persist for a long time.

Secondly, there was a powerful political economy argument: free societies could not stand heavy, persisting unemployment. In the long run we may have full employment. But in the long run we are dead; and in the short run we may have revolution if we allow mass unemployment to develop. This, as we have seen, was Keynes's answer to Hayek.

Thirdly, although most economists rejected any simple idea of 'secular stagnation', they were powerfully influenced by Keynes's thought that investment opportunities would flag in rich societies, while saving habits continued unchanged. So they were continually haunted by the prospect of depression even when economies were booming. The boom, Keynes himself had predicted, could not last.

These were all backward-looking ideas. The fourth, which looked to the future, was summed up in Keynes's phrase 'Joy through Statistics'. With Keynes this was something of a wisecrack. He was always deeply sceptical about statistics used for forecasting. But his followers took it seriously. From the crude beginnings of national income accounts they developed a faith that Keynesian policy could be made completely scientific, or 'automatic' as James Meade put it. This faith enabled them to finesse the problem to which anti-Keynesians constantly directed unwelcome attention: the fact that economic policy was bound to be run by politicians, with political aims and ambitions. These pre-scientific disturbances were simply removed from the Keynesian picture, their place taken by forecasting models, with more and more equations.

In time, all these assumptions, faiths, hopes, started to break down. Some of the problems started with the theory itself; others in the way it was accepted; others in the way it was applied. Some had nothing to do with Keynes or Keynesianism at all, though he got blamed nonetheless. All contributed to a 'counter-revolution' in both theory and policy which got under way in the late 1960s. In the course of it, some old truths were properly rediscovered, some new truths improperly ignored.

Keynes's 'general theory of employment' was not quite as general as he believed. For one thing, it left out the many causes of unemployment apart from demand-deficiency, particularly those to do with labour immobility and slowness of adaptation to change. Unemployment can occur even when there is enough aggregate demand. Hubert Henderson always emphasised the structural character of Britain's inter-war unemployment problem. Keynes was aware of 'structural unemployment', but it was not the subject of his theory. In that sense the *General Theory* was an unbalanced book, and it left an unbalanced legacy. This meant that little attention was paid to 'supply side problems' in the golden age; and they tended to cumulate, raising, as it was later said, the 'natural' rate of unemployment. It is inconceivable that Keynes would not have wanted to attack them. But he was no longer there, and his book was.

The deeper problem was with his theory itself. For Keynes mass unemployment, or underutilisation of available resources, was a logical possibility rooted in uncertain expectations. But economists had never understood how unemployment could persist, even occur, if workers were always willing to price themselves into jobs, and they felt that Keynes had not properly explained how this might be so, even though the fact could not be gainsaid. So the mainstream in the profession fell back on traditional explanations. Powerful unions and social legislation prevented the required wage flexibility and worker mobility which would have enabled economies to adjust fairly painlessly to shocks. 'Classical theory' was right after all in its claim that unemployment could not occur if wages and prices were perfectly flexible; it just happened not to be terribly relevant. The so-called 'neoclassical synthesis' of the 1950s thus reaffirmed 'classical theory' as the 'general case', with Keynesian theory as a 'special case of classical theory where wages are rigid'.[3] However, the special case was the actual case in the modern world. So there remained a substantial role for Keynesian *policy* in moving the economy from an inferior to superior equilibrium, or preventing the emergence of an inferior equilibrium.

This compromise with classical theory seemed to leave economics in a mess. The unexplained assumption of sticky wages and prices seemed to contradict the much more powerful axiom on which economics itself rested – that economic agents are rational utility maximisers. There was evidently a deal of theoretical clearing up to do. This clearing up took an anti-Keynesian form once the promise of Keynesian policy started to fade.

The second Keynesian thesis which ran aground was that of the long-run tendency to stagnation and unemployment. The post-war boom proved exceptionally strong and was prolonged all over the 'free' world, even after post-war reconstruction was finished. At the time this was attributed to Keynesian policies themselves, but this turns out to be unproven. True enough, both the British and US governments 'targeted' unemployment. But the targets were repeatedly revised downwards as actual results exceeded the targets. Low unemployment, it seemed, was not caused by the pursuit of low unemployment targets; the low unemployment targets were caused by low unemployment.

What then was it that made the 1950s and 1960s so 'golden'? A large part of the explanation is 'catch-up', the potential for growth given by 'a large back-log of unexploited technology. The principal part of this back-log ... consisted of methods of production and of industrial and commercial organization already in use in the United States at the end of the war, but not yet employed in the other countries of the West.'[4] In the inter-war years, it could be said, 'catch-up' was 'frustrated by the irregular effects of the Great War and of the years of disturbed political and financial conditions that followed, by the uneven impacts of the Great Depression itself and of the restrictions on international trade'. During the Second World War, the productivity gap between the United States and the rest of the world widened. After the war 'the three elements required for rapid growth by catching up came together ... large technological gaps; enlarged social competence ... and conditions favoring rapid realization of potential'.[5]

To what extent full employment policy itself was one of these conditions remains uncertain. As John Hicks put it in 1974: 'The combination of more rapid technical progress (surely a fact) with the socialist tendencies which increased demand for collective goods (surely also a fact) could have produced such a boom without the added stimulus of Keynesian policies. It is still unclear how much is to be attributed to the one and how much to the other.'[6]

The post-war trading and monetary regimes undoubtedly facilitated the diffusion of best-practice technology. Keynes's handiwork can be found in the setting up of both, but the ideas which inspired them – trade liberalisation, fixed exchange rates, currency convertibility – were not of specific Keynesian provenance. They reflected the American conviction that the troubles of the inter-war years had been brought about by currency and trade wars.

Keynes's own specific, the doctrine of 'creditor adjustment', was not accepted at Bretton Woods. This meant that the 1944 Agreement provided no mechanism for dealing with the post-war 'dollar gap'. Following the failure of the bilateral loans to Britain and France in 1945, the Bretton Woods Agreement was put into cold storage for almost fifteen years; the International Trade Organization was similarly aborted. Far from being the 'foundation upon which [post-war] world trade, production, employment and investment were gradually built', as one historian has claimed,[7] the Bretton Woods rules and institutions played little part in the golden-age experience. Their cornerstone, currency convertibility at fixed exchange rates, was not restored in the main European countries till 1959, by which time the golden age was in full flower.

The dollar scarcity, which had filled the British with apprehension in the run-up to Bretton Woods, was eliminated, not by the 'invisible hand', which was Keynes's somewhat despairing alternative to 'bancor', but by the very visible US commitment to keep western Europe and Japan free of communism. This led the United States to acquiesce in the large sterling, franc and deutschmark devaluations against the dollar in 1949; it led to Marshall Aid, later supplemented by large private outflows; it led the USA to promote a European Payments Union and to allow it to discriminate against American goods which it had sought to deny Britain. The trend in the balance of payments in turn enabled exchange rates to be gradually stabilised and currency convertibility re-established. This promoted the reduction in trade barriers, which in turn fuelled economic growth. By 1960 J. P. Morgan partner Russell Leffingwell, in the last year of his life, was writing:

> Wisely we undertook to set the world to rights. We gave money and know-how to our foreign friends, we made fixed foreign investments, and we policed the world against the Russians and Communist Chinese with foreign bases and foreign based troops and ships and planes. All this involved spending immense sums of dollars abroad.
>
> We and our friends abroad had been so obsessed by the thought of the ... dollar gap ... that until recently few noticed that the dollar shortage had disappeared and a dollar glut had taken its place. Our foreign aid has been successful beyond our dreams. Western Europe and Japan had fully recovered and were in hot competition with us here and abroad. So our favorable trade balance had dwindled to little or nothing.
>
> We are still spending abroad billions more than our income from abroad, and the resulting deficit is reflected in our loss of gold and increased short term debt to abroad.... For the first time in more than a quarter of a century we are being subjected, willy nilly, to the discipline of the gold standard.[8]

Any influence of Keynes in all this? These American policies, we may say, had Keynesian effects; they were not undertaken for Keynesian reasons.

But there is more to be said. The Keynesian background became more important as the great boom continued through the 1950s. In 1937 Keynes had sketched his technique of 'boom control'. Governments should run fiscal surpluses while avoiding dear money 'like hellfire'. This strategy of fiscal surpluses and (relatively) cheap money was pursued by most governments in the first fifteen years after the war. It might well have sustained the post-war boom over a far longer period than would otherwise have happened. By the early 1960s it had started to break down, as governments lost control of both fiscal and monetary levers.

Fiscal policy as a method of boom control was disabled by three developments: the more ambitious – but unsuccessful – use of the government's budget to boost growth rates; the explosion of welfare entitlements; and, superimposed on these, the inflationary US financing of the Vietnam War. The result was a chronic tendency to excess global demand, generated by budget deficits and through the growing deficit in the US balance of payments. At the same time monetary policy was used to accommodate trades union-led wage push. In combination, loose fiscal and monetary policy led to rising inflation. At the same time acquiescence in growing rigidities on the 'supply side' of the economy produced a steadily worsening trade-off between unemployment and inflation, so that over successive cycles unemployment and inflation tended to rise together. In the 1970s the

Keynesian system of political economy disintegrated, in face of 'shocks', whose origins lay partly at least in fiscal and monetary mismanagement. The Bretton Woods system of fixed exchange rates collapsed in 1971 as a result of the flight from the once-mighty dollar; three years later came the quadrupling of energy costs. Attempts to bottle up excess demand by means of price and wage controls – a reversion to the wartime methods Keynes had rejected in 1940 – broke down in face of trades union opposition.

It was the Keynesian Revolution itself which was blamed for this débâcle – notably by Milton Friedman, a leading light of the anti-Keynesian Chicago school. Friedman resurrected the idea of a 'natural' equilibrium – he called it the 'natural' rate of unemployment – towards which economies gravitated, and which was determined by the institutional characteristics of the labour market. Unlike Keynes, but like the classical economists, he thought of this as full employment. He then went on to argue that policies of demand expansion could improve on this equilibrium only in the very short-run, and at the cost of rising inflation. The scene was set for the revival of the quantity theory of money, faith in markets, and the de-regulating 'supply-side' policies of the 1980s. At the end of that decade the collapse of communism completed the triumph of anti-Keynesian, free market liberalism.

Yet there was something incomplete in the new magic. The contractionary fiscal and monetary policies adopted in the early 1980s to eliminate inflation left in their wake heavy and persisting unemployment – just as Keynes would have predicted. The regime of floating exchange rates and increasingly liberated private capital flows which followed the collapse of the Bretton Woods system in 1971 led to short-run currency volatility and prolonged currency misalignments which inflicted heavy losses on many countries, though the currency wars of the 1930s did not repeat themselves. In response to these unexpected consequences of the 'counter-revolution', Keynesianism started to revive – in new theories to explain sticky prices and in the renewed attention policymakers paid to 'output gaps'. Today most governments practise stabilisation policies, even though their chosen instrument is interest rates. No governments aim to balance their budgets annually; and while many economists are anti-Keynesian, no economists are pre-Keynesian.

IV. LIFE AFTER DEATH

The successes and failures of Keynes's prescriptions for diseased economies were outside his widow's interests and beyond her understanding. She now lived entirely in the past. Angelica Garnett describes going to see her with

Duncan Grant early in January 1972, in her seventy-ninth year: 'The light
was on, and Lydia came out at once peering out of the door exactly like Mrs
Mole – tiny and round, with an extraordinary knitted helmet on her head of
a tawny colour. As soon as she saw Duncan making his way towards her she
was delighted, and warmly embraced him – a couple of lamp-lit old moles
hugging each other.' At eighty she could still lift each leg straight as high as
her head. But, a couple of years after this, she was knocked out by a severe
bout of viral pneumonia. Following this, she started to lose both her memory
and her mobility. She and Logan would sit for hours in Tilton's spacious
hall, facing the front door. Lydia sipped wine most of the day. Angelica
Garnett's daughter Henrietta visited her on 1 May 1975:

> Lydia and Logan were sitting opposite one another on sturdy armchairs,
> beneath an over-hanging electric element.... She was more shrivelled
> and more shrunken. Her head was wrapped, as always, in several
> scarves; her tiny feet were thrust into a pair of short orange rubber
> boots. She wore a dark-green nylon jacket, buttoned to her chin, which
> made her look even more Russian than ever.... We exchanged several
> kisses. Logan levered himself up from his chair: his leg had grown
> gammy.
>
> As usual, I was offered a glass of Sauternes, and, as usual, I accepted
> it. As usual, too, the conversation rattled swiftly to the subject of ballet.
> '... it was a good school, my dear. We were taught. They do not
> teach you now. Not like that. And the food was good: that is so
> important.'[9]

One of the last sightings of Lydia at Tilton was by Maynard's grand-
nephew Simon Keynes, who, coming down for the night with his parents,
met Lydia for the first time in September 1975. He found her and Logan
Thomson sitting, as always, in the hall, which was now 'very tidy'. She was
'dressed in the most extraordinary clothes – a greyish woollen suit of skirt
and jacket, with loose rings of wool dangling (intentionally) from every part
of its area; an odd woollen hat; a pair of boots, coming about 9 inches up
her legs'. She boasted that the outfit had cost only £20, and removed her
jacket to show off the lining. Logan feared there would be nothing under-
neath; mischievously aware of the general anticipation, Lydia tried to engage
Anne Keynes in discussion about the fullness of her (Lydia's) breasts. In
disconnected fragments, and with much repetition, Lydia talked about
Diaghilev and Nijinsky and Massine and about Bloomsbury, particularly
Leonard Woolf. She did not mention Maynard. She was very keen to give
them a meal and at 6.15 fetched a melon and tried to lead them into the
dining room. Simon Keynes was sad not to have seen Lydia when she was
completely *compos mentis*. 'But her unique character is quite plainly evident
– her sense of mischievousness ... her devotion to ballet and the arts ...
her good but not perfect grasp of English which produces highly original

expressions curiously supported by magnificent gestures with her hands and face.'[10]

Lydia was transferred to a nursing home in Seaford in 1976. That October, James Callaghan, Labour Prime Minister of Britain, made a speech to the Party Conference, announcing the end of Keynesian economics. 'The option of spending our way out of recession no longer exists.' It had worked in the past only by 'injecting bigger and bigger doses of inflation into the economy'. By 1984, Britain's Conservative Chancellor of the Exchequer Nigel Lawson was stating the new orthodoxy in his Mais Lecture: the job of macro-economic policy was to fight inflation; unemployment was to be handled by microeconomic policy – the reverse of what Keynesians had come to believe, though Keynes himself might, by then, have had some sympathy with the idea.

Lydia survived into the Thatcher era, dying on 8 June 1981, at the age of eighty-nine. Her ashes were scattered by Richard Keynes from the same spot on the Downs where his father Geoffrey Keynes had scattered Maynard's ashes thirty-five years earlier. But ideas do not disperse so quickly; and Keynes's will live so long as the world has need of them.

Bibliography and Sources

1. MANUSCRIPT COLLECTIONS CONSULTED

Manuscript collections are listed by location. Where cited papers have been consulted, the reference is to the collection alone; for example, references to the Keynes Papers, located at King's College, Cambridge, will be to KP. (See References, after the Bibliography, for the code.)

KING'S COLLEGE, CAMBRIDGE
Keynes Papers (KP), Lydia Lopokova Keynes (LLKP), Charleston Papers, Kahn Papers, Sheppard Papers, E. M. Forster Papers, Sebastian Sprott Papers, Nathaniel Wedd Papers, College Papers, Miscellaneous Papers.

The Keynes Papers contain both his 'personal papers' and his 'economic papers'. The latter were deposited at the Marshall Library until 1986, when they were transferred to King's College to join the 'personal papers'. A fraction of the 'economic papers' have been published in *The Collected Writings of John Maynard Keynes* (see next section). The personal papers are now all classified as PP. Any other reference to the Keynes Papers will be to the unpublished economic papers.

There will be no reference to source in citations from four important 'runs' of correspondence:
JMK and his parents
JMK and Lydia Keynes
JMK and Lytton Strachey
Lydia Keynes and JMK's parents.
They are all in KP at PP/45 and LLKP (LK5).

BANK OF ENGLAND
Thompson-MacCausland Papers, ADMIN 14
Norman's Diary, ADM 20
Governor's Papers, G1
Sir Charles Addis's Papers, A11M 16
Otto Niemeyer's Papers, OV9
The Macmillan Committee, File KID 1/2
Home Finance, EID 4

UNIVERSITY OF BIRMINGHAM
Austen Chamberlain Papers

BODLEIAN LIBRARY, OXFORD
Brand Papers; Hammond Papers; MSS of the Society for the Protection of Science and
Learning; Asquith Papers; Gilbert Murray Papers

BRITISH LIBRARY, LONDON
Strachey Papers, Add. MSS 60655–734; Lytton Strachey and Duncan Grant correspon-
dence 1902–31, Add. MSS 57932–3; Lytton Strachey and James Strachey 1905–31,
Add. MSS 60706–12; JMK and Duncan Grant 1908–46, Add. MSS 57930–1; JMK and
Macmillan & Co., Add. MSS 55201–4; JMK's letters to O. T. Falk, Add. MSS 57923;
Christabel Maclaren Papers (Letters from Samuel Courtauld), Add. MSS 52432–5; C.
Y. Scott Papers, Add. MSS 50906–9
India Office Papers

CAMBRIDGE UNIVERSITY LIBRARY
Add. 7827f. JNK's Diary 1864–1917.
Various items of correspondence relating to JNK, FAK, Geoffrey Keynes, Margaret
Hill, Alfred Marshall. Where I have quoted from these, the catalogue number is given
in the individual reference
Kennet Papers

CHURCHILL COLLEGE, CAMBRIDGE
Reginald McKenna Papers; Cecil Spring-Rice Papers; Ralph Hawtrey Papers

COLUMBIA UNIVERSITY, NEW YORK
Herbert H. Lehman Papers; there are letters from JMK to J. M. Clark, M. A. Copeland,
Albert H. Hart, Lewis L. Lorwin, Marie M. Meloney, Wesley C. Mitchell, Allan Nevins,
E. R. A. Seligman and E. A. Vanderlip

ETON COLLEGE
Records of the College Debating Society (College 'Pop')

HARVARD UNIVERSITY
Thomas Lamont Papers; J. A. Schumpeter Papers

HOUSE OF LORDS
Lloyd George Papers; Bonar Law Papers; J. C. C. Davidson Papers

HUMANITIES RESEARCH CENTER, AUSTIN, TEXAS
Letters from JMK and Clive Bell to Barbara Bagenal, J. L. Garvin, Mary Hutchinson,
Mary MacCarthy, Dora Carrington, Ottoline Morrell

UNIVERSITY OF ILLINOIS
H. G. Wells Papers

UNIVERSITY OF KENTUCKY
Vinson Papers

LIBRARY OF CONGRESS
Felix Frankfurter Papers; Emmanuel Goldenweiser Papers; Oscar Crosby Papers

LONDON SCHOOL OF ECONOMICS, BRITISH LIBRARY OF POLITICAL AND
ECONOMIC SCIENCE
Edwin Cannan Papers; Dalton Papers; Durbin Papers; Meade Papers

MARSHALL LIBRARY
J. M. Keynes Papers; Marshall Papers

NEW YORK PUBLIC LIBRARY, BERG COLLECTION
Correspondence between JMK and Lytton Strachey for 1906, between JMK and
Leonard Woolf, and Lytton Strachey and Leonard Woolf

NUFFIELD COLLEGE, OXFORD
Henry Clay Papers; Hubert Henderson Papers; Sir Stafford Cripps Papers

PRINCETON UNIVERSITY
Harry Dexter White Papers; Bernard Baruch Papers; John Dulles Papers

PUBLIC RECORD OFFICE, KEW
Treasury Papers; Foreign Office Papers; Cabinet Papers. Papers from JMK's private
office are in T247; others dealing with JMK in T160, T172 and T236 classes; Sir Otto
Niemeyer Papers T176; Sir Richard Hopkins Papers T175; Sir Frederick Phillips Papers
T177

FRANKLIN D. ROOSEVELT LIBRARY, HYDE PARK, NEW YORK
Morgenthau Diaries; Franklin D. Roosevelt Papers

ROYAL OPERA HOUSE, COVENT GARDEN
Archive

SCOTTISH RECORD OFFICE, EDINBURGH
Lothian Papers

SUSSEX UNIVERSITY LIBRARY
Leonard Woolf Papers; Monk's House Papers

TATE GALLERY, LONDON
Vanessa Bell's letters to Roger Fry 1920–32

TRINITY COLLEGE, CAMBRIDGE
Edwin Montagu Papers; F. Pethick-Lawrence Papers; R. C. Trevelyan Papers

WISCONSIN UNIVERSITY LIBRARY
J. R. Commons Papers

STIRLING MEMORIAL LIBRARY, YALE UNIVERSITY
Irvin Fisher Papers; R. C. Leffingwell Papers; Walter Lippmann Papers; Paul M.
Warburg Papers; Edward House Papers; the *Yale Review* in the Beinecke Rare Book
and Manuscript Library

BORTHWICK INSTITUTE OF HISTORICAL RESEARCH, UNIVERSITY OF YORK
Halifax Diary

PRIVATE SOURCES

Peter Bareau: Paul Bareau Papers

Edward Birnberg: Naomi Bentwich's 'Lucifer by Starlight: A Human Document
    Depicting a Spiritual Adventure'

Mark Bonham Carter: The Diary of Margot Asquith (in the care of the Warden of
    Nuffield College, Oxford)

Mrs Roland Falk: O. T. Falk Papers

Michael Finlay: letters from JMK to R. H. Dundas

Lady Ford: R. H. Brand's letters to his wife

Henrietta Garnett: JMK letters to Duncan Grant; Duncan Grant's Diary 1917–18;
    material relating to Grant's application for exemption from war service on
    grounds of conscientious objection. Grant's letters to Vanessa Bell. Cited HC

Richard Garnett: The Diary of David Garnett 1915, 1917–18

Lady Harmer: the Diary of Sir Frederic Harmer 1945

Mrs Clarissa Heald: Harold Bowen's Diary

Polly Hill: correspondence between JNK and his parents, FAK and her parents, FAK
    and JNK. Cited PH

Richard and Anne Keynes: letters

Simon Keynes: files relating to Keynes–Brown family history, including notes of
    JMK's own research into the family tree, correspondence arising from it, and
    Simon Keynes's schoolboy essay 'The Dissemination of a Norman Family', and a
    note of his visit to Tilton in 1975. Cited SK

Stephen Keynes: JMK's Eton Diaries 1900–2. The 1899 volume is at King's College

Donald MacDougall: Donald MacDougall's wartime diary

Peter Plesch: 'Few Excuses, No Regrets', concerning Janos Plesch

Richard Shone: correspondence between JMK and Duncan Grant 1907–46. Cited RS

Tuesday Club: Records of Meetings and Recollections

2. PUBLISHED PRIMARY SOURCES

The main published source is *The Collected Writings of John Maynard Keynes*, 30
volumes, including Bibliography and Index, published by Macmillan/Cambridge
University Press for the Royal Economic Society, 1971–89. Volumes XV to XVIII were
edited by Elizabeth Johnson, the remainder by Donald Moggridge. They include
practically all Keynes's published writings, including journalism, as well as a generous
proportion of his unpublished economic correspondence, notes, memoranda, lectures
and speeches. They do not include his personal papers, except for a few excerpts
from his letters to his parents and his wife. All references to Keynes's published
writings are to this edition, though the text is not always identical to the originals –

for example, capital letters are used more sparingly. References will also be given to the published versions of the manuscript materials, rather than to the originals. Where reference is given to the Keynes Papers themselves, this is to material which has not been published.

The other main published primary sources are:

A. O. Bell (ed.), *The Diary of Virginia Woolf,* Hogarth Press, 1977–84

J. Morton Blum (ed.), *From the Morgenthau Diaries,* i: *Years of Crisis 1928–1938,* ii: *Years of Urgency 1938–1941,* iii: *Years of Achievement 1941–1945,* Boston: Houghton Mifflin, 1959, 1965, 1967

Roger Bullen and M. E. Pelly (eds), *Documents on British Policy Overseas,* series 1, iii, *Britain and America: Negotiation of the United States Loan 3 August–7 December 1945,* HMSO, 1986

Lord D'Abernon, *An Ambassador of Peace: Pages from the Diary of Viscount D'Abernon,* 3 vols, Hodder and Stoughton, 1929

Foreign Relations of the United States, 1941, iii; *1945,* vi, State Department

Max Freedman (ed.), *Roosevelt and Frankfurter: Their Correspondence 1928–1945,* Bodley Head, 1968

John Harvey (ed.), *The Diplomatic Diaries of Oliver Harvey, 1937–1940,* i; *1941–45,* ii; Collins, 1970, 1978

Polly Hill and Richard Keynes (eds), *Lydia and Maynard: Letters between Lydia Lopokova and John Maynard Keynes,* André Deutsch, 1989

Susan Howson and Donald Moggridge (eds), *The Wartime Diaries of Lionel Robbins and James Meade, 1943–45,* Macmillan, 1990

—— (eds), *The Collected Papers of James Meade, The Cabinet Office Diary 1944–6,* iv, Unwin Hyman, 1990

Joseph P. Lash, *From the Diaries of Felix Frankfurter,* New York: W. W. Norton, 1975

Norman MacKenzie (ed.), The Letters of Sidney and Beatrice Webb, 2 vols, Cambridge University Press/LSE, 1978

—— and Jeanne MacKenzie (eds), *The Diary of Beatrice Webb,* 4 vols, Virago/LSE, 1982–5

Perry Meisel and Walter Kendrick (eds), *Bloomsbury/Freud: The Letters of James and Alix Strachey 1924–5,* Chatto and Windus, 1986

Keith Middlemas (ed.), *Thomas Jones, Whitehall Diary 1916–30,* 2 vols, Oxford University Press, 1969

Nigel Nicolson (ed.), *Harold Nicolson: Diaries and Letters, 1930–9,* i; *1939–45,* iii, Collins, 1966, 1967

—— (ed.), *The Letters of Virginia Woolf, 1936–41,* Chatto and Windus, 1980

—— (ed.), assisted by Joanna Trautmann, *The Letters of Virginia Woolf,* 6 vols, Hogarth Press, 1975–80

Ben Pimlott (ed.), *The Second World War Diary of Hugh Dalton 1940–45,* Jonathan Cape/LSE, 1986

——, *The Political Diary of Hugh Dalton, 1918–20, 1945–60,* Jonathan Cape, 1986

Elliott Roosevelt (ed.), *FDR, His Personal Letters 1928–45,* 2 vols, Harrap, 1949

Royal Commission on the Depression of Trade and Industry: *Third Report,* Appendix C, 1888

T. K. Rymes (ed.), *Keynes's Lectures 1932–5: Notes of a Representative Student,* Macmillan, 1989

David Scrase and Peter Croft, *Maynard Keynes, Collector of Pictures, Books and Manuscripts*, Fitzwilliam Catalogue, 1983

Frederic Spotts (ed.), *The Letters of Leonard Woolf*, Weidenfeld and Nicolson, 1989

Denys Sutton (ed.), *Letters of Roger Fry*, 2 vols, Chatto and Windus, 1972

G. H. Wright (ed.), with intro., assisted by B. F. McGuinness, *Ludwig Wittgenstein: Letters to Russell, Keynes and Moore*, Basil Blackwell, 1974

The First Interim Report of the Committee on Currency and Foreign Exchanges after the War (Cunliffe Committee), Cmd 9182, 1918

Report of the Committee on the Currency and Bank of England Note Issues (Chamberlain–Bradbury Committee), Cmd 2993, 1924–5

Memoranda on Certain Proposals Relating to Unemployment, Cmd 3331, May 1929

Report on the Committee on Finance and Industry (Macmillan Committee), Cmd 28897, 1932. *Minutes of Evidence*, 2 vols, Treasury, 1931

White Paper on *Employment Policy*, Cmd 6527, HMSO, May 1944

3. SECONDARY SOURCES

BOOKS AND CHAPTERS IN BOOKS

Dean Acheson, *Present at the Creation: My Years in the State Department*, Hamish Hamilton, 1970

Peter Ackroyd, *T. S. Eliot*, Hamish Hamilton, 1984

Paul Addison, *The Road to 1945: British Politics and the Second World War*, Jonathan Cape, 1975

Derek H. Aldcroft, *From Versailles to Wall Street 1919–1929*, Allen Lane, 1977

——, *The British Economy between the Wars*, Philip Allan, 1983

Edward J. Amadeo, *Keynes's Principle of Effective Demand*, Edward Elgar, 1989

Christopher Andrew and Oleg Gordievsky, *KGB: The Inside Story of its Foreign Operations from Lenin to Gorbachev*, Hodder & Stoughton, 1990

Noel Annan, *Leslie Stephen: His Thought and Character in Relation to his Time*, MacGibbon & Kee, 1951

——, *Our Age: Portrait of a Generation*, Weidenfeld & Nicolson, 1990

——, *The Dons: Mentors, Eccentrics and Geniuses*, HarperCollins, 1999

——, 'The Intellectual Aristocracy' in J. H. Plumb (ed.), *Studies in Social History – a Tribute to G. M. Trevelyan*, Longmans, 1955

Ian Anstruther, *Oscar Browning: A Biography*, John Murray, 1983

Pier Francesco Asso, *The Economist behind the Model: The Keynesian Revolution in Historical Perspective*, Quaderno di Ricerche, No. 18, 1990

A. J. Ayer, *Part of My Life*, Collins, 1987

Jürgen Backhaus, 'Die "Allgemeine Theorie": Reaktionen deutscher Volkewirte', in Harald Hazemann and Otto Steiger (eds), *Keynes' General Theory nach funfzig Jahren*, Berlin: Duncker & Humblot, 1988

Thomas Balogh, *Unequal Partners*, ii, Blackwell, 1963

John Barnes and David Nicolson (eds), *The Empire at Bay: The Leo Amery Diaries 1929–1945*, Hutchinson, 1988

Correlli Barnett, *The Audit of War: The Illusion & Reality of Britain as a Great Nation*, Macmillan, 1986
——, *The Lost Victory: British Dreams, British Realities 1945–1950*, Macmillan, 1995
Geoffrey Barraclough, *An Introduction to Contemporay History*, Penguin Books, 1967
Norman Barry, *Hayek's Social and Economic Philosophy*, Macmillan, 1979
Bernard Baruch, *The Public Years*, Odhams, 1961
——, *The Making of the Reparation and Economic Sections of the Treaty*, New York: Harper, 1920
Basileon, A Magazine of King's College, Cambridge, 1900–14 Scolar Press, 1974
Bradley W. Bateman and John B. Davis (eds), *Keynes and Philosophy: Essays on the Origin of Keynes's Thought*, Edward Elgar, 1991
Charles A. Beard, *President Roosevelt and the Coming of the War 1941*, New Haven: Yale University Press, 1948
C. W. Beaumont, *Diaghilev Ballet in London: A Personal Record*, Putnam, 1940
Lord Beaverbrook, *Politicians and the War, 1914–1916*, Thornton Butterworth, 1928
——, *Men and Power, 1917–18*, Hutchinson, 1956
Sybille Bedford, *Aldous Huxley*, 2 vols, Chatto & Windus/Collins, 1973–4
Clive Bell, *Civilisation*, Chatto & Windus, 1928
——, *Old Friends*, Cassell, 1956 (1988 edn)
——, *Poems*, Hogarth Press, 1921
Quentin Bell, *Bloomsbury*, Weidenfeld & Nicolson, 1968
——, *Virginia Woolf, A Biography: vol. i: Virginia Stephen, 1882–1912*, 1972; *vol. ii: Mrs Woolf, 1912–1941*, Hogarth Press, 1972
——, *Elders and Betters*, John Murray, 1995
Hugh Hale Bellot, *University College, London, 1826–1926* London University Press, 1929
D. M. Bensusan-Butt, *On Economic Knowledge: A Sceptical Miscellany*, Australian National University, 1980
Michael Bentley, *The Liberal Mind 1914–1929*, Cambridge University Press, 1977
Michael Bentley and John Stevenson (eds), *High and Low Politics in Modern Britain*, Clarendon Press, 1983
Isaiah Berlin, *Personal Impressions*, Hogarth Press, 1980
William H. Beveridge, *Full Employment in a Free Society*, Allen & Unwin, 1944
Leonard Bickel, *Rise up to Life: A Biography of Howard Walter Florey*, Angus & Robertson, 1972
Robert John Bigg, *Cambridge and the Monetary Theory of Production*, Macmillan, 1990
The Earl of Birkenhead, *The Prof in Two Worlds*, Collins, 1961
Robert Blake, *The Unknown Prime Minister: The Life and Times of Andrew Bonar Law, 1858–1923*, Methuen, 1955
Mark Blaug, *Great Economists before Keynes*, Wheatsheaf, 1986
——, *Great Economists since Keynes*, Wheatsheaf, 1985
——, *John Maynard Keynes: Life, Ideas, Legacy*, Macmillan, 1990
Wilfrid Blunt, *John Christie of Glyndebourne*, Geoffrey Bles, 1968
Andrew Booth and Melvyn Pack, *Employment, Capital and Economic Policy: Great Britain 1919–1939*, Basil Blackwell, 1985
George Borrow, *Wild Wales*, Fontana/Collins, n.d.
John Bowle, *Viscount Samuel*, Gollancz, 1957
Andrew Boyle, *The Climate of Treason*, Hutchinson, rev. edn, 1980

——, *Montagu Norman*, Cassell, 1967

Lord Bridges, *The Treasury*, Allen & Unwin, 1964

S. Broadberry, *The British Economy between the Wars: A Macroeconomic Survey*, Basil Blackwell, 1986

—— and Peter Howlett, 'The United Kingdom: "Victory at all Costs"', in Mark Harrison (ed.), *The Economics of World War II: Six Great Powers in International Comparison*, Cambridge University Press, 1998

Frances M. Brookfield, *The Cambridge 'Apostles'*, Pitman, 1906

Neville Brown, *Dissenting Forbears: The Maternal Ancestors of J. M. Keynes*, Phillimore, 1988

Oscar Browning, *Memories of Sixty Years at Eton, Cambridge and Elsewhere*, John Lane, 1910

J. M. Buchanan, John Burton and R. E. Wagner, *The Economic Consequences of Mr. Keynes*, Institute of Economic Affairs, 1978

Richard Buckle, *Diaghilev*, Weidenfeld & Nicolson, 1978

Alan Bullock, *The Life and Times of Ernest Bevin*, 2 vols, Heinemann, 1960, 1967

Robert E. Bunselmeyer, *The Cost of the War 1914–1919: British Economic War Aims and the Origins of Reparations*, Hamden, Conn.: Archon Books, 1975

Kathleen Burk, 'The House of Morgan in Financial Diplomacy 1920–1930', in B. J. McKercher (ed.), *The Struggle for Supremacy: Anglo-American Relations in the 1920s*, Macmillan, 1988

Philip M. Burnett, *Reparations at the Paris Peace Conference from the Standpoint of the American Delegation*, 2 vols, New York: Columbia University Press, 1940

J. MacGregor Burns, *Roosevelt: The Soldier of Freedom 1940–1945*, Weidenfeld & Nicolson, 1971

John Burton (ed.), *Keynes's General Theory: Fifty Years On*, Institute of Economic Affairs, 1986

Alec Cairncross, *The Price of War: British Policy on German Reparations 1941–1949*, Basil Blackwell, 1986

——, *The Years of Recovery: British Economic Policy 1945–51*, Methuen, 1985

—— and Nina Watts, *The Economic Section 1939–1961: A Study in Economic Advising*, Routledge, 1989

John Campbell, *Lloyd George: The Goat in the Wilderness 1922–1931*, Jonathan Cape, 1977

Anna M. Carabelli, *On Keynes's Method*, Macmillan, 1988

David Carlton, *Anthony Eden*, Allen Lane, 1981

W. Carr, 'John Maynard Keynes and the Treaty of Versailles', in A. P. Thirlwall (ed.), *Keynes as a Policy Adviser*, Macmillan, 1982

Miranda Carter, *Anthony Blunt: His Lives*, Macmillan, 2001

Hugh and Mirabel Cecil, *Clever Hearts: Desmond and Molly MacCarthy: A Biography*, Victor Gollancz, 1990

James Chace, *Acheson: The Secretary of State who Created the American World*, Simon & Schuster, 1998

A. Chandavarkar, *Keynes and India: A Study in Economics and Biography*, Macmillan, 1989

John Charmley, *Churchill: The End of Glory: A Political Biography*, New York: Harcourt Brace, 1993

D. N. Chester (ed.), *Lessons of the British War Economy*, Cambridge University Press, 1951

Rupert Christiansen (ed.), *Cambridge Arts Theatre*, Granta Editions, 1998

Winston S. Churchill, *The Second World War*, 6 vols, Cassell, 1948–54

Kenneth Clark, *The Other Half: A Self-Portrait*, John Murray, 1977

Ronald W. Clark, *The Life of Bertrand Russell*, Jonathan Cape/Weidenfeld & Nicolson, 1975

Peter Clarke: *Liberals and Social Democrats*, Cambridge University Press, 1978

———, *The Keynesian Revolution in the Making 1924–1936*, Clarendon Press, 1988

———, 'The Politics of Keynesian Economics, 1924–1931', in Michael Bentley and John Stevenson (eds), *High and Low Politics in Modern Britain*, 1983, Clarendon Press

Sir Richard Clarke, *Anglo-American Economic Collaboration in War and Peace 1942–49*, ed. Alec Cairncross, Clarendon Press, 1982

S. V. O. Clarke, *Central Bank Cooperation 1924–1931*, Cambridge University Press, 1971

Henry Clay (ed.), *The Interwar Years and Other Papers: A Selection from the Writings of Hubert Douglas Henderson*, Oxford University Press, 1955

John Coates, *The claims of commonsense: Moore, Wittgenstein, Keynes and the social sciences*, Cambridge University Press, 1996

Alan Coddington, *Keynesian Economics: The Search for First Principles*, Allen & Unwin, 1983; reviewed by John Fender, *EJ*, December 1983, 914–16

Douglas Cooper, *The Courtauld Collection*, with a memoir of Samuel Courtauld by Anthony Blunt, Athlone Press, 1954

B. A. Corry, *Money, Saving and Investment in English Economics 1800–1850*, Macmillan, 1962

Maurice Cowling, *The Impact of Labour 1920–1924*, Cambridge University Press, 1971

Derek Crabtree and A. P. Thirlwall (eds), *Keynes and the Bloomsbury Group*, Macmillan, 1980

Maurice Cranston, 'Keynes: His Political Ideas and Their Influence', in A. P. Thirlwall (ed.), *Keynes and Laissez-Faire*, Macmillan, 1978

Bernard Crick, *George Orwell, A Life*, Penguin, 1980

C. A. R. Crosland, *The Future of Socialism*, Jonathan Cape, 1956

N. J. Crowson (ed.), *Fleet Street, Press Barons and Politics: The Journals of Collin Brooks 1932–1940*, Royal Historical Society, 1998

Robert Dallek, *Franklin D. Roosevelt and American Foreign Policy*, Oxford University Press, 1979

Hugh Dalton: *Call Back Yesterday*, Frederick Muller, 1953

———, *High Tide and After: Memoirs 1945–60*, Frederick Muller, 1962

Nicholas Davenport, *Memoirs of a City Radical*, Weidenfeld & Nicolson, 1974

———, *The Split Society*, Gollancz, 1964

Paul Davidson, *Financial Markets, Money and the Real World*, Edward Elgar, 2002

Joseph S. Davis, *The World between the Wars 1919–39*, Johns Hopkins University Press, 1975

Marcello de Cecco, *Money and Empire*, Blackwell, 1974

Richard Deacon, *The Cambridge Apostles*, Robert Royce, 1985

Phyllis Deane, *The Life and Times of J. Neville Keynes: A Beacon in the Tempest*, Edward Elgar, 2001

Jan Dejnozka, *Bertrand Russell on Modality and Logical Relevance*, Ashgate, 1999, see ch. 10

R. W. Dimand, *The Origins of the Keynesian Revolution*, Edward Elgar, 1988

Alan P. Dobson, *US Wartime Aid to Britain*, Croom Helm, 1986

Frances Donaldson, *The Royal Opera House in the Twentieth Century*, Weidenfeld & Nicolson, 1988

Armand van Dormael, *Bretton Woods: Birth of a Monetary System*, Macmillan, 1978

Gilles Dostaler and Bernard Maris, 'Dr Freud and Mr Keynes on money and capitalism', in John Swithin (ed.), *What is Money?*, Routledge, 2000

Ian M. Drummond, *British Economic Policy and the Empire 1919–1939*, Allen & Unwin, 1972

——, *The Floating Pound and the Sterling Area 1931–1939*, Cambridge University Press, 1981

Bruce Duffy, *The World as I Found it*, Secker & Warburg, 1987

Elizabeth Durbin, *New Jerusalems: The Labour Party and the Economics of Democratic Socialism*, Routledge & Kegan Paul, 1985

David Dutton, *Simon: A Political Biography of John Simon*, Aurum Press, 1992

John Eatwell and Murray Milgate (eds), *Keynes's Economics and the Theory of Value and Distribution*, Duckworth, 1983

—— and Peter Newman (eds), *The New Palgrave: A Dictionary of Economics*, 4 vols, Macmillan, 1987

Leon Edel, *Bloomsbury: A House of Lions*, Hogarth Press, 1979

Barry Eichengreen, *Golden Fetters: The Gold Standard and the Great Depression 1919–1939*, Oxford University Press, 1992

—— (ed.), *The Gold Standard in Theory and Practice*, Methuen, 1985

——, 'The Capital Levy in Theory and Practice', in Rudiger Dornbusch and Mario Draghi (eds), *Public Debt Management: Theory and History*, Cambridge University Press, 1990

Paul Einzig, *Hitler's New Order in Europe*, Macmillan, 1941

Howard Elcock: *Portrait of a Decision, The Council of Four and the Treaty of Versailles*, Methuen, 1972

Eprime Eshag, *From Marshall to Keynes: An Essay on the Monetary Theory of the Cambridge School*, Basil Blackwell, 1963

Keith Feiling, *The Life of Neville Chamberlain*, Macmillan, 1946

C. H. Feinstein, *National Income, Expenditure and Output of the United Kingdom 1865–1965*, Cambridge University Press, 1972

Herbert Feis, *1933: Characters in Crisis*, Boston/Toronto: Little, Brown, 1966

George R. Feiwel (ed.), *Joan Robinson and Modern Economic Theory*, i, Macmillan, 1989

David Felix, *Keynes: A Critical Life*, Westport, Connecticut: Greenwood Press, 1999

John Fforde, *The Bank of England and Public Policy 1941–1958*, Cambridge University Press, 1992

Carole Fink, *The Genoa Conference: European Diplomacy, 1921–1922*, Chapel Hill: University of North Carolina Press, 1984

Irving Fisher, assisted by Harry G. Brown, *The Purchasing Power of Money: Its Determination and Relation to Credit, Interest and Crises*, New York: Macmillan, 1911

Penelope Fitzgerald, *The Knox Brothers*, Macmillan, 1977

Athol Fitzgibbons, *Keynes's Vision: A New Political Economy*, Clarendon Press, 1988

Gordon Fletcher, *Understanding Dennis Robertson: The Man and His Work*, Edward Elgar, 2000

P. Sargant Florence and J. R. L. Anderson (eds), *C. K. Ogden: A Collective Memoir*, Elek: Pemberton, 1977

Inga Floto, *Colonel House in Paris: A Study of American Policy at the Paris Peace Conference, 1919*, Aarhus, 1973

Margot Fonteyn, *Autobiography*, W. H. Allen, 1975

Michael Foot, *Aneurin Bevan 1897–1945*, MacGibbon & Kee, 1962

E. M. Forster, *Goldsworthy Lowes Dickinson*, Edward Arnold, 1934

James Fox, *Five Sisters: The Langhornes of Virginia*, Simon & Schuster, 2000

H. E. Fraser, *Great Britain and the Gold Standard*, Macmillan, 1933

Sir James Frazer, *The Golden Bough*, Macmillan, abr. edn, 1924

M. Freeden, *Liberalism Divided*, Clarendon Press, 1986

M. Friedman and A. J. Schwartz, *The Great Contraction 1929–1933*, Princeton University Press, 1965

David Gadd, *The Loving Friends, A Portrait of Bloomsbury*, New York: Harcourt Brace Jovanovich, 1974

J. K. Galbraith, *A Contemporary Guide to Economics, Peace, and Laughter*, Boston: Houghton Mifflin, 1971

——, *A Life in Our Times*, André Deutsch, 1981

——, *Money: Whence It Came, Where It Went*, André Deutsch, 1975

——, *The Great Crash 1929*, André Deutsch, 3rd edn, 1973

R. N. Gardner, *Sterling–Dollar Diplomacy*, Oxford University Press, 1969 edn

Angelica Garnett, *Deceived with Kindness: A Bloomsbury Childhood*, Chatto & Windus, 1984

David Garnett, *Great Friends*, Macmillan, 1979

——, *The Golden Echo*, Chatto & Windus, 1954

——, *The Flowers of the Forest*, Chatto & Windus, 1955

John A. Garraty, *The Great Depression*, New York: Harcourt Brace Jovanovich, 1986

J. C. Gilbert, *Keynes's Impact on Monetary Economics*, Butterworth Scientific, 1982

Mary Glasgow, *The Nineteen Hundreds: A Diary in Retrospect*, Oxford University Press, 1986

Sean Glynn and Alan Booth (eds), *The Road to Full Employment*, Allen & Unwin, 1987

Robert Graves and Alan Hodge, *The Long Weekend: A Social History of Great Britain 1918–1939*, Faber & Faber, 1950

Martin Green, *Children of the Sun: A Narration of 'Decadence' in England after 1918*, Constable, 1977

P. J. Grigg, *Prejudice and Judgment*, Jonathan Cape, 1948

Phyllis Grosskurth, *John Addington Symonds, A Biography*, Longmans, 1964

Claude Guillebaud, *The Economic Recovery of Germany 1933–8*, Macmillan, 1938

G. Haberler, *Prosperity and Depression*, New York: Lake Success, 1946

Ian Hacking, *The Emergence of Probability*, Cambridge University Press, 1978

Frank Hahn, *Money and Inflation*, Basil Blackwell, 1982

Peter A. Hall (ed.), *The Political Power of Economic Ideas: Keynesianism across Nations*, Princeton University Press, 1989

O. F. Hamouda (ed.), *Controversies in Political Economy: Selected Essays of G. H. Harcourt*, Wheatsheaf, 1986

W. K. Hancock and M. M. Gowing, *British War Economy*, HMSO, 1949

W. K. Hancock, *Smuts: The Sanguine Years, 1870–1919*, Cambridge University Press, 1962

W. K. Hancock and Jean van der Poel, *Selections from the Smuts Papers*, vol. iv, Cambridge University Press, 1966

Steve H. Hanke and Kurt Schuler, 'Keynes's Russian Currency Board' in Steve H.

Hanke and Alan Walters (eds) *Capital Markets and Development*, San Francisco, Institute for Contemporary Studies Press, 1991

Lord Hankey, *The Supreme Control at the Paris Peace Conference, 1919*, Allen & Unwin, 1963

Alvin H. Hansen, *A Guide to Keynes*, McGraw-Hill, 1953

G. H. Harcourt (ed.), *Keynes and His Contemporaries*, Macmillan, 1985

——, *The Microeconomic Foundations of Macroeconomics*, Macmillan, 1977

Gerd Hardach, *The First World War 1914–1918 vol. 2: History of the World Economy in the Twentieth Century*, Allen Lane, 1977

G. H. Hardy, *A Mathematician's Apology*, Cambridge University Press, 1940

José Harris, *William Beveridge: A Biography*, Clarendon Press, 1977

Seymour Harris, *John Maynard Keynes*, New York: Scribners, 1955

R. F. Harrod, *The Life of John Maynard Keynes*, Macmillan, 1951

——, *The Prof: A Personal Memoir of Lord Cherwell*, Macmillan, 1959

R. M. Hartwell, 'Can We Escape?', in Ralph Harris and Arthur Seldon (eds), *The Coming Confrontation*, Institute of Economic Affairs, 1978

Arnold Haskell, *Balletomania: The Story of an Obsession*, Victor Gollancz, 1934

R. G. Hawtrey, *The Art of Central Banking*, Longmans, 1932

——, *Currency and Credit*, Longmans, 1919; reviewed by JMK, *E J*, September 1920, CW, xi, 411–14

F. A. Hayek, *The Road to Serfdom*, Routledge, 1944 (paperback edn 1962)

——, *Money, Capital, and Fluctuations*, Routledge, 1984

——, *New Studies in Philosophy, Politics, Economics and the History of Ideas*, Routledge, 1978

——, *Prices and Production*, Routledge, 1931

——, *A Tiger by the Tail*, Institute of Economic Affairs, 2nd edn, 1978

John Earl Haynes and Harvey Klehr, *Venona: Decoding Soviet Espionage in America*, New York: Yale University Press, 1999

Cameron Hazlehurst, *Politicians at War, July 1914 to May 1915*, Jonathan Cape, 1971

Burton J. Hendrick, *The Life and Letters of Walter Hines Page*, Heinemann, 1928

Charles H. Hession, *John Maynard Keynes: A Personal Biography of the Man who Revolutionized Capitalism and the Way We Live*, New York: Macmillan, 1984

J. R. Hicks, *Critical Essays in Monetary Theory*, Clarendon Press, 1979 edn

——, *The Crisis in Keynesian Economics*, Blackwell, 1974

—— (ed), *Sir Dennis Robertson: Essays in Money and Interest*, London: Fontana Library, 1966

Gertrude Himmelfarb, *Victorian Minds: A Study of Intellectuals in Crisis and of Ideologies in Transition*, New York: Harper, 1970

Michael J. Hogan, *Informal Entente: The Private Structure of Cooperation in Anglo-American Economic Diplomacy 1918–1928*, University of Missouri Press, 1977

Christopher Hollis, *Eton*, Hollis & Carter, 1960

Martin Hollis, *The Cunning of Reason*, Cambridge University Press, 1987

Michael Holroyd, *Bernard Shaw*, 4 vols, Chatto & Windus, 1988–92

——, *Lytton Strachey*, 2 vols, Heinemann, 1967–8; Penguin edn repr. with revs, 1979

Michaela Honicke, '"Prevent World War III": An Historiographical Appraisal of Morgenthau's Programme for Germany', in Robert A. Garson and Stuart S. Kidd (eds), *The Roosevelt Years: New Perspectives on American History 1933–1945*, Edinburgh University Press, 1999

Alistair Horne, *Macmillan 1894–1956*, Macmillan, 1988

Calvin Hoover, *Memoirs of Capitalism, Communism, and Nazism*, Duke University Press, 1965

J. Keith Horsefield, *The International Monetary Fund 1945–1965*, i and ii, Washington DC: IMF, 1969

T. E. B. Howarth, *Cambridge between the Wars*, Collins, 1978

Susan Howson, *British Monetary Policy 1945–51*, Clarendon Press, 1993

——, 'Cheap Money and Debt Management in Britain 1932–1952,' in P. L. Cottrell and D. E. Moggridge (eds), *Money and Power: Essays in Honour of L. S. Pressnell*, Macmillan, 1988, 227–89

—— and Donald Winch, *The Economic Advisory Council 1930–1939*, Cambridge University Press, 1977

David Hubback, *No Ordinary Press Baron: A Life of Walter Layton*, Weidenfeld & Nicolson, 1985

Cordell Hull, *The Memoirs of Cordell Hull*, New York: Macmillan, 1948

T. W. Hutchison: *A Review of Economic Doctrines, 1870–1929*, Oxford University Press, 1953

——, *Keynes and the 'Keynesians'*, with commentaries by Lord Kahn and Sir Austin Robinson, Institute of Economic Affairs, 1977

——, *On Revolutions and Progress in Economic Knowledge*, Cambridge University Press, 1978

——, *The Politics and Philosophy of Economics*, Basil Blackwell, 1981

Michael Ignatieff, *Isaiah Berlin, A Life*, Chatto and Windus, 1998

Geoffrey Ingham, *Capitalism Divided? The City and Industry in British Social Development*, Macmillan, 1984

Gilbert E. Jackson and Philip Vos (eds), *The Cambridge Union Society Debates, April 1910–March 1911*, Dent, 1911

Allan Janik and Stephen Toulmin: *Wittgenstein's Vienna*, Weidenfeld & Nicolson, 1973

Erin E. Jacobsson, *A Life for Sound Money*, Clarendon Press, 1979

Harold James, *International Monetary Cooperation since Bretton Woods*, IMF, Oxford University Press, 1996

Harold James, 'Post-War German Currency Plans', in Christoph Buchheim, Michael Hutter, Harold James (eds), *Zerrissene Zwisschenkriegszeit: Wirtschafthistorische Beiträge*, Knut Borchardt, 1994

——, *The German Slump: Politics and Economics 1924–1936*, Clarendon Press, 1986

Douglas Jay, *Change and Fortune: A Political Record*, Hutchinson, 1980

Roy Jenkins, *Asquith*, Collier, 1964

——, *Baldwin*, Collier, 1987

Elizabeth S. Johnson and Harry G. Johnson, *The Shadow of Keynes: Understanding Keynes, Cambridge, and Keynesian Economics*, Basil Blackwell, 1978

E. L. Jones, *The European Miracle: Environments, Economics and Geopolitics in the History of Europe and Asia*, Cambridge University Press, 1981

J. H. Jones, *Josiah Stamp, Public Servant: The Life of the First Baron Stamp of Shortlands*, Pitman, 1964

L. E. Jones: *A Victorian Boyhood*, Macmillan, 1955

Denis Judd, *Lord Reading*, Weidenfeld & Nicolson, 1982

Richard Kahn, *The Economics of the Short Period*, Macmillan, 1989

——, *The Making of Keynes' General Theory*, Cambridge University Press, 1984; reviewed by A. P. Thirlwall, *TLS*, 20 July 1984

N. Kaldor, 'Keynes as an Economic Adviser', in A. P. Thirlwall (ed.), *Keynes as a Policy Adviser*, Macmillan, 1980

Arnold P. Kaminsky, 'The India Office in the Late Nineteenth Century' in Robert I. Crane and N. Gerald Barrier (eds), *British Imperial Policy in India and Sri Lanka 1858–1912 – A Reassessment*, New Delhi: Heritage Publishers, 1981

Julie Kavanagh, *Secret Muses: The Life of Frederick Ashton*, Faber & Faber, 1996

J. M. Kenworthy, *Sailors, Statesmen – and Others: An Autobiography*, Rich & Cowan, 1933

Daniel J. Kevles, *In the Name of Eugenics, Genetics, and the Uses of Human Heredity*, New York: Knopf, 1985

F. A. Keynes, *By-Ways of Cambridge History*, Cambridge University Press, 1947

——, *Gathering up the Threads*, Heffer, 1950

Geoffrey Keynes, *The Gates of Memory*, Oxford University Press, 1981

J. N. Keynes, *Studies and Exercises in Formal Logic*, Macmillan, 1906 ed.

——, *The Scope and Method of Political Economy*, Macmillan, 1891

M. Keynes (ed.), *Essays on John Maynard Keynes*, Cambridge University Press, 1975

—— (ed.), *Lydia Lopokova*, Weidenfeld & Nicolson, 1983

Warren F. Kimball, *The Most Unsordid Act: Lend–Lease 1939–1941*, Johns Hopkins University Press, 1969

——, *The Juggler: Franklin Roosevelt as Wartime Statesman*, Princeton University Press, 1991

Charles P. Kindleberger, *The World in Depression 1929–1939*, Allen Lane, 1973

King's College Cambridge, *John Maynard Keynes 1883–1946: A Memoir*, Cambridge University Press, 1949

E. D. Klemke, *Studies in the Philosophy of G. E. Moore*, Chicago: Quadrangle Books, 1965

Leszek Kolakowski, *Positivist Philosophy: From Hume to the Vienna Circle*, Penguin Books, 1972 edn

Gabriel Kolko, *The Politics of War: The World and the United States' Foreign Policy 1943–1945*, New York: Random House, 1968

David Kynaston, *The City of London*, iii, *Illusions of Gold 1914–1945*, Chatto & Windus, 1999

David Laidler, *Fabricating the Keynesian Revolution: Studies of the Inter-war Literature on Money, the Cycle and Unemployment*, Cambridge University Press, 2001

John Laughland, *The Tainted Source: The Undemocratic Origins of the European Idea*, Little, Brown, 1997

Dan, H. Laurence (ed.), *Bernard Shaw: Collected Letters 1926–50*, Max Reinhart, 1988

F. Lavington, *The English Capital Market*, Frank Cass, 1921

——, *The Trade Cycle*, P. S. King, 1925

Tony Lawson, 'Keynes and the Analysis of Rational Behaviour', in R. M. O'Donnell (ed.), *Keynes as Philosopher-Economist*, Macmillan, 1991

—— and Hashem Pesaran (eds), *Keynes' Economics: Methodological Issues*, Croom Helm, 1985

Melvin P. Leffler, *The Elusive Quest: America's Pursuit of European Stability and French Security 1919–1933*, University of North Carolina Press, 1979

Axel Leijonhufvud, *On Keynesian Economics and the Economics of Keynes*, New York: Oxford University Press, 1966

Sir Frederick Leith-Ross, *Money Talks: Fifty Years of International Finance*, Hutchinson, 1968

Robert Lekachman, *The Age of Keynes: A Biographical Study*, Penguin, 1967

—— (ed.), *Keynes's General Theory: Reports of Three Decades*, St Martin's Press/ Macmillan, 1964

Douglas LePan, *Bright Glass of Memory: Memoirs*, McGraw-Hill Ryerson, 1979

A. P. Lerner, *The Economics of Employment*, McGraw-Hill, 1951

Paul Levy, *G. E. Moore and the Cambridge Apostles*, Weidenfeld & Nicloson, 1979

W. Arthur Lewis, *Economic Survey 1919–1939*, Allen & Unwin, 1949

Arthur S. Link, *Wilson: Campaigns for Progressivism and Peace, 1916–1917*, Princeton University Press, 1965

D. Lloyd George, *The Truth about Reparations and War-Debts*, William Heinemann, 1932

——, *War Memoirs*, 6 vols, Nicholson & Watson, 1933–6

Wm. Roger Louis, *In the Name of God, Go: Leo Amery and the British Empire in the Age of Churchill*, New York: W. W. Norton, 1992

Percy Lubbock, *Shades of Eton*, Jonathan Cape, 1929

F. L. Lucas, *Tragedy in Relation to Aristotle's Poetics*, Hogarth Press, 1927

R. B. McCallum, *Public Opinion and the Last Peace*, Oxford University Press, 1944

Desmond MacCarthy, *Portraits*, Putnam, 1931

Nesta MacDonald, *Diaghilev Observed by Critics in England and the United States 1911–1929*, Dance Horizons, NY/Dance Books, London, 1975

Sir Donald MacDougall, *Don and Mandarin*, John Murray, 1987

Walter A. McDougall, *France's Rhineland Diplomacy 1914–1924*, Princeton University Press, 1978

Sir Andrew MacFadyean, *Recollected in Tranquillity*, Pall Mall Press, 1964

Alasdair MacIntyre, *A Short History of Ethics*, Routledge, 1967

——, *After Virtue: A Study in Moral Theory*, Duckworth, 1981

R. M. Mackiver, *The Modern State*, Clarendon Press, 1926

R. McKenna, *Post-War Banking Policy*, William Heinemann, 1928

Stephen McKenna, *Reginald McKenna, 1863–1913: A Memoir*, Eyre & Spottiswoode, 1948

B. J. C. McKercher, *Transition of Power: Britain's Loss of Global Pre-Eminence to the United States 1930–1945*, Cambridge University Press, 1999

David S. McLellan, *Dean Acheson: The State Department Years*, New York: Dodd, Mead, 1976

Harold Macmillan, *Winds of Change 1914–1939*, Macmillan, 1966

Rita McWilliams-Tullberg, *Women at Cambridge*, Gollancz, 1975

Charles S. Maier, *Recasting Bourgeois Europe: Stabilization in France, Germany, and Italy in the Decade after World War I*, Princeton University Press, 1975

Etienne Mantoux, *The Carthaginian Peace or The Economic Consequences of Mr. Keynes*, Oxford University Press, 1946

Sally Marks, *The Illusion of Peace: International Relations in Europe 1918–1939*, Macmillan, 1976

David Marquand, *Ramsay MacDonald*, Jonathan Cape, 1977

A. Marshall, *Industry and Trade*, Macmillan, 1919

——, *Money, Credit and Commerce*, Macmillan, 1923

——, *Principles of Economics*, Macmillan, 8th edn, 1920

——, *Memorials*, ed. A. C. Pigou, Macmillan, 1925

——, *Official Papers*, ed. J. M. Keynes, Royal Economic Society, 1926

——, *Early Economic Writings, 1867–1890*, ed. J. K. Whittaker, Royal Economic Society/Macmillan, 1975

Kingsley Martin, *Editor: A Volume of Autobiography 1931–1945*, Hutchinson, 1968
———, *Father Figures*, Hutchinson, 1966
Léonide Massine, *My Life in Ballet*, Macmillan, 1968
Arno Mayer, *Politics and Diplomacy of Peace-Making, Containment and Counter-Revolution at Versailles, 1918–1919*, Weidenfeld & Nicolson, 1968
James Meade, *An Introduction to Economic Analysis and Policy*, Oxford University Press, 1936
Robert Medley, *Drawn from Life: A Memoir*, Faber & Faber, 1983
James Meenan, *George O'Brien: A Biographical Memoir*, Gill and Macmillan, 1980
Carl Melchior, *Carl Melchior: Ein Buch des Gedenkens und der Freundschaft*, with a foreword by Dr Jurt Seiveking, Tübingen: Mohr, 1967
Allan H. Meltzer, *Keynes's Monetary Theory: A Different Interpretation*, Cambridge University Press, 1988
Keith Middlemas and John Barnes, *Baldwin: A Biography*, Weidenfeld & Nicolson, 1969
Roger Middleton, *Towards the Managed Economy: Keynes, the Treasury and the Fiscal Policy Debate of the 1930s*, Methuen, 1985
Murray Milgate, *Capital and Employment: A Study of Keynes's Economics*, Academic Press, 1982
Piero V. Mini, *Keynes, Bloomsbury, and The General Theory*, Macmillan, 1991
H. P. Minsky, *John Maynard Keynes*, Macmillan, 1976; reviewed by B. A. Corry, *EJ*, June 1977, 335–6
Dmitri Mirsky, *The Intelligensia of Great Britain*, trans. Alec Brown, Victor Gollancz, 1935
J. S. Mill, *Autobiography*, 1873
Franco Modigliani, 'Liquidity Preference and the theory of interest and money', *Econometrica*, 1944, repr. in Henry Hazlitt (ed.), *The Critics of Keynesian Economics*, University of America Press, 1973 edn
D. E. Moggridge, *British Monetary Policy 1924–1931: The Norman Conquest of $4.86*, Cambridge University Press, 1972
———, *Keynes*, Macmillan, 1976; paperback, Fontana Great Masters Series, 1976; reviewed by B. A. Corry, *EJ*, June 1977, 335–6
——— (ed.), *Keynes: Aspects of the Man and his Work*, Macmillan, 1974
———, *Maynard Keynes: An Economist's Biography*, Routledge, 1992
———, 'Keynes and the International Monetary System 1909–1946,' in J. S. Cohen and G. C. Harcourt (eds), *International Monetary Problems and Supply-Side Economics: Essays in Honour of Lorie Tarshis*, Macmillan, 1986
———, *The Return to Gold, 1925: The Formulation of Economic Policy and Its Critics*, Cambridge University Press, 1969
Sir Alfred Mond, *Industry and Politics*, Macmillan, 1927
Ray Monk, *Ludwig Wittgenstein: The Duty of Genius*, Jonathan Cape, 1990
G. E. Moore, *Philosophical Studies*, Routledge, 1922
———, *Principia Ethica*, Cambridge University Press, 1971 edn
———, *Some Main Problems of Philosophy*, Allen & Unwin, 1953
E. V. Morgan, *Studies in British Financial Policy 1914–1925*, Macmillan, 1952
K. O. Morgan, *Consensus and Disunity: The Lloyd George Coalition 1918–1922*, Clarendon Press, 1979
———, *Labour in Power 1945–1957*, Oxford University Press, 1985
Lady Ottoline Morrell: *Ottoline: The Early Memoirs*, ed. Robert Gathorne-Hardy, Faber & Faber, 1963

———, *Ottoline at Garsington: Memoirs 1915–1913*, ed. Robert Gathorne-Hardy, Faber & Faber, 1974

John E. Moser, *Twisting the Lion's Tail: Anglophobia in the United States 1921–48*, Macmillan, 1999

Sir Oswald Mosley, *My Life*, Nelson, 1968

C. L. Mowat, *Britain between the Wars 1918–1910*, Methuen, 1955

J. H. Muirhead, *The Platonic Tradition in Anglo-Saxon Philosophy*, Allen & Unwin, 1931

H. G. Nicholas (ed.), *Washington Despatches 1941–1945*, Weidenfeld & Nicolson, 1981

Harold Nicolson, *Some People*, Constable 1927

Walter Nimocks, *Milner's Young Men: The 'Kindergarten' in Edwardian Imperial Affairs*, Hodder & Stoughton, 1968

Douglass North and Robert Paul Thomas, *The Rise of the Western World: A New Economic History*, Cambridge University Press, 1973

D. P. O'Brien, *The Classical Economists*, Oxford University Press, 1975

D. P. O'Brien and J. R. Presley (eds), *Pioneers of Modern Economics in Britain*, Macmillan, 1981

R. M. O'Donnell, *Keynes: Philosophy, Economics and Politics*, Macmillan, 1989

———, (ed.), *Keynes as Philosopher-Economist*, Macmillan, 1991

———, 'Continuity in Keynes's Conception of Probability', in D. E. Moggridge (ed.), *Perspectives on the History of Economic Thought*, iv, Edward Elgar, 1990

C. K. Ogden and I. A. Richards, *The Meaning of Meaning*, Kegan Paul, 1923

R. W. Oliver, *International Economic Cooperation and the World Bank*, Macmillan, 1975

Mancur Olson, *The Rise and Decline of Nations: Economic Growth, Stagnation, and Social Rigidities*, New Haven: Yale University Press, 1982

Frances Partridge, *A Pacifist's War*, Hogarth Press, 1978

———, *Memories*, Victor Gollancz, 1981

Don Patinkin, *Anticipations of the General Theory*, Basil Blackwell, 1982; reviewed by Susan Howson, *EJ*, December 1983, 912–14

———, *Keynes's Monetary Thought: A Study of Its Development*, Duke University Press, 1976; reviewed by Edward Nevin, *EJ*, June 1977, 333–4

———, 'John Maynard Keynes', in John Eatwell, Murray Milgate, Peter Newman (eds), *The New Palgrave Dictionary of Economics*, Macmillan, 1987, vol. 3

——— and J. Clark Reith (eds), *Keynes, Cambridge, and the General Theory*, Macmillan, 1977

D. Pears, *Wittgenstein*, Fontana Modern Masters, 1971

G. C. Peden, *British Rearmament and the Treasury 1932–1939*, Scottish Academic Press, 1979

———, *Keynes, the Treasury and British Economic Policy*, Macmillan, 1986

———, *The Treasury and British Public Policy 1906–1959*, Oxford University Press, 2000

———, 'Keynes, the Economics of Rearmament and Appeasement', in Wolfgang J. Mommsen and Lothar Kettenadker (eds), *The Fascist Challenge and the Policy of Appeasement*, Parsons, 1983

E. F. Penrose, *Economic Planning for Peace*, Princeton University Press, 1953

Frances Perkins, *The Roosevelt I Knew*, Hammond, 1947

A. C. Pigou, *Aspects of British Economic History 1918–1925*, Macmillan, 1947

———, *Economics in Practice*, Macmillan, 1935

——, *Keynes's 'General Theory': A Retrospective View*, Macmillan, 1950
——, *The Theory of Unemployment*, Macmillan, 1933
——, *Unemployment*, Home University Library, 1913
Ben Pimlott, *Hugh Dalton*, Jonathan Cape, 1985
——, *Labour and the Left in the 1930s*, Cambridge University Press, 1977
John Plesch, *Janos: The Story of a Doctor*, Victor Gollancz, 1947
Jean van der Poel, *Selections from the Smuts Papers*, v and vii, Cambridge University Press, 1973
Sidney Pollard (ed.), *The Gold Standard and Employment Politics between the Wars*, Methuen, 1970
J. R. Presley, *Robertsonian Economics*, Macmillan, 1978
L. S. Pressnell, *External Economic Policy since the War*, i: *The Post-War Financial Settlement*, HMSO, 1986
Frank Plumpton Ramsey, *The Foundation of Mathematics and Other Logical Essays*, ed. R. B. Braithwaite, with a preface by G. E. Moore, Macmillan, 1931
Gwen Raverat, *Period Piece: A Cambridge Childhood*, Faber & Faber, 1952
David Rees, *Harry Dexter White: A Study in Paradox*, Macmillan, 1973
Lord Riddell, *My Intimate Diary of the Paris Peace Conference and After, 1918-1923*, Gollancz, 1933
Lionel Robbins, *Autobiography of an Economist*, Macmillan, 1971
——, *The Economic Problem in Peace and War*, Macmillan, 1947
——, *The Great Depression*, Macmillan, 1934
——, *The Theory of Economic Policy in English Classical Political Economy*, Macmillan, 1952
Andrew Roberts, *Holy Fox*, Weidenfeld & Nicolson, 1991
D. H. Robertson, *Banking Policy and the Price Level: An Essay in the Theory of the Trade Cycle*, P. S. King, 1926
——, *Lectures on Economic Principles*, Fontana Library, 1963
——, *Money*, Nisbet, 1923; rev. edn, 1928
——, *A Study of Industrial Fluctuation*, P. S. King, 1915; rev. edn, LSE, 1948
Joan Robinson, *Collected Economic Papers*, Basil Blackwell, 1960
——, *Contributions to Modern Economics*, Basil Blackwell, 1979
——, *The Economics of Imperfect Competition*, Macmillan, 1933
——, *Introduction to the Theory of Employment*, Macmillan, 1937
——, *The Rate of Interest and Other Essays*, Macmillan, 1952
C. H. Rolph, *Kingsley: The Life, Letters and Diaries of Kingsley Martin*, Victor Gollancz, 1973
W. Ropke, *Crises and Cycles*, William Hodge, 1936
——, *International Economic Disintegration*, William Hodge, 1942
E. Rosenbaum and A. J. Sherman, *M. M. Warburg & Co., 1798–1938, Merchant Bankers of Hamburg*, Hamburg, 1979
S. P. Rosenbaum, *Victorian Bloomsbury: The Early Literary History of the Bloomsbury Group*, i, Macmillan, 1987
—— (ed.), *The Bloomsbury Group: A Collection of Memoirs, Commentary and Criticism*, Croom Helm, 1973
Henry Roseveare, *The Treasury: The Evolution of a British Institution*, Allen Lane, 1969
Sheldon Rothblatt, *The Revolution of the Dons: Cambridge and Society in Victorian England*, Faber & Faber, 1968

Roy J. Rotheim, 'Interdependence and the Cambridge Tradition', in B. Gerrard and J. Hillard (eds), *The Philosophy and Economics of J. M. Keynes*, Edward Elgar, 1992

——, 'Marx, Keynes and the Theory of a Monetary Economy', in G. A. Caravale (ed.), *Marx and Modern Economic Analysis*, Edward Elgar, 1991

Benjamin M. Rowland (ed.), *Balance of Power or Hegemony: The Interwar Monetary System*, Lehrman Institute, New York University Press, 1976

Peter Rowland, *Lloyd George*, Barrie & Jenkins, 1975

A. L. Rowse, *Glimpses of the Great*, Methuen, 1985

——, *Mr. Keynes and the Labour Movement*, Macmillan, 1936

Herman J. Rupieper, *The Cuno Government and Reparations 1922–1923*, Martinus Nijhoff, 1979

Bertrand Russell, *Autobiography*, i and ii, Allen & Unwin, Allen & Unwin, 1967–8

——, *My Philosophical Development*, Allen & Unwin, 1959

——, *Our Knowledge of the External World*, Allen & Unwin, 1914; 5th imp. 1969

——, *The Principles of Mathematics*, Allen & Unwin, 1903, 1937

——, *The Problems of Philosophy*, Williams & Norgate, 1913

Alan Ryan, *Bertrand Russell: A Political Life*, Allen Lane, 1988

Arthur Salter, *Slave of the Lamp*, Weidenfeld & Nicolson, 1967

R. S. Sayers, *The Bank of England 1891–1944*, 2 vols, Cambridge University Press, 1976

——, *Financial Policy 1939–1945*, HMSO, 1956

B. Schefold, 'The General Theory for a Totalitarian State? A Note on Keynes's Preface to the German Edition of 1936', repr. in John Cunningham Wood (ed.), *John Maynard Keynes: Critical Assessments*, ii, 416–17, Croom Helm, 1983

P. A. Schilpp (ed.), *The Philosophy of Bertrand Russell*, La Salle, Ill.: Open Court, 1971

Arthur M. Schlesinger Jr, *The Coming of the New Deal*, William Heinemann, 1959

J. B. Schneewind, *Sidgwick's Ethics and Victorian Moral Philosophy*, Oxford University Press, 1977

Stephen A. Schuker, *The End of French Predominance in Europe*, University of North Carolina Press, 1976

——, 'American Policy Toward Debts and Reconstruction at Genoa, 1922', in Carole Fink, Axel Frohn and Jurgen Heideking (eds), *Genoa, Rapallo and European Reconstruction in 1922*, Cambridge University Press, 1991

J. A. Schumpeter, *Capitalism, Socialism, and Democracy*, Allen & Unwin, 3rd edn, 1952

——, *History of Economic Analysis*, Allen & Unwin, 1954

——, *Ten Great Economists*, Allen & Unwin, 1952

Jordan A. Schwarz, *The Speculator, Bernard M. Baruch in Washington, 1917–1965*, Chapel Hill: University of North Carolina Press, 1981

G. L. S. Shackle, *The Years of High Theory: Invention and Tradition in Economic Thought 1926–1939*, Cambridge University Press, 1967

Robert E. Sherwood, *The White House Papers of Harry L. Hopkins: An Intimate History*, 2 vols, Eyre & Spottiswoode, 1948

Richard Shone, *Bloomsbury Portraits*, Phaidon, 1976

A. and E. M. Sidgwick, *Henry Sidgwick: A Memoir*, Macmillan, 1906

Henry Sidgwick: *Methods of Ethics*, 1874; University of Chicago Press, 1962

Andrew Sinclair, *The Red and the Blue*, Weidenfeld & Nicolson, 1986

Osbert Sitwell, *An Autobiography*, 5 vols, Macmillan, 1947–50

Robert Skidelsky, *John Maynard Keynes vol. 1: Hopes Betrayed 1883–1920*, Macmillan,

1983, New York: Viking, 1986; *John Maynard Keynes vol. 2: The Economist as Saviour 1920–1937*, Macmillan, 1992, Papermac, 1994, Allen Lane, The Penguin Press, 1995; *John Maynard Keynes vol. 3: Fighting for Britain*, Macmillan, 2001; *Fighting for Freedom*, Viking 2002

——, *Keynes*, Oxford University Press, 1996

——, *Oswald Mosley*, Macmillan, 1975; 3rd edn paperback, 1990

——, *Politicians and the Slump*, Macmillan, 1967; Papermac, 1994

—— (ed.), *The End of the Keynesian Era*, Macmillan, 1977

——, 'A Tale of Two Houses', in Hugh Lee (ed.), *A Cézanne in the Hedge and Other Memories of Charleston and Bloomsbury*, Collins & Brown, 1992

——, 'El Festeig de Lydia', in Marta Pessarrodona (ed.), *El Grup de Bloomsbury*, Fundacio Caixa de Pensions, 1988

——, with Marcus Miller and Paul Weller, 'Fear of Deficit Financing – Is it Rational?', in Rudiger Dornbusch and Mario Darghi (eds), *Public Debt Management: Theory and History*, Cambridge University Press, 1990

——, 'Keynes and Bloomsbury', the Joyce Brown Memorial Lecture, in Michael Holroyd (ed.), *Essays by Divers Hands*, Royal Society of Literature, 1982

——, 'Keynes and his Parents', in Stephen R. Graubard (ed.), *Generations*, W. W. Norton, 1978

——, 'Keynes and the Quantity Theory of Money', in Mark Blaug (ed.), *The Quantity Theory of Money from Locke to Keynes and Friedman*, Edward Elgar, 1995

——, 'Keynes and the State', in D. Helm (ed.), *The Economic Boundaries of the State*, Oxford University Press, 1989

——, 'Keynes and the Treasury View: The Case for and against an Active Unemployment Policy 1920–1939', in W. J. Mommsen (ed.), *The Emergence of the Welfare State in Britain and Germany*, 1981

——, 'Keynes e Sraffa: un caso di non-communicazione', in Riccardo Bellofiore (ed.), *Tra Teoria Economica e Grande Cultura Europea: Piero Sraffa*, Franco Angeli, 1986

——, 'Keynes's "Concluding Notes"', in G. C. Harcourt and P. A. Rich (eds), *A 'Second Edition' of The General Theory*, i, Routledge, 1997

——, 'Keynes's Philosophy of Practice', in R. M. O'Donnell (ed.), *Keynes as Philosopher-Economist*, Macmillan, 1991

——, 'Keynes's Political Legacy', in A. Kilmarnock (ed.), *The Radical Challenge*, André Deutsch, 1987

——, 'Keynes's Political Legacy', in Omar F. Hamouda and John N. Smithin (eds), *Keynes and Public Policy after Fifty Years*, Edward Elgar, 1988

——, 'Les possibilitats econòmiques per als nostres néts', in Marta Pessarrodona (ed.), *El Grup de Bloomsbury*, Fundacio Caixa de Pensions, 1988

——, 'Some Aspects of Keynes the Man', in Omar F. Hamouda and John N. Smithin (eds), *Keynes and Public Policy after Fifty Years*, Edward Elgar, 1988

——, 'The American Response to Keynes', in A. P. Thirlwall (ed.), *Keynes and Laissez-Faire*, Macmillan, 1978

——, 'The Conditions for the Reinstatement of Keynesian Policy', in Luigi Pasinetti and Bertram Schefold (eds), *The Impact of Keynes on Economics in the 20th Century*, Edward Elgar, 1999

——, 'The Political Meaning of the Keynesian Revolution', in R. Skidelsky (ed.), *The End of the Keynesian Era*, Macmillan, 1977

——, 'The Reception of the Keynesian Revolution', in Milo Keynes (ed.), *Essays on John Maynard Keynes*, Cambridge University Press, 1975

——, 'The Revolt against the Victorians', in R. Skidelsky (ed.), *The End of the Keynesian Era*, Macmillan, 1977

——, 'The Role of Ethics in Keynes's Economics', in Samuel Brittan and Alan Hamlin (eds), *Market Capitalism and Moral Values*, Edward Elgar, 1995

——, 'Thinking about the State and the Economy', in S. J. D. Green and R. C. Whiting (eds), *The Boundaries of the State in Modern Britain*, Cambridge University Press, 1996

Mark Skousen (ed.), *Dissent on Keynes: A Critical Appraisal of Keynesian Economics*, Praeger, 1992

Boris Sokoloff, *The Story of Penicillin*, New York: Ziff Publishing 1945

Lydia Sokolova, *Dancing for Diaghilev*, ed. Richard Buckle, John Murray, 1960

Felix Somary, *The Raven of Zurich*, Hurst, 1960

Frances Spalding *Duncan Grant: A Biography*, Chatto & Windus, 1997

——, *Roger Fry: Art and Life*, Granada Publishing, 1980

——, *Vanessa Bell*, Weidenfeld & Nicolson, 1983

Bartholomew H. Sparrow, *From the Outside In: World War II and the American State*, Princeton University Press, 1996

George Spater and Ian Parsons, *A Marriage of True Minds: An Intimate Portrait of Leonard and Virginia Woolf*, Jonathan Cape/Hogarth Press, 1977

P. Stansky and W. Abrahams, *Journey to the Frontier*, Constable, 1966

Ronald Steel, *Walter Lippmann and the American Century*, Boston: Little, Brown, 1980

Herbert Stein, *The Fiscal Revolution in America*, University of Chicago Press, 1969

Adrian Stephen, *The 'Dreadnought' Hoax*, L. & V. Woolf, 1936

Michael Stewart, *Keynes and After*, Penguin, 3rd edn, 1986

Barbara Strachey, *Remarkable Relations: The Story of the Pearsall Smith Family*, Gollancz, 1980

John Strachey, *Revolution by Reason*, Leonard Parson, 1925

——, *The Coming Struggle for Power*, Victor Gollancz, 1932

Lytton Strachey, *Eminent Victorians*, Chatto & Windus, 1918

——, *The Really Interesting Question and Other Papers*, ed. Paul Levy, Weidenfeld & Nicolson, 1972

Michael Straight, *After Long Silence*, Collins, 1983

B. Taper, *Balanchine, A Biography*, University of California Press, 3rd edn, 1984

André Tardieu, *The Truth about the Treaty*, Hodder & Stoughton, 1921

A. J. P. Taylor, *English History 1914–1915*, Oxford University Press, 1965

——, *The Origins of the Second World War*, Penguin edn, 1964

——, *Politics in Wartime*, Hamish Hamilton, 1964

Arthur J. Taylor, *Laissez-Faire and State Intervention in Nineteenth-Century Britain*, Macmillan, 1972

Peter Temin, *Did Monetary Forces Cause the Great Depression?*, New York: W. W. Norton, 1976

A. P. Thirlwall, *Nicholas Kaldor*, Wheatsheaf, 1987

—— (ed.), *Keynes and International Monetary Relations*, Macmillan, 1976

—— (ed.), *Keynes as a Policy Adviser*, Macmillan, 1982

—— (ed.), *Keynes and Laissez-Faire*, Macmillan, 1978

Seth P. Tillman, *Anglo-American Relations at the Paris Peace Conference of 1919*, Princeton University Press, 1961

Nicholas Timmins, *The Five Giants: A Biography of the Welfare State*, HarperCollins, 1995

Jim Tomlinson, *Employment Policy: The Crucial Years 1939–1955*, Clarendon Press, 1987

Marc Trachtenberg, *Reparation in World Politics*, Columbia University Press, 1980

Keith Tribe, *Strategies of Economic Order: German Economic Discourse 1750–1950*, Cambridge University Press, 1995

Rexford Tugwell, *The Democratic Roosevelt: A Biography of Franklin D. Roosevelt*, Doubleday, 1957

Marjorie S. Turner, *Joan Robinson and the Americans*, M. E. Sharpe Inc., 1989

Ninette de Valois, *Come Dance with Me: A Memoir 1898–1956*, Hamish Hamilton, 1957

S. Waley, *Edwin Montagu: A Memoir and an Account of his Visit to India*, Asia Publishing House, 1964

Immanuel Wallerstein, *The Modern World-System, Capitalist Agriculture and the Origins of the European World-Economy in the Sixteenth Century*, Academic Press, 1974

G. J. Warnock, *English Philosophy since 1900*, Oxford University Press, 1958

Simon Watney, *The Art of Duncan Grant*, John Murray, 1990

Sidney and Beatrice Webb, *The Decay of Capitalist Civilisation*, Allen & Unwin, 1923

Allen Weinstein and Alexander Vassiliev, *The Haunted Wood: Soviet Espionage in America – The Stalin Era*, Random House, 1999

Paul Wells, '"Mr. Churchill" and *The General Theory*', in J. S. Cohen and G. C. Harcourt (eds), *International Monetary Problems and Supply Side Economics: Essays in Honour of Lorie Tarshis*, Macmillan, 1986

Benjamin Welles, *Sumner Welles: FDR's Global Strategist*, Macmillan, 1997

Antony West, *H. G. Wells: Aspects of a Life*, Hutchinson, 1984

Knut Wicksell, *Interest and Prices: A Study of the Causes Regulating the Value of Money*, trans. from the German by R. F. Kahn, with an introduction by Bertil Ohlin, Macmillan, 1936 (first published 1898)

Martin J. Wiener, *English Culture and the Decline of the Industrial Spirit, 1850–1980*, Cambridge University Press, 1981

L. W. Wilkinson, *A Century of King's 1873–1972*, KCC, 1980

——, *Kingsmen of a Century 1873–1972*, KCC, 1980

Raymond Williams, 'The Significance of "Bloomsbury" as a Social and Cultural Group' in Derek Crabtree and A. P. Thirlwall (eds), *Keynes and the Bloomsbury Group*, 1980

John Williamson, 'Keynes and the International Economic Order', in G. D. N. Worswick and J. Trevithick (eds), *Keynes and the Modern World*, Cambridge University Press, 1983

Philip Williamson, *National Crisis and National Government: British Politics, the Economy and Empire 1926–1932*, Cambridge University Press, 1992

——, 'Financiers, the Gold Standard and British Politics 1925–1931', in John Turner (ed.), *Businessmen and Politics: Studies of Business Activity in British Politics 1900–1945*, William Heinemann, 1984

David Wilson, *Penicillin in Perspective*, Faber & Faber, 1976

Francesca Wilson, *Rebel Daughter of a Country House*, Allen & Unwin, 1967

Thomas Wilson, *Churchill and the Prof*, Cassell, 1995

Norbert F. Wilty, 'The Congruence of Weber and Keynes', in Randall Collins (ed.), *Sociological Theory*, Jossey-Bass, San Francisco, 1983

John G. Winant, *A Letter from Grosvenor Square*, Hodder & Stoughton, 1947

Donald Winch, *Economics and Policy: A Historical Study*, Collins/Fontana, 1972 edn

Esmé Wingfield-Stratford, *Before the Lamps Went Out*, Hodder & Stoughton, 1945

D. A. Winstanley: *Late Victorian Cambridge*, Cambridge University Press, 1947

Ludwig Wittgenstein, *Note-Books 1914–1916*, eds G. H. von Wright and G. E. M. Anscombe, Basil Blackwell, 1969

——, *Tractatus Logico-Philosophicus*, trans. from the German by C. K. Ogden, assisted by F. Ramsey, Routledge & Kegan Paul, 1922

John Cunningham Wood (ed.), *John Maynard Keynes: Critical Assessments*, 4 vols, Croom Helm, 1983

Neal Wood, *Communism and British Intellectuals*, Victor Gollancz, 1959

E. L. Woodward, *British Foreign Policy in the Second World War*, HMSO, 1971

Sir Earnest Llewellyn Woodward, *Great Britain and the War of 1914–1918*, Methuen, 1967

Leonard Woolf, *Autobiography*: vol. i: *Sowing*; vol. iii: *Beginning Again*; vol. iv: *Downhill All the Way*; Hogarth Press, 1960–7

Virginia Woolf, *Moments of Being*, ed. Jeanne Schulkind, Chatto & Windus, 1978

David Worswick and James Trevithick (eds), *Keynes and the Modern World*, Cambridge University Press, 1983

H. E. Wortham, *Victorian Eton and Cambridge, being the Life and Times of Oscar Browning*, Arthur Barker, 1956 edition

Harold Wright (ed.), *University Studies, Cambridge, 1933*, Nicholson & Watson, 1933

Q. Wright (ed.), *Unemployment as a World Problem*, University of Chicago Press, 1931

Warren Young, *Interpreting Mr. Keynes: The IS-LM Enigma*, Polity Press, 1987

A. J. Youngson, *The British Economy 1920–1957*, Allen & Unwin, 1960

ARTICLES AND MONOGRAPHS

Moses Abramovitz, 'Catching up, Forging Ahead, and Falling Behind', *Journal of Economic History*, 46, June 1986

James W. Angell, 'Monetary Theory and Monetary Policy: Some Recent Discussions', *Quarterly Journal of Economics*, February 1925, 267–99

Denise Artaud, 'À Propos de l'Occupation de la Ruhr', *Revue d'Histoire Moderne et Contemporaine*, January–March 1970, 1–21

Giacomo Beccattini, 'L'Acclimatamento del Pensiero di Keynes in Italia: Invito ad un Dibattito', *Passato e Presente*, April 1983, 85–104

D. K. Benjamin and L. A. Kochin, 'Searching for an Explanation of Unemployment in Interwar Britain', *Journal of Political Economy*, 87, 1979, 441–78

Bernard Bergonzi, 'Who are You?' (critique of Bloomsbury Group), *New Review*, November 1974, 50–4

William Beveridge, 'Mr. Keynes's Evidence for Overpopulation', *Economica*, February 1924, 1–20

R. D. Collison Black, 'Ralph George Hawtrey 1879–1975', *Proceedings of the British Academy*, vol. 63, 1977, 363–98

Sir George Bolton, 'Where the Critics Are as Wrong as Keynes Was', *Banker*, November 1972

Alan Booth, 'The "Keynesian Revolution" in Economic Policy-Making', *Economic History Review*, 2nd series, 36, 1983, 103–23
——, 'Simple Keynesianism and Whitehall, 1936–1947', *Economy and Society*, 15, 1986
Knut Borchardt, 'Keynes' Nationale Selbstgenügsamkeitp von 1933', *Zeitschrift für Wirtschafts und Sozialwissenschaften,* January 1988, 271–84
R. H. Brand, 'A Banker's Reflections on Some Economic Trends', *Economic Journal*, December 1953, 761–70
Karl Britton, 'Recollections of Cambridge 1928–32', *Cambridge Review*, ciii, no. 2270, 1982
S. Broadberry, 'Aggregate Supply in Interwar Britain', *Economic Journal*, June 1986, 467–81
Kathleen Burk, 'Economic Diplomacy between the Wars', *Historical Journal*, 4, 1981, 1003–15
——, 'J. M. Keynes and the Exchange Rate Crisis of July 1917', *Economic History Review*, 2nd series, xxxii, 3 (1979) 405–16
——, 'The Diplomacy of Finance: British Financial Missions to the United States, 1914–1918', *Historical Journal*, xxii, 2 (1979) 351–72
Neville Cain, 'Cambridge and its Revolution: A Perspective on the Multiplier and Effective Demand', *Economic Record,* June 1979, 108–17
——, 'Hawtrey and the Multiplier Theory', *Economic Record,* June 1981, 68–78
E. Cannan, 'The Meaning of British Bank Deposits', *Economica,* January 1921
George Catephores, *Keynes as a Bourgeois Marxist*, Discussion Paper No. 91–23, University College London Discussion Papers in Economics, 1991
J. H. Chau and R. S. Woodward, 'John Maynard Keynes' Investment Performance: A Note', *Journal of Finance*, March 1983, 232–5
S. G. Checkland, 'Economic Opinion in England as Jevons Found it', *Manchester School,* xix (May 1951), 143–69
Colin Clark, 'Public Finance and Changes in the Value of Money', *Economic Journal*, 55, December 1945
A. W. Coats, 'The Role of Authority in the Development of British Economics', *Journal of Law and Economics*, vii–viii (1964) 85–106
——, 'Sociological Aspects of British Economic Thought (1880–1930)', *Chicago Journal of Political Economy*, lxxv, October 1967, 706–29
——, 'The Historicist Reaction in English Political Economy, 1870–1890', *Economica*, xxi (May 1954), 143–53
Tim Congdon, 'Are We Really All Keynesians Now?', *Encounter*, April 1975, 23–32
Thomas F. Cooley and Lee E. Ohanian, 'Postwar Economic Growth and the Legacy of Keynes', *Journal of Political Economy*, 105, no. 3, 1996
John Milton Cooper, Jr, 'The British Response to the House–Grey Memorandum', *Journal of American History*, lix (1973) 958–71
——, 'The Command of Gold Reversed: American Loans to Britain, 1915–1917', *Pacific Historical Review*, xlv (May 1976) no. 2, 212–30
F. C. Costigliola, 'Anglo-French Financial Rivalry in the 1920s', *Journal of Economic History*, December 1977, 911–34
L. Cuyvers, 'Keynes's Collaboration with Erwin Rothbarth', *Economic Journal,* September 1983
Paul Davidson, 'The elephant and the butterfly; or hysteresis and Post-Keynesian economics', *Journal of Post-Keynesian Economics*, 1993

——, 'Sensible Expectations and the Long-Run Non-Neutrality of Money', *Journal of Post-Keynesian Economics*, Fall 1987, 146–53

E. G. Davis, 'The Correspondence between R. G. Hawtrey and J. M. Keynes on the *Treatise*: The Genesis of Output Adjustment Models', *Canadian Journal of Economics*, November 1980, 716–24

Sir Piers Debenham, 'The Economic Advisory Council and the Great Depression', *Sir Hubert Henderson*, Oxford Economic Papers Supplement, 1953, 28–47

Maurice Dobb, 'A Sceptical View of the Theory of Wages', *Economic Journal*, December 1929, 506–19

Charles P. Dunbar, 'The Reaction in Political Economy', *Quarterly Journal of Economics*, i (October 1886), 1–27

J. T. Dunlop, 'The Movement of Real and Money Wage Rates', *Economic Journal*, September 1938, 413–34

Sir Wilfrid Eady, 'Maynard Keynes at the Treasury', *Listener*, 7 June 1951

B. Eichengreen, 'Sterling and the Tariff 1929–1932', *Princeton Studies in International Finance*, no. 48, September 1981

W. Fellner, 'Saving, Investment and the Problem of Neutral Money', *Review of Economic Statistics*, November 1938, 185–93

Giuliano Ferrari Bravo, '"In the Name of Our Mutual Friend...": The Keynes-Cuno Affair', *Journal of Contemporary History*, January 1989, 147–67

Geoffrey Fishburn, 'Keynes and the Age of Eugenics', *The Age Monthly Review*, June 1983

H. S. Foxwell, 'The Economic Movement in England', *Quarterly Journal of Economics*, ii (1888) 84–103

J. Franklin, 'Resurrecting Logical Probability', *Erkenntnis* 55: 277–305, 2001

W. R. Garside, 'The Failure of the "Radical Alternative": Public Works, Deficit Finance and British Interwar Unemployment', *Banco di Roma*, Winter 1985, 537–55

D. A. Gillies, 'Keynes as a Methodologist', *British Journal for the Philosophy of Science*, 39, 1988, 117–29

Sean Glynn and Alan Booth, 'Unemployment in Interwar Britain: A Case for Re-learning the Lessons of the 1930s?', *Economic History Review*, 2nd Series, 36, 1, 1983, 329–18

A. G. Gruchy, 'The Philosophical Basis of the New Keynesian Economics', *Ethics*, July 1948, 235–44

C. W. Guillebaud, 'Hitler's New Economic Order for Europe', *Economic Journal*, 50, December 1940

Gottfried Haberler, 'The Great Depression of the 1930s: Can it Happen Again?', American Enterprise Institute, Reprint No. 118, January 1981

Bjorn Hansson, 'Keynes's Notion of Equilibrium in the *General Theory*', *Journal of Post-Keynesian Economics*, Spring 1985, 332–40

R. F. Harrod, 'Mr. Keynes and Traditional Theory', *Econometrica*, January 1937, 74–86

——, 'Clive Bell on Keynes', *Economic Journal*, December 1957, 692–9

——, 'An Essay in Dynamic Theory', *Economic Journal*, 49, June 1939, 294–300

A. G. Hart, 'An Examination of Mr. Keynes's Price Level Concepts', *Journal of Political Economy*, October 1933, 625–38

R. G. Hawtrey, 'Public Expenditure and the Demand for Labour', *Economica*, March 1925, 38–48

——, Review of *A Tract on Monetary Reform*, *Economic Journal*, June 1924, 227–35

F. A. Hayek, 'The London School of Economics 1895–1943', *Economica*, February 1946, 1–31

——, review of *A Treatise on Money, Economica*, August 1931, 270–95, February 1932, 22–44

——, 'A Rejoinder to Mr. Keynes', *Economica*, November 1931, 398–403

Faith Henderson, 'Editing the Nation', *Sir Hubert Henderson*, Oxford Economic Papers Supplement, 1953, 7–27

George C. Herring Jr, 'The United States and British Bankruptcy 1944–1945', *Political Science Quarterly*, 86, 1971

J. R. Hicks, 'Dennis Holme Robertson 1890–1963', *Proceedings of the British Academy*, vol. 50, 1964, 305–16

——, 'Mr. Keynes and the "Classics": A Suggested Interpretation', *Econometrica*, April 1937, 147–59

——, 'Mr. Keynes's Theory of Employment', *Economic Journal*, June 1936, 238–53

Sir Richard Hopkins, *Tributes*, Church [of England] Information Board, 1957

Susan Howson, 'The Management of Sterling 1932–1939', *Journal of Economic History*, 40, 1975

——, 'A Dear Money Man? Keynes on Monetary Policy, 1920', *Economic Journal*, June 1973, 456–64

——, 'The Origins of Dear Money, 1919–20', *Economic History Review*, 2nd series, 27, 1974, 88–107

David Hubback, 'Sir Richard Clarke, 1910–1975: A Most Unusual Civil Servant', *Public Policy and Administration*, 3, no. 1, Spring 1988

Syed Anwar Husain, 'The Administrative Departments of the India Office, 1858–1919', *Indian Journal of Public Administration*, xxvii, no. 2 (April–June 1981), 430–43

T. W. Hutchison, 'The Collected Writings of John Maynard Keynes, vols. i–vi and xv–xvi', *Economic History Review*, 2nd series, xxvi (February 1973) 141–52

Elizabeth Johnson, 'Keynes' Attitude to Compulsory Military Service', with 'A Comment by Sir Roy Harrod', *Economic Journal* (March 1960), 160–7

Byrd L. Jones, 'The Role of Keynesians in Wartime Policy and Postwar Planning 1940–46', in 'The Second Crisis of Economic Theory and Other Selected Papers', from the Annual Meeting of the American Economic Association, 27–29 December, 1971

Bill Jordan and Mark Drakeford, 'Major Douglas, Money and the New Technology', *New Society*, 24 January 1980

R. F. Kahn, 'The Relation of Home Investment to Unemployment', *Economic Journal*, June 1931, 173–98

——, 'Some Aspects of the Development of Keynes's Thought', *Journal of Economic Literature*, June 1978, 544–58

N. Kaldor, 'Professor Pigou on Money Wages in Relation to Unemployment', *Economic Journal*, December 1937, 745–53

J. N. Keynes, 'Obituary of Sidgwick', *Economic Journal* (1902) 586–91

Warren F. Kimball, 'Lend–Lease and the Open Door: The Temptation of British Opulence 1937–1942', *Political Science Quarterly*, 86, 1971

William Kingston, 'Ideas, Civil Servants and Keynes', *Economic Affairs*, January 1985

Meir Kohn, 'Monetary Analysis, the Equilibrium Method, and Keynes's "General Theory"', *Journal of Political Economy*, 94, 1986, 1191–1224

J. A. Kregel, 'Monetary Production, Economics, and Monetary Policy', *Économies et Sociétés*, April 1984, 221–32

David Laidler, 'Skidelsky's Keynes: A Review Essay', *European Journal of the History of Economic Thought*, vol. 9, no. 1, March 2002, 97–110.

Paul Lambert, 'The Evolution of Keynes's Thought from *The Treatise on Money* to *The General Theory*', *Annals of Public and Cooperative Economy*, 1969, 243–63

Tony Lawson, 'Keynes and Conventions', *Review of Social Economy*, vol. 51, no. 2, Summer 1993, 174–200

——, 'Probability and Uncertainty in Economic Analysis', *Journal of Post-Keynesian Economics*, Fall 1988, 38–63

——, 'Realism and Instrumentalism in the Development of Econometrics', *Oxford Economic Papers*, 91, 1989, 236–58

——, 'Uncertainty and Economic Analysis', *Economic Journal*, December 1985, 909–27

Q. D. Leavis, 'Henry Sidgwick's Cambridge', *Scrutiny* (December 1947) 3–11

Axel Leijonhufvud, *Keynes and the Classics*, Institute of Economic Affairs, 1969

J. Bradford Delong, Review of Skidelsky's *John Maynard Keynes: Fighting for Britain*, in *Journal of Economic Literature*, vol. XL (March 2002), 155–162

A. P. Lerner, 'Functional Finance and the Federal Debt', *Social Research*, 10, no. 1, February 1943

Bruce Littleboy, 'The Wider Significance of "How to Pay for the War"', *History of Economics Review*, 25, Winter–Summer 1996

—— and V. Mehta, 'Patinkin on Keynes' Theory of Effective Demand', *History of Political Economy*, Summer 1987, 311–28

Rodney Lowe, 'The Erosion of State Intervention in Britain, 1917–1924', *Economic History Review*, 2nd series, 21, 1978, 270–86

Donald M. McCloskey, 'The Literary Character of Economics', *Daedalus*, Summer 1984, 97–119

——, 'The Rhetoric of Economics', *Journal of Economic Literature*, June 1983, 481–517

Andrew MacDonald, 'The Geddes Committee and the Formulation of Public Expenditure Policy, 1921–1922', *Historical Journal*, 32, 2, 1989, 643–74

Walter A. McDougall, 'Political Economy versus National Sovereignty: French Structures for German Economic Integration after Versailles', *Journal of Modern History*, March 1979, 56–67

T. P. McLaughlin, 'The Teaching of the Canonists on Usury', *Mediaeval Studies*, 1, 2, 1939, 1940

Sally Marks, 'Reparations Reconsidered: A Reminder', *Central European History*, December 1969, 356–65

K. P. G. Matthews, 'Was Sterling Overvalued in 1925?', *Economic History Review*, 2nd series, 39, 1986, 572–87

Allan H. Meltzer, 'Keynes's General Theory: A Different Perspective', *Journal of Economic Literature*, March 1981, 34–65

Raymond F. Mikesell, 'The Bretton Woods Debates: A Memoir', *Princeton Essays in International Finance*, 192, March 1994

Murray Milgate, 'Keynes and Pigou on the Gold Standard and Monetary Theory', *Contributions to Political Economy*, March 1983, 39–48

Lawrence Minard, 'The Original Contrarian', *Forbes*, 26 September 1983

D. E. Moggridge, 'From the *Treatise* to *The General Theory*: An Exercise in Chronology', *History of Political Economy*, Spring 1973, 72–88

——, 'Rescuing Keynes from the economists?: The Skidelsky trilogy', *European Journal of the History of Economic Thought*, vol. 9, no. 1, March 2002, 111–123

—— and Susan Howson, 'Keynes on Monetary Policy 1919–1946', *Oxford Economic Papers*, July 1974, 227–47

G. Mongiovi, 'Keynes, Hayek and Sraffa: On the Origins of Chapter 17 of *The General Theory*', *Économique Appliquée*, tome XLIII, 1990, 131–56

O. Mosley, 'Revolution by Reason', Independent Labour Party, 1925

Larry Neal, 'The Economics and Finance of Bilateral Clearing Agreements: Germany 1934–8', *Economic History Review*, 2nd series, 32, 1979

J. S. Nicholson, 'The Vagaries of Recent Political Economy', *Quarterly Review*, ccxix, no. 437 (1913), 406–25

R. M. O'Donnell, 'Keynes on Mathematics: Philosophical Foundations and Economic Applications', *Cambridge Journal of Economics*, March 1990, 29–47

——, 'Mixed Goods and Social Reform', *Cahiers d'économie politique*, no. 30–31, L'Harmattan, 1998

Bertil Ohlin, 'The Reparation Problem: A Discussion: I. Transfer Difficulties, Real and Imagined', *Economic Journal*, June 1929, 172–8

——, 'Mr. Keynes' Views on the Transfer Problem: A Rejoinder', *Economic Journal*, September 1925, 400–4

Redvers Opie, 'Marshall's Time Analysis', *Economic Journal*, June 1931, 198–215

D. Wayne Parsons, 'Keynes and the Politics of Ideas', *History of Political Thought*, Summer 1983, 367–92

——, 'Newton the Man and Keynes the Economist', *Papers in Public Policy*, Series I, Number 3, 1991, Public Policy Research Unit, Queen Mary and Westfield College, London University

Talcott Parsons, 'Wants and Activities in Marshall', *Quarterly Journal of Economics*, xlvi, November 1931, 101–40

——, 'Economics and Sociology: Marshall in Relation to the Thought of His Time', *Quarterly Journal of Economics*, xlvii (February 1932) 316–47

Don Patinkin, 'The Chicago Tradition, the Quantity Theory, and Friedman', *Journal of Money, Credit and Banking*, February 1969, 46–70

——, 'The Collected Writings of John Maynard Keynes: From the *Tract* to *The General Theory*', *Economic Journal*, June 1975, 249–69

——, 'Friedman on the Quantity Theory and Keynesian Economics', *Journal of Political Economy*, September/October 1972, 883–905

——, 'In Defence of IS-LM', *Banca Nazionale del Lavoro Quarterly Review*, March 1990, 119–34

——, 'In Search of the "Veil of Money" and the "Neutrality of Money": A Note on the Origin of Terms', *Scandinavian Journal of Economics*, 91, 1989, 131–46

——, 'On Different Interpretations of *The General Theory*', *Journal of Monetary Economics*, 26, 1990, 205–43

Karl Pearson, 'Influence of Parental Alcoholism', *Journal of the Royal Statistical Society* (January 1911) 221–9

G. C. Peden, 'Sir Richard Hopkins and the "Keynesian Revolution" in Employment Policy 1929–45', *Economic History Review*, 2nd series, 36, 1983

——, 'The Treasury and Unemployment Policy in the later Nineteen-Thirties', *Oxford Economic Papers*, 32, no. 1, March 1980

——, 'Keynes, the Treasury and Unemployment in the Late 1930s', *Oxford Economic Papers*, March 1980, 1–18

A. F. W. Plumptre, 'Keynes in Cambridge', *Canadian Journal of Economics*, August 1947, 366–71, repr. in J. C. Wood (ed.), *John Maynard Keynes: Critical Assessments*, i, Croom Helm, 1983, 147–53

Pier Luigi Pona, 'Piero Sraffa 1898–1983', *Rivista Internationale di Scienze Economiche e Commerciale*, January 1984, 14–20

Jean-François Ponsot, 'Keynes and the "National Emission Caisse" of North Russia: 1918–1920', *History of Political Economy*, vol. 34, no. 1, 2002

J. R. Presley, 'J. M. Keynes and D. H. Robertson: Three Phases of Collaboration', *Research in the History of Economic Thought and Methodology*, 6, 1989, 31–46

——, 'J. M. Keynes and the Real Balance Effect', *Manchester School*, March 1986, 22–30

——, 'Marcel Labordère: A Neglected French Contribution to Trade Cycle Theory', *Kyklos*, vol. 2, 1979, 803–11

Frank Ramsey, 'Note on J. M. Keynes's *Treatise on Probability*', in *Cambridge Magazine*, Decennial Number 1912–21, 3–5

Melvin W. Reder, 'The Anti-Semitism of Some Eminent Economists', *History of Political Economy*, Vol. 32, no. 4, Winter 2000, pp. 833–56

J. P. Roach, 'Victorian Universities and the National Intelligentsia', *Victorian Studies* (December 1959) 131–50

D. H. Robertson, Review of JMK's *Economic Consequences of the Peace*, *Economic Journal*, March 1920, 77–84

——, 'Mr. Keynes's Theory of Money', *Economic Journal*, September 1931, 395–411

——, 'Some Notes on Mr. Keynes's General Theory of Employment', *Quarterly Journal of Economics*, November 1936, 169–91

H. M. Robertson, 'J. M. Keynes and Cambridge in the 1920s', *South African Journal of Economics*, September 1983, 407–18

E. A. G. Robinson, 'John Maynard Keynes 1883–1946', *Economic Journal*, March 1947, 1–68, repr. in John Cunningham Wood (ed.), *John Maynard Keynes: Critical Assessments*, i, Croom Helm, 1983, 86–143

——, 'Keynes', *Dictionary of National Biography 1941–50*, 452–7

——, *John Maynard Keynes: Economist, Author, Statesman*, British Academy Lecture, Oxford University Press, 1971, 3–20

Joan Robinson, 'The International Currency Proposals', *Economic Journal*, 53, June 1943

——, 'A Parable of Saving and Investment', *Economica*, February 1933, 75–84

S. P. Rosenbaum, 'Keynes, Lawrence and Cambridge Revisited', *Cambridge Quarterly*, xi (1982) 252–64

——, 'The Intellectual Origins of the Bloomsbury Group', *Times Higher Educational Supplement*, 29 October 1982

W. W. Rostow, 'The Terms of Trade in Theory and Practice', *Economic History Review*, 2nd series, 3, 1950, 1–20

Roy J. Rotheim, 'Keynes and the Language of Probability and Uncertainty', *Journal of Post-Keynesian Economics*, Fall 1988, 82–99

Jacques Rueff, 'Mr. Keynes's Views on the Transfer Problem', *Economic Journal*, September 1929, 388–408

Bertrand Russell, Review of JMK's *Treatise on Probability*, in *Mathematical Gazette*, July 1922

Roger J. Sandilands, 'Guilt by Association? Lauchlin Currie's Alleged Involvement with Washington Economists in Soviet Espionage', *History of Political Economy*, 32, no. 3, 2000

Roberta and David Schaefer, 'The Political Philosophy of J. M. Keynes', *Public Interest*, Spring 1983, 45–61

Stephen A. Schuker, 'The Collected Writings of John Maynard Keynes, volumes 17 and 18', *Journal of Economic Literature*, March 1980, 124–6

R. Skidelsky, 'Keynes and the Reconstruction of Liberalism', *Encounter*, April 1979, 29–39

———, 'Verdicts on Versailles', review of vols 17 and 18 of JMK's Collected Writings, *Times Literary Supplement*, 13 September 1978

Gregor W. Smith and R. Todd Smith, 'Stochastic Process Switching and the Return to Gold 1925', *Economic Journal*, March 1990, 164–73

Arthur Smithies, 'Keynes Revisited', *Quarterly Journal of Economics*, August 1972, 463–75

———, 'Schumpeter and Keynes', *Review of Economics and Statistics*, May 1951, 163–9

P. Sraffa, 'Dr. Hayek on Money and Capital', *Economic Journal*, March 1932, 42–53; F. A. Hayek, 'Money and Capital: A Reply', *ibid.*, June 1932, 237–49; P. Sraffa, 'A Rejoinder', *ibid.*, 249–51

———, 'The Laws of Return under Competitive Conditions', *Economic Journal*, December 1926, 535–50

George Steiner, 'Reflections: The Cleric of Treason', *New Yorker*, 8 December 1980

Richard Stone, *Keynes, Political Arithmetic and Econometrics*, Seventh Keynes Lecture in Economics, British Academy, 1978

L. Tarshis, 'Changes in Real and Money Wages', *Economic Journal*, March 1939, 150–4

Stephen Toulmin, 'Moore: G. E. Moore and the Cambridge Apostles by Paul Levy', *New Republic*, 30 August 1980

Richard Toye, 'Keynes and the Labour Movement, and "How to Pay for the War"', *Twentieth Century British History*, 10, no. 3, 1999

J. A. Trevithick, 'Keynes, Inflation and Money Illusion', *Economic Journal*, 86, March 1975

Sean Turnell, 'A Clearing Union or a Stabilising Fund? Australian Economists and the Creation of the IMF', Macquarie Economics Research Papers, no. 11/98

Thorstein Veblen: Review of *The Economic Consequences of the Peace*, in *Political Science Quarterly*, xxxv (October 1920) 467–72

David Vines, Review of R. Skidelsky, *Keynes* vol. iii, in *Economic Journal*, June 2003

Jens Warming, 'International Difficulties Arising out of the Financing of Public Works during a Depression', *Economic Journal*, June 1932, 211–24

N. Wedd, 'Goldie Dickinson: The Latest Cambridge Platonist', *Criterion*, xii, no. xlvii (January 1933) 175–83

Bernard Williams, 'The Point of View of the Universe: Sidgwick and the Ambitions of Ethics', *Cambridge Review*, 7 May 1982

Philip Williamson, 'A "Bankers' Ramp"?: Financiers and the British Political Crisis of August 1931', *English Historical Review*, October 1984, 770–806

E. G. Winslow, 'Keynes and Freud: Psychoanalysis and Keynes's Account of the "Animal Spirits" of Capitalism', *Social Research*, Winter 1986, 549–78

———, 'Bloomsbury, Freud and the Vulgar Passions', *Social Research*, Winter 1990, 785–819

———, '"Human Logic" and Keynes's Economics', *Eastern Economic Journal*, Autumn 1986, 413–30

———, 'John Maynard Keynes's "Poetical Economy"', *Journal of Psychohistory*, Fall 1989, 179–94

UNPUBLISHED WORK

Peter Barberis, 'The Keynesian Revolution in Whitehall: An Assessment', Manchester Polytechnic, September 1987

Paul Bareau, 'Anglo-American Financial Relations during and since the War', four lectures delivered at the LSE, 1951. In the possession of Peter Bareau

Ingo Barens, 'From the "Banana Parable" to the Principle of Effective Demand', Bergische University, Wuppertal, Germany, undated

Edward M. Bernstein, 'Reflections on Bretton Woods', first of three papers on 'The Fortieth Anniversary of the Bretton Woods Conference', 18 May 1984

Russell Brent Jones, 'The Wages Problem in Employment Policy 1936–48', M.Sc. (Bristol University), 1983

N. Brown, 'Reminiscences of Keynes', speech at the University of Essex, 14 December 1971

Bruce Craig, 'Treasonable Doubt: The Harry Dexter White Case', PhD, American University, 1999

J. A. Hemery, 'The Emergence of Treasury Influence in the Management of British Foreign Policy', M. Phil., Cambridge, 1982

Toshiaki Hirai, 'A Study of Keynes: From *A Treatise on Money* to *The General Theory*', 1988

Jesper Jesperson, 'Introduction to the Papers on New Interpretations of Keynes' Economic Theory and Method', Roskilde University, November 1990

Bruce Littleboy, 'Conventions: Their Role in Keynes's System and their Broader Significance', 1990

———, 'Why Economists Disagree about Keynes', 1989

Donald Markwell, 'John Maynard Keynes and International Relations: Idealism, Economic Paths to War and Peace, and Post-war Reconstruction', DPhil, Oxford University, 1995

Marcus Miller and Alan Sutherland, '"Speculative" Anticipations and the Return to Gold in 1925', University of Warwick and Centre for Economic Policy Research, February 1991

R. M. O'Donnell, 'Keynes: Philosophy and Economics: An Approach to Rationality and Uncertainty', D.Phil., Cambridge University, 1982

T. J. O'Shaughnessy, 'Short-Period and Long-Period Interpretations of the Principle of Effective Demand', King's College, Cambridge, 1984

Don Patinkin, 'On the Chronology of *The General Theory*,' Hebrew University of Jerusalem, March 1992

Lorie Tarshis, 'The Keynesian Revolution: What it meant in the 1930s', undated

VENONA: http://www.nsa.gov:8080/docs/venona

Richard Wright, 'On "Madmen" and "Defunct Economists"', Cambridge University, June 1987

References

These reference notes are intended to be used in conjunction with the Bibliography. Books or articles listed in the Bibliography have been cited by author alone – or if the author has several works listed, by author and short title. The following abbreviations have been used:

ACP – Austen Chamberlain Papers
AER – *American Economic Review*
BE – Bank of England
BL – British Library
BLH – Baker Library, Harvard University
BUL – Birmingham University Library
CAB – Cabinet Papers
CAMJE – *Cambridge Journal of Economics*
CC – Churchill College, Cambridge
CEH – *Central European History*
CJE – *Canadian Journal of Economics*
CMP – Christabel Maclaren Papers
CP – Charleston Papers
CR – *Cambridge Review*
CUL – Cambridge University Library
CW – *The Collected Writings of John Maynard Keynes + vol.*
DG – Duncan Grant
DGP – Duncan Grant Papers
DNB – *The Dictionary of National Biography*
ECP – *The Economic Consequences of the Peace*
EcHR – *Economic History Review*
EJ – *Economic Journal*
EGP – Emmanuel Goldweiser Papers
EMFP – E. M. Forster Papers
ER – *Economic Record*
FAK – Florence Ada Keynes
FDRP – Franklin Delano Roosevelt Papers
FFP – Felix Frankfurter Papers
FO – Foreign Office Papers

FRUS – *Foreign Relations of the United States*
GLK – Geoffrey Langdon Keynes
GLS – Giles Lytton Strachey
HBD – Harold Bowen's Diary
HC – Henrietta Couper
HCP – Henry Clay Papers
HDHP – Hubert Henderson Papers
HGWP – H. G. Wells Papers
HLL – House of Lords Library
HPE – *History of Political Economy*
IFP – Irving Fisher Papers
IJE – *Indian Journal of Economics*
ILR – *International Labour Review*
JASA – *Journal of American Statistical Association*
JASP – J. A. Schumpeter Papers
JBS – James Strachey
JEL – *Journal of Economic Literature*
JF – *Journal of Finances*
JGP – J. L. Garvin Papers
JMH – *Journal of Modern History*
JMK – John Maynard Keynes
JNK – John Neville Keynes
JNKP – J. N. Keynes Papers
JPE – *Journal of Political Economy*
JRCP – J. R. Commons Papers
JRHP – J. R. Hammond Papers
JRSS – *Journal of the Royal Statistical Society*
JTSP – J. T. Sheppard Papers
KC – King's College, Cambridge
KP – Keynes Papers
LBMR – *Lloyd's Bank Monthly Review*

LGP – Lloyd George Papers
LK – Lydia Keynes
LL – Lydia Lopokova
LLKP – Lydia Lopokova Keynes Papers
MD – Morgenthau Diaries
MG – Mathematical Gazette
MHP – Monk's House (Woolf) Papers
MLK – Margaret Keynes (later Hill)
MP – Marshall Papers
MPP – Macmillan Publishers Papers
MS – Manchester School
NBER – National Bureau of Economic
    Research
NP – New Palgrave Dictionary of
    Economics
NWP – Nathaniel Wedd Papers
OEP – Oxford Economic Papers
OMP – Ottoline Morrell Papers
OTFP1 – O. T. Falk Papers (British
    Library)
OTFP2 – O. T. Falk Papers (in possession
    of Mrs Roland Falk)
PBA – Proceedings of the British Academy
PH – Polly Hill
PI – Public Interest
PLP – Pethick-Lawrence Papers
PQ – Political Quarterly
PREM – Premier's Papers
PRO – Public Record Office
PSIF – Princeton Studies in International
    Finance
PSQ – Political Science Quarterly
q. – quoted in

QJE – Quarterly Journal of Economics
QR – Quarterly Review
RBP – Robert Brand Papers
RES – Review of Economic Studies
RF – Roger Fry
RFKP – Richard Kahn Papers
RHBP1 – Brand Papers (in Bodleian)
RHBP2 – Brand Papers (in possession of
    the Ford family)
RHETM – Research in the History of
    Economic Thought and
    Methodology
RHP – Ralph Hawtrey Papers
RLP – Russell Leffingwell Papers
RS – Richard Shone
RSE – Review of Social Economy
SAJE – South African Journal of
    Economics
SK – Simon Keynes
SP – Strachey Papers
SR – Social Research
SRO – Scottish Record Office
SSP – Sebastian Sprott Papers
TC – Tuesday Club
TCC – Trinity College, Cambridge
TLP – Thomas Lamont Papers
TLS – The Times Literary Supplement
T – Treasury
TP – Treasury Papers
VB – Vanessa Bell
VBP – Vanessa Bell Papers
VW – Virginia Woolf
WLP – Walter Lippmann Papers

1. Dynastic Origins

1. P. H. Reaney: *A Dictionary of British Surnames* (3rd Imp., 1966).
2. This is JMK's version. Dr Simon Keynes in 'The Dissemination of a Norman Family' (unpublished schoolboy essay) omits the intermediate Ralph.
3. SK, JMK to Mrs Keynes, Kenynton, S. Australia, 20 May 1907.
4. *Ibid.*
5. FAK, *Gathering*, 3.
6. *Ibid.*, 46.
7. *Ibid.*, 45.
8. Bellot, 298.
9. JNK Diary, 1 June 1870.
10. PH, Anna Keynes to JNK, 13 February 1871.
11. JNK Diary, 21 January 1873.

12. PH, JNK to John Keynes, 19 October 1872, to Anna Keynes, 20 October 1872.
13. JNK Diary, 20 February 1873.
14. *Ibid.*, 16 August 1873.
15. *Ibid.*, 13 March 1875.
16. *Ibid.*, 13 June 1874.
17. *Ibid.*, 26 January 1875.
18. CUL. Add. 7562, Item 7.
19. JNK Diary, 16 March, 31 August 1875.
20. *Ibid.*, 10, 11 August 1876.
21. 'Woman's Hour', transcript of FAK's interview with Ruth Drew, 1951; published in *The Listener*, 12 July 1951.
22. FAK, *Gathering*, 29–32.
23. GLK, *Gates*, 12.
24. PH, FAK typescript 'On Growing Old'.
25. FAK, *Gathering*, 33.
26. The information is pieced together from John Keynes's will and JNK's Diary.
27. JNK Diary, e.g. 22 September 1881, 28 July 1882.
28. *Ibid.*, 25 June, 18 July 1882.
29. *Ibid.*, 5 October 1881.
30. *Ibid.*, 21 February 1882.
31. *Ibid.*, 7 February 1881.
32. *Ibid.*, 31 August, 15, 16 September 1881.
33. *Ibid.*, 31 December 1881.
34. *Ibid.*, 24 January 1882.
35. *Ibid.*, 23 July 1882, reference to 1881.
36. *Ibid.*, 25 January 1882.
37. *Ibid.*, 21 October 1881.
38. *Ibid.*, 13 June 1881.
39. *Ibid.*, 28 February, 13 March 1881.
40. *Ibid.*, 25–27 February 1882.
41. *Ibid.*, 30 April 1882.
42. *Ibid.*, 30 April 1882.
43. *Ibid.*, 30 July 1882.
44. PH, Ada Brown to FAK, 17 October 1882.
45. JNK Diary, 13 October 1882.
46. *Ibid.*, 30 July 1882.
47. *Ibid.*, 8 August 1882.
48. *Ibid.*, 10 August 1882.
49. *Ibid.*, 13 August 1882.
50. *Ibid.*, 30 September 1882.
51. *Ibid.*, 11 October 1882.
52. KP, PP/45, John Brown to FAK, 6 June 1883.

2. Cambridge Civilisation: Sidgwick and Marshall

1. Mill, *Autobiography*, 225–6.
2. Quotations from Paley, Sedgwick and Whewell all from Schneewind, 105, 124,

150. This book has influenced my discussion of the Victorian search for 'doctrine'.
3. Rothblatt *The Revolution of the Dons: Cambridge and Society in Victorian England*.
4. See for example Wiener.
5. Schneewind, 163–6.
6. Sidgwick, 463–4.
7. A. and E. M. Sidgwick, 347.
8. *Ibid.*, 466–7.
9. Harrod, *Keynes*, 2, 214–5.
10. *CW*, x, 167.
11. Foxwell, 'Economic Movement in England'.
12. JNKP, 3:81, JSN to JNK; 27 July 1890.

3. Growing up in Cambridge

1. GLK in M. Keynes, *Essays*, 26.
2. JNK Diary, 8 July 1883.
3. *Ibid.*, 10 January 1889.
4. FAK, *By-Ways*, xix.
5. JNK Diary, 12 June 1895.
6. *Ibid.*, 26, 30 September, 3 October 1896.
7. *Ibid.*, 27 July 1898.
8. *Ibid.*, 22 February, 17 March 1890.
9. *Ibid.*, 9 December 1883.
10. *Ibid.*, 30 June, 10 November 1895.
11. FAK, *Gathering*, 65.
12. Marshall, *Principles* (8th edn.), 59.
13. JNK Diary, 30 March 1891.
14. *Ibid.*, 18 June 1883.
15. *Ibid.*, 5 February 1885.
16. *Ibid.*, 9 April 1886.
17. KP, PP/45, JNK to JMK, 13 July 1891.
18. JNK Diary, 10 February 1884.
19. *Ibid.*, 11 November 1885.
20. KP, PP/45, JNK to JMK, 29 January 1901.
21. For Neville's attitude to Florence's C.O.S. work see JNK Diary, 6 February 1897.
22. *Ibid.*, 25 October 1883.
23. Professor D. D. Merrill to author, 22 June 1999.
24. JNK Diary, 1 February 1885.
25. *Ibid.*, 6 June 1885.
26. q. *ibid.*, 2 June 1885.
27. Marshall, *Early Writings*, i, 18.
28. JNK Diary, 13, 14 January 1888.
29. *Ibid.*, 28 January 1888.
30. JNKP, 1:27, Foxwell to JNK, 15 January 1888.
31. JNK Diary, 21 April 1888.
32. JNKP, 3:B0, JNK to F. Edgeworth, 14 December 1890.

33. F. Y. Edgeworth, 'The Method of Political Economy', *Nature*, 26 February 1891, 387.
34. JNK Diary, 14 June 1891.
35. *Ibid.*, 17 January 1891.
36. JNKP, 1:101, Marshall to JNK, 18 March 1891.
37. JNK Diary, 26 March 1892.
38. CUL, Add. 7562: 72.
39. JNK Diary, 6, 10 June 1883.
40. PH, FAK to JNK, 31 July 1883.
41. JNK Diary, 4 November 1885.
42. Interview with GLK, 6 September 1979.
43. JNK Diary, 21 October 1894.
44. GLK, *Gates*, 19.
45. See JNK Diary, 31 August 1889, 18 April, 26 July, 15 August 1890; 14 June, 7 November 1891.
46. M. Keynes, *Essays*, 28–9.
47. GLK, *Gates*, 24.
48. JNK Diary, 11 August 1889.
49. *Ibid.*, 11 March 1885.
50. *Ibid.*, 11 February 1888.
51. *Ibid.*, 19 August 1888.
52. *Ibid.*, 2 December 1888.
53. *Ibid.*, 13, 17 April 1889.
54. *CW*, x, 213.
55. M. Keynes, *Essays*, 29.
56. JNK Diary, 14 March, 28 September 1892.
57. *Ibid.*, 30 April 1893.
58. *Ibid.*, 6 October 1893.
59. q. *ibid.*, 4 April 1896.
60. *Ibid.*, 5 November 1895.
61. M. Keynes, *Essays*, 29.
62. JNK Diary, 26 June, 28 June 1897.
63. *Ibid.*, 4–8 July 1897.
64. KP, PP/45, JNK, Diary, 23 August 1897.

4. Eton

1. L. E. Jones, 152, 176f.
2. *Ibid.*, 165.
3. Crick, 48.
4. M. Keynes, *Essays*, 31.
5. This was what Hope-Jones, one of Maynard's election, told Sir Roy Harrod; see Harrod, *Keynes*, 16–17.
6. q. Harrod, *Keynes*, 50.
7. KP, PP/45. The letter is addressed to 'Adolphe', which was Keynes's name for Knox.
8. JMK to DG, 22 December 1908.
9. JMK to JNK, 20 May 1900.

10. Dr G. E. Hale to FAK, 9 November 1900.
11. JMK to JNK, 21 October 1900.
12. JNK to JMK, 28 October 1901; S. G. Lubbock to Nathaniel Wedd, 9 May 1901. (Wedd Papers, III).
13. JMK to JNK, 17 December 1901, quoting from Leigh's letter.
14. Harrod, *Keynes*, 45.
15. JNK Diary, 31 March 1902.
16. *Ibid.*, 16 July 1902.
17. KC unclassified, B. W. Swithinbank, 'Note on Eton in JMK's Time' dated 9 March 1948.
18. JMK to FAK, 10 July 1902.

5. The Cambridge Undergraduate

1. Browning, 15.
2. Wingfield-Stratford, 145.
3. KP, PP/45.
4. Wilkinson, *Century*, 13.
5. Wingfield-Stratford, 151.
6. JNK Diary, 15 October 1902.
7. KP, PP/45, JMK to Swithinbank, 10 December 1902.
8. *Ibid.*, 17 December 1902.
9. JNK Diary, 12, 18 February 1903.
10. Levy, 66.
11. Russell, i, 66.
12. Stephen Toulmin, reviewing Levy's *Moore* in the *New Republic*, 30 August 1980.
13. JMK to GLS, 18 October 1905.
14. *Granta*, 28 November 1903; JNK Diary, 29 November 1903.
15. JNK Diary, 12 September 1903.
16. *Granta*, 28 January 1905.
17. JNK Diary, 15, 16 June 1904.
18. C. R. Fay in M. Keynes, *Essays*, 37.
19. Russell, i, 71.
20. JMK to GLS, 20 July 1904.
21. Russell, i, 72.
22. L. Woolf, *Sowing*, 201.
23. KP, PP/45, G. M. Trevelyan to JMK ?1904.
24. q. Holroyd, *Lytton Strachey*, ii, 211–12.
25. *Ibid.*, 213; Holroyd calls Hobhouse 'Sir Edgar Duckworth'.
26. Russell, i. 74.
27. KP, PP/45.
28. *CR*, 16 March 1905.
29. JNK Diary, 20 June 1905.

6. My Early Beliefs

1. MacIntyre, *After Virtue*, 63.
2. q. Levy, 223–5.
3. L. Woolf, *Sowing*, 131.
4. Russell, i, 64.
5. Russell to Alys Pearsall Smith, 18, 21 February 1894, q. Levy, 125–6.
6. Levy, 105.
7. *Ibid.*, 179–81.
8. *CW*, x, 444, 'My Early Beliefs'.
9. *Ibid.*, 438.
10. KP, PP/45, Norton to JMK c. 1906.
11. q. Levy, 198–9.
12. *Ibid.*, 145.
13. Moore, *Principia Ethica*, 188.
14. *Ibid.*, 189.
15. *Ibid.*, 27.
16. *CW*, x, 436.
17. *Ibid.*, 436–7.
18. *Ibid.*, 442.
19. *Ibid.*, 445–6.
20. *Ibid.*, 447–9.
21. *Ibid.*, 446.
22. *Ibid.*, 447.
23. Russell, i, 70–1; L. Woolf, *Sowing*, 148–9.
24. Harrod, *Keynes*, 76–81.
25. In M. Keynes, *Essays*, 242–6.
26. Leavis, 'Keynes, Lawrence and Cambridge', reprinted from *The Common Pursuit* (1953) in Rosenbaum, 391.
27. KP, UA/21.
28. *Ibid.*, paper to Apostles 'read again' on 22 January 1921.
29. KP, UA/20.
30. *Ibid.*, 16–7, 95.
31. *Ibid.*

7. Cambridge and London

1. JMK to GLS, 15 October 1905.
2. JMK to GLS, 20 January 1906.
3. JMK to GLS, 24 October 1905.
4. GLS to JMK, 4 November 1905.
5. JMK to GLS, 6 November 1905.
6. *CW*, xv, 2.
7. JMK to GLS, 3 February 1906.
8. KP, PP/45.
9. GLS to DG, 24 March 1906.
10. JMK to GLS, 1 March 1907.

11. JMK to JNK, 1 March 1907.
12. JMK to FAK, 17 March 1907.
13. KP, PP/45, R. C. Trevelyan to JMK, 16 March 1907.
14. JMK to GLS, 13 July 1907.
15. JMK to JNK, 4 September 1907.
16. KP, JMK, *The Principles of Probability*. The quotation is from the 1908 version of his thesis.
17. *CW*, xv, 15–17; KP, PP/45, TP/B, 1 July 1908.
18. BL, India Office Library, Public Works Dept. Orders and Memoranda, L/P/WD 528, no. 133.
19. *CW*, xv, 17.

8. Lytton, Duncan, Maynard

1. Holroyd, *Lytton Strachey*, i., 262.
2. GLS to JBS, 14 July 1908.
3. Holroyd, *Lytton Strachey*, i, 338.
4. JMK to DG, 24 July 1908.
5. JMK to JNK, 13 September 1908.
6. RS, 'Maynard Keynes as a Picture Buyer', Notes for BBC talk by Grant.
7. JMK to DG, 24 October 1908.
8. GLS to JBS, 27 October 1908.
9. JBS to GLS, 2 November 1908.
10. GLS to JBS, 23 November 1908.
11. JMK to DG, 20 November 1908.
12. JMK to DG, 24 November 1908.
13. JNK Diary, 4 December 1908.
14. JMK to DG, 22 December 1908.
15. JMK to DG, 31 January 1909.
16. JMK to MLK, 7 January 1909.
17. JMK to DG, 26 December 1908.
18. JMK to DG, 22 January 1909.
19. JMK to DG, 8 February 1909.

9. Pre-War Economic Interests

1. JMK to JNK, 10 April 1908.
2. *CW*, xv, 46–7.
3. Hutchison, *EcHR*, February 1973.
4. KP, PP/45.
5. JMK to Dundas, 30 September 1905.
6. *CW*, ii, 6.
7. Dalton, *Call Back Yesterday*, 157–8.
8. CUL, Add. 7562, Item 229.
9. JMK to DG, 19 January 1909.
10. JMK to DG, 20 January 1909.
11. JMK to DG, 24 October 1909.

12. JMK to DG, 16 February 1909.
13. KP, UA/34, 'Can We Consume our Surplus or the Influence of Furniture on Love', Paper read to Apostles *c.* 1909.
14. KP, Correspondence L/12. Angell to JMK, 19 February 1912.
15. See Presley, 37–8.
16. Marshall, *Principles of Economics*, 51.
17. *CW*, xii, 701–2, 730–1.
18. *Ibid.,* 760.
19. *Ibid., 696.*
20. *Ibid.,* 714–18.
21. *Ibid.,* 764.
22. *Ibid.,* 707–8.
23. *CW*, xiii, 2–14.
24. *CW*, xii, 755.
25. Stone, 7th Keynes Lecture, 3 May 1978.
26. *CW*, xi, 8.
27. JMK to DG, 18 December 1908.
28. *CW*, xi, 104f.
29. *CW*, viii, 349. See R. M. O'Donnell, ch. 10 for an illuminating discussion.
30. *CW*., xii, 767.

10. Private Lives

1. Dennis Robertson in *Basileon,* June 1911.
2. JMK to DG, 11 February 1909.
3. Wilkinson, *A Century of King's*, 51.
4. SP, Add. MSS 60668, DG to JBS, 22 April 1909.
5. GLS to JBS, 25 June 1909.
6. GLK's memoir of Henry James's visit, 'Henry James at Cambridge' (1967), is reproduced in *Gates*, 64–80.
7. JBS to GLS, 1 October 1909.
8. CUL, Hilton Young, 'In and Out', 25: Kennet Papers, 82/1.
9. Virginia Stephen to Vanessa Bell, 19 April 1911, N. Nicolson (ed.), *The Letters of Virginia Woolf,* i, 462.
10. Clarke, *Liberals and Social Democrats*, 132.
11. Jackson and Vos, 79–87.
12. The quotations from Virginia Woolf are from her *Moments of Being,* 164, 169, 172.
13. CP, Box 3, Item 30.
14. V. Woolf, *Moments of Being,* 126.
15. CP: Box 18, Item 7.
16. L. Woolf, *Beginning Again*, 35–7.
17. DG to JMK, 28 February 1910.
18. CP, Box 12, Item 1.
19. Garnett, *Golden Echo*, 207.
20. *CW*, viii, 241.
21. JMK to DG, 13 August 1910.
22. JBS to GLS, 29 August 1911.

23. JMK to JNK, 14 July 1911.
24. JMK to JNK, 29 June 1911.
25. JMK to GLS, 17 July 1911.
26. JMK to GLS, 8 September 1911.
27. JMK to DG, 7 September 1911.
28. JMK to DG, 12 March 1911.
29. KP, PP/45, JMK correspondence with Sarkar.
30. JMK to FAK, 24 September 1911.

11. An Indian Summer

1. KP, PP/45 (unclassified), G. H. Luce to JMK, 7 October 1913.
2. JMK to DG, 12 February 1913, 19 September 1912; JMK to FAK, 17 September 1912.
3. KP, L31, Waterlow to JMK, 6 October 1931; JMK to GLS, 13 October 1912.
4. JMK to DG, 15 November 1912.
5. KP, PP/45, Wittgenstein to JMK, 16 July 1913.
6. KP, PP/45, Rose to JMK.
7. Holroyd, *Lytton Strachey*, ii, 28.
8. KP, PP/45, JMK to MLK, 12 February 1911.
9. JMK to DG, 12 February 1913.
10. Q. Bell, *Virginia Woolf*, i, 175.
11. CP: Box 12, Item 9, V. Bell to C. Bell, 11 October 1911.
12. Virginia Stephen to Ottoline Morrell, 9 November 1911; to L. Woolf, 2 December 1911; N. Nicolson (ed.), *The Letters of Virginia Woolf*, i, 480, 484.
13. GLK, *Gates*, 115.
14. V. Woolf to K. Cox, 4 September 1912, N. Nicolson (ed.), *The Letters of Virginia Woolf*, ii, 6.
15. JMK to DG, 3 February 1911.
16. KP, Correspondence L/12, Leaf to JMK, 8 February 1912.
17. JMK to DG, 23 November 1911.
18. *CW*, xv, 62.
19. JMK to M. Macmillan, 12 August 1910, BL, Add. MSS 55201.
20. JMK, *Indian Currency and Finance*, *CW*, i, 51.
21. *Ibid.*, 124-6.
22. *Ibid.*, 165-6.
23. *Ibid.*, 255.
24. Austen Chamberlain to JMK, 12 August 1913, *CW*, xv, 100.
25. Editor's summary of Abraham's memo, *CW*, xv, 131.
26. JMK to JNK, 13 August 1913.
27. q. B. Strachey, 289; see also Holroyd, *Lytton Strachey*, ii, 90.
28. *CW*, xv, 143.
29. For the whole memo, see 'An Indian State Bank', *CW*, xv, 151–203.
30. JMK to JNK, 11 January 1914.
31. FAK, *Gathering*.
32. *CW*, xv, 258–63.
33. A. Marshall to JMK, 9 March 1914, *CW*, xv, 268.
34. q. Shone, 135.

35. *Ibid.*, 101.
36. In her obituary of Diaghilev, repr. in M. Keynes, *Lopokova.*
37. Sitwell, 209.
38. JMK to JNK, 28 July 1914.

12. Adapting to War

1. *CW*, xvi, 7–15.
2. *Ibid.*, 16–19.
3. Morgan, 15–18; for the deeper issues, see De Cecco, ch. 7.
4. JMK, *EJ*, September 1914, 472; cited Morgan, 30.
5. KP, MPI:67. Cf. Sir Felix Schuster's letter to JMK of 30 November 1914 in KP, L/ 14, in which he assured Keynes that it had been the pressure of himself and Holden which had prevented the suspension of specie payments which was being urged by the Governor of the Bank of England.
6. *CW*, xi, 318–19; reprinted from *EJ*, November 1914.
7. TP, Montagu papers, 2072(1), JMK to Montagu, 4 September 1914.
8. *CW*, xvi, 36.
9. KP, PP/45. JMK to DG, 10 October 1914; JMK to Hardman, 25 October 1914.
10. Holroyd, *Lytton Strachey*, ii, 117.
11. GLS to JMK, 24 September 1914.
12. q. JNK Diary, 22 January 1915.
13: q. JNK Diary, 30 January 1915.
14. Garnett Diary, 1, 2 February 1915.
15. HLL, Bonar Law Papers, 107/2/67, JMK to Bonar Law, 10 October 1922.
16. *CW*, xvi, 67.
17. Quotations from a lecture 'The Civil Service and Financial Control' that JMK gave to the Society of Civil Servants in 1921, *CW*, xvi, 296–307.
18. Cited Harrod, *Keynes*, 201.
19. Garnett, *Flowers*, 21–3
20. Holroyd, *Lytton Strachey*, ii, 160.
21. CUL, Kennet Papers, 28/8, DG to Hilton Young, ?April 1915.
22. CP: Box 12, Item 118, V. Bell to C. Bell, Monday? 1915.
23. Clark, *Russell*, 260–1; Morrell, *Ottoline at Garsington*, ed. Gathorne-Hardy, 60.
24. A. E. Bell (ed.), *The Diary of Virginia Woolf*, i, 17, 13 January 1915.
25. Hazlehurst, 232.
26. *Ibid.*, 297.
27. Morrell, *Ottoline at Garsington*, ed. Gathorne-Hardy, 50.

13. Keynes and the First World War

1. See Lloyd George's speech in the Commons, 4 May 1915, q. Hazlehurst, 224.
2. *DNB*, 'McKenna'.
3. *CW*, xvi, 104. See also PRO: CAB 37/129/29.
4. *Ibid.*, 125–8. See also PRO: T 170/73.
5. Morgan, 355–6.
6. *CW*, xvi, 110–15.

7. *Ibid.*, H7–25; final version in PRO: T. 17085. See also JMK's note for the PM on the Financial Position, 30/10/15 in Asquith Papers (31–4).
8. Cooper, 'Command of Gold', 212.
9. Lloyd George, *War Memoirs*, ii, 684.
10. *CW*, xvi, 154.
11. Jenkins, *Asquith*, 388.
12. *Ibid.*, 387.
13. C. Bell, *Old Friends*.
14. KP, PP/7. This file contains all the material relating to Keynes's conscientious objection.
15. Holroyd, *Lytton Strachey*, ii, 172.
16. Garnett, *Flowers*, 97.
17. Jenkins, *Asquith*, 389.
18. q. Holroyd, *Lytton Strachey*, i, n, 172.
19. In M. Keynes, *Essays*, 68.
20. Holroyd, *Lytton Strachey*, ii, 172.
21. Levy in M. Keynes, *Essays*, 68
22. GLS to JBS, 22 February 1916.
23. Woodward, 220; see also Cooper, 'British Response'.
24. CP: Box 4:18.
25. Garnett, *Flowers*, 121.
26. *Ibid.*, 122.

14. Touch and Go

1. CP: Box 14: 6, C. Bell to V. Bell, ?May 1916.
2. Morrell, *Ottoline at Garsington*, ed. Gathorne-Hardy, 107.
3. q. Bedford, i, 69.
4. JMK to JNK, 5 June 1916.
5. *CW*, xvi, 213.
6. *Ibid.*, 189–96. See also PRO: CAB 37/151/9.
7. N. Nicolson (ed.), *The Letters of Virginia Woolf*, ii, 95, V. Woolf to V. Bell, 14 May 1916.
8. JMK to FAK, 29 October 1916.
9. Garnett, *Flowers*, 144–5; see also his *Great Friends*, 136.
10. *CW*, xvi, 197–209. JMK memoranda are dated 10, 24 October 1916.
11. Lloyd George, *War Memoirs*, ii, 854–5.
12. *CW*, xvi, 198.
13. *Ibid.*, 215–21.
14. MacFadycan, 64.
15. JMK to FAK, 30 March 1917.
16. Hemery, 90.
17. S. H. Hanke and Alan Walters (eds), *Capital Markets and Developments*, 43–63.
18. JMK to JNK, 29 May 1917.
19. *CW*, x, 34, JMK, 'Andrew Bonar Law'.
20. For an account see Burk, *EcHR*, 1979, 405–16.
21. *CW*, xvi, 249–50.
22. *Ibid*, 253–4. See also TP 172/443: 61–2.

23. Burk, *EcHR*, 415.
24. *CW*, xvi, 255–63.
25. Blake, 351–4.
26. JMK to FAK, 10 July 1917.
27. FAK to JMK, 1 August 1917.
28. JMK to FAK, 19 August 1917.
29. JMK to FAK, 28 September 1917.
30. 'He has been my mainstay out here in finance and has given me most valuable assistance.' Reading to Bonar Law, q. *CW*, xvi, 264.
31. CC, Spring Rice Papers, 2/13, n.d.
32. HLL: LGP, F. 23/1/25; F. 23/4/43, 8.
33. Blackett to Hamilton, 1 January 1918, q. *CW*, xvi, 264.
34. JMK to FAK, 15 December 1917.
35. JMK to DG, 15 December 1917.
36. JMK to Blackett, 30 January 1918, q. *CW*, xvi, 264.
37. For the whole memo see *CW*, xvi, 274–85.
38. JMK to Chalmers, 30 April 1918. *CW*, xvi, 290–3.
39. *CW*, xvi, 289–90.
40. *Ibid.*, 287.
41. JMK to FAK, 14 November 1917.
42. JMK to FAK, 24 December 1917.
43. FAK to JMK, 26 December 1917.
44. JMK to FAK, 10 February 1918.
45. For Maurice Debate, see Beaverbrook, *Men and Power*, 248–64.
46. JMK to FAK, 14 April 1918.
47. N. Nicolson (ed.), *The Letters of Virginia Woolf*, ii, 208, V. Woolf to Margaret Llewellyn Davies, 2 January 1918.
48. See JMK to DG, 26 June 1918. Duncan's commission fell through.
49. CP: Box 18, JMK to V. Bell, 23 March 1918.
50. JMK to FAK, 22 March 1918.
51. CP: Box 14: 44.
52. *Ibid.*, Box 17.
53. JMK to FAK, 3 November 1918.

15. Zigzagging: Keynes at the Paris Peace Conference

1. *CW*, xvi, 313–34.
2. *Ibid.*, 341.
3. *Ibid.*, 'Memorandum by the Treasury on the Indemnity Payable by the Enemy Powers for Reparation and Other Claims', 348, 357, 375, 378.
4. Bunselmeyer, 16.
5. Hancock and Poel, iv, Doc. 876.
6. *Ibid.*, iv, Doc. 871.
7. *CW*, x, 398, 'Dr Melchior'.
8. *Ibid.*, 399.
9. *Ibid.*, 395, 403.
10. *Ibid.*, 402–3.
11. For the 1924 dispute see BUL, ACP, AC 35/7/4–11; also *CW*, xvi, 406–15.

12. *CW*, xvi, 422.
13. BLH: TLP, 170–15, Reports of Admiral Hope and T. W. Lamont on meetings held at Spa, 4 and 5 March 1919.
14. *Ibid.*
15. *CW*, x, 413–15, 'Dr Melchior'.
16. *Ibid.*, 409.
17. *Ibid.*, 422–3.
18. *Ibid.*, 425–6.
19. JMK to FAK, 12 February 1919.
20. *CW*, x, 390, 'Dr Melchior'.
21. CP: Box 18, JMK to V. Bell, 16 March 1919.
22. BLH: TLP, 164–15; Norman Davis, 'Peace Conference Notes', 5 July 1919.
23. HLL, LGP, F/30/3/27.
24. Tillman, 239.
25. TCC, Montagu Papers, 249(1), memorandum by Montagu, 4 April 1919.
26. Lothian Papers, G040/17/64.
27. HLL, LGP, F/213/59.
28. q. Tillman, 241.
29. For the text of the Smuts memorandum see Hancock and Poel, iv, pp. 926–8.
30. See Hancock and Poel, vii, Doc. 841 Smuts to R. F. Harrod, 24 March 1949. Harrod's letter of inquiry to Smuts is in the Smuts Papers vol. 89, No. 5, 26 February 1949. I am indebted to Dr Iain Smith for giving me a copy of the Harrod letter.
31. BLH: TLP, 168–4, T. W. Lamont, 'Note of a Conversation with Woodrow Wilson', 3 April 1919.
32. John Foster Dulles Papers, Box 2, 79.
33. BLH: TLP, 166–11, 'Memorandum of Conference held 5 April at the President's House'. Present were Clemenceau, Klotz, Loucheur and de la Chaume (France), Lloyd George, Lord Sumner and Col. Hankey (G.B.); Col. House, Baruch, Davis, Lamont and McCormick (USA); and Orlando and Crespi (Italy).
34. *Ibid.*, 164–20. Typed copy of Florence C. Lamont's Diary.
35. *Ibid.*, 164–20. Florence C. Lamont's Diary, 4 May 1919; Diary of Vance McCormick, 22 May 1919.
36. Hancock, *Smuts*, i, 515.
37. CP: Box 18: 11. JMK to V. Bell, 20 January 1919.
38. Hancock and Poel, iv, Doc. 936.
39. *CW*, xvi, 418.
40. Hancock and Poel, iv, Doc. 943.
41. HLL: LGP, F/7/2/27; Austen Chamberlain to Lloyd George, 17 April 1919.
42. *CW*, xvi, 429–31.
43. *Ibid.*, 436.
44. BLH: TLP, 165–12; T. W. Lamont, 'Comments upon the so-called Keynes Memorandum as to European Credits'.
45. *CW*, xvi, 439; JMK to Bradbury, 4 May 1919.
46. q. *CW*, xvi, 441.
47. *Ibid.*, 442.
48. *Ibid.*, 450–6.
49. Tardieu, 120.
50. *Ibid.*, 298.

51. Hancock and Poel, iv, Doc. 962.
52. Bernard Baruch Papers, Section IV, Diary, 2 June 1919.
53. *CW*, x, 429, 'Dr Melchior'.

16. Civilisation Under Threat

1. Hancock and Poel, iv, Doc. 1012.
2. *Ibid.*, 1054.
3. q. *CW*, xvii, 4.
4. KP, PP/45.
5. Garnett, *Great Friends*, 140.
6. In KP, PP/45.
7. JMK to FAK, 23 September 1919.
8. KP, PP/45.
9. JMK to FAK, 3 September 1919.
10. *CW*, xvii, 5–6, Salter to JMK, 14 October 1919.
11. *Ibid.*, 6–7, JMK to Salter, 18 October 1919.
12. *Ibid.*, 7.
13. KP, EC/1/4
14. *CW*, ii, 9.
15. *Ibid.*, 7, 9–10.
16. *Ibid.*, 11–12.
17. *Ibid.*, 13.
18. *Ibid.*, 146.
19. *Ibid.*, 35.
20. *Ibid.*, 18.
21. *Ibid.*, 32.
22. *Ibid.*, 26.
23. *CW*, x, 23–4, *Essays in Biography*.
24. *CW*, ii, 34.
25. *Ibid.*, 91.
26. *Ibid.*, 126.
27. *Ibid.*, 164–5.
28. KP, PP/45.
29. KP, EC/1.
30. FAK Scrapbook, *New Europe*, 1 January 1920, xiii, 168.
31. *The Times*, 5 January 1920.
32. FAK Scrapbook. An editorial in the *Liverpool Courier*, 15 January 1920, referring to a speech by JMK to the Liverpool Branch of the League of Nations Union, said he had failed to mention the League once, and that his appearance on a League platform was likely to destroy confidence in the League. In *ECP* (*CW*, ii, 163–5) JMK doubted whether the League could become an effective instrument for revising the Treaty.
33. FAK Scrapbook, *TLS*, 15 January 1920.
34. Vance McCormick's remark is in a letter to Dulles dated 16 March 1920, in Dulles Papers, Box 3. For a symposium of Wilsonian views, see the *Bulletin* of the League of Nations Association, April 1920.

35. Baruch, 6, 8. For Keynes's review in the *Manchester Guardian* of 2 December 1920, see *CW*, xvii, 91–8. For the genesis of Baruch's book, see Schwarz, 153–60.
36. Poel, v, Doc. 32, JMK to Smuts, 22 October 1920.
37. *CW*, iii, 103–4.
38. Mantoux, 21–2.
39. *Ibid.*, 122–3.
40. *Ibid.*, 126.
41. *Ibid.*,121.
42. Harrod, *Keynes*, 276.

17. Keynes in the 1920s

1. E. A. G. Robinson, an ex-RAF pilot who had come up to Christ's College to read economics, recalled the 'burning sense of the world's stupidities which animated the lecturer'. In 'John Maynard Keynes 1883–1946'. *EJ*, March 1947, 1; repr. Wood (ed.), *John Maynard Keynes*, i, 102.
2. Steel, *Walter Lippmann*, 40.
3. JMK to LK, 12 November 1925.
4. GLS to VW, 28 September 1919; q. Holroyd, *Lytton Strachey*, ii, 372.
5. VW to Barbara Bagenal, 23 December 1920; Letter 1160 in N. Nicolson (ed.), *The Letters of Virginia Woolf*, ii.
6. CP, JMK to VB, 8 January 1919.
7. GLS to Carrington, 31 May 1920; q. Holroyd, *Lytton Strachey*, ii, 387.
8. SP, GLS to JBS, 26 November 1921.
9. A. E. Bell (ed.), *The Diary of Virginia Woolf*, ii, 33.
10. *Ibid.*, 69.
11. *Ibid.*, 120.
12. RLP: File 103–15.
13. WLP, File 1312.
14. *CW*, ix, p. xvii.
15. For details see *CW*, xvii, 148f.
16. Roseveare, *The Treasury*, 261f.
17. Bernard Baruch's *The Public Years* is a compendium of complaints against Keynes.
18. See *CW*, xx, 17.
19. Hubback, *No Ordinary Press Baron*, 64.
20. See *CW*, xii, 2.
21. Davenport, *Memoirs of a City Radical*, 50.
22. Roger Fry told Margery Fry on 21 June 1923 that Vanessa and Duncan 'always inspire his [Maynard's] picture purchases'. (Sutton (ed.), *Letters of Roger Fry*, ii. 453.) Keynes later said that he bought his Seurat from a 'bird of passage dealer' who told him it came from a Swiss or German collection. KP, PP/45, JMK to Félix Fénéon, 1 June 1936.

18. The Transition to Peace

1. GLS to Carrington, 4 September 1920; q. Holroyd, *Lytton Strachey*, ii, 389.
2. CP, DG to VB, 6 October 1920.
3. JMK to GLS, 20 May 1920.
4. CP, DG to VB, 20 September 1920.
5. C. H. Broad has written that 'we owe the publication of Johnson's great work to his pupil Miss Naomi Bentwich. It is unlikely that he would ever have brought himself to undergo the drudgery of preparing his scattered manuscripts for the press had she not relieved him of the labour, and almost driven him to face the task.' *PBA*, January 1931.
6. JMK, 'The Economic Chaos of Europe' from *Harmsworth's Universal History of the World*, 25 June 1929, q. *CW*, xi, 354.
7. *First Interim Report of the Committee on Currency and Foreign Exchanges after the War*, Cmd 9182, 1918.
8. Original in ACP, 35/1/8; also in *CW*, xvii, 179. Keynes wrote: 'I believe that the Treasury Minute, if it is maintained, must logically end in a very high bank rate and corresponding rate for Treasury Bills.'
9. Pigou, *Aspects of British Economic History*, 191.
10. OTFP1, OTF to JMK, 30 March 1920. In his letter Falk cited Blackett's 'optimism' about getting bank rate up, but thought this would be delayed.
11. Basil Blackett, the controller of finance at the Treasury, had already invested £400 with Keynes outside the Syndicate. There was obviously a potential clash of interest here.
12. *CW*, xii, 7.
13. JMK to FAK, 23 December 1920. The story of the speculation can be followed in KP, File SY.
14. E. V. Morgan, *Studies in British Financial Policy*, 209.
15. KP, UA/6.
16. Lloyd George, *The Truth about Reparations and War-Debts*, 33–53.
17. *CW*, xvii, 208–12.
18. *Ibid.*, 219–20, 216.
19. J. F. Dulles writing in the *New Republic*, 12 March 1921.
20. Lloyd George, *The Truth about Reparations and War-Debts*, 62.
21. q. Marks, 'Reparations Reconsidered: A Reminder', *CEH*, 1969, 358.
22. Lord D'Abernon's diary, 29 June 1921, q. *CW*, xvii, 240. Lord D'Abernon was British Ambassador to Germany.

19. Probability and Goodness

1. KP, UA/19. JMK, 'Ethics in Relation to Conduct', unpublished paper read to the Apostles, 23 January 1904. Moore's argument is on pp. 152–4 of his *Principia Ethica*. Keynes reproduces the gist of his 1904 paper in *Treatise on Probability*, 341–2.
2. See also O'Donnell, *Keynes: Philosophy, Economics and Politics*, 117–18.
3. *CW*, viii, 103–4.
4. *Ibid.*, 32.

5. *Ibid.*, 356.
6. *Ibid.*, 348.
7. *Ibid.*, 285.
8. *Ibid.*, 428.
9. Moore, *Principia Ethica*, 188–9.
10. *Ibid.*, 208f.
11. KP, UA/35.
12. Keynes's 1910/1921 paper to the Apostles, 'On the Principle of Organic Unity', is in KP, UA/35. JMK's letter to F. L. Lucas of 19 March 1928 is in KP, PP/45. In fact, Keynes's 'solution' was suggested by Moore, *Principia Ethica*, 219.
13. B. Russell, *MG*, xi, July 1922.
14. C. P. Sanger, *New Statesman*, 17 September 1921; *Spectator*, 24 September 1921.
15. KP, TP/1. JMK to C. D. Broad, 31 January 1922. KP, TP contains a collection of material relating to his TP.
16. *Ibid.*
17. Ramsey, *The Foundations of Mathematics*, 289.
18. *Ibid.*, 161.
19. *Ibid.*, 186.
20. *Ibid.*, 182.
21. Hollis, *The Cunning of Reason*, 106.
22. Ramsey, *The Foundations of Mathematics*, 192–9.
23. Braithwaite in Wright (ed.), *Cambridge University Studies*, 25.
24. Kolakowski, *Positivist Philosophy*, 237.
25. *CW*, x, 336–9.

20. Russian and German Affairs

1. *CW*, xvii, 245, 248–9.
2. JNK to JMK, 11 September 1921.
3. JMK to C. P. Scott, 14 September 1921; *CW*, xvii, 319.
4. JMK to VB, 12 December 1921.
5. Chandavarkar, *Keynes and India*, 49–50, is clearly pained by Keynes's last-minute withdrawal from the Commission, and explains that Keynes had been required to stay in India longer than he had planned. In fact, *CW*, xvii, 331–3, makes it plain that Keynes had asked to be released from the Commission before any extension of his service was mooted. Harrod, *Keynes*, 308–9, rightly surmised that the main motive for his withdrawal was that he had fallen in love with Lydia.
6. Beaumont, *Diaghilev Ballet in London*, 141, 139.
7. *Ibid.*, 117, 140.
8. Sokolova, *Dancing for Diaghilev*, 74.
9. JMK to VB, 24 February 1922.
10. JRHP, V.1.34, C. P. Scott to J. L. Hammond, 11 March, 24 January 1923.
11. 'The Theory of the Exchanges and Purchasing Power Parity' and 'The Forward Market in Foreign Exchanges'.
12. KP, GS/1/2.
13. OTFP1: Add. MS. 57923, JMK to OTF, 26 October 1921.

14. His articles were also carried by the *Daily Express* in London, by the *New York World* and by a number of European newspapers.
15. Hogan, *Informal Entente*, 44–5.
16. Schuker, *The End of French Predominance in Europe*, 16; Rupieper, *The Cuno Government and Reparations*, 9–10.
17. *CW*, xvii, 363–9.
18. Eichengreen (ed.), *The Gold Standard in Theory and Practice*, 202–3.
19. *CW*, xvii, 372–3.
20. D'Abernon, *An Ambassador of Peace*, ii, 91.
21. *CW*, xvii, 388.
22. *Ibid.*, 390–4.
23. D'Abernon, *An Ambassador of Peace*, i, 255.
24. A. O. Bell (ed.), *The Diary of Virginia Woolf*, ii, 26 May 1921, 120.
25. VBP, VB to RF, 11 April 1922.
26. A. O. Bell (ed.), *The Diary of Virginia Woolf*, ii, 19 July 1922, 183.
27. Lloyd George, *The Truth about Reparations and War-Debts*, 66–7.
28. Leffler, *The Elusive Quest*, 78.
29. *CW*, xviii, 17.
30. *Ibid.*, 39–43, 34.
31. Rowland, *Lloyd George*, 586.
32. D'Abernon, *An Ambassador of Peace*, ii, 122–3, 126–9. KP, F1/31/
33. *CW*, xviii, 71.
34. JMK to FAK, 22 December 1922.
35. *CW*, xviii, 97–9.
36. *Ibid.*, 86.
37. D'Abernon, *An Ambassador of Peace*, ii, 140.
38. Trachtenberg, *Reparation in World Politics*, 287.
39. *CW*, iii, 113.
40. *CW*, xviii, 103.
41. Grigg, *Prejudice and Judgment*, 101; q. Boyle, *Montagu Norman*, 156–7.
42. Marks, *The Illusion of Peace*, 50.
43. Ferrari Bravo, *Economic Diplomacy*, 11.
44. *CW*, xviii, 136.
45. *Ibid.*, 143.
46. *Ibid.*, 143–4.
47. *Ibid.*, 148.
48. *Ibid.*, 156.
49. Middlemas and Barnes, *Baldwin*, 180–1.
50. Ferrari Bravo, *Economic Diplomacy*, 52.
51. *CW*, xviii, 165.
52. 'Events of the Week', *Nation*, 16 July 1923; *CW*, xviii, 165.

21. Monetary Reform

1. Broadberry, 'Aggregate Supply in Inter-war Britain', *EJ* 1986; Pigou, *Aspects of British Economic History*, 63, 81. Pigou thought 'efficiency' had fallen since 1913 owing to 'war weariness'.
2. *CW*, xvii, 265.

3. *CW*, xix, 65–7.
4. Faith Henderson, 'Editing the Nation', 8.
5. KP, NS/1/1. Walter Layton to JMK, 17 February 1923.
6. Ackroyd, *T. S. Eliot*, 132.
7. MHP: E. M. Forster to Leonard Woolf, 15 May 1923. I am indebted to S. P. Rosenbaum for drawing my attention to this.
8. For the 'row' see HDHP: Box 21 for Leonard Woolf to Hubert Henderson, 26 September 1923, and Henderson's reply on 29 September 1923; also DGP for Vanessa Bell to Duncan Grant, 8 October 1923.
9. VBP, 80.10.8.352, VB to RF (undated).
10. The quarrel is recounted in HBD; see also KP, LLK1/1 for Vera Bowen to JMK 9 August 1923, and JMK's reply 12 August 1923. The gist of it was about whether Vera should pay Lydia a salary, or whether Lydia should pay Vera one.
11. HBD, 11, 17 June 1923.
12. The two quotations are from A. O. Bell (ed.), *The Diary of Virginia Woolf*, ii, 266, and N. Nicolson (ed.), *The Letters of Virginia Woolf*, iii, Letter 1432.
13. HBD, 22 September 1923.
14. LL to JMK, 28 October 1923; JMK to LL, 28 October, 2 November 1923.
15. *CW*, xix, 100, 101.
16. BE, ADM 16/34. On the other hand, Reginald McKenna, one of Keynes's staunchest allies, told Montagu Norman on 20 June that 'our Rates are too low & diff[eren]ce between 3 and 4% cd not really affect trade ...' (Montagu Norman's Diary, BE, ADM 20/10). *The Economist* under Walter Layton also thought the rise in bank rate would make little or no difference to actual interest rates.
17. *CW*, xix, 100.
18. *Ibid.*, 104
19. *Ibid.*, 107–12.
20. *Ibid.*, 111, 112.
21. *Ibid.*, 116.
22. Letter to *The Times*, 14 February 1923; *CW*, xix, 79.
23. W. Beveridge, *Economica*, February 1924.
24. *CW*, xix, 121.
25. *Ibid.*, 134, 124.
26. JMK to LL, 26 October 1923.
27. *CW*, xix, 151–2, 153, 155.
28. JMK to LL, 4 December 1923; LL to JMK, 24 November 1923.
29. *CW*, xix, 158–62.
30. *The Economist*, 4 June 1983.
31. The discussion of the effects of a changing price level was not novel in Cambridge. See Lavington, *The English Capital Market*, 54; D. H. Robertson, *Money*, 9.
32. *CW*, iv, 34.
33. *Ibid.*, 36.
34. *Ibid.*, 61.
35. *Ibid.*, 65.
36. *Ibid.*, 68.
37. *Ibid.*, 65–7. Cf. Kahn, *The Making of Keynes' General Theory*, 54.
38. *CW*, iv, 148–9.

39. *Ibid.*, 126.
40. *Ibid.*, 128.
41. *Ibid.*, 132–4.
42. *Ibid.*, 121.
43. *Ibid.*, 155.
44. *Ibid.*, 149–53.
45. *Ibid.*, 158–9.
46. R. G. Hawtrey, *EJ*, June 1924, 227.
47. *CW*, iv, 138.
48. *Ibid.*, 16.
49. *Ibid.*, 56–7.
50. Harrod, *Keynes*, 339.
51. J. C. Stamp in *JRSS*, 24 May 1924.
52. *TLS*, 17 January 1924.
53. See *Manchester Guardian*, 22 December 1923; *Westminster Gazette*, 19 January 1924.
54. JMK to LL, 27 January 1924.
55. KP, NS/1/1, JMK to Prof. Kurt Singer, 23 April 1925.

22. Gold and Marriage

1. LL to JMK, 19 January 1924.
2. KP, PP/45, G. L. Keynes to JMK, 16 February 1923.
3. LL to FAK, 21 February 1924.
4. LL to JMK, 14 January 1924.
5. HBD, 1 April 1924.
6. LL to JMK, 5 May 1924.
7. JMK to LL, 14 May 1924.
8. JMK to LL, 15 May 1924.
9. JMK to LL, 1 June 1924.
10. HBD, 15 June 1924.
11. Schumpeter, *Ten Great Economists*, 271–2n.
12. N. Nicolson (ed.), *The Letters of Virginia Woolf*, iii, VW to J. Raverat, 8 June 1924, 115.
13. A lecture on 'The State and Foreign Investment', delivered before the University of Cambridge on 11 February 1924, was shortened and amended for a talk to the Liberal Summer School at Oxford on 2 August 1924; it was published in the *Nation* on 9 August, with a further comment in the *Manchester Guardian Commercial* Supplement on 21 August. The series concluded with a lecture on foreign investment to the Edinburgh Chamber of Commerce on 12 December 1924. The two unpublished lectures are in KP, PS/2.
14. *CW*, xix, 285–8. In his Cambridge lecture Keynes said, 'In short, the nineteenth century, as in so many other respects, came to look on an arrangement as normal which was really most abnormal. To lend vast sums abroad for long periods of time without any possibility of legal redress if things go wrong, is a crazy construction; specially in return for trifling extra interest.'
15. *Ibid.*, 283.
16. KP, PS/2; *CW*, xix, 275–84.

17. *CW*, xix, 219–23, 225.

18. *Ibid.*, 228–9.

19. The cruelty of the British ruling class was the main thesis of Nicholas Davenport, then City editor of the *Nation*, in e.g., *The Split Society* (1964), and *Memoirs of a City Radical* (1974). He attributed it to fox-hunting. Keynes's references to Freud are to be found in *A Treatise on Money*, ii, 258–9, in a section headed 'Auri Sacra Fames' – Sacred Hunger for Gold.

20. Grigg, *Prejudice and Judgment*, 182, 185.

21. TP, T 160/197, File 7528. Evidence of Sir Felix Schuster, 75–6; see also Norman's Evidence, 15.

22. *Ibid.*, Written Evidence of the Federation of British Industries, 29 July 1924.

23. *Ibid.*, Norman's Evidence, 6.

24. *Ibid.*, TP 172/1499B. M. Norman, 2 February 1925, in reply to Churchill's 'Exercise'.

25. KP, PS/6. JMK notes for a lecture, 1924, undated, but wrongly filed.

26. TP, T 160/197, File, 528, 10.

27. *CW*, xix, 250, 255, 257.

28. *Ibid.*, 268–72.

29. JMK to LL, 31 October 1924; see also Meisel and Kendrick, (eds) *Bloomsbury Freud*, JBS to Aux Strachey, 2 November 1924.

30. q. S. V. O. Clarke, *Central Bank Cooperation*, 71.

31. BE, ADM 16/3.

32. KP, PS/3.

33. BE, ADM 16/3.

34. TP, T 172/1499B, Bradbury to Niemeyer, 5 February 1925.

35. *Ibid.*, Churchill to Niemeyer, 6 February 1925.

36. *Ibid.*, Churchill to Niemeyer, 22 February 1925.

37. *Ibid.*, Niemeyer to Churchill, 2 February 1925.

38. *Ibid.*

39. Grigg, *Prejudice and Judgment*, 184.

40. Keynes made a rare mistake, in his published account on Churchill's decision, supposing that the Bank of England would not be required to import gold, only export it. This 'prudent' provision led him to mitigate his criticism of the return to gold. A week later he had to admit he had made a mistake: the Bank of England was obliged, as before, to buy gold in unlimited quantities which 'strips away most of the reasons for consolation I found last week'. *Nation*, 2 and 9 May 1925; *CW*, xix, 357–65.

41. *CW*, xix, 359–40.

42. *Ibid.*, 365, 373–4, 436–7.

43. *Ibid.*, 396–7.

44. *Ibid.*, 419.

45. *CW*, ix, 218–20.

46. *Ibid.*, 222–3.

47. *Ibid.*, 225–8.

48. *Ibid.*, 223–4.

49. Moggridge, *The Return to Gold*, 79–80.

50. KP, PP/45, L. Wittgenstein to JMK, 18 October 1925; see also JMK to LK, 23 October 1925.

51. LK to JMK, 26 May 1929, recalling the incident.

52. KP, PP/45, JMK to L. Wittgenstein, 29 March 1924.
53. JMK to LK, 15 November 1925.
54. M. Dobb, *New Statesman*, 18 June 1971. I am indebted to Brian Pollitt for bringing this reference to my attention.
55. For JMK's speeches see *CW*, xix, 434–42. Also KP, A/25.
56. A. O. Bell (ed.), *The Diary of Virginia Woolf*, iii, 24 September 1925, 43–4.
57. GLS to D. Carrington, q. Holroyd, *Lytton Strachey*, ii, 516–17. The house was not Tilton, as Holroyd says.
58. E. M. Forster was not the only one to notice JMK 'much softened & nicened by his marriage'. EMFP: Gen. Corr., EMF to Ada Borchgrevink, 15 November 1925.
59. VBP, VB to RF, 13 August 1927.
60. LK to JMK, 18 January 1926; JMK to LK, 18 January 1926.
61. LK to JMK, 2 November 1925, 24 April 1926.
62. LK to JMK, 25, 26 October 1925.
63. A. O. Bell (ed.), *The Diary of Virginia Woolf*, iii, 9 May 1925, 18; for LK's comment, see LK to JMK, 9 May 1925.
64. VBP, VB to RF, 25 September 1925.
65. LK to JMK, 26 November 1928.
66. Kavanagh, *Ashton*, 116.
67. KP, LK/5, LK to FAK, 8 September 1926.
68. VBP, VB to RF, 13 August 1927.
69. N. Nicolson (ed.), *The Letters of Virginia Woolf*, iii, VW to VB, 15 May 1927, 376.

23. Keynes's Middle Way

1. Hubert Henderson, editorial, *Nation*, 5 May 1923.
2. *CW*, ix, 276.
3. *Ibid.*, 283–4.
4. *Ibid.*, 288.
5. *Ibid.*, 291–2.
6. *Ibid.*, 289.
7. JRCP, JMK to JRC, 26 April 1927. For Keynes's observations on 'organised' capitalism see Richard Wright: 'On "Madmen" and "Defunct Economists"', unpublished paper, Cambridge University, 1987.
8. *CW*, ix, 303–5.
9. *Ibid.*, 305–6.
10. Olson, *The Rise and Decline of Nations*, 1982.
11. *CW*, ix, 306.
12. *CW*, xix, 441.
13. *CW*, ix, 302.
14. *Ibid.*, 310.
15. *Ibid.*, 296–7.
16. *Ibid.*, 299.
17. KP, PS/6. Unpublished fragment, undated, but wrongly catalogued.
18. *CW*, ix, 295. This passage was left out of *Essays in Persuasion*.
19. In the *Nation* of 20 February 1926; *CW*, ix, 309.
20. Crosland, *The Future of Socialism*, 353.
21. *CW*, ix, 297.

22. KP, PS/4.
23. *CW*, ix, 299.
24. *Ibid.*, 311.
25. JBS to Alix Strachey, 18 June 1925, q. Meisel and Kendrick (eds), *Bloomsbury/Freud*, 289.
26. *CW*, ii, 12–13.
27. *CW*, ix, 258.
28. *Ibid.*, 269, 271.
29. OMP: JMK to Ottoline Morrell, 2 May 1928.
30. The first version of 'EPOG' was read to the Chameleon Club in Cambridge on 10 February 1928. JMK then took it to the Essay Society of Winchester College on 17 March 1928, having been asked down by its secretary, Charles Gifford, who later read economics at Cambridge. The paper had another airing at the Political Economy Club in Cambridge on 22 October 1928, where Plumptre probably heard it, and Keynes read it to the Apostles on 31 May 1930. He then undertook a major revision for a lecture in Madrid in June 1930, which was published in the *Nation* on 11 and 18 October 1930. It was substantially this version that appeared in *Essays in Persuasion*. The main revision was to incorporate a reference to the great depression, which had started in 1929.
31. *CW*, ix, 322–6.
32. *Ibid.*, 329.
33. 'It seems to us', wrote D. R. Gadgill, reviewing *Essays in Persuasion* in *IJE* April 1933, 'that in his forecasts about the future Mr Keynes has too exclusively confined his attention to Western Europe and the USA and has especially neglected the heavily congested tracts of China, India, and Japan. Is the economic problem going to be solved for the whole world or only for the most fortunate countries of the West? And would it be possible to have any stable position with the economic problem solved for only half the world?' This is fair comment, but it is interesting that the world, even for Indians in the 1930s, did not include Africa.
34. *CW*, ix, 330.
35. *CW*, x, 382–4. See also KP, L/R2, DHR to JMK, 30 August 1929. 'I ran into the Prof. [Pigou] and Tom Gaunt on the way to Zermatt, and also made acquaintance with the latter's attractive negroid wife and her overdressed mama. They are a curious party. How hard it seems to be not to murder Jews.'
36. Letter from Neville Brown to the author, 20 February 1993.
37. KP, L/33, Max Radin to JMK, 12 September 1933; JMK to MR, 2 October 1933.

24. Working with Lloyd George

1. *CW*, xix, 446.
2. KP, PP/74, JMK 'History of the London Artists' Association' (?1929).
3. VBP, VB to RF, 8 September 1926.
4. Henderson's four articles ran between 19 December 1925 and 9 January 1926.
5. LK to JMK, 16 October 1926.
6. KP, L/26, JMK to HNB, 27 October 1926.
7. KP, PP/45, BW to JMK, 22 February 1926.
8. CP, DG to VB, 18 April 1926; V. Woolf confirmed the effect of *My Apprenticeship*

in a letter to Margaret Llewellyn Davies on 2 September 1926, repr. in N. Nicolson (ed.), *The Letters of Virginia Woolf*, iii, 289.

9. Keynes's review is in *CW*, ix, 315–20.
10. N. Nicolson (ed.), *The Letters of Virginia Woolf*, iii, VW to VB, 19 May 1926, 265.
11. *CW*, xix, 525–9.
12. For Birkenhead's proposals, see the *Nation*, 26 June 1926.
13. In 'Dr Melchior: A Defeated Enemy', *CW*, x, 419.
14. The JMK–Margot Asquith correspondence is in KP, PP/45.
15. KP, L/26, Thomas T. Tweed to JMK, 23, 28 June 1926.
16. *CW*, xix, 540.
17. MacKenzie and MacKenzie (eds), *The Diary of Beatrice Webb*, iv, 93–4.
18. HGWP, HG 10, JMK to HGW, 11 October 1926.
19. *CW*, xix, 654–60.
20. *Ibid.*, 585–8.
21. RHBP: Liberal Inquiry, Files 118(ii), 119(i); also *Britain's Industrial Future*, chs vi and vii.
22. RHBP: Liberal Inquiry, Files 118(ii), 119(i).
23. *Britain's Industrial Future*, 66.
24. *Ibid.*, 64–5.
25. *Ibid.*, 64.
26. *Ibid.*, 112–13.
27. *Ibid.*, 122, 123.
28. *Ibid.*, 410.
29. *Ibid.*, 414–15.
30. *Ibid.*, 422–5.
31. JMK to HGW, 18 January 1928, HGWP, HG 10.

25. *The Riddle of Savings*

1. Fletcher, *Understanding Dennis Robertson*, 96–7.
2. *Ibid.*, 98.
3. *Ibid.*, 53, 294.
4. D. H. Robertson, *A Study of Industrial Fluctuation*, 254.
5. The quotations are from the English translation of Labordère's essay, which is reproduced in French in the 1948 edn of *A Study of Industrial Fluctuation*. I am grateful to Prof. Presley for providing me with the translation. The Keynes–Labordère correspondence is in KP, PP/45.
6. D. H. Robertson, *Banking Policy and the Price Level*, 23.
7. *CW*, v, pp. i, 269.
8. D. H. Robertson, *Banking Policy and the Price Level*, 49, 50n, ch. v generally. The Keynes–Robertson exchanges on induced lacking can be followed in *CW*, xiii, 29–41. Keynes wrote on 28 May 1925: 'In assuming that the public as a whole has to reduce its current consumption when inflation takes place you overlook the fact that whilst some depositors may as a result of the inflation have less real resources at the bank, other depositors have more.' Inflation cannot create extra resources for investment, Keynes was led to insist, unless or until 'someone is induced ... to do *some new* hoarding out of current income'. This might come about either because those hit by inflation were

more interested in maintaining the 'real' value of their cash balances than in maintaining the 'real' value of their consumption; or because inflation has redistributed income into the hands of those 'whose incentive and ability to hoard is greater than those from whom it is taken'; or because ' a higher bank rate may increase the incentive to hoard'. On the other hand, inflation produces some powerful incentives to dishoard, or dissave. 'The new equilibrium of prices, as a result of a given percentage of inflation, depends upon the resultant of these forces.' Keynes thought that prices would go on rising until one of the 'incentives to new hoarding' came into play. But, he told Robertson, the decision to increase the money value of his cash balances was by no means *forced* on the individual: 'it remains just as voluntary as any other form of saving; it is the result of individual decisions balancing the advantage of maintaining hoards at certain levels as against those of maintaining consumption at a certain level'. In June 1925, Robertson capitulated: 'I think I am now convinced on the point of substance, viz. that the new real Hoarding and the new Short Lacking are the same (like Mrs Do-as-you-would-be-done-by and Mrs Be-done-by-as-you-did in the Water Babies').' Presley, in 'J. M. Keynes and the Real Balance Effect', *MS*, 1986, 28, holds that 'Robertson, and by implication Keynes, was using the real balance effect to explain the nature of the adjustment to a new equilibrium position when the absolute price level deviated from its equilibrium value.' This is confirmed in *CW*, xiii, 36–7. But it cannot be said that Keynes got very far in his 'stability analysis'. His discussion with Robertson was really about something else: whether inflation might be a way of increasing saving.

9. *CW*, xiv, 94–5.
10. *CW*, xiii, 273.
11. JMK to LK, 21 February 1927.
12. MPP, JMK to Daniel Macmillan, 22 September 1926.
13. JMK to LK, 27 April 1927.
14. *CW*, xiii, 770–2.
15. McKenna, *Post-War Banking Policy*, 122, 129–31.
16. *CW*, xiii, 90–1.
17. *Ibid.*, 51.
18. MPP, JMK to Daniel Macmillan, 10 December 1928.
19. For reminiscences of Cambridge in the 1920s see H. M. Robertson, 'J. M. Keynes and Cambridge in the 1920s', *SAJE*, 1983, 407–18, and E. A. G. Robinson, 'Keynes and His Cambridge Colleagues', in Patinkin and Clark Reith (eds), *Keynes, Cambridge, and the General Theory*, 25–37. The quotation about Joan Robinson comes from George R. Feiwel in 'Joan Robinson Inside and Outside the Stream', in George R Feiwel (ed.), *Joan Robinson and Modern Economic Theory*, 2.
20. E. A. G. Robinson, 'Keynes and His Cambridge Colleagues', in Patinkin and Clark Reith (eds), *Keynes, Cambridge, and the General Theory*, 26.
21. JMK to LK, 28 November 1927.
22. KP, L/S, PS to JMK, 23 November 1924.
23. JMK to LK, 31 OCtober 1925.
24. See Annan, *Our Age*, 179–80; Sinclair, *The Red and the Blue*, 26–30; N. Wood, *Communism and British Intellectuals*, 150–5.
25. From Alethea Graham's diary, 9 May 1930, published in the *Charleston Maga-*

zine, Summer/Autumn 1992, 24. Alethea Graham was up at Girton College from 1927 to 1930.

26. JMK to LK, 14 November 1926.
27. JMK to LK, 29 January 1928.
28. JMK to LK, 6 May 1927.
29. Harrod, *Keynes*, 400.
30. P. Clarke, *The Keynesian Revolution in the Making*, esp. chs 3 and 4.
31. *CW*, xix, 761–6.
32. P. Clarke, *The Keynesian Revolution in the Making*, 51–4.
33. *Ibid.*, 64, see also TP, 175/26, Memorandum by Sir Frederick Leith-Ross, 3 August 1928.
34. *CW*, xiii, 52–9.
35. *CW*, xix, 805.
36. Williamson, *National Crisis and National Government*, ch. 1, argues that the 'hastily produced' Lloyd George pledge was designed to 'pre-empt' similar schemes being canvassed in the Conservative and Labour Parties, and in fact inhibited both Conservative and Labour radicalism on unemployment. He cites the Joynson–Hicks and Steel–Maitland plans, as well as the fact that Snowden approved of a big public works programme 'early in 1929' (p. 40). But these plans – speculations really – which remained private, were similar to the Liberal one only in phraseology. The Conversative ministers' suggestions collapsed the moment the Treasury got to work on them, and Labour's would have as well, whereas the Liberal pledge was a public commitment, with administrative detail and intellectual guts behind it. There is simply no comparison with the vague proposals floating round the two other parties. Also the timing is wrong. The Lloyd George pledge was first mooted in a speech by Seebohm Rowntree in York in October 1928. Far from being 'hastily produced' it was a political crystallisation of the Liberal Industrial Inquiry, the work by the Rowntree Committee and estimates of both primary and secondary employment. Rowntree wrote to JMK on 31 January 1929, 'I am coming to the opinion that if it were possible for the Liberal Party to make a specific pledge with regard to the reduction of unemployment the results might be surprising. I propose to suggest to the Conference at Churt that such a pledge should be given. . . . We have the schemes ready, and we have what neither of the other Parties has, a leader with the imagination and drive to put a great scheme of this kind through.' (KP, L/29.)
37. McKenna's annual speech to the shareholders of the Midland Bank, as reported in the *Nation*, 26 January 1929, 599. See also *We Can Conquer Unemployment*, 55.
38. *CW*, ix, 117.
39. *Ibid.*, 106–7.
40. *Ibid.*, 125.
41. *CW*, vi, 132.
42. *CW*, v.
43. *Ibid.*, 273.
44. *Ibid.*, 160.
45. *CW*, vi, 299.
46. *Ibid.*, 304.

26. The Slump

1. D'Abernon, *An Ambassador of Peace*, ii, 51–2n.
2. LK to FAK, 1 August 1929.
3. Taper, *Balanchine*, 126.
4. See JMK to FAK, 20 September 1929. The film, directed by Sinclair Hill, is about David, a sculptor (Stewart Rome), who believes his wife Laura (Frances Doble) has taken as a lover Anton, a musician (Hugh Eden). He sees the ballet, given as an entertainment in a country house, in which the husband (Dolin) returns while the wife (Lydia) is with her lover (Balanchine), and cuts off her hands with an axe. Laura has asked her husband to take a cast of Anton's beautiful hands, and the ballet gives the sculptor the idea of embedding the supposed lover's hands in plaster and telling him he will cut them off unless he goes away for ever. Even without the fire, the film would not, one suspects, have achieved immortality. The only extant copy was tracked down by the ballet writer Deirdre McMahon in the attic of a film buff in Co. Galway, Ireland, in 1984.
5. Partridge, *Memories*, 163.
6. *CW*, xx, 2–3.
7. Somary, *The Raven of Zurich*, 146–7; q. Skousen, 'Keynes as a Speculator', in Skousen (ed.), *Dissent on Keynes*, 163. Skousen is an able critic of Keynes from the 'Austrian' viewpoint.
8. Davis, *The World between the Wars*, 136.
9. Kenworthy, *Sailors, Statesmen – and Others*, 304.
10. Robbins, *The Great Depression*, 52–3.
11. *CW*, xiii, 349.
12. JMK, 'Is There Inflation in the United States?', 1 September 1928; repr. in *ibid.*, 52–9.
13. KP, L/28.
14. *CW*, xiii, 71.
15. *CW*, vi, 170–7.
16. See *CW*, xii, 11, 15–17.
17. JMK to LK, 2 March 1930.
18. JMK to LK, 3 May 1930.
19. *CW*, xx, 38. Editorial comment.
20. *Ibid.*, 41–2.
21. *Ibid.*, 46.
22. *Ibid.*, 49.
23. *Ibid.*, 50–1.
24. *Ibid.*, 67.
25. *Ibid.*, 3–16. This followed a suggestion by Maurice Dobb, Cambridge's resident Marxist economist, whose 'A Sceptical View of the Theory of Wages' appeared in the *EJ*, December 1929. The talk was first given at Bedford College, London, on 24 October 1929. It was published as 'The Question of High Wages' in *PSQ*, January–March 1930.
26. *CW*, xx, 56.
27. *Ibid.*, 79–80.
28. *Ibid.*, 95.

29. *Ibid.*, 84–5.
30. *Ibid.*, 75.
31. RHBP, File 198, JMK to RB, 12 May 1930.
32. *CW*, xx, 72.
33. *Ibid.*, 127.
34. *Ibid.*
35. *Ibid.*, 99–102.
36. *Ibid.*, 102.
37. *Ibid.*, 109–13.
38. *Ibid.*, 113, 117.
39. *Ibid.*, 115.
40. *Ibid.*, 116, 120–1.
41. *Ibid.*, 130.
42. *Ibid.*, 130–1.
43. *Ibid.*, 138.
44. *Ibid.*, 151.
45. *Ibid.*, 157.
46. *Ibid.*, 153.
47. *Ibid.*, 156.
48. BE, G1/426. E. M. Harvey to Montagu Norman, 19 December 1929.
49. Macmillan Committee, Minutes of Evidence, Q3516. For JMK's description of Montagu Norman see A. O. Bell (ed.), *The Diary of Virginia Woolf*, iv, 208.
50. Boyle, *Montagu Norman*, 258.
51. Macmillan Committee, ME 3339.
52. *Ibid.*, 3382.
53. For the construction of the Bank's brief, see P. Clarke, *The Keynesian Revolution in the Making*, 131–5.
54. Macmillan Committee, ME 8733.
55. *Ibid.*, 7690.
56. *Ibid.*, 7783.
57. *Ibid.*, 7647.
58. *Ibid.*, 7653, 7836.
59. *CW*, xx, 345.
60. Macmillan Committee, ME 5565.
61. *Ibid.*, 5690.
62. KP, EA/4, JMK to James Ramsay MacDonald, 10 July 1930.
63. Howson and Winch, *The Economic Advisory Council*, 40.
64. For a discussion of such proposals see especially Booth and Pack, *Employment, Capital and Economic Policy*; Pollard (ed.), *The Gold Standard and Employment Policies between the Wars*; and Glynn and Booth (eds), *The Road to Full Employment*.
65. *CW*, xx, 359. Henderson wrote (p. 358), 'where there are solid grounds for expecting that a certain event will happen, and the grounds are of a kind which the business community can understand, then the results of that event begin to take effect in advance'.
66. Clay (ed.), *The Interwar Years*, Memorandum to the Committee of Economists, 18 September 1930, 69–70.
67. Robbins, *Autobiography of an Economist*, 134–5.
68. KP, PP/45.

69. KP, BR2, JMK to C. A. Siepmann, 4 January 1933.
70. *CW*, vii, 30n.
71. Robbins, *Autobiography of an Economist*, 154.
72. J. H. Jones, *Josiah Stamp*, 222. Stamp to his wife, 11 March 1924.
73. Macmillan Committee, ME 3716–18, 3972–3.
74. LK to JMK, 14 February 1930. The broadcast is repr. in *CW*, xx, 315–25.
75. *CW*, xiii, 179.
76. *Ibid.*, 183.
77. *Ibid.*, 180.
78. *Ibid.*, 181.
79. *Ibid.*, 186.
80. *Ibid.*, 187–9.
81. *Ibid.*, 192.
82. *Ibid.*, 185.
83. *CW*, xx, 431–2. Robbins had used Rueff's correlation between changes in unemployment and changes in the dole to persuade the Committee. See Dimand, *The Origins of the Keynesian Revolution*, 113.
84. *CW*, xx, 437–43; quotations from 441–2.
85. *Ibid.*, 443–8.
86. Henderson, 'Drift of the Draft Report', 13 October 1930; repr. *CW*, xx, 452–6.
87. JMK to LK, 9 October 1930.
88. Robbins, *Autobiography of an Economist*, 151.
89. Pimlott (ed.), *The Political Diary of Hugh Dalton*, 123.
90. Robbins, *Autobiography of an Economist*, 151; *CW*, xx, 463–6.
91. Pimlott (ed.), *The Political Diary of Hugh Dalton*, 124.
92. Howson and Winch, *The Economic Advisory Council*, 72.
93. Robbins's dissenting report is repr. *ibid.*, 227–31; the Keynes remark is from his *Autobiography of an Economist*, 155.
94. Pimlott (ed.), *The Political Diary of Hugh Dalton*, 124; Williamson, *National Crisis and National Government*, 68.
95. Howson and Winch, *The Economic Advisory Council*, 76.
96. *Ibid.*, 78.
97. *Ibid.*, 166–7.
98. *Ibid.*, 148.
99. KP, CO/1, JMK to Ryan, 7 September 1930.
100. Economists' Report, para. 5, q. Howson and Winch, *The Economic Advisory Council*, 180.
101. A. J. P. Taylor, *English History*, 286.
102. q. Skidelsky, *Politicians and the Slump*, 241.
103. OTFP1: JMK to OTF, 9 September 1930, 'A Note on This Phase of the Credit Cycle'.
104. *CW*, ix, 332.
105. LK to JMK, 25 May 1930.
106. M. Keynes (ed.), *Lydia Lopokova*, 117.
107. KP, LLK/1, AH to JMK, 12 December 1930.
108. Haskell, *Balletomania*, 185.
109. LK to JMK, 6 March 1931.
110. KP, LLK/5, LK to SC, undated, February 1931; SC to LK, 27 February 1931.
111. JMK to LK, 19 January 1931.

112. JMK to LK, 10 May 1931.
113. *Nation*, 13 December 1930; *CW*, xx, 474.
114. *CW*, ix, 137–9.
115. *CW*, xx, 484.
116. *Ibid.*, 486. Keynes was sending him regular financial appreciations at this time.
117. Editor's comment, *CW*, ix, 231.
118. JMK to LK, 9 March 1931.
119. *New Statesman*, 14 March 1931.
120. OTFP1: JMK to OTF, 22 June 1931.
121. Wright (ed.), *Unemployment as a World Problem*: Reports of Round Tables, vol. 1.
122. *CW*, xx, 591–3.
123. *New Statesman*, 15 August 1931; repr. in *CW*, ix, 141–5.
124. Marquand, *Ramsay MacDonald*, 610–11; Williamson, *National Crisis and National Government*, 294, cites MacDonald's letter to D'Abernon of 10 September 1931, showing that the Prime Minister thought Keynes had fallen in line with the other advice he was getting.
125. *CW*, xx, 611–12.
126. Feiling, *The Life of Neville Chamberlain*, 191; Bowle, *Viscount Samuel*, 271.
127. *CW*, xx, 598.
128. *CW*, ix, 238–42.
129. *CW*, xx, 598–602.
130. *CW*, ix, 145.
131. *CW*, xx, 605.
132. *Ibid.*, 609–11.
133. q. Skidelsky, *Oswald Mosley*, 268.
134. q. Rolph, *Kingsley*, 164; see also *New Statesman*, 27 September 1931; *CW*, xx, 245–6.
135. *LBMR*, April 1932; *CW*, xxi, 68–9.
136. TLP, Box 104–29.
137. WLP, File 1312.
138. KP, PP/45.
139. MacKenzie and MacKenzie (eds), *The Diary of Beatrice Webb*, iv, 260; LK to FAK, 22 September 1931.
140. JMK to MacDonald, 1 October 1931; *CW*, xx, 619.

27. Portrait of an Unusual Economist

1. This is the title of ch. 3 of Moggridge's *Keynes* (1976). Moggridge writes that when Marshall retired in 1907 he thought that 'the fundamental principles of the subject were fixed beyond dispute' (p. 46). In 1915, Keynes described the Cambridge school of economics as combining 'general agreement on principles with much variety on outlook, sympathies and methods'. For the Cambridge Economic Handbooks, see *CW*, xii, 855–60.
2. See the illuminating essay by R. M. Hartwell in Harris and Seldon (eds), *The Coming Confrontation*.
3. Annan, *Our Age*, 10.
4. Moore, *Principia Ethica*, 167.

5. *CW*, x, 173, 187.
6. *Ibid.*, 108.
7. *Ibid.*, 110, 114–16, 121–2, 139, 146, 155.
8. *Ibid.*, 365.
9. In his review of the 4th edn of S. Jevons's *Theory of Political Economy*, *EJ*, March 1912; *CW*, xi, 516.
10. *CW*, x, 131.
11. Marshall, *Principles of Economics*, 8th edn., 85; for JMK on Jevons, see *CW*, x, 198; the JMK remark is quoted in Pigou, *Economics in Practice*, 22.
12. *CW*, x, 256.
13. *Ibid.*, 272.
14. *Ibid.*, 262–3.
15. JMK letter in the *Nation*, 29 August 1925; *CW*, xviii, 392–3.
16. Introduction to JMK's Galton Lecture, 1937. KP, PS16.
17. *CW*, vi, 193.
18. KP, CO/2, JMK to D. Macmillan, 1 March 1932; see also JMK's correspondence iwith Larranaga in L/32. JMK to M. C. Rorty, 3, 29 February 1932, is in CO/6. See CO/2 for JMK to D. Macmillan on McGregor; L 35 for JMK to D. B. Copland, 14 January, 1 May 1935, and to I. M. Sutherland, 14 January 1935, on Sutherland.
19. KP, CO/1, JMK to W. Stark, 9 April 1942.
20. *CW*, x, 86.
21. *CR*; *CW*, x, 107.
22. KP, PS/2. This speech was to the annual dinner of the Political Economy Club at Gatti's Restaurant, London, 2 April 1924. Keynes must have got the letter from *EJ*, 1907, 274, where it had been printed by Foxwell. The fact that Keynes was aware of the Malthus of 'effective demand' as early as 1924 casts further doubt on the idea of the editor of *CW*, x, 71n. that Keynes picked up this side of Malthus only 'when his own thinking about these issues had already taken final shape'.
23. *CW*, x, 100–1.
24. Marshall's Inaugural Lecture, q. *CW*, x, 196.
25. Kahn, *The Making of Keynes's General Theory*, 28–9.
26. As told in Hamouda (ed.), *Controversies in Political Economy*, 194 n. 2.
27. Marshall, *Principles of Economics*, 291.
28. *CW*, x, 97–8.
29. *Ibid.*, 98.
30. *CW*, xviii, 328.
31. Moggridge, 'Keynes: The Economist', in Moggridge (ed.), *Keynes: Aspects of the Man and His Work*, 62. See also E. A. G. Robinson, 'John Maynard Keynes 1883–1946', *EJ*, 1947; repr. in Wood (ed.), *John Maynard Keynes*, i, 89; and his 'John Maynard Keynes: Economist, Author, Statesman', 8–9.
32. In *QJE*, August 1972, 463–4.
33. Moggridge (ed.), *Keynes: Aspects of the Man and His Work*, 57.
34. *CW*, vii, 350.
35. Coates, *Common Sense*, 5.
36. *CW*, vii, p. xxiii.
37. *CW*, ix, 138.
38. *CW*, xxviii, 399.

39. See *CW*, xx, 157–65. The 'discovery' turned out to be a hoax, but who was fooling whom is not clear.

28. The Practical Visionary

1. CP, VB to Clive Bell, 10 October 1931.
2. *CW*, ix, p. xix.
3. *The Times*, 4 December 1931.
4. A. O. Bell (ed.), *The Diary of Virginia Woolf*, iv, 27 December 1931, 56.
5. SP, Add. MS. 60672, JMK to JBS, 19 November 1933.
6. A. O. Bell (ed.), *The Diary of Virginia Woolf*, iv. 27 December 1931, 56.
7. DGP, VB to DG, 7 August 1930.
8. Howson and Winch, *The Economic Advisory Council*, 100–5.
9. In *EJ*, September, 1932, repr. in *CW*, xxi, 114.
10. JMK to J. R. MacDonald, 12 July 1931; *CW*, xviii, 379.
11. q. Eichengreen, 'Sterling and the Tariff 1929–32', *PSIF*, 1981, 32.
12. In *The Times*, 28 September 1931; *CW*, ix, 243; cf. Howson and Winch, *The Economic Advisory Council*, 98. JMK called tariffs 'a first-class curse' on 19 April 1932, *CW*, xxi, 103.
13. JMK, Memorandum to F. Leith-Ross, 16 November 1931; *CW*, xxi, 17.
14. In JMK's 'Report of the Australian Experts', *Melbourne Herald*, 27 June 1932, but written on 17 April 1932; *CW*, xxi, 98.
15. KP, A/32, JMK to Clive Baillieu, 14 July 1932.
16. Drummond, *British Economic Policy and the Empire*, 98–9.
17. *CW*, xxi, 110.
18. *Ibid.*
19. CMP, Add. MS. 52432, Samuel Courtauld to Christabel Aberconway, 1 September 1932.
20. JMK to Walter Case, 2 November 1931; *CW*, xxi, 9–10.
21. JMK's talk, on 11 December 1931, was to the Society for Socialist Inquiry and Propaganda, started by G. D. H. Cole. A version of his talk was printed in *PQ*, April–June 1932, of whose board he was a member. The phrase in inverted commas was from the talk but was left out of the published essay: see KP, A/32.
22. *CW*, xxi, 135.
23. Booth and Pack, *Employment, Capital and Economic Policy*, 144.
24. A. L. Rowse, *Adelphi*, April 1932.
25. KP, GTE/1/5, JMK to A. L. Rowse, 12 May 1936; see Durbin, *New Jerusalems*, ch. 7.
26. *CW*, xxi, 45.
27. P. Clarke, *The Keynesian Revolution in the Making*, 230.
28. Patinkin makes this point on pp. 18–19 of his *Anticipations of the General Theory*.
29. *CW*, xxi, 213.
30. JMK to L. F. Giblin, 2 July 1932; *CW*, xxi, 99: 'it may be that prices are related to costs after the same fashion as a cat to her tail'. He turned down an invitation at this time to visit Australia for six months for £2500, all expenses paid.
31. *CW*, xiii, 151.
32. *Ibid.*, 143–5.

33. *CW*, v, 125.
34. *CW*, xiii, 340n.
35. *Ibid.*, 270.
36. D. H. Robertson, 'Mr Keynes's Theory of Money', *EJ*, September 1931, 402n., 407.
37. Kahn, *The Making of Keynes's General Theory*, 182.
38. JMK, 'A Pure Theory of Money: A Reply to Dr. Hayek', *Economica*, November 1931; *CW*, xiii, 243, 252.
39. *CW*, xiii, 266.
40. Hayek, *New Studies*, 283, 287.
41. *CW*, xiii, 276.
42. P. Jacobsson's diary, 2 August 1932, q. Erin E. Jacobsson, *A Life for Sound Money*, 107.
43. Rymes, *Keynes's Lectures*, 126.
44. Ibid., 66–7, 70.
45. *CW*, xiii, 405.
46. Rymes, *Keynes's Lectures*, 123–7.
47. *Ibid.*, 78. (See also *CW*, xiii, 401.)
48. Rymes, *Keynes's Lectures.*, 122.
49. Cain, 'Cambridge and Its Revolution', *ER* 1979, 113. Warming's article, 'International Difficulties Arising out of the Financing of Public Works during a Depression', appeared in *EJ*, June 1932.
50. Rymes, *Keynes's Lectures*, 102.
51. JMK to R. F. Harrod, 30 August 1936; *CW*, xiv, 85.
52. Letter to author, 22 May 1993.
53. *New Statesman and Nation*, 24 December 1932; *CW*, xxi, 210–11.
54. See his article on the 'Kaffir Boom', *Daily Mail*, 7 February 1933; *CW*, xxi, 228.
55. Salter, *Slave of the Lamp*, 87–8.
56. Howson and Winch, *The Economic Advisory Council*, 122.
57. *CW*, xxi, 138–40.
58. *CW*, ix, 335–6. The introduction was added for the pamphlet. This is the American version, with the multiplier.
59. *Ibid.*, 339.
60. *Ibid.*, 342.
61. Kahn, *The Making of the Keynesian Revolution*, 97.
62. *CW*, ix, 347.
63. *Ibid.*, 356.
64. *Ibid.*, 348.
65. *Ibid.*, 358 and n.
66. *Ibid.*, 349.
67. *CW*, xxi, 203–4.
68. *Ibid.*, 215–6.
69. In the *Daily Mail*, 17 February 1933; *CW*, xxi, 229–30.
70. *CW*, ix, 358.
71. *Ibid.*, 365–6.
72. TP, T 175/70 Pt 1, 21 March 1933.
73. *Ibid.*, T 175/17, 14 March 1933.
74. HDHP, Suppl. Box 68m, Henderson to Sir F. Phillips, 16 March 1933; see also Howson and Winch, *The Economic Advisory Council*, 129.

75. HDHP: Box 8.
76. *CW*, xxi, 184.
77. BE, EID 4/103: J. A. C. Osborne to H. C. B. Mynors, 6 April 1933; cf. BE, G1/15 for R. N. Kershaw's Note on Keynes's reply.
78. For a summary see Middleton, *Towards the Managed Economy*, 176–80.
79. *CW*, xxi, 238.
80. *Ibid.*, 236.
81. *Ibid.*, 240–1.
82. *Ibid.*, 242–3.
83. Mosley, *My Life*, 247–8n.
84. JMK to FAK, 23 April 1933.
85. LK to JMK, 27 May 1933. See also the transatlantic broadcast discussion between JMK and Walter Lippmann, published in the *Listener*, 13 June 1933; *CW*, xxi, 251–9.
86. *CW*, xxi, 264–8. This closely followed the proposals adopted by the Committee on Economic Information, 16 May 1933. See Howson and Winch, *The Economic Advisory Council*, 120.
87. *Ibid.*, 273–7.
88. *Ibid.*, 281–2.

29. New Deals

1. Mini, *Keynes, Bloomsbury, and The General Theory*, ch. 1.
2. This interpretation of the 'meaning' of fascism has been influenced by Barraclough, *An Introduction to Contemporary History*, esp. 30–33.
3. *CW*, ii, 2.
4. See e.g. JMK's comment on French economists in a letter to M. Pierre Jerôme, 7 October 1932, in KP, CO/6.
5. Garraty, *The Great Depression*, 141.
6. KP, PS/5. The auspices were the journal *Der Deutsche Ökonomist* and the Studiengesellschaft für Wahrungstragen. One of the organisers, Dr Dahlberg, was an advocate of devaluation, which was apparently enough to damn him in the eyes of JMK's ultra-respectable Liberal friends.
7. *CW*, xxi, 244, 285.
8. KP, L/33. JMK to A. Spiethoff, 25 August 1933. The German translation omitted the passage criticising totalitarian regimes.
9. KP, MM/19 'Melchior', L. Rosenbaum to D. E. Moggridge, 13 November 1971.
10. KP, L/33, JMK to Wallenberg, 12 April 1933.
11. *CW*, xxi, 243–4, 245, 246.
12. JMK to LK, 22 October 1933; cf. *CW*, xviii, 16–19.
13. KP, LLK/5, LK to FAK, 11 December 1932, 14 August 1934.
14. JMK to LK, 3 March 1933.
15. Schlesinger, *The Coming of the New Deal*, 17, 19.
16. *CW*, xxi, 252.
17. In his speech at Amherst, 11 November 1933, q. Steel, *Walter Lippmann and the American Century*, 307.
18. *CW*, xxi, 289–97; an extended version of the Open Letter was published in *The Times*, 2 January 1934.

19. Stein, *The First Revolution in America*, 147–8.
20. Dimand, *The Origins of the Keynesian Revolution*, 61f.
21. Schlesinger, *The Coming of the New Deal*, 188.
22. KP, AV:1.
23. A. O. Bell (ed.), *The Diary of Virginia Woolf*, iv, 235. JMK blamed the captain, John W. Binks.
24. FFP, Reel 66, Frankfurter to Tom Corcoran, 7 April 1934.
25. Perkins, *The Roosevelt I Knew*, 183.
26. Roosevelt to Frankfurter, 11 June 1934, in Freedman (ed.), *Roosevelt and Frankfurter*.
27. q. Harrod, *Keynes*, 20.
28. Tugwell, *The Democratic Roosevelt*, 275.
29. Stein, *The Fiscal Revolution in America*, 150.
30. FFP, Reel 66.
31. KP, PS/6.
32. *CW*, xiii, 456–68.
33. FDRP, OF 264, David King to Louis Howe, 27 September 1934.
34. WLP, M5 326, Box 82, Folder 1217, WL to JMK, 9 January 1935.
35. *CW*, xxi, 321–2, for Szeliski's letter; KP, AV: 1, JMK to Szeliski, 2 June 1934, for the reply.
36. A. O. Bell (ed.), *The Diary of Virginia Woolf*, iv, 236–7.
37. JMK to LK, 12 November 1933.
38. A. O. Bell (ed.), *The Diary of Virginia Woolf*, iv, 209.
39. Stansky and Abrahams, *Journey to the Frontier*, 211.
40. See M. Keynes (ed.), *Lydia Lopokova*, 219–23.
41. q. *ibid.*, 223.
42. Straight, *After Long Silence*, 185.
43. Annan, *Our Age*, 235–6.
44. KP, PP/45.
45. A. O. Bell (ed.), *The Diary of Virginia Woolf*, iv, 19 April 1934, 208.
46. Letter, 11 August 1934; *CW*, xviii, 25–7.
47. A. O. Bell (ed.), *The Diary of Virginia Woolf*, iv, 272.
48. *CW*, xxviii, 38–41. See also JMK's correspondence with Susan Lawrence, on NEC of Labour Party, 15 January 1935, in KP, L/35.
49. KP, PP/45.
50. KP, PP/45, Dorothy Elmhirst to JMK, 19 October 1935, in which she quoted these passages from her son's letter. The published version is in Straight, *After Long Silence*, 66.
51. Straight, *After Long Silence*, 67.
52. *CW*, xii, 97.
53. *Ibid.*, 10–12.
54. A. N. L. Munby, 'The Book Collector', *John Maynard Keynes*, KC, 31, 34.
55. KP, PP/80.
56. *Ibid.*, Sean O'Casey to David Garnett, 25 October 1935.
57. For details of the Cambridge Arts Theatre, see KP, PP/80; also Norman Higgins's account in M. Keynes (ed.), *Essays on John Maynard Keynes*, 272–9.
58. KP, LLK/5, LK to FAK, 26 May 1935.
59. JMK to Harrod, 9 August 1935; *CW*, xiii, 538.
60. Harrod to JMK, *ibid.*, 550.

61. *Ibid.*, 537.
62. *Ibid.*, 548.
63. *Ibid.*, 540.
64. *Ibid.*, 552, 559.
65. *CW*, vii, 179.
66. *CW*, xiv.
67. See Skidelsky, *Keynes*, i, 218. The book was *Gold, Prices and Wages*.
68. JMK to J. A. Hobson, 31 July 1935.
69. KP, LLK/5, LK to FAK, 25 December 1935.

30. Firing at the Moon

1. *CW*, vii, 293.
2. *Ibid.*, 129.
3. *CW*, vi, 139–40.
4. *CW*, xxix, 83; Rymes, 92.
5. Hicks, 'Mr Keynes's Theory of Employment', *EJ*, 1936, repr. in Wood (ed.), *John Maynard Keynes*, ii, 40.
6. *CW*, vii, 247.
7. *Ibid.*, 27; for alternative formulation, see 96.
8. Quoted in Murray Milgate, *Capital and Employment*, 77.
9. Don Patinkin, *NP*, iii, 25.
10. *CW*, vii, 210.
11. *Ibid.*, 149.
12. *Ibid.*, 150, 161–3.
13. *Ibid.*, 161.
14. *Ibid.*, 163–4.
15. *Ibid.*, 161.
16. *Ibid.*, 168.
17. *Ibid.*, 202–3, 207–8.
18. *Ibid.*, 268.
19. *Ibid.*, 299–30.
20. *Ibid.*, 394–412.
21. *Ibid.*, 175.
22. *Ibid.*, 179–82.
23. *Ibid.*, 307.
24. *Ibid.*, 249–54. 'Notes on the Trade Cycle' 320f.
25. *Ibid.*, 327.
26. *Ibid.*, 235.
27. *CW*, xxix, 87.
28. *CW*, vii, 379.
29. *Ibid.*, 383.
30. In a letter to Dennis Robertson, 20 September 1936; *CW*, xiv, 87.
31. A. C. Pigou, *Economica*, 3 May 1936, repr. in Wood (ed.), *John Maynard Keynes*, ii, 18.
32. *Ibid.*, 26, 28, 29–30.
33. Pigou, *The Theory of Unemployment*, 100f.

34. See the exchanges between Hawtrey and Keynes, February–April 1936, in *CW*, xiv, esp. 6, 23.

35. JMK to LK, 3 May 1936, repr. in *CW*, xxix, 218.

36. HDHP, Box 10, Robertson to Henderson, 21 June 1936. For the summary together with Keynes's reply see *CW*, xxix, 219–24.

37. HDHP: Box 10, Henderson to R. F. Harrod, 2 April 1936; Harrod to Henderson, 9 April 1936.

38. Henderson's (much revised) paper is reprinted in *The Interwar Years and Other Papers*, ed. Henry Clay. The quotation is from p. 167.

39. Clay (ed.), *The Interwar Years and Other Papers*, 170, 173.

40. *CW*, xxix, 218–31.

41. Robertson to JMK, 28 September 1936; *CW*, xxix, 63–4.

42. JMK to Robertson, 20 September, 1936; *CW*, xiv, 88.

43. Gordon Fletcher, *Understanding Dennis Robertson*, 288–9. See also D. H. Robertson, 'Industrial Fluctuation and the Natural Rate of Interest', *EJ*, December 1934, 650–6, repr. in J. R. Hicks, *Sir Dennis Robertson: Essays in Money and Interest.*

44. *CW*, xiv, 91.

45. *Ibid.*, 94.

46. *Ibid.*, 98.

47. *Ibid.*, 207. In his article 'Alternative Theories of the Rate of Interest', published in *EJ*, June 1937.

48. *CW*, xxix, 166.

49. JMK to Austin Robinson, 22 March 1938; *CW*, xxix, 168.

50. *Ibid.*, 179.

51. See Moggridge, 599, 603, for an account of the tensions in the Economics Faculty in the late 1930s.

52. *QJE*, November 1936, repr. in Wood (ed.), *John Maynard Keynes*, ii, 86–7.

53. F. M. Knight, *CJE*, February 1937, repr. in Wood (ed.), *John Maynard Keynes*, ii, 141.

54. J. A. Schumpeter, *JASA*, December 1936, repr. in Wood (ed.), *John Maynard Keynes*, ii, 125–8.

55. JMK to V. W. Bladen, 13 March 1937; *CW*, xxix, 217–18. The correspondent was the editor of the journal, who asked Keynes whether he wanted to reply. Keynes refused. On the question of the priority of Keynes's and Knight's theory of uncertainty, see O'Donnell, *Keynes: Philosophy, Economics and Politics*, 262–3.

56. Patinkin, *Anticipations of the General Theory*, ch. 2. Patinkin claims that the Swedish school's emphasis on price adjustments disqualifies it as an independent precursor of the theory of effective demand, that is, the equilibrating role of changes in the level of output. But Patinkin's own interpretation of the Keynesian Revolution – roughly 'quantities adjust, not prices' – has often been challenged, most recently by Amadeo, *Keynes's Principle of Effective Demand*, 21–3, 117f.

57. Patinkin, *Anticipations of the General Theory*, 37.

58. Tarshis, 'The Keynesian Revolution: What it meant in the 1930s', unpublished.

59. In Lekachman (ed.), *Keynes's General Theory*, 332.

60. Galbraith, *Money: Whence It Came, Where It Went*, 229–30.

61. JMK to G. F. Shove, 15 April 1936, *CW*, xiv, 2.

62. Young, *Interpreting Mr Keynes*, 10.
63. *Ibid.*, 14, 17, 18.
64. Kahn, *The Making of Keynes's General Theory*, 159.
65. *CW*, xiv, 85.
66. *Ibid.*, 79–82.
67. *Ibid.*, 107.
68. *Ibid.*, 121.
69. *Ibid.*, 185–9.
70. *Ibid.*, 299–300.
71. *Ibid.*, 307, 309, 318.

31. Curing Invalidism

1. JMK to LK, 9, 11 October, 2 November 1936.
2. JMK to LK, 18, 25 October 1936.
3. JMK to LK, 15, 16 November 1936.
4. R. F. Harrod, 'An Essay in Dynamic Theory', *EJ*, June 1939, 294–300.
5. *CW*, xxi, 426, JMK to Henderson, 14 November 1937.
6. *CW*, xxviii, 87, JMK to K. Martin, 29 September 1937.
7. M. Keynes (ed.), *Lydia Lopokova*, 34.
8. Nicolson (ed.), *Letters of Virginia Woolf*, vi, Virginia Woolf to Vanessa Bell, 6 October 1937.
9. *Ibid.*, Virginia Woolf to JMK, 23 December 1937.
10. *CW*, xxi, 426.
11. *CW*, xii, 28.
12. Nicolson (ed.), *Letters of Virginia Woolf*, vi, Virginia Woolf to Angelica Bell, Christmas Day 1937.
13. A. O. Bell (ed.), *Diary of Virginia Woolf*, v, 129.
14. JMK to Richard Khan, 5 March 1938.
15. *CW*, xii, 38.
16. *CW*, xii, 47.
17. CMP: S. Courtauld to Christabel Aberconway, 27 June 1938.
18. Q. Bell, in Crabtree and Thirlwall (eds), *Keynes and the Bloomsbury Group*, 82, 83. For other reminiscences by Quentin Bell of Tilton, see his *Elders and Betters*, ch. 6.
19. R. C. Trevelyan Papers: 18, 96–8.
20. A. O. Bell (ed.), *Diary of Virginia Woolf*, v, 168–9.
21. *CW*, xxi, 390–1, 393.
22. *Ibid.*, 385.
23. *Ibid.*, 407.
24. *Ibid.*, 394, 408–9.
25. OTFP2 (unclassified).
26. *CW*, xxi, 408, 409.
27. *CW*, xiv, 207–10, 229.
28. *CW*, xxi, 449, 453.
29. *Ibid.*, 402–3.
30. Howson and Winch, *Economic Advisory Council*, 109, 140–2.

31. *Ibid.*, 343–55.
32. Howson, *British Monetary Policy*, 29.
33. JASP: 4.8, Box 2, JAS to K. Bode, 19 May 1937.
34. Rolph, *Kingsley*, 249, 244–5.
35. OTFP2 (unclassified): OTF to R. Boothby, 4 March 1947.
36. Markwell, 'Keynes and International Relations', 227.
37. *Ibid.*
38. q. Skidelsky, *Keynes*, ii, 62.
39. *CW*, xxviii, 100, 102.
40. *CW*, xxi, 499.
41. *CW*, xxviii, 48–50; *New Statesman*, 8 August 1936.
42. *CW*, xxviii, 62–4.
43. *Ibid.*, 72–3.
44. For an excellent account of American anglophobia see Moser, *Twisting the Lion's Tail*, esp. chs 4 and 5. The comment on the Nye Committee is on p. 91.
45. This letter is misdated by Keynes as 29 August 1938. It should be 29 September 1938.
46. *CW*, xxviii, 122–3.
47. *Ibid.*, 126, *New Statesman*, 'Mr Chamberlain's Foreign Policy'.
48. KP, PP/80, T. S. Eliot to JMK, 15 November 1938.
49. *CW*, xxi, 491–500, 'Democracy and Efficiency'.
50. KP, PP/45, JMK to B. G. Catterns, 30 April 1942.
51. Plesch, *Janos*, 424–5, 459–60, 504, 453–6.
52. RBP, File 198.
53. Sokoloff, *Story of Penicillin*, 69.
54. *CW*, xxi, 528–32; *Listener*, 1 June 1939.
55. *CW*, xxi, 564, 'Borrowing by the State'.

32. The Middle Way in War

1. RFKP, 13/57/434, JMK to RFK, 1 September 1939; *CW*, xxii, 3, letters to Roy Harrod and Lord Stamp, 7, 15 September 1939.
2. *CW*, xxii, 7.
3. *Ibid.*, 13.
4. KP, W/2, JMK to Henderson, 21 September 1939.
5. *Ibid.*, JMK to W. Beveridge, 30 September 1939.
6. OTFP1: JMK to OTF, 24 September 1939.
7. Laurence (ed.), *Bernard Shaw: Collected Letters 1926–50*, 537.
8. *CW*, xxviii, 132.
9. Laurence (ed.), *Bernard Shaw: Collected Letters 1926–50*, G. B. Shaw to JMK, 5 October 1939; see also KP, PP/45.
10. *CW*, xxii, 36–7.
11. KP, PP/45, correspondence between JMK and Lord Macmillan, 14–19 December 1939; Keynes tried again with John Reith, director-general of the BBC, in March 1940, with equal lack of success.
12. KP, PP/80.7, JMK to Fred Ashton, 8 December 1939; R. A. Butler to JMK, 29 February 1940; JMK to Raymond Mortimer, 14 January 1940.

13. *CW*, xxii, 38, JMK to A. B. Ramsay, 24 November 1939.
14. KP, L/39, Henderson to JMK, 26 November 1939.
15. *CW*, xxii, 31, letter to *The Times*, 28 September 1939.
16. Trevithick argues that the lag was due to sticky contracts, not money illusion. See J. A. Trevithick, 'Keynes, Inflation and Money Illusion', *EJ*, 85, March 1975, 104.
17. Moggridge (*Keynes: An Economist's Biography*, 629) writes that Keynes discussed it at 'a dinner meeting of officials, MPs and Ministers' on 27 October, but gives no reference.
18. *CW*, xxii, 50–1. The articles are reproduced *ibid.*, 41–51.
19. KP, HP/6, G. Dawson to JMK, 20 November 1939.
20. KP, HP/4, F. A. Hayek to JMK, 3 March 1940.
21. KP, HP/3, JMK to Henderson, 31 October 1939.
22. HDHP: Box 22/A/1, R. H. Brand to Henderson, 26 December 1939.
23. KP, HP/3, JMK to R. H. Brand, 27 November 1939.
24. *Ibid.*, JMK to R. H. Brand, 5 January 1940.
25. RBP: File 198, JMK to R. H. Brand, 27 April, 3 May 1940; R. H. Brand to JMK, 2 May 1940; Sayers, *Financial Policy*, 194.
26. KP, HP/3, Lord Stamp to JMK, 30 October 1939.
27. KP, HP/2, correspondence between JMK and C. R. Attlee, 24–31 October 1939.
28. *Daily Express*, 17 November 1939.
29. *Manchester Guardian*, 17 November 1939; KP, HP/2, Ernest Bevin to Seebohm Rowntree, 29 December 1939.
30. KP, HP/3, JMK to Lord Stamp, 12 January 1940.
31. Sayers, *Financial Policy*, 34.
32. Howson, *British Monetary Policy*, 74–7.
33. See Skidelsky, *Keynes*, i, 346.
34. KP, W/2, JMK to S. Courtauld, 10 December 1939.
35. A. O. Bell (ed.), *The Diary of Virginia Woolf*, iii, 255–6.
36. See Cooley and Ohanian, 'Postwar British Economic Growth and the Legacy of Keynes', *JPE*, 439–72.
37. KP, HP/3/75–84, 160–3; 4/32–3 for details of these suggestions, and Keynes's responses.
38. *Spectator*, 24 November 1939.
39. *CW*, xii, 93; KP, HP/2. JMK to Lord Stamp, 29 January 1939.
40. KP, HP/3, JMK to R. McKenna, 28 January 1940.
41. KP, HP/2/88–100; 3/176–88.
42. *CW*, ix, 394–6, JMK, *How to Pay for the War*.
43. *Ibid.*, 406–8.
44. *Ibid.*, 412–13.
45. *Ibid.*, 399–402.
46. *Ibid.*, 407.
47. KP, PP/45.
48. A. O. Bell (ed.), *Diary of Virginia Woolf*, iii, 283.
49. Quentin Bell, *Elders and Betters*, 101.
50. *CW*, xxii, 122–3, letter to *The Times*, 18 April 1940.
51. *CW*, xxii, 101–4, JMK to G. Dawson, 11 March 1940.
52. TP175/17.Pt 1, unsigned note dated 15 March 1933.
53. Kynaston, *City of London*, iii, 464.

54. Sayers, *Financial Policy*, 68.
55. *CW*, xxii, 66–73, for JMK's *EJ* article, March 1940; for correspondence with Rothbarth and Kaldor on this matter, see KP, W/4.
56. KP, W/4, E. Rothbarth to JMK, 29 November 1939; JMK to E. Rothbarth, 21 January 1940. Readers interested in the development of the concepts underlying the accounting identities, and how they diverged from those of Colin Clark, are referred to the discussion in Cuyvers, 'Keynes's Collaboration with Erwin Rothbarth', *EJ*, 629–36.
57. There are many versions of these calculations which do not tally exactly; Keynes also habitually rounded up figures by £50m to emphasise the inexact nature of the calculations. The figures above are summarised from *CW*, ix, 381–93, JMK, *How to Pay for the War*, and from *CW*, xxii, 60–1.
58. Sayers, *Financial Policy*, 33–4.
59. The phrase comes from Sir Richard Hopkins's 'Draft Statement on War Finance for the National Joint Advisory Council', 6 December 1939.
60. *CW*, xxii, 133.

33. The Dragons of War

1. KP, A/40, JMK to Bruce Bliven, 29 June 1940.
2. *CW*, xxii, 181–3, JMK to Brendan Bracken, 12 June 1940.
3. Sayers, *Financial Policy*, 233.
4. KP, W/3, JMK to Lord Stamp, 22 February 1940; JMK to Sir F. Phillips, 22 February, 4 March 1940.
5. *CW*, xxii, 162.
6. *Parliamentary Debates* (House of Commons), 9 April 1940, vol. 359, no. 50 col. 465.
7 KP, W/3, JMK to R. Boothby, 11 April 1940.
8. RFKP, 13/57/441, JMK to RFK, 9 May 1940; BE: G1/15, 9 May 1940; Kynaston, *City of London*, iii, 469–70.
9. For details see *CW*, xxii, 156–82.
10. KP, PP/45, A. C. Pigou to JMK, ? June 1940; JMK to A. C. Pigou, 18 June 1940.
11. *CW*, xxii, 191, JMK to F. C. Scott, 23 July 1940.
12. KP, PP/45, JMK to A. C. Pigou, 3 July 1940.
13. *CW*, xxii, 432–54, 197–212, 394–401; *CW*, xxiii, 2–10.
14. *CW*, xxii, 197–215.
15. A. O. Bell (ed.), *Diary of Virginia Woolf*, v, 314.
16. *CW*, xxii, 218–22, 223–7, 234–40.
17 *Ibid.*, 273, 'Revised Proposal for a War Surcharge', 5 January 1941.
18. Sayers, *Financial Policy*, 77.
19. *CW*, xxii, 276.
20. TP171/355, Sir H. Wilson, 'The Next Budget', 10 January 1941.
21. *Ibid.*, Sir K. Wood to Sir H. Wilson, 'The Next Budget', 14 January 1941.
22. *Ibid.*, 'Note by the Board of Inland Revenue on Mr. Keynes's revised proposal for a war surcharge', 15 January 1941; *CW*, xxii, JMK to Sir R. Hopkins, 19 January 1941.
23. *CW*, xxii, 277–9, JMK to Sir R. Hopkins, 19 January 1941.

24. TP171/355, Sir K. Wood, 'The Next Budget', 1 February 1941.
25. Sir Richard Hopkins, 'Mr. Keynes on the Budget Problem', 17 July 1940, q. Peden, *Keynes, the Treasury and British Economic Policy*.
26. *CW*, xxii, 260, 264–5, 'A Supplementary Note on the Dimensions of the Budget Problem', 26 December 1940.
27. *Ibid.*, 326–7, L. Robbins to JMK, October/November 1940.
28. R. Stone, 'The Use and Development of National Income and Expenditure Estimates', in Chester (ed.), *Lessons of the British War Economy*, 85; see also Harrod, *Keynes*, 501.
29. Sayers, *Financial Policy*, 69.
30. See *CW*, xxii, 355–63.
31. *Ibid.*, 383–5.
32. *Ibid.*, 390, 16 January 1945.
33. *Ibid.*, 402–8; Sayers, *Financial Policy*, 210–18.
34. *CW*, xxii, 410–20.
35. A. O. Bell (ed.), *Diary of Virginia Woolf*, v, 346.
36. Peden, *Keynes, the Treasury and British Economic Policy*, 40.
37. Sayers, *Financial Policy*, 73.
38. *CW*, xxii, 218, 'Notes on the Budget I', 21 September 1940.
39. q. Sayers, *Financial Policy*, 91.
40. Cooley and Ohanian, 'Postwar British Economic Growth and the Legacy of Keynes', *JPE*, 439–72.

34. Envoy Extraordinary

1. Halifax, Secret Diary, 17 February 1941.
2. *Ibid.*, 25 June 1941.
3. Arthur M. Schlesinger Jr, *The Coming of the New Deal*, 253.
4. Cordell Hull, *Memoirs*, i, 530.
5. Blum, *Morgenthau Diaries*, ii, 171.
6. Kimball, *Most Unsordid Act.*, 173.
7. *Ibid.*, 96.
8. TP160/995/19422, Lord Lothian to PM, 28 November 1940.
9. *CW*, xxiii, 13–26.
10. TP160/995/19422, Sir F. Phillips, 23 November 1940.
11. Feis, *1933*, 107.
12. Blum, *Morgenthau Diaries*, ii, 171.
13. Churchill, *The Second World War*, iii, 493–501.
14. TP175/121, Sir F. Phillips to Sir R. Hopkins, 14 January 1941.
15. Sherwood, *White House Papers of Harry L. Hopkins*, 245.
16. *CW*, xxiii, 41–2.
17. *FRUS*, 1941, iii, 2, Churchill to Roosevelt, 2 January 1941.
18. *Ibid.*, 4, memo of conversation by Secretary of State, 11 January 1941.
19. TP175/122, JMK, 'The Course of Sir Frederick Phillips' Negotiations', 18 March 1941; see also Dormael, *Bretton Woods*, 13.
20. Blum, *Morgenthau Diaries*, ii, 209.
21. Kimball, *Most Unsordid Act*, 104.
22. MD, vol. 404, 86.

23. *CW*, xxiii, 46–8, JMK to Nigel Roland.
24. *Ibid.*, 54–8.
25. *Ibid.*, 75.
26. *Ibid.*, 61–2, JMK to Lord Catto and Sir H. Wilson, 2 April 1941.
27. Lucius Thompson's diary of 8–11 May 1941, in TP247/113.
28. Harrod, *Keynes*, 557.
29. Reviewing Roy Harrod's biography in *The Times*, 31 January 1951.
30. MD, vol. 397, 221–4.
31. *CW*, xxiii, 87–8, JMK to Sir H. Wilson, 'The Course of my Negotiations', 19 May 1941.
32. *Ibid.*, 74–7, JMK to H. Morgenthau, 16 May 1941.
33. TP175,121, E. Playfair to S. D. Waley, 16 May 1941.
34. KP, PP/80/9, JMK to P. A. S. Hadley, 10 September 1941.
35. *CW*, xxiii, 154.
36. *Ibid.*, 122, JMK, 'The Course of my Negotiations: III'.
37. *Ibid.*, 130. For the whole letter see *ibid.*, 130–3.
38. MD, vol. 410, 19 June 1941, 103f.
39. *Ibid.*, 106–11, 119–29.
40. *CW*, xxiii, 147–8, 149, JMK to H. Morgenthau, 2 July 1941. McCoy is English slang for 'the real thing'; McCoy was also an official at the War Department.
41. Sayers, *Financial Policy*, 400–1.
42. TP160/955/19422, Sir F. Phillips, 2 November 1941.
43. TP247/67, JMK 1 January 1942.
44. KP, L/43, JMK to David Low, 25 April 1943, congratulating him on having spotted it.
45. TP175/121, E. Playfair to S. D. Waley, 16 May 1941.
46. Cairncross, *Years of Recovery*, 5.
47. Blum, *Morgenthau Diaries*, ii, 243.
48. TP247/113, JMK to S. D. Waley, 18 June 1941; JMK to Harry Hopkins, 27 June 1941.
49. *CW*, xxiii, 138–40.
50. *Ibid.*, 125 and n.
51. TP247/113, Sir K. Wood to JMK, 5 July 1941.
52. See Dobson, *US Wartime Aid to Britain*, 36–8; Moggridge, *Keynes: An Economist's Biography*, 660.
53. *CW*, xxiii, 145–6, JMK to Treasury, ? June 1941.
54. *FRUS*, 1941, iii, 21–2.
55. Kimball, 'Lend–Lease and the Open Door', 252–3. See also editor's summary, *CW*, xxiii, 143–4.
56. This account is conflated from Acheson, *Present at the Creation*, 30, and Acheson's 'Memorandum of Conversation', 28 July 1941, copy in FDR Library, PSF Box 16, File LL(3).
57. *CW*, xxiii, 151–2; Sayers, *Financial Policy*, 394–5.
58. Sayers, *Financial Policy*, 397.
59. WLP, MS 326, Box 82/1217; KP, P/45, JMK to WL, 28 April 1942.

35. Keynes in Wartime

1. *CW*, xxiii, 149, JMK to Sir H. Wilson, 2 July 1941.
2. LePan, *Bright Glass of Memory*, 62.
3. Clarke, *Anglo-American Economic Collaboration*, 71.
4. Partridge, *A Pacifist's War*, 140.
5. Chester (ed.), *Lessons of the British War Economy*, 9.
6. *Ibid.*, p. ix. See also *ibid.*, 31 for its remit.
7. KP, W/4, JMK to C. Clark, 23 January 1942.
8. Cairncross and Watts, *Economic Section*, 29.
9. *Ibid.*, 26–8.
10. *Ibid.*, 53.
11. *CW*, xxii, 382, JMK to FAK, 28 March, 10 April 1943.
12. Isaiah Berlin, citing a story told him by Lionel Robbins, in M. Keynes (ed.) *Lydia Lopokova*, 171–2.
13. He was so called by Lionel Robbins, *Autobiography*, 173.
14. *Ibid.*, 187.
15. *Ibid.*
16 *CW*, xxv, 102.
17. KP, L/B, R. H. Brand to JMK, 18 May 1943.
18. Obituary, 13 August 1943, repr. in *CW*, x, 330.
19. Sir W. Eady to FAK, 3 June 1951.
20. Eady, 'Maynard Keynes at the Treasury'.
21. *Ibid.*
22. Cairncross and Watts, *The Economic Section*, 54.
23. *Ibid.*, 53–4.
24. *CW*, xxiii, 316–23.
25. Moggridge, *Keynes: An Economist's Biography*, 663.
26. *John Maynard Keynes* (KCC), 26; Eady, 'Maynard Keynes at the Treasury'.
27. Eady, 'Maynard Keynes at the Treasury'.
28. Interview with the late Sir Frederick Harmer, 19 March 1987.
29. TP247/6, 'South American Correspondence'. For Playfair's letter see TP175/121.
30. KP, L/K 147, JMK to RFK, 31 October 1941.
31. TP247/4, JMK to S. D. Waley, 23 February 1942; to Lord Catto, N. E. Young, S. D. Waley, 3 March 1942.
32. TP247/5, JMK memo, 26 April 1945.
33. See KP, PP/45 for correspondence with Ray Milburn about Madrid; KP, W/9 for correspondence with Stanley Jevons on Ethiopia.
34. E. A. G. Robinson, 'Keynes', *DNB 1941–50*, 456. See *ibid.*, 456–7 for a good account of Keynes's 'practical genius'.
35. Hubback, 'Sir Richard Clarke', 77.
36. LePan, *Bright Glass of Memory*, 62.
37. RBP: File 198, R. H. Brand to Barbara Wootton, 29 November 1946.
38. Skidelsky, *Keynes*, ii, 213, 509–10.
39. Kingsley Martin reviewing Harrod's biography in the *New Statesman*, 3 February 1951.
40. JMK to FAK, 23 February 1943.
41. RFKP, 13/57/479, JMK to RFK, 8 December 1943.

42. KP, L/42, JMK to Joan Robinson, 9 December 1942.
43. JTSP: 6.13, JMK to JTS, 15 February 1946.
44. KP, PP/45, Quentin Keynes to JMK, 16 April 1943; JMK to Quentin Keynes, 29 April 1943.
45. KP, L/43, JMK to E. Tillyard, 25 June 1943.
46. KP, PP/79, JMK to G. Rylands, 3 December 1943.
47. Spalding, *Grant*, 375.
48. Harrod, *Keynes*, 193–4.
49. See Spotts (ed.), *Letters of Leonard Woolf,* 348 and n.
50. KP, PP/45, JMK to Ivor Brown, 4 October 1942.
51. KP, L/42, JMK Reader's Report, 17 June 1942.
52. *Ibid.*, correspondence with J. H. Clapham May/September 1942.
53. KP, CO/1, 'Dr. W. Stark'.
54. KP, L/43, correspondence May/June 1943.
55. KP, CO/10, JMK to Joan Robinson, 20 August 1942.
56. KP, L/45, JMK to Cyril Connolly, 22 February 1945.
57. KP, GE/1/1, JMK to W. Hope-Jones, 25 August 1940.
58. KP, GE/1/2, JMK to Claude Elliott, 26 August 1942.
59. KP, GE/1/2, Claude Elliott to JMK, 11 August 1942; see also JMK to R. E. Marsden, 9 November 1942. KP, GE/1/3, JMK to R. E. Marsden, 12 March 1943.
60. KP, GE/1/4, J. Ridley to JMK, 8 March 1944; JMK to J. Ridley, (undated) March 1944.
61. In *DNB 1951–60*, 202.
62. KP, GE/2, JMK to F. Cruso, 6, 24 February 1941.
63. KP, W/4, Sir G. Schuster to JMK 4 February 1943; JMK to Sir G. Schuster, 7 February 1943.

36. Keynes's 'New Order'

1. KP, W/1, JMK to Dean Acheson, 17 October 1941.
2. See TP175/123.
3. For an account of this see Dobson, *US Wartime Aid to Britain*, chs 3 and 4.
4. *CW*, xxv, 20.
5. *Ibid.*, 2.
6. Einzig, *Hitler's New Order in Europe*, 66.
7. *CW*, xxv, 8–9.
8. *Ibid.*, 16–19.
9. Eichengreen, *PSIF*, 'Sterling and the Tariff', 32.
10. JMK, *The General Theory of Employment, Interest and Money, CW*, vii, 348–9. Hubert Henderson agreed: 'Of the various expedients which different Governments employed in the 1930s, none produced more unfortunate results than deliberate exchange depreciation. It was the least helpful to countries which tried it, and the most harmful to other countries': q. Dormael, *Bretton Woods*, 129.
11. TP247/121, Henderson memorandum, 3 September 1941.
12. FFP, F. Frankfurter to JMK, 19 September 1941; RFKP, 13/57/472, JMK to RFK, 9 September 1941.
13. q. Kynaston, *City of London*, iii, 483.

14. HCP: M. Norman to H. Clay, 19 June 1946.
15. *CW*, xxv, 67, D. H. Robertson to JMK, 27 November 1941.
16. The first draft of the International Currency Union is reproduced in *CW*, xxv, 21–40. In my summary of Part I, I have rearranged the four sections in what, to me, seems a more logical order.
17. Moggridge, *Keynes: An Economist's Biography*, 674.
18. The progress of the Treasury 'sandwich' can be traced in TP247/121.
19. TP247/122, Bank of England memo on Post-War Trade and Financial Policy, 17 October 1941; B. G. Catterns to Sir R. Hopkins, 4 November 1941; Bank memo, 4 November 1941. Keynes identified G. L. Bolton as the author of the last. Bank of England reactions can also be followed in BE, ADMIN 14/1–2.
20. TP247/122, JMK, 'Bank of England Memorandum on Post-War Trade and Financial Policy', 22 October 1941.
21. *Ibid.*
22. TP247/121, D. H. Robertson, 26 September 1941, 22 August 1941.
23. *Ibid.*, Note on Treasury memo, 12 October 1941.
24. *Ibid.*, undated.
25. *Ibid.*, 16 October 1941.
26. *Ibid.*, 'Post-War Currency', 21 September 1941.
27. *Ibid.*, Note on Treasury Memo, 13 November 1941.
28. *Ibid.*, 'Notes on Memorandum . . .', 17 November 1941.
29. *Ibid.*, Henderson to Sir R. Hopkins, 22 October 1941.
30. BE, ADMIN 14/1, H. A. Siepmann, 'Results of Two Conversations with Keynes', 14 November 1941; G. L. F. Bolton's additions, 15 November 1941.
31. TP247/16, 'Mr. Keynes's Proposal,' 15 October 1941.
32. *Ibid.*, 24 December 1941.
33. RBP: File 198, R. H. Brand to JMK, 10 October 1941.
34. TP247/116, J. E. Meade to JMK, 9 October 1941.
35. C.1 and C.2 of the 18 November draft, *CW*, xxv, 65. This was not in the first draft.
36. Penrose, *Economic Planning for Peace*, 15–16.
37. *CW*, xxv, 91.
38. TP247/121. Both letters written on 26 November 1941.
39. *CW*, xxv, 66.
40. In TP247/116.
41. These phrases are from a memorandum Harrod sent to Keynes on 4 April 1942 (TP247/67), but he had been preaching this gospel throughout the autumn of 1941.
42. TP247/121, RFH, 'Notes on Memorandum . . .', 17 November 1941; 'Note on Points Made in Discussion', 26 November 1941. See TP272/63 for the development of Harrod's views.
43. *CW*, xxv, 149, JMK to Harrod, 19 April 1942.
44. TP247/122, JMK to M. Norman, 19 December 1941.
45. *CW*, xxv, 69–94, third draft of Proposals for an International Currency Union.
46. TP247/116, Roy Harrod to Sir R. Hopkins, 18 December 1941.
47. *Ibid.*, Sir R. Hopkins to Roy Harrod, 24 December 1941.
48. KP, L/K/163.
49. TP247/116.
50. Pressnell, *External Economic Policy since the War*, i, 78.

51. TP247/118. JMK to Sir R. Hopkins, 29 January 1942; Robbins Note, ? February 1942.
52. FO371/32450, C. Baring to N. Ronald, 6 February 1942, q. Dormael, *Bretton Woods*, 48.
53. B. Pimlott (ed.), *Second World War Diary of Hugh Dalton*, 406; *CW*, xxv, 140–3; Bullock, *Bevin*, ii, 204.
54. *CW*, xxv. 143, JMK to RFK, 11 May 1942.

37. The Strange Case of Harry Dexter White

1. TP247/116, Roy Harrod to Sir R. Hopkins, 4 December 1941.
2. *CW*, xxvii, 111, JMK to Sir R. Hopkins, 15 April 1942.
3. *Ibid.*, 122–34.
4. TP247/110, JMK to Sir F. Phillips, 6 January 1943.
5. *Ibid.*, 100. See also T247/2.
6. TP247/2, JMK, 'Post-War Commercial Policy', 15 January 1943.
7. *Ibid.* Details of the discussions on the Commercial Union are in TP247/2.
8. q. Dormael, *Bretton Woods*, p.40.
9. Oliver, *International Economic Cooperation and the World Bank*, 110–11.
10. Mikesell, 'Bretton Woods Debates', 5–6.
11. M. Bordo and Anna J. Schwartz, 'From the Exchange Stabilization Fund to the International Monetary Fund' NBER, 2001
12. Craig, 'Treasonable Doubt: The Harry Dexter White Case', 596–7.
13. Rees, *Harry Dexter White*, 100–2, 118, 143, 301–2.
14. See Keynes's comment in *CW*, xxv, 356.
15. The H. D. White Papers, Box 8, contains his drafts for the IMF and Reconstruction Bank.
16. Harrod, *Keynes*, 540.
17. For details, see Horsefield, *International Monetary Fund*, i, 21–5, iii, 41–82.
18. *CW*, xxv, 158–9. JMK to Sir R. Hopkins, 3 August 1942; JMK to Sir F. Phillips, 3 August 1942.
19. *Ibid.*, 160–7, JMK, 'Notes on the Memorandum . . . transmitted by Sir F. Phillips'.
20. RFKP, L/K/203, JMK to RFK, 28 August 1942.
21. Horsefield, *International Monetary Fund*, i, 30.
22. FO371/31516, Sir F. Phillips to Treasury, 8 October 1942.
23. Penrose, *Economic Planning for Peace*, 48–9.
24. KP, L/K/237, JMK to RFK, 13 November 1942.
25. Dormael, *Bretton Woods*, 67–8.
26. *CW*, xxv, 210, JMK speech to meeting of European Allies, London, 26 February 1943.
27. FO371/3530, JMK to N. Ronald, 25 February 1943.
28. *CW*, xxv, 238, JMK to Sir F. Phillips, 16 April 1943.
29. TP160/1281/18885/1, JMK, 'The Berle Memorandum', 18 February 1943 – as the White Plan was then called.
30. Horsefield, *International Monetary Fund*, i, 45–6.
31. TP160/1281/18885/3, JMK memo, 16 April 1943.
32. *CW*, xxv, 268, JMK to Roy Harrod, 27 April 1943.
33. TP160/18885/1, JMK to Lord Catto, Sir W. Eady, D. Proctor, 2 April 1943.

34. Dormael, *Bretton Woods*, 77.
35. TP160/1281/18885/5, Lord Halifax to FO 13, June 1943.
36. q. Gardner, *Sterling–Dollar Diplomacy*, 78.
37. BLH: TLP: Folder 104–1, 1943–4, 'Bancor and Unitas', 3 June 1943.
38. q. Rowland (ed.), *Balance of Power or Hegemony*, 221.
39. 'Memoranda on Axis-Controlled Europe', no. 60, Review of the Foreign Press, Series A, 3 August 1943, Research Department Foreign Office. This copy is in BE 14/9.
40. *CW*, xxv, 258–9.
41. TP160/1281/18885/5, JMK to D. H. Robinson, 2 June 1943.
42. *CW*, xxv, 269–80.

38. Building a Better Britain

1. KP, PP/45, JMK to William Temple, 3 December 1941.
2. Harris, *Beveridge*, 386; Bullock, *Bevin*, ii, 226.
3. *CW*, xxvii, 219, JMK to W. Beveridge, 25 June 1942.
4. *Ibid.*, 237.
5. *Ibid.*, 230, 238–9.
6. HDHP: Box 3, Beveridge File, Henderson to Sir Alexander Roger, 17 February 1943; to Sir R. Hopkins, 22 December 1942.
7. Cairncross and Watts, *Economic Section*, 71.
8. *CW*, xxvii, 271, JMK to Henderson and Sir R. Hopkins, 8 April 1942. For Henderson's paper see CAB 87/55.
9. *CW*, xxvii, 314–15.
10. Pre-1914 figures are based on the records of trade unions that paid benefits to their members. The shortcomings of the data as a measure of unemployment in the labour force are well known. (See Feinstein, *National Income, Expenditure and Output of the United Kingdom*, 225.) What matters is how Keynes interpreted them. Even so, the percentages varied considerably across the cycle, from 2 per cent to 7.8 per cent (*ibid.*, 57). So the figure of 5 per cent is an average, not a minimum.
11. *CW*, xxvii, 280–1, 299, 301, JMK, 'National Income and Expenditure after the War', 28 May 1942; JMK to Henderson, 3 June 1942.
12. Cairncross and Watts, *Economic Section*, 91–2.
13. *CW*, xxvii, 299, JMK to Henderson.
14. *Ibid.*, 381, JMK to W. Beveridge, 16 December 1944.
15. In Howson and Moggridge (ed.), *Collected Papers of James Meade*, iv, 63.
16. *CW*, xxvii, 225.
17. *Ibid.*, 227, JMK to Sir R. Hopkins and others, 15 May 1942; *ibid.*, 368, 'Post-War Employment Policy: Note by Lord Keynes on the Report of the Steering Committee', 14 February 1944; *ibid.*, 410–11, 'The Concept of a Capital Budget', 21 June 1945.
18. *Ibid.*, 405–6.
19. *Ibid.*, 352–3, JMK to Sir W. Eady, 10 June 1943; see also *ibid.*, 376–7, JMK to A. Barlow, 15 June 1944.
20. *Ibid.*, 226–8.
21. *Ibid.*, 319–20, JMK to James Meade, 25 April 1943.

22. KP, CO/2. Keynes attacked Lerner's paper 'Functional Finance and the Federal Debt', *Social Research,* February 1943, vol. 10, no. 1, in Washington in 1943. See JMK to Fritz Machlup, 24 October 1944; JMK to J. H. G. Pierson, 22 October 1943.

23. Wilson, *Churchill and the Prof,* 164–5.

24. For this shift see Tomlinson, *Employment Policy.*

25. Clark, 'Public Finance and Changes in the Value of Money', 371.

26. *CW,* xxvii, 206, 208.

27. *Ibid.,* 317, James Meade to JMK, 19 April 1943.

28. *Ibid.,* 310, JMK to James Meade, 25 August 1942.

29. *Ibid.,* 319–20, JMK to James Meade, 25 April 1943.

30. *Ibid.,* 322, 'The Long-Term Problem of Full Employment', 25 May 1943.

31. Henderson's paper is reproduced in Henderson, *The Inter-War Years and Other Papers.*

32. *CW,* xxvii, 321–4; see also *ibid.,* 350, JMK to Josiah Wedgwood, 7 July 1943.

33. 'Economic Possibilities for Our Grandchildren' is published in *CW,* ix, 321–32. For a discussion, and critique, see Skidelsky, *Keynes,* ii, 236–8.

34. *CW,* ix, 384.

35. See Moggridge, *Keynes: An Economist's Biography,* 711.

36. *CW,* xxvii, 325–6.

37. *Ibid.,* 358.

38. Peden, 'Sir Richard Hopkins and the "Keynesian Revolution"', LEcHR, 289.

39. q. Booth, 'Simple Keynesianism and Whitehall'.

40. Beveridge's *Full Employment in a Free Society* was published in 1944.

41. *CW,* xxvii, 371–2, 'Note by Lord Keynes on the Report of the Steering Committee', 14 February 1944.

42. *Ibid.,* 366–7.

43. *Ibid.,* 336–42.

44. *Ibid.,* 354–7.

45. HDHP: Box 3, 'Brave New Worlds: Internal and External', 22 March 1944; 'The Employment Policy', 27 March 1944, 'Employment Policy and the Balance of Payments', 31 March 1944.

46. *CW,* xxvii, 373–4, JMK to Sir W. Eady, Sir R. Hopkins, 28 March 1944.

47. JMK to Austin Robinson, 5 June 1944, q. Moggridge, *Keynes: An Economist's Biography,* 709.

48. *CW,* xxvii, 385.

49. Hayek, *Road to Serfdom,* 90–1.

50. E.g. Barbara Wootton, *Freedom under Planning,* 30, 62, as q. Durbin, *New Jerusalems,* 269.

51. *CW,* xxvii, 385–8, JMK to F. A. Hayek, 28 June 1944.

52. KP, PP/84(1), R. A. Butler to JMK, 17 December 1941.

53. See Mary Glasgow, 'The Concept of the Arts Council', in M. Keynes (ed.), *Essays on John Maynard Keynes,* 260–1, 262; also Glasgow, *Nineteen Hundreds,* 188.

54. Mary Glasgow, in M. Keynes (ed.), *Essays on John Maynard Keynes,* 267.

55. See Clive Bell, *Old Friends,* 56–8.

56. Kenneth Clark, *Other Half,* 27; Mary Glasgow in M. Keynes (ed.), *Essays on John Maynard Keynes,* 267.

57. Glasgow, *Nineteen Hundreds,* 192–3.

58. A large file on 'Entertainments Tax' can be found in KP, PP/84(6).

59. Mary Glasgow in M. Keynes (ed.), *Essays on John Maynard Keynes* 266–7.
60. KP, PP/84 (5), JMK to Sir Alfred Barker, 23 January 1943.
61. *CW*, xxviii, 360, JMK, 'The Arts in War-time', *The Times*, 11 May 1943.
62. Mary Glasgow in M. Keynes (ed.) Essays on *John Maynard Keynes*, 269.
63. KP, PP/84 (5), JMK to A. Dukes, 18 May 1943; for the antecedents to this row see also KP, PP/80(9).
64. KP, PP/84 (3) for these exchanges with R. A. Butler, February–April 1943.
65. KP, PP/84 (5).
66. KP, PP/84(3), JMK to R. A. Butler, 6 April 1945.
67. KP, PP/84 (8).

39. The Great Compromise

1. Penrose, *Economic Planning for Peace*, 120.
2. Howson and Moggridge (eds), *Wartime Diaries of Robbins and Meade*, 52.
3. *CW*, xxv, 292, D. H. Robertson, 'Notes', 3 June 1943.
4. *Ibid.*, 267, JMK to Roy Harrod, 27 April 1943; *ibid.*, 296, JMK to D. H. Robertson, 11 June 1943.
5. Dormael, *Bretton Woods*, 90–1; see also *CW*, xxv, 317.
6. *CW*, xxv, 303, JMK to D. H. Robertson, 9 July 1943.
7. *Ibid.*, 318–19, 321, JMK to Sir W. Eady, 13 July 1943; JMK to J. Viner, 9 June 1943.
8. So Keynes told the Australian economist Herbert Coombs, who saw him in London that summer. See Turnell, 'A Clearing Union or a Stabilising Fund? Australian Economists and the Creation of the IMF', 7. Coombs was also promoting the Australian 'employment approach' – that members of the SF should commit themselves to full employment policies.
9. MD, vol. 654, 95, telegram from J. Winant, 5 August 1943; see also Dormael, *Bretton Woods*, 89–91.
10. Howson and Moggridge (eds), *Wartime Diaries of Robbins and Meade*, 76.
11. *CW*, xxv, 305–7, JMK to S. D. Waley, 22 June 1943; see also Moggridge, *Keynes: An Economist's Biography*, 724.
12. FO371/35336, R. Opie note of 23 August 1943.
13. Howson and Moggridge (eds), *Wartime Diaries of Robbins and Meade*, 97.
14. TP160/1281/18885/6, JMK to E. Playfair, Sir W. Eady, 5 August 1943.
15. Howson and Moggridge (eds), *Wartime Diaries of Robbins and Meade*, 93.
16. *Ibid.*, 100.
17. *Ibid.*, 104, 109, 110.
18. TP160/1281/18885/6, 'Note of Plenary Session', 21 September 1943.
19. Howson and Moggridge (eds), *Wartime Diaries of Robbins and Meade*, 105.
20. FO371/3536, R. Campbell to FO, 15 September 1943, contains JMK's report of the conversation. See also *CW*, xxv, 340.
21. Gardner, *Sterling–Dollar Diplomacy*, 112.
22. Howson and Moggridge (eds), *Wartime Diaries of Robbins and Meade*, 130.
23. Dormael, *Bretton Woods*, 101.
24. Interview with Edward Bernstein, 10 April 1989.
25. *CW*, xxv, 334.
26. The phrase is from Pressnell, *External Economic Policy since the War*, 139.

27. Pimlott (ed.), *Second World War Diary of Hugh Dalton*, 631.
28. TP160/1281/18885/6.
29. Pimlott (ed.), *Second World War Diary of Hugh Dalton*, 648; also TP160/1281/18885/6, Telegrams 4174, 6356, 4274, 6702.
30. For Varvaressos's role, see Horsefield, *International Monetary Fund*, i, 58.
31. Howson and Moggridge (eds), *Wartime Diaries of Robbins and Meade*, 123.
32. *Ibid.* For Meade's comment on Thompson-McCausland, see *ibid.*, 121; for the Bank's instructions to him, *ibid.*, 150.
33. BE, ADMIN 14/9.
34. For Keynes's reasons, and plan, for monetising unitas, see *CW*, xxv, 321, 318–19, 341–4, 346–8; also L. P. Thompson-McCausland, 'Difference beween S. F. and Monetised Unitas . . .', 29 September 1943, in BE, ADMIN 14/9.
35. Howson and Moggridge (eds), *Wartime Diaries of Robbins and Meade*, 122.
36. *Ibid.*, 127.
37. MD, vol. 664, 30.
38. *CW*, xxv, 360–4, JMK to Sir W. Eady, 3 October 1943.
39. Howson and Moggridge (eds), *Wartime Diaries of Robbins and Meade*, 135.
40. *Ibid.*, 133; *CW*, xxv, 371.
41. MD, vol. 722, 17.
42. For the various documents resulting from the talks, see *CW*, xxv, 377–92. The comparisons are with the *CW*, xxv draft and the 10 July 1943 draft as reprinted in Horsefield, *International Monetary Fund*, iii, 83–96.
43. *CW*, xxv, 368, 369, JMK to Sir W. Eady, 8 October 1943.
44. Harrod, *Keynes*, 567–8.
45. For JMK's comments, see *CW*, xxv, 354, 356, 363–4.
46. Harry White Papers: Washington Section, 1944 folder. Information supplied by James Boughton.
47. TP160/1281/18885/7, JMK memo, 17 January 1944.
48. Pimlott (ed.), *Second World War Diary of Hugh Dalton*, 670.
49. Dobson, *US Wartime Aid to Britain*, 173.
50. LePan, *Bright Glass of Memory*, 61.
51. MacDougall, *Don and Mandarin*, 40.
52. *CW*, xxv, 399–408, JMK 'The Main Objects of the Plan'.
53. *Ibid.*, 409.
54. *Ibid.*, 410–13, JMK to Sir J. Anderson, 23 February 1944.
55. q. Kynaston, *City of London*, iii, 503, from a 'Note on Commercial Policy', BE, G 18/3, 20 March 1945.
56. Pimlott (ed.), *Second World War Diary of Hugh Dalton*, 710–12.
57. MacDougall, *Don and Mandarin*, 39.
58. For JMK's exchange with Beaverbrook 8–11 March, see *CW*, xxv, 415–18. For JMK's distinction between currency and commercial bilateralism, see his letter to Sir W. Eady, 29 March 1943, *ibid.*, 430, and his correspondence with D. H. Robertson, *CW*, xxvi, 23–6.
59. TP160/1287/18885/10, Hopkins to Chancellor, 3 April 1944.
60. Pimlott (ed.), *Second World War Diary of Hugh Dalton*, 735–6.
61. Dobson, *US Wartime Aid to Britain*, 173–4.
62. *CW*, xxvi, 3, JMK to F. Pethick-Lawrence, 16 May 1944.
63. As Balogh recalled in Thirlwall (ed.), *Keynes and International Monetary Relations*, 66.

64. LePan, *Bright Glass of Memory*, 101.
65. Letters to *The Times*, 10, 18 May 1943.
66. *CW*, xxvi, 29–30, JMK to L. Pasvolsky, 24 May 1944.
67. *Ibid.*, 9–21.
68. Pasvolsky, q. Dormael, *Bretton Woods*, 160.

40. The American Way of Business

1. *CW*, xxiv, 28–9, JMK to E. R. Stettinius, 18 April 1944.
2. See Moggridge, *Keynes: An Economist's Biography*, 657–60; *CW*, xxiii, ch. 8.
3. *CW*, xxiv, 1–18.
4. *Ibid.*, 64.
5. Howson and Moggridge (eds), *Wartime Diaries of Robbins and Meade*, 158–9, Robbins Diary, 24 June 1944.
6. *CW*, xxvi, 48–54, JMK, 'The Bank for Reconstruction and Development', 9 June 1944.
7. *Ibid.*, 61, 64, JMK to Sir R. Hopkins, 25 June 1944; see also FO371/40948, 40589.
8. Howson and Moggridge (eds), *Wartime Diaries of Robbins and Meade*, 166.
9. *CW*, xxvi, 86–7.
10. *Ibid.*, 109, JMK to Sir W. Hopkins, 22 July 1944.
11. JMK to Sir W. Eady, 1 March 1945.
12. EGP, BW Conference, Box 4.
13. Horsefield, *International Monetary Fund*, i, 95; Mikesell, 'The Bretton Woods Debates', 35–8.
14. MD, vol. 754, 20–30.
15. MD, vol. 753, 122–6.
16. *Ibid.*, 143–4; vol. 754, 4.
17. Eady in the *Listener*, 7 June 1951.
18. EGP, Box 4.
19. From Malcolm MacDonald's *People and Places*, 1969, reproduced in M. Keynes (ed.), *Lydia Lopokova*, 178–9.
20. *CW*, xxiv, 97–107, JMK to Sir J. Anderson, 10 August 1944; Sayers, *British Financial Policy*, 351–8; JMK to FAK, 7 August 1944.
21. *CW*, xxiv, 114–126.
22. Rees, *Harry Dexter White*, 251; see *ibid.*, 239–51 for the episode; also Penrose, *Economic Planning for Peace*, ch. 14.
23. KP, L/44, JMK to WL, 13 August 1944; MD, vol. 764, 90, H. D. White to H. Morgenthau, 20 August 1944.
24. Cairncross, *Price of War*, 27; *CW*, xxvi, 348–73.
25. Blum, *Morgenthau Diary*, iii, 369; Dobson, *US Wartime Aid to Britain*, 194.
26. Woodward, *British Foreign Policy*, 476.
27. Dobson, *US Wartime Aid to Britain*, 195–6.
28. Churchill, *Second World War*, vi, 139; Penrose, *External Economic Policy since the War*, 255.
29. MD, vol. 773, 74.
30. *CW*, xxiv, 187, Frank Lee to F. E. Harmer, 6 December 1944.
31. *Ibid.*, 129, JMK to Sir J. Anderson, 1 October 1944.

32. *Ibid.*, 132, JMK to Sir J. Anderson, 4 October 1944.
33. *Ibid.*, 133–4; Halifax Diary, 2 November 1944; Penrose, *External Economic Policy since the War*, 255.
34. *CW*, xxiv, 186–7, Frank Lee to F. E. Harmer, 6 December 1944.
35. *Ibid.*, 214–15, JMK to Sir J. Anderson, 12 December 1944.
36. MacDougall Diary, 24 October 1944.
37. Isaiah Berlin, in M. Keynes (ed.), *Lydia Lopokova*, 172–3. Berlin was stationed in Washington for most of the war.
38. *CW*, xxiv, 139, JMK to Sir J. Anderson, 21 October 1944.
39. For the Berlin story, see M. Keynes (ed.), *Lydia Lopokova*, 173. A variant is given in a transcript of an interview with Michael Ignatieff, 5 June 1994.
40. *CW*, xxiv, 160.
41. In M. Keynes (ed.), *Lydia Lopokova*, 184.
42. *CW*, xxiv, 204, 217, 218, JMK to Sir J. Anderson, 12 December 1944.
43. Ben Pimlott (ed.), *Second World War Diary of Hugh Dalton*, 818.
44. Dobson, *US Wartime Aid to Britain*, 211. For Roosevelt's change of mind, see *ibid.*, 206–11.
45. *CW*, xxiv, 220–1, JMK to Sir J. Anderson, 12 December 1944.

41. Temptation

1. Howson and Moggridge (eds), *Collected Papers of James Meade*, 55.
2. KP, PP/45, JMK to Sir C. Gregg, 9 April 1945.
3. See T. P. McLaughlin, 'The Teaching of the Canonists on Usury', *Mediaeval Studies*, 1, 1939.
4. For the British draft see *FRUS*, 1945, vi, 56–60; For Keynes's views, see *ibid.*, 19–21, J. Winant to Cordell Hull, 8 February 1945; Currie Report on conversations with British officials, *ibid.*, 38.
5. *CW*, xxiv, 249.
6. *FRUS*, 1945, vi, 28–9, 36–44.
7. LePan, *Bright Glass of Memory*, 69.
8. *CW*, xxiv, 272.
9. *Ibid.*, 276–9.
10. *Ibid.*, 281.
11. *Ibid.*, 292.
12. *CW*, xxiv, 277.
13. TP247/49, Sir W. Eady to JMK, 27 March 1945; cf. though JMK's comment to Brand on 3 May, that Eady was against an 'interim arrangement' with the US based on 'temporary borrowing', *CW*, xxv, 326.
14. TP247/49, comments by E. Rowe-Dutton, 3 April 1945; S. D. Waley, 5 April, 12 April 1945; C. F. Cobbold, 13 July 1945. Notes of meeting of Overseas Finance Division, 18 April, with JMK in the chair. Present: Waley, Rowe-Dutton, G. S. Pinsent, Norman Young, H. E. Brooks, A. T. K. Grant, R. W. B. Clarke, E. Jones.
15. *CW*, xxiv, 332, R. H. Brand to JMK, 14 May 1945.
16. Brand repeatedly emphasised this point: *ibid.*, 307–8, 332, 369.
17. *Ibid.*, 308, R. H. Brand to JMK, 5 April 1945.
18. *Ibid.*, 318, R. H. Brand to JMK, 25 April 1945.
19. *Ibid.*, 318, 321, 333.

20. Churchill, *Second World War*, vi, 498, 500–1.
21. TP247/49, 'Towards a Balance of Payments', 11 May 1945; repr. in Clarke, *Anglo-American Economic Collaboration*, 96–122.
22. TP247/49, Sir W. Eady to JMK, 4 August 1945.
23. *CW*, xxiv, 366–7, JMK to Sir W. Eady, R. Clarke, 9 July 1945.
24. Clarke, *Anglo-American Economic Collaboration*, 6.
25. LePan, *Bright Glass of Memory*, 72.
26. *Ibid.*, ch. 2. See particularly quotations at 56, 91.
27. *FRUS*, 1945, vi, 54–6, Clayton to F. Vinson, 25 June 1945.
28. Pimlott, *Dalton*, 426.
29. *CW*, xxiv, 370, R. H. Brand to JMK, 23 June 1945.
30. *FRUS*, 1945, vi, 79–86, Memorandum of Conversation, 3 August 1945.
31. *Ibid.*, 90–2, 94–7, J. Winant to US Secretary of State, 11 and 16 August 1945.
32. *Ibid.*, 97–101, J. Winant to James F. Byrnes, 17 August 1945. A slightly different version is in the Vinson Papers, Box 148.
33. Bullen and Pelly (eds), *Documents on British Policy Overseas*, Series 1, iii, 44–9.

42. Averting a Financial Dunkirk

1. *CW*, xxiv, 398–411, 'Our Overseas Financial Prospects', 13 August 1945.
2. Bullen and Pelly, 72–7.
3. *Ibid.*, 73–4, n. 4; for American reactions, see *FRUS*, 1945, vi, 110.
4. Howson and Moggridge (eds), *Wartime Diaries of Robbins and Meade*, 223.
5. Lamont Papers: File 104–5, R. C. Leffingwell to C. Gifford, 31 August 1945.
6. Bullen and Pelly, 117, E. Hall-Patch to Sir A. Cadogan, 8 September 1945.
7. Howson and Moggridge (eds), *Collected Papers of James Meade*, iv, 132.
8. Bullen and Pelly, 128–32, and notes at 132–3.
9. So Moscow was informed on 29 October 1945. See Weinstein and Vassiliev, *Haunted Wood*, 168.
10. Bareau, Lecture II, 6.
11. In the *Washington Daily News*, 4 December 1945.
12. Bareau, Note of meeting of Joint Finance Committee, 19 September 1945.
13. *Ibid.*, Note of meeting of 20 September 1945.
14. Pressnell, *External Economic Policy since the War*, 279–81.
15. Howson and Moggridge (eds), *Collected Papers of James Meade*, iv, 224.
16. Halifax Diary, 25 September 1945; Bullen and Pelly, 154, Lord Halifax to Ernest Bevin, 26 September 1945.
17. Bareau, Lecture II, 8.
18. *CW*, xxiv, 503–8, JMK, 'Terms of Assistance'; see also Bullen and Pelly, 155 n. 3; 158–9 n. 4.
19. *CW*, xxiv, 514, JMK to Hugh Dalton, 1 October 1945.
20. Pimlott, *Dalton*, 430.
21. See comments in Halifax Diary, 26 September, 5, 9, 11 October 1945.
22. Bullen and Pelly, 196–9, Hugh Dalton to Lord Halifax, 8 October 1945.
23. *Ibid.*, 210–14, JMK to Hugh Dalton, 9 October 1945; *CW*, xxiv, 543.
24. *CW*, xxiv, 542, JMK to Sir W. Eady, 12 October 1945.
25. Halifax Diary, 13 October 1945; Harmer Diary, 8 October 1945.
26. Pressnell, *External Economic Policy since the War*, 285.

27. Bullen and Pelly, 223–4, Lord Halifax and JMK to Hugh Dalton, 16 October 1945.
28. *Ibid.*, 227–32, JMK to Hugh Dalton, 18 October 1945.
29. Halifax Diary, 18 October 1945; Bullen and Pelly, 243–4, JMK to Hugh Dalton, 20 October 1945.
30. Harmer Diary, 8 October 1945; *CW*, xxiv, 541, JMK to Sir W. Eady, 12 October 1945.
31. Bullen and Pelly, 224, n. 5, JMK to Sir E. Bridges, 19 October 1945.
32. Robbins, *Autobiography*, 208–9.
33. Harmer Diary, 27 October 1945.
34. Howson and Moggridge (eds), *Collected Papers of James Meade*, iv, 163.
35. *Ibid.*, 164.
36. *CW*, xxiv, 584, JMK to Sir W. Eady, 7 November 1945.
37. Bullen and Pelly, 259–60, Hugh Dalton to British Mission, 27 October 1945.
38. Pressnell, *External Economic Policy since the War*, 296.
39. Dalton, *High Tide and After*, 72, 77.
40. Bullen and Pelly, 289–92, Hugh Dalton to Lord Halifax and JMK, 6 November 1945; see also Howson and Moggridge (eds), *Collected Papers of James Meade*, iv, 165–6.
41. Bullen and Pelly, 302–4, 7 November 1945.
42. Bareau Note, 12 November 1945.
43. Bullen and Pelly, 320–1, E. Hall-Patch to J. E. Coulson, 15 November 1945.
44. Halifax Diary, 15 November 1945.
45. Bareau Note, 16 November 1945.
46. Bullen and Pelly, 335, British Mission to Hugh Dalton, 21 November 1945.
47. *CW*, xxiv, 591.
48. KP, PP/45, JMK to Janos Plesch, 6 January 1946.
49. Bullen and Pelly, 368–70, British Mission to London, 26 November 1945.
50. *Ibid.*, 372–4, British Mission to Hugh Dalton, 27 November 1945.
51. *Ibid.*, 386–7, Hugh Dalton to Lord Halifax and JMK, 28 November 1945.
52. Richard Kahn, in Thirlwall (ed.), *Keynes and International Monetary Relations*, 57.
53. Bullen and Pelly, 389–94, 395–8, Annex to Cabinet Conclusions, 29 November 1945.
54. *Ibid.*, 405–6, British Mission to London, 30 November 1945.
55. *Ibid.*, 409, PM and Hugh Dalton to Lord Halifax, 30 November 1945.
56. Howson and Moggridge (eds), *Wartime Diaries of Robbins and Meade*, 241.
57. Bareau Note, 5 December 1945.
58. Howson and Moggridge (eds), *Wartime Diaries of Robbins and Meade*, 241.
59. q. Pimlott, *Dalton*, 437–8.
60. Bullen and Pelly, 430, Sir E. Bridges to PM, 5 December 1945.
61. KP, L/45, Frank Lee to JMK, 26 December 1945.
62. q. Barnes and Nicolson, *Empire at Bay*, 1052.
63. Robbins, *Autobiography*, 210.
64. *CW*, xxiv, 605–24.
65. Howson and Moggridge (eds), *Collected Papers of James Meade*, iv, 166.
66. James, *International Monetary Cooperation*, 70–1.
67. Howson and Moggridge (eds), *Collected Papers of James Meade*, iv, 63.
68. Clarke, *Anglo-American Economic Collaboration*, 57.

43. The Light is Gone

1. Jay, *Change and Fortune*, 139.
2. JMK to FAK, 28 December 1945.
3. Howson and Moggridge (eds), *Collected Papers of James Meade*, iv, 196.
4. This paper was published posthumously, *EJ*, June 1946.
5. Johnson and Johnson, *Shadow of Keynes*, 132–4.
6. KP, PP/45, G. Rylands to JMK, 27 December 1945.
7. *Ibid.*, JMK to Molly McCarthy, 2 January 1946.
8. *Ibid.*, JMK to Walter Lippmann, 29 January 1946.
9. *CW*, xxvii, 463.
10. Howson and Moggridge (eds), *Collected Papers of James Meade*, iv, 216.
11. *CW*, xxvii, 467.
12. *Ibid.*, 465–81, 'Political and Military Expenditure Overseas', 11 February 1946.
13. JTSP, 6–13, File 42–6, JMK to JTS, ? 1946.
14. JMK to FAK, 23 February 1946.
15. MD, Presidential Diary, vol. 8, 2 and 3 March 1946.
16. Dormael, *Bretton Woods*, 287, from H. D. White Papers, Box 7, Item 27c.
17. *CW*, xxvi, JMK to Treasury, 7 March 1946, 211.
18. KP, L/46, JMK to Lord Halifax, 18 March 1946.
19. Bareau Note on 'Inaugural Meeting', 11 March 1946.
20. Keynes's speech is reproduced in *CW*, xxvi, 215–17.
21. Cited in Gardner, *Sterling–Dollar Diplomacy*, 266 n. 4.
22. Horsefield, *International Monetary Fund*, i, 134.
23. *CW*, xxvi, 218–19.
24. *Ibid.*, 225.
25. KP, PP/45, JMK to Janos Plesch, 20 March 1946.
26. *CW*, xxvi, 482–7, 'Random Reflections from a Visit to the USA'.
27. RBP, Box 197, Sir W. Eady to R. H. Brand, 23 April 1946.
28. Howson and Moggridge (eds), *Collected Papers of James Meade*, iv, 251. Interview with J. E. Meade, 9 August 1980.
29. KP, PP/45, G. B. Shaw to JMK, 8 January 1946.
30. JMK's tribute is reproduced in *CW*, x, 375–81. It was published in June 1946 as *GBS at 90*, edited by S. Winsten.
31. HCP, H. Clay to M. Norman, 11 June 1946; M. Norman to H. Clay 19 June 1946.
32. KP, PP/45, JMK to A. V. Hill, 15 April 1946.
33. Texas University, Clive Bell to Mary Hutchinson, 23 April 1946. I am grateful to James Beechey for sending me a copy of this letter.
34. KP, PP/45, FAK, 'In Memoriam'.
35. Harrod, *Keynes*, 645; Clive Bell to Mary Hutchinson, 23 April 1946; Moggridge, *Keynes: An Economist's Biography*, 836. Keynes was sixty-two when he died, not sixty-three as Moggridge says.
36. G. L. Keynes to Sydney Cockerell, 28 April 1946. I am grateful to Fiona MacCarthy for sending me a copy of this letter.
37. Schumpeter, *Ten Great Economists*, 274.

Epilogue: Keynes's Legacy

1. Polly Hill and Richard Keynes (eds), *Lydia and Maynard*, published in 1989.
2. The account of Lydia which follows is based partly on the indispensable *Lydia Lopokova* edited by Milo Keynes; partly on Lydia Lopokova's correspondence in the Keynes Papers, especially LLK/5; partly on information supplied by members of the Keynes family and those who looked after her.
3. For a succinct discussion, see A. Leijonhufvud, esp. 12–18.
4. Moses Abramovitz, 'Catching Up, Forging Ahead, and Falling Behind', 385.
5. *Ibid.*, 395–6.
6. Hicks, *Crisis in Keynesian Economics*, 3.
7. Dormael, *Bretton Woods*, 307.
8. WLP: File 1316, R. C. Leffingwell to Walter Lippmann, 2 March 1960.
9. Henrietta Couper, 'Tea at Tilton', M. Keynes (ed.), *Lydia Lopokova*, 192.
10. Simon Keynes, 'Lydia at Tilton', September 1975, unpublished.

Dramatis Personae

Abbreviations: JMK for John Maynard Keynes; LK for Lydia Keynes; KCC for King's College, Cambridge; TCC for Trinity College, Cambridge; ECC for Emmanuel College, Cambridge; DNB for Dictionary of National Biography; EJ for Economic Journal.

'Wrangler' is someone who obtains first–class honours in mathematics at Cambridge University.

An 'Apostle' is a member of Cambridge University's most famous (though supposedly secret) society.

All are British unless otherwise identified.

ABRAHAMS, LIONEL (1869–1919), civil servant. Financial Secretary, India Office, 1902–11, when JMK was a junior clerk there.

ACHESON, DEAN (1893–1973), American lawyer, Democrat. Assistant Secretary of State 1941–5; Secretary of State 1949–53. An Anglophile friend and admirer of JMK. After JMK's death, he played a key role in developing the 'Truman doctrine' of resistance to Soviet aggression.

ADDIS, SIR CHARLES (1861–1945), banker. Joined Hongkong and Shanghai Bank 1880, London manager 1905–21. Director of the Bank of England 1918–25. Jousted with JMK at the Tuesday Club, and over the return to the gold standard, but sympathetic to JMK's argument for delay.

AFTALION, ALFRED (1874–1956), French business-cycle theorist, who influenced D. H. Robertson. JMK (in 1932) called him 'hopelessly old-fashioned on the theoretical side'. This was typical of JMK's view of French economics.

AINSWORTH, ALFRED (1879–1959), civil servant. Ed. Dulwich College and KCC. Apostle, 1899. Spent most of his career at the Board of Education.

ALTSCHUL, FRANK (1887–1981), American investment banker, philanthropist and bibliophile. JMK met him at the Paris Peace Conference in 1919; in 1932 called him an 'early Victorian curio'.

AMERY, LEOPOLD (1873–1955), Conservative politician and author. Secretary of State for India 1940–5, and a leading supporter of imperial preference in Churchill's government. DNB wrote of him that 'had he been half a head taller and his speeches half an hour shorter', he might have been prime minister.

AMOS, SIR MAURICE (1872–1940), lawyer. Ed. TCC. First in moral sciences 1893. Served in the Egyptian judiciary. On his visit to Egypt in 1913, JMK stayed with him in Cairo.

ANDERSON, SIR JOHN, Viscount Waverley (1882–1958), civil servant. Lord President of the Council 1940–3; Chancellor of the Exchequer 1943–5, Chairman Covent Garden Opera Trust 1946–58. The greatest public servant of his age, he was known as 'Pompous John'.

ANGELL, JAMES WATERHOUSE (1898–1985), American economist. Foreign Economic Administration 1943–5; Technical Advisor, US delegation to Bretton Woods, 1944.

ANGELL, SIR NORMAN (1874–1967), journalist. His best-known book was *The Great Illusion* (1910) which claimed that war had become obsolete because it did not pay. Awarded the Nobel Peace Price 1933. Much bruised at a meeting of JMK's Political Economy Club in Cambridge in 1912.

ANREP, BORIS (1883–1969), artist. Designed the mosaic floors at the Tate and National Galleries. His wife, Helen, née Maitland (1885–1965), left Anrep for Roger Fry, with whom she lived until his death in 1934. Anrep was a friend of LK.

ARUNDELL, DENNIS (1898–1988), actor, composer, theatrical producer. Cambridge educated, and much involved in Cambridge theatrical life, he acted with LK, and has left a fine account of her as an actress in Milo Keynes (ed.) *Lydia Lopokova*.

ASHLEY, WILLIAM JAMES (1860–1927), economic historian, Professor of Commerce, Birmingham University 1901–25. He and JMK produced a 'Memorandum on the Effect of an Indemnity', dated 2 January 1916, which Lloyd George (q.v.) claimed, falsely, gave politicians the idea of making Germany pay great sums over many years.

ASHTON, FREDERICK (1904–88), choreographer and ballet dancer. Choreographed for Marie Rambert, then for the Camargo Society, for whom he created *Façade* in 1931. Found JMK terrifying, but adored LK.

ASQUITH, EMMA MARGARET ('Margot') (1865–1945), Asquith's second wife. After Asquith's death, the friendship between Margot and JMK started up again and he was attentive to her in her impoverished old age. She wrote to him on 26 July 1934: '[Asquith] always delighted in yr society, & said you had *real genius* (rare praise from a man of *no* extremes).'

ASQUITH, HERBERT HENRY, Lord Oxford and Asquith (1852–1928), lawyer and Liberal politician. Ed. City of London School and Balliol College, Oxford, where he took a first in classics. Home Secretary 1892–5, Chancellor of the Exchequer 1906–8, Prime Minister 1908–16. JMK got to know him well in WW1, playing bridge at No.10, and spending weekends at the Wharf. His break with Asquith in 1926 was the most painful political rupture of his life.

ATKIN, GABRIEL (1897–1937), songwriter, painter. Great-nephew of Leigh Hunt. Boyfriend of Sebastian Sprott, Siegfried Sassoon and JMK. Married Mary Butts (1893–1937). Rupert Hart-Davis called him 'half-frivolous and wholly pleasure-loving', a 'talented drunken freak without strength of character to steer him through the shoals of intellectual Bohemia'. JMK bought two of his paintings, and gave him money.

ATTLEE, CLEMENT (1883–1967), Labour politician, Leader of the Labour Party 1935–1955, Prime Minister 1945–51. A laconic entry suits this laconic man.

ATTOLICO, BERNARDO (1880–1942), lawyer. Italian representative on the Wheat,

Dramatis Personae

War Purchase, and Maritime Transport Committees in London in WW1. Legal counsel to the Italian delegation to the Paris Peace Conference, and member of the Supreme Economic Council 1919. Italian Ambassador to Berlin 1935–40, not a good time.

AUDEN, WYSTAN (1907–73), poet and playwright. JMK staged two plays he wrote with Christopher Isherwood (q.v.) – *The Ascent of F6* (1937) and *On The Frontier* (1938) – at the Cambridge Arts Theatre. JMK thought that Auden's nail-bitten fingers explained something 'infantile' in his work.

BAGENAL, BARBARA, née Hiles, (1891–1994). One of the Bloomsbury bunnies or 'cropheads'. Studied at the Slade School 1913–14; employed at the Hogarth Press 1918–19. She had a brief affair with David Garnett, a fling with JMK, a lifelong friendship with Sidney Saxon-Turner, and looked after Clive Bell in his old age. She married Nicholas Bagenal in 1918, by whom she had a daughter and two sons.

BALANCHINE, GEORGE (1904–83), Russian-born American choreographer. Invented the balletic equivalent of 'stream of consciousness' in fiction. Became Diaghilev's ballet-master and choreographer in 1925, settled in the USA in 1934. Visited JMK at Tilton in 1929, in connection with the filming of *Dark Red Roses*, for which he composed the ballet sequence.

BALDWIN, STANLEY, Earl Baldwin of Bewley (1867–1947), Conservative politician. Prime Minister 1923, 1924–9, 1935–7. A monument to inaction. Middlemas and Barnes (p. 1075) write in their biography that he 'believed it was rarely possible to solve problems'. JMK said that he 'sentimentalises over his own stupidity'. But JMK liked him and, according to Beatrice Webb (Diary, 19 June 1936), 'was always citing Baldwin as a model statesman who could bring about a modified socialism if his party would let him'. JMK also approved of his foreign policy (or lack of it) in the mid-1930s.

BALFOUR, ARTHUR, Lord Riversdale (1873–1957), businessman. Chairman of the Committee on Industry and Trade, 1924–9, to which JMK gave evidence. Served with JMK on the Economic Advisory Council 1930–1.

BALFOUR, ARTHUR JAMES, Earl of (1848–1930), Conservative politician, nephew of Lord Salisbury, and dabbler in philosophy. Ed. Eton and TCC. Studied moral philosophy under Sidgwick, who married his sister Eleanor, subsequently Principal of Newnham College. Prime Minister 1903–5, First Lord of the Admiralty 1915–16, Foreign Secretary 1916–19, President of the Council 1919–20, 1925–9. The Balfour Declaration of 1917 led to the state of Israel; the Balfour Note of 1922 led to the American debt settlement. In WW1, JMK briefed him on the anti-conscriptionist cause, to which he inclined. But Balfour's inclinations were never very strong in any direction. To JMK he seemed 'perfectly poised between the past and the future'. The most striking summary is by Hugh Kingsmill: 'Men of affairs admired him as a philosopher. Philosophers admired him as a man of affairs. Thinkers of plebeian origin were flattered that an aristocrat should condescend to enquire into the mystery of things; and aristocrats were heartened by the rumour that one at least of their order was capable of sustained thought.'

BALOGH, THOMAS, Lord (1905–85), Hungarian-born British economist. Member of the Institute of Economics and Statistics, Oxford, 1940–5, Fellow of Balliol College, Oxford, 1945–73. Worked for 'Foxy' Falk in the City in the 1930s, then taken up by

Hubert Henderson. The leading left-wing 'Schachtian', who opposed the Bretton Woods Agreement and the American loan. JMK had him in mind when he complained to Halifax on 1 January 1946 of the Labour Government's 'Jewish economic advisers (who, like so many Jews, are either Nazi or Communist at heart . . .)'.

BAREAU, PAUL (1901–2000), Belgian-born financial journalist. Attached to the Treasury 1944–5.

BARLOW, SIR ALAN (1881–1968), civil servant. Under-Secretary, Treasury 1934–8; Joint Second Secretary, Supply, 1938–48. JMK persuaded him to agree a Treasury grant to support the Royal Opera House, Covent Garden, in 1944.

BARUCH, BERNARD (1870–1965), American financier, prominent Democrat, friend and admirer of Winston Churchill. Member of the American Commission to Negotiate Peace, and Supreme Economic Council, 1919. Famous for getting out of Wall Street just before the 1929 crash. Never forgave JMK for his attack on Woodrow Wilson (q.v.).

BEAUMONT, COMTE ETIENNE DE (1883–1956), French impresario who tried to imitate Diaghilev. He put on *Les Soirées de Paris* in 1924, in which LK danced.

BEAVERBROOK, LORD, Maxwell Aitken (1879–1964), Canadian-born newspaper proprietor (*Daily Express, Evening Standard*) and British politician. Minister of Information 1918, Minister of Aircraft Production 1940–1, Lord Privy Seal 1943–5. He and JMK opposed the return to the gold standard, and the *Evening Standard* published JMK's 'The Economic Consequences of Mr. Churchill' in 1925. A strong imperialist, he opposed JMK's internationalist plans in WW2.

BEKASSY, FERENC (1893–1915), poet, son of Hungarian landowner. Ed. Bedales and KCC, where he read history. Apostle, 1912. Served as lieutenant in the 5th Honved Hussars; killed at Bukovina 25 June 1915. King's put up a (separate) memorial to him in its chapel. JMK visited him in Hungary in 1912.

BELL, ANGELICA (b.1918), daughter of Vanessa Bell and Duncan Grant. JMK was her godfather.

BELL, CLIVE (1881–1964), art critic. Ed. Marlborough and TCC. A sportsman with a passion for modern French painting and good living, but regarded as a lightweight in Bloomsbury. Married Vanessa Stephen in 1907 and invented the aesthetic theory of 'significant form'. Vanessa lost interest in him and he lived with a succession of female companions, notably Mary Hutchinson. Virginia Woolf wrote of his book *Civilisation* (1928): 'He had great fun in the opening chapters, but in the end it turns out that civilisation is a lunch party at 50 Gordon Square'. JMK and Clive Bell saw each other constantly at Gordon Square and Charleston, but in his memoir, *Old Friends,* Bell implied that old friends might not always be best friends.

BELL, JULIAN (1908–37), poet. Elder son of Clive and Vanessa Bell. Ed. Leighton Park, KCC. Apostle, 1928. JMK established warm relations with Julian when he went up to Cambridge in 1927. Killed driving ambulance for Republicans in Spanish Civil War.

BELL, QUENTIN (1910–96), art historian, decorator, writer. Younger son of Clive and Vanessa Bell. Largely self-educated, he occupied chairs of fine arts at Leeds, Oxford and Sussex universities.

BELL, VANESSA, née Stephen (1879–1961), painter. Elder daughter of Leslie and Julia Stephen. After the failure of her marriage to Clive Bell, she had a succession of affairs, notably with Roger Fry and Duncan Grant. After WW1, Clive, Vanessa and Duncan divided their time between Bloomsbury, Charleston and (after 1938) Cassis in Provence. JMK's taking Lydia as his mistress, later his wife, broke up the Charleston 'family'. Vanessa resented Lydia, initially prompted by Clive. The feud was incomprehensible to the younger generation.

BELLERBY, JOHN RUTHERFORD (1896–1977), economist. Fellow of Gonville and Caius College, Cambridge, 1927–30. Economic adviser to Mosley's (q.v.) New Party 1931. Much involved in early discussions of JMK's monetary theory, he then faded out of the Keynesian revolution, and is now virtually unknown.

BENTWICH, NAOMI (1891–1988). Read moral sciences at Newnham College, Cambridge, 1915–17, and helped W. E. Johnson prepare the three volumes of his *Logic*. JMK's secretary 1920–21, she believed he had 'kindled' love for him in her, and suffered a mental breakdown when he denied it. She recovered in 1927 and married Jonas Birnberg.

BERENSON, BERNARD (1865–1959), art collector and historian. JMK visited him and his wife Mary Pearsall Smith (see PEARSALL SMITH family) at I Tatti outside Florence in 1906 and again in 1920, when, in a well-documented prank, JMK and Duncan Grant (q.v.) changed identities.

BERGSON, HENRI (1859–1941), French philosopher, whose theories of the mind influenced 'stream of consciousness' fiction. His doctrine of the *élan vital* influenced Bernard Shaw. A central cultural figure of the early twentieth century. JMK thought 'there is nothing in Bergson's logic, but something quite interesting in his ideas, if only one could get at them clearly'.

BERLE, ADOLF (1895–1971), American lawyer. Assistant Secretary of State 1938–44. A New Deal 'brains truster', Berle (with Gardiner C. Means) made an important contribution to economics with his book, *The Modern Corporation and Private Property* (1932), which traced the consequences of the divorce of management from ownership. An intellectual married to an Anglophobic wife, he was described by JMK as a 'queer unattractive figure in disequilibrium with himself and the world'.

BERNSTEIN, EDWARD (1904–71), American economist. Assistant Director of Monetary Research at the US Treasury 1941–6. He often infuriated JMK with his scholasticism, but got on famously with Dennis Robertson.

BEVERIDGE, SIR WILLIAM, Lord (1879–1963), British statistician and administrator. Director of the LSE 1919–37. One of the Liberal Party's 'social experts', his famous report of 1942 laid the foundations of the post-war welfare state. He and JMK disagreed about population (1923), tariffs (1931) and about method in economics, but shared the Edwardian ideal of reform 'above class' carried out by a benevolent state staffed with technocrats. Beveridge was interested not in people, but in society, and hoped that parliaments and dictators would be succeeded by 'enlightened professional administrators who would control the psychological and physical conditions'. He believed that 'one could indefinitely expand the powers of the state without thereby modifying any of the basic structures of political, social, and family life' (DNB). José Harris has written an outstanding biography of this unlovable man.

BEVES, DONALD HOWARD (1896–1961), lecturer in French literature and fellow of KCC. Produced and acted in many plays in Cambridge and elsewhere.

BEVIN, ERNEST (1881–1951), trade union leader and Labour politician. General Secretary of the Transport and General Workers Union 1921–40, Minister of Labour 1940–5, Foreign Secretary 1945–50. 'A turn-up in a million' was how he described himself. JMK educated him in economics on the Macmillan Committee in 1930–1, but failed to win his support for deferred pay in 1940.

BIBESCO, PRINCESS ELIZABETH (1897–1945), daughter of Asquith by his second wife Margot, married the Rumanian diplomat Prince Antoine Bibesco in 1919, but flirted with JMK. 'Her suffisance and utter idiocy are fit only for a Restoration comedy,' wrote Lytton Strachey to Mary Hutchinson on 21 October 1921, after lunching with her at the Savoy. 'She insisted on stuffing herself and unfortunately also me with pâté de foie gras and some very thick and sugary white wine, which she declared was Maynard's favourite.'

BIRRELL, FRANCIS (1889–1935), writer and translator, son of the Liberal politician, Augustine Birrell. Ed. Eton and KCC, where he read history. 'A tousled, gnome-like creature in spectacles' (David Garnett), he charmed JMK and appalled D. H. Lawrence, making him dream of beetles. In 1920 he and Garnett started a bookshop in London, Birrell and Garnett Ltd, with JMK's assistance. In his Founder's Day speech at KCC in 1926, JMK said, 'nothing but financial stringency ever brought Birrell's parties to an end'.

BLACKETT, SIR BASIL (1882–1935), financial administrator. Ed. Marlborough and University College, Oxford. Entered the Treasury in 1904. Secretary of the Royal Commission on Indian Finance and Currency 1913–14, on which JMK served. Treasury representative in USA 1917–18. As controller of finance at the Treasury 1919–22, Blackett's work 'gave rise to criticism' and in 1922 he went to India as Finance Member of the Viceroy's Council, where he effected 'a rigorous retrenchment of expenditure', but earned the hostility of Indian politicians (DNB). Director of the Bank of England in 1931. A career in the City, started in 1931, failed, perhaps due to his 'impulsive temperament', and he was killed in a motoring accident. Blackett was JMK's closest associate in the Treasury and partner in speculation. In the early 1930s Blackett publicly supported JMK's reflationary plans.

BLUNT, ANTHONY (1907–83), art historian. Elected an Apostle 1927, fellow of TCC 1932–6, director of the Courtauld Institute 1947–74, Surveyor of the Queen's Pictures 1952–72. Revealed as a Soviet spy 1979.

'BOLSHIES'. The name JMK and LK gave to three Russians who moved easily between the USSR and the UK and were often to be found at LK's Sunday lunches in the late 1920s. Paul Haensel was an economist whom JMK met in Moscow in 1925. He tried unsuccessfully to get JMK's 'A Short View of Soviet Russia' published in Moscow. JMK described him as 'Financial Adviser to the Bolshie Treasury, but very anti-Bolshie himself. He has, rather oddly, written a standard treatise on English death duties'. Schumpeter eventually got him a job in the USA. Prince Dmitri Mirsky was a convinced Marxist. He used to refer to his 'beloved Stalin'; his published study of the British intelligentsia seems to have been conducted largely at 46 Gordon Square. The third was P. Kupalov, a scientist.

BOLTON, SIR GEORGE (1900–82), banker. Adviser to the Bank of England 1941–8. Organised Bank's preparations for exchange control before WW2 and strongest advocate of their continuation after the war. Favoured JMK's 'Starvation Corner' option in 1945.

BOND, HENRY (1853–1938), friend of John Neville Keynes. Master of Trinity Hall, Cambridge, 1919–29.

BONHAM CARTER, LADY VIOLET (1887–1969), British politician, daughter of Asquith, married Sir Maurice Bonham Carter ('Bongie'). Defended Asquith against JMK in 1926.

BOOTHBY, ROBERT (1900–86), Conservative politician. An early and leading parliamentary 'Keynesian', he was a 'Schachtian' in WW2, mainly because of his intense hostility to the gold standard. The title of the first edition of his autobiography *I Fight to Live* was misprinted as *I Fight to Love*.

BOWEN, VERA (1889–1971), Russian-born choreographer and producer of plays and ballets. LK's closest woman friend in the 1920s. Born in the Ukraine, she finished her studies in Switzerland, where she married her first husband, a Swiss doctor called Victor Donnet, who divorced her on the grounds that she 'read too much, to the detriment of her marital duties'. She moved to Paris, where she met Diaghilev, and settled in London in 1914, marrying Harold Bowen (1896–1956) in 1922. He was a fine Arabic scholar and younger son of a tycoon who had made his fortune in South America. A woman of many talents, with a good sense of humour and excellent taste in clothes, she was Lydia's artistic as well as personal mainstay before her marriage to JMK in 1925. Later their friendship cooled, Lydia complaining that Vera was too critical of everything: Belgravia, not Bloomsbury.

BOWLEY, ARTHUR (1869–1957), statistician. Professor of Statistics at London University 1919–36. The main source of the data on which JMK relied for his 'intuitions'.

BRACKEN, BRENDAN (1901–58), journalist and politician. One of Churchill's intimates, he was Minister of Information 1940–5.

BRADBURY, SIR JOHN, Lord (1872–1950), civil servant. Joint Permanent Secretary, Treasury, 1913–19; British delegate to the Reparation Commission 1919–25. Treasury notes issued in WW1 were known as 'Bradburies'. One of the main architects of the return to the gold standard. JMK clashed with him about this at the time and on the Macmillan Committee in 1930.

BRAILSFORD, HENRY NOEL (1873–1958), socialist journalist. As editor of the *New Leader*, journal of the Independent Labour Party, 1922–6, he familiarised its readership with JMK's ideas on monetary reform, to no avail, though he himself was a follower of J. A. Hobson. Brailsford and JMK corresponded in the mid-1920s, but there was no meeting of minds – too much socialist baggage on one side, too much Cambridge baggage on the other.

BRAITHWAITE, RICHARD (1900–86), philosopher. Apostle, 1921. Fellow of KCC 1924; Knightbridge Professor of Moral Philosophy 1953. A good, but not close friend of JMK. He had a barking voice, and Lytton Strachey found his conversational method 'rather trying'.

BRAND, ROBERT HENRY, Lord (1878–1963), banker and public servant. Son of

Viscount Hampden. Ed. New College, Oxford, took a first in history. Became a fellow of All Souls College, Oxford, and a member of Milner's 'Kindergarten' in South Africa. Director of Lazard Bros 1909–60. JMK first got to know him at the Paris Peace Conference in 1919, where he was financial adviser to Lord Robert Cecil. A 'man of the utmost charm, with a soft voice and a mild, shortsighted appearance', he was 'uniquely fitted to find a meeting point' between JMK and City orthodoxy on the Macmillan Committee, 1930 (DNB). He was based in Washington after 1941 as head of the British Food Mission 1941–4, chairman of the British Supply Council 1942, and Treasury Representative 1944–6. One of the first-class brains whom Britain threw into the financial struggle with the USA, Brand was dazzled, but not overwhelmed, by JMK's brilliance. Their friendship was durable, though not intimate. His *Times* obituary (24 August 1963) called him 'an outstanding example of a species which has dwindled in numbers over the years – the London private banker who is an economist, philosopher, and, within a certain range, a statesman'.

BRIDGES, SIR EDWARD (1892–1969), civil servant. Secretary to the Cabinet 1938–46; Permanent Secretary, Treasury, 1945–56. Took over from JMK in the final week of the American loan negotiations in 1945.

BROAD, CHARLES DUNBAR (1887–1971), philosopher. Knightbridge Professor of Moral Philosophy, Cambridge 1933–53. The 'stockbroker' of Cambridge philosophy between the wars, he reviewed JMK's *Treatise on Probability*.

BROOKE, REV. ALAN ENGLAND (1863–1933), clergyman. Provost of KCC 1926–33. The 'compromise' candidate between JMK and Clapham.

BROOKE, JUSTIN (1885–1963), fruit farmer. Ed. Bedales, Abbotsholme and ECC, where he read law. Founder of the Marlowe Dramatic Society 1907; friend of Rupert Brooke.

BROOKE, RUPERT CHAWNOR (1887–1915), poet. Ed. Rugby and KCC. Apostle 1908. Fellow 1913. Died of blood poisoning at Skyros while on active service, 23 April 1915. Brooke's physical beauty, though not his mind, enchanted Bloomsbury, whose members he later came to despise. He and JMK were good, but not intimate friends, Brooke being closer to JMK's brother Geoffrey, a fellow Rugbeian. Brooke's younger brother Alfred, who came to KCC in 1909, was also killed in the war.

BROWN family, the family of JMK's mother. DR JOHN BROWN (1830–1922), father of Florence Ada Keynes and grandfather of JMK. Minister, Park Chapel, Cheetham Hill Road, Manchester,1855–64; Minister, Bunyan Meeting, Bedford, 1864–1903; Chairman of the Congregational Union 1891, he was author of numerous works on Puritanism, including *John Bunyan, His Life, Times, and Work* (1885). He married ADA HAYDON FORD (1837–1929) in 1859, by whom he had three sons and three daughters. Apart from JMK's mother, there were ALICE BROWN (1864–1947), a doctor; JESSIE (1866–1949), who married Albert Lloyd; WALTER LANGDON-BROWN (1870–1946), known to the Keynes children as Uncle Walrus, an eminent physician; HAROLD BROWN (1873–1957), a businessman, 'the nicest of the Browns', and KENNETH BROWN (1879–1958), a solicitor. NEVILLE BROWN (1904–95), a businessman, was the son of Harold Brown. Secretary of the Political Economy (Keynes) Club at Cambridge 1923–4, he provided JMK with useful information about conditions in the cotton industry in 1926, and in the USA on the occasion of his visit in 1934.

BROWNING, OSCAR (1837–1923), schoolmaster and famous Cambridge character. Ed. Eton and KCC, Apostle, 1858. Assistant master at Eton, 1860–75, he was dismissed by the headmaster, Dr Hornby, on 'unsubstantiated charges of misconduct' (DNB), involving in particular George Nathaniel Curzon, the future Foreign Secretary. He returned to KCC, where he became a lecturer in history 1880. Died in Rome.

BRUNING, HEINRICH (1885–1970), German politician. Chancellor 1930–2. JMK saw him in Berlin in 1932, when he told JMK that he would not give up deflation 'within a hundred yards of the finishing post'.

BRYCE, ROBERT (1910–97), Canadian economist and civil servant. His notes of JMK's lectures while a student at St John's College, Cambridge, 1932–4, are an important source of the genesis of JMK's *General Theory*. He introduced JMK's new theory to the LSE in 1935. Canadian Ministry of Finance 1938–45. JMK complained to him (10 July 1935) about the 'appalling scholasticism' of economists 'which allows them to take leave of their intuitions altogether'.

BURGESS, GUY (1910–63), diplomat and Soviet spy. Ed. Eton and TCC. Apostle. Defected to the USSR in 1951.

BUTLER, HAROLD BERESFORD (1883–1951), international civil servant. Ed. Eton and Balliol College, Oxford. Fellow of All Souls 1905–12. Schoolfriend of JMK.

CAIRNCROSS, ALEXANDER, later Sir Alec (1911–98), economist and civil servant. Ed. Glasgow University and TCC. Attended JMK's lectures 1932–5. Cambridge University lecturer in economics 1935–9. Economic Adviser HM Government 1961–4; Head, Government Economic Service, 1964–9.

CANNAN, EDWIN (1861–1935), economist. Professor of Political Economy, LSE, 1907–26. Cannan's old-fashioned monetary theory made him a leading opponent of 'monetary reformers' like JMK in the 1920s. His correspondence with JMK in WW1 is an important source of JMK's monetary ideas, for example JMK's letter to Cannan of 17 October 1917, which implied that the Treasury had no control over the money supply, but that it varied automatically in response to the requirements of business.

CANNY, SIR GERALD (1881–1954), civil servant. Chairman of the Board of Inland Revenue 1938–42. Canny aborted JMK's scheme for an income-tax surcharge to pay for the war, but JMK's compromise with Canny on income tax credits made possible the 1941 budget.

CARRINGTON, DORA HOUGHTON (1893–1932), painter. At the Slade School, Mark Gertler fell violently in love with her. She developed an implausible passion for Lytton Strachey in 1915 which consumed the rest of her life. They set up house together, first at the Mill House, Tidmarsh, after 1924 at Ham Spray, near Hungerford, though this did not stop her marrying Ralph Partridge in 1921, and having numerous affairs with men and women. At the Mill House 'one of her favourite visitors was Maynard Keynes and although she was completely ignorant of economics and politics ... she loved listening to him talk about the affairs of the great world when she took up his breakfast' (J. H. Doggart). She reminded Ottoline Morrell of a 'wild moorland pony'. Soon after Strachey's death in 1932, she committed suicide.

CASE, WALTER (1885–1937), American investment banker. Founder, 1916, president and director of Case, Pomeroy & Co. Inc., a private New York investment house with a specialised research organisation. JMK sent him regular reports on the economic situation in the early 1930s, and he used the firm's office as his New York base on his US trips in 1931 and 1934. Critic of the New Deal.

CASSEL, SIR ERNEST (1852–1921), financier. Helped rescue JMK from his currency speculations with a loan of £5,000 in 1920.

CASSEL, GUSTAV (1866–1945), Swedish economist. His textbook, *Theory of Social Economy* (1918), which presented the Walrasian system of general equilibrium in highly simplified form, was 'probably the most widely read textbook of economics in the interwar years' (Blaug). Inventor of the 'purchasing-power parity' theory of exchange-rates, Cassel served with JMK on the Committee of Experts in Berlin in 1922, but later became a critic of Keynes's economics.

CATTERNS, BASIL GAGE (1886–1969), banker. Deputy Governor of the Bank of England 1936–45.

CATTO, THOMAS, Lord (1879–1959), banker. Financial adviser to the Treasury 1940–4 (where he was 'Catto' to JMK's 'Doggo'); Governor of the Bank of England 1944–9. A working-class Scottish boy who made it to the top of the City 'through a combination of innate qualities and grasping opportunities wherever they offered' (DNB). Very short in stature. Some felt, when he became Governor of the Bank, that he had 'gone native' at the Treasury.

CECCHETTI, ENRICO (1850–1932), Italian ballet dancer and famous teacher. He opened a ballet school in London in 1918, at which LK, who had trained under him before the war, took private lessons, until he retired to Italy in 1923.

CHALMERS, SIR ROBERT, Lord (1858–1938), civil servant. Ed. City of London School and Oriel College, Oxford. Permanent Secretary at the Treasury 1911–13, Governor of Ceylon 1913–16, Joint Permanent Secretary at the Treasury 1916–19, Master of Peterhouse, Cambridge, 1924–31. 'His pomposity and cynicism concealed sensitivity and many benefactions' (DNB).

CHAMBERLAIN, SIR AUSTEN (1863–1937), Conservative politician, eldest son of Joseph Chamberlain. Ed. Rugby and TCC. Chairman of the Royal Commission on Indian Finance and Currency 1913–14, when JMK first got to know him, concluding that his intellect might be adequate for the premiership. Chancellor of the Exchequer 1919–21, first Chairman of the Chamberlain–Bradbury Committee on the Currency and Bank of England Note Issue 1924–5, Foreign Secretary 1924–9. Asquith wrote to Christabel Maclaren on 17 August 1921: 'Austen C. is a curious mixture – woolly brained, wooden tongued, with a quick & rather malignant temper, and unattractive manners. But he is not a bad-hearted creature, and is at times quite an effective Parliamentary performer. He is not even a chip off the old block.' Beaverbrook's verdict: 'He always played the game and he always lost it.'

CHAMBERLAIN, NEVILLE (1869–1940), Conservative politician. Chancellor of the Exchequer 1932–7, Prime Minister 1937–40. His policy of balanced budgets in the 1930s enraged JMK, though they may have created the confidence necessary to recover from the depression. JMK shared his unwillingness to fight Hitler, but not his eagerness to reach an agreement with him.

CHAMPERNOWNE, DAVID (1912–2000), economist. Ed. Winchester and KCC.

Fellow of KCC 1937–48, Professor of Economics and Statistics, Cambridge, 1969–78. One of the most eminent of JMK's students, whose notes on his lectures of 1934 have survived. His family sold Dartington Hall to the Elmhirsts (q.v.).

CHERWELL, LORD, Frederick Alexander Lindermann (1886–1957), scientist. Known as the 'Prof', he was head of the PM's Statistical Branch in WW2 and Paymaster-General 1942–5. Apart from his support for weapons research, he specialised in criticising departmental statistics and providing Churchill with short digests of complicated matters, supplemented by coloured graphs and charts. 'His loyalty to Churchill was absolute, his influence on him profound' (DNB). Believed that the pastoralisation of Germany would solve Britain's export problem. Worked with JMK during Stage II negotiations in Washington in 1944.

CHICHERIN, GEORGI VASILEVICH (1872–1936), Soviet diplomat. Foreign Minister when JMK met him at the Genoa conference in 1922. His old-world courtesy gave spurious respectability to Soviet aims.

CHRISTIE, JOHN (1882–1962), founder of Glyndebourne Opera 1934. His cultural ambitions brought him into conflict with JMK in 1945.

CHURCHILL, WINSTON SPENCER (1874–1965), Liberal and Conservative politician and war leader. Chancellor of the Exchequer 1924–29, Prime Minister 1940–5, 1951–5. Churchill's respect for JMK dated from 1925, when JMK opposed the return to the gold standard, which Churchill came to regard as his greatest mistake. In 1927 JMK was elected to the Other Club, founded by Churchill and F. E. Smith in 1911, a very English institution which combined political enmity with personal friendship, and met monthly for the purpose of dining and wagering. During WW2 the two met frequently at club dinners.

CITRINE, SIR WALTER (1887–1983), trade union leader. General Secretary of the Trades Union Congress 1926–46. He stayed at Tilton in 1931, 'flirting' (politically!) with JMK.

CLAPHAM, JOHN (1873–1946), economic historian. Vice-Provost of KCC 1933–46. Attacked 'empty box' method of formal economics, which JMK said was based on a misunderstanding.

CLARK, COLIN (1905–89), Australian statistician. Ed. Oxford, LSE. Staff, Economic Advisory Council 1930–1, helping Richard Kahn with first sketch of multiplier theory. Lecturer in statistics, Cambridge, 1930–7. His pioneering work on national income statistics was the basis of JMK's *How to Pay for the War*, 1940. His thesis that 25 per cent of national income was the safe upper limit of peacetime taxation appealed to JMK just before he died. JMK thought him 'a bit of a genius – about the only economic statistician I have ever met who seems to me quite first-class'.

CLARK, KENNETH, Lord (1903–83), arts administrator and connoisseur. Ed. Winchester and Trinity College, Oxford. Director of the National Gallery 1934–45, served on the Council of CEMA under JMK. Clark thought that JMK 'displayed his brilliance too unsparingly'.

CLARKE, RICHARD ('Otto') (1910–75), civil servant. Ed. Christ's Hospital and Clare College, Cambridge, first in mathematics. Served in various WW2 ministries before being appointed Assistant Secretary, Treasury, 1945. Dazzled by JMK, but the most incisive Treasury critic of his loan negotiation strategy in 1945. JMK's death left him the most formidable of the Treasury 'knights', because of his great speed in drafting. Supported Bank's Robot scheme to float the pound in 1952.

CLAY, SIR HENRY (1883–1954), economist. Ed. Bradford Grammar School and University College, Oxford. Economic Adviser to the Bank of England 1933–44, Warden of Nuffield College, Oxford, 1944–9. 'He was a Gladstonian liberal who, whilst recognizing that he was living in the twentieth century, felt that the liberty of the individual would be endangered by the continued growth of government economic activities.' (DNB). Despite this, Clay was generally a supporter of JMK, arguing – in his contribution to JMK's *Manchester Guardian*'s Reconstruction Supplement no. 9 – that the analogy between the individual and the state was 'profoundly wrong'. The individual had to curtail expenditure in bad times, but, if the government did so, it did not 'save' money, because unemployment consumed its 'saving'. JMK first started saying this in 1929! 'Gentle, scholarly, sensitive, and undogmatic' (DNB), he was called 'Feet of Clay' by Dalton.

CLAYTON, WILLIAM (1880–1966), American cotton merchant from Texas. Assistant Secretary of State 1944–5, Under–Secretary for Economic Affairs 1945–7. A self-made southern businessman of liberal views, he represented his Secretary of State, James Byrnes, in the loan negotiations of 1945. 'Will Clayton was tall, strikingly handsome, beautifully attired, articulate, affable, assured and stubbornly his own man to the extent that he was not controlled by his always stubbornly liberal wife.' (J. K. Galbraith). JMK found him too keen on 'business analogies' in the loan negotiations.

CLEMENCEAU, GEORGES (the 'Tiger') (1841–1929), French politician. Prime Minister of France 1917–19 and President of the Paris Peace Conference. JMK encountered him in extreme old age, not as the translator of John Stuart Mill and fiery Radical deputy of the early days of the Third Republic.

COBBOLD, CAMERON ('Kim') (1904–87), banker. Executive director, Bank of England 1938–45; Deputy Governor 1945–9; Governor 1949–61. Chief Bank of England negotiator of the Tripartite Agreement of 1936. Protégé of Montagu Norman.

COHEN, BENJAMIN (1894–1963), American lawyer. A protégé of Felix Frankfurter. Adviser to the US Ambassador to London 1941, when JMK discussed with him a loan, with Britain's North American securities put up as collateral.

COLE, ARTHUR FREDERICK ANDRE (1882–1968), barrister and bibliophile. Ed. Clifton College and KCC. Lifelong correspondent with JMK on book-collecting.

COLE, GEORGE DOUGLAS HOWARD (1889–1959), socialist writer and economist. Member of the Economic Advisory Council and Committee on Economic Information 1930–9. JMK called him 'a writer of great ability, but a prolific journalist who does not exercise much self-criticism'.

COMMONS, JOHN ROGER (1862–1945), American institutional economist. Professor of Economics, University of Wisconsin 1904–34. Foremost American critic of *laissez-faire*, who influenced JMK in the 1920s. Commons's writings were an attempt to give 'collective action', conceived as a set of controls (or laws), its due place in economic theory. A monetary reformer, he believed with JMK that economics should combine statistical data with 'insight', defined as 'Illumination, Understanding, and an Emotional Sense of the fitness of things'.

COOKE, SIDNEY RUSSELL (1895–1930), stockbroker. Partner in Rowe and Pitman. One of JMK's closest friends as a KCC undergraduate, co-director with him of the National Mutual Life Assurance Society in the 1920s. Committed suicide in 1930. 'A good-looking young man with dark brown hair and brown eyes, an aristocratic nose and the somewhat arrogant manner of the upper class' (Nicholas Davenport).

COOLIDGE, CALVIN (1872–1933), American politician. President of the United States 1925–9. Opposed forgiving Allied war debts: 'We hired them the money, didn't we?'

COUE, EMILE (1857–1926), French psychologist, whose theory of auto-suggestion enjoyed a vogue between the wars. He had his patients say, 'Every day, in every way, I am getting better and better.' Among converts were the insomniac Lord Curzon (q.v.) and JMK's friend, Robert Brand (q.v.).

COURTAULD, SAMUEL (1876–1947), industrialist, picture collector, philanthropist. His family were Huguenot silversmiths, who came to England in the seventeenth century. Became chairman of the family firm of artificial silk manufacturers (by the viscose process) in 1921, introducing enlightened industrial practices. A great friend and admirer of LK, he was JMK's closest contact with the business world, and with JMK co-guarantor of the London Artists Association. Collected Impressionist paintings, but disliked Post-Impressionism. Gave £50,000 for the purchase of French paintings to the Tate Gallery in 1923, and founded the Courtauld Institute of Art. His wife ELIZABETH ('Lil') (d. 1931), daughter of Edward Kelsey, financed three seasons at Covent Garden 1925–7, and started the Courtauld-Sargent Concert Club in 1929. LK frequently dined at the Courtaulds' house at 20 Portman Square, London, complaining of heavy meals.

COX, KATHERINE LAIRD ('Ka') (1887–1938), civil servant. Ed. Newnham College, Cambridge. A 'neo-pagan' friend of Rupert Brooke. In 1919 she married William Arnold-Foster.

COX, OSCAR (1905–66), American lawyer. General Counsel Lend–Lease Administration 1941–3, Foreign Economic Administration 1943–5. In 1943 JMK called him 'the sole survivor of our old friends' in the Lend–Lease business, but warned that 'he often tells one, as though it was accepted policy, his wishes rather than the unadorned facts'.

CRAVATH, PAUL DRENNAN (1861–1940), American lawyer. Advisory Counsel, American Mission to the Inter-Ally Council for War Purchases and Finance, London and Paris 1918.

CRIPPS, SIR RICHARD STAFFORD (1889–1952), lawyer and Labour politician. Member of Churchill's WW2 Coalition, President of the Board of Trade 1945–7, Chancellor of the Exchequer 1947–50. Member of London's ministerial team handling the loan negotiations in 1945. With his 'gaunt, uncompromising face exactly like that of a Puritan saint' (Nicholas Davenport), Cripps symbolised the post-war age of austerity.

CROSBY, OSCAR TERRY (1861–1947), American businessman. Director of a streetcar company, he became Assistant Secretary of the US Treasury, and President of the Inter-Ally Council for War Purchases and Finance 1917–19. Author of *The Electrical Railway in Theory and Practice* (1926).

CROWLEY, LEO (d.1972), American businessman. Head of the Foreign Economic Administration 1943–5. Of Irish descent, he was widely suspected by the British of manipulating Lend-Lease to Britain's disadvantage. JMK described his face as like 'the buttocks of a baboon'.

CUNLIFFE, LORD (1855–1919), banker. Governor of the Bank of England 1913–18. Dismissed by Bonar Law, he chaired the Cunliffe Committee which advocated the restoration of the gold standard.

CUNO, WILHELM (1876–1933), German businessman and politician. Chancellor 1922–3. Cuno's and JMK's connections with Melchior enabled JMK to play the role of unofficial go-between between the British and German governments in 1923.

CURRIE, LAUGHLIN (1902–93), Canadian-born American economist and civil servant. Administrative assistant to the President 1939–45; Deputy Administrator Foreign Economic Administration 1943–5. A supporter of Keynesian economics, Currie agreed with US Treasury policy of policing Lend–Lease to restrict Britain's gold and dollar reserves. JMK thought him anti-British, especially on India. Probably a Soviet agent, though there is still reasonable doubt about this.

CURZON, GEORGE NATHANIEL, Marquess of (1859–1929), British politician. Viceroy of India 1899–1905, Foreign Secretary 1919–24.

D'ABERNON EDGAR, Viscount(1857–1941), financier and diplomat. British Ambassador in Berlin 1920–6, when JMK went there as a member of the Committee of Experts, and strong supporter of JMK's views on reparations. Left one of the cleverest, most amusing records of a diplomatic mission in his book *An Ambassador of Peace*, 1929.

DALTON, HUGH (1887–1962), economist and Labour politician. Ed. Eton and KCC, where he studied economics under Pigou and JMK. Always known as 'Daddy' in JMK's circle. As Reader in Economics, LSE, 1923–36, he combined a belief in redistributive taxation with strict adherence to free trade and the quantity theory of money. Minister of Economic Warfare 1940–2, President of the Board of Trade 1942–5, Chancellor of the Exchequer 1945–7. He supported JMK over Bretton Woods and endorsed his department's free-trade outlook, but as Chancellor wobbled over the American Loan Agreement negotiated by JMK in 1945. Some respect, but little affection between the two men. Possessed of a booming voice. Dalton was once heard shouting in an ante-room when Churchill came in. 'Who's that shouting?' he demanded. 'It's Dalton. He's speaking to Edinburgh.' 'Why on earth doesn't he use the telephone?' said Churchill.

DARWIN family. CHARLES DARWIN (1809–1882) had three sons who became prominent in science, all of them graduates of TCC. SIR GEORGE DARWIN (1845–1912), Professor of Astronomy at Cambridge, SIR FRANCIS DARWIN (1848–1925), a botanist, and SIR HORACE DARWIN (1851–1928), an engineer and designer of scientific instruments. Sir George's daughter GWEN (1885–1957) married the painter JACQUES RAVERAT (1885–1925); her sister MARGARET (d.1974) married JMK's brother Geoffrey in 1917; Sir Francis's daughter FRANCES (1886–1960) married the classical scholar FRANCIS CORNFORD (1874–1943). It was of Sir George Darwin that JMK wrote to his father in 1899: 'His hands certainly looked as if he might be descended from an ape.'

DAVENPORT, ERNEST HAROLD ('Nicholas') (1893–1979), financial journalist and stockbroker. Ed. Cheltenham and Queen's College, Oxford, took a first in history. As City editor of the *Nation 1923–30*, of the *New Statesman* after 1930, and director of the National Mutual Life Assurance Society from 1931 to 1969, he worked with JMK for most of the interwar years. Founded the XYZ Club in 1932 to educate the Labour party in finance. He shared JMK's cheap-money outlook, but JMK opposed his plans to 'bolshevise' the British war economy, as expounded in his book *Vested Interests or Common Pool* (1941). His *Memoirs of a City Radical* is the best account of JMK in the City. Davenport thought that in his speculations JMK was more interested in testing his theory of probability than in making money. When JMK 'carried you away on his flights of fancy or argument, it was as exhilarating as listening to a Mozart symphony' (p. 48).

DAVIDSON, JOHN COLIN CAMPBELL (1889–1970), politician and famous political 'fixer'. JMK got to know him at the Treasury in WW1 when Bonar Law was Chancellor, and used him as a conduit to Bonar Law and Baldwin afterwards.

DAVIDSON family. There were five brothers altogether, four of whom were at Cambridge in the early 1920s. Dadie Rylands writes: 'The eldest was a Scottish laird; ALISTAIR had a career in the Navy – possibly a vice-admiral, MALCOLM was a singer – not very successful, the two Bloomsbury ones ANGUS and DOUGLAS were at Cambridge with me (Magdalene) and my friends – Douglas a close friends always. Angus [1898–1980] wrote a life of Edward Lear and translated from the Italian ... he worked briefly (like the rest of us) at the Hogarth Press. Douglas was a protégé of Vanessa and Duncan – a painter and designer, who decorated my south room [at KCC]. We lodged in Gordon Square when we went down. We gave a memorable summer party with Philip Ritchie ... attended by Bloomsbury, entire Russian ballet, Margot Asquith, Ottoline, Mary Pickford and Douglas Fairbanks.'

DAVIES, CLEMENT (1884–1962), Liberal politician. MP for Montgomeryshire 1929–62. 'At the beginning of the war in 1939 [he] became the chairman of an action committee in the House of Commons which sought the most effective prosecution of the war and which was supported by members of the three main parties in the House' (DNB).

DAVIES family. The Rev. John Llewelyn Davies (1826–1916), a graduate of TCC, follower of F. D. Maurice and noted preacher and theologian, had two sons CROMP-TON (1868–1935) and THEODORE (1870–1905), who were both Apostles of the Moore–Russell generation. Their sister MARGARET (1861–1944), a supporter of women's rights, was Virginia Woolf's friend. Their aunt SARAH EMILY (1830–1921) was founder of Girton College, Cambridge.

DAVIS, NORMAN HEZEKIAH (1878–1944), American banker. Assistant Secretary of State US Treasury 1917; member of the American Commission to Negotiate Peace and Supreme Economic Council 1918–9. Active in US financial and disarmament diplomacy between the wars.

DAWES, CHARLES GATES (1865–1951), American businessman and banker. Chairman of the Dawes Committee 1923–4, which led to the Dawes Loan to Germany.

DAWSON, GEOFFREY (1874–1944), journalist. Editor of *The Times* 1923–44. Refused to publish articles by JMK on economic topics in the 1920s, opened his columns to JMK in 1930s. JMK disliked his line over Munich, but in November 1939 Dawson gave him the platform for the articles which were turned into the pamphlet *How to Pay for the War. The Times* was the weathercock of the British Establishment under his editorship.

DENT, EDWARD (1876–1967), British musicologist. Fellow of KCC 1902–8, Professor of Music, Cambridge, 1926–41. He hoped to do for opera what Ninette de Valois had done for ballet – develop a 'British' repertory and style, initially by getting operas sung in English. JMK brought him on to the Covent Garden Opera Trust in 1944.

DE VALERA, EAMON (1882–1975), Irish politician. Prime Minister of Ireland in 1933 when JMK visited Dublin, hoping to talk him out of his 'insane wheat schemes'.

DIAGHILEV, SERGE (1872–1929), Russian ballet impresario. A major cultural influence on JMK's generation. LK and JMK always referred to him as 'Big Serge', and JMK used to see him in both London and Monte Carlo.

DICKINSON, GOLDSWORTHY LOWES (1862–1932), humanist and philosopher. Ed. Charterhouse and KCC. Apostle, 1885. Fellow of KCC 1887–1932. Best known for his books *A Greek View of Life* (1896), *Letters from John Chinaman* (1901), and *The International Anarchy* (1926), the last an investigation into the causes of WW1. Sheppard thought that this book would be recognised as 'the greatest contribution Cambridge ever made to historical research'. JMK wrote to E. M. Forster (26 August 1933), 'I had a lot of letters from Goldie at different times, but was apt to thrown them away out of dislike for the paper and the typing.'

DOBB, MAURICE (1900–76), economist. Lecturer in economics and fellow of TCC 1924–67. A Marxist, he played little part in the development of the Keynesian Revolution, but JMK was influenced by his article 'A Sceptical View of the Theory of Wages', which appeared in the *Economic Journal*, December 1929.

DOBSON, FRANK (1888–1963), sculptor. Sculpted a bust of LK in 1924.

DOGGART, JAMES HAMILTON (1900–1989), opthalmic surgeon. Ed. KCC. Apostle 1919, but preferred rugby to philosophy. His recollections of the Cambridge Apostles of his day are in the Miscellaneous Papers at KCC Library.

DOLIN, ANTON (1904–1983), ballet dancer and choreographer. Born Sydney Francis Patrick Chippendall Healey-Kay. Partnered LK and danced with the Camargo Society. LK thought him too silly to be a really great dancer.

DOUGLAS, MAJOR CLIFFORD HUGH (1879–1952), engineer turned economist, founder of Social Credit. The most famous economic 'crank' of the interwar years, his A+B theorem inspired a passionate political following in the farming communities of Australia, Canada and New Zealand, by promising a cure for deflation and unemployment. JMK included him in the 'brave army of heretics'.

DRAKE, FRANCIS COURTNEY (1868–1915), civil servant. Ed. Winchester and New College, Oxford. Assistant Secretary, Revenue and Statistical Department, India Office 1907–12.

DULLES, JOHN FOSTER (1888–1959), American lawyer and politician. Advisory Counsel to the Commission to Negotiate the Peace and member of the Supreme Economic Council 1918–19. US Secretary of State 1952–9.

DUNDAS, ROBERT HAMILTON (1884–1957), classics don. Ed. Eton and New College, Oxford. Lecturer in Greek History and Censor, Christ Church, Oxford. Eton friend of JMK.

DUNLOP, JOHN THOMAS (1914–), American economist. His article, 'The Movement of Real and Money Wage Rates' (with L. Tarshis), *EJ*, September 1938, attracted a reply from JMK. The *New Palgrave* entry on Dunlop is wrong to say that his article 'caused Keynes to admit that the *General Theory* was wrong on the relation between them over the cycle'. JMK only suggested the need for further study of the relationship.

DURBIN, EVAN (1906–48), economist and Labour politician. LSE-trained critic of JMK's *General Theory*. In his efforts to persuade Labour to support *How to Pay for the War*, JMK (inexplicably) ignored Durbin and other Labour economists.

DURNFORD, SIR WALTER (1847–1926), Provost of KCC 1918–26. His nephew, HUGH DURNFORD, was made domus bursar in 1919. JMK liked him, but had to pension him off in 1935, as he kept making a mess of the accounts.

EADY, SIR WILFRID (1890–1962), civil servant. Ed. Clifton and Jesus College, Cambridge. Chairman of the Board of Customs and Excise 1940–2, Second Secretary, Treasury, 1942–52 in charge of overseas finance. Admired JMK, but JMK was exasperated by his lack of technical acumen. Eady opposed JMK's strategy for the American loan negotiations, and came close to wrecking the negotiations themselves in November 1945.

ECCLES, MARRINER (1890–1977), American banker, from Utah. Chairman, US Federal Reserve Board 1936–48. JMK encountered his stentorian assurance and provincialism in the loan negotiations of 1945. He said of him: 'No wonder that man is a Mormon. No single woman could stand him.'

EDEN, ANTHONY, later Lord Avon (1897–1977), Conservative politician. Foreign Secretary 1935–8, 1940–5, Prime Minister 1955–7. JMK supported his policy of 'heroic cunctation' in the 1930s, but was unallured by him in WW2 and thought that Sir John Anderson (q.v.), not Eden, should succeed Churchill as PM.

EDGEWORTH, FRANCIS YSIDRO (1845–1926), economist. Drummond Professor of Political Economy at Oxford 1891–1922. JMK's co-editor of the *Economic Journal* 1911–26, and subject of one his best 'essays in biography'.

EINSTEIN, ALBERT (1879–1955), German-born physicist, Nobel prizewinner, and one of the greatest cultural influences on the JMK generation. His theory of relativity shook the certainties of the Victorian world by suggesting that the universe was unstable. JMK met him in Berlin in 1926, described him in 1933 as 'Charlie Chaplin with the brow of Shakespeare', and visited him again at Princeton in 1941, where LK described him in bed with a big toe sticking out. When JMK described the classical theory of employment as a 'special case' of a 'general theory' of employment, he consciously modelled his language on Einstein's distinction between the special (Newtonian) and the general theory of relativity. (JMK also drew a parallel between classical economists and Euclidean 'geometers' in a non-Euclidean world.)

EINZIG, PAUL (1897–1973), German-born financial journalist and prolific author on monetary questions. Political correspondent of the *Financial News* 1939–45. His leak of the White Plan precipitated the publication of both the Keynes and White Plans on 7 April 1943.

ELIOT, THOMAS STEARNS (1888–1965), American-born poet. His poem *The Wasteland* (1922) captured the mood of the post-war generation. He was JMK's first choice as literary editor of the *Nation*, and JMK, though an atheist, developed increasing sympathy for Eliot's social cricitism, and defence of culture, from a High Anglican position. JMK increasingly came to see his own economic theory as a secular application of Christianity.

ELMHIRST family. LEONARD (1893–1974) and DOROTHY (1887–1967), an Anglo-American philanthropic team. He was a mystic, agricultural economist and Chairman of Political and Economic Planning (PEP); she was a wealthy idealist. Dorothy and her first husband Whitney Straight (d.1918) financed the American liberal weekly, *New Republic*, started with Herbert Croly as editor in 1914, which took many of JMK's articles between the wars. In 1931 the Elmhirsts founded a utopian community at Dartington in Devon, which they bought from the Champernownes (q.v.) in 1925 and which housed a progressive school and the avant-garde Jooss ballet company after it left Germany. MICHAEL STRAIGHT (b.1916), Dorothy's son by her first marriage, attended the Keynes Club while reading economics at TCC 1934–7 (he got a first in economics), became an Apostle in 1936, and was torn between JMK's economics and his friends' communism. The Elmhirsts brought JMK news of the US Administration's views on the European war in 1939.

EPPS, SIR GEORGE (1885–1951), actuary. Government Actuary 1936–44. With JMK considered the affordability of the Beveridge Report in 1942.

EVANS, IFOR (1897–1952), historian and economist. Principal, University College of Wales, Aberystwyth 1934–52. Served under JMK on CEMA.

FALK, OSWALD TOYNBEE (1881–1972), actuary and stockbroker, his family being of German origins. Ed. Rugby and Balliol College, Oxford. Served with JMK in 'A' Division, Treasury 1917–19. JMK's closest associate in the City, a major influence on his understanding of the psychology of businessmen, and one of the most perceptive judges of his mind and character. Founded the Tuesday Club 1917. JMK's co-director of the National Mutual Life Assurance Society and several investment trusts. Partner in the stockbroking firm of Buckmaster and Moore 1919–32, his clients 'either made a killing in the market or [were] wiped out completely' (Nicholas Davenport). Collector of Post-Impressionist paintings and a ballet-lover. In 1930 he circulated a memorandum saying British industry was obsolete, and that investors should sell their British securities and buy American ones. JMK's public disagreement in *The Times* of 11 March 1930 led to a cooling of their friendship. In 1933 he started his own firm of merchant bankers, O. T. Falk & Co, to which he recruited bright young men like the economist Thomas Balogh (q.v.) and the physicist Lancelot Law Whyte. 'Their brains make them dangerous, for they arrive at their errors more rapidly' (*Fortune*, September 1933). Falk was fond of quoting, 'Genius does not consist in an infinite capacity for taking pains, but in the power to survive the taking of infinite pains with zest undiminished and sensitiveness unimpaired.' Looking back on his youth in 1950, he wrote that 'when the storm broke in 1914 we believed that it was merely an interlude to be followed by another and even more secure nineteenth century'. By this time he had come to believe Western civilisation was finished and that the torch would pass to China.

FAWCETT, HENRY (1833–84), economist. Ed. King's College School, London, and Peterhouse College, Cambridge. A family friend of JMK's grandfather. Blinded by his own father in a shooting accident, he was Professor of Political Economy, Cambridge, 1863–84, Postmaster-General under Gladstone 1880–4. An orthodox expositor of the doctrines of Ricardo and John Stuart Mill.

FAY, CHARLES RYE (1884–1961), economic historian. Ed. Merchant Taylors' School and KCC. Took a first in history. Fellow and lecturer of Christ's College, Cambridge, 1908–22. Professor of Economic History, Toronto University, 1921–30, before returning to Cambridge as a Reader. First met JMK when they were freshmen at KCC in 1902. After JMK's death, he called him 'the most brilliant man I have ever met or can hope to meet', but in 1927 he described JMK as 'the wizard, part medicine man, part devil of the economic world'. JMK thought Fay's essays on money were mainly off the point.

FERGUSSON, SIR DONALD (1891–1963), civil servant. Permanent Secretary, Ministry of Agriculture and Fisheries 1936–45, Ministry of Fuel and Power 1945–52. Organised the policy of reviving British farming and increasing food production in the war. Attacked JMK's buffer stock plan in 1942, opposed trade liberalisation schemes. JMK called his objections 'barmy'.

FISHER, IRVING (1867–1947), American economist. Professor of Political and Social Science, Yale University, 1898–1935. Founder of the modern quantity theory of money, his 'compensated dollar' was designed to eliminate price fluctuations. JMK regarded him as 'the true leader and pioneer' of the monetary reform movement. Fisher's reputation and fortune (made from patenting a card-index system) both collapsed with the stock market crash of 1929, which he had declared was inconceivable.

FLANDERS, ALAN (1910–65), industrial economist. Corresponded with JMK on *How to Pay for the War* in 1940.

FORSTER, EDWARD MORGAN (1879–1970), writer. Ed. Tonbridge and KCC. Apostle, 1901. His main Cambridge friends were Dickinson and H. O. Meredith. Brought up in a 'haze of elderly ladies', he grew up into a sharp and demure old maid. His *A Passage to India* (1924) helped shape post-WW1 attitudes to colonialism, but had no effect on JMK. JMK helped get him a supernumerary fellowship at KCC in 1927.

FOXWELL, HENRY SOMERTON (1848–1936), economist and bibliographer. Ed. Wesleyan College Institute, Taunton, University College, London, and St John's College, Cambridge. Senior Moralist 1870. Professor of Political Economy, London University, 1881–1928. Foxwell collected nearly 60,000 books, pamphlets, and rare MSS on economics, which were sold to Goldsmith's Library in London and also to Harvard University. On his engagement to Olive Dorrington in 1897 he wrote to Neville Keynes: 'I grieve to add that Miss Dorrington is not a bit advanced or cultured, knows no political economy ... and couldn't possibly pass in any tripos except perhaps modern languages. On the other hand, she doesn't sing, which is a great comfort...' JMK's favourite character among the economists of Marshall's generation, and the subject of an affectionate essay by him.

FRANKFURTER, FELIX (1882–1965), American lawyer and legal philosopher, US Supreme Court Justice 1939–62. Met JMK at the Paris Peace Conference, developing for Woodrow Wilson 'the scorn that the tough-minded have for the high-minded' (Joseph Lash, p. 23). In a letter to Walter Lippmann (11 July 1919) he referred to 'some brave like Keynes ... who resigned because of the utter breach of faith the Treaty involved'. A member of Roosevelt's 'Brain Trust', he used his great manipulative skills in the service of the New Deal, and was one of the main conduits for JMK's ideas to Washington.

FREUD, SIGMUND (1856–1939), Austrian-born founder of psychoanalysis. A central influence on twentieth-century consciousness, he undermined JMK's pre-WW1 faith in rationality. Members of JMK's circle, notably James Strachey and Frank Ramsey, went to Vienna for psychoanalysis. Strachey was analysed by Freud himself, subsequently producing an English edition of his writings. He was particularly struck by Freud as a 'dazzling artistic performer ... Almost every hour is made into an organic aesthetic whole.' His brother Lytton Strachey wrote to him on 24 November 1920, 'I wish to God he could have analysed Queen Victoria. It's quite clear, of course, that she was a martyr to anal eroticism: but what else? What else?' JMK wrote an appreciative comment on Freud, and used Freudian insights in discussing 'love of money'.

FRY family. SIR GEOFFREY STORRS FRY (1888–1960), ed. Harrow and KCC, barrister. Served under JMK in 'A' Division at the Treasury, 1917–19, and accompanied him to Paris as secretary in 1919. As private secretary to Bonar Law and Baldwin he gave JMK access to both. JMK rented Oare House, Marlborough, from him in 1922. His cousin ROGER ELIOT FRY (1866–1934) was a painter, art critic and friend of JMK, famous for his formalistic theory of aesthetics. Ed. Clifton and KCC. First in Parts I and II of the natural science tripos. Apostle, 1887. Slade Professor of Art at Cambridge 1933–4. 'The greatest influence on taste since Ruskin' (DNB). Scientific about pictures, but credulous about everything else.

FUNK, WALTHER (1890–1960), German Economics Minister 1937–45. Author of the Funk Plan for the European 'New Order'. 'A notorious homosexual and habitual drunkard, the greasy-looking dwarfish Minister of Economics ... proved after 1938 to carry little weight in the upper echelons of the [Nazi] Party' (Robert Wistrich).

FURNESS, ROBERT ALLASON (1883–1954), civil servant. Ed. Rugby and KCC. First in classics. JMK's closest undergraduate friend at KCC. Egyptian Civil Service 1906–23; thereafter a variety of posts in Egypt. JMK stayed with him in Egypt in 1913.

GAGE, VISCOUNT, HENRY RAINALD (1895–1982), landlord of Tilton, which JMK rented in 1925. Member of the East Sussex County Council 1924–74, one of the country's leading experts on sewage systems 'Many of the Bloomsbury Group were his tenants ... He received them all at Firle and touched their diverse activities with his tolerance, and his own informal, but strong Christian beliefs, fortified by a considerable knowledge ... of the Scriptures.' (Obituary in *The Times*, 3 March 1982.)

GARNETT, DAVID ('Bunny') (1892–1981), writer. Ed. Royal College of Science, S. Kensington. Friend of JMK and one of his main defenders in the Bloomsbury Group. JMK described him as 'earthy'. His best novel, *Lady into Fox*, which made use of his knowledge of biology, was published in 1922. In 1924 he acquired Hilton Hall in

Huntingdonshire. JMK paid for the education of his two sons by Ray Marshall, whom he married in 1921. Married Angelica Bell in 1942. In 1933 he visited JMK at Tilton, flying his own aeroplane.

GARVIN, JAMES LOUIS (1868–1947), journalist. Editor, the *Observer* 1908–42. Strong supporter of Lloyd George and admirer of JMK. Called him (aptly) an 'ungovernable soda-water syphon' in response to an attack on him in the *Nation*. Curiously, JMK never wrote for the *Observer*, despite its great influence at this time.

GIANNINI, AMEDEO (1886–1960), Italian lawyer and diplomat. JMK met him at the Paris Peace Conference in 1919.

GIBLIN, LYNDHURST FAULKNER (1875–1951), Australian economist. Read mathematics at KCC. JMK corresponded with him in the early 1930s. Independently invented the (foreign trade) multiplier in the late 1920s.

GLASGOW, MARY (1905–1983), civil servant, arts administrator. Secretary-General of CEMA and the Arts Council 1939–51. JMK wrote to her almost every day 1942–6, but always on arts business.

GODLEY, JOHN ARTHUR, first Lord Kilbracken (1847–1932), civil servant. Ed. Rugby and Balliol College, Oxford. Permanent Under-Secretary of State for India 1883–1909. JMK's boss at the India Office.

GOLDENWEISER, EMMANUEL (1883–1953), American statistician. Director, Division of Research and Statistics, Federal Reserve Board 1926–45.

GOODENOUGH, FREDERICK (1866–1934), banker. Chairman, Barclays Bank, during debate on return to the gold standard.

GRANT, JAMES DUNCAN CORROW (1885–1978), painter. Ed. St Paul's School, London, Westminster School of Art, Slade, studied under Jacques-Emile Blanche in Paris. JMK's lover and lifelong friend. Portrayed as the painter Duncan Forbes in D. H. Lawrence's *Lady Chatterley's Lover* – 'that dark-skinned taciturn Hamlet of a fellow with straight black hair and a weird Celtic conceit of himself'. Cousin of Lytton Strachey, emotional lynch-pin of the Bloomsbury Group. Decorated JMK's rooms at KCC and Gordon Square, and designed a number of ballets in which LK appeared. JMK supported the London Artists' Association, which he and Vanessa Bell dominated. His reputation declined in the 1930s, and JMK settled a lifelong income on him in 1937.

GREENWOOD, LEONARD HUGH (1880–1965), classical scholar from New Zealand. Ed. KCC. First in classics. Apostle, 1902. Fellow and Director of Studies at ECC 1906–65.

GREGG, SIR CORNELIUS (d.1959), actuary. Chairman, Board of Inland Revenue 1942–58. Fellow member, with JMK, of the National Debt Enquiry Committee 1945. JMK told him that usury was the same as his liquidity preference theory of the rate of interest.

GREGORY, SIR THEODORE (1890–1970), German-born economist. Cassel Professor of Economics, LSE, 1927–37. Served with JMK on the Macmillan Committee 1930–1. Supported the return to the gold standard and doubted JMK's view that monetary policy could eliminate trade fluctuations.

GRENFELL, EDWARD ('Teddy') (1870–1941), banker. He and his wife FLORENCE ('Florrie'), née Henderson (1888–1971), were among LK's closest friends in the 1920s.

GRIGG, PERCY JAMES (1890–1964), civil servant. PPS to Winston Churchill at the time of the return to the gold standard, he left the only account of the dinner given by Churchill before the decision for JMK, McKenna, Niemeyer and Bradbury.

GUILLEBAUD, CLAUDE (1890–1971), economist. Alfred Marshall's nephew and Fellow of St John's College, Cambridge, 1915–71. Provided JMK with most of his information about Nazi Germany's economic system.

GULICK, LUTHER (1892–1993), American economist. Special Assistant, US Treasury 1941–3, Gulick's proposal for an International Development Agency may have been a common influence on both the Keynes and White Plans for post-war monetary institutions, leading eventually to the creation of the International Bank for Reconstruction and Development.

GUTT, CAMILLE (1884–1971), Belgian journalist and politician. First Managing Director of the IMF 1946–51.

HABERLER, GOTTFRIED (1900–95), Austrian-born economist. His attempt to synthesise the main business-cycle theories in his book *Prosperity and Depression* (1937) brought a complaint from JMK (31 October 1934) who had seen an early draft: 'I cannot believe that the solution can be reached by bringing together in selected packets excerpts from the views of large numbers of writers, each differing from the other more or less on fundamentals. The answer must lie somewhere much deeper down...' After publication of the *General Theory*, JMK and Haberler clashed over the concept of the 'identity' of saving and investment.

HALDANE, J. B. S. (1892–1964), geneticist. In 1925, he was dismissed from his Readership in biochemistry at Cambridge University for 'immorality' (being cited as co-respondent in a divorce case). JMK supported him and he was reinstated. A noted Cambridge communist in the 1930s, he resigned from the party in 1950 'because of Stalin's interference with science' (DNB) – one of his lesser crimes.

HALIFAX, EDWARD WOOD, Lord (1881–1959), Conservative politician. Ed. Eton and Christ Church, Oxford. President, Board of Education 1922–4, Viceroy of India 1925–31, Foreign Secretary 1938–40, British Ambassador to the USA 1941–6. Established a close relationship with JMK on his missions to Washington, based on mutual respect which ripened into affection. Spent much time with JMK gossiping about Eton. Exercised a calming influence on JMK in the American loan negotiations.

HALL-PATCH, EDMUND (1896–1975), civil servant. Assistant Secretary, Treasury, 1935–44; Assistant Under-Secretary, Foreign Office, 1944–6. Part of British team in the American loan negotiations.

HAMILTON, GRANVILLE, *see* PROBY.

HANSEN, ALVIN (1887–1975), American economist. Professor of Political Economy, Harvard University, 1937–62. An early American convert to JMK's *General Theory*, tirelessly promoted Keynesian economics in the USA, especially in its 'secular stagnation' form.

HARDMAN, FREDERICK MCMAHON (1891–1914). Ed. Eton and KCC. JMK taught him economics. Lytton Strachey said that he belonged 'to the small, chiselled, fair and futile type – with an infinitely aristocratic voice'. Killed in action, October 1914.

HARMER, FREDERIC (1909–95), civil servant and businessman. Ed. Eton and KCC. Apostle, 1925. First in mathematics and economics. Lytton Strachey found his face a cross between a Pre-Raphaelite painting and a wicked sheepdog. Temporary Assistant Secretary, Treasury, 1943–5. JMK's personal assistant during the American loan negotiations. His diary is an important source for JMK's moods during the negotiations.

HARDY, GODFREY HAROLD (1877–1947), mathematician. Ed. Cranleigh, Winchester and TCC. Apostle, 1898, Fourth Wrangler 1898. Sadlerian Professor of Pure Mathematics, Cambridge, 1931–42. Wrote a well-known autobiographical essay, *A Mathematician's Apology* (1940), defending mathematics as at least harmless.

HARRIS, FRANK (1858–1931), journalist and (by his own account) prodigious lover. Interviewed JMK at Genoa in 1922 for *Pearson's Magazine*, but JMK hated Harris's account so much that he refused to allow publication.

HARROD, ROY (1900–78), economist and philosopher. Student (i.e. Fellow) of Christ Church, Oxford, 1924–67. After graduating from Christ Church in 1922, with firsts in both Greats and modern history, he studied economics (money and international trade) at Cambridge under JMK in the autumn of 1922. His main contribution to Keynes's *General Theory* came in 1935, with comments on drafts of JMK's book. His concept of the 'warranted rate of growth', a dynamic extension of Keynes's theory (1938), attempted to define an equilibrium growth path at which a community's saving would be continually absorbed into investment. Keynes thought him (in a letter to Harold Macmillan, 21 February 1939) 'the best man at Oxford', but 'a little inclined to over-write'. In WW2 served in the PM's Statistical Branch 1940–2. Reshaped JMK's Clearing Union in a more liberal direction, but failed to get the Treasury job which he coveted. His official biography of JMK appeared in 1951. Harrod 'increasingly ... regarded himself as being not only a disciple of Keynes, but the disciple on whom the responsibility for continuity had especially fallen' (obituary in *The Times*, 10 March 1978).

HAWKINS, HARRY (1894–1975), American State Department official in charge of trade negotiations with Britain in WW2. An enthusiastic executant of Cordell Hull's free trade policies, he ran into the full barrage of JMK's evasive tactics.

HAWTREY, RALPH (1879–1975), civil servant and economist. Ed. Eton and TCC. Nineteenth Wrangler, 1898. Apostle, 1900. Entered the Treasury 1904, and for most of his time as its Director of Financial Enquiries (1919–45) was its only professional economist. Occasionally the Treasury remembered he was still there. Anticipated JMK in seeing changes in prices as results, not causes, of changes in output and employment, JMK calling him one of his 'grandparents in errancy', the other being Dennis Robertson. In WW2, wrote enormous memoranda on early drafts of JMK's Clearing Union plan.

HAYEK, FRIEDRICH (1899–1991), Austrian-born economist, philosopher of liberalism and Nobel prizewinner. Tooke Professor of Economic Science and Statistics, LSE, 1931–1950. In a cultural and historical, rather than technical, sense was JMK's outstanding opponent. He later wrote, 'If I have succeeded ... in building up something like a fairly systematic body of opinion on economic policy that is not least due to the circumstance that all this time I had to be content with the role of a spectator and had never to ask what was politically possible ...' During WW2, JMK helped him get a home in Cambridge, and sponsored his election to the British Academy. Hayek approved of JMK's *How to Pay for the War*; JMK approved of Hayek's *Road to Serfdom* (1944) with reservations. The debate between the two on how much government intervention is compatible with a free society was never properly joined, because JMK died. It would have been a battle of giants.

HENDERSON, SIR HUBERT (1890–1952), economist and civil servant. Ed. Rugby and ECC. Fellow of Clare College, Cambridge, and Lecturer in Economics 1919–23. A student of Keynes before WW1, his main inter-war association with JMK was as editor of the *Nation* 1923–30, and joint secretary of the Economic Advisory Council 1930–4. Fellow of All Souls College, Oxford, 1934. The high point of his intellectual partnership with JMK was the pamphlet 'Can Lloyd George Do It?' (1929). Thereafter they fell out over theory and policy. Henderson was not in JMK's class as a theorist, but he was a shrewd judge of JMK's character, and had a strong sense of what was practicable. Much of his economic credo is contained in a letter he wrote to JMK on 10 July 1925: 'it is fearfully dangerous to advocate anything which depends for its success on conditions of clear-sighted resolution in execution, which are most unlikely to be forthcoming, and which otherwise will be a visible and dramatic failure ... The moral is that one should only advocate ideas, which would do more good than harm, if applied in a feeble and wavering way.' Both attached to the Treasury in WW2, JMK and Henderson continued their sparring, Henderson setting out to torpedo 'utopian' schemes for post-war improvement. Alec Cairncross wrote, 'He carried realism to the point of contra-suggestibility, reacting critically to proposals rather than devising ways of making the best of what was to hand.' Isaiah Berlin called him 'a man of deep convictions, which he held with clarity and a kind of tranquil passion'.

HICKS, JOHN (1904–89), economist and Nobel prizewinner. Lecturer, LSE, 1926–35, Fellow of Gonville and Caius College, Cambridge, 1935–8, Professor of Political Economy, Manchester University, 1938–46. His 'generalisation' of JMK's *General Theory* by means of the IS-LM model was crucial in getting a version of it accepted by economists. The most powerful synthesising, mathematical mind in twentieth-century British economics, Hicks was held in only moderate esteem by JMK.

HIGGINS, NORMAN (1898–1974), Manager, Managing Director and Trustee of the Cambridge Arts Theatre 1935–69.

HILL, ARCHIBALD VIVIAN (1886–1977), physiologist and Nobel prizewinner. He married JMK's sister MARGARET (1885–1970). Their daughter MARY EGLANTYNE ('Polly') (b.1914) studied economics at Cambridge, though not under JMK. She worked as a temporary civil servant during the war and, for a period, slept in the basement of 46 Gordon Square. She became a noted anthropologist.

HINDLEY-SMITH, JAMES (1894–1974), connoisseur. Helped guarantee the London Artists' Association with JMK and Samuel Courtauld.

HITLER, ADOLF (1889–1945), German dictator and war leader. Chancellor of Germany 1933–45. In the late 1930s JMK viewed him, much as did A. J. P. Taylor, as a rational opportunist. But on 22 August 1939 he wrote that 'he seems to show in high degree what Scotland Yard says is particularly characteristic of all criminals, namely an inability to vary his methods'.

HOBSON, JOHN ATKINSON (1858–1940), economist and journalist. Ed. Derby School and Lincoln College, Oxford. Best-known for his doctrine of underconsumption, and as a critic of imperialism who influenced Lenin. He failed to get a university job, remarking 'I hardly realised that in appearing to question the virtue of unlimited thrift I had committed the unpardonable sin.' JMK, who savaged his views before WW1, made handsome amends in the *General Theory*. J. A. Hobson's older brother, ERNEST WILLIAM HOBSON (1856–1933), taught JMK mathematics at Cambridge. Hobson's nephew, OSCAR RUDOLF HOBSON (1886–1961), was a City journalist, who studied at KCC before the war. 'Like all the Hobsons', JMK said of this one, 'he will always put justice before expediency.'

HOBHOUSE, ARTHUR (1886–1965), solicitor and farmer. Ed. Eton and TCC. Apostle, 1905. Friend of JMK. 'Really Arthur is a triumph ... of hereditary muddles' (JMK to Lytton Strachey, 10 December 1905).

HOLDERNESS, SIR THOMAS WILLIAM (1849–1924), civil servant. Secretary, Revenue, Statistics and Commerce Department of the India Office, 1901–12. Permanent Under-Secretary 1912.

HOOVER, CALVIN (1897–1974), American agricultural economist. LK said of him that he 'always goes into an upheavled country and scribbles its effects' – this in reference to his studies of the Soviet and Nazi economic systems. JMK had dinner with him in Washington in 1934; they corresponded on German reparations in 1945.

HOOVER, HERBERT (1874–1974), American politician. In charge of US relief to Europe during WW1 and Armistice; member of the Supreme Economic Council 1919. President of the United States 1929–33.

HOPKINS, HARRY (1890–1946), American politician and wheeler-dealer. Special Adviser to Roosevelt 1940–5.

HOPKINS, SIR RICHARD VALENTINE (1880–1955), civil servant. Ed. King Edward's School, Birmingham, and ECC. First in classics and history. Chairman of the Board of Inland Revenue 1922–7; Controller of Finance, Treasury, 1927–32; Second Secretary, Treasury, 1932–42; Permanent Secretary 1942–5. JMK's toughest Treasury adversary before the Macmillan Committee. Brought JMK into the Treasury 1940. JMK had great respect and affection for 'Hoppy', who in turn was shifted from his pre-war fiscal and monetary orthodoxies. Hopkins realised that JMK reinforced the Treasury's wartime position and kept him on a loose rein.

HOUSE, EDWARD MANDELL (Colonel) (1858–1938), American businessman. President Wilson's special adviser and *éminence grise*. Represented Wilson on the American Commission to Negotiate Peace and the Supreme War Council 1918–19.

HUDSON, ROBERT (1886–1957), Conservative politician. Minister of Agriculture and Fisheries 1940–5. Achieved a revolution in agricultural production, decentralising powers and introducing guaranteed prices and markets. Opposed JMK's buffer stock plan and trade liberalisation.

HUGHES, WILLIAM MORRIS (1862–1952), Australian politician. Born in London of Welsh parents, educated in Llandudno, he emigrated to Australia and was Federal

Prime Minister 1915–23. A strong supporter of a total Australian war effort, he expected Australia to be fully compensated by Germany for its sacrifices. According to Bernard Baruch (q.v.) he 'insisted that every Australian who had placed a mortgage on his house to buy a war bond was as definitely entitled to reparation as was every Frenchman whose house had been burned by the Germans'.

HULL, CORDELL (1871–1955), American politician. Secretary of State 1933–44. His main personal war aim was to dismantle Britain's imperial preference system and in Article VII of the Lend–Lease Agreement found the instrument to do so. JMK regarded him not so much as wrong as monomaniacal in pursuit of this objective to the exclusion of any other.

HURST, GILBERT HARRISON JOHN (1872–1930), schoolmaster, later lawyer. Ed. Eton and KCC. Second Wrangler. Taught JMK mathematics at Eton.

HUTCHINSON, MARY (1889–1977), wife of the barrister St John Hutchinson, mistress of Clive Bell till 1927. LK wrote to her on 17 February 1937 soliciting support for the Cambridge Arts Theatre: 'You are an important element in all sets 1) the high brow, 2) the smart set, 3) the mezzo world where we all live. Can you entice all the people to come and see us?'

IDZIKOVSKY, STANISLAS (1894–1972), Polish-born ballet dancer who often part-nered LK.

ISHERWOOD, CHRISTOPHER (1904–80), writer. Visited Tilton with W. H. Auden in 1937 to discuss staging their play *On The Frontier* at the Cambridge Arts Theatre.

JAMES, HENRY (1843–1916), American-born novelist, much admired by Blooms-bury Group. JMK gave a breakfast party for him in Cambridge in 1909. On his deathbed he is supposed to have called his secretary, saying 'I wish to dictate a few faint and faded words...' – after which he never spoke again.

JAY, DOUGLAS (1907–96), Labour politician and early Labour 'Keynesian'.

JEVONS, WILLIAM STANLEY (1835–82), economist and logician. Ed. University College, London, 1851, Professor of Political Economy, UCL, 1876–81. Famous for his theory of marginal utility and the sunspot theory of trade depressions. Subject of one of JMK's 'essays in biography'. JMK found his style of writing electrifying.

JOHNSON, WILLIAM ERNEST (1858–1931), logician. Ed. Perse School, Liverpool Royal Institution and KCC. Eleventh Wrangler 1882, first in moral sciences 1883. Fellow of KCC and Sidgwick Lecturer in Moral Sciences 1902–31. His *Logic* appeared in three volumes between 1921 and 1924. The most ingenious problems in Neville Keynes's *Studies and Exercises in Formal Logic* were devised by Johnson whose fertility in producing problems on the syllogism seemed inexhaustible. As a boy, JMK would fidget as his father and Johnson discussed logical problems over lunch, but JMK's theory of probability was influenced by his work. 'A merciful release', JMK wrote to LK on his death, 'as his mind had broken down completely...'

JOHNSTON, THOMAS (1881–1965), Labour politician. JMK debated socialism with him at the Liberal Summer School, 1928. Never knew Britain could leave the gold standard.

JONES, JESSE (1874–1955), Texas businessman. Administrator, Federal Loan Agency, 1939–45, Secretary of Commerce 1940–5. The 'Jesse Jones Loan' was one of JMK's achievements. 'I had been brought up', Jesse Jones once said, 'in the belief that the three most necessary things to a satisfactory life were family, religion, and money.' Arthur Schlesinger comments, 'Some might wonder whether this accurately stated the priority; but people learned not to fool with Jesse Jones.'

JONES, THOMAS (1870–1955), civil servant and prime ministerial confidant. Secretary of the Pilgrim Trust 1930–45.

JOOSS, KURT (1901–79), German-born ballet dancer and choreographer. Exiled from Germany, he founded the Ballets Jooss, based at Dartington Hall. JMK brought his ballet to Cambridge in December 1939. 'He was the first choreographer of international renown to attempt a synthesis of classical and modern dance . . .' (*The Concise Oxford Dictionary of Ballet*).

KAHN, RICHARD FERDINAND (1905–89), economist, JMK's 'favourite pupil'. Ed. St Paul's School and KCC. First in part II of the economic tripos 1928, Fellow of KCC from 1930 onwards. Outstanding contribution to the Keynesian Revolution was his multiplier theory, 1931, but his own particular interest was to link the theory of imperfect competition associated with Sraffa and Joan Robinson to the macroeconomic revolution initiated by JMK. Sheppard called him 'a very nice boy'. Preferred to remain behind the scenes, helping with the work of others rather than bringing his own to fruition. A temporary civil servant in WW2, first at Board of Trade, then as economic adviser to Oliver Lyttleton in the Middle East, then back in London at the Ministry of Supply, then the Ministry of Production. JMK failed to get him into the Treasury, and their close working relationship was suspended for most of the war. After the war, he was one of the two trustees of JMK's estate.

KALDOR, NICHOLAS (1908–86), Hungarian–born British economist. First in economics, LSE,1930. Lecturer, LSE, 1932–47. One of the most powerful 'intuitive' economists of twentieth century. His article 'Professor Pigou on Money Wages in Relation to Unemployment', *Economic Journal*, December 1939, was important in converting economists to Keynes's theory. Kaldor spent most of WW2 in Cambridge, went on to become fellow of KCC 1949–86, and Professor of Economics, Cambridge, 1965–75. JMK liked and respected him.

KALECKI, MICHAL (1899–1970), Polish economist. 'Acknowledged posthumously as an independent creator of many of the elements of the 'Keynesian' system' (Blaug). In WW2 suggested comprehensive rationing as an alternative to JMK's budgetary approach of *How to Pay for the War*. Leffingwell (q.v.) described his scheme as a 'communist system to put everyone on the breadline. . . '. After WW2 taught economics in Poland.

KAPITSA, PETER (1895–1984), Soviet physicist. Nobel prizewinner, 1978. JMK met him several times in the 1920s when he was working under Rutherford at Cambridge's Cavendish Laboratory – work which contributed to the 'splitting of the atom'. The Kapitsa Club, based on Trinity College, Cambridge, mingled scientific and political discussion, and helped spread communism among young Cambridge scientists in the 1920s.

KARSAVINA, TAMARA (1885–1978), classical ballerina. Settled in London 1918; a great friend of LK.

KEELING, FREDERIC HILLERSDON ('Ben') (1886–1916). Ed. Winchester and TCC. Refounded University Fabian Society 1906. Killed on the Somme.

KENNEDY, GEORGE (1882–1954), architect. Friend of JMK, who got him a number of commissions, including the rebuilding of KCC, reconstruction of Tilton, and building of the Cambridge Arts Theatre. Against the modern functionalist movement, he specialised in alterations to private houses.

KEYNES, FLORENCE ADA (1861–1958), JMK's mother. Eldest daughter of the Revd John and Ada Haydon Brown. Ed. privately and at Newnham College, Cambridge, 1878–80. Married J. N. Keynes 1882. Secretary, Cambridge branch of Charity Organisation Society 1894–1928. Chairman, Cambridge Board of Guardians 1907. Founder and Chairman of National Union of Women Workers 1912. First woman member, Cambridge Borough Council 1914; Alderman 1931, Mayor 1932–3. Founded Papworth Village Settlement 1917. President, National Council of Women, 1930. Started Cambridge Juvenile Employment Exchange. Hon. Fellow Newnham College 1954. 'The busiest woman in Cambridge'.

KEYNES, SIR GEOFFREY LANGDON (1887–1982), surgeon, bibliographer, author. JMK's younger brother. Ed. Rugby and Pembroke College, Cambridge. First in natural sciences. He had a distinguished surgical career at St Bartholomew's Hospital. In the world of letters he is best known for his bibliographies of William Blake and editions of his works. In WW2 was acting Air Vice-Marshal, and senior consulting surgeon, RAF. Married MARGARET, née Darwin (1890–1974), in 1917. JMK took an avuncular interest in their four sons RICHARD (b.1919), QUENTIN (b.1921), MILO (b.1924) and STEPHEN (b.1927).

KEYNES, JOHN MAYNARD (1883–1946), the subject of this biography.

KEYNES, JOHN NEVILLE (1852–1949), JMK's father. Logician and university administrator. Only son of JOHN KEYNES of Salisbury (1806–78) and ANNA MAYNARD KEYNES (1821–1907), though he had a half-sister FANNY MARIA PURCHASE, née Keynes (1836–1933). Ed. Amersham Hall, University College, London, and Pembroke College, Cambridge. Senior Moralist 1875. Fellow of Pembroke College 1876–82; Hon Fellow 1911. University Lecturer in Moral Sciences 1884–1911; Assistant Secretary of the Local Examinations and Lectures Syndicate 1882–92; Secretary 1892–1910; Registrary, Cambridge University, 1910–25. Author of *Studies and Exercises in Formal Logic* (1884) and *Scope and Method of Political Economy* (1891).

KEYNES, LYDIA, née Lopokova (1892–1981), ballerina, wife of JMK.

KIDDY, ARTHUR WILLIAM (1868–1950), financial journalist. Member of the Tuesday Club.

KINDERSLEY, SIR ROBERT (1871–1954), banker. Partner in Lazard Bros and chairman of the National Savings Committee 1920–46. Opposed JMK's compulsory savings plan.

KLOTZ, LOUIS-LUCIEN (1868–1930), French lawyer and politician. Minister of Finance 1910, 1911, 1917–20; played a leading part in drawing up the financial clauses of the Versailles Treaty. His career was ended by a financial scandal. Clemenceau called him 'the one Jew I know with no capacity whatever for finance'.

KNIGHT, FRANK (1885–1972), American economist. Professor of Economics, Chicago University, 1928–55. First to develop crucial distinction between risk and uncertainty (1921), but bitterly opposed to JMK's *General Theory*. JMK referred to his 'passionate, expiring cries'.

KNOX, DILLWYN (1885–1943), classical scholar and cryptographer. Ed. Eton and KCC. A schoolfriend of JMK. At the KCC Founder's Day Feast 1926, JMK said, 'It is not fitting that the best Greek scholar in the world, a card player of genius, a dear and beloved card himself, should languish in some obscure government office.' At Station X, Bletchley Park, Knox (together with Oliver Strachey) played a key part in breaking the German 'Enigma' cipher in WW2.

KREUGER, IVAR (1880–1932), Swedish match-king, uncovered as a fraud, and committed suicide. JMK saw him as more victim than criminal.

LABORDERE, MARCEL (1869–1946), French financial journalist. First got in touch with JMK in 1911 and they corresponded until JMK died, mainly on money and stock-market psychology. They both thought of each other as poets of economics. JMK's letters to Labordère have disappeared.

LAMBERT, CONSTANT (1905–51), composer and conductor. Conductor of the Camargo Society, wrote music for Fred Ashton's ballets. Friend of LK and regular guest at her Sunday lunches. A great drinker, he found the hospitality at Tilton too frugal for his taste.

LAMONT, THOMAS WILLIAM (1870–1948), American banker, partner in J. P. Morgan & Co. 1911–40. Was chiefly responsible, with Henry P. Davison, for organising financial assistance to Britain and France before USA came into WW1. US Treasury representative on American Commission to Negotiate Peace 1918–19. Much engaged in financial negotiations between the wars. Conservative critic of JMK's theories.

LASKI, HAROLD (1893–1950), jurist and academic. Professor of Political Science, LSE, 1926–50. JMK defended his freedom to utter nonsense in 1934. His garrulous presence in Labour's inner circle was an obstacle to the loan negotiations in 1945. 'A period of silence on your part would be welcome', Attlee told him.

LASTEYRIE, CHARLES, Comte de (1879–1936), French civil servant and archivist. An Inspecteur des Finances, he represented the French Treasury at the conferences at Trèves, Spa and Paris 1919. Minister of Finance 1922–4. JMK thought he represented France's 'grasping' spirit.

LAVINGTON, FREDERICK (1881–1927), economist. Ed. ECC. First in economics 1910–11. After working at the Board of Trade in WW1, he returned to Cambridge as Girdler's Lecturer in Economics 1920, and Fellow of Emmanuel College 1922. He was the most orthodox of the Cambridge economists of the 1920s, his favourite dictum being 'It's all in Marshall.' On the other hand, his notion of the rate of interest as a 'payment for uncertainty' sounds very Keynesian.

LAW, ANDREW BONAR (1858–1923), Conservative politician. Chancellor of the

Exchequer 1916–18, Prime Minister 1922–3. JMK got on very well with him, partly because he was 'almost devoid of Conservative principles'. During his short premiership Bonar Law was influenced by JMK on reparations and the American debt. JMK summarised Bonar Law's character as 'too pessimistic to snatch present profits and too short-sighted to avoid future catastrophe'.

LAW, RICHARD (1905–80), politician, son of Andrew Bonar Law (q.v.). Parliamentary Under-Secretary, Foreign Office, 1941–3, Minister of State, Foreign Office, 1943–5, Minister of Education 1945. JMK got on as well with the son as with the father. Technically head of the British delegation at the Washington monetary and commercial talks in September–October 1943. Published *Return from Utopia* (1950), an anti-planning polemic.

LAWRENCE, THOMAS EDWARD (1888–1935), 'Lawrence of Arabia'. JMK spent enough time with him at the Paris Peace Conference to consider him a friend and be consulted on his character by David Garnett when Garnett came to edit his letters.

LAYTON, WALTER (1884–1966), Cambridge-educated economist, editor of *The Economist* 1922–38. Chairman of the Liberal Industrial Inquiry 1926–8. A Liberal mandarin; one of the 'Old Dogs' who met with JMK at 46 Gordon Square in the autumn of 1939, later employed in the Ministries of Supply and Production.

LEAF, WALTER (1852–1927), classical scholar and banker. Chairman of the Westminster Bank 1919–27. JMK opposed his conservative views in debate on return to the gold standard.

LEE, FRANK (1903–71), civil servant. Ed. Downing College, Cambridge. Member, Treasury Delegation, Washington, 1944–6. Left glowing accounts of JMK performances.

LEFFINGWELL, RUSSELL (1870–1960), American lawyer and banker. Director, J. P. Morgan, 1940–59. Provided a running, but acute, critique of JMK's personality and policies from a conservative point of view from the Paris Peace Conference onwards.

LEISCHING, SIR PERCIVALE (1895–1973), civil servant. Second Secretary, Board of Trade, 1942–6. Led for Britain in trade negotiations with the USA. 'A bit of a Tory no doubt, and a little solemn, solid and conventional. But good brains and a good Whitehall reputation . . .' (Dalton Diary).

LEITH-ROSS, SIR FREDERICK ('Leithers') (1887–1968), civil servant. Long-standing Treasury official, with anomalous status of Chief Economic Adviser to the government 1932–46. Director-General, Ministry of Economic Warfare, 1939–42; Chairman of the Inter-Allied Post-War Requirements Committee 1941–3; Deputy-Director UNRRA 1944–5. To JMK he typified Britain's 'Lady Bountiful' attitude – giving away money it did not have.

LENIN, VLADIMIR ILYICH (1870–1924), Russian revolutionary leader, who seized power in the Bolshevik Revolution of 1917 and established the Soviet state. JMK worked out his remedies for capitalism under Lenin's gigantic shadow.

LePAN, DOUGLAS (1914–98), Canadian author and diplomat. Joined the Canadian High Commission in London in 1945, having fought in Italy as a volunteer gunner. His book *Bright Glass of Memory* (1979) contains a memorable chapter on JMK.

LERNER, ABBA (1903–82), Russian-born economist. Student and assistant lecturer at the LSE 1930–37, he was one of a number of Hayek's students who deserted to the Keynesian camp. His theory of 'functional finance' (1943) was a logical application of Keynesian ideas to public finance, shocking in its starkness. The first principle of functional finance was that fiscal policy should be judged solely by its effect on the economy, not by its effect on the government's budget. This was not 'dressed up' enough to suit JMK.

LEVER, SIR SAMUEL HARDMAN (1869–1947), accountant. Treasury Representative in the USA 1917–19.

LIPPMANN, WALTER (1889–1974), American journalist. Columnist for the *New Republic* 1913–19, *New York World* 1922–31, *New York Herald Tribune* 1931–65. The most influential newspaper columnist of this century; he was educated by JMK in economics and educated JMK in the realities of American politics. 'My friendship with Keynes was one of the happiest of my life', Lippmann recalled, but, according to his biographer Ronald Steel, he never knew 'how to connect the Bloomsbury Keynes with the government adviser and economic theorist'.

LLOYD GEORGE, DAVID, Earl Lloyd George of Dwyfor (1863–1945), Liberal politician and war leader. Chancellor of the Exchequer 1908–15, Minister of Munitions 1915–16, Secretary of State for War 1916, Prime Minister 1916–22. In WW1, JMK detested Lloyd George for his commitment to total victory and his deviousness. In *Old Friends* (1957), Clive Bell remembers (p. 47) JMK 'cutting from a French paper . . . a photograph of 'the goat' . . . in full evening dress and smothered in ribbons, speaking at a banquet in Paris; and . . . writing under it 'Lying in State'. He pinned it up in the dining room at forty–six [Gordon Square]'. JMK was reconciled to him in 1926, and provided the intellectual substance for Lloyd George's pledge to 'conquer unemployment' in 1929. JMK called him the 'Professor of Political Practice' in a speech to the Cambridge University Liberal Club in 1928.

LOPUKHOV family. LK's parents were FEDOR (d. 1914?) and CONSTANZA ('Karlusha') (1860–1942). Her elder sister EVGENIA (1885–1943), her elder brother FEDOR (1886–1973) and her younger brother ANDREI (1898–1947) were all ballet dancers. They stayed in Russia. Fedor was a noted choreographer with the Maryinsky (later Kirov) theatre, and its director from 1922–30 and again after WW2.

LOTHIAN, MARQUESS OF, Philip Kerr (1882–1940), writer and politician. Very successful ambassador to Washington 1939–40, despite his 'appeasing' past. Converted to Christian Science by Nancy Astor. This holds that all illnesses are mental, and all doctors quacks. He therefore refused to see a doctor for a kidney complaint, and died.

LOUCHEUR, LOUIS (1872–1931), French industrialist and politician. Minister of Munitions 1917–18, Minister of Reconstruction 1918–20.

LUBBOCK, SAMUEL GURNEY (1873–1958), schoolmaster. Ed. Eton and KCC. First in classics. JMK's Tutor at Eton.

LUCAS, FRANK LAURENCE ('Peter') (1894–1967), classicist and anti-Leavisite literary critic. Ed. Rugby and TCC. Apostle, 1914. Fellow of KCC 1920–67. Gassed and wounded on active service in WW1. Married the novelist E. B. C. ('Topsy') Jones in 1921, and secondly Prudence Wilkinson in 1932. JMK greatly admired his book

Tragedy in Relation to Aristotle's Poetics (1922). A would-be man of action with the 'sensitive face of a poet'.

LUCE, GORDON HANNINGTON (1889–1979), poet and teacher. Ed. Dean Close, Cheltenham and ECC. First in classics 1911. Apostle, 1912. Professor of English, University of Rangoon. Lifelong friend of JMK to whom he dedicated his *Poems* (1920), published by Macmillan at JMK's expense.

LUXMOORE, HENRY ELFORD (1839–1926), schoolmaster. Ed. Eton and Pembroke College, Oxford. Taught JMK classics at Eton.

McADOO, WILLIAM GIBBS (1863–1941), American lawyer and businessman. Married Eleanor Wilson, daughter of President Wilson, 1914. Secretary of the Treasury 1913–1918. Successfully floated four Liberty Loans, collecting over $18bn. Later a US Senator and a leader of the Democratic party.

MACAULAY, WILLIAM HERRICK (1858–1936), mathematician, bursar of KCC. JMK got money out of his brother Reginald for the rebuilding of KCC in 1925.

MacCARTHY, DESMOND (1877–1952), literary and dramatic critic. Ed. Eton and TCC. Apostle, 1896. Literary editor, *New Statesman*, 1920–7; senior literary critic, *Sunday Times*, 1928–52. Leonard Woolf thought him 'perhaps the most charming man I have ever met'. A marvellous raconteur, he never wrote the great book which his friends expected. His wife MARY ('Molly') (1882–1953) started the Memoir Club to get him to write it.

MacDONALD, JAMES RAMSAY (1866–1937), Labour politician. Prime Minister 1924, 1929–35 (after 1931 leading a 'National Government'). Used JMK as an adviser after 1929, but was too pessimistic to take his advice, preferring the more cautious Hubert Henderson. His brainchild the Economic Advisory Council faded away in the 1930s.

MacDONALD, MALCOLM (1908–81), politician. UK High Commissioner in Canada 1941–6, where he was JMK's host on several missions. After the war, much involved in winding up the British Empire, which he did with tact and charm.

MacDOUGALL, DONALD (b.1912), economist. PM's Statistical Branch 1940–5, where he supplied the coloured charts and graphs favoured by Winston Churchill. Accompanied Cherwell (q.v.) to Quebec and Washington 1944, taking part in Stage II negotiations.

MacFADYEAN, SIR ANDREW (1887–1974), civil servant. Ed. University College School, London, and University College, Oxford. First in literary humanities 1909. Appointed to 'A' Division of the Treasury 1917, but spent most of the next two years as Treasury representative in the USA. Secretary, Reparation Commission, 1922–4; Secretary, Dawes Commission, 1924.

McKENNA, REGINALD (1863–1943), Liberal politician and banker. Ed. King's School, London, and Trinity Hall, Cambridge, where he read mathematics. President of the Board of Trade 1907–8, First Lord of the Admiralty 1908–11, Home Secretary 1911–15, Chancellor of the Exchequer 1915–16, Chairman of the Midland Bank 1922–43. JMK and McKenna were allies against Lloyd George's great gun programme in 1915–16 (when McKenna tried to convince Lloyd George that 'the same man could not at the same time be in the navy and the army, in a factory and an arsenal and down a mine'), against the return to the gold standard in 1925, against deflation in the late 1920s, and on the Macmillan Committee in 1930–1, but JMK felt that 'McKenna always lets you down in the end' – notably by not resigning over conscription in 1916, and by backing down over the gold standard. The two men kept in friendly touch until McKenna's death.

MACMILLAN, DANIEL DE MENDI (1886–1965), publisher. Ed. Eton and Balliol College, Oxford. Director Macmillan & Co. 1911, Chairman and Managing Director 1936–63. Eton friend and publisher of JMK.

MACMILLAN, HAROLD (1894–1986), Conservative politician, Daniel Macmillan's younger brother, and also a friend of JMK. Prime Minister 1956–63.

McTAGGART, JOHN ELLIS (1866–1925), Idealist philosopher. Ed. Clifton College and TCC. Apostle, 1886. Fellow of TCC 1891–1923. His breakfasts were notorious for their lack of food and conversation. C. D. Broad wrote that 'McTaggart, though an atheist, could never have been anything but an Anglican'.

MADGE, CHARLES (1912–96), social scientist. Founded Mass Observation with Tom Harrisson 1937. His studies of working-class savings habits and attitudes to compulsory saving were used by JMK in arguing for deferred pay in 1940–1.

MAINE, BASIL (1894–1972), music critic. LK's 'platonic lover', who played her the piano. Later became a clergyman.

MAISKY, IVAN (1884–1975), Soviet diplomat, surprisingly long-lived. Ambassador to Britain 1932–43. JMK first encountered him in 1922 in connection with the *Manchester Guardian* Reconstruction Supplements, when he was Chief of the Press Department of the Russian Foreign Office. JMK and LK cultivated him mainly for the protection of her relatives, but he was unable to arrange for them to come to the West, following the defection of Balanchine.

MALKIN, SIR WILLIAM (1883–1945), lawyer. Legal Adviser, Foreign Office 1929–45. Chaired the Malkin Committee on German Reparations 1943–4, on which JMK served.

MARCHANT, SIR STANLEY (1883–1949), musician. Member of CEMA and the Arts Council under JMK, trustee of the Royal Opera House.

MARSHALL, ALFRED (1842–1924), economist. Ed. Merchant Taylors School and St John's College, Cambridge. Second Wrangler. Fellow of St John's 1868–77, Principal of University College, Bristol, 1877–8, Professor of Political Economy, Cambridge, 1883–1907. One of the great Victorian synthesisers, he published his *Principles* (1890), which reconciled classical cost of production to Jevons's marginal utility, abstract theory to history, and science to morals. JMK thought him 'a very great man, though I suppose rather a silly one . . .' On the other hand, JMK loved his wife and widow MARY PALEY MARSHALL (1850–1944), of whom he wrote a touching memorial which ended: 'Modest as the Morn; as Mid-day bright;/Gentle as Ev'ning; cool as Night'.

MARTEN, SIR CLARENCE HENRY KENNETT (1872–1948), schoolmaster. Ed. Eton and Balliol College, Oxford, where he took a first in modern history. Taught JMK history at Eton and Queen Elizabeth II history when she was a girl. Provost of Eton 1945–8, succeeding 'Linky' Quickswood (q.v.).

MARTIN, KINGSLEY (1867–1969), journalist. Edited the *New Statesman* 1931–62. Frequently clashed with JMK, who was chairman of the board, and who thought the *NS* was too muddled and left-wing (he often took these two terms as synonymous).

MASSINE, LEONIDE (1896–1979), Russian-born dancer and choreographer. He choreographed *The Good-Humoured Ladies* and *La Boutique Fantasque*, in which LK made her mark in London in 1918–19, and they danced together in the early 1920s. LK found him selfish as a dancer, and his witty choreography gave little scope for her dramatic talents.

MEADE, JAMES (1907–95), economist and Nobel prize winner. Ed. Malvern College and Oriel College, Oxford. First in PPE, 1930. Fellow and Lecturer in economics at Hertford College 1930–7. Spent a postgraduate year at Cambridge, 1930, as a member of JMK's 'Circus'. Meade's contribution to the Keynesian Revolution was, firstly, 'Mr. Meade's Relation', an extension of Kahn's original multiplier theory; second, his 'A Simplified Model of Mr. Keynes's System', *Review of Economic Studies*, 4, 1937. JMK 'considered [Meade] to be of excellent promise' in 1932. Meade served in the Economic Section of the War Cabinet 1940–7, while working part-time at the Board of Trade. After JMK, the most fertile constructive mind in Whitehall, with key papers on national income statistics, employment policy and Commercial Union. JMK was often in vigorous dispute with Meade, who nevertheless regarded him as 'God'. Meade would rarely be diverted from the logic of an argument by questions of political practicability, and he had (to modern eyes) a ludicrous faith in the power of statistics to substitute for judgement.

MELCHIOR, CARL (1877–1933), German banker. Partner in the Hamburg merchant bank, M. M. Warburg & Co. A member of the Wilhelmine 'Kaiserjuden' establishment, Melchior had served the German government on special missions in Eastern Europe during WW1. His meetings with JMK early in 1919 during the armistice negotiations are the subject of the latter's memoir 'Dr. Melchior: A Defeated Enemy', read to Bloomsbury's Memoir Club in 1920, in which JMK praised Melchior for his courage and dignity in defeat. JMK's estimate of German capacity to pay reparations was identical to that put forward by Melchior at Paris. As *persona grata* to the Allies, particularly the British, Melchior played a key part in the reparation diplomacy of the early 1920s, he and JMK working together to try to bring about an Anglo-German financial agreement in 1923. The only German to be elected to the League of Nations' Financial Committee, Melchior became its chairman in 1930.

MEREDITH, HUGH OWEN ('Hom') (1878–1964), economist. Ed. Shrewsbury and KCC. First in classics part I and in history part II. Apostle, 1900. Girdler's Lecturer in Economics 1908–11, Professor of Economics, Queen's University, Belfast 1911–45. Friend of Lowes Dickinson, E. M. Forster and G. E. Moore. Oscar Browning told him, 'You are very brilliant, but you will never do anything.' Meredith suggested to G. E. Moore 'the whole plan of the last chapter of *Principia Ethica*'. Praised JMK's *General Theory*.

MONICK, EMMANUEL (1893–1984), French public servant. Inspector–general of Finance 1920–45; financial attaché in London 1934–40; governor of the Bank of France 1945–9. Prominent in the financial diplomacy of the 1930s. JMK saw him in London before the fall of France. One of the two Frenchmen he liked, the other being Labordère.

Dramatis Personae

MONTAGU, EDWIN SAMUEL (1879–1924), Liberal politician. Ed. Clifton College, City of London School, and TCC. As President of the Cambridge Union (1902), he gave JMK the first of many helping hands in his career. Private Secretary to Asquith 1906–10, Parliamentary Under-Secretary of State for India 1910–14, Financial Secretary to the Treasury 1914–16, Chancellor of the Duchy of Lancaster 1915, Minister of Munitions 1916, Secretary of State for India 1917–22. L. E. Jones remembers that, as an undergraduate, 'his long, ugly bony face was pockmarked like a photograph of the moon, but his eyes held me: sombre, patient, unhappy eyes of extraordinary intelligence'. Waley (q.v.) called him 'the most melancholy and gayest of friends'. JMK called him a 'natural tool and victim'.

MOORE, GEORGE EDWARD (1873–1958), philosopher. Ed. Dulwich College and TCC. Apostle,1894. Fellow of Trinity 1894–1904, University Lecturer in moral science 1911–25, Professor of Philosophy, Cambridge University, 1925–39. In professional philosophy famous as the leader, with Russell, of the revolt against Idealism. But to JMK and his friends he was the author of the 'religion' of *Principia Ethica.*

MORGENTHAU, HENRY (1891–1967), American politician, intimate of Roosevelt. Secretary of the Treasury 1934–45. Morgenthau's support for Britain in WW2 coexisted with his determination to keep Britain dependent on the USA. His attitude started to change in 1944, but in Roosevelt's last months he was in eclipse. He and JMK started off frostily, but in 1944 JMK won Morgenthau over at Bretton Woods. Morgenthau did not understand finance. This meant he could be manipulated by Harry Dexter White (q.v.).

MORRELL, LADY OTTOLINE (1873–1938), famous pre-war Bloomsbury hostess. Half-sister of the sixth Duke of Portland, married Philip Morrell (1870–1943), a Liberal MP. Lover of Bertrand Russell, protector and butt of Bloomsbury. In WW1 her house in Garsington, Oxford, provided a refuge for pacifists and conscientious objectors. JMK went on seeing her during the inter-war years.

MORTIMER, RAYMOND (1895–1980), literary critic, member of post-war Bloomsbury Group. He stayed with JMK and LK at Studlands, Dorset, 1923, contributed reviews and articles to the *Nation,* and became literary editor of the *New Statesman* in 1935.

MOSLEY, SIR OSWALD (1896–1980), politician. Chancellor of the Duchy of Lancaster 1929–30, leader of the New Party 1930–2, and the British Union of Fascists 1932–40. The first British 'Keynesian'. In his *Revolution by Reason* (1925), Mosley anticipated JMK by identifying 'lack of effective demand' as the cause of unemployment, and stating the task of policy was to close the 'output gap'. JMK was in sympathetic contact with him till 1931. LK once dreamt she was being seduced by him!

MUIR, RAMSAY (1872–1941), historian. One of the architects of post-1918 liberalism, he was, in effect, rejected by JMK as editor of the *Nation* in 1923. 'He dealt in fine generalities, but he was perhaps deficient in the saving ballast of particulars' (DNB).

NEWBOLD, JOHN TURNER WALTON (1888–1943), writer and politician. A Manchester man, with a Quaker, agricultural and trade background. Communist MP 1922–3, resigning from the party in 1924; a member of the Macmillan Committee

1929–31. JMK found him interesting but woolly. Newbold affectionately appreciated JMK as (he hoped) a failed saviour of capitalism.

NICHOLSON, JOSEPH SHIELD (1850–1927), economist. Won the Cobden Prize (over Neville Keynes) in 1877. Professor of Political Economy, Edinburgh University, 1880–1927. Pioneer of economic history in Scotland. 'On questions of imperial policy and currency and banking he attained a position of exceptional authority.' (DNB).

NORMAN, MONTAGU, Lord (1871–1950), banker. Governor of the Bank of England 1920–42. JMK clashed with Norman on the American debt settlement 1923, the return to the gold standard 1925, and – before the Macmillan Committee 1930–1 – the effects of monetary policy on employment, but they agreed on German reparations. JMK supported Norman's initiative in setting up the Bank for International Settlements in 1931, and relations between the two thawed in the run-up to and during WW2. Norman was an obsessively shy, secretive man, who travelled abroad as Mr Skinner – the name of his secretary. Whereas he wrought his alchemy by his prolonged silences, JMK spun his magic with his flow of words. Norman's final assessment of JMK: 'A great economist, but a bad banker.' JMK on Norman: 'Montagu Norman, always absolutely charming, always absolutely wrong.'

NORTON, HENRY TERTIUS JAMES (1887–1936), mathematician. Ed. Eton and TCC, of which he became a fellow in 1910. Apostle, 1906. Brilliant and excitable friend of JMK, he eventually gave up mathematics after a nervous breakdown.

OLIVIER family. SYDNEY HALDANE, LORD OLIVIER (1859–1943), Fabian, civil servant and politician, had four daughters, MARGERY (1887–1974), BRYNHILD (1887–1935), DAPHNE (1889–1950), and NOEL (1892–1969). JMK rode with Brynhild, 'the outstanding beauty of the four' (David Garnett), who married Hugh Popham, and whose daughter ANNE OLIVIER (b.1916) married Quentin Bell. Garnett wrote of the four sisters, who were his childhood friends: 'They were all aristocratic creatures; pride was the moving force of their lives; they felt contempt easily; pity did not come naturally, except for animals. Their minds were free; but though loving discussion of all things and eager to hear all sides, they were violently prejudiced and swayed by their emotions and the views in which they had been brought up.' The Oliviers were a link between the Fabians and the Bloomsbury Group.

OPIE, REDVERS (1900–84), economist, later naturalised American citizen. Counsellor and economic adviser, British Embassy, Washington, 1939–46. Married daughter of American economist F. W. Taussig. Kept JMK informed of Washington gossip.

PAISH, SIR GEORGE (1897–1957), statistician and writer. Adviser to the Chancellor of the Exchequer, 1914–16. JMK wrote, 'As usual, however, Mr. Lloyd George soon got bored with him and stopped reading his lengthy memoranda.'

PASVOLSKY, LEO (1893–1953), American economist. Special Assistant to US Secretary of State 1939–46.

PEACOCK, SIR EDWARD (1872–1962), Canadian-born British merchant banker. Director of Baring Bros, 1924–54; Bank of England, 1929–46. Involved with JMK in Jesse Jones Loan, 1941.

PEARSALL SMITH family. ROBERT (1827–99) and HANNAH (1832–1911), Quakers from Philadelphia, who settled in England in 1880s, had three children, MARY,

LOGAN and ALYS. Mary (1864–1945) married Benjamin Francis Costelloe (1855–99), by whom she had two daughters, RACHEL 'RAY' CONN (1887–1940) and KARIN ELIZABETH CONN (1889–1938), both of whom went to Newnham College, Cambridge. Rachel married Lytton Strachey's elder brother Oliver (1874–1960) in 1911 and took up women's causes. Karin, who Russell thought had 'more philosophical capacity than I have ever before seen in a woman', married Adrian Stephen in 1914. Mary Costelloe became the mistress and then the wife of the art dealer Bernard Berenson (1867–1959), and then lived at I Tatti, outside Florence. Logan (1865–1946) was a writer. Alys (1867–1951) was Bertrand Russell's first wife. JMK first met the sisters Ray and Karin on his motor-tour of Italy with their mother in 1906. The Pearsall Smiths were 'one of the most interesting intersection points between the Fabians and what became the Bloomsbury Group' (Norman Mackenzie).

PEARSON, KARL (1857–1936), statistician and eugenicist, a pioneer of applying statistical methods to human behaviour. Ed. University College School, London, and KCC. Professor of Applied Mathematics 1884, Geometry 1891, and Eugenics 1911 at University College, London. JMK had a big statistical row with him in 1911. David Garnett describes him as a 'tall stiff man who wore one of those hard hats with straight sides and a flat top, and had a very blank and wooden face with thin, compressed lips'.

PENROSE family. Three Quaker brothers were part of JMK's Cambridge circle in the early 1920s. ALEC (1896–1950), KCC, Apostle, 1919, designed the scenery for the *Oresteia*, 1921, and produced Lytton Strachey's play, *The Son of Heaven*, 1925, in which Dennis Robertson acted the part of the head eunuch. LIONEL (1898–1972), St John's College, Cambridge, Apostle, 1921, was an eminent geneticist, who married the daughter of Pavlov. ROLAND (1900–83), Queen's College, Cambridge, was a painter, art critic and biographer of Picasso. A fourth brother, BERNARD ('Beakus'), came up to Cambridge a few years later, after a spell in the Royal Navy. Lytton Strachey wrote, 'His existence is of a sordid insignificance which ... opens up vistas in human pointlessness hitherto undreamt of.'

PETHICK-LAWRENCE, FREDERICK (1871–1961), Labour academic and politician. Ed. Eton and TCC. Fellow of Trinity College, Cambridge, 1897–1903. Financial Secretary, Treasury, 1929–31; Secretary of State for India 1945–7. Old-fashioned Liberal, driven to the left by social problems. Supported Bretton Woods Agreement. He and JMK were in occasional touch during WW2. He had no real influence in the Labour Party.

PHILLIPS, SIR FREDERICK (1884–1943), civil servant. Ed. Aske's School and ECC. He took a first in mathematics, a first in natural sciences, and was first in the civil service examination in 1908, when he entered the Treasury. Under-Secretary 1932. Represented the Treasury in Washington, 1940–43, where he got on famously with Morgenthau. Very dry, puffed away silently at his pipe. JMK got on well with him.

PIGOU, ARTHUR CECIL (1877–1959), economist. Ed. Harrow and KCC, first in history, 1899, and in part II, moral science, 1900. Fellow of KCC, 1902; succeeded Marshall as Professor of Political Economy, Cambridge, 1908–48. Pioneer of welfare economics, in which 'he elaborated Marshall's invention of the concept of externalities into a general economic theory of government intervention' (Blaug). Served on the Cunliffe (1919) and Chamberlain–Bradbury (1924) Committees on Currency, and with JMK on the Committee of Economists, 1930. A misogynist, Pigou never married, being happiest in the company of his male students. He took them mountain-climbing, wrote them letters laced with Italian couplets, and with a favoured few, like Donald Corrie, indulged in 'Cumberland wresting ... in the seclusion of the grass area on the north of the Chapel at dead of night'; after his 'heart attack' in 1927, he became a physical shadow of his former self. Wrote one of the most hostile reviews of JMK's *General Theory*, but made a handsome retraction in 1949. Kept Cambridge Economics Faculty going in WW2, complaining to JMK about Joan Robinson 'parrot-ing' JMK's theories.

PLAYFAIR, EDWARD (1909–99), civil servant. Ed. Eton and KCC. Treasury 1934–58. A lively source for JMK's Washington visit of 1941.

PLESCH, JANOS (1870–1950), Hungarian-born doctor. Started treating JMK for heart disease in March 1939. A mixture of genius and charlatan, JMK credited him with having restored him to 'active life'.

PLUMPTRE, ARTHUR FITZWALTER WYNNE (1907–77), Canadian-born economist and civil servant. A student of JMK at KCC in 1920s.

POINCARE, RAYMOND (1860–1934), French politician from Lorraine. PM at the time of the French occupation of the Ruhr, 1923; Finance Minister 1926–8 at the time of the French undervaluation of the franc.

PROBY, GRANVILLE (1883–1947), lawyer. Contemporary and friend of JMK at Eton, whom JMK knew as Granville Hamilton, his father changing his name to Proby by deed poll.

PURVES, PATRICK JOHN CHESTER (1890–1960), international civil servant. Ed. Fettes and KCC. Worked with League of Nations and later WHO and UNESCO. Cambridge friend of JMK.

PURVIS, ARTHUR (1890–1941), businessman, who made his business career in Canada. From 1939–41, as head of the Anglo-French (subsequently British) Purchas-ing Board, and first Chairman of the British Supply Council, he controlled British procurement of munitions and war-related goods in the USA. Is said to have influenced the size of the first Lend–Lease appropriation. Tragically killed in an aeroplane accident on 14 August 1941. To Morgenthau, he was not only the 'ablest British representative in Washington, but one of the rarest persons I have ever known'.

QUICKSWOOD, HUGH CECIL ('Linky'), Lord (1869–1956), politician and High Churchman. He was the (increasingly eccentric) Provost of Eton (1936–44) during JMK's time as a Fellow there. He resigned in 1944 with the classic words: 'I go to Bournemouth in lieu of Paradise.'

RAMSEY, FRANK PLUMPTON (1903–30), extraordinarily precocious, short-lived philosopher and economist. Ed. Winchester and TCC. First in parts I and II of the mathematical tripos; Apostle, 1921; Fellow of KCC 1924–30. JMK thought him a genius, and his criticism of JMK's *Treatise on Probability* edged JMK away from his view of probability as an 'objective relation'. His article 'A Mathematical Theory of Saving' (*EJ*, December 1928), produced the 'Ramsey rule' that 'the rate of saving, multiplied by the marginal utility of consumption, should always be equal to the amount by which the total net rate of of enjoyment of utility falls short of the maximum possible rate' (David M. Newbery in *The New Palgrave*). Summed up the message of Wittgenstein's *Tractatus* as 'What you can't say, you can't say, and you can't whistle either.'

RASMINSKY, LOUIS (1908–98), Canadian economist. Chairman, Foreign Exchange Control Board, 1940–51. JMK worked with him in London, Atlantic City, Bretton Woods and Savannah.

RATHBONE, ELEANOR (1872–1946), social reformer. Independent MP 1929–46. Helped persuade JMK to include family allowances in his *How to Pay for the War*.

REDDAWAY, WILLIAM BRIAN (1913–2002), economist. Ed. KCC, where he studied economics under JMK, obtaining a first in part II, 1934. Fellow of Clare College, Cambridge 1934. Professor of Political Economy, Cambridge, 1969–80. JMK called him 'by far the best economist of his year'.

RIDLEY, JASPER (1887–1951), banker. Ed. Eton and Balliol College, Oxford. Chairman, Coutts and National Provincial Bank. Served with JMK on Eton's Governing Body in WW2.

ROBBINS, LIONEL (1898–1984), economist. Professor of Economics, LSE, 1929–61. Defended free trade and the policy of diminishing public spending in a slump against JMK, their quarrel coming to a head on the Committee of Economists, 1930. On the first he believed he was right; on the second he acknowledged he was wrong. Director, Economic Section of the War Cabinet Office, 1941–5, and staunch ally of JMK in pushing through the Bretton Woods Agreement and in the American loan negotiations. His attitude to JMK remained ambiguous. In his autobiography he argued that economics as a study of 'remoter effects' was still a better guide to policy than the 'gay reminder' that 'in the long run we are all dead'. Admired JMK as an artist, but mistrusted his reasoning and panaceas. JMK thought him 'difficult and queer'.

ROBERTS, WILLIAM (1895–1980), painter, influenced by Futurism and Cubism; he painted a much reproduced portrait of JMK and LK in 1931–2. JMK greatly admired his work, bought six of his paintings and continued to subsidise him after the end of the London Artists' Association in 1934.

ROBERTSON, DENNIS HOLME (1890–1963), economist. Ed. Eton and TCC. First in classics part I, 1910, and in economics part II, 1912. Fellow of Trinity College 1914–38. Temporary civil servant at the Treasury 1939–44, when he left to become Pigou's successor as Professor of Political Economy at Cambridge. A buttoned-up, repressed bachelor don, he was JMK's chief intellectual stimulus in the 1920s, but rejected JMK's 'revolution' in the 1930s, with bad effects on their personal relationship. He thought that industrial fluctuations were an inevitable, and necessary, accompaniment of economic progress; the use of money aggravated, but did not cause them; monetary policy should be used to limit them to what was 'appropriate' or 'warranted'. Had a greater belief in the price mechanism than did JMK. Robertson regarded JMK's *General Theory* as the theory of a one-off, deep slump, not a 'general' analysis of the working of the capitalist system, and rejected its stagnationist presuppositions. He wrote in a playful, but on the whole private, language, spiced with quotations from *Alice in Wonderland*; his ideas were typically too subtle for most to grasp; and he had little impact outside Cambridge.

ROBINSON, EDWARD AUSTIN GOSSAGE (1897–1993), economist. Ed. Marlborough and Christ's College, Cambridge. Fellow of Sidney Sussex College, Cambridge, 1929–93; University Lecturer in Economics 1929–49; Professor of Economics, Cambridge, 1950–65. Assistant editor, *Economic Journal*, 1934–44, Joint Editor 1944–70. Member of the Economic Section of the Cabinet Office, 1939–42. A member of JMK's 'Circus' 1930–1, he was a superb university politician and excellent chronicler of the Keynesian Revolution but he did not play much part in it.

ROBINSON, JOAN, née Maurice (1903–83), economist, wife of Austin Robinson. Studied economics at Girton College, failing to get a first in 1925. Appointed Assistant Lecturer, 1931. One of the most outstanding minds and powerful personalities in Cambridge economics for half a century, she made her reputation with her first book, *The Economics of Imperfect Competition* (1933), helped by Richard Kahn, with whom she had her most intense intellectual and emotional relationship. JMK thought increasingly highly of her, and she was one of the most able expositors, as well as simplifiers, of his ideas. A favourite saying of hers was: 'As I never learnt mathematics, I have had to think.' The only woman (so far) among the great economists.

RONALD, NIGEL (1894–1973), diplomat. Ed. Winchester and Magdalen College, Oxford. Foreign Office official most involved with JMK's economic and financial negotiations.

ROOSEVELT, FRANKLIN DELANO (1882–1945), American politician. President of the United States 1932–45. JMK put his hopes in FDR for a democratic escape from the depression, and later to help Britain generously in WW2. He had four meetings with him, being, as were most, charmed by him, but noticing that his hands while 'firm and fairly strong' were 'not clever or with finesse'.

ROSE, CHARLES ARCHIBALD WALKER (1880–1961), diplomat and businessman. Ed. Bedford School and King's College, London. Came to KCC in 1911 as an Advanced Student, after thirteen years in consular service in China. Later joined the British-American Tobacco Company, and became a director of the Chartered Bank. JMK taught him economics and he taught JMK riding. His 'supreme gift was for friendship' (*KCC Annual Report*, 1961, pp. 55–7).

ROTHBARTH, ERWIN (1913–44), German-born statistician. JMK got him a job in the Institute of Statistical Research, Cambridge. He helped JMK with *How To Pay for the War*. Killed in action in 1944; JMK settled £200 a year on his widow.

ROTHSCHILD, VICTOR (1910–90), scientist, with distinguished career in scientific research, WW2, business, and public service. Ed. Harrow and TCC. Apostle, 1933. Prize Fellow of TCC 1935–9. In the 1930s, JMK used to dine frequently with Victor and his first wife Barbara, née Hutchinson, in the Rothschild family house in Newmarket.

ROWE–DUTTON, ERNEST (1891–1965), civil servant. Assistant, then Principal Assistant Secretary, Treasury, 1939–46.

ROWSE, ALFRED LESLIE (1903–97), eccentric Elizabethan historian and Fellow of All Souls College, Oxford, 1925–74. A strong advocate of JMK's ideas in the Labour

Party, but came strongly to disapprove of the *Economic Consequences of the Peace*, as leading to the appeasement of Germany.

RUNCIMAN family. JMK knew SIR WALTER RUNCIMAN (1870–1949), the Liberal politician, and his second son STEVEN (b.1903), the historian of the crusades, an Eton Scholar (with George Orwell), undergraduate and then Fellow of TCC. He much preferred the son to the father.

RUSSELL, BERTRAND ARTHUR WILLIAM, Earl (1872–1970), mathematician and philosopher. Ed. by tutors, at crammer, and TCC. Seventh Wrangler, 1893, and first in moral sciences, 1894. Apostle, 1892. Fellow of TCC 1895–1901 and Lecturer in Mathematics 1910–16. In latter years deprived of his lectureship after being convicted for writing and distributing a seditious anti-conscriptionist pamphlet. In his autobiography he wrote: 'What I most desired was to find some reason for supposing mathematics true.' Wrote *Principles of Mathematics* (1903) and (with A. N. Whitehead) *Principia Mathematica* (1910). In his autobiography (vol. I, 71) he wrote: 'Keynes's escape [into the great world] . . . was not complete. He went about the world carrying with him everywhere a feeling of a bishop *in partibus*. The salvation was elsewhere, among the faithful at Cambridge. When he concerned himself with politics and economics he left his soul at home.'

RYLANDS, GEORGE HUMPHREY WOLFERSTAN ('Dadie') (1902–99) ed. Eton and KCC. First in English literature. Apostle, 1922. Fellow 1927, and bursar 1939–47, of KCC. Shakespearean scholar, he was Cambridge's leading actor-director in the inter-war years, and closely involved with JMK's and LK's ballet and dramatic projects. Became a close friend of JMK only after his return to KCC in 1927, Sheppard having earlier – as he told JMK –'made it entirely impossible for me to know you or be known by you. I suppose unconsciously.' Lytton Strachey was 'luckily (*almost* entirely) immune from his yellow hair', but 'those who are not . . . ah! I pity them.'

SALANT, WALTER (1911–99), American economist. Cambridge student of JMK in the early 1930s; Office of Price Administration in Washington during the war. Clashed famously with JMK over inflation at a meeting of economists in Washington in 1941.

SALTER, SIR ARTHUR (1881–1975), civil servant and politician. General Secretary, Reparation Commission, 1920–2; director, Economic Section of the League of Nations, 1922–3; served on Committee of Economic Information 1931–7. A good example of the middle way in search of a theory.

SAMUEL, SIR HERBERT (1870–1963), Liberal politician. At the Founder's Feast at KCC, 6 December 1935, at which he was guest, JMK remarked tactfully, 'For myself working with him in the production of the famous Liberal Yellow Book I knew well the powers of his criticism and at the same time the justice and fairness of his mind.' Lloyd George's comment was tarter: 'When they circumcised him, they threw the wrong piece away.'

SANGER, CHARLES PERCY (1872–1930), statistician and barrister. Ed. Winchester and TCC. Second Wrangler, Apostle, 1902. Bridged the gap between the Russell and Keynes generations of Apostles. Virginia Woolf wrote of him in 1916: 'He is very red-eyed and wizened and overworked but he pumps up the most amazing quips and cracks, and his eyes glow and he looks like one of the dwarfs in the Ring.' According to Lowes Dickinson, he was of the type of Cambridge man 'unworldly without being saintly, unambitious without being inactive, warm-hearted without being sentimental.'

SCHACHT, HJALMAR (1877–1970), German banker. President of the Reichsbank 1923–30, 1933–9; Minister of Economics 1934–7. Creator of the 'Schachtian' system of bilateral barter for foreign trade to protect Germany's balance of payments position. Influenced Britain's system of foreign exchange controls in WW2, which temporarily attracted JMK as a solution to Britain's post-war problems.

SCHUMPETER, JOSEPH ALOIS (1883–1950), Austrian-born economist. Austrian Minister of Finance 1920; Professor of Economics at University of Bonn 1925–32, and Harvard 1932–50. The most wide-ranging, encyclopaedic economist of the twentieth century. 'In an astonishing book, *Theory of Economic Development* (1912), written at the early age of 28, he replaced Marx's greedy, blood-sucking capitalist by the dynamic, innovating entrepreneur as the lynchpin of the capitalist system, responsible not just for technical progress but the very existence of a positive rate of profit on capital' (Blaug). Schumpeter was scathing about the Anglo-Saxon tradition of not properly distinguishing between interest and profit, and investment and enterprise; and for concentrating on the conditions of static equilibrium. He had little sympathy, therefore, with JMK's method. Wrote one of the best biographical essays on JMK.

SCHUSTER, SIR FELIX (1854–1936), banker. Dominant in the City before WW1, his old-fashioned banking principles made him anathema to JMK, who largely blamed him for the 1914 banking crisis. Died in Ruthin castle in Wales just before JMK's arrival there.

SCOTT, CHARLES PRESTWICH (1846–1932), journalist. Editor of the *Manchester Guardian*, 1872–1929. JMK worked with him and his son EDWARD (1883–1932) on the *Manchester Guardian* Commercial Reconstruction Supplements 1922–3. C. P. Scott thought JMK brilliant but self-centred.

SCOTT, FRANCIS CLAYTON (1881–1979), chairman of the Provincial Insurance Company, on whose board JMK served.

SCOTT, GEOFFREY (1883–1929), writer. Ed. New College, Oxford. Friend of JMK and Mary Berenson. He married Lady Sybil Cutting in 1918, and had an affair with Vita Sackville-West.

SCOTT, WILLIAM ROBERTS (1868–1940), economic historian. Sponsored JMK, unsuccessfully, for election to the British Academy in 1920.

SHACKLE, ROBERT JONES (1895–1950), civil servant. Principal Assistant Secretary, Board of Trade, 1942–7. Involved in Anglo-American trade negotiations in WW2.

SHAW, GEORGE BERNARD (1856–1950), Irish-born playwright, philosopher, and self-proclaimed genius, who dazzled the first half of the twentieth century with his verbal pyrotechnics, which he nevertheless used to promote his ideal of socialism brought about by Nietzschean supermen. Despite the generation gap, and his obsolete economics, JMK loved GBS for his wit and his inexhaustible fancy, and wrote him probably the most quoted of all his letters in 1935 explaining the political purpose of the *General Theory*. GBS, in turn, thought JMK (at the age of fifty-nine), a 'bright and promising youth, frightfully handicapped by the Cambridge nullification process, with some inextinguishable sparks of culture' in him. JMK hated Shaw's article 'Uncommon Sense about the War', published in the *New Statesman* on 7 October 1939. When GBS told him that 'the difference between us is that you are English and I am Irish', he was not just referring to temperament. JMK's gracious ninetieth birthday tribute to GBS in 1946 was the last thing he wrote.

SHEPPARD, JOHN TRESSIDER (1881–1968), classicist. Ed. Dulwich College and KCC. Apostle, 1902. Fellow of KCC (1906) and University Lecturer in Classics 1908–33. Provost of KCC 1933–54. His reign was marked by the astonishing amount of attention he gave to the 'young men', whom Lytton Strachey described as 'exhalations whizzing in the air'. He was at his best at his Sunday evening 'at homes', where the 'hypnotic power of those slightly protruding eyes', and his mixture of dignity and clowning, snobbery and subversiveness 'made us feel a community with him in original sin' (Patrick Wilkinson). His life-long friend was Cecil Taylor, later a housemaster at Clifton, known in JMK's circle as 'Madame'. A character rather than a scholar, he was best known in the university for his productions of the triennial Greek plays, starting with *Oedipus Tyrannus* in 1912. A frequent visitor to JMK's country house, Tilton, between the wars and the pillar of JMK's position at KCC.

SHOVE, GERALD FRANK (1887–1947), economist. Ed. Uppingham and KCC. Switched from classics to economics, in which he got a first in 1911 on the strength of a few answers. Apostle, 1909. Generally silent and taciturn but with flashes of ebullience (as when he proposed the toast of 'The King, God damn him' at the Carbonari dinner of 1909) and moral passion. In 1915 he married FREDEGOND CECILY MAITLAND, daughter of Sir Frederic Maitland, the legal historian and cousin of Virginia Woolf. Became a Fellow of King's 1926. Between the wars, Cambridge's hardest working economics don. He relieved JMK of much of his teaching, but published almost nothing in consequence. JMK estimated that in the early 1920s he was doing five lectures and supervising fifty to sixty pupils a week. Shove's 1913 fellowship dissertation 'Notes on the Applications of G. E. Moore's System of Ethics to Some Problems of Political Theory' would repay study.

SICKERT, WALTER (1860–1942), painter. When he painted LK in 1924, he told her her head was like a pigeon's.

SIDGWICK, HENRY (1838–1900), philosopher and university reformer. Ed. Rugby and TCC. Apostle, 1856. Resigned his Fellowship at Trinity in 1869 to avoid 'dogmatic obligations' of a lost faith. Knightbridge Professor of Moral Philosophy 1882–1900. A leading late Victorian 'pious agnostic'. JMK wrote 'He never did anything but wonder whether Christianity was true and prove that it wasn't and hope that it was', but in the intervals of doubt he founded Newnham College.

SIEPMANN, HENRY ARTHUR (1889–1963), civil servant. Ex-Treasury official, he was appointed special adviser to the Bank of England in 1926.

SIMON, SIR ERNEST DARWIN (1879–1960), Liberal politician and social reformer. Leader of the post-WW1 Manchester liberalism which started the Liberal Summer Schools, he sat with JMK on the board of the *Nation*, served with him on the Liberal Industrial Inquiry, and so on.

SIMON, SIR JOHN, Lord (1873–1954), Liberal politician. Annoyed JMK by his legalistic attitude towards the General Strike. Chancellor of the Exchequer 1937–40. Lloyd George made the best quip about him: 'He has sat so long on the fence, the iron has entered his soul.'

SMUTS, JAN CHRISTIAN (1870–1950), South African lawyer, politician, philosopher. Ed. Christ's College, Cambridge, where he obtained a first in both parts of the law tripos. South African Minister of Defence 1910–19. Member of the British War Cabinet 1917–19, and of the British Empire Delegation to the Paris Peace Conference, where he and JMK became friends and allies over reparations.

SNOWDEN, PHILIP, Lord (1864–1937), Labour politician. As Chancellor of the Exchequer 1929–31, he was the main obstacle to a radical unemployment policy, Churchill remarking that 'The Treasury mind and the Snowden mind embraced each other with the fervour of two long-separated kindred lizards.'

SPICER, ROBERT HENRY SCANES (1897–1956), business economist and statistician. Apostle, 1919. One of JMK's favourites immediately after WW1.

SPOKES, ARTHUR HEWETT (1854–1922), lawyer. Friend of J. N. Keynes. Recorder of Reading, 1894.

SPRAGUE, OLIVER (1873–1953), American-born economist, adviser to the Bank of England 1930–33. He was the butt of one of JMK's typical sallies. Sprague had argued that deflation applied at the top of the boom would lessen the pain later. JMK: 'I suppose, my dear Sprague, that in that situation your pathological propensities would do less harm.'

SPRING-RICE, SIR CECIL (1859–1918), diplomat. British Ambassador to the United States 1913–18. Wrote words of hymn: 'I vow to Thee my country'. JMK thought he was senile, he thought JMK supercilious, when they met in Washington in 1917.

SPROTT, WALTER JOHN HERBERT ('Sebastian') (1897–1971), psychologist. Ed. Fellsted School and Clare College, Cambridge. First in moral sciences, 1922. Apostle, 1920. Demonstrator at Psychological Laboratory, Cambridge, 1922–5; Lecturer in Psychology at Nottingham University 1925; Professor of Philosophy, Nottingham, 1948–60. JMK's affair with Sprott after WW1 overlapped his courtship of LK. At Nottingham he was known for his wit and brilliant oratory. Wives of colleagues entertained in his house were served with great courtesy by discharged prisoners carrying small trays of wine in their fists.

SRAFFA, PIERO (1898–1983), Italian-born economist. Cambridge University Lecturer in Economics 1927–31; Assistant Director of Research in Economics 1935–63 – a job JMK invented to keep him in Cambridge, so great was his horror of teaching; Fellow of Trinity College 1934–83. A *curiosum* of twentieth-century economics. Arriving at Cambridge with a great reputation on the wings of his article, 'The Laws of Return under Competitive Conditions' (*EJ*, December 1926), he proceeded to spend thirty years editing an eleven-volume edition of Ricardo's works, paused briefly to demolish Hayek's theory of business cycles in 1932, and resurrected his reputation as a theorist with a largely incomprehensible ninety-nine-page book published in 1960, though mainly written in the 1920s. JMK used to 'potter with Piero' round the antiquarian bookshops on Saturday afternoons. Sraffa influenced both Joan Robinson and Wittgenstein, without accepting the ideas of either. Joan Robinson recalled 'having innumerable discussions with Piero Sraffa but they always consisted of his heading me off from errors; he would never say anything positive.' His strongest emotional attachment was to his mother. In 1944 JMK helped him track down papers in Ireland for his Ricardo edition.

STALIN, JOSEF (1879–1953), Soviet dictator and war leader. General Secretary of the Communist Party of the USSR 1924–53.

STAMP, SIR JOSIAH, Lord (1880–1941), statistician, foremost expert on the taxation system. 'A great gun loaded with statistics' is how Oswald Falk described him. One of the few in JMK's circle – or that of the interwar great and good – who had worked himself up from the ranks. Entering the Inland Revenue service as a boy clerk in 1896, he had proceeded via an external B.Sc. at London University in 1911 (in which he gained outstanding first-class honours) to occupy a series of top positions in the 'semi–public' corporations of the day, as well as serving on important advisory committees, like the Colwyn Committee on National Debt and Taxation, the Economic Advisory Council and the Committee of Economists. As British representative on the Dawes and Young Committees he played a crucial part in settling the reparation problem. Led the Stamp Survey into war preparations 1939–40, but was killed by a bomb in 1941. He was perhaps JMK's model for the businessman of the future – part technical expert, part public servant – required for managing business life in the 'age of stabilisation'.

STEPHEN family. One of the leading evangelical, intellectual and administrative families of Victorian England. SIR LESLIE STEPHEN (1832–1904), philosopher and man of letters, was educated at Eton, University College, London, and Trinity Hall, Cambridge, of which he became Fellow and Tutor, resigning in 1862 following religious doubts. According to Quentin Bell, his 'agnosticism made him not less, but more anxious to preserve the proprieties'. Sir Leslie had two sons THOBY ('the Goth') (1880–1906) and ADRIAN (1883–1948), both of whom went to TCC, and two daughters VANESSA (1879–1961), who married Clive Bell, and VIRGINIA (1882–1941), who married Leonard Woolf, by his second wife JULIA PATTLE. His elder brother was the lawyer SIR JAMES FITZJAMES STEPHEN (1829–94), author of a famous attack on John Stuart Mill. The Stephens exemplify the passage from pious agnosticism to impious atheism.

STIRLING, JOHN (1891–1965), civil servant. Assistant secretary, Board of Trade, during WW2. JMK 'stalled' his trade negotiations with Harry Hawkins of the US State Department on his mission to Washington in 1941.

STONE, JOHN RICHARD NICHOLAS (1913–91), economist and statistician. Central Statistical Office 1940–5. Fellow, KCC, 1945–91, and Professor of Finance and Accounting, Cambridge, 1955–80. JMK promoted and used his work on national income accounts.

STRACHEY family. Another central transitional family, with roots in Britain's imperial service. EDWARD STRACHEY (1774–1832), a judge in India, had six sons of whom three – SIR EDWARD STRACHEY (1812–1901), SIR RICHARD STRACHEY (1817–1908), and SIR JOHN STRACHEY (1823–1907) made their mark, the second and third in Indian administration. Sir Edward's son JOHN ST LOE (1860–1927) became editor of the *Spectator,* his son EVELYN JOHN ST LOE (1901–63) was the Labour politician who sought a 'revolution by reason' first with Mosley then with Marx. Sir Richard Strachey, soldier and scientist, had by his second wife JANE MARIA GRANT

(1840–1928) ten surviving children (she forgot one of them in her entry in *Who's Who*), of whom GILES LYTTON (1880–1932) was the eighth and JAMES BEAUMONT (1887–1945) was the youngest. The others in descending order were ELINOR (1860–1945), married to JAMES MEADOWS RENDEL, another Indian administrator; RICHARD (1861–1935), who served as a soldier in Borneo; DOROTHEA (1866–1960), translator and married to the French painter SIMON BUSSY; RALPH (1868–1923); PHILIPPA ('Pippa') (1872–1968), an 'inconspicuous but indefatiguable force at the centre of the constitutional women's movement' (Anne Olivier Bell); OLIVER (1874–1960), an historian and civil servant, who married RACHEL COSTELLOE; JOAN PERNEL (1876–1951), Principal of Newnham College, Cambridge 1923–41; and MARJORIE (1882–1969), a writer and teacher.

STRACHEY, GILES LYTTON (1880–1932), biographer and literary critic, who achieved fame with *Eminent Victorians*. Ed. Abbotsholme and TCC. Apostle, 1902. JMK's closest friend in the 1900s and a continued moral presence in his life. JMK's last few exchanges with Lytton are typical of the untroubled state their friendship had reached. 'My dearest Lytton', JMK wrote (3 December 1928), on receipt of Strachey's *Elizabeth and Essex*, 'Thank you most affectionately for Elizabeth . . . I don't believe it is essentially as good as Victoria. But the *natural pleasure* of reading it is enormous. You seem, on the whole, to imagine yourself as Elizabeth, but I see from the pictures that it is Essex whom you have got up as yourself. But I expect you have managed to get the best of both worlds.' 'Dearest Maynard', wrote Lytton (31 October 1930), on receipt of JMK's *Treatise on Money*, 'What a delightful and imposing present! Thank you for something more than Commodity Money, Managed Money, Fiat Money, State Money, Bank Money, Reserve Money and Current Money can buy. You see I have read the first chapter.'

STRACHEY, JAMES BEAUMONT (1887–1945), psychoanalyst. Ed. St. Paul's School and Trinity College, Cambridge. Apostle,1905. In the 1920s kept JMK in touch with Freud's theories.

STRAIGHT, MICHAEL – See ELMHIRST family.

STRAKOSCH, SIR HENRY (1871–1943), banker. Montagu Norman (q.v.) described him as a 'visionary arbitrageur'. JMK was involved with him in a number of projects relating to South African gold mining and banking immediately after WW1.

SWITHINBANK, BERNARD WINTHROP (1884–1958), administrator. Ed. Eton and and Balliol College, Oxford. Career civil servant in Burma. JMK's best friend at Eton.

SYDNEY-TURNER, SAXON (1880–1962), civil servant. Ed. Westminster and TCC. First in classics, parts I and II, and also a natural mathematician. Apostle, 1902. Disappeared into the Estate Duty Office, later the Treasury where he remained till retirement. The silent man of Bloomsbury, short, with straw-coloured hair. Leonard Woolf called him an 'atrophied Shelley', but he had a passion for Wagnerian opera, reputedly seeing over a hundred Tristans. Looked after by Barbara Bagenal (q.v.) later in life.

TARSHIS, LORIE (1911–93), Canadian economist. Attended JMK's lectures 1932–5. Spread JMK's ideas at Tufts and Harvard in late 1930s. His article 'Changes in Real and Money Wages', *EJ*, March 1939, written with Dunlop (qv), and showing that real and money wages moved pro-cyclically, was important in dispelling fears of the inflationary consequences of Keynesian policy.

TAUSSIG, FRANK WILLIAM (1859–1940), American economist. Professor of Economics, Harvard University, 1892–1935. His *Principles of Economics* (first edn 1911) is regarded as epitomising the classical school against which JMK wrote the *General Theory*. If discovered, JMK's letters to Taussig in 1914–15 might throw interesting light on JMK's attitude to WW1.

TAYLOR, CECIL FRANCIS (1886–1955), schoolmaster. Ed. ECC. Apostle, 1905. From 1912 till his retirement taught at Clifton College. He was Sheppard's (q.v.) lifelong friend. At Clifton, his nickname was 'Babe'.

THOMPSON-McCAUSLAND, LUCIUS (1904–84), banker and journalist. Ed. KCC, where he studied economics under JMK. Bank of England staff 1939–65. JMK's 'bag carrier' in Washington 1941.

THOMSON, LOGAN (d.1980), farmer. JMK's manager, subsequently partner, Tilton Farm (from 1936) and Charleston Farm (from 1940).

TINBERGEN, JAN (1903–94), Dutch economist and Nobel prizewinner. Professor, Netherlands School of Economics 1933–73. JMK had a famous controversy with him on the theory of econometrics 1938–9.

TOWERS, GRAHAM (1897–1965), Canadian banker. Governor of the Bank of Canada 1934–54. JMK suggested him as Governor of the Bank of England to succeed Montagu Norman in 1944. But Towers was not willing; Norman found him 'too much JMK & $'.

TREVELYAN family. The three sons of SIR GEORGE OTTO TREVELYAN (1838–1928), historian and Liberal politician, and CAROLINE PHILIPS, were SIR CHARLES PHILIPS TREVELYAN (1870–1958), Liberal and Labour politician, ROBERT CALVERLEY TREVELYAN ('Bob Trevy') (1872–1951), and GEORGE MACAULAY TREVELYAN (1876–1962). All three brothers were educated at Harrow and TCC, the last two were Apostles, in 1893 and 1895 respectively, as their father had been (1862). Bob Trevy and GMT were both friends of JMK; the former, a 'very scholarly but not very inspired poet' (Russell), but a great mimic; the latter an austere historian, Regius Professor of Modern History 1927–40, Master of TCC 1941–50, and pillar of the Liberal establishment. It was he who advised JMK to go into politics in 1904. All the Trevelyans were prodigious walkers.

TROUTON, RUPERT (1887–1965), economist and businessman. Served in the Treasury under JMK 1916–19, then read economics at KCC, gaining a first in both parts of the tripos, 1920–1. Stockbroker with Laurence, Keen and Gardener 1928–61; Director of the Hector Whaling Company, in which JMK invested. Economic adviser to Mosley's New Party 1931. Trouton alerted JMK to the falsity of shipping statistics 1941–2. He and his wife were frequent guests at Tilton.

TRUMAN, HARRY (1884–1972), American politician. President of the United States 1945–53. Cancelled Lend–Lease without warning on 19 August 1945.

VALOIS, NINETTE DE (1898–2001), British dancer, choreographer and founder of the Vic-Wells Ballet. JMK made possible the move of her ballet company to the Royal Opera House, Covent Garden, in 1946. A friend, but not a close friend, of LK.

VENN, JOHN (1834–1923), logician and historian. Fellow of Caius College, Cambridge, 1857, President 1912–23. A founder of the Cambridge moral science tripos. His book *Logic of Chance* (1866) was criticised by JMK in his *Treatise on Probability*, pp. 101–9.

VINER, JACOB (1892–1970), American economist. Professor of Economics, Chicago University, 1925–46. Consultant, State Department, 1943–52. 'A leading interwar price and trade theorist and quite simply the greatest historian of economic thought that ever lived' (Blaug). Viner's review of JMK's *General Theory* was one of the few critical notices JMK took seriously. It contained the famous remark: 'In a world organized in accordance with Keynes's specifications there would be a constant race between the printing press and the business agents of the trade unions, with the problem of unemployment largely solved if the printing press could maintain a constant lead . . .' JMK corresponded with him about the IMF in 1943.

VINSON, FREDERICK ('Judge') (1890–1953), American lawyer from Kentucky. Secretary of the Treasury 1945–6; appointed Chief Justice of US Supreme Court in 1946. JMK's two important passages of arms with him were at the Washington loan negotiations of 1945 and the Savannah Conference of 1946.

WALEY, SIGISMUND DAVID (1887–1962), civil servant. Principal Assistant Secretary, Under-Secretary, Treasury, 1939–46, and Head of the Overseas Finance Division. Involved in the gestation of JMK's Clearing Union Plan and preparations for the American loan negotiations.

WALLACE, HENRY (1888–1965), American politician. Roosevelt's Vice-President 1941–4; Secretary of Commerce 1945–6. On the left wing of the New Deal, and represented US agricultural interests. JMK tried to placate him with his Buffer Stock Plan.

WALRAS, LEON (1834–1910), French economist and failed engineering student. The founder of general equilibrium theory, in which equilibrium is a solution to a simultaneous-equations model of the economy. Became probably the most influential economist (in terms of method) of all time, especially following the translation of his *Elements of Pure Economics* (1874–7) into English in 1954. In Schumpeter's view, it is 'the only work by an economist that will stand comparison with the achievements of theoretical physics'. Others (including JMK) believed it led to a sterile formalism. It is interesting that Anglo-Saxon economics followed a style which is classically French.

WARD, DUDLEY (1885–1957), civil servant and banker. Ed. Derby School and St John's College, Cambridge. JMK taught him economics; he served under JMK in 'A' Division of the Treasury 1917–19, accompanying him to the Paris Peace Conference. Friend of Rupert Brooke.

WARRE, EDMOND (1837–1920), schoolmaster. Ed. Eton and Balliol College, Oxford. Headmaster of Eton 1884–1915. Much admired for improving its moral tone.

WEBB, BEATRICE, née Potter (1858–1943), wife of SIDNEY JAMES WEBB, Lord Passfield (1859–1947), leaders of the Fabian Society. JMK and LK developed a warm relationship with both, but especially Beatrice, between the wars, JMK being won over by her *My Apprenticeship*, published in 1926. To JMK, the two socialists embodied the spirit of disinterested public service, and he was moved by Beatrice's struggle to replace her lost Christianity by service to humanity. Beatrice admired his intellectual energy, but doubted his seriousness. Lydia reported on her visit to Passfield Corner in 1933: 'The old lady is magnificent, be it in a Dutch cap she wears in the afternoon, or lying on the sofa with black silks in the evening.' At a party in the early 1930s, Beatrice said to JMK: 'Ah, Mr. Keynes, we are awaiting with great interest your economic theory to cure unemployment', to which JMK replied, 'Oh, it's all in the Minority Report, Mrs Webb.'

WEBSTER, DAVID (1903–71), retailer. Worked closely with JMK in re-establishing Covent Garden 1945–6. General Administrator, Royal Opera House, 1946–70.

WELLS, HERBERT GEORGE (1866–1946), writer. Wells 'adored' JMK. JMK admired Wells's idea of a Samurai leading mankind to better things, but repeatedly pointed out to him that he gave them no idea of what to do.

WHITE, HARRY DEXTER (1892–1948), American economist and public servant. Director of Monetary Research at the US Treasury 1938–45. Joint author with JMK of the Bretton Woods system. An able, abrasive, ambitious man, he was JMK's most important American colleague during WW2, but there was more to Harry White than met the eye.

WICKSELL, KNUT (1851–1926), Swedish economist, founder of the Stockholm school. JMK referred to him as his 'great grandparent in errancy'. His distinction between the 'market' and 'natural' rates of interest (and their possible divergence) was adopted by JMK in his *Treatise on Money* (1930), but later discarded as suggesting a unique position of equilibrium. JMK underestimated Wicksell, thinking him too academic and formal, but did not know his work well. Like JMK, Wicksell combined free-thinking in private life (he was once imprisoned for blasphemy) with the attempt to stabilise the economic system, seeing the 'solution' of the economic problem as a necessary condition for an improved quality of life.

WILLIAMS, JOHN HENRY (1887–1980), American economist and banker. Author of the 'key currency' plan, the New York bankers' alternative to the IMF and Bretton Woods system.

WILSON, SIR HORACE (1882–1972), civil servant. Permanent Secretary, Treasury, 1932–42, when he retired, having reached the minimum retirement age.

WILSON, WOODROW (1856–1924), American politician. President of the United States 1912–20. Professor of Jurisprudence and Politics, Princeton University, 1897–1910. JMK thought better of him as a professor than as a president. His description of him as a 'blind and deaf Don Quixote' in *Economic Consequences of the Peace* alienated many of his natural liberal allies in the United States, though its contribution to US 'isolationism' has been greatly exaggerated.

WINANT, JOHN GILBERT (1889–1947), American public servant and politician. US Ambassador to London 1941–6. Committed suicide by shooting himself. A strong Anglophile and friend of JMK and LK.

WITTGENSTEIN, LUDWIG (1889–1951), Austrian-born philospher, probably the most important of the twentieth century. Born in Vienna, studied philosophy under Russell at TCC 1912–3. Apostle, 1912 – but didn't like it. JMK revered him as a genius but found his company wearying. Wittgenstein's relations with him were 'marred by his hypersensitivity and his neurotic propensity to misinterpret minor incidents as symptomatic of alienation or disloyalty' (*(Times Literary Supplement*, 18

October 1974). Frances Partridge writes that 'in mixed company [Wittgenstein's] conversation was often trivial in the extreme and loaded with feeble jokes accompanied by a wintry smile.' Wittgenstein's influence on JMK's epistemology has been frequently argued, notably by John Coates and Wayne Parsons. Parsons writes that they had a joint belief 'in the necessity of shared languages and "forms of life" as a prerequisite to the possibility of meaningful, if not rational discussion and communication' – that is, one had to 'see' things in the same way first, before discussion could be fruitful.

WOLFIT, DONALD (1902–68), actor-manager of the old school. JMK lectured him on his production of *Tis Pity She's a Whore*, which the Cambridge Arts Theatre was staging in April 1940, and once remarked that he was 'lone Wolfit'.

WOOD, SIR KINGSLEY (1881–1943), Conservative politician. Chancellor of the Exchequer 1940–3. He introduced the first 'Keynesian' budget in 1941.

WOOLF, LEONARD (1880–1963), author and publisher, husband of the writer VIRGINIA WOOLF, née Stephen (1882–1941). Ed. St Paul's School and TCC. First in classics part 1. Apostle, 1902. Colonial civil servant in Ceylon 1904–11. Wrote on 'international government' during WW1. With Virginia, founded the Hogarth Press in 1917. Literary editor of the *Nation* 1923–30. The Woolfs lived in Rodmell, a few miles from Tilton in East Sussex, and visited each other regularly. Virginia Woolf committed suicide there in April 1941. Leonard called JMK a 'lovable character' in his autobiography (*Sowing*, vol i, p. 144) but does not seem to have liked him that much. In her diary, Virginia Woolf was constantly critical of JMK and LK. The Woolfs' joint view was that JMK had a brilliant, even great, mind, but bad character – selfish, domineering, unreflective.

WRIGHT, HAROLD (1883–1934), economist. Ed. ECC. Staff of the *Nation* 1923–30, editor 1930–1. Wrote *Population* (1923) for the Cambridge Economic Handbooks series, of which JMK was editor. JMK's (unpublished) letter to him of 18 April 1923 on that book is a good example of his neo-Malthusianism at the time: 'I think you might rub in a little more the hopelessness of emigration as anything better than a temporary expedient on the ground that a country which is already feeling the strain of population is in no position to afford the breeding up of human beings to the productive age and then exporting them free of charge.'

YOUNG family. Had strong connections with Eton, Cambridge and administration. Of the three sons of SIR GEORGE YOUNG (1837–1930), a progressive civil servant and intrepid mountain climber, SIR GEORGE YOUNG (1872–1952) was a diplomat, GEOFFREY WINTHROP YOUNG (1879–1960) was assistant-master at Eton 1900–05, during JMK's time, and also a famous mountaineer, and EDWARD HILTON YOUNG (1879–1960), later first Baron Kennet of Dene, was a Liberal politician, who proposed to Virginia Woolf, and whom Desmond MacCarthy called a 'sphinx without a riddle'. JMK's Eton friend GERARD MACKWORTH YOUNG (1884–1963) was the son of SIR WILLIAM MACKWORTH YOUNG (1840–1924), an Indian civil servant and brother of the first Sir George Young above.

YULE, GEORGE UDNY (1871–1951), statistician. JMK was instrumental in getting him appointed University Lecturer in Statistics at Cambridge in 1912 on the strength of his *Introduction to the Theory of Statistics* (1911). His next book was in 1944.

Index

KEYNES, JOHN MAYNARD (*cont.*)
591–2, 688, 747; heart attack (1940), 598;
Treasury missions to US, 624–5, 628–31;
Lend-Lease, 624–8, 631–6, 655, 756–7;
768–9, 771, 775; work on Kingsley Wood
budget (1941), 605–11, 651; peerage, 641–2;
High Steward of Borough of Cambridge, 658;
Clearing Union Plan, 649, 651, 654, 659, 673,
674–95, 701, 708, 730–1; Fellow of Eton, 664;
Director of Bank of England, 674–5; Buffer
Stock Plan, 692–3, 694, 701, 757; response to
White Plan, 700, 702–3; White meeting
(1942), 701; CEMA, 708, 724–9; maiden
speech in Lords, 706–7, 710; sixtieth birthday,
707; Beveridge Report, 708–11; fiscal
attitudes, 714–18; on Post-War Employment
report, 719–20; Covent Garden Committee,
729, 827; US mission (1943), 732–47;
Monetary Group, 735–6; Washington
agreement, 748–55; US mission (1944),
760–1; in Atlantic City, 760–2; Bretton
Woods, 655, 762–7, 849; Canadian visit,
767–8; voyage to Canada, 768–9; in
Washington (1944), 771–5; preparing for
Stage III, 780–4; National Debt Enquiry
(1945), 712, 779, 823; Canadian colloquium at
KCC, 788–9; Clayton meetings, 791–2;
Downing Street emergency meeting (1945),
793–5; US mission (1945), 795–818; Lords
speech on Bretton Woods and loan, 819–20;
US trip (1946), 828; death, 832–3; cremation,
834; memorial services, 834; will, 836–7;
reputation, 846–51

APPEARANCE: as a child, 41; considers
himself ugly, 41, 103, 306; height, 41, 45; at
Eton, 51, 55, 63; as a Cambridge freshman, 69;
after WWI, 253; in 1920s, 253, 259; Virginia
Woolf's descriptions, 259, 357, 592; Naomi
Bentwich's description, 279; voice, 328, 349,
466, 729; clothes, 328, 359, 466, 471, 555,
630; in 1931, 474; recovery from illness, 565;
in 1941, 630; at Treasury, 649–50; in 1945,
788, 796, 798, 818

CHARACTER: attitude to religion, 54–5,
515–16; conversational style, 145; sense of
superiority, 207, 467; rudeness, 207, 264, 471,
653, 654, 745, 779–80; manners, 213; use of
language, 264, 469–70, 655–6, 745, 798;
attitude to Jews, 373–5, 746; self-confidence,
466, 468; talents, 467; intuition, 461, 467–8,
652; analytic skills, 468–9, 654; loyalty,
470–1, 656; taste, 471–2; confidence in
predictions, 472; optimism, 654, 796;
compromise, 654–5; negotiating style, 626,
820–1; will-power, 656

FINANCES: as economics lecturer, 110;
managing friends' money, 147; spending on

Bloomsbury causes, 147; stock market
investment, 163, 171, 265; discount market
lending, 177; Treasury income, 197;
resignation from Treasury, 234; currency
speculation, 234, 266, 272–4, 295–6, 520;
sales of *Economic Consequences of the Peace*,
244; support for Duncan Grant, 258; gifts,
258, 522; investment income, 265, 520;
academic income, 265, 520; income from
writing, 265, 490; directorships, 265, 266, 416;
commodity losses (1928), 417–18; Wall Street
crash, 417–18, 519; net worth (1936), 519;
investment gains, 519–20; commodity
speculation, 520; losses in slump, 563, 565;
Treasury requisition securities, 600

HEALTH: tongue-tied, 40; circumcised, 40;
delicate childhood, 41, 43, 44, 47; at Eton,
59–60; stammering, 45; takes quinine, 117;
influenza, 117; diphtheria, 168–9;
appendicitis, 184–5; pneumonia, 185;
influenza attacks, 202, 221; colds, 359, 401;
tooth problems, 443, 556; tonsillitis and
influenza, 443; pleurisy, 474, 556; wisdom
teeth out, 511; influenza (1935), 527; bilious
attack, 527; forgetfulness, 555; heart
problems, 556–8, 580; influenza (1936), 556,
557; heart attack, 361, 558; recovery at
Ruthin, 558–60, 564; treatment by Plesch,
578–80, 586, 594, 599, 608, 732, 753; strain of
war work, 594; heart attack (1940), 598, 599;
wartime lifestyle, 646; smoking, 656; effect of
US missions, 656, 761–2, 807, 825; in 1943,
706, 732; collapse in 1944, 753; exhaustion at
Bretton Woods, 766; in Washington (1945),
807, 814–15; recuperation at Tilton, 825; in
1946, 830, 831

HOMES: childhood at 6 Harvey Road, 31;
lodgings in King's Lane, 69; rooms at KCC, 76,
111, 116, 138; flat in St James's Court, 106,
117; room in Duncan Grant's flat, 142, 162; 38
Brunswick Square, 162, 178; rooms in 10
Ormond Street, 178–9, 183; 3 Gower Street,
183, 199; Gordon Square, 199, 256–7, 308,
360, 564, 604, 727, 788; Tilton, 360–3, 414,
415, 521, 522, 555, 561, 581, 660–1, 688; St
Edward's Passage, 598, 657, 838

HONOURS AND TITLES: CB, 202, 204, 341;
peerage, 641–2; High Steward of Borough of
Cambridge, 658; Fellow of Eton, 664 Fellow of
Eton, 664; Director of Bank of England, 674–5

INTERESTS: golf, 26, 33, 77, 108, 117, 137;
stamps, 32; book collecting, 33, 70, 108, 137,
522, 663; mediaeval Latin poetry, 58; sport,
58–9; debating, 70–1, 77; visual arts, 78, 107,
725; picture collection, 107, 137, 212, 266–7,
471, 519, 522, 662; reading, 107, 471;
gambling, 108, 137, 339; psychical research,